WORLD WIDE

ARcheology

photographs

Like in this

History Book.

Silkscreened

on all fa

made PRoducts.

World History

People and Nations

World History

People and Nations

Anatole G. Mazour
John M. Peoples

 Harcourt Brace Jovanovich, Publishers
Orlando   San Diego   Chicago   Dallas

AUTHORS **Anatole G. Mazour** was Professor of History at Stanford University for 25 years. He received an M.A. from Yale University and a Ph.D. from the University of California. His other books include *Russia: Past and Present; Finland Between East and West; The Rise and Fall of the Romanovs;* and *Russia: Tsarist and Communist.*

John M. Peoples taught world history and other social studies courses at Alameda High School in California for 35 years. Dr. Peoples received both an M.A. and a Ph.D. from the University of California.

Cover: Funeral mask of the Egyptian pharaoh Tutankhamen

Acknowledgments: For permission to reprint copyrighted material, grateful acknowledgment is made to the following sources:
American Heritage, a division of Forbes Inc.: From pp. 179 and 184 in *The Horizon History of Africa,* edited by Alvin M. Josephy, Jr. Copyright © 1971 by American Heritage Publishing Co., Inc. From p. 606 in *The American Heritage Picture Book of World War II* by C. L. Sulzberger. Copyright © 1966 by American Heritage Publishing Co., Inc. *Apt Books, Inc., on behalf of Asia Publishing House:* "The War Drum" from *Hymns from the Vedas,* English translation by Abinash Chandra Bose. © 1966 by Abinash Chandra Bose. *Atheneum Publishers, an imprint of Macmillan Publishing Company:* From pp. 135–136 in *Florence Nightingale* by Cecil Woodham-Smith. Copyright © 1951 by Cecil Woodham-Smith; copyright renewed 1979 by Charles Woodham-Smith and Mrs. John Bonython. *British Crown Copyright and Hansard:* From Prime Minister Winston Churchill's speech to the House of Commons, May 1940 in *Hansard.* *Cambridge University Press:* From "The Ten Commandments" in *The New English Bible.* Copyright © 1961, 1970 by the Delegates of the Oxford University Press and the Syndics of the Cambridge University Press. From *Life on an English Manor: A Study of Peasant Conditions, 1150–1400* by H. S. Bennett. Published by Cambridge University Press, 1937. From p. 33 in *The Stages of Economic Growth* by W. W. Rostow. © 1960 by Cambridge University Press. *Carnegie Endowment for International Peace:* From "The Political and Social Doctrines of Fascism" by Benito Mussolini in *International Conciliation* No. 306, January 1935. *Lionel Casson:* From pp. 64–73 in *Smithsonian,* June 1984. *Leon E. Clark and Richard H. Minear:* From "A Closed Society: 1600–1853" in *Through Japanese Eyes* by Richard H. Minear, edited by Leon E. Clark. © 1974, 1981 by Leon E. Clark and Richard H. Minear. *Columbia University Press:* From pp. 129–130 in *CHUANG TZU: Basic Writings,* translated by Burton Watson. Copyright © 1964 by Columbia University Press. From p. 115 in *Sources of Chinese Tradition,* Volume I, compiled by Wm. Theodore de Bary, Wing-tsit Chan, and Burton Watson. Copyright © 1960 by Columbia University Press. *Robert Lloyd Davis:* From "We Lose the Next War" by Elmer Davis. Originally published in *Harper's Magazine,* March 1938. *Dembner Books, a division of Red Dembner Enterprises Corporation:* From "About Kings" in *Isaac Asimov's Book of Facts* by Isaac Asimov. Copyright © 1979 by Red Dembner Enterprises Corp. *Doubleday, a division of Bantam, Doubleday, Dell Publishing Group, Inc.:* From p. 30 in *An Introduction to Haiku* by Harold G. Henderson. Copyright © 1958 by Harold G. Henderson. From *The Odyssey* by Homer, translated by Robert Fitzgerald. Copyright © 1961 by Robert Fitzgerald. *E. P. Dutton, a division of Penguin Books USA Inc.:* From the Preface and from pp. 152–154 in *Lost City of the Incas* by Hiram Bingham. Copyright 1948 by Duell Sloan and Pearce, renewed 1976 by Alfred Bingham. *Egypt Exploration Society:* From "The Hyksos Rule in Egypt" by Torgny Säve-Soderbergh in *Journal of Egyptian Archaeology,* Volume 37, 1951. *Kathleen Schmidgall Floria and Audrey A. Tiersam:* From p. 13 in *Sparks from the Anvil* by Carl Schmidgall. Copyright 1953 by Carl Henry Schmidgall. *Harcourt Brace Jovanovich, Inc.:* From pp. 16–17 in *Elizabeth and Essex: A Tragic History* by Lytton Strachey. Copyright 1928 by Lytton Strachey and the Curtis Publishing Company, renewed 1956 by James Strachey. *Harper & Row, Publishers, Inc.:* From pp. 145–146 in *A History of Their Own: Women in Europe from Prehistory to the Present,* Volume I, by Bonnie S. Anderson and Judith P. Zinsser. Copyright © 1988 by Bonnie S. Anderson and Judith P. Zinsser. From p. 307 in *Not In God's Image,* edited by Julia O'Faolain and Lauro Martines. Copyright © 1973 by Julia O'Faolain and Lauro Martines. From pp. 45, 172, and 193 in *DELIVERED FROM EVIL: The Saga of World War II* by Robert Leckie. Copyright © 1987 by Robert Leckie. From SS First Lieutenant Kurt Gerstein's handwritten account in *Never to Forget: The Jews of the Holocaust* by Milton Meltzer. Copyright © 1976 by Milton Meltzer. From pp. 78 and 79 in *Documents in World History, Volume I, The Great Traditions: From Ancient Times to 1500,* edited by Peter N. Stearns, et al. Copyright © 1988 by Harper & Row, Publishers, Inc. *D. C. Heath, a division of Raytheon Co.:* From Chapter 2, "Early India and China" in *World Civilizations* by F. Roy Willis. Copyright © 1982 by D. C. Heath and Company. *Heinemann Educational Books, Ltd.:* "The Election Results" (chart) from *History Broadsheets: Hitler & Germany 1919–1939* by Tony Edwards. © 1972 by Tony Edwards. *David Higham Associates Limited and Macmillan Press, Ltd.:* From "The Vietnam War: A Reporter with the Vietcong, near Hanoi, 10 December 1965" in *What a Way to Run the Tribe* by James Cameron. Published in 1968 by Macmillan & Co. Ltd. *Holt, Rinehart and Winston, Inc.:* From p. 68 in *Source Problems in World Civilization: China's Cultural Tradition* by Derk Bodde. Copyright © 1957 by Derk Bodde. From p. 188 in *The Quest for a Principal Authority in Europe, 1715–Present* by Thomas G. Mendenhall, Basil O. Henning, and Archibald S. Foord. Copyright 1948 by Holt, Rinehart and Winston, Inc. *Houghton Mifflin Company:* From pp. 15–16, 72–73, 86, 98, 218, 261, 352–353, 412–413 in *Sources of the Western Tradition, Vol. I: From Ancient Times to the Enlightenment* by Perry, Peden and Von Laue. Copyright © 1987 by Houghton Mifflin. From p. 180 in *Sources of the Western Tradition, Vol. II: From the Scientific Revolution to the Present* by Perry, Peden and Von Laue. Copyright © 1987 by Houghton Mifflin. *Indiana University Press:* From "The Story of Daedalus and Icarus" in *Metamorphoses* by Ovid, translated by Rolfe Humphries. *Jean Kistler Kendall, Executrix of the Estates of Elizabeth Bothwell Kistler and Jean Bothwell:* From pp. 40–41 in *The Story of India* by Jean Bothwell. Copyright 1952 by Harcourt Brace Jovanovich, Inc. *Alfred A. Knopf, Inc.:* From pp. 80–81 and 220 in *Ten Keys to Latin America* by Frank Tannenbaum. Copyright © 1959 by The American Assembly; copyright © 1960 by the Council on Foreign Relations, Inc; copyright © 1960, 1962 by Frank Tannenbaum. *Longman Group Limited:* From "The Breakneck Speed of Industrialisation" in *Stalin and Stalinism* by Martin McCauley. © 1983 by Longman Group Limited. Table from *The Modern World* by L. E. Snellgrove. © 1984 by Longman Group Limited. *Macmillan Publishing Company:* From *A Short History of the Near East, from the Founding of Constantinople (330 A.D. to 1922)* by William Stearns Davis. Copyright 1922 by the Macmillan Publishing Company, renewed 1953 by Alice R. Davis. From p. 1 in *The Guns of August* by Barbara W. Tuchman. © 1962 by Barbara W. Tuchman. From "Garibaldi's Report on the Conquest of Naples" in *Prologue: A Documentary History of Europe: 1846–1960,* edited by Christine Walsh. Originally published by Cassell, Australia, 1968. *David McKay Company, Inc., a division of Random House, Inc.:* From p. 5 in *Germany and the East-West Crisis: The Decisive Challenge to American Policy* by William S. Schlamm. Copyright © 1959 by William S. Schlamm. *National Geographic Society:* From "La Navidad, 1462: Searching for Columbus's Lost Colony" by Kathleen A. Deagan in *National Geographic Magazine,* November 1987. Copyright © 1987 by National Geographic Society. From "Viking Trail East" by R. P. Jordan in *National Geographic Magazine,* March 1985.   *(Acknowledgments continued on page R63)*

Printed in the United States of America
ISBN   0-15-373458-2

C·O·N·T·E·N·T·S

21

Reforms Swept Through Many Areas of the World in the 1800s *1794–1911* **542**

22

Unification of New Nations Added to Rising Tensions in Europe *1806–1913* **572**

The Great Depression Helped the Rise of Totalitarian Dictators *1919–1936* **664**

New Political Forces Emerged in Africa, Asia, and Latin America *1900–1938* **690**

UNIT SEVEN

*THE WORLD
SINCE 1945* **748**

29

Asian Nations Struggled to Gain Stability   *1945—the present* **774**

30

The Nations of Africa and the Middle East Became Independent   *1945—the present*   **806**

FEATURES

History Through the Arts

Connections: Then and Now

What If?

Building History Study Skills

Reading About History

MAPS

Atlas

CHARTS

Geography and World History: An Introduction

World History: People and Nations focuses on the story of the world's people from the very earliest times to the present. *History* describes the events that make up this story, while *geography* describes the places in which the events take place. History, then, represents the unfolding drama of people and events through the ages. Geography describes the stage on which this drama is played out.

History and geography are so intertwined that to separate them would leave the story only partially told. More than 350 years ago, English historian Peter Heylyn wrote some lines that beautifully describe the interconnection between these two disciplines. The language that Heylyn used was quite different from modern English, yet the message rings as true today as it did in the early 1600s.

> **"** As Geography without History, hath life and motion, but at randome, & unstable: So History without Geography, like a dead carkasse hath neither life nor motion at all &: as the exact notice of the place addeth a satisfactorie delight to the action: so the mention of the action, beautifieth the notice of the place. **"**

Time and Space

Even though history and geography are closely related, they are still two distinct subjects. The basic difference between them may be stated quite simply. As you study history, you acquire an orientation to time; as you study geography, you acquire an orientation to space. Geographers, then, organize their thoughts with respect to spatial arrangements and distributions over the earth's surface. Historians, on the other hand, organize their ideas with respect to time.

Although history is mostly concerned with time, and geography mostly with space, each subject employs aspects of the other as analytical tools. Historians know full well that events occur in place as well as in time. Events, like people, are widely distributed across the earth. In other words, events have a spatial, or geographic, dimension. And geographers, in examining distributions and arrangements throughout the world today, find that they often must look back in time in order to explain these current patterns.

World History: People and Nations tells the story of world history. Geography helps bring this story into focus. Therefore, understanding the special themes and tools of geography will be of great value to you as you read and think about the great personalities and events of the past.

The Five Basic Themes in Geography

Modern geography focuses on five basic themes, or topics: location, place, relationships within places, movement, and regions. Each of these five basic themes helps to clarify the relationship between the world's physical landscape and its human occupants. These relationships, of course, have a time as well as a spatial context.

Location. The first theme, location, has two aspects. Absolute location deals with the exact, or precise, spot on the earth that a place occupies. Relative location, on the other hand, describes the position of a place in relation to other places.

The latitude and longitude of a place best describe its absolute location. To calculate latitude and longitude, geographers use a grid formed by a series of imaginary lines drawn around the earth (see map, this page). The equator, an imaginary line that circles the earth halfway

Lines of latitude and longitude circling the earth

between the North and South poles, divides the earth into two halves, or hemispheres. Geographers call these hemispheres the Northern Hemisphere and the Southern Hemisphere. Several shorter imaginary lines—called parallels, or lines of latitude—circle the earth, parallel to the equator.

Geographers identify different parallels through a special numbering system based on degrees. In the Northern Hemisphere, the parallels number from zero degrees (0°) at the equator to ninety degrees north (90° N) at the North Pole. Similarly, in the Southern Hemisphere they run from 0° at the equator to 90° south (S) at the South Pole.

Another set of imaginary lines, called meridians, or lines of longitude, circle the earth from pole to pole. The prime meridian, which runs through the Royal Observatory, in Greenwich, England, serves as 0° longitude. The meridian directly opposite the prime meridian, on the other side of the globe, is the 180° meridian. The prime meridian and the 180° meridian together divide the earth into the Eastern and Western hemispheres. The Eastern Hemisphere includes the half of the earth that extends east of the prime meridian to the 180° meridian. The Western Hemisphere includes the half of the earth west of the prime meridian to the 180° meridian.

Together, parallels and meridians form an imaginary grid over the earth. Since each degree of latitude and longitude can be broken into 60 minutes ('), and each minute can be broken into 60 seconds ("), the grid fixes the precise location of any place on the earth's surface. For example, Houston, Texas, can be found at 33°46' North and 95°21' West. No other place on earth is located at exactly this same place.

The relative location of a place is often described in terms of direction and distance from another place. Houston's relative location, for example, might be expressed as 1,221 air miles southwest of Washington, D.C. Other ways of describing relative location include nearness to resources and accessibility to trade routes.

Place. The second basic theme of geography, place, grows directly out of location. Every location on earth has its own unique, or distinctive, physical and human characteristics. These physical characteristics include the shape of the land, climate, soils, vegetation, and animal life. Land use, street layout, architecture, and population distribution all constitute a location's human characteristics. Together, these physical and human characteristics make up a location's place identity. This identity changes through time and, therefore, is very important to an understanding of history.

Relationships within places. Throughout time, people have adapted their way of life to accommodate their environment. For example, people who live in hot climates often use pungent spices in their cooking. These spices cover the rancid taste of meat, which quickly becomes tainted in hot weather. People also have made changes to their physical environment. They have cleared forests, dug irrigation ditches, and built huge cities. Geographers define relationships within places as all the ways in which people interact with their natural environment.

The theme of relationships within places is of great importance to historians, for it includes not only how people interact with their physical surroundings but also the consequences of such interactions. For example, the decision to mine and use fossil fuels to produce energy had the negative consequence of polluting the environment. This con-

Tea fields in Sri Lanka

sequence, in turn, gave rise to a movement to protect the environment. Such movements are of great interest to historians.

Movement. The fourth theme of modern geography, movement, concerns the interactions of people with one another as they travel, communicate, and exchange goods and services on a worldwide basis. Movement also includes an examination of the spread of ideas and the great human migrations that have occurred through the centuries—two vital themes in the study of history.

Regions. In order to better study and understand the earth, geographers divide it into smaller units called regions. The fifth theme of geography concerns these regions. Geographical regions vary in size from those that cover an entire continent to those that include only a small part of a city, such as its retail shopping area. The particular features that characterize a region set it apart from other regions. A vast number of different characteristics may be used to define the regions of the world. As a result, any given area might be part of a great number of regions, and the boundaries of one region might overlap the boundaries of others. To make the study of regions less complex, however, the defining characteristics used include such physical features as climate or vegetation and such cultural features as economic activities or dominant religion or language.

Skyline of Houston, Texas

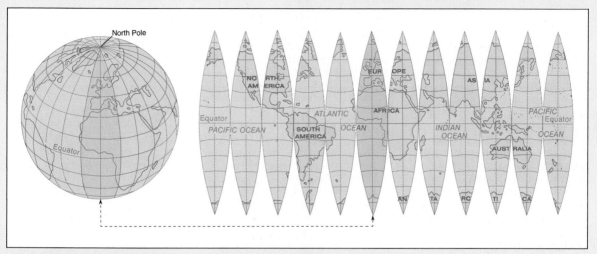

North Pole

Equator

Equator

NORTH AMERICA

EUROPE

ASIA

ATLANTIC OCEAN

AFRICA

PACIFIC OCEAN

PACIFIC OCEAN

SOUTH AMERICA

OCEAN

INDIAN OCEAN

Equator

AUSTRALIA

The making of a map projection

The Tools of Geography

To develop these five basic themes, geographers use a wide variety of tools. These tools include such modern and sophisticated items as aerial photographs, satellite images, and extremely intricate computer programs. However, the geographers' most basic and essential tools—globes and maps—have been used for centuries. Globes and maps, of course, are very familiar objects. Undoubtedly you have seen them in your classroom or school library and, perhaps, even in your home. Nevertheless, globes and maps are essential to the study of geography because they provide fairly accurate representations of the earth. However, globes and maps are not perfect models of the earth, and each has advantages and disadvantages as a geographical tool.

The most important advantage of a globe is its shape. It is the only model of the earth that is spherical like the earth. Because a globe's shape follows the spherical shape of the earth, the landmasses and bodies of water shown on it are correct in terms of shape and area. A globe also accurately shows distance and direction from one place to another.

In spite of its accuracy, the globe has some limitations. To begin with, a globe is bulky and awkward to carry. In addition, it makes it impossible to see the entire earth at once. For example, if you focus on South America, Australia is hidden from your view. When you turn the globe to find Australia, South America disappears. A globe's greatest problem, however, is that it lacks detail. Even the largest globes could not show the detailed features of the ancient Nile Valley. There would be no way to indicate the location of each of the 80 or more pyramids, the huge stone figure of the Sphinx, or the thousands of irrigation channels and reservoirs used by the farmers of the region.

In contrast, the intricate details shown on maps make them useful to geographers. Through the use of symbols and colors, a huge range of information can be shown clearly on a map. By comparing maps, geographers can see movements, relationships within places, and the locations of various physical and cultural regions. In addition, maps are far more manageable than globes. They can be rolled or folded and, therefore, are easy to carry.

Yet maps do have one serious drawback—they are never totally accurate. Regardless of the skill of the cartographer, or mapmaker, no map can accurately show the qualities of shape, area, distance, and direction at the same time. This is because mapmaking involves the difficult task of transferring the curved surface of the earth onto a flat piece of paper (see map, this page).

To appreciate the problems faced by cartographers, place a piece of paper directly over one of the Great Lakes of North America on a globe. Now trace the outline of the lake onto your paper. You should be able to trace its outline accurately without once bending or twisting your paper. Next, try tracing the outline of the entire North American continent. You can see immediately that some cutting or folding of the paper is required. Otherwise, you are going to have to drastically distort the outline of the continent. Yet in cutting or folding the map, you create other distortions.

Distortion, then, is a major problem for cartographers when transferring large areas of the earth's curved surface onto a flat map. Since maps cannot accurately show all four map qualities—shape, area, distance, and direction—at the same time, cartographers must decide which quality they want their maps to distort least. A variety of projections—methods by which the earth's surface is transferred, or projected, onto paper to create flat maps—enables them to do this.

Map Projections

Literally thousands of map projections exist. Each one distorts one or more of the four major map qualities. The projection that a cartographer chooses depends on the size and location of the area being projected and on the purpose of the map.

Cartographers often choose the Robinson projection (see map, right). The Robinson projection is unique because it is a compromise projection. It maintains no single property but minimizes overall distortion.

If true shape is the most important objective of the cartographer, he or she will select a conformal projection, such as the Mercator projection (see map, below). On a map using such a projection, the shapes of the land and water areas conform to, or look like, the shapes shown on a globe. If the purpose of the map is to show correct relative area, an equal-area projection, such as the Molleweide projection (see map, page xxix) or the Peters projection

The Robinson projection

The Mercator projection

(see map, below), will be used. Maps using projections that show correct distances between places are called equidistant maps. Equidistant maps work well for projecting areas of limited size, such as a city or a state. There is no way, however, that maps of the entire world can be equidistant, because it is impossible to show the lengths of lines of latitude and longitude on a flat map as accurately as they appear on a globe. Finally, maps using projections that show accurate compass directions are called azimuthal maps (see map at the bottom of this page).

The Molleweide projection

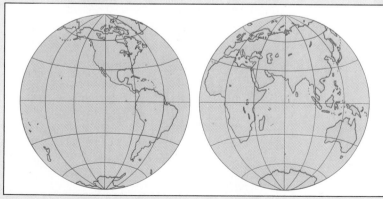

The Peters projection (top) and an azimuthal projection (bottom)

If you think about the types of projections described in the paragraphs above, you may see how and why each of them is used. Many people like to use a conformal map, for example, because the shapes of the continents and oceans look familiar and are, therefore, easy to recognize. Unfortunately, conformal maps often greatly distort distance and area.

Equal-area maps, on the other hand, are especially useful for comparing factors that may be affected by an area's size, such as temperature patterns, population size, or mineral production. The greatest drawback of equal-area maps is that they distort the shapes of the areas shown.

Equidistant projections are used for road maps because they allow the driver to get a clear and accurate picture of the distances to be traveled. Azimuthal maps, in contrast, are especially useful to navigators who must plot their courses along exact compass directions.

In spite of their drawbacks, then, there is indeed a map projection to meet every need. In studying maps, however, always remember to note the type of projection being used so that you will be aware of exactly how it is different from a globe, the one precise model of the earth. To aid you in this task, each of the maps in this book identifies the map projection being used.

LINKING PAST TO PRESENT

As you study the photographs on pages xxx-xxxvii of this Linking Past to Present feature, think of how understanding what went on thousands of years ago will help you understand the world today.

Photos: 1. Renaissance festival in Italy
2. concert for human rights in Los Angeles
3. opening ceremonies at the 1980 Winter Olympics in Lake Placid, New York
4. college football game
5. early baseball game
6. festival in Chile
7. Sudanese dancers
8. Nigerian wedding festival
9. Alvin Ailey dancers perform Orozo
10. Indian at the Inca Sun Festival in Peru
11. traditional stylized No drama in Japan
12. Mardi Gras celebration in Venice
13. Kabuki performance in modern-day Japan

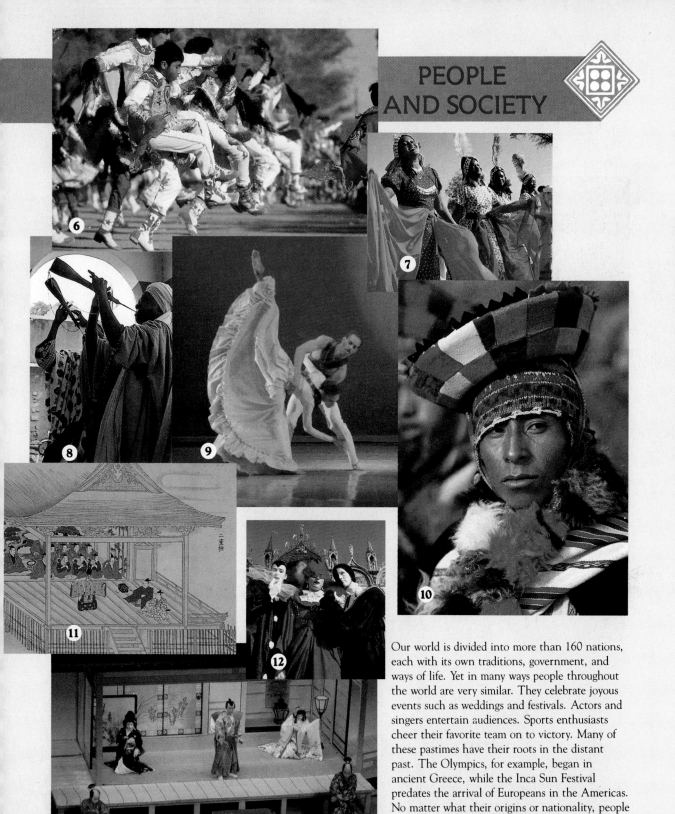

6

7

8

9

10

11

12

13

Our world is divided into more than 160 nations, each with its own traditions, government, and ways of life. Yet in many ways people throughout the world are very similar. They celebrate joyous events such as weddings and festivals. Actors and singers entertain audiences. Sports enthusiasts cheer their favorite team on to victory. Many of these pastimes have their roots in the distant past. The Olympics, for example, began in ancient Greece, while the Inca Sun Festival predates the arrival of Europeans in the Americas. No matter what their origins or nationality, people value their traditions—traditions that have their roots in thousands of years of history.

SCIENCE AND TECHNOLOGY

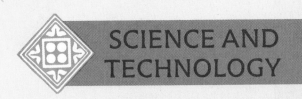

Photos: 1. underwater research vessel
2. Apollo moon landing
3. Formula 1 racing car
4. Arab dhow
5. medieval astronomer
6. microchips on a silicon wafer
7. bacteriologist Robert Koch
8. laser beam
9. reading a CAT scan
10. chemist Marie Curie

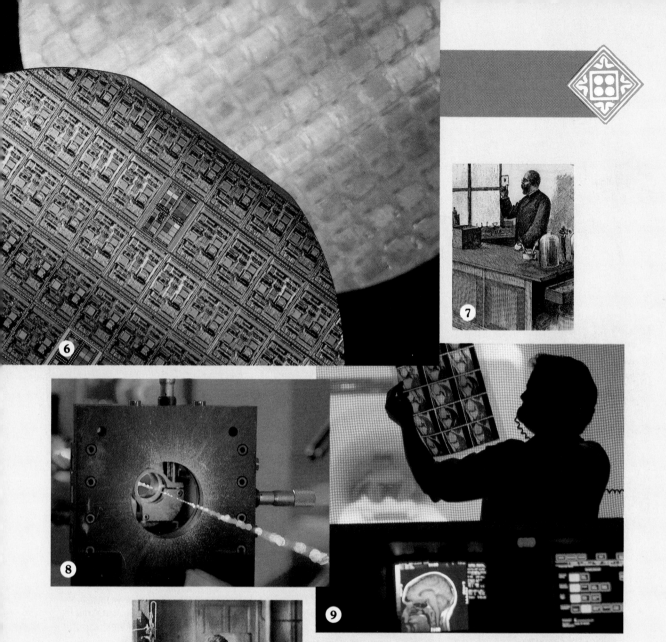

The last 30 years have seen many technological innovations and scientific discoveries. Although these developments seem special because they took place during our or our parents' lifetimes, they are but steps in a process that began thousands of years ago. The principles used to build a dhow helped to design the sleek lines of a Formula 1 racing car. And the space missions and explorations of the ocean floor had their beginnings in the work of the early astronomers who first began to chart the relationship between our world and the rest of the universe.

In the field of medicine, developments in the diagnosis and treatment of disease, such as the CAT scan and the laser, are part of a long history of medical innovation that includes such pioneers as Marie Curie and Robert Koch. Technological wonders like the microchip hold promise of even greater, more exciting, scientific and medical developments in the future.

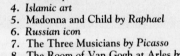

Photos: 1. *Japanese painting*
2. *prehistoric cave painting*
3. *Chinese print*
4. *Islamic art*
5. Madonna and Child *by Raphael*
6. *Russian icon*
7. The Three Musicians *by Picasso*
8. The Room of Van Gogh at Arles *by Van Gogh*; 9. *the Sphinx*
10. *Transamerica Building*
11. *Buddhist temple*; 12. *Chartres Cathedral*
13. *African mask*; 14. *Chinese carving*
15. *Picasso sculpture*
16. Pieta *by Michelangelo*

9

11

From the beginnings of time people have used art to express themselves. And in many cases, artists have drawn upon inspirations from the past as they crafted new works of art. The Transamerica Building in San Francisco, for example, reflects the towering elegance of the pyramids of ancient Egypt. A modern Picasso sculpture reflects the majesty of the Sphinx. A madonna by Raphael deals with the same subject as a pieta by Michelangelo and a Russian icon. In other ways, however, the art of a society reflects that society's unique contributions and ways of life and helps us understand societies at various points in time and place.

10

12

13

14

15

16

CUSTOMS AND BELIEFS

Photos: 1. Buddhist temple in Gansu, China
2. Hindu festival in India
3. Native American children at festival
4. Shinto priests in Japan
5. Muslim praying at mosque in Afghanistan
6. Jewish bar mitzvah at the Wailing Wall in Jerusalem
7. Easter procession in Guatemala
8. Jerusalem, a holy city to Muslims, Jews, and Christians
9. Protestant service at Christmas

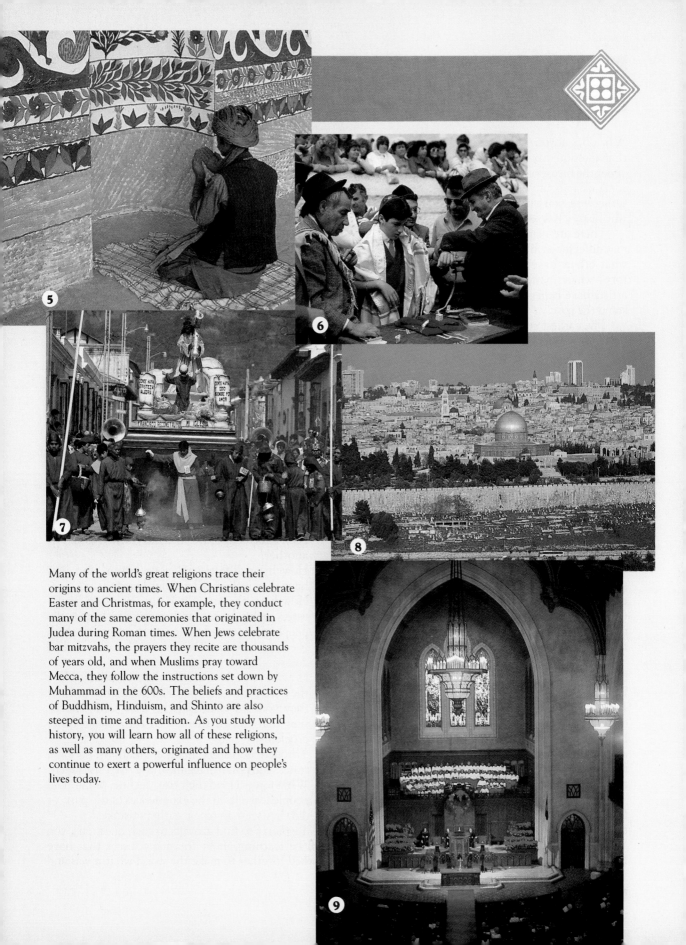

Many of the world's great religions trace their origins to ancient times. When Christians celebrate Easter and Christmas, for example, they conduct many of the same ceremonies that originated in Judea during Roman times. When Jews celebrate bar mitzvahs, the prayers they recite are thousands of years old, and when Muslims pray toward Mecca, they follow the instructions set down by Muhammad in the 600s. The beliefs and practices of Buddhism, Hinduism, and Shinto are also steeped in time and tradition. As you study world history, you will learn how all of these religions, as well as many others, originated and how they continue to exert a powerful influence on people's lives today.

Why does anyone bother to study history? Asking that question may seem a strange way to start a book about the history of the world, but you ought to have some idea about possible answers before you begin. Otherwise, you will have no idea what to look for, or why history has seemed important to all peoples.

There are many answers to the question. They may differ for each person. It is useful, though, to see what others have thought about the value of history—why so many writers, politicians, teachers, and artists have believed that it is important to understand the past.

The earliest audience for history consisted simply of people who liked a good story. The two words, story and history, are essentially the same, and the appeal of history for many was that it brought to life real people and events, rather than invented ones. Before long, though, these real-life stories came to have a moral purpose—they taught lessons about how one should behave. The brave and the good usually succeeded; the cowardly or evil did not.

History was also considered important because it could explain—even without moral teachings—how or why things turned out as they did. It could show how a war happened, why one side won, and what the results were. By studying the past, people could thus learn what mistakes to avoid and what good examples to follow.

Finally, history came to be seen as a way of understanding ourselves and our own world. We cannot understand why Americans place such faith in their Constitution, why Islam is so important to Iranians, or why the Chinese think their revolution is still continuing, if we do not understand their history.

These different reasons for studying the past can be contradictory. Someone who looks for the moral lessons of history may not reach the same conclusions as someone who wants to explain the success of certain policies. Sometimes, for example, immoral behavior has proved successful. The historian has to assess these matters, try to reach conclusions about them, and thus determine their significance for our times.

As you read this book, think of yourself as a historian. Try to figure out why some people or events of the past seem more interesting to you than others. What do they tell you about yourself and your times? By keeping such questions in mind, you will be able to form your own answer about the reasons for studying history.

It may also help you to realize that a number of powerful forces have helped shape history in all periods. If you read thoughtfully and critically, you can learn what these forces are by asking yourself questions like these:

1. How has geography influenced the course of history? Have people simply adjusted to their environment, or have they tried to modify it?
2. How have people worked and earned their living? In other words, how have they organized their economy? What roles have farming, trade, and manufacturing played? How has income been distributed?
3. How have people been governed? Has political power been held by a few, or by many? Have individuals had rights and liberties? How have rights and liberties been gained, protected, or lost? In what way were laws made and enforced? How have they worked in practice, and for whose benefit? Why and how have people changed their form of government?
4. How have people gained knowledge, and how have they passed it on to their descendants? Have they had a formal system of education? Who has been educated? Have societies learned from one another?
5. How have different religions arisen, and how have they influenced people's lives?
6. How have the arts—literature, painting, sculpture, architecture, and music—reflected the people who created them and the times in which they were produced? What arts have flourished and why?
7. How have nations settled their conflicts? Have they tried to reach peaceful solutions, or have they gone to war? Did the wars settle the issues that caused them? Did they create other problems?
8. Throughout history, many civilizations, national states, and political regimes have risen and fallen. What forces led to their rise, decline, or fall? Did people learn from the experiences of the past, or did they seem to repeat earlier mistakes?

If you try to find answers to such questions, you will be learning about the many forces that have worked together to make the world what it was and what it is. You will learn about the power of ideas, such as the belief that every human being has worth and dignity that must be respected. You can watch ideas like this appear, develop gradually, become strong, and finally be accepted by enough people to be put into practice. You will see other ideas decline and die out.

People have been pondering questions and ideas like these since earliest times. As you seek your own answers, you will be discovering what kind of person you are and want to be; you will be shaping your own role in the world of the future.

World History: People and Nations has been organized to help you seek the answers to these many questions.

Units. There are seven units, which group the chapters into broad historical periods. Each unit opens with a large illustration, symbolizing its contents, and with a list of the chapters it contains. Each chapter title is accompanied by the dates covered in the chapter so that you will easily recognize the time period. (See, for example, page 1.)

Unit Syntheses. Each unit of *World History: People and Nations* concludes with a six-page Unit Synthesis that highlights the major themes of the unit. You may use these syntheses to preview a unit or as a quick review before taking the unit test. (See pages 92–97.)

Chapters. The 33 chapters of *World History: People and Nations* are organized around definite periods or topics. Like the units, each begins with a single illustration symbolic of its contents. Above the illustration is a map of the world that locates the area or areas discussed in the chapter. The **Chapter Focus** allows you to briefly understand the place, time, and significance of what you are about to study and lists important terms, people, and places that you will be studying. The **Chapter Focus** concludes with a series of questions designed to guide your reading. (See pages 2–3.)

Chapter Sections. A chapter may contain from two to six sections, each numbered. At the end of each section is a **Section Review** to help you review and check your understanding of the material you have just read. (See page 13.)

Chapter Reviews. Every chapter ends with a two-page review. First there is a **Time Line,** which presents in graphic form the most important events—with their dates—discussed in the chapter.

It is followed by a **Chapter Summary,** which traces the main ideas of the chapter. The questions, activities, and research projects that complete the Chapter Review are divided into six parts: **Reviewing Important Terms, Developing Critical Thinking Skills, Relating Geography to History, Relating Past to Present, Applying History Study Skills,** and **Investigating Further.** (See pages 14–15.)

Unit Reviews. Each of the seven units ends with a two-page **Unit Review.** Here you will find a number of questions that will help you review what you learned in the unit. (See pages 90–91.)

Graphics. The 123 maps will give you the location of every place mentioned in the text as well as show you topography, the size of empires, the thrust of invasions, and the extent of alliances. Each map is placed as close as possible to the relevant text. (See page 18.) Important sequences of events or ideas are summarized in chart form. (See page 43.) The hundreds of illustrations show you how people and places looked throughout the history of the world.

Features. You will find six kinds of special features running throughout the book. Combining text and illustrations, they will give you additional insights into world history:

- **Building History Study Skills** Each of the 33 chapters includes a skill lesson designed to help you master a specific skill. (See page 12.)
- **History Through the Arts** is a series of 50 illustrated features that reveal how civilizations are reflected in their arts and literature. (See page 23.)
- **Connections: Then and Now** is a series of 18 illustrated essays that relate past to present by showing how familiar customs and traditions have existed throughout history. (See page 25.)
- **What If?** is a series of 15 features designed to stimulate discussion and to develop critical thinking skills. (See page 38.)
- **Perspectives: Legacies of the Past** is a series of seven two-page features that trace specific developments or concepts through time and analyze how these developments or concepts affect our lives today. (See pages 40–41.)
- **Linking Geography to History** is a series of eight features designed to build your understanding of geography. (See page 44.)

Reference Section. The **Reference Section** at the back of the book includes an **Atlas,** a **Glossary,** and an **Index.**

The Beginnings of Civilization

◀ *Egyptian wall painting in Luxor*   1

1

Cultures and Civilizations Began in Prehistoric Times

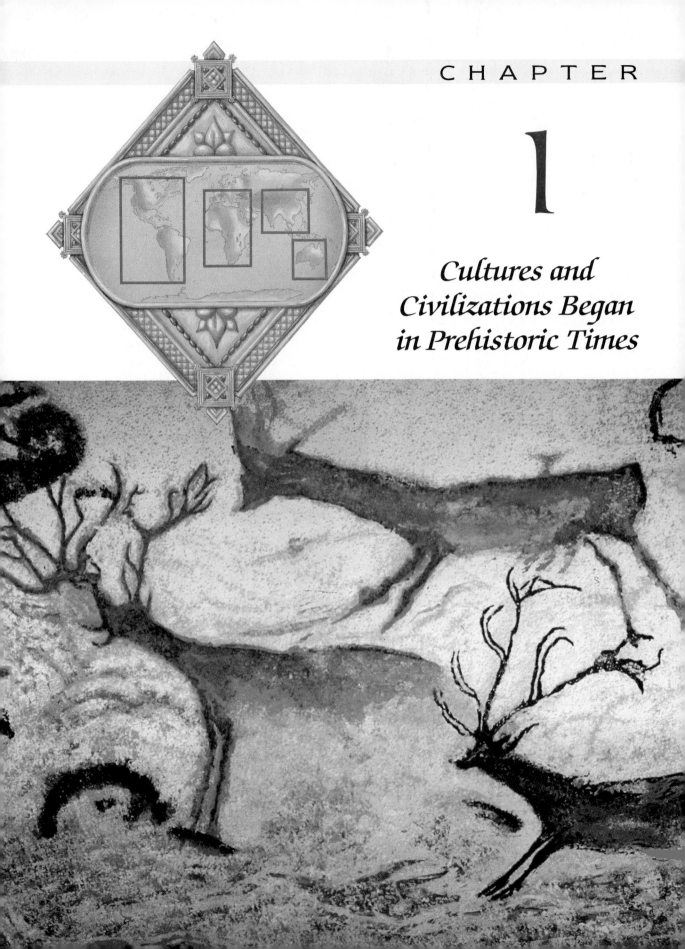

Place   Africa, Asia, Europe, the Americas, and Australia

Time   ca.*3,700,000 B.C.—1200 B.C.

3.7 mil. BC   4000 BC   AD 2100

Significance

This book deals primarily with **history**—the record of events since people first developed writing, about 5,000 years ago. Writing allowed people to leave permanent information, facts, descriptions, opinions, ideas, and literature. But evidence indicates that people lived on earth long before the development of writing, during the period known as **prehistory.**

Since we have no written records of prehistoric times, many of the events of that remote past remain cloaked in mystery. Nevertheless, we know that the lives of prehistoric people resembled ours in several important ways. For example, prehistoric people invented tools, produced beautiful art, built cities, and developed forms of government. They gradually created what we call **civilizations**—highly organized societies with complex institutions and attitudes that link a large number of people together.

With civilizations came the first forms of writing and thus the end of prehistory. Our main story, the story of history, could begin.

Terms to Define

history	culture
prehistory	migrate
civilization	glacier
anthropologist	agriculture
archaeologist	nomad
artifact	irrigation

People to Identify

Mary Leakey   Donald C. Johanson

Places to Locate

Laetoli	Nile River
Neander Valley	Tigris River
Jarmo	Euphrates River
Çatal Hüyük	Indus River

Questions to Guide Your Reading

1 What important discoveries did prehistoric people make?
2 In what great river valleys did civilization first develop?

*ca. stands for *circa* and means "about."

In 1978 in a remote, almost inaccessible region of northern Tanzania, the noted scientist Mary D. Leakey made a remarkable discovery. As she stared down into the rugged terrain, she was amazed to see that a simple series of footprints lay imbedded in the volcanic rock. What fascinated her was that these footprints had not been left earlier that day or even earlier that week. Instead, they were millions of years old. Made in the soft ash of a volcanic eruption, the prints had been preserved as the ash had hardened.

Although we will never know exactly who made these prints, Leakey believes that they belonged to one of the humanlike creatures who, according to her theory, preceded us on earth.

*❝*F*ollowing the path produces, at least for me, a kind of poignant time wrench. At one point, and you need not be an expert tracker to discern this, the traveler stops, pauses, turns to the left to glance at some possible threat or irregularity, then continues to the north. This motion, so intensely human, transcends time. Three million seven hundred thousand years ago, a remote ancestor—just as you or I—experienced a moment of doubt.* ❞

Leakey is only one of many dedicated scholars who have tried to piece together the distant past.

1 Prehistoric People Made Important Discoveries

How can we learn anything about what happened on the earth before people learned to keep written records? Surprisingly enough, we can find out a great deal.

Examining Prehistory

Researchers called **anthropologists** (an • thruh • PAHL • uh • jists) and **archaeologists** (ahr • kee • AHL • uh • jists) have discovered many things about prehistory, often by using scientific methods. Anthropologists study the skeletal remains of early humanlike creatures and people to determine how they looked, how long they lived, and other physical characteristics. Archaeologists excavate ancient settlements and study **artifacts**—material objects

◀ *Animal painting from Lascaux Cave in France*

shaped by human beings. Examples of artifacts include buildings, furniture, clothing, tools, weapons, works of art, coins, and toys. By studying these objects, archaeologists can piece together information on the cultures of early people. **Culture** is what a human group acquires through living together, and includes language, knowledge, skills, art, literature, law, and life styles.

To assign a date to prehistoric remains, scientists use a variety of scientific techniques, including **radiocarbon dating.** Each living thing contains radiocarbon atoms that begin to decay when the organism dies. Radiocarbon dating measures the rate of this decay for organic matter up to about 100,000 years old. For remains more than 100,000 years old, scientists usually use other methods that record the rate of decay of certain key elements and compounds. For example, the *amino acid racemization* method can be used to date items up to 1 million years old.

Despite these sophisticated methods, scientists still must rely on guesses. However, scientists usually are quite confident about the conclusions they reach. They can tell us when important changes took place thousands of years ago. They can also describe some of the ways the first human beings spent their lives.

Learning from Pictures   In Egypt an archaeologist traces an artifact for further study. What methods do archaeologists use to date prehistoric remains?

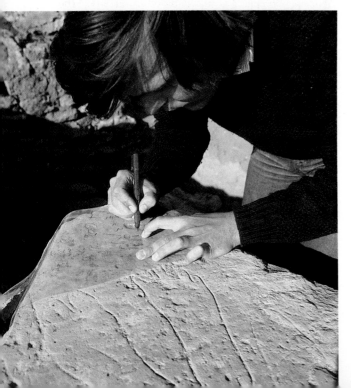

Early Humanlike Creatures

Anthropologists now know that humanlike creatures appeared on the earth millions of years ago. That period of prehistory is called the Old Stone Age, or Paleolithic (pay • lee • oh • LITH • ik) Age. The word *paleolithic* comes from the Greek words *palaios,* meaning "old," and *lithos,* meaning "stone." We call this period the Stone Age because almost all of the artifacts that have survived were made of stone.

In 1974 in Ethiopia, anthropologist Donald C. Johanson discovered female skeletal remains that may be 3 million years old. Although Johanson named his find Australopithecus (aw • struh • loh • PITH • uh • kuhs), the skeleton became known as "Lucy," after the Beatles' song "Lucy in the Sky with Diamonds," which was popular at the time of the discovery.

After examining the bones found at the excavation site, particularly fragments of her leg and foot, Johanson concluded that Lucy walked on two legs. In 1978 at Laetoli (lay • TOH • lee) in Tanzania (tan • zuh • NEE • uh), Mary Leakey unearthed the skeletons of other Australopithecines dating back 3.7 million years. These creatures also walked on two legs.

Creatures similar to the Australopithecines lived in eastern Africa 2 million years ago. In 1986, for example, Donald Johanson discovered the skeleton of a female who probably lived about 1.8 million years ago in Olduvai (OHL • duh • way) Gorge in Tanzania. Scientists also uncovered tools made of chipped stone when they found the bones.

Anthropologists are still not certain whether a relationship exists between these Australopithecines and the humans of today. But many believe that upright posture and the ability to make tools occurred very early in human development.

The First People

Despite the many findings of anthropologists, knowledge of early humans and of the humanlike creatures that preceded them on earth millions of years ago is based on fragmentary remains. Because these remains are very difficult to study, scientists often disagree on the significance of the bones and other materials found at excavation sites. Future discoveries may lead to theories different from those commonly held today.

Anthropologists have used the excavated bones to describe how the first people looked. These individuals were very strong and had powerful jaws, sharply receding chins, low foreheads, and heavy eyebrow ridges.

Scientists believe these early people sometimes used caves as shelters and probably ate vegetables and gathered seeds, fruits, nuts, and other edible plants. Later, people added meat to their diets as they began to hunt small animals. Eventually, humans hunted large animals. In order to hunt successfully, people had to work together, communicate with one another, and make tools. Inquiring minds—and hands freed by an upright posture—helped make these developments possible.

As humans became successful hunters, they moved, or **migrated,** over great distances in search of food. Their populations expanded from Africa to Asia. Paleolithic people lived in Asia as early as 1 to 1.5 million years ago. Archaeologists discovered the remains of prehistoric people on the Indonesian island of Java in 1891 and near Beijing (BAY • JING), China, in 1929. Scientists named these people Java people and Beijing people.

More recently, scientists have discovered the remains of Paleolithic people in other parts of Asia as well as in Europe and Africa. For thousands of years, however, periods of extremely cold weather limited the areas to which early people could migrate.

The Ice Age

Extremes of climate have greatly influenced human history and the history of the earth itself. Four times within the last 1.5 million years, the earth has had periods of extremely cold weather. Each time, the northern polar icecap (a permanent ice sheet near the North Pole) moved south and joined **glaciers**—large, slowly moving masses of snow and ice—that formed in the mountain ranges. Each of these four cold-weather periods lasted from 10,000 to 50,000 years. Together they are known as the **Ice Age.** Scientists believe that we now live in a warm era that began after the fourth period of the Ice Age, which ended between 10,000 and 25,000 years ago.

It is difficult to imagine the vastness of the great ice sheets of the Ice Age. Today ice covers about one-twelfth of the earth's land surface. During the third and longest period of the Ice Age, ice covered about one-third of the earth's surface. In some places the ice was several miles thick. Large areas of northern North America, Europe, and Asia lay engulfed in ice.

The Ice Age affected the earth in various ways. Some humans and animals migrated to warmer, ice-free areas. Many kinds of animals and plants disappeared completely. The grinding, chiseling effect of the moving ice changed the surface of the earth greatly. While ice covered much of the northern half of the earth, the rest of the earth received unusually large amounts of rainfall. Rivers and lakes rose. Inland seas formed. Former desert regions began to produce vegetation and support animal life.

On the other hand, the sea level dropped because so much water was frozen in the icecaps. As the sea level fell, underwater ridges became uncovered and formed "land bridges." These bridges linked certain continents and islands that are today separated by water. To escape the ice, many people and animals walked over some of these land bridges.

The icecap and glaciers gradually melted between glacial advances. Only when prehistoric peoples learned to use fire and craft warm clothing could they successfully settle in the colder regions of the earth.

Neanderthal People

In caves located in many parts of Europe, the Middle East, and Asia, anthropologists have found the remains of the Neanderthal (nee • AN • duhr • thawl) people—humans who lived some 30,000 to 100,000 years ago. These people were named after the Neander Valley in Germany, where Neanderthal remains were first found in 1856. Neanderthal skulls reveal that these people had powerful builds, heavy jaws, thick eyebrow ridges, and large noses.

Neanderthal people made more efficient tools than did the humans who preceded them. They lived in caves, wore clothing made of animal skins, and used fire.

Since the Neanderthals lived in cold regions, some anthropologists believe they were the first people to cook food. According to this theory, Neanderthals placed frozen meat on hot coals to thaw. When they discovered that the cooked meat tasted better than raw meat, they adopted cooking.

Neanderthal people differed from earlier humans in another very significant way—they buried their dead. What is more, they buried them with tools, weapons, and even food. Many scientists believe this practice shows that the Neanderthals expected these items to be useful to the dead person after his or her death. If the theories of these scientists are correct, this practice shows a belief in some form of life after death—a belief basic to many of the world's religions. Perhaps the Neanderthals were the first people to believe in a god or gods.

Many scientists also think that the Neanderthals nursed their sick instead of abandoning them to die as earlier humans apparently did. One Neanderthal skeleton is that of a man who was about 40 years old. Analyses of this skeleton show that the man suffered from severe arthritis and had lost most of his teeth. It would have been almost impossible for him to survive unless someone had cared for him.

Like earlier humans, Neanderthal people disappeared. We do not know why. Massive glaciers had again advanced southward and covered much of Europe and North America, and Neanderthal people may have perished because of the cold, hostile environment. Perhaps physically stronger or more mentally alert people overwhelmed and destroyed the Neanderthals.

Learning from Maps This map indicates where remains of prehistoric people have been discovered. In what four river valleys did prehistoric people settle?

Civilization in East Asia Reached New Heights   100–1644   **274**

Africa and the Americas Produced Complex Civilizations   1800 B.C.–A.D. 1500   **292**

Prehistoric Ivory Head

A Cro-Magnon artist carved this ivory head of a woman about 20,000 years ago, during the Old Stone Age. Found in France, it is small enough to hold in the palm of your hand. From works like this, we learn that some prehistoric peoples had an appreciation of beauty similar to our own. Such artifacts also tell us that some prehistoric groups had time for activities other than looking for food and making tools. This carving is one of the earliest known attempts to create a portrait. It may have been an object of worship that the owner could easily carry from place to place as he or she searched for food.

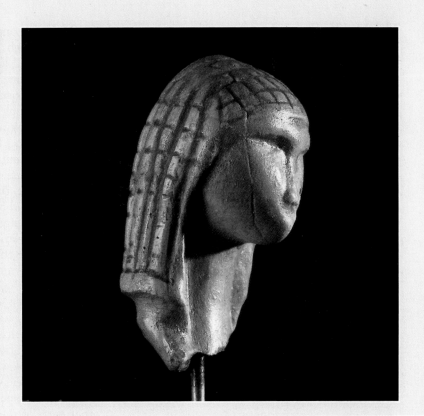

Cro-Magnon People

At just about the time Neanderthal people disappeared—some 30,000 to 35,000 years ago—a new kind of people appeared in Europe, perhaps having come from Africa or Asia. These new people were better equipped to survive than Neanderthal people were, for the new arrivals made better tools and weapons. Their invention of the spear, for example, made them more effective hunters. This new group of humans—Cro-Magnon people—are named for a cave in southern France where remains were first found in 1868 (see map, page 6).

By 20,000 years ago, humans had migrated to northeastern Europe, northern Asia, North America, and Australia. Scientists theorize that people crossed land bridges to reach the Americas and Australia.

We know much more about Cro-Magnon people than we do about any of the other early humans. For one thing, more Cro-Magnon remains have been found. Then, too, the Cro-Magnons themselves have "told" us more about themselves. They could not write, but they could draw and paint and were probably the first real artists. In Spain and southern France where Cro-Magnon people lived, paintings of the animals they hunted cover the walls of caves. There, in limestone caverns, hundreds of feet from the entrance, we can see paintings of bulls tossing their heads, wounded bison charging a hunter, herds of fleeing reindeer, and schools of swimming salmon and trout. Paintings of red and black horses six feet (1.8 meters) long leap majestically out of the darkness. And faint drawings of human hands and faces appear and disappear depending on the angle of light.

Scientists are uncertain about why the Cro-Magnons created these artworks. The art may have been a chronicle of the hunt or a means not only of teaching hunting techniques to the younger people but also of passing on tales about how the world began and how people and animals were created.

With high foreheads, well-defined chins, and small brow ridges, Cro-Magnon people looked almost the same as men and women living today. The Cro-Magnons lived on earth for many thousands of years. By the end of the Old Stone Age, however, the Cro-Magnon as a distinct type of people no longer existed. In appearance, people had become as they are today.

The Middle Stone Age

The period lasting from the end of the last Ice Age until the development of **agriculture,** or the raising of crops for food, is called the Middle Stone Age. Since people in different parts of the world developed agriculture at different times, the dates of the Middle Stone Age vary according to region. For example, the Middle Stone Age lasted from about 12,000 to about 10,000 years ago in Africa and Asia. In most of northern Europe, however, the era lasted until about 5,000 years ago. The era is also often called the Mesolithic Age, from the Greek words *mesos,* meaning "middle," and *lithos,* meaning "stone."

People made much progress during this short period. They **domesticated,** or tamed, the goat as a source of milk and meat. They also domesticated the dog, which proved valuable in hunting smaller animals. They invented the bow and arrow, as well as fishhooks, fish spears, and harpoons made from bones and antlers. By hollowing out logs, they made dugout canoes so that they could fish in deep water and cross rivers.

The New Stone Age

About 10,000 years ago, in certain parts of the world, basic changes occurred in the way people lived. The period that began then is called the New Stone Age, or Neolithic Age. Its scientific name comes from the Greek words *neos,* meaning "new," and *lithos,* meaning "stone."

In the Old Stone Age and Middle Stone Age, people chipped stone to produce an edge or a point. In the New Stone Age, people discovered a better way to make tools and weapons. They learned how to use a flat piece of sandstone to polish stones to a fine edge or a sharp point. They learned to make tools from wood and from many kinds of stone. With these new methods and materials, they could make special tools—awls, wedges, saws, drills, chisels, and needles.

But other far more important changes occurred during the New Stone Age. Earlier people had been **nomads,** or wanderers who travel from place to place in search of food. Neolithic people, however, began settling in permanent villages because of two important developments: (1) the taming of several additional kinds of animals, and (2) the development of agriculture.

Paleolithic and Mesolithic hunters never knew whether enough food would be available. They might have bad luck in hunting, or animals might starve or migrate. The food supply became much more certain once people domesticated animals. Mesolithic people had tamed dogs and goats, but Neolithic people also learned to raise cattle, horses, sheep, and pigs. They used the flesh of these animals for food and the hides for clothing.

The greatest advance Neolithic people made was agriculture, though exactly how people learned that seeds could be planted and made to grow year after year remains a mystery. In prehistoric times men went out in search of animals, while women remained near the campsite to care for the children. Women and children gathered plants and fruit from nearby areas for food. Perhaps a woman first noticed that seeds could be planted and grown. In any case, people somehow learned to plant wheat, barley, rice, and millet, a grass cultivated for grain. They also learned to use fertilizer and invented the plow.

Certain areas of the world became centers from which new domesticated plant species spread to other parts of the world. Wheat and barley originated in the Middle East, rice developed in southwestern Asia, and corn was first cultivated in the Americas. Other domesticated plants included bananas and yams in Southeast Asia and potatoes in South America.

The important shift from food gathering to food producing has often been called the **Neolithic Revolution.** (Although the word *revolution* is most often used to mean the overthrow of a government, it may also mean a very important change in people's lives.)

Having new sources of food permitted Neolithic people to build homes and settle permanently in one region. By 9,000 years ago, agricultural villages numbering up to about 200 inhabitants dotted the hills and valleys of many parts of the world. In Iraq, for example, archaeologists have unearthed the remains of a town called Jarmo that existed about 8,750 years ago. And in Turkey, scientists have excavated Çatal Hüyük (chah·TUHL hoo·YOOK), a town that had almost 3,000 residents 8,000 years ago. Evidence shows that the people of Çatal Hüyük built shrines to many gods and probably offered them food and other forms of wealth to win their favor or to express gratitude for past favors.

Learning from Pictures
Archaeologists discovered
kitchen utensils (right) in
the burial mounds (far
right) of Çatal Hüyük.

SECTION 1 REVIEW

1. **Define** history, prehistory, civilization, anthropologist, archaeologist, artifact, culture, radiocarbon dating, migrate, glacier, Ice Age, agriculture, domesticate, nomad, Neolithic Revolution
2. **Identify** Mary Leakey, Donald C. Johanson
3. **Locate** Laetoli, Neander Valley, Jarmo, Çatal Hüyük
4. **Understanding Ideas** What evidence left by prehistoric people tells us about their daily life?
5. **Identifying Ideas** List the advances made in the following periods: **(a)** Paleolithic, **(b)** Mesolithic, **(c)** Neolithic.
6. **Analyzing Ideas** Why is the development of agriculture considered a "revolution"?

2 The First Civilizations Began in Four Great River Valleys

By the end of the Stone Age, people had learned to make tools and weapons, use fire, create works of art, tame animals, grow their own food, and establish permanent settlements. However, not everyone developed this way of life during the Neolithic Age. For example, not all areas of the world had soil and climate suitable for farming. In some regions with grassy pasture lands, people maintained a herding culture in which they moved their flocks from one place to another to graze. They continued as nomads, wandering about in small groups or tribes and never settling down.

Moving into the River Valleys

Although Neolithic people settled in many areas, the settlements in four specific regions had particular importance in later human development. These four regions were: (1) the Nile River valley in Egypt, (2) the valley of the Tigris and Euphrates (yoo • FRAY • teez) rivers in southwestern Asia, (3) the Indus River valley in southern Asia, and (4) the Huang He (HWANG HOOH) valley in eastern Asia (see map, page 6).

In these four river valleys, people first developed the advanced form of culture known as civilization. All people have some sort of culture. Only when a culture becomes highly developed do we call it a civilization.

Most civilizations have at least five characteristics: (1) The people have advanced technical skills, such as the ability to use metals. (2) People have created cities with some form of government. (3) A **division of labor** exists, in which different people perform different jobs, instead of one person doing all kinds of work. (4) People have developed a calendar. (5) People have developed a form of writing.

Learning to Use Metals

People probably discovered metals by accident. It may have happened when someone built a fire over an area that contained the metal copper. Later, the fire builder might have noticed lumps of this metal in the ashes. People may then have learned how to shape the heated metal.

9

About 6,000 years ago, people in both the Nile and Tigris-Euphrates River valleys knew how to make copper weapons, tools, utensils, and jewelry. Copper tools and weapons proved unsatisfactory, however, mainly because the soft metal could not keep a sharp edge or be used in heavy work. In time, people learned to make a better metal—bronze. An alloy, or mixture, of copper and tin, bronze is harder than copper. People in Egypt and in the Tigris-Euphrates River valley knew how to make bronze jewelry and weapons as early as 5,000 years ago. People in India and China also used bronze at an early date. The invention of bronze tools marked the end of the Stone Age and the beginning of the Bronze Age.

A stronger metal than either copper or bronze, iron ore—the iron as it exists in the earth mixed with other minerals—exists in more places and in larger amounts than either copper or tin. Yet its use came much later, because separating the iron from the ore required an extremely long and difficult process. The invention of the forge, a kind of furnace in which forcing air through fire produces great heat, helped make the use of iron possible. After the extreme heat of the forge had softened the iron ore, the hot metal had to be hammered to eliminate impurities that would weaken the iron and render it useless.

We do not know when people discovered the process of making iron or who invented it. It may have originated separately in several different areas. We do know, however, that about 3,200 years ago people in southwestern Asia learned to make iron and craft it into stronger tools and weapons, more durable than those made of copper or bronze. The Iron Age had begun.

Irrigation, Government, and Cities

The valleys of the Nile, Tigris-Euphrates, Indus, and Huang He have a common feature that greatly influenced their early histories. Once a year their rivers rise and flood the valleys. Except for this rainy period, however, little if any rain falls. Hot, dry conditions prevail throughout the rest of the year.

This climate challenged the farmers of these valleys; somehow they had to get water to their crops during the dry season. Carrying water proved difficult, time-consuming, and backbreaking. At some point in the distant past, however, the farmers in these valleys learned to dig ditches and canals to transport needed water to their fields. Thus they developed the first systems of **irrigation.**

Violent floods occurred during the rainy season in three of the river valleys—the Tigris-Euphrates, the Indus, and the Huang He. Therefore, farmers in these valleys also had to build dikes to keep the rivers within their banks.

Farming in these river valleys, then, depended on irrigation and the ability to control floods. Because individuals working alone could not build large irrigation and flood-control projects, people had to learn to work together.

Governments may have developed gradually as a result of such cooperation. As people worked together, they needed rules to govern their behavior and to plan, direct, and regulate their work.

The first valley dwellers moved into their valleys in tribes. Each tribe settled in a village along the river. People lived together in the villages and worked the surrounding land. In time more and more people banded together to work on group projects and to defend their villages. Some of these village communities grew to become cities.

An increase in population, made possible by improved farming methods such as irrigation and better tools, also led to the growth of cities. Improved farming meant more and better food and, therefore, a healthier and more comfortable life for each person. The large number of people living in cities also provided the labor to create great palaces, temples, and other public buildings.

Division of Labor

As methods of farming improved, fewer people had to work in the fields in order to produce enough food for all. Some people could specialize in work other than farming. Expert toolmakers and weaponmakers could devote all their time to this type of work. They would then trade their products for food. Thus a class of skilled craftworkers called **artisans** appeared.

Other people became merchants and traders. They made their living by buying goods from farmers or artisans and then selling the goods for a profit to anyone who needed them, especially to people in the cities. Traders not only transported goods to be sold but also passed along ideas. For example, these early traders spread their systems of counting that

Learning from Pictures *These prehistoric monuments in Outer Hebrides, Scotland, are believed to be grave markers called dolmens.*

showed the number of articles bought and sold. Today we call the spread of certain parts of cultures from one area of the world to another **cultural diffusion.**

Developing a Calendar

The people in the great river valleys developed calendars early in their history. Because these people farmed, they carefully observed the changes of the seasons. They had to know, for example, when the yearly floods would start and stop. One way was to regard the time from flood to flood as a year and to divide the interval according to the phases of the moon. These changes in the moon's appearance were the most regular repetitions that early people could see in the sky.

The time from one new moon to the next new moon would be a month. Twelve of these lunar months would equal a year. But this system presented a major problem. A month based on the movement of the moon—on the time it takes the moon to revolve once completely around the earth—lasts only about 29 1/2 days. Twelve "moon" months thus equal 354 days. But by measuring the time it takes the earth to revolve once completely around the sun, we know a year has approximately 365 1/4 days. A calendar based on the moon, therefore, fell about 11 days short. As a result, the months came earlier each year, and 12 months did not fill the time until the next flood. As you read more about river-valley civilizations, you will see how early people coped with this problem. In addition to discussing the many ways early people used to identify the months of the year, in this book we will be using a system of dating years with the letters B.C. and A.D. (see *Building History Study Skills,* page 12).

Interpreting Visuals: Using a Time Line to Understand B.C. and A.D.

To understand history you need to be aware of when events happened. In this book we will be using a system of dating years from the birth of Christ. Years following Christ's birth are identified in numerical order and start with the letters A.D. The letters A.D. stand for the Latin phrase *Anno Domini,* which means "in the year of our Lord," or "since the birth of Christ." The year A.D. 1900 thus stands for 1,900 years after Christ's birth. Years before Christ's birth are identified in reverse numerical order and are followed by the letters B.C., which stand for "**B**efore the birth of **C**hrist." Thus the date 2000 B.C. means 2,000 years before Christ's birth.

To calculate how many years separate events in modern times from events in ancient history requires using both B.C. and A.D. For example, 5000 B.C. was 6,990 years before A.D. 1990 (5,000 + 1,990 = 6,990), while 1000 B.C. was about 2,500 years before A.D. 1500 (1,000 + 1,500 = 2,500).

The method of dating events from the birth of Christ is only one of several ways of calculating time. Muslims, Chinese, Jews, and Hindus count the years in different ways. For example, the Christian year A.D. 1900 corresponds with the Muslim year 1318, the Hebrew year 5660, and the Chinese year 4597.

How to Use a Time Line to Understand B.C. and A.D.

To help you understand when important events occurred, the Chapter Review in each chapter in this book includes a time line that shows the order, or sequence, of important events discussed in the chapter. A time line can also help you see relationships between certain events. In order to use a time line to understand B.C. and A.D., follow these steps.

1. Determine the length of time shown on the time line. Be certain to calculate the years that are B.C. and those that are A.D.

2. Read the time line from left to right so that you can determine the sequence of events.
3. Identify the important events that the time line shows. Which events occurred in B.C.? Which events occurred in A.D.?
4. Identify relationships in time between the events on the time line. For example, how many years before A.D. 158 was 1350 B.C.?

Developing the Skill

The time line at the bottom of this page includes several important events that you will study in later chapters of this book. The time line documents events that occurred between 1200 B.C. and A.D. 1988, a period of 3,188 years (1,200 + 1,988 = 3,188).

As you read the time line from left to right, notice that 1000 B.C. is earlier in time than 100 B.C. and that 500 B.C. is later in time than 800 B.C. This is true because the years before the birth of Christ (B.C.) are numbered in reverse numerical order. Also note that A.D. 1900 is later in time than A.D. 100 because the years after the birth of Christ (A.D.) are numbered in numerical order.

The time line helps you to understand the order in which events occurred. For example, the Bronze Age began in southwestern Asia in 1200 B.C.—447 years before the legendary founding of Rome (753 B.C.) and 739 years before the Age of Pericles in Athens (461 B.C.). Also note that the Bronze Age began about 2,976 years before the signing of the Declaration of Independence. You know that this is true because from 1200 B.C. to the end of the B.C. period was 1,200 years, and from the beginning of A.D. to A.D. 1776 was 1,776 years (1,200 + 1,776 = 2,976).

Practicing the skill. How many years after the beginning of the Bronze Age in southwestern Asia was George Bush elected President of the United States?

To apply this skill, see Applying History Study Skills on page 15.

Inventing Writing

With the many changes of late Neolithic times, life became increasingly complex. People in settled communities developed rules for living together and for protecting property. They also developed agreements for working together. Governments were established and with them taxes to pay the costs of government. Trade also developed between various communities.

Speech no longer sufficed as the only means of communication. People needed a written language to preserve and pass on ideas and information. Rulers wished to keep a permanent record of the events of their reigns and to keep tax records; parents wished to hand down lasting instruction to their children. The long and complex process of the development of writing may be summarized in four chief steps:

(1) *A picture represents a thing.* For example, a picture of a tree stands for the word *tree*. Picture signs of this sort are called *pictograms*. Pictograms have disadvantages, however. It is easy to show a tree or a person. But how would you represent an idea, such as "truth," "honesty," "liberty," or "life after death"?

(2) *A picture stands for an idea.* As time went on, people used symbols to stand for ideas. Suppose a farmer had orchards. In this case the farmer might use the drawing of a tree to represent the idea of "wealth." We call picture signs of this sort *ideograms.*

(3) *A picture stands for a sound, usually a syllable.* In using pictograms and ideograms, a great many pictures are needed. Fewer are required if a certain symbol can represent a sound, not just one meaning. Thus the tree symbol could stand not only for *tree* but also for the syllable *trea* in the word *treason.* We call signs of this sort *phonograms.*

(4) *A sign represents a single consonant or vowel.* These signs, or letters, form an alphabet. An alphabet marks the final step in the development of writing. Over the years two things happened to the tree symbol. First, it was simplified so that it became easier to draw. Second, it came to stand for the beginning sound of the phonogram, not the whole sound. Thus a simplified version of the picture—the letter *T*—came to represent just the first sound of *tree.* This story of the development of the letter *T* is an imaginary and simplified one, but it illustrates how people invented alphabets.

The Family in Early Civilizations

When civilization developed, men hunted less, and many became farmers. Women also continued to do some of the farming, such as planting and harvesting crops. In the early river-valley civilizations, men farmed and made metal products, such as weapons. Women managed the family, cared for the children, and made items necessary for survival. They prepared food, made clothing, and probably invented pottery and weaving.

Religion also played an important part in the lives of early families. Early people believed in many gods and in the unseen forces of nature. They believed that the gods and these forces controlled all aspects of their lives. People feared that the rains would not come and that their crops would not grow. Since crop failure would mean starvation, they begged their gods to provide water and to make seeds grow. Often these people offered sacrifices to their gods in order to ensure good harvests and offered thanks when they believed their prayers had been answered.

People in early civilizations lived in large families. In addition to mothers, fathers, and children, families included grandparents, aunts and uncles, and cousins. However, because of limited medical knowledge, many children died as infants. When people grew old, they expected their children to take care of them. People of all ages began to depend on their relatives for help in everyday affairs.

In most early civilizations, the father headed the family. But because the mother played a key role in running the family's daily life, she also had great authority. However, women's authority often did not extend into politics or religion.

SECTION 2 REVIEW

1. **Define**   division of labor, irrigation, artisan, cultural diffusion
2. **Locate**   Nile River, Tigris River, Euphrates River, Indus River, Huang He
3. **Seeing Relationships**   How did the need for irrigation and flood control lead to the development of governments?
4. **Analyzing Ideas**   Why were calendars important to people of early civilizations?
5. **Understanding Ideas**   (a) Why was written language needed?   (b) What were the four chief steps in developing a written language?

13

CHAPTER 1 REVIEW

BC ca. 3,700,000   ca. 2,000,000   ca. 1,600,000

First stone tools

Appearance of
Australopithecus

Appearance of
Java and
Beijing people

Chapter Summary

The following list contains the key concepts you have learned about the cultures and civilizations that began during prehistoric times.

1. The first humans left behind bones, artifacts, and pictures. From these, anthropologists have been able to determine what the first human beings looked like, what they ate, where they lived, and what some of their customs were.
2. Many scientists believe that during prehistoric times people gradually developed greater skills, such as producing more effective tools, learning to hunt more efficiently, and creating the earliest works of art.
3. Eventually, people learned to domesticate animals and to farm. As a result, they began settling in villages and gave up their nomadic life styles.
4. Changes during Neolithic times brought about one of the most important turning points in human history—the development of civilization.
5. People developed the first civilizations in four great river valleys in Africa and Asia. There, people learned how to use metals, build cities, promote economic activity, and establish governments.
6. One of the most significant developments was writing. The ability to keep written records gave civilizations continuity. It also allows us, for the first time, to find out what early people thought about their own times. With the development of writing, prehistory ended and history began.

On a separate sheet of paper, complete the following review exercises.

Reviewing Important Terms

Match each of the following terms with the correct definition in column two.

a. prehistory
b. civilization
c. artifact
d. history
e. division
   of labor
f. anthropologist
g. radiocarbon
   dating
h. glacier
i. agriculture
j. Neolithic
   Revolution

___ 1. Record of what has taken place in the world since the invention of writing
___ 2. Highly organized society with complex institutions and attitudes that link a large number of people together
___ 3. Period before the invention of writing
___ 4. Technique that measures the rate of decay of certain atoms present in organic matter
___ 5. Large, slowly moving mass of snow and ice
___ 6. The shift from food gathering to food producing
___ 7. Material object shaped by a human being
___ 8. System in which different people perform different jobs, instead of one person having to do all kinds of work
___ 9. Scientist who studies the skeletal remains of early humans to determine how they looked, how tall they were, how long they lived, and other physical characteristics
___ 10. The raising of crops for food

Developing Critical Thinking Skills

1. **Understanding Ideas** (a) Why do the events of prehistory remain cloaked in mystery? (b) What methods do archaeologists and anthropologists use to unlock these mysteries?
2. **Understanding Chronology** Place the items in each of the following three lists in chronological order from most ancient to most recent: (a) plow, upright posture, meat eaters, use of fire; (b) Beijing people, Australopithecus, Cro-Magnon people, Neanderthal people; (c) farming, hunting, herding of animals, gathering of fruits and seeds
3. **Seeing Relationships** How did the lives of early people change after they learned to domesticate animals and raise food crops?
4. **Contrasting Ideas** How did the people of the Neolithic Age differ from those of the Paleolithic Age in these categories: (a) method of obtaining food; (b) tools; (c) government?
5. **Synthesizing Ideas** (a) What are the five major characteristics of civilizations? (b) How does life in the United States today meet each of these five characteristics?

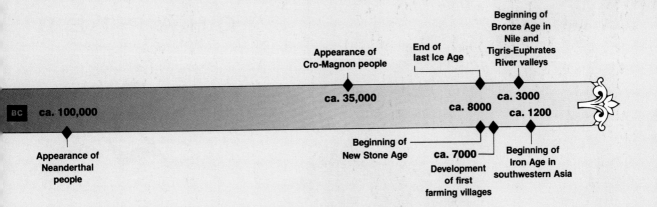

ca. 100,000 BC

Appearance of
Neanderthal
people

Appearance of
Cro-Magnon people

ca. 35,000

End of
last Ice Age

Beginning of
Bronze Age in
Nile and
Tigris-Euphrates
River valleys

ca. 3000

ca. 8000

ca. 1200

Beginning of
New Stone Age

ca. 7000

Development
of first
farming villages

Beginning of
Iron Age in
southwestern Asia

Relating Geography to History

Study the map of the sites of early human remains and the four river-valley civilizations on page 6. **(a)** List the large bodies of water that are closest to the four major river-valley civilizations. **(b)** Which two of these civilizations were most likely, because of their location, to have some trading contact with each other? **(c)** Which civilization seems the most isolated from the others?

Relating Past to Present

1. **(a)** What was the role of women in Neolithic society? **(b)** On what can we base this view? **(c)** How have the roles of women in the United States changed in the past 25 years? **(d)** What new inventions, developments, and attitudes have helped bring about these changes?
2. What do you think a civilization from outer space would learn of the culture of the United States today from investigating the contents of our garbage dumps, cemeteries, and junkyards?
3. Over thousands of years, prehistoric people discovered new skills and inventions that greatly changed their lives. Among these were methods of agriculture, the use of metals, and the calendar. **(a)** Choose a modern skill or invention and explain how it has changed our lives today. **(b)** Why do you think it took prehistoric people thousands of years to make a few important discoveries?

Applying History Study Skills

Before completing this activity, review Building History Study Skills on page 12.

Look again at the events shown on the time line in Building History Study Skills on page 12. Notice that some events occurred during B.C. and some during A.D. Remember that B.C. years are numbered in reverse numerical order before the birth of Christ. A.D. (*A*nno *D*omini) years are numbered in numerical order after the birth of Christ. Then use the time line to help you place the events in column two in the order in which they happened.

(a) Crucifixion of Jesus
(b) Election of George Bush as President of the United States
(c) Beginning of Bronze Age in southwestern Asia
(d) Legendary founding of Rome
(e) Age of Pericles in Athens
(f) Height of Buddhism in China
(g) Death of Alexander the Great
(h) Signing of the Declaration of Independence
(i) Voyage of Christopher Columbus

Investigating Further

1. **Writing a Report** In your school or local library, locate information about hunting and gathering societies in the world today. For example, you might read Elizabeth M. Thomas's *The Harmless People* (Random House), which is about the Bush people of southern Africa. Or you might choose to read about the Pygmies of Central Africa, who are described in Colin M. Turnbull's *The Forest People* (Simon and Schuster). Other groups that you might read about are New Guinea tribes, Amazon tribes, or Philippine tribes. Periodicals such as *National Geographic* and *Explorer* would be good sources for your research. Then write a report describing: **(a)** how the group is organized and governed; **(b)** the roles of men and women; **(c)** how food is obtained and distributed within the group; **(d)** the group's religious practices; **(e)** the physical environment and how it affects the way the people live; **(f)** the types of tools made and used.
2. **Making Comparisons** Use encyclopedias to locate information about one of these calendars—the Chinese, Hebrew, Muslim, or Hindu calendar. **(a)** How does each calendar calculate a one-month period? **(b)** How does this period compare with one month on the Christian calendar? **(c)** Why does each calendar have a different beginning of the year?
3. **Making Charts** Reread the information on inventing writing on page 13. Then use resources in your school or public library to find more information on the systems of writing that early people developed. Use the information you find to help you construct a chart illustrating the four major steps in the development of writing.

15

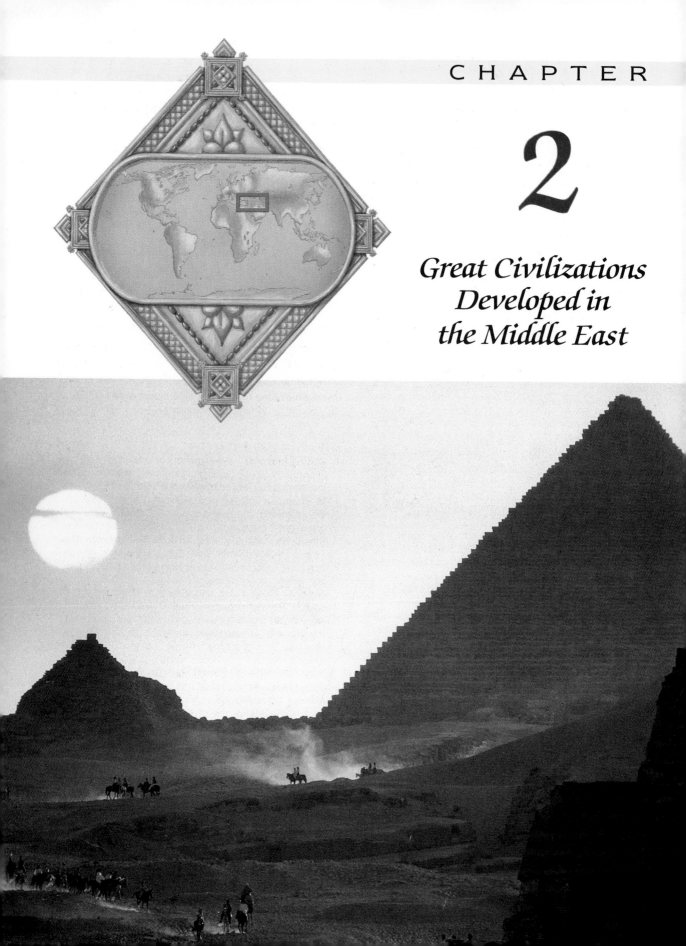

C H A P T E R

2

*Great Civilizations
Developed in
the Middle East*

Place   Egypt and Southwestern Asia

Time   ca. 6000 B.C.—586 B.C.

3.7 mil. BC   4000 BC   AD 2100

Significance

Civilizations first appeared in two great river valleys of the Middle East. In both of these river valleys—along the Nile River and along the Tigris and Euphrates rivers—people gradually developed complex societies with strong governments.

Although the two civilizations lay only about 600 miles (960 kilometers) apart and had some contact with each other, their societies developed very differently. One reason for these differences was the geography of the land.

Miles of scorching desert surrounded the Nile River and protected the communities along its banks from invasion. There the Egyptians created a very stable society and developed traditions in the arts, government, religion, and thought that lasted thousands of years.

Because invaders could easily enter the valley along the Tigris and Euphrates, a succession of less stable societies developed there. Each of these societies created its own institutions and culture. Many of these peoples spread beyond the valley, creating a series of powerful empires in the Middle East.

Terms to Define

dynasty	ziggurat
empire	cavalry
city-state	money economy

People to Identify

Menes	Darius
Cyrus	Hebrews

Places to Locate

Egypt	Tigris-Euphrates Valley
Fertile Crescent	Persia

Questions to Guide Your Reading

1 How did the Egyptians develop a civilization along the Nile River?
2 What were the major accomplishments of Egyptian civilization?
3 Why were the Sumerians important?
4 What empires arose in the Fertile Crescent?
5 What lasting contributions did the Phoenicians, the Lydians, and the Hebrews make to Western civilization?

Almost 4,000 years ago in the town of Sumer in the fertile valley of the Tigris and Euphrates rivers, a worried father turned to his son and gave the advice that would be repeated by generations of fathers down through the centuries of history.

❝*The father begins by asking his son:*
'Where did you go?'
'I did not go anywhere.'
'If you did not go anywhere, why do you idle about? Go to school, stand before your "school-father," recite your assignment, open your schoolbag, write your tablet, let your "big brother" write your new tablet for you. After you have finished your assignment and reported to your monitor, come to me, and do not wander about in the street. . . . Don't stand about in the public square, or wander about the boulevard.'❞

The story of the Sumerians, as well as of the other great civilizations of Egypt and southwestern Asia, shows how early people developed cultures and passed them on to future generations.

1 The Egyptians Built a Civilization Along the Nile River

Of all the ancient river-valley civilizations, Egypt is probably the best known because almost everyone has seen pictures of its ancient landmarks, such as the pyramids and the Sphinx. And even today in the nation of Egypt, many people maintain a culture similar to that developed by their ancestors more than 5,000 years ago.

The Physical Setting

The Egypt of 3000 B.C. probably looked very much like the Egypt of today. About the size of Texas and Oregon combined, Egypt is a large country, but sandy desert covers most of the land. An occasional **oasis,** or place in the desert where there is irrigation or an underground spring, dots the barren landscape. In this vast country, people can grow crops only in one long, narrow ribbon of land that averages only 12 miles (19 kilometers) in width—the valley of the Nile River.

◀ *The Pyramids of Giza, Egypt*

Learning from Maps *Today huge dams trap the silt that once flowed in the floodwaters of the Nile River. What hindered ancient Egyptian transportation on the Nile River?*

This river, the longest river in the world, begins near Lake Victoria in eastern Africa and flows north 4,187 miles (6,700 kilometers) before meandering through the Nile Delta and emptying into the Mediterranean Sea. Along its length lie six great cataracts where the river is forced into narrow channels cut through rock. The ancient Egyptians built their civilization along 750 miles (1,200 kilometers) downstream from the First Cataract because its swirling waters made river transportation through the cataract impossible.

"The gift of the Nile." Many centuries after the early period of Egyptian history, a Greek historian named Herodotus (hi•RAHD•uh•tuhs) wrote of his travels in Egypt. "All Egypt," he said, "is the gift of the Nile." His writings accurately describe a remarkable feature of Egyptian geography—the annual flood.

Until the construction of the Aswan Dam in 1971, each year from June to October, rain and

melting snow from the mountains at the source of the Nile caused the river to overflow. The floodwaters spread out over the flatland of the southern Nile Valley. As the waters receded, they left behind a layer of **silt,** or fertile soil carried as sediment in a river's waters.

From earliest times Egyptian farmers planned their work according to the flood. They knew when it would come every year. They harvested their crops, such as wheat and barley, before the flood began, and then waited for the water to soak the hard, dry earth before draining off and leaving its new, fertile soil.

Little or no rain falls in Egypt, so the moisture produced by the flood was sufficient for only one planting. Early in their history, however, the Egyptians learned to use water from the Nile for irrigation. Farmers dug networks of short canals to carry water to their fields. The water stored in the canals helped farmers grow two or even three crops a year, thus making it possible to feed a large population.

Other natural advantages. Even in ancient times the Nile Valley had other natural resources besides its fertile soil. Its sunny, frost-free climate, for example, nurtured many kinds of crops.

An interesting and important feature of the climate was, and still is, the prevailing wind that blows from the Mediterranean Sea into the Nile Valley. Because this prevailing wind in the Nile Valley blows southward, it blows upstream from the region of the Mediterranean Sea. Consequently a boat on the Nile can either go upstream with the wind by using a sail, or drift downstream against the wind, carried by the river current. This fact allowed the ancient Egyptians to make the Nile River a pathway of travel and trade that linked all parts of the Nile Valley. In addition, it helped the ancient Egyptians unite the region.

The Nile Valley also contains deposits of clay, granite, sandstone, and limestone. The Egyptians used these minerals for building because few forests to furnish lumber grew in the arid climate. Finally, the ancient Egyptians enjoyed one other natural advantage—the valley's location. Deserts and seas surrounded the Nile Valley and provided a natural protection against invaders. Only the Isthmus of Suez broke the natural barriers (see map, this page). The isthmus formed a land bridge between Asia and Africa. Throughout history it provided a route for traders, for the exchange of ideas, and even for invading armies.

18

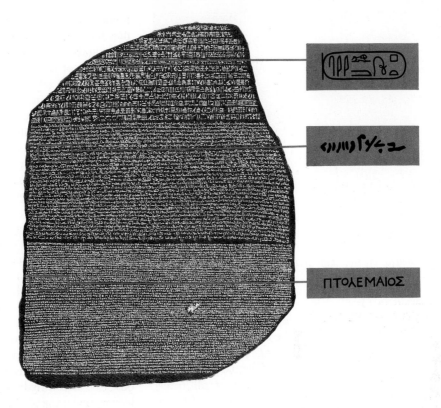

Learning from Pictures
Scholars translated the
Rosetta Stone and
discovered that the way the
birds in the script faced
determined whether the
symbols should be read
from left to right or
right to left.

Early Steps Toward Civilization

People have lived in the long valley of the Nile River since earliest times. Archaeologists have discovered Paleolithic remains in the Nile Valley, and a Neolithic culture probably developed there about 6000 B.C.

By about 3800 B.C. the people of the Nile Valley began to take important steps along the road to civilization. They learned to use copper to make needles, chisels, and jewelry. They discovered how to make bronze, the strong alloy of copper and tin. Evidence indicates that they invented the potter's wheel, a rotating disk that made it easier to make round pots and jars.

Egyptian writing. Writing developed along with the other major achievements of Egyptian civilization. By about 3000 B.C. the Egyptians had worked out a system of writing called **hieroglyphics** (hy • ruh • GLIF • iks). The word comes from the Greek words *hieros*, meaning "sacred," and *glyphe*, meaning "carving." Hieroglyphic writing used more than 600 hieroglyphic signs, pictures, or symbols to indicate words or sounds. The Egyptians did not develop a true alphabet, but they did progress

toward one. They developed 24 signs that each stood for only one sound—all consonants. In addition, about 80 signs contained two consonants. They developed no signs for vowels.

At first Egyptians carved hieroglyphics on slate and ivory, but this involved a long and difficult process. Searching for a better material on which to write, they discovered how to use the papyrus plant that grew in the marshes near the Nile. The Egyptians cut the stem of the plant into long, thin slices. They then placed the slices together and moistened and pounded them to form a mat with a smooth surface. The Egyptians called this product **papyrus,** from which we get our word *paper.*

Egyptians wrote on papyrus with ink made from soot, water, and vegetable gum, a sticky juice from certain trees and plants. The Egyptians diluted the gum with water before mixing it with soot. They used a sharpened reed as a pen.

Solving the hieroglyphic puzzle. Modern scholars learned to read the language of the ancient Egyptians through a clever bit of detective work. In A.D. 1798 a French army commanded by Napoleon Bonaparte invaded Egypt. The next year a French officer discovered a large stone with inscriptions

19

Learning from Pictures *The ancient Egyptians used many symbols to reflect their beliefs. The ankh above symbolizes life and immortality.*

written in Greek, hieroglyphics, and an Egyptian writing called *demotic*. The Rosetta Stone, named for the Rosetta branch of the Nile Delta where the officer stumbled upon the stone, provided the key to the language of the ancient Egyptians.

Scholars guessed that the text of all three kinds of writing had the same meaning. Almost 23 years after the discovery of the Rosetta Stone, a French language expert, Jean François Champollion (shan • paw • LYAWN), solved the mystery. Beginning with the Greek, which he could read, he deciphered the hieroglyphic inscription that described honors granted by the priesthood to the ruler Ptolemy (TAHL • uh • mee) V in 196 B.C. Champollion went on to translate the hieroglyphic symbols and establish the principles by which all other hieroglyphics could be read. Because scholars could now decipher hieroglyphics, they could read eyewitness accounts of Egypt's glorious history.

A United Kingdom

Over the centuries strong leaders united early Egyptian settlements to form two kingdoms—Upper Egypt and Lower Egypt. (A king or queen heads a **kingdom,** one of the earliest forms of government. Another name for *kingdom* is **monarchy.**) Upper Egypt lay farther south from the Mediterranean Sea, along the upper Nile River. Lower Egypt lay to the north, nearer the sea (see map, page 18).

Then, about 3100 B.C., a ruler known as Menes (MEE • neez) united all Egypt into one kingdom.

Menes and his successors crushed rebellions, gained new territory, regulated irrigation, and encouraged trade and prosperity.

Much of the power of these rulers came from their roles as religious as well as political leaders. The people regarded them as gods. In later years rulers took the title **pharaoh,** which means "great house," after the palace in which they lived.

The pharaohs' position as gods placed them far above ordinary people. They led the government and served as judges, high priests, and generals of the armies. Although the pharaohs had absolute, or unlimited, power, their duties included protecting and caring for their people.

Menes founded a **dynasty,** or family of rulers in which the right to rule passes on within the family, usually from father to son or daughter. This hereditary rule ends only when a family is overthrown, or when it dies out so that there is no one left to become ruler. In more than 2,500 years, beginning with the time of Menes and continuing to about 300 B.C., about 30 Egyptian dynasties rose and fell. Historians divide this span of time into four periods—the Old Kingdom, the Middle Kingdom, the New Kingdom, and the Late Period.

The Old Kingdom

The Old Kingdom—probably the greatest period of Egyptian history—existed from about 2700 B.C. to 2181 B.C. Many important discoveries in science and the arts took place during this time. For example, Egyptians of the Old Kingdom built the largest pyramids, which still stand as symbols of the glory of Egyptian civilization. For this reason historians sometimes call the period of the Old Kingdom the Pyramid Age.

In the early dynasties of the Old Kingdom, Egyptian society included only two main groups of people: (1) an upper class—the pharaoh, the royal family, and the priests and officials who helped govern the country—and (2) a lower class—everyone else. The majority of this lower class consisted of peasants, or farmers. They owed the pharaoh their services, such as duty in the army or work on the irrigation system or on the pyramids and public buildings.

As time passed, officials in the upper class gradually became a hereditary group of nobles. Toward the end of the Old Kingdom, the pharaohs grew weaker and the nobles grew stronger. For 125 years after the end of this period, civil wars divided the country as rivals claimed the throne.

The Middle Kingdom

In about 2000 B.C. a strong new line of pharaohs united Egypt again, beginning a period known as the Middle Kingdom. These pharaohs restored order and prosperity for a while. However, the difficulty of making and carrying out all decisions by themselves defeated all but the strongest rulers. Meanwhile, other officials became more powerful in the government. They also became wealthy. Once again the rise of a hereditary class of nobles and priests weakened the power of the pharaoh.

The Middle Kingdom ended in disorder around 1780 B.C., the victim of rivalries, conflicts, and the division of power. Then, about 1730 B.C., much of Egypt fell under the rule of an Asiatic people—the Hyksos (HIHK • sohs)—whose horse-drawn chariots overwhelmed the donkey carts the Egyptians used.

The story of the Hyksos' rule in Egypt provides an excellent example of differing interpretations of history. Historians investigate past events and interpret these events based on the evidence they find. Often, historians disagree as to exactly what happened.

According to Egyptian records written hundreds of years later, the brutal, warlike Hyksos savagely invaded Lower Egypt. As the Egyptian priest Manetho recorded in about 200 B.C.:

> **❝U**nexpectedly from the regions of the East invaders of obscure race marched in confidence of victory against our land. By main force they seized it without striking a blow; and having overpowered the rulers of the land, they then burned our cities ruthlessly, razed to the ground the temples of the gods, and treated all the natives with a cruel hostility, massacring some and leading into slavery the wives and children of others. **❞**

Based on this account and others from ancient Egyptian sources, some scholars believe that the Hyksos invaded and conquered Egypt.

Other scholars, however, point out that little evidence confirms the destruction of Egyptian temples during this period. They discount Egyptian stories of the Hyksos' brutality as explanations for why the Hyksos were able to conquer Egypt. After

EGYPT: THE NEW KINGDOM ca. 1450 B.C.

▲ Pyramid — — Trade route

LAMBERT CONFORMAL CONIC PROJECTION

Learning from Maps *The New Kingdom expanded Egypt's borders. Why did the New Kingdom expand to the northeast rather than to the west?*

all, how could a land ruled by a god fall under foreign rule unless those foreigners had mighty armies?

These scholars believe nomadic Hyksos migrated into the Nile Delta about 1800 B.C. In the confusion following the collapse of the Middle Kingdom, the Hyksos emerged as the most powerful people in the region and ruled most of Lower Egypt for about 150 years.

The New Kingdom

Although historians disagree about how the Hyksos came to rule Egypt, all agree that the proud Egyptians despised their foreign—and in Egyptian eyes, inferior—rulers. Eventually, rulers of Upper Egypt forged an army, rebelled against the Hyksos,

21

and drove them from the country. A number of strong pharaohs who lived in the city of Thebes far up the Nile ruled a reunited Egypt. The period in which they ruled—from about 1550 B.C. to about 1085 B.C.—is called the New Kingdom.

For a time, the pharaohs once more had absolute power. They kept strict control over the government and, adopting the horse-drawn chariots of the Hyksos, created a strong army. With the aid of this army, the pharaohs extended their territory to include land along the eastern end of the Mediterranean Sea and south into Nubia (see map, page 21). In doing so, they created an **empire,** a form of government that unites different territories and peoples under one ruler.

Like many other peoples, however, the Egyptians found it easier to conquer territory than to keep and govern it. Usually they allowed the local prince of a conquered region to act as governor. To be sure of his loyalty and obedience, they took his son back to Egypt as a hostage to be trained at the palace of Thebes.

Only the strongest pharaohs, however, could hold the empire together. Whenever the government of Egypt showed signs of weakness, some part of the empire would revolt and try to break away.

Hatshepsut rules Egypt. The first woman ruler about whom we have written records, Hatshepsut (hat • SHEP • soot), reigned as pharaoh from about 1500 B.C. to 1480 B.C. Although Egyptian queens often gained fame as wives of kings, few ever became pharaoh. Hatshepsut, however, proved an able ruler. More interested in the welfare of her country than in war and conquest, she ordered the construction of temples to the gods and other public buildings.

Hatshepsut first ruled with her husband, Thutmose (thoot • MOH • suh) II, who was also her half-brother. This marriage illustrates a unique custom of Egyptian rulers. As a god, the pharaoh could not marry an ordinary human being. Instead, he usually married his sister or half-sister. After Thutmose II died, his son, Thutmose III, took his place, but Hatshepsut continued to rule. Angry at Hatshepsut for refusing to give him power, Thutmose III had her name removed from all public monuments after she died.

Amenhotep and religious revolution. The pharaoh Amenhotep (ah • muhn • HOH • tep) IV ruled from about 1379 B.C. to 1362 B.C. Neither a famous conqueror nor a good ruler, Amenhotep is

Learning from Pictures *Nefertiti supported her husband, Akhenaton, in his social and religious revolution. Why did their religious reforms fail?*

remembered because he brought about a social and religious revolution.

Before Amenhotep became pharaoh, Egyptians believed in the existence of many gods. We call such a belief **polytheism** (PAHL • i • thee • iz • uhm), from the Greek words *polys,* meaning "many," and *theos,* meaning "god." The greatest of the Egyptian gods was Amon.

Amenhotep tried to change Egyptian religion. He believed in only one god—the sun, symbolized by a sun disk called the Aton—and that the pharaoh was the god's earthly son. We call this belief in only one god **monotheism** (MAHN • uh • thee • iz • uhm), from the Greek word *monos,* meaning "one," plus *theos.* To honor the Aton, pharaoh Amenhotep changed his own name to Akhenaton (ahk • uh • NAHT • uhn), which means "he who is beneficial to Aton."

The priests of Amon had become so powerful that they interfered in all affairs. To help break

Funeral Mask of a Pharaoh

One of the most beautiful treasures in the world is this life-sized funeral mask of the pharaoh Tutankhamen. The discovery of his tomb in 1922 captured the imagination of people around the world. What was extraordinary about the find was that the tomb's treasures had not been stolen. The tomb contained more than 5,000 works of art that revealed many aspects of Egyptian life.

The mask is made of beaten gold inlaid with jewels and colored glass. It shows Tutankhamen as the handsome youth he was when he died more than 3,200 years ago at the age of 18. The decorative beard on the mask is a symbol of Osiris, the god of the dead. On the headdress are symbols of the vulture and cobra goddesses. They represent Upper and Lower Egypt.

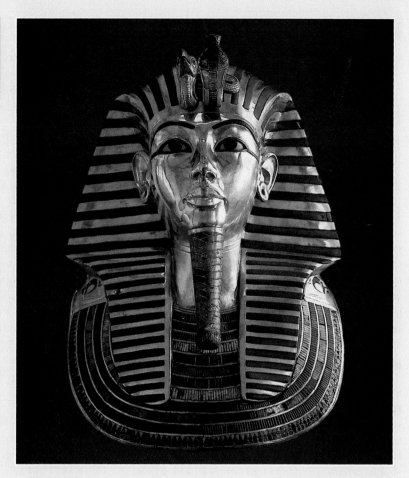

their power, Akhenaton moved his capital from Thebes, the site of the great temple of Amon, to a new city, Tell el Amarna. At Tell el Amarna, Akhenaton devoted his time to religion and neglected the ruling of the empire.

Akhenaton's actions infuriated the priests of Amon. The wealth that formerly came to them at their great temple of Thebes now went to the temple of the new god in the new capital. Their easy life suddenly ended. Appointments to high positions, which formerly went to the priests of Amon, now went to followers of Aton.

Akhenaton learned that he could not change all his people's religious beliefs by command. A bitter struggle between pharaoh and priests disrupted Egypt during the later years of his reign. When Akhenaton died, the priests of Amon reestablished their power, and the religious and cultural upheaval that Akhenaton had begun ended. His successor, Tutankhamen (too•tahn•KAHM•uhn), moved the capital back to Thebes. Polytheism was reinstated and the priests of Amon regained their influence.

After the death of Akhenaton, few strong pharaohs ruled Egypt. Ramses II, however, was a powerful leader who ruled from about 1304 B.C. to 1237 B.C. and held Egypt and the empire intact. His successors could not maintain the empire or prevent corruption in the government. Slowly Egypt slipped into the Late Period, a period of decline.

The Late Period

Beginning about 1100 B.C., Egypt grew steadily weaker. The empire crumbled, and foreign invaders, including the Nubians, the Assyrians, and the Persians, ravaged Egypt. Even during these times, however, dynasties of Egyptian pharaohs continued to reign. It was not until the 300s B.C. that native rule in Egypt finally came to an end.

2 The Culture of Ancient Egypt Reached Impressive Heights

Although dynasties rose and fell, the remarkably stable Egyptian culture extended over many centuries. This stability resulted partly from favorable conditions, particularly the regular Nile floods and Egypt's protected geographic location.

Farming and Trade

Farmland in Egypt was divided into large estates. Peasants did most of the farming, using crude hoes or wooden plows. The peasants, however, kept only part of the crop. The rest went to the pharaoh for rents and taxes.

Wheat and barley ranked as the chief grain crops. Farmers grew flax to be spun and woven into linen. They also raised cotton, as important an Egyptian crop in ancient times as it is today, to be woven into cloth.

Ancient Egypt produced more food than its people required. The Egyptians traded the surplus with other peoples for products that Egypt needed. Egyptians were among the first to build seagoing ships. These ships sailed into the Mediterranean and Aegean seas, the Red Sea, and along the African coast. On land, merchants riding donkeys and camels joined **caravans**—groups of people traveling together for safety over long distances—into western Asia and deep into Africa (see map, page 21).

Social Classes

For the most part, rigid divisions separated Egyptian social classes. Although people in the lower

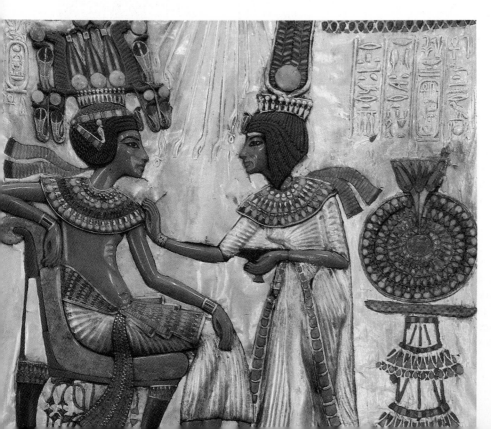

Learning from Pictures
The upper class, or nobles, in ancient Egypt followed many rituals. This painting depicts a wife anointing her husband.

Cotton

The painted figures on ancient Egyptian temple walls (below and right) and mummy cases wear draped garments of woven cotton cloth. Egypt has long been a major source of cotton, which is second only to food as the most important agricultural product in the world today. Egypt's warm climate and the irrigation provided by the Nile River combine to produce a highly desirable type of cotton. Because of its high quality, Egyptian cotton is exported throughout the world.

Cotton probably appeared first in India around 3000 B.C. Evidence also indicates that it existed long ago in Peru and in what is now Arizona. Some kinds of cotton are named after the places where they originated. For example, the cotton we know as madras is named after the port of Madras in India.

The fabric woven from the fluffy blossoms of the cotton plant absorbs moisture and remains cool even in hot weather. It is so comfortable that manufacturers today use it in clothing of all kinds, from pajamas to jeans. Cotton is used in many other products, too, such as bandages, life vests, and the stuffing for sofas. Its popularity spans thousands of years, and the demand for cotton is now greater than it has ever been.

class sometimes could improve their status, they almost never entered the ranks of the upper class.

Women, however, enjoyed many rights and ranked as the equals of their husbands in social and business affairs. An Egyptian woman could own property in her own right and could leave it to her daughter. In many ways, Egyptian women at that time had more privileges than women in other cultures of the Middle East.

Architecture and the Arts

When you think of Egypt, you probably first think of the huge stone figure of the Sphinx and the majestic pyramids, all of which still stand after nearly 5,000 years. Early Greek travelers named the huge limestone beast crouched in the sand near the present-day village of Giza the Great Sphinx. The statue has the 240-foot (73-meter) body of a lion, stands 66 feet (20 meters) tall, and has a human face measuring 13 feet (4 meters) across. Thought to be about 4,500 years old, the Great Sphinx represents the ancient Egyptian sun god.

The Egyptians built the pyramids as tombs for the pharaohs. Most of the 80 or so pyramids that still stand are clustered in groups along the west bank of the Nile. The best known soar above the scorching sands at Giza and include the Great Pyramid, which dates from about 2600 B.C. This gigantic structure measures more than half a mile (800 meters) in circumference at the base and is 450 feet (137 meters) high. It consists of more than 2 million blocks of stone, each of which weighs about 2.5 tons (2.3 metric tons).

The building of these pyramids obviously required skillful engineering. Egyptian architects and engineers ranked among the best in the ancient world. They built ramps, or sloping walkways, along which thousands of slaves pushed or pulled enormous stones into place. They also used levers for moving heavy objects.

The Egyptians perfected other art forms as well. In addition to large-scale works, sculptors also made small, lifelike statues of kings and sacred animals from copper, bronze, stone, or wood.

Egyptians decorated many of their buildings with paintings showing everyday life. Scenes included artisans at work, farmers harvesting grain, and people enjoying banquets. Egyptians developed a distinctive way of drawing the human figure. They showed the head in profile, the shoulders facing forward, and the feet in profile. Despite this angular, somewhat stiff interpretation, the surviving paintings provide colorful examples of the Egyptian enjoyment of life.

Science and Mathematics

Early in their history the Egyptians invented a lunar calendar, that is, one based on the moon's movements. Such a calendar caused difficulties because it did not fill the entire year. Then, somewhere in the Nile Valley, someone noticed that a very bright star began to appear above the horizon just before the floods came. The time between one rising of this star, which we now call Sirius, the Dog Star, and the next was 365 days, almost exactly a full year. The ancient Egyptians based their year on this cycle, dividing it into 12 months of 30 days each. This system left them with five extra days, which they used for holidays and feasting.

Numbering the years posed no great problem. At first, the Egyptians named years for an outstanding event—the year of the great flood or the year the locusts swarmed over the fields. Later, people used the years of the reigns of pharaohs to classify years; for example, the first, second, or twentieth year of the reign of a certain pharaoh. Using this method, we can trace the yearly record in Egypt to about 2780 B.C. Some historians believe that this is the earliest recorded date that can be firmly established in terms of our own system of dating.

The Egyptians developed a number system based on 10, similar to the decimal system we use today, and used fractions as well as whole numbers.

They also used geometry to calculate how to restore the boundaries of fields after floods and to determine how to lay out canals and irrigation ditches.

The Egyptians also made discoveries in medicine. They knew a great deal about the human body and used this knowledge in treating illnesses and in preserving bodies. *The Book of Healing Diseases,* written during the Old Kingdom, classified diseases according to symptoms and also prescribed treatments. Although the treatments included some "magic spells," many scientifically specified the use of herbs and medicine.

Education and Religion

The Egyptians could not have gathered and passed on their knowledge without a system of education. Religious instruction formed an important part of Egyptian education, and schools were usually in temples. Most education, however, focused on training clerks, or **scribes,** for the government.

Learning from Pictures   These papyrus-shaped pillars form the Great Hall of Pillars at the Temple of Amon in Luxor.

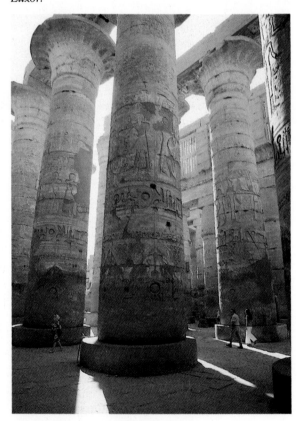

Religion formed an extremely important part of Egyptian life, specifically the worship of the sun and moon. The most important god of ancient Egypt was Amon, whose priests fought Akhenaton's attempt to replace Amon with Aton, the sun god. The people loved Osiris, god of the Nile River and lord of the Realm of the Dead, the most. His wife, Isis, the moon goddess, was also mother of the universe and queen of the world and the heavens. In early days each village and district had its local god or gods. In time people throughout the country accepted and worshiped some of these gods. Each god had an animal symbol that people considered sacred. Sacred animals included the cat, the bull, the crocodile, and the scarab (beetle).

The afterlife. At first Egyptians believed that only the pharaohs and a few others chosen by the pharaohs had an afterlife, or a life after death. Later, Egyptians believed that everyone, including animals, had a life after death. They thought that the spirit would be happier if the body were preserved. To do this, they developed a process called **mummification,** which involved treating the body with chemicals so that it would dry and remain preserved for centuries.

Workers placed the mummy in a tomb stocked with clothing, food, jewelry, tools, weapons, and even servants in the form of sculptured or painted figures. The number and richness of the articles in the tomb depended on the importance of the dead person. The Egyptians considered these articles necessary for the long journey to a place called "the Realm of the Dead." To guard the soul against attacks from vicious serpents and demons, the Egyptians placed in the tomb *The Book of the Dead*—a collection of hymns, prayers, and magic chants that formed a kind of guide to the afterlife.

When the soul reached the Realm of the Dead, it entered the Hall of Truth, where the god Osiris sat in judgment. Here the soul had to testify to the kind of life it had lived on earth. It had to take an oath that it had not lied, murdered, or been excessively proud.

When the soul had testified and had taken the oath, Osiris weighed it on a great scale against a feather, the symbol of truth. If the scales balanced, the soul had spoken the truth. It could then enter into the presence of the sun god and enjoy eternal happiness. But if it outweighed the feather, the soul was thrown to a horrible monster called "the Eater of the Dead." Ancient Egyptians emphasized the importance of having a good character and living a morally pure life because these qualities led to rewards in the afterlife.

Egyptian tombs. Because of the precious articles buried inside Egyptian graves, robbers constantly plundered them. Looters opened the pyramids built during the Old Kingdom and stole their contents. During the Middle Kingdom and New Kingdom, the Egyptians cut elaborate secret tombs into cliff walls. But thieves robbed most of these tombs also. In A.D. 1922, however, archaeologists discovered the previously unopened grave of Tutankhamen. This tomb, cut into rock, dated from the 1300s B.C. and contained gold, objects decorated with jewels, furniture, and household items that have taught us much about life in ancient Egypt.

3 Sumerian Civilization Arose Along the Tigris and Euphrates Rivers

The story of ancient Egypt described one people living in one place for generations. A very different story developed in the area of western Asia called the Fertile Crescent. Here, wave upon wave of invaders crisscrossed the land.

The Physical Setting

Look at the map of the Fertile Crescent on page 28. Note the green strip of land that begins at the Isthmus of Suez and arcs through the Middle East before dipping to the Persian Gulf. Much fertile land lies within this crescent-shaped area known as the Fertile Crescent.

As in Egypt, deserts and mountains surrounded the Fertile Crescent. One great difference in geography, however, made the history of the two areas quite different. The deserts and hills around the Fertile Crescent were not as barren as those around Egypt. Thus, grass and other plant life sustained tribes of wandering herders. Their way of life toughened these wild, fierce people. They envied the richer, easier life of the people who lived in the river valleys. At various times the people of the Fertile Crescent became less powerful and could not defend themselves. During these periods the herders came into the region, conquered it, and established empires. In time, these invaders, too, grew weak, and new waves of invaders conquered them. Thus the history of the Fertile Crescent provides a story of migration into the fertile valleys of the Tigris and Euphrates rivers.

The Tigris and Euphrates rivers both begin in the hills of Armenia. The Tigris flows about 1,100 miles (1,770 kilometers) to the Persian Gulf. The Euphrates, to the west, flows about 1,700 miles (2,740 kilometers) before reaching the Persian Gulf. At one point the two rivers come within 20 miles (30 kilometers) of each other and then spread apart until the valley between them—the Tigris-Euphrates Valley—widens to more than 150 miles (240 kilometers). They then flow together to form the Shatt-al-Arab near the Persian Gulf (see map, this page).

The Tigris has the greater amount of water. It cuts a deep path in the earth, lowering the water level below that of the land and making irrigation difficult. The Euphrates, too, creates problems for those who live along its banks. Its treacherous current carries five times the amount of silt the Nile does. Because this silt builds up at the bottom of the river, the Euphrates often overflows and sends floodwaters swirling across the surrounding land. Valley dwellers must dig canals and dikes to bring water to the fields and also to carry excess water back to the river after floods.

The flood of the Tigris and the Euphrates, unlike that of the Nile, cannot be predicted. It may come anytime between the beginning of April and the early part of June. Not only is the exact time of year unpredictable, but the extent of the flood cannot be estimated. Not surprisingly, the people of the valley viewed nature and the gods as angry and unreasonable. Their world differed greatly from that of the Egyptians, who generally saw only goodness in nature.

Various names have been given to certain regions of the Tigris-Euphrates Valley. The Greeks called the northern part Mesopotamia (meaning "between rivers"). The southern part of the valley has usually been known as Babylonia. Today, the nation of Iraq controls the entire valley.

Sumer and Its People

The lowest part of the Tigris-Euphrates Valley contains the rich soil the rivers carry as they pour into the Persian Gulf. In ancient times especially fertile soil covered this area, called Sumer (SOO•muhr). Here Neolithic people settled and grew crops. Joined by two groups of people from the east, the inhabitants created what we call Sumerian culture. We do not know much about the Sumerians except that a group of nomadic people probably migrated to Sumer and mingled with the original inhabitants. By 3000 B.C. these people knew how to use metal and had developed a kind of writing.

Learning from Maps The people of the Tigris and Euphrates River valleys used the rivers' waters for irrigation. Where do the Tigris and Euphrates meet?

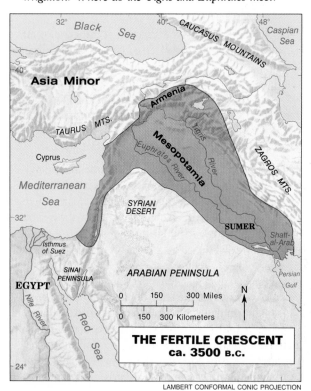

THE FERTILE CRESCENT ca. 3500 B.C.

LAMBERT CONFORMAL CONIC PROJECTION

Sacred Sumerian Animal

This beautiful statue of an animal peering through the branches of a flowering tree was crafted in Sumer about 4,500 years ago. It is made of wood decorated with gold, lapis lazuli, silver, and mother-of-pearl. Scholars think the animal may be a goat or a ram. The combination of the flowering tree and the animal leads some scholars to believe that the statue had an agricultural meaning. Sumer was located in an area of sparse rainfall and depended on water from the unpredictable flooding of the Tigris and Euphrates rivers. The animal may have been used in ceremonies to ensure the fertility of the fields.

The Sumerian culture was at least as rich and as advanced as that of Egypt. In many ways the Sumerians were even more original than the Egyptians. In fact, some historians believe that civilization first began in Sumer.

City-states

Early in their history the Sumerians developed a form of government called the **city-state,** which included a town or city and the surrounding land it controlled. The major city-states, including Ur, Erech, and Kish, had thousands of residents.

The people believed that much of the land in each of these early city-states belonged to a god or gods, while other land belonged to the palace, the temple, the nobles, or private citizens. Priests managed the gods' land, interpreted the gods' will to the people, and directed worship. Evidence indicates that kings ruled these city-states.

The many Sumerian city-states seldom united under a single government. Instead, the city-states competed, particularly over land boundaries and water rights.

Social Classes

The Sumerians had three distinct social classes. At the top stood a privileged class of nobles, including priests and government officials. Next came a group of merchants and artisans. Peasants and slaves made up the lowest class.

Sumerian Writing

Sumerian writing looked quite different from Egyptian writing. While Egyptian hieroglyphics consisted of symbols carved on slate or ivory or scribed on papyrus, Sumerian writing began mostly as marks pressed into clay tablets. Because the writers used a pointed stick called a stylus, most of the signs were combinations of wedge shapes. Today we call Sumerian writing **cuneiform** (kyoo • NEE • uh • fawrm) from the Latin word for "wedge," *cuneus.* The Sumerians had about 600 cuneiform signs.

The papyrus reed, which the Egyptians used to make paper, did not grow in Sumer, so the Sumerians did not learn to make paper. Instead, throughout their history, they wrote primarily on clay.

29

Learning from Pictures *Khuzistan Ziggurat is located in Choga Zanbil, Iran, and was built about 1250* B.C. *What important architectural designs did the Sumerians invent?*

They rolled out a lump of soft clay, made their wedge-shaped marks on it, and then allowed the clay tablet to dry until hard. Hardened clay would last for many years. It might shatter, but the pieces could usually be fitted together.

Farming and Trade

Most Sumerians farmed, growing grains, vegetables, and dates. Their domestic animals included cows, sheep, and goats, as well as oxen to pull plows and donkeys to pull carts and chariots. The Sumerians also developed a dairy industry, wove fine woolen goods, and raised flax for linen.

Sumer produced enough food to allow many people to work as traders and artisans. Before about 3000 B.C., Sumerians had begun trading with other peoples of the Middle East. Some merchants had agents in faraway places, while others traveled from city to city to sell Sumerian products.

Architecture, Engineering, and Science

The Sumerians used sun-dried clay bricks to build houses. Their brick structures did not last as long as the stone buildings of the Egyptians, but they were nonetheless well planned and well built.

The Sumerians may have invented several important architectural designs, including one of the strongest forms in building—the **arch,** a curved structure over an opening. By combining several arches, the Sumerians built rounded roofs in the shape of domes or vaults. They also knew how to use the ramp and even built sewers beneath their buildings.

The most striking Sumerian buildings were the temples, known as **ziggurats,** built on hills specially created on the flat land of the valley. Builders erected a ziggurat in layers, each one smaller than the one below, so that it looked somewhat like a wedding cake. They sometimes painted each story a different color. Usually a ziggurat soared seven stories, with the top one serving as the shrine of one of the gods.

Sumerian engineers and scientists made many important discoveries. Some scholars think that Sumerians were the first Neolithic people to develop and use the wheel. Later the Sumerians developed some of the principles of algebra. In mathematics they used a system of numbers based on 60. They stated large numbers in 60s—for example, they expressed 120 as two 60s and 180 as three 60s. They divided a circle into 360 degrees (six 60s), each degree into 60 minutes, each minute

◆READ
WRITE
INTERPRET
CONNECT
THINK

BUILDING HISTORY STUDY SKILLS

Reading About History: Identifying Sources of Evidence

Identifying sources of evidence—information used to support an explanation of the past—helps us interpret historical events. Two basic categories of sources are used as evidence. Primary sources include items such as artifacts, original documents, letters, diaries, and eyewitness accounts of an event or a period of history. Secondary sources are accounts written after the events by people who played no part in them.

How to Identify Sources of Evidence

To identify sources of evidence, follow these steps.

1. Identify the document or artifact. For example, is it a letter, diary, government record, work of art, building, or photograph?
2. Review the definitions of primary and secondary sources to determine the category of the evidence you have labeled.
3. Determine and then record the usefulness of the evidence. What question will it help you answer? Is a primary source always more reliable as evidence than a secondary source? Why or why not? Support your opinion with facts.

Developing the Skill

The work of art "The Royal Standard of Ur" was found in a Sumerian grave dated about 2700 B.C. It is made of shell, lapis lazuli (a semiprecious stone), and red stone inlaid on the sides of a wooden box. In the panel, the fruits of victory are being celebrated by the court. From this artifact depicting domestic animals, the wheel, leisure activities such as listening to music, and the banquet itself, historians can determine the sophistication of Sumerian society.

"The Royal Standard of Ur" is classified as a primary source. Sometimes a piece of evidence, however, can be classified as both a primary source and a secondary source, depending on the purpose for its use and the question that historians wish to answer. For example, Howard Carter's description of the opening of Egyptian pharaoh Tutankhamen's tomb can be classified as a primary source when the question posed concerns the discovery of the tomb. However, this same description is considered a secondary source when it is used to answer questions about Egyptian life during ancient times. Can you see the two applications of sources of evidence from the excerpt below?

❝ With suppressed excitement I carefully cut the cord, removed that precious seal, drew back the bolts, and opened the doors, when a fourth shrine was revealed . . . even more brilliant in workmanship than the last. . . . There, filling the entire area within . . . stood an immense yellow quartzite sarcophagus [stone coffin]. . . .

The tackle for raising the lid was in position. I gave the word. Amid intense silence the huge slab . . . rose from its bed. . . . The lid being suspended in mid-air, we rolled back those covering shrouds, one by one. . . . So gorgeous was the sight that met our eyes: a golden effigy of the young boy king. ❞

Practicing the skill. How might an account of the 1988 discovery of a Spanish galleon that sank off the coast of Florida in 1568 be considered both a primary and a secondary source?

To apply this skill, see Applying History Study Skills on page 47.

Sumerian Royal Standard of Ur

into 60 seconds. Today, when you look at a compass or a watch, you are seeing a principle the Sumerians developed thousands of years ago.

The Sumerians also developed a 12-month lunar calendar. When the passage of years made their calendar inaccurate, they added a thirteenth month to bring it back into line with the seasons.

Education and Religion

The Sumerians considered education very important, although only upper-class boys attended schools. Students learned to write and spell by copying religious books and songs. They also studied reading, history, mathematics, foreign languages, and mapmaking. Advanced education included law, medicine, and surgery. Students also spent much time trying to predict the future.

Like the Egyptians, the Sumerians practiced polytheism. They associated their gods with the forces of nature and with heavenly bodies, such as the sun and moon. Sumerians believed the gods had the same habits and feelings as ordinary humans but had much more power. Anu, lord of heaven, Enlil, god of air and storms, and Ea, god of the waters, ranked as the most important Sumerian gods.

Unlike the Egyptians, the Sumerians did not have a firm set of beliefs about an afterlife. They did not believe in reward in heaven or punishment in hell, but they did believe in some form of life after death. They also feared ghosts. They thought, for example, that if they did not bury personal objects such as jewelry with the dead, the spirits of the dead person would be displeased and would return to haunt the homes and families of the living.

SECTION 3 REVIEW

1. **Define** city-state, cuneiform, arch, ziggurat
2. **Identify** Sumerians
3. **Locate** Fertile Crescent, Tigris-Euphrates Valley, Persian Gulf, Mesopotamia, Babylonia, Sumer
4. **Understanding Ideas** Why did the inhabitants of the Tigris-Euphrates Valley regard nature as a hostile force?
5. **Summarizing Ideas** Describe the Sumerian contributions to architecture.
6. **Interpreting Ideas** Explain the mathematical ideas that originated in the Sumerian culture.
7. **Synthesizing Ideas** (a) How did the religious beliefs of the Sumerians resemble those of the Egyptians? (b) How were they different? (c) How do you account for the differences?

4 Several Empires Were Established in the Fertile Crescent

Sumerian city-states did not unite under one government. This lack of unity proved to be a fatal weakness.

The Akkadians Under Sargon

After 2400 B.C. the Akkadians (uh • KAYD • ee • uhnz), a people who also lived in Mesopotamia, conquered the Sumerians. Unlike the Sumerians, the Akkadians spoke a Semitic language closely related to modern Hebrew and Arabic. The most powerful of the Semitic kings, Sargon of Akkad, established a great empire that extended as far west as the Mediterranean (see map, this page). The Akkadian empire lasted about 100 years. When it ended, Sumerian city-states once again became prosperous, but new waves of invaders soon swept through the eastern Fertile Crescent. Another powerful

Learning from Maps The Akkadian Empire had its capital at the magnificent city of Akkad. What was the southernmost city in the Akkadian Empire?

AKKADIAN EMPIRE
ca. 2300 B.C.

LAMBERT CONFORMAL CONIC PROJECTION

Semitic state arose, this time centered at the large new city of Babylon.

The Lawgiving Babylonians

About 1792 B.C. a strong ruler named Hammurabi (ham•uh•RAHB•ee) came to power in Babylon and conquered most of the upper Tigris-Euphrates Valley (see map, this page). More than a great military leader, Hammurabi was a just political leader as well. He is best known for the Code of Hammurabi, a collection of laws passed under his direction.

The Code of Hammurabi consisted of 282 laws that controlled all aspects of life in Babylon. For example, the code carefully regulated agriculture. Farmers who failed to cultivate their fields or keep the irrigation canals and ditches in good condition were punished. Some laws concerned commerce and industry and included provisions regarding wages, hours, and working conditions. Other laws dealt with property rights, contracts, and bankruptcy. Still others dealt with marriage and divorce. Judges enforced the laws under the supervision of the king's advisers and officials.

The Code of Hammurabi provided for harsh punishments. For example:

> **❝** *I*f a man has accused another man and has brought a charge of murder against him, but has not proved it, his accuser shall be put to death. 22–23 If a man has committed robbery and is caught, that man shall be put to death. If the robber is not caught, the man who has been robbed shall formally declare whatever he has lost before a god, and the city and mayor in whose territory or district the robbery was committed shall make good to him his lost property. 229–30 If a builder has constructed a house for an *awilum* [man] but has not made his work strong, with the result that the house which he built collapsed and so caused the death of the owner of the house, that builder shall be put to death. If it has caused the death of the son of the owner of the house, they shall put to death the son of the builder. **❞**

The concept of "an eye for an eye, a tooth for a tooth" provided the basis of punishment. If a man caused another to lose an eye, then his own eye was put out.

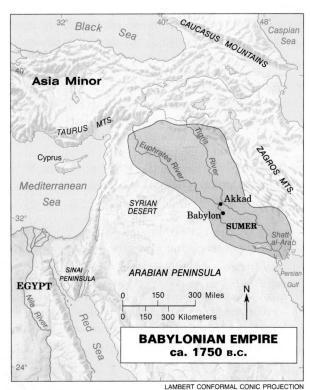

LAMBERT CONFORMAL CONIC PROJECTION

Learning from Maps A Hittite king eventually overthrew the Babylonian Empire, encountering little opposition. Who was Babylon's first strong military ruler?

Punishment often varied according to wealth, however. If a wealthy man destroyed the eye of a poor man, the wealthy man did not lose his eye but merely paid a fine. A thief who could not repay what was stolen was put to death. If the thief had money, however, the only punishment was to repay more than had been stolen.

Babylonian culture. Like the Sumerians, most Babylonians farmed. They domesticated animals, grew large amounts of food, and also wove textiles. As traders, however, the Babylonians surpassed the Sumerians. They traded with merchants from distant parts of the Fertile Crescent as well as from Egypt and even India.

The social organization of the Babylonians also resembled that of the Sumerians. A nobility including priests and government officials made up the upper class. Next came a middle class of artisans and merchants and a lower class of peasants and slaves.

Babylonian women probably had fewer privileges than Egyptian women, but they enjoyed a higher position in society than that of most women in ancient civilizations. Some ancient peoples considered women as property to be owned and treated as slaves. In contrast, Babylonian women had legal and economic rights, and laws protected their property. However, a man might sell his wife—or even his children or himself—to pay his debts.

Babylonian women could be traders and merchants and could work in other professions. They could even become priests. They possibly received as much pay as men for doing the same work.

Babylonian religion. The Babylonians adopted many Sumerian religious beliefs. Although Marduk, god of the city of Babylon, became the principal god, the old Sumerian gods remained. The Babylonians made many sacrifices to their gods for such things as good harvests or success in business. They believed in a gloomy, hopeless life after death spent in a place called "the Land of No Return."

Babylonian priests wielded as much power as Sumerian priests. They had great influence because of the spells they used against evil spirits. They also claimed they could predict the future.

The Invading Hittites

Many times in history, you will read of conquerors who adopted the culture of the people they conquered. This was certainly true of the Babylonians after they conquered the Sumerians. However, it was definitely not true of the Hittites, a warlike people who invaded the Tigris-Euphrates Valley from Asia Minor about 1600 B.C.

The Hittites were the first people to make extensive use of iron weapons. Their most important achievement, however, lay in their laws, which were less brutal than the Code of Hammurabi. Only major crimes, such as rebellion, warranted execution. Hittite law called for a person to pay a fine for causing damage or injury. For example, if you broke someone's arm, you paid 20 pieces of silver rather than having your own arm broken. In determining the punishment, the law also considered such factors as premeditation—whether a person intended beforehand to commit the crime.

When the Hittites invaded the Tigris-Euphrates Valley, they conquered and looted Babylon itself. The Hittites were too far from their homeland to control Babylonia permanently, however, and soon withdrew to the western part of the Fertile Crescent. They remained a powerful force in the west until about 1200 B.C.

LAMBERT CONFORMAL CONIC PROJECTION

Learning from Maps *The last Assyrian army was defeated six years after Nineveh was destroyed. What city survived the changing empires of the Fertile Crescent?*

The Conquering Assyrians

Following the decline of the Hittites, Babylon suffered further invasions by mountain peoples. Then about 900 B.C., the fiercest, cruelest, and most warlike of all ancient peoples—the Assyrians—overwhelmed Mesopotamia.

The Assyrians first settled along the Tigris River, northwest of Babylonia. There they built the city-state Assur, named for their chief god. Both the region, Assyria, and the people took their name from the word *Assur*. From Assur they spread throughout the region until they controlled Syria, Babylonia, and even Egypt (see map, this page).

The Assyrians excelled in warfare. Instead of chariots they used **cavalry**—a military unit of riders on horses. They also used many iron weapons and invented the battering ram to break through the brick walls of cities they attacked.

And how cruel they were! Often using savage methods, the Assyrians killed the enemies they captured in battle. They enslaved conquered peoples and deported them to other areas, replacing them with Assyrian colonists. In this way the Assyrians easily controlled conquered lands and gained many slaves. About 700 B.C. the Assyrians captured Babylon, looted it, and finally destroyed it completely. They even changed the course of the Euphrates River to flow over the site. Such acts of destruction earned the Assyrians the hatred and fear of people throughout the ancient world.

Assyrian government. The Assyrian king had total power. Priests and government officials took orders from him and answered to him. The monarch was responsible only to the god Assur, whose representative on earth he claimed to be.

The Assyrians created an extremely efficient government, building roads so that troops could move about quickly and establishing a postal service to speed news of rebellions to the army. Governors ruled conquered lands, collected high taxes, and made regular and frequent reports to the king. To ensure loyalty, inspectors checked on the governors' activities. The king always stationed an army in a conquered area to keep the people under control. This army sometimes consisted of large groups of **mercenaries**—professional soldiers paid to serve in a foreign army.

The Assyrians were the first people to develop an effective method of governing an empire, and all other empires of the ancient Middle East modeled their governments after it. In other fields, however, the Assyrians contributed little to civilization.

Assyrian greatness and decline. After the Assyrians became powerful, they made the city of Nineveh (NIN • uh • vuh) their capital. Nineveh symbolized the pride and cruelty of the Assyrians. Attempting to make it the most fortified city in the world, the Assyrians constructed a huge double wall, 50 feet (15 meters) thick and 100 feet (30 meters) high, that stretched for seven miles (11.2 kilometers) around the city. The wall had 15 gates, each beautifully decorated and strongly defended. To assure a supply of water, the Assyrians diverted 18 mountain streams to flow through Nineveh. Within the city the Assyrians built a large library in which scholars collected clay tablets from all over Assyria and Babylonia, preserving these literary works for future generations.

Powerful Nineveh was not powerful enough to resist Assyria's many enemies, however. Finally, in 612 B.C., a group of opponents led by the Chaldeans (kal • DEE • uhnz) and the Medes (MEEDZ) captured and destroyed Nineveh.

The Chaldeans

The Chaldeans took control of much of the territory that the Assyrians had ruled. Under the leadership of a wise ruler named Nebuchadnezzar (neb • uh • kuhd • NEZ • uhr), who ruled from the rebuilt capital city of Babylon between 605 B.C. and 562 B.C., the Chaldeans conquered most of the Fertile Crescent (see map, this page).

The Chaldeans of Babylon enjoyed a high standard of living and surrounded themselves with beautiful buildings. The enormous palace of Nebuchadnezzar, perhaps the most impressive building in the city, contained a very unusual feature—the Hanging Gardens. According to legend, Nebuchadnezzar's wife had lived in the mountains and was homesick on the flat plains of Babylonia. To please her, the king planted thousands of brightly colored tropical plants and flowers on the roof of the palace. The Greeks and other peoples of the ancient world regarded the Hanging Gardens of Babylon as one of the Seven Wonders of the World.

Learning from Maps *Under the Chaldeans, Babylon once again became the center of civilization in the Fertile Crescent. What was the other major city of the Chaldean Empire?*

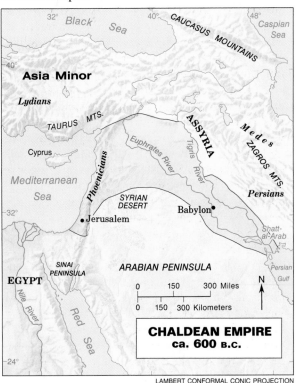

LAMBERT CONFORMAL CONIC PROJECTION

All the strength of the Chaldeans seemed to lie in the leadership ability of Nebuchadnezzar. One of his successors, a religious fanatic, opposed the priests, who then betrayed the city to the Persians. Within 30 years after Nebuchadnezzar's death, the Chaldean Empire fell.

Like the Assyrians, the Chaldeans contributed little to civilization. An exception was their deep interest in astronomy, which enabled them to calculate the length of a year to within seven minutes.

The Mighty Persians

The Persians who conquered Babylon in 539 B.C. spoke an Indo-European language and, like the Medes, had migrated into what is today Iran about 1800 B.C.* The region became known as Persia and Media after these two tribes.

---

*The Indo-Europeans originally lived in the region north of the Caspian and Black seas. Other Indo-European peoples included the Hittites and the ancestors of the Greeks and Romans.

Cyrus, Darius, and Xerxes. About 550 B.C. Cyrus, a Persian and one of the greatest leaders in all history, led a successful revolt against the Medes. Cyrus then began a series of conquests, capturing Babylon and conquering the rest of the Fertile Crescent and Asia Minor.

A later Persian ruler, Darius the Great, added regions south and east of Persia as far as the Indus River in India as well as parts of southeastern Europe (see map, this page). Both Darius and his son Xerxes (ZUHRK•seez) invaded Greece in the 400s B.C. but failed to conquer it. Nevertheless, the Persians ruled the mightiest empire known up to that time.

Persian government. The early Persian kings distinguished themselves not only as great generals but also as wise rulers. Although all-powerful in government, they showed great concern for justice. They collected taxes and administered justice fairly.

Persian rulers chose the best officials they could find, often from among the conquered peoples, to govern their huge empire. They paid close attention to local customs and allowed the conquered peoples

Learning from Maps *Persian emperors relied on the corps of Persian soldiers called the "10,000 Immortals" to protect the huge empire. How far was Susa from Persepolis?*

ROBINSON PROJECTION

Learning from Pictures
Darius the Great is shown here in a stone carving receiving homage in his palace at Persepolis.

to keep their own religions and laws. This tolerant practice won the favor of the priests and the loyalty of the people.

The Persians copied some things from the Assyrians, especially the kinds of officials used to govern the empire. Inspectors called "the King's Eyes and Ears" helped Persian rulers. The Persians also extended the Assyrian road system. The most famous road, the Royal Road, extended from Sardis, in Asia Minor, to Susa, one of the capitals of the empire. The Persians built these roads mainly for the army and postal riders, but merchants also used them. As a result, these roads aided the process of cultural diffusion in the empire by promoting the exchange of customs and ideas.

Persian religion. The greatest cultural contribution of the Persians concerned religion. At first, like other early peoples, the Persians worshiped many gods. Then about 600 B.C. a great prophet and religious reformer named Zoroaster (ZOHR•uh•was•tuhr) completely changed their religious ideas.

Zoroaster taught that on earth people received training for a future life. In the world the forces of good and evil struggled savagely, and people could choose between good and evil. Those who chose good (symbolized by light) would be rewarded with eternal life. Those who chose evil would face darkness and misery after death. In the distant future, the forces of good would triumph. Then the earth would disappear, having served its purpose as the stage on which the great conflict had taken place.

The ideas of Zoroaster, called Zoroastrianism, strongly influenced the lives of the Persians. According to this prophet, nothing was more shameful than lying. The Persians taught their children that they must always tell the truth. They also considered getting into debt a form of lying and therefore a disgrace.

Zoroaster's idea of a struggle between good and evil is similar to that of the Hebrews and, later, of the Christians. Zoroastrian ideas also taught that final judgment was based on reward or punishment and, according to what some people believed, depended on human choice.

The decline of the Persians. The Persian kings who followed Darius and Xerxes lacked strength and wisdom. Therefore, both the government and the army grew weak. In 331 B.C., more than 200 years after Cyrus led the revolt against the Medes, Alexander the Great led his army out of Greece and conquered the Persian Empire.

SECTION 4 REVIEW

1. **Define**   cavalry, mercenary
2. **Identify**   Sargon of Akkad, Hammurabi, Babylonians, Chaldeans, Nebuchadnezzar, Cyrus, Darius, Xerxes, Zoroaster
3. **Locate**   Syria, Babylon, Asia Minor, Nineveh, Persia, Caspian Sea, Black Sea, Royal Road, Sardis, Susa
4. **Summarizing Ideas**   **(a)** List five laws in the Code of Hammurabi.   **(b)** How did the Hittite laws vary from the Code of Hammurabi?
5. **Understanding Ideas**   Describe the treatment of women in Babylonian society.
6. **Evaluating Ideas**   **(a)** List briefly the accomplishments of the Babylonians, the Hittites, the Assyrians, the Chaldeans, and the Persians.   **(b)** Which accomplishment do you believe was the most important?   **(c)** Why?

5 Phoenicians, Lydians, and Hebrews Made Lasting Contributions

The peoples who lived in the western end of the Fertile Crescent and in western Asia Minor did not create large empires, but they had a great influence on the modern world. This narrow strip of land along the Mediterranean Sea today forms portions of the nations of Egypt, Israel, Jordan, Lebanon, Syria, and Turkey. In ancient times, however, people called the northern part Phoenicia (fi • NEESH • ee • uh) and Lydia (LID • ee • uh). The southern section had different names during the course of history, including Canaan, Israel, and Palestine. Between about 1200 B.C. and 500 B.C. the peoples of this region—the Phoenicians, Lydians, and Hebrews—made important contributions in economics and religion.

The Phoenicians

Phoenicia consisted of a loose union of city-states, each governed by a different king. Although Phoenicia had hills and mountains, its lack of fertile land made large-scale farming impossible. Blocked by the high ridges of the Lebanon Mountains, the Phoenicians did not migrate eastward. Instead, they turned to the sea and to commerce for their living. On the map on this page, notice the cities of Tyre (TYR) and Sidon (SYD • uhn). Both of these seaports became world famous.

The Phoenicians built seagoing ships that today would seem small and frail, but the Phoenicians proved skillful and fearless sailors. Propelled by sails and oars, Phoenician ships plied the Mediterranean Sea. Some historians believe that the Phoenicians sailed as far as Britain in search of tin and may also have sailed around Africa. In time the Phoenicians became the greatest traders in the ancient world.

Articles of trade. Phoenicia had only one important natural resource—lumber taken from the beautiful cedar trees of the Lebanon Mountains. Many ancient peoples used this lumber for building.

Because of the lack of local mineral resources, the Phoenicians bought metals from other regions. They became highly skilled in creating beautiful objects of gold, silver, copper, and bronze. They also learned how to make exquisite glass.

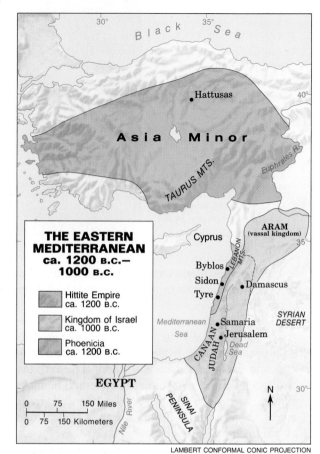

THE EASTERN MEDITERRANEAN ca. 1200 B.C.–1000 B.C.

- Hittite Empire ca. 1200 B.C.
- Kingdom of Israel ca. 1000 B.C.
- Phoenicia ca. 1200 B.C.

0   75   150 Miles
0   75   150 Kilometers

LAMBERT CONFORMAL CONIC PROJECTION

Learning from Maps Because of their location along the sea, the territories of the eastern Mediterranean depended on trade. Which region had the most centers of trade?

Along their seacoast the Phoenicians found a shellfish called murex, which they used to make purple dye. People throughout the ancient world prized Phoenician woolen cloth, dyed purple. So expensive that only the wealthy could afford it, purple—the royal purple—became the color worn by kings and queens.

Phoenician colonies. Between 1000 and 700 B.C., conditions favored the Phoenician traders. The Hittite Empire had disintegrated, and Egypt

---

What If?
The Phoenician Alphabet
Phoenician trade helped spread the alphabet throughout the Mediterranean region. How might the history of writing have been different if the Phoenicians had not been traders?

was in decline. Tyre united the Phoenician city-states under its leadership, and the Phoenicians began to establish colonies throughout the Mediterranean region.

These new colonies, on the islands of Sicily, Sardinia, and Malta and throughout the Mediterranean Sea, served as centers for trade. Farther west, beyond the Mediterranean Sea, the Phoenicians also established a colony on the site of the modern city of Cádiz, Spain.

Phoenician culture. The Phoenicians imitated the cultures of other peoples. They patterned their government and most of their customs after the Egyptians and the Babylonians. Through trading the Phoenicians indirectly spread Egyptian and Babylonian culture throughout the Mediterranean area.

Phoenician religion offered the people few comforts. Phoenicians did not believe in an afterlife and sometimes sacrificed their own children to win favor from the many gods they worshiped.

The Phoenicians made one very important contribution to Western civilization—the alphabet. Earlier alphabets had been developed in Canaan, the Sinai Peninsula, and northern Syria, but the Phoenicians developed the alphabet that became the model for later Western alphabets.

The spread of the alphabet provides a good example of how commerce can speed the process of cultural diffusion. The practical Phoenicians used writing in their businesses for recording contracts and drawing up bills. Phoenician commerce made it possible for the knowledge of alphabetical writing to spread throughout the Mediterranean world.

The Greeks adopted and improved the Phoenician alphabet by adding signs for vowel sounds. Later, the Romans copied this alphabet from the Greeks and developed the Roman alphabet we use.

The Lydians

Like the Phoenicians, the Lydians of Asia Minor made a significant contribution to civilization based on trade. About 600 B.C., the Lydians became the first people in history to use coined money. Before this invention, traders had to rely on **barter,** or exchanging one good or service for another. Barter, however, limited trade because two people could strike a bargain only if each had a good or service that the other wanted. The use of money allowed traders to set prices for various goods and services and to develop a **money economy,** an economic

system based on the use of money rather than on barter.

Like the Phoenicians, the Lydians did not rule an empire. Through trade, however, they passed on the concept of a money economy to the Greeks and the Persians, who in turn helped spread this concept to other parts of the world.

The Physical Setting

To the south of Phoenicia lay a small strip of land known as Canaan that had no forests and few minerals or other natural resources. As you can see on the map on page 38, Canaan consisted of two regions. The Jordan River watered the northern valley. There the fertile soil helped farmers grow grains, olives, figs, and grapes. Desert covered most of the southern region, around and south of the Dead Sea. (The sea was called *dead* because the high salt content of the water killed all marine life.) This arid plateau had poor and rocky soil.

Canaan lay along the great land bridge between Asia and Africa. In one way, this location gave the people an advantage, because the merchants who carried goods and ideas between Egypt and the Fertile Crescent traveled this route.

In another way, however, Canaan's location was a disadvantage, because armies also passed along the route. The people of Canaan lacked powerful armies, and at one time or another the Egyptians, Hittites, Assyrians, Chaldeans, and Persians conquered Canaan.

The Hebrews

Just as in the eastern part of the Fertile Crescent, a series of peoples inhabited Canaan. The Hebrews, or Jews, however, had the greatest influence on their own times and on all of later history. The Hebrews did not always live in Canaan. Abraham, the leader of the Hebrew people according to the Bible, once lived in Sumer. After leaving there, he led his nomadic people through the desert to the borders of northern Canaan and farther south across the Isthmus of Suez into Egypt. They settled in the "Land of Goshen," east of the Nile Delta, where the Nile flows into the Mediterranean Sea.

These Hebrews lived peacefully in Egypt for some time, but eventually they fell from favor. Some scholars believe that one group of Hebrews

Text continues on page 42.

What is money? Quite simply, it is any object that people are willing to accept as payment for goods or services.

Throughout history, money has taken many different forms, but its definition has changed in only one way: Today money is accepted as payment by all people; in the past it was accepted only by some.

Early societies—people who hunted, fished, and farmed for their own needs—used a barter system. One family might trade a basket of fish for another family's extra vegetables. This system was extremely burdensome, however. If the farmer did not want fish that day, the fisher would have to make several trades to get the needed vegetables.

To make trade easier, people began to look for objects with a common value. To work well, the object had to be useful to everyone, rare enough to be valuable, and small and light enough to be carried. One of the first kinds of this "commodity money" people tried was salt. In the ancient Middle East, people carried salt in small containers and traded it for other objects. Early Roman emperors gave salt to their

soldiers as a type of travel allowance. In fact, our word "salary" comes from the Roman word "salarium" or "salt place." Salt was also used in Africa, Abyssinia and parts of Asia. But this money was useful only in areas where salt was rare. The ancient Greeks, Romans, Egyptians, and early Europeans also used cattle as money.

A most impractical form of money was employed on the island of Yap in the South Pacific. People there used wheel-shaped boulders as money until the mid-1900s.

To carry their money, two people had to pass a pole through a hole in the middle and rest it on their shoulders. Unlike cattle, the stones had no other practical use, but because they came from the distant islands of Guam and Peleu, they were greatly prized. Even today, many Yaps place these large stones in front of their houses, and smaller stones are still used as currency.

Seashells were another widely accepted form of money. In southern Asia, the Pacific Islands, and parts of the Middle East and Africa, people used the colorful cowrie shell. But the shell money with which Americans are most familiar is "wampum." These carefully cut and highly polished black and white shells were both beautiful and rare.

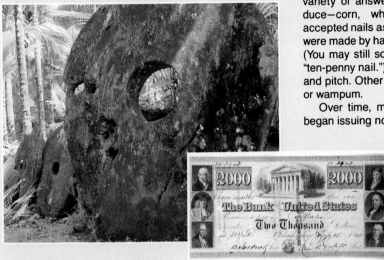

For hundreds of years, Indians in what is today the northeastern United States used these tiny, hard objects, strung together on their belts and jewelry, as their only money.

Easy to carry, durable, and scarce, shells made excellent money. But in other parts of the world, another object—metal—met these requirements. By 800 B.C., parts of China and the Middle East were using gold, silver, and copper shaped as long bars or even lumps. Farmers of early Rome used crude copper or bronze bars. Since the metal was exchanged for its actual value, it was weighed at every transaction, and eventually merchants began to mark the weight on each bar.

As the countries around the Mediterranean Sea began to trade with one another, they needed to find a kind of money that was guaranteed in value and was light enough to be carried on ships without sinking them. About 700 B.C., the king of Lydia, in what is now called Turkey, came up with the idea of stamping his personal mark on small kidney-bean-shaped pieces of electrum (a mixture of gold and silver). These "staters" are usually considered to be the first coins. Within 100 years, Greece began minting coins. About 200 B.C., Rome came out with the silver "denarius," which became one of the most widely accepted coins in the world.

The early American colonists were unable to use coins. Few of the settlers who first arrived in the British colonies were wealthy, and the money they had brought with them soon flowed back to Europe to buy supplies. When the colonists tried to mint their own money, such as the Massachusetts Pine-tree Shilling, the British government stopped them.

Faced with these problems, what were the colonists to use for money? The inventive colonists came up with a variety of answers to this question. In addition to produce—corn, wheat, peas, and rye—many colonies accepted nails as money. Scarce and costly because they were made by hand, nails were valued in terms of a penny. (You may still sometimes hear the terms "two-penny" or "ten-penny nail.") The Carolinas accepted rice, indigo, tar, and pitch. Other colonies used Indian corn, beaver skins, or wampum.

Over time, many governments throughout the world began issuing notes or IOUs for their coins. Unlike earlier forms of money, the notes had no value themselves. The government simply agreed to pay the owner the face value of the note in gold or silver. These early forms of paper money, first used in China more than 1,000 years ago, became common all over the world by the 1700s. But the value of paper money depended on the confidence people had in the government that issued it. After the Civil War, for example, Confederate "scrip" issued by the South became totally worthless.

Coins today are little more than symbols themselves. The face value stamped on the coin is far more than the coin's metal is worth. Beginning in 1965 dimes and quarters minted by the United States contained no silver at all.

Today, with automated banking and computerized checking, we think little about the problems of storing, handling, and transporting our money. However, not so long ago a cow would have gotten you a lot further than a credit card.

Photos   Page 40: wampum belt (top), Swiss bank worker (bottom left), manufacturing coins (bottom right); Page 41: Yap money (top), early United States paper money (middle), ancient coins (bottom)

Learning from Pictures *In their siege on the Canaanite city of Jericho, the Hebrews carry the ark of the covenant containing the Ten Commandments around the walls of the city.*

entered Egypt along with the Hyksos in the 1700s B.C. When the Egyptians finally expelled the Hyksos in the 1500s B.C., the pharaohs enslaved the Hebrews.

Establishing a homeland. A great leader, Moses, later arose among the Hebrews and led his people out of slavery and into the deserts of the Sinai Peninsula. The books of Exodus, Numbers, and Deuteronomy in the Bible describe Moses and the escape from Egypt.

According to the Bible, Moses climbed to the top of Mount Sinai and returned to the Hebrews bearing the **Ten Commandments**—the moral laws the Hebrew god Yahweh (YAH•way) revealed to him. These commandments emphasize the Hebrew principles of self-restraint; the importance of the family, human life, and formal worship; and the nature of the monotheistic religion. As the Bible records:

"God spoke, and these were his words: I am the LORD your God who brought you out of Egypt, out of the land of slavery.

[1] You shall have no other god to set against me.

[2] You shall not make a carved image for yourself nor the likeness of anything in the heavens above, or on the earth below, or in the waters under the earth. . . .

[3] You shall not make wrong use of the name of the LORD your God; the LORD will not leave unpunished the man who misuses his name.

[4] Remember to keep the sabbath day holy. You have six days to labour and do all your work. But the seventh day is a sabbath of the LORD your God; that day you shall not do any work. . . .

[5] Honour your father and your mother. . . .
[6] You shall not commit murder.
[7] You shall not commit adultery.
[8] You shall not steal.
[9] You shall not give false evidence against your neighbour.
[10] You shall not covet your neighbour's house; you shall not covet your neighbour's wife . . . or anything that belongs to him. **"**

Moses claimed that Canaan was a promised land and that Yahweh had commissioned him to found a holy nation. Inspired by his words, the Hebrews set out for Canaan. According to the Bible, Moses and his followers wandered in the desert for many years. Finally, a new generation of Hebrews entered Canaan.

The Hebrews who had come from Egypt joined those who had lived for so long on the borders of northern Canaan. By this time the harsh desert life had hardened the Hebrews into tough desert tribes. But establishing a homeland in Canaan proved difficult. A people known as the Canaanites held the northern Jordan Valley, while the Philistines lived along the southern coast. Both groups vigorously defended their land in a struggle that lasted more than 100 years. The Hebrews first conquered the Canaanites, making it possible for some of the Hebrews to settle in the Jordan Valley. The Philistines proved fiercer opponents. The Hebrews drove them closer to the seacoast but never conquered them completely.

A new government and new customs. As nomads the Hebrews had been divided into 12 tribes. During the long years of fighting, the tribes united under the rule of one king. The first king of this united kingdom called Israel was Saul. David, and then Solomon, succeeded Saul.

David occupied the city of Jerusalem and made it a capital and a religious center. His son, Solomon, built palaces there and a great temple for Yahweh, but the enormous cost overburdened the poor country. The government levied high taxes and forced many people to work on these great buildings without pay.

At the end of Solomon's reign in 922 B.C., the 10 northern tribes revolted, and the kingdom divided into two parts. The northern part became the kingdom of Israel, with its capital at Samaria. The southern part, situated around the Dead Sea, became the kingdom of Judah, with Jerusalem as its capital (see map, page 38).

These two Hebrew kingdoms lacked the strength to withstand invasions from the east. About 722 B.C. the Assyrians ravaged Samaria and conquered Israel, capturing many Hebrews and deporting them as slaves. Later, in 586 B.C., the Chaldeans captured Judah and its capital, Jerusalem (see chart, this page). They destroyed Solomon's temple and took the southern Hebrews into captivity. Cyrus, the Persian king, conquered the Chaldeans and allowed the Hebrews to return to their homeland to rebuild the temple at Jerusalem. Thereafter, however, one people after another conquered the Hebrews.

The Old Testament and Jewish Law

The great Hebrew work of literature is the Old Testament of the Bible. Its 39 books tell the story of the creation of the world, the special mission of the Hebrews, their escape from slavery in Egypt, and the progress of their history and beliefs over 1,000 years. About one-third of the books tell the history. The remainder includes poetry, religious instruction, prophecy, and laws.

The Hebrews did not think of **prophets** as people who predicted the future, though some prophets claimed that they could. Rather, they viewed the prophets as great religious and moral thinkers—the nagging conscience of the people. The messages that prophets conveyed in such phrases as "A soft answer turneth away wrath," "There is no peace unto the wicked," and "Thou shalt love thy neighbor as thyself" have remained the foundation for moral and ethical behavior.

Kingdoms and Empires of the Fertile Crescent	
ca. 3000 B.C. – 2400 B.C.	Sumerians
ca. 2400 B.C. – 2300 B.C.	Akkadians
ca. 1800 B.C. – 1600 B.C.	Babylonians
ca. 1600 B.C. – 1200 B.C.	Hittites
ca. 1200 B.C. – 586 B.C.	Hebrews
ca. 1000 B.C. – 700 B.C.	Phoenicians
ca. 900 B.C. – 612 B.C.	Assyrians
ca. 700 B.C. – 547 B.C.	Lydians
612 B.C. – 539 B.C.	Chaldeans
550 B.C. – 331 B.C.	Persians

The Amazing Variety of the Earth's Surface

Plains, plateaus, hills, mountains, canyons, valleys, and ridges are but a few of our planet's amazing variety of landforms, or shapes on the earth's surface. As you read about these landforms, think about the ones that can be seen in the area where you live.

Types of Landforms

By and large, geographers recognize four general types of landforms —plains, plateaus, hills, and mountains. Geographers categorize these landforms in terms of such characteristics as slope and local relief. Slope refers to the slant of the land. Local relief refers to a landform's elevation. Elevation is a place's distance above or below sea level. The difference in elevation between the highest and lowest points in an area is that area's local relief.

Plains. Geographers classify landforms with nearly level or gently rolling land as plains. This type of landform has little slope and, by definition, a local relief of less than 500 feet (150 meters). Most plains occur at low elevations—less than 1,000 feet (305 meters) above sea level. The Gulf Coastal Plain of the United States, for example, stretches from the Gulf of Mexico to southern Illinois, but no part of it rises higher than 500 feet (150 meters) above sea level. A few plains, such as the western Great Plains of the United States, however, are located at higher elevations.

Plateaus. A plateau is a generally flat area that rises far above the surrounding land on at least one side. Tableland—another name for plateau —provides a helpful image of the characteristics of this landform. Like a table, a plateau has a flat surface high off the ground.

Among the most distinguishing feature of plateaus is their high elevation. The Colorado Plateau of the western United States, for example, lies 7,000 to 8,000 feet (2,135 to 2,440 meters) above sea level. The Plateau of Tibet in China rises more than 15,000 feet (4,572 meters) above sea level. Some plateaus, however, occur at relatively low elevations.

The land at the top of a plateau is usually broad and flat. On some plateaus, deep canyons break up this pattern. These canyons have high slope and high local relief. For example, the Grand Canyon, which the Colorado River carved into the Colorado Plateau, has a local relief of more than 5,000 feet (1,525 meters).

Hills. Geographers classify as a hill any generally rounded landform that rises at least 500 feet (152 meters) above the surrounding area. The slope of hills varies from very gentle to very steep. By definition, however, the local relief of a hill must be less than 2,000 feet (610 meters).

Mountains. A dramatic type of landform that rises sharply from the surrounding land to heights thousands of feet above sea level is called a mountain. Mountains have steep slope and local relief of at least 2,000 feet (610 meters). The summit, or highest point, of a mountain typically appears smaller and sharper than the summit of a hill. High elevations also distinguish mountains from other landforms. For example, the highest mountain in the world, Mount Everest in the Himalayas in Asia, soars to an elevation of 29,028 feet (8,848 meters) above sea level.

Landforms and History

Throughout history landforms have had an important impact on human activity. For example, the fertile plains areas of North Africa and the Middle East nurtured the growth of the early civilizations you have read about in this chapter. In addition, huge mountain barriers have isolated some civilizations from outside influence for thousands of years. However, you should note that landforms only influence history, they do not determine it. In fact, one of the most important themes of history concerns the ways in which people have altered their physical environment to suit their way of life.

The majestic Austrian Alps

Learning from Pictures *At the Synagogue of the Home for the Aged in Tel-Aviv, this elderly man reads about the teachings of Judaism.*

The first five books of the Old Testament, known as the Torah, listed the Hebrew, or Jewish, code of laws. This code of laws, named for Moses, was called Mosaic law and included the Ten Commandments and laws developed during later periods. Mosaic law, like the Code of Hammurabi, demanded "an eye for an eye," but it set a much higher value on human life. Although Mosaic law accepted slavery as the custom of the ancient world, the law demanded kindness for slaves. Mosaic law also preached kindness toward the poor and toward strangers, as did Babylonian law. Mosaic law reserved the most severe punishments for witchcraft and sacrifices to idols, crimes punished by death.

Mosaic law reflected the belief that all people, regardless of their station in life, deserved kindness and respect. This belief was based on the idea that Yahweh had created each person in his image. In later centuries, Christians adopted this same belief as part of their religion.

Judaism

Judaism, the religion of the Hebrews, survived partly because it changed throughout history. The early Hebrews worshiped Yahweh as a god who belonged to them alone and believed that people needed only to trust in Yahweh. They believed that Yahweh protected them from their enemies, took

their side in battle, and provided them with food and water. According to the Ten Commandments, Yahweh was a jealous god. If people sinned against Yahweh, not only would they be punished but also their children and succeeding generations would suffer. The Hebrews therefore viewed Yahweh not only as their protector and provider but also as a god to fear.

This concept of Yahweh slowly changed, partly because of the Hebrews' many sufferings and partly because of the teachings and writings of their prophets. In general, the prophets insisted that Yahweh was more concerned with a person's moral behavior than with religious rituals. Like the Zoroastrians, the Hebrews believed that people had a choice between good and evil. The Hebrews also believed that Yahweh held them responsible for their choices.

These ideas led the Hebrews to think of Yahweh as a loving father—a god who lived in the hearts of his worshipers and the god of all peoples. Other ancient peoples thought of their gods as having human qualities, but as being more powerful than humans. The Hebrews viewed Yahweh as a spiritual force rather than as a human being. The kings of other ancient peoples claimed to be gods or the representatives of gods in order to gain power. Hebrew kings were not gods. Only Yahweh was divine.

Because of its emphasis on ethics, or proper conduct, the Hebrew form of monotheism is often called **ethical monotheism.** It ranks as the most important contribution of the ancient Jews to Western civilization.

SECTION 5 REVIEW

1. **Define** barter, money economy, Ten Commandments, prophet, ethical monotheism
2. **Identify** Phoenicians, Hebrews, Abraham, Moses, Saul, David, Solomon
3. **Locate** Phoenicia, Lydia, Tyre, Sidon, Israel, Canaan, Sinai Peninsula, Jordan River, Samaria, Judah, Jerusalem
4. **Evaluating Ideas** **(a)** How did Phoenician sea trade benefit the peoples of the Mediterranean? **(b)** How did the invention of coined money make trade easier?
5. **Analyzing Ideas** **(a)** Why did the Hebrews leave Egypt? **(b)** Why was it difficult for the Hebrews to conquer Canaan?
6. **Summarizing Ideas** What were three of the most important contributions of the Hebrews to our civilization?

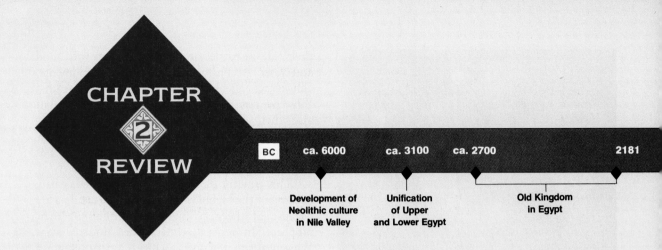

CHAPTER 2 REVIEW

BC	ca. 6000	ca. 3100	ca. 2700	2181

Development of Neolithic culture in Nile Valley

Unification of Upper and Lower Egypt

Old Kingdom in Egypt

Chapter Summary

The following list contains the key concepts you have learned about the great civilizations that developed in the Middle East.

1. Because of its geography and climate, Egypt created a long-lasting and distinctive civilization whose monuments have endured to this day.
2. About 3100 B.C. Upper and Lower Egypt were united into a single kingdom ruled by pharaohs. The successive dynasties of pharaohs made Egypt a considerable power for some 2,000 years.
3. The Egyptians developed a remarkable society and culture. The arts, literature, science, and religion became sophisticated, and a complex and effective agricultural system evolved. At the same time, strict divisions were maintained between social classes. It was a very rigid but also an extremely inventive society.
4. In the Fertile Crescent a succession of conquests and empires led to a variety of societies and cultures.
5. The Sumerians organized city-states, invented a new form of writing, and made many discoveries in architecture and engineering.
6. The Babylonians were famous for their laws, written in the Code of Hammurabi.
7. The Assyrians were fierce warriors and extended their conquests farther than any previous empire.
8. The Persians developed a complex and effective government for their empire. They also adopted an influential new religion called Zoroastrianism.
9. The Phoenicians were the world's first great sea traders. They organized a loose union of cities and colonies around the Mediterranean that were linked by the sea. The alphabet that the Phoenicians developed became the model for later Western alphabets.
10. The Lydians of Asia Minor were the first to use coined money.
11. The Hebrews developed Judaism—a system of laws and a religious faith that has had a major influence on Western civilization. The great written work of Judaism, the Old Testament, introduced the concept of ethical monotheism, which has shaped Western history ever since.

On a separate sheet of paper, complete the following review exercises.

Reviewing Important Terms

Match each of the following terms with the correct definition below.

a. hieroglyphics f. scribe
b. pharaoh   g. barter
c. dynasty   h. ziggurat
d. monotheism   i. Ten Commandments
e. caravan   j. prophet

____ 1. family of rulers
____ 2. exchange of a good or service for another good or service
____ 3. Sumerian temple
____ 4. great religious and moral thinker
____ 5. leader of Egyptian government
____ 6. belief in one god
____ 7. writing that uses pictures or symbols to indicate words or sounds
____ 8. clerk who read or wrote for those who could not
____ 9. moral laws revealed to Moses
____ 10. group of people traveling together for safety over long distances

Developing Critical Thinking Skills

1. **Contrasting Ideas** How did the civilization that arose along the banks of the Nile in Egypt differ from that of the Fertile Crescent?
2. **Understanding Ideas** (a) List the peoples of the Fertile Crescent. (b) Next to the name of each group, write down that group's most important achievements.
3. **Analyzing Maps** (a) Using the maps in Chapter 2, name the geographic barriers between the ancient civilizations of the Middle East. (b) How do you think the peoples of these early civilizations overcame these geographic barriers?
4. **Comparing Ideas** (a) Compare the legal systems of the Babylonians, the Hittites, and the Hebrews. (b) Under which system would you have preferred to live? Explain your choice.

46

Beginning of Hammurabi's reign

New Kingdom in Egypt

Division of Israel into kingdoms of Israel and Judah

• Lydian invention of coined money

• Beginning of Zoroastrianism

586 Chaldean conquest of Jerusalem

BC

ca. 2000   1792   ca. 1550   1085   922   ca. 600

       1780   1500   ca. 900   ca. 722   612

Middle Kingdom in Egypt

Exodus of Hebrews from Egypt

Assyrian conquest of Mesopotamia

Assyrian conquest of Israel

Destruction of Nineveh

ca. 605 – 562 Nebuchadnezzar's reign

Relating Geography to History

The environment has an enormous impact on how a group of people lives and on the ideas and attitudes it holds. Choose two groups of people in this chapter and show how the environment affected **(a)** their ways of life, **(b)** their ways of making a living, and **(c)** their ideas and attitudes.

Relating Past to Present

1. **(a)** Look up the word *justice* in a dictionary. How would you define it? **(b)** How does the concept of justice in the United States today compare with the concept of justice shown in Hammurabi's code? **(c)** Which concept of justice do you think would be more effective in combating crime?
2. **(a)** Throughout history, trade has been an important source for the spread of ideas from one culture to another. How does trade in the world today help the spread of ideas from one culture to another? **(b)** What effects do you think movies and records from the United States might have on other cultures? **(c)** Can you give other examples of cultural diffusion?
3. In this chapter you read about the pharaoh Akhenaton's conflict with the priests of the god Amon. This was an early example in history of a conflict between governmental authority and religion. Review how the First Amendment to the United States Constitution deals with the relationship between church and state in the United States.
4. Economic power is an important part of being a major empire. **(a)** Explain the basis of the economic power of ancient Egypt. **(b)** What was the basis of the economic power of the Fertile Crescent? **(c)** Explain the economic power of oil-producing countries today. How does this affect the political and military power of the United States and the Soviet Union?
5. **(a)** Cotton continues to be an important crop in Egypt and many other parts of the world, including the southeastern United States. Using encyclopedias and statistical abstracts, find out about the size and nature of the cotton industry in the United States. **(b)** What are some of the items produced from the cotton crop in the United States?

Applying History Study Skills

Before completing this activity, review Building History Study Skills on page 31.

Look again at the definitions of a primary source and a secondary source. Then review the guidelines for identifying sources of evidence.

Select a historical event that occurred in the last 100 years. For example, you may be interested in a particular aspect of the Great Depression, World War II, or the Vietnam War. If possible, interview a person who experienced that event. You may wish to prepare a list of questions ahead of time.

After you have discussed the historical event with an "eyewitness," locate a secondary source, such as a magazine article, on the same topic. Then compare the information you have available. Did both sources present a similar point of view? What advantages or disadvantages can you identify regarding the use of primary sources and secondary sources? Which type of evidence is more useful?

Investigating Further

1. **Making Comparisons** Use encyclopedias in your school or public library to write a report comparing Judaism, Christianity, Zoroastrianism, and the religion of ancient Egypt. You should write about the beliefs each religion has regarding the struggle between good and evil. Conclude your report by discussing why the conflict between good and evil is a persistent theme in most religions.
2. **Writing a Report** The pyramids are among the most impressive structures left by any civilization. Research and write a report on the techniques of Egyptian building. You might use the following books as sources: Ahmed Fakhry's *The Pyramids* (University of Chicago Press), and James Finch's *The Story of Engineering* (Doubleday), which has a chapter titled "The Chief Works of Ancient Egypt."
3. **Contrasting Ideas** Find pictures of modern Egyptian cities that also show ancient Egyptian structures. Write a paragraph contrasting the modern structures with the ancient structures.

47

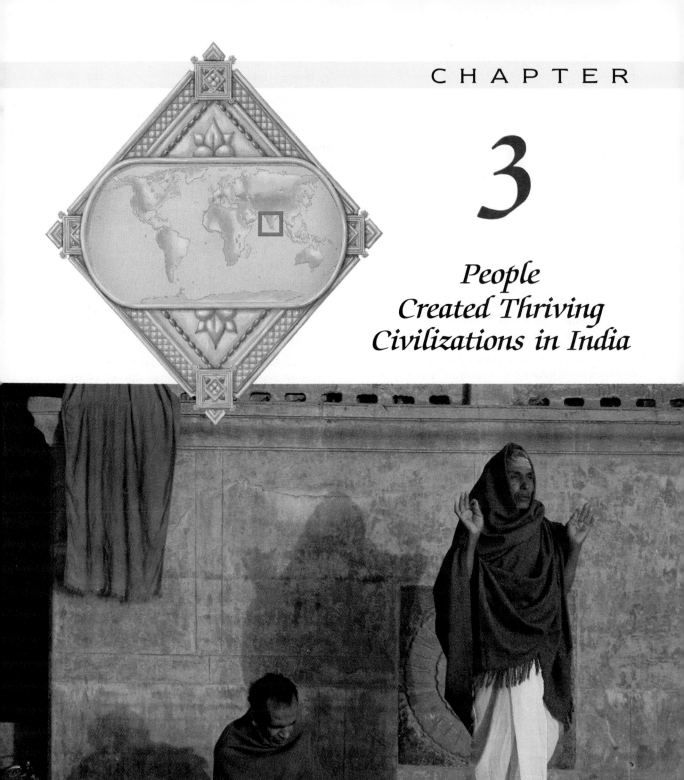

3

People Created Thriving Civilizations in India

CHAPTER ✦ FOCUS

Place   India

Time   ca. 2500 B.C.—A.D. 535

3.7 mil. BC   4000 BC   AD 2100

Significance

In some ways the Indus River valley civilization that developed in India resembled the early civilizations of the Nile and Tigris-Euphrates valleys. For example, the early people of India learned to farm, developed a written language and calendars, and created a complex civilization that included trade, cities, and a sophisticated government. Through philosophy and religion they tried to understand the mysterious forces of nature, the mind, and the soul.

Important differences existed between Eastern, or Oriental, civilizations and those of the West, however. For example, the ideals and beliefs of the Egyptians, Sumerians, and Babylonians vanished long ago. In contrast, the customs and traditions developed in the East in ancient India remain a part of Indian life today. Hindu priests still recite the same prayers that their ancestors did. Cows are still sacred, and people continue to practice the specialized crafts common 4,000 years ago. While the problems of East and West have often been similar, the people of the two regions have frequently found different ways to solve them.

Terms to Define

monsoon   monism
citadel   reincarnation
caste system   yoga

People to Identify

Aryans   Chandragupta I
Buddha   Guptas

Places to Locate

Ganges River   Mohenjo-Daro
Indus River   Harappa

Questions to Guide Your Reading

1 How did the geographic features of India affect the civilization that arose in the Indus Valley?
2 What contributions did the Aryans make to Indian civilization during the Vedic Age?
3 How did Buddhism and Hinduism influence the structure of Indian society during the Epic Age?
4 What cultural imprint did the dynasties and empires of ancient India leave on Indian society?
5 Why did ancient Indian civilization flourish from the Epic Age to the Golden Age of the Gupta Empire?

◀ *Hindus praying on the banks of the Ganges River*

The Hindu religion of India contains many unique practices and rituals. One of these is the practice of yoga in which an individual or yogi attempts to make contact with the divine spirit. To succeed the yogi must first concentrate on ignoring everything going on around him. Only then can the yogi continue his search for the divine spirit. The following is an excerpt from the famous Hindu sacred text, the Bhagavad-Gita (Song of the Lord). Here the Lord Krishna, a Hindu god, discusses the practice and meaning of yoga.

> “*A* yogi should always try to concentrate his mind in absolute solitude, having retired to a secret place. . . . Having in a clean place firmly fixed his seat neither too high nor too low, and having spread over it the sacred grass, and then a deerskin, and then a cloth, he should practice yoga . . . restraining his thoughts and senses, and bringing his mind to a point. Sitting firm he should hold his body, head, and neck erect and still, and gaze steadfastly on the point of his nose, without looking around. Serene and fearless, steadfast in the vow of celibacy, and subdued in mind, he should sit in yoga, thinking on me and intent on me alone. ”

Although many Hindu rituals no longer exist in India, some, such as walking across a bed of hot coals or lying on a bed of nails, are still practiced to gain forgiveness of sins or to build spiritual control. They continue to intrigue outsiders who have never experienced the rich cultural diversity of India.

1 The First Indian Civilization Arose in the Indus Valley

The first Indian civilization developed in the Indus Valley of northern India about 4,500 years ago. In time people settled throughout the entire subcontinent* of India, a region that includes the modern countries of India, Pakistan, Bangladesh (bahn • gluh • DESH), Nepal, Bhutan, and Sri Lanka (SREE LAHNG • kuh).

---

*A subcontinent is a large landmass that is smaller than a continent.

The Physical Setting

The northern border of the Indian subcontinent nestles in the Himalayas (him • uh • LAY • uhz), the tallest mountains on earth. Half as large as the United States, India has a wide diversity of both terrain and climate. Dense rain forests, great fertile plains, high plateaus, dry deserts, narrow coastal plains, and vast rivers sprawl across this subcontinent of timeless beauty in South Asia.

Physical regions. Geographically, the Indian subcontinent can be divided into four main regions. Each region has its own geographic features, climate, and natural resources. While reading about each region, look carefully at the map of India on this page.

(1) *The northern mountains.* Three mountain ranges, the Himalayas, the Karakorums (kar • uh • KOHR • uhms), and the Hindu Kush, loom in the north. The Himalayas, named for the Hindi word meaning "place of the snow," consist of a series of

Learning from Maps *Heavy flooding accompanies the monsoon season in the Ganges River valley. What other river empties into the Bay of Bengal?*

THE INDIAN SUBCONTINENT

⟵ Summer monsoon   ⟵ Winter monsoon

HINDU KUSH
Khyber Pass
KARAKORUM RANGE
PLATEAU OF TIBET
Indus River
-30°
H I M A L A Y A S
INDO-GANGETIC PLAIN
Ganges R.
Brahmaputra R.
THAR DESERT
VINDHYA MTS.
Narbada R.
-20°
DECCAN
Arabian Sea
WESTERN GHATS
PLATEAU
GHATS
Bay of Bengal
EASTERN GHATS
-10°
N
INDIAN OCEAN
0   200   400 Miles
0   200   400 Kilometers
Sri Lanka (Ceylon)
70°   80°   90°

LAMBERT CONFORMAL CONIC PROJECTION

parallel mountain ranges that stretch east and southeast for more than 1,500 miles (2,400 kilometers). Massive glaciers rest in the mountain valleys. Avalanches careen down the rugged mountainsides, and winds up to 100 miles (160 kilometers) per hour lash the towering peaks. Few usable mountain passes penetrate the formidable mountain walls.

The majestic Karakorums meet the Himalayas in the east and the Hindu Kush in the west. Forbidding peaks, many as high as 22,000 feet (6,600 meters), jut boldly to the sky. The Karakorums compose part of the mountain chain that forms a wall between the Indian subcontinent and the rest of Asia.

Not quite as rugged as the other mountain ranges of northern India, the Hindu Kush lie to the northwest of the Karakorums. Several usable passes, including the famous Khyber (KY • buhr) Pass, provided migrating and invading tribes access to India.

(2) *The Indo-Gangetic Plain.* Two great rivers lie south of the three mountain ranges. The Ganges (GAN • jeez) River flows to the southeast through an immensely fertile valley, while the Indus River flows southwest through drier lands. Only a low divide, or ridge, separates the northern ends of the two river valleys. Think of the two valleys as one broad plain stretching more than 1,500 miles (2,400 kilometers) from west to east. After immigrants and invaders traveled through the narrow mountain passes, they spread out along this broad plain and established contact with the earlier settlers in this area.

(3) *The Deccan.* The interior region of the vast Indian subcontinent lies south of the Indo-Gangetic Plain. This high plateau is called the Deccan, meaning "southland." A range of hills—the Vindhya (VIN • dyah) Mountains—separates the Deccan from the Indo-Gangetic Plain. Historically this mountain range has formed a cultural barrier between northern and southern India.

At the western edge of the Deccan lie the Western Ghats, a low mountain range that slopes gradually eastward to the inland plateau. A lower mountain range called the Eastern Ghats marks the eastern edge of the Deccan.

(4) *The Coastal Plain.* The Coastal Plain extends around southern India, facing the Arabian Sea on the west and the Bay of Bengal on the east. Not far from the sea, the abrupt rise of the Western

Learning from Pictures *Mount Everest and Mount Kala Paltar in the Himalayas rise above the clouds. What happens when the monsoon arrives late in India?*

Ghats isolates the Coastal Plain's narrow western rim. The broader eastern rim slopes gradually upward toward the Eastern Ghats.

The people of the Coastal Plain turned to the sea very early in their history. Those in the west traded with the people of the Fertile Crescent, Egypt, and the Mediterranean region. Those in the east traded with the people living in what is now Sri Lanka (Ceylon) and Southeast Asia. The coastal people had more contacts with people overseas than they did with the people of the Indo-Gangetic Plain.

The climate. Two features dominate India's climate—the monsoons and the high temperatures. **Monsoons** are seasonal winds named for the direction in which they blow or the season in which they occur. From late September until the end of the following March, the monsoon blows from the north and northeast. Any moisture it carries falls onto the northern slopes of the Himalayas before reaching the rest of India.

Beginning in late May or early June, the monsoon swings around and blows from the southwest. As the southwest monsoon crosses the Indian Ocean, it picks up moisture, which drops unevenly throughout India in the form of rain. Heavy rains fall along the Coastal Plain, while sparse rainfall is typical of the land behind the Western Ghats. The lower Ganges Valley and the eastern Himalayas receive the heaviest rainfall because they lie directly in the path of these winds.

In most of India, the rainfall for the entire year comes during the four months when the monsoon comes out of the southwest. The timing of the monsoon is critical. If the monsoon arrives late, or if little rain falls, crops wither and starvation threatens India. If the monsoon brings too much rain, destructive floods rage across the countryside. When the monsoon brings the right amount of rain, however, farmers can grow two or more crops in one year.

The second important feature of India's climate is the high temperature. Although temperatures seldom soar on the Coastal Plain or on the Deccan, scorching heat plagues the Indo-Gangetic Plain. Here, temperatures in the winter months of December, January, and February remain cool, but during the rest of the year they become stifling, with many days in May and early June averaging 120°F (49°C).

Seals from the Indus Valley

Much of our knowledge of Harappan civilization comes from tantalizing bits and pieces. Seals like the ones shown here are the most puzzling of the remains that archaeologists have unearthed. Such objects are the only known examples of the picture writing of the Harappans. Scholars have been unable to translate this writing, but a widely held opinion is that the Harappans used the seals to stamp property or to identify their owners.

Many of the pictures on the seals seem to have a religious meaning. The most common carving is that of a bull, an object of worship throughout the ancient world. Many seals also show seated figures that may represent gods. Because Harappan seals have been found in the Tigris-Euphrates region near the site of Sumerian civilization, scholars think that the people of the Indus Valley traded with the people of the Middle East.

Early Civilization in the Indus Valley

An impressive civilization appeared in the Indus River valley about 2500 B.C., not long after Egypt and Sumer developed civilizations. Although our knowledge of this early civilization is incomplete, archaeologists have unearthed much information in the past 100 years. Scholars now believe that this civilization flourished until about 1500 B.C.

The twin cities. The ruins of two cities, Mohenjo-Daro (moh • hen • joh-DAHR • oh) and Harappa (huh • RAP • uh), provide the most complete evidence of this early Indus Valley civilization. Harappa became so important to this civilization that historians often call it the Harappan civilization.

For their day, Harappa and Mohenjo-Daro represented miracles of city planning and design. Wide streets, laid out in a regular pattern, intersected at right angles. Each city had a water system, complete with public baths, and a covered brick sewer system for private homes. The brick homes of the wealthy appear to have been two stories tall, equipped with bathrooms and garbage chutes.

The people of Harappa and Mohenjo-Daro designed their buildings for use, not beauty. In many of these buildings, they used bricks superior to those used in Sumer. Many of the bricks, baked in kilns, or ovens, instead of being sun-dried, have remained intact over the centuries.

The two cities seem to have been twin capitals and not rivals. Each had a strong central fortress, or **citadel,** built on a platform of bricks. At Harappa, farmers stored enough grain in large storehouses to feed the city's population of about 35,000 people.

Indus Valley culture. Agricultural regions surrounded Harappa and Mohenjo-Daro. The Indus River, with its swift current of heavy silt, probably made irrigation difficult. But archaeologists do not know how the Indus Valley people solved these problems, because since then silt deposits have raised the level of the plain around the two cities as much as 12 feet (3.66 meters).

City dwellers worked primarily in industry or trade. As early as 2300 B.C., they traded with people of the Tigris-Euphrates Valley. Indus Valley artisans produced fine articles, including cotton cloth, pottery, bronze items, and gold and silver jewelry.

These early Indus Valley people also developed a written language. Pictograms dating from about 2300 B.C. have been found, but scholars have not yet deciphered the language, partly because most are personal seals believed to be signatures. Although additional writing has been found on clay pots and fragments, scholars have established no connection with any other language.

Scholars know little about Indus Valley religion, but studies indicate that it was a form of **animism,** a belief that spirits inhabit everything —trees and other natural objects, animals, and even

◆READ
WRITE
INTERPRET
CONNECT
THINK

BUILDING HISTORY STUDY SKILLS

Reading About History: Classifying Information

Classifying information involves grouping ideas, objects, or people according to the things they have in common. Grouping ideas or events within a category enables you to organize and understand large amounts of information and give added meaning to isolated bits of information. When data are organized, conclusions can be drawn and comparisons can be made.

How to Classify Information

To classify information, follow these steps:

1. Read the information or items.
2. Sort the information into similar groups.
3. Assign a category to each group.
4. Place the information within broader categories.
5. Formulate a statement clarifying the meaning of the information.

Developing the Skill

Read the following description of Mohenjo-Daro and Harappa to determine the characteristics of Harappan society.

❝ Innumerable artifacts of this civilization have been found, including copper, bronze, gold and jeweled tools. . . . Sculpted figures . . . depicted gods and priest-kings. More than a thousand carved seals, possibly used as signatures on clay tablets, depict the humped bull, rhinoceros, and sometimes a three headed god. . . . Mohenjo-Daro was laid out in strict rectangular blocks, in a north-south direction that took advantage of prevailing winds. Its houses were usually composed of a first floor of furnace baked bricks . . . with an upper floor of wood. Almost every house had a bathroom, in which the family would shower by pouring water over themselves with jugs. The runoff was funneled through drainpipes in the floor into the city drainage system that ran through all the streets. Chutes in the wall provided an outlet for garbage to bins in the streets, where it was presumably collected by the city authorities. The houses were topped by waterproof roofs built from mud spread over layers of bamboo and rush mats. The government buildings were clustered on a mud-brick mound, thirty feet in height and twelve hundred feet in length. Grain, mostly barley, was stored in a government granary. An open colonnaded courtyard may have been a kind of college. A vast bath or swimming pool, forty feet long and eight feet deep, was probably used for sacred absolutions [remission of sins] or bathing. Elaborate palace buildings suggest the presence of powerful rulers, who . . . were also religious leaders. ❞

Study the chart below to learn how the characteristics of the Harappan civilization can be grouped into four major categories.

Government	Religion	Technology	Economy
government buildings	seals	drainage systems	grain production
city services	sacred pool	bathrooms	grain storage
elaborate palaces	sacred animals	sewer systems	public works

Studying the chart enables you to draw conclusions about the civilization of Mohenjo-Daro. The civilization was concerned with cleanliness. This is evident in the elaborate technology devoted to cleanliness—bathrooms, sewers, the drainage system, and the swimming pool for sacred washing. In addition, we know that the government protected the people's welfare because it performed extensive public services. A connection between religion and politics seems to exist. The government seals were religious, and the government buildings seem to have been connected to powerful religious leaders. This was a highly developed urban civilization, as evidenced by the technology, the city services, and the layout of the city.

Practicing the skill. Use the categories in the chart to list the major characteristics of society in your town or city.

To apply this skill, see Applying History Study Skills on page 67.

The excavation site at Mohenjo-Daro

Learning from Maps *Natural river highways encouraged exchange as well as unity in Harappan civilization. Where did the Aryan invaders cross into India?*

people. The Harappans believed these spirits influenced a person's life; therefore, they tried to control them and please them.

Although archaeologists have found no temples, shrines, or religious writings, they believe that the people of the Indus Valley also worshiped animals associated with physical power and fertility, such as bulls, crocodiles, and snakes. One of the most important symbols was the unicorn, a fabled animal with a single long horn jutting from its forehead. Other evidence indicates that a sacred tree and a mother goddess symbolized fertility.

Scholars do not know why the Indus Valley civilization declined. They speculate that tribes from outside lands conquered the valley. More recent evidence indicates that the salt content of underground water increased. Such an increase probably made agriculture impossible and may have disintegrated the baked bricks of the buildings.

Some evidence suggests that major earthquakes and floods struck the region about 1700 B.C. The discovery of several unburied skeletons, together with homes and personal belongings hastily abandoned, seems to indicate some disastrous event at Mohenjo-Daro. The evidence needed to verify this theory, however, remains incomplete.

SECTION 1 REVIEW

1. **Define**   monsoon, citadel, animism
2. **Locate**   Himalayas, Indo-Gangetic Plain, Indus River, Deccan, Coastal Plain, Harappa
3. **Summarizing Ideas**   Name and briefly describe the four main geographical regions of India.
4. **Interpreting Ideas**   What do archaeological findings in the Indus Valley suggest about the political, economic, and social aspects of city life?

2 Aryan Invaders Ruled India's Northern Plain During the Vedic Age

About 1500 B.C. a new group of people flooded through the Khyber Pass into India. They came from the region north of the Black and Caspian seas and spoke an Indo-European language.

The Conquering Aryans

We call the many Indo-European tribes that forced their way into northwestern India, one after another, Indo-Aryans, or Aryans (see map, this page). As one historian observed:

❝*T*here is no ancient record of that first successful trip to India. We do not know how difficult the journey was when the Aryan invaders first led their people down . . . beyond the snowline to the hot, rock-strewn [narrow passage] and out onto the broad grasslands which they had come seeking. We have no way of knowing how the animals felt, and whether or not their owners knew that horses would die unless their noses bled at the top of the Pass, to relieve the pressure of the height. We know only that enough people and animals survived that rugged experience to change the course of Indian history.❞

The nomadic Aryans herded sheep and cows. In fact, their word for "war" meant "a desire for more cows." Many strong and brave Aryan archers followed horse-drawn chariots into battle. Skillful fighters, they conquered the Indus Valley and then moved eastward along the Ganges until they controlled the entire northern plain.

Aryan Civilization During the Vedic Age

Neither traders nor builders, the Aryans did nothing to improve the cities they conquered. They simply left the ruins of the cities to decay. Their early history remains vague because they had no written language. What we do know of the Aryans comes from the Vedas (VAY • duhz), the great literature of the Aryan religion. For centuries people memorized the Vedas and handed them down by word of mouth. Later, with the development of writing, scholars wrote them in the Aryan language, Sanskrit. So important are the Vedas to Indian history that we call the period from 1500 B.C. to 1000 B.C. the Vedic Age.

Aryan religion. The earliest gods mentioned in the Vedas include elements of nature, such as the sky, sun, earth, light, fire, wind, storms, water, and rain. The Vedas personified these natural objects and forces—that is, they regarded or represented them as people. Thus, the sky became a father, the earth a mother. Although the Vedas mention gods and goddesses, a very important hymn celebrating the creation of the universe suggests a concept of a supreme god, called "That One," who created universal order out of the original chaos.

The Vedic religion constantly changed and developed, as shown in the story of the god Varuna. He began as the heavens. His garment was the sky, his breath the storm. As the spiritual beliefs of his worshipers changed, so did Varuna. He watched over the world through his eye, the sun. He rewarded good and punished evil. Thus he became the guardian and enforcer of an eternal law of morality—of right and wrong.

Like the Persians, the early Aryans believed in immortality. After death Varuna either thrust the soul into a dark pit of eternal punishment or raised it into a heaven filled with earthly joy. Through repeated ritual sacrifices and correct ritual action, a person reached this heaven free of his or her earthly body.

Apparently, no temples or images characterized the early Vedic religion. Rituals consisted of building fires on newly constructed altars and pouring the juice of the soma plant and liquid butter into the sacred fire. The important point was to perform the ceremony properly. The good qualities of the person performing it did not matter.

As time passed, the rituals of sacrifice became more complicated. The spoken language of the Indian people also changed, until it became quite different from the Sanskrit of the first Aryan invaders. Since they emphasized the importance of proper observance, priests who knew the proper forms and could read and write Sanskrit also became more important. These priests, called **Brahmans,** prepared the proper ceremony for almost every occasion in life and charged heavily for their services.

Early Aryan society. The Aryans had the habits and customs of wanderers. They eventually settled in the Indo-Gangetic Plain, however, where they found one of the richest and most fertile areas

Learning from Pictures In this relief from Ghandara, two young Brahmans raise their hands in a gesture meaning "do not fear." What did Brahmans do in Aryan society?

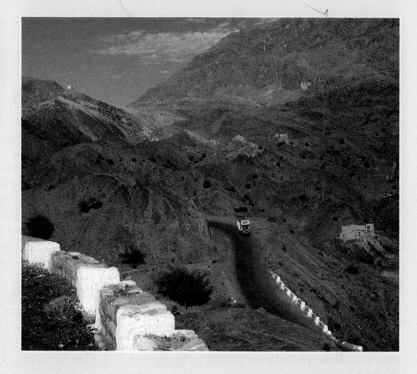

Atharva-Veda

The Aryans who surged through the Khyber Pass (right) later developed literary works called the Vedas. The word *veda* means "knowledge" or "wisdom" in Sanskrit. The Vedas—books of sacred knowledge that make up the body of Hindu scripture—consist of collections of religious rituals and hymns to the gods.

Only four major collections have survived: (1) the *Rig-Veda,* hymns of praise; (2) the *Sama-Veda,* melodies or chants; (3) the *Yajur-Veda,* rituals of sacrifice; and (4) the *Atharva-Veda,* chants and magic spells.

The Vedas cover an amazing variety of subjects. The *Rig-Veda,* the greatest of the Vedas as literature, contains more than 1,000 hymns of praise to all the objects of Aryan worship. Some are straightforward prayers for good crops or long life. Some show a simple, child-like wonder: Why doesn't the sun fall very rapidly once it begins to slip downward? Still others are as eloquent and beautiful as the Psalms of the Bible.

The *Atharva-Veda* has chants for a variety of purposes—to obtain children, to ward off evil, to prolong life, and to destroy enemies. The excerpt below is a chant to bring victory on the battlefield.

> Speak to our enemies, O Drum,
>   faintheartedness and discord of minds;
> We bring upon our adversaries
>   hatred, division, and panic.
>
> Trembling in the mind, in the eye,
>   in the heart, let our enemies
> flee in fright, in consternation,
>   as soon as our oblation is made.
>
> Wrought out of wood, compact
>   with leather-straps, dear to the whole clan,
> besprinkled with molten butter,
>   speak thou terror to our enemies.
>
> As animals of the forest flee,
>   panic-stricken, from a man,
> so do thou, Drum, roar out to our enemies,
>   and frighten them, and then confound their minds.
>
> As from a wolf goats and sheep
>   run away greatly terrified,
> so do thou, Drum, roar out to our enemies,
>   and frighten them and then confound their minds.
>
> As from a hawk birds in the sky fly in terror
>   day by day, as if from the roaring of a lion,
> so do thou, Drum, roar out to the enemies,
>   and frighten them and then confound their minds.
>
> May all the Devas who control
>   the fortunes of the battle-field,
> frighten away our foes with the Drum
>   and the skin of the antelope.
>
> Let those our enemies who go
>   in battalions be terrified
> with the sound of feet and the shadows
>   with which Indra makes his sport.
>
> May the clang of bowstrings and Drums
>   cry out to the direction where
> the defeated hosts of our enemies
>   flee in full battalions.
>
> O Sun, take away their sight!
>   Beams of Light, follow them close:
> Let these cling to foot-bound hosts
>   when their valour has ebbed away.
>
> You mighty Maruts, Sons of Prishni,
>   allied with Indra, crush our enemies!
> May King Soma, King Varuna,
>   Mahādeva, Mrityu, and Indra,
>
> may these embattled Devas
>   bright as the sun, united in mind,
> conquer our enemies. All hail!

in the world. Here, along with farming and a settled life style, they also developed simple forms of government.

In time Aryan tribes joined to form small city-states. A **rajah,** or prince, ruled each city-state. He acted as military leader, chief priest, lawmaker, and judge. A royal council of friends and relatives assisted the rajah. For hundreds of years, the city-states enjoyed peace and independence.

Several physical and social differences existed between conquerors and conquered. The light-skinned Aryans had been nomads. The dark-skinned Indus Valley people had been city dwellers. Although the original Indus Valley people outnumbered them, the Aryans believed in maintaining their separate identity. To do so they passed laws prohibiting marriages between Aryans and the valley dwellers.

Class divisions began to form during the Vedic Age, but not until later did fixed hereditary classes appear. The early Aryans considered warriors to be among the most admirable and important members of society. But when peace came, and farmers needed to ask religious leaders for help against the hostile forces of nature, Brahman priests gained importance.

In addition to providing information about Aryan religion, the Vedas provide a great deal of information about family life in the Vedic Age. Marriages took place by kidnapping, by purchase, or by mutual consent. A woman considered it a great compliment to be stolen. To be bought and paid for was more flattering than to be married by consent. Men could marry more than one woman and owned their wives and children.

The wife had a primary duty to produce sons who would help the father care for their herds of cattle and other animals. Fathers also expected their sons to go to battle to bring honor to their families, and to perform the correct rituals at their fathers' funerals.

The Aryan economy. When the Aryans began farming the Indo-Gangetic Plain, they raised barley as their principal crop. Rice, the most important food in India today, was apparently unknown in Vedic times. Each village divided its land among its families, but the whole village shared the responsibility for irrigation. Land could not be sold to outsiders and could be willed only to male heirs. Most Aryans owned their land. They considered working for someone else a disgrace.

Although poor transportation and trading methods limited trade, handicrafts gradually appeared in the villages. Early traders bartered, often exchanging cattle for goods.

The Aryan invaders made significant contributions to the civilization of the Indian subcontinent. These contributions included a new social order of classes, a new language, and new religious interpretations of how the world works. In time Aryan contributions blended with the previous civilization of Indus Valley people. Farmers gradually displaced herders. Religious values changed, and social classes became more rigid and closely identified with ritual purity.

3 Buddhism and Hinduism Took Hold in India

During the Vedic Age, a new social structure appeared in India. In time this system formed the foundation of Indian society.

The Great Epics

The Vedic Age was named after the Vedas, collections of religious rituals and hymns to the gods. The **Epic Age,** the period from 1000 to 500 B.C., also takes its name from religious literature.

Brahman priests interpreted the rituals and hymns of the Vedas and became increasingly influential in Aryan society. During the Epic Age, the Brahman priests gained even more importance when they composed the *Upanishads* (oo • PAHN • i • shahdz), complex philosophical explanations of the Vedic religion.

Ordinary people did not understand the *Upanishads* any more than they could the Vedas. But they could understand simple stories that made these ideas about Vedic religion clearer. These stories, retold from generation to generation, were eventually combined into two **epics,** or long poems describing heroes and great events. These epics are the *Mahabharata* (muh·HAH·bah·ruh·tuh) and the *Ramayana* (rah·MAH·yuh·nuh).

Sacred Hindu scripture includes the longest epic poem in literature, the *Mahabharata,* or "Great War." It tells the story of a great civil war in a kingdom near Delhi, in what is today northern India. The last 18 chapters of this epic, known as the *Bhagavad-Gita,* or "Lord's Song," stress that doing one's moral duty according to one's responsibilities marks the highest fulfillment in life. In the *Bhagavad-Gita,* Krishna, a human incarnation of the god Vishnu, also explains that love and devotion to Vishnu can lead to salvation in the afterlife.

The *Ramayana* tells the story of two royal heroic figures—Rama (another human incarnation of the god Vishnu) and his devoted wife, Sita. Because of their faithfulness to duty and their devotion to each other and the people of their kingdom, Rama and Sita symbolize the ideals of Indian manhood and womanhood.

From the *Mahabharata* and the *Ramayana,* and from the *Upanishads* and the Vedas themselves, scholars have pieced together the origins of the two most important influences in Indian history—the caste system and Hinduism.

The Caste System

The **caste system,** a form of social organization unlike any developed elsewhere in the world, began in northern India when the invading Aryans laid down rules prohibiting marriages between themselves and the peoples they had conquered. During the Epic Age, four distinct classes emerged in Indian society. At the top of the social scale stood the rulers and warriors called Kshatriyas (kuh·SHA·tree·yuhz). Next came the priests, scholars, and wise men called Brahmans. During the Epic Age, the Brahmans and the Kshatriyas changed positions within society, with the Brahmans becoming most important. The class of Vaisyas (VYSH·yuhz), which included merchants, traders, and owners of small farms, came third. The

Sudras—peasants bound to work the fields of large landowners—stood at the foot of the social ladder.

A fifth group of people in Indian society did not even appear on the ladder. These people were called "untouchables" because the other people in Indian society thought that merely touching them would make one impure. Indians considered many of the conquered peoples untouchables.

As time passed, the caste system emerged as the original four groups divided into smaller groups called castes. Eventually, some 3,000 hereditary castes developed. Each had its own fixed social position and rules about eating, marriage, labor, and worship. For example, people could not eat or drink with someone of a lower caste, but they could perform services that were consistent with the duties of their caste for other people. They could work only at those occupations recognized as fitting for members of their caste, and they could not marry outside their caste.

Hinduism

Hinduism, India's major religion, developed through Brahman priests' interpretations of the Vedas. According to the *Upanishads,* a basic divine essence known as Brahman fills everything in the world. Atman, or self, refers to the essence of an individual person. When Hindus say that Brahma and Atman are one and indivisible, they mean that God and human beings are one. We call this idea **monism.**

According to Hinduism, the world known to our senses is merely an illusion called Maya, which betrays people, giving them sorrow and pain. People can be delivered from their suffering if they can identify Maya. However, this requires lifetimes of experience. Hinduism explains that **reincarnation**—the transmigration or rebirth of the soul—provides this experience. According to this belief, the soul does not die with the body but enters the body of another being, either human or animal, and thus lives again and again.

Two major elements in the theory of reincarnation are known as dharma and karma. **Dharma** is fulfillment of one's moral duty in this life so that the soul can make progress toward deliverance from punishment in the next life. **Karma** is the belief that the present condition of a person's life reflects what a person did or did not do during a previous

The God Siva

Along with Brahma and Vishnu, Siva is one of the three great gods of Hinduism. Siva had many roles but is best known as the destroyer whose actions bring forth new life. The god is also worshiped as time, justice, and the sun. This bronze statue emphasizes the role of destroyer. Around the edge of the circular frame and in one left hand are the flames of destruction. The other left hand points to a dwarf, an enemy overcome by Siva as the lord of death.

Another of Siva's roles is shown by a hand raised in a gesture that means "do not fear." It represents the god's kindliness. A fourth hand holds a drum, the instrument that made the first sound in the universe. The power of meditation is symbolized by a third eye, engraved on the forehead. Siva is often shown dancing and is worshiped as the god of dancers.

life. Ultimately, each person hopes to end the repeated transmigrations and enable the soul to reunite with the soul of Brahma.

According to Hinduism, good persons are rewarded and evil ones are punished. Reward means that the soul enters the body of someone of a higher caste. Punishment occurs when the souls of evil people are reborn in the bodies of people of lower castes or of insects. Since Hindus believe that all souls make up part of the Universal Soul, or Brahman, Hindus respect the sacredness of life in all forms. Members of the Brahman, or highest caste, have to be particularly careful not to bring injury or violence to any living thing.

Hindu religious practices. Hindus commonly practice **yoga,** a physical and mental discipline harmonizing body with soul. A Hindu practicing one form of yoga might, for example, sit for many hours in a certain position in order to free the mind of bodily concerns.

The Brahman priests teach that people can achieve salvation by fulfilling one's dharma and uniting with the Universal Soul or Brahman. Brahman's characteristics include a basic trinity, or three closely related persons or things. The Brahman trinity includes (1) Brahma the Creator, (2) Vishnu the Preserver, and (3) Siva the Destroyer. Below these come many other gods, represented in the spirits of trees, animals, and people.

Some Hindus pay special reverence to certain animals. For example, they consider cows especially sacred because cows provide the power for the plow and the cart and produce food (milk and butter) and fuel (dung). For these reasons most Hindus will not eat beef.

To Westerners this religion of many gods sounds polytheistic. However, Hindus insist that it is monistic—that the basic trinity and all the other gods are merely different representations of the oneness of the universe.

Establishment of the caste system and Hinduism ranked as the most important developments of Indian history during the Epic Age—or of any other age in Indian history. These two ideas became interwoven in the fabric of Indian society.

The Early Life of Buddha

Another of the world's great religions—Buddhism—also arose in India. Buddhism's founder, Gautama, who became known as Buddha, or the "Enlightened One," was born about 563 B.C. and died about 483 B.C. The son of an Indian prince, he lived in luxury, shielded from the ordinary people of his native city. At the age of 29, he ventured into the city streets. What he saw—an old decrepit man, a very sick man covered with boils, and a corpse about to be cremated—profoundly disturbed him. He wondered about the great problems of life and asked "Why does suffering exist? What is the value of life and death?"

Gautama decided to spend the rest of his life seeking answers to these questions. In what is called the Great Renunciation, he put aside all his possessions, left his wife and infant son, and set out to search for the truth.

Gautama followed all the practices recommended to attain wisdom. He lived as a hermit and a scholar and practiced the mental and physical discipline of yoga so strictly that he almost died. He tried fasting—not eating for a specified amount of time—and self-torture. But none of these practices gave him the answers he longed for so much.

One day, after six years of searching, as Gautama meditated under a fig tree, he felt that he understood the truth which formed the basis of life. In that moment, according to his followers, he became Buddha—the "Enlightened One." He spent the remainder of his life teaching the Enlightenment, the Way of Life.

Buddha's Teachings

Buddha accepted the Hindu belief that the progress of the soul depends on the life a person leads and that good is rewarded and evil punished. Departing from Hindu beliefs, however, Buddha said that since only deeds, good or bad, count, salvation cannot come through self-torture or from the sacrifice of animals. According to Buddha, salvation comes from knowing the Four Noble Truths and following the Eightfold Path.

The Four Noble Truths. The Four Noble Truths were as follows: (1) all human life contains suffering and sorrow; (2) a greedy desire for only pleasure and material things causes suffering and sorrow; (3) renouncing desire frees people from suffering and helps their souls attain **nirvana,** or the perfect peace, which frees the soul from the endless cycle of reincarnation; and (4) following the Eightfold Path leads to renunciation, or denial of desire and attainment of nirvana.

The Eightfold Path. The Eightfold Path consists of eight guides to thought and conduct. It includes (1) right views, or seeing life as it really is, with all its imperfections; (2) right intentions; (3) right speech, or avoiding lying and gossiping; (4) right action, or avoiding committing crimes and instead, seeking to be honest; (5) right living, by which Buddha meant working at a job that did not harm others; (6) right effort, or working to prevent evil; (7) right mindfulness, or constant awareness of one's self; and (8) right concentration to direct the mind in meditation.

Buddha stressed ethics, a code of morals and conduct, rather than ceremonies. Unselfishness formed the key to his ethics, and he gave definite rules for unselfish behavior. A person should not kill, steal, lie, gossip, find fault with others, use profanity, or become greedy.

Buddha did not accept the Hindu gods. According to Buddha, only people could change good to evil and evil to good. They did not need the help of gods, priests, temples, or idols to follow the Eightfold Path. Buddha taught that only two kinds of people exist—the good and the bad. Although he did not attack the Hindu caste system openly, he did not accept it.

The Spread of Buddhism

Buddha gained some followers in his lifetime, but not many. Over several centuries, however, his teachings won wide acceptance (see map, page 61).

By the 100s B.C., Buddhism had split into two branches—Hinayana (HEE • nuh • yahn • uh) and Mahayana (MAH • huh • yahn • uh). Hinayana followed the traditional beliefs of Buddhism and regarded Buddha simply as a teacher. In time this

MODIFIED OBLIQUE CONIC CONFORMAL PROJECTION

Learning from Maps *Buddhism spread to China over major trade routes about* A.D. *250. According to the map, how long did it take for Buddhism to spread?*

form of Buddhism spread to countries outside India, including Burma, Thailand, and Cambodia.

Believers in the Mahayana form of Buddhism regarded Buddha as a god and savior. They developed Buddhism into a religion with priests, temples, creeds, and rituals. Mahayana Buddhism spread over a wide area, including Afghanistan, central Asia, China, Korea, and Japan.

In India itself the priestly Brahmans opposed Buddhism. Their high position depended on people's acceptance of their role in performing rituals. The Brahmans opposed any religion that taught that people, regardless of caste, could reach nirvana without help if only they were good.

Despite the strong opposition of the Brahmans, Buddhism gained many followers in India over several centuries and then slowly declined. Buddhism achieved greater acceptance in other areas of Asia.

SECTION 3 REVIEW

1. **Define** Epic Age, epic, caste system, monism, reincarnation, dharma, karma, yoga, nirvana
2. **Identify** Krishna, Rama, Sita, Universal Soul, Enlightened One
3. **Locate** Afghanistan, China, Korea, Japan
4. **Identifying Ideas** (a) What was the origin of the caste system? (b) What five groups had emerged in India by the beginning of the Epic Age?
5. **Analyzing Ideas** According to Hindus, how can a soul reach salvation?
6. **Comparing Ideas** (a) Which Hindu ideas did Buddha accept? (b) Which did he reject?
7. **Summarizing Ideas** Explain the Four Noble Truths and the principles of the Eightfold Path.

61

4 Dynasties and Empires Rose and Fell in Ancient India

Neither the Persians nor the Greeks conquered the Indian subcontinent, although both had conquered land as far as the Indus River. Darius, the Persian ruler, sent an army to invade the Indus Valley in the 500s B.C. and organized the area as a part of the Persian Empire. Indian kingdoms slowly reduced Persian control of northwestern India as the Persian Empire began to decline. The kingdom of Magadha (mah·GAH·duh), in northeastern India, finally absorbed this region. Magadha rule ended in 322 B.C.

The Maurya Empire

A new kingdom arose in India in 322 B.C. as a result of the conquests of a powerful young adventurer named Chandragupta (chuhn·druh·GOOHP·tuh). He established the Maurya Empire that lasted almost 150 years.

Chandragupta Maurya. We know a good deal about Chandragupta Maurya from a fascinating book written by a Greek ambassador to his court. According to this account, Chandragupta was an able administrator. He took control of Pataliputra (pah·tah·li·POOT·rah) on the Ganges River and made it a magnificent and beautiful city. He learned the science of government and methods of warfare from the Macedonians who had conquered Persia. Chandragupta raised a huge army of 700,000 soldiers, with 10,000 chariots and 9,000 elephants. He maintained an efficient postal service that moved swiftly over the empire's excellent roads, and he united northern India from the delta of the Ganges to the region west of the Indus. Eventually, he conquered all of northwestern India up to the Hindu Kush.

An able but harsh ruler, Chandragupta made many enemies. Some of these enemies dug tunnels under his palace in their attempts to kill him. To avoid assassination, he slept in a different room each night and employed food tasters as protection against poisoning. Finally, Chandragupta abdicated the throne in favor of his son.

Asoka. Perhaps one of India's greatest rulers was Asoka (uh·SHOH·kuh), Chandragupta's grandson, who came to the throne about 270 B.C.

In military campaigns that took 100,000 lives and 150,000 captives, Asoka enlarged the empire until it included all of India except the southern tip of the subcontinent.

This slaughter so sickened Asoka that he renounced war and became a devout Buddhist. He did not force the Indian people to accept Buddhism, although many did. He sent his brother as a missionary to what is now Sri Lanka (Ceylon) and other missionaries to Tibet, China, Burma, Indonesia, and even to Egypt, Syria, and Macedonia.

After his conversion to Buddhism, Asoka thought constantly of piety and duty. He urged religious toleration and relaxed the harsh laws that had supported the unlimited power of his father and grandfather. He pardoned prisoners and forbade animal sacrifices.

When Asoka died about 230 B.C., the Maurya Empire quickly began to crumble. Following the assassination of the last Maurya ruler in 184 B.C., a series of foreign rulers took control of northern India.

The Gupta Rulers

The next great rulers of India were the Guptas, who came to power in A.D. 320. The Guptas first ruled in the Ganges Valley, but through intermarriage and conquest they extended their power over a wide area of India (see map, page 63). The first three Gupta rulers—Chandragupta I (no relation to the earlier Chandragupta of the Maurya dynasty), Samudragupta (sam·oo·drah·GOOHP·tah), and Chandragupta II—used their great powers for the good of society.

The Guptas, believing the gods had appointed them to rule, favored Hinduism over Buddhism, because Hinduism stressed the gods and Buddhism did not. By the end of the Gupta period, Buddhism had declined in India, while it gained strength in many other parts of Asia. Hinduism, now somewhat influenced by Buddhism, again became the dominant religion of India and remains so today.

The time during which the Guptas ruled has been called a golden age because of the brilliant civilization that flourished then. Gupta rule ended in A.D. 535, however, when once again invaders stormed into the subcontinent and brutally ravaged northern India.

Southern India

Because few of the Indian empires controlled southern India, its history developed quite differently from that of northern India. Location and natural resources played a major role in this history. Separated from the north by the Vindhya Mountains, southern Indians, particularly those along the coast, turned to trade and commerce. As traders they became wealthy because they had products, such as cotton, spices, ivory, and gold, that brought high prices.

Hinduism penetrated the region sometime after the 600s B.C. The first recorded date in the history of southern India is 250 B.C., when Asoka sent Buddhist missionaries to the Deccan. During the period of Maurya decline, beginning around 230 B.C., the Andhra dynasty arose in the south. The Andhras created an empire that eventually included a large part of southern India. When the empire declined, about A.D. 225, the south broke up into a number of small, warring states.

Learning from Maps The Gupta rulers made Pataliputra their capital. What bodies of water border the Gupta Empire?

GUPTA EMPIRE, ca. A.D. 400

BACTRIA
HINDU KUSH
Khyber Pass GANDHARA
PLATEAU OF TIBET
HIMALAYAS
Indus River
30°
INDIA
Ganges R.
Ayodhya
Brahmaputra R.
Pataliputra (Patna)
Nalanda
MAGADHA
VINDHYA MTS.
Narbada R.
Ajanta
20°
Arabian Sea
DECCAN PLATEAU
ANDHRA
Bay of Bengal
N
0   200   400 Miles
0   200   400 Kilometers
10°
Tamils
INDIAN OCEAN
Sri Lanka (Ceylon)
70°   80°   90°

LAMBERT CONFORMAL CONIC PROJECTION

SECTION 4 REVIEW

1. **Identify** Asoka, Guptas, Chandragupta I
2. **Locate** Ganges River
3. **Summarizing Ideas** What did Chandragupta Maurya and Asoka accomplish as rulers?
4. **Analyzing Ideas** Why did the Guptas favor Hinduism over Buddhism?
5. **Determining Cause and Effect** Why did northern and southern India develop differently?

5 Civilization Flourished in Ancient India

Indian civilization reached new heights from the Epic Age to the Golden Age of the Gupta Empire. India has indeed left the world a rich legacy in the areas of art, literature, mathematics, and science. These ancient societies also established the cultural traditions of India. Their impact reached beyond the borders of India, endured through the centuries, and still influences Indian society today.

Economy and Social Life

From ancient times the land had provided a living for nearly all the people of northern India. For a limited few at the top of the caste system, the land provided great luxury. Nevertheless, most people eked out a meager existence. During the Epic Age, the rajahs in theory owned all the land and took what they wanted from the farmers. By the time of the Guptas, the rulers claimed one-sixth of the agricultural produce as their share.

Many people in southern India made their living from commerce or trade with foreign nations. Foreign trade also flourished in northern India under the Guptas. In the ancient world, Indian goods such as silks, spices, precious gems, muslins, and cashmere could be found in areas as widely scattered as the Far East, the Middle East, and Europe.

Women's freedom in India became more restricted as empires rose and fell. Women enjoyed some measure of freedom in Aryan society, and Hindu laws allowed women certain rights. However, in Gupta India a woman's status was lower than a man's. The *Mahabharata* called a man's wife his "truest friend," but a Gupta legal treatise recommended that the wife worship her husband as a god. **Polygamy,** or marriage to more than one person, became common in the Epic Age and widespread under the Guptas. Another practice that became common during the Gupta period, especially among the upper castes, was **suttee.** In this practice a widow would commit suicide by throwing herself on top of her husband's flaming funeral pyre.

Literature

In addition to the *Mahabharata* and *Ramayana*, people enjoyed the stories of the *Panchatantra* (pahn • chah • TAN • trah), a series of fables from the Gupta period. These stories contained underlying morals and emphasized desirable traits such as adaptability, shrewdness, and determination. The *Panchatantra* includes stories about Sinbad the Sailor, Jack the Giant Killer, the Magic Mirror, and the Seven League Boots—stories known throughout the world today. Next to the Bible, the *Panchatantra* is the most widely translated book in the world today.

Indian drama developed greatly under the Guptas. Indian plays, which always had happy endings, offered little action and used different dialects, or regional variations of language, for different characters. Actors, who formed a distinct caste, performed these plays in a courtyard, using only simple scenery.

Art and Architecture

We know little about Indian art before the reign of Asoka in the 200s B.C. because these artists used perishable materials such as wood. Asoka, however, set up pillars with his laws carved on them throughout his empire and possibly built 84,000 stupas. A **stupa** was a hemisphere or dome-shaped shrine that held artifacts and objects associated with Buddha.

Early images of Buddha showed foreign influence. However, during the rule of the Guptas, Indian sculptors developed their own more rigid and formal style, which still characterizes Indian art. As Hinduism increased in importance, Indians also created a distinctive style of Hindu temple—a square building with heavy walls enclosing the statue of a god.

Mural paintings in caves tell us something about the artistic style of early Indian painters. However, we know most about mural painting in the time of the Guptas. Today people continue to visit the caves at Ajanta in central India to admire the paintings of Buddha and his followers. These paintings provide a valuable source of information about the daily life of Indian people under the Gupta rulers.

Education

In India formal schooling began at the age of nine. Although poor children learned only crafts or trades, upper-class Indian children received a formal education. Indian children read the *Upanishads*, the *Mahabharata*, and the *Ramayana*.

By the time of the Guptas, Nalanda, a famous Buddhist monastic university, had become the chief center of Indian education. Located in the lower Ganges Valley, it attracted students from as far away as Tibet, China, and Korea. Nalanda had more than 100 lecture halls, 3 large library buildings, dormitories, a model dairy, and an observatory. The curriculum included religion, philosophy, medicine, art, architecture, and agriculture.

Mathematics and Astronomy

Indian mathematicians learned to deal with abstract numbers. Indians actually invented the numeral system we call Arabic—1 through 9 and the zero. Arab traders brought it to the West from India. People in India used these so-called Arabic numerals as early as A.D. 595.

Indians also understood negative numbers (numbers preceded by a minus sign), without which algebra could not exist. They calculated the square root of 2 and prepared a table of sines, or the ratio of the side opposite the angle and the longest side of the triangle, used extensively in trigonometry. Aryabhata (ahr • yuh • BUHT • uh), who lived in the A.D. 400s, computed the value of π (pi) and also solved algebraic equations.

Indian astronomers identified the seven planets that can be seen without the aid of a telescope. They knew that the planets and the moon reflected the sun's light. They understood the daily rotation of the earth on its axis, predicted eclipses, calculated the diameter of the earth, and developed a theory of gravity.

Fairy Tales

"Once upon a time . . ." is a phrase we all recognize from fairy tales we heard as children. These stories occur in every culture, and a number of them are familiar to us all.

The Jataka Tales, ancient Indian stories taken from Buddhist writings, tell of animal and human kindness (top). Their theme is good versus evil. The same theme underlies the story of Cinderella (bottom). Her fairy godmother represents good; the wicked stepmother and stepsisters represent evil. In the Chinese version of this tale, a talking fish plays the fairy godmother's role, but the slipper, the prince, and the wedding are all there. In the Algonquin Indian version, the gods, rather than the prince, search for the true Cinderella. One collector of fairy tales estimates that there may be almost 300 different versions of the Cinderella story.

Another worldwide theme is that of the sleeper and the awakening. A wicked witch or fairy gives a curse, and the sleeper sleeps until awakened by a person of good will. We know this theme in Sleeping Beauty. In an Indian story, the Lord Krishna awakens the Hindu king Muchukunda.

A third universal theme is that of magical transformation, usually brought about by love. Pinocchio turns from a wooden puppet into a donkey, and finally into a real boy. In a Chinese fairy tale, Mrs. Number Three is turned into a donkey.

Psychologists see fairy tales as a way in which societies pass their values along to their young. Such tales also provide vivid examples of different kinds of human character. And they communicate eternal human concerns, dreams, and fears—the triumph of good, the power of nature, and the chance of success even for the most unlikely people.

Medicine

Indian physicians understood the importance of the spinal cord, and their surgery included bone setting and plastic surgery. They perfected the technique of inoculation—infecting a person with a mild form of a disease so that he or she will not fall ill with the more serious form. For example, Indian physicians used relatively harmless cowpox germs to inoculate against deadly smallpox, a method unknown in the Western world until the end of the 1700s.

Indian rulers built free hospitals in the early 400s. Susruta (suhs•ROO•tuh), a great Indian doctor, practiced strict cleanliness before an operation and also sterilized wounds, a procedure unknown in the West until modern times.

SECTION 5 REVIEW

1. **Define** polygamy, suttee, stupa
2. **Identify** Aryabhata, Susruta
3. **Locate** Ajanta, Nalanda
4. **Summarizing Ideas** **(a)** From what books did Indian children learn to read? **(b)** What subjects were studied at Nalanda?
5. **Classifying Ideas** What contributions did the early Indians make in the fields of mathematics, astronomy, and medicine?

CHAPTER 3 REVIEW

| BC | ca. 2500 | ca. 1500 | 1000 |

Development of Harappan civilization

Decline of Harappan civilization

Rule of Aryan invaders during the Vedic Age

Chapter Summary

The following list contains the key concepts you have learned about the ancient civilizations of India.

1. The Indian subcontinent is divided roughly into four geographical regions—the northern mountains, the Indo-Gangetic Plain, the Deccan, and the Coastal Plain.
2. Monsoons and oppressive heat dominate India's climate.
3. About 2500 B.C. an impressive civilization, the Harappan civilization, appeared in the Indus Valley. Industry and trade were centered in such cities as Harappa and Mohenjo-Daro. The Harappans developed a written language and a form of animistic religion.
4. About 1500 B.C. the Aryans began to enter the Indus Valley. Because the Aryans lacked a written language, knowledge of their early history comes mainly from the Vedas, their sacred books, which describe their religious beliefs. Originally herders and nomads, the Aryans became farmers and founded small tribal states. Intermarriage with the original Indus Valley people was prohibited, and class divisions began to form during the Vedic Age.
5. The Aryans of India developed a caste system. Each caste had its own fixed position in society and its own rules about eating, marriage, labor, and worship. Caste remains an important part of social organization in India today.
6. Brahman scholars composed the *Upanishads* to explain the Vedic religion. From these explanations grew a complex set of ideas known as Hinduism, which remains the major Indian religion.
7. Hinduism teaches that the world of the senses is an illusion. Only through reincarnation can a person gain the experience needed to escape suffering and be reunited with the Universal Soul.
8. Gautama, an Indian prince who became known as Buddha, taught that people could attain salvation by accepting the Four Noble Truths and following the Eightfold Path. These teachings, which became known as Buddhism, exerted an even more powerful influence on the rest of Asia than on India itself.
9. From 322 B.C. to 184 B.C., the Maurya Empire ruled India. Asoka, a Mauryan emperor, was one of India's greatest rulers. He embraced Buddhism, relaxed harsh laws, and urged toleration for the many religions of India.
10. The Gupta dynasty lasted from A.D. 320 to A.D. 535. This period is known as the "Golden Age" in India. The first three Gupta rulers, Chandragupta I, Samudragupta, and Chandragupta II, used their great powers for the good of society. It was during this period that Hinduism became the major religion of India.
11. Indian culture reached new heights during ancient times. Great epics, such as the *Mahabharata* and the *Ramayana,* and the famous fables of the *Panchatantra* were written at this time. Many of India's greatest dramatists and poets wrote plays and poems during this time. Great advances were made in the areas of mathematics, astronomy, and medicine. Indians invented Arabic numerals, computed the value of π (pi), identified seven planets, and practiced surgery and inoculation.

On a separate sheet of paper, complete the following review exercises.

Reviewing Important Terms

Supply the term that correctly completes each sentence.

1. A _____ is a seasonal wind named for the direction in which it blows.
2. A _____ is a strong central fortress.
3. _____ is a belief that spirits inhabit everything, even people.
4. Indian priests were called _____ .
5. In Aryan times princes, or _____ , ruled each city-state.
6. The _____ _____ in Indian history lasted from 1000 B.C. to 500 B.C. and takes its name from religious literature.
7. The Hindu belief that God and human beings are one and indivisible is called _____ .
8. Marriage to more than one person is called _____ .
9. The Hindu belief in the transmigration or rebirth of the soul is called _____ .
10. _____ is the belief that the present condition of a person's life is wholly the result of what was done or not done during a previous life.

Life of Buddha

Asoka became
ruler of the
Maurya Empire

Rule of the
Gupta dynasty—the
"Golden Age" in India

BC
1000   ca. 563 483   270   AD   320   535
                      500   322 184   220   ca. 400

Epic Age in India   Establishment   Assassination   Beginning of   • Aryabhata, Indian
                           of Maurya Empire   of last   chaotic period of   mathematician, computed
                                                 Maurya ruler   100 years in India   the value of π
                                                                                            • Free hospitals built in India

11. Hindus commonly practice _____ , a physical and mental discipline designed to harmonize the body with the soul.

Developing Critical Thinking Skills

1. **Summarizing Ideas** What changes did the Aryans bring to the Indus Valley civilization?
2. **Describing Ideas** Describe the geographical features of India that were barriers to the spread of Indian culture.
3. **Determining Cause and Effect** How does climate influence agricultural production in the four geographic regions of India?
4. **Making Charts** Make a chart showing the major accomplishments of the Indus Valley civilization and the Aryans.
5. **Analyzing Information** **(a)** What differences and similarities can you find between the civilizations of the Indus Valley and the civilizations that you read about in Chapter 2? **(b)** How would you account for these differences?

Relating Geography to History

(a) Trace a map of India. **(b)** Indicate the areas that have heavy rainfall. **(c)** Indicate the areas that need irrigation in order to grow crops. **(d)** Show the desert areas that might be used for grazing. **(e)** Indicate the wind direction for summer and fall monsoons and for winter winds.

Relating Past to Present

1. Animism is the term used to describe the ancient religious beliefs of the Harappan civilization. **(a)** List some of their ideas and practices and compare them with what people today call "superstitions." **(b)** What are some of the symbols considered "lucky" and "unlucky" today?
2. **(a)** What city-planning problems did the people of Harappa and Mohenjo-Daro solve? **(b)** What are some modern city-planning problems that were

unknown to the people of these ancient civilizations? **(c)** How are these city-planning problems being solved?

Applying History Study Skills

Before completing this activity, review Building History Study Skills on page 53.

The *Rig-Veda*, the Aryan collection of hymns, consists of stanzas of praise to the Aryan gods. This literature helps us to understand the religious beliefs and the society of the early Indian people. Study the names and functions of the gods listed below. Then construct a chart in which you classify the gods according to the characteristics they share.

Varuna—directed the cosmos; god of justice and order
Soma—god of immortality
Indra—victorious war god
Rudra—storm god
Agni—god of fire, healing, and the home
Ushas—god of the dawn
Surya—god of the sun
Vac—goddess of speech
Tad Ekam—"That One," the source of all creation

Investigating Further

1. **Presenting an Oral Report** Present an oral report on the achievements, mysterious beginnings, and sudden end of the Harappan civilization. Good sources for your report are "The Valley of the Indus" in *The Horizon Book of Lost Worlds* by Leonard Cottrell (American Heritage) and "India's Forgotten Civilization" in *Readings in World History* by Leften S. Stavrianos et al. (Allyn and Bacon).
2. **Writing a Report** Using encyclopedias, find out more about Chandragupta Maurya and Asoka. Prepare a written report on the life and accomplishments of one of these Indian rulers.
3. **Constructing a Model** Use resources in your school or public library to find more information on the architecture of Mohenjo-Daro or Harappa. Then construct a model showing what the city might have looked like.

Ancient Chinese Civilization Developed Lasting Traditions

CHAPTER ✦ FOCUS

Place   China

Time   1500 B.C.—A.D. 589

3.7 mil. BC   4000 BC   AD 2100

Significance

Throughout much of the world in the 500s B.C., many great civilizations struggled in the first stages of development. Some of these civilizations would survive, and some would not. In all of them, people tested ideas and created traditions that most of the nations of the world today still share.

Chinese civilization began in the vastness of the North China Plain, to the northeast of the rugged, snowcapped peaks of the Himalayas. As in India, many of the customs and traditions developed in ancient China remain a part of Chinese life today. One reason for this continuity is the enduring influence of two great leaders, Gautama Buddha and Confucius, on Chinese life. In one of the great coincidences of history, both leaders lived at about the same time, in the 500s B.C. As you have read, Buddhism, the religion founded by Gautama Buddha, began in India and spread throughout Asia. Confucius, on the other hand, lived and taught in China. Both leaders influenced the lives of millions of people in China, the Middle East, and other parts of Asia.

Terms to Define

loess   calligraphy
silt   oracle bones
Mandate of Heaven   civil service

People to Identify

Shang   Wu Di
Zhou   Kongzi
Qin   Laozi

Places to Locate

Huang He   China Proper
Chang Jiang   Xi Jiang

Questions to Guide Your Reading

1 What geographic and cultural features helped shape Chinese history?
2 How did the first Chinese civilization flourish under the Shang dynasty?
3 How did Chinese civilization evolve through changing dynasties?
4 What philosophies emerged in ancient China?
5 How did China develop under the rule of the Zhou, Qin, and Han dynasties?

Not long ago, in 1974, some modern Chinese farmers near the ancient city of Xian made a momentous discovery. As the farmers were digging new wells to bring badly needed water to their village, they uncovered a life-sized figure of an ancient Chinese knight. Soon the farmers began to uncover other life-sized figures lined up in a vast underground cavern.

News of this discovery spread quickly, and archaeologists launched a large-scale excavation. As work progressed, they found row after row of knights, horses, servants, chariots, and weapons—thousands in all. But who had created these sculptures? And why were there so many? Although scholars still cannot answer these questions, many believe that an early Chinese emperor, Shi Huangdi (SHUHR HWAHNG • DEE), had them made to help him in his conquests in the afterlife. These sculptures provide just one example of the magnificent accomplishments of the ancient Chinese civilization.

1 Geographic and Cultural Features Helped Shape Chinese History

Paleolithic people lived near what is today the city of Beijing (BAY • JING). Later Neolithic developments along the Yellow River, or Huang He* (HWANG HOOH), resembled those in other parts of the world. The people domesticated many kinds of animals, improved their tools and weapons, developed agriculture, and eventually settled in permanent communities.

Before continuing the story of China, however, it is helpful to do two things. First, we must examine the geography of China. Second, we must learn about the basic patterns of Chinese history.

The Physical Setting

Intersecting mountain ranges crisscross China (see map, page 70). The great mountain ranges of the west, northwest, and southwest slope down to high desert or semi-desert plateaus. In the south the plateaus give way to a region of many low hills and valleys. In

---

*The words *He* and *Jiang* are Chinese for "river." Throughout this book we will be using the Pinyin system of spelling Chinese names. For an explanation of the Pinyin system, see page R22.

◀ *The Great Wall of China*

the north the plateaus slope gradually down to the North China Plain, a coastal plain along the Pacific Ocean. Much smaller than the plain that stretches across northern India, the North China Plain became the center of early Chinese civilization.

Look again at the map on this page. Notice the range of mountains that cuts from west to east across the center of China. This range separates the valleys of the two greatest rivers of China—the Huang He and the Chang Jiang, or Yangtze River. Known as the Qin Ling (CHIN LING), it marks the boundary between North and South China. The range also marks the boundary between the two major agricultural areas of China. In the north, where relatively little rain falls, wheat is the principal crop. In the center and south, where rainfall is more plentiful, rice is the leading farm product.

Throughout its history China has also been divided politically into two main sections. The smaller and more important section lies along the seacoast and stretches inland up the valleys of the Huang He and Chang Jiang. We call this region China Proper—the heart of China.

The second section surrounds China Proper with a great semicircle of regions, including Tibet, Xinjiang (SHIN·JAHNG), Mongolia, Manchuria, and Korea. At various times throughout their history, the Chinese conquered and ruled these regions, usually to protect themselves from attack. On a few occasions, nomads from one or another of these outlying regions conquered and ruled China's heartland.

The rivers of China. China has many rivers, but the Huang He, the Chang Jiang, and the Xi (SHEE) Jiang have played particularly important roles in its history. The Huang He meanders for more than 2,900 miles (4,600 kilometers) across China before emptying into the Gulf of Chihli. The climate in the Huang He valley includes long, cold winters and short, hot summers. Duststorms

Learning from Maps The Chang Jiang flows 3,434 miles (5,494 km) from west to east, emptying into the East China Sea. What river in China crosses the Tropic of Cancer?

MODIFIED OBLIQUE CONIC CONFORMAL PROJECTION

70

sweep across the valley in the spring. Yet enough rain falls to nourish most crops. More importantly, the region has extraordinarily fertile yellow soil called **loess** (LES).

Most rivers carry only 2 to 3 percent of their weight as **silt,** or moist soil carried as sediment in a river's waters. In contrast the Huang He carries between 10 and 40 percent. The Chinese often call the Huang He the Yellow River because the loess gives the water a yellowish tint.

Early Chinese farmers in the Huang He valley built earthen dikes to protect their crops from periodic floods. These dikes, however, caused the Huang He to deposit loess on the river bottom. Over the years so much silt accumulated that the river level reached the tops of the dikes. Even moderate rains brought the Huang He to flood stage, sending torrents of water raging over the dikes and into the fields. Successive generations of Chinese farmers responded to the threat of floods by building higher dikes. As a result, today the Huang He flows from 10 to 40 feet (3 to 12 meters) above the land outside the dikes.

The higher dikes did not end the flooding, however. Every few years the Huang He still broke through the dikes, and the rampaging floodwater destroyed everything in its path. The floodwater remained on the land until it evaporated—sometimes for as long as three years—because it could not drain back into the higher riverbed. Such devastating floods led the ancient Chinese to nickname the river "China's Sorrow."

The Chang Jiang, in central China, flows for 3,400 miles (5,400 kilometers) and cuts a deep channel. In modern times large oceangoing ships have been able to navigate 600 miles (960 kilometers) upstream to the great city of Wuhan (WOO • HAHN). Smaller ships can travel as far as Chongqing (CHOOHNG • CHING), about 1,300 miles (2,000 kilometers) from the sea.

The Xi Jiang, in southern China, is more than 1,200 miles (1,900 kilometers) long. Like the Chang Jiang, it forms an important commercial waterway. Large ships can navigate the Xi Jiang as far as Zangwu (ZAHNG • WOO), about 220 miles (350 kilometers) inland.

China's isolation. Civilization in China developed in relative isolation from the civilizations of India and the West. Great distances, the towering mountains of central Asia, and formidable deserts such as the Gobi (GOH • BEE) made China almost inaccessible. As a result, China developed and retained its own distinctive culture. Although the Chinese did adopt some of the ideas and skills of other peoples, they probably owed less to outside influence than any other people in ancient times.

Until modern times China's only regular contact with foreigners was with the nomads from the dry lands to the north and northwest. These peoples spoke their own languages and had their own tribal religions. Usually they traded peacefully with the Chinese, exchanging livestock for grain and other agricultural products. Sometimes, however, they organized bands of mounted warriors and attacked Chinese settlements. The Chinese called these nomadic peoples "barbarians" and considered them culturally inferior.

Lack of contact with foreigners helped give the Chinese a strong sense of identity and superiority. They regarded their land as the only civilized land and called it *zhongguo* (JOOHNG • GWAH), or the Middle Kingdom. To the Chinese it represented the center of the world. In their eyes other people could become civilized only by learning the Chinese language and adopting Chinese customs. Even when outsiders overran China, as sometimes happened, the Chinese believed that the strangers would in time lose their identity and be absorbed into China's vast population. "China," they said, "is a sea which salts all rivers that run into it."

Patterns of Chinese History

In reading about Chinese civilization, you will encounter many ideas and customs that differ from those of your own civilization. These differences exist because of two basic patterns of Chinese history—the dynastic cycle and cultural evolution.

The dynastic cycle. From the beginning of its recorded history until the early A.D. 1900s, a succession of dynasties ruled China. The first dynasty, the Shang, came to power about 1500 B.C. The last dynasty, the Qing (CHING), ruled China from A.D. 1644 to A.D. 1912. Some dynasties lasted only a few years; others held power for centuries. No matter how long they lasted, however, all went through a dynastic cycle consisting of several stages.

The first stage involved the founding of the dynasty. By defeating military rivals in war, an individual leader gained control of China. The right to rule the country then became hereditary within the leader's family, and a new dynasty emerged. Next

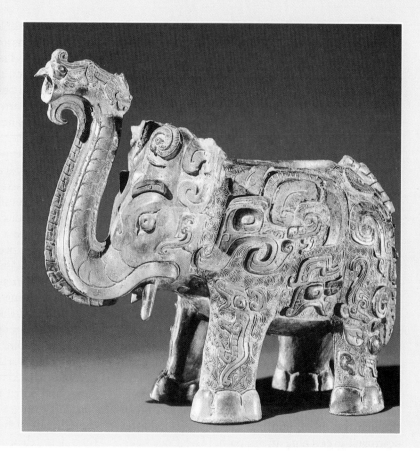

Ancient Chinese Elephant

This small, boldly decorated bronze elephant is a container that probably once held food. It was buried as an offering to the spirit of a river or mountain near where it was found in Hunan Province in China.

Containers such as this one give us an idea of the importance of nature to the Chinese. Spiral designs representing clouds and rain cover the elephant. Use of these symbols was widespread during the Shang dynasty, when the container was made. Real and imaginary animals also decorate the container. The animals stood for the spirits of nature or for particular families. These ceremonial containers are extraordinary examples of bronze casting, a craft the Chinese developed into a great art.

came a period of internal peace, expansion, and great power. The new dynasty collected taxes and labor services from the people. The dynasty used its wealth to improve roads and irrigation systems, to support education and the arts, and to build splendid palaces to enhance its prestige.

A period of regression marked by decline followed the period of great power. During this stage the rulers thought less of the people and more about living in luxury. It raised taxes whenever it could, creating hardship among the people. The government stopped maintaining dikes and irrigation systems, increasing the risk of floods. The ruling dynasty gradually became unable to defend the frontiers of China, and nomadic invasions increased. When its decline reached a low point, with chaos and rebellion in many parts of the land, the dynasty collapsed. A new leader emerged, and another dynastic cycle began.

Cultural evolution. The dynastic cycle describes the political history of China, but it does not explain many other aspects of China's history. Beneath the recurring pattern of events in politics was a continuous evolution, or development, of culture over the centuries. For example, structures such as the family, the farm, and the village developed their own patterns of change. During some stages of the dynastic cycle, the pace of cultural evolution quickened; during others, it slowed. Over the centuries, however, civilization in China maintained a steady pattern of growth as institutions and ideas became more complex.

SECTION 1 REVIEW

1. **Define** loess, silt
2. **Locate** Huang He, Chang Jiang, Qin Ling, China Proper, Tibet, Xinjiang, Mongolia, Manchuria, Korea, Xi Jiang, Gobi Desert
3. **Interpreting Ideas** Explain why the Huang He has been called "China's Sorrow."
4. **Evaluating Ideas** Why did the Chinese consider all other people to be "barbarians"?
5. **Analyzing Ideas** What was meant by the statement, "China is a sea which salts all rivers that run into it"?
6. **Summarizing Ideas** Describe the stages of China's dynastic cycle.

2 Chinese Civilization Flourished Under the Shang Dynasty

The Chinese placed great importance on explanations of the distant past and on China's role in history. Many legends about the beginnings of the world and about ancient China and its people lend vivid illustrations to centuries of Chinese history.

Legends of Ancient China

The legends of ancient China tell of Pan Gu (BAHN GOO), the first man, who worked for 18,000 years to create the universe. They tell of hero-kings who ruled for more than 100 years each and personally created such institutions and inventions as marriage, music, painting, and the wheel. The legends also tell of the Xia (SHAH) dynasty, which ruled the Huang He region from about 2000 B.C. to about 1500 B.C.

Unfortunately, these legends contain very few proven facts. Whether or not the Xia dynasty existed, however, scholars do not doubt that the people of the Huang He valley made great advances during those 500 years. The Chinese improved their methods of agriculture, and some evidence indicates they began to use written symbols. With the development of writing, the history of China became more concrete.

China's first historic dynasty, the Shang, began about 1500 B.C. along the Huang He. Although scholars do not know how the Shang rulers established power, legend tells us that the Shang were immigrants, not natives. Before the Shang dynasty, the people of the valley had no government to regulate irrigation, drainage, or flood control. They lived well in good years but starved when droughts or floods struck. Many scholars believe that the Shang introduced simple irrigation and flood control systems to their people. Control of these systems meant control of the region.

Government During the Shang Dynasty

The first Shang rulers probably conquered 1,800 city-states. Apparently, the Shang moved their capital many times, either because it was difficult to defend or because of floods. During the last centuries of Shang rule, the capital was situated near what is today the city of Anyang (AHN • YAHNG).

Shang rulers created a relatively simple government. A hereditary king gave land to his principal followers. In return the followers pledged loyalty, performed certain services, and paid dues. Less advanced peoples lived on the borders of the kingdom. The Shang used war chariots and bronze weapons to maintain their power over these peoples. Shang military force enabled them to gain territory and to spread the knowledge of their more advanced civilization. At one point, they ruled most of northern and central China (see map, this page).

The Chinese believed that their ruler symbolized the direct link between the people and heaven, where the gods of nature and fertility lived. The gods gave the monarch the right to rule, a right known as the **Mandate of Heaven.** People believed that the gods helped their ruler in war and in planning for good crops. However, the ruler had to produce results, and rebellions broke out when he failed. Poor crops or defeat in battle meant the ruler had lost the Mandate of Heaven and thus the right to rule. Throughout Chinese history, when rebels overthrew a dynasty, they justified their actions by saying the old dynasty had lost the Mandate of Heaven.

Learning from Maps *Shang rulers interpreted the calendar to predict the best times for planting and harvesting. Which city on the map is closest to the Huang He?*

MODIFIED OBLIQUE CONIC CONFORMAL PROJECTION

Learning from Pictures *Bronze castings of the Shang dynasty are considered some of the most remarkable achievements in metal craft of ancient history.* †

Culture During the Shang Dynasty

Shang rulers held the Mandate of Heaven from about 1500 B.C. to 1122 B.C. During this time the Chinese people made new discoveries and developed new skills while refining the discoveries and skills of earlier periods.

Economy and handicrafts. The Shang economy was based mainly on agriculture. The chief crops included a grain called millet and barley. Though farmers also grew some rice, they imported most rice from the south.

Domesticated animals included cattle, horses, sheep, pigs, chickens, and dogs. In addition, the Shang used elephants from southern Asia in battle and for some other kinds of work. Sometime during the Shang dynasty, the Chinese learned to raise silkworms, to spin thread from their cocoons, and to weave silk cloth from the thread.

Not all the Chinese farmed, however. Many merchants and artisans lived in the cities. Some merchants made clothing from silk, and others made cord from hemp. Artisans crafted jewelry by carving jade and also inlaid turquoise in ivory and bone.

Shang artisans established the foundation for all later Chinese ceramic art, including every form and shape used in Chinese ceremonial vases. Shang potters learned to use kaolin (KAY•uh•luhn), a fine white clay, and to shape items on a potter's wheel. They also glazed some of their pottery to give it a shiny, durable finish.

Today people throughout the world regard the bronze castings of Shang artisans as outstanding works of art. The Chinese may have learned the technique of casting from the Middle East, possibly Sumer. However, the forms of the vessels and the designs of the decorations were uniquely Chinese. Chinese artisans probably imported copper and tin ores and mixed the bronze themselves. They cast small figures as well as large ceremonial vessels whose surfaces featured delicate relief work characterized by elevations in the metal.

Astronomy and the calendar. An accurate calendar meant as much to Shang farmers and their

† (middle photo) Courtesy of the *Freer Gallery of Art*, Smithsonian Institution, Washington D.C. 43.9 Chinese Bronze: 12th–11th Cent. B.C. Shang Middle-late An-yang. Ceremonial vessel of type ku. 29.3 × 16.7 overall (11-9/16 ×6-9/16)

rulers as it did to the peoples of Egypt and the Fertile Crescent. The Chinese based their calendar on the movement of the moon. The shortest period in the calendar consisted of 10 days. Three such periods, sometimes shortened by a day, made a month. Six 10-day periods made a "cycle." Six cycles made a year of up to 360 days. To provide enough days for a full 365-day year, responsible and skilled priest-astronomers employed by the government added days as needed. Since the king's popularity depended on the success of the harvest, which in part depended on the time of planting as determined by the calendar, the priest-astronomers played a very important role.

Shang astronomers predicted eclipses of the moon so accurately that even an error of 24 hours alarmed the authorities. Because of their skill with the calendar, the astronomers were given the duty of keeping other records. Thus the Chinese had "official historians" very early in their history.

Language and writing. The Chinese rank as one of the few peoples who developed an original written language. To understand the ancient Chinese writing system, one must first understand some characteristics of spoken Chinese.

First, almost all ancient Chinese words consisted of one syllable. To express a new or more complicated meaning, the Chinese would combine two or more simple words. Thus the word for *magnet* was made up of three one-syllable words meaning "pull-iron-stone." Each word-syllable kept just as much of its original meaning as was needed to accurately define the compound word. This compound word was something new, not just a collection of the three things named.

Second, the ancient Chinese language did not include as many variations or uses of the same word as some other languages. For example, the same noun could be either singular or plural.

Because of the characteristics of their language, the Chinese did not need a phonetic system of writing. Instead they assigned a special symbol, or character, to every word in their language. At first these characters were pictograms, or drawings of objects. Later, as their culture and therefore their language became more complex, the Chinese developed ideograms and phonograms. Many written characters then consisted of two parts. One was a significant, or "idea sign." It gave a clue to the meaning of the character. The other was a phonetic, or "sound sign." It told how to pronounce the character.

The Chinese developed their system of writing in an effective way, and they could combine signs to invent new characters. However, because each character had to be memorized, it took years of painstaking study to learn to read and write. For centuries a well-educated Chinese person had to know more than 10,000 characters. Thus, until the Chinese developed a simplified version of the language in recent times, only a small percentage of Chinese people could read and write.

Unlike the Aryans of India, the early Chinese used writing to compose and preserve literary works. They used a brush to write characters in lines that ran from the top to the bottom of a page, beginning on the right side. Writing itself became an art, called **calligraphy** (kuh•LIG•ruh•fee). Even today the Chinese admire beautiful calligraphy as much as they admire beautiful paintings.

Religion in the Shang period. The religion that developed during the Shang dynasty combined animism and ancestor worship. People believed in an all-powerful and kindly dragon that lived in the seas and rivers and could rise into the clouds. They believed that dragons fighting in the heavens caused the summer thunderstorms that brought rain. In time this good dragon became the symbol of Chinese rulers.

The Chinese held great religious festivals in the spring and autumn. In spring, the planting season, the ruler plowed the first furrow to ensure good crops. In autumn the people thanked the gods for the harvest.

In addition to animistic beliefs, the Chinese revered the elders and ancestors of their families. They regarded the family as both earth-dwelling and spirit-dwelling, believing that all members of the family—the living and the dead—were united forever through their religion. A child's obligation to a parent was most important. In Chinese writing the character that symbolizes the honor and reverence owed to parents shows a son supporting his aged father as he walks.

Priests played an important role in Chinese religion. Some worked as priest-astronomers. Others foretold the future in order to learn the wishes of the spirits, especially of the spirits of ancestors. The priests wrote questions on **oracle bones,** the shoulder bones of cattle or the bottoms of tortoise shells, into which they thrust a heated metal rod. They used the pattern of cracks that formed to interpret the answers, which the priests then inscribed on

Learning from Pictures *Some oracle bones, unlike the one above, were never burned with rods. They contain written records of receipts and historical events dealing with the Shang royal court.*

the bone or shell. The inscriptions often included the name of the ruler who asked the questions. These recorded questions and answers have helped scholars solve many of the historical and cultural mysteries of the Shang dynasty.

Fall of the Shang Dynasty

The Shang kingdom collapsed in 1122 B.C., apparently because the last king was busy trying to expand his boundaries south to the Chang Jiang. He failed to guard the northwest frontier, where a tribe of soldier-farmers called the Zhou (JOH) led a rebellion. The Zhou ultimately conquered the Shang, claiming that the last Shang king had lost the Mandate of Heaven because he was a monster of corrupt wickedness and cruelty. Yet another dynastic cycle had begun.

3 Chinese Civilization Evolved Through Changing Dynasties

The Zhou conquest of China in 1122 B.C. marked the beginning of a dynamic era in Chinese history. Under the rule of three successive dynasties—the Zhou (JOH), the Qin (CHIN), and the Han—China gradually became a large and powerful empire. Great technological and economic growth occurred in China during this first imperial age, or age of an empire. Tremendous philosophical activity also took place, as the Chinese formulated ideas and theories of lasting importance to their civilization. Eventually, internal weaknesses and foreign invasions brought this imperial age to an end.

The Zhou Dynasty

The most enduring Chinese dynasty—the Zhou—lasted almost 800 years, from 1122 B.C. to 256 B.C. Originally less advanced than the Shang, the Zhou quickly adopted many aspects of Shang culture and later developed some of their own.

Zhou rulers called themselves Sons of Heaven. Like the Shang rulers, they claimed to rule by the Mandate of Heaven, which obligated them to keep the gods contented, perform rites to ensure the fertility of the soil, and control the rivers.

During the many years of Zhou rule, internal trade expanded, and copper coins came into use as money. The introduction of iron, which helped transform Chinese agriculture, probably ranks as the most important development. Using iron farm tools and plows pulled by oxen, Chinese peasants cultivated new lands and produced more grain than ever before. They built canals, dikes, and reservoirs for irrigation, among them the Grand Canal, which irrigated approximately 1,000 square miles (2,600 square kilometers) of land. As a result, China's population grew steadily. By the 700s B.C., China probably ranked as the most densely populated land in the world.

The Zhou rulers did not create a unified empire. They established a central government first in the capital city of Hao and later in Luoyang (LOH • YAHNG), but many independent city-states also existed. Although they owed certain obligations to the Zhou, these city-states could also act on their own.

ZHOU DYNASTY, ca. 1000 B.C.

GOBI (DESERT)

(Yellow R.)

Huang He

NORTH CHINA PLAIN

Wei He Huang He

Fêng • Hao • Luoyang

Chang Jiang

Xi Jiang

Yellow Sea

East China Sea

South China Sea

N

0   200   400 Miles
0   200   400 Kilometers

MODIFIED OBLIQUE CONIC CONFORMAL PROJECTION

QIN DYNASTY, 210 B.C.

GOBI (DESERT)

Great Wall

(Yellow R.)

K A N S U

Huang He

NORTH CHINA PLAIN

Wei He Xianyang Huang He

• Luoyang

Chang Jiang

Xi Jiang

Yellow Sea

East China Sea

South China Sea

N

0   200   400 Miles
0   200   400 Kilometers

MODIFIED OBLIQUE CONIC CONFORMAL PROJECTION

Learning from Maps *First the Zhou and later the Qin dynasties lost the Mandate of Heaven after their rulers put personal interests before those of the kingdom. In what part of China did the emperors have the Great Wall built? Why?*

In the early days of the Zhou dynasty, the heads of the city-states sent military and financial assistance to the Zhou rulers whenever requested to do so. Crisis struck the Zhou, however, in 771 B.C. The frivolous King You (YOO) had entertained his favorite princess by lighting the warning fires which signaled the nobles that nomadic raiders were attacking. The princess and the king enjoyed watching the powerful nobles gallop into town to protect the capital. But the false alarms had infuriated the nobles. When an army of nomads really appeared, the nobles ignored the warning fires. The nomads killed King You and then ransacked the capital.

After You's death the city-states grew rebellious. The warring states, as they were called, began to fight among themselves to expand their territories. By the 400s B.C., the Zhou rulers had no real power outside their own city-state. Instead, local rulers wielded great power. Zhou rulers continued to hold the Mandate of Heaven, however, until a new dynasty, the Qin, replaced them.

The Qin Dynasty

The Qin dynasty came to power in 221 B.C. by using cavalry armed with bows and arrows, a military technique new to the Chinese. Shi Huangdi, which means "first emperor," founded this new dynasty.

From its beautiful capital at Xianyang (SHEE • EN • YAHNG), the Qin dynasty ruled a larger area than did either of the preceding dynasties and controlled it more firmly. Although the Qin dynasty lasted only a short time, until 207 B.C., it unified China under a strong central government for the first time in history. This dynasty, from whose name the Western name for China comes, created the first Chinese empire, standardized weights, measures, and coinage, and established a uniform system of writing.

Not satisfied with ruling northern China and parts of the Chang Jiang valley, Shi Huangdi sent his armies far to the south. In a brilliant military campaign, he soon conquered the central part of

77

southern China as far as the delta of the Xi Jiang River (see map, page 77). He also tore down the walls of the many city-states, disarmed their rulers, and ended their independence. The emperor divided China into military districts ruled by governors who used stern military and civilian authority. The Code of Qin replaced conflicting local laws with a uniform system of laws. Shi Huangdi also implemented a single tax system throughout the country, ending chaos in tax collecting.

The Qin as builders. To guard against invasion from the north and west, the Chinese over the years had built several walls. The Qin completed and connected these walls to form the Great Wall of China. This massive structure, much of which still stands today, was 25 feet (7.5 meters) high and extended 1,400 miles (2,250 kilometers) from Gansu (GAHN • SOO) province to the sea (see map, page 77). It was 15 feet (4.5 meters) wide, with a road along the top that enabled soldiers to travel quickly to any threatened area of the frontier.

Understanding the importance of transportation and communication, Shi Huangdi built broad, tree-lined highways. He set a standard width for the axles of carts and other vehicles so that they could pass each other easily on roads and bridges.

Harshness of the Qin. The Qin maintained order in their empire, but they established an **autocracy** in which the emperor held total power. Like autocrats ever since, Shi Huangdi saw the danger of allowing scholars to investigate and discuss problems freely. He began his attack on the scholars by burning two important books called the *Classic of Songs* and the *Classic of Documents*. When scholars did not heed this warning, Shi Huangdi had 460 of them executed.

Discontent spread quickly under the rule of the Qin dynasty. A great gap existed between the ruler, supported by his warriors, and the mass of people. Almost 700,000 workers had been brutally driven to build the Great Wall—it is said that each of its stones cost a life—and peasants resented the heavy taxes they had to pay. In 207 B.C. a general of peasant background, Liu Bang (LEE • OO BAHNG), led a revolt against the Qin. He overthrew the empire and in 202 B.C. founded the Han dynasty.

Learning from Pictures *The imperial tomb of Shi Huangdi is housed in the Army Vault Museum and contains terra-cotta statues of warriors, horses, and the emperor's royal guards.*

MODIFIED OBLIQUE CONIC CONFORMAL PROJECTION

Learning from Maps   *By appointing friends and family as administrators of the empire, Liu Bang almost caused its breakup. What is the easternmost point of the Silk Route?*

The Han Dynasty

The new dynasty took its name from the Han River, where Liu Bang had been stationed as a general for several years. Like the Qin, the Han dynasty ruled a centralized and expanding empire. Unlike the Qin, however, it was less autocratic and succeeded in maintaining its power for almost 400 years. Han rulers so influenced China that even today many Chinese refer to themselves as "Sons of Han."

The most famous Han emperor, Wu Di (WOO DEE), ruled from 140 B.C. to 87 B.C. He established his capital at Chang'an (CHAHNG • AHN), now called Xian (SHEE • AHN), and extended Chinese territory north into Manchuria and Korea, south into Indochina, and west into central Asia (see map, this page).

The civil service system. The Han dynasty established the Chinese civil service system. A **civil service** administers the day-to-day business of gov-

ernment, and its members usually receive their appointments based on the results of competitive examinations. The philosopher Confucius, who believed that only educated and virtuous people should enter government service, originated the idea for civil service examinations. These long and difficult examinations tested candidates for civil service positions on their knowledge of the great classics of Chinese literature and law. As a result, the best scholars in the country became government officials. Civil service examinations remained important to the Chinese government until the early A.D. 1900s.

In theory anyone could take the examinations, and cases in which a poor boy rose to great heights in the civil service were not unknown. Since education cost a great deal of money, however, few peasant families could afford to send their sons to school. Generally, only the sons of wealthy landowning families had a chance to become civil servants.

79

Learning from Pictures
Under the Han Empire, education and the arts flourished. This bronze flying horse was made around 150 B.C., at about the same time the first Chinese dictionary was published.

Leveling. Wu Di began an economic policy known as leveling because the rise and fall of prices of farm products had caused endless hardships for peasants. Under this policy, in years of good harvests government agents bought and stored surpluses to keep prices from falling. In years of poor harvests, the agents sold the stored food to prevent scarcity and high prices.

The Pax Sinica. Wu Di fought vigorous battles with the nomadic Huns of central and eastern Asia who threatened the frontiers of his empire. He later established what historians call the *Pax Sinica,* or "Chinese Peace," through much of Asia.

During this period of peace, merchants opened the famous Silk Route from China across central Asia to the Mediterranean region (see map, page 79). Long camel caravans carried silk, jade, and other valuable Chinese goods to be sold to wealthy Greeks and Romans. They returned with glass, amber, asbestos, and wool and linen textiles.

China's population grew to more than 60 million during the Han dynasty. The imperial capital at Chang'an became a huge city, with imposing palaces and broad avenues and a population of 250,000. On its many side streets stood the shops of merchants and artisans. There one could find luxury goods from lands throughout the world as well as many products from China, including two

of the greatest of all Chinese inventions, paper and porcelain. Both of these inventions spread from China to the Western world in later centuries and had a profound impact on Western life. Even today we call porcelain, or highly glazed ceramic ware, china.

None of Wu Di's successors in the Han dynasty matched his leadership abilities. Still, with the exception of one brief interruption, the Han dynasty ruled China until A.D. 220, when a revolt overthrew the last Han emperor.

For hundreds of years, countless nomadic tribes swept across China, ravaging the countryside and terrorizing the people. Not until A.D. 589 did a Chinese general unify China once again.

SECTION 3 REVIEW

1. **Define**   autocracy, civil service
2. **Identify**   Liu Bang, "Sons of Han," Wu Di
3. **Locate**   Chang'an
4. **Summarizing Ideas**   Describe the government under the rule of the Qin dynasty.
5. **Contrasting Ideas**   Two emperors, Shi Huangdi and Wu Di, are considered among China's greatest. What did each do to earn his reputation?
6. **Classifying Ideas**   How were Chinese government officials chosen during the Han dynasty?

4 The Ancient Chinese Created Unique Philosophies

Although political disunity and almost constant warfare marked the last years of the Zhou dynasty, this period marked one of the most creative in the history of Chinese philosophy. As in other ancient civilizations of the same period, new political, economic, and social problems prompted many new ideas and theories. Scholars classify these theories into four important groups—Naturalism, Confucianism, Legalism, and Daoism.

Naturalism

Like all other Chinese philosophers of the period, the Naturalists were far more interested in human beings and the real world than in divine or spiritual matters. They tried to explain the workings of nature by certain cosmic principles—principles that applied to the whole universe. One of their basic ideas concerned the dualism, or two-sidedness, of nature. Naturalists defined this dualism of nature as its *yin* and *yang*. *Yin* was female, dark, cold, and passive. *Yang* was male, light, hot, and active.

Yin and *yang* did not conflict with each other, however, as did the concepts of good and evil in Western civilization. Rather they depended on one another and constantly maintained a balance. Day, which was *yang*, gave way to night, which was *yin*. Summer gave way to winter.

The Naturalists also believed that balance in human affairs was inevitable. For example, extremes such as a harsh government or an anarchy (no government) could not exist for long.

Confucianism

Westerners know Kongzi (KOOHNG • ZUH), meaning "Kong the Philosopher," or "Reverend Master Kong," as Confucius. Left in poverty at the age of three when his father died, Confucius, who lived from about 551 B.C. to 478 B.C., still managed to receive a good education. At age 22, Confucius began teaching and soon gained many followers. In time his ideas and teachings, as written by his followers in a collection of writings called *Analects*, became known as Confucianism. The philosophy of Confucianism exerted a more powerful influence on later Chinese beliefs and life styles than did any other philosophy.

Confucius was not a religious prophet and had little to say about the gods, the meaning of death, or the idea of life after death. Instead, he taught about the importance of the family, respect for one's elders, and reverence for the past and one's ancestors. These three concepts formed the basis of Confucian philosophy.

Confucius had a primary interest in politics and wanted to end the political disorder of his time. He believed this could be accomplished in two ways. First, every person should accept an assigned role in society and perform the duties of that role. Second, government should be virtuous. Instead of relying

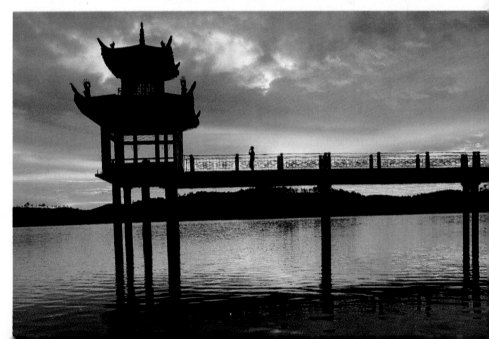

Learning from Pictures
This Chinese pagoda in Kunming in southern China emphasizes the Chinese ideal of harmony with nature—an ideal that was part of the Chinese philosophy of naturalism.

on military power, rulers should be honest and have concern for others. Only well-educated and extremely virtuous officials should be appointed to run the government.

Confucius taught that government should set a good example, believing that the people would willingly obey a ruler who lived and governed virtuously. Virtue, in Confucian teaching, consists of correct behavior toward others. This basic principle resembled the Christian Golden Rule, although stated negatively: "What you do not like when done unto yourself, do not do unto others."

Confucius hoped to put his ideas into practice by becoming adviser to a local ruler. According to legend, he worked as minister of crime in his native province of Shandong (SHAHN • DOOHNG), and within a year crime had almost disappeared. Neighboring rulers became jealous, however, and forced Confucius to retire. He spent the rest of his life teaching, and eventually his teachings took on religious significance. In 195 B.C., for example, Liu Bang, founder of the Han dynasty, visited the tomb of Confucius and offered a sacrifice to his spirit. In A.D. 58 the emperor of China ordered schools to offer sacrifices to Confucius.

Daoism

Laozi (LOW • ZUH), thought to have lived in the 500s B.C., founded a philosophy called Daoism (DOW • iz • um). Daoism got its name from its central idea, Dao, which can be defined as the "Way of Nature." Laozi saw Dao as an indescribable force that governed the universe and all nature. Only by withdrawing from the world and contemplating nature could people understand Dao and live in harmony with it.

According to Laozi, people should not strive for learning, riches, or power. Rather they should try to bring themselves into harmony with Dao by being quiet, thoughtful, and humble. As Laozi said, "He who overcomes others is strong; he who overcomes himself is mighty." Unlike Confucius, Laozi shunned politics and advised people not to participate in public affairs.

Daoism became second only to Confucianism in its importance to the Chinese. Daoism appealed to the masses of peasants because of its concern with nature and natural forces. It also appealed to many artists and poets because it encouraged artistic expression as a means of understanding Dao.

Daoism appealed to many Confucianists as well because it added balance to their lives. Some Confucianists believed that being concerned only with politics and social problems was too restrictive. Even officials and the emperor needed a temporary escape from governing the country. They found the escape they desired within the Daoist contemplation of nature.

Like *yin* and *yang*, Daoism and Confucianism came to be complementary parts in Chinese culture. Each supplied what the other lacked.

Legalism

Like Confucianism, the school of philosophy known as Legalism concerned itself with politics. Its teachings, however, differed greatly from the teachings of Confucianism. The Legalists believed in power, not virtue, and in harsh laws. In their view, people were by nature selfish and untrustworthy. Peace and prosperity could be achieved only by threatening severe punishment if people failed to do what the laws expected of them.

The first Qin emperor, Shi Huangdi, followed the ideas of Legalism. He succeeded in creating a powerful empire, but his dynasty ruled for a very short period. Later Chinese philosophers believed that the Qin dynasty failed because of its extremely cruel methods. The Qin failed to maintain a proper balance between *yin* and *yang*.

The government of the Han dynasty was Legalist in structure—that is, it was highly centralized and powerful. However, it was Confucian in operation, since educated officials who believed in the ethical principles of righteousness and compassion controlled it. The Han dynasty lasted as long as it did because it achieved a balance.

Buddhism in China

Another great influence on Chinese thought and religious belief came not from China but from India—from the teachings of Buddha. Missionaries from India first brought Buddhism to China during the Han dynasty.

As the Han dynasty collapsed and nomads from the north raided China, Buddhism found many converts, especially among the peasants. People looking for consolation in this time of crisis found it in Mahayana Buddhism, with its worship of Buddha as a savior and its promise of an eventual

●READ
WRITE
INTERPRET
CONNECT
THINK

BUILDING HISTORY STUDY SKILLS

Reading About History: Analyzing a Statement

To analyze a statement, you must take it apart in order to find its meaning, identify the main idea, see relationships, or determine the importance of the information. Analysis has a specific goal. For example, you would analyze a statement so that you could understand the author's thoughts and relate them to a movement, idea, or situation. You may tie together the various parts of a theory by analyzing the statements.

How to Analyze a Statement

To analyze a statement, follow these steps.

1. Determine the goal or purpose of the analysis.
2. Read the statement carefully.
3. Identify the key words in the statement.
4. Explain what the statement means.
5. Determine how the statement relates to other ideas.

Developing the Skill

Read the following statements. The first is attributed to Laozi and the second to Zhuan Zu. Both were founders of Daoist thought in the 500s B.C. By analyzing both statements, you will be able to understand the meaning of Daoism and its impact on Chinese thought and institutions.

> He who knows others is learned;
>   He who knows himself is wise.
> He who conquers others has power of muscles;
>   He who conquers himself is strong.
> He who is contented is rich.
>   He who is determined has strength of will.
> He who does not loose his center endures;
> He who dies yet (his power) remains has long life.
> (Laozi)

> Once long ago a bird alighted in the suburbs of the Lu capital. The ruler of Lu was delighted with it, had a . . . sacrifice prepared for it to feast on, and . . . music performed for its enjoyment. But the bird immediately began to look unhappy, and dazed, and did not dare to eat or drink. This is what is called trying to nourish a bird with what would nourish you. If you want to nourish a bird with what will nourish a bird, you had best let it roost in the deep forest, float on the rivers and lakes, and live on snakes—then it can feel at ease.
> (Zhuan Zu)

The key words in Laozi's statement are *learned, wise, strong, strength of will, endures,* and *long life.* These are desired virtues or states of being that Laozi believes people will acquire when they learn self-mastery. One develops this self-mastery through knowledge and determination.

The key words in Zhuan Zu's statement are *unhappy, nourish, roost,* and *float.* These words refer to being natural and finding happiness through discovering one's own nature. Zhuan Zu is pointing out that every person must realize his or her own human nature in order to be healthy, creative, and happy.

Both statements illustrate one of the key beliefs of Daoism—the importance of internal harmony or peace, which can only be reached through self-realization, or knowledge of one's self.

Practicing the skill. Using the steps for analyzing a statement, find and analyze a statement or quote made by a famous person in the 1900s.

To apply this skill, see Applying History Study Skills on page 89.

Miniature house from the Han Dynasty

Learning from Pictures
*These three jade Buddhas
are in a temple in Shanghai,
China. What other philos-
ophies had the greatest
influence in ancient China?*

escape from the miseries of the world in nirvana. Buddhist temples and ceremonies also offered a sense of comfort and tranquillity in turbulent times.

Of all the philosophies of ancient China, those of Confucius, Laozi, and Buddha had the greatest influence on Chinese attitudes. Confucianism, with its reverence for the past and emphasis on the family, won the most followers. The Chinese had always revered their ancestors and worshiped the emperor as almost a divine being, and these practices continued. Other ideas contained in Daoism and Buddhism—humility, contentment, loyalty, justice, wisdom, and obedience—were absorbed into Chinese culture and helped make the Chinese a patient and enduring people.

SECTION 4 REVIEW

1. **Identify** Kongzi, Laozi
2. **Comparing Ideas** Explain the concept of *yin* and *yang.*
3. **Analyzing Ideas** **(a)** What are the basic teachings of Confucianism? **(b)** How did the ideas of Daoism complement the ideas of Confucianism?
4. **Classifying Ideas** List the ideas of Legalism.

5 Culture Reached New Heights During the Zhou, Qin, and Han Dynasties

Chinese society rested on the Confucian principle that the family was of key importance to the welfare of the state. The values that governed family life—reverence for one's family, respect for age, and acceptance of the decisions made by one's superiors—governed national life as well as Chinese social and cultural life, including the economy, education, literature, and science.

Family and Social Life

The family, not the individual, constituted the most important unit in Chinese society. A man rose or fell in the social system not because of wealth or personal accomplishments but because of his family's position. Each family consisted of the father, his wife, the sons with their wives and children, and the unmarried daughters. Often all members of a family lived in the same house and shared day-to-day tasks.

Harvest Festivals

When Americans sit down for Thanksgiving dinner each year, they are repeating a celebration found in almost every society in the world. All peoples find a way to give thanks when they have finished gathering the harvest. The summer is over, and the food has been grown. There is a feeling of gratitude that the earth has once again provided grain, vegetables, and fruits, such as at the Irish strawberry festival (right).

Long ago the ancient Hebrews celebrated a fall thanksgiving, a holiday called *Succoth* that Jews today still celebrate.

As early as the Shang dynasty, there were harvest gods in China (below). Later the Chinese celebrated the Harvest Moon Festival, and they saw a rabbit's form in the moon. They ate cakes in the shape of rabbits and moons, and gave thanks at altars adorned with wheat. In Japan today the harvest is honored by placing the produce of the earth on altars. The Japanese also

hold large parades and carry giant fish to thank the ocean for the food it provides.

Among the early American Indians there were many rituals of planting and harvest (above). The ancient

wish to give thanks when the farmer's work is done, and when the earth gives up its harvest, continues. The forms differ from place to place, but the importance of the land is the same for people all over the world.

The Chinese father ruled the family. The older he was, the more authority he had, for the Chinese respected age as a source of wisdom. Respect for one's aged parents and especially for one's father was an important virtue. Each family kept a careful genealogy, or record of their family tree, even including third cousins. When family members died, they became honored ancestors. Most families constructed altars where they worshiped their ancestors as links between the family's past, present, and future.

The Chinese father arranged his children's and his grandchildren's marriages, decided how much education his sons would receive, and even chose his sons' careers. Women were subordinate to men and had no property rights of their own. After marriage a young wife became almost a servant in the household of her husband's family. Before her wedding she often cried, not because she did not yet know her husband but because she did not know how her new family would treat her. With motherhood and age, however, the wife became an important figure in the family.

The Economy

Despite the growth of cities and towns, the vast majority of Chinese people continued to eke out meager existences as farmers in small villages. On the one hand, they had to contend with nature. If too much or too little rain fell, their crops might be ruined and they would starve. On the other hand, they had to contend with government. In addition to paying taxes, peasants also had to perform labor. For about one month each year, they left their farms and worked on roads, canals, or other local construction projects.

Just as during the Shang dynasty, farmers grew millet and wheat in the north and rice in the south. In both northern and southern China, about eight families worked fields in common. They used ox-drawn plows and complex systems of irrigation and flood control. These systems were so well constructed that Chinese farmers still use some built in the 200s B.C.

Although trade was never very important to the Chinese economy, it increased early in the

Learning from Pictures The ancient Chinese used sailboats called junks to trade throughout East Asia. Even today junks ply the rivers of China.

Zhou dynasty, when the northern Chinese began migrating into southern China. Items of trade between northern and southern China included leather goods, silk, jade, jewelry, screens, and couches. Trade improved when the Qin dynasty standardized the currency system and weights and measures. Trade increased further when the Silk Route linked China with the Mediterranean region during the Han dynasty.

Education

The Chinese did not consider education the responsibility of government, on either the national or the local level. Instead, families hired private tutors. If a family could not afford to do so, the children went uneducated. Even as late as the year 1900, not more than 5 percent of the Chinese people could read or write. Both the expense of paying a tutor and the difficulty of learning Chinese reading and writing caused this low rate of literacy.

Literature

The most important works of Chinese literature and the basis for all Chinese education were the Five Classics. We do not know who wrote these works or when they were written, but we do know that they were already important by the time of the Zhou dynasty. Officials used two of the Five Classics in civil service examinations: the *Classic of Songs*, containing more than 300 songs about love, joy, politics, and domestic life; and the *Classic of Documents*, containing semihistorical speeches and documents about government. The other three classics included the *Classic of Changes*, about the art of foretelling the future; *Spring and Autumn Annals*, a record of events in the important city-state of Lu from 722 B.C. to 481 B.C.; and *Ceremonies and Rituals*, about etiquette and ceremonies.

Shi Huangdi ordered the burning of the *Classic of Songs* and the *Classic of Documents* and tried to ban the reading of the other three. Toward the end of the Qin dynasty, this ban was lifted and the texts restored to their present form. In A.D. 175 the Five Classics were carved in stone to ensure that they would never again be destroyed.

Learning the Five Classics became essential for every well-brought-up young man of China. The Chinese also expected such young men to know many of the *Analects* of Confucius.

Science and Technology

As early as 444 B.C., Chinese astronomers had computed the year at 365 1/4 days. During the Han dynasty, scientists refined these calculations even further. In 28 B.C. astronomers in China first observed sunspots, which Europeans did not discover until the A.D. 1600s.

Sometime before A.D. 100, Chinese astronomers built special instruments to observe the orbit they believed the sun followed. Using these instruments, an early astronomer estimated the number of stars at 11,520. Other scientific achievements included the invention of a primitive seismograph that registered earthquakes so faint that royal officials did not even notice them.

The Chinese also invented paper. First produced in A.D. 105 from hemp, old rags, fishing nets, and the bark of mulberry trees, the paper was a bright yellow. The use of paper had spread throughout Asia by A.D. 700 and also to Europe, where it replaced papyrus as the main writing material. The Chinese also invented the sun dial, the water clock, and printing.

Perhaps the most widely known Chinese contribution to medicine is the therapy known as **acupuncture.** Its development stemmed from the Daoist belief that good health depends on the movement of a life-force energy through the body and that illness or pain results when something interferes with that movement.

In acupuncture the doctor inserts needles into certain points of the body to enable the life-force energy to move properly. Some modern researchers believe that these needle-insertion points have less electrical resistance than other parts of the body and thus may affect the nervous system. Today the Chinese use acupuncture as a general anesthetic in most types of surgery. Many Americans use it to relieve the pain of arthritis, cancer, and neuralgia.

SECTION 5 REVIEW

1. **Define** acupuncture
2. **Understanding Ideas** Explain the important role that the family played in Chinese government and social life.
3. **Interpreting Ideas** (a) What were the Five Classics? (b) the *Analects*?
4. **Analyzing Ideas** (a) How did the Chinese educate their children? (b) Why did so few Chinese learn to read and write?

CHAPTER 4 REVIEW

Rule of the Shang dynasty

BC ca. 1500

1122

Rule of the Zhou dynasty

Chapter Summary

The following list contains the key concepts you have learned about the great civilization of China.

1. China is divided into two main sections—China Proper and the vast semicircle of regions that surround it. These regions include Tibet, Xinjiang, Mongolia, Manchuria, and Korea.
2. The major rivers of China include the Chang Jiang, the Huang He, and the Xi Jiang. Because of devastating floods, the Huang He is often referred to as "China's Sorrow."
3. China's political history involves a succession of ruling dynasties that rose and fell in a recognizable pattern or cycle. China's cultural history concerns the gradual evolution of civilization over the centuries.
4. The Shang was the first historic Chinese dynasty. During their rule simple irrigation and flood control systems, a calendar, and an original written language were developed.
5. The Zhou, Qin, and Han dynasties had an important and enduring influence on the development of Chinese government and thought.
6. China's most influential philosopher was Confucius, who taught that emphasizing family and choosing virtuous rulers led to a healthy society. Confucianism became the most important philosophy in China. It later evolved into a religion.
7. Laozi, the founder of Daoism, taught that people should withdraw from the world and try to achieve harmony with nature. In time Daoism became the second most important philosophy in China.
8. Two other significant schools of Chinese philosophy were Naturalism and Legalism. Naturalism explained nature through the principles of *yin* and *yang*. Legalism stressed political power and harsh laws.
9. The most important unit in Chinese society was the family. Age was highly respected, and fathers had great authority.
10. Many cultural and technological advances occurred during the Zhou, Qin, and Han dynasties. The Five Classics became the most important works of Chinese literature. Technological advances included the invention of paper as well as scientific instruments and the medical technique of acupuncture.

On a separate sheet of paper, complete the following review exercises.

Reviewing Important Terms

Supply the term that correctly completes each sentence.

1. In an _____ the ruler wields unlimited power.
2. _____ is the art of beautiful writing.
3. _____ _____ administers the government on a day-to-day basis, and its members are usually appointed based on the results of highly competitive examinations.
4. The yellowish silt carried in the waters of the Huang He is called _____ .
5. The gods gave the Chinese monarch the right to rule, a right known as the _____ _____ _____ .
6. During the Shang dynasty, priests wrote questions on _____ _____ , the shoulder bones of cattle or the bottoms of tortoise shells.
7. _____ is a Chinese therapy in which doctors insert needles into certain points of the body to enable life-force energy to move properly.
8. _____ is moist soil carried as sediment in a river's waters.

Developing Critical Thinking Skills

1. **Seeing Relationships** Describe the geographical barriers of China that limited the spread of Chinese culture.
2. **Making Charts** Make a chart listing the accomplishments of the Shang dynasty.
3. **Classifying Ideas** Put each of the following names or ideas in one of these four categories: literature, technology, philosophy, government.
   (a) leveling
   (b) Pax Sinica
   (c) civil service examinations
   (d) *yin* and *yang*
   (e) standard width of axle for carts
   (f) Great Wall
   (g) uniform law code
   (h) teachings of Confucius

ca. 551–478
Life of
Confucius

Chinese
computation of
length of year

221–207
Rule of the
Qin dynasty

Rule of the
Han dynasty

BC
563

444

256

202

140   87

AD

105

220

589

Birth
of Buddha

Rule of Wu Di,
most famous
Han emperor

Invention of
paper

Reunification
of China

(i) large-scale irrigation and flood control
(j) *Classic of Songs* and *Classic of Documents*
(k) acupuncture
(l) Naturalism

4. **Evaluating Ideas** Which dynasty—the Zhou, the Qin, or the Han—did the most to advance Chinese culture? Give evidence to support your answer.

5. **Analyzing Ideas** (a) Compare the ideas of Confucianism and Legalism regarding how society should be changed. (b) Are any of these ideas or values used in our society today? Give examples from newspapers to support your opinion.

6. **Synthesizing Ideas** (a) Why did the Chinese call their country the Middle Kingdom? (b) How do you think the attitude the Chinese held toward foreigners might have affected ancient Chinese history? (c) How might it affect China today?

Relating Geography to History

(a) Trace the map of eastern Asia on page 70. Then use atlases to complete the following activities. (b) Indicate the areas that have heavy rainfall. (c) Indicate the areas that need irrigation in order to grow crops. (d) Show the desert area (the Gobi Desert) that might be used for grazing.

Relating Past to Present

1. Animism is the belief that spirits inhabit everything—rocks, plants, animals, and even people. Scholars believe that the people who lived in China during the Shang dynasty were animists. (a) List some of these animistic ideas and practices and compare them with what people today call "superstitions." (b) What are some of the symbols considered "lucky" and "unlucky" today?

2. It is sometimes said that a culture can be judged by the people to whom the greatest honor is paid. (a) Which people were most honored in ancient China? (b) Which people do you think people in the United States today respect or honor most? (c) What qualities make people in the United States regard these people so highly?

Applying History Study Skills

Before completing this activity, review Building History Study Skills on page 83.

Look again at the steps for analyzing statements. Then complete the following exercise.

Read the following statement from the Confucian book *The Great Learning*. Then analyze the statement by answering the questions below.

❝ The ancients who wished clearly to exemplify ... virtue throughout the world would first set up good government in their states. Wishing to govern well their states, they would first regulate their families. Wishing to regulate their families, they would first cultivate their persons. Wishing to cultivate their persons, they would first rectify their minds. Wishing to rectify their minds, they would first seek sincerity in their thoughts. Wishing for sincerity in their thoughts, they would first extend their knowledge. ❞

1. What is the purpose of the statement?
2. One of the key words in the statement is *cultivate*. (a) What does the word mean? (b) What are the other key words in the statement?
3. (a) According to Confucius, how is harmony in society achieved? (b) Do you agree? Why or why not?

Investigating Further

1. **Presenting an Oral Report** Learn how to write 10 characters of the Chinese language as an art form. You may use *Chinese Calligraphy* by Chiang Yee (Harvard University Press) as a source. Report to the class the skills learned in the use of the brush.

2. **Writing a Report** Find pictures of bronze items from the Shang dynasty in reference books in your school or public library. Study the pictures to determine the religious functions and the aesthetic value of the bronzes. Write a report describing your findings.

3. **Interviewing** Visit a Chinese restaurant in your community and interview one of the employees to find what types of food are typically Chinese. How do these foods differ from American food? How are they prepared differently than American foods?

Unit Summary

The following list contains the key concepts you have learned about ancient civilizations.

1. Using bones, artifacts, and pictures, anthropologists study early human behavior, customs, and skills.
2. During Neolithic times, people in four great river valleys developed the first civilizations.
3. Protected by geographic barriers, the Egyptians developed a remarkable culture that included literature, science, art, complex agricultural practices, hieroglyphics, and elaborate religious rituals.
4. In the Fertile Crescent, a succession of empire builders formed societies and cultures. Major developments included cuneiform (Sumerians), codification of law (Babylonians), effective methods of government (Persians), the alphabet (Phoenicians), invention of money (Lydians), and ethical monotheism (Hebrews).
5. About 2500 B.C. people in the Indus Valley cities of Harappa and Mohenjo-Daro developed a complex civilization. In 1500 B.C. nomadic Aryans swept through the Khyber Pass and settled in India. By 1000 B.C. they had developed the rigid caste system that regulated everyday contacts between more than 3,000 hereditary classes.
6. The religious books of Hinduism, the *Upanishads,* outline the path of reincarnation each soul must take to be reunited with the Universal Soul.
7. Gautama founded Buddhism. According to this religion, people can reach salvation by accepting the Four Noble Truths and following the Eightfold Path.
8. Geographical barriers isolated China as its civilization evolved along the Huang He. The Chinese built irrigation ditches and dikes and developed a lunar calendar and written language.
9. During the Zhou, Qin, and Han dynasties, philosophy flourished, with Naturalists, Confucianists, Legalists, and Daoists developing systems of thought.

On a separate sheet of paper, complete the following review exercises.

Reviewing Concepts

1. Supply the term that correctly completes each sentence.
   (a) Belief in many gods is _____ .
   (b) _____ are books of sacred knowledge in India.
   (c) Skilled craftworkers are called _____ .
   (d) A _____ is a town or city and the surrounding land it controlled.
   (e) _____ is the Sumerian form of writing.
2. Identify the specific society or culture with which each of the following ideas or facts is associated:
   (a) Constructed pyramids as royal tombs
   (b) Built large granaries to store food for city-state
   (c) Worshiped in seven-story temples called *ziggurats*
   (d) Permitted women to own property in their own right
   (e) Lacked direct contact with other great civilizations and believed peoples of other cultures were barbarians
   (f) Had a religion that placed emphasis on earthly struggle between good and evil
   (g) Developed the alphabet that became the model for later Western alphabets
   (h) Believed that Canaan was their promised land
3. Explain the beliefs about God (or gods) and an afterlife in three of the following civilizations: (a) Egyptian, (b) Sumerian, (c) Hebrew, (d) Buddhist, (e) Aryan, (f) Shang, (g) Persian

Applying Critical Thinking Skills

1. **Understanding Ideas** Discuss how cultural diffusion took place in the Fertile Crescent.
2. **Analyzing Ideas** (a) Describe some of the laws included in the Code of Hammurabi and in Mosaic law. (b) Explain why such codes of law became important as people began living together in groups.
3. **Evaluating Ideas** Choose two of the following leaders: Akhenaton, Hammurabi, Moses, Darius, Buddha, Asoka, Shi Huangdi, Wu Di, or Confucius. (a) Describe each person's accomplishments. (b) Do you think that these leaders achieved their goals? Why or why not?
4. **Synthesizing Ideas** Using evidence from the civilizations explained in Unit One, discuss the following statement: "Cultures obtain more ideas and ways of doing things from other cultures, rather than creating ideas and methods that are unique to themselves."

Relating Geography to History

The earliest civilizations developed in four great river valleys—the Huang He, the Nile, the Indus, and the Tigris-Euphrates. Almost all other civilizations also originally developed in river valleys. (a) Why do you think this was so? (b) What advantages did rivers provide to the people of early civilizations?

Writing About History

1. Write a dialogue to take place within one of the following groups of people:
   (a) the pharaoh of Egypt and his advisers, deciding which countries they wish to be allies with and which countries they wish to attack. The dialogue should be taking place in the year 1000 B.C.
   (b) a Hebrew prophet, a follower of Zoroastrianism, a Buddhist priest, and a Brahman, arguing about the

role of religion in shaping the values of their particular societies.

2. Write a newspaper story dated A.D. 536, summarizing the great accomplishments of the Gupta rulers.

Further Readings

Bothwell, Jean. *Dancing Princess.* San Diego: Harcourt Brace Jovanovich. Describes the life of a young woman in ancient India.

Casson, Lionel. *Daily Life in Ancient Egypt.* New York: American Heritage. Describes daily life during the New Kingdom.

Everyday Life in Bible Times. Washington, D.C.: National Geographic Society. Describes the history of Judaism.

Hall, Alice J. "Special Treasures from a Chinese Tomb." *National Geographic,* May 1974: 661–681. Describes life during the Han dynasty.

The World's Last Mysteries. Pleasantville, New York: Reader's Digest Association. Analyzes mythical ancient kingdoms and peoples that mysteriously vanished.

Weaver, Kenneth F. "The Search for Our Ancestors." *National Geographic,* May 1975: 560–629. Describes the recent discoveries that anthropologists and archaeologists have made.

Unit One Chronology

Date	Political and Social Developments	Technological and Scientific Advances	Visual Arts and Literature	Religious and Philosophical Thought
6000 B.C.– 3000 B.C.	Prehistoric times 1* River valley civilizations 1	Neolithic culture 1	Cave paintings 1	
3000 B.C.– 2000 B.C.	Sumerian civilization 2 Egyptian Old Kingdom 2 Mohenjo-Daro 3	Egyptian irrigation 2 Egyptian pyramids 2 Sumerian ziggurats 2 Hieroglyphics 2 Cuneiform 2 Sumerian arch 2	Egyptian calendar 2 *The Book of the Dead* 2	Polytheism in Egypt 2 Animism in India and China 3, 4
2000 B.C.– 1000 B.C.	Egyptian Middle Kingdom 2 Hammurabi's Code 2 Aryan invasions 3 Xia dynasty 4 Shang dynasty 4	Hittites use iron weapons 2	Chinese bronze casting 4 Chinese pottery 4 Chinese calendar 4	Amenhotep; Israelites develop monotheism 2 Indian Vedic religion 3 Chinese ancestor worship 4
1000 B.C.– 500 B.C.	Phoenicians and trade 2 Solomon in Israel 2 Indian caste system 3 Chinese Zhou dynasty 4	Assyrians use cavalry 2 Iron in China 4 Chaldean math and astronomy 2	Nineveh library 2 Phoenician alphabet 2 *Upanishads* 3	Zoroaster in Persia 2 Jewish ethical monotheism 2 Hinduism 3
500 B.C.–0	Qin dynasty 4 Pax Sinica 4 Han dynasty 4 Persian Empire 2 Maurya Empire and Asoka 3	Great Wall 4 Chinese civil service 4 Chinese calendar 4 Chinese astronomy 4	Ajanta cave painting 3 Stupas constructed 3	Buddhism in India 3 Confucius 4 Laozi 4
0–A.D. 500	Gupta rulers 3 Huns invade China 4	Indian numeral system 3 Chinese paper 4	Indian *Sakuntala* 3	

* Indicates chapter in which development is discussed

The Beginnings of Civilization

1 Cultures and Civilizations Began in Prehistoric Times

Scholars believe that people lived on earth long before the development of writing, during the period known as prehistory. Although unable to write, prehistoric people made significant discoveries and advances.

Prehistoric Discoveries

Based on scientific studies, researchers have concluded that humanlike creatures appeared on the earth millions of years ago during a period of prehistory called the Old Stone Age, or Paleolithic (pay • lee • oh • LITH • ik) Age. Centuries later, the first prehistoric people migrated to many parts of the world. Long periods of extremely cold weather known as the Ice Age, however, prevented these early people from moving into the colder regions of the earth. It was only when prehistoric peoples such as the Neanderthals and later the Cro-Magnons learned to use fire and to craft warm clothing, that they could successfully settle in the colder regions of the earth.

Both the Neanderthals and the Cro-Magnons had been nomads who traveled from place to place in search of food. About 10,000 years ago, in the period called the New Stone Age or Neolithic Age, however, people began to settle in villages. Two important developments—the domestication, or taming, of several kinds of animals and the development of agriculture—helped make permanent settlements possible.

The First Civilizations

Although Neolithic people settled in many regions, the settlements in the Nile River valley in Egypt, the valley of the Tigris and Euphrates (yoo • FRAY • teez) rivers in southwestern Asia, the Indus River valley in southern Asia, and the Huang He (HWANG HOOH) valley in eastern Asia had particular significance. In these four river valleys, people first developed civilizations.

The people of these civilizations became the first in the world to develop advanced technical skills, such as the ability to use metals. In addition, an increase in population, made possible by improved farming methods, encouraged the growth of cities. Eventually the people of these communities developed calendars to predict when crops should be planted and harvested.

With the many changes of late Neolithic times, life became increasingly complex. People in settled communities developed rules for living together and for protecting property. They also developed governments and traded with other communities. To keep government records and to better communicate with one another, the people of these civilizations developed the first forms of writing. The development of writing marked the end of prehistory and the beginning of history.

2 Great Civilizations

Civilizations first appeared along the Nile River and along the Tigris and Euphrates rivers.

The Egyptians

Along the narrow ribbon of fertile land that straddles the Nile River in Egypt in northeastern Africa, people created a thriving civilization. Each year the river swept over its banks and deposited a layer of fertile silt in the valley. This fertile silt enabled the early inhabitants of the valley to establish agriculture.

The people of the Nile Valley learned to use copper to make needles, chisels, and jewelry. They discovered how to make bronze, the strong alloy of copper and tin. They also developed a system of writing known as hieroglyphics about 3000 B.C.

Over the centuries early Egyptian settlements were united to form the two kingdoms of Upper Egypt and Lower Egypt. Then, about 3100 B.C., a ruler known as Menes (MEE • neez) united all Egypt into one kingdom and took the title pharaoh.

In more than 2,500 years, beginning with the time of Menes and continuing to about 300 B.C., there were about 30 Egyptian dynasties. This span of time is divided into four periods—the Old Kingdom, the Middle Kingdom, the New Kingdom, and the Late Period.

Egyptian Culture

The Egyptians created great monuments to their gods and rulers. These monuments included the great Sphinx near Giza and the pyramids, designed as tombs for the pharaohs. In addition to large-scale works, sculptors also made small, lifelike statues of kings and sacred animals from copper, bronze, stone, or wood.

The Egyptians developed an accurate calendar with 12 months of 30 days each. This system left them with five extra days, which they used for holidays and feasting. The Egyptians also developed a number system based on 10, used geometry, made significant advances in medicine, and developed an excellent educational system.

Sumerian Civilization

To the east of Egypt, the fertile valley of the Tigris and Euphrates rivers nurtured equally brilliant civilizations. There, in a region known as the Fertile Crescent that stretches from the Mediterranean Sea to the Persian Gulf, many civilizations rose and fell. The earliest was that of Sumer.

Early in their history the Sumerians developed a form of government called the city-state, which included a town or city and the surrounding land it controlled. Unlike Egypt, the many Sumerian city-states were seldom united.

The Sumerians used sun-dried clay bricks to build houses and may have invented several important architectural designs. These included the arch, the ramp, and the dome. The most striking

The pyramids

Sumerian buildings were the temples known as ziggurats. Built on hills that were specially created on the flat land of the valley, a ziggurat was constructed in layers, each one smaller than the one below.

The Sumerians developed a form of writing known as cuneiform and considered education very important, although only upper-class boys were educated. Students learned to write and spell by copying religious books and songs. They also studied reading, history, mathematics, foreign languages, and mapmaking.

Empires of the Fertile Crescent

The disunity of the Sumerian city-states proved to be a fatal weakness.

The Akkadians. After 2400 B.C. the Akkadians (uh • KAYD • ee • uhnz) conquered the Sumerians and established a great empire that lasted about 100 years. When it ended, new waves of invaders swept through the region.

The Babylonians. About 1792 B.C. a strong ruler named Hammurabi (ham • uh • RAHB • ee) came to power in Babylon and conquered the upper Tigris-Euphrates Valley. Hammurabi's greatest accomplishment was the Code of Hammurabi, a collection of 282 harsh laws that controlled all aspects of life in Babylon.

The Hittites. About 1600 B.C. the Hittites invaded the Tigris-Euphrates Valley from Asia Minor. The Hittites were the first people to make extensive use of iron for weapons. Their most important achievement, however, was their laws, which were less brutal than the Code of Hammurabi. The Hittites were too far from their homeland to control

Babylonia permanently, however, and soon withdrew to the western part of the Fertile Crescent.

The Assyrians. Following the decline of the Hittites, Babylon suffered further invasions. Then about 900 B.C., the fiercest, cruelest, and most warlike of all ancient peoples—the Assyrians—overwhelmed the region.

The Assyrians were specialists in warfare. Often using savage methods, the Assyrians killed the enemies they captured in battle, enslaved conquered peoples, and deported them to other areas.

The Assyrians were the first people to develop an effective method of governing an empire, and all other empires of the ancient Middle East were modeled after it. In other fields, however, the Assyrians contributed few new ideas to civilization. And in 612 B.C., a group of opponents captured and destroyed the Assyrian capital of Nineveh.

The Chaldeans. A people known as the Chaldeans took control of much of the territory that the Assyrians had ruled. Under the leadership of a wise ruler named Nebuchadnezzar (neb • uh • kuhd • NEZ • uhr), who ruled from the rebuilt capital city of Babylon between 605 and 562 B.C., the Chaldeans conquered most of the Fertile Crescent.

All the strength of the Chaldeans seemed to lie in the ability of Nebuchadnezzar. Within 30 years of Nebuchadnezzar's death, the empire fell.

The Persians. About 550 B.C. Cyrus, a Persian and one of the greatest leaders in all history, began a series of conquests, capturing Babylon, and conquering the rest of the Fertile Crescent and Asia Minor. A later Persian ruler, Darius the Great, added regions south and east of Persia as far as the Indus River in India, as well as parts of Europe.

The Persians ruled the mightiest empire known up to that time. Although all-powerful in government, Persian rulers showed great concern for justice. Tax collection and the administration of justice were fair. And rulers chose the best officials they could find, often from among the conquered peoples, to govern their huge empire.

The Phoenicians, Lydians, and Hebrews

The peoples who lived in the western end of the Fertile Crescent and in western Asia Minor did not create large empires, but they made important contributions in economics and religion.

Because of a lack of good farmland, the Phoenicians turned to the sea and to commerce for their living. The most important contribution of the Phoenicians was the alphabet upon which our alphabet is patterned.

The Lydians of Asia Minor made a significant contribution to civilization that was based on trade. About 600 B.C., they became the first people in history to use coined money.

Just as in the eastern part of the Fertile Crescent, a series of peoples inhabited Canaan to the south of Phoenicia. The people who had the greatest influence on their own times and on all later history were the Hebrews, or Jews.

Judaism, the religion of the Hebrews, is the Hebrews' most important contribution. Judaism was the first major example of monotheism—the belief in one supreme god. To the Hebrews, their god, Yahweh, was not like a human being but was a spiritual force. The kings of many other ancient peoples claimed to be gods, but Hebrew kings were not gods. Other ancient peoples worshiped statues or idols. To the Hebrews, only Yahweh was divine. Because of its emphasis on ethics, or proper conduct, the Hebrew form of monotheism is often called ethical monotheism.

3 People Created Thriving Civilizations in India

In India early people learned to farm, developed a written language and calendars, and created a complex civilization.

Harappan Civilization

The first Indian civilization developed in the Indus Valley about 2500 B.C., not long after Egypt and Sumer developed civilizations. This early Indus Valley civilization is best seen in the ruins of two cities, Mohenjo-Daro (moh • hen • joh-DAHR • oh) and Harappa (huh • RAP • uh). Harappa was so important to this civilization that historians often call it Harappan civilization.

The areas surrounding Harappa and Mohenjo-Daro were agricultural regions. City dwellers worked primarily in industry or trade. These early Indus Valley people also developed a written language before the civilization's mysterious collapse about 1700 B.C.

Aryan Invaders

About 1500 B.C. a new group of people, the Aryans, invaded the Indus Valley. Although outnumbered by the original Indus Valley people, the Aryans believed they had to maintain their identity. To do so they passed laws prohibiting marriages between Aryans and the valley dwellers. In later centuries, this class system evolved into a rigid social organization known as the caste system.

Hinduism and Buddhism

Two of the world's great religions—Hinduism and Buddhism developed in ancient India.

Hinduism. According to Hinduism, the world known to our senses is an illusion called Maya, which betrays people, giving them sorrow and pain. People can be delivered from their suffering if they can identify Maya, but this requires lifetimes of experience. Hinduism explains that this experience is provided through reincarnation—the transmigration or rebirth of the soul. According to this belief, the soul does not die with the body but enters the body of another being, either human or animal, and thus lives second, third, and more lives. Ultimately each person hopes to be the one who ends the repeated reincarnations and enables the soul to be reunited with the soul of Brahma.

Buddhism. The other great religion of India, Buddhism, was founded by an Indian prince named Gautama and known as Buddha, or the "Enlightened One." Buddha accepted the Hindu belief that the progress of the soul depends on the life a person leads and that good is rewarded and evil punished. Departing from Hindu beliefs, however,

Religious pilgrims in India

Buddha said that salvation came from following the guidelines for conduct embodied in the Four Noble Truths and the Eightfold Path.

Empires in Ancient India

The subcontinent of India was never conquered by the Persians or Greeks, although both had conquered land as far as the Indus River.

The Maurya Empire. A kingdom arose in India in 322 B.C. as a result of the conquests of a powerful young adventurer named Chandragupta (chuhn • druh • GOOHP • tuh). He established what is called the Maurya Empire. Chandragupta's grandson Asoka (uh • SHOH • kuh), who came to the throne about 270 B.C., enlarged the empire until it included all of India except the southern tip.

The Gupta rulers. The next great rulers of India were the Guptas, who came to power in A.D. 320. The time during which the Guptas ruled has been called a golden age because of the brilliant civilization that flourished then. Gupta rule ended in A.D. 535, however, when once again invaders stormed into the subcontinent and brutally ravaged northern India.

Indian Culture

India has indeed left the world a rich legacy in the areas of art, literature, mathematics, and science.

Economy and social life. From ancient times the land had provided a living for nearly all the people of India. For a limited few at the top of the caste system, the land provided great luxury. Nevertheless, most people were poor.

Literature. Throughout Indian history the most popular writings were the two great epics, the *Mahabharata* and *Ramayana*. People also enjoyed the stories of the *Panchatantra* (pahn • chah • TAN • trah), a series of fables from the Gupta period.

Architecture and art. Much Indian architecture and art reflects religious influences. For example, stupas, hemispheres or dome-shaped shrines, held artifacts and objects associated with Buddha. Indians also created a distinctive style of Hindu temple—a square building with heavy walls that enclosed the statue of a god.

Mathematics and astronomy. Indians actually invented the numeral system we call Arabic—1 through 9 and the zero. Arab traders brought it to the West from India. Indians also understood negative numbers and prepared a table of sines, or the ratio of the side opposite the angle and the longest side of the triangle, used extensively in trigonometry.

Indian astronomers identified the seven planets that can be seen without the aid of a telescope. They knew that the planets and the moon reflected the sun's light. They understood the daily rotation of the earth on its axis. They also predicted eclipses, calculated the diameter of the earth, and developed a theory of gravity.

Medicine. Indian physicians understood the importance of the spinal cord, and their surgery included bone setting and plastic surgery on ears, noses, and lips. They perfected the technique of inoculation.

4 Ancient Chinese Civilization Developed Lasting Traditions

Great distances, the towering mountains of central Asia, and such formidable deserts as the Gobi (GOH • BEE) made China almost inaccessible. As a result, China developed and retained its own distinctive culture in relative isolation.

The Shaping of Chinese History

From the beginning of its recorded history until the early 1900s, a succession of dynasties ruled China. Each dynasty went through a dynastic cycle consisting of four major stages. The first stage involved the founding of the dynasty. Next came a period of internal peace, expansion, and great power. A period of regression marked by decline followed the period of great power. When its decline reached a low point, with chaos and rebellion engulfing many parts of the land, the dynasty collapsed. A new leader emerged, and another dynastic cycle then began.

Beneath the recurring pattern of the dynastic cycle lay a continuous evolution, or development, of culture over the centuries. For example, structures such as the family, the farm, and the village developed their own pattern of change. During some stages of the dynastic cycle the pace of cultural evolution quickened; during others it slowed.

The Shang Dynasty

China's first historic dynasty, the Shang, began about 1500 B.C. along the Huang He. Shang government was relatively simple. A hereditary king granted land to his principal followers. In return they pledged loyalty, performed certain services, and paid dues. Although the Shang economy was based mainly on agriculture, Shang artisans established the foundation for all later Chinese ceramic art, including the development of every form and shape used in Chinese ceremonial vases.

Changing Dynasties

In 1122 B.C. a new dynasty—the Zhou (JOH) overthrew the Shang. The Zhou dynasty was the most enduring Chinese dynasty, lasting almost 800 years, from 1122 B.C. to 256 B.C. During the many years of Zhou rule, internal trade expanded, and copper coins came into use as money. But probably the most important development was the introduction of iron, which helped transform Chinese agriculture. Using iron farm tools and plows pulled by oxen, Chinese peasants cultivated new lands and produced more grain than ever before.

The Qin dynasty. The Qin (CHIN) dynasty came to power in 221 B.C. by using cavalry armed with bows and arrows, a military technique new to the Chinese. The dynasty's founder was Shi Huangdi (SHUHR HWAHNG • DEE), which means "first emperor." Although the Qin dynasty lasted only a short time, until 207 B.C., it succeeded in unifying China under a strong central government for the very first time. It was also noted for standardizing weights, measures, and coinage, and for establishing a uniform system of writing. To guard against invasion from the north and west, the Qin completed the Great Wall of China, much of which still stands today.

The Han dynasty. In 202 B.C. a general of peasant background, Liu Bang (LEE • OO BAHNG), founded the Han dynasty. Like the Qin, the Han dynasty ruled a centralized and expanding empire. Unlike the Qin, however, it succeeded in maintaining its power for almost 400 years. Han influence was so great that even today many Chinese refer to themselves as "Sons of Han."

The Han dynasty established the Chinese civil service system to administer the government on a day-to-day basis. Candidates for civil service

The Great Wall of China

positions had to pass rigorous tests based on their knowledge of the great classics of Chinese literature and law. As a result, the best scholars in the country became government officials.

Chinese Philosophies

Although political disunity and almost constant warfare marked the last years of the Zhou dynasty, this period was one of the most creative in the history of Chinese philosophy.

Naturalism. Like other Chinese philosophers, the Naturalists were far more interested in human beings and the real world than in divine or spiritual matters. One of their basic ideas concerned the dualism, or two-sidedness, of nature. The Naturalists defined this dualism of nature as its *yin* and *yang*. *Yin* was female, dark, cold, and passive. *Yang* was male, light, hot, and active.

Confucianism. Kongzi, (KOOHNG • ZUH), meaning "Kong the Philosopher," or "Reverend Master Kong," is known to Westerners as Confucius. Confucius was not a religious prophet and had little to say about the gods, the meaning of death, or the idea of life after death. Instead, he taught about the importance of the family, respect for one's elders, and reverence for the past. These three concepts formed the basis of Confucian philosophy.

Daoism. Daoism (DOW • iz • um) got its name from its central idea, Dao, which can be defined as the Way of Nature. Laozi (LOW • ZUH), the founder of Daoism, believed that only by withdrawing from the world and contemplating nature could people live in harmony with nature.

Legalism. Like Confucianism, the school of philosophy known as Legalism was concerned with politics. Its teachings, however, were very different

from the teachings of Confucianism. The Legalists believed in power, not virtue. They also believed in harsh laws. In their view, people were by nature selfish and untrustworthy. Peace and prosperity could only be achieved by threatening severe punishment if people failed to do what was expected.

Chinese Culture

The family, not the individual, was the most important unit in Chinese society. The Chinese father was the source of all family authority. He arranged his children's and his grandchildren's marriages, decided how much education his sons would receive, and even chose his sons' careers. Women were subordinate to men and had no property rights of their own.

The most important works of Chinese literature and the basis for all Chinese education were the Five Classics. Two of the Five Classics were used in civil service examinations: the *Classic of Songs*, containing more than 300 songs about love, joy, politics, and domestic life; and the *Classic of Documents*, containing semihistorical speeches and documents about government.

As early as 444 B.C., Chinese astronomers had computed the year at 365 1/4 days. During the Han dynasty these calculations were refined even further. Sometime before A.D. 100, Chinese astronomers built special instruments to observe the orbit they believed the sun followed. Using these instruments, an early astronomer estimated the number of stars at 11,520. Other achievements included the invention of a primitive seismograph that registered earthquakes so faint they were unnoticed by the royal court, and the invention of paper in A.D. 105.

SYNTHESIS REVIEW

1. **Classifying Ideas** What advances were made by the people of the earliest civilizations?
2. **Contrasting Ideas** How was Egyptian civilization different from that of the Fertile Crescent?
3. **Understanding Ideas** What were the major beliefs of Hinduism and Buddhism?
4. **Analyzing Ideas** Why did Chinese civilization develop in relative isolation?
5. **Synthesizing Ideas** What characteristics of Indian, Chinese, and Egyptian cultures made them civilizations?

Civilizations of the Mediterranean World

◀ *A panoramic Roman mosaic of the Nile*   99

Greek City-states Developed in the Mediterranean Region

Place   Greece and Asia Minor

Time   2000 B.C. – 404 B.C.

3.7 mil. BC   4000 BC   AD 2100

Significance

The rugged Balkan Peninsula juts crooked fingers southward from Europe into the northeastern part of the Mediterranean Sea. On the southern end of this peninsula, as well as in Asia Minor and on the nearby islands, one of the greatest civilizations the world has known—Greek civilization—developed.

At first glance it might seem puzzling that the people of this region, the ancient Greeks, created such an important civilization. A quarrelsome people, they could never agree among themselves for any length of time. Nor were they great empire-builders. We take a special interest in them, however, because much of **Western civilization**—the civilization that in later centuries evolved in Europe and spread to the Americas—had its foundations in early Greece. For example, the Greeks were the first people to experiment successfully with the idea that citizens could govern themselves, an idea that the United States and many other countries have since adopted and refined.

Terms to Define

Western civilization   popular government
polis   democracy
chora   helot
myth   metic
aristocracy   rhetoric

People to Identify

Mycenaeans   Solon
Homer   Pericles

Places to Locate

Crete   Sparta
Athens   Peloponnesus

Questions to Guide Your Reading

1 Why did early Greeks settle in city-states?
2 How did Greek government and society become more varied?
3 How did the city-states of Sparta and Athens develop differently?
4 What were the major features of daily life in Athens?
5 What challenges did Greek civilization face during the 400s B.C.?

When the world's best athletes test their skills at the Olympic Games every four years, they repeat a tradition that began thousands of years ago among the rocky hills of Greece. As historian Lionel Casson noted:

> *One midsummer day in the year we calculate to have been 776 B.C., a 200-meter dash was run in a rural backwater in southwestern Greece, and a young local named Coroebus won it. It was an obscure event in an obscure spot but it earned him immortality: he is the first Olympic victor on record.*

Over time, the ancient Olympics became a ritual of Greek life with ceremonies honoring the winners.

> *Winners formed a procession and marched to the Temple of Zeus [the chief Greek god]. . . . At the temple, each was handed what ancient athletes considered the most precious object in the world, the victor's olive wreath. . . .*
> *Winning was everything; there were no seconds or thirds, no Greek equivalents of silver or bronze medals. . . . Losers were jeered and, hiding their heads in shame, slunk away. Even their mothers treated them with scorn. 'The wreath or death' was their motto.*

The Olympic Games are only one of the many traditions we owe to the people of ancient Greece.

1 Early Greeks Settled in City-states

Geography influences history. This has certainly been true in Greece, where the location and surroundings of each city influenced its growth, development, and ultimate fate.

The Physical Setting

At the extreme northeastern end of the Mediterranean, the Aegean (i•JEE• uhn) Sea separates the Balkan Peninsula from Asia Minor. The southern tip of the Balkan Peninsula consists of many small peninsulas that form the mainland of Greece. In addition,

◀ *The Temple of Athena at Delphi*

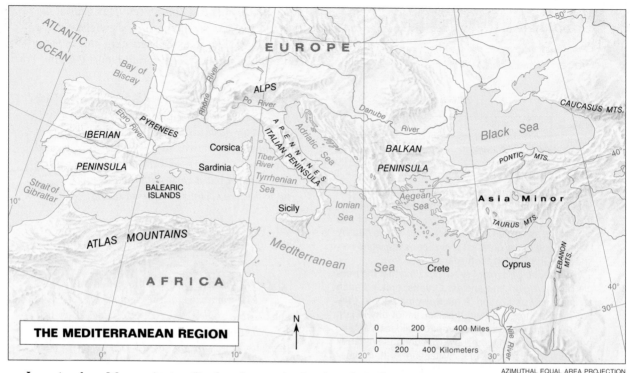

THE MEDITERRANEAN REGION

N

0   200   400 Miles

0   200   400 Kilometers

AZIMUTHAL EQUAL AREA PROJECTION

Learning from Maps   *Ancient Greek civilization developed on the Balkan Peninsula.*
What other two peninsulas extend southward into the Mediterranean Sea?

many small islands dot the Aegean Sea and are considered part of Greece.

In many ways nature did not smile kindly on the Greeks. Look at the map of the Mediterranean region on this page. Notice that short mountain ranges cut up the Greek mainland. These mountains separated communities and prevented them from developing a sense of unity. Also notice that Greece had no important rivers such as those along which the ancient civilizations of Egypt and Mesopotamia developed. Despite these disadvantages Greece had a mild climate, enough good soil, and sufficient rainfall to grow grain, grapes, and olives in the small valleys and in the foothills of the mountains. The foothills also provided pasture for sheep and goats. Still Greece could not produce the amount or the variety of food that its increasing population needed. Many Greeks became traders, both to improve their quality of life and to make their fortunes. The invention of coined money in the 500s B.C. also stimulated trade by making it easier to buy and sell goods.

Greece's geography encouraged the development of trade. The long, irregular coastline allowed every part of the mainland to be close to the sea,

and both the mainland and the islands had many good harbors. With the sea so much a part of their lives, the Greeks became fishers, sailors, traders, and eventually colonizers of new lands.

These early sailors and traders traveled throughout the eastern Mediterranean. From Egypt and the Fertile Crescent, people brought knowledge and ideas to the Aegean Islands, to the mainland of Greece, and to the Aegean shores of Asia Minor.

Minoan Civilization

Look again at the map on this page and locate the long, narrow island of Crete in the Aegean Sea. For centuries Greek myths told of a great and powerful civilization that had existed there before about 1500 B.C. Many scholars, however, doubted that the barren, sandy soil of the island could have supported a great civilization. Then in 1898 British archaeologist Arthur Evans discovered the ruins of a great palace with more than 800 rooms. Evans believed he had unearthed Knossos (kuh • NAHS • uhs), the palace of Minos (MY • nuhs), the legendary king of Crete. Evans named this civilization Minoan (mi • NOH • uhn) in honor of its king, who

102

Stadiums

Millions of sports fans jam stadiums each year to watch their favorite teams compete. The idea of a big "bowl" with terraced steps on which people can sit goes back nearly 3,000 years, to the time of the ancient Greeks. When the first Olympic Games were held, the events took place in a magnificent stadium built for the occasion in the city-state of Olympia. Many ancient stadiums still stand, such as the one in Tunisia (top).

The Greeks, and later the Romans, erected many of these arenas, which often were used for other entertainments. Circuses were held there, and plays were performed on a stage at one end.

Today stadiums continue to have various uses. Yankee Stadium in New York City, for example, is mainly a place to play baseball. Yet it has also held huge crowds attending a concert or seeing the pope during his visit to the United States.

Ancient stadiums were smaller than modern stadiums. One of the largest, the Colosseum in Rome, could hold perhaps 40,000 people. Modern stadiums have room for many more. For example, the soccer stadium in Rio de Janeiro, Brazil, can hold 200,000 people, and one in Prague, Czechoslovakia, has a capacity of 240,000.

In the United States, the football stadium in Los Angeles, California (center), has room for 100,000, and the Astrodome (bottom), the indoor stadium in Houston, Texas, can hold 60,000. Putting a roof over a stadium is a modern innovation. It solves the one problem that makes scheduling events in the open air so difficult: bad weather.

The appeal of sports thus goes back thousands of years. So, too, does the need to provide a place where a large number of people can watch an event at the same time. The stadium remains the best way of meeting that need.

allegedly protected a giant creature—half human and half bull—called the *Minotaur*.

Since Evans's discovery, other archaeologists have unearthed artifacts showing that a great civilization did indeed flourish on the island. Although the Minoans developed writing, scholars have not been able to decipher all of the script. As a result, much of what we believe about this civilization is theory.

Evidence indicates that Minoan civilization reached its height between 2000 B.C. and 1400 B.C. Although the great civilizations of nearby Egypt and the Fertile Crescent influenced Minoan civilization, the Minoans added ideas of their own. Ruins excavated in Knossos show that the royal palace and the homes of the nobles had running water and walls decorated with colorful **frescoes**—paintings made on wet plaster walls. Minoan artisans made beautiful, delicately carved figures from ivory, stone, gold, silver, and bronze. These artifacts show the Minoans as a cheerful people who enjoyed festivals, who worshiped the bull and an earth goddess, and who accorded women many rights.

Since the soil of Crete was unsuitable for growing many kinds of crops, the Minoans turned to the sea for their livelihood. They controlled the Aegean Islands and probably founded colonies both there and in Asia Minor. Excellent sailors, they built ships powered by both oars and sails. The Minoans also traded widely, bringing much of the art and civilization of Egypt and the Fertile Crescent back to Crete. The kings of Crete had so much confidence in the strength of their navy that they did not bother to fortify their cities. They overlooked the forces of nature, however.

About 1500 B.C. a volcanic explosion on a nearby island sent giant tidal waves crashing across Crete, causing great destruction and loss of life. Soon after, warriors from Greece conquered the weakened civilization. The glory of the Minoans was soon forgotten, but through trade they had influenced the peoples of mainland Greece.

Early Migrations into Greece

At the same time that the Minoan civilization developed, important changes took place on the Greek mainland. Beginning about 2000 B.C., new people entered Greece from the north. They spoke an Indo-European language that was an early form of Greek.

Learning from Pictures   *The dangerous ritual of leaping over bulls was popular among young Minoans. How was the bull perceived in Minoan society?*

Learning from Pictures
Mycenaean artists crafted delicate works of gold such as this ornate mask (right), ceremonial cup (top), and dagger depicting a lion hunt (bottom). What other talents did the Mycenaeans share with the Minoans?

The invaders were organized into clans and tribes. Several related families formed a clan headed by a chief. A number of clans made up a tribe, which had its own chief. The clan chiefs formed a council to help in governing. In Greece these wandering people learned how to grow grain, grapes, and olives. They also learned how to sail and often became pirates.

The Mycenaeans (my • suh • NEE • uhnz)* dominated the Greek mainland from about 1600 B.C. to 1200 B.C. They built fortified cities in the Peloponnesus (pel • uh • puh • NEE • suhs), the southern part of Greece. These included Mycenae (my • SEE • nee), Tiryns, and Pylos (see map, page 106). A warlike people who carried out raids throughout the eastern Mediterranean, the Mycenaeans conquered Crete and, in turn, adopted many elements of Minoan civilization.

Like the Minoans, the Mycenaeans had a written language. However, only a few of their documents have survived. Continual warfare probably weakened the Mycenaeans. By 1200 B.C. most of their major cities, including Mycenae, had been destroyed. According to tradition, the destruction of the city of Troy in Asia Minor also took place about this time. Perhaps these cities perished in the general upheaval caused by other migrating tribes, the legendary Sea Peoples.

After the collapse of Mycenaean society about 1200 B.C., more-primitive Greeks—the Dorians—moved into the fertile areas of the Peloponnesus, Crete, and southwestern Asia Minor. The newcomers were illiterate, and knowledge of writing disappeared when the Mycenaeans fell. A dark age descended on Greece until Phoenician traders introduced an alphabet about 750 B.C.

The City-states of Greece

Influenced by the geography of Greece and their own tribal organization, the early Greeks established city-states, such as Athens and Sparta (see map, page 110), in the 800s B.C. and 700s B.C. The Greek word for city-state—**polis**—originally meant a fort, a refuge in time of danger. As a village or city grew up around the fort, *polis* came to mean not only the fort but also the city, its surrounding region including the **chora,** or land outside the city walls, and the government. Our words *police, politics,* and *policy* all come from the Greek word *polis.*

---

*The Mycenaeans were part of the Achaean (uh • KEE • uhn) tribe. We call them Mycenaeans after Mycenae (my • SEE • nee), one of their principal cities.

All Greek city-states shared certain physical features: (1) *Small size.* Athens at its greatest extent was smaller than Rhode Island. Sparta, the largest city-state, was only three-fourths the size of Connecticut. (2) *Small population.* The Greeks considered the ideal city-state population to be 5,000 to 10,000 citizens, not including slaves and other noncitizens. Only adult males had all the rights of citizenship because the Greeks did not count women or children. A few city-states had populations of more than 10,000 citizens, but most had fewer. One exception was Athens, which at its height had approximately 40,000 citizens. (3) *The original polis.* In most city-states the fort stood on an **acropolis** (uh · CRAHP · uh · luhs), a hill or mountain, together with temples and other public buildings. (4) *A public meeting place,* or **agora** (AG · uh · ruh), where all citizens could gather. In almost all city-states the agora was the city marketplace.

Although physically similar, the Greek city-states developed different forms of government. These differences helped make each of the city-states unique as they developed between 1000 B.C. and 500 B.C.

Learning from Maps *Mycenae was the center of Aegean civilization. What other fortified cities did the Mycenaeans build?*

SECTION 1 REVIEW

1. **Define** Western civilization, polis, chora, acropolis, agora
2. **Identify** Mycenaeans, Dorians
3. **Locate** Balkan Peninsula, Aegean Sea, Crete, Mycenae, Troy, Athens, Sparta
4. **Interpreting Ideas** How did geography influence the way of life of the early Greeks?
5. **Summarizing Ideas** What were the accomplishments of Minoan civilization?
6. **Comparing Ideas** **(a)** What four things did all Greek city-states have in common? **(b)** How do these characteristics compare to those of modern cities in the United States?

2 Greek Government and Society Became More Varied

Between about 1000 B.C. and 700 B.C., chiefs ruled the tribal systems of Greece. Later, as the independent Greek city-states emerged, a variety of governments developed throughout Greece.

The Age of Kings

Little is known about Greek civilization between 1000 B.C. and 700 B.C. We do know that the city-states had similar forms of government based on the tribal systems introduced during the early migrations. These tribal systems gradually developed into small kingdoms, or monarchies, during a period often called the *Age of Kings.* The city-states constantly waged war among themselves, and as a result little trade took place.

The Greeks of this period did not have a very advanced civilization. Few people could write. Most communication was oral, with poets wandering from village to village, singing or reciting folk songs, ballads, and **epics**—long poems describing heroes and great events.

Sometime during the 700s B.C., much of this oral poetry was gathered together and woven into two great epics—the *Iliad* (IL · ee · uhd) and the *Odyssey* (AHD · uh · see). According to tradition the blind poet Homer composed them. Scholars

The *Odyssey*

Homer's *Odyssey* details the many adventures of Odysseus and his crew as they made their way home from the Trojan Wars. In one adventure they landed on the island of the Cyclopes, legendary one-eyed giants known for their cruelty. A Cyclops named Polyphemus (pahl·uh·FEE·muhs) captured Odysseus and part of his crew and viciously devoured some of the men. Through a clever trick, however, Odysseus saved the remaining crew members.

“ Three bowls I brought him, and he poured them down.
   I saw the fuddle and flush come over him, then I
sang out in cordial tones:
                            'Cyclops,

you ask my honorable name? Remember
the gift you promised me, and I shall tell you.
My name is Nohbdy: mother, father, and friends,
everyone calls me Nohbdy,'
                          And he said:

'Nohbdy's my meat, then, after I eat his friends.
Others come first. There's a noble gift, now.'

Even as he spoke, he reeled and tumbled backward,
his great head lolling to one side; and sleep
took him like any creature. Drunk, hiccuping,
he dribbled streams of liquor and bits of men.

Now, by the gods, I drove my big hand spike
deep in the embers, charring it again,
and cheered my men along with battle talk
to keep their courage up: no quitting now.
The pike of olive, green though it had been,
reddened and glowed as if about to catch.
I drew it from the coals and my four fellows
gave me a hand, lugging it near the Cyclops
as more than natural force nerved them; straight
forward they sprinted, lifted it, and rammed it deep
in his crater eye, and I leaned on it
turning it as a shipwright turns a drill
in planking, having men below to swing
the two-handled strap that spins it in the groove.
So with our brand we bored that great eye socket

while blood ran out around the red-hot bar.
Eyelid and lash were seared; the pierced ball
hissed broiling, and the roots popped. . . .
The Cyclops bellowed and the rock roared round him,
and we fell back in fear. Clawing his face
he tugged the bloody spike out of his eye,
threw it away, and his wild hands went groping;
then he set up a howl for Cyclopes
who lived in caves on windy peaks nearby.
Some heard him; and they came by divers ways
to clump around outside and call:
                    'What ails you,

Polyphemus? Why do you cry so sore
in the starry night? You will not let us sleep.
Sure no man's driving off your flock? No man
has tricked you, ruined you?'
                      Out of the cave

the mammoth Polyphemus roared in answer:

'Nohbdy, Nohbdy's tricked me, Nohbdy's ruined me!'

To this rough shout they made a sage reply:

'Ah well, if nobody has played you foul
there in your lonely bed, we are not use in pain
given by great Zeus. Let it be your father,
Poseidon Lord, to whom you pray.'
                      So saying

they trailed away. And I was filled with laughter
to see how like a charm
the name deceived them. . . . ”

often refer to this period as the *Homeric Age* because of Homer's magnificent description of it.

The Trojan* War provided a backdrop for the Homeric epics. Legends told how Paris, a Trojan prince, stole Helen, the beautiful wife of a Mycenaean king. The Mycenaeans then sent a great sea expedition against Troy. After years of fighting, Troy was defeated by a clever trick. The Mycenaeans built a giant wooden horse outside Troy's walls. Then, after secretly filling the horse with soldiers, they broke camp and left. Thinking the Mycenaeans had given up the fight, the unsuspecting Trojans dragged the horse into the city as a trophy. But when night fell, the soldiers inside the horse burst out and threw open the city gates. The rest of the Mycenaean forces poured into Troy and destroyed it.

The *Iliad* describes incidents in the tenth year of the Trojan War. The *Odyssey* relates the many adventures of the Mycenaean hero Odysseus on his long journey home from the war. According to legend several gods, angered by Odysseus' trickery, condemned him to wander for 10 years before finally arriving home.

The *Iliad* and the *Odyssey* supposedly describe the Mycenaeans of the 1200s B.C. But they actually provide our best and richest source of information about the life, customs, and ideals of the Greeks between 1000 B.C. and 700 B.C.

Religious and moral beliefs. The religion that developed among the Greeks during the Homeric Age differed greatly from the religions of the Egyptians, Persians, and Hebrews. The Greeks asked three things of their religion: (1) an explanation for such mysteries of the physical world as thunder, lightning, and the change of the seasons; (2) an explanation of the passions that could make people lose the self-control that the Greeks considered necessary; and (3) a way to gain such benefits as long life, good fortune, and abundant harvests.

Greek religion did not focus on morality. The Greeks did not expect their religion to save them from sin, to bring them any spiritual blessings, or to ensure a life after death. Their religion contained no commandments.

Greeks of the Homeric Age were not as concerned, for example, as the Egyptians were about what happened to them after death. Often they cremated, or burned, their dead with only a simple ritual. They thought that with few exceptions the spirits of all people went to a gray and gloomy place—the underworld—ruled by the god Hades (HAY·deez). The "house of Hades" was not a place of punishment except for extremely evil people.

The Greek gods. The Egyptians worshiped the sun and the moon, attributed both human and animal characteristics to many of their gods, and believed their pharaoh represented these gods. In contrast the Greeks attributed human qualities and personal characteristics to all of their gods and goddesses.

The Greeks thought of gods as having weaknesses and wants much like their own but on a larger scale. Greek gods lived not in some remote heaven but on the top of Mount Olympus, a peak in northern Greece (see map, page 106).

To explain their world, the Greeks developed **myths**—traditional stories about the deeds and misdeeds of gods, goddesses, and heroes. The Greeks believed in many gods and goddesses, all more or less equal to one another. Zeus (ZOOS), god of the sky, was the king of the gods and the father of some humans. Hera, his sister and wife, protected women and marriage. Poseidon (poh·SY·duhn), brother of Zeus, was god of the sea—a particularly important god to the seafaring Greeks. Hades ruled the underworld.

Athena, daughter of Zeus, was the goddess of wisdom, womanly virtue, and technical skill—the special protector of the great city-states, especially Athens, which was named in her honor. Aphrodite (af·ruh·DYT·ee), another daughter, reigned as goddess of love and beauty. Apollo was god of light, music, and poetry, as well as the symbol of manly beauty. Dionysus (dy·uh·NY·suhs) was the god of fertility and wine.

Religious practices. At special sanctuaries called *oracles*, the Greeks believed that the gods spoke through priests or priestesses, usually in answer to questions about the future. The most famous oracle was that of Apollo at Delphi in the rugged mountains north of the Gulf of Corinth (see map, page 110).

Because displays of strength and courage supposedly pleased the gods, the Greeks held athletic

---

*For centuries scholars believed Homer's epics were mere legend. Then in 1870 the German archaeologist Heinrich Schliemann unearthed the ruins of a city in Asia Minor that scholars determined was Troy. Schliemann later discovered the ruins of Mycenae, Troy's chief enemy.

Greek Funeral Stele

By the time of the sculptor Phidias, in the 400s B.C., the Greeks did not have a very religious attitude about death. The Greeks held funerals without priests, hymns, or prayers. They emphasized the memory of the deceased. The Greeks erected steles (STEE • leez), or stone slabs, to commemorate their dead permanently and publicly. The earliest steles were rough pillars used only to mark grave sites. In time steles became more elaborate, with stylized figures symbolizing how the dead person had lived and worked— for example, as a soldier, a farmer, or a politician. By 400 B.C. simple scenes showing the deceased with their families, in courageous feats, or preparing for death decorated steles.

This grave stele of Hegeso was done in the late 400s B.C. It captures the lovely Athenian woman as she carefully selects a precious jewel from a jewelry box held by her servant. Perhaps Hegeso is planning to wear the jewel on her journey to the next world. The stele is set inside an

architectural frame, typical of the classic style. Symmetry and balance, so important in Greek art, are evident in this stele. Hegeso's right hand is located precisely in the center of the relief. In keeping with the Greek idealization of human beings, the unknown sculptor suggests that Hegeso was beautiful in spirit as well as in body.

contests in their honor. Most famous were the games at Olympia, held every fourth year in honor of Zeus. Only men, however, could compete in and attend the Olympic Games. Women had their own events, dedicated to the goddess Hera.

At first the Olympic Games consisted only of footraces. Later the Greeks added jumping, javelin and discus throwing, boxing, wrestling, and horse and chariot racing. At the games winners received only wreaths of wild olive branches, but when they returned home their fellow citizens showered them with honors, money, and valuable gifts. The games became so important that the Greeks used them as the basis for dating events. Beginning in 776 B.C., they figured time in four-year periods called *Olympiads.*

Rise of the Nobles

About 700 B.C. the nobles—the chief landowners —began to have more influence on the kings. One reason for the nobles' importance was that they supplied cavalry to the military forces. Another reason was that although the population steadily increased, the amount of land that could be farmed did not. Farmers with small plots of land had trouble providing their families with enough food. When the harvest was meager, these farmers frequently had to mortgage or sell their land to a noble. Nobles often sold farmers who could not pay their debts into slavery.

Some of the unemployed farmers and laborers moved to the cities, where a commercial class of

109

merchants developed. Although the merchants could become wealthy, they always remained beneath the nobles in social position.

The nobles encouraged discontented peasants and laborers to establish colonies outside Greece. This drive to colonize proved very successful because the Greeks usually chose leaders, laws, and forms of government in advance. Greek colonies, set up as city-states like those on the mainland, were established on islands and shorelines throughout the Black, Aegean, and Mediterranean seas (see map, this page). In this manner Greek culture spread throughout the Mediterranean region.

Colonization also promoted trade. The new colonies often imported goods from and exported grain and other products to the mainland. An **import** is a good or service brought from another country or region. An **export** is a good or service sold to another country or region.

The nobles controlled many Greek city-states called **aristocracies.** (Today the word *aristocracy*

Learning from Maps *The ancient Greek city-states established colonies to relieve overcrowding on the mainland and to increase the food supply. Where were the Greek colonies located?*

LAMBERT CONFORMAL CONIC PROJECTION

often means a privileged social class.) Eventually, changes took place that weakened the nobles' power. Foot soldiers became more important in war, eliminating the need for the nobles' cavalry. Nobles fought among themselves. Many people became discontented with the rule of the nobles and looked for leaders who could promise them a better life.

The Age of Tyrants

The leaders who appeared with those promises were called **tyrants.** The ancient Greeks defined a tyrant as someone who seized power by force and ruled alone. Tyrants always promised to bring peace and prosperity and to defend the poor against the nobles and officials. Many of the tyrants governed well because their interest in commerce made them want peace. They put an end to the nobles' struggles for political power, encouraged trade, and passed laws that were just.

The height of tyranny, or rule by tyrants, occurred in many of the Greek city-states between 650 B.C. and 500 B.C. As time went on, some of these leaders became harsh and unjust, giving the word *tyrant* its present meaning—a ruler who exercises absolute power brutally and oppressively.

Popular Government

As Greek government changed first from monarchy to aristocracy and then to tyranny, the idea of **popular government**—that people could and should rule themselves rather than be ruled by others—began to take root in many city-states. Some cities that ousted their tyrants restored the old monarchies or aristocracies. Others developed the form of government called **democracy**—a government in which all citizens take part. Even in monarchies and aristocracies, however, a council of citizens limited the power of the rulers.

At this time many factors might have led the Greeks to unite. All spoke the same language, which they regarded as a common tie. They referred to peoples who did not speak Greek as "barbarians." The ancient Greeks also believed they all were descended from the same ancestor, the hero Hellen. They called themselves Hellenes and their country Hellas. They also shared a common religion, and great festivals such as the Olympic Games brought them together. They joined in common management of certain temples, such as those of Zeus at Olympia and Apollo at Delphi.

However, other factors kept the Greeks apart. One factor was geography. The rugged mountains separated the small valleys and their populations from one another. Another factor was the fierce spirit of independence that made Greeks so proud of their own city-states and so distrustful of others. Each city-state had its own laws, calendar, money, and system of weights and measures. Citizens loved their city-state and would willingly give up their lives for it.

SECTION 2 REVIEW

1. **Define** epic, myth, import, export, aristocracy, tyrant, popular government, democracy
2. **Identify** Homer, Zeus, Athena
3. **Locate** Mount Olympus
4. **Understanding Ideas** List three religious beliefs of the Greeks.
5. **Interpreting Ideas** **(a)** How did the nobles win power in Greece? **(b)** Why did they lose power? **(c)** What parts did tyrants play in the process?
6. **Evaluating Ideas** Name and discuss the many factors that might have led the Greeks to unite.

---

3 Sparta and Athens Developed Different Ways of Life

Greek city-states had both similarities and differences. The wide range of differences shows clearly in a comparison of the two city-states that became most important, Sparta and Athens.

Sparta: The Military Ideal

The Dorians moved south to the Peloponnesus about 1200 B.C. They conquered the city of Sparta and made it their capital (see map, page 110). The conquerors maintained their separate societies but forced the agricultural laborers, known as **helots** (HEL • uhts), to work for them. The Spartans constantly had to use force to control the rebellious helots, who outnumbered them by about five to one.

In spite of this danger, the Spartans built their city-state in a valley, without a wall to surround it. Spartans were boastful people, and one of their leaders said, "A city is well fortified which has a wall of men instead of brick." The Spartans

Learning from Pictures
The rugged mountains of Greece created a geographical barrier that hindered communication among the city-states, allowing each to develop its own unique way of life.

devoted their culture to this militaristic idea—this "wall of men."

Social groups. Three groups lived in Sparta. The first group consisted of citizens descended from the Dorian invaders; they controlled the government. To support these citizens and their families, the government in Sparta divided land equally among them. With each allotment of land went helots to work it.

The Spartans called the second group of people "neighbors." Although free, they did not have citizenship. They lived in the towns, and most of them worked in commerce and industry. Some "neighbors" became rich, but they could never be citizens.

The third group, the helots, ranked at the bottom of the social scale. Because the Spartans lived in constant fear of a helot revolt, they tried to prevent the helots from developing any leaders. Sometimes the Spartans killed helots who defied the government.

Government in Sparta. Sparta had an Assembly elected by all citizens, a Council of Elders that proposed laws, and two ceremonial kings. However, five **ephors,** or overseers, elected by the Assembly for one-year terms controlled the government. The ephors had unlimited power to act as guardians of the state, and they used that power harshly. For example, fearing the people would come to love money and luxuries, the ephors prohibited the use of gold and silver. Money was made of iron bars, which were too heavy to carry around and would not buy much. Fearing also that contact with outside peoples and ideas would weaken discipline and obedience, the ephors forbade citizens to travel and did not welcome foreign visitors.

The military machine. Sparta regulated the lives of its citizens from birth to death. All the rules had the same basic aim: to make every adult male citizen part of an efficient military machine designed to control the helots and extend Spartan power.

The development of Spartan fighting men, and of women fit to marry them, began at birth when a group of officials examined newborn babies. Any child who seemed weak, unhealthy, or deformed in any way was abandoned in the countryside to die. At the age of seven, boys went to live in military barracks. Although they learned to read and write, military training formed the basis of their education.

It was a harsh education. To develop endurance, boys wore only a single garment, summer and winter. They never wore shoes. Often they were beaten publicly so they would learn to bear pain without crying out. To teach them to feed themselves in wartime, the authorities provided coarse and scanty food. The boys had to steal food to keep from starving. Anyone caught received a severe punishment. The punishment, however, was not for stealing but for being clumsy enough to get caught.

The citizen began his military service at the age of 20, remaining in the army until the age of 60. At 30 a Spartan was expected to marry, but he had little family life. He devoted most of his time to military training, eating his meals and spending his leisure time in a military club. The authorities did not allow him to engage in any trade or business because business activities and love of money interfered with military discipline.

Spartan girls, as the future mothers of soldiers, had to be healthy, too. They received strict physical training to develop strength and endurance. They also had training in patriotic devotion.

The strict discipline of Sparta did lead to efficient government and an almost unconquerable army. The Spartans paid heavily for this military might, however. First, they sacrificed individual freedom to the state. Second, their society produced nothing in art, literature, philosophy, or science.

Athens: The Birth of Democracy

The early history of Athens differed greatly from that of Sparta. To begin with, Athens had no military class of conquering invaders imposing its rule upon a conquered people, as did Sparta.

Because Athens had rocky and unproductive soil, the Athenians became sea traders. They built their city inland to protect it against pirates and constructed Piraeus (py • REE • uhs) as its special port (see map, page 110). Athens itself was a typical polis built around the rocky, fortified hill of the Acropolis. In time of war, people from all the surrounding region took refuge within the city's strong walls.

Social groups. As in Sparta, three groups lived in Athens. At the top stood the citizens. In Athens, as a rule, one could be a citizen only if both parents were citizens. If only one parent had been a citizen, a person might become a citizen by decree.

BUILDING HISTORY STUDY SKILLS

Reading About History: Making Comparisons

Making comparisons helps you organize information. It helps you to remember ideas and facts because you are able to place the details in a historical context. Making comparisons means identifying the similarities and differences between events, ideas, and actions in order to understand them.

How to Make Comparisons

To make comparisons, follow these guidelines.

1. Identify the purpose of the comparison.
2. Select the categories to be compared, such as government, family life, or education.
3. Identify similarities and differences by asking questions about the categories.
4. Draw a conclusion based on the similarities and differences.

Developing the Skill

Read the following excerpts to make a comparison between life in ancient Athens and Sparta. The first excerpt, about Athens, is from Thucydides' account of a funeral oration that Pericles made. The second excerpt, which describes the Spartan system, is from a biography of the Spartan lawmaker Lycurgus (ly • KUHR • guhs) by Plutarch.

❝ Our constitution is called a democracy because power is in the hands not of a minority but of the whole people. When it is a question of settling private disputes, everyone is equal before the law, when it is a question of putting one person before another in positions of public responsibility, what counts is not membership of a particular class, but the actual ability which the man possesses. . . . And, just as our political life is free and open, so is our day-to-day life in our relations with each other. We do not get into a state with our next door neighbour if he enjoys himself in his own way. . . . We are free and tolerant in our private lives; but in public affairs we keep to the law. This is because it commands our deep respect. . . . When our work is over, we are in a position to enjoy all kinds of recreation for our spirits. . . . Our love of what is beautiful does not lead to extravagance; our love of the things of the mind does not make us soft. ❞

❝ Nor was it lawful, indeed, for the father himself to breed up the children after his own fancy; but soon as they were seven years old, they were to be enrolled in certain companies . . . where they lived under the same order and discipline. . . . Reading and writing they gave them, just enough to serve their term; their chief care was to make them good sub-

jects, and to teach them to endure pain and conquer in battle. To this end, as they grew in years, their discipline was proportionately increased. . . . No one was allowed to live after his own fancy; but the city was sort of a camp, in which every man had his share . . . of businesses set out, and looked upon himself not so much born to serve his own ends as the interest of his country. ❞

The first step in comparing life in ancient Athens with life in Sparta is to establish categories for analysis. The categories here are the relationship of the citizen to the government, and the value system.

You can discover the similarities between Athens and Sparta by asking questions. For example: What was the purpose of government in each city-state? The purposes were similar in that the good of the group and the strength of the state were important to both societies. Both valued obedience to the law and loyalty to the government. The relationship of the citizen to the state, however, was different. Individuals in Athens could pursue their own interests freely as long as they obeyed the law. Sparta allowed no private interest apart from the state. Individuals were trained to think of the city-state above themselves. In addition, the Spartans valued the body over the mind; the strong body better protected the state. The Athenians felt that the mind should be cultivated so that the individual initiative could develop and the state would be stronger.

What conclusion can you draw about Sparta and Athens by comparing the two societies? Sparta denied the individual full development, while the Athenian was encouraged to be creative and develop the mind.

Practicing the skill. What other conclusion can you draw about life in Athens and life in Sparta?

To apply this skill, see Applying History Study Skills on page 123.

Greek cavalry

113

The government rarely issued such decrees, however. Although women could have citizenship, they could not vote or hold office and were regarded legally as minors.

Next came the aliens—non-Athenians—called **metics.** Most metics worked as merchants or artisans. Although free they could not own land or take part in government, even though they paid the same taxes as citizens.

At the bottom stood the slaves, whom the Athenians—just as all Greeks—considered a necessity and part of the natural order of things. At the time of Athens' greatest glory, more than half its population consisted of metics and slaves. In Athens, as in all of Greece, people regarded slaves as property, dependent on their master's will. An Athenian master could not treat his slaves brutally, nor did he have the power of life and death over them. However, if a slave complained or was killed, the court accepted the word of the master. If the master agreed, the slave might acquire property and even become wealthy. A freed slave became a metic.

Early government in Athens. After the Age of Kings, Athens had an aristocratic government. Only those citizens who had a certain amount of land could vote.

The voters met in an Assembly and elected nine **archons,** or rulers, each of whom served a one-year term. The archons appointed all officials and made all the laws, but they did not write these laws down. The judges, always a group of nobles, interpreted the laws and applied them in each case. The laws, by the way, always seemed to favor the nobles.

Four reformers. Four rulers—Draco, Solon, Pisistratus (pi • SIS • truht • uhs), and Cleisthenes (KLYS • thuh • neez)—strongly influenced the political development of Athens. Each ruler helped Athens move closer to democracy.

Draco, who served as archon in 621 B.C., is known for his code of laws. Although harsh and severe, these laws were written down so that everyone could know them. Today we call a harsh law a Draconian law.

Overall, conditions in Athens remained unsatisfactory under Draco. Nobles and metics became wealthy from trade, but small farmers grew poorer. More and more citizens were sold into slavery to pay off their debts. The poor began to demand that their debts be canceled and that the land be divided

Learning from Pictures Solon was a poet as well as a political leader. What economic reform did Solon make to settle the debts of the poor?

equally. Creditors and landowners opposed both demands.

In this emergency Solon, a trusted business leader, took control of Athens. Solon, who served as archon about 594 B.C., took a moderate position in the dispute between debtors and creditors. He canceled the debts of the poor, outlawed enslavement for debt, and freed those who had been enslaved for nonpayment.

Most citizens could vote, although only wealthier citizens could hold office. To limit the power of the judges, Solon set up a court, composed of a large number of citizens, to which a citizen could appeal an unfavorable decision.

Under Solon's rule, however, Athens still suffered much unrest. The nobles formed rival political groups and struggled for control of the government. Then Pisistratus, a wealthy aristocrat and a relative of Solon, developed a following among the lower classes. About 560 B.C. he became a tyrant and remained one off and on until 527 B.C. Pisistratus lessened opposition by exiling nobles who disagreed with him, seizing their estates and dividing the estates among peasants.

About 510 B.C. Cleisthenes seized power in Athens. Although a man of wealth and high social position, Cleisthenes cared about the welfare of the common people. He opposed class divisions based on wealth and instead divided citizens into 10 tribes based on where they lived. All male citizens over 20 years of age became members of the Assembly. Cleisthenes set up the Council of 500 with 50 members from each tribe, selected from all male citizens over 30 years of age. The council took over many of the powers and duties the archons formerly held.

A democratic state. Cleisthenes' reforms moved Athens even closer to democracy. The Assembly had much power. It chose archons and generals and could punish them for wrongdoing. The Council of 500 proposed laws to the Assembly.

Athens even had democratic courts. Jurors and some officials were chosen by lot, in keeping with the Athenian belief in the equality and fitness of all citizens for government service. Each man could plead his own case, and no judge presided. The jury of citizens made up the entire court, and each juror voted by secret ballot.

Athenian democracy under Cleisthenes was what we call **direct democracy.** That is, all citizens participated directly in making decisions. In contrast, present-day democratic nations such as the United States are **representative democracies,** in which the citizens elect representatives to run the government for them.

SECTION 3 REVIEW

1. **Define** helot, ephor, metic, archon, direct democracy, representative democracy
2. **Identify** Solon, Cleisthenes
3. **Locate** Piraeus
4. **Summarizing Ideas** (a) How was Sparta governed? (b) How did Spartans try to prevent helot revolts?
5. **Analyzing Ideas** (a) Describe the features of Athens' early government. (b) What reforms occurred to transform this government into a democracy?
6. **Synthesizing Ideas** Why would direct democracy be impractical in the United States today?

4 Daily Life in Athens Combined Recreation and Public Duties

The citizens of Athens and the other Greek city-states lived in much the same way. Their lives consisted of work, recreation, and the fulfillment of their responsibilities to the city-state.

Farming

Farming was the most honored occupation for an Athenian citizen. More than half of all citizens farmed, including many who owned the small plots of land that they worked. Unlike small farmers and peasants in most other societies, however, Athenian citizens could vote and hold public office.

Although some areas of Greece had good farmland, the soil around Athens was poor, and fields had to lie unplanted every second year so the soil could regain fertility. To make matters worse, much of the level land proved unsuitable for raising grain. Thus farmers concentrated instead on growing olives, grapes, and figs on terraced hillsides. (**Terracing** means creating small, flat plots of land by building low walls around the hillsides and filling the space behind them with soil.) Athens exported olive oil and wine and imported much of the grain needed to feed its people.

The principal domestic animals were sheep and goats. People used goat's milk for making cheese, and they valued sheep for their wool and meat. However, Athenians did not eat much meat. Fish and cheese made up most of their diet.

Manufacturing and Trade

Athenian manufacturing took place in small workshops. The largest shop was a shield factory, owned by a metic, which employed 120 workers. However, Athenians considered a shop with 20 workers large. Many artisans worked in their homes, where family members labored side by side with slaves and free employees. Today people throughout the world value Athenian vases and household utensils for their simple grace and beauty and their extraordinarily high quality. Yet ordinary citizens rather than famous artists made most of these objects.

The Athenian economy depended on trade. The desire to increase the food supply influenced

115

Learning from Pictures *Highly valued Athenian pottery was often exported. In what kind of activity might these Greeks be engaged?*

came from open pans that held burning coals. Lamps that burned olive oil furnished a dim light. Houses had neither plumbing nor running water. Instead residents carried water in large jars from wells or springs.

The narrow, crooked streets were usually dirty because people threw rubbish into them. The city had neither sidewalks nor paving, no sewage system, and no services such as garbage collection and street cleaning.

Family Life

Athenians considered marriage a very important institution. Its main purpose was the bearing and rearing of children. The parents always arranged the marriages. A girl married early, typically at age 13 or 14 and to a man who was at least twice her age. Many women died in childbirth because of poor medical knowledge. And if a family could not afford to raise a baby, they abandoned it to die. More females than males were abandoned.

A married woman had few legal rights. She could not make a contract or bring a suit in court. Also, when a man died, his wife did not inherit his property. In social life, too, Athenians considered women inferior to men. Their duties included managing the household and the slaves and raising the children. They rarely appeared in public, and then only with the permission of their husbands. During banquets or entertainment in the home, the wife stayed out of sight.

In many Athenian households, the mother, aided by a woman slave, took care of both the boys and the girls until they were six. At the age of six, a boy was placed in the care of a male slave, or **pedagogue,** who taught the boy manners and went everywhere with him, including to school. Girls stayed at home, where they learned how to run a household but received no other schooling.

Education and Recreation

Most Greeks were poor and hardworking. They toiled long hours at monotonous work, with little time off. The rich did no work with their hands, preferring the pursuit of intellectual and physical excellence. They spent most of their time engaging in politics, gossip in the marketplace, conversations with friends, and athletic activities.

all government policy. It made foreign trade a necessity and led to the building of the Athenian fleet and the establishment of colonies. Athenian ships went everywhere in the Mediterranean world, from the Black Sea in the east to Spain in the west.

Homes and Streets

Although the Athenians built magnificent temples and other public buildings, they lived in simple homes. Athenians believed money should be spent on buildings to benefit the whole community, not on private homes.

Houses made of sun-dried brick sat close to the street and usually were one story high. The street wall was plain except for a door leading into an open court. From the court other doors opened into the living room, dining room, bedrooms, storerooms, and kitchen. Athenians paid little attention to the appearance of the house itself, and it contained simple furnishings. The only heat

Learning from Pictures *Greek artists depicted scenes from everyday life, such as baking bread (bottom) and hunting (top). What was the Athenian ideal of life?*

The citizens of Athens knew that for their democracy to succeed, its leaders had to receive an education. Boys therefore attended elementary schools, which charged fees.

Students in these elementary schools studied grammar, music, and gymnastics. Grammar included arithmetic, reading, and writing, done on a wax-covered wooden tablet. Much of the reading consisted of Homer's *Iliad* and *Odyssey*. Boys also learned to sing and to play musical instruments.

The Athenian ideal stressed a sound mind in a healthy body. Grammar and music developed the mind and the emotions. Gymnastics developed the body. In open fields at the edge of the city, boys practiced running, jumping, boxing, and throwing the discus and the javelin.

Men who called themselves Sophists, from the Greek word *sophos*, meaning "wise," conducted schools for older boys. Here the boys studied poetry, government, ethics, geometry, astronomy, and rhetoric (RET•uh•rik). **Rhetoric** was the study of oratory, or public speaking, and debating.

Today the term *rhetoric* means the art of speaking or writing effectively.

At the age of 18, a boy received a year of military training. At 19, in an impressive public ceremony, he became a full citizen. After becoming a citizen, a young man who could afford to pay for weapons and armor served in the army for a year. The poor served the city by rowing the warships of the Athenian fleet.

Education played an important role in the spread of both the Greek language and Greek civilization throughout the Mediterranean world. Traders commonly spoke Greek, which was a second language for educated non-Greeks everywhere. Even today we use many words derived from Greek. We can hardly write or talk about government without using such Greek terms as *politics*, *democracy*, and *aristocracy*. Most terms used in medicine come from Greek. For example, the Greek ending *-itis* means "an inflammation" and is part of the words *appendicitis* and *tonsillitis*, among many others.

SECTION 4 REVIEW

1. **Define**   terracing, pedagogue, rhetoric
2. **Analyzing Ideas**   **(a)** Why was the Athenian economy so dependent on trade?   **(b)** How did this dependence on trade lead the Greeks to found colonies?
3. **Understanding Ideas**   **(a)** Describe a typical home in ancient Athens.   **(b)** Why were the homes not more elaborate?
4. **Interpreting Ideas**   Describe Greek attitudes toward women, as shown in marriage customs, the rights of citizenship, and social life.

5 Greek Civilization Defended Itself and Expanded

The Greek city-states and their colonies around the Aegean, Black, and Mediterranean seas developed for a long time without interference from the empires of the Middle East. Then the powerful Persian Empire intervened in Greek affairs, leading to war between the city-states and the Persians. Once they defeated the Persians, however, the Greeks warred among themselves.

The Persian Wars

In 546 B.C. Cyrus of Persia conquered the Greek city-states on the western shores of Asia Minor. The Persians did not treat the Greeks cruelly and permitted the Greeks to keep their own local governments. Nevertheless, the conquered Greeks had to pay tribute to Persia and consequently resented Persian rule. In 499 B.C. revolts broke out in several city-states of Asia Minor (see map, this page). These rebellions, which Athens aided, began a series of conflicts that lasted until 479 B.C. Together these conflicts are known as the Persian Wars.

Darius, Cyrus' son, easily crushed the revolts. However, he wanted to punish Athens for its support of the Greek rebels and to control the city-states on the Greek mainland as well as those of Asia Minor.

With this goal in mind, Darius sent a Persian army and a fleet toward Greece in 492 B.C. (see map, this page). Fortunately for the Greeks, a violent storm destroyed the fleet and the invasion attempt failed. Still determined to defeat the Greeks, Darius launched another invasion in 490 B.C. The Persians landed on the coast of Attica and set up camp on the plain of Marathon, some 20 miles (32 kilometers) from Athens.

Learning from Maps Thebes remained neutral during the Persian Wars. What city-states revolted against the Persians in 499 B.C.?

The Greek historian Herodotus wrote that the Persians outnumbered the Athenians 10 to 1. Although he may have exaggerated, it is certain that the smaller Athenian army attacked bravely and drove out the Persians.

For 10 years an uneasy peace existed. Then in 480 B.C., the dreaded news spread throughout Greece—Darius' son Xerxes was coming with a vast army and fleet from every part of the Persian Empire. Herodotus, who loved a good story, wrote that the Persian army was so large that when it drank water, whole rivers ran dry. The exaggeration pointed to the truth—Xerxes was marching with little opposition through Thrace and Macedonia toward northern Greece.

To advance from northern Greece into central Greece, the Persians had to march through the narrow mountain pass of Thermopylae (thur • MAHP • uh • lee). There King Leonidas of Sparta, with a force of 300 Spartans and about 6,000 allies, met the 200,000 Persians.

Aware that the Greek forces could not possibly survive the attack, Leonidas allowed only soldiers who had sons to carry on the family line to remain at Thermopylae. It was these soldiers who valiantly held the narrow pass against the entire Persian army for three days. Finally a Greek traitor showed the Persians a secret pass through the mountains. Surrounded, the Spartans and their allies refused to surrender and fought until every one of their soldiers was killed.

With the pass cleared, the Persians had an unobstructed route to Athens, which itself was in turmoil. The able Greek general Themistocles (thuh • MIS • tuh • kleez) persuaded the Athenians to abandon their city and to sail to the island of Salamis. With Athens evacuated, Xerxes' army entered the city and destroyed it.

Themistocles next tricked Xerxes into attacking the Athenian fleet in the Strait of Salamis. The narrow waters of the strait gave the light, maneuverable Greek ships an advantage over the lumbering Persian ships. From his throne high atop the coastal plain, Xerxes watched in horror as the Athenian ships rammed and sank many of the Persian ships.

After abandoning the naval attack, Xerxes withdrew most of his army and returned home. The next year, 479 B.C., a combined Greek army defeated the remnants of the Persian army at Plataea (pluh • TEE • uh). The Persian Wars were over.

Importance of the Greek Victories

Winning the Persian Wars did not immediately seem like a great victory for Greece. The Persian Empire remained powerful, and its rulers continued to meddle in Greek affairs. The Greek cities of Asia Minor fell under Persian rule again, and the Persians actively worked to prevent any unity in Greece.

From a long-range viewpoint, however, the battles of Marathon, Salamis, and Plataea are considered important and decisive in history. Success against the Persians gave the Greeks confidence and made them believe that their way of life was superior to that of others. Athens took credit for the defeat of Persia and created an empire in the Aegean. The wealth of this empire helped usher in an unprecedented Golden Age for Athens.

Athens as Leader

After these destructive wars, the Athenians completely rebuilt their city with even more magnificent temples and public buildings. Although the remnants of Xerxes' army had been defeated, the threat of invasion from the Persian Empire continued as long as Xerxes lived. Unity among the Greek city-states seemed necessary for survival.

Sparta wanted Greek unity under its own leadership. The Spartans tried conquest, but fear of helot revolt kept them from sending expeditions far from home. Even their strong army could not extend Spartan power beyond the Peloponnesus.

Athens was much more successful, using diplomacy to form the Delian League, a system of alliances among some 140 other city-states. Each city-state contributed either ships or money to the alliance. No city-state could withdraw from the league without unanimous consent. The league's

What If?
The Persian Wars
The Greek victory over Persia ensured the survival of the Greek way of life and government. As a result the Greek ideal of democracy, rather than the Persian concept of rule by an absolute monarch, was passed on to the Western world. How do you think a Persian victory in the war would have affected the course of world history?

funds were deposited on the island of Delos (from which the name *Delian* is derived). As the league's leading city-state, Athens had the power to decide how many ships and how much money other city-states would contribute.

With the death of Xerxes in 465 B.C., the threat of Persian invasion ended. The Delian League, however, continued under Athens' domination. By the 450s B.C., it had become an Athenian empire.

The Age of Pericles

During this time Pericles (PER • uh • kleez), the greatest of Athenian leaders, rose to power. His ability and reputation for honesty commanded such awe that he was chosen general for 16 successive years. Even when he did not hold this official position, he was the most influential speaker in the Assembly.

Pericles led Athens for more than 30 years—from 461 B.C. to 429 B.C.—the time of its greatest power and prosperity. So significant was his rule that this period of Athenian history is called the *Age of Pericles*.

Under Pericles, Athenian democracy reached its height. (The chart below shows the major steps in the growth of Athenian democracy.) All citizens could hold public office, and officeholders received salaries, ensuring that even poor citizens

Democracy in Athens	
621 B.C.	Draco drew up code of laws.
594 B.C.	Solon abolished enslavement for debt, permitted most citizens to vote, established court of appeals.
560 B.C.–527 B.C.	Pisistratus abolished landowning requirement for citizenship, divided estates among landless peasants.
510 B.C.–508 B.C.	Cleisthenes abolished class divisions based on wealth, broadened Assembly membership, established Council of 500.
461 B.C.–429 B.C.	Pericles opened offices to all citizens, provided that officeholders be paid.

could take an active role in government. For those allowed to participate, Athens was probably the most completely democratic government in history. However, more than half of the residents did not hold citizenship. And many Athenians could contribute so much time and service to government because slaves supported them.

The Empire Under Pericles

In foreign affairs Pericles enlarged the Delian League by forcing more city-states to join. He moved the league treasury from Delos to Athens, openly using the money to benefit Athens. Athenian forces crushed revolts by other city-states against these policies. Although Athenian government within the city-state was democratic, the Athenians did not extend these rights to others. As the historian Thucydides (thoo • SID • uh • deez) warned:

> **"** *Y*ou entirely forget that your empire is a despotism and your subjects disaffected conspirators, whose obedience is insured not by your suicidal concessions, but by the superiority given you by your own strength and not their loyalty. **"**

Even Athens could not unify the Greek city-states, however. Quarrels with Athens' commercial rival, Corinth, as well as with Sparta increased tensions in the region, until a devastating war broke out in 431 B.C. The war is called the *Peloponnesian War* because much of the fighting took place in the Peloponnesus, where Sparta and Corinth are located.

The Peloponnesian War

Athens and Sparta shared responsibility for the Peloponnesian War. There was, of course, economic and commercial rivalry among a number of city-states. But Athens and Sparta had a long-standing social and cultural rivalry. Athens was progressive, commercial, and culturally advanced; Sparta was conservative, agricultural, and culturally backward. Athenians considered Spartans rude and ill-mannered; Spartans considered Athenians money-mad.

The Spartans started the fighting, but the Athenians had provoked them into action. Neither side tried very hard to avoid war. Thucydides wrote:

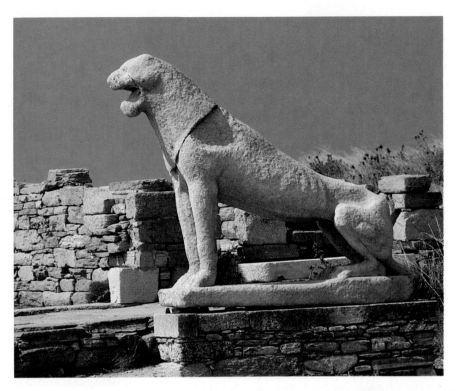

Learning from Pictures
Many lions like the one here guard the temples on the island of Delos. The Greeks carved them from rough marble.

"The Peloponnesus and Athens were both full of young men whose inexperience made them eager to take up arms."

The Spartans invaded Attica, the region surrounding Athens, and destroyed fields and villages. The Athenian army and the entire population of the city withdrew behind the walls and the fortifications of Athens. The Spartans and their allies could not starve them out because Athens controlled the sea. However, a terrible plague broke out among the Athenians, killing many people, including Pericles.

The war went on for a generation, with great loss of life. Even during a period of peace, Athens could not resist the temptation to attack the great city of Syracuse in Sicily. There, however, Athens suffered a great defeat. After that some Athenians lost faith in democracy and allowed aristocrats to seize power in the city. They were soon overthrown and democracy was restored, but Athens' prestige was shaken. Athens finally surrendered to the Spartans in 404 B.C.

Greek Disunity

After the defeat of Athens, first Sparta and then Thebes tried to dominate Greece. The Spartans proved even harsher than the Athenians. Thebes then defeated Sparta and tried to control all of Greece. But Theban rule was not successful, and the ruinous wars continued.

All the city-states realized that unity was necessary, but each wanted to dominate any union that might be formed. Some promised democratic rule, others aristocracy, but all practiced tyranny. Some Greeks believed union could come only under a foreign power, and Persia seemed the logical choice. The power that brought unity, however, was not to appear for more than a generation. In the meantime, as you will read in Chapter 6, Greek civilization reached new heights.

SECTION 5 REVIEW

1. **Identify** Darius, Xerxes, Themistocles, Pericles
2. **Locate** Thrace, Thermopylae, Salamis, Delos
3. **Interpreting Ideas** Why are the battles of Marathon, Salamis, and Plataea considered decisive in the history of the world?
4. **Analyzing Ideas** **(a)** What was the Delian League? **(b)** How did Athens use it? **(c)** Why did other Greek city-states fear Athens?
5. **Understanding Ideas** What qualities gave Pericles his great hold over the people of Athens?

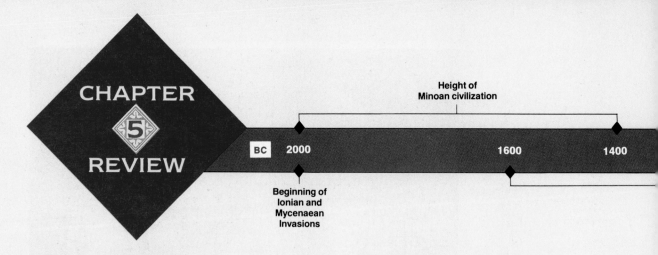

CHAPTER 5 REVIEW

Height of Minoan civilization

BC 2000   1600   1400

Beginning of Ionian and Mycenaean Invasions

Chapter Summary

The following list contains the key concepts you have learned about the Greek city-states.

1. The geography of Greece was not as favorable to settlement as that of the great river valleys.
2. The Greeks became traders to increase their food supply and to improve the quality of their lives.
3. The Minoan culture of Crete was an important early influence on the Greeks.
4. Around 2000 B.C. various invaders entered Greece. The period during which these invaders dominated Greece is called the Mycenaean Age.
5. The polis was the basic political unit of ancient Greece.
6. After being ruled by kings, nobles, and tyrants for hundreds of years, many cities adopted popular governments, or democracies.
7. Sparta was a powerful militaristic state in which a select few inhabitants were considered citizens and ran the government.
8. Athens gradually adopted a democratic government.
9. The Athenian economy depended on farming, manufacturing, and trade.
10. After the Greeks defeated the Persian invaders, Athens became the leader of the Delian League.
11. Athens enjoyed a Golden Age under the rule of Pericles. Although more than half of its population could not participate in government, those who did participate enjoyed one of the most complete democracies the world has ever seen.
12. Rivalries among the city-states led to the disastrous Peloponnesian War, which lasted from 431 B.C. to 404 B.C. and left much of Greece in ruins.

On a separate sheet of paper, complete the following review exercises.

Reviewing Important Terms

Supply the term that correctly completes each statement.

1. The civilization that evolved in Europe and spread to the Americas is called _____ _____ .
2. The Greek word for city-state was _____ .
3. City-states governed by nobles were _____ .
4. To the ancient Greeks, a _____ was someone who seized power by force rather than inheriting it.
5. The idea that people could and should rule themselves rather than be ruled by others is called _____ _____ .
6. A government in which all citizens take part is a _____ .
7. A system in which people select representatives to run the government is a _____ _____ .
8. _____ means creating small, flat plots of land by building walls and filling the space behind them with soil.

Developing Critical Thinking Skills

1. **Understanding Chronology** Place the following events in the correct chronological order: **(a)** Mycenaean civilization, **(b)** early aristocratic city-states, **(c)** Minoan civilization, **(d)** early age of democracy, **(e)** Age of Tyrants.
2. **Determining Cause and Effect** In each of the following sets of three statements, one statement may be considered the cause and the other two the results. List the cause first and then the results:
   (a) The Mediterranean became the center of early Western civilization.
   The Mediterranean borders on Asia, Africa, and Europe.
   The Mediterranean was a pathway for trade and ideas.
   (b) Tyrants promised to bring peace and prosperity.
   Nobles proved to be poor leaders.
   People became discontented with the rule of the nobles.
   (c) Athens exported olive oil and wine.
   Poor soil made the growing of grain difficult.
   Athens built a large navy and established colonies throughout the Mediterranean.
3. **Comparing Ideas** **(a)** Compare the government in Sparta with the government in Athens in the 400s B.C. **(b)** How do you account for the differences?
4. **Interpreting Ideas** **(a)** How did democracy develop in Athens? **(b)** How did slavery fit into Athenian democracy?

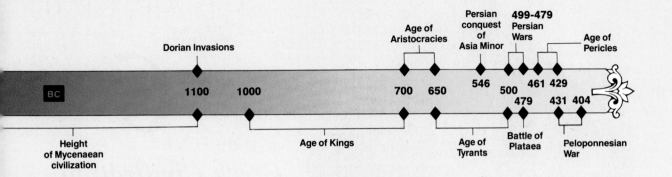

Dorian Invasions

BC

Height of Mycenaean civilization

1100   1000

Age of Kings

Age of Aristocracies

700   650

Age of Tyrants

Persian conquest of Asia Minor

546   500
       479

Age of Tyrants   Battle of Plataea

499-479 Persian Wars

461   429
500   431   404

Age of Pericles

Peloponnesian War

5. **Analyzing Primary Sources** Reread the excerpt from Thucydides on page 120. **(a)** Why do you think the Athenians championed democratic ideals in their city-state but denied them to other members of the Delian League? **(b)** How might this have contributed to the eventual defeat of Athens?

Relating Geography to History

Study the maps on pages 102, 106, 110, and 118. How did the geography of Greece influence the patterns of settlement and the types of government that the ancient Greeks developed?

Relating Past to Present

1. Sports were important in the culture of ancient Greece, where the Olympic Games originated. The modern Olympics trace their origins to these ancient Greek games. **(a)** How does the importance of sports and physical fitness in our society compare with that in ancient Greece? **(b)** In what ways do the modern Olympics differ from the ancient Greek Olympics?
2. Compare the ideas and practices of Greek democracy with the democratic ideals of American government in the following areas: **(a)** right of citizenship, **(b)** right to hold public office, **(c)** right to vote, **(d)** passage and review of laws.

Applying History Study Skills

Before completing this activity, review Building History Study Skills on page 113.

Read the following descriptions of the treatment of women in Athens and Sparta. Then answer the questions below to compare the two societies' views of the status and role of women.

Athens

❝ Since the indoor and outdoor tasks demand labour and attention, God from the first adapted the woman's nature . . . to the indoor and man's to the outdoor tasks and cares. . . . To the woman, since he had made her body less capable of such endurance . . . God has imposed on her the nourishment of the infants . . . the protection of the stores. . . . And besides, the law declares those tasks to be honour-able for each of them wherein God had made them to excel the other. Thus, to the woman, it is more honourable to stay indoors. . . . ❞
(Xenophon, *Oeconomicus*)

Sparta

❝ The truth is, he [Lycurgus] took in their case, also, all the care that was possible; he ordered the maidens to exercise themselves with wrestling, running, throwing the quoit, and casting the dart. . . . Hence it was natural for them to think and speak as Gorgo, for example, the wife of Leonidas, is said to have done, when some foreign lady . . . told her that the women of Lacedaemon were the only women of the world who could rule men; 'With good reason,' she said, 'for we are the only women who bring forth men.' ❞
(Plutarch, *The Library of Original Sources*)

1. **(a)** What are the similarities between the role and status of women in Athens and the role and status of women in Sparta? **(b)** What are the differences?
2. Do you think Spartan women were more respected than Athenian women? Why or why not?
3. How does the status of women in Athens and in Sparta compare with that of women in the United States today?

Investigating Further

1. **Writing a Report** In your school or public library, use the card catalog or the *Readers' Guide to Periodical Literature* to find books or magazine articles about the excavations at Mycenae. Then write a report on this important archaeological site. Be certain to discuss what archaeologists were involved.
2. **Making Comparisons** Compare Greek religion with the religions of the Egyptians, Persians, and Hebrews that you studied in Chapter 2. What are the differences and similarities?

123

6

Greek Civilization Triumphed During the Golden Age and the Hellenistic Age

Place   Greece, the Middle East, Egypt, and Persia

Time   478 B.C.—146 B.C.

3.7 mil. BC   4000 BC   AD 2100

Significance

Greek culture reached new heights during the 400s B.C., a period so magnificent we call it the *Golden Age*. It may seem astonishing that in such a short time one group of people created so many enduring contributions in art, thought, and politics. Their achievements appear even more remarkable if we consider that they took place when the Greek city-states were engaged in fierce military struggles among themselves and also faced serious danger from enemies outside Greece.

In the 300s B.C. an outside power, Macedonia, conquered the Greek city-states. An extraordinary commander, Alexander the Great, established a vast empire. By creating a much larger area within which Greek ideas and art could thrive, Alexander made possible the development of the **Hellenistic culture,** a new culture founded on Greek ideas and features from other cultures of the Mediterranean region. Remarkable advances in philosophy, science, mathematics, medicine, and astronomy dramatically changed the way people thought. These achievements molded ideas about the physical universe and influenced Western civilization for centuries.

Terms to Define

Hellenistic culture   infantry
philosophy   phalanx
drama   orator

People to Identify

Socrates   Demosthenes
Plato   Alexander
Aristotle   the Great

Places to Locate

Macedonia   Susa
Thebes   Syria

Questions to Guide Your Reading

1 How did Greek art represent the ideals of Greek civilization?
2 In what ways did philosophers and writers add to the heritage of Greece?
3 How did Alexander the Great create an empire?
4 How did Hellenistic culture spread throughout the Mediterranean region?

History records the feats of the Macedonian conqueror known as Alexander the Great primarily in terms of military conquest. But those who knew Alexander witnessed more than history in the making. They saw the soul of the man, the melting eyes, the emotion inspired by poetry and music, the uncontrollable temper, the grief he bore when his army suffered, and the frenzied excitement of victory.

A natural athlete, Alexander became a swift runner, an agile fencer, an accomplished archer, and a fearless hunter. He also exhibited an uncanny ability as a horseman. Alexander's prowess emerged when, as a young boy, he tamed a horse that reared, thrashed its hooves, and shied away from everyone. Alexander watched the horse and noticed that it was afraid of its own shadow. Soothing the spirited animal, Alexander turned it to face the sun and quickly mounted the horse, called Bucephalas (byoo • SEF • uh • luhs).

Seeing his young son's success, Philip of Macedon turned proudly to Alexander and said "My son, Macedonia is too small for you; seek out a larger empire, worthier of you." Philip saw something in the young prince that day that historians can write about but never define—the elements of greatness that shape human history. These qualities in Alexander the Great sparked the spread of Greek culture throughout the Mediterranean world.

1 Greek Art Represented the Ideals of Greek Civilization

After the Persian Wars, the wealth and power of Athens attracted artists and teachers from throughout Greece to the city. As Greece's center of art and culture, Athens inspired many people whose artistic and literary contributions exerted a lasting impact on Western civilization. The peak of cultural activity in Athens occurred during the 400s B.C.—a period called the Golden Age.

Architecture

The Athenians surrounded themselves with beauty. They showed their love of Athens and their pride in it by erecting impressive temples, gymnasiums, and theaters. They decorated these structures with their finest works of art, especially sculpture.

◀ *The Battle of Issus*

125

Learning from Pictures *Athenians built their major temples on the easily defended and centrally located Acropolis. Why is the Parthenon the finest example of Greek architecture?*

The Acropolis, the location of the original polis, provided the backdrop for special artistic creations. A magnificent gate graced the entrance to the path up the hill. Inside the gate towered a huge bronze statue of the goddess Athena that stood 70 feet (21 meters) high. As the special protector of the city of Athens, she bore a shield and a spear.

At the top of the Acropolis stood the Parthenon, a white marble temple built in honor of Athena. Begun in 447 B.C. and completed about 14 years later, it is considered the finest example of Greek architecture. This splendid structure measures 230 feet (69 meters) long, 100 feet (30 meters) wide, and 65 feet (19.5 meters) high. Its exquisite beauty lay not in its great size but in its graceful design and balanced proportions—the relation of length to width, and of length and width to height. The structure represents a Greek ideal known as the Golden Mean—a midpoint between two extremes—"Nothing in excess, and everything in proportion."

Like most Greek temples, built as shrines rather than meeting places for worshipers, the Parthenon had doors but no windows. A series of columns, or a colonnade, encircled the structure. Sculptured figures painted in a variety of vivid colors adorned the slabs of marble above the columns. Inside the Parthenon stood a large statue of Athena, with a surface delicately carved of ivory and draped in gold studded with jewels. Today people consider this type of sculpture and architecture one of the greatest gifts of the Greeks to Western civilization.

Painting

Because many of the originals have been lost or severely damaged, our knowledge of Greek painting comes mainly from literary descriptions and from later Roman copies. The best-preserved Greek paintings are those found on vases. Greek vase painters illustrated scenes from everyday life as well as mythological events. These artists delighted in showing the graceful and natural movements of their subjects. Some of these vase painters could depict light and shade on the pottery, a technique used to show contour and depth.

Other Greek painters decorated public buildings with murals, or wall paintings. Mural painters often chose to illustrate scenes from the *Iliad* or the *Odyssey*. On one of the public buildings of Athens, for example, an artist painted *The Sack of Troy*. With a true sense of tragedy, he did not depict the massacre at the moment of the Greek victory but the silence of the following day, with the bodies of the defeated lying amid the ruins of the once magnificent city.

Sculpture

As with Greek painting, few original works of Greek sculpture still exist. What we know about Greek sculpture has come chiefly from studying the copies made during Roman times.

Myron and Phidias (FID • ee • uhs), two of history's greatest sculptors, lived during the Golden Age. Myron sculpted the famous figure called *The Discus Thrower*. Phidias created the two exquisite statues of Athena in the Parthenon. His greatest work, however, was the statue of Zeus at the Temple of Olympia. Greeks who attended the Olympic Games viewed the statue with awe. In ancient times people considered this statue one of the Seven Wonders of the World.

Praxiteles (prak • SIT • uh • leez), who lived about 100 years after Phidias, from 385 B.C. to 320 B.C., created quite a different kind of sculpture. While Phidias created large, formal, dignified works appropriate for the gods, Praxiteles created more delicate, lifelike, often life-sized figures. Though more graceful than those of Phidias, these figures did not inspire awe and reverence, as had the works of the earlier master. Above all, the works of Praxiteles expressed the Greek admiration for the beauty of the human body.

Learning from Pictures
Praxiteles' admiration for the beauty of the human body is seen here in his statue of the god Hermes holding the god Dionysus as a child.

The Nature of Greek Art

Throughout Greek history architecture, painting, and sculpture reflected the Greeks' view of themselves and the world. Four characteristics in particular helped establish the style of this great art.

First, Greek art glorified humans as the most important creatures in the universe. Much of the painting and sculpture portrayed gods and goddesses, but the Greeks thought the gods existed for the benefit of the people. When humans glorified the gods, then, they glorified themselves. To gain this effect, the Greek painter or sculptor idealized the subject, omitting any blemishes. The faces and figures of men and women represented the Greek ideal of beauty. The statues also suggested other ideal traits admired by the Greeks—strength, intelligence, pride, grace, and courage.

Second, Greek art symbolized the peoples' pride in their city-states. At the same time, it honored the gods, thanked them for life and fortune, and tried to win their favor. Thus, in giving Athena a beautiful shrine in the Parthenon, the Athenians showed their love for their city and their hope for its continuing good fortune.

Third, all Greek art expressed Greek ideals of harmony, balance, order, and moderation. By moderation the Greeks meant simplicity and restraint—qualities that they emphasized in their day-to-day lives.

Finally, the Greeks believed in combining beauty and usefulness. To them, the useful, the beautiful, and the good were closely bound together. They wanted their art and even their furniture and kitchen utensils to be both serviceable and beautiful.

SECTION 1 REVIEW

1. **Define** Hellenistic culture
2. **Identify** Myron, Phidias, Praxiteles
3. **Locate** Athens
4. **Interpreting Ideas** Briefly explain the meaning of the following quotation: "Nothing in excess, and everything in proportion."
5. **Understanding Ideas** (a) What do the paintings on Greek vases depict? (b) How is the subject matter different from that of sculpture?
6. **Comparing Ideas** How did the style of Phidias differ from that of Praxiteles?
7. **Analyzing Ideas** (a) List the four main characteristics of Greek art. (b) How did each reflect Greek ideals?

2 Philosophers and Writers Added to the Heritage of Greece

The Greeks have been honored through the ages for their artistic and intellectual achievements. No people before them—and few since—have demonstrated so clearly the capacity of the human hand and mind.

Socrates

Socrates (SAHK • ruh • teez), one of history's greatest thinkers and teachers, lived in Athens from 469 B.C. to 399 B.C. Trained as a sculptor, Socrates left that profession to become a teacher.

Socrates criticized Athenian education, especially the teachings of the Sophists, who taught in most Athenian schools. He believed that they boasted of their wisdom, too often inspiring conceit in their pupils. He would not allow himself to be called a Sophist, preferring the term *philosopher*, a Greek word that means "lover of wisdom." From this term comes our word **philosophy,** or the study of the most fundamental questions of reality and human existence.

Socrates wanted people to think for themselves and not imitate their elders. Only then could they acquire wisdom, which would lead to "right living." According to Socrates, only evil could result from ignorance. People should depend on reason and logic to guide their lives.

Unlike the Sophists Socrates did not use the teaching method of memorizing. Instead he asked questions of anyone he met, anywhere. His purpose was not to receive information but to make people think in order to answer the questions. Constantly repeating his motto "know thyself," Socrates tried to teach people to understand what love, friendship, duty, patriotism, honor, and justice really meant. He urged each person to find his or her own answers to these and other questions. This way of teaching became known as the "Socratic method."

Although greatly loved because of his wisdom, honesty, and kindness, Socrates also had enemies. His questions often made public officials look foolish. He also criticized democracy. He believed it unwise to elect unskilled people to positions of power, and he distrusted the wisdom of the Assembly. After all, he said, we do not elect doctors or ship pilots—why should we elect rulers? Crowds of young followers gathered to hear Socrates mock democracy and its leaders, who did not find him so amusing.

Though Socrates honored the gods of Athens, his enemies accused him of denying the existence of many Greek gods. The Athenian leaders brought him to trial on charges of teaching false religion and corrupting the minds of Athenian youth.

At his trial Socrates said that his conscience made him teach. If allowed to live, he would continue to teach because his conscience would compel him to do so. Found guilty and condemned to die by drinking a poison made from the hemlock plant, Socrates faced his fate cheerfully. He believed in the immortality of his soul and persisted in his search for truth until his death.

Plato

Although Socrates never recorded his ideas, later generations learned of them from the writings of Plato, a wealthy young aristocrat and the greatest of his students. After the death of Socrates, Plato traveled throughout the Mediterranean region. He then returned to Athens and began to teach philosophy on the grounds of the Academy, a public park and athletic field.

Plato wrote dialogues, or imaginary conversations among several people, covering such topics as government, education, justice, virtue, and religion. In each dialogue Socrates usually appeared as the primary speaker and asked questions of the others. The dialogues, however, expressed many of Plato's theories as well.

In one such dialogue, Socrates asked "What is justice?" To answer the question, Plato wrote the *Republic*, a long dialogue describing his concept of the ideal form of government. People, he said, should do the work for which they are best suited. For example, those noted for their bravery should be in the army. People interested in material things such as food, clothing, and luxuries should conduct the business and perform the labor. Plato's ideal government was an aristocracy—a government ruled by an upper class. However, it was not an aristocracy of birth or of wealth but one based on intelligence, reasoning, education, and high ideals. Plato's ideal "aristocrats" were philosophers, chosen for their wisdom, ability, and "correct" ideas about justice.

Aristotle

Among Plato's students in the Academy was a young man named Aristotle, who founded his own school at Athens in 335 B.C. An accomplished scientist as well as a great philosopher, Aristotle vigorously embarked upon the task of investigating every kind of knowledge and collected as many facts as possible. He then organized these facts into systems, comparing one fact with another to find what each meant or showed. Aristotle demonstrated a special skill for defining words and grouping similar or related facts. This process of organization forms an important part of modern scientific thinking.

Aristotle almost accomplished his goal of investigating every known field of knowledge in his time. He collected, described, and classified plants and animals. For his book *Ethics*, Aristotle examined the acts and beliefs of individuals to learn what brought them the greatest happiness. He concluded that the Greek ideal of style in the arts—balance, order, and restraint—also represented the ideal in terms of human behavior. In his work *Poetics*, he studied Greek drama to show the differences between a good play and a bad one. In his *Logic* he attempted to define the principles of correct reasoning. Aristotle studied the political organization of 150 city-states in order to describe the principles of government, and he recorded his conclusions in a book called *Politics*. He concluded that the best type of government contained a middle class—those people neither wealthy nor poor—who played an important role. He wrote:

❝ *T*he middle class is least likely to shrink from rule, or to be overambitious for it; both of which are injuries to the state. . . . But a city ought to be composed, as far as possible, of equals and similars; and these are generally the middle classes. . . .

Thus it is manifest that the best political community is formed by citizens of the middle class, and that those states are likely to be well administered in which the middle class is large, and stronger if possible than both the other classes, or at any rate than either singly; for the addition of the middle class turns the scale, and prevents either of the extremes from being dominant. ❞

Aristotle's political writings, like those of other great philosophers of the Golden Age, reflected his study of Greek culture and his experiences in public life. Aristotle believed that although pure monarchy, aristocracy, and democracy were equally good forms of government, each could easily be corrupted. For example, he believed that the power of the people in a democracy could easily lead to a dictatorship of the "mob." Therefore, the best government should include aspects of each form of government—a powerful leader, aristocratic advisers, and a democratic assembly.

Aristotle's belief in division of power among different levels of government contrasted with Plato's belief that one level of government should control a person's life for the benefit of the whole state. According to Plato, people of the lower classes could never rise above their position in society and achieve success in life without the guidance of intellectual leaders who represented a higher level of authority.

Mathematics and Science

In the 500s B.C., the philosopher and mathematician Pythagoras (puh • THAG • uh • ruhs), who was born on the island of Samos in the Aegean Sea, wrote that everything could be explained or expressed with numbers. He is probably best known for the Pythagorean theorem, the geometric theory that states that the square of the hypotenuse of a right triangle equals the sum of the squares of the other two sides.

The Greeks of the Golden Age also made some advances in science. However, Greek scientific achievements did not develop fully until a later period. Aristotle laid the foundations for the development of botany, zoology, and anatomy. The Greek philosopher Democritus (di • MAHK • ruht • uhs) believed that moving atoms—small particles that could not be divided—compose all matter. Scientists have since proved that the atom can be divided, but they still accept the theory that all matter consists of atoms.

One of the greatest scientists of the Golden Age was Hippocrates (hip • AHK • ruh • teez). Considered the founder of medicine, he taught that all disease comes from natural causes, not as punishment from the gods. He believed that rest, fresh air, and a proper diet made the best cures. Hippocrates recorded his ideas in his *Regimen of Health*. He wrote:

> "In winter it is beneficial to counteract the cold and congealed season by living according to the following regimen. First, a man should have one meal a day only, unless he have a very dry belly; in that case let him take a light luncheon. The articles of diet to be used are such as are of a drying nature, of a warming character, assorted and undiluted; wheaten bread is to be preferred to barley cake, and roasted to boiled meats . . . vegetables should be reduced to a minimum, except such as are warming and dry."

Hippocrates had high ideals for physicians. Today physicians still take the Hippocratic oath, a pledge to follow the code of medical ethics based on Hippocrates' teachings.

History

The Greeks became the first people to take the writing of history seriously. Herodotus, an enthusiastic traveler and the first great historian of the western world, visited Babylonia, Phoenicia, and Egypt. He included his impressions of these countries and their people in his histories.

A fascinating writer and a wonderful storyteller, Herodotus exaggerated at times, but always carefully distinguished between the things he had personally seen or investigated and those he had been told. He often expressed doubt about legends but reported them for whatever they were worth. Historians still consult his writings for information about the world during his time, and he is often called the "Father of History."

Another Greek historian, Thucydides (thoo • SID • uh • deez), became famous for his *History of the Peloponnesian War* (see Chapter 5). Thucydides wanted his account of history to reflect his belief that studying the past yields an understanding of human nature. He also hoped that his scientific approach to history would serve as a guide for future political leaders.

Learning from Pictures   *During the Festival of Dionysus, plays were held in this well-preserved theater at Epidaurus.*

Greek Drama

Greeks living in Athens during the Golden Age wrote a surprising number of the world's greatest works of literature. A tremendous flood of creative writing occurred during that brief period. Greek literature still endures today because of its simple, beautiful, and realistic portrayal of people.

The Greeks were the first people to write **dramas,** or plays containing action or dialogue and usually involving conflict and emotion. They excelled in this form of literature. They always wrote plays in poetic form, and two or three actors and a chorus, or a group of singers and dancers who described the scenes, spoke or sang the lines in front of an audience.

Reflecting the idea of harmony with nature, the Greeks carved outdoor theaters into hillsides noted for beauty and serenity. The Greeks frequently built seats for the audience into the slopes of these hillsides. The base contained the *orchestra,* the area where the chorus changed and the actors performed. Greek theaters did not have raised stages as the Romans would use for plays. Also, unlike the "sets" of many plays today, sets for Greek dramas featured little scenery. Audiences relied on choral descriptions to set the time and place of various scenes.

The male actors, their voices trained to produce variety in tone and pitch, also played women's roles. They wore elaborate padded costumes and thick-soled boots to make them look larger than life. Actors also used masks to indicate the characters and emotions they portrayed.

Learning from Pictures *This comic mask belonged to a Greek actor around 300 B.C. Why did actors use masks in their performances?*

Performed in connection with religious festivals, the plays often focused on a religious theme. Each spring and winter, such festivals were held in honor of Dionysus (dy•uh•NY•suhs), the god of fertility and wine. At the winter Festival of Dionysus, three plays were presented each day for three successive days. Each day the audience selected the best play, judging it by the beauty of the language and the wisdom of its ideas. The winning author received a crown of ivy, the traditional Greek symbol of victory.

Tragedies. In Greek **tragedies** the main character struggled against fate. Often a combination of outside forces overcame this central character, who assumed that he or she had the same knowledge or ability as the gods. Such an assumption, known as **hubris** (HYOO•bruhs), insulted the gods and doomed the character to a tragic fate.

Three great writers of tragedy lived during the 400s B.C. One writer, Aeschylus (ES•kuh•luhs), wrote of the old religious beliefs concerning the relationship between gods and people. His three most famous plays centered on the murder of

Agamemnon, the king who led the Greeks against Troy, and the revenge that followed.

Another writer of tragedies, Sophocles (SAHF•uh•kleez), defended traditional values. Aristotle called Sophocles' most famous play, *Oedipus the Tyrant,* a perfect example of tragedy.

Euripides (yoo•RIP•uh•deez), the third playwright, was more of a realist than Aeschylus or Sophocles. Like Socrates he questioned many old beliefs and ideas. Earlier writers often glorified war for its deeds of courage and heroism. In *The Trojan Women,* Euripides showed the reality of war, exposing all its pain and misery.

Comedies. Greek **comedies,** which also originated at the festival honoring Dionysus, mocked ideas and people. The comedies usually introduced both tragic and comic figures. Unlike their counterparts in tragedies, however, the central characters in comedies succeeded in solving their problems.

No person or institution could escape the wit of Aristophanes (ar•uh•STAHF•uh•neez), the greatest Greek writer of comedies. In *The Clouds* he poked fun at Socrates for his theories about educating the youth of Athens. Aristophanes also disliked war and used comedy to make Athenians think about its causes and consequences. In some of his plays, women controlled the government or persuaded their husbands to make peace during war. This amused the Athenians because of their low opinion of women.

SECTION 2 REVIEW

1. **Define** philosophy, drama, tragedy, hubris, comedy
2. **Identify** Socrates, Plato, Aristotle, Pythagoras, Democritus, Hippocrates, Thucydides, Aeschylus, Sophocles, Euripides, Aristophanes
3. **Understanding Ideas** **(a)** Why did Socrates criticize the Sophists? **(b)** What teaching method did Socrates use? **(c)** What was its purpose?
4. **Summarizing Ideas** What were the main characteristics of the ideal government described in Plato's *Republic?*
5. **Interpreting Ideas** **(a)** Why is Aristotle considered a scientist as well as a philosopher? **(b)** List the major ideas presented in *Politics, Ethics, Poetics,* and *Logic.*
6. **Contrasting Ideas** In what ways did Aristotle's view of government differ from Plato's view of government?
7. **Synthesizing Ideas** Why would the comedies of Aristophanes have been impossible to perform in Sparta?

3 Alexander the Great Created a Huge Empire

Between 404 B.C. and 362 B.C., Sparta and then Thebes attempted to dominate Greece. However, unsuccessful leadership and continuous Persian interference in Greek affairs prevented unity. Wars raged, and although Persia seemed the most logical victor, another foreign power—Macedonia— brought unity to Greece.

Philip of Macedon

The power that finally unified Greece came from an unexpected direction. Look at the map on page 134. A mountainous land called Macedonia lies north of Greece. In the 300s B.C., the Macedonians, a hardy, warlike people closely related to Greeks, inhabited this land. The Macedonians lived in small villages, each ruled by a powerful noble. Macedonia also had a king, but the extent of his power depended on his own leadership abilities and on the help of the nobles.

In 359 B.C. a remarkable young man known as Philip of Macedon became king. Captured by the Thebans in his youth, Philip remained a hostage in Thebes for three years. During that time he came to admire both the Greek life style and the organization of the Theban military.

Philip wanted to be a strong king and to control the unruly Macedonian nobles and people. Instead of depending on the nobles to supply troops for an army, Philip recruited the first regular paid army in Macedonian history.

He drilled his force of 10,000 soldiers into the most powerful army Europe had ever known. Landowners, serving as cavalry, rode massive horses and underwent extensive training that taught them to fight in close formation. In addition, Philip organized hunters and peasants into an **infantry**—a group of soldiers trained and equipped to fight on foot. Philip organized part of the infantry into phalanxes (fuh • LAN • jeez) similar to those used by the armies of the Greek city-states. A **phalanx** (FAY • langks) consisted of 16 rows of tightly spaced soldiers equipped with lances 21 feet (6.4 meters) long. Weighted at the back, each lance became a deadly weapon when hurled.

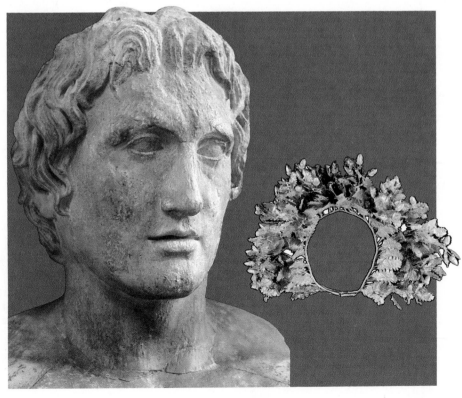

Learning from Pictures
The gold crown (far right) found in the city of Vergina in Macedonia may have belonged to Alexander the Great (right). Alexander had his own silver coin minted (above) since traders in the empire accepted silver as the medium of exchange.

After unifying his own kingdom, Philip used his army to conquer surrounding peoples. He first gained control of some towns in northern Greece that Athens claimed as colonies. He then turned south and began unifying the Greek city-states under his rule.

The Greeks had varying opinions of Philip. Some people regarded him as a savior who could bring unity to Greece. Others opposed him as a menace to liberty. Demosthenes (di•MAHS•thuh•neez), one of the greatest **orators,** or public speakers, in all Athenian history, led the opposition to Philip in Athens.

Demosthenes tried to make Athenians aware of the danger he believed Philip of Macedon posed. He bitterly attacked Philip in a series of speeches to the Assembly and tried to get Athens to lead the Greeks once more in a fight for liberty. Demosthenes did spur the Athenians to action. As so often happened in Greek history, however, the city-states failed to present a unified defense. As Philip and his army relentlessly marched south, traitors betrayed some city-states, supporting Philip's belief that "No fortress is inaccessible if one can only introduce within it a mule laden with gold." One by one, other city-states fell to Philip's army. Finally it defeated the forces of Thebes and Athens at the battle of Chaeronea (ker•uh•NEE•uh) in 338 B.C. (see map, this page), and Philip became master of Greece.

The Greeks were at last united, but they had lost their freedom. Although Philip organized the cities into a league to support his plans for an invasion of Persia, he never achieved his goal. At his daughter's wedding in the summer of 336 B.C., an army officer whom Philip had refused to help with a dispute assassinated him. His 20-year-old son Alexander, known to history as Alexander the Great, succeeded him.

Alexander the Great

Alexander proved to be even more remarkable than his father. Although very much alike, Alexander

Learning from Maps Alexander conquered Persepolis before turning north to conquer the rest of Persia. Which city did he conquer first, Susa or Persepolis?

ALEXANDER THE GREAT'S EMPIRE AND DEPENDENT STATES, 323 B.C.

◆ City founded by Alexander

✴ Major battle site

← Route of Alexander and his armies

ROBINSON PROJECTION

CONNECTIONS: THEN AND NOW

Memorials

What is the name of your school? Many schools, libraries, colleges, and towns are named for famous people. In this way we remember individuals and honor their contributions long after they have died. In the United States, our two most famous leaders are honored by the Washington and Lincoln Memorials in Washington, D.C., in the state and cities called Washington, and in the 19 American cities and towns named Lincoln.

In all history Alexander the Great probably has been memorialized more than anyone else. As he conquered cities and towns, he gave many of them his name (right). Beginning in Alexandria, Egypt, his route can be traced eastward by following the towns having his name or that of *Iskander,* his name in Arabic.

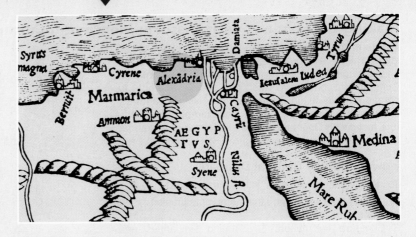

Although in the ancient world cities were generally named after living people, the cities memorialized that person after his or her death.

Names sometimes change with history. For example, Idlewild Airport in New York was renamed Kennedy Airport in honor of John F. Kennedy.

Notice the names of places in your town. Perhaps you can think of other people who have been memorialized in this way.

and Philip rarely agreed and often quarreled bitterly. Despite their differences, however, Philip did everything to give his son the best training and education possible. Alexander received his military training in the Macedonian army and his formal education from the great Greek philosopher Aristotle. The opportunity to cultivate both military skills and an appreciation for his cultural heritage prepared Alexander for leadership and made him a lifelong admirer of Greek culture.

As a military commander, Alexander was even more skilled than his father. His military campaigns rank among the greatest in history. Physically strong and brave to the point of rashness, Alexander's dramatic acts in battle so captured the imagination of his troops that they willingly followed him into unknown lands.

Alexander's plan. Alexander dreamed of a Hellenistic empire—a world empire that would connect East and West and blend the best features of the Greek and Persian cultures into a new culture. He planned to create his vast empire in three ways. First, he wanted to found new cities and rebuild old ones as cultural centers of his empire. He actually established more than 70 cities, many of them named Alexandria in his honor. Groups of Greeks and Macedonians settled in each one.

Second, Alexander planned to merge the Macedonians and the Persians into one ruling group in order to run his empire more efficiently. He married the Persian princess Roxana and also required his generals to marry Persian royalty.

Third, Alexander wanted his subjects to consider him a divine monarch, a god-king. He became convinced that his real father was not Philip but the god Zeus-Ammon. Alexander insisted that all of his subjects honor him as being part human and part divine. The Persians did not believe in god-kings, but the Egyptians did; and the Greeks thought that some heroes became gods.

Alexander's conquests. Having developed a plan to create his empire, Alexander put his plan into action by crushing rebellions in the Greek city-states and declaring himself master of Greece. He then set out to conquer the world. By 331 B.C. he had conquered Asia Minor, Syria, Egypt, Mesopotamia, and the once mighty Persian Empire (see map, page 134).

135

READ
WRITE
INTERPRET
●CONNECT
THINK

BUILDING HISTORY STUDY SKILLS

Making Connections with History: Identifying Cultural Diffusion

The term "cultural diffusion" refers to the exchange of ideas, values, and products between societies and the changes that result from such cross-cultural contacts. Cultural diffusion occurs when one society attempts to spread its own culture or results from military ventures, trade, or the migration of people. For example, Greek culture fused with Oriental cultures as a result of Alexander the Great's conquests.

How to Identify Cultural Diffusion

To identify cultural diffusion, follow these steps.

1. Identify the cultures and the method of diffusion.
2. Identify the subject.
3. Compare the cultures by stating similarities and differences.
4. Determine the connection between the cultures.

Developing the Skill

Study the sculptures in the photographs on this page and note their similarities and differences. The statue on the left illustrates classic Greek sculpture. The statues above reveal the cultural diffusion Alexander the Great promoted through military conquests.

Sculpted by Myron in the 400s B.C., "The Discus Thrower" mixes idealism and realism. The human body is depicted as it appears to the human eye, but the sculpture stresses the Greek ideals of perfection and self-restraint. The artist captures the athlete at the moment before he makes his supreme effort. He appears dynamically poised and in full control. Yet he represents the Greek ideal rather than an individual. He symbolizes the balance between the individual and the community so characteristic of the Greeks.

The product of cultural diffusion, the Hellenistic statues of a woman and a boy reflect the Greek ideal in that the proportions of the figures are correct. But these statues take realism a step further and represent particular people.

How do the Hellenistic statues show cultural diffusion? First, the statues retain the technical excellence and emphasis on proportions that characterize the Greek ideals. But they also emphasize the individual by focusing on the material aspects of life rather than on perfection.

Practicing the skill. Locate photographs of sculptures and paintings depicting ancient Egyptian culture and ancient Sumerian and Babylonian culture about 2000 B.C. Explain how the statues of Babylon show the influence of Egyptian and Sumerian cultures.

To apply this skill, see Applying History Study Skills on page 141.

Although Alexander now ruled a huge territory, he longed to acquire more. Beyond Persia lay India, the "end of the world," as the people around the Mediterranean Sea then called it. For almost four years he led his troops east, meeting little resistance and going as far as the Indus River. From there he wanted to march on to the Ganges River and so control the entire vast plain of northern India. After four years, however, Alexander's long-suffering army had finally had enough fighting. For three days he pleaded with them, but his exhausted soldiers would not follow. Reluctantly, Alexander turned back in 326 B.C.

Alexander led his army to the Indian Ocean, where he divided his troops. Half of them traveled west by sea, explored the shores of the Persian Gulf as far as the mouth of the Euphrates, and sailed inland to meet Alexander at Susa. Alexander led the rest of his army through the desert, where many of his troops died from scorching heat and searing thirst. Throughout this ordeal Alexander shared the hardships with his troops. At one point a soldier brought him water in a helmet, but Alexander poured the water on the ground, refusing to drink it because his soldiers had none. According to Arrian, a second-century Greek historian, "So extraordinary was the effect of this action that the water wasted by Alexander was as good as a drink for every man in the army."

The tattered remnants of his forces finally reached Susa in the spring of 324 B.C. Although Alexander's fleet suffered only minor losses and joined the king at Susa, the great army would never be reassembled. Alexander and his soldiers had spent years in Asia and had suffered greatly. Amid the growing discontent in his army, Alexander withdrew to a lonely life dominated by suspicions of his soldiers' disloyalty.

One night shortly after his return to Babylon in 323 B.C., Alexander became ill with a fever now thought to be cholera or malaria. In the early evening of the eleventh day of his raging fever, Alexander the Great died at the age of 33.

In 13 years Alexander had never lost a battle and had conquered much of the world known to him. Although his dream of ruling the entire world remained unfulfilled and his empire soon crumbled, Alexander's reign spread Hellenistic culture throughout much of the world. So great was the influence of this culture that we refer to the time between Alexander's death and the Roman conquest of Greece in 146 B.C. as the Hellenistic Age.

The Breakup of Alexander's Empire

After Alexander's death his generals murdered his family and divided the "one world" that composed his empire. A fierce power struggle raged until 301 B.C., when the last attempt to hold the empire together under one ambitious general failed. The three surviving generals, honored as god-kings, divided Alexander's empire into three main kingdoms—Macedonia, Egypt, and Syria. The three kingdoms, often at war with one another, used the cities of Greece as pawns in their struggles. They wasted much wealth and energy on war. After 200 B.C. a new people, the Romans, filtered into Greece, and over a span of more than 150 years they conquered the three kingdoms.

SECTION 3 REVIEW

1. **Define**   infantry, phalanx, orator
2. **Identify**   Philip, Demosthenes, Alexander the Great
3. **Locate**   Macedonia, Indus River, Ganges River, Susa, Egypt, Syria
4. **Evaluating Ideas**   Why did Demosthenes and other Athenians oppose Philip of Macedon?
5. **Summarizing Ideas**   Describe Alexander's three goals for his empire.
6. **Analyzing Ideas**   How did Alexander's generals divide his empire after his death?

4 Hellenistic Culture Spread Throughout the Mediterranean Region

The conquests of Alexander the Great brought Greek culture to Egypt and other lands of the Middle East, up to the border of India. Greek culture continued to influence these areas long after Alexander's death. At the same time, the ideas that Alexander's followers brought from other lands modified Greek culture at home. Although the greatest achievements of Hellenistic culture included new advances in philosophy and science, writers also made important contributions that influenced Western thought for centuries.

The Economy

Throughout the Hellenistic world, rulers or governments owned much land. Wealthy aristocrats usually held most of the privately owned land, while slaves or poorly paid free laborers did the work. Hellenistic society included a small class of very wealthy people and a large class of miserably poor people. Still the middle class thrived because of the many opportunities for acquiring wealth.

Trade, the most profitable activity, originated from the main trading centers in the cities of Alexandria, in Egypt; Rhodes, on the island of Rhodes, off the coast of Asia Minor; and Antioch, in Syria. Trade routes now connected the entire Mediterranean world, reaching as far east as India. Bigger and better ships contributed greatly to this increase in trade.

The cities Alexander had built or rebuilt became the wonders of the Hellenistic world. Carefully planned and laid out, these cities included market squares and large public buildings such as theaters, schools, or gymnasiums, where men exercised and discussed important issues. Homes of the wealthy included elaborate furniture, running water, and drain pipes. Alexandria, in Egypt, with a population of almost 1 million, became the largest city. Its museum and its library, which housed 750,000 papyrus rolls, made Alexandria a great center of learning and an important center of commerce.

Changing Attitudes

As the middle class expanded, education became widespread. Novels gained popularity. The old and now less respected values of Greece faded. The status of women improved. Hellenistic women appeared more often in public and acquired more rights regarding property and divorce.

Another major change centered on a new definition of what it meant to be a Greek. A Hellenized Egyptian or Syrian was considered a "Greek." Nevertheless, tensions still surfaced when Greeks, Hellenized Greeks, and non-Greeks lived side by side, because the old Greek bias against "barbarians" did not actually decrease; more of the world became Greek.

Philosophy

Hellenistic philosophers concerned themselves more with ethics than with the basic questions of reality and human existence. Three chief schools of philosophy existed—the Cynic, the Stoic, and the Epicurean schools.

The Cynics taught that people should seek virtue only. They scorned pleasure, wealth, and social position. Many stories exist about the best known Cynic, Diogenes (dy • AHJ • uh • neez). One story concerns the meeting of Diogenes and Alexander the Great. "If I were not Alexander, I would prefer to be Diogenes," the conqueror said. But Diogenes growled in reply, "If I were not Diogenes, I would prefer to be any man except Alexander." Today the word *cynic* means a sarcastic person who believes that selfish and insincere motives underlie people's actions.

Zeno established the Stoic philosophy in Athens in the late 300s B.C. He and his followers believed that divine reason directed the world. For example, they believed that whatever fate dictated was right. In their opinion, people should not complain but should learn to accept whatever nature might bring. They should be indifferent to grief, fear, pain, and pleasure.

The Stoics greatly influenced Roman and Christian thinking. Today the word *stoic* means much the same as it meant in Hellenistic times— one who remains outwardly unaffected by pain or pleasure.

Epicurus, founder of the Epicurean philosophy, taught that the aim of life focused on seeking pleasure and avoiding pain. Pleasure to him was intellectual, not physical. After his death, however, his followers sought physical pleasures as well. Their motto became "Eat, drink, and be merry, for tomorrow may bring pain or death." Today the word *epicure* means a person who enjoys the pleasures of the senses, particularly someone who enjoys fine food and chooses to postpone worry.

Mathematics and Physics

Greeks of the Hellenistic Age became outstanding scientists and mathematicians. Euclid contributed extremely important work to the field of mathematics. He developed geometry into a system by showing how geometric statements of truth, or theorems, develop logically from one another. His *Elements* textbook, used for more than 1,000 years, is the basis for many of today's geometry books.

Archimedes (ahr • kuh • MEED • eez), considered the greatest scientist of the Hellenistic period, used geometry to measure spheres, cones, and cylinders. He also calculated the value of pi (π)—the ratio of the circumference of a circle to its diameter—and used mathematics to explain the principle of the lever, building many machines that employed levers. His inventions included the compound pulley (or block and tackle) and cogged wheels used as gears.

Medicine

Hellenistic scientists greatly enhanced the medical knowledge of the Greeks. Alexandria became the center for the study of medicine and surgery. By dissecting the bodies of executed criminals physicians learned much about human anatomy. Studies by Alexandrian physicians revealed that the brain is the center of the nervous system. These and other advances in medicine allowed Hellenistic physicians to perform delicate surgery on patients, using anesthetics (painkillers).

Astronomy and Geography

Hellenistic scientists added to the knowledge of astronomy. They used mathematics to calculate the daily position of stars and planets. Aristarchus (ar • uh • STAHR • kuhs) of Samos believed that the earth and other planets moved around the sun, but he failed to convince other scientists of his day. Hipparchus (hip • AHR • kuhs) of Rhodes, the first scientist to systematically use trigonometry, calculated the times of eclipses of the sun and the moon and the length of the year according to both the sun and the moon.

Hellenistic geographers knew that the earth was round. At Alexandria Eratosthenes (er • uh • TAHS • thuh • neez) calculated the diameter of the earth to within 50 miles (70 kilometers) of the actual figure. He also claimed that people could reach India by sailing west around the world. However, no ship built then could risk so long an ocean voyage.

Characteristics of Hellenistic Science

Two characteristics of Hellenistic science remain particularly remarkable. First, scientists learned so much using simple instruments. They had no microscopes, telescopes, compasses, or delicate balances for weighing small quantities.

Second, the Hellenistic Greeks made little effort to apply their scientific knowledge in practical

Learning from Pictures An unknown sculptor carved Winged Victory on the island of Samothrace to commemorate a successful Greek naval battle.

ways, except perhaps in the field of geography. They valued knowledge for its own sake and had no interest in inventions or mechanical progress. For example, an Alexandrian scientist named Hero invented a steam engine, but people regarded it only as an interesting toy. One explanation for this attitude stems from the fact that slavery served as the basis for Hellenistic civilization. These labor-saving inventions would have helped the slaves, and the Greeks did not think it necessary or fitting to improve the slaves' situation.

SECTION 4 REVIEW

1. **Identify**   Diogenes, Zeno, Epicurus, Euclid, Archimedes, Aristarchus, Hipparchus, Eratosthenes
2. **Summarizing Ideas**   What people were considered Greek during the Hellenistic Age?
3. **Classifying Ideas**   What were the main ideas of the three major Hellenistic philosophies?
4. **Evaluating Ideas**   Why did Hellenistic Greeks have relatively little interest in the practical application of science?

139

CHAPTER 6 REVIEW

BC

447-433
400s 399 375   338 336 320

Construction
of Parthenon

Defeat of the
Greeks by
Philip of Macedon
at Chaeronea

Conquest of
vast empire by
Alexander the Great

Golden
Age of
Greece

Death
of Socrates

Life of
Phidias

Chapter Summary

The following list contains the key concepts you have learned about Greek civilization and the Hellenistic Age.

1. The peak of cultural activity in Athens occurred in the 400s B.C.—a period known as the Golden Age.
2. Athenians surrounded themselves with beauty and showed their love for Athens by building temples, gymnasiums, and public theaters adorned with sculpture and other fine works of art.
3. The Parthenon, a shrine constructed in honor of the goddess Athena, still stands atop the Acropolis, the hill where the original polis was located.
4. Greek art glorified humans, symbolized the pride of Greeks, honored the gods, expressed the ideals of balance and order, and combined beauty with usefulness.
5. The works of Greek philosophers and writers, such as Aristotle and Plato, remain among the world's greatest works of literature.
6. Philip of Macedon invaded Greece, conquered all the city-states, and united them under his rule.
7. Philip's son, Alexander the Great, went on to conquer the entire Persian Empire and more. He hoped to rule the world, but he died before he could accomplish his goal. In time his empire was divided into three separate kingdoms.
8. As a result of Alexander's conquests, Greek culture, known as Hellenistic culture, spread throughout the Mediterranean area.
9. Hellenistic contributions to our understanding of ethics, mathematics, and science—especially geometry, physics, medicine, and astronomy—remained influential for more than 1,000 years.

On a separate sheet of paper, complete the following review exercises.

Reviewing Important Terms

Supply the term that correctly completes each statement.

1. The new culture founded on Greek ideas and features from other cultures of the Mediterranean is known as _____ _____.
2. _____ is the inquiry into the most fundamental questions of reality and human existence.
3. A play containing action and dialogue and usually involving conflict and emotion is called a _____.
4. The Greeks called an assumption that a person had the same knowledge or ability as the gods _____.
5. A Greek _____ showed the main character struggling against a fate that resulted in a sad ending.
6. A _____ is a form of Greek drama that mocks ideas and people.
7. _____ is a term for soldiers trained and equipped to fight on foot.

Developing Critical Thinking Skills

1. **Evaluating Ideas**   How did the architecture and art of the Golden Age in Athens reflect the values of Greek culture? Include specific examples to support your answer.
2. **Contrasting Ideas**   How does Socrates' concept of the ideal form of government, as described in Plato's *Republic*, differ from modern democratic governments?
3. **Applying Ideas**   How might Aristotle's views of the importance of the middle class be reflected in the governments of many nondemocratic nations today?
4. **Classifying Ideas**   In what ways did the Hellenistic world follow the models set by Alexander?
5. **Interpreting Ideas**   How did middle-class expansion change Greek attitudes during the Hellenistic Age?
6. **Comparing Ideas**   How did the views of Greek philosophers of the Golden Age differ from the views of philosophers of the Hellenistic Age?
7. **Relating Ideas**   How might Thucydides' approach to history apply to other contributions of Greek culture?

Relating Geography to History

Compare the map on page 134 with a modern map of the same area.   **(a)** What countries now lie in the land that once formed Alexander's empire?   **(b)** What geographic barriers prevented Alexander from conquering the Indian subcontinent?

Relating Past to Present

1. The architects of many of the public buildings in our nation's capital, Washington, D.C., were influenced by

the architecture of ancient Greece. In your school or local library, find a book with photographs of buildings located in Washington, D.C. Find another book with photographs of ancient buildings still standing in Greece today. Compare the buildings shown in each book. **(a)** List the ways in which the buildings shown are similar and the ways in which they are different. **(b)** What functions did the ancient Greek buildings serve? **(c)** What functions do the modern buildings in Washington, D.C. serve?

2. Explore the history of your town or city to find streets, parks, or buildings named after people. Which of these people have been memorialized in other parts of the United States?

3. Give examples of how Hellenistic culture influenced the governments and economies of the regions with which it came in contact. What aspects of American culture have spread to other countries today?

Applying History Study Skills

Before completing this activity, review Building History Study Skills on page 136.

Look again at the steps explaining how to identify cultural diffusion. Then read the following selections from Plato's *Republic* and Epicurus' *The Prudent Pursuit of Pleasure* to answer the questions below.

❝ Unless either philosophers become kings in their countries or those who are now called kings and rulers come to be sufficiently inspired with a genuine desire for wisdom; unless, that is to say, political power and philosophy meet together . . . there can be no rest from troubles . . . for states, nor yet, as I believe, for all mankind. ❞

(Plato)

❝ When, therefore, we maintain that pleasure is the end, we do not mean . . . continuous drinkings and revellings, . . . but sober reasoning, searching out the motives for all choice and avoidance, and banishing mere opinions, to which are due the greatest disturbance of the spirit.

Of all this the beginning and the greatest good is prudence [self-discipline] . . . for from prudence are sprung all the other virtues, and it teaches us that it is not possible to live pleasantly without living prudently and honourably and justly. ❞

(Epicurus)

1. **(a)** How are the purposes of these two writers similar? **(b)** How do their goals differ?

2. How does Plato's philosophy represent a response to a polis or city-state?

3. How does Epicurus' philosophy represent a response to a society that is multiracial and a center of trade?

4. What evidence of cultural diffusion is present in the quotes by these two philosophers?

Investigating Further

1. **Preparing an Oral Presentation** Read selections from Plato's *Republic.* Then choose one idea from his work on each of the following subjects: **(a)** education, **(b)** the role of women, **(c)** the organization of society, **(d)** the definition of a state. Prepare an oral report on the ways these ideas were reflected in the city-state governments of ancient Greece.

2. **Conducting an Interview** Choose one of the mathematicians or scientists, such as Hippocrates or Aristarchus, mentioned in this chapter. Interview a math or science teacher to learn how the ideas of these ancient scholars were developed and are used today. Investigate the work of other mathematicians or scientists who may have tried to prove them wrong.

3. **Writing a Report** Report on the speeches that Demosthenes made in defense of Athens and discuss the arguments that he advanced against Philip of Macedon. You can locate the appropriate speeches in Lewis Copeland and Lawrence Lamm's *The World's Great Speeches* (Dover), or in the book by Houston Peterson, *Treasury of the World's Great Speeches* (Simon and Schuster).

4. **Studying Literature** During the Golden Age in Athens, women were subordinate to men in matters of education, legal rights, government participation, and business affairs. Yet during this same period Euripides composed great plays about strong women (for example, *Medea*), and Sophocles wrote *Antigone*. What role did these women play in Greek tradition?

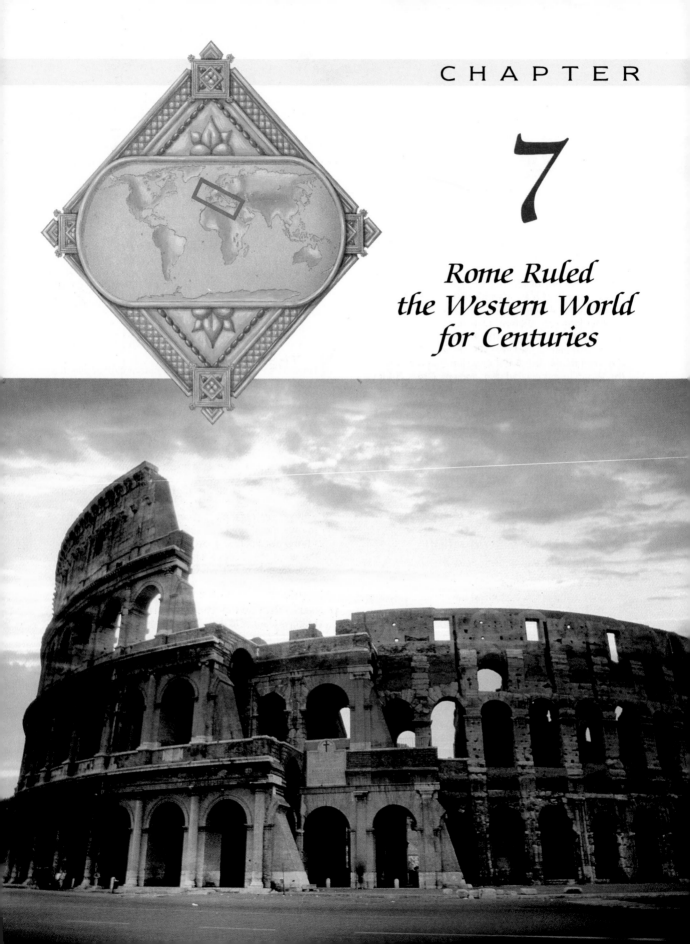

CHAPTER

7

*Rome Ruled
the Western World
for Centuries*

Place   Italy and the Mediterranean region

Time

1000 B.C.–A.D. 476

3.7 mil. BC   4000 BC   AD 2100

Significance

The date 146 B.C. is often given as the end of the Hellenistic Age because by that year the Romans had extended their power over a large part of the eastern Mediterranean. But who were the Romans? How did they become powerful enough to gain control of the Mediterranean region and much of Europe as well? And why are they important to us today?

To answer these questions, we must look west of Greece to the shores of the Tiber River, on the rugged Italian Peninsula. There the settlement that would in time become the imperial city of Rome was founded about 750 B.C. In contrast to the genius of the Greeks, which lay in the development of philosophy, the genius of the Romans lay in politics and law. Even today we trace the origins of many of our legal and political institutions to those of ancient Rome.

Terms to Define

republic	indemnity
consul	latifundia
veto	Pax Romana
patrician	inflation
plebeian	anarchy

People to Identify

Julius Caesar	Jesus
Octavian	Constantine
Cicero	Diocletian

Places to Locate

Italian Peninsula	Judea
Rome	Nicaea
Carthage	Constantinople

Questions to Guide Your Reading

1 How did the geography of Italy influence the rise of Roman power?
2 How did the Roman Republic expand its territory to include the entire Mediterranean region?
3 How was the Roman Republic transformed into an empire?
4 What features of Roman society and culture helped the Romans build and maintain their empire?
5 Why did Christianity take root in Judea?
6 What problems led to the decline and fall of the Roman Empire in the west?

No one knows exactly when the city of Rome was founded, but several colorful legends exist. The most famous legend holds that Romulus, the son of a priestess and Mars—the god of war—founded the city. Romulus and his twin brother, Remus, were allegedly abandoned by their mother and left to die. Good fortune saved the infants, a wolf mothered them, and a shepherd raised them. As adults the brothers founded villages on separate hills—the Palatine and the Aventine. The brothers soon quarreled, and Remus—to show how little he thought of Romulus' village—jumped over its unfinished wall. Furious, Romulus killed his brother and swore to do the same to "whoever else shall leap over my walls." Rome, the city formed when the two villages eventually united, was named after Romulus.

1 The Romans Founded a Republic on the Italian Peninsula

The geography of Italy and the location of Rome itself had a great deal to do with the rise of Roman power. In time Rome became the heart of a vast empire. Like most empires, it took shape gradually.

The Physical Setting

Italy is the central peninsula of the three great peninsulas in the Mediterranean region. On the map on page 144, note that Italy resembles a boot, with its top nestled in the Alps to the north and its toe and heel jutting into the Mediterranean Sea to the south. The toe of Italy rests only about 2 miles (3 kilometers) from Sicily, which is only 80 miles (128 kilometers) from Africa. Italy lies at the center of the Mediterranean region, slicing the sea nearly in half. Because of its location, Italy is also the obvious base from which to control both the eastern and the western halves of the region.

At first glance the snowcapped Alps separating Italy from the rest of Europe seem to be good protection against invasion. However, for centuries invaders have streamed through several passes that cut through the jagged mountains. Italy's location also makes it vulnerable to sea invasion, for invaders can land anywhere along the peninsula's long, rugged seacoast.

Geographical factors made unity possible in Italy, whereas in Greece the geography prevented it. Notice on the map that the Apennine Mountains, which run the full length of the boot, divide the peninsula. Because the Apennines are less rugged than the mountains of Greece, they did not hinder trade and travel. In addition, although Italy has a long coastline, it has fewer good harbors than Greece has. For these reasons the people living in the early coastal settlements turned inland for trade and growth rather than toward the sea as the Greeks had done.

Except for the long coastal plain to the west and the great valley of the Po River to the north, mountains dominate the landscape of Italy. Heavy rains easily wash away the sandy soil, and most land can be used only for grazing. Nevertheless, Italy's pleasant climate and plentiful winter rains enable

Learning from Maps *Rome was in an ideal location to become the leading city and the center of power on the Italian Peninsula. On what island did the Greeks establish a colony?*

ANCIENT ITALY, ca. 600 B.C.

AZIMUTHAL EQUAL AREA PROJECTION

farmers to raise vegetables, olives, grapes, and citrus fruits.

Italy's rivers are short and shallow. Soil that washes down from higher land partially blocks the mouths of most of these rivers, making the surrounding regions swampy. Throughout history epidemics of malaria and other fevers carried by mosquitoes that thrive in these marshes have plagued the people of Italy.

Early Peoples in Italy

People lived in Italy as early as the Old Stone Age, and a Neolithic culture had developed there before 3000 B.C. After 2000 B.C. waves of invaders swept through the mountain passes and overran the peninsula. As in Greece these invaders came from north of the Black and Caspian seas.

About 1000 B.C. the Latins entered the peninsula and settled in the west-central plains region called Latium (LAY•shee•uhm). Some of the Latin settlers built villages along the Tiber River. In time these villages united to form the city of Rome (see map, this page).

In the late 600s B.C., Etruscans (ih•TRUHS•kuhnz) from north of the Tiber River captured the plains of Latium, including Rome, and controlled the area for about 100 years. They were later absorbed into the mixture of peoples who came to be known as Romans.

Although the Etruscans disappeared as a people, their culture continued to influence the Latins. The Etruscans had developed a written language using an alphabet based on Greek characters. Although scholars have not yet deciphered the script, many believe that the Romans patterned their alphabet after the Etruscan alphabet.

The Etruscans also made fine clothing and jewelry and were skilled workers in metal, pottery, and wood. From the Etruscans the early farmers of Latium learned how to pave roads, drain unhealthy marshes, and build sewers.

The Etruscans introduced to the people of Rome the triumph, a splendid parade held for a conquering military leader returning victorious from battle. Preceded by the spoils and prisoners of war, the leader rode in a special chariot at the head of the troops. To keep the leader from being completely carried away by the cheers of the people, a servant rode in the chariot and constantly repeated, "Remember that you are mortal."

Etruscan Archers and Discus Thrower

The Etruscans were a powerful people of ancient Italy. Skilled fighters and merchants whose wealth came from shipping, the Etruscans traded across the Mediterranean, especially with the Greeks and Egyptians.

Wealthy Etruscans built magnificent tombs for their dead. They filled the tombs with items they thought the dead might need in their future life. Much of our knowledge of Etruscan customs comes from objects found in these tombs. They tell us that Etruscans loved music, games, wrestling, horseback riding, and chariot races.

Metropolitan Museum of Art, Purchase, John Pulitzer Bequest, 1940. (40.11.3)

Sometimes the Etruscans cremated, or burned, their dead. The bronze funeral urn shown here was used to hold ashes. Etruscan funeral urns were decorated with scenes of real life. The discus thrower and four mounted archers may have been placed on the lid to represent pleasures the dead person had once enjoyed.

Some Greeks also settled in ancient Italy. Greek colonies in Sicily and southern Italy became city-states, as disunited and quarrelsome as those of the homeland. The Greek culture of these colonies strongly influenced the Romans.

A Strategic Location

Latins, Etruscans, and other peoples living around Rome gradually began to call themselves Romans. At first Rome was only one of many city-states on the plains of Latium. Rome's location, however, gave it an advantage over other city-states on the Italian Peninsula.

Locate Rome on the map on page 144. Built on seven hills along the Tiber River, Rome lies about 15 miles (24 kilometers) inland from the western coast of Italy. This location protected the Romans from sea invasions.

Rome's location gave the city economic advantages as well. The city lay along one of the shallowest parts of the Tiber, near a small island in the river. This location at the easiest river crossing for many miles put the city at the center of land trade routes that spread out in all directions.

Roman Government

When the Romans overthrew the last Etruscan king in 509 B.C., they set up a republic to govern Rome. A **republic** is a form of government in which voters elect their leaders. In the early Roman Republic, only adult male citizens were entitled to vote and participate in government.

Three groups of citizens helped govern Rome: the Assembly of Centuries, the Assembly of Tribes, and the Senate.

The Assembly of Centuries took its name from a military formation of 100 men. The formation was called a "century" after the Latin word *centum,* which means "hundred." The Assembly declared war and peace and elected three kinds of magistrates, or public officials, to oversee the daily affairs of government.

First, two **consuls** were elected for one-year terms. They served as the chief executives who ran the government and as army commanders. Each could **veto,** or refuse to approve, acts of the other. (The Latin word *veto* means "I forbid.") Although powerful, the consuls governed with the advice of the Senate. This division of power was an example of the principle of **checks and balances** that prevented any one part of the government from becoming too powerful. Many nations of the modern world, including the United States, later adopted the principle of checks and balances as well as the veto.

Second, **praetors** (PREET • uhrz) served as military commanders and judges. They became very important because they actually created most of the laws of Rome through their decisions in court cases.

Third, **censors** registered people according to their wealth to determine how much they should pay in taxes.

The Assembly of Tribes. Citizens grouped into 35 tribes according to where they lived made up the Assembly of Tribes. The Assembly elected 10 officials called **tribunes.** Although they did not take part in day-to-day government, the 10 tribunes became the most important officials without administrative authority in Rome. They could veto Senate bills and the actions of public officials if they believed that the acts were contrary to the public interest.

The Senate. The most important and powerful of the three governing bodies—the Senate—included 300 men. The Senate controlled public funds, determined foreign policy, and sometimes acted as a court. In times of emergency, the Senate could propose that a citizen be named **dictator.** If the consuls agreed, the Senate gave the dictator absolute power for a term limited to six months.

The composition of the assemblies and responsibilities of the elected officials changed throughout the life of the republic. The changes stemmed from the common people's attempts to win more rights, conflicts known as "the struggle of the orders."

The Struggle of the Orders

In the earliest days of Rome, most men farmed. No one was very rich, and no one was miserably poor. As time passed, however, the distinctions among social classes became greater. A powerful aristocratic class, the **patricians,** gained control of the government. All other citizens were **plebeians** (pli • BEE • yuhnz).

Plebeians suffered discrimination for many years. Laws prevented them from holding public office or marrying patricians. They could not even know what the laws said because the laws were not written down. In court, a judge stated and applied all laws, and only patricians served as judges.

Gradually the plebeians increased their power by making demands and by leading strikes. They gained the right to marry patricians and to hold office in the government. In one of their greatest victories, they forced the government to write the laws down. About 450 B.C. the Romans engraved these laws on tablets known as the Twelve Tables and placed them in the Forum—the chief public square—for all to view.

Over the years the plebeians won additional rights. Laws banned debt slavery and permitted plebeians to fill public offices, including that of consul.

By about 300 B.C. wealthy and powerful plebeians had joined with the patricians to form the Roman nobility. From that time on, the distinction between patricians and plebeians was of little importance. Although the common people had the right to elect officials and make laws, they did not exert much influence. Since no official received a salary, only the wealthy nobles could afford to hold office. The nobles controlled the Assembly of Centuries and the Senate. The Senate overshadowed the magistrates. And ambitious tribunes, hoping for higher office, sometimes cooperated with the Senate in using their veto power. Therefore, through skillful political maneuvering, the nobles dominated the republic.

Roman Expansion

For more than 200 years after the founding of the republic, the Romans fought many wars against neighboring peoples in Italy. By 265 B.C. the Romans controlled all of Italy south of the Rubicon River on the northeast coast. Both military organization and wise policies helped the Romans achieve their victories.

The army. Roman law obligated every adult male citizen to serve in the army. Discipline was strict, and the soldiers themselves enforced it. No man could be a candidate for high office until he had served at least 10 years in the army, and for many centuries only citizens could serve.

The most important military unit of the Roman army was the **legion,** consisting of 4,500 to 6,000 men called legionnaires. Because of excellent organization, training, and high morale, the Roman legions eventually defeated even the great Macedonian army.

Learning from Pictures *On the battlefield Roman soldiers wore army tunics (right) and ornate helmets like this one (left), which shows battle scenes of Troy.*

Wise policies. To ensure the loyalty of their subjects, the Romans shared citizenship and political power with the people they conquered. The Romans granted full citizenship to the inhabitants of nearby Italian cities and partial citizenship to the inhabitants of more distant cities, including the Greek city-states in Italy. Partial citizens could own property and marry under Roman law, but they could not vote. The Romans also made treaties of alliance with more distant cities. The allies remained independent, but they promised to provide military assistance to the Romans and to support Rome's foreign policy.

The early Romans did not care to obtain tribute or slaves, but did expect subject peoples to provide land for Roman farmers' resettlement. This land settlement policy enabled the Romans to maintain military control over their conquests and to spread the Latin language, Roman law, and other aspects of Roman culture throughout Italy.

The Family

As the center of religion, morals, and education, the family became the most important unit in Roman society during the days of the republic. A Roman family included all unmarried children, married sons and their families, all dependent relatives, and the family slaves.

The father, known as the **paterfamilias** (pat • uhr • fuh • MIL • ee • uhs), had absolute authority. He conducted religious ceremonies, made all important decisions, and supervised his sons' education. Roman women enjoyed a higher status than did Greek women. The mother managed the household, did the buying, and helped her husband entertain guests.

Religion

The early Romans believed that spirits inhabited everything. The spirits of the home were the most important. These included the *lares* (LAR • eez), who were ancestral spirits, and *penates* (puh • NAYT • eez), guardians of the storeroom. Family worship focused on Vesta, guardian of fire and hearth. Other spirits governed every aspect of farm life.

Contacts with other peoples, however, changed Roman beliefs. Jupiter, for example, was at first an Indo-European sky god. The Etruscans gave Jupiter a human form. Later, after the Romans conquered the Greeks, Jupiter took on the characteristics of the chief Greek god, Zeus. From the Etruscans the Romans also adopted the practice of trying to learn a god's will by observing the internal organs of animals or the flight of birds.

In time the old family religion became a state religion with temples, ceremonies, and processions. The high priest, elected for life by a special assembly of 17 tribes, was called the Pontifex Maximus.

SECTION 1 REVIEW

1. **Define** republic, consul, veto, checks and balances, praetor, censor, tribune, dictator, patrician, plebeian, legion, paterfamilias
2. **Identify** Romulus, Pontifex Maximus
3. **Locate** Po River, Latium, Tiber River, Rome, Rubicon River
4. **Understanding Ideas** What did the Latins learn from the Etruscans?
5. **Interpreting Ideas** How was Rome ideally located for trade?
6. **Analyzing Ideas** (a) Name the three groups of citizens that helped govern Rome during the Republic. (b) Which group was the most powerful? (c) Why? (d) How were the nobles able to control the government?

2 The Roman Republic Expanded into the Entire Mediterranean Region

By the middle 200s B.C., the Roman Republic had extended its power over all of the Italian Peninsula south of the Rubicon River. The addition of so much land and so many new people to the republic increased its power and strength, but the burden of defending the republic also increased.

Rome Versus Carthage

Rome soon came into contact with Carthage, a large and powerful city on the coast of North Africa (see map, page 149). Originally a Phoenician colony, Carthage became a great commercial power with an empire that spanned the western Mediterranean. The Carthaginians boasted that the Mediterranean was a "Carthaginian lake," in which people could not so much as wash their hands without Carthage's permission.

After the Romans occupied southern Italy, Carthage feared that they would also try to take Sicily, with its Carthaginian colonies and markets. The Romans feared that the Carthaginian navy would close the Adriatic Sea and the narrow Strait of Messina between Italy and Sicily. These fears sparked a series of devastating wars between the two cities.

Rome and Carthage fought three wars which, despite intervals of peace, lasted from 264 B.C. to 146 B.C. We call them the Punic Wars because the Latin adjective for "Phoenician" was *punicus*.

The opponents were well matched. Rome had the better army; Carthage had the better navy. Carthage had more wealth. Roman lands were more compact and more easily defended. At first Carthaginian military commanders had greater skill, but later Rome also acquired able generals.

The First Punic War. The First Punic War began in 264 B.C. Initially Rome had no navy, but soon built one using a captured Carthaginian vessel as a model. The Romans used land tactics at sea, equipping their ships with "boarding bridges." The Romans would ram their ship into a Carthaginian ship and then let down the bridge so that heavily armed soldiers could stampede across and take the enemy. This clever Roman tactic succeeded, and in 241 B.C. Carthage asked for peace. The Romans made Carthage pay a large **indemnity**—money for the damages it had caused—and forced Carthage to give up control of Sicily. Within a few years, the Romans conquered all of Italy and had major overseas holdings. But the Carthaginians thirsted for revenge.

The Second Punic War. The Second Punic War began in 218 B.C. In Spain Hannibal, one of the greatest generals of all time, assembled an army including an infantry, a cavalry, and 50 war elephants. They marched across what is now southern France and began the job of crossing the Alps into Italy in August. The crossing proved to be an incredible disaster, made doubly difficult by early snows and landslides. Almost half the army and most of the elephants perished. At the end of September, Hannibal led his remaining soldiers, half-starved and half-frozen, into the Po Valley (see map, page 149).

Despite the condition of Hannibal's army, the Roman armies were no match for him. He defeated several of the Roman armies, which then retreated to their fortified cities. Since Hannibal had no

THE GROWTH OF THE ROMAN REPUBLIC
509 B.C.–133 B.C.

- Roman territory, 509 B.C.
- Territory added, 508 B.C.–265 B.C.
- Territory added, 264 B.C.–133 B.C.
- ← Hannibal's route, 218 B.C.–203 B.C.
- ✹ Battle site

AZIMUTHAL EQUAL AREA PROJECTION

Learning from Maps The destruction of Carthage made Rome the greatest power in the Mediterranean. What territories did Rome acquire after 265 B.C.?

siege equipment, he could not attack the cities. Instead he spent 15 years ravaging the southern Italian countryside. He also tried to win away the Roman Republic's allies. The Roman policy of sharing citizenship and political power proved its value, however, and the majority of the republic's allies remained loyal.

Finally the Romans turned the tables by invading Africa and threatening Carthage. Hannibal's

What If?
Hannibal

Hannibal's army suffered devastating losses as they crossed the Alps. Even so, the Roman legions were no match for the remnants of the once-mighty Carthaginian forces. How do you think the course of world history would have been different if Hannibal had lost none of his men or war elephants when he crossed the Alps?

government ordered him home to defend the city. In Africa he finally met his match—the Roman general Scipio (SIP • ee • oh). In 202 B.C. at the battle of Zama, near Carthage, the brilliant Scipio defeated Hannibal and his army, ensuring the supremacy of Greco-Roman civilization in the Mediterranean (see map, this page).

Once more Carthage asked for peace and had to pay a huge indemnity. It also gave up its Spanish colonies. The city of Carthage remained independent, but it had lost all its power.

The Third Punic War. Although Carthage no longer threatened the power of Rome, some Roman war veterans passionately hated Carthage. Under pressure from these groups, the Senate finally decided to crush Carthage. On a flimsy excuse, Rome declared war against Carthage in 149 B.C. After a bitter siege, the city fell in 146 B.C. The Romans razed Carthage and sold the surviving population into slavery.

Conquest of the Hellenistic East

During the Second Punic War, Macedonia had been allied with Carthage. Out of revenge Rome started a war against Macedonia and defeated it in 197 B.C. The Greek cities now came under Roman "protection." The Romans soon defeated the Seleucid king and gave parts of his territory in Asia to their allies. By 146 B.C., after more conquests, Rome's supremacy in the east was total.

Problems of Roman Expansion

The Roman state had grown from a loose alliance of Italian cities into a great Mediterranean power. The expansion, however, created many problems for the Roman Republic.

Government. Rome itself retained a republican form of government. But the operation of the government changed in certain ways to accommodate the problems of ruling a larger territory. The Senate controlled the army, finances, foreign affairs, and the new territories. The nobles gained even more power.

The provinces. The Romans governed the recently organized territories, called provinces, poorly. They did not grant the people of the provinces citizenship, nor did they make them allies as they did with the people of conquered Italian cities. Instead the Romans taxed the people of the provinces without mercy.

Provincial cities became centers of local government, and new cities sprouted in rural regions throughout the republic's territories. The provinces became a collection of city-states, each one subject to Rome. Each province had a Roman governor called a *proconsul,* appointed by the Senate and backed by a Roman army of occupation. Because his term of office lasted for only one year and he received no salary, the proconsul often took bribes and neglected the needs of the people.

The proconsuls were not the only Romans who became wealthy by stealing from the provinces. In Rome the censors contracted with officials called *publicans,* who agreed to collect the taxes and pay a fixed amount to the Roman treasury. The publicans could then keep whatever they collected in excess of this fixed sum. This system of collecting taxes, called *tax farming,* provided another example of the widespread corruption that plagued the provinces.

Changes in agriculture. Rome's annexation of distant territories lessened the role of the small citizen-farmer in Roman life. The Roman government owned much land in the new provinces and leased it in very large estates, or *latifundia* (lat • uh • FUHN • dee • uh), to anyone who could pay the price. Only wealthy people could afford to rent the land and buy the slaves who did the work. As time passed Rome came to depend on the provinces for grain, Rome's chief food staple.

The Punic Wars also contributed to changes in agriculture. The farmer-soldiers who returned from the Punic Wars were sickened to find their livestock killed, their homes in ruins, olive groves or vineyards uprooted or burned, and the land untended. The farmers did not have enough money to bring the war-torn land back into cultivation, nor could they compete with the low price of imported grain. They sold their land to wealthy people who then combined the small fields into huge latifundia.

Many of the now landless farmers moved to the cities. Not all of them could find jobs there, however, and they depended on the government for food. To make matters worse, the displaced farmers could no longer serve in the army because the republic allowed only landowners to fight. All that these landless veterans could do was sell their votes to the highest bidder.

Growth of commerce. As farming declined in Italy, trade within Rome's vast empire increased. The businesspeople of Rome formed a class called **equites** (EK • wuh • teez). They had great wealth but little political power. In addition to wealth from trade, they made money from contracts for public works, tax farming, and the loot of war.

Social change. The decline of the independent farmers and the growth of jobless masses in the cities weakened the ideals of discipline and devotion to the state. Romans now judged people by their wealth rather than their character.

Other changes had also taken place. As Rome expanded, victorious generals enslaved their enemies. Many of these slaves enjoyed relatively humane treatment. For example, owners often let skilled slaves keep part of what they earned to buy their freedom later. And by Roman law a freed slave became a citizen.

Other slaves led miserable lives. They often revolted. The most brutal revolt, led by a slave named Spartacus, began in 73 B.C. More than 70,000 slaves took part in this revolt. However, by

Baths

Ancient peoples were just as fond of taking a plunge into water as we are. The Romans were particularly fond of bathing and built many large public pools and baths. These pools and baths were often filled with water of different temperatures, heated either by natural hot springs or by furnaces. The Roman bather would go from one pool to the other, combining dips with exercises followed by massages with fine oils.

Some of the Roman bath houses also contained libraries, sports facilities, and shops. The public bath was a social gathering place where people could meet, gossip, and even do business. The largest public bath in Rome is credited as the main achievement of its builder, the Emperor Caracalla, who ruled in the A.D. 200s.

The Romans built baths wherever they settled. One such place in England, which had natural hot springs, became known as the city of Bath (top). People enjoyed its refreshing waters long after the Romans left England.

Today public baths are used as neighborhood gathering places and are extremely popular throughout Japan. There is also a very ornate public bath in Moscow, the capital of the Soviet Union, and in Budapest, Hungary (below). In the United States, outdoor and indoor public swimming pools provide the same enjoyment and recreation the ancient Romans knew.

71 B.C. the Roman army had crushed the uprising. The generals crucified Spartacus and 6,000 of his followers. **Crucifixion,** in which the accused was tied to a cross and left to die a slow and agonizing death from suffocation, was a common Roman method of execution.

SECTION 2 REVIEW

1. **Define** indemnity, latifundia, equites, crucifixion
2. **Identify** publican, Spartacus
3. **Locate** Carthage, Sicily, Zama
4. **Summarizing Ideas** (a) How were Rome and Carthage in competition with each other? (b) What were the final results of the Punic Wars?
5. **Determining Cause and Effect** (a) How did the government of Rome change as a result of the conquest of new territories? (b) What effect did the Punic Wars have on Roman agriculture?

3 The Roman Republic Was Transformed into an Empire

By 133 B.C. the Roman Republic faced many problems. Although courageous leaders attempted reform, the days of the republic were numbered.

The Gracchi

Two brothers, Tiberius and Gaius Gracchus (GRAK • uhs), were among the first to attempt reforms. Elected tribune in 133 B.C., Tiberius saw that some senators used public land for their own benefit. He therefore limited the amount of public land they could use. He also moved many landless citizens from the cities to work the land confiscated from

151

the senators. Although this policy made him popular with the masses, it angered and frightened many senators. A mob of senators and their sympathizers clubbed Tiberius and 300 of his followers to death.

His brother Gaius, elected tribune in 123 B.C., tried to increase the power of the Assembly of Tribes. Gaius used public funds to purchase grain to be sold to the poor at low prices. Other measures improved the political status of the equites. Again these policies outraged the senators. They soon gathered together 3,000 supporters of Gaius, killed them, and declared Gaius an enemy of the republic. To escape a public trial, Gaius committed suicide.

The violent deaths of the Gracchi marked a turning point in Roman history. From this point on, violence became the primary tool of Roman politics and replaced respect for the law.

Marius and Sulla

Gaius Marius (MER • ee • uhs), a military hero, also attempted reform. In 105 B.C. Marius defeated Germanic invaders and changed the course of Roman history. To fill his legions, he signed up any citizen, regardless of whether he had land or not. The soldiers served not only for pay but also for booty—whatever they could steal from the enemy and all the slaves they could bring home. When they were discharged, the soldiers expected their general to reward them with public land. In other words Marius had substituted a professional army for an army of draftees. As other generals followed these practices, armies became loyal to their leaders instead of to the Roman government.

The consul Lucius Cornelius Sulla showed what an ambitious general could do with a professional army. He led his legions from Asia Minor to Rome and drove out Marius, who had seized the city. A bloody civil war then broke out between the followers of Marius and Sulla. By 82 B.C. Sulla had triumphed. With terrible brutality and complete disregard for the law, Sulla executed thousands of Roman citizens.

Sulla ruled as a military dictator until 79 B.C. He placed all the powers of government in the hands of the Senate, which he enlarged by 300 members. Increasingly, however, army commanders who could count on the loyalty of their troops could force the Senate to do their bidding.

The First Triumvirate

Julius Caesar, a nephew of Marius, gained popularity during this period. An opponent of Sulla's, Caesar narrowly escaped assassination by bribing the guards Sulla sent to kill him. After Sulla's retirement, Caesar used spellbinding oratory and lavish gifts of grain to build a huge following among the poor citizens of Rome.

Realizing that his popularity with the people had made him many enemies in the Senate, Caesar joined forces with two popular generals, Pompey (PAHM • pee) and Crassus, in 60 B.C. The three formed a political alliance that became known as the First Triumvirate. (The word triumvirate means "rule of three.") With the support of the other triumvirs, Caesar became consul in 59 B.C.

Caesar in Power

Caesar realized that he could not win power without a loyal army, so he made himself proconsul of Gaul, a region in what is today France (see map, page 149). In his 10 years as proconsul, Caesar brought all Gaul under Roman rule and showed his superb abilities as a military leader and organizer. Caesar issued written reports about his campaigns and victories to keep the people of Rome informed. Students of Latin still read these clearly detailed reports known as Commentaries on the Gallic Wars.

Crassus died in battle in 53 B.C. Pompey, meanwhile, grew jealous of Caesar's rising fame. To head off his rival, Pompey had himself made sole consul. He then persuaded the Senate to order Caesar to return home without his army. Caesar refused to give up his military command and take second place to Pompey. Instead he led his army toward Rome in 49 B.C.

When Caesar reached the Rubicon River (the border between Cisalpine Gaul and Italy), a messenger from the Senate met him with the decree that he would be declared a rebel if he crossed the river with his army. Caesar hesitated a short time, and then made his decision. He ordered his army to march on to Rome. Today when people make an irreversible decision, we say they have "crossed the Rubicon."

Pompey and his followers fled to Greece, leaving the way open for Caesar to assume power. He first secured his power in Italy and Spain and defeated Pompey in Greece. He then went to Egypt, which had increasingly come under Roman domination. There Caesar put Cleopatra, a daughter of the ruling Ptolemy (TAHL • uh • mee) family, on the throne as an ally of Rome.

In 46 B.C. Caesar returned to Rome, where the Senate appointed him dictator for life. Caesar kept the republican form of government, but he was king in everything but name.

Caesar proved to be an able politician as well as general. He granted citizenship to many people in the provinces and gave public land to veterans and grain to the poor. Caesar reduced the Senate to the position of an advisory council and raised its membership to 900 senators. He also ordered the establishment of a calendar of 365 1/4 days, which was used in Europe until A.D. 1582.

The conservative families of Rome did not welcome Caesar's new status. Some 60 men who envied his great power formed a conspiracy against him. Two of these were men Caesar considered friends: Gaius Cassius and Marcus Brutus. On the stormy Ides of March (March 15), 44 B.C., the conspirators stabbed Caesar to death in the Senate.

The Second Triumvirate

Although Caesar had chosen his 18-year-old grandnephew Octavian as his heir, a scramble for power erupted after Caesar's death. While Octavian was in Greece, Marc Antony, a general and an ally of Caesar, and Lepidus (LEP • uh • duhs), Caesar's second-in-command, drove out the conspirators and took control in Rome. The three men—Octavian, Marc Antony, and Lepidus—then formed the Second Triumvirate in 43 B.C.

Antony led an army east and reconquered Syria and Asia Minor from the armies of Brutus and Cassius. Then, having fallen in love with Cleopatra, he joined her in Egypt. Meanwhile Octavian forced Lepidus to retire from political life and built up his own power in Italy.

Octavian: the First Augustus

Antony and Octavian divided the Roman world. Antony took the east and Octavian the west. In time, however, Octavian persuaded the Senate to declare war on Antony and Cleopatra. In 31 B.C., in a great naval battle at Actium in Greece, Octavian defeated their fleet. The following summer

Learning from Pictures *Augustus considered himself a citizen and tried to exemplify good citizenship, even using his own money to restore temples.*

Octavian captured Alexandria. Seeing that they could not escape, both Antony and Cleopatra committed suicide. The wars had finally ended, but so had the republic.

Determined to avoid his granduncle's fate, Octavian proceeded cautiously. The Senate appointed Octavian sole ruler, but he carefully preserved the outward appearance of the republic.

The Senate gave Octavian the title *Augustus*, which means "set aside for religious purposes" or "sacred." He has been known ever since as Augustus Caesar, or simply Augustus. Many later Roman rulers used the name *Caesar* as part of their titles.

Historians generally refer to Augustus as the first Roman emperor, although he did not actually use the title. Beginning with the reign of Augustus, the Roman state became the Roman Empire. Under his rule Rome's territory stretched from Spain in the west to Syria in the east and from the Rhine and Danube rivers in the north to Egypt and the Sahara in the south.

153

Writing About History: Formulating a Thesis Statement

The first step in writing an essay is to determine what you wish to describe, explain, or prove. The information or the data you have gathered helps you to complete this step. You can then use the information you have collected and your stated purpose to formulate a thesis statement. A thesis statement expresses the main idea of your essay. It serves the same function as the topic sentence of a paragraph, which expresses the main idea of the essay.

A thesis statement follows these criteria:

- It is a generalization.
- It uses significant data to express a point of view.
- It measures how the various parts of the data interact with or relate to each other.

How to Formulate a Thesis Statement

To formulate a thesis statement, follow these steps.

1. Choose a topic of interest. Begin to collect facts about the general topic and keep detailed notes.
2. Begin to refine the topic. Look for related facts. Make a generalization based on the related facts.
3. Organize the collected facts. Discard those facts that have no bearing on the general statement, or refine the statement even further to include the facts.
4. Write a thesis statement using the characteristics given above. Refine the generalization, turning it into a thesis statement that can be proven and that meets the criteria listed above.

Developing the Skill

Study the data below about significant events during the Roman Republic. As you read the data, think about what thesis statement you can formulate.

- The Senate, the Assembly of Centuries, and the Assembly of Tribes helped govern Rome.
- Over hundreds of years, the plebeians gained many rights.
- After the Punic Wars, slavery became widespread, and a new class of urban poor was created.
- The gap between the rich and the poor widened.
- Although the common people of Rome had many rights, the nobility dominated the government.
- The attempts by the Gracchi to bring about land and government reform failed because of resistance from wealthy landowners.
- After Marius promised his soldiers booty from their campaigns, soldiers began to be more loyal to their generals than to Rome.
- Julius Caesar became so powerful that the Senate named him dictator for life.
- Civil war followed Caesar's assassination, and the republic ended with the reign of Octavian.

The facts all relate to conditions during the Roman Republic. The first two statements show that the republic gave many rights to its citizens and that many groups shared in governing Rome. The next eight facts, however, detail events that led to the end of the republic. A generalization relating all these facts might be: The Roman Republic had a democratic government, but various events combined to end the republic. Another way of formulating this generalization, thus turning it into a thesis statement, is:

Although many people were allowed to take part in Roman government, the power of the landowning nobility and the growth of a professional army loyal to generals doomed the Roman Republic.

Practicing the skill. What other thesis statement can you formulate from this data?

To apply this skill, see Applying History Study Skills on page 175.

An upper-class banquet in Pompeii

154

The Julian Emperors

Augustus died in A.D. 14. For the next 54 years, relatives of Julius Caesar, called the Julian Emperors, ruled the empire (see chart, page 156). Tiberius, who reigned from A.D. 14 to A.D. 37, was the adopted son of Augustus. Tiberius proved to be an adequate ruler. His brutal and insane successor Caligula (kuh • LIHG • yuh • luh)—who even appointed his favorite horse as consul—was murdered.

Claudius, an intelligent and scholarly man who administered the empire wisely, followed Caligula. During his rule the Roman legions conquered Britain. But even Claudius could not escape the violence that almost always marked the imperial succession.* According to reports, his wife Agrippina poisoned him, perhaps with tainted mushrooms, in A.D. 54.

A disastrous fire swept Rome during the reign of Nero (A.D. 54–A.D. 68). Many people believed that the emperor started the fire. Whether or not the emperor was to blame, the Romans hated him because of his cruel and unpredictable policies. Facing certain assassination, Nero committed suicide in A.D. 68.

The Good Emperors

After the death of Nero, a number of emperors supported by the army ruled Rome. Then, in A.D. 96, Emperor Nerva came to the throne. He was the first of a group of five, known as the Good Emperors, who ruled Rome for almost 100 years. A Spanish general, Trajan, ruled from A.D. 98 to A.D. 117 and added new territories that brought the empire to its greatest size—about the size of the United States today (see map, page 159).

Hadrian, Trajan's successor, supported art and proved an able ruler. Born in Spain, he understood the provinces and spent much time organizing and Romanizing them. To help protect the boundaries of the empire, Hadrian built fortifications along the frontiers and encouraged frontier peoples to enter the army. He disapproved of conquering neighboring regions and gave up the areas that Trajan had acquired in Asia.

---

* The Romans never developed a formal policy of succession. Although many emperors named their successors, the Roman army often refused to accept the new emperors and assassinated them.

After the uneventful reign of Antoninus Pius, Marcus Aurelius, the last of the Good Emperors, began his reign in A.D. 161. A well-educated man who preferred studying Stoic philosophy to fighting wars, he nevertheless had to defend the empire against invaders from the north and east. These invaders would play a key role in the future of the empire.

SECTION 3 REVIEW

1. **Identify** Marius, Sulla, Pompey, Cleopatra, Marc Antony, Nero, Hadrian, Marcus Aurelius
2. **Locate** Actium
3. **Summarizing Ideas** **(a)** What was the First Triumvirate? **(b)** Why was it formed?
4. **Interpreting Ideas** **(a)** Why was Julius Caesar so popular with the common people of Rome? **(b)** Why was he killed?
5. **Analyzing Ideas** **(a)** Why was the Second Triumvirate formed? **(b)** What caused it to break apart?
6. **Understanding Ideas** What powers did Augustus hold as ruler of the Roman Empire?

---

4 The Romans Developed a Distinctive Society and Culture

Several essential characteristics helped the Romans build their empire and maintain it in peace. The Romans had a talent for ruling others and maintained their authority through an efficient government both at home and abroad. Law, military organization, and widespread trade and transportation held the empire together and brought peace for more than 200 years.

The period from the beginning of Augustus' reign until the death of Marcus Aurelius (27 B.C. to A.D. 180) is known as the time of the **Pax Romana,** or the "Roman Peace." The world has rarely known such continuing unity, peace, and stability.

Government

The Roman government provided the strongest unifying force in the empire and ruled a population of about 100 million people. The government maintained order, enforced the laws, defended the

155

Emperors of the Pax Romana 27 B.C.—A.D. 180	
27 B.C.—A.D. 14	Augustus
A.D. 14—A.D. 68	Julian Emperors Tiberius (14–37)* Caligula (37–41) Claudius (41–54) Nero (54–68)
A.D. 68—A.D. 69	Army Emperors Galba, Otho, Vitellus (Chosen by various legions during a succession crisis)
A.D. 69—A.D. 96	Flavian Emperors Vespasian (69–79) Titus (79–81) Domitian (81–96)
A.D. 96—A.D. 180	The Good Emperors Nerva (96–98) Trajan (98–117) Hadrian (117–138) Antoninus Pius (138–161) Marcus Aurelius (161–180)

*Indicates dates of reign

frontiers, and provided relief when fires or earthquakes damaged areas.

The position of emperor was a demanding one. He had to make all policy decisions. He appointed the officials who controlled the provinces and ran the entire government. The role of emperor entailed too many responsibilities for all but the ablest people, however. If a weak, incompetent, or selfish emperor reigned, effective government depended on the strength of the other government officials.

From the time of Augustus on, emperors appointed and promoted government officials on the basis of their ability alone. The positions were highly desired not only for the salary but also for the honor.

The Provinces

The provinces were governed more efficiently during the time of the Pax Romana than they had been under the republic, partly because the government in Rome kept a closer check on provincial governors. Any citizen in the provinces could appeal a governor's decision directly to the emperor.

The western provinces, especially Gaul and Spain, benefited greatly from their closeness to Roman civilization. The Romans constructed many new cities in the western provinces, each a small version of imperial Rome, complete with a senate building, theaters, and public baths. Most of the cities had aqueducts—bridgelike structures that carried water from the mountains. Most cities also had paved streets and sewer systems. Wealthy citizens of the provinces took great pride in their cities. They donated large sums of money for public buildings, streets, schools, and entertainment.

Law

Roman law also unified the empire. The code of the Twelve Tables had been created in a small agricultural society, and these laws had to be changed to address the many needs of a huge empire.

The Romans modified and expanded the Twelve Tables in two ways. First, the government passed new laws as needed. Second, judges interpreted the old laws to fit new circumstances. Both ways ensured that Roman law could adapt to fit the customs of all peoples throughout the provinces.

Roman judges helped develop the belief that certain basic legal principles apply to all humans. For example, Roman law established an idea we believe in today—that an accused person is considered innocent unless proven guilty.

In later years the Roman system of law became the foundation for the laws of all the European countries that had been part of the Roman Empire. Roman law also had a strong influence on the laws of the Christian Church.

The Army

Augustus had reorganized the Roman army. The Praetorian Guard—first organized by Augustus to guard the praetorium, or headquarters of the commander-in-chief—was a small, elite force stationed in Rome to protect the emperor. Citizens who served for 20 years made up the legions that were stationed in great fortified camps along the frontiers. People often settled around these camps, and these settlements eventually grew into towns and cities.

Other forces from the provinces or the border tribes aided the Roman army. The soldiers enlisted for 25 years in return for the promise of Roman citizenship at the end of their enlistment. Thus a population of trained soldiers was established to help guard the frontiers. An estimated 250,000 to 300,000 soldiers guarded the empire at the time of Augustus' death. Although this number increased under later emperors, the total number of Roman soldiers probably never exceeded 500,000.

In some regions the Romans built great lines of fortifications for protection. In Britain, for example, Hadrian's Wall stretched entirely across the island in the north. A line of forts ran between the Rhine and Danube rivers. Between the great camps of the legions lay protective ditches, fortresses, and walls. Many portions of these walls still stand as reminders of Roman military glory.

Trade and Transportation

Throughout the time of the Pax Romana, agriculture remained the primary occupation of people in the empire. In Italy itself most farmers worked on large estates devoted to vineyards or livestock. The provinces contained more small farms.

A new type of agricultural worker, a tenant farmer known as a **colonus**, began to replace slaves on the large estates. Each of these farmers received a small plot of land from the owner. The colonus had to remain on the land for a certain period and had to pay the owner of the land with crops. A colonus worked long, hard hours and had little to show for it.

The vast empire provided great opportunities for commerce, and the exchange of goods was easy. Taxes on trade remained low, and people everywhere used Roman currency. Rome and Alexandria became the empire's greatest commercial centers.

From the provinces Italy imported grain and raw materials such as meat, wool, and hides. From Asia came silks, linens, glassware, jewelry, and furniture to satisfy the tastes of the wealthy. India exported many products such as spices, cotton, and other luxury products that Romans had never known before.

Manufacturing also increased throughout the empire. Italy, Gaul, and Spain made inexpensive

Learning from Pictures A grooved channel, cut into the top of the aqueducts, carried fresh water from distant springs to large Roman cities.

pottery and textiles. As in Greece most work was done by hand in small shops.

Transportation greatly improved during the early period of the empire. An estimated 180,000 miles (288,000 kilometers) of paved highways joined military outposts with cities in the interior, and highways linked all provincial cities to Rome—the origin of the saying, "All roads lead to Rome." Bridges spanned rivers, and an imperial post carried correspondence from the emperor and his officials to all parts of the empire. However, even with improved transportation and communications, it took a Roman messenger at least 10 weeks to cross the empire, traveling at top speed and using every known means of transportation.

Living Conditions

The Pax Romana provided prosperity to many people, but citizens did not share equally in this wealth. The rich citizen usually had both a city home and a country home. Each residence included many conveniences, such as running water and baths.

The lives of the wealthy included much time for leisure—rest, exercise, public baths, and banquets. Reclining on couches, many wealthy Romans ate and drank enormous quantities at banquets. These lavish banquets frequently offered exotic foods. For example:

Appetizers
Jellyfish and eggs
Patina of brains cooked with milk and eggs
Boiled tree fungi with peppered fish-fat sauce
Sea urchins with spices, honey, oil and egg sauce

Main Course
Fallow deer roasted with onion sauce, rue,
Jericho dates, raisins, oil and honey
Boiled ostrich with sweet sauce
Turtle dove boiled in its feathers
Roast parrot
Dormice stuffed with pork and pine kernels
Ham boiled with figs and bay leaves, rubbed
with honey, baked in pastry crust
Flamingo boiled with dates

Dessert
Fricassee of roses with pastry
Stoned dates stuffed with nuts and pine
kernels, fried in honey
Hot African sweet-wine cakes with honey

Most Romans, however, ate three simple meals each day, including foods such as bread, cheese, and fruit. Many ate only cereal and vegetables.

Extreme differences separated the lives of the wealthy from those of the poor. The average Roman lived with very little furniture. The bed was the main piece of furniture, and chairs were chiefly camp stools or benches. Many of the 1 million residents of Rome lived in crowded three- or four-story concrete apartment houses, where fire posed a constant threat because of the candles and torches used for light. The massive wooden beams used in construction made the fires more intense. These fires, as well as the collapse of cheaply constructed buildings, often claimed hundreds of lives.

Most Romans were poor and hardworking. Some worked as artisans or farmers, but they had little security because of frequent unemployment and low wages. In Rome landlords charged high rents, but the government provided free grain to residents of the capital. This helped, but no one could survive on free grain alone.

The number of slaves in the empire declined greatly during the Pax Romana. With the end of

Learning from Pictures *Romans enjoyed music and games. This mosaic from Pompeii shows a group of musicians that includes a female flutist.*

THE HEIGHT OF THE ROMAN EMPIRE
A.D. 117

AZIMUTHAL EQUAL AREA PROJECTION

Learning from Maps   The Romans controlled the largest empire in the ancient world. What territories did the Romans acquire between 133 B.C. and A.D. 117?

foreign conquests, the Romans no longer captured and enslaved prisoners of war. As a result, the price of slaves rose dramatically. In addition, most people could not afford to feed, clothe, and care for a slave. An owner of a large estate might find it more profitable to free a slave and make that slave a colonus.

Amusements

Romans enjoyed the theater, especially light comedies and satires. Performers such as mimes, jugglers, dancers, acrobats, and clowns became quite popular. Romans also enjoyed savage and brutal sports. They made Greek sports such as boxing bloodier by using brass knuckles. As many as 250,000 spectators watched chariot racing in the huge Circus Maximus of Rome, a kind of racetrack. Organized "fan clubs" for the popular chariot racers had many members.

Thousands of Romans also enjoyed spectacles in the Colosseum, the great amphitheater in Rome. Wild beasts, made more savage by hunger, fought one another in the arena. Sometimes humans fought against animals. Often condemned criminals or slaves were thrown into the arena to be killed by the beasts.

Combats between gladiators—trained fighters who were usually slaves—drew the largest crowds. The gladiators sometimes fought animals, but they often fought one another. The fights usually ended in death for one or both fighters. When a gladiator was wounded, he appealed for mercy to the crowd, who signaled whether he should be killed or spared.

Science, Engineering, and Architecture

The Romans were less interested in scientific research to increase knowledge than in collecting and organizing information. Galen, a physician

159

who lived in Rome during the A.D. 100s, wrote several volumes that summarized all the medical knowledge of his day. For centuries people regarded him as the greatest authority on medicine. People also accepted Ptolemy's theories in astronomy. A scientist from Alexandria, Ptolemy believed that the earth lay at the center of the universe. Most people accepted this theory until the A.D. 1600s.

The practical Romans applied the scientific knowledge they gained from the Greeks in planning cities, building water and sewage systems, and improving farming and livestock breeding. Roman engineers surpassed all other ancient peoples in their ability to construct roads, bridges, aqueducts, amphitheaters, and public buildings.

The most important contribution of Roman architects was the use of concrete, which made large buildings possible in terms of both cost and engineering. Architects designed great public buildings—law courts, palaces, temples, amphitheaters, and triumphal arches—for the emperor, imperial officials, and the government. The Romans often based their buildings on Greek models. However, unlike the Greeks, the Romans knew how to build the arch and vaulted dome, and emphasized size as well as pleasing proportion.

Education

The Romans trained their children to be loyal citizens and to be obedient to their elders and superiors. They received their early education at home. The Roman father taught the sons farming and the duties of citizenship. The mother instructed the children in reading, writing, and arithmetic. Children also memorized the Twelve Tables.

The matron of the family taught her daughters to manage a household. In wealthy households girls also learned to sing, dance, paint, and play musical instruments. And although most Roman women did not receive a formal education, many upper-class women were well educated.

Every important town or city throughout the Roman Empire had elementary, secondary, and higher level schools. A boy or girl of the free classes entered elementary school at the age of seven and studied reading, writing, arithmetic, and music. At about the age of 13, boys entered a secondary school, where they studied grammar, Greek, literature, composition, and expressive speech. Former Greek slaves often taught the courses.

In rhetoric schools, where the chief subjects included oratory, geometry, astronomy, and philosophy, students received the equivalent of our college education. Students entered a school of rhetoric at the age of 16 and stayed as long as they liked. Wealthy students often continued their education at specialized schools such as the ones at Athens for philosophy, Alexandria for medicine, and Rhodes for rhetoric. In the Athenaeum at Rome, students could listen to the great orators of the day. Students in all schools paid fees for their educations.

Literature

Augustus and several of the Good Emperors encouraged the development of art and literature. Although the Greeks strongly influenced Roman artists and writers, a number of Romans produced works of great originality, particularly in the field of literature.

One of the most important writers of the late republic was Cicero, a great orator noted for his political works. Virgil, who lived during the reign of Augustus, ranked as the greatest Roman poet. He wrote the epic poem, *Aeneid,* a sort of sequel to Homer's *Iliad.* It tells the story of Aeneas, a prince of Troy and a supposed ancestor of the Latins. When the Greeks captured Troy, Aeneas fled and, after many adventures, came to Italy. His descendants Romulus and Remus founded Rome. Another Roman poet, Horace, wrote of human emotions in odes, satires, and epistles (letters). Yet another poet, Ovid, wrote love lyrics and the *Metamorphoses,* a collection of legends written in verse (see page 161).

Tacitus, one of the greatest Roman historians, wrote *Annals,* a history of Rome under the Julian Emperors, which shows his criticism of the government established by Augustus. He worried about the luxurious living of the wealthy and the lack of public virtue. Another of his works, *Germania,* provides the best account of the Germanic tribes along the borders. However, Tacitus may have exaggerated the virtues of the Germanic peoples because he wrote the book to shame the Romans for their low moral standards.

Plutarch, a Greek, wrote *Parallel Lives.* This work includes a series of biographical sketches, one of a famous Greek followed by one of a Roman whose life in some way resembled the Greek's life.

The *Metamorphoses*

Ovid, who lived from 43 B.C. to A.D. 17, was one of the best-known Roman poets. Although he wrote many works, his most famous was the *Metamorphoses,* 15 books of mostly Greek and some Roman mythology. With this work Ovid produced a masterpiece, or great work, for which he was hoping to become immortal. Using lively descriptions, he particularly demonstrates the richness of Greek mythology. Generations of poets and painters used his work for inspiration. The selection below recounts the story of Daedalus and Icarus, whom the legendary King Minos of Crete held prisoner.

DEDALE PERD SON FILS ICARE
Icare c'est en vain que ta foiblesse aspire
Au Sacré cabinet des Merveilles des Dieux,
La seule foy te peut guinder iusques aux Cieux,
Autrement tu fondras ton aisleron de Cire.

❝ Homesick for homeland, Daedalus hated Crete
And his long exile there, but the sea held him.
'Though Minos blocks escape by land or water,'
Daedalus said, 'surely the sky is open,
And that's the way we'll go. Minos' dominion
Does not include the air.' He turned his thinking
Toward unknown arts, changing the laws of nature.
He laid out feathers in order, first the smallest,
A little larger next it, and so continued,
The way that panpipes rise in gradual sequence.
He fastened them with twine and wax, at middle,
At bottom, so, and bent them, gently curving,
So that they looked like wings of birds, most surely.
And Icarus, his son, stood by and watched him,
Not knowing he was dealing with his downfall,
Stood by and watched and raised his shiny face
To let a feather, light as down, fall on it,
Or stuck his thumb into the yellow wax,
Fooling around, the way a boy will, always,
Whenever a father tries to get some work done.
Still, it was done at last, and the father hovered,
Poised, in the moving air, and taught his son:
'I warn you, Icarus, fly a middle course:
Don't go too low, or water will weigh the wings down;
Don't go too high, or the sun's fire will burn them.
Keep to the middle way. And one more thing,
No fancy steering by star or constellation,
Follow my lead!' That was the flying lesson,
And now to fit the wings to the boy's shoulders.
Between the work and warning the father found
His cheeks were wet with tears, and his hands trembled.

He kissed his son (*Good-by,* if he had known it),
Rose on his wings, flew on ahead, as fearful
As any bird launching the little nestlings
Out of high nest into thin air. *Keep on,*
Keep on, he signals, *follow me!* He guides him
In flight—O fatal art!—and the wings move
And the father looks back to see the son's wings moving.
Far off, far down, some fisherman is watching
As the rod dips and trembles over the water,
Some shepherd rests his weight upon his crook,
Some plowman on the handles of the plowshare,
And all look up, in absolute amazement,
At those airborne above. They must be gods!
They were over Samos, Juno's sacred island,
Delos and Paros toward the left, Lebinthus
Visible to the right, and another island,
Calymne, rich in honey. And the boy
Thought *This is wonderful!* and left his father,
Soared higher, higher, drawn to the vast heaven,
Nearer the sun, and the wax that held the wings
Melted in that fierce heat, and the bare arms
Beat up and down in air, and lacking oarage
Took hold of nothing. *Father!* he cried, and *Father!*
Until the blue sea hushed him, the dark water
Men call the Icarian now. And Daedalus,
Father no more, called 'Icarus, where are you!
Where are you, Icarus? Tell me where to find you!'
And saw the wings on the waves and cursed his talents,
Buried the body in a tomb, and the land
Was named for Icarus. ❞

Language

The Romans learned the Greek alphabet from the Etruscans and later changed some of the letters. The Roman, or Latin, alphabet of 23 letters, plus the *J*, *Y*, and *W*, which the English added after Roman times, is the alphabet we use today.

Long after the end of the Roman Empire, the Latin language continued to be used, with some changes, in most of Europe. Most medieval European universities used Latin in their classes, and the Roman Catholic church conducted services in Latin until the 1960s. For centuries all governments in western Europe wrote their laws and decrees in Latin. Latin is the parent of the modern Romance (a word derived from *Roman*) languages—Italian, French, Spanish, Portuguese, and Romanian.

Many scientific terms have either Latin or Greek origins. Although the English language developed mainly from the language of the early Germanic peoples, more than one-third of all English words have Latin origins.

SECTION 4 REVIEW

1. **Define** Pax Romana, aqueduct, colonus
2. **Identify** Praetorian Guard, Galen, Ptolemy
3. **Understanding Ideas** How did the army contribute to the protection and expansion of the Roman Empire?
4. **Interpreting Ideas** How did farming change during the period of the Roman Empire?
5. **Analyzing Ideas** (a) Why did trade expand so rapidly throughout the empire? (b) What products were traded and where did they come from?
6. **Summarizing Ideas** Name three important Roman writers and describe the writings of each.

---

5 Christianity Took Root in Judea

The Romans respected the various religions practiced in the provinces, if only to keep peace. However, as Roman power expanded, the Roman emperor became more widely regarded as a divine monarch. The Romans expected every resident of the empire to honor the gods of Rome and the "divine spirit" of the emperor. Such a ritual act, the Romans believed, would demonstrate the people's loyalty to the state.

Jews and the Roman Empire

In Roman times most Jews lived in Judea, which became a Roman province in A.D. 6. As monotheists believing in a single god, Jews could not honor the Roman gods or the "divine spirit" of the emperor, and the Romans excused them from doing so.

Many Jews in Judea hoped they could win their independence and have a king in the tradition of David. They yearned for a king like David—for a Messiah. (Each Jewish king was anointed, or smeared with oil, as part of his coronation. The word *Messiah* means "the Anointed One.")

As the years of Roman rule continued and independence became increasingly unlikely, the Jews began to think of the Messiah as a divinely appointed liberator. Various individuals claiming to be Messiahs appeared from time to time in Judea, but the Romans usually executed them as rebels. Occasionally the Jews would turn to radical measures and revolt against the Romans. After the great revolt of A.D. 66–A.D. 70, the Romans sacked Jerusalem, slaughtered thousands of Jews, and destroyed the Second Temple. Only the western wall of the Temple withstood the onslaught. Today Jews consider this wall, also known as the Wailing Wall, the most sacred site of Judaism.

The destruction of the Second Temple marked a major turning point in Jewish history. With the Temple gone, priests ceased to be the religious leaders of Judaism. **Rabbis**—scholars learned in the scriptures and in commentaries on religious law—filled their role.

Under the rule of the emperors Trajan and Hadrian,* more Jewish revolts erupted in Judea. In the last one, led by Simon bar Kokhba, the Jews struggled fiercely against Emperor Hadrian. After the Romans brutally suppressed the revolt in A.D. 135, they banned all Jews from Jerusalem. Jewish communities outside Jerusalem, however, carried on the Jewish faith and culture.

Christianity, the religion founded by the Jewish teacher known as Jesus of Nazareth, arose out of this setting. Christianity drew on the expectations

---

*Hadrian changed the name of the region from Judea to Palestine.

for a Messiah common in the region during these centuries.

The Life and Teachings of Jesus

Roman histories say very little about Jesus and the early Christians. Our knowledge of Jesus comes mainly from the Gospels of Matthew, Mark, Luke, and John—the first four books of the New Testament of the Bible.

According to the Gospels, Jesus was born in Bethlehem, near Jerusalem, and grew up in the town of Nazareth. He was said to have been a carpenter and a student of the writings of the Jewish prophets. In time he began preaching. As he traveled through the villages of Judea, he gathered a small group of disciples, or followers. From these he chose 12, the Apostles, to help him preach.

Jesus spoke of "my Father in heaven," and his followers believed that Jesus was the Messiah. He traveled with his disciples as a wandering rabbi, depending on the charity of the people for his needs. According to the Gospels, he created great excitement among the people, performing miracles of healing and defending the poor and the oppressed.

The teachings of Jesus have become one of the greatest influences on the Western world.

He accepted the Ten Commandments as guides to right living but gave them further meaning. According to the Gospel of Matthew, Jesus said:

> *"Don't misunderstand why I have come—it isn't to cancel the laws of Moses and the warnings of the prophets. No, I come to fulfill them, and to make them all come true.*"

He summarized the 10 rules in two great commandments: People must love God above all else, and they must love others as they love themselves. His many teachings include:

(1) God cares more for people than for their laws. He desires a new relationship between himself and humans based on his love, to which people respond in faith.

(2) Jesus saw himself as the link that would reestablish the loving relationship that God desires. Jesus called this new relationship the "Kingdom of God." The "Kingdom of God" would be both here on earth and in an eternal life beyond this world.

(3) God will forgive people their sins if they will admit the wrong and ask to be forgiven. People must also forgive one another in recognition of what God has already done for them and must not seek revenge.

Learning from Pictures
This Christian mosaic depicts Jesus on the road to Calvary to be crucified.

The Death of Jesus

Jesus claimed that he was the Son of God. When he traveled to Jerusalem in about A.D. 30, many Jews there hailed him as the Messiah and as "King of the Jews." Others, especially the conservative priestly class of Jews, denied that he was the Messiah and regarded him as a revolutionary.

The Romans feared that Jesus wanted to lead an uprising, and they considered him an enemy of the state. Jesus was tried before Pontius Pilate, the Roman governor. Pilate acted reluctantly, apparently because he feared the trial would ignite yet another revolt. Eventually, however, he agreed to Jesus' crucifixion.

The Spread of Christianity

According to the Gospels, Jesus arose from the dead, remained on earth for 40 more days, and then ascended into heaven. His followers believed that the resurrection and the ascension proved that Jesus was the Messiah, calling him Jesus Christ, after the Greek word for messiah—*Christos*. The resurrection became the central message of Christianity. Through the death of Jesus Christ, the Son of God, who had died for the sins of the human race, all people could achieve redemption. The disciples of Jesus set out to spread this message. At first the disciples worked mainly in the Jewish communities of the Middle East.

One of the people who did the most to spread Christianity was a Jew named Saul. Born in the town of Tarsus in Asia Minor, Saul converted to Christianity, took the name Paul, and became a great Christian missionary. Paul carried on his work not only among Jews but among all peoples. Between about A.D. 45 and A.D. 65, he journeyed throughout the eastern Mediterranean region, spreading the teachings of Jesus and founding Christian communities. Paul visited Rome, where, according to tradition, he was put to death.

Paul's Epistles, or letters, to Christian congregations in Greece and Asia Minor form an important part of the New Testament. Paul insisted that Jesus was not just the Jewish Messiah but a divine universal savior who would soon return to judge the entire human race. By following the teachings of Jesus, all people could be saved from the consequences of their sins. They could avoid damnation and instead enjoy the bliss of salvation in paradise after death.

Christianity and Its Rivals

Christianity spread slowly, but its appeal increased as life in the Roman Empire became more difficult. Emperor worship and many of the old religions of the empire no longer offered comfort to many people. The Persian cult of Mithras did promise happiness after death, but it excluded women. The cult of Cybele (SIB • uh • lee) in Asia Minor and the Egyptian cult of Isis worshiped goddesses, but it was expensive to belong to these cults.

Christianity, on the other hand, accepted everyone and charged nothing. It welcomed the poor and rich alike and promised salvation after death. In this world Christians were expected to be good citizens and to obey the laws. They were encouraged to practice charity and to care for the poor and outcast.

Persecution of the Christians

At first the Roman government viewed Christians as a Jewish sect and thus freed them from the obligation to worship the emperor. However, by the A.D. 100s it recognized the difference, and Christians had to make a difficult choice.

The early Christians were good citizens. Their religion taught them to respect government, but they refused to worship the emperor as a god.

To the emperors this refusal defied Roman religion and law, and they outlawed Christianity, seized Christian property, and executed many Christians. Sometimes the Romans used the Christians as scapegoats,* blaming them for natural or political disasters. As the Roman writer Tertullian (tuhr • TUHL • yuhn) reported: "If the Tiber floods or the Nile fails to, the cry goes up: the Christians to the lions!" Many Christians became **martyrs,** put to death because they refused to renounce their beliefs. The Roman efforts, however, failed to stop the spread of Christianity.

In the A.D. 200s, civil wars shook the Roman Empire, and many people turned to Christianity. City dwellers of the middle and upper classes suffered greatly, and many of them converted to this new religion, which gave them hope. By the end

---

*Many ancient religions sacrificed goats to their god or gods in order to obtain forgiveness. The term *scapegoat* came to mean a person or thing bearing blame for the actions of others.

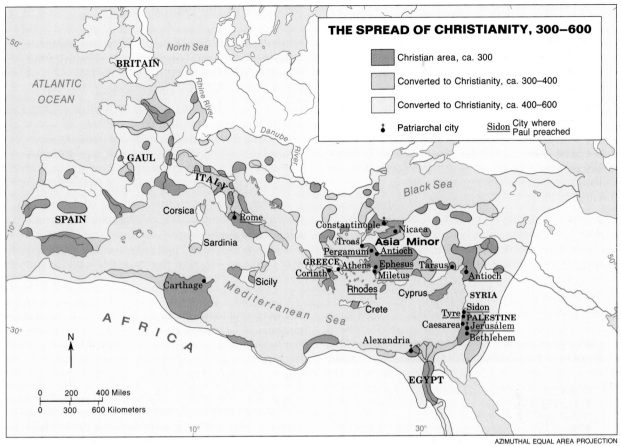

THE SPREAD OF CHRISTIANITY, 300–600

- Christian area, ca. 300
- Converted to Christianity, ca. 300–400
- Converted to Christianity, ca. 400–600
- Patriarchal city
- Sidon — City where Paul preached

AZIMUTHAL EQUAL AREA PROJECTION

Learning from Maps *Christianity grew from a small sect to become the state religion of the Roman Empire. What patriarchal city lies due north of Jerusalem?*

of the A.D. 200s, the Christian Church had become too large for the government to punish all its members, and Roman law accepted Christianity as a religion.

The Success of Christianity

The position of the Christians vastly improved when Emperor Constantine became a supporter of Christianity. According to Constantine, in A.D. 312 he was leading his army into battle when he saw a blazing cross in the sky. Beneath it were the words *In Hoc Signo Vinces*, Latin words meaning "By this sign you will conquer." He placed himself and his army under the protection of the Christian God. After his victory he protected Christians and converted to Christianity on his deathbed in A.D. 337.

Constantine's successor, Theodosius (thee • uh • DOH • shuhs), banned pagan worship. Christian

emperors persecuted the pagans, ordered the pagan temples destroyed, and abolished the Olympic Games because of their pagan rites. Within 400 years, Christianity had spread from its birthplace in Judea to all parts of the huge empire (see map, this page).

Organization of the Church

During the first few years after the crucifixion of Jesus, Christians saw little need for church organization. Christians lived together in groups, sharing their possessions and holding all property in common. They selected certain members to hold church services, preach, and help the sick and needy.

By the last years of the Roman Empire, a more definite church organization developed. The priests conducted services and performed baptisms and marriages. Above the priests were the bishops, who

165

were considered to be the successors of the apostles. A bishop headed the church in each city.

Five of the empire's cities—Rome, Constantinople, Alexandria, Antioch, and Jerusalem—gained special importance as administrative centers for the Christian Church. The bishops of these cities were called **patriarchs.** Over time the patriarch of Rome assumed the title of **pope** (from a Latin word meaning "father") and claimed supremacy over the other patriarchs. As successors of Peter, whom Jesus had named as his successor on earth, later bishops of Rome claimed broad powers.

Church councils also played an important role in strengthening the early Christian Church. In A.D. 325 the council at Nicaea (ny•SEE•uh) proclaimed the doctrine of the Trinity, the existence of three persons—God the Father, the Son, and the Holy Spirit—in one god, as a main article of faith. Today the concept of the Trinity is a central belief of Christians throughout the world.

SECTION 5 REVIEW

1. **Define**   rabbi, martyr, patriarch, pope
2. **Identify**   disciples, Constantine, Theodosius
3. **Locate**   Bethlehem, Jerusalem, Nazareth, Tarsus
4. **Summarizing Ideas**   (a) What did Jesus believe his mission to be?   (b) State three teachings of Jesus.
5. **Analyzing Ideas**   (a) What factors encouraged the spread of Christianity?   (b) Why did the Romans persecute the Christians?
6. **Organizing Ideas**   How was the early Christian Church organized?

6 A Weakened Roman Empire in the West Declined and Fell

The western part of the Roman Empire grew constantly weaker until it collapsed in the A.D. 400s. To understand this long period of decline, we must turn back to the time of the Good Emperors.

When Marcus Aurelius picked his successor in A.D. 180, he failed to show his usual wisdom. He appointed his weak, spoiled son Commodus (KAHM•uh•duhs). The end of the reign of Marcus Aurelius marked the beginning of the disintegration of the empire.

Problems of the Empire

Many capable soldier-emperors, including Septimus Severus, Diocletian (dy•uh•KLEE•shuhn), and Constantine, helped slow the decline of the empire. Even the best emperors, however, had to face population decline, unrest within the empire, and attacks from outside forces.

During most of the A.D. 200s, the empire experienced dreadful confusion and civil war. Between A.D. 235 and A.D. 284, for example, 20 emperors reigned. All but one died violently. The legions, moreover, did not perform their job of defending the frontiers. Barbarian tribes invaded every frontier of the empire.

The civil wars and barbarian invasions affected many aspects of Roman life. Travel became unsafe, and merchants hesitated to send goods by land or sea. The rural population grew even poorer than before. Population decreased throughout the empire, partly because a great plague spread through the provinces and caused several million deaths.

It became very difficult to collect taxes. Money was so scarce that people often paid taxes in grain. In A.D. 212 the government granted citizenship to all the peoples of the empire in order to collect from everyone the inheritance tax that citizens had to pay.

While taxes rose, money declined in value. The end of Roman expansion meant no new sources of gold. In addition, gold was being transported out of the empire because the rich continued to buy luxuries from abroad. To maintain the money supply, emperors minted new coins containing copper or lead as well as gold. When people realized that their coins had less gold in them, they refused to accept them at their face value.

In order to receive the same amount of gold as before, merchants raised their prices. We call the rise in prices caused by a decrease in the value of the exchange medium **inflation.** Inflation became so severe in some parts of the empire that people stopped using money and reverted to barter.

Only the major landowners remained relatively prosperous. As small farmers were forced to sell their land, large estates grew even larger. Many landowners left the cities and moved to their country estates. They organized and paid private armies and defied the government officials who came to collect taxes. With the decline in population, a danger that there might not be enough farmers

Learning from Pictures
This relief sculpture shows a Roman legionary and an attacking barbarian. How did barbarian invasions affect Roman life?

arose. The emperor refused to permit farmers who inherited their land to leave it.

The people in the cities fared no better. Many artisans tried to leave their jobs in the cities to find work in the country. To prevent this the government made use of the workers' trade associations, called **collegia** (kuh • LEE • jee • uh). A law made workers' membership in the collegia compulsory. The government required members of the collegia to stay at their jobs and to perform certain public services. When some people tried to resign from the collegia, another law made membership not only compulsory but also hereditary.

Diocletian

The Roman Empire would probably have collapsed in the late A.D. 200s except for the efforts of two able emperors, Diocletian and Constantine. Their reforms and reorganizations postponed the collapse for nearly 200 years.

The son of a peasant, Diocletian had risen through the ranks of the army to become a general. The army made him emperor in A.D. 284, and he proved to be an able administrator.

Diocletian reorganized the administration of the empire. Realizing that the empire had grown too large for one person to manage, Diocletian appointed a co-emperor. Each co-emperor, known as an *augustus*, chose an assistant, called a *caesar*, to help him rule and to be his successor.

Although the empire was not officially divided, each augustus administered approximately half of its territory. Diocletian ruled in the east, while Maximian ruled in the west.

Although Diocletian shared his power with others, he held supreme authority. He ended lawlessness within the empire and drove out the invading barbarian tribes. Diocletian also tried to improve commerce and manufacturing and to increase the wealth of the empire. However, his achievements did not endure. His policies proved impractical and difficult to enforce, and Rome drifted closer to economic ruin.

Constantine

The system of divided rule Diocletian established did not work well after he retired in A.D. 305. The rivalry between the co-emperors and their caesars became intense, and civil war racked the empire. Constantine, who came to power as a caesar in A.D. 306, became sole emperor in A.D. 324. His reign is known for two great achievements: his protection of the Christian religion and his creation of a new capital on the site of the former Greek city of Byzantium. Named Constantinople, the new capital was dedicated in A.D. 330. Today it is the Turkish city of Istanbul.

After Constantine's death in A.D. 337, the empire enjoyed some 50 years of stability. However, inefficiency and corruption plagued the government, and the poor suffered greatly. The Spanish emperor Theodosius was the last ruler to control a unified empire. After his death in A.D. 395, his two weak sons shared the throne. By A.D. 400, two empires existed, one in the west and one in the east. The one in the west grew constantly weaker. Power had shifted to the east, the center of wealth. Although the empire in the west collapsed in the A.D. 400s, the empire in the east remained until 1453 (see Chapter 8).

The Germans

It might seem that the western Roman Empire would have fallen apart from inner weaknesses alone. However, pressures from the outside also mounted as enemies attacked every frontier of the empire. The most important of these outsiders were the Germans, who lived beyond the Rhine and north of the Danube rivers. One Germanic tribe, the Ostrogoths, eventually migrated southeast to settle north of the Black Sea. Another tribe, the Visigoths, occupied land north of the Danube River (see map, page 169).

Germans in the empire. The northern frontier of the Roman Empire along the Rhine and Danube rivers had strong fortifications designed to stop the Germans. As early as the reign of Augustus, however, many Germans began crossing the frontier peacefully.

About A.D. 375 the Huns, an Asiatic tribe, began moving into the region north of the Black Sea. The nomadic Huns lived by raiding and plundering, and their fierceness terrified the people of Europe.

Pressure by the Huns pushed many German tribes into the empire. Roman officials mistreated the new settlers, however, and in A.D. 378 the Visigoths revolted. In a battle at Adrianople, they destroyed a Roman army and killed its leader, the eastern emperor Valens.

An ambitious leader named Alaric now became king of the Visigoths. In A.D. 401 he led the Visigoths west into Italy (see map, page 169). Alaric captured Rome in A.D. 410 and savagely sacked the city. Amid the destruction, the Senate issued a momentous decree:

> 66*T*he devastations of Alaric the Barbarian have destroyed imperial Rome, burnt its records, and ransacked its treasuries. You can no longer rely on Rome for finance or direction. You are on your own. 99

Final invasions of the west. The two parts of the empire drifted further apart. The east revived and gained strength, while the west sank into ruin as barbarians poured in everywhere (see map, page 169). One tribe of barbarians, the Vandals, so savagely destroyed everything in their path that today we use the word *vandal* to mean one who causes senseless destruction.

In the mid-400s Attila, a fierce leader of the Huns, led an attack on Gaul. An army of Romans and Visigoths defeated the Huns in a great battle at Châlons in A.D. 451. Attila himself died two years later. His army quickly broke up, and the Huns no longer threatened the empire. But it was now too late to save the western Roman Empire, which was weakened and shattered beyond repair.

A barbarian commander overthrew Romulus Augustulus, the last Roman emperor in the west, in A.D. 476. Because of this event, people sometimes refer to the "fall" of the Roman Empire in A.D. 476. Actually, no such thing as a single "fall" occurred, but instead the empire had gradually disintegrated.

Results of Rome's Decline

European civilization suffered a grave setback when the western Roman Empire collapsed. The Germans who invaded the west established tribal kingdoms, but they proved incapable of ruling an empire. The result was **anarchy**—the absence of any government at all.

Wandering bands of barbarians regularly attacked towns and cities. Most people left the cities in search of both food and greater safety. In the country, however, soldiers often trampled crops during battles, and weeds choked the fields. Learning declined, for no government existed to set up

BARBARIAN INVASIONS, 340–476

- Western Roman Empire, 395
- Eastern Roman Empire, 395
- ★ Battle site
- Huns 450 Tribe and invasion date

Picts 400
North Sea
Scots 376–500
Jutes 450
Angles 450
Saxons 450
BRITAIN
Baltic Sea
ATLANTIC OCEAN
Franks 428
Rhine River
443
Huns 450
Lombards 400
Châlons 451
GAUL
Burgundians
Huns 450
Ostrogoths 340–481
Vandals 409
416–507
Visigoths
Visigoths
Danube River
Huns 400
Black Sea
Corsica
Rome
Visigoths 400
376–395
Adrianople, 378
Constantinople
ARMENIA
Caspian Sea
SPAIN
BALEARIC ISLANDS
Sardinia
410
455
Sicily
Visigoths
Asia Minor
PERSIA
Tigris River
Euphrates River
Vandals 429
Carthage
Mediterranean Sea
Crete
Cyprus
SYRIA
A F R I C A
EGYPT
Nile River
Red Sea

0 200 400 Miles
0 300 600 Kilometers

AZIMUTHAL EQUAL AREA PROJECTION

Learning from Maps During the A.D. 300s and A.D. 400s, Germanic invaders threatened the frontiers of the Roman Empire. What Germanic group first invaded the empire?

and maintain schools. Libraries, with their great stores of knowledge, were destroyed. The number of literate and learned people grew smaller and smaller. Knowledge of the world and the past declined and was replaced by ignorance and superstition. Without cities, trade, communication, and literacy of some kind, civilization could not survive.

Why Rome Declined

But *why* did Rome decline? How did this mighty empire that accomplished so much disappear? For centuries historians have debated these questions. Some historians have stressed the institution of slavery as the initial cause of Rome's decline. Slavery produced a class of people who were always discontented and often in revolt. It tended to make slave owners brutal, selfish, and lazy. However, the

number of slaves decreased greatly during the period of the empire.

The army also has been blamed as a weakening factor. After the time of the Good Emperors, poor leaders and lax discipline plagued the once mighty legions. Military interference in the choice of an emperor made the government unstable.

Barbarian invasions played an important role in Roman collapse. However, tribes of barbarians lived on the frontiers throughout the time of both the Roman Republic and the Roman Empire. Their numbers were small compared to the millions of people who lived within the empire. Not until the empire had declined were the mass of barbarians able to break through the frontiers.

The important point to remember is that no one factor caused Rome to decline. Like many other complex movements and events in history,

169

Aristotle's Views of World Geography

People have always been curious about the world, and since the beginnings of time they have tried to describe it. The Greek philosopher Aristotle, for example, was the first to use observation to prove that the earth was round. He pointed out that when the shadow of the earth crosses the moon during an eclipse, the edge of that shadow is circular. He also recognized that the height of some stars along the horizon increases as one travels north. Aristotle correctly stated that this could only occur if the observer was traveling over the curved surface of a sphere. Curiously enough, even though he surely had many opportunities to observe the disappearance of ships over the horizon, he never wrote about this most obvious proof of the earth's spherical shape.

Some people saw Aristotle as the essence of the armchair explorer, for he used logic alone to explain his theories. He saw no need to verify his premises through experimentation. For example, Aristotle believed that he could explain the habitability of the earth solely as a function of distance north or south of the equator. He based this theory on observations of people who lived around the shores of the Mediterranean Sea. He saw no reason to explore north or south of the Mediterranean to gather further ideas.

According to Aristotle, if the earth is a sphere and the sun is revolving around it, those parts of the earth where the sun is most directly overhead—around the equator—must be far hotter than elsewhere on earth. Aristotle knew of the excessively high temperatures recorded in North Africa along the southern shores of the Mediterranean. If it became so hot and unbearable some 30° north of the equator, Aristotle reasoned life must actually be impossible at the equator.

Aristotle called those uninhabitable parts of the earth close to the equator the *torrid zone*. Further, he suggested that areas of the earth far from the equator composed a *frigid zone*. This frigid zone, Aristotle surmised, would be perpetually frozen and therefore totally uninhabited. According to Aristotle, the *temperate zone,* a region lying between the uninhabitable torrid and frigid regions, composed the habitable portion of the earth.

Aristotle believed that a south temperate zone existed to balance the north temperate zone in which he lived. However, he assumed that travel between the temperate zones would be impossible because of the intense heat of the torrid zone that separated them. Some of Aristotle's followers also accepted the existence of a south temperate zone, but they believed that it would be uninhabited because people there would have to walk upside down.

Aristotle certainly would be surprised by the modern world. Indonesia, one of the most populous nations on earth, sits in the middle of the torrid zone. Alaska, Canada, and Finland, located in the heart of the frigid zone, enjoy pleasant, warm summers filled with sunshine. And the people of Argentina, Australia, and New Zealand, who live in the south temperate zone, walk on the ground just as people in the north do.

Like Aristotle, modern-day geographers use logic to develop new theories. However, their theories are also based on statistics gathered over long periods of time. They test the accuracy of these theories through experimentation and careful observation. Today, compared to the clear, accurate vision offered by modern geographers, Aristotle's view of the world seems rather fanciful.

Ptolemy, the celebrated mathematician, astronomer, and geographer, used the observations of Aristotle and other Greek philosophers to develop the Ptolemaic System. This represented a stationary earth in the center of the universe with the sun, moon, and stars revolving around it.

the disintegration of the empire resulted from a combination of different forces. Between A.D. 200 and A.D. 400, no aspect of Roman life—political, economic, or social—escaped decay, each one acting upon the others.

Political weakness. Rome tried to control the entire Mediterranean world with a government designed for a small city-state. The miracle is that it worked for 600 years. In an age of slow transportation, the empire grew too fast and became too large for the kind of governmental organization the Romans had set up.

Another political weakness was the lack of civilian control of the military. Many emperors did win the loyalty of the army, but the emperor had to be strong to keep the legions loyal. Ambitious generals often seized control, assassinated the emperor, and assumed the throne. The common soldiers lost a sense of loyalty to Rome and instead served anyone who could pay them more.

Economic decline. The economic decline proved even more devastating than the political decline. Government expenses were heavy. Taxes had to finance the construction of public buildings, the maintenance of the army, and, later, the cost of two capitals—one in the west and one in the east. Heavy taxes could not support the government. For centuries the Roman government maintained itself on rich plunder from foreign wars. After Trajan, however, this source of revenue was exhausted.

Some emperors tried to fix prices and regulate business activity, but they failed. Decreased revenue for the government resulted in unrepaired roads and bridges and increased banditry. The greater danger in travel led in turn to a decrease in trade. When trade declined, manufacturing suffered and both eventually disappeared. Agriculture suffered the same fate as trade and commerce. Small farmers—once the strength of the empire—gradually lost their lands to a few very powerful landowners.

The Roman economy did not produce enough wealth to support a great civilization permanently. Wealth was concentrated in too few hands, and poverty steadily increased.

When the barbarians invaded the empire, Roman armies fought heroically, but when they lost, the empire lacked the leadership to recover. Moreover, morale collapsed because of the grinding oppression of the government. Taxes and public

service crushed the urban middle class. The farmers were now *coloni* (plural of *colonus*) and paid heavy taxes, while the great landowners did not pay their share of taxes. The corrupt courts did not serve justice. Yet the government seemed to be locked into this system and unable to change it.

Social decay. A third force of great importance was social decay. Early Romans may have been rude and uncultured, but they were stern, virtuous, hardworking, and patriotic. They had a strong sense of duty and believed in serving their government. Romans of the later empire lost this patriotism, took little interest in government, and lacked political honesty. For example, at a time when barbarians threatened every frontier, thousands of soldiers deserted, and countless legions abandoned frontier posts.

The Roman Heritage and Christianity

In the ruins of the Roman world, two key ideas did survive in the west—the Roman heritage and the presence of Christianity. The barbarians whose kingdoms had once been part of the Roman Empire were influenced by its customs and civilizations. The leaders of the barbarian peoples remembered that unity under an emperor had once existed. Ambitious rulers in later centuries tried to regain this unity.

At the same time, Christianity became the official church, that is, the one religion recognized by the state. Its leaders would play key roles in the post-Roman world. In addition, the Christian Church became the main preserver of Roman ideas and civilization.

SECTION 6 REVIEW

1. **Define** inflation, collegia, anarchy
2. **Identify** Commodus, Ostrogoths, Visigoths, Huns, Alaric, Attila, Romulus Augustulus
3. **Locate** Constantinople, Black Sea, Rhine River, Danube River, Adrianople, Châlons
4. **Understanding Ideas** Describe the economic problems of the Roman Empire under the rule of Diocletian and Constantine.
5. **Interpreting Ideas** (a) What was the system of divided rule? (b) What were the problems caused by this organization?
6. **Synthesizing Ideas** (a) What was the major reason for the collapse of the Roman Empire in the west? (b) Give examples to support your answer.

The Roman Empire collapsed more than 1,500 years ago. But in many ways it never died. Instead, it continues to influence people throughout the world even today.

Take language, for example. The Romans based their alphabet on that of the Greeks—who had borrowed theirs from the Phoenicians. But the modern letters that you see on this page are a direct gift from the Romans. So are Roman numerals. Even the planets of our solar system show the influence of imperial Rome because they bear the names of Roman gods—Mars, Mercury, and Venus, for example. Our calendar is based on the one developed by Julius Caesar in 46 B.C. July bears the name of Julius Caesar himself, August that of his successor, Augustus Caesar. The last day of the week, Saturday, honors the Roman god Saturn.

Latin, the language of the Romans, developed directly into the Romance languages of Italian, Romanian, French, Spanish, and Portuguese. The common origins of these languages becomes evident when you examine a few of their words. For example, the Latin word *luz*, meaning "light" is similar to the Italian word *luce,* and the French word *lumière*. And the Spanish word *luz* is exactly the same as the Latin word. Although the English language is a mixture of Old Norse, Old German, Latin, and Norman French, 60 percent of English words have Latin origins. For example, the word "republic" comes from *res publica,* Latin for "things belonging to the people." "Senate" came from the Roman council of elders, the *senatus.* Rome's legacy remains highly visible throughout the countryside of southern Europe, North Africa, and the Middle East. Roman bridges still span French and Spanish rivers, and roads that once connected Rome with its provinces survive today. In each city they conquered, the Romans added their own urban plan—a grid system of roads, temples, a central forum, baths, and theaters. Many cities that flourished under the Romans, such as Alexandria, Antioch, and the rebuilt Carthage, owe their layout to Roman engineers.

The ruins of Roman buildings, themselves largely based on Greek models, inspired generations of architects. Michelangelo used Roman models to design St. Peter's Basilica in Rome in 1547. And Thomas Jefferson studied Roman architecture when he built his home, Monticello, in 1770. Roman law left its imprint on the world, too. Codified in the second and third centuries, Roman laws were adopted by many countries in Europe and the East after the empire fell. Through Spain, Roman law became the foundation of the law of New Spain and remained in force when the territories became Texas and New Mexico. France's Napoleonic Code was based on Roman law. It was this law that the former French province of Louisiana used even after it became a state.

In hundreds of ways, Rome speaks to us all. But why? Why not the Persian or the Ottoman Empire? What made Rome so special? For one thing, the Roman Empire was huge. It once included what is today Italy, France, Spain, Portugal, Switzerland, Austria, Greece, Romania, Asia Minor, Libya, Syria, Morocco, and Tunisia, as well as parts of Great Britain and Germany. Across its far-reaching roads Rome sent not just legions but also commerce and culture.

Rome also lasted a long time. Founded, according to legend, in 753 B.C., it lived over 1,200 years, until the last Roman emperor, Romulus Augustulus, was deposed in A.D. 476. When Rome fell, the city of Constantinople laid claim to the entire Roman world. The Eastern Roman, or Byzantine, Empire carried on the heritage and organization of Rome for another 1,000 years, until it fell to the Turks in 1453.

The East was not the only place to keep the Roman tradition alive. The Germanic rulers who overran the empire saw themselves as successors to the Romans. The Frankish ruler Charlemagne, who spoke fluent Latin, was crowned "Emperor of the Romans" in A.D. 800, wearing a Roman toga and sandals.

In 962 Otto the Great founded the Holy Roman Empire, uniting the lands of Germany and Italy into a loose confederation of states. This empire lasted almost 1,000 years, until the reign of Napoleon.

Not to be outdone, Napoleon Bonaparte crowned himself Emperor of the Romans in 1804. He based his Napoleonic Code on Roman laws and encouraged a style of clothing and architecture modeled after ancient Rome.

Roman influence lived on not only in politics but also in religion. Christianity, first scorned by Roman authorities, was made an official state religion in the fourth century and took on many Roman features. Church structure and organization were modeled after Roman government. Roman law became the model for canon, or church, law, and the pope became the center of Christianity. Christian churches were styled after Roman government centers or "basilicas."

Over the centuries, our Roman heritage has been idealized, romanticized, and often sanitized. While much about Rome was corrupt and unappealing, it was Rome's sense of grandeur, its power, and its organization that made everybody want to be a Roman, and that ultimately passed its legacy down to us.

Photos *Page 172: Charlemagne (top), Roman Senate (bottom left), United States Congress (bottom right); Page 173: Monticello (top left), St. Peter's Basilica (top right), Roman Colosseum (bottom left), Roman theatrical masks (bottom right)*

173

CHAPTER 7 REVIEW

Legendary founding of Rome

Establishment of Roman Republic

BC 1000   900   753   509

Latin invasion of Italy

Etruscan rule of Italy

Chapter Summary

The following list contains the key concepts you have learned about Rome.

1. The early inhabitants of Italy included the Latins, the Etruscans, and the Greeks.
2. The Romans dominated the entire Mediterranean region by the 100s B.C.
3. Early Rome was a republic. The most important governing bodies were the Senate, the Assembly of Centuries, and the Assembly of Tribes.
4. After the struggle of the orders, the plebeians had many rights. The nobility, however, actually controlled the republic.
5. The growing importance of the army brought the Roman Republic to an end as military commanders repeatedly gained control of Rome's government. The last and most successful of these military leaders was Julius Caesar.
6. Caesar's grand-nephew Augustus, who succeeded him, became the first emperor. From the 20s B.C. onward, Rome was an empire, not a republic.
7. The abilities of the emperors varied greatly, but they all maintained internal stability and a continued expansion of Roman territory until the late A.D. 100s.
8. Education and literature flourished, as did engineering and architecture. However, corruption and political disorder gradually increased.
9. One of the world's great religions—Christianity—began in Judea. It was based on the teachings of Jesus.
10. Despite persecutions, Christianity spread.
11. About A.D. 300 two reforming emperors, Diocletian and Constantine, helped restore the empire.
12. Political, economic, and social factors all led to the collapse of the Roman Empire in the west.
13. The Christian Church helped preserve Roman civilization after the western half of the empire lost its strength and was overrun by invaders in the A.D. 400s. Only in the east did the descendants of the Romans preserve their independence in an empire centered on the city of Constantinople.

On a separate sheet of paper, complete the following review exercises.

Reviewing Important Terms

Match each of the following terms with the correct definition below.

a. latifundia
b. consul
c. veto
d. indemnity
e. inflation
f. Pax Romana
g. patriarch
h. republic
i. crucifixion
j. checks and balances

_____ 1. The rise in prices that a decrease in the value of the exchange medium causes
_____ 2. "Roman Peace"
_____ 3. Bishop of one of the five most important early Christian cities
_____ 4. Form of government in which voters elect their leaders
_____ 5. Refuse to approve
_____ 6. Money for the damages of war
_____ 7. Large estate during the later Roman Republic and the Roman Empire
_____ 8. One of the two chief executives who ran the government and who was also an army commander during the Roman Republic
_____ 9. Method of execution in which the accused is tied to a cross and left to die a slow and agonizing death from suffocation
_____ 10. Principle that prevents any one part of the government from becoming too powerful

Developing Critical Thinking Skills

1. **Understanding Chronology** Place the three items in each of the following lists in chronological order:
   (a) The First Triumvirate, the Third Punic War, the Julian Emperors
   (b) The German invasions, the life of Jesus, the reign of Julius Caesar
   (c) The Hun invasions, the Carthaginian invasions, the Etruscan invasions
   (d) The letters of Paul, Virgil's *Aeneid,* the battle of Adrianople
   (e) Reforms under the Gracchi, founding of Constantinople, division of the empire

Tiberius Gracchus as consul

Formation of First Triumvirate

Formation of Second Triumvirate

Rule of Good Emperors

306–337 Rule of Constantine

Formal division of Roman Empire

Overthrow of last Roman emperor in the west

BC 264   146   133   60   43   44   AD ca. 30   96   180   284   305   395   394   476   410

Punic Wars

Assassination of Julius Caesar

Crucifixion of Jesus

45–65 Journeys of Paul

Rule of Diocletian

Outlawing of pagan rites

Sack of Rome by Visigoths

2. **Contrasting Ideas** How did the government of the Roman Republic differ from that of the Roman Empire?

3. **Interpreting Ideas** How did the use of written law help to strengthen the Roman government?

4. **Analyzing Ideas** (a) What do you consider to be the most important contribution that the Romans made to civilization today? (b) Give reasons to support your answer.

5. **Analyzing Primary Sources** Reread the decree of the Roman Senate on page 168. (a) Why did the Senate issue the decree? (b) If you had been a Roman citizen, how would you have reacted to the decree?

6. **Comparing Ideas** Compare the role of citizens in Athenian democracy with that of citizens in the Roman Republic. What are the similarities and differences? (You may wish to refer to Chapters 5 and 6 for information on Athenian democracy.)

Relating Geography to History

Compare the extent of Roman territory shown on the maps on pages 149, 159, and 169. (a) What was the farthest extent of Roman territory to the east? (b) When did these boundaries represent the farthest extent of Roman territory?

Relating Past to Present

1. The Roman Republic had a citizen army instead of a professional army. (a) What kind of army do we have in the United States today? (b) What are the advantages and disadvantages of each type of army?

2. (a) Discuss how the persecution of the Christians in Rome affected the spread of Christianity. (b) Choose a country where religious persecution exists today. What effect does this have on the members of the religious group being persecuted? (c) On the religion worldwide?

3. The Roman historian Tacitus used his treatise *Germania,* which is about the Germanic tribes, to criticize the corruption and immorality of Roman society. Choose a modern book, play, or movie that comments on contemporary events or people and describe the "message" that is being put forward.

Applying History Study Skills

Before completing this activity, review Building History Study Skills on page 154.

Study the following data on the policies and practices of Julius Caesar. Then formulate a thesis statement based on the data.

- Caesar resettled landless soldiers throughout Gaul.
- Caesar employed people on public works.
- Caesar tried to reduce the debt of farmers.
- Caesar expanded Roman citizenship to the peoples outside Italy.
- The Senate declared Caesar dictator for life.
- Senators who felt that Caesar was trying to destroy the republic assassinated him on the Ides of March, 44 B.C.

Investigating Further

1. **Determining Historical Accuracy** Read Shakespeare's play *Julius Caesar.* (a) How did Shakespeare depict Caesar? (b) How did Shakespeare depict Cassius? (c) Based on what you have read about Caesar in this chapter, is the character in the play historically accurate? (d) Was Caesar really trying to become a dictator? (e) According to the play, how did Brutus justify his role in the assassination of Caesar?

2. **Writing a Report** In A.D. 79 an eruption of Mount Vesuvius destroyed the city of Pompeii in southern Italy. The volcanic ash that buried Pompeii preserved the ruins, and from them we can learn much about daily life during the period. Prepare a written report on the destruction of Pompeii. Include information that clearly indicates that the citizens of Pompeii were caught by surprise when the volcano erupted. Two useful sources are the article "Last Moments of the Pompeians" (*National Geographic,* November 1961) and Ron and Nancy Goor's *Pompeii: Exploring a Roman Ghost Town* (Harper & Row Junior Books).

3. **Dramatizing History** Use resources in your school or public library to find more information on the plot to assassinate Julius Caesar. Then write a script of a scene in which the conspirators decide when they will kill Caesar.

UNIT 2 REVIEW

Unit Summary

The following list contains the key concepts you have learned about the civilizations of the Mediterranean world.

1. The Minoans and the Mycenaeans created the first Greek civilizations.
2. The polis, or city-state, was the basic political unit of ancient Greece. The ancient Greeks were fiercely loyal to their own city-state, and they could seldom unite for very long.
3. The two most famous city-states were Sparta and Athens. Sparta was a militaristic state, while Athens gradually evolved into a democracy.
4. After stopping two Persian invasions, the city-states united under the leadership of Athens. This union was short-lived, however, and the city-states soon fought the devastating Peloponnesian War. Only when an outside invader, Philip of Macedon, conquered Greece was the region once again united.
5. Against the background of the Peloponnesian War, Athens underwent an unprecedented Golden Age. Athenian ideals of art, literature, and democracy were valuable contributions to Western civilization.
6. Alexander the Great created an empire that included Egypt, Asia Minor, and Persia. During this empire classical Greek culture merged with eastern cultures to form Hellenistic culture.
7. On the Italian Peninsula, the Latins, Etruscans, and Greeks influenced the culture of Rome. In time the Romans conquered the entire Mediterranean region and became a great empire.
8. The Romans made many contributions to Western civilization. Engineers constructed aqueducts; artists, sculptors, and writers created many original works; and architects first used concrete to build public buildings. Roman law formed the basis of our legal code, and from the Latin language emerged our present Romance languages.
9. Christianity developed in Judea and spread throughout the Roman Empire.
10. Although the Roman Empire in the west collapsed in A.D. 476, the empire in the east preserved the Roman heritage and traditions.

On a separate sheet of paper, complete the following review exercises.

Reviewing Concepts

Name the individuals who might have made the following statements. Explain why each statement is significant.

1. "King Philip of Macedon should not be allowed to rule over the Greeks."
2. "If I succeed at Salamis, I will have victory over all the Greeks."
3. "All the world should enjoy the benefits of Hellenistic culture under my rule."
4. "We must make Athens a center of culture, beauty, and good government."
5. "You must love God first and then love your neighbor as yourself."
6. "I wish to extend the *Pax Romana* to all the world and eliminate all possible rivals to my position as the first consul."
7. "I will write of the great legends of the ancient Greeks and how they conquered Troy."
8. "I believe that all information should be classified so that study will be rational and knowledge will advance."
9. "I will invade Italy from the north and conquer Rome with my elephants from North Africa."
10. "I will spread the teachings of Jesus throughout the world and write letters to answer people's questions about ethics."

Applying Critical Thinking Skills

1. **Comparing Ideas**   In what way did the concept of Greek democracy differ from the Roman concept of a republic?
2. **Interpreting Ideas**   (a) Trace the development of written law from Draco to Pericles to the Twelve Tables to Roman imperial law. Consider the individual rights of citizens, women, and slaves.   (b) Why was Roman law considered superior to Greek law?
3. **Analyzing Ideas**   How did sculpture, architecture, painting, mosaics, drama, and poetry reflect the religions and philosophies of Greece and Rome?
4. **Synthesizing Ideas**   What do these two periods in history have in common: Athens under the rule of Pericles and Rome under the rule of Augustus?

Relating Geography to History

(a) How was the geography of ancient Greece different from that of ancient Italy?   (b) How was the geography of these two countries similar?
(c) How did the geography of each region influence the civilization that developed?

Writing About History

1. Assume that you are either a member of the Greek Council of 500 or a Roman noble during the reign of Caesar Augustus. Write a diary describing what you did during a typical week. Describe the major landmarks you passed, the people you met, and the government activities in which you took part. Include a description of your home and family and any family activities in which you participated. Also, describe your job and friends.

2. Write an essay describing the Greek and Roman contributions to the development of government in the United States. Focus especially on the separation of powers, checks and balances, the role of citizens, and the powers of the legislature.

Further Readings

Bowra, C. M., ed. *Classical Greece.* New York: Time-Life Books. Shows the famous buildings, sculptures, and reliefs of ancient Greece.

Brion, Marcel. *Pompeii and Herculaneum: The Glory and the Grief.* New York: Crown Publishing. Describes these two ancient cities as they look today.

Bulfinch, Thomas. *Bulfinch's Mythology.* New York: Avenel Books. Describes various Greek myths, gods, and goddesses.

Hadas, Moses, ed. *Imperial Rome.* New York: Time-Life Books. Describes the history of the Roman Empire.

Lane Fox, Robin. *The Search for Alexander.* New York: Little, Brown and Company. Analyzes the life of Alexander the Great.

Unit Two Chronology

Date	Political and Social Developments	Technological and Scientific Advances	Visual Arts and Literature	Religious and Philosophical Thought
3000 B.C.— 1500 B.C.	Minoan civilization **5*** Mycenaean invasion of Greece **5**		Minoan art **5**	Minoan bull worship **5**
1500 B.C.— 500 B.C.	Latin invasion of Italy **7** Trojan War **5** Greek Age of Kings **5** Etruscans rule Italy **7** Draco's law codes **5**	Hippocrates and medicine **6** Pythagoras **6**	*Iliad* and *Odyssey* **5**	Greek polytheism **5**
500 B.C.— 250 B.C.	Roman Republic begins **7** Cleisthenes **5** Golden Age of Greece **6** Persian Wars **5** Peloponnesian War **5** Alexander the Great **6**	*Elements* (Euclid) **6** Greek temples **6**	Sophocles **6** Parthenon **6** *Republic* **6** *Politics* **6** Euripides **6**	Roman lares and penates **7** Socrates **6** Cynicism, Stoicism, Epicureanism **6**
250 B.C.— 0	Punic Wars **7** Rome invades Greece and Egypt **7**	Roman roads **7**	Virgil's *Aeneid* **7** Ovid's *Metamorphoses* **7**	
0— A.D. 250	Pax Romana **7** Caesar Augustus **7**	Galen and medicine **7** Ptolemy **7** Colosseum in Rome **7**	Tacitus' *Germania* **7** Plutarch's *Parallel Lives* **7** Paul's Epistles **7**	Roman emperor worship **7** Christianity and Paul's mission **7**
A.D. 250— A.D. 500	Roman civil wars **7** Constantine moves to Byzantium **7** Barbarian invasions of West **7** Rome falls **7**			Christianity official religion **7**

*Indicates chapter in which development is discussed

Civilizations of the Mediterranean World

5 Greek City-states Developed in the Mediterranean Region

On the southern end of the mountainous Balkan Peninsula, as well as in Asia Minor and on the nearby islands, one of the greatest civilizations the world has ever known—Greek civilization—developed.

Early Greek City-states

A great civilization—Minoan civilization—flourished on the island of Crete in the Mediterranean Sea between about 2000 B.C. and 1400 B.C. Although the great civilizations of nearby Egypt and the Fertile Crescent influenced Minoan civilization, the Minoans added ideas of their own. Remains show that they equipped the royal palace and the homes of the nobles with running water. They were decorated with colorful frescoes—paintings made on wet plaster walls. Artisans made beautiful, delicately carved figures of ivory, stone, gold, silver, and bronze.

While Minoan civilization was developing, important changes were taking place on the Greek mainland. Beginning about 2000 B.C. a warlike people known as the Mycenaeans entered Greece from the north. The Mycenaeans conquered Crete and were in turn influenced by Minoan civilization. By 1200 B.C., however, the major Mycenaean cities had been destroyed and more primitive Greeks—the Dorians—moved into the peninsula.

Because of the geography of Greece and their own tribal organization, the early Greeks established city-states, such as Athens and Sparta, in the ninth and eighth centuries B.C. The Greek word for city-state—polis—originally meant a fort, a refuge in time of danger. As a village or city grew up around the fort, *polis* came to mean not only the fort, but also the city and its surrounding region.

Greek Government and Society

The early city-states were monarchies that constantly waged war among themselves. Despite this warfare, the Greeks gradually made significant advances. For example, they developed religious beliefs that sought to explain the mysteries of the physical world, the passions that could make people lose self-control, and how to gain such benefits as long life, good fortune, and abundant harvests. Because the gods were thought to be pleased by displays of strength and courage, the Greeks held athletic contests in their honor. Most famous were the games at Olympia, held every fourth year in honor of Zeus.

Over time, the Greeks developed new forms of government. First, nobles—the chief landowners—began to govern many city-states in a form of government known as aristocracy. As the Greek people chafed under the rule of aristocracies, many city-states adopted tyrannies in which a strong leader—a tyrant—seized power. Tyrants were not always harsh rulers. To the contrary, many of the tyrants were excellent rulers who encouraged trade and passed just laws.

As Greek government changed from monarchy to aristocracy to tyranny, the idea of popular government—that people could and should rule themselves and not be ruled by others—began to take root in many city-states. When cities ousted their tyrants, some restored the old monarchies or aristocracies. Others developed the form of government called democracy—a government in which all citizens took part.

Sparta and Athens

Similarities and differences existed among Greek city-states. The wide range of differences shows clearly in a comparison of the two city-states that became the most important, Sparta and Athens.

Sparta. The population of Sparta was divided into three groups. The citizens descended from the Dorian invaders controlled the government. The Spartans called the second group of people by the Greek word that meant "neighbors." They were free, but were not citizens. They lived in the towns, and most of them worked in commerce and industry. Some "neighbors" became rich, but they could never be citizens. The lowest group were the helots. Because the Spartans lived in constant fear of a helot revolt, they tried to prevent the helots from developing any leaders.

Sparta regulated the lives of its citizens from birth to death. All the rules had a single basic aim: to make every adult male citizen part of an efficient military machine designed to control the conquered people and extend Spartan power.

Athens. As in Sparta, the population of Athens was divided into three groups. First were the citizens. Next came the aliens—those who were not Athenians—who were called metics. Most metics were merchants or skilled workers. They were free but could not own land or take part in government. Metics, however, paid the same taxes as citizens and moved about freely. At the bottom were the slaves.

After the Age of Kings, Athens had an aristocratic government. However, four rulers—Draco, Solon, Pisistratus (pi • SIS • truht • uhs), and Cleisthenes (KLYS • thuh • neez)—helped change the political development of Athens. Each ruler helped Athens move closer to democracy until Cleisthenes established what we call direct democracy. That is, all citizens participated directly in making decisions.

Daily Life in Athens

The citizens of Athens and the other Greek city-states lived in much the same way. Their lives consisted of work, recreation, and the fulfillment of their responsibilities to the city-state.

Farming was the most honored occupation for an Athenian. More than half of all citizens were farmers. Foreign trade and manufacturing were also important to the Athenian economy.

Although the Athenians built magnificent temples and other public buildings, their private homes remained simple. Athenians believed that money should be spent on buildings to benefit the whole community, not on private homes.

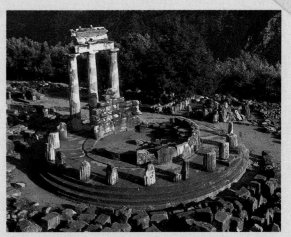

Temple of Athena at Delphi

Expansion of Greek Civilization

In 546 B.C. Cyrus of Persia conquered the Greek city-states on the western shores of Asia Minor. Then three Persian emperors—Cyrus, Darius, and Xerxes—sent huge armies to conquer the mainland Greeks. However, by 479 B.C. a combined Greek army had defeated the remnants of the Persian army at Plataea (pluh • TEE • uh).

After these destructive wars, the Greek city-states made several attempts to unify. The most notable was the Delian League under the leadership of Athens.

During this time Pericles (PER • uh • kleez) rose to power in Athens. Under his rule Athens became a complete democracy.

Even the firm control of Athens under Pericles could not unify the Greek city-states, however. Tensions between the city-states rose until a devastating war known as the Peloponnesian War broke out. After almost a generation of warfare, Athens finally surrendered to Sparta in 404 B.C.

6 Greek Civilization Triumphed During the Golden Age and the Hellenistic Age

Greek culture reached new heights during the 400s B.C., a period so magnificent we call it the *Golden Age.*

Greek Art

After the Persian Wars, the wealth and power of Athens attracted artists and teachers from throughout Greece to the city.

Architecture. The Athenians made beauty a part of their daily life. They showed their love of Athens, and their pride in it, by erecting many impressive public buildings such as temples, gymnasiums, and theaters. They decorated these structures—such as the magnificent Parthenon that crowned the Acropolis—with their finest works of art, especially sculpture.

Painting. The best-preserved Greek paintings are those used to decorate vases. Vase painters illustrated everyday life as well as myths. They delighted in showing graceful and natural movements of their subjects.

Sculpture. Three great sculptors typify Greek sculpture. First was Myron, whose most famous figure is the Discus Thrower. The second was Phidias (FID • ee • uhs), who created the two wonderful statues of Athena in the Parthenon. The third was Praxiteles (prak • SIT • uh • leez), who crafted delicate, lifelike, and often life-sized figures.

The nature of Greek art. Greek art reflected how Greeks viewed themselves and the world. First, Greek art glorified humans as the most important creatures in the universe. Second, Greek art symbolized the pride of the people in their city-states. At the same time, it honored the gods, thanked them for life and fortune, and tried to win their favor. Third, all Greek art expressed Greek ideals of harmony, balance, order, and moderation—the qualities of simplicity and restraint. Finally, the Greeks believed in combining beauty and usefulness. To them, the useful, the beautiful, and the good were closely bound together.

Philosophers and Writers

The Greeks were eager to learn all they could and to think through everything that the human mind is capable of understanding. These characteristics are clearly shown in the record of the Greek thinkers and writers.

Socrates. One of the greatest thinkers and teachers of all time was Socrates (SAHK • ruh • teez), who lived in Athens from 469 B.C. to 399 B.C. Socrates wanted people to learn to think for themselves and not imitate their elders. Only

Battle of Issus

then could they learn wisdom.

Socrates inspired great love among his followers, but he also made enemies. Even though Socrates honored the gods of the city, his enemies accused him of denying the existence of the many Greek gods. He was found guilty of teaching false religion and corrupting the minds of Athenian youth and was sentenced to death.

Plato. After Socrates' death, his student Plato began to teach in the grounds of the Academy, a public park and athletic field. One of Plato's major works is the *Republic*, in which he described his belief that the ideal government would be led by the most intelligent people of the polis.

Aristotle. Among Plato's students in the Academy was a young man named Aristotle, who founded his own school at Athens in 335 B.C. In order to describe the principles of government, Aristotle studied the political organization of 150 city-states and recorded his conclusions in a book called *Politics*. He concluded that the best government was one in which the middle class—those people who were neither wealthy nor poor—played an important role.

Mathematics and science. In the 500s B.C., before the Golden Age, Pythagoras (puh • THAG • uh • ruhs), a philosopher and mathematician, wrote that everything could be explained or expressed with numbers. He is probably best known for the Pythagorean theorem, the geometric theory which states that the square of the hypotenuse of a right triangle is equal to the sum of the squares of the other two sides.

History. The Greeks were the first people to take the writing of history seriously. Herodotus and Thucydides were the first great historians of the Western world.

Greek drama. The Greeks were the first people to write dramas—plays usually involving conflict and emotion through action and dialogue. It is in this form of literature that they excelled. Playwrights wrote both tragedies—showing the major character struggling unsuccessfully against fate—and comedies, in which the central characters succeeded in solving their problems.

Alexander the Great

In 359 B.C. a remarkable young man known as Philip of Macedon became king of Macedonia to the north of Greece and proceeded to conquer the quarrelsome Greek city-states. But it was Philip's son Alexander who had a lasting impact on history. By 331 B.C. Alexander had conquered Asia Minor, Syria, Egypt, Mesopotamia, and the Persian Empire and was attempting to conquer India. After a long campaign, however, he turned back and started the long journey home. On the journey, in 323 B.C., Alexander died in Babylon.

Although Alexander's empire broke up shortly after his death, his policies had long-lasting impact. Greek culture spread rapidly, and merged with other cultures to become what is known as Hellenistic culture.

Hellenistic Culture

Hellenistic society included a small class of very wealthy people and a large class of miserably poor people. However, the middle class grew because of the many opportunities for wealth.

Trade, the most profitable activity, radiated from the main trading centers in the cities of Alexandria, in Egypt; Rhodes, on the island of Rhodes off the coast of Asia Minor; and Antioch, in Syria. Trade routes now connected the whole Mediterranean world and even reached as far east as India.

The philosophers of the Hellenistic Age were more concerned with ethics than with fundamental questions of reality and human existence. There were three chief schools, or groups—the Cynics, the Stoics, and the Epicureans. The Cynics taught that people should seek virtue only. Stoics believed that divine reason directed the world. Epicureans taught that the aim of life was to seek pleasure and avoid pain.

Greeks of the Hellenistic Age were outstanding scientists. For example, Euclid developed geometry into a system by showing how geometric statements of truth, or theorems, develop logically from one another. And Archimedes (ahr • kuh • MEED • eez) used geometry to measure spheres, cones, and cylinders. He also calculated the value of π (pi)—the ratio of the circumference of a circle to its diameter—and used mathematics to explain the principle of the lever.

7 Rome Ruled the Western World for Centuries

The date 146 B.C. is often given as the end of the Hellenistic Age because by that year the Romans had extended their power over a large part of the eastern Mediterranean.

The Roman Republic

Although many peoples inhabited the Italian Peninsula in ancient times, the people who had the greatest impact on world history were the Romans. Early in their history, the Romans set up a republic, a form of government in which voters elect their leaders. Three groups of citizens helped govern Rome: the Assembly of Centuries, the Assembly of Tribes, and the Senate.

For more than 200 years after the founding of the Republic, the Romans fought many wars against neighboring peoples in Italy. By 265 B.C. the Romans controlled all of Italy south of the Rubicon River on the northeast coast. Both military organization and wise policies helped the Romans achieve their victories.

Roman Expansion in the Mediterranean

Rome soon came into contact with Carthage, a large and powerful city on the coast of North Africa. In a series of three wars, called the Punic Wars, the Romans completely destroyed their rival city. At the same time, Rome conquered the Hellenistic East.

Rome's annexation of distant territories lessened the role of the small citizen-farmer in Roman life. As land and slaves became more expensive, many citizen-farmers lost their lands and moved to the cities where they joined the unemployed masses.

181

From Republic to Empire

By 133 B.C. the Roman Republic faced many problems. Although leaders such as Tiberius, Gaius Gracchus (GRAK • uhs), Gaius Marius (MER • ee • uhs), and Lucius Cornelius Sulla attempted reforms, their programs met with little success.

Julius Caesar, who became dictator for life in 46 B.C., had the most impact. Although Caesar kept the republican form of government, he was king in everything but name. The conservative families of Rome did not welcome Caesar's new status, however, and he was assassinated in 44 B.C.

A scramble for power between Caesar's chosen heir Octavian and Marc Antony erupted soon after Caesar's death. But by 31 B.C. Octavian had defeated Marc Antony and taken the title *Augustus*, which means "set aside for religious purposes" or "sacred." He has been known ever since as Augustus Caesar, or simply Augustus, and is considered the first Roman emperor.

Roman Society and Culture

Law, military organization, and widespread trade and transportation held the empire together and brought peace for over 200 years—a period known as the Roman Peace, or Pax Romana.

Trade and transportation. Throughout the time of the Pax Romana, agriculture remained the primary occupation of people in the empire. In Italy itself most farmers worked on large estates devoted to vineyards or livestock. The provinces contained more small farms.

The vast empire provided great opportunities for commerce, and the exchange of goods was easy. Taxes on trade were low, and Roman currency was used everywhere. Rome and Alexandria in Egypt became the empire's greatest commercial centers.

Manufacturing also increased throughout the empire. Italy, Gaul, and Spain made inexpensive pottery and textiles. As in Greece, most work was done by hand in small shops.

Living conditions. The Pax Romana provided prosperity to many people, but wealth was not evenly distributed. The rich citizen usually had both a city home and a country home. Each residence included many conveniences, such as running water and baths. In contrast, the average Roman lived in a poorly constructed apartment building with very little furniture.

Science, engineering, and architecture. The Romans were less interested in scientific research to increase knowledge than in collecting and organizing information. Galen, a physician, wrote several volumes that summarized all the medical knowledge of his day. Ptolemy's theories in astronomy were also widely accepted. A scientist from Alexandria, Ptolemy believed that the earth was the center of the universe. Most people accepted this theory until the A.D. 1600s.

Education. Every important town or city throughout the Roman Empire had elementary, secondary, and higher level schools. A boy or girl of the free classes entered elementary school at the age of seven and studied reading, writing, arithmetic, and music. At about the age of 13, boys entered a secondary school, where they studied grammar, Greek, literature, good writing, and expressive speech. Greeks who had been slaves often taught the courses.

Literature. Although Greek influence was strong, a number of Romans produced literary works of distinction. For example, students still study the works of Cicero, Tacitus, Virgil, Ovid, and Plutarch to catch a glimpse of how the Romans thought and lived.

Christianity

One of the world's great religions—Christianity—began during the Roman Empire in the Roman-controlled territory of Judea. It was founded by a Jew known as Jesus of Nazareth.

Roman histories do not refer to Jesus at all. Our knowledge of Jesus comes mainly from the Gospels of Matthew, Mark, Luke, and John—the first four books of the New Testament of the Bible.

According to the Gospels, Jesus was born in Bethlehem, grew up in Nazareth, worked for a time as a carpenter, and began preaching as a young adult. Jesus spoke of "my Father in heaven," and his followers believed that Jesus was the Messiah, the Son of God.

The teachings of Jesus have become one of the greatest influences on the Western world. He accepted the Hebrew Ten Commandments as guides to right living but gave them further meaning. He summarized the 10 rules in two great commandments: People must love God above all else, and they must love others as they love themselves. His many teachings include:

The Colosseum in Rome

(1) God cares more for people than for laws.

(2) Jesus saw himself as the link that would reestablish the loving relationship that God desires. Jesus referred to this new relationship the "Kingdom of God."

(3) God will forgive people their sins if they will admit that they are wrong and ask to be forgiven.

The Romans feared that Jesus wanted to lead an uprising, and they considered him an enemy of the state. Consequently, Jesus was tried before Pontius Pilate, the Roman governor, who sentenced him to be crucified.

According to the Gospels, Jesus arose from the dead, remained on earth for 40 more days, and then ascended into heaven. His followers believed that the resurrection and the ascension proved that Jesus was the Messiah, calling him Jesus Christ, after the Greek word for messiah—*Christos*. The resurrection became the central message of Christianity. Through the death of Jesus Christ, the Son of God, who had died for the sins of the human race, all people could achieve redemption. The disciples of Jesus set out to spread this message, and within 400 years, Christianity had spread from its birthplace in Judea to all parts of the huge Roman Empire.

As Christianity spread, it developed a strict organization. Priests conducted services and performed baptisms and marriages. Above the priests were the bishops, who were considered the successors of the apostles. A bishop headed the church in each city. Over time, the bishop of Rome assumed the title of pope and claimed supremacy over the church.

The Collapse of the Empire in the West

During most of the A.D. 200s, the empire experienced dreadful confusion, civil war, and barbarian invasions. Travel became unsafe, and merchants hesitated to send goods by land or sea. People fled the cities. The rural population grew even poorer than before. Population decreased throughout the empire, partly because of a great plague that spread through the provinces and caused several million deaths.

The Roman Empire would probably have collapsed in the late 200s except for the efforts of two able emperors, Diocletian (dy • uh • KLEE • shuhn) and Constantine. Their reforms and reorganizations revived the empire. Nevertheless, their reforms could not postpone the collapse forever, and by A.D. 476 German barbarians had sacked imperial Rome—the empire was finished.

But *why* did Rome decline? How did this mighty empire that accomplished so much disappear? For centuries, historians have debated these questions. Some cite political weaknesses; the empire was too large to be governed efficiently. Others cite economic decline, including spiraling inflation. Still others cite social decay, the growth of the empire eroded the traditional values of the Romans. The important point to remember, however, is that no one cause was responsible for Roman decline. Like many other complex movements and events in history, it resulted from a combination of political, economic, and social forces.

In the ruins of the Roman world, however, two key ideas did survive in the West—the Roman heritage, including language and law, and the presence of Christianity. Both forces continue to influence life today—1,500 years after the collapse of the mighty Roman Empire.

SYNTHESIS REVIEW

1. **Summarizing Ideas** What were the three forms of government developed by the Greeks?
2. **Analyzing Ideas** How did Greek art reflect the ideals of Greek society?
3. **Interpreting Ideas** How did foreign conquests weaken the Roman Republic?
4. **Synthesizing Ideas** Why were the Romans able to establish a great empire, while the Greeks could never unify for very long?

183

The World in Transition

◀ *Marco Polo leaving Venice*   185

8

The Byzantine Empire Preserved the Heritage of Rome

Place Eastern Europe, Asia Minor, and Russia

Time A.D. 395—A.D. 1589

3.7 mil. BC   4000 BC   AD 2100

Significance

In the West the collapse of the Roman Empire resulted in fragmentation—the disappearance of strong governments and the division of land into isolated regions that were cut off from one another. However, the Roman Empire in the East maintained its traditions and kept out barbarian invaders. This new eastern empire took its name—the Byzantine Empire—from Byzantium, the ancient name for Constantinople. The empire lasted more than 1,000 years, from the formal split of the Roman Empire in 395 to the Turkish conquest of Constantinople in 1453. It created a distinct culture and a distinct branch of Christianity—the Byzantine church, later called the Eastern Orthodox church.

The Byzantines had the greatest influence upon Kievan Rus (KEE•ef•uhn ROOS), a land that eventually became known as Russia. As the Rus and other peoples of the territory struggled for political identity, they looked to the Byzantine Empire for religious and cultural inspiration. Although the Mongols plundered Kievan Rus in the 1200s, the Mongol influence was more political than cultural. As a result, the people of the area continued their Byzantine traditions.

Terms to Define

dowry	steppe
icon	boyar
iconoclast	metropolitan
heresy	taiga
mosaic	czar

People to Identify

Justinian	Methodius
Theodora	Vladimir I
Cyril	Ivan IV

Places to Locate

Constantinople	Kiev
Volga River	Lithuania

Questions to Guide Your Reading

1 How did the Byzantine Empire help preserve Western civilization?
2 How did the Byzantine Empire influence Kievan Rus?
3 How did Russia develop?

◀ *Hagia Sophia in Istanbul*

Amid the ruins of the Roman world, the magnificent city of Constantinople rose to become a great cultural and economic center. One historian noted the city's splendor.

" *A*round A.D. 1000 Christian Constantinople undoubtedly boasted over 500,000 inhabitants and may well have approximated 1,000,000. It was incomparably the largest city in Christendom, and, since the waning of the splendors of Baghdad, probably surpassed any other in the known world. . . .

Strangers were lost in . . . eloquence when describing the magnificence of New Rome [Constantinople] and the impression which a visit to it produced upon them. Its denizens [residents] took this homage as a matter of course. To them their capital was not only 'The City guarded by God,' it was 'The City' —as if all other communities in the world were merely secondary towns. "

Constantinople, head of the Byzantine Empire, preserved the traditions of the Greco-Roman world for future generations.

1 The Byzantine Empire Helped Preserve Western Civilization

While barbarians plundered the Western Roman Empire in the 400s and 500s, the Byzantine Empire in the East thrived. Although surrounded by enemies, the Byzantine Empire maintained its independence for more than 1,000 years.

The Reign of Justinian

In the year 500, the Eastern Roman Empire included Greece and the northern Balkan Peninsula, Asia Minor, Syria, Palestine, Egypt, and Cyrenaica. Although Germanic tribes had attacked the eastern empire even before marching on the western empire, the East had withstood the attacks. By the early 500s, the Western Roman Empire had broken down into a group of Germanic tribal kingdoms (see map, page 188). The Eastern Roman Empire, on the other hand, had ousted the barbarians and was primed for a great political, economic, intellectual, and artistic revival.

North
Sea
0°
Baltic Sea
20
N
Anglo-
Saxons   Saxons
Thuringians
50°
ATLANTIC
OCEAN
F r a n k s
Alemanni
Lombards
Burgundians
Suevi
Ostrogoths
•Rome
EASTERN
V i s i g o t h s
V a n d a l s
ROMAN
Mediterranean
EMPIRE
Vandals
Sea

0   300   600 Miles
0   300   600 Kilometers

A F R I C A
30°

GERMANIC KINGDOMS, 526

AZIMUTHAL EQUAL AREA PROJECTION

Learning from Maps   The Germanic invaders established kingdoms as far south as northern Africa. What group controlled northern Italy?

Emperor Justinian, who ruled from 527 to 565, led this revival and accomplished so much that the 37 years of his reign marked one of the most splendid periods in Byzantine history. Justinian's uncanny instinct for judging the abilities of others allowed him to choose exceptional people to help him rule the empire. Two wise choices were his wife, Theodora, and the commander-in-chief of his army, Belisarius (bel • uh • SAR • ee • uhs).

Theodora. The Byzantine Empire had several famous empresses, but the most extraordinary was Justinian's wife, Theodora. Theodora spent her early childhood with the circus, where her father trained bears. A pretty, witty, and intelligent girl, Theodora became an actress in her early teens. Soon she met and fell in love with Justinian. Although Byzantine law forbade marriage between high imperial officials and actresses, Justinian ignored the law and married Theodora in 523.

With Theodora's encouragement, Justinian changed Byzantine law to improve the status of women. Justinian decreed that a husband could not beat his wife and that a woman could sue for divorce if her husband mistreated her. Justinian changed the law prohibiting women from owning property. The new law allowed a woman to own property equal to the value of her **dowry,** the money or goods that she brought to her husband when the couple married. Furthermore, Justinian repealed an old law that forced a widow to surrender her children to a male relative. The new law allowed the widow to raise her own children.

Theodora's most dramatic contribution to her husband's success took place in 532. A group of senators, angry about high taxes, had organized a revolt known as the Nika Rebellion. As the leaders of the rebellion threatened to crown a new emperor, a cowering Justinian prepared to flee Constantinople. However, Theodora urged him to stay and fight. In a fierce battle, Justinian's troops hacked 30,000 rebels to death, ensuring that he would remain on the throne.

Belisarius. Justinian's appointment of Belisarius as commander-in-chief of the army proved as successful and unconventional as his choice of a wife. An officer of peasant stock who had little money, Belisarius had very little military experience. He was a friend of Theodora, however, and he had made a name for himself leading the troops that crushed the Nika Rebellion.

While the new Germanic kingdoms in the west quarreled among themselves, Justinian's armies, under the capable leadership of Belisarius, regained many territories in the Mediterranean region. As a result of these conquests, the Byzantine Empire reached its greatest territorial extent during Justinian's reign (see map, page 189).

The legacy of Justinian. After Justinian's death in 565, the empire suffered almost 50 years of civil wars, made worse by attacks from the outside. From the East came the Persians, whom Justinian's successors defeated in the late 500s. Meanwhile, an Asiatic group, the Avars, and a European people, the Slavs, invaded the Balkan Peninsula. The Lombards sacked Italy. By the early 600s, Germanic tribes had won back most of the territory that Justinian's armies had spent so much time conquering.

During the 600s the Byzantine Empire faced a new and highly energetic force—the armies of the Muslim Empire (see Chapter 9). The Muslims soon conquered Armenia, Syria, Palestine, and much of North Africa, including Egypt. After 650 the eastern empire consisted of little more than Asia Minor, the southern Balkan Peninsula, parts of Italy, and the nearby islands.

THE BYZANTINE EMPIRE
526–565

Byzantine Empire, 526

Justinian's conquests,
527–565

AZIMUTHAL EQUAL AREA PROJECTION

Learning from Maps *Justinian, perhaps the greatest of the Byzantine emperors, reunited most of the lands around the Mediterranean coast. What parts of the former Western Roman Empire did he reconquer?*

Strengths of the Empire

Several factors helped the Byzantine Empire survive for more than 1,000 years. It had political, military, and economic strength, and its people adapted skillfully to change.

Political strength. A highly centralized and autocratic government headed by an all-powerful emperor ruled the Byzantine Empire. Well-paid, efficient, skillful, and usually loyal officials carried out imperial commands and policies. Even during times of weak emperors or civil war, these officials made sure the empire ran smoothly.

The Byzantines practiced especially shrewd diplomacy. Their excellent intelligence service kept the emperor well informed of important foreign developments. They often bribed foreign officials to obtain information. To cement alliances Byzantine emperors often arranged marriages between

Byzantine princesses and foreign princes. The Byzantines also routinely provoked one neighbor to attack another in order to prevent either one from attacking the empire. Today we use the term *byzantine* to describe tricky or devious policies.

Military strength. Byzantine rulers developed effective frontier, infantry, cavalry, and engineering corps to defend the empire. The government provided its soldiers with medical services and rewarded them with land grants. The military developed instruction manuals and established schools to teach leaders the latest strategies. It also replaced the bow and lance with the sword and javelin and designed a more protective armor.

During the 600s the Byzantines built a strong navy. Ships had battering rams, but the sailors' secret weapon was a flammable liquid called "Greek fire," which they hurled to set enemy ships ablaze. So carefully did the Byzantines guard their secret

189

Egyptian Christian Cloth

The power of the Byzantine Empire helped spread Christianity throughout the lands around the Mediterranean Sea, including Egypt. The Copts, as Egyptian Christians were called, combined aspects of Christian art that had developed in Italy and Byzantium with traditional Egyptian styles to form Coptic art.

In this ancient woven fabric, we see an excellent example of Coptic art. An elegant Byzantine woman, surrounded by a spiral of waves, gazes out from the cloth. This spiral design is one of the oldest in Mediterranean culture. It was being used as a decorative form long before the time of Jesus. The ducks that fill the circles on four sides typify the deco-

ration used by early Egyptian artists, who portrayed all kinds of animal and plant life.

The face of the woman, stylized and two-dimensional, resembles the early portraits on Egyptian coffins

and mummy cases. However, the woman's headdress, jewels, and robe look very much like the mosaic picture of a Byzantine empress in an early Christian church in Ravenna, Italy.

---

that even today no one knows its exact formula. The best guess is that Greek fire contained a combination of naphtha, sulphur, and saltpeter (potassium nitrate).

Economic strength. Because of its abundant agriculture, manufacturing, and trade, the East had always been the richest part of the Roman Empire. At the heart of the empire lay Constantinople, a city of grandeur with a population of 1 million inhabitants. Its advantage lay in its location. Situated on the border of Asia and Europe, the city overlooked the strategic Bosphorus, the narrow straits that linked the Black and Mediterranean seas (see map, page 191). Such a location allowed the Byzantines to control the vital trade routes linking Europe and Asia.

Merchandise from as far away as Scandinavia, China, and India poured into the markets of Constantinople. There and throughout the empire, the government regulated trade and manufacturing to produce large tax revenues. The emperor used the taxes to pay government officials and soldiers and to build great public buildings.

The Christian Church

Important figures in the early Christian Church included the patriarchs of Rome, Constantinople, Alexandria, Antioch, and Jerusalem. In time the pope and the church in Rome gained supreme authority in the West. However, the Byzantines did not recognize this authority. In the East the patriarch of Constantinople came to be the most important church leader.

The Byzantine faith provided a source of both weakness and strength for the Byzantine Empire. Because Christianity formed such a vital part of Byzantine life, the Byzantines argued bitterly and endlessly about minute details of ritual and doctrines concerning beliefs. Often, Byzantine leaders considered these arguments more important than broad matters of imperial policy, such as taxes or defense.

The most significant religious argument concerned holy pictures of Jesus, the Virgin Mary, and the saints, called **icons**, from *eikon*, the Greek word for "portrait." Many Byzantines revered icons, which they kept in their homes and worshiped at church. Some Byzantines, however, were **iconoclasts,** who felt that the presence of icons constituted idol worship and should be suppressed.

The **iconoclastic controversy,** the argument between the supporters and the opponents of icons, rocked the empire for more than a century. In 730 Emperor Leo III outlawed the use of icons in an attempt to curb the power of the church and monasteries, which owned most of the icons. However, largely because people refused to give up their icons, the Byzantine emperors abandoned their efforts to suppress icon worship in 843. In the meantime the controversy had drastically affected the empire's relations with Europe.

Most people in western Europe, unlike those in the Byzantine Empire, could not read or write. Western clergy, therefore, considered visual images essential in teaching about Christianity. After

Learning from Pictures This Byzantine wood carving depicts the Empress Irene, who ruled the Byzantine Empire between 780 and 802.

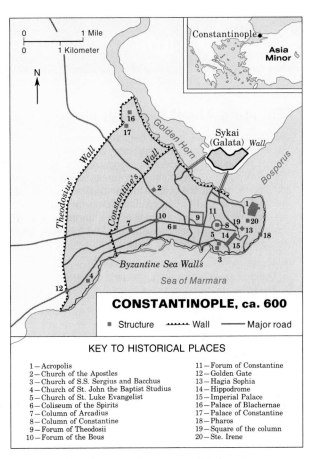

KEY TO HISTORICAL PLACES

1 — Acropolis	11 — Forum of Constantine
2 — Church of the Apostles	12 — Golden Gate
3 — Church of S.S. Sergius and Bacchus	13 — Hagia Sophia
4 — Church of St. John the Baptist Studius	14 — Hippodrome
5 — Church of St. Luke Evangelist	15 — Imperial Palace
6 — Coliseum of the Spirits	16 — Palace of Blachernae
7 — Column of Arcadius	17 — Palace of Constantine
8 — Column of Constantine	18 — Pharos
9 — Forum of Theodosii	19 — Square of the column
10 — Forum of the Bous	20 — Ste. Irene

Learning from Maps Constantinople's location on vital trade routes made it a great commercial center. What bodies of water protected the city?

Emperor Leo III forbade the use of icons in the Byzantine Empire, the pope called a council of bishops. The council declared opposition to icons a **heresy,** or an opinion that conflicts with church doctrine, and excommunicated the iconoclasts. **Excommunication** entails barring a person from church membership and excluding the person from taking part in any church ceremonies, including baptism, marriage, and communion.

The declaration of iconoclasm as a heresy led to friction between the pope and the patriarch of Constantinople. The friction grew steadily worse over the years until finally the Christian Church split in 1054. In the West it became known as the Roman Catholic church, with the pope as its head. In the East it became known as the Eastern Orthodox church, with the patriarch of Constantinople as its head. This division between Roman Catholic and Eastern Orthodox Christendom still exists.

191

Thinking About History: Identifying Bias

Bias is a word that often has negative connotations. People often equate bias with *prejudice,* a negative (or positive) opinion that is based on ignorance or is without foundation in truth. In its simplest sense, however, bias is nothing more than the outlook that a speaker or writer presents. Thus to identify bias means to determine whether a speaker or writer has a positive or a negative attitude toward the subject being discussed. The following three sentences demonstrate the point.

- The emperor addressed the Senate.
- The brilliant emperor addressed the Senate.
- The silly emperor addressed the Senate.

The first statement is a simple report of an action. The statement is not biased; it shows neither favor nor disfavor. In the second statement, the word *brilliant* conveys a positive feeling toward the emperor. In the third statement, the word *silly* creates a negative feeling.

Being able to identify bias in writing and in speeches is an important skill to have, not only as you study history, but also as you read newspapers and magazines or watch newscasts on television. It helps you decide whether you are reading a factual report or one that shows the author's biased opinion.

How to Identify Bias

To identify bias, follow these steps.

1. Look for clues. Check for words or phrases that convey a positive or negative attitude.
2. Assess the evidence. Decide for yourself whether you agree or disagree with the bias on the basis of the evidence presented.

Developing the Skill

Procopius, an official in Constantinople, wrote *The Secret History* describing the rule of Justinian and Theodora. Read the excerpt below in order to identify bias.

> ❝ They were a pair of blood-thirsty demons. . . .
> For they plotted together to find the easiest and the swiftest means of destroying all races of men and all their works, assumed human shape, became man-demons, and in this way convulsed the whole world. . . . He never even gave a hint of anger or irritation to show how he felt towards those who had offended him; but with a friendly expression on his face and without raising an eyebrow, in a gentle voice he would order tens of thousands of quite innocent persons to be put to death, cities to be razed to the ground, and all their possessions confiscated for the Treasury. . . . His ambition being to force everybody into one form of Christian belief he wantonly destroyed everyone who would not conform, and that while keeping up a pretense of piety. For he did not regard it as murder, so long as those who died did not happen to share his beliefs. ❞

The excerpt includes many words that condemn Justinian and Theodora. For example, *bloodthirsty demons* and *man-demons* give the impression that they were truly evil people.

Practicing the skill. Read an article in your local newspaper and determine whether the article shows bias.

To apply this skill, see Applying History Study Skills on page 203.

Empress Theodora

Emperor Justinian I

Byzantine Culture

The Byzantine Empire performed a great service for civilization. Although its scholars produced little that was original, they did preserve and pass on the classical learning of Greece, Rome, and the Orient. For more than 1,000 years, while western Europe struggled to develop a new way of life, Constantinople served as the center of a brilliant civilization.

Not only did the Byzantines preserve the culture of the Mediterranean world, they also carried it beyond the borders of their empire. Cyril (SIR • uhl) and Methodius (muh • THOH • dee • uhs), two brothers who lived in the 800s, illustrate the role of the Byzantines in this cultural diffusion. As missionaries the brothers worked to convert the Slavs of central and eastern Europe to Christianity. Cyril wanted to teach the Slavs to read the Bible, but the Slavs had no written language. So Cyril created an alphabet that evolved into the Cyrillic (suh • RIL • ik) alphabet. Today many Slavic peoples of central and eastern Europe, including the Russians, still use the Cyrillic alphabet or one derived from it.

Cyril and Methodius converted many Slavs to Christianity. Descendants of these converts still follow the Eastern Orthodox faith.

Art. Byzantine art glorified religion. Murals covered the walls and ceilings of churches. Floors, walls, and arches glistened with colored **mosaics**—pictures or designs formed by inlaid pieces of stone, glass, or enamel. Artists used both painting and mosaics to create icons. The location of a particular person's image in the church indicated that person's importance to church doctrine. For example, an image of Jesus always occupied the dome of the church.

The subjects of Byzantine art, whether angels, saints, or martyrs, appeared stiff and artificial. The calm, meditative faces resembled Buddhist art in their purpose—to inspire reverence and to emphasize the importance of renouncing the pleasures of this life to prepare for the afterlife.

Architecture. Architecture, especially religious architecture, was the greatest form of Byzantine art. The finest Byzantine building ever built —indeed, one of the architectural masterpieces of the world—is the church of Hagia Sophia (meaning "holy wisdom") in Constantinople.

Justinian ordered the construction of Hagia Sophia in 532. A huge building in the form of a cross, the church measures 240 feet (73 meters) wide by 270 feet (82 meters) long. The interior once glittered with breathtaking decorations that reflected the sunlight streaming through lofty windows. Murals, mosaics, stone carvings, and metalwork covered every surface. Insets of ivory, silver, and jewels adorned the pulpit. The patriarch's throne was solid silver.

A huge dome, 165 feet (50 meters) high, dominates the cathedral. Resting on massive columns instead of walls, the dome illustrates the talent of Byzantine architects, who first solved the difficult problem of placing a round dome over a rectangular building.

Learning from Pictures   *Today the Turkish government maintains the church of Hagia Sophia as a museum. What art covered the walls and ceilings of Byzantine churches?*

What If?
The Byzantine Empire
The Byzantine Empire helped preserve the Greco-Roman heritage of the ancient world. How do you think the course of world history would have changed if the Germanic tribes had toppled the Byzantine Empire at the same time they plundered the imperial city of Rome?

When Hagia Sophia was completed in 537, one Byzantine writer called it a church "the like of which had never been since Adam, nor ever will be." And the great Byzantine historian Procopius (pruh•KOH•pee•uhs) described his feelings after first entering the church.

" The church . . . is distinguished by indescribable beauty, for it excels both in its size and in the harmony of its proportion. . . . It is singularly full of light and sunshine; you would declare that the place is not lighted by the sun from without, but that the rays are produced within itself, such an abundance of light is poured into this church. . . .

The entire ceiling is covered with pure gold, which adds glory to its beauty, though the rays of light reflected upon the gold from the marble surpass it in beauty. . . . Who could tell of the beauty of the columns and marbles with which the church is adorned? One would think that one had come upon a meadow full of flowers in bloom: who would not admire the purple tints of some and the green of others, the glowing red and glittering white . . . ? Whoever enters there to worship perceives at once that it is not by any human strength or skill, but by the favour of God that this work has been perfected; his mind rises sublime to commune with God, feeling that He cannot be far off, but must especially love to dwell in the place which He has chosen. "

Justinian himself solemnly consecrated the church. As he first entered Hagia Sophia, he exclaimed, "O Solomon, I have outdone thee!" He was referring to King Solomon of Israel, who built a magnificent temple in Jerusalem. The splendor of Solomon's temple is described in the Bible.

The Preservation of Roman Law

Probably the greatest Byzantine contribution to civilization was the preservation of Roman law. Early in his reign, Justinian ordered his scholars to collect and organize all Roman law. The entire collection is known as the *Corpus Juris Civilis* (Latin for "Body of Civil Law"). It is also called Justinian's Code and includes four parts—the *Code,* the *Digest,* the *Institutes,* and the *Novels.*

The *Code* was a collection of Roman laws, omitting repetitions, inconsistencies, and statutes dealing with Roman religion. The *Digest* consisted of a summary of the writings of the great Roman legal experts, organized alphabetically by ideas. The *Institutes* was a textbook on the basic principles of Roman law. Justinian's own laws were included in both the *Institutes* and the *Novels.* In western Europe Roman law was studied chiefly from the *Digest* and *Institutes.* Justinian's Code forms the basis of many modern European legal systems.

Decline of the Empire

In the 1000s the Seljuk Turks, originally a nomadic people from central Asia, captured most of Asia Minor. This vital area included the Byzantine Empire's "breadbasket" and the source of soldiers for its army. When the Turks prepared to attack Constantinople, the Byzantine emperor appealed to the West for help. Western Europeans responded in 1096 and 1097 with the First Crusade, recapturing western Asia Minor for the Byzantines (see Chapter 11). During the Fourth Crusade in 1204, however, the crusaders attacked the Byzantine Empire and captured Constantinople.

After 50 years of Western rule, the Byzantines recaptured the city and reorganized the empire. Although the empire continued to exist for almost 200 years, it never regained its former strength. In the 1400s a new Asiatic people, the Ottoman Turks, rose to power in the region. When they captured Constantinople in 1453, the Byzantine Empire finally came to an end.

SECTION 1 REVIEW

1. **Define** dowry, icon, iconoclast, iconoclastic controversy, heresy, excommunication, mosaic
2. **Identify** Justinian, Greek fire, Slavs, Hagia Sophia
3. **Locate** Constantinople
4. **Analyzing Maps** (a) Using the map on page 189, describe the area of the Roman Empire in the west that Justinian had conquered by 565. (b) What peoples were affected by these conquests?
5. **Understanding Ideas** What factors enabled the Byzantine Empire to survive as long as it did?
6. **Evaluating Ideas** What did Cyril and Methodius contribute to the civilization of central and eastern Europe?

Spices

Do you realize that when you have a bowl of chili you are eating food seasoned with the same kinds of spices that the Incas in Peru used 2,000 years ago? Whether you eat at home or in a restaurant (top right), at almost every meal, you are enjoying the taste of a spice—ginger in ginger ale or gingerbread, oregano in spaghetti sauce, anise in licorice, and mint in peppermints.

More than 800 years ago, the Aztecs in Mexico ground hot chili peppers and mixed them with other spices to make chili powder. Today hot peppers are used throughout the world. People in tropical countries believe that hot food stimulates the liver and promotes good health.

Black and white pepper can give us almost the same zing found in hot chilis. The black peppercorn is the whole berry, which is picked while it is green and set out to dry. White pepper is made from the core of the ripe berry. Pepper was originally grown on the western coast of India and was brought to Europe by traders who often passed through the markets of Constantinople on their journey.

When barbarians pillaged Rome in 410, the ransom they demanded included pepper as well as gold and silver. Pepper was later used as money, and dock workers had to have their pockets sewn shut so they would not steal it from the ships they were unloading.

In the 1400s spices from the East were in great demand in Europe. Explorers began to search for new and faster routes to bring pepper and other spices from India to Europe. Columbus hoped to find such a route to India when he sailed west and landed at Santo Domingo.

As trade has become international, so has the taste for foreign dishes and flavors. Today, spices are sold all over the world, as in these markets in the Middle East (center and bottom right).

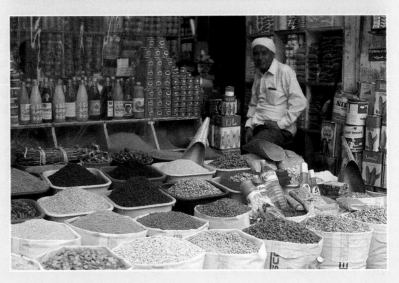

195

2 Kievan Rus Developed Strong Ties with the Byzantine Empire

During the early days of the Byzantine Empire, the Slavs who lived north of the Black Sea began to trade with Constantinople. The Byzantines greatly influenced the political and social lives of these Slavs.

The Physical Setting

A vast, grassy, almost treeless plain called the **steppe** stretches across eastern Europe and central Asia. It extends from the Arctic Ocean and the Baltic Sea south to the Black and Caspian seas, and from the Carpathian (kahr • PAY • thee • uhn) Mountains in Europe east to Manchuria in eastern Asia. Only the Ural (YOOR • uhl) Mountains, which run north and south and separate the continents of Europe and Asia, break the plain. Because the two continents form a single great landmass, they are sometimes called Eurasia.

The European part of the steppe is generally known as eastern Europe. Three mountain ranges —the Carpathians in the west, the Urals in the east, and the Caucasus (KAW • kuh • suhs) in the south—border the region (see map, page 197). Black, fertile soil makes the grassy steppe ideal for farming, especially in the area now known as the Ukraine.

A number of large rivers crisscross the steppe and provide a network of transportation within the region. The Dvina (duh • vee • NAH) and the Vistula (VISH • chuh • luh) rivers flow directly into the Baltic Sea. The Dniester (NEES • tuhr), the Dnieper (NEE • puhr), and the Don rivers empty into the Black Sea. The Volga and Ural rivers, because they flow into the landlocked Caspian Sea, are much less useful for trade than the other rivers of the steppe.

Slavic and Viking Influences

People have lived in the southern part of eastern Europe since Neolithic times. According to Herodotus, Greek merchants traded with the peoples north of the Black Sea. Later, Asian barbarians invaded the region. Beginning in the A.D. 200s,

Slavs settled much of eastern Europe. Because the Slavs were peaceful and had only a very loose political organization, other invading peoples, including the Huns, Avars, and Magyars, often conquered them and made them pay tribute.

During the 800s Vikings from Scandinavia swept into eastern Europe. However, they came more as traders than as conquerors. Each fall they sailed up the rivers from the Baltic Sea and from Lake Ladoga (see map, page 197). When winter came, they loaded their ships on large sleds and hauled them across the snow to one of the rivers that flowed into the Black Sea. When the ice melted in the spring, they sailed south to trade in the Black Sea region. After trading their goods, they retraced their route to their Scandinavian homeland.

Kievan Rus

Several cities sprang up along the Viking trade routes. Two such cities were Novgorod (Russian for "new fort"), south of Lake Ladoga, and Kiev, on the Dnieper River. Kiev prospered because of its strategic location astride the rich trade route that extended from Constantinople to the Baltic Sea (see map, page 197).

According to legend, in the 860s the people of Novgorod asked Rurik, a Viking military leader, to help defend their city. Rurik and his successors became rulers of Novgorod and other principalities, including Kiev. The Slavs called both the Vikings and the area they controlled Rus. The word *Russia* is probably derived from this name.

Kiev grew to be the most important principality in Rus. The city of Kiev served as the capital of Rus from about 882 to 1169. Although the rulers of individual principalities paid tribute to the prince in Kiev in exchange for military protection, the degree of their loyalty varied, depending on the Kievan prince's power. Many of the smaller towns remained semi-independent.

Government

The prince of each of the cities of Kievan Rus at times ruled with the advice of a council of **boyars,** or nobles. Another important institution widely used in both Kiev and Novgorod was the *veche,* or town meeting. Here, at the request of the prince, the heads of all of the households met in the public

Learning from Maps *Kievan Rus controlled semi-independent principalities. What geographic feature lies south of the Ural Mountains?*

marketplace. They considered such matters as calls to war, disputes between princes, and special emergency laws proposed by the prince.

Kievan Rus's greatest period came during the reign of Yaroslav I, called Yaroslav the Wise, who ruled from 1019 to 1054. Yaroslav's domain included about 7 million people. He issued Rus's first law code, the *Pravda Russkaia,* which remained in force in parts of the region until 1550.

Religion

In the 980s Vladimir I of Kiev invited missionaries from several faiths to address his boyar council and offer reasons why his people should convert to their religion. The prince rejected Islam because it prohibited the drinking of wine (see Chapter 9). He rejected Judaism because the Romans had expelled the Jews from Palestine in 135, leading Vladimir to believe that the Jews' god lacked political power.

Christian services in Germany failed to impress Vladimir's envoys, but those who went to Constantinople and attended services in Hagia Sophia reported the following:

“*W*e know not whether we were in heaven or on earth. For on earth there is no such splendor or such beauty, and we are at a loss how to describe it. We only know that God dwells there among men. . . . Every man, after tasting something sweet, is afterward unwilling to accept that which is bitter, and therefore we cannot any longer remain pagans.”

Influenced by the reports of his envoys and by his desire to marry Anna, the Byzantine emperor's sister, Vladimir converted to Christianity in 988. He immediately ordered the baptism of Kievans and the destruction of pagan statues. Although many Kievans continued to worship the spirits of their

Learning from Pictures *This Russian icon shows Christ the Pantocrator, or almighty ruler, his right hand raised in a gesture of benediction.*

ancestors and ancient gods of nature, the Byzantine church became increasingly important as a spiritual force. When the Christian Church split in 1054, the Kievan church became a part of the Eastern Orthodox church; the patriarch of Constantinople chose the chief bishop, or **metropolitan,** of the Kievan church. New monasteries, which soon became great centers for social services, education, and artistic expression, further strengthened the church.

Religious feelings and subjects dominated Kievan culture in this period. Although authors wrote epic poems and historical chronicles about wars and the personal tragedies associated with war, religious hymns and sermons constituted the bulk of Kievan literature. Icon painting became the dominant Kievan art form. However, artists made no attempt to show figures as three-dimensional. The Kievans believed that the second of the Ten Commandments, "You shall not make a carved image for yourself," prohibited any art resembling sculpture. Thus they chose mosaics, frescoes, and

icons—which were two-dimensional—as the only correct representations of religious subjects.

The Kievan Economy

Agriculture and trade were the most important economic activities in Kievan society.

Agriculture. Kievan Rus contained two major agricultural regions. In the north lay the forest zone known as the **taiga** (TY•guh). Although the taiga received abundant rainfall, the brutally cold, long winters limited the growing season to about four months each year. Because of the need to grow and harvest crops in such a short time, everyone worked long hours.

In the steppe to the east and south of the taiga, less rain fell and less vegetation grew. However, the milder climate permitted a growing season of six months, giving the people more time to sow, cultivate, and harvest their crops of grain.

Trade. Kievan Rus traded agricultural goods, wood, iron, salt, and other products with the Byzantine Empire. The most important of these goods were fur, wax, honey, animal hides, flax, hemp, burlap, and hops. Kievan Rus also furnished slaves for the Byzantines. In return the people of Kievan Rus obtained wine, silk, religious art objects, spices, precious stones, steel blades, and horses from the Byzantines. From western Europe the Rus received textiles, glassware, and metals. By the early 1000s, trade had helped make Kievan Rus as strong and wealthy as any western European power. Scholars estimate that Kiev's population was larger than that of Paris, which was the most populous city in western Europe.

Kievan Social Classes

In the varied economy of Kievan Rus, several social classes emerged. The highest class included the local princes and their families. Below the princes came the boyars. Next were the artisans and merchants, who lived in the towns and devoted themselves entirely to trade.

The clergy formed another important group in Kievan society. They not only performed religious ceremonies but also ran schools, hospitals, and other charities.

The largest social class, however, consisted of peasants. The peasants lived in small villages and produced the agricultural output of Kievan Rus.

SECTION 2 REVIEW

1. **Define** steppe, boyar, metropolitan, taiga
2. **Identify** Vikings, Rurik, Yaroslav the Wise, *Pravda Russkaia*
3. **Locate** Arctic Ocean, Baltic Sea, Black Sea, Caspian Sea, Ural Mountains, Dvina River, Vistula River, Volga River, Novgorod, Kiev
4. **Analyzing Ideas** Why did Vladimir I choose Byzantine Christianity?
5. **Seeing Relationships** What ties did Kievan Rus have with the Byzantine Empire?
6. **Contrasting Ideas** What were the differences between the northern and southern agricultural regions in Kievan Rus?
7. **Classifying Ideas** Describe the social classes in Kievan Rus.

3 The Mongols Established a Vast Empire in Eurasia

After the rule of Yaroslav the Wise ended in 1054, Kiev declined in power and wealth. The Kievan rulers gave their younger sons outlying towns to rule as independent principalities. These princes and their descendants fought among themselves and with the ruler of Kiev to expand their own territories. Kiev's trade declined because of raids by the Polovtsy, Asiatic peoples who controlled the region south of Kiev after 1055. Also, the Italians developed new trade routes throughout the Mediterranean region that competed with the Kievan routes.

After a group of princes sacked Kiev in 1169 and again in 1203, the city's prosperity ended. As these princes continued to fight among themselves, new invaders took advantage of Kiev's weakness. These new invaders, the Mongols, came from the Asian steppe west of the Urals.

The Mongols in Eastern Europe

The Mongols first attacked eastern Europe in force in 1237. Kievan resistance proved too weak to halt the Mongols, and by 1240 they had conquered and burned almost every city in Kievan Rus.

The Mongols pushed on across the Carpathian Mountains into Hungary and across the plains into Poland. After defeating the Hungarian and Polish armies, however, the Mongol leader rushed back to the Mongolian capital in central Asia to help choose a new ruler. Thus Hungary and Poland, although terribly damaged by war and savage plundering, escaped continuing Mongol rule. The Kievan region, however, remained under Mongol control until the late 1400s.

Society Under the Rule of the Mongols

The Mongols did not try to impose their way of life on the people they conquered. They wanted only to collect taxes. Taxes were often harsh, but as long as they were paid, the Mongols allowed the people to retain their own government and customs. The local landlord collected taxes and administered justice. Peasants had two obligations to their landlords—labor at specified times and a payment either in money or in goods. The second obligation was considered more important. Most peasants in the north, the area between the Volga and Oka rivers, did not have landlords and paid taxes directly to the government.

The Mongols grazed their flocks on the steppe north of the Caspian Sea and the Sea of Azov, where they had little contact with the Slavs. Although they formed only a small ruling class, the Mongols did influence the society of the Eastern Slavs in several ways. They built important roads and improved methods of taxation and communication. Some of their words filtered into the language that came to be called Russian.

Learning from Pictures *Genghis Khan, a leader of the Mongols, was a skilled politician. He won a faithful following by rewarding those loyal to him.*

Learning from Pictures *The Byzantines influenced the religion and architecture of the Eastern Slavs. The Russians modified the dome style into an onion shape.*

During the time of Mongol rule, the Slavs of eastern Europe had little contact with central and western Europe. Lithuania and Poland took territory from the northern part of Kievan Rus in the late 1300s, forming a kingdom hostile to the Eastern Slavs. Religious conflicts also existed. The Poles had been converted to Western Christianity. The Eastern Slavs clung to their Orthodox faith, which set them apart from both the Poles and the Mongols. The Eastern Slavs grew suspicious of Europeans and their influence. This suspicion became a deep-seated one that has not disappeared to the present day.

The Rise of Moscow

In time Mongol rule grew weaker, and the princes of the region became more independent. During the early 1300s, Moscow, or Muscovy, became the strongest principality, partly because it cooperated with the Mongols. In return for this cooperation, the Mongols awarded Prince Ivan I, who ruled Moscow from 1325 to 1341, the title of Grand Prince. Ivan's power increased further when the chief metropolitan of the Orthodox church moved to Moscow in 1328.

By the time of Ivan III, who ruled as Grand Prince from 1462 to 1505, Moscow was so powerful that it refused to pay taxes to the Mongols. In 1480 Ivan III overthrew Mongol rule. He united many principalities and emerged as the first ruler of an independent state called Russia.

In 1533, at the age of only 3, Ivan IV became ruler of Russia. Because of Ivan's youth, however, the boyars wielded power. The young boy watched powerlessly as the boyars fought each other, tortured captive opponents, and murdered political prisoners.

In an impressive ceremony in 1547, Ivan declared himself the heir of the Roman and Byzantine empires and took the title **czar,** the Russian word for "caesar." As czar, Ivan IV reformed Yaroslav's laws, reestablished trade with western Europe, and opened Siberia for Russian settlement.

When Ivan's wife died mysteriously, he blamed the boyars for her death. He immediately formed a secret police who dressed in black uniforms and rode black horses. These fearsome agents carried broomsticks to show how they would sweep the streets of trouble and execute all traitors.

Ivan used the secret police to control Russia. They arrested boyars and distributed the boyars' land to Ivan's supporters. Ivan later sent the secret police to execute the metropolitan of Moscow and routinely ordered the massacres of all the residents of villages. In a fit of rage, he even killed his own son. Such ferocious acts of cruelty earned Ivan IV the nickname "Ivan the Terrible," or "Ivan the Awesome." Nevertheless, Ivan IV established the nature of the new Russian state. The state would be huge, including old Kievan Rus and Siberia. And it would be autocratic, with one person ruling as czar.

The Growth of the Church

As in western Europe, the church in Russia continued to expand its landholdings, primarily through gifts from people who saw these donations to the church as a guarantee of spiritual salvation. By 1500 the Orthodox church owned as much as one-fourth of all cultivated land in Russia.

During the Mongol period, the Russian Orthodox church became increasingly independent of the patriarch of Constantinople. In 1448 the metropolitan of the Orthodox church in Moscow took office without the authority of Constantinople. The final break with Constantinople occurred in 1589, when Moscow's metropolitan was crowned patriarch and proclaimed equal with those of other Eastern Orthodox churches.

The Russians rewrote the history of how their country had been Christianized to give the Russian

History Through the Arts

PAINTING

Sacred Icons

As Christianity spread into Kievan Rus in the 900s, the people were baptized and told to destroy their pagan idols. Holy pictures, or icons, were hung in lavish new churches. Gold- or silver-painted backgrounds made the icons easier to see in dimly lit interiors. Troops marching into battle also carried icons. In this icon from Kiev, we see three popular Byzantine saints: St. Vassilios; the eloquent St. John Chrysostom; and St. Grigorios Theologos, who was often shown shedding blood into the sacrificial chalice or cup.

Despite their flat, two-dimensional style, icons conveyed both individuality and a sense of godliness. Byzantine artists were expected to lead pure lives to demonstrate this feeling of holiness. Only then were they worthy enough to transfer God's goodness to men and women.

Orthodox church important theological support for its independence. The Russians now claimed that Andrew, one of the original 12 apostles of Jesus, brought Christianity to Russia directly from Jerusalem. They confidently proclaimed Moscow as the "third Rome." In 1510 a Russian abbot wrote that the first Rome had fallen because of heresy and the second Rome (Constantinople) had fallen because of infidels, or people who were not Christians. The third Rome (Moscow), he said, was destined to be the final one that would bring spiritual light to the whole world.

This new confidence affected Russian architecture and art. The Cathedral of the Assumption in Moscow exemplifies the artistry and religious fervor of the period. The church has the domed-roof style so popular in both the Byzantine and Russian cultures. Every inch of the church's interior walls exhibited some form of artwork. Sparkling chandeliers and candles illuminated every alcove. The face of Jesus adorned the highest central dome. The cathedral, full of grandeur and beauty, was designed to produce a strong mystical response from the people. Even today, people marvel at this early Russian masterpiece.

SECTION 3 REVIEW

1. **Define** czar
2. **Identify** Polovtsy, Mongols, third Rome, Ivan III, Ivan IV
3. **Locate** Sea of Azov, Lithuania, Poland, Moscow
4. **Determining Cause and Effect** What were some of the reasons for Kievan Rus's isolation from, and suspicion toward, western Europe?
5. **Summarizing Ideas** How did the Mongol rulers maintain control over the Kievan territories?
6. **Understanding Ideas** What two obligations did the peasants have to their landlords?
7. **Analyzing Ideas** How did Muscovy become independent from Mongol rule?

201

Official split of Roman Empire

Reign of Justinian

Iconoclastic controversy

AD   395   527   565   726

532   537

Nika Rebellion

Completion of Hagia Sophia

Chapter Summary

The following list contains the key concepts you have learned about the Byzantine Empire and its heritage.

1. A brilliant and sophisticated civilization, the Byzantine Empire helped preserve the heritage of Greco-Roman civilization.
2. Justinian, one of the most famous Byzantine emperors, survived the Nika Rebellion, extended the borders of the empire, and ordered the building of Hagia Sophia.
3. The Byzantine Empire survived for 1,000 years because of political, military, and economic strengths.
4. In 1054 the Christian Church split into two churches—the Roman Catholic church and the Eastern Orthodox church.
5. The main inheritor of Byzantine traditions was Kievan Rus, located on the vast, almost treeless steppe of eastern Europe.
6. Kievan Rus became a flourishing society based on agriculture and trade.
7. Although the Mongols conquered Kievan Rus, they had little long-lasting influence on local institutions and culture in the region around Kiev and Novgorod.
8. As Mongol control weakened, a strong state, centered in Moscow, started to emerge in the 1400s.
9. In the 1500s Ivan the Terrible took the title *czar* and firmly established the large Russian state.

On a separate sheet of paper, complete the following review exercises.

Reviewing Important Terms

Supply the term that correctly completes each sentence.

1. The money or goods that a bride brings to her husband when the couple is married is called a _____ .
2. Holy pictures of Jesus, the Virgin Mary, and the saints, typically used in devotions, are called _____ .
3. _____ felt that the presence of icons constituted idol worship and should be suppressed.
4. The argument between the supporters and the opponents of icons was called the _____ _____ .
5. Church leaders label an opinion that conflicts with church doctrine _____ .
6. _____ entails barring a person from church membership and excluding the person from taking part in any church ceremonies such as baptism, marriage, and communion.
7. _____ are pictures or designs formed by inlaid pieces of stone, glass, or enamel.
8. In Kievan Rus, the princes sometimes ruled with the advice of a council of _____ , or nobles.
9. Much of eastern Europe consists of a grassy, almost treeless plain called the _____ .
10. When the Christian Church split in 1054, the Kievan church became a part of the Eastern Orthodox church, with its chief bishop, the _____ , chosen by the patriarch of Constantinople.
11. The forest zone in northern Kievan Rus was known as the _____ .
12. Ivan IV declared himself the heir of the Roman and Byzantine empires and took the title _____ , the Russian word for "caesar."

Developing Critical Thinking Skills

1. **Classifying Ideas** Classify each of the following statements as characteristic of the Byzantine Empire, Kievan Rus, the Mongol Empire, or Muscovite Russia.
   (a) Justinian established Law Code.
   (b) Princesses married foreign princes to help cement alliances.
   (c) The *veche* settled disputes.
   (d) First Russian law code compiled.
   (e) Ivan III united territories into Russia.
   (f) Semi-independent city-states developed.
   (g) Rulers gave younger sons outlying towns to rule independently.
   (h) Government regulated trade and manufacturing to produce large tax revenues.
2. **Summarizing Ideas** (a) Describe Byzantine art, architecture, and law. (b) What features of Byzantine culture did the people who eventually formed Russia adopt?
3. **Relating Cause and Effect** (a) In eastern Europe, how did the Viking trade routes affect the growth of

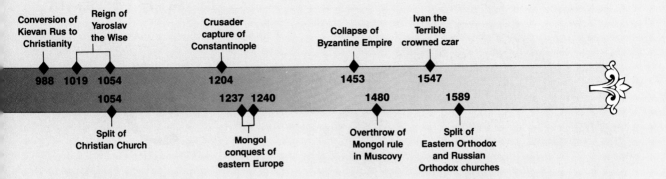

Conversion of Kievan Rus to Christianity	**Reign of Yaroslav the Wise**		**Crusader capture of Constantinople**	**Collapse of Byzantine Empire**	**Ivan the Terrible crowned czar**

988   **1019**   **1054**   **1204**   **1453**   **1547**

1054   **1237 1240**   **1480**   **1589**

Split of Christian Church

Mongol conquest of eastern Europe

Overthrow of Mongol rule in Muscovy

Split of Eastern Orthodox and Russian Orthodox churches

cities such as Kiev? **(b)** What effects did the Mongol invasion have on Kievan Rus?

4. **Analyzing Ideas** **(a)** How did the Russian Orthodox church branch out from the Eastern Orthodox church? **(b)** How was the Eastern Orthodox church in the region of Kievan Rus strengthened during Mongol rule?

5. **Understanding Chronology** Indicate whether each of the following events occurred between 300 and 600, 600 and 900, 900 and 1200, or 1200 and 1500.
   (a) Mongols capture Kiev.
   (b) Justinian rules the Byzantine Empire.
   (c) Yaroslav I rules.
   (d) Eastern church splits from the Roman Catholic church.

 ## Relating Geography to History

(a) On an outline map of the present-day Soviet Union, trace the rivers mentioned in this chapter and label the body of water into which each river flows. **(b)** Using the maps on page 197 and Chapter 12, page 281, compare the territories of Kievan Rus with the Kipchak Empire (Golden Horde). What areas overlap? What territory of Kievan Rus is not included in the Kipchak Empire?

Relating Past to Present

1. Use either *The Statesman's Yearbook* or a world almanac from your library to obtain a list of products that the Soviet Union and Turkey import and export today. Compare this list with what was traded between the Byzantine Empire and Kievan Rus.

2. Visit a Greek or Russian Orthodox church and a Roman Catholic church. Write a report on the types of art, architecture, and decorative pieces you observe. Try to explain any similarities or differences you observe between these modern churches and the descriptions of the ancient churches in this chapter.

Applying History Study Skills

Before completing this activity, review Building History Study Skills on page 192.

Read the following excerpt from *Of the Buildings of Justinian* by Procopius. Then identify whether the author is neutral, biased in favor of Justinian, or biased against Justinian. Provide evidence, such as words or phrases that convey positive or negative attitudes, that supports your conclusions.

“ The Emperor Justinian . . . succeeding to the throne when the state was decayed, added greatly to its extent and glory by driving out from it the barbarians. . . . As for religion, which he found uncertain and torn by various heresies, he destroyed everything which could lead to error, and securely established the true faith upon one solid foundation. Moreover, finding the laws obscure through their unnecessary multitude, and confused by their conflict with one another, he firmly established them by reducing the number of those which were unnecessary, and in the case of those which were contradictory, by confirming better ones. ”

Investigating Further

1. **Writing a Report** Use encyclopedias or books about the Byzantine Empire to prepare a written report about the emperor Justinian. Include in your report a description of his life and his accomplishments.

2. **Interviewing People** Interview someone from Eastern Europe (Greece, Russia, Turkey, or the Ukraine) to gather information on the celebrations of special religious occasions, such as Christmas, Easter, weddings, baptisms, and funerals. Present your findings in an oral report to the class. Ask members of the class to compare this information with their own experiences on similar occasions.

3. **Drawing a Building Plan** Using pictures in encyclopedias and the photograph on page 186 of this chapter as models, draw a building plan of the church of Hagia Sophia. Display your plan on the bulletin board.

4. **Researching** Use resources in the school and public libraries to undertake a research project on Yaroslav the Wise's law code, the Pravda Russkaia. Make special note of its similarities to Justinian's Code. Be prepared to present an oral report on your findings to the class.

9

Islam Became a Powerful Force from Spain to India

3.7 mil. BC   4000 BC   AD 2100

Significance

In the 600s the prophet Muhammad founded Islam, the youngest of the world's major religions. In only a few decades, this young religion captured the fervent support of millions of people and spread from Muhammad's homeland of Arabia west into the Mediterranean region and east into India.

Military conquest contributed greatly to the success of Islam. Indeed, Muhammad preached that the followers of Islam—known as Muslims—had to fight for their beliefs. "The sword is the key of heaven and hell," he said. However, Muhammad also offered spiritual teachings, encouraging people to lead humble, generous, and tolerant lives. Many who sought religious faith to guide their lives received and accepted this powerful messages.

As Islam spread, it encouraged the establishment of well-organized and vigorous states. Economic and cultural life flourished. Islamic philosophers, scientists, and artists created works that greatly influenced Western and Muslim cultures.

Terms to Define

hegira   imam
mullah   caliphate
mosque   dower
caliph   sultan

People to Identify

Muhammad   Babur
Abu Bakr   Akbar
Janissaries   Shah Jahan
Tamerlane   Aurangzeb

Places to Locate

Jiddah   Cairo
Mecca   Cordova
Medina   Delhi
Baghdad   Samarkand

Questions to Guide Your Reading

1 How did Islam and the Muslim Empire spread outward from Arabia?
2 What characteristics of their culture allowed the Muslims to create an advanced civilization?
3 What important changes did Muslim and Mogul rulers bring to India?

A story in Muslim literature tells of a sultan named Schariar (shahr • i • YAHR). Each night he married a new wife, and each morning he ordered her execution because he believed that no wife would remain loyal. However, one of these wives, Scheherezade (shuh • her • uh • ZAHD), told him an entertaining story which pleased him so much that he did not order her execution the following day. Night after night she continued to charm him with her stories. After a thousand and one nights of her storytelling, the sultan became convinced that this wife would remain forever faithful, and he abandoned all thoughts of executing her.

The collection of the "thousand and one" folk stories and fairy tales of Indian, Persian, or Arabic origin were translated from Persian into Arabic as early as 850 and have been enjoyed by people throughout the world for centuries. But it was not until the late 1700s that they were brought together in the collection we know today as the Thousand and One Nights, or Arabian Nights.

The collection includes the Sinbad stories, "Aladdin and His Magic Lamp" and "The History of Ali Baba" (source of the familiar phrase "Open Sesame"). These stories and others from the Thousand and One Nights are among the most widely read in history.

1 Islam and the Muslim Empire Spread Outward from Arabia

While the Byzantines ruled Asia Minor and the Balkan region, a new empire—the Muslim, or Arab, Empire—took shape to the south and east. The Muslims, like the Byzantines, developed a civilization that for centuries far surpassed that of Western Europe. It began in Arabia.

The Physical Setting

South of the Fertile Crescent lay the great peninsula of Arabia. Most of it consisted of a desert plateau with such sparse vegetation that it could only support herders and their flocks of sheep. These herders, called Arabs or Bedouins (BED • uh • wuhnz), lived as nomads, moving their flocks from one grazing area to another. They were organized into tribes, each

◀ *Dome of the Rock in Jerusalem*

ruled with an iron hand by a sheikh (SHEEK), or chief.

Some coastal regions of Arabia with greater rainfall could support more people. Here towns grew up. The Arabs who lived in these centers became traders. Goods from Asia and Africa entered the port of Jiddah (JID•uh) and then were taken overland to Mecca, the starting point of a caravan route running north to Syria. Consequently the Arabs who lived in towns met people of other cultures and were more influenced by the mainstream of civilization in the Fertile Crescent than the nomadic Bedouins.

The Life of Muhammad

Muhammad, the founder of Islam,* was born in Mecca about 570. Orphaned at an early age, Muhammad spent his youth in poverty. Having had little formal education, Muhammad probably never learned to write. As a young man, he became a camel driver and a caravan trader.

Because Muhammad lived in a major trading city that had contact with the outside world, he was exposed to Judaism and Christianity. As he met foreign traders and traveled to Christian and Jewish areas north of Mecca, Muhammad began to think seriously about religious and ethical questions. Although the Arabs worshiped many gods, meditation and prayer convinced Muhammad that there was only one god, whom he called Allah.

When he was about 40 years old, Muhammad had a great religious experience. He believed that Gabriel the archangel, or chief angel, approached him and ordered him to preach the word of Allah to the Arabs. Muhammad did not claim to have any supernatural powers. Like Moses, he considered himself a prophet and teacher.

Mecca's rulers bitterly opposed Muhammad's preaching. Mecca, an important center of trade, was also the site of a yearly pilgrimage that Arabs made to worship in the sacred Kaaba (KAHB•uh), a small stone building filled with the statues of many gods. The travelers brought income to many of Mecca's merchants. The rulers feared that Muhammad's preaching of a new religion would threaten the pilgrimage and cause the merchants to lose money.

---

*In Arabic the word *Islam* means "submission to the will of God."

Fearing for his life, Muhammad took his little band of followers to the nearby town of Medina. The event became known as the **hegira** (hi•JY•ruh), meaning "flight." It remained such an important event in Muhammad's life that the date, 622, became the first year of the Muslim calendar.

In Medina, Muhammad converted many people to Islam and established himself as the community leader. A few years later, he returned to Mecca at the head of an army and captured the city. He destroyed the idols in the Kaaba and made it Islam's holiest place. The only symbol he left in the temple was the Black Stone. Muhammad believed that Abraham had built the Kaaba and placed in it, as a sign of Allah's power, the stone sent from heaven.

The fall of Mecca convinced many Arabs that Muhammad was a prophet too strong to oppose. With a combination of wise policies, tolerance, and force, he converted many of the Bedouin tribes to his new religion. By 632, when Muhammad died, a large part of Arabia had accepted Islam (see map, page 209).

The Faith of Islam

The central belief of Islam is "There is no God but Allah, and Muhammad is his prophet." Like most religions, Islam has a holy book, definite rules for its believers, and emphasis on certain moral teachings.

The holy book of Islam is the Koran (meaning "recital"). The Koran presents Muhammad's most important teachings and includes many concepts and teachings also found in the Bible and the Torah. For example, the Koran recounts the creation of the world and the teachings of major prophets and of Jesus. Muhammad accepted the Bible and the Torah as part of Allah's revelations, and he taught respect for Christians and Jews. Muhammad also taught that the Koran was Allah's guide for all people and that it had existed in heaven, but he believed that no person before himself had been worthy of receiving it.

All Muslims recognize the Koran as their sacred book. Because it was written in Arabic, and because Arabs discouraged its translation into other languages, Arabic became the common language of Muslims in matters of religion, law, and literature.

According to the Koran, a Muslim must meet five important obligations known as *The Pillars of Faith:* (1) Recite the words of witness, "There is no

Learning from Pictures *Islam's holiest shrine is the Kaaba located in Mecca, where Muslims go to fulfill the Third Pillar of Faith.*

God but Allah, and Muhammad is his prophet." (2) Pray five times a day facing Mecca, the holy city of Islam. (3) If possible, make a pilgrimage to Mecca at least once in a lifetime. (4) Give alms—money or food—to the needy. (5) Fast, or go without food and drink, from sunrise to sunset during the month of Ramadan—the ninth month of the Muslim year. The month is considered sacred because it was the month in which Muhammad had his vision of the archangel Gabriel and received Allah's instructions, later written in the Koran.

Muhammad required and emphasized the virtues of temperance, humility, justice, generosity, tolerance, obedience to authority, and courage. Islam allowed a Muslim man to have as many as four wives, but only if he treated them all with equal kindness. The faith also permitted slavery, but slaves had to be treated humanely. Muslims were forbidden to drink alcoholic beverages or to eat pork, believing, as the Jews did, that pigs were unclean.

In contrast to the teachings of Jesus, Muhammad praised what he called the jihad (ji • HAHD), or holy war—fighting to defend or spread the faith of Islam. According to Muhammad a fallen warrior's sins were forgiven and he received promised rewards in heaven.

Islam permits no religious images, such as statues, because Muhammad forbade his followers to make representations of human or animal forms. No elaborate ceremonies characterize the faith, and no formal priesthood exists. However, **mullahs,** men learned in Islamic faith and law, perform priestly duties. At a service in a Muslim temple, or **mosque,** the people pray together under the guidance of a leader. On Friday, the holy day in the week, all male worshipers must gather at noon for prayer and a sermon. The faith requires women to offer the same prayers at home or in a special section of the mosque set aside for them. A woman must also obey her husband, care for his children, and manage his household.

The Spread of Islam

When Muhammad died in 632, an assembly of Muslims chose Abu Bakr (UH • boo BAK • uhr), his father-in-law and probably his first convert, as his

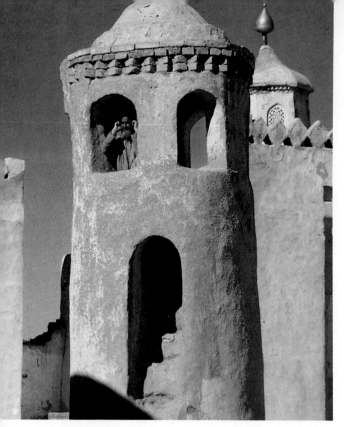

In less than 100 years after the death of Muhammad, the Islamic prophet's followers had swept through Arabia, Palestine, Syria, Armenia, Mesopotamia, Persia, part of India, and all of North Africa, including Egypt (see map, page 209). Then they took to the sea and eventually conquered the islands of the Mediterranean, from which they controlled the vital trade routes of the southern Mediterranean.

An attempt to take Constantinople failed. However, at the western end of the Mediterranean Sea, Muslims successfully entered Europe. A people of North Africa, called the Berbers, had recently converted to Islam and eagerly sought conquest. In 711 a Berber general named Tariq led an expedition

Learning from Pictures *A muezzin, or crier, calls the hour of daily prayers from the minaret of a mosque in Turkestan.*

successor. Abu Bakr used the title **caliph,** meaning "successor to the prophet." When Abu Bakr died, an assembly chose his friend and counselor, Umar, as caliph. To avoid civil wars over the succession, both Abu Bakr and Umar followed a policy aimed at conquering neighboring territories of non-Muslims. This policy diverted attention from the selection of the new caliph.

Fortunately for the caliphs, the Arabs had many opportunities for conquest in the 600s. Years of conflict had weakened both the Byzantine and Persian empires.

The Arab policy toward conquered peoples made their conquests easier. Fierce and fearless in battle, the Arabs were generous in victory. Non-Muslims who surrendered could choose either to accept Islam or to pay an annual tribute, or tax. However, some who refused to do either received the death penalty. Few of the conquered chose to die; they either paid the tribute or converted to Islam. Those who paid the tribute could keep their religion and customs but could not hold government office.

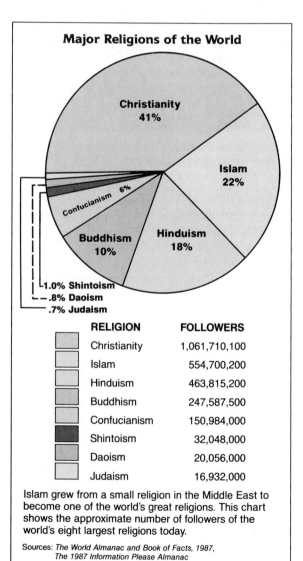

Major Religions of the World

Christianity 41%

Islam 22%

Confucianism 6%

Buddhism 10%

Hinduism 18%

1.0% Shintoism
.8% Daoism
.7% Judaism

RELIGION	FOLLOWERS
Christianity	1,061,710,100
Islam	554,700,200
Hinduism	463,815,200
Buddhism	247,587,500
Confucianism	150,984,000
Shintoism	32,048,000
Daoism	20,056,000
Judaism	16,932,000

Islam grew from a small religion in the Middle East to become one of the world's great religions. This chart shows the approximate number of followers of the world's eight largest religions today.

Sources: *The World Almanac and Book of Facts, 1987, The 1987 Information Please Almanac*

What If?
Constantinople

The Muslims attempted to conquer Constantinople in 718, but Byzantine armies successfully defended the city. How do you think the course of history would have been different if the Muslims had toppled the Byzantine Empire?

against the Visigoths in Spain, past the great rock that guards the strait between Africa and Europe. The rock became known as Jabal-al-Tariq, the "Mountain of Tariq." Europeans later altered the name to Gibraltar.

Spain was an easy conquest, and within seven years the Moors, Muslims of Spain, had passed beyond the Pyrenees to raid the plains of what is now central France. In 732 the Franks defeated them near the town of Tours (see map, this page). Driven back into Spain, the Moors continued to rule there for over 700 years.

In the 1800s the American author Washington Irving traveled throughout Spain. After visiting the Alhambra, the beautiful palace of the Moorish kings in Granada, a province of southern Spain, Irving wrote:

❝*T*heir career of conquest, from the rock of Gibraltar to the cliffs of the Pyrenees, was as rapid and brilliant as the Moslem victories of Syria and Egypt. Nay, had they not been checked on the plains of Tours, all France, all Europe, might have been overrun with the same facility as the empires of the East. . . .

Where are they? Ask the shores of Barbary and its desert places. . . . They have not even left a distinct name behind them, though for nearly eight centuries they were a distinct people. . . . A few broken monuments are all that remain to bear witness to their power and dominion, as solitary rocks, left far in the interior, bear testimony to the extent of some vast inundation. Such is the Alhambra; . . . an elegant memento of a brave, intelligent, and graceful people, who conquered, ruled, flourished, and passed away.❞

Learning from Maps   *Two of the most important Islamic cities were Cordova and Baghdad. Where is Islam's holiest city?*

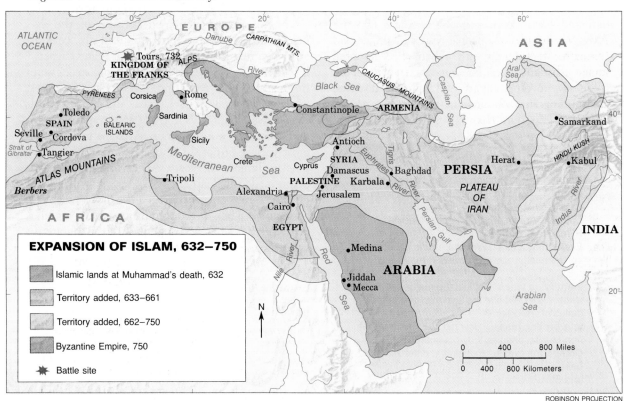

EXPANSION OF ISLAM, 632–750

- Islamic lands at Muhammad's death, 632
- Territory added, 633–661
- Territory added, 662–750
- Byzantine Empire, 750
- ★ Battle site

ROBINSON PROJECTION

Islam Divides

Early in the history of Islam, rival groups began to emerge. Disputes arose over Muhammad's successors and over differing interpretations of the Koran. These divisions have persisted into modern times.

One group, the Sunnis (SOON • neez), claimed that the only intercessor between believers and Allah was the Koran. Another group, the Shiites (SHEE • yts), believed that a person, rather than the Koran itself, was the proper intermediary between Allah and believers. Shiites looked to this person, called the **imam,** as having both spiritual and secular authority. In countries where the Shiite sect dominated, the supreme religious authority also led the government.

The interpretation of the Koran by the faithful remained basic to both Islamic groups. According to Islamic belief, the Koran could not contain errors because Allah had dictated it directly to Muhammad. However, in order to establish the authority needed for the particular community, a decision had to be made concerning which verses or ideas took precedence over others.

As Islam spread beyond Arabia, numerous opportunities arose for direct contact with Christian and Jewish concepts and practices. By the 700s, Muslim mystics, people who said they could communicate directly with Allah, had adopted some Christian values. For example, they accepted voluntary poverty, a part of Christian doctrine maintaining that the amount of money a person has is less important than his or her faith in God.

SECTION 1 REVIEW

1. **Define** hegira, mullah, mosque, caliph, imam
2. **Identify** Bedouin, Muhammad, Allah, jihad, Abu Bakr, Berbers, Jabal-al-Tariq, Moors
3. **Locate** Arabia, Jiddah, Mecca, Medina, Pyrenees, Tours
4. **Evaluating Ideas** Why did Arabic become the common language of Muslims in matters of religion, law, and literature?
5. **Identifying Ideas** **(a)** List the major beliefs of Islam. **(b)** Describe the five chief obligations or duties of a Muslim.
6. **Interpreting Ideas** How did Muslims treat the non-Muslim peoples they conquered?
7. **Comparing Ideas** Explain the differences in beliefs and practices between Sunni Muslims and Shiite Muslims.

---

2 Muslims Created an Advanced Civilization

The tightly organized Islamic government gave its rulers great authority. Within the stable society that developed, both economic and cultural activity flourished.

Government and Economy

The caliph, the supreme civil, military, and religious leader of the vast Muslim Empire, headed the government. Although an elected office at first, the position of caliph later became hereditary. The territory of the empire, then organized into provinces, came under the leadership of Arabs.

Because the empire became more and more difficult to rule, it was later divided into three parts, or **caliphates,** ruled by caliphs in Baghdad, Cairo, and Cordova.

The Arabs had long been traders, and Muhammad had encouraged commerce. India and China sent goods across the Indian Ocean to the Persian Gulf and the Red Sea, then overland to the ports of Syria and to Cairo and Alexandria in Egypt.

Manufacturing increased because of the demands of trade. The empire produced silk, cotton, and linen textiles, as well as tapestries and carpets. Luxuries such as jewelry, perfumes, and spices were in great demand. Metal products included objects made of gold, silver, steel, brass, and copper. Steel swords from Damascus in Syria and from Toledo in Spain became world-famous. Artisans produced a great variety of pottery and glassware. Other artisans in Tangier in North Africa and Cordova in Spain made fine leather goods.

The Arabs also encouraged the development of agriculture. They introduced fruits, vegetables, and other products native to one part of the empire to other areas where they might grow.

Society and Art

In Islamic families, as in many other cultures and religions, the father was the absolute head of the household. The family provided the individual with both economic security and physical protection. Muslims respected the elderly and showed concern for the needs of all members of the extended

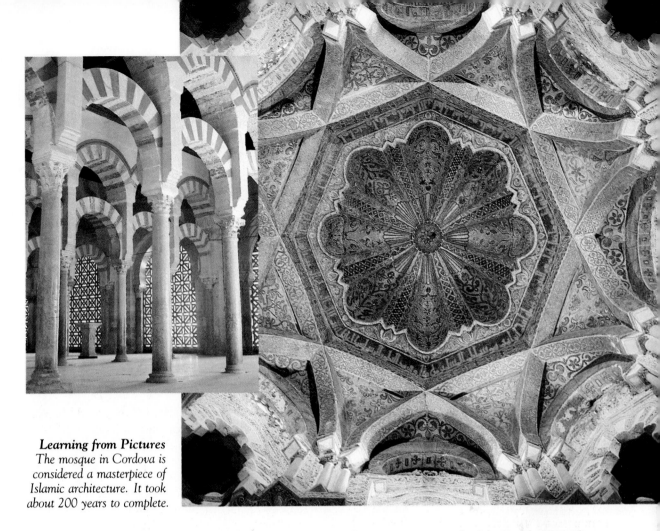

Learning from Pictures
The mosque in Cordova is considered a masterpiece of Islamic architecture. It took about 200 years to complete.

family—parents, children, grandparents, aunts, uncles, and cousins.

Women had a clearly defined position in Islamic society. The Koran says, "Good women are obedient." A father or husband accepted responsibility for a woman's behavior. Parents arranged marriages for their children, and the groom gave his bride a special marriage gift called a *sadaq* or *mahr*, meaning **dower.** This gift did not represent a purchase price, but rather a gesture of love. In the event of a divorce, the bride kept this money.

The Koran extended more rights to women than they had received under traditional Arab law. For example, many Muslim women obtained an education and owned property. The Koran also forbade the killing of unwanted infant girls, a traditional Bedouin custom. And if a man divorced his wife, he had to continue to support her. She also was free to remarry. Although Muslim women later lost many of these rights, they still received the protection of either their husbands or brothers.

State governments had large educational systems, but the family and the mosque also took responsibility for education in Islamic society. The abilities to speak well and to write were considered the standards for an educated person. Subjects of required study were based on the Koran. A person with a superior intellect might be expected to memorize as many as 300,000 religious quotations.

Because Islamic law prohibited the use of the human form to depict Allah, the decorative arts and calligraphy assumed a special importance. Islamic art often used geometric and floral designs. Pictures of people showed only non-religious subjects, such as hunting or fighting battles.

Advances in Science and Mathematics

Though divided politically, the Muslim world remained united in one great civilization. The Arabs adopted the best ideas, customs, and institutions they found. For example, they combined the

CONNECTIONS: THEN AND NOW

Medicine

Who was the first person in your life to set eyes on you? Most likely it was a doctor (below). Doctors and medicine have existed since ancient times. Early Egyptian books contain directions for setting fractures, and X-rays of mummies reveal healed bones.

We believe the Greeks were the first people to record their scientific research so that others could use it. They had medical centers where people could go, first to be cured, and then to offer sacrifices to the gods in thanks. The Romans established a medical school in Egypt. There Galen, a famous Greek physician, conducted studies whose results were used in Europe for the next 1,300 years.

In the Middle East, the Arabs developed their own interests in medicine. Legend says that in 765

the founder of Baghdad had incurable indigestion, so the doctors sought help from a Persian medical school. From then on, Persian doctors practiced in Baghdad and taught the Muslims about surgery performed with anesthesia. They established traveling clinics whose doctors went from place to place by camel, caring for the sick (above).

When the Muslims invaded Spain, they brought their medical knowledge to the Spanish universities. From there it soon spread to other European centers of learning. Monks in Italy had preserved the old medical knowledge, and now, combined with the new learning, medicine was taught at Italian universities. Farther north, young men studied medicine at the universities of Paris, Oxford, and Cambridge. These colleges are still well known for medical studies.

scientific and philosophical ideas of Greece, Rome, and Asia.

Muslim scientists wrote handbooks and encyclopedias on many subjects. Their geographers and navigators, known as the finest in the world, perfected the astrolabe, a small instrument used to determine latitude by calculating the positions of planets and stars. And from the Chinese, Muslims learned the art of papermaking.

Muslims added much medical knowledge to that developed by Hippocrates and Galen. At Baghdad in the early 900s, Rhazes (RAY•zeez), a

Muslim physician, wrote about surgery, diseases of the eye, smallpox, and measles. He compiled a huge medical encyclopedia which, translated into Latin, was used in Europe for centuries.

About the same time that Rhazes wrote, Avicenna (av • uh • SEN • uh), an Arabian philosopher and physician, used ancient Greek sources to write the *Canon of Medicine,* a medical textbook organized like an encyclopedia. Then in the 1100s, Averroës (uh • VER • uh • weez), a Spanish-Arabian physician and philosopher, wrote highly regarded commentaries based on Aristotle's works and on Plato's *Republic.* His interpretations of Aristotle influenced later Jewish and Christian writers.

Muslims excelled at mathematics and perfected algebra as a science. Our word *algebra* comes from the Arabic words *al-jabr,* meaning "the reunion of broken parts." Mathematicians of India developed the system of Arabic numerals, but the Arabs transmitted the system to the West. The Arabs also contributed the concept of zero to mathematics.

Arab scholars were particularly influential in the development of geography as a science. They used the observations of travelers as well as astronomical calculations to perfect mapmaking. Arab geographers adopted a Hindu idea that each hemisphere of the world had a center, or summit, equally distant from the four cardinal points of north, south, east, and west. Christopher Columbus based his conclusion that the earth was not flat on this theory.

The Spread of Muslim Culture

Europeans encountered Muslim culture in two ways. One was through contact with Spain, where the Muslim culture flourished. The cities of Cordova and Toledo became famous centers of learning, and Seville was known for art and luxury. Christian and Jewish scholars then carried Muslim learning from Spain into western Europe. Europe was also affected by Muslim culture through the Crusades—the attempts by Europeans to recapture the Holy Land from the Muslims from about 1100 to about 1300 (see Chapter 11). In Palestine and other Muslim regions, the crusaders learned of Muslim achievements and later returned home with ideas that greatly influenced European culture.

The great era of Muslim culture, however, lasted from about 700 to 1000. After that time those who believed in "following the letter of the Koran" rose to power in the Muslim world. These people opposed free thought and foreign ideas. At the same time, Turk and Mongol invaders disrupted trade and destroyed cities throughout the Muslim world. Only in Spain, which remained independent from the rest of the Muslim world, did Muslim culture continue to flourish.

The Turks

In the late 900s, the Seljuk Turks of central Asia migrated to Baghdad, where they adopted Islam.

Learning from Pictures
This Muslim astronomer uses a quadrant to calculate the altitude of a meteor. What navigational instrument did Muslim scientists perfect?

Oriental Carpets

People have been weaving rugs for at least 3,000 years. Used first as protection against cold, carpets soon had other purposes as well. They became symbols of wealth and popular items of trade. In Turkey, Persia, and central Asia, rug weaving became a great art. Many Oriental carpets remain unsurpassed for their texture, richness of color, and beauty of design.

Through the centuries, Muslims who could afford them have knelt and prayed on beautiful rugs. During prayer, the rug must be placed on the floor so that the arch in the design points toward Mecca, Muhammad's birthplace. The prayer rug shown here was woven in Turkey during the late 1600s or early 1700s. Typical of almost all Oriental carpets, it has a border of wide and narrow stripes and various geometric and stylized designs. The parts of the carpet have specific meanings. The color red, for example, stands for happiness and wealth. The trees above the arches are probably symbols of the tree of life.

During the 1000s they seized much of Asia Minor from the Byzantines and extended their rule into the Muslim territories of Syria and Mesopotamia. For the next 200 years, conflicts among Arabs, Turks, Byzantines, and Crusaders raged throughout the eastern Mediterranean area.

During the first half of the 1300s, a group of Turks called Ottomans (after their first ruler, Osman) surged through Asia Minor before invading Europe and establishing a capital at Adrianople, northwest of Constantinople. In the late 1300s they moved against Constantinople itself. Although the Mongols temporarily halted the Ottoman advance, the Turks eventually captured the city in 1453 and made it the capital of the Ottoman Empire.

The Ottoman rulers allowed conquered non-Muslims to practice their own religion. Religious minorities, grouped into communities called **millets,** exercised some self-government. They could establish their own schools, administer a civil government with its own courts, and collect taxes. However, any Muslim involved in a crime was not subject to the millet's authority.

A group of slaves called Janissaries* contributed to the Ottoman successes in battle and in government. The Janissaries, carefully instructed in

---

*Most of the Janissaries had been taken as prisoners of war. In later times, children taken from conquered Christians were often raised as Janissaries.

Islamic beliefs and laws, were organized into a standing army of disciplined, trained infantry. As bodyguards to the Turkish rulers, the **sultans,** they became influential in the government. Encouraged by promotions for merit and by a system of rewards and punishments, they represented a source of great strength. Later they gained much power and became a danger to the government, somewhat like the Praetorian Guard of the Roman Empire.

SECTION 2 REVIEW

1. **Define** caliphate, dower, millet, sultan
2. **Identify** Rhazes, Ottomans, Janissaries
3. **Locate** Baghdad, Cairo, Cordova, Damascus, Toledo, Tangier, Seville
4. **Summarizing Ideas** What items were manufactured in various locations throughout the Islamic Empire?
5. **Describing Ideas** Describe the organization of an Islamic family.
6. **Classifying Ideas** List what you consider to be the three most important scientific contributions of Islamic culture.
7. **Evaluating Ideas** How did the Ottoman Turks use the Janissaries in the organization of their government?

3 Muslim and Mogul Rulers Brought Important Changes to India

Islam also had profound effects far to the east of Arabia. Gupta rule in India came to an end in the 500s. At that time the Huns swept through the mountain passes and conquered all of northern India. Disorder and confusion disrupted the region until a ruler named Harsha brought peace.

Harsha's Rule

By the early 600s, the Huns had been overcome, and three warring states controlled the Ganges Valley. In 606 Harsha became the rajah in one of these kingdoms and built an effective army that included a cavalry and an infantry, as well as trained war elephants that wore enormous armor plates.

In six years Harsha conquered what had been the Gupta Empire. The Deccan, the rugged hill country south of the Narbada River, proved unconquerable, and Harsha never subdued it. Instead he settled down to govern his empire in northern India, which for a long time he did wisely and well. A Chinese Buddhist pilgrim to India wrote of the excellence of Harsha's early reign. He reported that the law-abiding people enjoyed low taxes, a high standard of living, and an excellent educational system.

Evil advisers victimized Harsha in the last years of his reign, and he became cruel and suspicious. By 647 his rule became so oppressive that the army had him assassinated.

The Rajputs

After Harsha's death northern India split into numerous small states, ruled over by the Rajputs (RAHJ • poots).* Descended from tribes that had migrated from central Asia into northern India during the 400s and 500s, the Rajputs claimed divine origins. They intermarried with Hindus, adopted the Hindu religion with its caste system, and took control of the small states.

Rajput rule was generally stable. Literature of the time included codes of conduct stressing respect for women, fair fighting in combat, and mercy for fallen warriors. Advanced codes of law also governed Rajput society. Courts used the testimony of sworn witnesses or written statements to decide civil cases. A man's children inherited his property, and his family supported his widow. The Rajputs also strictly enforced the caste system. Marriages could be arranged only between persons of similar caste.

Northern Indians under the Rajputs took great pride in their land. One visitor wrote that Indians "believe that there is no country but theirs, no nation like theirs, no kings like theirs, no religions like theirs, no science like theirs."

As it always had been and would long remain, agriculture in the small, self-sufficient villages served as the foundation for the economy of northern India. Villagers worked their own small plots of land, but policy required that they give free labor to the government once a month. Trade thrived, with people exchanging goods and services both within the village and between villages. And overseas trade flourished—with some trade monopolies, groups that controlled a good or a service, reaping large profits.

---

* *Rajput* means "son of a king."

Muslim Invasions of India

In the early 700s, Indian pirates from the Indus Valley began attacking Muslim ships in the Arabian Sea. About 712 the Muslims struck back by conquering the Indus Valley. They governed the valley as a Muslim province but gave the Indians considerable freedom. Muslim criminal law applied to everyone, but courts cited Indian law in civil cases.

For about 300 years, the Muslims made no further conquests in India. Meanwhile, Turkish Muslims had occupied the area now called Afghanistan, northwest of the Indus River. About the year 1000, the Turks surged through the northwest mountain passes into India. One by one the small states of the Rajput princes fell to the conquerors. In battle the Indians always outnumbered the Turks and used their lumbering war elephants. However, the Muslims, adopting tactics originally developed by Alexander the Great, used their cavalry to stampede the elephants back upon the Indian troops. In 1193 the Muslims occupied Delhi, and by 1236 they controlled all of northern India.

The Delhi sultans. In 1206 one Muslim leader, a Turkish slave-general, founded the Mamluk dynasty. Because the Mamluk rulers used Delhi as their capital, they are called the Delhi sultans. Although the sultans were fanatical and cruel, they kept northern India unified for about 300 years. Early in the 1300s, one of the Delhi sultans conquered the Deccan. By 1320, resistance to the Muslims had collapsed throughout most of the Indian subcontinent.

Two Delhi sultans represent the worst and the best of Muslim rule in India. Probably the worst was Muhammad Tughluq (tuhg • LUHK), who ruled from 1325 to 1351. He murdered his father and fed the flesh of a rebel nephew to the rebel's wife and children. He once ordered the evacuation of Delhi and forced its inhabitants to march 600 miles south to a new capital.

Perhaps the best of the Delhi sultans was Firuz Shah, a social reformer and cultured man, who reigned from 1351 to 1388. He laid out more than 2,000 gardens and built five large canals. He also set up an employment agency for young men and a marriage bureau for young women. The bureau not only found husbands for the young women but also gave them marriage gifts.

Tamerlane. First civil wars and then the devastating onslaught of the Mongol leader Tamerlane interrupted the rule of the Delhi sultans. Tamerlane (Timur the Lame), born in Afghanistan in 1336, claimed to be descended from Genghis Khan, a great Mongol leader, and was as ferocious as his supposed ancestor. Following the usual pattern of Asiatic nomad warriors, he created an army and established his power in central Asia, with his capital at Samarkand. Then, about 1380, he began a career of conquest. After defeating the Golden Horde—Mongols who had invaded eastern Europe in the 1200s—north of the Caspian Sea, he led his army into India.

Tamerlane captured Delhi in 1398 and is said to have slaughtered about 100,000 of its inhabitants. When his campaign ended, he returned to Samarkand, taking with him all of Delhi's surviving artisans and leaving the city to die. Tamerlane reportedly said of the deserted capital, "For two whole months, not a bird moved in the city." After returning to Samarkand, Tamerlane moved westward again. He captured and looted Baghdad and Damascus and massacred their inhabitants. In 1402, his forces defeated the Ottoman Turks and captured the sultan in a great battle at Angora (modern Ankara) in Asia Minor. At the time the Turks were threatening what was left of the Byzantine Empire. Their defeat at the hands of the Mongols saved Constantinople for another 50 years.

In his late 60s, Tamerlane planned a campaign against China, wanting to conquer it as Genghis Khan had. However, Tamerlane died in 1405 before he could accomplish his goal.

Tamerlane's successors in India ruled until 1450. At that time the Delhi sultans regained power and maintained their rule until 1526.

Results of Muslim Rule

Despite the interruption of Tamerlane and his Mongol successors, the first period of Muslim rule in India had important and lasting consequences. Most northern Indians and nearly all southern Indians were Hindus. At first the Muslims ruthlessly slaughtered Hindus. Later they seemed content to confiscate land, leaving village life to go on as it had in the past. Even so, many Hindus converted to Islam, either to gain favor with the conquerors or to escape from the Hindu caste system.

Profound religious differences separated Muslims and Hindus. The Hindu worship of many gods

BUILDING HISTORY STUDY SKILLS

Reading About History: Understanding Sequence

A sequence is the order in which things happen in time. Sequencing events, then, is arranging these events in the order in which they occurred. Sequencing helps you to organize information. From the pattern of the data, you can determine how events are related to each other. The relationship among these events can help you to identify other important ideas such as cause and effect and historical significance.

How to Sequence Information

To sequence information, follow these steps.

1. Identify what you hope to learn by sequencing the information being studied.
2. Look for calendar references, clue words, and time periods. Calendar references include centuries, years, and dates. Clue words include *first, second, after, before, meanwhile,* and *later.*
3. Determine whether there is an implied sequence or a cause-and-effect relationship. For example, could one event have happened without the other taking place?
4. List the events in sequence.
5. Make a statement about the relationship between the items, actions, or events included. What is the significance of the pattern of data?

Developing the Skill

You can better understand the expansion of Islam by organizing significant events sequentially. The following statements about the spread of Islam are not listed in the order they occurred. As you read the list, try to determine the proper sequence.

1. Muhammad's preaching was opposed, and in 622 he fled to Medina.
2. By 632, when Muhammad died, a large part of Arabia had accepted Islam.
3. Muhammad's successors pursued a policy aimed at conquering the territory of non-Muslims.
4. Muhammad considered himself a prophet and a teacher, and believed that there is only one god, Allah.
5. Muhammad became the leader of the community in Medina.
6. The Muslims were generous toward conquered peoples, who had to accept the religion of Islam or pay a tribute.
7. In 732, the Franks defeated the Moors and drove them back to Spain.
8. Less than a century after the death of Muhammad, his followers had conquered Palestine, Syria, Mesopotamia, part of India, Egypt, and the rest of North Africa.

The correct sequence of events would be: 4, 1, 5, 2, 3, 8, 6, and 7. The first statement (4) establishes Muhammad as the leader. Muhammad's beliefs are an implied part of the sequence. Muhammad has to be preaching something in order to be expelled from Mecca (1). Muhammad then became the leader of Medina (5). The date 632 completes Muhammad's achievements (2). His successors (3) would have to follow after his death. They conquered neighboring territories and then went to India, Egypt, and the rest of North Africa (8). Their conquering policy (6) is then explained as an implied part of the sequence. The Franks prevented the Muslim expansion into other parts of Europe in 732 (7).

Practicing the skill. Using the guidelines for sequencing information, make a list of important events at your school and arrange them in sequence. Include events such as special assemblies, school-sponsored club activities, and sports competitions.

To apply this skill, see Applying History Study Skills on page 221.

Muhammad's son-in-law, Imam Ali, in battle

and of idols repelled the Muslims. Hindus used music in their religious ceremonies; Muslims did not. The Hindu caste system contradicted Muslim belief in the equality of all people before Allah. Muslims introduced the seclusion of women— called *purdah*—into India. They also introduced the harem of several wives, which Hindus rejected. The Muslims ate the cows so sacred to the Hindus, while Hindus ate pork, which the Muslims thought unclean. In addition, Hindus drank fermented beverages that Muslims rejected.

However, the Muslims made several contributions to Indian life. They introduced a new and important language, Urdu. This language combined Persian and Arabic words with Hindu grammar and was used in addition to other official languages. Indian architects learned from the Muslims how to build the dome and the arch. Also, the

Learning from Maps Babur defeated the Delhi sultans at the battle of Panipat. What two cities on the west coast of the subcontinent remained independent from Mogul rule?

THE MOGUL EMPIRE, 1526–1707

LAMBERT CONFORMAL CONIC PROJECTION

Muslims borrowed paper, gunpowder, and the art of making porcelain from the Chinese and introduced it to India.

The Mogul Empire

As the Delhi sultanate grew weaker, Rajput princes again struggled for control of India. Thus, as in the time of Tamerlane, India lay open to Mongol attack. It came under the leadership of the youthful and talented "Babur the Tiger," a descendant of Tamerlane. He captured Delhi in 1526 and brought the Rajputs under his control. Then he set up the Mogul Empire (see map, this page), which lasted until 1761.*

Although Babur died in 1530, a series of energetic and talented rulers controlled the empire he had founded and united northern and southern India. While Tamerlane had made Indians fear Mongol rulers, the Moguls encouraged unity, orderly government, and the arts.

Babur's grandson, Akbar, considered the greatest of the Mogul emperors, reigned from 1556 to 1605. He fostered toleration for all religions, one of his greatest contributions to Indian civilization. Akbar repealed the special tax that non-Muslims had been forced to pay. He took a Hindu wife and encouraged Hindu as well as Muslim artists. These artists, supported by the royal household, created delicate and colorful miniature paintings based on the styles of Persia.

The rule of the Mogul emperor Shah Jahan, from 1628 to 1658, was outstanding. He is best known for ordering the construction of two famous buildings—the magnificent Taj Mahal at Agra and the Hall of Private Audience in the Red Fort at Delhi. The Taj Mahal, made of marble inlaid with semiprecious gems and built as a tomb for Shah Jahan's favorite wife, remains one of the architectural wonders of the world. In the cornices of the Hall of Private Audience are carved these famous lines: "If on earth be an Eden of Bliss, It is this, it is this, it is this."

These great buildings of marble were enormously expensive both in monetary and in human terms. Their cost became a grinding tax burden on

---

*In 1761 the Afghans pillaged Delhi. Although Mogul rulers continued to use the title of emperor until 1858, they had no power. Therefore, historians usually list the year 1761 as the end of the Mogul Empire.

Learning from Pictures *The Taj Mahal's decorative details, gardens, and pools typify the blending of Muslim and Hindu cultures.*

Shah Jahan's subjects. It took 22,000 workers 22 years to finish the Taj Mahal.

The Moguls attempted a grand synthesis of Hindu and Muslim cultures. In the late 1400s, Nanak, a mystic prophet who was born a Hindu, attempted to bring about a total union of these two faiths. Out of his teachings grew a new religion— the Sikh (SEEK) faith. This faith stressed loving devotion to one god and the brotherhood of all, ideas that conflicted with Hindu beliefs. Nanak became the first guru (leader or teacher) of the Sikh faith. By the late 1600s, the Sikhs had become militant. As their military power developed, they became fierce enemies of the Mogul Empire and the Muslims.

In 1658, Aurangzeb (AWR • uhng • zeb), Shah Jahan's son, had his ailing father imprisoned and declared himself emperor. A fanatical Muslim, Aurangzeb began a campaign of persecution against people of other faiths, an act which led to revolts throughout his empire—by Sikhs and Rajputs in the north and among the peoples of the Deccan to the south.

Although the Mogul Empire reached its greatest territorial extent under Aurangzeb, his policies of persecution seriously weakened it. After his death in 1707, the empire began to disintegrate.

SECTION 3 REVIEW

1. **Identify** Harsha, Rajputs, Tamerlane, Urdu, Babur, Mogul, Akbar, Shah Jahan, Nanak
2. **Locate** Delhi, Samarkand, Angora, Agra
3. **Evaluating Ideas** Why were Turkish Muslims and the Mongols able to conquer northern India?
4. **Contrasting Ideas** What differences between Muslims and Hindus led to antagonisms?
5. **Identifying Ideas** Why was Akbar considered the greatest of the Mogul emperors?

CHAPTER 9 REVIEW

Timeline:
- **622** Hegira
- **Death of Muhammad**
- **Great era of Muslim culture**
- AD ca. 570
- 606
- **632**
- ca. 700
- 711 732
- ca. 1000
- **Birth of Muhammad**
- **Beginning of Harsha's rule in India**
- **Tarik's expedition in Spain**
- **Defeat of Moors in France**

Chapter Summary

The following list contains the key concepts you have learned about Islam.

1. The rise of Islam transformed much of Asia and parts of Africa and Europe. Its early believers spread the Islamic faith aggressively, resulting in the most rapid spread of a new religion the world has ever seen.
2. Although the first wave of Muslim conquests died down in the 700s, the Muslims made further advances in India 400 years later.
3. A new Muslim expansionist force, the Ottoman Turks, rose to prominence in the 1300s and 1400s.
4. The faith of Islam emphasized humility and obedience. The result was the creation of stable states throughout the Muslim world.
5. The Muslims encouraged economic activity, and they became great traders, linking east and west.
6. The stable Islamic societies also promoted notable advances in science, philosophy, and art. Muslim contributions to medicine, mathematics, and geography had considerable influence on later scientific work.
7. In India the Muslim presence was felt at first in the 700s. It came to be of major significance only in the 1100s, when the Muslims conquered northern India.
8. Muslim rule brought new ideas and a new language, Urdu, to India. It also brought unrest and upheaval. The Muslims came as conquerors, and they persecuted the Hindus.
9. The Mogul Empire that conquered India in the 1500s was much more peaceful than earlier Muslim rulers. The Moguls encouraged the arts, most notably represented by the building of the Taj Mahal.

On a separate sheet of paper, complete the following review exercises.

Reviewing Important Terms

Supply the term that correctly completes the sentence.

1. Muhammad's flight to Medina is known as the _____ .
2. _____ are learned in Islamic faith and law and perform priestly duties.
3. A _____ is a Muslim temple.
4. The successor to the prophet was called a _____ .
5. Shiites believed that _____ were intermediaries between Allah and the people.
6. The Muslim Empire was divided into three parts called _____ .
7. Communities of religious minorities were called _____ .
8. _____ were bodyguards to Turkish rulers.

Developing Critical Thinking Skills

1. **Classifying Ideas** (a) Discuss the effects of the Muslim conquest on Indian culture. (b) Which effects do you think were positive? (c) Which were negative?
2. **Analyzing Ideas** How did trade in the ancient world influence Muhammad's ideas?
3. **Comparing Ideas** In what ways is the Koran similar to the Bible and the Torah?
4. **Synthesizing Ideas** Although the Muslim world was politically divided, it developed a high level of civilization. Using evidence from the textbook, explain how Muslims made advances in trade, art, math, science, and education.
5. **Interpreting Ideas** Why was Muslim Spain important to Europe's cultural development?
6. **Contrasting Ideas** Compare the treatment of non-Muslims in the Ottoman Empire and the Mogul Empire.
7. **Understanding Chronology** In each of the groups below, place the three events in chronological order.
   (a) Battle of Tours
       Hegira of Muhammad
       Muslim conquest of Spain
   (b) Taj Mahal built
       Delhi sultanate established
       Harsha's conquest of Gupta Empire
   (c) Delhi conquered by Tamerlane
       Hindus and Sikhs persecuted by Aurangzeb
       Mogul Empire established by Babur
   (d) Christian values adopted by Muslim mystics
       Abu Bakr named first caliph
       Constantinople captured by Ottoman Turks
8. **Evaluating Ideas** Why did the Mogul Empire begin to disintegrate?

Muslim occupation
of Delhi

Delhi captured
by Tamerlane

Defeat of
Ottoman Turks
by Tamerlane

Rule of
Mogul Empire

1193   1398 1402   1526   1761

ca. 1100   ca.1300   1453   1556   1605 1658 1707

Crusades

Ottoman
capture of
Constantinople

Rule of
Akbar

Rule of
Aurangzeb

Relating Geography to History

Write a general description of the territorial changes that occurred in North Africa, southern and eastern Europe, and western Asia from about 550 to 1450. Use these maps for comparison: the Byzantine Empire in 565 (page 189) and Expansion of Islam (page 209).

Relating Past to Present

1. In early Islamic society, women were expected to be obedient and were kept in seclusion. Discuss the roles of women today in Muslim countries such as Egypt and Turkey. Compare these roles with the more traditional roles of women in such countries as Saudi Arabia and Iran. Use current sources to obtain information.

2. Many English words have been borrowed from other languages. For example, the coffee tree was introduced in Arabia in the 1400s. Coffee made from ground and roasted coffee beans became a favorite beverage of the Arabs. From Arabia, coffee spread to Egypt and Turkey and then to Europe and North America. Look up the word *coffee* in your dictionary. Where does it come from? Then research the origin and the use of tea. What can you conclude about the relationship between borrowed words and trade?

Applying History Study Skills

Before completing this activity, review Building History Study Skills on page 217.

All Muslims are expected to make at least one pilgrimage to Mecca during their lifetime. The following selection describes the events that occur during this pilgrimage. Read the selection. Then list the events in sequence.

66 Scarcely had the first smile of morning beamed . . . when we arose, bathed, and proceeded in our pilgrim garb to the sanctuary [the Kaaba]. We entered by the principal northern door, descended two long flights of steps, traversed the cloister, and stood in the sight of the Bait Allah [House of God]. . . . We proceeded to the open pavement . . . where we performed the usual two prostrations in honor of the mosque. This was followed by a cup of holy water and a present to the . . . carriers, who for the consideration distributed a large earthen vaseful in my name to poor pilgrims. We then advanced toward the eastern angle of the Kaabah, in which is inserted the Black Stone, and standing about ten yards from it, repeated with upraised hands, 'There is no God but Allah alone, Whose covenant is truth, and Whose servant is victorious. . . .' After which we approached as close as we could to the stone. . . . Then commenced the ceremony of Tawaf, or circumambulation, our route being the . . . low oval of polished granite immediately surrounding the Kaabah. . . . At the conclusion of the Tawaf, it was . . . advisable to kiss the stone. . . . In the evening, . . . I again . . . repaired to the . . . [Kaaba]. 99

Investigating Further

1. **Writing a Report**   An important event in a Muslim's life is a pilgrimage to Mecca, the birthplace of Muhammad. In some years more than 400,000 Muslims visit the ancient city. Using encyclopedias, magazine articles, or other library reference materials, prepare a report on the holy places in Mecca and the religious ceremonies that take place during the pilgrimage. How do these ceremonies differ from religious ceremonies of other religions such as Christianity, Judaism, and Hinduism?

2. **Preparing an Oral Report**   Oriental carpets made in Persia (Iran) have long been popular in the United States. Research and report to the class on the history and background of these rugs. Include the following information in your report:
   (a) How were the rugs made?
   (b) What were the importance and symbolic meaning of rugs in the Persian home?
   (c) How did the subject matter and design of the rugs reflect Islamic teaching?
   Among the books you might use are *Oriental Rugs: Antique and Modern* (Dover) by Walter Hawley and *Oriental Rugs: A Comprehensive Guide,* edited by Murray L. Eiland (N.Y. Graphic Society).

10

Feudal Lords and the Church Dominated Medieval Europe

Time   432–1328

| 3.7 mil. BC | 4000 BC | AD 2100 |

Significance

While the Byzantine and Muslim empires flourished in the East, no strong empire emerged in what had been the western part of the Roman Empire. The Roman Empire did not end with a sudden crash, however. Rather, it slipped away a little at a time. A border fort would be abandoned. Mail would no longer come to a city. Slowly, what had been a magnificent empire became splintered ruins.

The period in western European history following the collapse of the Roman Empire, from about 500 to about 1500, is called the **Middle Ages,** or the **medieval** period. (The word *medieval* comes from the Latin words *medius,* meaning "middle," and *aevum,* meaning "age.")

The people of that time never thought of themselves as living in a "middle age." They thought of human history as a chain of events that had begun in the Biblical era and continued to their own time. Although these people had little understanding of the past, they developed new customs and institutions to suit the conditions under which they lived.

Terms to Define

Middle Ages	serf
feudalism	Inquisition
manor	Magna Carta

People to Identify

Charlemagne	William the Conqueror
Vikings	Hugh Capet

Places to Locate

Papal States	Hastings
Normandy	Worms

Questions to Guide Your Reading

1 How did Frankish rulers gain control of western Europe?
2 Why was medieval life organized around feudalism and the manorial system?
3 What was the role of the church during the Middle Ages?
4 What prompted conflict between kings and nobles in France and England?
5 Why did popes and emperors clash over Germany and Italy?

In the Middle Ages, most Europeans were peasants who eked out a meager living in the fields, often working from dawn to dusk. As one historian noted:

❝*T*he sun rose early, . . . but not much earlier than the peasants of the little village of Belcombe. . . . Within most of the houses men were stirring . . . taking a look at the sky before they ate a brief meal . . . of a lump of bread and a draught of ale. . . . Then they . . . fetched their scythes and rakes from the sheds, and started off. . . . On entering the field the peasants broke up in little groups, some going to one and some to another part of the meadow. . . .

In one corner of the field John Wilde and his two sons, Richard and Roger, kept to their tasks for some time without pause. . . . All three continued until the sun was getting well up into the heavens, when they stopped their work and left the field together with many others. As they passed the church John glanced at the Mass clock on its wall near the door, and saw by the shadow . . . that they had good time before the service, as it was not yet eight.❞

These hardworking peasants formed the backbone of a society attempting to restore order out of the chaos that followed the collapse of the Roman Empire in the West. In time a new social and political order emerged.

1 Frankish Rulers Governed Much of Western Europe for Centuries

After the Roman Empire in the west collapsed, many Germanic tribes, including Visigoths, Vandals, Burgundians, and Ostrogoths, plundered Europe and established several small kingdoms. Most tribes, however, did not create strong governments. Of all the Germanic tribes, the Franks played the greatest role in European history. The Franks first entered the Roman Empire near the mouth of the Rhine River in the A.D. 300s. They settled in the area of northern Gaul that corresponds roughly to the present-day nations of Belgium and the Netherlands.

◀ *King John signing the Magna Carta*

Clovis and the Merovingians

In 481 an able ruler named Clovis became king of one of the Frankish tribes. He and his successors were called Merovingians because Clovis traced his family back to an ancestor named Meroveg. Although brutal, cruel, and apparently without a conscience, Clovis excelled as a military leader. His troops conquered the other Frankish tribes and soon controlled all of northern Gaul.

A few years after Clovis became king, an important event took place. Influenced by his Christian wife, he vowed to accept her religion if he won a certain battle. When he won the battle, he not only kept his vow but also ordered 3,000 of his warriors to receive baptism. Clovis became a strong supporter of Christianity, and he and the Franks gained the support of the Church.

Later, Clovis seized southwestern Gaul from the Visigoths. Even though he ruled most of what is today France (which took its name from the Franks), Clovis failed to pass on to his successors either his strong leadership qualities or his united kingdom. In accordance with Frankish custom, Clovis's sons divided the kingdom among themselves.

The later Merovingian kings thought only of the pleasures and luxuries of palace life. One writer of the period tells of a Merovingian king who spent his time combing his long yellow curls with a jeweled comb. Because these "do-nothing kings" left the business of governing to palace officials, the chief of the royal household, called the mayor of the palace, became the real ruler. About 700, Pepin II, the mayor of the palace of one kingdom, succeeded in making the office of mayor hereditary. His successors were Frankish kings in everything but name.

Charles Martel and Pepin the Short

Pepin's able son, Charles Martel (meaning "Charles the Hammer"), succeeded Pepin as the mayor of the palace. In 732 Spanish Moors invaded France. Charles Martel's cavalry defeated the Moors near Tours, in central France, thus halting the Muslim advance in western Europe and removing an immediate danger and a constant menace.

When Charles Martel died in 741, he left a large and strong kingdom for his son Pepin III, or Pepin the Short. In 751 an assembly of Franks took

What If?
Battle of Tours
The Frankish victory at Tours in 732 halted Muslim expansion in Europe. How do you think modern European culture would be different if the Moors had won the battle?

the throne from the Merovingian king and elected Pepin king of the Franks. Three years later the pope traveled to France and personally crowned Pepin "king by the grace of God." Later popes claimed this action established a precedent, or an example to be followed in the future, which gave the popes the authority to install and depose kings.

While the pope was in France, he asked Pepin for help against the Lombards, a Germanic tribe that was ravaging central Italy and threatening Rome. Pepin led an army of Franks into Italy and defeated the Lombards. He then took territory around Rome from the Lombard king and gave it to the pope. This gift of land, called the Donation of Pepin, created the Papal States, a region that would be ruled by popes for centuries.

History does not record whether the pope and Pepin made an agreement that Pepin would defend Rome in exchange for his coronation by the pope. Certainly, however, these events began an alliance between the Franks and the pope that greatly strengthened both sides. The way now opened for the greatest of all Frankish kings, Charlemagne (SHAHR • luh • mayn).*

Charlemagne's Empire

Pepin's son Charlemagne assumed the Frankish throne in 768 and ruled until 814. Although he had little formal education, this deeply religious and highly intelligent king became one of history's outstanding rulers.

Like many kings of his day, Charlemagne spent much of his life at war. He defeated the Lombards in Italy, the Saxons in northern Germany, and the Avars in central Europe. Although he failed in his attempt to conquer all of Muslim Spain, he drove the Moors back across the Pyrenees, thus gaining a

---

*Charlemagne's Latin name was *Carolus Magnus* (from which comes the name of his dynasty, *Carolingian*). The Germans called him *Karl de Grosse*. Translated into English, all these names mean "Charles the Great."

Government. Charlemagne's empire consisted of several hundred regions, each ruled by a representative called a count. Each count raised an army and administered the laws within his own lands. Charlemagne established his capital at Aix-la-Chapelle (AYK-SLAH-shuh • PEL), which today is Aachen (AHK • uhn), West Germany, but he traveled extensively throughout his empire. He also appointed officials called *missi dominici* (MI • see dohm • i • NEE • chee), Latin for "the lord's messengers." The missi dominici traveled throughout the empire to listen to complaints, to review the effectiveness of the laws, and to make certain the counts served the emperor rather than themselves.

The government levied no direct taxes on land or people because the emperor's vast estates produced enough revenue to cover most of the government's low expenses. Each person who lived in the

Learning from Maps *Charlemagne conquered much of Europe before his death in 814. Where did he establish his capital?*

CHARLEMAGNE'S EMPIRE 768–814

- Frankish Kingdom at the death of Pepin, 768
- Territories added by Charlemagne, 768–814
- ⊛ Charlemagne's capital

AZIMUTHAL EQUAL AREA PROJECTION

Learning from Pictures *Charlemagne was a patron of learning and encouraged the development of art, science, and literature.*

small strip of Spanish territory. By the end of his reign, Charlemagne controlled much of western Europe (see map, this page).

On Christmas Day in the year 800, Charlemagne knelt at worship in St. Peter's Church in Rome. Pope Leo III placed a crown on Charlemagne's head and declared him "Emperor of the Romans." The new title had little to do with the Frankish Empire, but it signified that Charlemagne, who had united much of Europe for the first time in 400 years, was regarded by many people as the successor to the emperors of Rome. Charlemagne's coronation by the pope also dramatized the close ties between the Frankish people and the Christian Church.

empire contributed to the army in some way. Wealthy lords provided the cavalry, and free peasants usually served as soldiers three months a year. Thus the emperor had an army at no expense to himself or the government.

Education and learning. Greatly interested in education, Charlemagne founded a school at the palace for his own children and the other young nobles. He invited learned scholars from throughout western Europe to teach in the school. The emperor also assembled scholars from all over Europe to produce a readable and authentic Bible. He ordered bishops to create libraries by copying ancient Latin manuscripts and to organize schools for the children of nobles and for intelligent children from the lower classes.

Although Charlemagne never learned to write, he could read. One of his favorite books, St.

Learning from Maps Lothair's kingdom, with many important cities, was the first kingdom to break up. In what kingdom was Paris located?

Augustine's *City of God,* urged all Christians to love God, and Charlemagne vigorously encouraged people throughout the empire to convert to Christianity. Sometimes he even forced people to convert, giving them a choice between baptism and execution.

The Decline of the Frankish Empire

Charlemagne's energy, ability, and personality unified the empire during his lifetime. But the empire crumbled during the reign of Charlemagne's only surviving son, Louis the Pious. After Louis died, his three sons agreed to divide the empire into three parts: the eastern kingdom, the middle kingdom, and the western kingdom (see map, this page). Their agreement, signed in 843, was called the Treaty of Verdun.

Poor leaders, Charlemagne's descendants fought among themselves instead of uniting against powerful and ambitious local rulers. By 870 the middle kingdom broke up and was divided between the eastern and western kingdoms. But the great lords of these two kingdoms no longer obeyed the Carolingian monarchs. Instead they chose their own kings.

Charlemagne's empire splintered not only because of internal feuds but also because invaders swarmed into the empire from every direction. In the late 800s, Europe suffered from invasions more terrible than the invasions of the 400s (see map, page 227).

The Muslims came from North Africa and terrorized the Mediterranean coast, conquering Sicily, Sardinia, and Corsica. From the east came the Slavs, who pressed into central Europe. From Asia came a new group of nomads, the Magyars (MAG • yahrz). Magyar tactics so resembled those of the earlier Huns that Europeans called them Hungarians. After a century of terrifying raids, the Magyars settled down and established a kingdom in what is now the country of Hungary.

The Vikings

The most feared of all invaders, however, came from Scandinavia, in the north. The Germanic peoples of what are now the countries of Norway, Sweden, and Denmark called themselves Vikings. The English called them Danes, while other Europeans called them Northmen, or the Norse.

map labels

20° 10° 60° 0° 10° 20° 30° 40° 50°

Vikings

North
Sea

Celts

Celts

Anglo-Saxons

Celts

Volga
River

Baltic Sea

Jutes

Angles

ATLANTIC

OCEAN

London

Saxons

Elbe

*Western
Slavs*

Vistula
R.

Dnieper
River

*Eastern
Slavs*

Don
River

Kiev

Normans

Paris

Rhine

F r a n k s

R.

CARPATHIAN MTS.

Alemanni

Burgundians

ALPS

*L
o
m
b
a
r
d
s*

Magyars

Slavs

CAUCASUS MTS.

Danube

Bulgars

River

Black Sea

Basques

PYRENEES

Adriatic Sea

S o u t h   S l a v s

Iberians

Visigoths

Corsica

Rome

Italians

Constantinople

Asia Minor

Moors

Sardinia

Greeks

AFRICA

N

0   200   400 Miles

0   200   400 Kilometers

Sicily

Mediterranean Sea

**PEOPLES OF EUROPE
600–1000**

⟵ Viking invasions and migrations

⟵ Magyar migrations

AZIMUTHAL EQUAL AREA PROJECTION

Learning from Maps   *The Vikings migrated from the north to all parts of Europe. What body of water separated the Viking homeland from the Western Slavs?*

Although the Vikings had kings and nobles, their government was surprisingly democratic for its time. The Vikings honored work, and all classes worked. Most people owned their own land, and few large estates existed. Assemblies of landowners made the laws.

During the 800s climate changes and a growing population apparently caused a serious food shortage in Scandinavia. Many Vikings sailed from their homeland in search of food and treasure. Sturdy Viking ships, propelled partly by sails but mostly by oars, skirted the coasts of Europe and plied the rivers of Germany, France, and the eastern Baltic area. They sailed across the Atlantic Ocean to Iceland, then on to Greenland and North America. In time the Vikings settled in England, Ireland, France, eastern Europe, and later, elsewhere in Europe. A large settlement of Vikings in northwestern France gave the region its name, Normandy, from the French word *Normans,* for "Northmen."

As chaos engulfed medieval Europe, the Vikings continued their conquests, trading with the strong and pillaging the weak. Skilled in siege operations, they sometimes captured strongly fortified towns. Savage and cruel people, the Vikings seem to have enjoyed battle. They used their axes and swords to strike terror into people everywhere. A Viking once complained that "peace lasted so long that I was afraid I might come to die of old age, within doors, on a bed."

The Vikings' customs and myths centered on god-heroes, who led their people bravely in life and symbolically sailed away in death. Archaeologists have excavated Viking burial mounds in Europe that include boats and implements to be used in the afterlife. Sometimes the Vikings placed the dead person in a boat, set the boat adrift, and burned it. In 922 Ibn Fadlan, an Arab, attended the funeral of a Viking chieftain along the Volga. A historian wrote the following about Fadlan's experience:

"*A* girl slave volunteered to be burned with her master, Ibn Fadlan relates. His ship was hauled onto land and wood placed beneath. A tent was raised on deck and a brocaded mattress set on it. The richly clothed corpse was seated on the mattress. . . .

On the day of the burial, . . . the slave girl said, 'Lo, I see my lord and master . . . he calls to me. Let me go to him.' Aboard the ship waited the old woman called the Angel of Death, who would kill her. The girl drank from a cup of nabidh and sang a long song. She grew fearful and hesitant. At once the old woman grasped her head and led her into the tent.

Inside the tent the girl died beside her master by stabbing and strangling. Then the ship was fired. "

SECTION 1 REVIEW

1. **Define** Middle Ages, medieval
2. **Identify** Franks, Clovis, Merovingians, Charles Martel, Pepin the Short, Charlemagne, Louis the Pious, Magyars, Vikings
3. **Locate** Papal States, Aix-la-Chapelle, Normandy
4. **Summarizing Ideas** **(a)** What were the accomplishments of Clovis? **(b)** of Charles Martel?
5. **Interpreting Ideas** **(a)** How did Pepin the Short become king of the Franks? **(b)** What precedent did the crowning of Pepin establish?
6. **Organizing Ideas** How did Charlemagne change government and education in his empire?
7. **Determining Cause and Effect** Give two reasons for the breakup of Charlemagne's empire.

2 Medieval Life Was Based on Feudalism and the Manorial System

On the continent of Europe, organized government again disappeared within a century after Charlemagne's death in 814. Europe became a continent of small, independent local governments. We call the political system that evolved in Europe feudalism. **Feudalism,** a political system in which kings and powerful nobles granted land to other nobles in return for loyalty, military assistance, and services,

was firmly established in northern France by the end of the 900s. By the mid-1000s, it had become the way of life throughout most of western Europe.

Feudalism

Feudalism arose when powerful nobles began to govern their own lands in the absence of a strong central government. In return for needed military help, weak kings granted the nobles the use of land from the royal estates. The strong nobles, who often had more land than they needed, granted part of this land to less powerful nobles in return for military help and other services. Many small landholders who needed protection gave their land to more powerful nobles. The small landholder retained the right to occupy and work the lands but had to provide military service to the noble.

The person who granted land was a lord. The person who held land in return for services was a **vassal.** The grant of land was called a **fief.** This term comes from the Latin word *feudum,* which gave rise to the word *feudal.* The granting and holding of a fief was really a contract between lord and vassal.

In time the fief became hereditary. Legal ownership passed from the lord to his son, while legal possession and use passed from the vassal to his son. Since a fief could not be divided, the eldest son always inherited it—a system called **primogeniture** (pry•moh•JEN•uh•chuhr). However, many lords held more than one fief.

Women could influence society and politics, but their legal property rights were limited. A woman could include fiefs in her dowry. However, her husband would take over the dowry, and she controlled it only if he died.

Local lords held many of the powers of government, and the king became just another feudal lord. In theory every holder of land became a vassal to the king, but in practice the king had power only over those who lived on the king's feudal lands.

The church, too, became part of the feudal system. By the 900s the church owned vast amounts of land, some of which it granted as fiefs to nobles in return for military protection.

Feudal relationships. Keeping three things in mind will help you understand the relationship between lord and vassal:

(1) It was an honorable relationship between legal equals. Only nobles could be vassals. The greater lords were vassals and tenants of the king.

Learning from Pictures *This stained glass window depicts the relationship between a lord and his vassal. In the feudal relationship, who had more obligations, the vassal or the lord?*

The less powerful lords were vassals and tenants of the greater lords, and so on down.

(2) The same man might be both vassal and lord—vassal to a more powerful lord above him and lord to a less powerful vassal below him.

(3) It was a very personal relationship. Each man owed loyalties and obligations only to the lord immediately above him or to the vassal immediately below him.

Obligations of feudalism. Under the feudal contracts, the vassal had more obligations than the lord. The vassal promised to provide the lord a certain number of fully equipped cavalry riders and infantry soldiers, and he agreed to pay their expenses while at war.

The vassal had to make special payments to help cover the lord's extraordinary expenses such as ransom if the lord became captive in war. The vassal also had to house and feed the lord and his companions for a certain number of days a year, attend such ceremonies as the marriage of the lord's daughter, and serve on the lord's court to administer justice.

Feudal justice. Feudal justice differed from Roman justice. Decisions at trials were made in one of three ways:

(1) *Trial by battle.* The accused and the accuser, or men representing them, fought a duel. The outcome of the duel determined guilt or innocence.

(2) *Compurgation, or oath-taking.* The accused and the accuser each gathered a group of people who swore that "their" man was telling the truth. Compurgators, the oath-takers, were similar to the character witnesses in today's trials.

(3) *Ordeal.* The accused carried a piece of hot iron in his hand, or walked through fire, or plunged his arm into a pot of boiling water to pick up a hot stone. If his wounds healed rapidly, he was judged innocent; otherwise he was guilty.

Warfare. Frequent wars plagued the medieval period. Sometimes two kingdoms fought. Other times a king tried to subdue a powerful, rebellious vassal. Most wars, however, stemmed from private fights between feudal lords or between lords and vassals.

In the early Middle Ages, the knight, or fighting man, wore an iron helmet and a shirt of chain mail—small metal links hooked together to form flexible armor. The knight carried a sword, a large shield, and a lance. Armor became complicated in later medieval times, as metal plates replaced chain mail. Metal armor was so heavy that a knight often had to be hauled or boosted onto his horse.

For nobles, wars represented opportunities for glory and wealth, but to the rest of society, wars brought suffering and famine. The church tried to limit private wars. It issued decrees, known together as the Peace of God, which set aside certain places, such as churches, where fighting was not permitted. The church tried to get all lords to accept another decree, known as the Truce of God, which forbade fighting on weekends and holy days. Gradually more days were added to the Truce of God, until only 80 legal fighting days a year remained. Restrictions on fighting, however, could almost never be strictly enforced. Private wars continued until kings became strong enough to stop them.

The Manorial System

While feudalism was essentially a governmental and military system, the manorial system became the economic system. The **manor,** a large estate that included the manor house, pastures, fields, and a village, became the economic unit of the early Middle Ages, just as the fief had become the

229

Learning from Pictures *Manorial banquets or feasts were often held at the end of the harvest season. What items did the manor import?*

A typical manor village, usually on a stream that furnished water power for its mill, had houses clustered together for safety a short distance away from the manor house or castle. The land of the manor extended out from the village and included vegetable plots, cultivated fields, pastures, and forests.

The cultivated land of the manor was often divided into three large fields for growing grain. Only two of the three fields were planted each year so that the third field could lie fallow, or unplanted, to regain its fertility. The three large fields in turn were divided into small strips. Peasants had their own strips in each field. If the lord's domain was divided, he too had strips in each field.

Peasant Life

Most of the peasants on a manor were **serfs,** or people bound to the land. Serfs could not leave the land without the lord's permission, and the price of his permission was usually more money than they could afford. Serfs were not slaves, for they could not be sold away from the land. If the land was granted to a new lord, the serfs became the new lord's tenants.

Manors had some free people who rented land from the lord. Free people included the skilled workers necessary to the village economy, such as millers, blacksmiths, and carpenters. Most villages also had a priest to provide for the spiritual needs of the villagers.

Long hours spent doing backbreaking work in the fields made daily life very hard. The laborers' meager diet consisted mainly of coarse black bread, cabbage and a few other vegetables, cheese, and eggs. Beer was plentiful in northern Europe, and wine in the grape-growing regions of the south. People rarely ate meat because they needed animals to help them work the fields and because they were not allowed to hunt on the lord's land.

We know little about the life of ordinary people in medieval times. However, historians tell us that because of diseases and starvation, the average life expectancy was probably less than 40 years. Because people in their forties were regarded as old, medieval society was a much younger society than ours. People could become prominent by their twenties, and a bright child would be encouraged at an early age. When a village priest found a particularly intelligent boy, he could arrange to have him

governmental unit. While a small fief had only one manor, large fiefs had several.

Because no central authority or organized trade existed, each manor tried to be self-sufficient—or able to produce everything it needed. Most manors produced their own food, clothing, and leather goods. Only a few items, such as iron, salt, and tar, were imported.

The lord and several peasants shared the land of a manor. The lord kept about one-third of the manor land, called the **domain,** for himself. The domain was often divided into several plots, although it might form one large block near the lord's house. The peasants paid to use the remaining two-thirds of the land. In exchange they gave the lord part of their crops, worked on his land, performed other services on the manor, and paid many kinds of taxes.

educated for a career in the church, and thus a life in the wider world.

However, people rarely escaped the village. People usually died where they had been born. If a terrible disaster struck, such as a famine that lasted many years, villagers might flee. Usually, however, they stayed on, struggling to keep small families alive.

One of the few things we know about family life during these early years of the Middle Ages is that a child's status was sometimes determined by the mother rather than by the father. If a serf married a woman from a free family, for example, the couple's children might be considered free people rather than serfs.

The Life of the Nobility

When people today think of the Middle Ages, they sometimes picture luxurious castles and knights in shining armor. However, the nobles did not necessarily lead luxurious or even easy lives.

A castle, or a fortified home for a lord, served as a base for protecting the surrounding countryside and enforcing the lord's authority. Most people today picture a castle as a great stone structure. Actually, stone castles were not constructed until much later in the Middle Ages. Throughout the early medieval period, castles were relatively simple structures built of earth and wood.

Located on hills or in other places that were easy to defend, castles were built for defense, not for pleasant living. If a castle had to be built in flat country, a ditch often filled with water, called a moat, surrounded the outer walls. A drawbridge across the moat enabled people to reach the gate to the courtyard inside the walls. In case of an attack, the drawbridge was raised.

The main part of the castle was the keep—a strong tower that contained storerooms, barracks, and workshops, as well as the lord's living quarters. In the great hall, the lord received visitors. Here the family also lived during the day. The lord and his family usually had a separate bedroom, but everyone else slept in the great hall. There was little furniture. The thick walls, with their small, usually glassless windows, made the rooms dark, damp, and chilly. Fowl, dogs, and other small animals ran across the filthy, straw-covered floors.

The lord spent most of his day looking after his land and dispensing justice to his vassals and serfs.

He might have to spend some time each year fighting, either to help his own lord or to resolve a quarrel with another lord.

The lord and the head of a peasant family each depended a great deal on help from his wife and children. Medieval people viewed marriage as a way to advance one's fortunes, perhaps by inheriting new lands. Marriage also produced children, who had to be cared for. A lord had to provide a dowry for a daughter. For a son he had to provide either land or a position serving the church or the king.

When not fighting, the nobles and vassals amused themselves with mock battles called tournaments. In early medieval times, tournaments often led to loss of life, but later they became more like pageants.

Chivalry

During the 1100s **chivalry,** a code of conduct for knights, changed feudal society. The word *chivalry* comes from the French word *cheval,* meaning "horse." A knight usually rode a horse when he performed deeds demanded by the code of chivalry.

In the early days, becoming a knight was quite simple. Any noble, after proving himself in battle, could be knighted by any other knight. As time passed, chivalry became much more complex.

To become a knight, a boy had to go through two preliminary stages of training supervised by a knight. First, at the age of seven, a boy became a page, or knight's attendant, learning knightly manners and beginning his training in the use of weapons. Then, in his early teens, the boy became a squire, or knight's assistant. He continued his training in both manners and weapons. He took care of the knight's horses, armor, weapons, and clothing. When he was considered ready, the squire accompanied the knight into battle. After the squire proved himself worthy in battle, an elaborate religious ceremony initiated him into knighthood.

Chivalry required a knight to be brave—sometimes foolishly brave. He had to fight fairly. Tricks and strategy were considered cowardly. A knight had to be loyal to his friends, keep his word, and treat conquered foes gallantly. In addition, he had to be especially courteous to women.

Chivalry greatly improved the rough and crude manners of early feudal lords. Behavior, however, did not become perfect by any standards. The knight extended courtesy only to people of his own

◆ READ
WRITE
INTERPRET
CONNECT
●THINK

BUILDING HISTORY STUDY SKILLS

Thinking About History: Distinguishing a Fact from a Value Statement

A fact can be verified or proved. A value statement is an opinion that represents a particular point of view. For example, a writer can state that Charlemagne was a successful ruler. That statement is a value statement because it is based upon the writer's definition of "successful."

Sometimes a fact and a value statement may be included in the same sentence. For example, in the book *Life of Charlemagne,* the author states that Charlemagne spoke Latin and Greek and was so eloquent that he could have taught both languages. Charlemagne's mastery of the two languages is a fact that can be verified. However, the degree of his mastery of the languages is a value statement. In your study of history, and later as you assume the responsibilities of citizenship, such as voting, it is important for you to be able to distinguish between facts and value statements.

How to Distinguish a Fact from a Value Statement

To distinguish a fact from a value statement, follow these steps.

1. Review the difference between a fact and a value statement.
2. Identify clue words that suggest values. For example, adjectives such as *great, wonderful,* and *horrible* are "feeling" words. "I" statements such as *I believe* or *In my opinion* indicate a point of view.
3. Ask questions about the sentence. Is it open to different interpretations? Does it contain "feeling" words or "I" statements?

Developing the Skill

The statement below tells how feudalism is best defined. Which sentences contain facts? Which sentences contain value statements?

> ❝ The simplest way will be to begin by saying what feudal society was not. Although the obligations arising from blood-relationship played a very active part in it, it did not rely on kinship alone. . . . Feudal ties . . . developed when those of kinship proved inadequate. . . .
>
> European feudalism should therefore be seen as the outcome of the violent dissolution of older societies. It would in fact be unintelligible without the great upheaval of the great Germanic invasions which, by forcibly uniting two societies originally at very different stages of development, disrupted both of them and brought to the surface a great many . . . social practices of an extremely primitive character. ❞

In the quotation, the author emphasizes the social and economic aspects of feudalism. He begins by stating a fact: it (feudalism) did not rely on kinship alone. You know from reading this chapter that this statement is a fact because lord-vassal relations often did not depend on kinship. The value statements are developed by the use of words such as *simplest, unintelligible,* and *primitive.* These statements are open to interpretation and depend on definitions and data the author provides.

Practicing the skill. Select a newspaper article about a person or a current event. Then identify the facts and the value statements.

To apply this skill, see Applying History Study Skills on page 247.

Farming on the manor

class. Toward all others his attitude and actions were likely to be coarse and arrogant.

In addition to codes of conduct, other traditions originated in feudal times. As early as the 1000s, knights carried personal symbols mounted on banners or shields into battle. In the 1100s it became customary for sons to inherit these banners and shields from their fathers. Later, three-dimensional crests, mostly of aggressive animals such as lions and hawks, were added to helmets. In time these crests became badges of nobility.

By the 1200s the crest, helmet, and shield had been incorporated into a family coat of arms. When a knight stayed at an inn, he hung his coat of arms outside. In later times coats of arms such as Richard II's white heart or the rose and crown of England were incorporated into signs that identified the inn where the person had stayed.

SECTION 2 REVIEW

1. **Define** feudalism, vassal, fief, primogeniture, manor, domain, serf, chivalry
2. **Summarizing Ideas** (a) What was feudalism? (b) Why did it develop?
3. **Classifying Ideas** What were the obligations of vassals and lords under the feudal relationship?
4. **Interpreting Ideas** Explain the three methods of trial under feudal justice.
5. **Evaluating Ideas** Describe the ways in which land on a manor was divided and used.
6. **Sequencing Ideas** Under the rules of chivalry, what were the steps leading to knighthood?

3 The Church Had Many Roles in the Middle Ages

Central governments in medieval Europe were weak or did not exist at all. Therefore, the church performed many of the responsibilities of modern governments. In one way or another, the church touched the lives of most medieval people.

The Church Hierarchy

Members of the clergy were organized in ranks according to their power and responsibilities. The levels of this hierarchy (HY • uh • rahr • kee), starting at the bottom, were as follows:

(1) *The parish priest.* The parish priest, usually of peasant origin, had little formal education. He served the people in his parish, the smallest division of the church. The poorest clergy member, the priest could hardly be distinguished from the peasants among whom he lived.

Though at the bottom of the hierarchy, the priest was in one sense the church's most important officer, for he administered five of the seven sacraments. The **sacraments** consisted of special ceremonies at which the participants received the direct favor, or grace, of God to help them ward off the consequences of sin. By the 1100s leaders of the church recognized seven ceremonies as sacraments—baptism, Holy Eucharist (communion), confirmation (admission to church membership), penance (acts showing repentance for sins), ordination (holy orders), matrimony, and extreme unction (the anointing of the dying). The parish priest conducted church services in his parish and administered all the sacraments except confirmation and ordination. He supervised the moral and religious instruction of his people and the moral life of the community. Often, however, the beliefs of villagers were as much pagan and superstitious as they were Christian. For example, the villagers sometimes relied on local "wise women" and "cunning men" for spiritual help.

(2) *The bishop.* A number of parishes made up a diocese (DY • uh • suhs), which the bishop managed. The cathedral church, or official church of the bishop, was located in the most important city of the diocese. (*Cathedra* is the Latin word for the bishop's throne, or chair.) The king or great nobles usually controlled the selection of a bishop. Bishops, frequently chosen for their family connections and political power, were often feudal lords or vassals who had vassals themselves.

(3) *The archbishop.* An archbishop managed a diocese and had all the powers of a bishop. In addition, he exercised some authority over the other dioceses and bishops in his province, which consisted of several dioceses. An archbishop could summon provincial councils of the clergy to decide questions of church belief and policy.

(4) *The pope and his curia.* The pope had a group of counselors, called the curia, to advise him. Cardinals, the most important members of the curia, advised the pope on legal and spiritual matters. Beginning in 1059 the cardinals elected the new pope.

Learning from Pictures *These Benedictine monks are reading in the relaxed atmosphere of a monastery's garden.*

Only in the church hierarchy could a commoner rise in the world. It did not happen often, but a man of great ability, regardless of birth, might rise to great heights in the church. For example, Callistus I was originally a slave of a Christian master in Rome. He was later freed, and in time he became a bishop. From about 217 to 222 he served as pope.

Monasticism

The medieval church was much like a present-day government. Everyone became a member, just as we become citizens. Priests, bishops, and the pope belonged to what was called the secular clergy. They lived *in saeculo,* a Latin phrase meaning "in the world," or "among ordinary people." They administered the sacraments and preached the gospel. A second group of church people, called regular clergy because they lived according to a strict rule, or *regula,* was the monastics—monks and nuns.

Monks and nuns believed that one of the best ways to live a perfect Christian life was to withdraw from the world and its temptations and serve God through prayer, fasting, and self-denial. At first each monk lived alone. Later, monks gathered in religious communities called monasteries and nuns lived in convents. The way of life in monasteries and convents was called **monasticism.**

Monasticism lacked organization and direction until the early 500s. About that time Benedict, a young Roman noble, became disgusted with worldly corruption and left Rome to become a hermit. In time his reputation for holiness attracted so many followers that he established a monastery at Monte Cassino in central Italy. Benedict drew up a set of standards to regulate the lives of the monks. Monasteries throughout Europe adopted this set of standards, called the Benedictine Rule.

According to the Benedictine Rule, a monk could own absolutely nothing. Everything he used or wore belonged to the community of monks. The **abbot,** the elected head of the community, controlled and distributed all property. The monks promised to obey the abbot in all things.

Monks spent several hours every day in prayer, but they were also expected to work. The abbot assigned each monk certain tasks in and around the monastery.

Monasteries fulfilled the intellectual and charitable needs of medieval society. Monks were often the most learned scholars of the time, and the monastery libraries were the main preservers of the literature of ancient civilizations and the early church. Several monasteries also ran schools to train the clergy.

Over the years monasteries became very rich. As an act of piety, a noble might leave his land to a monastery. Or a monastery might receive a large gift in return for accepting a young man as a monk. There were fewer convents than monasteries, and the convents were not as rich as monasteries. Like the monasteries, however, convents usually gave some of their wealth to the needy in nearby communities. Monks and nuns often cared for the sick, fed the hungry, and clothed the poor.

Some monks left the monasteries to become missionaries, a practice that existed long before the time of Benedict. St. Patrick in Ireland and St. Augustine in England were among those who did important missionary work.

Christianity in Ireland and England

Christian missionaries arrived in Ireland in the 400s. St. Patrick, the best known missionary,

Lindisfarne Gospels

During the early Middle Ages, monks were among the few people in Europe who could read and write. In monastery workshops they copied by hand almost all the books dating from this period. In this age of great faith, the work that was copied most often was the Bible. The monks were painstakingly careful, for a manuscript containing the word of God was considered a sacred object whose visual beauty should reflect the importance of its contents. To glorify God, the monks illuminated, or illustrated, the pages with gold leaf and intricate designs.

The Lindisfarne Gospels, among the most beautiful of the early illuminated books, were produced around 700 in the monastery of Lindisfarne. Now called Holy Island, Lindisfarne is a peninsula that becomes an island at high tide. One of England's early centers of learning, Lindisfarne lies off the northeastern coast of England.

The beginning of the Gospel According to St. John, part of the

New Testament shown here, features a decorative border of interlaced ribbons, circles, and other designs. The Latin words mean, "In the beginning was the Word, and the Word was with God."

began his work there in 432. Several monastic schools provided the basis of an advanced culture that lasted from about 500 to about 800. Missionaries and teachers from Irish schools went to all parts of the British Isles and to the royal families on the continent of Europe. During this time Ireland became the greatest center and preserver of ancient and Christian culture in western Europe.

About 600 Pope Gregory I sent missionaries to England. Led by a monk named Augustine, the missionaries converted many people. Soon all England accepted Christianity. Augustine, made the first archbishop of Canterbury, eventually became known as St. Augustine of Canterbury. Canterbury became the center of the Christian Church in England.

The Church and Medieval Life

Both the secular and the regular clergy played a leading part in medieval institutions and in life. The church sought the most intelligent people among all classes to become members of the clergy. During the early Middle Ages, church leaders were almost the only educated people in Europe.

Since printing was unknown in the early Middle Ages, all books had to be copied by hand. Monks did most of this work. To relieve the tedious work of copying and to beautify the texts, the monks often added small paintings at the beginning of a page or in the margins. The gold leaf and brilliant colors they used brightened the pages so much that such works are called illuminated manuscripts.

These manuscripts were the finest artistic works produced during the early Middle Ages.

Political role. The church also became a political force during the Middle Ages. In the Papal States, the pope was both the political and spiritual ruler. Many popes claimed supreme political power for the church. They decreed that all monarchs in Europe had to obey the pope. Church leaders also held positions of power as feudal lords and as advisers to kings and nobles. The church preached that people should obey the laws of kings unless these laws conflicted with church laws.

The church had its own code of law, called **canon law,** and its own courts where members of the clergy were tried. The church enforced its laws by using excommunication and interdict.

Excommunication cut an individual off from the church. He or she could not receive the sacraments or be buried in sacred ground. All Christians had to avoid the excommunicated person, and the state treated him or her like a criminal. An excommunicated person was thought to be surely damned after death.

To punish an entire region, the church issued an **interdict.** No religious services could be held in the region, and only the sacraments of baptism and extreme unction could be administered. Everyone who lived in the region was in danger of eternal damnation.

As do present-day national governments, the church in the Middle Ages had the power of taxation. Through the parish priest, the church collected the **tithe,** or one-tenth of a person's income, from all Christians. In England and Scandinavia, the church collected "Peter's Pence," a tax of one penny a year on every household. The church also received fines collected by its courts and fees charged for the performance of ceremonies such as baptism and marriage. Finally, the church received vast income from church-owned lands. In the early 1200s, when the church reached the peak of its power, it had a larger income than all the kings of Europe combined.

Economic life. The moral ideas of the church affected all economic life. The church opposed people gaining wealth by exploiting others. It insisted that labor was in keeping with the dignity of free people.

Monks were leaders in agriculture. They developed new ways of raising crops, breeding cattle, and cultivating fruit. They cleared forests, drained swamps, and built dikes and roads to increase the amount of land that could be farmed.

Monasteries carried on widespread trading activities. They owned their own pack animals, ships, markets, and warehouses. Their trade routes were carefully mapped.

Social role. The church considered the family a sacred institution. It forbade divorce and took responsibility for all widows and orphans. It also took complete charge of all social work, such as relief for the poor.

To relieve the sick and distressed, the church established hospitals, orphanages, and poorhouses. Special religious orders provided hospital care, care of lepers, burial of the poor, and general charity.

Problems of the Church

At the peak of its power, the church faced several problems.

(1) *Lay investiture.* The tremendous wealth of the church created a problem, especially after church leaders became feudal lords and vassals. Nobles often rewarded their loyal friends or relatives by appointing them bishops and abbots, a procedure known as lay investiture. No one questioned a king's or a noble's right to grant a bishop or an abbot a fief and to have him become a vassal. The church, however, did object to kings and nobles naming bishops and abbots. Church leaders firmly believed that only a church member could grant spiritual authority to another member of the church. In the case of a bishop, a ring and crosier, or staff, symbolized this authority. A king or lord who granted a new bishop his fiefs often insisted on giving him his ring and crosier as well.

(2) *Worldly lives of the clergy.* Some members of the clergy lived in luxury. People criticized them because they seemed more interested in wealth than in holy living.

(3) *Simony.* In feudal times people often paid to get positions in the church, a practice called **simony** (SY • muh • nee). The purchaser expected to make money through his position, either from church income or by charging high fees for performing religious services.

(4) *Heresy.* The church did not permit anyone to question the basic principles, or doctrines, that served as the foundation of the Christian religion. People who denied the truth of these principles or preached unauthorized doctrines were considered

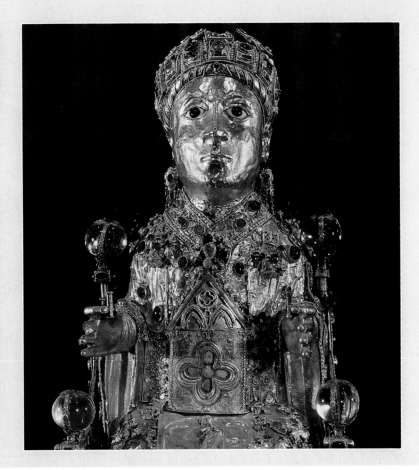

Reliquary of St. Faith

This golden image of St. Faith illustrates an important feature of medieval religion. It shows the devotion Christians had for the relics, or remains, of saints. During the last Roman persecution of Christians, in the early 300s, the Romans killed Faith, a French girl. Almost 500 years later, tales of miracles she had performed began circulating, and the church declared Faith a saint. Pilgrims soon flocked to the church in France where some of her remains had been taken. Many of these pilgrims made offerings of gold, jewels, and other valuables. In about 985, these precious metals and stones were used to make this reliquary, a container for relics. St. Faith's skull is in a cavity in the back, wrapped in a covering of silver.

heretics, or unbelievers, guilty of the unpardonable sin of heresy, which brought eternal damnation. Heresy threatened the church itself, as treason does a modern government.

Attempts at church reform were made by many church leaders and lay rulers who tried to solve church problems through various measures. Two religious groups, or orders, established in the 1200s dedicated themselves to reform. They were the Franciscans, founded by St. Francis of Assisi in 1209, and the Dominicans, founded by St. Dominic in 1216. Members of both of these religious orders lived and preached among the people instead of secluding themselves in monasteries as members of most other religious orders did.

In the mid-1200s the pope ordered the Dominicans to seek out heretics and to eliminate heresy. During this search, known as the **Inquisition,** anyone suspected of heresy could be tried in secret and tortured in order to force a confession. Heretics who confessed they had been wrong were required to perform penance. The Inquisition condemned heretics who did not reform and turned them over to the civil government to be punished, usually by burning at the stake. The church thought these severe penalties were necessary to save the souls of heretics and to prevent the spread of heresy throughout Christendom.

SECTION 3 REVIEW

1. **Define**   sacrament, monasticism, abbot, canon law, interdict, tithe, simony, Inquisition
2. **Identify**   curia, cardinals, St. Francis of Assisi, St. Dominic
3. **Summarizing Ideas**   Name the positions in the church hierarchy and briefly describe the duties of each position.
4. **Classifying Ideas**   In what three ways did the medieval church resemble a state?
5. **Evaluating Ideas**   How did the church contribute to medieval life?
6. **Interpreting Ideas**   (a) What four major problems faced the church during the Middle Ages?   (b) How do you think each problem hurt the power and status of the church?

4 Kings and Nobles Struggled for Power in England and France

In Europe before the 1000s, kings and lords often struggled for power in a kind of feudal tug of war. Some great lords, as powerful as the kings themselves, served them only when it was convenient. However, a number of kings were able to impose their will on their subjects. From this struggle gradually emerged such kingdoms as England and France, where the king's authority grew stronger than that of the lords.

Anglo-Saxon England

About 450, not long after the last Roman legions left Britain, several Germanic tribes invaded the island. Although they first came as raiders, they soon began to settle. Two of these tribes, the Angles and the Saxons, became so powerful that we refer to their descendants as Anglo-Saxons even today. Even though the Saxons came to dominate the Angles and the other tribes, the Angles gave their name to the land. The word *England* comes from *Engla-land*, meaning "land of the Angles." The name *England* refers to the eastern island of the British Isles, except for Scotland in the north and Wales in the west.

The Anglo-Saxons in Britain formed several small independent kingdoms. Later these kingdoms combined into three important ones: (1) Northumbria, in what is now southern Scotland and northern England; (2) Mercia, in central England; and (3) Wessex, in southern England. In time the Anglo-Saxons divided these kingdoms into governmental districts called **shires.** Officials known as shire-reeves (which became the word *sheriffs*) governed these districts.

Alfred the Great. By the early 800s, the Wessex kings controlled practically all of England. However, their rule was soon challenged by the ferocious raiders from the north, the Vikings. At first the Danes—as the Anglo-Saxons called the Vikings—met little resistance, and they quickly conquered much of England. Then, in 871, Alfred the Great came to the throne of Wessex determined to drive the Danes from English soil. First, he persuaded them to leave Wessex by paying them a huge tribute, or sum of money. He spent the next five years reorganizing his army and building a fleet of

Learning from Pictures *Although tortured to death, St. Edmund, an Anglo-Saxon king, never renounced his faith. Here he gives alms to the poor.* †

ships. In 876, when he felt that his forces were strong enough, he attacked the Danes. The war raged for a decade, and in 886 the Danes sued for peace. The peace treaty limited Danish settlement to northeast Mercia and much of Northumbria. In this region, called the Danelaw, the Danes could live under their own laws and govern themselves.

Although best known as a warrior-king, Alfred the Great made many contributions to learning. An educated and scholarly man, he wanted his people to be educated also. To this end he established a number of schools and invited the best scholars from Ireland and Europe to teach in them. Alfred himself undertook the translation of a number of books from Latin to Anglo-Saxon. And at his command, scholars began a history of England from the earliest times. Work on this history,

†St. Edmund as alms giver, M736 F. 9r.: The Pierpont Morgan Library, New York

known as the *Anglo-Saxon Chronicle,* continued for some 250 years after Alfred's death in 899.

Danish rule. During the 900s Alfred's successors won back much of the remaining Danish-held land in England. At the same time, they unified the country, strengthened its government, and spread Christianity throughout the land. However, by the end of the century, England once again came under attack from the Danes. By 1013 they had conquered the whole of the country.

In 1019, under the rule of King Canute of Denmark, England became part of a large kingdom that included most of Scandinavia. Canute, who spent much of his time in England, ruled wisely. Canute's sons, however, had neither his intelligence nor his skill, and they proved to be weak rulers. By 1042 the Danes had been driven from England and the Anglo-Saxon nobles had chosen Edward the Confessor, as their new king.

The Norman Conquest

Edward the Confessor's background—part Anglo-Saxon and part Norman—created problems upon his death. When he died childless in 1066, Duke William of Normandy, a distant relative, claimed the English throne. The Anglo-Saxon nobles refused to recognize William's claim, selecting Edward's brother-in-law, Harold of Wessex, instead. So in 1066 William gathered a fleet of ships and an army of nobles and landed at Hastings, on the southeastern coast of England. In short order he defeated the Anglo-Saxon forces and declared himself King William I of England.

It took William, usually called William the Conqueror, several years to overcome Anglo-Saxon resistance. It took many more years for the Norman conquerors to overcome the hatred of the defeated Anglo-Saxons. The Anglo-Saxons did not adopt Norman ideas, customs, or language willingly. Anglo-Saxon, a Germanic language, remained the language of the people. Norman French, a Romance language based on Latin, became the language of the nobles. As time went on, however, the culture of England, including laws and customs, became as much Norman as Anglo-Saxon.

Feudalism in England

William the Conqueror, who ruled from 1066 to 1087, imported feudalism from France to England.

However, he carefully altered feudalism in England so that the king, rather than the nobles, held the authority. To weaken the lords and prevent them from uniting, William gave his followers fiefs scattered throughout England.

William the Conqueror laid the foundation for a centralized government by requiring each feudal lord to swear allegiance directly to him. Thus all the feudal lords became vassals of the king.

To determine the population and wealth of England, William sent out commissioners to gather information on everyone in the country. This information helped to determine taxation. The survey became known as the *Domesday Book* (or *Doomsday Book*) because people said that it would be easier to escape doomsday, God's final judgment, than to avoid the royal commissioners.

Reforms Under William's Successors

One of William the Conqueror's sons, Henry I, ruled from 1100 to 1135. He made the central government more efficient by setting up a new department known as the Exchequer (eks • CHEK • uhr) to handle the kingdom's finances. Henry's other contribution was in the legal system. He wanted to weaken the feudal lords by having cases tried in the king's courts rather than in feudal courts. He sent traveling judges out to hold court sessions throughout the country.

Henry II, who reigned from 1154 to 1189, further increased royal authority. He allowed nobles to pay him instead of doing military service, then used the money to hire mercenaries. In this way he had an army loyal to him rather than to the nobles. He later raised a national army by requiring every freeman to obtain arms and serve. Henry reorganized the Exchequer to keep careful accounts of the government's finances.

Henry II made great use of the traveling judges. He established definite circuits, or routes, on which the judges were to travel. Thus they became known as circuit judges.

To let the judge know what cases should be tried, the king appointed groups of men called juries in each district. A grand jury consisted of 25 or more men who submitted the names of suspected criminals to the judge. In the 1200s the petit (PET • ee) jury of 12 developed. (*Grand* is the French word for "large," and *petit* the French word for "small.") At first petit juries decided only civil

Learning from Pictures
King Henry II is shown doing penance at Thomas Becket's shrine.

cases, such as disputes over land. The feudal procedures of ordeal and combat still tried criminal cases. In time, however, petit juries decided criminal cases, too. In this way the king's law replaced feudal law.

In his efforts to increase royal authority, Henry II sought to transfer trials of certain members of the clergy from church courts to royal courts. The Archbishop of Canterbury, Thomas Becket, refused to allow this transfer, and the two men, once the best of friends, became bitter enemies. Four of the king's knights, thinking they were doing the king a great favor, murdered the archbishop in his cathedral.

Henry II denied any part in the assassination of Thomas Becket. Faced with papal excommunication, however, he was forced to abandon further attempts to reduce the power of the church. Thomas Becket became a saint, and his shrine in Canterbury became the most popular holy place in England for pilgrims to visit.

The last years of Henry II were troubled. His sons plotted against each other and united to plot against their father. His marriage to Eleanor of Aquitaine was stormy. Because he had received lands in France as part of Eleanor's dowry, England became further embroiled in wars in France. Nevertheless, Henry II helped consolidate the powers of the crown over the feudal lords. Later kings built upon his government and judicial institutions.

King John and the Magna Carta

One son of Henry II, King John, is famous for bringing on a revolt among the nobles of the realm by forcing them to pay taxes that they considered unjust. On June 15, 1215, the English nobles forced John to accept a document known as the **Magna Carta** (Latin for "great charter"), which protected the liberties of the nobles. Some provisions of the Magna Carta, however, dealt with the rights of England's ordinary people. These provisions have come to be considered the most important ones in the document.

King John made several promises. He agreed not to collect any new or special tax without the consent of the Great Council, a body of important nobles and church leaders who advised the king. He promised not to take property without paying for it, and he agreed not to sell, refuse, or delay justice. The king also promised to grant any accused person a trial by a jury of peers, or equals. The Magna Carta meant that the king was not above the law—the king had to obey the law just as his subjects did, or they would be free to rebel against him.

Although the charter was not considered significant at the time, later political thinkers regarded many of its clauses as important precedents. Today the Magna Carta is considered one of the world's great documents, spelling out the rule of the law.

The Magna Carta forms part of the British Constitution, a series of great documents and acts of Parliament rather than one document such as the Constitution of the United States. Although the Magna Carta was a feudal document, it served as the basis for the establishment of parliamentary democracy in England and for the War of Independence that followed in the American colonies.

The original purpose of the Magna Carta was to protect the nobles, not to establish a constitutional government. Because the nobles were powerful, the rights they claimed were later extended to other classes of people. The document became the cornerstone of constitutional government and representative democracy.

Parliament and Common Law

In the century that followed the signing of the Magna Carta, the two most important developments in English history were the evolution of Parliament and the growth of common law.

Parliament. In the 1260s nobles revolted against King Henry III. The leader of the nobles, Simon de Montfort, ruled England for several months. He hoped to get greater support for the nobles' cause by broadening the representation in the Great Council.

In 1265 de Montfort summoned representatives of the middle class to meet with the higher nobles and clergy in the Great Council. There were two knights from each shire and two burgesses, or citizens, from each of several towns.

Learning from Pictures *The Magna Carta established the principle of limited government by restraining the power of the English monarch.*

De Montfort was killed in battle and the revolt was crushed, but the precedent of including knights and burgesses in the Great Council had been set. Later monarchs found it simpler to do business with a representative body of knights and burgesses than with crown officials. In time this representative body came to be called Parliament. It was eventually divided into two parts, or houses. The upper house consisted of nobles and clergy and was called the House of Lords. The lower house was made up of knights and burgesses and was called the House of Commons. Within a few years, this was the accepted form of representation.

The early Parliament did not have the power to pass laws, but it did have the important right of refusing to agree to new and special taxes. As the cost of running the central government increased, new taxes were necessary, and Parliament's approval became vital. Over the years Parliament used this power to its advantage.

Common law. One of England's greatest monarchs, Edward I, who ruled from 1272 to 1307, divided the king's court into three branches. The Court of the Exchequer kept financial accounts and tried tax cases. The Court of Common Pleas tried cases between private citizens. The Court of the King's Bench heard cases that concerned the king or the government.

Each of the three royal courts handed down many verdicts. Each year the courts collected the most important verdicts and wrote them down. These written decisions became the basis for future decisions made in the king's courts and in the circuit courts. This type of law, based on judges' decisions rather than on a code of statutes like Roman law, is known as **common law.** It received this name because it was common to all of the people of England. Common law forms the basis for the present-day legal systems in the United States and in England.

Rise of the Capetian Kings in France

When the last Carolingian king of France died without an heir in 987, an assembly of nobles chose Hugh Capet (kuh • PAY), a French noble, as king. Capet and his descendants, called the Capetians (kuh • PEE • shuhnz), ruled for more than 300 years.

As king, Hugh Capet ruled only a small region around Paris called the Ile-de-France (EEL-DUH-FRAHNS). *Ile* is the French word for "island," and this region was indeed an island of royal authority in the midst of feudal lands. Even in the Ile-de-France, the king's vassals resisted his authority.

The rest of what is today France was divided into provinces ruled by feudal lords (see map, this page). The Capetians set out to unite these provinces and to develop a strong central government.

The Capetian kings' method of succession allowed them to outlast many other noble families, including the Carolingian kings. Instead of dividing their kingdom among their sons, the Capetians allowed only the eldest son of a king to inherit. This method worked for more than 300 years.

The history of the Capetian kings demonstrates the feudal struggle for power. Strong kings increased royal lands and authority. Weak kings

Learning from Maps The growth of France took place from the center, the Ile-de-France. What were the English possessions in France in 1328?

THE GROWTH OF FRANCE, 1035–1328

0 — 150 — 300 Miles
0 — 150 — 300 Kilometers

French royal domain

Fiefs of French kings

English possessions in France

MODIFIED AZIMUTHAL EQUAL AREA PROJECTION

242

allowed nobles to regain power. Fortunately for the Capetians, enough strong kings ruled to outweigh the losses of the weaker kings.

The strong Capetian kings increased their power in three ways: by adding to the royal lands, by developing a strong central government, and by increasing the revenue from taxes.

The growth of royal territory. Kings sometimes married the daughters of great feudal lords to add to the royal lands. By doing so, they gained fiefs that were often included in the daughters' dowries. Kings also increased their royal territory by claiming the lands of those noble families that died out.

After 1066, when William of Normandy conquered England, the territorial problems of the Capetians became even more complicated. For centuries the English kings owned vast territories in France. Strong Capetians watched for a chance to regain these lands. The shrewd Philip Augustus, king of France from 1180 to 1223, seized much English-owned land in France. By 1328, when the last Capetian king died, the only major English land-holdings in France included parts of the provinces of Aquitaine and Gascony (see map, page 242).

Central government. To maintain a strong government, the Capetians needed loyal, well-trained officials. They could not rely on feudal lords. Philip Augustus sent out loyal inspectors to investigate, hear complaints, report to the King's Council, and conduct government affairs.

The Capetians set up two new government departments. A Chamber of Accounts collected the taxes, and a supreme court, called the Parlement of Paris, heard appeals from all parts of the kingdom. Trained officials, like those in the King's Council, staffed and ran these departments.

Revenues. A strong central government needed money to pay the army, government officials, and other expenses. The expanding royal territory produced more wealth, as did fees and fines from royal courts. Because a wealthier country would produce more revenue from taxes, the Capetians encouraged the growth of towns, trade, and manufacturing. This policy caused townspeople to support the Capetians against the feudal lords. By the early 1300s, France was a strong, well-organized country, and the power of the king was greater than that of the nobles. However, the three sons of Philip IV died without a male heir, and in 1328 the long line of the Capetians ended.

SECTION 4 REVIEW

1. **Define**   shire, Magna Carta, common law
2. **Identify**   Anglo-Saxons, Alfred the Great, Edward the Confessor, Normans, William the Conqueror, Thomas Becket, Eleanor of Aquitaine, Simon de Montfort, Hugh Capet
3. **Locate**   Hastings, Canterbury, Ile-de-France, Aquitaine, Gascony
4. **Interpreting Ideas**   **(a)** Name four of the main provisions of the Magna Carta.   **(b)** Why was the Magna Carta important?
5. **Evaluating Ideas**   How did each of the following develop in England: **(a)** Parliament, **(b)** common law.
6. **Classifying Ideas**   **(a)** What problems did the Capetian kings of France face?   **(b)** What advantage did the kings have?
7. **Analyzing Ideas**   Explain how the strong Capetian kings added to their power.

5 Popes and Emperors Clashed over Germany and Italy

Although people throughout Europe recognized the spiritual authority of the church, many conflicts arose over the church's temporal authority, or its role in worldly affairs. The greatest threat to the power of the medieval popes came from the German rulers of the revived Holy Roman Empire.

The Holy Roman Empire

Part of Italy had belonged to Charlemagne's empire. After Charlemagne's death in 814, Italy fell into a state of feudal anarchy. Several of Charlemagne's descendants held the title of "Emperor of the Romans" or "Holy Roman Emperor," without really ruling Italy. Later no one had even the title. The pope ruled the Papal States. The Byzantine Empire held some parts of Italy. Muslims held the island of Sicily and often invaded the Italian mainland.

In Germany the great feudal lords elected Otto I, known as Otto the Great, as king in 936. A powerful and forceful ruler, he might have developed a strong kingdom in Germany, like that of the Capetians in France, had he not been more interested in Italy.

Learning from Pictures *Emperor Otto had his son crowned as co-emperor by Pope John XIII. Who had Otto's title of Holy Roman Emperor 162 years before this coronation?*

Otto seized some territory in northern Italy. Then Pope John XII begged Otto's help in his struggle with the Roman nobles. Otto supported the pope, who crowned him "Emperor of the Romans" in 962. Otto later made his own secretary pope, and for the next 40 years, German kings chose the popes.

Although Otto's title was the same as that given Charlemagne 162 years earlier, he ruled a much smaller area—just Germany and northern Italy. This empire, called the Holy Roman Empire, was a shadowy sort of empire, but it lasted, in name at least, for centuries. It established a unique relationship between Germany and Italy that continued for more than 800 years, to the great harm of both regions.

The power of the Holy Roman Emperors reached a high point under Emperor Henry III, who reigned from 1039 to 1056. Like Charlemagne, Henry regarded the church as a branch of the royal government that should do what the emperor expected. During Henry's reign three different men claimed to be pope. Henry III deposed all three of these claimants and had a German "elected" to the papacy. He also chose the next three popes.

Struggle with the Papacy

Henry III's son, Emperor Henry IV, was only six years old when his father died. Powerful nobles in Germany took advantage of Henry's youth and reestablished their feudal powers. At the same time, the church increased its powers. After Henry IV became old enough to rule, Gregory VII, one of the great medieval church leaders, became pope.

The new pope sought to restore the papacy to power. He believed that as God's representative he had supreme power not only over the church but also over all temporal rulers and their subjects. As pope, Gregory used the most terrible punishments of the church—excommunication and interdict—in his conflicts with emperors, kings, and nobles. Gregory's greatest struggle was with Henry IV.

The struggle between Gregory VII and Henry IV concerned the issue of lay investiture. Henry IV insisted that he had the right to appoint bishops within the Holy Roman Empire. Gregory disagreed and excommunicated the emperor. He released all of Henry's subjects from their oaths of allegiance and urged them to elect another emperor.

Fearing rebellion, Henry decided to appeal to the pope for mercy. During the bitter winter of 1077, he set off to meet the pope at the castle of Canossa, high in the mountains of northern Italy.

At great risk Henry and his attendants reached the rugged Alpine summit. The most dangerous part of the journey, however, was the descent down the ice-covered jagged peaks. Cautiously the travelers slipped and slid a few feet at a time. The queen and her attendants sat on makeshift slides made of oxen skins, as guides directed their descent. Some horses were also placed on makeshift slides, and others were dragged across the ice and through crevices to the mountain base.

When Gregory learned that Henry had defied the cruel weather to make his treacherous journey, he ordered him to come to the castle at Canossa. When Henry arrived, he laid his royal regalia down and stood humbly, barefoot and dressed as a pilgrim, waiting for the pope's invitation to enter the castle. For three days Henry suffered the piercing chill of the freezing weather. On the fourth day, he was admitted to the castle. He agreed to several conditions of his forgiveness, and Gregory absolved his excommunication.

The struggle over lay investiture, however, continued during the reign of Henry's son. Finally, in

1122 at the German city of Worms (VAWRMS), an assembly of church leaders, nobles, and representatives of the Holy Roman Emperor reached an agreement known as the Concordat of Worms. The emperor agreed to grant only lands and secular powers to church officials. The church officials should elect bishops and grant them their spiritual powers. The emperor promised not to try to influence the elections.

Even though the Concordat of Worms established the popes as spiritual leaders, the bitter struggle between popes and emperors did not end. The emperors still meddled in Italian politics and continued to threaten the popes' rule in the Papal States. The popes therefore opposed all attempts of the Holy Roman Emperors to rule any part of Italy.

Frederick Barbarossa

Frederick I, called Frederick Barbarossa (meaning "Frederick of the Red Beard"), ruled Germany from 1152 to 1190. Like the emperors who preceded him, Frederick could have made a determined effort to unite the empire, but he was more interested in Italy.

The rich city-states of Lombardy in northern Italy—Bologna, Parma, Padua, Verona, and Milan —had become increasingly independent trade centers. Each city-state had a wealthy merchant class. Frederick knew that if he could capture these rich city-states he would be a very rich ruler. So he sent representatives to take over the governments in the cities. When Milan refused to receive his representative, Frederick captured the city, destroyed it, and drove out its people.

The other Lombard city-states, aided by the pope, united to form the Lombard League. They raised an army and defeated Frederick in 1176. According to the peace settlement, the cities recognized Frederick as overlord in return for his agreement that they could govern themselves.

Innocent III and Papal Power

Innocent III, who was pope from 1198 to 1216, led the papacy to the height of its prestige and power. A learned and intelligent man, Innocent wrote books about law, theology, and Christian discipline. He was also a skillful diplomat and one of the greatest political leaders in all church history.

Innocent III made even more sweeping claims and enforced them more successfully on behalf of papal power than had Gregory VII. Innocent III believed himself supreme over the clergy and all temporal rulers. To Innocent, emperors and kings were merely servants of the church. Thus Innocent claimed the right to settle all political and religious problems. No person or group could do more than advise him.

Innocent intervened in disputes throughout Europe and made free use of his powers of excommunication and interdict. In a quarrel with King John, Innocent placed England under interdict. To have the interdict lifted, John had to become the pope's vassal and pay money every year to Rome. Innocent dominated all of Italy. In Germany he overthrew two kings and put his own choices on the throne.

Innocent III dominated almost all of Europe because of his seemingly superhuman ability and energy. Even so, he was successful partly because conditions in Europe were favorable to his claims and activities. Later popes were less skillful, and circumstances were less favorable. Thus they did not attain the power or influence that Innocent had possessed.

Nevertheless, Germany and Italy never united. The Holy Roman Emperor Frederick II attempted to unite the two areas in the early 1200s. Like earlier emperors, however, Frederick failed.

The attempts to unite Germany and Italy not only failed but also prevented either country from being united. Germany remained a jumble of independent cities and feudal states over which the emperor had little authority. Italy was fragmented too, with the Lombard cities in the north, the Papal States in the central region, and the Kingdom of Sicily in the south. Neither Germany nor Italy became a unified nation until the 1800s.

SECTION 5 REVIEW

1. **Identify** Otto I, Pope John XII, Henry III, Frederick Barbarossa, Frederick II
2. **Locate** Canossa, Worms
3. **Identifying Ideas** (a) What was the major issue in the conflict between Gregory VII and Henry IV? (b) How was the issue resolved?
4. **Classifying Ideas** What were the provisions of the Concordat of Worms?
5. **Analyzing Ideas** Why was the papacy of Innocent III so important?

CHAPTER 10 REVIEW

741
Death of
Charles Martel

Beginning of
St. Patrick's
missionary work
in Ireland

Defeat of
the Moors
near Tours

Rule of
Charlemagne

AD

432

481

732

768 814

754

800

Beginning of
Clovis's rule
of the Franks

Founding
of Carolingian
dynasty by
Pepin the Short

Charlemagne
declared Emperor
of the Romans

Chapter Summary

The following list contains the key concepts you have learned about feudal lords and the church in medieval Europe.

1. After the Roman Empire declined, Germanic tribes plundered Europe and established a series of short-lived kingdoms.
2. Clovis, king of a Frankish tribe, and the Merovingians who succeeded him created a large kingdom in France. The greatest Frankish king, Charlemagne, created an empire that included much of western Europe.
3. Two important medieval institutions were feudalism and the manorial system. Feudalism was a political system in which lords granted fiefs to vassals in return for military duty and other services. The manorial system was an economic system based on the self-sufficient manor, worked mainly by serfs.
4. During the Middle Ages, the church performed many functions. The church had its own laws and the power of taxation.
5. Monasticism attracted many people. Both secular and regular clergy played important roles in education, politics, economics, and social life.
6. Certain difficulties and problems, such as lay investiture, the worldly lives of the clergy, simony, and heresy, plagued the medieval church.
7. During the rule of the Anglo-Saxons in England, the people accepted Christianity and the Danes (Vikings) invaded. Although the Anglo-Saxons drove the Danes out of England, the Normans soon arrived.
8. The English ruler himself was made subject to the law when King John was forced to accept the Magna Carta. Parliament and common law developed in England during the 1200s.
9. French kings gradually extended their authority. The Capetians—Hugh Capet and his descendants—added territory, developed a strong central government, and increased tax revenues.
10. Holy Roman Emperors, who struggled for power with the papacy, controlled much of Germany and Italy.

On a separate sheet of paper, complete the following review exercises.

Reviewing Important Terms

Supply the term that correctly completes the sentence.

1. The period in western European history following the collapse of the Roman Empire, from about 500 to about 1500, is called the _____ _____ .
2. _____ was the political system that flourished in Europe during the medieval period.
3. The person who held land in return for services was called the _____ .
4. A _____ was a grant of land.
5. The custom of allowing only the eldest son to inherit land is called _____ .
6. Under the manorial system, the lord kept about one-third of the manor land, called the _____ .
7. In medieval Europe most peasants who lived on manors were _____ , or people bound to the land.
8. The code of conduct for knights was known as _____ .
9. Special rites or ceremonies at which participants receive the grace of God to help ward off the consequences of sins are called _____ .
10. The elected head of a community of monks was called an _____ .
11. _____ occurred when the church punished an entire region.
12. In feudal times people often paid to get positions in the church, a practice called _____ .

Developing Critical Thinking Skills

1. **Identifying Ideas** Why were the Franks the most important Germanic tribe in western Europe?
2. **Interpreting Ideas** Why was Charlemagne's title as "Emperor of the Romans" significant?
3. **Evaluating Ideas** (a) How did the church become part of the feudal system in Europe? (b) In what ways was the church independent of the feudal system?
4. **Contrasting Ideas** Discuss the conflicts between church and state that arose in the disputes between (a) Henry II and Thomas Becket (b) Henry IV and Gregory VII.
5. **Sequencing Information** Give the correct date for each of the following events and arrange them in chronological order.

Timeline:

- Treaty of Verdun — **843**
- Election of Otto I as King of Germany — **936**
- Coronation of Otto I as Emperor of the Romans — **962**
- Beginnings of feudalism in Europe — **ca. 1000**
- **1066–1087** Rule of William the Conqueror — **1066**
- Norman Conquest of England — **1066**
- Concordat of Worms — **1122**
- **1152 / 1154** Rule of Frederick Barbarossa in Germany
- **1190 / 1189** Rule of Henry II in England
- **1215** Signing of Magna Carta
- **1198–1216** Innocent III served as pope
- Death of last Capetian king in France — **1328**

(a) Concordat of Worms signed
(b) Clovis became king of Frankish tribe
(c) Invasion of England by William the Conqueror
(d) Battle of Tours
(e) Charlemagne crowned Emperor of the Romans
(f) Capetian line of kings founded
(g) Signing of Magna Carta

6. **Analyzing Ideas** In both England and France, kings increased their power at the expense of the nobility. **(a)** List the ways in which William the Conqueror and his successors and the French Capetian kings added to their power and developed central governments. **(b)** Explain how these measures increased royal authority and decreased the nobles' power.

Relating Geography to History

Compare the map of Charlemagne's Empire on page 225 with the map of territorial changes resulting from the Treaty of Verdun on page 226. Then write a paragraph describing how Charlemagne's death affected the boundaries of his empire.

Relating Past to Present

1. Compare life on a medieval manor with life on a modern American farm. In which place would you find greater self-sufficiency? You may want to refer to books or magazines in your library for information about life on American farms.
2. Use a book on American civics or government to find the following information: **(a)** What kinds of cases go before a modern-day grand jury? **(b)** Why do some cases use a petit jury while others use only a judge? **(c)** What is the role of the judge? **(d)** What are the different types of courts in your state? Now compare your findings with the information in this chapter about the beginning of the court system in England.

Applying History Study Skills

Before completing this activity, review Building History Study Skills on page 232.

Read the following quotations about the role and status of women during the Middle Ages. Then identify one fact and one value statement in each quotation.

❝ In addition to providing for their families' physical survival, peasant women also provided moral, emotional and spiritual sustenance. . . . There would be much in the harshness of life to justify and explain. As the daughter, as the female, the peasant woman's life would never be without responsibility. She would be the first child picked to work and the one always expected to assist in the maintenance of the family. ❞

❝ The women of the ninth century enjoyed an increased capacity to share in the inheritance of property. Women had always been eligible to receive certain movable goods from either their own relatives or from their husbands but now law and practice allowed women to inherit immovables. A reason for this trend may be discerned from a deed from the eighth century in which a doting father left equal shares of his property to his sons and daughters. ❞

Investigating Further

1. **Analyzing Ideas** Read the medieval play *Everyman* (Dutton). **(a)** Describe five of the main characters. **(b)** What values does the church want people to cherish the most? **(c)** What is the importance of good deeds?
2. **Writing a Report** Obtain a copy of Eileen Power's *Medieval People* (Harper & Row), which tells the story of a peasant's life during the reign of Charlemagne. Read the selection "Madame Eglentyne," in which the author describes everyday life in a nunnery. Then prepare a written report that answers the following questions: **(a)** What religious duties were performed by the nuns? **(b)** What evidence of "worldliness" is given?
3. **Constructing a Model** Use resources in your school or public library to find more information about medieval manors. Then construct a scale model showing a typical manor.

Trade Revived and Nations Developed in Europe

Place Western Europe

Time 1000–1500

```
3.7 mil. BC    4000 BC                    AD 2100
```

Significance

In a world where changes occur rapidly and mass media bombard us with a steady stream of information, it is difficult to imagine a time when change was slow and information scarce. During the Middle Ages, however, news traveled by word of mouth, few books existed, and most people could not read.

During the Middle Ages, Europe provided a world of striking contrasts. On the one hand were faith and chivalry; on the other hand, drudgery, violence, and ancient pagan and magical beliefs. Dark, filthy streets surrounded a majestic cathedral. Serfs lived in miserable huts below the noble's hilltop castle.

Great changes occurred during the Middle Ages, too. Cities became powerful centers of social and political change. Trade revived as people began to look outward, away from Europe.

Christians and Muslims came into conflict in the Middle East. Crusader armies fought the Muslims and returned to Europe, little realizing that they themselves had been conquered—by new and remarkable ideas that still influence the world today.

Terms to Define

capital
market economy
craft guild
apprentice

People to Identify

crusaders
Louis VII
Joan of Arc
Charles VII

Places to Locate

Venice
Avignon

Questions to Guide Your Reading

1 In what ways did the Crusades change the lives of the people of Europe?
2 What was the economic impact of the increase in trade in the late Middle Ages?
3 How did the growth of towns bring about great social and political change?
4 In what ways did the culture of the Middle Ages flourish in towns and cities?
5 What were the results of the spread of patriotism throughout western Europe?
6 How was the temporal power of the church challenged and weakened?

The Song of Roland *is one of the earliest and best-known epic poems of medieval Europe. Written in the 1000s, the poem depicts the death of Roland, a courageous and loyal knight in Charlemagne's army. When the army fought the Moors in Spain, Roland was fatally wounded in an ambush of Charlemagne's rear guard. The following verse describes the last act of the dying hero:*

> *With deadly travail, in stress and pain,*
>   *Count Roland sounded the mighty strain. Forth from his mouth the*
>   *bright blood sprang,*
> *And his temples burst for the very pang.*
> *On and onward was borne the blast,*
> *Till Karl [Charlemagne] hath heard as*
>   *the gorge he passed,*
> *And Naimes and all his men of war.*
> *'It is Roland's horn,' said the Emperor,*
> *'And, save in battle, he had not blown.'*

By the later Middle Ages, knights from all over Europe, like Roland, were answering the call to battle in foreign lands.

1 The Crusades Changed the Lives of the People of Europe

During the Middle Ages, Christians regarded Palestine, where Jesus had lived and taught, as the Holy Land. The Arabs conquered Palestine in the 600s. Although most Arabs were Muslims, they usually tolerated other religions. If Christians or Jews paid their taxes and observed other regulations, they could live in Palestine and practice their religion openly. For centuries Christian pilgrims visiting Palestine met with little interference from the Arab rulers. European traders could generally do business there.

During the 1000s, however, the Seljuk Turks, a warlike people from central Asia who had adopted the Muslim faith, conquered Palestine and attacked Asia Minor, a part of the Byzantine Empire. When the Turks threatened the capital city of Constantinople, the Byzantine emperor appealed to the pope in Rome. Because Christian pilgrims to Palestine came home with reports of persecutions at the hands of the Turks, the Byzantine emperor's appeal for help found a warm reception in Europe.

◀ *Building a medieval cathedral*

The Pope's Call for a Crusade

Pope Urban II was eager to regain the Holy Land from the Muslims. He called a great meeting of church leaders and French nobles at Clermont, France, in 1095. At the meeting he urged the powerful feudal nobles to stop fighting among themselves and to join in one great war against the "unbelievers."

Urban's plea fired his listeners with enthusiasm, and they joined in one mighty cry, "God wills it!" From Clermont people traveled throughout France preaching the cause. Those who joined the expeditions sewed a cross of cloth on their garments. They were called crusaders, from the Latin word *cruciata,* meaning "marked with a cross."

People joined the **Crusades,** the expeditions to regain the Holy Land, for many different reasons. The lure of lands and plunder in the rich Middle East dazzled the knights. Merchants saw a chance to make money. The pope promised both heavenly

and earthly rewards. Those who died on a Crusade were said to go straight to heaven. The pope also guaranteed church protection of the crusader's property and family during his absence. Debtors who joined a Crusade had their debts canceled. Criminals were relieved of punishment. Thus the Crusades appealed to a love of adventure and the promise of reward—the desire to escape debts or punishment.

The First Crusade

French and Norman nobles led the First Crusade, which lasted from 1096 to 1099. In three organized armies, they marched across Europe to Constantinople (see map, this page).

Not surprisingly, the crusaders received a hostile reception in Constantinople. The Byzantine emperor had asked for some assistance, but now, seeing three armies approaching the city, he feared they might capture and plunder the capital. After

Learning from Maps Most of the Crusades were launched from France. Which Crusade took the longest route to the Holy Land?

THE MAJOR CRUSADES, 1096–1204

First Crusade 1096–1099
Second Crusade 1147–1149
Third Crusade 1189–1192
Fourth Crusade 1202–1204

Major Religions in 1096:
Roman Catholicism
Eastern Orthodoxy
Islam

Area of map, page 251

AZIMUTHAL EQUAL AREA PROJECTION

much discussion the Byzantines allowed the crusaders to pass through Constantinople to begin their long, hot march across Asia Minor toward Palestine.

In their wool and leather garments and their heavy armor, the crusaders suffered severely from the heat. Because they had few pack animals, a shortage of food and water plagued them. Additional problems erupted when the leaders quarreled over fiefs in the lands they captured. Despite these difficulties, however, the crusaders forged on to capture the city of Antioch. Then they marched toward Jerusalem. If the Turks had not also been quarreling and disunited, the expedition would have failed.

Conditions improved as the crusaders marched down the seacoast toward Palestine. Fleets of ships from the Italian cities of Genoa and Pisa brought reinforcements and supplies. The crusaders captured Jerusalem after a short battle and slaughtered the Muslim inhabitants. One leader wrote to the pope that his horse's legs had been bloodstained to the knees from riding among the bodies of the dead Muslims.

In the Middle East the crusaders set up four small states: the County of Edessa, the Principality of Antioch, the County of Tripoli, and the Kingdom of Jerusalem (see map, this page). They introduced European feudalism and subdivided the land into fiefs controlled by vassals and lords. For almost a century, the Europeans occupied these lands. Brisk European trade, with goods carried mostly in Italian ships, sprang up. Christians and Muslims lived in close proximity and grew to respect each other. Many Christians adopted Eastern customs and came to prefer Eastern food and clothing.

The Second Crusade

The Second Crusade began in 1147, after the Turks had recaptured the important city of Edessa and threatened the Kingdom of Jerusalem. In this Crusade King Louis VII of France and the Holy Roman Emperor Conrad III led their armies across Europe to the Holy Land.

The armies of the two monarchs met many misfortunes on the march to the Holy Land. They fought separately and did not join forces until they reached Damascus, which the Turks held. Even then the large combined forces of Louis and Conrad failed to capture the city. After only two years, their armies returned to Europe in disgrace.

MODIFIED AZIMUTHAL EQUAL AREA PROJECTION

Learning from Maps *The Turks eventually conquered the crusader states. What crusader state did the Third Crusade attempt to reconquer?*

The Third Crusade

In 1187 the news reached Europe that the Muslim leader Saladin (SAL•uh•din) had recaptured Jerusalem. Europe responded with the Third Crusade, the "Crusade of the Three Kings," from 1189 to 1192. King Richard the Lion-Hearted of England, King Philip Augustus of France, and Emperor Frederick Barbarossa of the Holy Roman Empire each started out at the head of a great army to regain the Holy Land.

Once again the Europeans failed. Barbarossa drowned on the way to the Holy Land, and most of his army turned back. Philip and Richard quarreled, and Philip took his army home to seize English lands in France. Several times Richard might have gained the whole Kingdom of Jerusalem by diplomacy, but he preferred military attempts. In the end he made no significant gains. As a result of this Crusade, an estimated 300,000 Christians and Muslims lost their lives.

251

Learning from Pictures *Pilgrims arriving in the Holy Land (inset) built castles to protect themselves and to keep control of the land. Belvoir was built overlooking the Sea of Galilee.*

Later Crusades

Pope Innocent III persuaded a group of French knights to embark on the Fourth Crusade in 1202. The city-state of Venice provided transportation, at the same time persuading the crusaders to attack Zara, a city on the Adriatic coast. Zara, a Christian city, was also a commercial rival of Venice. After the crusaders captured Zara, Pope Innocent excommunicated the entire army for attacking a Christian city.

Next the Venetians and the crusaders planned an attack on Constantinople. Although it, too, was a Christian city, its capture offered irresistible plunder to the crusaders and commercial advantages to Venice.

In 1204 the crusaders looted Constantinople, sending many sacred relics back to the West. Although the Byzantines regained Constantinople and a part of their lands after 50 years, they never

regained their strength. The once-mighty empire finally collapsed when the Turks seized Constantinople in 1453.

A tragic episode in the story of the Crusades occurred in 1212, when a group of young children, believing they could triumph where their elders had failed, undertook their own march to the Holy Land. This Children's Crusade had untrained leaders and no equipment. The pope turned back some of the children. Others reached Marseilles in France, only to be tricked into boarding ships that carried them off to be sold to Muslim slave traders.

Additional Crusades were undertaken after 1204, although historians differ on how many took place. The Crusades continued until 1291, when the Muslims captured the last Christian stronghold, in Acre (AHK • ruh). For 200 years a constant flow of Europeans streamed into the Holy Land. Over that period, however, the religious zeal of the crusaders had steadily dwindled.

Results of the Crusades

From a military standpoint, all the Crusades except the first failed. The Muslims eventually recaptured Jerusalem and the rest of Palestine.

However, Europeans learned about many things of military importance, including the crossbow, a sophisticated bow and arrow held horizontally and fired by pulling a trigger. The crusaders also learned to use carrier pigeons as messengers. From the Byzantines the Europeans learned new siege tactics such as undermining walls and using catapults to hurl stones. In addition, they may have learned about gunpowder from the Muslims, who probably acquired their knowledge of this explosive from the Chinese.

In Europe the Crusades increased the power of kings and decreased the power of feudal lords. Kings imposed new taxes and led armies drawn from their entire countries. Many nobles died fighting, while others sold political liberties to towns in order to raise money to go on a Crusade. The church also assumed more political power because of its leadership role in initiating the Crusades.

The Crusades had other important results. For example, the status of women changed. With their husbands absent, many wives managed feudal estates. Europeans were influenced, too, by the ideas exchanged among the crusaders from different countries and between the crusaders and the other peoples they met.

Commercial changes also occurred. Italian cities benefited from their role in transporting crusading armies. Europeans discovered products from the Middle East—rice, sugar, lemons, apricots, and melons, among other things—which stimulated trade in such goods. Cotton cloth was also introduced into Europe in the form of muslin (cloth of Mosul, a city in Persia) and damask (cloth of Damascus).

SECTION 1 REVIEW

1. **Define** Crusade
2. **Identify** Urban II, Louis VII, Conrad III, Saladin
3. **Locate** County of Edessa, Principality of Antioch, County of Tripoli, Kingdom of Jerusalem
4. **Analyzing Ideas** Why did people join the Crusades?
5. **Interpreting Ideas** The Crusades are sometimes called "successful failures."
   (a) What is meant by this description?
   (b) Do you agree or disagree? Why?

2 Trade Increased in Europe

Trade nearly died out in western Europe after the 400s. Manors became increasingly self-sufficient, growing or making nearly everything they used. Towns and cities, which depended on trade and manufacturing, decreased in both population and size. Some towns disappeared completely.

Those who wanted to trade faced many obstacles—little money, poor roads, and few bridges. Each feudal lord charged tolls for the use of roads and bridges in his territory. Thieves on land and pirates at sea made travel dangerous.

Church laws also made trade difficult. The church insisted on a "just price" that did not permit the seller to make a large profit. The church prohibited the purchase of articles for resale at higher prices—in other words, retail selling. It also prohibited **usury** (YOOZH·uh·ree), which at that time meant the charging of interest on loans. Although people discovered various ways to overcome these prohibitions, restrictions still hampered the growth of trade.

Trade Routes

Trade first began to revive in Italy, largely because neither trade nor towns had declined as much there as elsewhere. Also, the geographic location of the Italian Peninsula favored trade. Italy lay between northern Europe, where people were becoming interested in goods from Asia, and the Middle East, where such goods could be bought. The Italians became the great European distributors, acting as go-betweens for traders from Asia, on the one hand, and traders from central and northern Europe, on the other.

During the late 900s and early 1000s, Italian traders began to make contacts with the Middle East. By a combination of force and negotiation, the Italian city-states of Venice, Genoa, and Pisa won trading rights in Constantinople, Syria, Palestine, and North Africa.

At the time of the Crusades, ships from Italian city-states carried crusaders to the Holy Land and brought back rich cargoes from the East. From Italian seaports these goods traveled by pack train through northern Italy and across the Alps into

Tolls

Toll roads are not modern inventions. If you had been part of a camel caravan in the Middle Eastern city of Petra more than 2,000 years ago, you would have paid a stiff toll before leaving the city.

About this time the Romans built a network of highways extending from the Wall of Hadrian in northern England to the Persian Gulf. Repairs were financed by the collection of tolls at the city gates. Many of the roads were still in use in the Middle Ages (right).

In medieval times some tolls were collected by barring the road with a pike, or pole, and then turning the pike to allow the traveler to pass. Early in the development of the North American colonies, private companies built "turnpikes" and charged travelers tolls to use them. Now the states build roads, either with money from the federal government or with tolls collected from users of those roads. And some states, such as Florida, charge tolls for driving on the beach (far right).

Rivers and canals have also provided natural opportunities for toll stations. By the year 1300, there were more than 35 places along the Rhine River, in Germany, where fees were collected. In England travelers were charged for passage both over and under London Bridge. Today ships pay tolls to go through Canada's Welland Canal and through the Suez and Panama canals.

---

central and northern Europe. This overland trade route led to the growth and increasing wealth of cities in Germany, Lombardy, and southern France.

Trade also revived in northern Europe. Before the year 1000, Viking traders from Kiev, in what is now the Soviet Union, traveled regularly to the Black Sea and on to Constantinople to collect goods from the East. They transported these items to the cities of northern Europe.

The region of Flanders, today part of Belgium and northern France, gained importance. It was the meeting point of trade routes that led across France, down the Rhine River from Germany, across the English Channel from England, and south from the coasts of the Baltic Sea. Moreover, people throughout Europe eagerly sought the fine woolen cloth that was the chief product of Flanders. During the 1200s Flanders became the textile headquarters of Europe. Cities such as

Ghent and Bruges became thriving centers of population and wealth.

Hamburg, Lübeck, and Bremen became the most important commercial cities on the North and Baltic seas. Because Germany lacked a strong central government, these trading cities formed an alliance called the Hanseatic League. Eventually the league had more than 70 member cities. It became a powerful influence on the commerce of northwestern Europe during the 1300s and 1400s.

The Hanseatic cities set up permanent trading posts in Flanders, Scandinavia, England, and Russia. Any member that failed to abide by league agreements lost its trading privileges. If a ruler revoked the privileges of any Hanseatic traders, the league stopped all shipments of goods to that country. Sometimes league members waged small-scale wars in order to regain trading rights.

Learning from Pictures *Bruges, known as the "City of Bridges," was one of the chief Hanseatic cities and became the financial hub of northern Europe. Other cities in northern Europe also became trading centers.*

Articles of Trade

By far the most profitable trade for medieval merchants was in luxury goods from Asia and the Middle East. Because these highly valued articles were in short supply, merchants could charge exorbitant prices and make enormous profits. The Crusades caused a great increase in demand for spices, medicines, perfumes, dyes, and precious gems from Asia. Manufactured goods included silk, cotton, and linen fabrics, as well as gold, silver, and ivory art objects. The Middle East also supplied textiles, rugs, grain, and fruit.

Europe offered various products in exchange for Asian goods. The Baltic region supplied fur, timber, fish, and grain. From Spain came wine, oil, leather, and weapons and armor. Other European products included metal goods and glassware from Venice, fine woolen cloth from England and Flanders, and wine from France.

Markets and Fairs

As trade grew, merchants needed places where they could exchange goods. Many villages had weekly market days, but these local markets did not attract large crowds. Some merchants began to sell goods during religious festivals. Then some feudal lords established fairs for the sale of imported goods. They realized that they could become wealthy by charging fees, or taxes, on the merchandise sold. The feudal lords guaranteed special protection to merchants who held a fair.

Champagne, a region in northeastern France that lay directly along the trade route between Italy and northern Europe, held the most important and best-known fairs. In Champagne traders exchanged the textiles, wool, and wines of Europe for Asian luxury goods. Six fairs, each lasting four to seven weeks, were held annually at four towns in the region. Held at different times, the fairs provided a central marketplace for all of Europe.

A simple **barter economy**—that is, one in which goods and services are exchanged for other goods and services without the use of money—could not meet the needs of fairs as large and elaborate as those of Champagne. Even though little money might actually change hands at a fair, the value of goods had to be fixed in terms of a common medium of exchange. Since many different kinds of coins existed, a special class of money changers became important at the fairs. They estimated the value of the currency of one region in relation to the currency of another. In this way the money changers helped in the exchange of goods.

Fairs helped to create ties between regions and to broaden the narrow outlook of the people. Travelers came from great distances to attend large fairs, which offered entertainment in addition to the opportunity to buy and sell. Jugglers, clowns, and musicians entertained the crowds just as they do at county and state fairs today.

Manufacturing, Banking, and Investment

Three important developments resulted from the revival of European trade—a manufacturing system, a banking system, and the practice of investing capital.

Manufacturing grew out of trade. In a new method of production called the **domestic system,** manufacturing took place in workers' homes rather

Medieval Tapestry

The large stone castles of the Middle Ages were cold, dark, and damp. To make their homes warmer and more cheerful, nobles often hung tapestries on the walls. These skillfully woven fabrics were both decorative and practical. They not only gave protection against the cold but also could easily be packed up and moved. The hangings were woven so that they could be cut into smaller pieces and resewn to fit rooms of various sizes.

The weavers of France and Flanders were especially skilled. They made tapestries with complicated pictures—usually with religious, historical, or mythological themes. The

tapestry shown here, "A Walk on the Bank of the Loire," was woven in France around 1500. Flowers form the background for scenes illustrating the daily life of the nobles. Tapestries such as this one are highly valued for the skill with which even the smallest details are woven.

than in a shop or factory. A good example of the domestic system was the woolen industry. In this system an individual would buy wool and then distribute it to several workers. For an agreed price, each worker performed a particular job, such as spinning, weaving, or dyeing. The individual who owned the wool then collected the finished cloth and sold it for the highest price possible. The domestic system began in towns, but by the end of the Middle Ages, it had spread to the countryside.

Banking also developed in the later Middle Ages. In addition to evaluating and exchanging various currencies, money changers now began to provide other services. The word *bank* comes from the Italian word *banca*, meaning the "money changer's table."

Lending money was the most important service early bankers performed. Rulers, nobles, and merchants often needed to borrow funds to finance their activities. During the early Middle Ages, Jews had done much of the moneylending because the Christian Church forbade usury. By the mid-1200s, however, many Christians became involved in moneylending.

Officially these Christian moneylenders did not charge interest. Instead they paid themselves by collecting rents and fees for services and damages. They also eased the transfer of funds from one place to another by developing special notes, called letters of credit, to be used instead of money. A person could take a letter of credit issued by a banker in Ghent and cash it with another banker in Venice. This somewhat resembled our modern-day checking accounts.

With the growth of trade also came **capital,** which is wealth earned, saved, and invested in order to produce profits. People with capital began investing it in businesses such as shipping companies. With the increase in trade, shipbuilding and the financing of voyages became good investments. Each investor contributed part of the cost and received a share of the profits.

These three factors laid the foundation for the emergence of a **market economy,** an economy in which land, labor, and capital are controlled by individuals. It was the market economy that formed the basis of the modern capitalist system (see Chapter 19).

256

SECTION 2 REVIEW

1. **Define** usury, barter economy, domestic system, capital, market economy
2. **Locate** English Channel, Flanders, Ghent, Bruges, Hamburg, Lübeck, Bremen
3. **Determining Cause and Effect (a)** What caused trade to decline during the early Middle Ages? **(b)** What effect did this have on western Europe?
4. **Summarizing Ideas** Why were fairs important in medieval society?
5. **Understanding Ideas (a)** What is capital? **(b)** How was capital invested in medieval Europe?

3 The Growth of Towns Brought Great Social and Political Change

The growth of towns and cities accompanied the revival of trade in the Middle Ages. In fact, trade and cities always grow together. In a town or city, we find all the conditions needed for exchanging goods and services.

Beginning in the late 900s, existing towns began to grow larger. New towns grew at locations important for trade—natural harbors, the mouths of rivers, and transfer points, where cargo was shifted from oceangoing ships to river barges.

The Rights of Townspeople

As towns grew, it became clear that the town dweller did not fit into the manorial system. Townspeople made their living by manufacturing and trade. They played little part in the villages' agricultural economy.

Townspeople wanted to control their own governments. Under feudalism, however, lords controlled the town and would give up control only in exchange for something. Sometimes townspeople won rights of self-government by peaceful means. In some cases, however, they resorted to violence and even war.

Some lords granted political liberties to towns in order to encourage their development. Sometimes towns bought charters of liberties—written statements of their rights—from their lords.

Town and city charters differed widely from place to place. In time, though, everyone who lived in a town in Europe was assured of at least four basic rights:

(1) *Freedom.* No matter what their birth or origin, people who lived in a town had a chance to become free. If officials did not challenge them for a year and a day, they became free. This broke all ties to a manor or manor lord. A serf who escaped to a town could thus become free.

(2) *Exempt status.* Inhabitants of towns were exempt, or free, from having to perform any services on the manor.

(3) *Town justice.* Towns had their own courts, made up of prominent citizens familiar with local customs, which tried cases involving townspeople.

(4) *Commercial privileges.* Townspeople had the right to sell goods freely in the town market and to charge tolls to all outsiders trading there.

Guilds

As trade increased and towns grew larger and wealthier, medieval merchants began to unite in associations. Because of the dangers of travel, traders often assembled convoys—groups that travel together for safety. Arranging such convoys, however, took much planning and money. Gradually merchants founded associations called guilds.

In each town a **merchant guild** gained a monopoly—the sole right to trade there. Merchants from other towns or foreign nations could not trade in that town unless they paid a fee. The guilds also set standards of quality for manufactured goods. In addition, guilds acted as charitable organizations. They made loans to members and looked after those who were in any kind of trouble. For example, they supported the widows and children of deceased members.

In time the skilled workers who were engaged in manufacturing formed **craft guilds.** Each of these guilds included all of the people engaged in one particular craft, such as shoemaking or weaving. These guilds regulated wages and set hours and conditions of labor. They also set prices and conditions for selling the goods, disciplined workers, looked after ill or disabled members, and supervised the training of skilled workers. A master worker, or fully accepted member of the guild, had to be a male.

A candidate for membership in a craft guild went through two preliminary stages of training which took years to complete. In the first stage, he served as an **apprentice.** When he was still a boy,

Learning from Pictures *Guilds monitored the quality of products, such as cabinets. Guilds also decided whether a journeyman could become a master.*

his parents apprenticed him—bound him by legal agreement and often after paying a hefty fee—to a master worker to learn a trade. He lived at the home of the master. The master gave the apprentice food, clothing, training, and moral guidance. The apprentice promised to obey his master, to keep the secrets of his craft, and to behave properly. The period of apprenticeship varied from 3 to 12 years.

After completing his apprenticeship, a young man became a journeyman. A **journeyman** was a skilled artisan who worked for a master for daily wages. After working for wages for some time, he could become a master by submitting proof of his skill—a "masterpiece," or piece of work judged worthy of a master. If the guild masters approved his work, the journeyman could open a shop of his own.

Toward the end of the Middle Ages, the line between masters and journeymen became much more distinct and much harder to cross. The journeyman usually remained a wage earner all his life. Increased prosperity turned masters into an industrial aristocracy. Often the master's son inherited the business and position without performing the required apprenticeship.

The Rise of the Middle Class

A new class of merchants, master workers, and skilled workers emerged in medieval society. The members of this class were called *burgesses* in England, *bourgeoisie* (boorzh • wah • ZEE) in France, and *burgers* in Germany—all from the word *burg*, or *borough*, meaning "town."

The rise to prominence of this class during the later Middle Ages transformed European society. Townspeople tended to want stable and uniform governments that would protect trade and property, so they usually favored kings over nobles. To gain their support, kings began to consult them and to employ them in government positions.

Life in Medieval Towns

Medieval towns and cities, small by modern standards, had from 5,000 to 10,000 people. According to some estimates, in the 1300s Paris had a population of about 80,000. Ghent and Bruges, with about 50,000 inhabitants each, were considered huge. London, with about 35,000, was far above average size.

Physically compact, the medieval city often stood on top of a hill or at the bend of a river so that it could be defended easily. Because city land was scarce and valuable, houses were built five or six stories high. To increase the space inside a building, each story projected out a little farther than the one below. Thus at the top the houses almost met in the middle of the street. Each city had some particularly fine buildings such as a cathedral, a town hall, and the guild halls.

A medieval city would have offended the eyes and noses of people today. Sewage littered dark, filthy streets and was dumped into open gutters that were cleared only when it rained. Epidemics ran rampant. There was no street lighting. Servants accompanied law-abiding people who ventured out at night to protect them from robbers, for there were no police. Despite the uncomfortable conditions, however, life in a medieval city was not completely unpleasant. The medieval city was a busy and interesting place, alive with activity and an array of people—peddlers, lawyers, merchants, strolling actors, musicians, and jugglers.

The Decline of Serfdom

As the number of townspeople increased, the number of serfs declined. The growing towns offered serfs a chance to improve their hard lives. They might escape to the town and become free. Even if they did not, the town changed their way of living. Because the town needed food, serfs could sell their produce for money. Thus they could pay for the use of their lands in money rather than in labor.

Changes in agricultural methods also caused the number of serfs to decline. In England, for example, some landowners fenced off part of their land for sheep pastures, eliminating the need for shepherds. This action left some serfs without work and forced them into the cities. A devastating epidemic that began in the mid-1300s also contributed to the decline of serfdom.

The Black Death

In 1346 the bubonic plague, which Europeans called the Black Death, swept into Europe. It was brought to Genoa, Italy, by infected rats on board a merchant ship from a port on the Black Sea. The plague was transmitted to humans in two forms, the bubonic plague and the pneumonic plague. The bubonic plague erupted when rats infected with a bacterium became infested with fleas. The fleas bit people, and these people soon showed symptoms of the plague—infected lymph glands accompanied by painful swelling and high fever. Often, black spots broke out on the body, which might have been the reason for the name Black Death. The pneumonic plague, which attacks the lungs, was transmitted directly from one infected person to another. This horrible disease was almost always fatal to anyone contracting it.

It is difficult to estimate the total number of deaths throughout Europe. They happened so rapidly that often the survivors could not keep up with burying the dead. Bodies were loaded on carts and dumped in common graves outside the town. Entire villages and towns were emptied. Some estimates say that as many as one-third of Europe's population died and as many as 75 million people died worldwide. England lost one-third of its population. These devastating losses disrupted the continent's social, economic, and religious institutions. Europe was left in a decline from which it did not recover for 100 years.

SECTION 3 REVIEW

1. **Define** merchant guild, craft guild, apprentice, journeyman
2. **Analyzing Ideas** Why are towns and cities essential to trade?
3. **Interpreting Ideas** (a) How did townspeople gain the rights of self-government? (b) What were the most important of these rights?
4. **Comparing Ideas** What were the differences between merchant guilds and craft guilds?
5. **Determining Cause and Effect** (a) What caused the growth of towns? (b) How did this growth contribute to the decline in the number of serfs? (c) How did the Black Death affect these towns?

4 The Culture of the Middle Ages Flourished in Towns and Cities

Civilization developed only after early humans settled in towns and cities. In a similar way, the culture of the Middle Ages did not flourish until city life revived.

Language and Literature

After the Roman Empire collapsed, Latin became the written language of western Europe. For centuries most educated people spoke a form called Medieval Latin. During the Middle Ages, however, the common people began to speak **vernacular languages,** or "everyday" speech that varied from place to place. These languages included English, Italian, French, German, and Spanish.

Vernacular literature. In time writers also began to use vernacular languages. The troubadours' songs were one of the first forms of vernacular literature. **Troubadours,** or traveling singers, wrote lyrical poems of love and chivalry, which they sang in the castles and courts of feudal lords. They also went from town to town singing, in this way helping to spread the vernacular language.

Another form of vernacular literature was the national epic. An English epic about King Arthur and his Knights of the Round Table became popular throughout Europe. France had its *Song of Roland.* Germans had the *Nibelungenlied,* a legend of how the hero Siegfried captured a magic treasure guarded by a dragon.

259

The Canterbury Tales

The pilgrims in Geoffrey Chaucer's *The Canterbury Tales* represent almost every social class in English society. In the *Prologue* Chaucer parades a colorful cast of characters, each with an interesting story to tell, before the reader. The rhyming poetry and subtle satire of *The Canterbury Tales* make them fun to read even today. The following verses from the *Prologue* show Chaucer's mastery of description and satire:

There was a *Knight,* a most distinguished man,
Who from the day on which he first began
To ride abroad had followed chivalry,
Truth, honour, generousness and courtesy. . .

There also was a *Nun,* a Prioress,
Her way of smiling very simple and coy.
Her greatest oath was only 'By St. Loy!'
And she was known as Madam Eglantyne.
And well she sang a service, with a fine
Intoning through her nose, as was most seemly,
And she spoke daintily in French extremely . . .

A *Monk* there was, one of the finest sort
Who rode the country; hunting was his sport.
A manly man, to be an Abbot able;
Many a dainty horse he had in stable. . . .

There was a *Merchant* with a forking beard
And motley dress; high on his horse he sat,
Upon his head a Flemish beaver hat
And on his feet daintily buckled boots.
He told of his opinions and pursuits . . .

They had a *Cook* with them who stood alone
For boiling chicken with a marrow-bone, . . .
But what a pity—so it seemed to me,
That he should have an ulcer on his knee. . . .

A *Doctor* too emerged as we proceeded;
No one alive could talk as well as he did
On points of medicine and of surgery, . . .

This *Pardoner* had hair as yellow as wax,
Hanging down smoothly like a hank of flax.
In driblets fell his locks behind his head
Down to his shoulders which they overspread;
Thinly they fell, like rat-tails, one by one.
He wore no hood upon his head, for fun . . .

Now I have told you shortly, in a clause,
The rank, the array, the number and the cause
Of our assembly in this company
In Southwark, at that high-class hostelry . . .

The growth of towns created an audience for a new kind of literature that the French called *fabliaux* (FAB • lee • oh), which were short comic stories written in rhymed verse. The fabliaux mocked the lofty ideals of chivalry, ridiculed human foolishness, and criticized the clergy in particular. Animal stories or fables like that of Reynard the Fox grew increasingly popular among the more worldly and cynical people who lived in the towns and cities.

Another form of vernacular literature that developed during the Middle Ages was the mystery play, or **miracle play.** These short dramas on religious or biblical subjects were first written in Latin and enhanced the church services at Easter and Christmas. Later, as towns grew, miracle plays were written in vernacular languages, lengthened, and presented to large audiences in town marketplaces. One very popular miracle play was *Noye's Fludde* (Noah's Flood). It told the story of how Noah built his ark, collected pairs of all creatures, and kept them and his family safe during the great flood.

Dante and Chaucer. Two great writers, Dante and Chaucer, represent the flowering of medieval vernacular literature. Dante Alighieri (DAHN • tay al • uhg • YER • ee) was born in Florence, Italy, in 1265. He wrote his scholarly works in Latin. When writing poetry, however, he preferred the Italian dialect of his native Tuscany. Because Dante used the Tuscan dialect in his most famous works, which were widely read throughout Italy, it became the written language of all Italy. Thus Dante is considered the father of modern Italian.

Dante's greatest work is *The Divine Comedy*. It tells of a pilgrimage on which Dante is guided by the Roman poet Virgil. Together the two pass through hell, purgatory, and heaven. They meet the souls of famous people, both good and evil. A work of this sort gave Dante the opportunity to criticize the society of his own time, and he used it fully. *The Divine Comedy* reflects the period in which Dante lived.

Geoffrey Chaucer was born in England in 1340. He wrote his *Canterbury Tales* in the form of a series of stories told by a group of pilgrims on their way to Thomas Becket's shrine in Canterbury. Chaucer used the Midland dialect of English to poke good-natured fun at the English and to satirize the clergy. Because of the popularity of his writings, this dialect became the forerunner of modern English.

Education

During the early Middle Ages, only a few nobles and some clergy were educated, mainly at monasteries or by teachers in the church. Gradually, however, schools admitted any males who wanted to study. Located in prosperous towns, these schools had simple beginnings. A teacher could set up a place of instruction and try to attract students, who enrolled in the school by paying a fee. This educational system resembled that of Athens when Plato and Aristotle taught.

As teachers and students increased in number, they united to form guilds for both protection and privileges. Such a guild was called a *universitas*, a Latin word meaning "an association of people." Gradually the word *university* came to mean an association of people organized for the purpose of teaching and learning.

Learning from Pictures In The Divine Comedy *Dante reflects on the fate of his soul. Here Dante and his beloved Beatrice are in Paradise.*

Four great universities developed between 1000 and 1200. Those at Paris and at Oxford, in England, specialized in theology, or the study of religious doctrine, and the liberal arts, which included Latin grammar, logic, rhetoric, arithmetic, geometry, astronomy, and music. The University of Bologna, in Italy, taught Roman law and canon, or church, law. The University at Salerno, also in Italy, specialized in medicine. By the 1300s towns throughout western Europe had universities.

In time medieval universities established standard courses of study, with uniform requirements for the various stages of progress. These stages were represented by academic degrees. The degree of bachelor of arts showed that a student had finished the apprenticeship. After further study and examination, the student qualified for the degree of master of arts and could then teach. The student was admitted to the guild of teachers at a ceremony that

READ
WRITE
INTERPRET
●CONNECT
THINK

BUILDING HISTORY STUDY SKILLS

Making Connections with History: Linking Literature to History

The literature of a society as found in novels, poems, and stories gives us information about the values and culture of a people. The content is fiction, but the ideas often indicate what the people of that society believed and what they felt was important. Literature helps us understand the intangible or underlying values and beliefs of a society.

How to Link Literature to History

To link literature to history, follow these steps.

1. Identify the source. Is the selection a novel, a poem, or a story? When was it written? Why was it written?
2. Explain the contents. What is the selection about? What is the main theme? Who are the characters?
3. Identify the values or beliefs being expressed.
4. Connect the literature to history. Does the literature represent an ideal, or does it describe a real event? Does it support or contradict the historical facts?

Developing the Skill

The troubadours' love songs focused on courtship. In the following poem, the troubadour Cercamon sings of his lady. Read the poem and attempt to explain the historical link.

> 66 Now that the air is fresher
> and the world turned green,
> I shall sing once more
> of the one I love and desire,
> but we are so far apart
> that I cannot go and witness
> how my words might please her.
>
> I sing of her, yet her beauty
> is greater than I can tell,
> with her fresh color, lovely eyes,
> and white skin, untanned
> and untainted by rouge.
> She is so pure and noble
> that no one can speak ill of her.
>
> But above all, one must praise,
> it seems to me, her truthfulness,
> her manners and her gracious speech,
> for she never would betray a friend;
> and I was mad to believe
> what I heard tell of her
> and thus cause her to be angry.
>
> I never intended to complain;
> and even now, if she so desires,
> she could bring me happiness
> by granting what I seek.
> I cannot go on like this much longer,
> for since she's been so far away
> I've scarcely slept or eaten. 99

Written in the 1100s, the poem is about romantic love. The young man has lost his love because he listened to lies about her. Now he is sorry about their separation.

The poem reflects the age in which it was written, with the woman represented as an ideal—pure, noble, gracious, and loyal, with "lovely eyes, white skin, untanned and untainted. . . ." It demonstrates the attitude of men toward women during the age of chivalry. Women were regarded as the weaker sex and, according to the code of chivalry, had to be protected and defended. The poem describes the woman in idealistic terms and places her on a pedestal.

Practicing the skill. Using the information on linking literature to history, choose a poem or novel written by a 20th-century author and find characteristics in the work that reflect modern times.

To apply this skill, see Applying History Study Skills on page 273.

An English knight

was called the commencement because it signified the beginning of work as a teacher. Only then could the student study one of the specialties offered at medieval universities—theology, law, or medicine.

Philosophy

During the Middle Ages, the classic works of the ancient Greek and Roman philosophers came to the attention of western Europe by way of the Moors in Spain. As a result, European scholars spent much time trying to reconcile Aristotle's ideas with those of the early church writers. Aristotle emphasized human reason. The early church writers, however, emphasized faith. The attempt of medieval philosophers to reconcile early church writers' faith and Aristotle's reason is often called **scholasticism.** The aim of the scholastic philosophers was to discover how people could improve themselves in this life by reason and also ensure salvation in the life to come.

Peter Abelard (AB•uh•lahrd), who taught in Paris in the 1100s, was an important scholastic philosopher. In his book *Sic et Non* (*Yes and No*), he raised many questions about church doctrine. After each question he placed his opinions of scripture from the Bible, decrees of the popes, and the writings of church philosophers. Many of these opinions conflicted with one another. Abelard made his students think and inquire. His motto was "By doubting we come to inquiry, and by inquiring we perceive the truth."

Probably the greatest of all medieval philosophers was Thomas Aquinas, a Dominican friar. His principal work, *Summa Theologica*, written in the late 1200s, summarizes Christian thought at that time. In it Aquinas examined each point of church doctrine and tried to show that it could be arrived at by logic or reason as well as by faith. Today the *Summa* forms one of the bases for the teaching of theology in Roman Catholic schools.

Science

Medieval thinking was deductive, leaving little room for scientific progress. In other words, an idea was taken from an authority, usually the Bible, accepted as true, and used as a basis for reasoning. Classical writings, like those of Galen and Ptolemy, formed the basis of much medieval science.

While the Arabs preserved the great accomplishments of Hellenistic science, only two subjects received serious attention in the West: mathematics and optics (the study of light). Europeans regarded mathematics as important because of its use in counting, calendars, trade, and measuring. They considered optics important because of their belief that God's influence was carried by light. In these subjects some important work was done, especially in the 1200s, 1300s, and 1400s. It was not until the 1550s, however, that major interest in science reappeared and led to vast changes in the understanding of the physical world.

Art and Architecture

During the Middle Ages, most artists dedicated themselves to glorifying God. Church architecture became the primary art form, and the other arts embellished or beautified it.

Between 1000 and 1150, most architects used the arches, domes, and low horizontal lines characteristic of Roman architecture. This style later came to be called *Romanesque* (meaning "similar to the Roman"). Because of the enormous weight of the domed stone roof, the walls of a Romanesque church could have only a few small windows. The style resulted in very dark, eerie interiors, but the simple style of the columns and arches gave the building dignity and serenity. Romanesque churches contained little sculpture, but frescoes adorned the walls.

During the mid-1100s, master builders in western Europe developed a radically different style of church architecture. Critics ridiculed this style because it did not conform to the standards of classical architecture. These critics called the new style *Gothic,* after the barbarian Goths. Despite the origin of the name, Gothic has come to be considered one of the most beautiful styles of architecture ever developed.

In contrast to the low, heavy Romanesque churches, the spires of Gothic churches soared delicately above the roofs of the surrounding town. Outside the walls, builders used rows of supporting ribs, called flying buttresses, which they connected to the church with arches. Because the buttress carried part of the weight of the roof, the walls could be high and thin, with large windows. Everything in Gothic churches—pointed arches, tall spires, and high walls—reached toward heaven.

Learning from Pictures *The flying buttresses of Notre Dame support the high walls used in Gothic architecture. Reims' Cathedral (inset) provides a beautiful example of lofty Gothic interiors.*

The inside of the Gothic church also differed from that of the Romanesque church. Statues of saints and rulers lined the interiors, sculpture in relief adorned the walls, and stained-glass windows let in shafts of sunlight.

In many ways Gothic churches exemplified the changing world of the late Middle Ages. The tall structures rose above the growing town. Marketplaces in the shadows of their walls teemed with traders. Religious pageants and miracle plays were performed both within the churches and outside their carved doors. All the skills of the medieval world went into building these monuments to God.

SECTION 4 REVIEW

1. **Define** vernacular language, troubadours, miracle play, scholasticism
2. **Identify** Dante, Chaucer, Abelard, Aquinas
3. **Comparing Ideas** How did the *fabliaux* differ from the epics?
4. **Summarizing Ideas** How did the church teach the Bible's stories to those who could not read?
5. **Organizing Ideas** What was the organizational structure of medieval universities?
6. **Comparing Ideas** What were some of the differences between the Romanesque and Gothic styles of architecture?

264

5 Patriotic Feelings Spread Throughout Western Europe

Under feudalism in the early Middle Ages, the people of a country did not look to a central government for defense or help, nor did they feel any loyalty toward the country as a whole. Instead, their loyalty lay with a local feudal lord, a manor village, or a town.

Gradually, however, nations began to form. The development of a nation usually started with the growth of patriotism among its people. **Patriotism** is a feeling of loyalty to the country as a whole. It gives the feeling of belonging to a large society rather than to only a small locality.

England

The authority of the English king, although partially restricted by Parliament, increased in various ways. These included the development of a single system of law and courts and an increase in revenue as the country grew more prosperous. Also, the military strength of a professional army and the support of the townspeople strengthened the king's position against the feudal lords.

Consequently, the power of feudal lords decreased. Manors began to disappear as the number of serfs declined. Increasingly, villages and farms of free peasants dotted the English countryside.

The Hundred Years' War. English prosperity and the development of a strong national government suffered a setback during a long war with France. The Hundred Years' War, which began in 1337, had three basic causes. First, the English king Edward III claimed the provinces of Aquitaine and Gascony in France. Second, he tried to seize the French throne when the last male Capetian died. Third, England and France competed for control of commercially rich Flanders. The war brought two important developments.

(1) The use of two new weapons—the longbow and the cannon—weakened feudalism. The English longbow was 5 or 6 feet (1.5 or 1.8 meters) long, with a range up to 400 yards (360 meters). English foot soldiers armed with longbows completely defeated a French feudal cavalry at Agincourt (AJ•uhn•kohrt) in 1415. Knights on horseback were no match for foot soldiers with longbows.

AZIMUTHAL EQUAL AREA PROJECTION

Learning from Maps The English defeated the French for control of the English Channel in 1340, at the battle of Sluys. What battle did the French win in the south?

Europeans may have learned the use of gunpowder from the Muslims during the Crusades. To this knowledge they added the use of the gun. At first the gun was only a crude tube of wood and metal out of which exploding gunpowder hurled stones or chunks of metal. Cannons developed from these rather simple weapons. Castles no longer provided strong protection for the feudal lord and his soldiers. One powerful blast from a cannon could break through a castle's thick walls.

(2) The English Parliament temporarily gained more power over the king. Through its right to grant or withhold tax revenues, Parliament forced some weak English kings during time of war to agree to a number of rights: (a) Parliament, as well as the king, had to approve any restatement or

265

change of a law; (b) Parliament gained the right to levy all taxes, and any new tax had to be proposed first by the House of Commons rather than by the House of Lords; and (c) the king could spend money only for the purpose for which Parliament had appropriated it.

Despite many English victories, when the Hundred Years' War ended in 1453, England had lost all of its lands in France except Calais (see map, page 265). Actually, these losses helped England in the long run. Now the English king could pay attention to governing his own country.

The Wars of the Roses. A struggle for the throne between the York and Lancaster families began in 1455 and delayed the emergence of a strong centralized government in England. In this civil war—the Wars of the Roses—the Yorkists used a white rose as their badge, and the Lancastrians used a red rose. Small bands of nobles and their vassals did most of the fighting. The monarchy benefited because of the chaos caused by the fighting and because many of the great nobles of England were killed.

In 1485 Henry Tudor, a member of the House of Lancaster, ended the wars by defeating the Yorkist king, Richard III. He seized the throne of England and married a daughter of the House of York. He became Henry VII, founder of the Tudor dynasty. The English people, tired of war and disorder, willingly accepted the strong government that Henry VII established.

France

The history of France during the 1300s and 1400s resembled that of England. Capetian kings had developed a strong monarchy, although the Hundred Years' War with England caused French kings to lose some of their power. France suffered much more than England during that war because much of the fighting took place on French soil. Bands of robbers ravaged the already devastated French countryside. Even during the periods of relative peace, starvation plagued the citizens. The following excerpt describes the misery of the people in 1421:

❝ *A* nd in truth when good weather came, in April, those who in the winter had made their beverages from apples and sloe plums emptied the residue of their apples and their plums into the street with the intention that the pigs of St. Antoine would eat them. But the pigs did not get to them in time, for as soon as they were thrown out, they were seized by poor folk, women and children, who ate them with great relish, which was a great pity, each for himself; for they ate what the pigs scorned to eat, they ate the cores of cabbages without bread or without cooking, grasses of the fields without bread or salt. ❞

Joan of Arc. During the Hundred Years' War, rivalry broke out between two branches of the royal family—Burgundy and Orléans—making it difficult for the French to fight the English. Defeat followed defeat. However, French fortunes in the war were revived by an uneducated peasant girl in her teens, Joan of Arc. Joan said she had heard voices telling her to leave her small village and help defend the city of Orléans, which was under English attack. She persuaded the French authorities of her sincerity and made her way to the city. In 1429, inspired to greater efforts by Joan's presence, the weary French troops rallied and saved the city. That same year Joan helped the heir to the French throne take the crown as Charles VII.

Enemy forces captured Joan and turned her over to English authorities. A church council tried and convicted her of heresy and witchcraft. She was burned at the stake by the English in 1431. As the sentence was being carried out, an English leader cried, "We are lost! We have burned a saint!"

Joan's fate created a strong patriotic feeling among the French. Her example helped to bring about the successful conclusion of the war in 1453. The French finally drove the English out and reestablished a strong monarchy.

The Estates-General. In 1302 Philip IV established the Estates-General, a representative assembly resembling the English Parliament. It took its name from the groups that attended the meetings: members of the clergy (First Estate), nobles (Second Estate), and townspeople (Third Estate). During the Hundred Years' War, when France lacked a strong king, the Estates-General controlled finances and passed laws. For a time during the war, it looked as if the Estates-General might become the real ruler of France. When the war ended, however, Charles VII emerged strong enough to rule without the Estates-General, which seldom met thereafter. It never gained the right to approve taxes, which was so important for the English Parliament. In France the king could levy taxes on his own authority.

Louis XI. Louis XI, one of the most remarkable French kings, further strengthened the French monarchy during his reign from 1461 to 1483. Louis avoided war except as a last resort, preferring to use diplomacy, at which he was a master. His opponents called him "The Spider." He used any methods to get what he wanted. His administration was harsh and taxes were heavy, but he used the money to strengthen the kingdom.

Louis XI used diplomacy to build an alliance against the powerful Duke of Burgundy, Charles the Bold. He did so by persuading the leaders of Switzerland, an independent nation, that a strong Burgundy would threaten Swiss freedom.

The Swiss did Louis's fighting for him. They armed themselves with pikes, long poles with metal spearheads. These Swiss pikes proved highly effective against cavalry charges, and, like the English longbows, they helped end the military supremacy of feudal knights. In 1477 the Duke of Burgundy was killed in battle. Since the duke had no son, Louis XI seized much of the territory of Burgundy.

The French king soon met with more good luck. French nobles now ruled various provinces that had once been part of the royal territory. Louis claimed their lands because several of these nobles died without heirs. In this way he obtained the provinces of Anjou, Maine, and Provence for the crown. He gained Brittany by marriage. Thus all of France was unified under the monarchy.

As the power of French kings increased, the power of French feudal lords declined. However, French nobles remained rich and influential until the middle of the 1700s. They had many privileges, including exemption from taxes.

As feudalism declined, French peasants did not gain as much personal freedom as the English did. Unlike the English, they still had to pay many dues and owed services to the manor and its lord.

Spain

By 1400 four principal Christian kingdoms—Portugal, Castile-León, Navarre, and Aragón—had emerged on the Iberian Peninsula (see map, this page). Granada, the last stronghold of the Moors in Spain, also shared the peninsula.

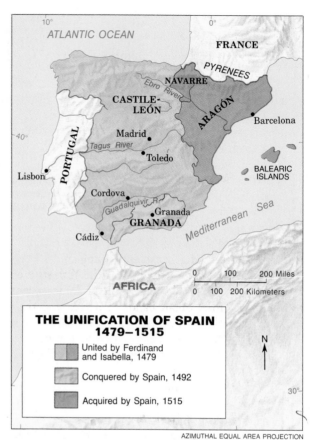

AZIMUTHAL EQUAL AREA PROJECTION

Learning from Maps The fall of Granada completed the reconquest of Spain. In what year did Spain acquire Navarre?

The first real step toward unification of the peninsula came in 1469, when Isabella of Castile-León married Ferdinand of Aragón. The two kingdoms remained separate, but their rulers joined forces in a war against the Moors, capturing Granada in 1492. In the 1500s Ferdinand and Isabella united Castile-León and Aragón to form the new nation of Spain and added the kingdom of Navarre to its territories.

Ferdinand and Isabella made Spain a powerful monarchy. They took powers away from the church courts and the nobles. Ardent Catholics, they looked with displeasure at the many Moors and Jews in their kingdoms. Even after the fall of Granada, Moors had continued to live peacefully in Spain. Jews had been there from the time of the Roman Empire.

In 1492 Ferdinand and Isabella ordered all Jews within their two kingdoms to become Christians or leave. Several years later they offered the

267

AZIMUTHAL EQUAL AREA PROJECTION

Learning from Maps *In 1500 the Holy Roman Empire included lands in Italy as well as in Germany. However, local rulers held most of the power. What countries border the Holy Roman Empire?*

Moors the same choice. Most people of both groups chose to leave rather than accept Christianity. In the long run, this policy weakened Spain because the Moors and Jews had been leaders in industrial and commercial activity.

The Holy Roman Empire

England, France, and Spain each formed strong nations after 1100. However, Germany and Italy— the regions that made up the Holy Roman Empire—did not become unified nations until the 1800s. The Holy Roman Emperor lacked the power to exercise complete control.

In the early days, the rulers of many German states elected the Holy Roman Emperor. Gradually, the number who could vote for emperor decreased. Finally, by a decree in 1356, Emperor Charles IV

ruled that only seven electors would choose the emperor.

The electors feared giving too much power to one of their own group or to any other powerful prince. As a result, for many years they elected only princes who had little land or power. The Holy Roman Emperor had no real authority, but he did have prestige. For this reason the election became an occasion for bribery and the trading of political favors.

Around 1300 a member of the Hapsburg family, which ruled a small state in what is now Switzerland, was elected emperor. The Hapsburgs, although only weak princes with little land, used the prestige of the title of Holy Roman Emperor to arrange marriages with powerful families. Through marriage the Hapsburg family gained control of the duchy of Austria and nearby lands. Many other well-planned marriages eventually gave them control of vast amounts of territory in the empire.

After 1437 the Hapsburgs maneuvered cleverly enough to ensure that the Holy Roman Emperor was always a member of their family. However, even the most powerful Hapsburg emperor did not rule all of Germany, but only the family lands. Germany, made up of more than 300 separate and independent governments, remained a nation in name only.

Italy, too, suffered from being a part of the Holy Roman Empire. Another problem that delayed Italian unification was that the country was divided, as by a belt across the middle, by the Papal States ruled by the pope.

SECTION 5 REVIEW

1. **Define** patriotism
2. **Identify** Joan of Arc, Charles VII, Estates-General, Charles the Bold, Ferdinand, Isabella, Hapsburgs
3. **Locate** Burgundy, Orléans, Portugal, Castile-León, Navarre, Aragón, Granada
4. **Summarizing Ideas** (a) What were two important results in England of the Hundred Years' War? (b) What ruler brought to an end the Wars of the Roses and established a strong monarchy in England?
5. **Analyzing Ideas** (a) Why was the reign of Louis XI important to France? (b) What territory did he gain?
6. **Interpreting Ideas** Explain why Italy and Germany failed to become unified nations during the later Middle Ages.

6 The Temporal Power of the Church Was Challenged

Innocent III, the most powerful of all the popes, made himself both the supreme ruler of the church and the judge of political questions throughout Europe. After his time, however, the temporal, or worldly, power of the church began to weaken. This occurred for two major reasons.

First, Europe was changing. Kings developed strong national governments with rich treasuries. The importance of townspeople grew, and they often felt that the restrictions of church laws hindered trade and industry.

Second, the wisdom of the Muslims and the pagan Greeks appeared in Europe as a "new learning." However, much of it conflicted with the teachings of the church. As a result a spirit of skepticism, or questioning, began to develop. People criticized the church because of its great wealth, its methods of raising money, and the worldly lives of some members of the clergy.

Boniface VIII Versus Philip IV

A serious clash between the church and secular authority erupted over the issue of whether the clergy had to obey national laws or pay taxes. In 1294 Philip IV of France (Philip the Fair) demanded that the clergy pay taxes to the national treasury. His demand angered Pope Boniface VIII. Although the pope was educated and cultured, he was proud, tactless, and eager for power. The pope argued that the clergy did not have to pay taxes. As the struggle wore on, Philip the Fair summoned the first meeting of the Estates-General in 1302. On this occasion Philip accused the pope of simony and heresy and protested Boniface's demands. He also demanded that a general council of the church bring Boniface to trial. The French king then had his envoy in Italy seize the pope and hold him prisoner. Although quickly released, Boniface died soon afterward. After his death the political power of the papacy lessened.

The Babylonian Captivity

Shortly after Boniface's death, Philip IV managed to have one of his French advisers elected pope. The new pope moved the headquarters, of the papacy from Rome to Avignon (a • veen • YOHN), in southern France. The next six popes were also French, and Avignon remained the papal capital for nearly 70 years.

This period of papal history—from 1309 to 1377—is known as the Babylonian Captivity, named after the Hebrew captivity in Babylonia. For 1,000 years, Rome had been the center of the church in the West. With the pope living in France, people in other countries became suspicious of the French monarch's control of the church. The French popes seemed more interested in their luxurious households than in the spiritual welfare of Christians. Rome fell into lawlessness in the pope's absence.

The World of Arab Geographers

Between 900 and 1400, people's knowledge of the world greatly increased. This expanded understanding, in large part, resulted from the travels of a number of Arab geographers. Ibn-Haukal, one of the earliest of these Arab geographers, explored some of the most remote parts of Africa and Asia between 943 and 973. On one of his voyages along the east coast of Africa, he reached a point just 20°N of the equator. He noted that thousands of people lived in those latitudes. This finding disproved Aristotle's theory that areas near the equator would be totally uninhabitable.

Other Arab geographers made important discoveries about the climates of the world. In fact, the Arabs published the world's first climatic atlas in the 900s. It included observations about temperature patterns from places south of the equator and proved emphatically that Aristotle's *torrid zone* did not exist. Then in 985 a geographer named Al-Maqdisi drew a map showing 14 world climatic regions in place of the three identified by Aristotle. Al-Maqdisi noted that climates varied not only with latitude, but also with location east and west. In addition, he suggested that much of the Southern Hemisphere consisted of oceans, while most of the Northern Hemisphere consisted of land.

During the mid-1100s, Edrisi, a Muslim who lived in Palermo, Sicily, began to compile the huge volume of data accumulated by Arab travelers. When Edrisi doubted the accuracy or precision of information about the location of a mountain, river, or coastline, he sent out trained geographers to make careful observations. With this fund of accurate information, Edrisi wrote what he called a *new geography*. Completed in 1154, it bore the interesting title of *Amusement for Him Who Desires to Travel Around the World*.

Edrisi's book corrected a number of mistaken notions. For example, he refuted the ideas that land completely encircled the Indian Ocean and that the Caspian Sea was a gulf of the world ocean. Unfortunately for the European explorers of the 1500s, Edrisi's book was not translated from Arabic into Latin until 1619.

Ibn-Batuta, born in Morocco in 1304, ranks among the greatest geographers and explorers of all time. At the age of 21, Ibn-Batuta set out on a pilgrimage to Mecca. During his journey he became increasingly intrigued with the people he met and the lands he saw. Before he reached Mecca, Ibn-Batuta committed himself to a life of travel, determining never to take the same route twice.

His journeys took him to practically every part of the known world. He sailed along the Red Sea, visited Ethiopia, and continued south along the shores of Africa's east coast. He went as far as Kilwa, 9°S of the equator. Ibn-Batuta then headed northward to explore the lands surrounding the Black Sea. From there he trekked across the vast grasslands of the Russian steppes, finally arriving in the fabled caravan city of Samarkand. Still impatient to see more, he climbed the snow-covered peaks of Afghanistan and crossed into India. He also visited a number of islands in the Indian Ocean and explored part of what today is Indonesia. Ultimately he reached China.

Not content with having seen more of Asia than any person of his time, Ibn-Batuta next visited Spain. He then returned to Africa and journeyed across the Sahara, traveling all the way to Tombouctou. During his nearly 30 years of traveling, he covered more than 75,000 miles (280,000 kilometers).

He finally settled in Morocco, not far from his native home, where he wrote his great work, *The Travels of Ibn-Batuta.* Thus, beginning with Ibn-Haukal and ending with Ibn-Batuta, the geographers of the Muslim world kept the light of geographic knowledge burning brightly for more than 400 years.

Arab geographers in Istanbul

The Great Schism

The 1370s were an especially difficult time for the papacy. A French pope was persuaded to leave Avignon and return to Rome, where he died. The threats of a Roman mob forced the College of Cardinals to elect an Italian pope. But in 1378 the French cardinals elected a French pope, who remained at Avignon. The Italian pope excommunicated the French pope and cardinals; the French pope excommunicated the Italian pope and cardinals.

The period from 1378 to 1417 is known as the Great Schism (SIZ • uhm), meaning a division into hostile groups. For political reasons each of the two popes had the support of certain national rulers. Generally, the people and clergy of a country followed the choice of their ruler.

In 1414 a church council met at Constance in Germany to attempt to heal the schism and to consider reforms of all the weaknesses of the church. The council quickly dealt with the schism by deposing both the Italian and French popes. It agreed that a new pope should be elected, but not until a program of reforms had been adopted.

The Council of Constance had more difficulty agreeing on a program of reforms. Everyone agreed that corruption in the church and immorality among the clergy must end. However, when a definite plan was proposed to deal with a problem, the delegates disagreed so strongly that no conclusion could be reached.

After long and bitter debate, the council decided that church councils should be called regularly to deal with problems, including needed reforms. The council drew up a statement of reforms and the cardinals then elected a new pope.

Continued Criticism of the Church

The Babylonian Captivity and the Great Schism weakened the authority and prestige of the papacy and increased criticism of the church. Some of this criticism came from within the church itself.

In 1324 two members of the Franciscan order, Marsilius of Padua and John of Jandun, wrote an influential work called *Defender of the Peace.* According to the writers, the pope was only the elected head of the church and had no other power. The authors believed that all power belonged to the members of the church, who could delegate this power only to a general church council. A council had authority to make broad reforms in the entire church, including the papacy.

John Wycliffe. John Wycliffe, a member of the clergy and a teacher at Oxford University, adopted and spread these beliefs in England in the late 1300s. He attacked the wealth of the church, immorality among the clergy, and the pope's claim to absolute authority. He also said that Jesus Christ could save one's soul without the aid of a priest and that the means of salvation was in the Bible, not in the clergy. It is believed that in about 1382 Wycliffe encouraged the translation of the Bible from Latin into English. This enabled people to read scripture for themselves and learn what to believe and how to act.

John Huss. Wycliffe's books were widely read both in England and in Europe. His writings influenced John Huss of Bohemia, a teacher at the University of Prague. Huss became popular with the people of Bohemia by denouncing abuses in the church, but he angered the clergy and was excommunicated in 1410. Huss appeared before the Council of Constance to answer charges of heresy. In 1415 the council tried and condemned him as a heretic and ordered him burned at the stake.

By the end of the 1400s, the church seemed to have weathered the worst of its troubles. The demand for councils had died away, and the popes, wealthier than ever, held unchallenged authority over the church. The accusations of Wycliffe and Huss that the church ignored spiritual needs made little impact. Yet those spiritual needs later caused far greater problems for the popes than had the Babylonian Captivity and the Great Schism.

SECTION 6 REVIEW

1. **Identify** Boniface VIII, Babylonian Captivity, Great Schism, John Wycliffe, John Huss
2. **Locate** Avignon, Constance, Prague
3. **Analyzing Ideas** What caused the decline of the church's temporal power after the reign of Innocent III?
4. **Interpreting Ideas** Describe the dispute between Boniface VIII and Philip IV.
5. **Summarizing Ideas** (a) What were the Babylonian Captivity and the Great Schism? (b) Why did they weaken the church?
6. **Understanding Ideas** (a) Explain the importance of the ideas of *Defender of the Peace.* (b) How were these ideas further developed by both Wycliffe and Huss?

Development of Gothic architecture

Birth of Dante

AD 1096

ca. 1150

1265

1291

Crusades

Chapter Summary

The following list contains the key concepts you have learned about the revival of trade and the rise of nations in medieval Europe.

1. The Crusades were organized by Christians chiefly to regain the Holy Land from the Muslims. They had several important effects on Europe: the introduction of new weapons, increased royal power, the weakening of feudal lords, and intellectual and commercial stimulation.
2. Even before the Crusades, trade had begun to revive in Europe. Italians acted as distributors for traders from Asia and from central and northern Europe. Flanders had great commercial importance, as did the Hanseatic League. Trade was enhanced by fairs and led to the development of a monetary and banking system.
3. Towns grew as trade revived. Townspeople gained important rights including freedom, town justice, and commercial privileges. Merchants and artisans organized guilds.
4. Medieval culture flourished with the revival of towns. Vernacular languages developed and were used by such writers as Dante and Chaucer. At great universities scholastic philosophers, including Abelard and Aquinas, sought to reconcile faith and reason. Examples of outstanding medieval architecture are the Romanesque and Gothic churches.
5. National governments continued to grow stronger. After the Hundred Years' War and the Wars of the Roses, England's government became centralized under Henry VII, founder of the Tudor dynasty.
6. In France, Joan of Arc and the French victory over the English in the Hundred Years' War spurred patriotism. Louis XI added much land to the royal territory and helped unify France.
7. In Spain Ferdinand and Isabella created a strong monarchy but weakened the country by driving out the Moors and Jews. Germany and Italy remained disunited until the 1800s.
8. A quarrel between Philip IV of France and Pope Boniface VIII weakened papal authority. The reformers Wycliffe and Huss criticized the church.

On a separate sheet of paper, complete the following review exercises.

Reviewing Important Terms

Supply the term that correctly completes each sentence.

1. Everyday speech is called _____ _____ .
2. _____ was the attempt of medieval philosophers to reconcile faith and reason.
3. A method of production in which the workers performed their jobs in their homes was called the _____ _____ .
4. _____ were expeditions by Christians to regain the Holy Land from the Muslims.
5. In a _____ _____ , goods are exchanged for other goods without the use of money.
6. A skilled artisan who worked for a master for daily wages was a _____ .
7. In a _____ , land, labor, and capital are controlled by individuals.
8. In the Middle Ages, the church prohibited _____ , or the charging of interest on loans.
9. In medieval towns, the organization that gained a monopoly, the sole right to trade there, was called a _____ _____ .
10. In the late Middle Ages, the skilled workers who were engaged in manufacturing formed _____ _____ .
11. _____ _____ were short dramas on religious or biblical subjects first written in Latin to enhance the church services at Easter and Christmas.
12. _____ is a feeling of loyalty to the country as a whole.
13. _____ was the first stage of training in a craft.
14. _____ were traveling singers who wrote love poems.

Developing Critical Thinking Skills

1. **Summarizing Ideas** What were the effects of the Crusades on Europe?
2. **Analyzing Ideas** How did the teachings of Peter Abelard and Thomas Aquinas build upon those of Plato and Aristotle?
3. **Comparing Ideas** (a) Describe the Romanesque and

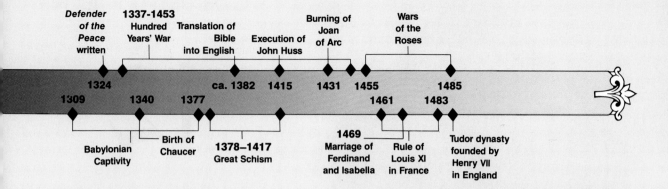

Defender of the Peace written — 1309

1324 — Babylonian Captivity

1337-1453 Hundred Years' War

1340 — Birth of Chaucer

Translation of Bible into English

1377

1378–1417 Great Schism

ca. 1382

Execution of John Huss — 1415

Burning of Joan of Arc — 1431

1469 Marriage of Ferdinand and Isabella

Wars of the Roses

1455

1461 — Rule of Louis XI in France

1483

1485 — Tudor dynasty founded by Henry VII in England

Gothic styles of church architecture. **(b)** Why was the name *Gothic* used for the newer style?

4. **Understanding Cause and Effect** **(a)** What caused trade to increase in Europe in the late Middle Ages? **(b)** In what ways did the increase in trade affect the economy of Europe?

5. **Interpreting Ideas** **(a)** Why was the Black Death so devastating to Europe? **(b)** Why did European recovery take such a long time?

Relating Geography to History

Use the map of the Crusades on page 250 and the map of Europe today on page R12 in order to do the following exercises.

1. List the bodies of water, cities, and islands that Richard's fleet passed through or visited.

2. List the cities and bodies of water crusaders passed through in the First and Fourth Crusades.

Relating Past to Present

1. In the late Middle Ages, the longbow, the cannon, and the pike changed the nature of warfare and contributed to the decline of feudalism. Read Chapter 3 in James Burke's *Connections* (Little, Brown) to find out more about medieval weapons. **(a)** Then name some of the weapons developed in the 1900s. **(b)** What effects have these weapons had on the modern world?

2. Consult your village, town, or city planning agency to obtain the following information:
   (a) What are some of the major building code regulations for housing?
   (b) How are sewage, clean water, and garbage removal provided for or regulated?
   (c) Compare your information with what you have learned about towns and cities in the Middle Ages.

Applying History Study Skills

Before completing this activity, review Building History Study Skills on page 262.

Read the following poem written by a French noble in the 1100s. Then answer the questions that follow.

> I love the springtide of the year
> When leaves and blossoms do abound,
> And well it pleases me to hear
> The birds that make the woods resound
> With their exulting voices.
> And very well it pleases me
> Tents and pavilions pitched to see,
> And oh, my heart rejoices
> To see armed knights in panoply [full armor]
> Of war on meadow and on lea [pasture]. . . .
>
> And well I like a noble lord
> When boldly the attack he leads,
> For he, whene'er he wields his sword,
> Inspires his men by his brave deeds,
> Their hearts with courage filling.
> When tide of battle's at the flood,
> Each soldier then, in fighting mood,
> To follow should be willing,
> For no man is accounted good
> Till blows he's given and withstood.

1. Why does the poet long for the springtime?
2. How does he feel about the fighting lord?
3. What is the theme of the poem, and which sentences help you to identify the theme?
4. **(a)** How is the poem similar to the troubadour's love song on page 262? **(b)** How is it different?

Investigating Further

1. **Writing a Report** Using encyclopedias or books on the Middle Ages, collect additional information about one of the Crusades. You might find "Triumph of the First Crusade to the Holy Land," *National Geographic* (December 1963), helpful in your research. Then pretend you are a crusader and write an imaginary diary of your experiences on your journey to the Holy Land.

2. **Presenting an Oral Report** Read *Song of Roland* in Gerald Simons's *Barbarian Europe* (Time-Life), which depicts the values of chivalry and the love of battle. Present an oral report on your findings to the class.

12

Civilization in East Asia Reached New Heights

CHAPTER ✦ FOCUS

Place   China, Indochina, Japan, and Korea

Time

100—1644

3.7 mil. BC   4000 BC   AD 2100

Significance

From about 500 to 1644, great civilizations flourished in East Asia. The Chinese and Japanese established complex patterns of government, society, and culture. The attitudes and institutions they developed influenced Korea and Indochina as well as other neighboring countries and have lasted into modern times.

The Chinese developed a remarkably inventive civilization, even though the region experienced a considerable amount of political unrest during this period. Chinese culture extended far beyond the country's borders. Korea and Indochina felt China's strong influence, although they managed to maintain their own political and cultural identities.

A different civilization emerged on the islands of Japan. Although enormously influenced by Chinese culture, the Japanese developed their own distinct culture and created traditions as long-lasting as those of China.

Through their literature, art, religion, and political structure, these two countries, over more than a thousand years, advanced to a level of social and intellectual achievement that the West could well envy.

Terms to Define

shogun   Bushido
samurai   daimyo

People to Identify

Li Bai   Kublai Khan
Du Fu   Rabban Bar Sauma
Genghis Khan   Ashikaga

Places to Locate

Grand Canal   Karakorum
Chang'an   Kyoto
Beijing   Kamakura
Hangzhou   Korea

Questions to Guide Your Reading

1 In what ways did China flourish under a restored empire?
2 Who were the central Asian nomads who invaded China and the West?
3 In what ways did the Japanese develop their own politics, society, and culture?

Written in the late 1500s or early 1600s, a strict code of chivalry and conduct called Bushido acted as a guide for the Japanese samurai, or warriors. Reminiscent of the standards expected of the knights during the medieval period in Europe, one part of the code stated:

“*One who is a samurai must before all things keep constantly in mind, by day and by night, from the morning when he takes up his chopsticks to eat his New Year's breakfast to Old Year's night when he pays his yearly bills, the fact that he has to die. That is his chief business. If he is always mindful of this, he will be able to live in accordance with the paths of Loyalty and Filial Duty, will avoid myriads of evils and adversities, keep himself free from disease and calamity and moreover enjoy a long life. He will also be a fine personality with many admirable qualities.*”

1 China Flourished Under a Restored Empire

In the West the Roman Empire never recovered after its collapse in the late 400s. In the East, however, the Chinese defeated the Huns and other invaders from Tibet and Mongolia and established a unified empire. By the 600s this empire emerged stronger, wealthier, and grander than the Han dynasty.

The Sui and Tang Dynasties

The short-lived Sui (SWEE) dynasty succeeded in reuniting China in 589. In their brief period of power, Sui rulers oversaw the building of one of the engineering marvels of the ancient world—the Grand Canal. By skillfully using existing waterways between the Huang He and Chang Jiang, and also by digging new ones, the Chinese successfully linked North and South China for the first time in history. This efficiency in engineering did not extend to governing, however, for the Sui rulers proved overambitious and unskilled in administration. They tried unsuccessfully to conquer southern Manchuria and northern Korea and were defeated by invading Turks in 615. An uprising in

◀ *Shogun Yoritomo Minamoto*

THE TANG EMPIRE, 751

——— Silk route
- - - - Other trade route
⊛ Imperial capital

Learning from Maps In 751 the Muslims defeated the Chinese on China's western frontier at the Battle of Talas. Which city on the Silk Route is located in the Tien Shan?

618 ended the Sui dynasty and ushered in a new dynasty—the Tang.

Expansion under the Tang. The early Tang rulers defeated the invading Turks to the north and west and extended China's frontiers farther west than ever before (see map, this page). Tang rulers made contact with India and the Muslim Empire, and Chinese ideas greatly influenced China's eastern neighbors, Korea and Japan. This contact with other peoples also influenced and enhanced the culture of China.

The Tang established their capital at Chang'an (CHAHNG·AHN). During the 700s and 800s, about 2 million people lived in and around Chang'an, making it the largest city in the world at that time. The city served not only as the center of government but also as a center of culture. People from many parts of the world made Chang'an their home. In its marketplaces Arabs, Persians, Jews, Greeks, and native Chinese shopped side by side.

Like the Han dynasty centuries earlier, the Tang gave China a golden age. Although the Tang dynasty itself lasted only until 906, it began a 1,000-year period during which China could be described as the most powerful, the most sophisticated, and the wealthiest country in the world.

Literature under the Tang. During the Tang dynasty, numerous Chinese poets created an abundance of beautiful literature. Later Chinese anthologies, or literary collections, include more than 48,900 poems by more than 2,300 Tang poets. Although exact opposites in terms of personality, two writers of the 700s represent the best of these poets.

Li Bai (LEE BY), a Daoist, spent a great deal of his life seeking pleasure. His writings—happy, light, and elegant—described the delights of life. According to Chinese legend, Li Bai became tipsy and drowned while reaching from a boat for his reflection in the moonlit water.

Tang Camel

This lively ceramic figure of a two-humped camel, approximately 2.5 feet (.75 meters) tall, was used as a tomb figure during the Tang dynasty (618–906). The practice of burying pottery replicas of servants and favorite animals was widespread in ancient times. It replaced the older, more primitive custom of killing slaves and cattle in order to provide

the dead person with company and food in the afterworld.

In addition to servants and animals, the Chinese also buried figures of musicians, dancers, bodyguards, and grooms. Although tomb figures were made long before the Han dynasty (202 B.C.–A.D. 220), the realistic horses and camels of the Tang period are regarded as the finest.

The brilliant colors, the sense of drama, and the joyous pose of this camel are typical of the rebirth in art that took place under Tai Zong (TY ZOOHNG), the second Tang emperor. During his reign China experienced great prosperity and expanded its borders. Ceramists began to borrow colors and motifs from Persia, India, and Syria, becoming more international in style.

Du Fu (DOO FOO), on the other hand, possessed a serious, even solemn, nature and devoutly followed the teachings of Confucius. His carefully written lyrics showed his deep concern about the suffering and tragedy of human life.

Religion in Tang China. Missionaries from India introduced Buddhism into China during the Han dynasty. Under the Tang dynasty, Buddhism reached its peak there. Wealthy believers donated land for monasteries. Many different sects developed, the most famous of which is known by its later Japanese name, Zen. Zen Buddhism stressed meditation as a means to enlightenment and showed a marked similarity to Daoism. Many Chinese peasants found Buddhism and Daoism closely related. Inspired by the example of Buddhism, the people organized Daoist sects and parishes so that Daoism became a religion. In later centuries the religion of the common people in China contained a complicated blend of Buddhist and Daoist teachings.

In time the growing wealth of Buddhist monasteries began to alarm government officials. They tried to tax the monastery lands and sometimes seized the monasteries' precious art objects for the emperor's treasury. In the middle of the 800s, an insane, fanatically anti-Buddhist emperor began to persecute Buddhists. He destroyed 40,000 shrines and 4,600 monasteries and forced 260,000 monks and nuns to give up their religious duties and return to ordinary life. Buddhism continued to exist as a

religion in China, but it never again became as important a force in Chinese life.

A revival of Confucianism occurred during the Tang dynasty. The government further developed civil service examinations so that once again Chinese scholars stressed the Confucian classics. The construction of temples for worshiping Confucius reinforced this emphasis on Confucian philosophy, and it continued as the main religion of China's governing classes until the early 1900s.

The decline of the Tang dynasty. The Tang dynasty reached its height about 750 and then gradually declined under weak emperors. By 900, tax revenues had diminished, nomadic peoples had invaded, and governors in the provinces had challenged the emperors' power. The Tang dynasty was overthrown in 906 when the last emperor, a child, was murdered.

China Under the Song Dynasty

In 960 Zhao Kuangyin (JOW KWAHNG • YIN) established the Song (SOOHNG) dynasty. Like the Tang, the Song faced foreign invasions and civil wars.

By the mid-900s the principal foreign pressure came from Mongols called the Khitan, in the north. They had occupied Chinese territory in southern Manchuria and in time invaded as far south as the Huang He. When the Khitan threatened the Song capital at Kaifeng (KY • FUHNG), the Song emperors kept the peace only by paying a

THE SONG AND JIN EMPIRES
ca. 1150

Jin Empire	⊛ Capital city
Song Empire	

Mongols

GOBI (DESERT)

MANCHURIA

KOREA

Huang He (Yellow River)

Great Wall

⊛ Beijing

Yellow Sea

Kaifeng

Wei He

CHINA

Chang Jiang (Yellow River)

⊛ Ping-Chiang
⊛ Hangzhou (Lin-an)

Rao

East China Sea

Fuzhou

Taiwan

Xi Jiang

Guangzhou (Canton)

South China Sea

Hui-ning

N

0 200 400 Miles
0 200 400 Kilometers

MODIFIED OBLIQUE CONIC CONFORMAL PROJECTION

Learning from Maps Foreigners established the Jin dynasty in the north, dividing China and forcing the Song south. What city became the capital of the Song?

huge tribute. By 1042 these tributes cost the Song more than 200,000 ounces of silver annually, a tremendous burden.

Another central Asian people, the Jurchen, moved into Manchuria and took over northern China. This again divided China. The Jurchen established the Jin dynasty in the north, with its capital at Beijing (BAY•JING), while Hangzhou (HAHNG•JOH) became the capital of the Song dynasty in the south (see map, this page).

Culture. Despite the problems of the Song emperors, Chinese civilization remained at a high level under their rule. Foreign trade expanded, boosting the hard-pressed treasury. Overseas commerce centered on Hangzhou and Guangzhou (GWAHNG•JOH). A thriving caravan trade also brought goods in from central Asia and India.

A Chinese customs list of the year 999 shows exports of gold, silver, and copper "cash" (a small

coin). It also lists porcelain—a fine, translucent pottery—which from this period on was one of China's most valuable exports. Song artisans perfected the art of making porcelain, creating delicate vases as thin as eggshell.

Song artists also produced beautiful landscape paintings. Inspired partly by the Daoist love of nature, they painted scenes of natural grandeur, with jagged mountain peaks rising above misty hills and rushing water. Many of these landscapes were painted on silk.

The civil service system. The Chinese further improved their civil service system during the Song dynasty. Examinations took place in the capital every three years. To qualify for these, an individual first had to pass an examination at the local level. Fewer than 10 percent of those who tried this succeeded, and fewer than 10 percent of that group passed the national examination.

Because of the intense competition for civil service employment, steps had to be taken to prevent cheating and corrupt practices by government officials, who might accept bribes or be swayed by friends. Candidates were identified by numbers, not names, and guards watched them take the examination. Clerks then copied the candidates' papers so that no one's handwriting would be recognized. Finally, three judges read each paper.

Great inventions. The Chinese invented gunpowder during the Tang dynasty but used it at that time only in firecrackers. They first used it for warfare as an explosive around the year 1100.

Printing was an even greater invention of the Chinese. They had learned very early how to make ink and paper. The first step toward printing probably came in A.D. 175, during the Han dynasty, when the Chinese classics were carved in stone. Artisans could copy these writings by carefully fitting damp paper over the stone inscription and patting the flat surface with soot. This resulted in a white-on-black image of the original.

The next step in printing probably came with seals of metal or wood on which an inscription was carved in reverse. By the 600s such seals had become quite large, and the images they created resembled today's block prints.

The oldest printed book is the *Diamond Sutra*, a Buddhist religious text printed in China in 868, during the Tang dynasty. It was made in the form of a roll of six sheets of paper pasted together. Carved blocks were used to print the words on the roll.

Movable type, by which separate characters can be arranged freely to form words and sentences, apparently came into China from Korea about 1030. The characters were made of wood, porcelain, or copper. This technique did not become common in China, however. Since the Chinese language consists of so many characters, printers would have had to make about 40,000 separate movable blocks to represent them all. For this reason the Chinese preferred blocks carved with an entire page of text.

Peasant life. By about 1050 China's population may have exceeded 100 million. The population consisted mostly of peasants, who lived and worked in the countryside. Two important changes took place in peasant life during the Tang and Song dynasties.

One change stemmed from technological improvements in agriculture. Many extensive water-control projects had been built in South China. As a result, the number of irrigated fields where rice could be grown increased. In addition, a new kind of quick-ripening rice from Southeast Asia made it possible to grow two crops of rice each year instead of only one. Also from Southeast Asia came an entirely new crop, tea, which soon became a popular drink throughout China.

Thus agricultural productivity greatly increased, especially in South China. Peasants had more work to do than ever before, but they also had a greater chance to produce surplus food. That surplus could be sold in the many small market towns found in rural areas.

The second important change in the life of the peasants resulted from a change in the agricultural tax system during the Tang dynasty. In the past, individuals had been taxed. Every peasant owed the government a certain amount of agricultural produce and labor each year. However, peasants living on the tax-free estates of high officials did not have to pay taxes. After the 700s the land itself was taxed, and tax-free estates no longer existed. Taxes had to be paid in produce according to the amount of land a person owned.

The government benefited from this change, but the peasants did not. They could not escape to

Learning from Pictures
The Chinese emperor had important administrative and ceremonial obligations (right). The Song emperors relaxed at the Lotus Pavilion (above).

tax-free estates when they produced too little to pay taxes. Instead they had to sell their land and become tenant farmers. As tenant farmers they paid the landlords high rents, sometimes half the crops they raised. From Song times on, the power of landlords became a serious problem in China. It was not solved until the 1900s.

For many Chinese peasants, the new tax system made life a struggle for survival. To avoid losing their land, they had to stay out of debt. If they lost their land and became tenant farmers, they worried about not having enough food to eat after paying their rent. During the growing season, they worked in the fields from early morning until sundown. During the winter they repaired their simple tools and wove cloth. Young children were kept busy collecting firewood, bringing in water, and watching the family's chickens or pigs. Only for a short time each winter could they go to school—if their village had one—to learn a little writing and arithmetic.

Two or three times a year, peasant families had a chance to relax at festivals held in the villages. Everyone would gather to watch jugglers or acrobats and to enjoy feasting and music. Then the daily routine of hard work would begin again.

City life. During the Song period, a larger share of China's population than ever before came to live in cities and towns. Hangzhou, the capital of the dynasty after 1127, had a population of almost 1 million. Marco Polo, a merchant and explorer from Venice, visited the city in the 1200s and recorded his amazement at its size and beauty. In addition to Hangzhou, several smaller cities and many towns were scattered throughout the empire. Although outnumbered by rural peasants, the city dwellers dominated Chinese society and culture.

The cities of Song China bustled with activity. Huge shipments of rice, fish, and vegetables arrived daily in the marketplaces. Streets were jammed with traffic—carts for transporting goods, sedan chairs in which wealthy people were carried along by servants, peddlers with their goods on bamboo poles, and large numbers of pedestrians. Boats and barges jammed the canals that crisscrossed many cities in South China. Shops specializing in luxury goods—embroidered silks, pearl necklaces, chess sets, and printed books—lined the main streets. Shops selling noodles, candles, and other articles of everyday use lined the narrow side streets and alleyways. Amusement quarters provided puppet shows, plays, and performances by dancers and acrobats.

Officials and wealthy merchants lived in fine homes surrounded by gardens and artificial lakes. Ordinary people lived in crowded apartments, with only one or two rooms for an entire family. Some people had no homes at all. They begged for food and slept wherever they could find shelter. The government set up hospitals and orphanages to help the poor. It also gave food and money to the needy after disasters. However, poverty remained a serious problem in China's cities. In times of great floods or famines, peasants would crowd into the cities and increase the numbers of poor.

Chinese food. Many of the foods found in Chinese homes and restaurants today were also served during the Song dynasty. The development of agriculture in South China made rice the basic food of the Chinese diet. Ordinary people ate rice three times a day, with small portions of dried fish or pork on the side. Wealthy people enjoyed a healthier diet. They could afford fresh fruits and vegetables and greater quantities of fish and meat.

Whether rich or poor, the Chinese prepared their food in the same way. Because of a scarcity of firewood, food had to be cooked as quickly as possible. Meat and vegetables were cut into small pieces first and then stir-fried for only a few minutes. The Chinese used chopsticks instead of forks and knives, probably because they served the food already cut into bite-sized pieces. Various spices and seasonings added flavor. For centuries the Chinese had believed in the concept of "the five flavors"—bitter, salty, sour, hot, and sweet. They tried to achieve a mixture of these flavors in the meals they cooked, which made even simple peasant food varied and interesting in taste.

SECTION 1 REVIEW

1. **Identify** Li Bai, Du Fu, Zen, *Diamond Sutra*
2. **Locate** Grand Canal, Chang'an, Kaifeng, Beijing, Hangzhou
3. **Organizing Ideas** List the names of the four dynasties established in China from 589 to the 1200s.
4. **Interpreting Ideas** **(a)** How did a person qualify for the civil service exams? **(b)** How were the exams administered?
5. **Expressing Ideas** Describe the invention and development of printing in China.
6. **Summarizing Ideas** What were two important changes in the lives of Chinese peasants that took place during the Tang and Song dynasties?

2 Central Asian Nomads Invaded China and the West

The nomadic peoples who lived in central Asia, to the north and northwest of China proper, inhabited lands not well suited to farming. As a result, they raised horses and sheep and spent their lives moving their herds from one pasture to another. Often they covered vast distances in a year. The hardships of outdoor life made these nomads sturdy and self-reliant. They were also fierce warriors. A strong leader could organize these rival clans of nomads into a disciplined fighting force ready to conquer vast lands.

Such leaders emerged among the Huns and other central Asian nomadic tribes. Many invaded China over the centuries, but the greatest nomadic

leader of all times was Genghis Khan (JENG•guh SKAHN). With his fighting force of Mongols, he created the largest empire the world has ever known (see map, this page).

The Mongol Empire

The Mongols inhabited the area to the northwest of China, a region now called Mongolia. At most, they numbered 2 million people. At its height the Mongol army consisted of about 130,000 cavalry troops. Usually no more than 30,000 of these troops engaged in any one campaign. With their superior military technology and battle tactics, however, they were able to conquer vast and heavily populated territories.

Before the invention of firearms, warriors on horseback had a great advantage over soldiers on foot. Mongol troops, who took extra horses with

Learning from Maps *Mongol cavalries captured much of Asia. The Mongol's armada, however, was not very successful. What country did the Mongols try to invade across the East China Sea?*

THE MONGOL EMPIRE, 1294

⟵ Route of Mongol invasion
◄--- Route of Marco Polo
⟶ Subdivisions of the Empire

0   750   1500 Miles
0   750   1500 Kilometers

ROBINSON PROJECTION

them on campaigns, could cover up to 90 miles (145 kilometers) in one day. Specially designed saddles and iron stirrups enabled them to fire arrows with deadly accuracy while moving at full speed. On the open plains of central Asia, they learned to make good use of their speed and mobility on horseback. In battle seemingly endless columns of Mongol riders surrounded the enemy in the same way that they surrounded wild game. Equally important, the Mongolian soldiers enjoyed combat. It provided a test of their abilities and a way to acquire riches, honor, and personal power.

In the early 1200s, Mongols under Genghis Khan swept down from Karakorum (kar•uh•KOHR•uhm), their headquarters. They captured Beijing and renamed it Khanbalik (kahn•buh•LEEK). They then turned westward, conquering central Asia and most of Persia. Under Kublai Khan (KOO•bluh KAHN), a grandson of Genghis Khan, the Mongols completed their conquest of China. The Mongols also conquered Korea and tried unsuccessfully to conquer Japan.

Another grandson of Genghis Khan, Batu, invaded Europe, sweeping with his troops across Russia, Poland, and Hungary to the outskirts of Vienna. They plundered city after city, either killing the inhabitants or taking them as slaves. To terrified Europeans, the Mongolian forces became known as the Golden Horde—"golden" for all the riches they acquired and "horde" after the Mongolian word *ordo,* which means "elite cavalry force." The Mongols eventually left Poland and Hungary, but they controlled Russia for almost 200 years.

The Mongol Empire was divided into four parts (see map, page 281). These four parts remained united for about a century and then slowly began to drift apart.

In 1260 Kublai Khan was given the title of Great Khan and recognized as the head of the whole Mongol Empire. He incorporated the cultural refinements of the Chinese in his personal manners and at his court. In addition to the magnificent palace in Beijing, he also owned a lavish summer palace north of the city, described by the English poet Samuel Taylor Coleridge:

“ *I*n Xanadu did Kubla Khan
A stately pleasure-dome decree,
Where Alph, the sacred river, ran
Through caverns measureless to man
Down to a sunless sea. ”

Life under Mongol rule. In 1271 Kublai Khan established the Yuan (YOO•AHN) dynasty in North China with Beijing as his capital. Yuan forces defeated the Song dynasty in South China in 1279 and ruled all of China until 1368.

Under Mongol rule China made notable economic progress. During more than a century of invasion and warfare, its population had declined from 100 million to only 59 million. With the restoration of peace, however, the population began to increase.

Kublai extended the Grand Canal from the Huang He to Beijing in order to ship rice from South China to his new and expanding capital city. Next to the canal he built a stone-surfaced highway that stretched for 1,100 miles (1,770 kilometers) between Hangzhou and Beijing. A messenger could cover this distance in 40 days. Kublai also linked China to India and Persia by post roads or mail routes, which greatly improved trade.

Contacts with Europeans. During Mongol rule Europeans and Chinese became better acquainted with one another. Among the Europeans living in China at this time were Russian artisans and soldiers captured by the Golden Horde, a Parisian goldsmith kidnapped in what is now Yugoslavia, and the nephew of a French bishop.

King Louis IX of France and the pope in Rome sent ambassadors to China during the 1200s. Christian missionaries, as well as the famous Venetian merchant Marco Polo, also traveled to China. Polo's Chinese counterpart, Rabban Bar Sauma of Beijing, journeyed across Asia to Persia, then to Constantinople, and eventually to Italy, where he talked with the pope. Bar Sauma also went to France, where he met King Philip IV and visited the University of Paris.

Chinese-Mongol differences. The Yuan dynasty had brought certain benefits to China. But a natural antagonism existed between the conquerors and the conquered that resulted from the striking differences between Mongol and Chinese ways of living. To begin with, their languages differed. As warriors, the Mongols valued action. The Chinese, on the other hand, valued accomplishment in literature and the arts. The Chinese disliked the smell and appearance of the invaders, who did not wash often. They also objected to the freedom Mongol women were allowed.

When Kublai Khan died in 1294, he left China to weak successors. Seven Mongol emperors ruled

Learning from Pictures *This tranquil scroll painting from the Yuan dynasty illustrates the Mongol's admiration of horses.*

China over the following 26 years. During this period the country experienced many problems. The Huang He flooded, destroying crops and causing famine throughout the land. Many secret organizations calling for revolution sprang up. Finally, in 1368, the Yuan dynasty came to an end with the overthrow of the last Mongol emperor.

Later Chinese historians denounced the Mongols as savages. They claimed that the Yuan dynasty had no lasting effect on China. The Mongols did, however, influence China in important ways. Among other things, they improved communications and made local governments directly responsible to the central government in Beijing. Later Chinese dynasties built upon the Mongols' political reforms by concentrating greater power in the hands of the emperor.

Civilization Developed in Indochina

Historically Indochina consists of the countries of Cambodia, Laos, and Vietnam. However, geographers include the countries of Burma, Malaysia, and Thailand as well. Indochina is located on a peninsula that borders China on the north and India on the northwest. As a result, the region shows the influences of both of these cultures. During much of their history, the countries of Indochina were part of the Chinese Empire. At times, however, they were able to maintain their independence because of their location far from the center of Chinese rule.

Buddhism, which was adopted from the Chinese, helped shape the culture of Indochina. Daoism and Confucianism also were transplanted from China. And, for the most part, the countries of Indochina adopted the Chinese political structure. However, they retained their own languages.

Early in the history of Indochina, people from India settled in the region, bringing their language, art, and religion. Evidence of their cultural impact can still be found in the southern part of the peninsula. Religious art, temples, and sculpture show this influence. In present-day Cambodia (Kampuchea), ruins of the city of Angkor Thom (ANG • kawr TAHM), particularly at the huge temple of Angkor Wat, offer reminders of Indian influence. Reliefs with scenes from the Hindu epics adorn this structure, one of the architectural wonders of the Far East. Although Hinduism was strong in this area due to the Indian influence, Buddhism remained the main religion of most of the people.

During the late 1300s, a form of writing easier than Chinese developed in Indochina. Also at this time, a national literature and a native style of art arose in parts of the region.

SECTION 2 REVIEW

1. **Identify** Genghis Khan, Kublai Khan, Batu, Golden Horde, Rabban Bar Sauma
2. **Locate** Karakorum, Indochina
3. **Understanding Ideas** How were the Mongols able to conquer so much land in Asia so quickly?
4. **Analyzing Ideas** (a) Why did the Chinese despise the Mongols? (b) What were some of the good features of Mongol rule?
5. **Organizing Ideas** How did Kublai Khan improve communications in China?
6. **Summarizing Ideas** How were the countries of Indochina able to maintain their own identities?

283

3 Japan Developed Its Own Government, Society, and Culture

Japan consists of a chain of islands in the Pacific Ocean off the northeast coast of Asia. Most of the country's large population lives on the four main islands—Honshu (HAHN•shoo), Kyushu (kee•OO•shoo), Shikoku (shi•KOH•koo), and Hokkaido (hah•KYD•oh).

The Physical Setting

Because it is so mountainous, only about one-sixth of the area of Japan can be used for farming. However, this farmland produces more food than do most other places in the world, thanks to abundant rainfall, plentiful sunlight, long growing seasons, and the diligence of Japanese farmers. The plentiful water supply provides easy irrigation and, in modern times, is also a source of electric power. The rains also support heavy timber growth. Nature is not entirely kind to Japan, however. Earthquakes, tidal waves, and typhoons often strike the islands, causing extensive damage.

Until modern times the seas surrounding Japan shielded the islands from foreign influences. This protection allowed the Japanese to choose whether they wanted to have contact with other peoples. At times in their history, they have been very interested in the outside world, especially China. At other times they have preferred to live in isolation.

The Mongols under Kublai Khan tried several times to conquer Japan, but they failed. In 1281, for example, a Mongol fleet of 3,500 ships carrying more than 100,000 soldiers assembled to invade Japan. However, an extraordinarily powerful typhoon, or "Divine Wind," which the Japanese call the *Kamikaze,* dispersed the fleet.

Japan's Beginnings

Long ago the people of Japan migrated to the islands from the Asian mainland. The two oldest and most basic characteristics of their society have been the ancient Shinto religion and a deep reverence for their emperor.

Shinto means "the way of the gods." It teaches that spirits live in such objects as sand, waterfalls, and great trees. Shintoism lacks established scripture, specific doctrine, and priests. It contains, however, numerous gods called *Kami,* meaning "superior." The Kami help especially in promoting fertility in families and crops. From one viewpoint Shinto is not so much a religion as a set of prayers and rituals to satisfy the Kami.

Reverence or respect for the emperor is also a foundation of Japanese life. According to tradition, Jimmu, the first emperor, was crowned in 660 B.C. The Japanese chose this date in A.D. 601 by counting back 1,260 years, a period of time borrowed from the Chinese as representing a major historical cycle.

Jimmu probably was a mythical figure. The first real, or historic, emperor, Sujin, reigned in the 300s. He, and his successors, claimed divine descent from the sun goddess. Official denial of this belief was not announced until 1945, after the Japanese defeat in World War II. In the entire history of Japan, only one imperial family has ruled, making it the longest unbroken dynasty in the history of the world.

Early History of Japan

Only sketchy records of early Japanese history exist. The Chinese, however, knew about Japan before A.D. 100. Chinese writing was introduced and adopted in Japan about 405. Another Chinese influence filtered in about 550, when a monk brought Buddhism to Japan. At first the emperor's conservative advisers opposed the new religion. One of them even threw a statue of Buddha into a canal. But soon after, when an epidemic broke out, the advisers interpreted the illness as a sign of the new religion's power, and the emperor allowed several Buddhist monasteries to be built. Buddhism then won many converts among nobles at the emperor's court.

In later centuries Buddhism spread among the common people and became an important part of Japanese life. It did not replace Shinto, however. For most of Japanese history, the two religions coexisted peacefully, and people believed in both religions at the same time. They celebrated important events, such as births and marriages, according to Shinto rituals. They held funerals according to Buddhist rituals.

Japanese adoption of Chinese writing and Buddhism led to the introduction of other Chinese

Parks and Gardens

There are times when you just want to "get away from it all." When this happens to people in Japan, many seek a garden such as this one (bottom left) to refresh their spirits. Gardens in Asia are designed to imitate nature. They are miniature representations of the world, where rocks stand for mountains, ponds represent oceans, and sand and gravel are rivers. Frequently the gardens are open and in harmony with the hills around them.

In contrast, some gardens, particularly in China, are completely walled. Inside, visitors enjoy special views that change with the time of day or the seasons. Sometimes there are platforms where one can sit and look at the moon.

Some private homes and many public parks in Japan have tea gardens with paths leading to small houses. There tea is served with great ceremony. The public parks are lined with rows of cherry trees, and in springtime families have picnics under the blossoms. The Japanese sent similar cherry trees, now planted around the Tidal Basin in Washington, D.C., so that Americans could enjoy them, too.

You may have camped out in one of the many national or state parks in the United States. People who live in or near cities visit Central Park in New York, the Public Gardens in Boston, Grant Park in Chicago, or Golden Gate Park in San Francisco. The people of Victoria, British Columbia, enjoy walking and sitting in the Butchart Gardens (below right). The Tivoli Gardens (above) in Copenhagen, Denmark, and the Prater in Vienna, Austria, have giant Ferris wheels and other entertainments. A number of parks in the United States have special themes. Sometimes they contain animals and are game preserves.

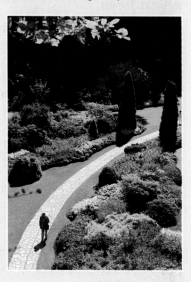

ideas and ways of life. The Japanese also adopted Chinese artistic designs, road engineering, medical knowledge, a system of weights and measures, and styles of clothing.

The Japanese sent their first ambassadors to China in 607. Japanese students returning from China in the 640s believed Japan inferior in various ways and worked to have other aspects of Chinese culture adopted in their country.

In 702 Japan's emperor issued a law code modeled on one from China's Tang dynasty. The code regulated all aspects of life in Japan and established a highly centralized government under the emperor. In 794 the Japanese built a capital named Heian-kyo (HAY • ahn-KYOH), which became the modern city of Kyoto. In Heian-kyo members of the ruling class began to modify some of the practices that had been adopted from China, creating their own distinctive culture. For example, earlier poetry had been written in Chinese. Japanese poets now began writing in their own language.

Women enjoyed a high position in upper-class society in Heian-kyo. They could own property, and they played an important role in the literary life of the capital. Several women wrote diaries. Around the year 1000, Lady Murasaki Shikibu (moohr • uh • SAHK • ee SHEE • kee • boo) wrote *The Tale of Genji*, the world's first novel. It tells the story of Prince Genji, the perfect courtier. Written in a quiet, sensitive style and filled with poems about the beauties of nature, it became one of the masterpieces of Japanese literature.

Feudal Japan

Although emperors continued to reign in Heian-kyo, after the early 800s the centralized political system adopted from China gradually fell into decline. In its place Japan developed a system of local power that in many ways resembled feudalism, the system that governed Europe at this time.

In Japan the feudal system contained two conflicting sources of power. One was an indirect form of central government under which an important family held power in the name of the emperor. The other source of power existed outside the control of the central government. It consisted of military units that had authority in the territories they occupied.

Central government. The first family to gain control over the emperor and to use his power to

their advantage were the Fujiwara (foo • jee • WAH • rah). By holding important government offices and by marrying into the emperor's family, the Fujiwara controlled the central government from the early 800s to the mid-1100s.

After a long power struggle, the Minamoto (mi • nah • MOH • TOH) family took control of the government in 1185. They held power until 1338. In 1192 the Minamoto introduced a new kind of official called the **shogun.** On paper the shogun was the chief officer of the emperor and was expected to be dutiful to him. In practice he was the agent of the Minamoto and of the powerful families that succeeded them. From this time on, gaining control of the shogunate, or office of shogun, became the major aim of any ambitious family.

The shogun also was the chief military officer of the central government. In addition, he controlled finance, law, the courts, and appointments to office. He often governed from his military headquarters at Kamakura. In 1338 the Ashikaga (ah • shee • KAH • gah) family took over the shogunate from the Minamoto. They controlled the office for more than 200 years.

Local military rule. The leading families and their shoguns had power, but they were not strong enough to extend this power to local levels. There, warrior-landlords called **samurai** (SAM • uh • ry) led the military units. The power of a samurai rested on his control of land, on his descent from earlier local leaders, and on his ability with the sword. The samurai followed a code called **Bushido** (BOOH • shee • doh) that stressed bravery, loyalty, and honor. Samurai had to endure great physical hardship without complaint and could have no fear of death. They regarded **seppuku** (se • POO • koo), a form of ceremonial suicide also known as hara-kiri, or "belly slitting," as the honorable way to avoid torture, execution, or defeat in battle.

In time, the samurai developed an order of ranking among themselves. At the top were the **daimyos** (DY • mee • ohz), who gained the loyalty of the lesser samurai. As the power of the daimyos increased and they became like petty kings, the samurai lost both power and prestige.

Life in Feudal Japan

Rival military units competed for power at the local level, and leading families competed for the shogunate, making warfare a frequent occurrence in

Learning from Pictures
Japanese people often prepare food at the dinner table as they eat. What was the purpose of the tea ceremony?

feudal Japan. Nevertheless, considerable economic and cultural growth took place during the feudal period.

Instead of weakening the country, warfare seems to have enriched it. The daimyos encouraged peasants to grow larger crops, since larger crops meant more taxes for the daimyos. They also promoted and taxed trade, financing their military campaigns with the money they received.

For ordinary people, the frequent warfare offered a chance to rise in the world. Any man who could use a sword or a lance could join a daimyo's army. If he proved himself a good fighter and leader, he might be promoted to a higher rank. Or he might even lead a revolt against his daimyo and become a daimyo himself.

The spread of Buddhism. A religious awakening occurred during the feudal period in Japan. Buddhists established new sects, including several that taught that salvation could come through faith alone. According to the older Buddhist sects, a person had to make contributions to monasteries and study Buddhist scriptures to achieve salvation. Only wealthy people could afford that. The new sects appealed to ordinary people.

Zen Buddhism, a sect introduced from China in the late 1100s, particularly interested warriors. Zen stressed salvation through enlightenment, not faith. To achieve enlightenment, a person had to engage in long hours of meditation and rigorous self-discipline. Warriors found that practicing Zen gave them the courage they needed to fight.

Zen and Japanese culture. The Ashikaga shoguns strongly supported Zen Buddhism. They built Zen monasteries throughout the country and encouraged the artistic efforts of Zen monks. Several new art forms inspired by Zen developed during the late 1300s and early 1400s, at the height of Ashikaga power. One was landscape architecture, the art of designing gardens. By the careful arrangement of rocks, trees, and water, Zen believers tried to represent the essential beauty of nature.

Another new art form was the tea ceremony, a ritual designed to produce spiritual calm. A few people gathered in a small, simply furnished room that overlooked a garden. They sat quietly while one of them slowly and deliberately made tea. Then they drank the tea, admired the pottery bowls in which it was served, and enjoyed the beauties of nature in the garden outside.

BUILDING HISTORY STUDY SKILLS

Interpreting Visuals: Reading a Chart

Charts are visual ways of organizing information in order to show relationships. For example, a time line is a chart for recording the order of events. A classification chart groups information so that it can be compared easily. An organization chart shows relationships within a system or group. Lines are connected to show who has authority over whom. A flow chart illustrates the steps in a process, and a family tree diagrams the structure of a family.

How to Read a Chart

To read a chart, follow these steps.

1. Identify the type of chart and its purpose.
2. Identify the details.
3. Relate the details to each other.

Developing the Skill

The following chart is an organization chart. It records the structure of Japanese society under the feudal system. The emperor is at the top of the feudal structure. Under him is the shogun. The daimyos are under the shogun, the samurai under the daimyos, and the merchants, peasants, farmers, and craft workers are on the bottom of the chart.

The dotted lines show weak or formal rule. The solid lines show real power. The relationship of the samurai to the daimyo can be seen, as can the relationship of the daimyo to the shogun and that of the shogun to the emperor. By reading the chart, you can see clearly that the daimyos possessed the real power in feudal Japan.

Practicing the skill. Using the above information on charts, draw an organization chart that shows the structure of the United States government. You may need to use an American history textbook to find the information necessary to practice this skill.

To apply this skill, see Applying History Study Skills on page 291.

A samurai warrior on horseback

Feudal Society in Japan

Emperor
(figurehead)

Shogun
(chosen by most powerful daimyos)

Daimyos

Samurai   **Samurai**

merchants, peasants, farmers, craft workers

Learning from Maps *The Koreans built a great wall on the northern frontier to protect themselves from invasion. What body of water separates Japan and Korea?*

Another artistic expression of Zen was the *No* play. First performed in the 1300s, *No* plays were highly stylized dance dramas, usually on religious subjects. Like Greek plays, *No* plays were performed on a bare stage by male actors wearing masks, while a chorus chanted the story.

The Ashikaga retained control of the shogunate until 1573 but had no political influence after about 1460. Real power rested with the many daimyos, who now began to fight among themselves for supremacy. For about a century, Japan had no central government.

Civilization Developed in Korea

Korea occupies a peninsula on the eastern border of the Chinese mainland (see map, this page). China controlled the peninsula for much of Korea's history and, as a result, greatly influenced Korea's political and cultural development. China first invaded Korea in 200 B.C., during the Han dynasty. At this time the Chinese began to transmit their culture to Korea.

After the fall of the Han dynasty, three independent kingdoms, with shifting boundaries, took control of the peninsula. The kingdom of Silla (SI•luh) eventually emerged as the strongest and unified the country in 668. During the Tang dynasty, Korea once again became a colony of China but kept its own ruling dynasty. Buddhism was introduced to Korea during this period. Then Korea became part of the Mongol Empire, and when the Mongols were expelled, a new dynasty, the Yi (YEE), was founded in 1392. This dynasty survived until 1910, when Japan annexed Korea.

Buddhism had the most important religious influence on Korea. Its teachings can be seen in the country's culture, philosophy, and morality. In 845 Buddhism was made the state religion. Scholars studied the Confucian classics, and the government adopted the Chinese civil service system, based on the teachings of Confucius. The Koreans did not, however, completely copy the Chinese. They retained both their native dress and their own language. Sejong (SA•ZHONG), a Yi emperor who ruled in the mid-1400s, directed the development of a Korean alphabet. The Koreans also invented a method of printing using movable metal type that the Chinese later adopted.

SECTION 3 REVIEW

1. **Define**   shogun, samurai, Bushido, seppuku, daimyo
2. **Identify**   Shinto, *The Tale of Genji*, Ashikaga, Sejong
3. **Locate**   Kyoto, Kamakura, Korea
4. **Comparing Ideas**   Compare the favorable and unfavorable features of Japanese geography.
5. **Interpreting Ideas**   What were China's major contributions to and influences on Japan?
6. **Organizing Ideas**   **(a)** Name the two centers of power in Japanese feudalism.   **(b)** How did they complement each other?   **(c)** How did they conflict with each other?
7. **Analyzing Ideas**   How did Zen Buddhism influence Japanese culture?
8. **Identifying Cause and Effect**   What effect did years of Chinese domination have on Korean culture?

289

CHAPTER 12 REVIEW

AD

Buddhism introduced in Japan	Tang dynasty established in China	Height of Buddhism in China		Buddhism made state religion in Korea
550	618	700		845
589	668		794	868

Sui dynasty established in China — Kingdom of Silla united Korea — Japanese capital built at Heian-kyo (Kyoto) — *Diamond Sutra* printed

Chapter Summary

The following list contains the key concepts you have learned about the civilizations of China, Indochina, Japan, and Korea.

1. A unified empire was reestablished in China in 589 by the Sui dynasty. Soon China was stronger and wealthier than ever before.
2. During the Tang and Song dynasties, the Chinese civil service system was perfected. Important inventions, such as gunpowder and printing, were made.
3. In the 1200s the nomadic Mongols of central Asia were united into a powerful fighting force under Genghis Khan and, later, his grandson Kublai Khan. They conquered China, Persia, and much of eastern Europe.
4. Mongol rule brought economic growth to China. Also under the Mongols, population increased, roads and canals were built, and trade developed with other peoples. The Chinese resented the Mongols. However, later Chinese dynasties used the Mongol's political method of concentrating greater power in the hands of the emperor.
5. The countries of Indochina were controlled by China during much of their histories. As a result, Chinese culture greatly influenced these countries.
6. Japan was influenced by China but created its own distinct culture. Its island location made it safe from foreign invasion. The difficult terrain encouraged a political system in which there was both central and local power.
7. Two of the most basic characteristics of Japanese society are the Shinto religion and a deep reverence for the emperor. The Shinto religion lacks established scripture, doctrine, and priests. It contains numerous gods called Kami. Japanese emperors claimed divine descent from the sun goddess. In all of its history, Japan has been ruled by only one imperial family.
8. Japan developed a feudal political system. The central government was controlled by the shogun, who held power in the name of the emperor. At the local level, power was in the hands of the samurai, warrior-landlords. The most powerful samurai were the daimyo.
9. Korea, although dominated by China for most of its history, managed to develop its own culture. The Koreans had their own native dress as well as their own language and developed their own alphabet. Movable type was invented in Korea.

On a separate sheet of paper, complete the following review exercises.

Reviewing Important Terms

Supply the term that correctly completes each sentence.

1. _____ was a ceremonial suicide in Japan.
2. The chief officer of a Japanese emperor who was always careful to be dutiful to him was the _____ .
3. At the top of the samurai were the _____, who, as their power increased, became petty kings.
4. _____ were warrior-landlords in Japan.

Developing Critical Thinking Skills

1. **Understanding Cause and Effect** **(a)** What were the steps in the development of printing? **(b)** What effect did the invention have on China and eventually the rest of the world?
2. **Analyzing Ideas** **(a)** What agricultural improvements took place in China during the Tang and Song dynasties? **(b)** What part of China was most affected by these changes? **(c)** How did these changes influence city life in China?
3. **Interpreting Ideas** **(a)** Explain the tax reforms introduced during the Tang dynasty. **(b)** Why was this change good for the government and bad for the peasants?
4. **Summarizing Ideas** Why was the position of shogun established in Japan?
5. **Comparing Ideas** How was the role of emperor in Japan different from the role of emperor in China?
6. **Analyzing Ideas** In what ways did the Chinese influence the culture of Korea?

Relating Geography to History

Using the map of China on page 70 and the map of the Tang Empire on page 276, list the physical obstacles a merchant would have to overcome while traveling along the Silk Route.

290

Song dynasty established in China — 960

1000 — The Tale of Genji written

First use of gunpowder in warfare by Chinese — 1100

1185 — Minamoto family in power in Japan

Yuan dynasty in China — 1271 / 1368

1338 — Ashikaga shogunate in Japan

Emperor Sejong directed the development of the Korean alphabet — ca. 1450

1573

Relating Past to Present

1. Consult an American history textbook to learn how and why the United States government introduced civil service examinations in the late 1800s. Compare the beginnings of the American civil service exam to the beginnings of the civil service exam in China.
2. Describe the development of printing in early China. How are today's copy machines similar to the block prints of early China? What impact have mass-produced paperback books had on our society today?

Applying History Study Skills

Before completing this activity, review Building History Study Skills on page 288.

Look again at the steps for reading a chart. Then complete the following exercise.

Study the chart in column 2 of this page. It shows the Confucian Five Relationships and how they operate. Then answer the following questions.

1. What type of chart is it?
2. **(a)** According to the chart, what does a son owe to a father? **(b)** A father to a son? **(c)** What is the obligation of a younger brother to an older brother? **(d)** What is the obligation of a wife to a husband? **(e)** What is the obligation of a husband to a wife?
3. Would you characterize the relationships as unequal or as complementary? Why?
4. Which of the five relationships relate to the family? Why?
5. What is the purpose of the five relationships?

Investigating Further

1. **Writing a Report** Read poems by the Chinese poets Li Bai and Du Fu. One possible source is Cyril Birch's *Anthology of Chinese Literature* (Grove Press). What do these poems tell you about life in China?
2. **Presenting an Oral Report** Find out more about Marco Polo's impressions of the Chinese people. You might want to read Ronald Latham's *The Travels of Marco Polo* (Penguin) to learn about Chinese life and social customs. Report your findings to the class.

Confucian Five Relationships

The Five Relationships and the attitudes they involve can be set out as follows:

Father Is kind Gives protection Provides education	**Son** Shows respect Accepts father's guidance Cares for him in old age and performs the customary burial ceremonies
Elder Brother Sets an example of refinement and good behavior	**Younger Brother** Respects the character and experience of the elder
Husband Carries out his family duties Is honorable and faithful Provides for his wife and family	**Wife** Looks after the home Is obedient Diligently meets the needs of her husband and children
Elder Gives encouragement Shows consideration toward younger people Sets a good example	**Junior** Shows respect Defers to the advice of those with more experience Is eager to learn
Ruler Acts justly Strives to improve the welfare of his people Is worthy of loyalty	**Subjects** Are loyal Serve their ruler Honor their ruler because of his position and character

291

CHAPTER

13

Africa and the Americas Produced Complex Civilizations

CHAPTER ✦ FOCUS

Place Africa and the Americas

Time

1800 B.C.—A.D. 1500

3.7 mil. BC   4000 BC   AD 2100

Significance

Because we have few written records of peoples who lived in Africa south of the Sahara and in the Americas, we know much less about events before 1500 in those regions than we do about events in Europe and Asia. Often we must reconstruct early African and American history from artifacts and ancient folk traditions. As a result, our historical knowledge of Africa and the Americas remains fragmentary.

Despite the lack of written records, we know that complex, highly sophisticated societies, remarkable for their political forms and their cultural achievements, developed in both Africa and the Americas. On these continents archaeologists are only beginning to uncover the walls of elaborate cities and fortresses and the foundations of huge temples.

Although the early peoples of Africa and the Americas had little influence on or contact with other parts of the world, understanding these vigorous and varied societies will help you to understand human history. These societies exhibit both contrasts and similarities between European and Asian societies of the same period.

Terms to Define

jungle   adobe
savanna   chinampa
linguist   quipu

People to Identify

Karanga   Olmecs
Mansa Musa   Maya
Sunni Ali   Aztecs

Places to Locate

Niger River   Ghana
Sahara   Andes Mountains
Axum   Yucatán Peninsula

Questions to Guide Your Reading

1 How did historians uncover Africa's early history?
2 What major city-states and kingdoms arose throughout Africa?
3 How did people migrate from Europe and Asia to the Americas?
4 What were the major accomplishments of the empires in Mexico and Peru?

◀ *Machu Picchu, Peru*

On July 24, 1911, in the Peruvian Andes, the American archaeologist Hiram Bingham uncovered the fabled lost city of the Incas—one of the greatest civilizations of the Americas. Bingham marveled at what he saw:

“ *S uddenly I found myself confronted with the walls of ruined houses built of the finest quality of Inca stone work. It was hard to see them for they were partly covered with trees and moss, the growth of centuries, but in the dense shadow, hiding in bamboo thickets and tangled vines, here and there walls of white granite . . . carefully cut and exquisitely fitted together. . . .*

Surprise followed surprise in bewildering succession. . . . Suddenly we found ourselves standing in front of the ruins of two of the finest and most interesting structures in ancient America. Made of beautiful white granite, the walls contained blocks of Cyclopean size, higher than a man. The sight held me spellbound. . . .

I could scarcely believe my senses as I examined the larger blocks . . . and estimated that they must weigh from ten to fifteen tons each. Would anyone believe what I had found? ”

Bingham's discovery, called Machu Picchu, was only one of many glorious cities built by the peoples of the Americas. At the same time, African peoples were creating equally spectacular civilizations.

1 Many Methods Uncovered Africa's Early History

Written records, surviving monuments, and ruins provide evidence of the great civilizations that thrived in North Africa before 1500. Equally important developments were taking place in the rest of Africa—the vast portion of the continent south of the Sahara known as SubSaharan Africa.

The Physical Setting

Most of the vast expanse of SubSaharan Africa rests on a high plateau. Here and there, however, basins and deep valleys dent this plateau.

Learning from Maps *The Sahara covers most of northern Africa. Between what rivers is the Kalahari Desert located?*

The plateau. The great plateau of SubSaharan Africa straddles the equator like a giant inverted bowl, uplifted in the center and then dropping sharply to the shoreline. Only in Liberia, Ghana (GAHN•uh), and the Ivory Coast—on Africa's western bulge—and in Mozambique (moh•zuhm•BEEK)—in the east—does the slope rise more gently.

The steep shoreline contains few harbors. Most major rivers, including the Niger (NY•juhr), Zaïre (zah•EER), or Congo, and the Zambezi (zam•BEE•zee), are navigable only for relatively short distances into the interior because of numerous rapids. Although these rivers limited trade, they also protected many parts of Africa from invasion. The

absence of good natural harbors and navigable rivers has also hindered communication and contact among the African peoples.

Rain falls irregularly throughout much of Africa. In the north lies the enormous Sahara, and in the south, the Kalahari (kal•uh•HAHR•ee) Desert (see map, this page). In contrast, some areas of western and central Africa receive more than 100 inches (254 centimeters) of rain each year. There, vast forests called **tropical rain forests** thrive. People often mistakenly call these forests jungles. However, a **jungle** is a thick growth of plants found in a tropical rain forest wherever sunlight penetrates the dense umbrella of tall trees and reaches the forest floor.

The wet climate of the rain forests provides fertile breeding grounds for insects that carry deadly diseases. For example, mosquitoes transmit malaria and yellow fever, and the tsetse (SET • see) fly carries sleeping sickness. Although modern medicine can treat these diseases, many Africans perished from them in earlier centuries.

Although no mountain ranges break the plateau, isolated mountain peaks dot its eastern part. Some, such as Mount Kenya and Mount Kilimanjaro (kil • uh • muhn • JAHR • oh), jut thousands of feet above the plateau.

The basins. Five deep basins dent the plateau. Each more than 600 miles (965 kilometers) wide, these basins sink more than 5,000 feet (1,525 meters) below the top of the plateau.

The Rift Valley. Perhaps the most remarkable geographic feature of SubSaharan Africa is the Great Rift Valley. Formed thousands of years ago when a part of the plateau sank, this steep-sided structural crack runs north and south near the plateau's eastern edge. Today many long, narrow lakes lie in the rift valley.

The Sahel. A vast area of relatively dry grasslands called **savannas,** dotted with a few trees and thorny bushes, stretches across Africa immediately south of the Sahara. In this region, known as the Sahel (suh • HAYL), sparse, unpredictable rainfall often results in severe droughts.

Rediscovering the African Past

Scholars rely on a variety of methods to understand the African past during the time before the people there developed writing. For example, **linguists**—scholars who study languages—have used computers and mathematics to compare the roots of words and common vocabulary. This technique—lexicostatistics—has helped solve the mystery of how Bantu, a family of closely related languages spoken in many parts of Africa, spread. The study suggests that for centuries wave upon wave of peoples have migrated throughout SubSaharan Africa.

An original "cradle land" of the Bantu language was in the southeastern region of what is today Nigeria. From there, beginning perhaps 2,000 years ago, Bantu-speaking people began to migrate southward into what are today the countries of Cameroon and Gabon. By the A.D. 700s, Bantu was spoken in central Africa as well as on the island of Zanzibar, in the Indian Ocean off the coast of Africa (see map, page 298).

The study of **oral traditions**—poems, songs, or stories passed by word of mouth from one generation to another—has been another source of information about specific African clans, villages, and dynasties. Africans have always had a strong sense of their own history. Individual families or villages preserved the memory of important events by incorporating them into poetry or song. People then passed these stories on from one generation to the next, with each generation adding to the tradition. In a similar way, the royal households of African kingdoms paid professional reciters to record in song the important events of a dynasty. Anthropologists and historians have now written down much of this oral tradition.

Other fields of scholarship have also helped unlock the secrets of Africa's past. For example, scholars who study music have discovered similarities in the design and tuning of xylophones found in East Africa and Indonesia, in Southeast Asia. These similarities suggest that at some early date, people migrated from Asia to Africa. Similarly, scientists have studied the spread to Africa of the banana, a plant that grows in Southeast Asia. And linguists have studied the Malagasy language, spoken on the island of Madagascar in the Indian Ocean off the east coast of Africa. Malagasy has many words in common with languages spoken on the islands of Indonesia. From these fields of study—the study of music, plants, and language—scholars have determined that people from Indonesia migrated to East Africa about A.D. 300.

Scholars have also discovered that the people of SubSaharan Africa were particularly adept at coping with their often harsh environment. Although wheat and barley could not be cultivated south of the Sahara near sea level, the people there were able to domesticate a variety of crops. For example, the people of the Sahel domesticated millet, sorghum, pennisetum, and eleusine. In later centuries these grains became the staple crops of the people of SubSaharan Africa. In addition, farmers cultivated sesame, which through the process of cultural diffusion was introduced in Sumer about 2350 B.C.

Although the people of SubSaharan Africa domesticated various crops, changes in the climate of the Sahel soon altered patterns of agriculture. Between about 2500 B.C. and 2300 B.C. the region became much drier. As a result the people of the region relied increasingly on herding.

Trumpets

The sound of trumpets has been echoing around the world for thousands of years. The first trumpets were made from hollow branches or reeds. They were used to frighten away evil spirits, to make mournful sounds at funerals, and in the evening to appeal to the sun to return the next day. In some parts of Switzerland, the alpenhorn still sounds the evening prayer. In Romania and Tibet, men play long wooden trumpets at funerals.

Early Africans used horns to send messages over long distances (far right). In present-day Nigeria, horns are still sounded at celebrations (above). The Aztecs used trumpets to call the rain gods, and horns of silver, copper, and wood were used by the Incas in Peru. Incas also had clay trumpets with bells shaped like jaguar heads.

Both the Egyptians and the Hebrews used metal trumpets to attract the attention of the gods. The Bible says that when Joshua fought the battle of Jericho, the blast of seven trumpets made the walls fall down. Today, at the ceremony to celebrate the Jewish New Year, the *shofar*

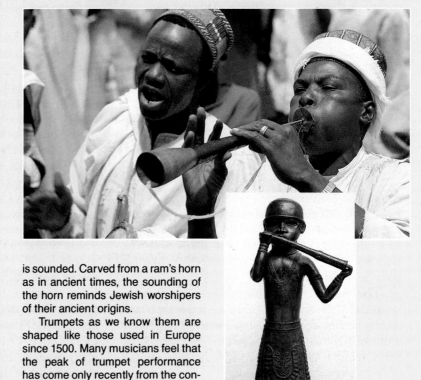

is sounded. Carved from a ram's horn as in ancient times, the sounding of the horn reminds Jewish worshipers of their ancient origins.

Trumpets as we know them are shaped like those used in Europe since 1500. Many musicians feel that the peak of trumpet performance has come only recently from the contributions of America's great jazz musicians, such as Wynton Marsalis (below left) and Chuck Mangione (below right).

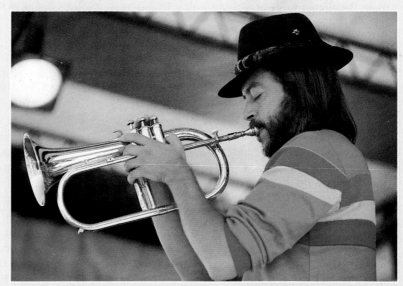

Archaeology has also added much to our understanding of African history. Excavation sites throughout the continent have revealed details of daily life in early Africa. Much of this work has helped to either support or disprove what has been learned from oral traditions and other sources.

Patterns of Life

Based upon the scholarly studies of the African past, experts have drawn several conclusions about patterns of life in early Africa. They believe that most Africans lived in small, independent villages and were farmers or herders. Relationships of kinship, age, and sex provided the ties that bound the different societies together. Within this system women played a crucial role. As laborers they performed much of the agricultural work. In Great Zimbabwe women worked in the mines. Scholars believe that societies in many parts of SubSaharan Africa were matrilineal. In **matrilineal** (ma • truh • LIN • ee • uhl) societies, people trace their ancestors through their mothers rather than their fathers. In such societies, a boy inherited from his mother's brother rather than from his father.

Chiefs or elders usually exercised authority over the village. However, since land was plentiful and migration became a real choice for those who were unhappy, a chief's rule had to be fair. Life in the African villages was closely bound to the agricultural cycles of planting and harvesting. Through the rise and fall of numerous kingdoms, the village survived as the basic unit of society and the economy. Its persistence makes it a vital part of the African heritage.

SECTION 1 REVIEW

1. **Define** tropical rain forest, jungle, savanna, linguist, oral tradition, matrilineal
2. **Locate** Niger River, Zaïre (Congo) River, Zambezi River, Sahara, Kalahari Desert
3. **Linking Geography and History** **(a)** What geographic factors made contact difficult among peoples in Africa's interior? **(b)** How did the geography of Africa influence patterns of settlement?
4. **Summarizing Ideas** What nonwritten evidence identifies early African developments?
5. **Understanding Ideas** What conclusions have scholars reached about patterns of life in early Africa?

2 City-states and Kingdoms Arose Throughout Africa

A remarkable variety of kingdoms, empires, and small city-states arose in the different areas of Africa before 1500. These kingdoms were as diverse as the African geography.

Cush

Along the Nile River, south of the major centers of ancient Egypt, lies an area known as Nubia. A source of gold, granite, and timber, it also thrived as an important trade center. Here, caravans hauled goods from the Red Sea to barges on the Nile. And here arose a powerful kingdom known as Cush (see map, page 298).

Cush traces its roots to the city of Kerma, a trading center of southern Nubia that the Egyptians founded about 1800 B.C. The Egyptians greatly influenced this region. Nevertheless, the pottery, jewelry, and other ornaments uncovered in this area show that a distinctly local Nubian culture emerged.

Learning from Pictures *These ruins of the kingdom of Cush are located in the Sudan.*

Learning from Maps *African civilizations were thriving during the height of the Roman Empire. How many years does the map cover?*

AFRICAN KINGDOMS AND EMPIRES
ca. 200 B.C.–A.D. 1500

- Cush, ca. 200 B.C.
- Nok, ca. A.D. 100
- Axum, ca. A.D. 500
- Ghana, ca. A.D. 900
- Mali, ca. A.D. 1300
- Benin, ca. A.D. 1400
- Songhai, ca. A.D. 1500
- ← – – Trade route
- ← Bantu migrations

SINUSOIDAL PROJECTION

Over the next centuries, Cush became a distinct kingdom. It had its own dynasty and a capital at Napata (NAP•uht•uh), a city upstream from Kerma. But it maintained close cultural and economic ties with Egypt. By the 1100s B.C., Cush had become virtually independent of Egypt, and about 750 B.C. it conquered Upper Egypt. For about 100 years—until the Assyrians, armed with iron weapons, invaded in 671 B.C.—a Cush dynasty ruled a unified Egypt.

With the Assyrian invasion, the Cush kingdom weakened. Following the Assyrian plunder of Napata in 591 B.C., the kingdom reorganized itself around a new capital at Meroë (MER•uh•wee) and

began a new period of growth and cultural achievement. Meroë was one of the earliest centers of iron working in Africa. Today, the remains of huge heaps of slag, the waste from smelting, rise out of the desert, indicating the importance of this ancient activity.

The Cush kingdom also controlled trade routes from the Red Sea to the Nile. Caravans brought Hellenistic, Persian, and Indian influences that the people of Meroë adapted to their own culture.

The brilliant Cush civilization reached its height from 250 B.C. to A.D. 150. The people erected impressive pyramids and temples and crafted exquisite pottery and ornaments. Then the

READ
● WRITE
INTERPRET
CONNECT
THINK

BUILDING HISTORY STUDY SKILLS

Writing About History: Paraphrasing Information

As you study world history and perfect your writing skills, you will use many primary and secondary sources. You might either quote or paraphrase these sources. *Quoting* is repeating exactly the words of the author or speaker. *Paraphrasing* is translating something into your own words. Putting something into your own words often helps you think about what you have read and makes it easier to understand and remember, especially for tests. If you are writing a report, paraphrasing will help you to avoid plagiarizing, or copying the words and ideas of others without acknowledging the source.

How to Paraphrase Information

To paraphrase information, follow these steps:
1. Define the main idea of the selection.
2. Indicate the details—bits and pieces of information related to the main idea.
3. Put the main idea and details in your own words.
4. Compare your statement with the original selection by asking questions:
   - Have you written a complete thought?
   - Does it make sense?
   - Does it have new information that focuses on meaning?

Developing the Skill

The following document describes the founding of the East African city of Kilwa. Read the document. Then define the main idea and paraphrase the document in a few sentences.

Arab dhows sailing

❝ The story goes that there was a Sultan of Shiraz named Hasan bin Ali. . . . One day he saw a vision of a rat with an iron snout nibbling and gnawing at the walls. From this he foreboded the ruin of the country, and so, . . . the whole family, seven in number, sailed away from the doomed country in as many ships. Of these it was the sixth that came to Kilwa. At the time of the immigration Kilwa was an island only at high tide. . . . The new-comers found a Muslim already settled there with his family, and a mosque. From him they learned that the country belonged to the chief of the neighboring district, who was then absent on a hunting expedition. After a few days, he returned to Kilwa, and the stranger, being pleased with the island, offered, through the mediation of the friendly Muslim, to buy it. The chief named his terms, which were that the stranger should surround the whole island with colored cloth. This was soon done, and the chief took the cloth and surrendered the island. All the while, however, he cherished the secret intention of returning with an armed force to destroy the immigrants and carry off their goods. This was guessed by the Muslim, who had acted as interpreter, so he warned the strangers to provide for their safety in time. Accordingly, as soon as the chief's back was turned, they set to work and dug a trench in the neck of the land joining Kilwa to the continent. . . . The chief . . . waited for the tide to go down and leave a dry passage to Kilwa; but the water never subsided, so he returned to his own country defeated and disappointed. ❞

The topic of the selection is the founding of the East African city of Kilwa. The details focus on why the sultan fled his home, how he took possession of Kilwa, and how he secured the island. A paraphrased statement of the selection might be:

According to legend, the Sultan of Shiraz had a vision telling of impending ruin for his country. He gathered his family, and they fled in seven ships. One of the ships landed at Kilwa, where a sympathetic Muslim helped the sultan buy the area from the local chief. Warned that the chief was going to invade, the sultan and his family dug a deep trench to protect Kilwa. Since Kilwa was now an island, the chief abandoned it. And that is how Kilwa became an island.

Practicing the skill. Reread the selection by Hiram Bingham on page 293 and put it into your own words.

To apply this skill, see Applying History Study Skills on page 313.

Cush civilization mysteriously declined. Although scholars do not know why, many believe that it involved the rise of a rival state—Axum.

Axum

Situated in the Ethiopian Highlands south of Cush, Axum straddled the trade routes from the Red Sea into Egypt and the interior of Africa (see map, page 298). As Cush declined, Axum became a major competitor for control of this trade and sent war elephants, rhinoceros horns, tortoise shells, incense, and spices to the Mediterranean world by way of Egypt.

Finally, in A.D. 325, King Ezana (AH • zah • nah) of Axum inflicted a crushing defeat on Cush and established a thriving kingdom. During his reign Ezana converted to Christianity, and the religion, which incorporated many elements of the people's traditional beliefs, has remained an important influence in the region.

For the next 400 years, Axum controlled the African side of the Red Sea trade. Its influence beyond this region, however, ended with the rise of Islam. By the early 700s, Muslim forces controlled both the Arabian and the African sides of the Red Sea.

East Africa and Trade

No large kingdoms like Cush and Axum emerged on the coast of East Africa. Instead, a series of city-states that dominated coastal trade in the Indian Ocean arose. The seasonal monsoon winds provided a reliable means of travel. Sailors explored the seas and developed trade routes linking all shores of the Indian Ocean. Africans exported gold, slaves, ivory, hides, and tortoise shells and imported porcelain and weapons.

The spread of Islam to northeastern Africa also created favorable conditions for trade. Along the East African coast, a golden age began in the 700s and lasted through the 1300s. The opportunity to make money in Africa attracted merchant families, adventurers, and refugees fleeing the Shiite-Sunnite conflicts in Arabia and Persia. They settled on islands and easily defensible spits of land, where they soon established several thriving trading centers.

Over several generations a unique African culture—Swahili (swah • HEE • lee)—developed on the

Learning from Pictures This ritual charm discovered in the present-day nation of Zaire belonged to Bantu-speaking people.

East African coast. The people of this culture spoke Swahili, a Bantu language with Arabic and Persian influences. Although the Swahili were not a unified ethnic group, their common pursuits—especially trade—and language bound the people together.

The earliest of the city-states—Mogadishu (mahg • uh • DISH • oo), Lamu, Pate (PAH • tay), and Malindi—lay in the north. Gradually, commercial activity shifted southward. By the 1100s Kilwa, the most famous city-state, was the leading port along the African coast.

Under Kilwa's leadership, coastal civilization flourished. Ibn Battuta (IB • uhn bah • TOO • tah), a famous Muslim traveler of the 1300s, described Kilwa as one of the most beautiful and well-constructed towns in the world. Recent archaeological excavations have uncovered a massive trade center and a large mosque that reveal the city's wealth and achievements.

Central Africa and Great Zimbabwe

Kilwa grew as a port for the shipment of gold mined along the Zambezi River in central Africa. For centuries gold and other goods had reached the coast from there, passing eastward through small-scale

Royal Figure from West Africa

The people of Ife, in what is now southwestern Nigeria, began making life-sized bronze heads more than 600 years ago. Historians believe that the original inhabitants of the region—the Yoruba (YAWR•uh•buh) people—had crafted terra cotta sculpture for centuries.

About 700 years ago, however, immigrants from the northeast swept into the area and founded the city of

Ife. It was these immigrants who taught the Yoruba the intricate art of making bronze sculptures and introduced the concept of divine kingship.

The magnificent example of bronze casting shown here depicts one of these kings. The beaded crown tells us that the head is that of a very important king. The vertical lines represent ritual scarring—a practice still followed by people in some parts of Africa. A beard and a mustache were attached to the holes around the mouth.

After a king died, the bronze head was attached to a wooden body and carried throughout the city. The ceremony indicated that although the king was dead, the power of the office lived on in his successors.

trade networks based on the exchange of essential items such as salt, tools, or cloth.

The growth of Indian Ocean trade after the 900s dramatically increased the demand for gold. With this increased demand came a consolidation of control over the mining of gold and its shipment to the coast. In about 800 the Karanga, a people who immigrated onto the plateau land of what is today Zimbabwe (zim•BAHB•wee), achieved this control. Gradually, the Karanga asserted control over local peoples and mining activities. Archaeologists have located more than 7,000 mine shafts, indicating the importance of mining to the local economy.

Although we have little definite information about the Karanga people, scholars believe they built fortified enclosures and probably attained great wealth and power. Great Zimbabwe, the largest and most famous of these fortresses, became the administrative and religious center of the Karanga state. Its 32-foot- (10-meter-) high and 17-foot- (5-meter-) thick walls consist of some 900,000 large granite blocks and show the advanced construction methods this society used.

Excavation of the site revealed a rapid and seemingly mysterious decline in the 1400s. Scientists now believe that the area may have experienced an ecological disaster. One theory is that the population grew so quickly that it outpaced dwindling water and food resources. Without enough

food and water, people starved, and the brilliant civilization declined.

Kingdoms and Cultures of West Africa

In West Africa, between Lake Chad and the Atlantic Ocean, important African kingdoms flourished. They included Ghana, Mali (MAHL•ee), and Songhai (SAWNG•hy). Knowledge of these kingdoms comes largely from oral tradition and from the writings of African scholars and Muslim traders.

The wealth and strength of these kingdoms depended on control of the trade routes across the Sahara. At the desert's edge, traders exchanged gold, extracted from the forest zone south of the Sahel, for salt, mined in the Sahara. The people of the Sahel needed the salt to flavor and preserve their food. The traders from the north wanted the gold for coins and for buying goods from Europe. At the site where this gold-for-salt exchange took place, important commercial cities grew and flourished. Indeed, West Africa produced most of the world's gold until 1500. In time traders in these cities also exchanged ivory and slaves for horses, textiles, linen, books, paper, and weapons.

In these civilizations monarchs ruled, assisted by officials. Often adorned with gold, these monarchs presided over elaborate ceremonies and administered justice. According to the Muslim historian Al-Bakri, trial by wood was common:

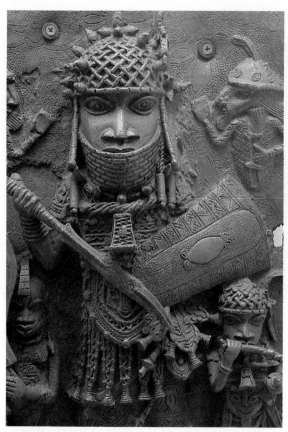

Learning from Pictures *This bronze plaque depicting soldiers wearing helmets and decorative robes is from the kingdom of Benin in West Africa.*

66 *W* hen a man is accused of denying a debt or having shed blood or some other crime, a headman takes a thin piece of wood, which is sour and bitter to taste, and pours upon it some water which he then gives to the defendant to drink. If the man vomits, his innocence is recognized and he is congratulated. If he does not vomit and the drink remains in his stomach, the accusation is accepted as justified. 99

Below the royal family and government officials on the social scale came merchants, farmers, fishers, and cattle breeders. Slaves, whose numbers remained small, ranked at the bottom of the social scale.

Ghana. Ghana, the earliest of these kingdoms, traced its origin to Kumbi Saleh, a trading village founded in the 200s and situated in the southeastern part of modern Mauritania (mawr • uh • TAY • nee • uh). Ghana was at its peak in the

900s, but its period of prosperity was short-lived. In the 1000s a Muslim religious revival and the preaching of a Holy War stirred up Berber tribes, who had once controlled trade in the Sahara. They invaded Ghana. The kingdom never recovered from this attack and in 1235 ceased to exist.

Mali. The rise of a successor kingdom—Mali—followed the fall of Ghana. This new kingdom came to power in the region that had been Ghana, as well as in vast areas to the north and west and along the upper Niger River. Under Mansa Musa, who ruled from 1307 to 1332, Mali's power reached its peak. When Mansa Musa made his pilgrimage to Mecca, 60,000 other pilgrims, including 500 slaves each carrying a 4-pound (1.8 kilogram) bar of gold, accompanied him. Upon his return, Musa supported education, the arts, and building. His capital, Tombouctou (tohn • book • TOO), became an important center of Muslim learning, with a large university that attracted scholars from Egypt and Arabia.

When Ibn Battuta visited Mali shortly after Mansa Musa's death, the wealth and peace of the kingdom astounded him. He wrote:

66 *T* hey [the people of Mali] are seldom unjust and have a greater abhorrence of injustice than any other people. Their Sultan shows no mercy to any one guilty of the least act of it. There is complete security in their country. Neither traveler nor inhabitant in it has any thing to fear from robbers or men of violence. They do not confiscate the property of any white man who dies in their country, even if it be uncounted wealth. On the contrary, they give it into the charge of some trust-worthy person among the whites, until the rightful heir takes possession of it. 99

Although disputes over dynastic succession weakened Mali, it managed to maintain control over the desert trade routes until the 1400s. Then in 1468 Sunni Ali, leader of a region that had broken away from Mali's authority, captured Tombouctou, beginning the age of the third kingdom—Songhai.

Songhai. The kingdom of Songhai was centered on the important trading city of Gao (GOH). From there it controlled a kingdom about the size of all western Europe. Sunni Ali, its most important ruler, hoped to avoid a succession crisis after his death. Therefore, he established a government designed to ensure tighter control over his subjects. He divided the kingdom into provinces, each with a governor and officials who reported directly to the king in his capital at Gao. He also built a fleet of warships to enforce peace along the Niger River, which had become a major route of African commerce. His policies made Songhai a powerful and efficient kingdom that continued to thrive until the Moroccans invaded in 1591.

SECTION 2 REVIEW

1. **Identify**   Mansa Musa, Sunni Ali
2. **Locate**   Kerma, Napata, Meroë, Kilwa, Lake Chad, Ghana, Mali, Tombouctou, Songhai, Gao
3. **Summarizing Ideas**   What metals were mined in the ancient kingdoms of Africa?
4. **Understanding Ideas**   What factors helped make East Africa a center for trade?
5. **Analyzing Ideas**   (a) Give evidence to support the idea that Ghana, Mali, and Songhai were powerful, wealthy kingdoms.   (b) What role did trade play in their development?

3 People Migrated from Asia to the Americas

From the beginning of history until about 500 years ago, the peoples of the Eastern and Western hemispheres had virtually no contact with each other. Although daring Viking explorers landed at several places on the coast of North America around the year 1000, accounts of their voyages were not well known, and other explorers did not follow up their journeys. Old European maps show a vast blank space or fanciful islands where what we now call the Western Hemisphere lies. Europeans seemed unaware that millions of people already inhabited that vast region of the world.

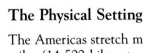

The Physical Setting

The Americas stretch more than 9,000 miles (14,500 kilometers) from Greenland in the north to Cape Horn at the southern tip of South America. Not surprisingly, geographic contrasts typify this enormous expanse of land.

Almost every type of climate and terrain can be found somewhere in the Americas. Jagged mountains curve like a rugged backbone near the western coast of the Americas. Known as the Rocky Mountains in North America, they extend through Mexico and into South America, where they are called the Andes Mountains. To the east of the mountains on both continents are flatter lands dotted here and there by mountains.

The Americas also include two of the world's great river systems. In North America the Mississippi River drains much of the continent and provides a major transportation route. In South America the Amazon River, second only to the Nile in length, flows almost 3,900 miles (6,275 kilometers) from the Andes through dense rain forests before emptying into the Atlantic Ocean.

The Great Migrations

While the Ice Age still gripped the earth, people migrated from Asia to the Americas across what is now the Bering Strait, off the coast of Alaska. This strait marks the narrowest point between the continents of Asia and North America. During several periods in the past, a "bridge" of land stood there. Even when water covered the land, the strait spanned only a few miles, and people in boats could have crossed it easily.

Neither a single large migration nor a continuous flow of people from Asia populated the Americas. Rather, over the centuries a series of waves of different peoples crossed to the Americas. Changes in Asia's climate may from time to time have forced people northeastward and across the strait. From there they drifted toward warmer climates. Finding some areas already inhabited by earlier immigrants, they would move on, looking for a favorable place to settle.

Some people moved into the eastern and central areas of North America. Others drifted farther south, through Mexico and Central America and

What If?
The Bering Strait
Prehistoric peoples migrated across a land bridge linking Asia and North America. How do you think the course of world history would have been different if this land bridge still existed?

303

INDIAN PEOPLES OF NORTH AMERICA, 1400

AZIMUTHAL EQUAL AREA PROJECTION

Learning from Maps *Many cities in North America are named after Indian tribes. What Indian people settled along the Bering Strait?*

across the narrow Isthmus of Panama. From there all South America spread out before them.

The Development of Agriculture

The first people to reach the Americas were nomads who lived by hunting and gathering. Their descendants, however, discovered a new way of life—farming. The earliest traces of farming in the Western Hemisphere have been found in parts of

south-central and northeastern Mexico, along the coast of Peru, and in the southwestern United States. Scholars believe that the first farmers planted sunflowers (for seeds), corn, beans, squash, and a variety of other crops. In South America and on the islands of the Caribbean, farmers raised various root crops, mainly manioc and other crops similar to sweet potatoes. In the highlands of Peru, the potato was the most important food. As archaeologist Hiram Bingham stated:

“ *F*ew Americans realize how much we owe to the ancient Peruvians. Very few people appreciate that they gave us the white potato, many varieties of Indian corn, and such useful [medicines] as quinine. . . . ”

Farming began at about the same time in both hemispheres but developed more gradually in the Americas. The plow was not invented in the Americas partly because animals large enough to pull it, such as horses, were not available there. For the same reason, the ancient people of the region did not use wheeled implements in agriculture, although ancient toys unearthed in Mexico show that the people did know of the wheel. In the highlands farmers used digging sticks to plant rows of seeds. They also used dead fish as fertilizer.

Agriculture produced enough to support village life and the beginnings of towns. By the time of Columbus's voyage in 1492, people as far north as the northeastern United States and Canada and as far south as Argentina depended on farming for much of their food supply. In Mexico and in the Andes Mountains, agriculture and food storage formed the basis of civilizations as advanced as those of Egypt and Sumer.

The North Americans

In what is today the United States and Canada, many different cultures and some highly organized societies thrived (see map, page 304). The cultures of these peoples often depended on the geography of the region they inhabited.

Southwest. The Pueblo (poo • EB • loh) people created a well-developed culture in what is now the southwestern United States. These farmers lived in permanent settlements and used **adobe**, a sun-dried brick, to build communal houses—ancient versions of our apartment houses. They erected many multi-storied houses, some with as many as 800 rooms, and clustered others together beneath overhanging cliffs so they could be better defended.

Northwest. Several tribes with economies based largely on fishing lived on the northwest coast of North America. Expert woodworkers and weavers, these people crafted majestic totem poles—great wooden carvings of people and beasts that symbolized tribal history.

Great Plains. An entirely different culture flourished in the Great Plains, which stretch between the Rocky Mountains and the Mississippi River. Here, tribal peoples lived by hunting the

Learning from Pictures
The Tsimshian Indians of the Northwest, known for their expert woodwork, carved these two ceremonial masks.

Learning from Pictures *This cliff dwelling in Mesa Verde National Park, Colorado, is sheltered by a spruce forest and is named the Spruce Tree House Ruin.*

huge herds of wild buffalo that roamed the land. The Plains peoples ate the meat of the buffalo and used its hide to make clothing and to build their cone-shaped tents, called **tepees.** Skilled fighters, they placed a high value on deeds of bravery.

Eastern Woodlands. The Eastern Woodlands stretch from what is now Canada to the Gulf of Mexico and from the Atlantic Ocean to the Mississippi River. There one of North America's most sophisticated cultures flourished. The peoples of the region are sometimes called the Mound Builders because of the many earthen mounds they constructed throughout the area.

The tools, jewelry, and weapons found in mounds built as burial places reveal that these peoples had highly developed artistic skills. Some of the mounds are in the shapes of animals. One such mound in Ohio, the Great Serpent Mound, extends more than 1,300 feet (400 meters) in length. Although archaeologists recognize that building the mounds obviously required cooperative effort, they do not know what happened to the builders.

SECTION 3 REVIEW

1. **Define** adobe, tepee
2. **Identify** Pueblo people, Plains people
3. **Locate** Rocky Mountains, Andes Mountains
4. **Understanding Ideas** What may have motivated early peoples to migrate to the Americas?
5. **Summarizing Ideas** **(a)** List the important crops grown in the Americas. **(b)** What factors limited farmers' productivity?
6. **Contrasting Ideas** How did the various cultures of North America differ?

4 Empires Rose and Flourished in Mexico and Peru

By about 1500 B.C., the peoples along the coast of Peru and in central Mexico lived in villages. In another 500 years, ceremonial and trading centers, made possible by the food surplus of many villages, began to appear. Unlike cities in other regions of the world, the central areas of these cities were reserved for priests and high officials. The common people lived in nearby farming villages. The societies of these cities remain mysterious because scholars have not deciphered their hieroglyphic writings.

The Olmecs

The earliest of these cultures in Mexico, the Olmecs (OHL • meks), left giant stone heads and many objects made of jade. Carved from basalt that had to be transported from quarries 80 miles (129 kilometers) away, each stone head weighs 16 to 18 tons. Although scholars remain mystified about how the Olmecs moved the giant stones, they believe that only a highly sophisticated society could have developed the technology to do so. Scholars also believe that the Olmecs developed a priestly class and worshiped a god represented by the image of a jaguar. In the highlands of Peru and along its coast, a culture called Chavin (shuh • VEEN) developed about the same time. The Chavin also worshiped the jaguar. Both the Olmec and Chavin cultures mysteriously disappeared about A.D. 200.

The Maya

One of the most advanced cultures of the Americas was that of the Maya, who occupied the tropical lowlands of Central America considerably before 1000 B.C. (see map, this page). Skilled architects and engineers, the Maya built many steep pyramids. For example, recent excavations of the Mayan city of El Mirador in Guatemala show that one pyramid soared 18 stories and had a base about the size of three football fields.

The Maya also studied astronomy. They learned to predict solar eclipses and devised a calendar more accurate than the one used in Europe at the time. The Maya developed a counting system that was based on the number 20 and that included the zero. They also used a writing system based on pictograms, ideograms, and phonograms. Much of the Mayan script, however, remains undeciphered, and the Spaniards destroyed nearly all Mayan manuscripts. Nevertheless, the ruins of magnificent cities lead scholars to believe that the Maya used their writing and mathematical knowledge to record the dates of kings' reigns, their ritual ceremonies, and their knowledge of astronomy.

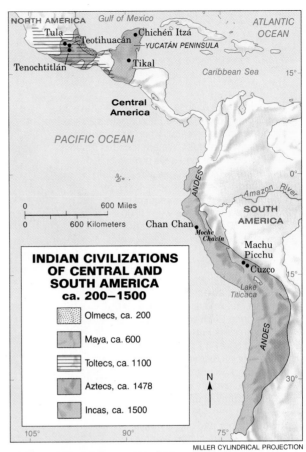

Learning from Maps The Toltecs controlled the largest Indian empire of North America. What Indian people controlled the west coast of South America?

The Maya produced a great deal of food, perhaps more efficiently than European farmers of the time. This food helped support noble and priestly classes, whose members did not perform any manual labor. The complex religion of the Maya involved astronomy and the worship of many gods who were thought to change their forms at will. Sometimes in periods of crisis, such as droughts, Mayan priests offered human sacrifices to the gods, hoping for rain.

About A.D. 900 a mysterious catastrophe struck the Mayan civilization. The population declined sharply and people fled the ceremonial centers. Although scholars can only speculate, any number of disasters could have caused this decline. The agricultural methods used by the Maya may have worn out the soil. A foreign invasion may have overwhelmed them, or possibly a peasant revolt may have overthrown the nobles and priests.

Text continues on page 310.

307

The calendar is a mess. Some months have 31 days, some have 30, and February has 28—except, of course, in "leap years," when February has 29 days instead of 28. We are told that it's easy to remember that leap days always occur in years divisible by four—such as 1984, 1988, and 1992. But the year 1900, although it was divisible by four, was not a leap year. Neither were 1700 and 1800. The year 2000 will be a leap year, but 2100 (4 × 525 = 2100) will not be.

For thousands of years people have tried to make the calendar as accurate as possible. Yet we still don't have it quite right. Each year is still 26 seconds off. Fortunately, that's not a lot—it's off by one day out of every 3,323 years.

As imprecise as this is, our calendar is better than what our ancestors put up with. The year 46 B.C. had 445 days. In A.D. 1582, October had only 21 days. And in 1752, Americans went to bed the night of September 2nd and awoke the morning of September 14th.

People have kept track of time for their own survival. To know when to plant or when to prepare for floods and storms, people learned to watch the movements of the sun, moon, and stars. Many early cultures worshiped these heavenly bodies and devised calendars to know when to hold religious festivals. A lunar month—from one full moon to the next—was one good measure of time everyone could *see*. But, because each solar year contains about 12.37 lunar months, the sun cycle and the moon cycle didn't fit together. People had to choose between the two or try to harmonize them.

The Babylonians may have been the first to use a formal calendar. Following the moon cycle, they alternated between 29- and 30-day months, which only added up to 364 days—not a full year. The ancient Chinese and, later, the Hebrews and Muslims also used the lunar cycle.

The Egyptians counted 365 days between the *annual* risings of the Nile and divided the year into 12 30-day months with 5 extra days. This was closer than the Babylonian calendar, and it compensated for the extra ¼ day each year has.

The ancestor of the calendar we use today was invented in Rome—although the early Romans were quite nonchalant about calendrical accuracy and made do with a 10-month, 304-day year. About 700 B.C., two new months were added—Januarius and Februarius—making the year 355 days long. By the time Julius Caesar came to power in 59 B.C., the Roman calendar was more than two months behind—and the spring festival was ridiculously being celebrated in July. With the help of the Greek astronomer Sosigenes, Caesar changed the calendar to 365 days, adding one extra day every fourth February. Caesar rewarded himself by changing the name of the month Quintilis to his own, Julius (July). His successor Augustus, not to be outdone, changed the next month, Sextilis, to Augustus.

Things went along pretty smoothly for the next 1,500 years until a pope in Rome noticed that the annual date for Easter—the first full moon after the spring equinox—was getting later and later in the year. He discovered that the Julian (Julius Caesar's) calendar was about 11 minutes too long. Over 1,500 years this had put an extra 10 days on the year. So in 1582 Pope Gregory XIII declared that the day after October 4 would be October 15. To prevent this problem from recurring, he had to find a way of eliminating three days about every 400 years. He did this by abolish-

ing leap day in all turn-of-the-century years except those divisible by 400. Therefore, 1600 remained a leap year, but 1700, 1800, and 1900 each lost the leap day. This made the calendar correct to within 26 seconds a year, or one day every 3,323 years.

Roman Catholic countries adopted the Gregorian calendar immediately. Protestant countries were reluctant. When England and its colonies, including America, finally adopted the calendar in 1752, they were 11 days behind. After Parliament announced that the day after September 2, 1752, would be September 14, angry people shouting

"Give us back our 11 days!" mobbed the House of Commons. Landlords protested losing two weeks' rents, and everyone protested changing dates for holidays and birthdays. But in America, Ben Franklin advised people not to regret the lost time but to rejoice that one could "lie down in peace on the second of the month and not . . . awake till the morning of the 14th."

In Orthodox Christian countries—Greece, Russia, Romania, Serbia, Bulgaria, and others—the Julian calendar continued. The Russian Orthodox church still follows the Julian calendar and celebrates Christmas 13 days later than western Christians. Russia kept the Julian calendar until the 1917 Communist Revolution. The ensuing loss of 13 days led to the oddity that the Communist "October Revolution" had to be celebrated in November.

Some people argue for a "world calendar." Each 52-week year would begin with Sunday, and leap days would be tacked on at the end of the year whenever necessary. Such a change is hard to make, and many people would protest, but it has been done before. "Time stops for no man," but time has frequently been rearranged—on paper.

Photos   Page 308: Jewish omer calendar (top); Pope Gregory XII presenting calendar (bottom); Page 309: Stonehenge (top); Egyptian calendar (middle); Aztec calendar (bottom)

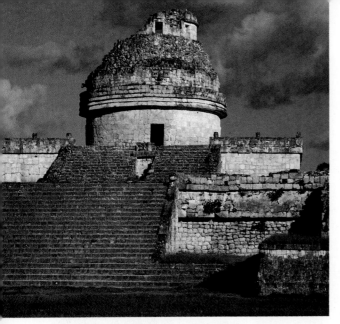

Learning from Pictures *This Mayan observatory is located in Chichén Itzá. What Toltec influences do the ruins of Chichén Itzá reflect?*

The Toltecs

About A.D. 650 a people called the Toltecs (TOHL • tecks) invaded central Mexico from the north. Ruled by a military class, the Toltecs built a capital city at Tula (TOO • luh) and by 1100 had spread their influence as far south as the Yucatán Peninsula (see map, page 307). There they encountered the Maya, who were rebuilding their civilization. The influence of Toltec religion and designs is noticeable in the ruins of Chichén Itzá (chuh • CHEN uht • SAH), the chief Mayan city.

Like the Maya, the Toltecs built pyramids. However, they never produced art as advanced as that of the Maya. The Toltecs extended trade much farther than had the Maya and introduced the working of gold and silver. The Toltecs also spread the worship of their god, Quetzalcoatl (ket • SAHL • kwaht • uhl), represented by a feathered serpent, and practiced human sacrifice.

The Aztecs

Around A.D. 1200 peoples from the north launched further invasions of central Mexico. Unlike the Toltecs, these peoples probably lived as hunters and gatherers at the time of their arrival. A number of these groups fought one another in central Mexico. Out of these struggles emerged the strongest group—the Aztecs.

The Aztecs had been wandering warriors. According to legend their priests had instructed them to settle where they saw a sign—an eagle sitting on a cactus and devouring a serpent. They finally saw the sign on one of a pair of islands in Lake Texcoco (tes • KOH • koh) in Mexico. There they built their city of Tenochtitlán (tay • nawch • tee • TLAHN).

From about 1325 on, the Aztecs increased their power until they dominated central Mexico. Conquered tribes paid them tribute in gold, turquoise, corn, animals, and slaves.

By building causeways and stone foundations, the Aztecs expanded Tenochtitlán to make room for great pyramid-temples, marketplaces, and palaces for the nobles and wealthy families. The city may have had more than 100,000 inhabitants at its period of greatest power and prestige in the 1400s.

The Aztecs incorporated into their culture the inventions of peoples they conquered or with whom they traded. They soon learned metalwork, weaving, pottery-making, the calendar, and mathematics. Their artisans produced finely finished pieces of art.

The Aztecs perfected farming on **chinampas**—artificial islands in the region's many lakes. The use of chinampas was perhaps the most productive form of agriculture in the world.

The military dominated Aztec society. Warfare carried great prestige and led to wealth and power. The Aztecs believed that the sun god and the god of war demanded human sacrifices in return for favors. Hundreds of captives from defeated tribes might be put to death each year. In 1487, at the height of their power, the Aztecs sacrificed 20,000 captives on their pyramid altars.

Just as the great Aztec civilization had grown rapidly, so it was to fall in a very short time. By the end of the 1400s, surrounding peoples who had been paying tribute to the Aztecs revolted. But the final blow to the Aztec Empire came from foreign conquerors—the Spanish explorers of the 1500s.

The Incas

At about the same period that the Aztecs built their civilization in Mexico, another group created a civilization in the Andes Mountains of South America. These people based their religion on sun worship. Their name—Incas—means "children of the sun."

Learning from Pictures
The gold earrings (above)
and the tapestry (right)
are examples of the
sophistication of the
artworks of the Incas.

The Inca Empire expanded steadily. By about 1470, it extended along most of the west coast of South America and far into the Andes, covering much of the present-day nations of Peru, Ecuador, Bolivia, and Chile. As in ancient Egypt, everything belonged to the ruler, and everyone owed absolute obedience to him. Although an autocrat, the emperor used his power to improve the empire.

The Inca capital was Cuzco (KOO • skoh), known as the "City of the Sun." The Incas built fortresses and irrigation systems and laid paved roads from one end of their realm to the other. Pack animals called *llamas* carried goods, and swift runners brought news to the Inca capital. The rulers of the empire prevented local famines by maintaining storehouses and by moving food supplies to villages when crops failed.

After conquering their neighbors, the Inca rulers sought to eliminate tribal diversity in their empire. In order to pacify and colonize newly conquered lands, they moved entire villages to the new lands. They established an educational system, particularly for the children of the nobility, that taught the Inca religion and history. Even today millions of native people in the five South American countries of Peru, Ecuador, Bolivia, Chile, and Argentina speak the Inca language—Quechua (KECH • wuh).

Although the Incas did not have a system of writing, they did keep records by means of the **quipu** (KEE • poo)—a kind of knotted string used to assist the memory. They were quite advanced in the practice of medicine, using anesthetics and even performing a primitive kind of brain surgery.

Just as they did with the Aztecs, the Spaniards conquered the Incas in the 1500s. Yet many aspects of this fabulous civilization lived on in the isolated highland valleys of the Andes.

SECTION 4 REVIEW

1. **Define**   chinampa, quipu
2. **Identify**   Olmecs, Chavin, Maya, Toltecs, Quetzalcoatl, Aztecs, Incas
3. **Locate**   Tula, Yucatán Peninsula, Chichén Itzá, Tenochtitlán, Cuzco
4. **Determining Cause and Effect**   What factors contributed to the growth of large populations in Mexico and Peru?
5. **Summarizing Ideas**   How did the Incas prevent famines?
6. **Comparing Ideas**   **(a)** How were the civilizations of the Maya, Aztecs, and Incas similar?   **(b)** How were they different?

311

Founding of Kerma

Cushite rule in Egypt

BC   1800   750   671

Chapter Summary

The following list contains the key concepts you have learned about civilizations in Africa and the Americas.

1. SubSaharan Africa lies on a great plateau, broken here and there by basins and the Great Rift Valley.
2. Scholars have used linguistics, oral traditions, music, and archaeology to unlock the African past.
3. Africans lived primarily in small villages where families were very important.
4. The great kingdoms of Cush and Axum dominated the interior of eastern Africa.
5. Independent city-states, noted for their trading activity, were established on Africa's eastern coast. The region experienced a golden age that lasted from the 700s through the 1300s.
6. In central Africa, Zimbabwe controlled a large area.
7. To the west, large kingdoms such as Mali, Ghana, and Songhai developed. These kingdoms controlled the vital gold-for-salt trade of the western Sudan.
8. Successive waves of immigrants from Asia settled the Americas. Many crossed the land bridge that linked Asia and the Americas.
9. North American tribes included the fishers of the Northwest, the hunters of the Plains region, the Pueblo farmers of the Southwest, and the Mound Builders of the Eastern Woodlands.
10. As agriculture and small towns developed, several great cultures arose—the Olmecs, Maya, Toltecs, and Aztecs of Mexico and Central America, and the Incas of Peru.

On a separate sheet of paper, complete the following review exercises.

Reviewing Important Terms

Match each of the following terms with the correct definition in column two.

a. savanna   f. adobe
b. linguist   g. tepee
c. oral traditions h. tropical rain forest
d. chinampa   i. jungle
e. quipu   j. matrilineal

___ 1. Scholar who studies languages
___ 2. Kind of knotted string developed by the Incas to keep records and assist the memory
___ 3. A vast area of relatively dry grasslands
___ 4. Artificial island that the Aztecs created for agriculture
___ 5. Poems, songs, or stories passed by word of mouth from one generation to another
___ 6. Cone-shaped tent made of buffalo hide
___ 7. Sun-dried brick
___ 8. Society in which people trace their ancestors through their mothers rather than their fathers
___ 9. Forest where annual rainfall exceeds 100 inches (254 centimeters)
___ 10. A thick growth of plants found in a tropical rain forest wherever sunlight penetrates the dense umbrella of tall trees and reaches the forest floor

Developing Critical Thinking Skills

1. **Classifying Ideas** Supply the name of the area or culture that completes each statement.

   (a) The _____ developed a counting system based on 20.
   (b) _____ was an early East African center of iron-working.
   (c) The first West African kingdom to build up gold-for-salt trade was _____ .
   (d) Tombouctou, the capital of _____, was a center of Muslim learning.
   (e) _____ became the most famous city-state for East African trade.
   (f) The _____ of Mexico farmed on floating artificial islands.

2. **Interpreting Ideas** (a) What evidence supports the claim that the Maya were one of the most advanced cultures of the Americas? (b) In what ways were the Maya as advanced as the Europeans of the same period?

3. **Evaluating Ideas** (a) How do the use of metals and the type of buildings that are constructed reflect the accomplishments of a civilization? (b) Give an example from one African and one American civilization to support your answer.

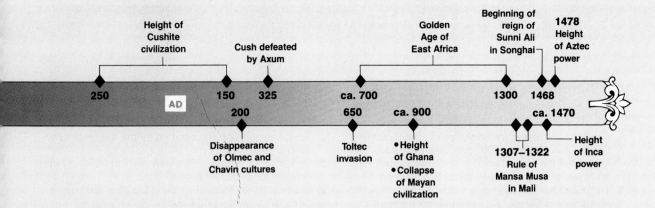

Height of Cushite civilization 250

AD 200

Disappearance of Olmec and Chavin cultures

Cush defeated by Axum 150 · 325

Toltec invasion 650

Golden Age of East Africa ca. 700

• **Height of Ghana**
• **Collapse of Mayan civilization** ca. 900

Beginning of reign of Sunni Ali in Songhai 1300 · 1468

1478 Height of Aztec power

ca. 1470

1307–1322 Rule of Mansa Musa in Mali

Height of Inca power

4. **Summarizing Ideas** (a) What types of trade developed across the Sahara and along the eastern coast of Africa? (b) What items were traded in the American civilizations? (c) Who traded with whom? (d) What similarities or differences in trade do you notice in all of these civilizations?

5. **Analyzing Ideas** Review the functions of the pyramid structures of the Maya, Toltecs, and Aztecs. What do these structures tell us about the cultures they represent?

Relating Geography to History

(a) Using information in this chapter, trace on maps of Africa and the Americas the migration routes of the peoples who later established the great civilizations. (b) What climatic and geographical obstacles did they have to overcome? (c) What approximate dates are given for these migrations?

Relating Past to Present

1. The Bush people of the Kalahari Desert and the Bantu-speaking peoples of East and South Africa live much the same way as their ancestors did hundreds of years ago. Use encyclopedias, history books, or other reference books on Africa to find out more about the culture of one of these groups.

2. Many English words have roots in Latin American cultures. Use your dictionary to find the origin of these words: *chocolate, hammock, potato, quinine, tapioca, tobacco, tomato, avocado.*

Applying History Study Skills

Before completing this activity, review Building History Study Skills on page 299.

Read the following excerpt in which Olauda Equiano describes his Nigerian home.

❝ In our buildings we study convenience rather than ornament. Each master of a family has a large square piece of ground, surrounded with a moat or a fence. . . . Within this, are his houses to accommodate his family and slaves, which if numerous, frequently present the appearance of a village. In the middle, stands the principal building, appropriated to the sole use of the master and consisting of two apartments; in one of which he sits in the day with his family, the other is left for the reception of his friends. . . . On each side are the apartments of his wives, who also have their separate day and night houses. The habitations of the slaves and their families are distributed throughout the rest of the enclosure. These houses never exceed one story in height; they are always built of wood . . . crossed with wattles and neatly plastered within and without. . . . ❞

1. What is the main idea of Equino's description?
2. In two complete sentences, paraphrase the main idea of the excerpt.

Investigating Further

1. **Writing a Report** In 1911 Hiram Bingham discovered the Inca city of Machu Picchu in the wilderness of the Andes Mountains. Read his account in *Lost City of the Incas* (Atheneum). Check other sources to determine if additional research has discovered new information about the purpose of this city, the organization of its society, the uniqueness of its buildings, or its methods of farming. Write a report discussing your findings. Conclude your report by discussing why this fabulous city remained undiscovered for so many centuries.

2. **Preparing an Oral Report** Form study groups to prepare oral reports on the Indians of North America. Each group can choose one Indian culture to research. Assign each member of the group a particular area of study, such as clothing, shelter, transportation, or religious beliefs. One source for your research is Alvin Josephy's *The Indian Heritage of America* (Knopf). Another source may be scholars at a local college or university.

3. **Constructing a Chart** Use resources in your school or public library to locate more information on the decline of the kingdoms of Africa and the Americas discussed in this chapter. Then prepare a chart that lists the reasons for the decline of these kingdoms in three categories: political, economic, and social.

313

UNIT 3 REVIEW

Unit Summary

The following list contains the key concepts you have learned about the world in transition.

1. A brilliant and sophisticated civilization, the Byzantine Empire survived for 1,000 years and preserved the heritage of the ancient world in the West. Kievan Rus and Muscovy adopted many Byzantine traditions.
2. The rise of Islam transformed much of Asia and parts of Africa and Europe. Its early believers spread the Islamic faith aggressively.
3. The great Frankish king Charlemagne created an empire that included much of western Europe.
4. Two important medieval institutions were feudalism and the manorial system.
5. During the Middle Ages, the church in western Europe performed many functions.
6. Kings in France and England gradually extended their authority in the late Middle Ages.
7. The Crusades were organized chiefly to regain the Holy Land from the Muslims.
8. Towns grew and medieval culture flourished as trade revived. Townspeople gained freedom from services on the manor, town justice, and commercial rights.
9. Under the rule of the Sui, Tang, and Song dynasties, the Chinese made notable achievements.
10. In the 1200s the nomadic Mongols of central Asia were united into a powerful fighting force under Genghis Khan.
11. Japan was influenced by China but created its own distinct culture.
12. From ancient times through the 1500s, a remarkable variety of societies arose on the African continent. The great kingdoms included Cush, Axum, Zimbabwe, Ghana, Mali, and Songhai.
13. Immigrants from Asia settled the Americas. Civilizations developed, particularly in Mexico and Peru.

Reviewing Concepts

Identify the person who might have made each of the following statements:

1. "I used my native Italian language to describe a spiritual pilgrimage through hell, purgatory, and heaven."
2. "I was crowned Emperor of the Romans in 800."
3. "I traveled extensively over the Mongol Empire as a trader, keeping a record of my experiences."
4. "I asked my followers to believe in one god, Allah, and accept me as his prophet."
5. "I conquered England in 1066 but also retained control over large territories of France."
6. "I was forced by my nobles to sign a charter protecting their rights and limiting my power."
7. "I showed religious tolerance by marrying a Hindu princess and repealing the special tax on non-Muslims."

Applying Critical Thinking Skills

1. **Classifying Ideas** Name the culture that each of the following statements describes.

(a) Artistic expression represented by the tea ceremony and *no* plays
(b) Spread from Arabia with a new religion believing in one god for all peoples
(c) Continued the Roman Empire in the east and helped Christianity spread into Russia
(d) Decided issues of peace or war at the *veche,* or town meeting
(e) Built steep pyramids as ceremonial centers; had a counting system based on 20 and a calendar that could predict solar eclipses
(f) Perfected civil service examinations
2. **Summarizing Ideas** (a) Explain why the Christian Church divided. (b) Identify its two branches. (c) What factors contributed to the split in Islam? (d) What two sects emerged?
3. **Synthesizing Ideas** Trade and city life are considered essential to the strength of a civilization. Defend or oppose this idea as it would apply to any three of the following: western Europe, China, Russia, western Africa.
4. **Comparing Ideas** Compare the western European culture of the Middle Ages to the Islamic culture of the same period with regard to scientific accomplishments, language and literature, and concepts of law and justice.

Relating Geography to History

Study the maps of Africa and the Americas on pages 294 and 304 and the map of the world on pages R2–R3. (a) What geographic factors isolated the peoples of SubSaharan Africa from people in the rest of the world? (b) What geographic factors isolated the peoples of North and South America from people in the rest of the world?

Writing About History

1. Work with other members of your class to write a scene from a play in which a representative from Mali, one of Charlemagne's lords, a Muslim mullah, a Song emperor, a Tokugawa shogun, and an Inca prince debate the merits of their civilizations.
2. Use encyclopedias and recent issues of periodicals such as *National Geographic* to write a report on archaeological excavations in the Americas and Africa.

Further Readings

Bengtsson, Frans G. *The Long Ships.* New York: New American Library. Discusses Viking life.

Holmes, George, ed. *The Oxford Illustrated History of Medieval Europe.* New York: Oxford University Press. Shows territorial changes in Europe, 400–1500.

Parker, Henry. *A History of Mexico.* Boston: Houghton Mifflin. Recounts events in history of Mexico.

Ritchie, Rita. *The Year of the Horse.* New York: Dutton. Details life in Genghis Khan's empire.

Stewart, Desmond. *Early Islam.* New York: Time, Inc. Recounts the history of the beginnings of Islam.

Tuchman, Barbara. *A Distant Mirror: The Calamitous 14th Century.* New York: Ballantine Books. Analyzes life in Europe during the 1300s.

Unit Three Chronology

Date	Political and Social Developments	Technological and Scientific Advances	Visual Arts and Literature	Religious and Philosophical Thought
0–A.D. 500	Angles, Jutes, and Saxons in England 10* Mayan civilization 13 Height of Cush kingdom 13 Cush defeated by Axum 13	Maya develop calendar and zero 13 Paper in China 12 Axum dry-stone construction 13 Mexican pyramids 13	Byzantine mosaics 8	St. Patrick in Ireland 10 Ezana converted to Christianity 13
500–750	Sui and Tang dynasties in China 12 Justinian's empire 8 Muslim invasion of Spain and Indus Valley 9 Battle of Tours 10 Feudalism begins 10	Beginning of Golden Age in East Africa 13	Hagia Sophia 8 Illuminated manuscript 10 Tang porcelain 12	Buddhism in Japan 12 Muhammad 9 Islam in East Africa 13
750–1000	Karanga state; Ghana civilization 13 Height of Mayan civilization 13 Charlemagne 10 Viking invasions 8 Alfred the Great 10 Song Dynasty 12	Norse navigational techniques 10 Three-field system 10 Stirrup 10 Arabs invent zero 9 Construction of Great Zimbabwe 13	Cyrillic alphabet 8 *Diamond Sutra* 12 *The Tale of Genji* 12 *Anglo-Saxon Chronicles* 10	Origins of scholasticism 11
1000–1250	Norman Conquest 10 Toltecs 13 Yaroslav I 8 Barbarossa 10 Innocent III 10 Magna Carta 10	Chinese gunpowder 12 Optics 11 Textile "home" industry 11 Flying Buttress 11	Gothic cathedrals 11 Nigerian bronze sculpture 13 Universities—Paris and Bologna 11 *Domesday Book* 10	Concordat of Worms 10 Division of Roman and Eastern churches 8 Crusades begin 11 Constantinople falls to crusaders 8
1250–1500	Mongols in Russia 8 100 Years' War 11 Tamerlane in Delhi 9 Yuan dynasty 12 Marco Polo 12 Fall of Constantinople 8 Bubonic plague 11 Mali and Songhai 13 Height of Aztec and Inca civilizations 13	Inca irrigation and roads 13 Incan quipus 13	*Defender of the Peace* 11 Wycliffe's English Bible 11 *The Divine Comedy* 11 *Canterbury Tales* 11	Babylonian Captivity 11 Great Schism 11 John Huss executed 11

*Indicates chapter in which development is discussed

The World in Transition

8 The Byzantine Empire Preserved the Heritage of Rome

In the West the collapse of the Roman Empire resulted in the disappearance of strong governments. However, the Roman Empire in the East—the Byzantine Empire—maintained its traditions and kept out barbarian invaders.

The Byzantine Empire

By the early 500s the empire in the West had broken down into a group of Germanic tribal kingdoms. The Eastern Roman Empire, on the other hand, had ousted the barbarians and had begun a great political, economic, intellectual, and artistic revival under the leadership of Emperor Justinian. Although many problems plagued the Byzantine Empire after Justinian's death, its political, military, and economic strengths helped it survive for more than 1,000 years.

The Church. In religion, the Byzantines recognized the patriarch in Constantinople rather than the pope in Rome as head of the Christian Church. Then after years of arguments over the role of icons, or holy pictures, in services, the Christian Church officially split in 1054. In the West, it became known as the Roman Catholic church. In the East, it became known as the Eastern Orthodox church.

Byzantine culture. Of all the Byzantine contributions to world civilization, the greatest was probably the preservation of Roman law. Early in his reign, Emperor Justinian ordered his scholars to collect and organize all Roman law. The entire collection is known as the *Corpus Juris Civilis* (Latin for "Body of Civil Law"). It is also called Justinian's Code. It remained in force until the Ottoman Turks toppled the empire and captured Constantinople in 1453.

Kievan Rus

A vast, grassy, almost treeless plain called the steppe stretches across eastern Europe and central Asia. On the western portions of the steppe, another civilization—Kievan Rus—arose.

Kiev, one of many city-states in the region, prospered because of its strategic location astride rich trade routes. In time, Kiev became the most powerful city in a region that included many semi-independent principalities.

Religion dominated Kievan culture. Although authors wrote epic poems and historical chronicles about wars and the personal tragedies associated with war, religious hymns and sermons constituted the bulk of Kievan literature. Icon painting became the most distinctive Kievan art form.

The Mongols

After the rule of Yaroslav the Wise ended in 1054, Kiev declined in power and wealth. By 1240 fierce Mongol invaders from Central Asia had conquered and burned almost every city in Kievan Rus. The Mongols retained control of the Kievan region until the 1400s.

In time, Mongol rule grew weaker and the princes of the region became more independent. During the 1300s Moscow, or Muscovy, became the strongest principality. By the late 1400s, Muscovy had overthrown Mongol rule and become the capital of an independent state called Russia.

9 Islam Became a Powerful Force from Spain to India

In the 600s the prophet Muhammad founded Islam, the youngest of the world's major religions.

Islam and the Muslim Empire

The central belief of Islam is: "There is no God but Allah, and Muhammad is his prophet." The holy book of Islam is the Koran (meaning "recital"). The Koran presents Muhammad's most important teachings and includes many concepts and teachings also found in the Bible and the Torah.

According to the Koran, a Muslim must meet five chief obligations known as *The Pillars of Faith*: (1) Recite the words of witness: "There is no God but Allah, and Muhammad is his prophet." (2) Pray five times a day facing Mecca. (3) If possible, make a pilgrimage, or a journey to a holy place, to Mecca at least once in a lifetime. (4) Give assistance to the needy. (5) Fast from sunrise to sunset during the month of Ramadan.

In contrast to the teachings of Jesus, Muhammad praised what he called the jihad (ji • HAHD), or holy war—fighting to defend or spread the faith of Islam. Following this principle, Muhammad's successors spread Islam throughout the Middle East and along the shores of the Mediterranean.

Muslim Civilization

The tightly organized Islamic government gave its rulers great authority. Within the stable society that developed, both economic and cultural activity flourished. Though the Muslim Empire later divided, the Muslim world remained united in one great civilization. The Arabs adopted the best ideas, customs, and institutions they found. For example, they combined the scientific and philosophical ideas of Greece, Rome, and Asia.

Muslim and Mogul Rulers in India

About the year 1000, the Turks surged through the northwest mountain passes and into India. One by one the small states of the local Rajput princes fell to the conquerors. In 1193 the Muslims occupied Delhi, and by 1236 they controlled all of northern India in what is called the Delhi sultanate.

First civil wars and then the devastating onslaught of the Mongol leader Tamerlane interrupted Muslim rule. Despite these interruptions, the first period of Muslim rule in India had important and lasting consequences. Many Indians converted to Islam, and the Muslims introduced a new and important language, Urdu.

Dome of the Rock in Jerusalem

As the Delhi sultanate grew weaker, Rajput princes again struggled for control of India. Thus, as in the time of Tamerlane, India lay open to Mongol attack. It came under the leadership of the youthful and talented "Babur the Tiger," a descendant of Tamerlane who set up the Mogul Empire, which lasted until 1761.

10 Feudal Lords and the Church Dominated Medieval Europe

The period in western European history following the collapse of the Roman Empire, between ancient times and the modern period (from about 500 to about 1500), is called the Middle Ages.

Frankish Rulers

After the Roman Empire collapsed, many Germanic tribes, including Visigoths, Vandals, Burgundians, and Ostrogoths, plundered Europe and established kingdoms. Of all the Germanic tribes, the Franks played the greatest role in history. The greatest Frankish ruler was Charlemagne, who assumed the throne in 768 and ruled until 814. By the end of his reign, he controlled much of western Europe.

Although Charlemagne was a powerful ruler who organized an efficient government, his empire soon crumbled not only because of internal feuds, but also because invaders—Muslims, Slavs, Vikings, and Magyars—swarmed into the empire from every direction.

Feudalism and the Manorial System

We call the political system that evolved in Europe after the death of Charlemagne feudalism. Feudalism, a political system in which kings and powerful nobles granted land to other nobles in return for loyalty, military assistance, and services, was firmly established throughout most of western Europe by the 1000s.

While feudalism was essentially a governmental and military system, the manorial system became the economic system. The manor, a large estate including a village, became the economic unit of the early Middle Ages.

The lord and several peasants shared the land of a manor. Most of the peasants on a manor were serfs, or people bound to the land. But serfs were not slaves, for they could not be sold away from the land.

The Church in the Middle Ages

Central governments in medieval Europe were weak or did not exist at all. Therefore, the church performed many of the responsibilities of modern governments.

Members of the clergy were organized in ranks according to their power and responsibilities. The levels of this hierarchy (HY • uh • rahr • kee), starting at the bottom, were the parish priest, the bishop, the archbishop, and the pope and his curia. In addition, monks and nuns provided valuable services for the church.

England and France

Kings and lords often struggled for power. From this struggle gradually emerged such kingdoms as England and France, where the king's authority grew stronger than that of the lords.

England. In 1066 Duke William of Normandy invaded and conquered England. One of William's successors, John, brought on a revolt among the nobles by forcing them to pay taxes that they considered unjust. In 1215 the nobles forced John to accept a document known as the Magna Carta (Latin for "great charter") in which he accorded them many rights. Although the charter was not considered significant at the time, later political thinkers regarded many of its clauses as important precedents.

King John signing the Magna Carta

In the century that followed the signing of the Magna Carta, the two most important developments in English history were the evolution of Parliament—the legislative body of England—and the growth of common law—the type of law based on judges' decisions.

France. In 987 an assembly of nobles chose Hugh Capet (kuh • PAY), a French noble, as king. Capet and his descendants, called the Capetians, ruled France for over 300 years and steadily increased royal power by adding to the royal lands, by developing a strong central government, and by increasing the revenue from taxes.

Germany and Italy

During the 1000s the Holy Roman Emperors who ruled what is today Germany and northern Italy often clashed with the papacy because the emperors claimed the right to appoint bishops. After years of conflict, the issue was finally settled in 1122 when an assembly of church leaders, nobles, and representatives of the Holy Roman Emperor reached an agreement known as the Concordat of Worms. The Concordat provided that only the church could select bishops.

11 Trade Revived and Nations Developed in Europe

During the Middle Ages people gradually began to look outward, away from Europe, seeking new products and new ways of making money.

The Crusades

During the 1000s the Seljuk Turks conquered Palestine and interfered with Christian pilgrims who were trying to visit the sites of the life of Jesus. In response, Pope Urban II called for a war to regain the Holy Land from the Muslims. The series of wars that followed is called the Crusades.

From a military standpoint, all the Crusades except the first failed. However, Europeans learned about many things of military importance, including the crossbow, a sophisticated bow and arrow held horizontally and set off by a trigger, and perhaps the use of gunpowder.

Trade

Trade nearly died out in western Europe after the 400s. Slowly, however, it began to revive—first in Italy where neither trade nor towns had declined as much as elsewhere. Later, trade revived in northern Europe as well.

Four important results of the revival of European trade were: a monetary system, a manufacturing system, a banking system, and the practice of investing capital.

The Growth of Towns

The growth of trade spurred the growth of towns. As the number of towns increased and their populations grew, a new class of merchants, master workers, and skilled workers emerged in medieval society. The rise of this class, in turn, encouraged the growth of nations. Townspeople tended to want stable and uniform governments that would protect trade and property, so they usually favored kings over nobles.

The Culture of the Middle Ages

Two great writers, Dante and Chaucer, represent the flowering of medieval literature. Dante Alighieri (DAHN • tay al • uhg • YER • ee) was born in Florence, Italy, in 1265. Dante's greatest work is *The Divine Comedy*. Geoffrey Chaucer of England wrote his *Canterbury Tales* in the form of a series of stories told by a group of religious pilgrims.

The later Middle Ages also witnessed the growth of universities. By the 1300s universities could be found in towns throughout western Europe. And in architecture, the soaring Gothic style replaced the earlier Romanesque style that had been based on Roman architecture.

Nations

In the late Middle Ages, European monarchs continued the process of national consolidation.

In England, the authority of the monarch, although partially restricted by Parliament, increased in various ways. These included the development of a single system of law and courts and an increase in revenue as the country grew more prosperous.

The history of France during the 1300s and 1400s resembled that of England. Philip IV, for example, established the Estates-General, a representative assembly resembling the English Parliament. But strong French kings curtailed its powers and seldom called it into session.

Spain had been divided into four kingdoms during the early Middle Ages. In the 1500s, however, Ferdinand and Isabella united Castile-León and Aragón to form the new nation of Spain, added the kingdom of Navarre to its territories, and made Spain a powerful monarchy.

Unlike England, France, and Spain, Germany and Italy—the regions that made up the Holy Roman Empire—did not become unified nations until the 1800s.

The Temporal Power of the Church

The late Middle Ages also witnessed changes in the status of the church. By the early 1300s, French kings named the popes, who ruled the church from

Building a cathedral

319

Avignon in southern France rather than from Rome. This period of papal history—from 1309 to 1377—is known as the Babylonian Captivity.

The situation for the church worsened after 1378 when two popes, one French and one Italian, claimed power during a period called the Great Schism. Although the conflict was resolved, both the Babylonian Captivity and the Great Schism weakened the authority and prestige of the papacy and increased criticism of the church.

12 Civilization in East Asia Reached New Heights

From the 100s to 1644 great civilizations flourished in East Asia.

China

The Sui dynasty succeeded in reuniting China in 589. In their brief period of power, Sui rulers oversaw the building of one of the engineering marvels of the ancient world—the Grand Canal. However, an uprising in 618 ended the Sui dynasty, which was replaced by the Tang dynasty.

Although the Tang dynasty itself lasted only until 906, it began a 1,000-year period during which China could be described as the most powerful, the most sophisticated, and the wealthiest country in the world. It was also during the Tang dynasty that the Chinese invented printing.

The next dynasty, the Song, faced both foreign invasion and civil wars. Nevertheless, Song rulers maintained Chinese civilization and expanded trade.

Nomadic Invasions

In the 1200s the Mongols under the leadership of Genghis Khan captured Beijing and renamed it Khanbalik (kahn • buh • LEEK). They then turned westward, conquering central Asia, most of Persia, and Korea.

Japan

Only sketchy records of early Japanese history exist. We do know that Chinese influences were very strong and that the centralized political system adopted from China gradually fell into decline after the early 800s. In its place Japan developed a system of local power that in many ways resembled feudalism, the system that governed Europe at this time.

In Japan the feudal system contained two conflicting sources of power. One was an indirect form of central government under which an important family held power in the name of the emperor. The other source consisted of military units that had authority in the territories they occupied.

In 1192 the Minamoto family introduced a new kind of official called the shogun. Officially he was the chief officer of the emperor and was always careful to be dutiful to him. In fact, however, he was the agent of the powerful families.

The leading families and their shoguns had power, but they did not control enough to extend this power to local levels. There, warrior-landlords called samurai (SAM • uh • ry) led the military units.

Japan's neighbor to the east, Korea, also developed civilization. There both Japanese and Chinese influences were evident.

13 Africa and the Americas Produced Complex Civilizations

Because we have few written records of peoples who lived in Africa south of the Sahara and in the Americas, we know much less about events before 1500 in those regions than we do about events in Europe and Asia. We do know that complex, highly sophisticated societies developed.

Shogun Yoritomo Minamoto

Machu Picchu, Peru

Africa's Early History

Experts have drawn several conclusions about life in early Africa. They believe that most Africans lived in small, independent agricultural villages ruled by chiefs. Relationships of kinship, age, and sex bound the different societies together. Within this system women played a crucial role.

African City-states and Kingdoms

Along the Nile River, south of the major centers of ancient Egypt, lies an area known as Nubia, which was the site of Cush. Cush maintained close cultural and economic ties with Egypt, and about 750 B.C. it conquered Upper Egypt. Later the kingdom of Axum arose in the Ethiopian highlands.

No large kingdoms like Cush and Axum emerged on the coast of East Africa. Instead, a series of city-states that dominated coastal trade in the Indian Ocean arose.

The growth of Indian Ocean trade after the 900s dramatically increased the demand for gold. The Karanga, a people who first immigrated onto the plateau land of what is today Zimbabwe (zim • BAHB • wee) about 800, achieved control of this trade.

In West Africa, between Lake Chad and the Atlantic Ocean, several important African societies developed. The most powerful included Ghana, Mali, and Songhai.

The Americas

While the Ice Age still gripped the earth, people migrated from Asia to the Americas across a land bridge that then linked the two continents near what is today the Bering Strait. These early immigrants lived by hunting and gathering. Their descendants, however, learned to farm.

In what is today the United States and Canada, many different cultures and some highly organized societies thrived. The cultures of these peoples often depended on the geography of the region they inhabited.

Empires in Mexico and Peru

Several cultures developed in Mexico. Early cultures included the Olmecs, the Maya, and the Toltecs. Then about A.D. 1200 peoples from the north launched further invasions of central Mexico. One of these groups, the Aztecs, soon dominated central Mexico. The Aztecs incorporated into their culture the inventions of peoples they conquered or with whom they traded. They soon learned the use of metals, weaving, pottery-making, the calendar, and mathematics.

At about the same period that the Aztecs built their civilization in Mexico, another group created a civilization in the Andes Mountains of South America. These people based their religion on sun worship. Their name—Incas—meant "children of the sun."

The Inca Empire expanded steadily. By the late 1400s it extended along most of the west coast of South America and far into the Andes, covering much of the present-day nations of Peru, Ecuador, Bolivia, and Chile.

The Emergence of Modern Nations

◀ *A European Renaissance seaport*

The Renaissance, Reformation, and Scientific Revolution Changed Europe

Place Europe

Time 1350–1700

3.7 mil. BC   4000 BC   AD 2100

Significance

If you were to think about the differences between medieval and modern times, you would probably think first of the great difference in the material goods available. Today we have compact disc players, VCRs, and other luxuries and conveniences that medieval people never dreamed of. However, another and perhaps even greater difference exists—a difference in attitudes. Beginning in the 1300s, people gradually began to look for new ways to explain what happened in the world in which they lived.

The changes in attitude that altered how people viewed themselves as well as their world did not occur overnight. Many historians believe that the changes grew out of a philosophical and artistic movement that began in Italy about 1350. Because it centered on a revival of interest in the classical learning of Greece and Rome, we call this movement the **Renaissance** (REN·uh·sahnts), a French word meaning "rebirth." Some scholars think of the Renaissance as merely a continuation and development of the Middle Ages. Others think of the Renaissance as a break with medieval life and medieval thought—as the beginning of modern times.

Terms to Define

Renaissance
perspective
Reformation
indulgences
Scientific Revolution
heliocentric theory

People to Identify

Leonardo da Vinci
Johann Gutenberg
Martin Luther
John Calvin
Nicolaus Copernicus
Galileo

Places to Locate

Florence
Worms

Questions to Guide Your Reading

1 What major works did Renaissance writers and artists create?
2 Why did the Reformation take place?
3 How did Calvinism and the Counter-Reformation affect religion in Europe?
4 How did popular culture change during the Renaissance and the Reformation?
5 Why was the Scientific Revolution important?

On November 4, 1966, newscasts across the world carried reports of a staggering natural disaster. In northern Italy the Arno River had burst over its banks, sending torrents of swirling floodwaters cascading through the museums, cathedrals, and libraries of Florence. When the waters receded, they left layer upon layer of sewage and muck. Within days, hundreds of people—mostly students—converged on the water-logged city to help with the massive cleanup.

Why would news of a flood in northern Italy electrify people across the world? Quite simply because that city of only 150,000 people contained the world's greatest store of Renaissance art and literature. As one reporter noted:

> **❝***I*t is fair to say that much of what we know today of painting and sculpture, of architecture and political science, of scientific method and economic theory, we owe to the artists, politicians, statesmen, bankers, and merchants of the Renaissance—that explosion of intellectual and artistic energy in Italy between 1300 and 1600. And Florentines stood at the turbulent center of the Renaissance.**❞**

Throughout Europe the outpouring of creativity that was the Renaissance changed the course of Western civilization.

1 Renaissance Writers and Artists Created Outstanding Works

Scholars use the term *Renaissance* to refer not only to a philosophical and artistic movement but also to the period during which it flourished. The period of the Renaissance saw many developments, including the invention of the printing press, advances in science, and a new emphasis on reason.

The Origins of the Italian Renaissance

A renewed interest in Roman literature and life characterized the Renaissance. In many ways it was natural that this interest would reawaken in Italy. Ruins of the mighty Roman Empire dotted the Italian countryside and served as constant reminders of Roman glory. The tradition of Rome as the capital city of a vast empire lived on in the popes, who made Rome the seat of the Roman

Catholic church. The Crusades and trade with the Middle East brought Italians into contact with Byzantine civilization, whose scholars had preserved much learning from classical Greece and Rome. Even before the fall of Constantinople in 1453, many Byzantine scholars had fled to Italy to escape the troubled political climate of their native land. These scholars brought with them a great appreciation and knowledge of the Greek and Roman classics.

Florence, Rome, Venice, Milan, and Naples were the most important cities of the Renaissance. These cities had grown rich through trade. Their citizens included many educated, wealthy merchants who saw themselves and their city as a reflection of the ancient polis. In Florence, for example, the Medici (MED • uh • chee) family grew wealthy first as bankers and then as rulers of the city-state. Lorenzo Medici, who was known as "the

Learning from Maps Many Italian cities became centers of Renaissance learning. Which major Renaissance city is on the northern Adriatic coast?

RENAISSANCE ITALY
ca. 1500

LAMBERT CONFORMAL CONIC PROJECTION

Magnificent," became a great patron of the arts and wanted to make Florence the most glorious city in Europe.

The Humanities

Beginning about the mid-1300s, a number of Italian scholars developed a lively interest in classical literature, particularly that of the Romans. Medieval scholars who had studied ancient times had tried to make everything they learned harmonize with Christian doctrine. The Italian scholars of the 1300s, on the other hand, studied the ancient world in an attempt to imitate its great achievements.

These Italian scholars stressed the study of grammar, rhetoric, history, and poetry, using classical texts. We call these studies the *humanities;* people who specialized in the humanities were called **humanists.** Humanists searched out Greek and Latin language manuscripts. Often they would find more than one copy of a work. If the copies differed, humanists compared the different versions to determine which was correct. In doing so they developed a critical attitude that had been lacking in much medieval scholarship.

As humanists studied classical manuscripts, they began to acquire a new outlook on life. They came to believe that it was important to know how things worked. This belief led them to emphasize education. However, they also wondered whether a life that consisted only of contemplation gave a person enough opportunities to lead a meaningful life. Humanists became more and more convinced that a person had to become actively involved in practical affairs such as politics or patronage of the arts.

Humanists viewed existence not only as a preparation for life after death but also as a joy in itself. They thought that men and women, despite all their faults, were intelligent beings who could make their own decisions. Along with a belief in individual dignity came an admiration for individual achievement. Many remarkable individuals of this period displayed a variety of talents. A person might be not only a poet and musician but also a scientist and painter.

Writers of the Italian Renaissance

One of the first humanists, the Florentine Francesco Petrarch (PEE • trahrk), lived from 1304 to 1374. Like many of the humanists, Petrarch became famous as a scholar and as a teacher. He

History Through the Arts

LITERATURE

The Book of the Courtier

In 1528 the Italian diplomat and writer Baldassare Castiglione (kahs·teel·YOH·nay) published what was probably the most famous book of the Renaissance, *The Book of the Courtier*. Castiglione's work is both a book on courtesy and an explanation of the role of the refined courtier as a successor to the coarse knight of the Middle Ages. The setting for the book is the court of the dukes of Urbino, an Italian city-state where the author lived many happy years. Castiglione's characters are real people who reflect in fictional conversations on how gentlemen and gentlewomen ought to act in polite society. Castiglione wrote:

❝ I would have him speak not always of serious subjects but also of amusing things, such as games and jests and jokes, according to the occasion. He should always, of course, speak out fully and frankly, and avoid talking nonsense. . . .

He should have a knowledge of Greek as well as Latin [and] he should be very well acquainted with the poets, and no less with the orators and historians, and also skilled at writing both verse and prose, especially in our own language. . . .

Gentleness is most impressive in a man who is a capable and courageous warrior. . . . He should . . . above all avoid affectation. Next let him consider well whatever he does or says, the place where he does it, in whose presence, its timing, why he is doing it, his own age, his profession, the end he is aiming at, and the means that are suitable. . . .

He will not speak evil. . . . Our courtier will avoid foolish arrogance; he will not be the bearer of bad news; he will not be careless in sometimes saying things that may give offence, instead of striving to please; he will not be obstinate. . . . He will not be an idle or lying babbler, nor a stupid flatterer or boaster, but will be modest and reserved. . . .

The courtier should . . . take great care to give a good impression of himself. . . . [There are men who are] convinced they are being terribly witty and amusing, [when] they use filthy and indecent language in the presence of noble ladies, and often to their face. And the more they make the ladies blush, the more they are convinced that they are being good courtiers. . . . The only reason they behave in such a beastly fashion is because they believe it makes them the life . . . of the party. . . . To acquire this reputation they indulge in the most shameful and shocking discourtesies. . . . Sometimes they push one another downstairs, belabor each other with sticks and bricks, throw handfuls of dust in each other's eyes, cause their horses to collapse on one another . . . then at table they hurl the soup, or the sauce or jelly, in one another's face, and they burst out laughing. . . .

[The lady must have] those virtues of the mind . . . in common with the courtier, such as prudence, magnanimity . . . and many others besides, and also the qualities that are common to all kinds of women, such as goodness and discretion, the ability to take good care . . . of her husband's belongings and house and children, and the virtues belonging to a good mother. . . . And her serene and modest behaviour . . . should be accompanied by a quick and vivacious spirit. . . .

She should know how to choose topics suitable for the kind of person she is addressing. . . . She should not introduce . . . jests and jokes into a discussion about serious things. She should not . . . [pretend] to know what she does not know, but should seek modestly to win credit for knowing what she does. . . . In this way she will be adorned with good manners. . . . Thus she will be not only loved but also revered by all. ❞

also wrote poetry, and his sonnets to Laura, the imaginary ideal woman, are considered some of the greatest love poems in literature.

Petrarch's main influence, however, stemmed from his ideas about virtue and about the Romans. He thought the Romans had set the best examples of ethical behavior and believed they could best be imitated if one studied their writings. This study of the writings of the ancients, particularly the Romans, came to be called *classical education*. A command of the Latin language, as written by ancient writers, became the mark of an educated person.

Although the humanists remained deeply committed to Christian teachings, they sometimes felt a tension between their commitment to the study of the Romans and their commitment to Christianity. Petrarch, for instance, agonized over his lust for fame (a well-known Roman ambition), which he feared would hurt his chances for salvation. Like most Italian humanists, Petrarch thought it important to lead a full and active life here on Earth, even if that meant devoting less time to purely spiritual concerns.

Niccolò Machiavelli (mahk • yah • VEL • lee) of Florence, a diplomat and historian who lived from 1469 to 1527, probably ranks as the most illustrious of the many Renaissance writers. In 1513 he wrote a famous essay, *The Prince*, which described government not in terms of lofty ideals but as Machiavelli felt government actually worked. He believed that in the real world, power counts much more than noble ideals. "It is safer to be feared than loved," he said.

The Prince advised rulers to maintain the safety of their states by whatever means they thought necessary and not to let considerations of honesty, justice, or honor hamper them. Today we use the word *Machiavellian* to describe people who use deceit and who have little regard for morality in their effort to get what they want.

Machiavelli can be considered a humanist because he looked to the ancient Romans for models and because such matters as the workings of politics interested him. However, his lack of concern for morality in *The Prince* set him apart from the other humanists, who considered virtue their main aim.

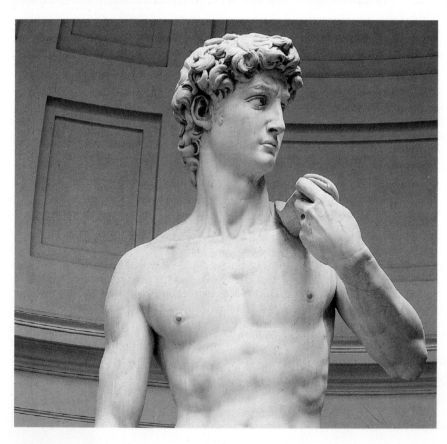

Learning from Pictures
Michelangelo, the famous Renaissance artist, sculpted this marble statue of David, king of ancient Israel. Michelangelo has been noted as one of history's greatest sculptors.

PAINTING

Realism and Perspective

The changes in painting from medieval to modern times can be seen in the work of the great early Renaissance artist Giotto. In this painting the angel of God tells St. Anne that she will have a child, Mary, who will be the mother of Jesus. Giotto makes us feel the scene is an actual event rather than a symbolic one by giving a three-dimensional quality to the lighted room, to the rooftops that recede into the dark, and to the faces of the women and the angel.

Giotto was an architect as well as an artist. His attention to architectural detail and perspective heightens the realism of his work. Note, for example, how he realistically portrayed the staircase leading to the balcony above the entrance. Like other Renaissance artists, Giotto was interested in showing a building or a landscape as it appeared through a person's own eyes. Later Renaissance painters developed perspective mathematically and portrayed distances with great accuracy.

Italian Renaissance Artists

Art as well as literature flourished during the Renaissance. In an outburst of creativity, Italian artists produced some of the world's most exquisite masterpieces.

Medieval paintings stressed the world beyond everyday life—a world associated with religious subjects—and depicted formal and stylized figures. The most noticeable characteristic of Renaissance painting, on the other hand, is its realism. Renaissance painters admired the intensely realistic art of the Romans, and they depicted realistic and lifelike human figures in Renaissance paintings. Even the backgrounds of these paintings differed from those of medieval paintings. Earlier artists had portrayed the Holy Land. Renaissance painters showed the rugged countryside that they knew.

Renaissance painters could make their works lifelike because they had learned a very important technique of painting called **perspective.** By making distant objects smaller than those in the foreground, and by arranging the objects in certain ways, an artist could create the illusion of depth on a flat canvas.

Giotto (JAW • toh), who lived from 1276 to 1337, and Masaccio (mah • ZAHT • choh), who lived from 1401 to 1428, pioneered the emphasis on realism. According to legend, a fly in one of Giotto's paintings looked so lifelike that an observer tried to brush it off the picture. Masaccio painted light and shadows to give the effect of depth to objects.

Italian painters of the late 1400s and early 1500s displayed such genius that historians often call this period the High Renaissance. Among the many great painters of this period, four made particularly outstanding contributions.

Leonardo da Vinci (duh • VIN • chee)—artist, musician, architect, mathematician, and scientist—lived from 1452 to 1519. He used his experiments

PAINTING

Lady with a Unicorn

The work of the great Italian artist Raphael reflected the intellectual and artistic ideals of the Renaissance. His paintings combined spirituality and artistry with the search for realism and truth that characterized his age. Raphael studied and worked in Florence, in the schools of Michelangelo and Leonardo da Vinci. He became so accomplished that he was called to Rome to help decorate the Vatican. Each year millions of visitors to Rome marvel at some of his most famous works.

In his paintings Raphael conveyed a feeling of balanced space, giving the viewer a sensation of tranquillity and joy. In this painting we see a Renaissance lady holding a baby unicorn. The unicorn is snugly enclosed in the lady's arms, yet relaxed in the spaciousness of her lap. The main figure takes up almost the entire canvas and the landscape stretches back into the distance; yet there is no sense of crowding. The glowing fabric of the lady's dress and the beauty of her pendant reveal the splendor of Renaissance taste.

Raphael's respect for antiquity are demonstrated in the little unicorn, a fabled animal that appeared in the art of ancient civilizations. During the Middle Ages, the unicorn was often used in Christian art as a symbol for the purity of Christ and the Virgin Mary.

in science to enhance his painting. Studies of anatomy helped him draw the human figure, and mathematics helped him organize the space in his paintings. People throughout the world still marvel at his mural, *The Last Supper*. Probably his most famous painting is the portrait called *Mona Lisa*.

Another master of Renaissance art, Michelangelo Buonarroti (my•kuh•LAN•juh•loh bwaw•nah•RAW•tee), lived from 1475 to 1564. Millions of people have visited the Sistine Chapel of the Vatican, the residence of the pope in Rome, and looked with wonder at the frescoes Michelangelo painted on the ceiling.

Although a brilliant painter, Michelangelo preferred sculpture. Both his paintings and his stone carvings of such biblical figures as David and Moses suggest a massive dignity. Almost as versatile as Leonardo, Michelangelo also wrote poetry and worked as an architect, helping design St. Peter's Basilica in Rome.

Raphael (raf•ee•EL), who lived from 1483 to 1520, became so popular in Florence that the pope hired him to help beautify the Vatican. His frescoes in the papal chambers include *The School of Athens*, which depicts the great philosophers of classical Greece. Raphael also painted exquisite madonnas, representations of the Virgin Mary.

Titian (TISH•uhn), who lived from about 1488 to 1576, spent most of his life in his native Venice. His works, such as *The Assumption of the Virgin*, portray a vivid sense of drama and are noted for their rich colors. The Holy Roman Emperor and the king of France sponsored many of Titian's works, and he became one of the first painters to become rich through his work.

Dozens of other artists prospered in Italy in the 1400s and 1500s. Princes supported many of these artists. The princes thought they would achieve lasting fame if they became patrons of the arts. One way a prince could be remembered was to have a great artist paint his portrait. Thus the patrons helped foster the enormous creativity of the period.

The Northern Renaissance

Humanist thought spread beyond Italy. Numerous mountain passes, such as the Brenner and the Great Saint Bernard, pierce the rugged Alps and allow people—and ideas—to pass from Italy to northern Europe. The Danube, Rhône, and Rhine rivers provide even easier routes. New ideas, often carried by northern European students who had studied in Italy, soon traveled to Germany, the Netherlands, France, and England.

Printing. A remarkable new process—printing—also helped ideas spread. Hundreds of years earlier, the Chinese had learned how to create a wooden block into which writing or pictures could be etched. Printers smeared ink on the block and pressed the block onto paper, which absorbed the ink. Then the block was reinked. In this way the writing or pictures could be reproduced many times. The Chinese had also learned how to assemble the block from separate pieces, or type, that could be used again and again.

The Arabs captured some Chinese people who knew how to make paper and perfected the production of paper. The Moors of Spain later introduced paper to Europe. In the 1400s printing began to appear in Europe, where it had its first great impact on intellectual life.

Scholars believe that in about 1450, Johann Gutenberg of Mainz, Germany, was the first European to use movable type to print books. Gutenberg developed a printing press on which he printed a copy of the Bible between 1453 and 1456. Many publishers adopted the printing press, and books soon helped spread new ideas to a large audience.

The Dutch scholar Desiderius Erasmus (i • RAZ • muhs) was the greatest humanist of northern Europe. He learned about the ideas of the Italian humanists from printed books. Erasmus, who lived from 1466 to 1536, entered a monastery as a young man but soon decided to spend his life studying the ancient Greeks and Romans.

Unlike the Italian humanists, Erasmus and other northern humanists were interested in the early Christian period as well as in early Roman and Greek culture. Erasmus believed that in its early years, Christianity had existed in harmony with classical civilization. He applied to his study of the Bible the critical method that the Italian humanists had developed, arguing for a return to the original, simple message of Jesus. Erasmus was saddened that the medieval scholars had made Christian faith less spiritual and more complicated and ceremonial. He published stinging criticisms of the church's lack of spirituality, a popular subject among the northern humanists.

Erasmus's most famous book, *In Praise of Folly,* ridiculed ignorance, superstition, and vice among the clergy and ordinary Christians. Erasmus criticized fasting, pilgrimages to religious shrines, and even the church's interpretation of some parts of the Bible.

Erasmus's friend Thomas More, the English humanist, took a similar view. In 1516 More published *Utopia,* a book in which he criticized the society of his day by describing an imaginary ideal society. According to More, the ideal society would consist entirely of free citizens who would elect their own governing officials. Conscientious citizens, not police, would enforce laws. Money and greed would vanish, and everyone would practice a simple, ethical religion. More's *Utopia* became so popular that today **utopia** means "an ideal place or society."

English literature. Renaissance literature in England reached its peak in the late 1500s and early 1600s in the plays of William Shakespeare. Like many other playwrights, Shakespeare often used familiar plots, but he built masterpieces of poetic drama around them.

Shakespeare's characters grapple with the questions that humanists asked about virtue and morality. Few writers have been able to portray personality and human emotions with Shakespeare's skill. The jovial Falstaff, the moody Hamlet, the young lovers Romeo and Juliet, and the tragic Macbeth seem as real today as when Shakespeare first created them.

Learning from Pictures *This painting by Dürer depicts the deposition of Christ. What possibilities did Dürer see for art in the mass production of books?*

Northern Renaissance Artists

The dynamic new painting techniques of Italian artists inspired artists outside of Italy. Northern European merchants carried Italian paintings home, and painters from northern Europe studied with Italian masters, thus spreading the arts of Italy to northern Europe.

Perhaps the most creative artists lived in Flanders; these artists perfected the technique of painting in oils on canvas. The brothers Hubert and Jan van Eyck, who lived in Flanders in the 1400s, paid great attention to detail in works such as *The Adoration of the Lamb*, the altarpiece of the cathedral at Ghent.

One of the greatest Flemish artists, Pieter Brueghel (BROO•guhl) the Elder, painted in the mid-1500s. Brueghel loved the countryside and the peasants of his native Flanders and painted lively scenes of village festivals and dances. He also used his paintings as a means to criticize the intolerance and cruelty he saw around him.

The German artist Albrecht Dürer (DYUR• uhr), who lived from 1471 to 1528, was famous for his copper engravings and woodcuts. During Dürer's lifetime the printing press made mass production of books possible. Dürer became one of the first to see the possibilities of printed illustrations in books.

Although a German, Hans Holbein the Younger (1497–1543) did most of his work in other countries. Holbein traveled throughout Europe to paint portraits of famous people, such as Erasmus, Thomas More, and King Henry VIII of England. This emphasis on portrait painting reflects the Renaissance interest in the individual and in fame among the political leaders of the time.

SECTION 1 REVIEW

1. **Define** Renaissance, humanist, perspective, utopia
2. **Identify** Francesco Petrarch, Niccolò Machiavelli, Leonardo da Vinci, Michelangelo, Johann Gutenberg, Desiderius Erasmus, Thomas More, William Shakespeare, Pieter Brueghel the Elder, Hans Holbein the Younger
3. **Locate** Florence, Venice, Milan, Flanders
4. **Interpreting Ideas** Why did the Renaissance begin in Italy?
5. **Analyzing Ideas** Why did humanism spread northward?
6. **Summarizing Ideas** (a) What was the most notable characteristic of Renaissance painting? (b) How was it achieved?

---

2 The Protestant Reformation Changed Religious Attitudes

About 1500 several northern humanists suggested that the Roman Catholic church had lost sight of the spiritual mission proclaimed by Jesus. Instead of setting an example of moral leadership, they said, popes acted as political leaders and warriors. Instead of encouraging inner piety, priests concerned themselves with the details of ceremonies. The church as a whole, the humanists claimed, seemed more interested in its income than in saving souls. The northern humanists sought a new emphasis on personal faith and spirituality. When the Catholic church ignored their concerns, a new generation of reformers urged believers who were unhappy with traditional religion to form a new church. This religious revolution, which split the church in western Europe and created several new churches, is called the **Reformation.**

The Origins of the Reformation

The first break with the Roman Catholic church occurred in Germany, where the political situation of the time helped lay the foundation for the Reformation. Unlike some countries during the early 1500s, Germany lacked a strong central government. Although Germany formed the core of the Holy Roman Empire, the empire included about 365 independent states. A number of imperial cities with a great deal of freedom existed side by side with principalities. The weak emperor could not control independent ideas about religion within the German states or keep the pope from demanding money.

Pope Leo X continued the rebuilding of St. Peter's Basilica in Rome. The pope charged an enthusiastic monk named Johann Tetzel with raising funds in northern Germany. Using a technique that had become accepted in the church, Tetzel asked people to buy **indulgences,** or pardons from punishment for sin.

Indulgences, part of the sacrament of penance, had originally been a reward for exceptionally pious deeds, such as helping a poor person go on a Crusade. Renaissance popes, however, sold indulgences simply to raise money.

This misuse of indulgences appalled the northern humanists, who wanted the church to become more spiritual. The concern grew especially strong in Germany, where political leaders gave sellers of indulgences great freedom of movement. One unhappy observer, Martin Luther, protested Tetzel's behavior in 1517.

Martin Luther's Protest

Martin Luther was born in 1483 to a moderately prosperous peasant family in the small mining community of Eisenleben in Saxony. Luther's family made sure he received a good education. Although he planned to become a lawyer, as a young man Luther considered himself a terrible sinner, and he desperately worried about the salvation of his soul. One summer day as he walked home, a sudden storm overtook him. A blinding bolt of lightning

struck close by. Luther cried out, "Help, dear Saint Anne, I will become a monk!" He gave up studying law in order to enter a monastery and spend his life in search of salvation.

Luther found that the church's methods for overcoming sin gave him no comfort. He did all the things required of him, including making a trip to holy places in Rome. Nothing, however, relieved his feeling of damnation.

One evening while Luther studied the Bible, a revelation, or new understanding, came to him. Suddenly Luther realized that all the ceremonies and good deeds made no difference in saving a sinner. The only thing that counted, Luther believed, was an inner faith in God. As long as people did

Learning from Pictures *This religious statue in a Renaissance village is being restored and blessed after it was mutilated during Reformation violence.*

Learning from Pictures *Even though Martin Luther had humble beginnings, he earned a degree from the University of Erfurt.*

not rely on their own actions, but believed God would save them, they could receive salvation by God's grace. Luther later described this revelation as the opening of the "doors into paradise."

On the basis of this new insight, he developed beliefs which later became known as Lutheranism. Luther believed that a simple faith could lead everyone to salvation. Thus he believed Tetzel committed a criminal act by asking poor people to give up their precious money for false promises of forgiveness.

In 1517 Luther challenged Tetzel by posting on the church door at Wittenberg **95 theses,** or statements, about indulgences. Sales of indulgences began to decline. The news quickly spread across Europe that a monk had publicly challenged the selling of indulgences.

Luther clearly considered himself a reformer within the main tradition of the church. Surprised at the widespread impact of his ideas, Luther had no wish to break with the church. But because his ideas challenged church practices, church leaders denounced him.

Luther's Break with the Medieval Church

By 1520 Luther openly disagreed with many church doctrines. The sole religious authority, he said, was the Bible. Popes and bishops should not tell a person what to believe. Luther believed that ceremonies did not counteract sins and that priests had no special role in helping people to salvation. God viewed all people with faith equally. Luther considered his church a "priesthood of all believers."

Taking advantage of the power of the printed word to spread ideas, in 1520 Luther wrote three publications that outlined his doctrines, attacked the pope, and called on all Germans to support his views. Pope Leo X declared Luther a heretic and excommunicated him.

To put the excommunication into effect, the new Holy Roman Emperor Charles V summoned Luther in 1521 to the Imperial Diet, a special meeting of the rulers of the empire, at the city of Worms (VOHRMZ). The emperor commanded Luther to renounce his ideas. When Luther refused, the Diet of Worms banished him from the empire and prohibited the sale or printing of his works. Luther was now considered an outlaw. Because Germany lacked a strong government, however, the powerless emperor could not enforce the Diet's ruling. The Elector of Saxony, Frederick the Wise, protected Luther and provided a place for him to hide while the uproar caused by the confrontation at the Diet of Worms died down.

In 1522, while under the protection of Frederick the Wise, Luther translated the New Testament of the Bible into German. By 1534 he had translated the entire Bible from Hebrew and Greek. Now all literate Christians in Germany could read the Bible for themselves.

Emperor Charles V continued to oppose Luther's doctrines and did what he could to keep Lutheranism from spreading. The princes who supported Luther protested the emperor's treatment of Lutheranism. Because of the protest, the followers of Luther and all later reformers came to be called "Protestants."

Luther's works continued to circulate, and his ideas continued to spread. In time he established a new church called the Lutheran church. Luther kept the organization of the new church as simple as possible. Lutheran clergy, called ministers, had no special powers; they served merely to guide their congregations to the true faith. Ministers also had less importance than Catholic priests had, because Luther permitted only the two sacraments mentioned in the Bible—baptism and communion—rather than the seven sacraments practiced in the Roman Catholic church.

The Spread of Protestantism

Luther had touched a very deep desire among the people of Europe for a simpler, more direct faith. Within a short time after he took his stand, many rulers in the German states established the Lutheran church within their domains. In addition, dozens of other reformers appeared who were dissatisfied with both the Roman Catholic church and the Lutheran church.

Charles V attempted to stop the spread of Protestantism, but for about 10 years he was too busy fighting the Ottoman Turks and the French. Then in 1544 he sent his armies against the Protestant princes in Germany for both religious and political reasons. The emperor won most of his battles with the princes, but in the end he could not defeat them or the Lutheran church. Charles V finally reached a compromise with the princes with the signing of the Peace of Augsburg in 1555.

One of the provisions of the Peace of Augsburg stated that each German ruler had the right to choose the religion for his state. His subjects had to accept the ruler's decision or move away. Almost all the princes of northern Germany accepted Luther's faith.

The sects. Hundreds of new religious groups emerged in much of Germany and Switzerland in the 1520s and 1530s. These groups, known as **sects,** did not form organized churches with clear-cut rules, authority, discipline, and membership. The sects were societies of a few people gathered together, usually with a preacher as their leader.

Most of the sects later died out. One that survived was known as the Anabaptists. The ancestors of the modern-day Baptist denomination, the Anabaptists believed that infants should not receive baptism because they could not understand the significance of the ceremony. Instead, they believed baptism should be offered only to adults who accepted the Anabaptist faith.

The Anglican church. In England the Protestant Reformation came about by entirely different means than in Germany. True, some Protestant ideas had filtered into England by the 1520s. The English also had a tradition of resistance to the popes that went back to John Wycliffe in the 1300s. However, King Henry VIII caused the break between England and the Roman Catholic church between 1529 and 1536. The break was a political move that had little to do with religious doctrine. In fact, before 1529 Henry VIII had defended the church so well against Martin Luther's ideas that the pope had granted Henry the title of "Defender of the Faith"—a title that the present monarch of England still bears.

England's break with Rome took place because Henry VIII wanted to divorce his wife, Catherine of Aragon, for not producing a male heir to the throne. The king believed that a continuing strong monarchy depended on having a son to succeed him. The royal couple had a daughter, Mary, but England had no tradition of a ruling queen. Furthermore, Henry had fallen in love with Anne Boleyn, a lady-in-waiting at the court, and wanted to be rid of Catherine.

Although the Catholic church forbade divorce, the pope could make exceptions. Pope Clement VII, however, refused to dissolve Henry's marriage. Clement made his decision in part because the troops of Catherine of Aragon's nephew, the Holy Roman Emperor Charles V, had captured and sacked Rome in 1527.

Pope Clement's refusal to grant the divorce infuriated Henry, who withdrew England from the Catholic church and created a new church. In a series of laws, Parliament created the Church of England with the king as its head. Although the Church of England, or Anglican church, slowly acquired some Protestant doctrines, it kept the organization and many of the ceremonial features of the Catholic church.

Of course, Henry VIII's church granted his divorce. The king married not only once again but five times. He finally fathered a son, the future Edward VI, although not by Anne Boleyn. More important, by creating the Anglican church and making England Protestant, he created a refuge for people who held the new religious ideas.

3 The Roman Catholic Church Met New Challenges

Lutheranism, the sects, and Anglicanism did not pose a major problem for the Catholic church except in a few areas of northern Europe. However, another reformer, the French-born John Calvin, and his followers challenged the Catholic church even in countries such as France, where the Catholic faith remained strong. After 1550 the followers of Calvin and a remarkable Catholic revival known as the Counter-Reformation dominated the religious conflict in Europe.

Calvin and Calvinism

Huldrych Zwingli (TSVING • lee), the vicar at the cathedral in Zurich in the early 1500s, was greatly influenced by the humanist writings of Erasmus, whom he met in 1516. Zwingli was leading the forces of religious reform in Switzerland when he heard about Luther's 95 theses. Zwingli and Luther met and discovered that they basically agreed on doctrine but disagreed about forms of worship and the use of images. Zwingli's supporters, for example, whitewashed wall decorations in churches.

In 1531 Zwingli died in a battle between Catholics and Protestants, but the French Protestant John Calvin carried on the work of the Reformation in Switzerland. Calvin founded a Protestant church that had a powerful and popular following. Calvin formulated a complete and clear set of beliefs, the *Institutes of the Christian Religion*, published in 1536. This work laid down exactly what the faithful ought to believe on every major question of religion. Calvin thus provided his followers, known as Calvinists, with a code that united them and gave them strength in the face of opposition and persecution.

In 1536 Calvin settled in the free city of Geneva, where Calvinism became the official religion. Calvin retained Luther's reliance on faith and on the Bible, but he placed a new emphasis on the community of believers. He believed that God had decided, at the beginning of time, who would be saved and who would be damned—a belief known as **predestination.** Those predestined (or chosen beforehand) for salvation were called "the elect." They formed a special community of people who were expected to live up to their position by following the highest moral standards. These standards included devoutness, dislike of frivolity, self-discipline, attendance at sermons for the purpose of denouncing one's sins, and complete dedication to God's wishes.

Calvin became almost all-powerful in Geneva. He made the city a **theocracy,** or a government ruled by a clergy claiming God's authority. By attaching such great importance to righteous living, Calvin regulated the conduct of the citizens down to the smallest detail. Laws prohibited dancing, card playing, showy dress, and profane language. Violation of these laws brought extremely severe punishment.

Calvinism soon spread to France, where its converts became known as Huguenots (HYOO • guh • nahts). Although France remained primarily Roman Catholic, by the mid-1550s Huguenots composed about one-fifteenth of the French population. Many high-ranking nobles and prosperous townspeople adopted the Calvinist doctrines. The Catholic French monarchs, who wanted a strongly united kingdom, considered the Huguenots a threat to national unity. To the kings of France, as to most European rulers of the time, a subject who differed with his or her king in matters of religion committed treason.

Beginning in 1562 the Huguenots defended themselves in a series of bloody civil wars with the Catholics. In 1598 King Henry IV issued a decree called the Edict of Nantes (NANTS), which gave the Huguenots freedom of worship and some political rights.

Calvinist minorities also existed in Poland and Hungary in eastern Europe. The Calvinists met with the most success, however, in Scotland, in the northern Netherlands, and in some parts of Germany. In these countries the strength of the Calvinists among ordinary people persuaded rulers to change their views. In a form called *Puritanism,* Calvinism would also play a vital role in England and in the English colonies of North America. By 1600 the Calvinist churches were the strongest of the many Protestant churches that had been established in Europe.

The Counter-Reformation

The Catholic church took a long time to realize that Protestantism posed a serious threat. The pope at first dismissed Luther's criticisms as "a monk's quarrel." However, a number of people within the Catholic church, including Erasmus, had called for internal reforms even before Luther appeared. As the breakup of the church continued, these reformers eventually convinced the pope of the drastic need for change.

In the 1530s a major reform effort known as the **Counter-Reformation,** or the Catholic Reformation, began in the Catholic church. Initially created to foster a more spiritual outlook in the Catholic church, the Counter-Reformation also clarified the doctrines of the church and pursued an aggressive campaign against Protestants.

Counter-Reformation tactics. Pope Paul III, who reigned as pope from 1534 to 1549, began the deliberate policy of reviving a more spiritual outlook in the Catholic church. He appointed devout and learned men as bishops and cardinals and required bishops to live and work in their home dioceses.

Pope Paul III brought the medieval Inquisition to Rome from Spain, where authorities had been trying and punishing so-called heretics since 1478. The Inquisition borrowed many of its cruel punishments, including burning at the stake, from governments, which had long used such methods against the worst criminals and traitors. The Inquisition viewed its chief purpose not as punishing Protestants but as keeping Catholics within the church.

In 1557 Pope Paul IV introduced another method of combating heresy. He established the *Index of Prohibited Books,* which forbade Catholics to read certain books. The Index was a recognition of the important part printing had played in spreading the Reformation. Before the printing press, the church could easily find and burn manuscript copies of heretical work. After printing was developed, it became far easier to prohibit what people could read than to try to burn all the books. The Catholic church maintained the Index as late as 1966, when the Second Vatican Council finally abandoned it.

The Council of Trent. Pope Paul III knew that no counterattack against Protestantism would be possible unless Catholic doctrines were well defined. Because church authorities often disagreed about complicated doctrines, such as the role of priests, heresy was difficult to oppose. In 1545 Paul summoned a council of church leaders to the Italian city of Trent. The Council of Trent, which met in three sessions from 1545 to 1563, defined official church doctrine with the same precision Calvin had used to define his faith.

Learning from Pictures Pope Paul III commissioned the Venetian painter Titian to record the Council of Trent in session.

BUILDING HISTORY STUDY SKILLS

Making Connections with History: Using Art to Understand Values

In 1508 Pope Julius II commissioned Michelangelo to paint the ceiling of the Sistine Chapel in Rome. Perched atop a new type of scaffolding that he had designed for the project, Michelangelo worked until 1512 to complete the commission. The result of his work has often been called the best example of Renaissance art in the world.

By studying the works of art produced during a specific period in history, we can learn much about the values of the people who lived during that period. Much of the art of the Middle Ages in western Europe, for example, reflects the religious nature of the society. The backgrounds of paintings focus not on real scenery but on heavenly backdrops, symbols, or gold reflections. People's faces reflect piety rather than individuality, and the figures themselves do not appear three-dimensional. Renaissance art retains religious themes while reflecting the humanistic and secular values of the time.

How to Use Art to Understand Values

To use art to understand values, follow these steps.
1. Identify when the artwork was produced. What historical period does the artwork represent?
2. Explain what major theme the artist is attempting to illustrate. Does the artwork depict a religious theme? Does it show daily life?
3. Identify the subject of the work of art and note the details.
4. Use the theme and the subject to help explain the values of the historical period in which the work was created.

Developing the Skill

The illustration at the bottom of this page shows details from Michelangelo's *The Creation of Adam* on the ceiling of the Sistine Chapel in Rome. The painting reflects the values of the southern Renaissance.

The painting has a religious theme, similar to paintings of the Middle Ages. The subject is God's creation of Adam; however, the details focus on the humanity and individuality of Adam. Michelangelo captures Adam at the very moment that God holds out his hand to give life to Adam, whom God has created in his own image. Michelangelo portrays Adam as weak—barely able to lift his arm to receive the gift of life from God. God, on the other hand, appears supremely powerful.

Based on the painting, what conclusions can you draw about values during the cultural explosion of the Renaissance? The painting shows the concern with religious themes, as does medieval art. Michelangelo, however, depicts figures as intensely human and realistic. The painting captures the beauty of Adam's face, his reflection of God's power and glory, and the heroic individualism at the beginning of life. The painting shows that during the Renaissance people were intensely religious. At the same time, they believed in the dignity of human beings.

Practicing the skill. Find an illustration of a modern work of art. How does this artwork reflect the values of modern society?

To apply this skill, see Applying History Study Skills on page 353.

The Council of Trent banned the sale of indulgences and tightened discipline for the clergy. In most cases, however, the council reaffirmed the importance of those doctrines that Protestants rejected. It emphasized the need for ceremonies, arguing that God ought to be worshiped with pomp and splendor. It noted that people must depend on priests because God granted forgiveness only through the church, not on personal merit. The council stressed that although everyone enjoyed free will, a person's fate after death depended not only on his or her faith, as Luther claimed, but on ceremonial church actions as well.

The decisions made at the Council of Trent worked effectively for the Catholic church. Many people found Protestantism's simplicity and austerity appealing, but many others took comfort from ancient ceremonies, beautifully decorated churches, the authority of priests, and the idea that one could perform good works to gain salvation. The Counter-Reformation thus had its effect. By the 1600s the Reformation had slowed down.

Soldiers of the Counter-Reformation

A new aggressiveness on the part of the Catholic church became a major reason for the success of the Counter-Reformation. This aggressiveness took many forms. Better-educated priests worked more forcefully for the church. The old religious orders reformed their rules, while new religious orders such as the Society of Jesus, known as Jesuits, formed.

Ignatius of Loyola founded the Jesuits in 1534. Loyola was a Spanish soldier who walked with a limp because his leg had been shattered fighting for Charles V against the French. Loyola's long period of recovery from his injury gave him time to read about the lives of Jesus and the saints. Like Martin Luther, Loyola wondered how he could attain salvation despite his sins. The answer came to him in a vision that he recorded in 1548 in his book *Spiritual Exercises.* According to Loyola, salvation could be achieved by self-discipline and a tremendous effort of will to do good deeds—in other words, by one's own actions. Loyola soon convinced six fellow students at the University of Paris—but not his fellow student John Calvin—to take religious vows and to follow him. In 1540 Pope Paul III recognized Loyola's group as an official order of the Catholic church.

Learning from Pictures *Loyola believed that educating and disciplining children were the best ways to prepare them for adult life.*

Loyola organized the Jesuits like a military body, with military discipline and the strictest obedience. He was the order's general; the members were his soldiers. The Jesuits quickly became the most disciplined and effective agents in spreading Catholicism. Within 16 years the Jesuits had 1,500 members. Their missions took them as far away as China and Japan. In Europe their preaching and their hearing of confessions slowed the spread of Protestantism in Poland, Germany, and France.

The Jesuits stressed education. They founded some of the best colleges in Europe, combining humanist values with theology to turn out learned, fervent supporters of the church.

The Jesuits opposed killing heretics because they believed that, given a chance to discuss religion with a Protestant, they could convert the person and thus gain a soul. Unfortunately, few other religious groups took such a nonviolent view in

EUROPEAN RELIGIONS, 1600

Lutheran	Roman Catholic
Calvinist	Orthodox
Anglican	Muslim
Roman Catholic with Protestant minorities	

AZIMUTHAL EQUAL AREA PROJECTION

Learning from Maps *The Reformation did not gain many converts in southern Europe. What religions were dominant in England? Sweden? Italy?*

the 1500s. The period from the 1530s through the mid-1600s was a time of devastating religious wars—sometimes interrupted by long truces—in Germany, Switzerland, France, and the Netherlands. Not until the mid-1600s, when the wars ended, could the results of the Reformation and the Counter-Reformation be fully seen.

Results of the Religious Upheaval

The most striking result of the great religious struggle of the 1500s was the emergence of many different churches in western Europe. In Italy, although Protestantism never made much headway as a broad movement, interest in church reform remained strong. Most of the people of southern and eastern Europe and the native population of Ireland remained firmly Catholic. France and the Netherlands had large numbers of Protestants. In Switzerland, northern Germany, England, Scotland, Norway, Denmark, and Sweden, various Protestant faiths became the established churches, backed by the central government (see map, this page).

Another far-reaching result of the Reformation and Counter-Reformation was a new interest in education. Many new universities had appeared in the 1400s and 1500s because of the humanists' concern for learning. After the mid-1500s enrollments increased dramatically, and the religious reformers supported this trend.

Protestants believed that people could find their way to Christian faith by studying the Bible. As a result, reading became increasingly important. In their schools the Jesuits and other new religious orders worked to strengthen the faith of the Catholics. Education did not mean tolerance of new ideas, however. Luther, Calvin, and their followers felt obliged to set up standards of faith and religious practice. Neither the Protestant nor the Catholic authorities permitted views that differed from their own.

The Reformation led to an increase in the power of national governments and to a decrease in the power of the pope. In Protestant regions each government took responsibility for the leadership of the official church. In Catholic areas rulers often obtained considerable control over their churches in return for remaining loyal to the pope.

SECTION 3 REVIEW

1. **Define**   predestination, theocracy, Counter-Reformation
2. **Identify**   Huldrych Zwingli, John Calvin, Pope Paul II, Ignatius of Loyola
3. **Locate**   Zurich, Geneva
4. **Understanding Ideas**   **(a)** What were the main ideas of John Calvin?   **(b)** Why did Calvinism spread so rapidly throughout Europe?
5. **Evaluating Ideas**   **(a)** Why was the Council of Trent summoned?   **(b)** What actions did it take?   **(c)** Do you think it was successful?
6. **Summarizing Ideas**   What role did the Jesuits play in the Counter-Reformation?

4 Popular Culture Took New Forms and Influenced Daily Life

The ideas that shaped the Renaissance, the Reformation, and the Counter-Reformation involved relatively few people. Ordinary people had their own views about themselves and the world around them.

Magic and Witchcraft

Most Europeans lived in small villages and spent their entire lives raising food and combating nature to survive. People close to the land could never predict what life would bring. They never knew when a cow might suddenly fall ill, when lightning might burn down a cottage, or when milk would fail to turn into butter.

The world of spirits. Since people considered God to be a distant, unknowable force, they thought spirits populated the world. Although good spirits abounded, demons, or devils, made life difficult. Because people believed in spirits, nothing was considered an accident. If lightning struck a house, a demon had caused it. If the butter would not form, a demon had prevented it. If a pitcher of milk spilled or a woman could not have a baby, the cause stemmed from the evil work of a demon. Many "superstitions," such as the belief that walking under a ladder might bring bad luck, began during this period.

Village priests usually tolerated these beliefs or at least pretended to ignore them. To the ordinary villager, the priest could offer no better explanations of how the world worked. The priest was likely to say that misfortune was God's will or God's punishment for sin. However, villagers often found certain of the priest's actions helpful. For example, every spring in a special ceremony, the priest would go out to the fields to bless the earth and pray for good crops. His blessing of a husband and wife at a wedding supposedly gave the couple a good start in life, and baptism was thought to safeguard a newborn child.

The priest, however, was not the only person to whom the villagers turned in times of trouble. They also looked to a so-called "wise" or "cunning" man or woman. This person, usually fairly old, was thought to have a special understanding of the way the world operated. Ordinary people would explain their problem—a lost ring, a cruel husband, a sick pig, or even an ominous sign—to these "wise" folk. Since people believed nothing happened by accident, anything unusual, such as a frog jumping into a fishing boat, was taken as a warning. The wise man or woman would explain what the warning meant and would sometimes recommend a remedy to ward off evil. The remedy might include a good-luck charm to wear, a strange spell to chant, or a potion to drink.

The belief in witchcraft. Wise people were often called "good witches." However, if their relationships with their neighbors turned sour, wise people might be accused of being "bad witches." In many cases the person accused of witchcraft would be an elderly widow. Perhaps too weak to work, with no husband or family to support her, she would be the most defenseless person in the community and an easy target for attack.

Stories about witches became more sensational as they spread throughout the countryside. Outrageous accusations were made; a person might be accused of flying on a broomstick, sticking pins into dolls, or dancing with the devil in the woods at night. When the majority of people believed an accusation, a wise person would be unable to convince a mob that the accusation was untrue. In some cases the priest might be asked to hold a ceremony to exorcise, or drive out, a demon that was thought to have taken over the witch's body. In other cases, the accused person might be dragged to a bonfire, tied to a stake, and burned, perhaps with the approval of the local lord.

"Witch hunting" signaled that the normal harmony and cooperation of village life had broken down. Witch hunting showed a dark side of the ordinary person's view of how the world worked.

An enormous outburst of witch hunting occurred in Europe in the mid-1500s and lasted for more than 100 years. Religious leaders were ready to attack witches, whom they regarded as rivals for their own position as advisers in times of trouble. Political authorities were eager to use law courts to prosecute witches. But as witch hunting began to lead to hysteria, religious and political authorities made a deliberate effort to slow down the prosecution of witches. After 1700 only a handful of cases came to trial, and very few of these trials resulted in the execution of the accused person.

Forms of Recreation

For most people, daylight meant work and night meant sleep. Because they had only crude farming methods, people needed all their daylight hours for raising food. Villagers limited evening activities because they were exhausted from working all day and because they could not afford the candles needed for light. Still, they did find time for relaxation.

Every village had a gathering place, such as the village green, where people came together to drink, sew, do simple chores, and tell stories. Some people played games such as skittles (a form of bowling) and dice. Occasionally traveling companies of actors passed through a village and put on a simple show. Holidays occurred frequently. The church decreed some holidays. Others honored a local saint or a local tradition. During the holidays, the

Games

People throughout the ages have played games for amusement and diversion. In some cultures, games gave children an opportunity to learn skills that would be useful to them in later life. In addition, games provided relief and relaxation from the routine of hard work in the home or the fields.

In ancient Greece a favorite game of children used knucklebones of sheep similar to the way that we use dice today.

More than 400 years ago, the Flemish artist Pieter Brueghel painted the large picture shown here (above). The picture is almost an encyclopedia of the games played by children of Brueghel's time. Brueghel loved to show the activities of peasants and working people. This painting depicts at least 80 games, including everything from marbles to hockey to ring-around-the-rosy and hoop rolling.

Many games are played by adults as well as by children. Baseball, for example, can be a pickup game in a neighborhood park or a schoolyard, or a competition among professional athletes. In recent years people of all ages have been fascinated by the new games and twists on old games that electronics and the computer have made possible.

The wide appeal of games to people of all ages may account for a feature of Brueghel's painting that has never been explained. Some people think that all the people playing games in his paintings look like adults. Perhaps Brueghel wanted to suggest that adult activities are no different from the games that children play. However, we cannot know for sure. What we do know is that many of these games and activities are still amusements today (left), for children as well as for grownups throughout the world.

343

villagers sometimes dressed up and would often put on their own ceremonies.

A favorite ceremony poked fun at the familiar sights and scenes of village life. In different parts of Europe, this ceremony had different names— "rough music," "charivari," "abbeys of misrule." The basic ceremony was always much the same. The young men of the village formed a procession and marched along, ridiculing the accepted customs or the foolish people of the village. For example, two young men would impersonate a couple known to everyone because the wife beat the husband. The impersonators would be pulled along in a cart and, as they passed by, the other villagers would jeer and hoot at them. The same sort of ridicule might be directed at an old man who had a young wife.

Sometimes the marchers had more serious targets; often they wanted to show how things would look if the poor or the weak had power. They would dress a fool like a bishop, or they would put the poorest man on a throne. At this point, the jokes lost their lightheartedness and symbolized the resentment the villagers felt about the hard lives they led and about the privileges of those who ruled them.

Violence and Protest in the Village

Villagers lived in close-knit communities. They could turn angrily on neighbors or on outsiders who seemed to upset their traditions or their sense of proper behavior. At times of hardship or famine, these neighbors or outsiders became the targets of more than jokes.

Sometimes people would burn an official's house and beat or kill the official. The women of the village often led these attacks. Since women were responsible for feeding their families, they felt strongly the impact of taxes or food shortages. Women dealt firsthand with bakers and other suppliers of food. If the women suspected that a baker hoarded bread or sent it elsewhere for higher profits, they might ransack the baker's shop.

The authorities sometimes tried to break up public gatherings because they feared the gatherings would result in violence. If the king sent troops to quiet a disturbance, the women would stand in the front line, because people knew that soldiers would be more reluctant to shoot at women than at men.

Printing and the Spread of Knowledge

In the 1500s the world beyond the village began to affect village life. Printed works and, in some areas, traveling preachers, inspired the changes.

Few ordinary villagers could read. Often even the village priest could not read. Nevertheless, soon after the invention of printing, publishers started selling popular works. Single printed sheets known as **broadsides** began to appear. A broadside usually had a picture and some verses that made fun of a favorite object of humor, such as monks. Books and broadsides arrived in the village in the packs of peddlers who brought goods from the outside world. When the villagers gathered around a fire in the evening, they enjoyed listening to someone read the latest book or a new broadside.

While romances and epics of the classical age appealed to the nobility, publishers quickly found subjects that appealed to country folk and produced cheap books for this new market. The most common books were **almanacs,** the ancestors of *The Farmer's Almanac* of today. Arranged like a calendar, an almanac made predictions about the weather and the prospects for growing crops. Almanacs also contained traditional superstitious advice about daily living, such as the warning that if you put on your left shoe before your right shoe in the morning, you would have bad luck all week. Almanacs became best-sellers because they reflected the beliefs about nature and life that made up the ordinary person's view of the world.

Soon after Luther's break with the church, new religious ideas reached the villages. Sometimes preachers came to visit. More often, different kinds of books came out of the peddlers' packs. Some of Erasmus's writings took the form of simple stories that attacked the church. Perhaps people heard the stories read in the evening at village get-togethers. Certainly the messages of Luther and Calvin traveled in this way, as did translations of the Bible.

As Protestants and Catholics battled for the loyalties of ordinary people, leaders of both sides encouraged the founding of primary schools in the villages and towns. Both Protestant and Catholic leaders believed that knowledge would lead a person to support the faith; but the leaders did not hesitate to encourage their followers to use force against their enemies, including religious opponents. It was better, many said, to kill a heretic than to allow a soul that was damned to live. In the

Learning from Pictures
By the end of the 1400s, Germany had become the center of printing in Europe. More than 60 German towns had printing presses.

long run, however, education assisted by the printing press helped people to understand that those of differing faiths could live together in peace and worship as they chose.

Changes in Daily Life

In addition to religious and political changes, economic changes resulted in a higher standard of living. The measure of the quality of life of a people or a country is called the **standard of living.** The standard of living is not strictly limited to income or economic output; it also includes working conditions, home life, the environment, health, and leisure.

Population and inflation. After the Black Death of the 1300s cut Europe's population by perhaps one-third, to about 50 million, the peasants prospered. Their goods and labor were in demand, and they enjoyed a relatively high standard of living.

By 1550, when the wars of religion had begun to ravage Europe, conditions changed. The population had grown tremendously, surpassing its pre-Black Death high of about 74 million in 1300 to reach about 78 million by 1550.

With the growth of the population came **inflation,** a rise in prices for goods. After 1550 wages could not keep up with the rise in prices, especially of farm products.

Diet. By 1700 half the population ate cereals rather than bread. White bread made from wheat was a rarity. Meat was scarce and expensive, but fish was not. Salt, needed to preserve fish and meats, had long been an important item of trade in Europe. Cheese and eggs, cheap sources of protein, were an important part of the diet everywhere. Western Europeans drank a lot of milk, but they complained that merchants sold watered-down milk. Butter, limited to northern Europe, was not widely used until the 1700s.

The spices that had earlier come to Europe from the East had been largely luxury items. By the 1500s the spice trade increased; Luther said Germany had more spices than grain. However, the spice trade declined by the late 1600s as traders introduced Europeans not only to new vegetables—asparagus, spinach, lettuce, green beans, tomatoes, and melons—but also to the new luxuries of coffee, tea, and chocolate.

Not everyone enjoyed the new and varied diets. Wealthy people in the cities could live better than

Learning from Pictures *This Brueghel painting captures a moment from a country dance—one of the few diversions for the common people.*

most of the peasants and the urban poor, who ate largely the same simple meals they had eaten for centuries.

The table settings and customs that we know today were not common in the 1300s and 1400s. People ate mostly with their fingers, picking what they wanted from one large dish which everyone shared. In some areas people ate from wooden plates. Guests brought their own knives; individual forks and spoons did not come into use until the 1500s. People drank beverages from a common cup passed around the table.

Housing. The growing cities of Europe began to use brick and stone in construction after the 1500s. In the countryside, however, peasants continued to live in thatched-roof cottages as they had in the Middle Ages.

Most rural houses were small. Because glass was expensive and sometimes not available even for the wealthy, most houses had shutters rather than glass windows.

Most peasants endured harsh living conditions. Their houses reflected the overwhelming poverty of rural life and contained few possessions—a large cooking pot, a table, a bench, and a few tools. Those who were fortunate had a bed; others slept on sacks filled with straw. Enmeshed in poverty, with little hope of escaping their fate, many peasants sought refuge in the cities.

The Decline of Traditional Culture

The migration from countryside to city further altered traditional popular culture. In the city, food came from a shop rather than from the fields. Local governments often helped out when disaster loomed. If famine struck, local government authorities distributed bread. If plagues broke out, the government set up hospitals and quarantines.

Gradually, more sophisticated attitudes began to take hold among the residents of towns and cities. In particular, people's understanding of how things happened in the world began to change. Demons and spirits no longer dominated views of daily life. People sought rational explanations for day-to-day events, and there now seemed less need for magic and "wise" folk. This development has been called the "disenchantment" of the world—the removal of "enchantment," or magic, from nature. One of the most important influences on the growth of this new attitude was the creation of modern science.

SECTION 4 REVIEW

1. **Define** broadside, almanac, standard of living, inflation
2. **Identify** "rough music"
3. **Understanding Ideas** Why were almanacs such popular books for country people?
4. **Analyzing Ideas** Why did the standard of living for many peasants decline after 1550?
5. **Interpreting Ideas** Why did traditional culture decline?

5 The Scientific Revolution Swept Europe

Unlikely though it may seem, belief in magic helped create the revolution in thinking that led to modern science. In the 1500s it was not only ordinary people who thought hidden forces controlled the world; the early scientists also hoped to discover what they called the secrets of nature. Alchemists were early scientists who used spells and magic formulas to try to change one substance into another—for example, lead into gold. Astrologers believed that the position of the stars in the sky affected human life.

What made the early scientists more than just alchemists or astrologers was that they had very general interests. They wanted to find out why stones fall, why the stars seem to move, or what

function the heart serves. They attempted to uncover the invisible structure of the universe by performing experiments and using mathematics—two methods that proved more effective than chants or spells.

The success of these early investigators in solving ancient problems in astronomy, physics, and anatomy created a new way of thinking that no longer relied on magic. This new way of pursuing knowledge is today called science. Before the 1600s the word *science* meant "knowledge." After the 1600s the meaning of the word evolved into the narrower, specialized meaning it has today.

Experiments and Mathematics

The Europeans' ideas about the universe had come to them from the ancient Greeks and Romans. People considered Aristotle and Galen to be absolute authorities who knew the truth. However, as the humanists unearthed more classical manuscripts, they found that even the respected writers of the ancient period did not all agree with each other. As people began to examine the world around them—for example, the movement of stars in the sky—they made observations that did not correspond to ancient beliefs.

As a result, people in the 1500s began to question traditional opinions. They began to observe and experiment for themselves. Most importantly, they described nature without any reference to previous beliefs. The foundation of this approach was the principle of doubt; nothing was to be believed unless it could be proved by experiment or mathematics. This approach became the new way of studying the world. The transformation in thinking that occurred during the 1500s and 1600s as a result of this new system of investigation is known as the **Scientific Revolution.**

The new approach relied heavily on the scientists' ability to conduct scientific experiments. Scientists did not have great research laboratories like those of today, where they could test and measure their experiments in a controlled environment. However, they did have newly invented instruments, such as the barometer, the microscope, and the thermometer, which improved their ability to observe and measure. At the same time, improved mathematical calculations became essential to investigations of nature. The method of inquiry that includes carefully conducted experiments and

347

mathematical calculations—to verify the results of the experiments—is called the **scientific method.**

Most Europeans in the 1500s and 1600s continued to believe in astrology, magic, and witchcraft. Educated people, however, began to adopt the scientific approach to evidence.

Astronomy, Physics, and Anatomy

New frontiers in science attracted people with interests in different fields of study. Five Europeans in particular—Copernicus, Kepler, Galileo, Vesalius, and Harvey—became pioneers of modern astronomy, physics, and anatomy.

Copernicus. For centuries astronomers had believed in the theory Ptolemy stated about A.D. 100: that the earth was the center of the universe and that the other planets and the sun moved around it. Ptolemy's theory is called the **geocentric** ("Earth-centered") **theory,** from the Greek words *geo*, meaning "Earth," and *kentron*, meaning "center."

In the early 1500s, a Polish scientist named Nicolaus Copernicus discovered ancient writings arguing that the sun was the center of the universe. This theory became known as the **heliocentric theory,** from the Greek word *helios*, meaning "sun." After a long period of study and observation, Copernicus became convinced that the heliocentric theory best explained all the known facts of astronomy of his time. In 1543 Copernicus published his conclusions in a book titled *On the Revolutions of the Heavenly Spheres*.

The book caused little excitement at the time. Few people believed in the heliocentric theory because it seemed to contradict the evidence of the senses. Anyone could "see" that the sun and planets moved around the earth. Anyone could "feel" that the solid earth did not move.

Learning from Pictures   *Along with his many other discoveries, the astronomer Galileo found that the sun's reflected light creates the moon's glow.*

Copernicus could not test and prove the heliocentric theory with the instruments or the mathematics available to him. Proof had to wait for the work of two later scientists, a German named Kepler and an Italian named Galileo.

Kepler and Galileo. Johannes Kepler, a brilliant mathematician who lived in the early 1600s, used mathematics to test the heliocentric theory of Copernicus. At first Kepler could not make the theory fit the observed facts. It is said that he calculated the problem 70 times before he discovered the error. Copernicus had written that the earth and other planets went around the sun in orbits, or paths in space, that were exact circles. Kepler discovered that the orbits were not exact circles but ovals called ellipses. Now other facts made sense. The heliocentric theory of the universe *could* be proved mathematically.

Because Kepler's proof could not be seen or observed, only mathematicians understood it. An Italian professor of mathematics, Galileo Galilei, provided proof that non-mathematicians could understand.

Galileo had read of a Dutch eyeglass-maker who put two glass lenses together in a tube to make a telescope. By looking through the telescope, a person could see distant objects more clearly. Galileo made a telescope for himself. By modern standards Galileo's telescope was only a small one, but it allowed him to see more of the heavens than anyone had ever seen. He could see the mountains and valleys of the moon and the rings around the planet Saturn. He observed sunspots. He proved that the earth rotated on its axis. His discovery that the moons of Jupiter revolve around the planet helped disprove the geocentric theory of Ptolemy by showing that not every heavenly body revolves around the earth.

Galileo published his findings in 1632 in a work called *Dialogue on the Two Great Systems of the World*. His work caused much more of an uproar than had the work of Copernicus. Many people now wanted telescopes. Many others believed telescopes to be the devil's work and refused to have anything to do with them. Scholars who accepted the authority of Ptolemy refused to believe the heliocentric theory. The church disapproved because the theory seemed to contradict the Bible. The church further insisted upon its right to condemn any scientific explanations that differed from Scripture. The Inquisition summoned Galileo to Rome, where it ordered him to renounce his belief that the earth moves around the sun. Galileo did so, but legend tells us that as he left the Inquisition room he said, "Yet it *does* move." The new ideas continued to advance.

Galileo was interested in physics as well as astronomy. Perhaps the most remarkable of his discoveries disproved the popular belief that heavier bodies fall faster than lighter ones. Galileo proved mathematically that, in the absence of air friction, all objects fall at the same speed regardless of their weight. This discovery laid the foundation for the modern science of mechanics, the study of matter in motion. Galileo further showed that the laws of physics operate in the heavens just as they do on Earth.

Vesalius and Harvey. Andreas Vesalius, a Flemish scientist, pioneered the study of anatomy. Vesalius refused to accept the descriptions of human muscles and tissues that Galen had written 1,400 years earlier. Vesalius conducted his own investigations to see how the human body was constructed. In 1543, the same year that Copernicus published his book, Vesalius published a landmark work in the history of medicine called *On the Fabric of the Human Body*.

Equally important was the work of William Harvey, an English physician. Using laboratory experiments, Harvey described the circulation of the blood through veins and arteries, the working of the body's most important muscle—the heart—and the function of the blood vessels.

The Triumph of Science

The effects of these discoveries were felt throughout Europe. So much had been accomplished. Knowledge had advanced so far that the scientists' methods became examples for everyone.

Just as new religious orders of the Counter-Reformation spread the revived faith in the church, scientific "orders" helped spread developments of the Scientific Revolution. Galileo belonged to the Accademia dei Lincei, founded in Rome in 1601. King Charles II granted a charter to the Royal Society in London in 1662, and Louis XIV established the French Academy of Sciences in 1666. The printing press helped the scientists just as it had the religious reformers. Most societies published journals so that scientists everywhere could read of work being done throughout Europe.

Learning from Pictures *Descartes wrote a book agreeing with Copernican theory, but he stopped its publication when Galileo was summoned by the Inquisition.*

Descartes. One of the most influential advocates of science was René Descartes (day • KAHRT), a French philosopher and scientist who lived from 1596 to 1650. Educated at a Jesuit college, Descartes decided to become a soldier in order to learn more about the world around him. He saw little fighting as a soldier and thus had ample time to think.

Descartes rejected everything based on anyone else's authority. He decided to start fresh with a new philosophy based on his own reason. In his *Discourse on Method* (1637), he argued that everything had to be proved. Descartes believed that the fact that he could think proved that he existed: "I think, therefore I am," he said. This was his first truth. From this basic truth, Descartes established a method of inquiry in which all thoughts would follow the clear, orderly progression of scientific reasoning.

Bacon and Pascal. Descartes's contemporary, the English philosopher Francis Bacon, put the case even more strongly. Science, Bacon thought,

would help humanity conquer nature and would end all the suffering in the world. Blaise Pascal, a French philosopher and scientist, opposed such ideas because they ignored the power of faith and the need to rely on God. Few people took notice of Pascal. Instead they made a hero of Isaac Newton, an English mathematician and philosopher who was considered the supreme example of the new reasoning powers of science.

Newton. In 1687 Newton, one of the greatest scientists of all time, published his *Mathematical Principles of Natural Philosophy.* It combined and related the contributions of Copernicus, Kepler, and Galileo. These early scientists had shown that the planets, including the earth, revolve around the sun. But they had not been able to explain *why* the planets moved as they did.

Newton's book contained his laws of motion and universal gravitation, which explained the movements of the planets. His law of universal gravitation states that all bodies attract each other with a force that can be measured. This force holds the whole system of sun and planets together by keeping them in their orbits.

Newton's work had a tremendous influence on the thinking of his own era and on all later scientific thought. The English poet Alexander Pope described Newton's great impact: "Nature and nature's laws lay hid in night; God said, 'Let Newton be,' and all was light."

Other scientific discoveries. New discoveries were made elsewhere in Europe. Working independently of each other, both Newton and Gottfried Wilhelm Leibniz (LYP • nits), a German philosopher and mathematician, developed calculus, a branch of mathematics that studies continuously changing quantities. A Dutch scientist, Anton van Leeuwenhoek (LAY • vuhn • hook), used the microscope, an invention of the late 1500s, to discover bacteria. The microscope enabled him to study a whole new world of life that could not normally be seen by the human eye.

Robert Hooke of England, who lived from 1635 to 1703, also worked with the microscope. The first person to identify cells in living matter, Hooke examined a thin slice of cork and noticed that it consisted of small rectangular "rooms." He called these "rooms" *cells* because they looked like the cells in which bees store honey.

The English scientist Robert Boyle is known as the founder of modern chemistry, the study of the

350

Learning from Pictures This painting, which hangs in the palace at Versailles, shows the establishment of the Academy of Science in 1666. It symbolizes the emphasis that people during the Enlightenment placed on science.

composition of materials and the changes they undergo. Another English chemist, Joseph Priestley, discovered the element later called oxygen. (Elements are the fundamental substances that make up matter.)

A French scientist, Antoine Lavoisier (luhv • WAHZ • ee • ay), named oxygen. Lavoisier showed that fire was not an element, as many had believed. He proved that fire was the result of the rapid combination of oxygen with another substance. Lavoisier also demonstrated that matter is indestructible; it can be changed from one form into another, but it cannot be created or destroyed. For example, when water boils, it does not disappear. It forms steam, which combines with the air. The water's form has changed, but the water has not disappeared. Lavoisier's discovery is known as the law of conservation of matter.

By the time Priestley and Lavoisier made their discoveries, the scientific point of view dominated European thought. Many Europeans of the 1700s spoke of their changing times as an "Age of Enlightenment."

SECTION 5 REVIEW

1. **Define** Scientific Revolution, scientific method, geocentric theory, heliocentric theory
2. **Identify** Nicolaus Copernicus, Johannes Kepler, Galileo, Andreas Vesalius, William Harvey, Isaac Newton, Joseph Priestley, Antoine Lavoisier
3. **Interpreting Ideas** How did Descartes and Bacon adapt the ideas of science to their writings?
4. **Summarizing Ideas** What were Newton's scientific contributions?

CHAPTER
14
REVIEW

Beginning
of Italian
Renaissance

Gutenberg's
printing
press

AD   ca. 1350   1450

Chapter Summary

The following list contains the key concepts you have learned about the Renaissance and the Reformation.

1. In the late 1300s, a literary and artistic movement known as the Renaissance swept Italy and then the rest of western Europe.
2. The humanists, such as Petrarch, Erasmus, and More, emphasized a renewed interest in classical learning, a critical spirit, and an enthusiasm for life in this world.
3. The Renaissance also inspired masterpieces in painting and sculpture.
4. In Germany, Martin Luther broke away from the Roman Catholic church and began the Protestant Reformation. The doctrines he developed, known today as Lutheranism, spread throughout northern Europe.
5. In England the Anglican church was founded under Henry VIII.
6. John Calvin's teachings spread from Switzerland to much of Europe.
7. In the 1530s the Roman Catholic church began a major revival effort known as the Counter-Reformation. At the Council of Trent, church leaders defined official doctrines. The church used the Inquisition and the Index to combat heresy. New religious orders, such as the Jesuits, tried to halt the spread of Protestantism.
8. The development of the printing press and the religious changes of the Reformation brought new ideas to the lives of ordinary people. New attitudes toward nature and toward the community took hold.
9. The Scientific Revolution transformed the methods and understanding of astronomy, physics, and anatomy. Europeans made important technological and scientific achievements. The new scientific attitude would dominate future European thought.

On a separate sheet of paper, complete the following review exercises.

Reviewing Important Terms

Supply the term that correctly completes each statement.

1. The creative movement that began in Italy in the mid-1300s and included a revival of interest in the classical learning of ancient Greece and Rome was called the _____ .
2. People who used classical texts to study grammar, rhetoric, history, and poetry were called _____ .
3. The painting technique in which painters make distant objects smaller than those in the foreground and arrange the objects in certain ways to make them appear more realistic is called _____ .
4. The religious revolution, which split the church in western Europe and created several new churches, is called the _____ .
5. The sale of _____ by the church in Germany sparked the Reformation.
6. Calvin made Geneva a _____ in which the government was ruled by a clergy claiming God's authority.
7. The _____ _____ marked the development of a new way of thinking about the world.
8. Nicolaus Copernicus caused controversy with the _____ _____ , which contradicted what most people believed about the relationship between the earth and the sun.

Developing Critical Thinking Skills

1. **Identifying Ideas**   Identify the historical figure who could have made each of the following statements.
   (a) "I think, therefore I am."
   (b) "The law of gravitation is a universal law."
   (c) "Salvation is possible through faith alone."
   (d) "All matter is indestructable."
   (e) "Individual actions can bring salvation."
2. **Evaluating Ideas**   Identify what each of the following people contributed to the humanist movement. Which person do you think made the greatest contribution? Why?   (a) Petrarch;   (b) Machiavelli;   (c) Erasmus;   (d) Shakespeare
3. **Summarizing Ideas**   Identify what Martin Luther's ideas were on each of the following: (a) salvation;   (b) the sacraments;   (c) the clergy.
4. **Interpreting Ideas**   (a) What was the Counter-Reformation?   (b) What did it try to accomplish?   (c) How successful was it?
5. **Understanding Ideas**   During the time of the Reformation, most people in Europe lived in small villages.

ca. 1530
Beginning of the
Counter-Reformation

1534
Founding
of Jesuits

Luther's
95 theses

Machiavelli's
The Prince

Council
of Trent

Galileo's
Dialogue

Newton's
*Mathematical
Principles of
Natural Philosophy*

1513 1517   1545   1563   1632   1687
1516 1521   1543 1555   1637

More's *Utopia;*
Erasmus's
In Praise of Folly

Diet
of Worms

1536
Calvin's
*Institutes of
the Christian
Religion*

Copernicus's *On
the Revolutions
of the
Heavenly Spheres*

Peace of
Augsburg

Descartes's
*Discourse
on Method*

Describe how villagers explained the natural events that occurred in their lives.

6. **Analyzing Ideas** How did the Scientific Revolution change the way people viewed themselves and their world?

Relating Geography to History

Study the map of Europe on pages R12–R13 in the Atlas. **(a)** Why was Italy ideally suited to establish trade with the Middle East? **(b)** How did the ideas of the Italian Renaissance spread to northern Europe?

Relating Past to Present

1. A Renaissance person is defined as one who is knowledgeable in both science and art. **(a)** Give an example of someone in today's world who might be called a Renaissance person. **(b)** What are the advantages and disadvantages of this combination of knowledge for an educated person?

2. **(a)** How did the invention of printing revolutionize the spread of knowledge and ideas in Europe during the time of the Reformation? **(b)** Describe how radio and television have changed our understanding of the world.

Applying History Study Skills

Before completing this activity, review Building History Study Skills on page 338.

Look again at Michelangelo's *The Creation of Adam* on page 338. Then look at the statue of Hermes by Praxiteles in column 2.

1. How do these works of art show similarities between the values of Greek and Renaissance societies?
2. How do they show differences?

Investigating Further

1. **Writing a Report** Leonardo da Vinci was one of the greatest geniuses of the Renaissance. Prepare a written report on Leonardo's talents and achievements.

You may use the following sources: "The Scope of Genius" in John Hale's *The Renaissance* (Time-Life Books) and "Leonardo da Vinci" in *Horizon Book of the Renaissance* (American Heritage).

2. **Preparing an Oral Presentation** The invention of the printing press caused a revolution in communication. Find out more about Gutenberg's invention and its development. Sources include: Douglas McMurtie's *The Book: The Story of Printing and Bookmaking* (Oxford University Press) and "The Birth of Printing" in Edith Simon's *The Reformation* (Time-Life Books). Present your findings to the class.

3. **Writing a Biography** In encyclopedias or biographies, read more about one of the Renaissance artists or writers that you read about in this chapter. Prepare a short biography of that person. Be certain that your biography discusses the person's major achievements.

353

Strong Monarchies Helped European States Expand

Place   Europe, Asia, North and South America

Time   1400–1800

3.7 mil. BC   4000 BC   AD 2100

Significance

In 1400 Europe's monarchs lacked the wealth and power of the rulers of China, India, Africa, the Americas, and even Europe's neighbor, the Ottoman Empire. Less than 400 years later, however, Europe had become the dominant civilization on earth. This remarkable transformation of relationships among the world's peoples is one of the most significant developments in history.

European expansion occurred only after technological, economic, and political changes had taken place in Europe. Central governments grew larger and more powerful, while local governments became weaker. By the 1600s a system of government called **absolute monarchy** had become more popular in Europe than those systems that favored representative government or local self-rule. In an absolute monarchy, the ruler determines policy without consulting either the people or their representatives.

Terms to Define

absolute monarchy	subsidy
mercantilism	triangular trade
favorable balance of trade	Middle Passage
tariff	balance of power

People to Identify

Vasco Núñez de Balboa	Peter the Great
Ferdinand Magellan	Catherine the Great
Ferdinand I	Maria Theresa

Places to Locate

Isthmus of Panama	St. Lawrence River
Versailles	Moscow

Questions to Guide Your Reading

1 What technological, political, and economic forces allowed European countries to embark upon overseas expansion?
2 Why did the Portuguese fail to maintain their large empire?
3 How did Spain's huge empire in the New World affect economic and political developments in Spain itself?
4 How did the kings of France go about establishing an absolute monarchy?
5 How were the reigns of Catherine the Great, Maria Theresa, and Frederick the Great similar?

◀ *A royal summit, Louis XIV and Philip IV*

Archaeologists believe the recently discovered ruins on Haiti's north shore may be those of the first Spanish settlement in North America—Christopher Columbus's lost colony, La Navidad. Kathleen A. Deagan, confident that her search for the colony has ended, writes:

❝*J*ust before midnight on Christmas Eve, 1492, a sleepy helmsman gave the tiller of Christopher Columbus's flagship, Santa Maria, to the ship's boy. . . . The hapless lad promptly ran the ship onto a coral reef off the north coast of Haiti. . . . Attempts to free the vessel failed, the planking opened, and the Admiral abandoned her for Niña. . . .

Columbus appealed for help to Guacanagari, the Indian . . . chief, whose village was about four miles from the wreck. The Indians helped unload supplies, . . . dismantle the ship's timbers and boards, and carry them . . . to the village. . . . Thus the tiny settlement—named for the infant child of Christmas, La Navidad—was established. . . . We can only speculate upon what happened next. When Columbus returned 11 months later, he found the settlement burned and all his men dead. . . . The site was forgotten for nearly 500 years. Now, . . . our team . . . believes we have found it again. ❞

Christopher Columbus was only one of many Europeans who spread Western civilization throughout the world.

1 Europeans Had New Reasons for Exploring Overseas

Before the 1400s Europeans had not been totally isolated. Marco Polo traveled to China, the crusaders tried to wrest the Holy Land from the Arabs, and other Europeans engaged in the spice trade. But most Europeans had neither the interest nor the ability to explore foreign lands. By the late 1400s, however, technology, politics, economics, and society had changed significantly. These changes sparked European interest in foreign lands and provided the opportunity to explore them. Soon adventurous Europeans discovered new routes to these lands. These discoveries opened up an era of exploration that lasted for the next 400 years.

Technological Advances

The first European explorers wanted to reach Asia to acquire spices, silks, and jewels—very valuable trading items, even in small amounts. A ship filled with spices had a cargo worth more than 100 times that of a ship filled with timber or grain.

Spices, silks, and jewels came mainly from India, China, and the islands of Southeast Asia. To compete successfully with powerful Arab and local traders, the Europeans needed better maps, navigation instruments, ships, and guns—in short, a more advanced technology.

Mapmaking. Mapmaking improved during the Renaissance because of the growing interest in the writings of ancient geographers and the desire for pictorial accuracy. Most scholars knew—as Ptolemy's maps had shown—that the world was round. Renaissance mapmakers added information

Learning from Pictures   The Dutch painter Vermeer painted this mapmaker at work. In the 1400s what did most scholars believe about the shape of the earth?

about Africa and Asia. Their early globes showed Madagascar, Java, and Japan, but not, of course, North and South America. Observers could see that the distance from Europe to Asia was shorter to the west—across the Atlantic Ocean—than to the east. Daring sea captains soon set out on their travels, opening up new worlds scarcely dreamed of before. In the meantime Italian sailors prepared even more accurate charts of coastlines. These charts were essential for explorers, who used them to record their routes so that others could follow.

Navigation instruments. Just as important, navigation instruments helped make it possible for ships to sail out of the sight of land without losing their bearings. One such instrument was the **compass.** As early as the 1100s, European navigators had learned that an iron needle rubbed against a piece of lodestone—a kind of magnetic rock—would become magnetized and turn toward the north. At first they floated the magnetized needle on a piece of cork in water. In the 1300s, by fixing the needle to a card marked with directions, they created a true compass.

Another important navigation instrument, the **astrolabe,** applied astronomy and geometry to navigation and allowed sailors to determine the relative height of stars and planets. Using this information they could calculate a ship's **latitude,** its distance north or south of the equator.

New ships. Long-distance exploration also required improvements in ships. In 1400 the Arabs, the Indians, and the Chinese were making better ships than the Europeans, but by 1600 European ships were the best in the world.

Before and even during the 1400s, long ships called **galleys** conducted most European coastal trade. Slaves or prisoners of war strained at the 50 or 60 oars that propelled the galley. In deeper ocean waters, traders used sailing ships. Before the late 1400s, however, these small and clumsy ships could sail only in the direction in which the wind blew.

In the late 1400s, ship designers in Portugal and Spain made important improvements. They reduced the width of ships in proportion to their length, made smaller and different-shaped sails, and moved the location of the rudder—a device used for steering—from the side to the rear, or stern, of the ship. These improvements allowed ships to sail against the wind, to travel quickly, and to be steered with reasonable accuracy.

A Mariner's Astrolabe

The process of determining a vehicle's position and directing its movement is called navigation. The word *navigation* comes from two Latin words—"navis," meaning "ship," and "agere," meaning "to drive."

The explorers of the 1500s sailed the oceans with only a few simple instruments such as the compass and the astrolabe to guide them. But with these, along with the stars and the sun, they navigated the world. They could plot and hold a course, measure their progress, and estimate their position in relation to land.

The bronze astrolabe shown here was an instrument used to measure latitude. It has an outer edge divided into degrees, and a movable center bar with pointers on each end. Grasping the astrolabe by the ring at the top, the viewer sighted along the bar, rotating it until one of the pointers aimed at the sun. The figure at the other end of the instrument indicated the correct latitude. This is the origin of the expression "shooting the sun."

The astrolabe became obsolete with the invention of the sextant, an instrument navigators use to measure the angular distance between two points such as the horizon and the sun.

The cannon. Europeans first used the cannon in war during the 1400s. Until this time naval warfare had consisted of ramming and boarding an enemy vessel. Shipboard cannons and the handguns sailors carried now helped Europeans defeat the vastly larger navies of their enemies.

Political Change

Technological advances alone could not have made successful explorations possible. Money provided by the stronger and more ambitious central governments that emerged in Europe in the 1400s and 1500s financed these expeditions.

By the 1400s and 1500s, dynastic ambitions and rivalries between countries often made the central governments enthusiastic supporters of new exploration and colonization. And governments appealed to the patriotism of their citizens to help build empires.

Economic Change

The development of new economic policies and methods also played an important part in carrying out exploration. In some cases developments that had already begun, such as the use of money and the services provided by banks, simply changed to accommodate the needs of exploration. In other cases the old methods of doing business became inadequate, and Europeans worked out new ones. The changes in the European economy were so extensive that some historians have referred to the period from 1400 to 1750 as the **Commercial Revolution.**

Standardized money. Money, essential to growth, had been in short supply. Also, its value had not yet been standardized—that is, the value of certain coins might change depending on the amount of precious metal used to make them. Until the 1400s the scarcity of precious metals from which coins were made, the great variety of coins in use, and the lack of a fixed value for money handicapped Europeans.

During the 1400s, however, Europeans developed standard systems of money. The Italian cities led the way in minting coins that had a fixed value. The gold florin of Florence and the ducat (DUHK • uht) of Venice became very dependable. Later, the Spanish kings used silver and gold shipped from the New World to pay debts owed their bankers. These payments helped relieve the shortage of precious metals in Europe.

The standardization of money made economic transactions much more reliable. Anyone who accepted a florin in payment for goods or services knew that the money was worth a certain amount and could be used to buy other goods or services.

357

Money

In early times any object that everyone accepted as valuable could serve as money. The Romans, for example, paid their soldiers with what was then a prized commodity, salt. From this custom we get the phrase "worth one's salt." Other items that have been used as money include shells, tobacco, feathers, and whale teeth.

Probably the first money made specifically as a medium of exchange appeared in China during the Shang dynasty. Because farmers often had traded spades and knives for other goods, this ancient money was shaped like spades.

Increasingly, rare metals, especially gold and silver, came to be used as money. They were fashioned into coins, which could be carried easily.

Governments jealously guarded the right to make coins and to establish their value. Often, however, government officials would clip pieces

off coins. Then they would melt these pieces down to make more coins so that they could buy more. During the 1500s this process brought on inflation and was stopped only when milled, or grooved, edges were put on coins (above). These edges enabled people to see at once if the coins had been clipped.

About this time, too, paper money became more common. The Chinese, the first to use both paper and movable type, were also the first to use paper money, about the year A.D. 1060. Paper money was even more convenient than coins and became especially useful as long-distance trade grew increasingly important.

This in turn encouraged the growth of international trade and banking. The large sums that banks now accumulated made it possible for them to loan money to governments and major trading companies who financed large overseas expeditions.

Joint-stock companies. Individual merchants often combined their resources in a new type of business organization called a **joint-stock company.** Such a company raised money by selling stock, or shares, in the company to investors. These shareholders became co-owners. Shareholders divided profits according to the numbers of shares of stock they owned. Joint-stock companies raised large amounts of money from people willing to invest in their activities.

Despite their contributions to the Commercial Revolution and the growth of capitalism, no Italian city-states such as Florence or Venice financed explorations or established overseas colonies. As the age of exploration began, economic leadership in Europe shifted. Trade that previously had been concentrated in the Mediterranean area and southern Germany now moved to the Atlantic nations. So in Portugal, Spain, and France, monarchs and their advisers not only financed voyages but also controlled exploration and the building of overseas empires. These monarchs understood what the great merchant families of Venice, Genoa, Florence, and Augsburg had not—that overseas possessions could bring power to their dynasties and great riches to their countries.

Mercantilism

The political and economic changes associated with overseas expansion also contributed to a new economic theory called **mercantilism.** According to this theory, the world contained only a fixed amount of wealth. To increase its share, a country had to take some wealth away from another country. More wealth meant more power. Therefore, a country's government had to do all it could to increase the country's wealth. For this reason many countries sought overseas possessions.

Balance of trade. A nation could gain wealth by mining gold and silver either at home or in its colonies. It could also get these precious metals by selling more goods than it bought in foreign countries, thus creating a **favorable balance of trade.** By bringing money into a country, a favorable balance of trade strengthened the country itself and weakened its foreign rivals, who paid for the goods they bought and thus depleted their supplies of gold and silver.

To gain a favorable balance of trade, a nation could take several measures:

(1) It could reduce the amount of goods imported into the country by imposing **tariffs,** or import taxes, on foreign goods. The importer paid the tax and added that amount to the selling price of the goods. The higher price discouraged people from buying foreign goods.

(2) It could try to increase the value of its exports. Manufactured goods were the most valuable kind of exports because they sold for more money than raw materials; woolen cloth, for instance, brought more than raw wool. Therefore, mercantilist nations encouraged manufacturers, exporters of manufactured goods, and shipbuilders. In many cases governments made grants of money called **subsidies** to help establish new industries and build ships.

(3) It could try to make itself self-sufficient by producing everything it needed, plus a surplus of goods for export. The self-sufficient nation did not have to depend on foreign countries, which were always rivals and might at any time become active enemies. The desire for self-sufficiency helped to stimulate the race for colonies.

The role of colonies. Colonies played an important part in mercantilism. Those that produced gold and silver were the most desirable. Next best were those which produced raw materials that could not be produced at home. By buying these materials in its colonies, a nation could avoid buying from a foreign rival. Thus money did not go out of the nation or empire, and it maintained complete control of its wealth.

Finally, mercantilist theory put a high value on colonies as markets for the manufactured goods of the home country. Governments passed strict laws to prevent colonists from buying foreign manufactured goods or selling their raw materials anywhere except the home country. In this way the home country kept strict economic control of its colonies.

Social Change

Government policies alone could not create a willingness to explore and settle overseas. Because of the changes in society, however, exploration and resettlement abroad became attractive to some people.

The great increase in the population during the 1400s and 1500s caused overcrowding on the land. As a result, many people sought better opportunities. One such prospect was a life at sea. Sailors were paid, fed, and given a place to stay. Other adventurous people hoped that, despite harsh living conditions in the colonies, settling overseas would give them a fresh start and a better life.

Many more people went to the colonies hoping to reap quick profits. Tales of gold and jewels and of fabulous cities like the legendary El Dorado in South America persuaded thousands that easy wealth lay overseas.

Others—like the French Huguenots and the English Puritans—went overseas to escape religious or political persecution at home. Those who went for other reasons, such as to spread Christianity or to expand Europe's trade, comprised a small minority. On the whole, hardships caused by social change prompted people to participate in Europe's expansion.

Sometimes a combination of reasons caused people to seek refuge in new lands. However, regardless of the reasons, thousands resettled during this period.

SECTION 1 REVIEW

1. **Define** absolute monarchy, compass, astrolabe, latitude, galley, Commercial Revolution, joint-stock company, mercantilism, favorable balance of trade, tariff, subsidy
2. **Summarizing Ideas** Describe the improvements in navigational instruments and ship construction that made long-range exploration possible.
3. **Analyzing Ideas** Why was the standardization of money important?
4. **Interpreting Ideas** What role did colonies play in mercantilism?
5. **Synthesizing Ideas** What were some of the reasons people left Europe to settle in the colonies?

Arctic Circle

Greenland

Baffin and Bylot, 1616

Hudson Bay

Hudson and Bylot, 1610–1611,

John Cabot, 1497

ENGLAND

NORTH
AMERICA

John Cabot, 1498

Cartier, 1535–1536

NETHERLA

FRANCE

*Champlain,
1603–1615*

Newfoundland

*Marquette and
Joliet, 1673*

Nova Scotia

Champlain, 1603–1615

Rodríguez and Espinoza, 1565

*La Salle,
1678–1680*

Hudson, 1609

PORTUGAL SPAIN

Lisbon

AZORES

Columbus, 1492–1493

Seville
Palos

*Coronado,
1540–1542*

St. Augustine

Verrazano, 1524

MADEIRA IS.

Tropic of Cancer

*De Soto,
1539–1542*

MEXICO

Drake, 1577–1580

Columbus, 1492–1493

Havana

BAHAMAS

Tenochtitlán
(Mexico City)

*Cortés,
1519*

YUCATÁN
PENINSULA

Cuba
San Salvador

Hispaniola

CAPE VERDE IS.

Acapulco

Villalobos, 1542–1544

PACIFIC

OCEAN

*Balboa,
1509–1513*

ISTHMUS OF
PANAMA

*Pizarro,
1531–1533*

Quito

*Orellana,
1541–1543*

ATLANTIC

OCEAN

BENI

Gulf of Guine

Magellan, 1519–1522

Vespucci, 1501

Drake, 1577–1580

Cabo (for Magellan), 1519

Da Gama, 1497–1499

Drake, 1577–

Equator

Mendaña and Quiros, 1595–1596

Cajamarca

Lima

PERU

SOUTH
AMERICA

BRAZIL

Bahia

Da Gama, 1497–1499

Magellan, 1519–1522

*Almagro,
1535–1537*

Rio de Janeiro

Cabral, 1500

Tropic of Capricorn

Drake, 1577–1580

Valdivia, 1540–1547

Buenos
Aires

Vespucci, 1501

Strait of Magellan

Cape Horn

N

| 0 | 1000 | 2000 Miles |
| 0 | 1000 | 2000 Kilometers |

Spanish-Portuguese
Demarcation line by the
Treaty of Tordesillas, 1494

Antarctic Circle

became ice bound here, for the winter.

Barents and Linschoten, 1596-1597

Borough, 1556

Barents and Linschoten, 1594-1595

Willoughby and Chancellor, 1553-1554

Moscow

ASIA

EUROPE

CHINA

JAPAN

PACIFIC OCEAN

Rodríguez and Espinoza, 1565

ARABIA

Hormuz

Diu

INDIA

AFRICA

Calicut
Cochin

Ceylon

Strait of Malacca

PHILIPPINES
Death of Magellan, 1521

Magellan, 1519-1522

Villalobos, 1542-1544

Malindi
Mombasa

Zanzibar

Kilwa

Luanda

Da Gama, 1497-1499

Cabral, 1500

INDIAN OCEAN

Malacca

Borneo

Sumatra

Batavia

Java

EAST INDIES

SPICE IS. (MOLUCCAS)

Mendaña and Quiros, 1595-1596

Drake, 1577-1580

Tasman, 1642-1643

Tasman, 1642-1643

Drake, 1577-1580

Tasman, 1644

Cabral, 1500

Da Gama, 1497-1499

Cano (for Magellan), 1519-1522

AUSTRALIA

Cape of Good Hope

Tasman, 1642-1643

EUROPEAN EXPLORATION, 1487–1682

- Portuguese exploration
- Spanish exploration
- French exploration
- English exploration
- Dutch exploration
- • Cities
- Spanish territory, 1600
- Portuguese territory, 1600

Spanish-Portuguese Demarcation line by the Treaty of Tordesillas, 1494

MILLER CYLINDRICAL PROJECTION

ANTARCTICA

2 Portugal and Spain Took the Lead in Exploration

Explorers sailing under the flags of Portugal and Spain made the first European voyages into unknown waters. Driven by curiosity and by religious and economic aims, and backed by their governments, they made discoveries throughout the world. The ventures of these early pioneers served as the foundation for future empire-building.

Portugal and Prince Henry

Perched at the southwestern corner of Europe, the small nation of Portugal was one of the first to become seriously interested in exploration. Prince Henry the Navigator, a member of the Portuguese royal family, was largely responsible for this interest. Henry wanted to start a crusade in Africa—in which he would join forces with Prester John, the king of a legendary Christian kingdom—to encircle and outflank the Muslims. He also wanted to acquire a share of the African slave trade, then controlled by the Muslims, and to begin trading with Asia.

To help accomplish these goals, Prince Henry founded a school that trained navigators. After 1418 his navigators began a series of explorations westward into the Atlantic and southward along the west coast of Africa. As they slowly worked their way south, they claimed for Portugal a number of islands, including the Azores in the Atlantic Ocean. Farther to the south, below the desert region of the Sahara, the Portuguese began to trade for slaves, gold, and ivory.

Further explorations brought the Portuguese even greater gains. In 1488 Bartolomeu Dias (DEE • ahsh) sailed around the Cape of Good Hope at the southern tip of Africa. Then in 1498 Vasco da Gama sailed beyond the Cape of Good Hope eastward across the Indian Ocean to India (see map, pages 360–61). He returned home with a fabulous cargo of spices and jewels that paid for his trip 60 times over.

Da Gama's successful voyage represented a tremendous stroke of good fortune for the Portuguese. Their ships could now sail to India and the East Indies and bring back rich cargoes of Asian goods. The direct ocean route saved the Portuguese money

Learning from Pictures *The Ciboney Indians welcome Christopher Columbus to Cuba in 1492. What country sponsored Columbus's voyage?*

because they could buy goods directly from Asia rather than from Arab traders or Italian merchants who charged very high prices. Ships could also carry cargoes more cheaply than could wagons or animals traveling overland. In addition, ships did not have to pay the tolls that frequently were levied on overland transportation.

Christopher Columbus

Spain, too, became interested in the search for new trade routes. Its rulers, King Ferdinand and Queen Isabella, decided to finance a voyage by Christopher Columbus, an Italian navigator. Inspired by the writings of Marco Polo and influenced by Ptolemy's description of the round earth, Columbus believed he could reach Asia quickly by sailing westward.

In August 1492 Columbus set sail from Palos, Spain, with three small ships—the *Niña,* the *Pinta,* and the *Santa Maria*—and crossed the Atlantic. In October his small fleet landed on a tiny island that Columbus named San Salvador (see map, pages 360–61). After visiting several other islands in the area, Columbus returned triumphantly to Spain in the spring of 1493 to report his discoveries. Because he believed the islands lay off the east coast of India, Columbus called them the "Indies" and their inhabitants "Indians." He had discovered the islands that were later to be known as the West Indies. Although Columbus made three more voyages to the "Indies" between 1493 and 1504, he believed until his death that he had landed off the coast of Asia.

Dividing the New Lands

In the early days of exploration, Spain and Portugal often claimed the same newly discovered lands. Finally, they agreed to let Pope Alexander VI settle their disputes. In 1493 he drew on a world map a line of demarcation down the middle of the Atlantic Ocean, from the North Pole to the South Pole. He granted Spain the rights to all newly discovered lands west of the line. Portugal could claim all those to the east of the line. A year later, the Treaty of Tordesillas (tawrd • uh • SEE • yuhs) between Spain and Portugal moved the line farther west (see map, pages 360–61).

Obviously, because the earth is round, if either Spain or Portugal had continued to explore and claim lands in the direction allowed, their claims would have eventually overlapped on the other side of the world. For practical purposes, however, the pope's line of demarcation worked well. For example, a Portuguese captain, Pedro Álvares Cabral (kuh • BRAHL), reached the east coast of South America by accident in 1500. He had sailed for India along da Gama's route, but strong winds had blown him far off course, forcing him westward. When he claimed what is now Brazil for Portugal,

Spain honored his claim because he had landed east of the line fixed by the Treaty of Tordesillas.

In 1529 Spain and Portugal agreed to extend the line completely around the globe. Thus Spain took control of most of Central and South America, while Portugal exploited Asia.

Vespucci, Balboa, and Magellan

Other explorers followed Columbus westward. Between 1497 and 1503, another Italian, Amerigo Vespucci (veh • SPOO • chee), took part in several Portuguese expeditions across the Atlantic. Vespucci became convinced that the land he saw was not part of Asia but was instead what he called a "New World." After reading Vespucci's writings, a German geographer named the new land America after Vespucci (whose first name, in Latin, is *Americus*).

In 1513 a Spaniard named Vasco Núñez de Balboa crossed the Isthmus of Panama and looked out on a vast ocean, which he called the South Sea and claimed for Spain. It now seemed clear that the

Learning from Pictures *Amerigo Vespucci uses an astrolabe as he works on maps. What did Vespucci conclude about the land he saw across the Atlantic?*

What If?
Christopher Columbus
Christopher Columbus reached the Americas and claimed the lands he discovered for Spain. How might the history of the world have been different if Columbus had sailed as a representative of the English monarch rather than the Spanish monarch?

New World really was a distinct landmass, separate from Asia. Ferdinand Magellan, a Portuguese navigator sailing for Spain, proved it.

In 1519, with five ships, Magellan set out from Spain, crossed the Atlantic to South America, and sailed along its eastern shore until he reached the southernmost tip. After passing through the strait now named for him, Magellan found himself in a great ocean. Because it appeared to be very calm, he named it the Pacific Ocean, from the Latin word *pacificus,* meaning "peaceful." This was the same ocean Balboa had named the South Sea.

Magellan sailed westward across the Pacific and reached the Philippine Islands, claiming them for Spain. There, in 1521, he died in a fight with the islanders. The crew sailed on. Only one ship and 18 crew members survived to finish the historic voyage, returning to Spain in 1522. For the first time, people had sailed completely around the earth.

Portuguese Expansion

After the voyages of Dias and da Gama, the Portuguese pursued Henry the Navigator's dream of dominating trade with Asia.

The Portuguese in the East. About 1510 the Portuguese conquered part of the southwest coast of India, making the port of Goa (GO • uh) their administrative center. From India they attacked and conquered Malacca (muh • LAHK • uh), a city on the southwest coast of Malaya. From there they moved east to take the fabled Moluccas (muh • LUHK • uhz), a group of islands that Europeans called the Spice Islands because cloves, nutmeg, and other spices grew there in abundance.

The Portuguese next gained footholds in China and Japan. They then turned their attention to the island of Ceylon (now Sri Lanka), off the southeast coast of India, adding it to their chain of trading bases. With its key location between Goa and Malacca and its tea and spices, Ceylon helped the Portuguese dominate European trade with the East Indies.

The Portuguese in the New World. Portugal's colonies in Asia, though important, were small trading bases. In the New World, however, the Portuguese founded a much larger colony in Brazil. They divided this huge country into enormous agricultural estates on which they grew sugar for export.

The Slave Trade

As they did in Asia, the Portuguese went to Africa to trade. At first the Portuguese, largely at the request of Christian missionaries who wanted to convert the continent's inhabitants, maintained friendly relations with the Africans. The Portuguese treated the monarch of the Kongo kingdom as a legitimate and "brother" king to the Portuguese ruler. In turn, the king of the Kongo welcomed the newcomers and accepted baptism. His advisers adopted European dress and manners. Envoys from the Kongo traveled to Europe, and the king corresponded with the pope. The cordial relations, however, soon collapsed when the economic interests of Portuguese traders became evident.

Portuguese economic interests in Africa centered largely on slavery, holding people in servitude. Slavery had been practiced since the earliest times. Europeans themselves had been used as slaves in the Byzantine Empire and in the Arab and Turkish empires. During the 1500s, however, the new overseas empires of the Europeans began to require slave labor.

The trade grew very gradually, beginning in earnest when the Portuguese set up sugar plantations on the islands of Príncipe and São Tomé off the coast of West Africa. To operate efficiently and profitably, these plantations required large numbers of slaves. Plantation owners acquired their slaves from the African mainland. As plantation agriculture spread to Brazil and the Caribbean islands, the demand for slaves increased. By the early 1600s, the slave trade served as the chief purpose of European relations with Africa.

The growth of the slave trade. The Portuguese began to lose their grip on international commerce when Spain annexed Portugal in 1580. The Dutch emerged as the leading naval power and took over some of Portugal's colonies, most notably the East Indies. In addition, the slave trade came under their control. Later, the English and the French also became involved in the slave trade.

Triangular trade. The transatlantic slave trade was just one aspect of a system known as the **triangular trade.** In the first stage of this system, merchants shipped cotton goods, weapons, and liquor to Africa, in exchange for slaves or gold. The second stage—called the **Middle Passage**—was the shipment of slaves across the Atlantic to the Americas. There the traders sold the slaves for produce from the plantations. To complete the triangle, merchants used the plantations' products, such as molasses and sugar, to make rum. The triangular trade began anew when they used the rum as well as cloth, metal, and guns to buy more African slaves.

Middle Passage. The Middle Passage had a brutal and dehumanizing effect on all involved. The traders chained the slaves in the overcrowded hold of the ship to prevent them from jumping overboard or organizing a rebellion aboard ship. The slaves had little food or water and no provision for sanitation. Many died before they ever reached their destination.

In the 1500s slave traders transported about 2,000 slaves a year from Africa. At the height of the trade in the 1780s, they seized as many as 80,000 slaves a year. Historians estimate that a total of 11 million to 14 million Africans lived through the horrible journey of the Middle Passage to become slaves in the Americas. Possibly as many died during the process of enslavement by fellow Africans and on the hard trip from the interior of Africa to the coast, where still other Africans sold the slaves to Europeans for shipment overseas. This tragic loss meant that Africa's population did not increase between 1650 and 1800, when Europe's population grew rapidly. Despite the tragedy of the slave trade, strong states arose that helped to protect their own people from slave raiders. In time these states conquered large areas of West Africa where most of the slave trade was centered.

In the late 1600s, for example, the Ashanti state developed on the Gold Coast bordering the Gulf of Guinea in West Africa. At about this time the economy of the Gold Coast experienced rapid change. The Europeans who had arrived in the late 1400s had been interested primarily in gold. But by the 1700s the traders actively engaged in the slave trade. Ashanti rulers responded to this trade by limiting the slaves traded to prisoners of war, and Ashanti flourished throughout the 1700s and 1800s.

To the east of Ashanti two other kingdoms—Benin and Dahomey—arose. These kingdoms pursued completely different policies toward the slave trade. Benin took little part in the trade after the early 1500s when the ruler outlawed the export of male slaves.

Since the Europeans were almost exclusively interested in male slaves to do manual work on colonial plantations, the ban effectively meant that Benin had nothing to do with the slave trade.

Although the ban was eased in the 1700s, the slave trade never became an important part of Benin's economy. In contrast, Dahomey based its economy in large part on the slave trade.

African slavery. Not all Africans participated in the slave trade with Europeans, but many Africans had practiced slavery well before the arrival of the Europeans. African slavery was very different from that of the Americas, however.

African slavery included a wide range of relationships, from voluntary service to enforced captivity of prisoners of war. While the slavers sold children captured in raids, Africans usually considered the children born to enslaved women as free because their fathers were often free men. Most slaves sold in the international slave trade were adult males, whose labor would be productive on plantations. African societies generally allowed slaves to buy back their freedom, and they treated slaves as people with a role in society. Europeans, on the other hand, considered slaves as property to be bought or sold for profit.

Because Europeans rarely ventured beyond Africa's coast, they needed the help of Africans in gathering and transporting slaves. Some African societies and individuals willingly joined in the slave trade to obtain arms and other goods from Europe. In turn, neighboring groups either had to participate in the trade or become its victims. The demand for slaves led to increased slave raiding that accelerated the cycle of violence in African life and had a disastrous effect on the future of the continent.

Weakness of the Portuguese Empire

Portugal rapidly acquired wealth and a vast empire, but the empire declined almost as swiftly as it rose. Three main factors hastened this decline. First, the Portuguese government, neither strong nor well organized, had difficulty controlling its officials at home and found it impossible to control them in its colonies.

Second, transporting products home from the colonies drastically reduced Portugal's population. Portuguese ships made enormous profits in trade, but they carried so much cargo that they were top-heavy and thus dangerous to sail. The voyage from Portugal to India took six to eight months. The ships, often manned by inexperienced sailors and usually in bad repair, might be beset by storms and

the crew lost to accident or disease. Each year Portugal sent out its strongest, most daring young men as sailors or traders. Sometimes only half of those who set out returned. Because Portugal had a small population to begin with, the losses could not easily be replaced.

Third, Spain annexed Portugal in 1580, and Portugal did not regain its independence until 1640. In the meantime Spain limited Portuguese trade and neglected the colonies that the Portuguese had established.

Taking advantage of these weaknesses, the Dutch and English captured much of the Asian trade from the Portuguese in the 1600s. Small Portuguese colonies survived in Africa, India, and China, but they no longer served as sources of great wealth. Only Brazil and Angola remained major Portuguese colonies.

SECTION 2 REVIEW

1. **Define**   triangular trade, Middle Passage
2. **Identify**   Prince Henry the Navigator, Prester John, Bartholomeu Dias, Vasco da Gama, Treaty of Tordesillas, Pedro Álvares Cabral, Amerigo Vespucci, Vasco Núñez de Balboa, Ferdinand Magellan
3. **Locate**   Azores, Cape of Good Hope, San Salvador, Brazil, Isthmus of Panama, Strait of Magellan, Philippine Islands, Malacca, Moluccas, Ceylon
4. **Interpreting Ideas**   **(a)** Why did Christopher Columbus set sail across the Atlantic Ocean? **(b)** What was the result of his exploration?
5. **Summarizing Ideas**   **(a)** What route did Magellan follow?   **(b)** What did Magellan and his crew accomplish?
6. **Synthesizing Ideas**   What weaknesses made it difficult for Portugal to maintain its colonial empire?

3 Spain Created a Vast Empire in Europe and Overseas

Throughout the 1500s Spain, the most powerful nation in Europe, had the largest overseas empire. However, within just 150 years, Spain's power declined. The reasons for the rise and rapid decline of the Spanish Empire are woven through an intricate network of historical events.

Learning from Pictures
Hernando de Soto discovered the Mississippi River and searched for gold in what is today Tennessee and Arkansas.

Spain's Colonial Empire

Portugal's main interests, with the exception of Brazil, lay in Africa and Asia. Spain, on the other hand, turned most of its energies to the Americas. In Asia only the Philippine Islands remained of any great interest to Spain as a colony.

Beginning with the voyages of Columbus and Balboa, Spaniards explored the West Indies, Central America, and parts of the mainland of North and South America (see map, pages 360–61). They failed to find the spices they sought and quickly learned that America was not Asia and that the lands they explored were not the East Indies. However, America's good climate, the fertile soil, and rich mineral resources provided other opportunities.

Spanish colonization of the New World began in the West Indies. From Santo Domingo, in what is today the Dominican Republic, Spanish explorers went forward to conquer Puerto Rico, Cuba, and parts of the South American coast. From Puerto Rico, Juan Ponce de León (PAHN • suh DAY lee • OHN) sailed northward in 1513 and explored what is today the state of Florida.

Other explorers went to Yucatán in Mexico and learned of the great Mayan civilization that had flourished there. In 1519, with 10 ships and 600 men, Hernando Cortés invaded Mexico. After defeating the Aztec ruler Montezuma (mahnt • uh • ZOO • muh), Cortés captured and destroyed the wealthy

ancient city of Tenochtitlán—on the ruins of which the Spanish built Mexico City—and eventually conquered the entire Aztec Empire. Horses and guns, unknown in the Americas, helped the small Spanish force overcome the much larger Aztec armies.

The Spaniards had also heard of a great and rich civilization in South America. In 1530 Francisco Pizarro led an expedition of 180 men and 27 horses from the Isthmus of Panama to the Inca Empire in what is now Peru and seized it for Spain.

In time Spain controlled a vast empire in the West Indies, Central America, southern North America, and a large part of South America. The Spaniards became colonizers in the true sense of the word. Unlike the Europeans in Africa and Asia, who became mainly traders, the Spaniards in the Americas established settlements.

Spain also developed a centralized form of government for its colonies. **Viceroys**, representatives of the monarch, reported to the Council of the Indies in Spain. The council carefully planned and directed the development of Spain's empire.

Spain grew enormously rich from its colonies and their valuable silver mines in the regions that are now Bolivia and northern Mexico. Although agriculture and trade retained their importance, mineral resources became the Spanish Empire's main asset.

The Europeans passed on diseases new to the Americas. The native inhabitants had no resistance
Text continues on page 370.

Greenland

ICELAND
(DENMARK)

North
DENMA
Sea
ENGLAND
NETHERLANDS
FRANCE

NORTH
AMERICA

Hudson Bay

ROCKY MTS

NEWFOUNDLAND

FRANCE

NOVA SCOTIA

Montreal
Quebec
Albany
Boston
New York
Philadelphia

NEW

LOUISIANA

ATLANTIC
OCEAN

PORTUGAL   SPAIN

AZORES   Lisbon   Seville
MADEIRA IS.   Ceuta   Melilla
CANARY IS.

Charleston
FLORIDA

MEXICO

Havana

Cuba   Hispaniola

Mexico City

Jamaica
BELIZE

Guadeloupe
Martinique
Barbados

Curaçao

CAPE VERDE IS.   St. Louis
Gambia

PACIFIC

OCEAN

Panamá

TASO

Elmina

GUIANA

SOUTH
AMERICA

Lima
PERU

Bahia

ANDES

ATLANTIC

OCEAN

PAMPAS

Strait of Magellan

Cape Horn

N

0   1000   2000 Miles

0   1000   2000 Kilometers

EUROPE

ASIA

CHINA

HIMALAYAS

ARABIA

INDIA

Ft. William
(Calcutta)

Bombay

Formosa

Macao

JAPAN

AFRICA

Goa

Madras
Pondicherry

Cochin

Ceylon

Manila

PHILIPPINES

PACIFIC
OCEAN

Strait of
Malacca

anda

Malindi
Mombasa
Kilwa

Malacca

Sumatra

Borneo

SPICE ISLANDS
(MOLUCCAS)

NGOLA

Mozambique

INDIAN

New Guinea

Batavia
(Jakarta)

Java

Madagascar

OCEAN

Timor

Mauritius
Bourbon (Réunion)

AUSTRALIA
(New Holland)

e Cape of
n Good Hope

30°-

NEW
ZEALAND

Tasmania

EUROPEAN OVERSEAS EMPIRES, 1700

Spanish territory

Dutch territory

Portuguese territory

French territory

English territory

MILLER CYLINDRICAL PROJECTION

ANTARCTICA

369

Learning from Pictures *The Hapsburgs were very enthusiastic hunters. Here Charles V observes the ladies as they take their turn at the hunt.*

to smallpox, and massive epidemics of this disease killed millions. In Mexico alone the native population had numbered about 10 million when the Spaniards arrived in 1519; by the 1600s only 1.5 million native Americans were left. Since the Spaniards needed workers for mines and farms, they imported slaves from Africa to compensate for the loss of Indian labor.

Raids on Spain's Treasure Ships

The Spanish government made every effort to keep the wealth of the Americas for Spain alone. It kept foreigners out of the Spanish colonies and decreed that silver and gold from the Americas could be carried only in Spanish ships and only to the Spanish port of Seville.

Making rules, however, proved easier than enforcing them. Spanish treasure ships became rich prizes and attractive targets for pirates who prowled the seas. Late in the 1500s, Spain developed a convoy system, with warships to escort the treasure vessels on the voyage across the Atlantic to Spain. For a time, at least, most of the treasure reached Spain safely.

Spain's colonial rivals—particularly England and France—envied Spain's American wealth and used various means to capture a share of it. They sold manufactured goods in American ports. And instead of trying to suppress piracy, these nations encouraged pirates to attack Spanish ships.

Spain's rivals also established colonies in the New World, paying no attention to the pope's line of demarcation. Some inroads were made on Spanish territory; for example, England, Holland, and France held islands in the West Indies. But the Spanish Empire in the New World remained otherwise intact until the early 1800s. Let us now turn to Spain itself and examine its rise and fall as a great European nation.

Charles V

As Spanish explorers created a great empire outside Europe, Spanish kings expanded their authority in Spain itself. Perhaps one of the greatest of these kings was Charles V, a member of the Hapsburg family.

The Hapsburgs successfully arranged marriages that increased their lands and power. Through a series of such marriages, Charles came to the Spanish throne in 1516. Three years later, the electors of the Holy Roman Empire chose him emperor. Though he was the first king named Charles to rule Spain, he was the fifth Charles with the title Holy Roman Emperor and is known in history as Charles V.

Charles V found that his titles and power brought with them problems and responsibilities. Born in Flanders, he spoke French as his first language. But as king of Spain, he had to acquire a Spanish viewpoint, and as head of the Holy Roman Empire, he had to support German aims. As the secular leader of Christian Europe, Charles also had to assume responsibility for defending Europe against the Ottoman Turks, who were invading central Europe and attacking European ships in the Mediterranean.

Charles V halted the Turkish penetration of central Europe by driving the Turks away from Vienna in 1529. Then in 1555, the Peace of Augsburg temporarily settled the religious wars between Lutherans and Roman Catholics in Germany. Nonetheless, the nearly continuous wars drained Spain's human and financial resources.

In addition, Spain lacked industries and the government did little to encourage them. It also had difficulty feeding its people, because so much land was devoted to raising sheep for wool. Food prices quintupled between 1500 and the mid-1600s. The Spanish government, though tightly controlled by the king, could not operate efficiently over a territory that included land scattered throughout Europe as well as colonies in the New World.

Charles V realized that this scattered empire had become too large for any one monarch to rule alone. In 1556 he gave up his throne and divided his vast territory between members of his family. Charles's son, Philip II, received Spain and its possessions, and his branch of the family became known as the Spanish Hapsburgs. Charles's brother, Ferdinand I, king of Hungary and Bohemia, became Holy Roman Emperor and founded the Austrian Hapsburgs.

Charles V retired to a monastery, where he continued to take an interest in political affairs. However, largely because of his rich and unhealthy diet, which consisted of sardine omelettes, eel pies, and pickled partridges, he did not live long.

Philip II

Unlike his father Charles V, Philip II was born and educated in Spain and proudly considered himself a Spaniard. Philip II had such a dedicated sense of responsibility to his country that he had almost no private life. No matter escaped his attention, and he worked long hours at the business of being king. He wanted to make Spain stronger at home so that it might continue as Europe's leading power. Philip II made the central government responsible only to the king, and he moved the capital to Madrid.

Philip II also saw himself as the leader of the Counter-Reformation. A very devout Catholic, Philip ordered the Spanish Inquisition to redouble its efforts to find and stamp out heresy at home.

Abroad, Philip became involved in wars to defend Catholicism and advance Spain's glory. These wars drained the Spanish treasury. Taxes never kept up with expenses, and the bankers charged more and more interest on loans they made to Spain. The government's financial problems grew worse, and Philip declared bankruptcy four times. Near the end of his reign, the national debt stood at 100 million ducats, and the interest payments alone on this sum took two-thirds of all government revenues.

Undeterred by these financial problems, Philip built a new royal residence, El Escorial, 30 miles from Madrid. From there Philip, surrounded by mountains of government papers, drew the reins of the government so tightly that he almost paralyzed the administration. Because he insisted upon approving every important decision personally, Philip's subjects called him "The Prudent King." In fact, Philip II's communication with his enormous empire became so slow that one of his governors wrote, "If Death had to come from Spain, I would live forever."

Philip found it impossible to subdue all the enemies of Spanish power and of Catholicism. His war with the Ottoman Empire in the Mediterranean ended in a draw. An attempted Spanish invasion of England in 1588 with an Armada, or huge fleet of ships, ended in disaster. And an attempt to invade France to prevent a Protestant from becoming king proved an expensive failure. The most costly disaster, however, resulted from Philip's policy toward the Netherlands.

The Rise of the Dutch

The 17 provinces of the Netherlands that Philip II inherited had been a great trading center and one of Europe's richest areas since the Middle Ages. Their people had a proud tradition of independence. By the 1550s Calvinism was already making headway in the area. Philip II's harsh treatment of his subjects in the Netherlands led to catastrophe for Spain.

The people of the Netherlands strongly distrusted Philip. Unlike his father Charles V, who had been born in the Netherlands, Philip was a Spaniard. Philip turned this distrust into outright rebellion by making three fundamental errors. First, he ignored the long tradition of self-rule of the Netherlands and insisted that he, not the local nobles, held all authority. Second, he taxed the

Text continues on page 374.

In the last decades of the 1700s, revolutions shook both sides of the Atlantic. In 1776 the 13 British colonies of North America declared their independence. In 1789 the French people overturned the absolute power of King Louis XVI and established a limited monarchy.

In both cases, important documents marked political change: the Declaration of Independence in the United States in 1776 and the Declaration of the Rights of Man in France in 1789. The two share many features and ideas.

Undoubtedly, the French were inspired by the American example. But the common elements are not just due to imitation. The documents resemble each other because both drew on similar ideas.

It was the time of the Enlightenment, also called the Age of Reason. People were beginning to question old institutions.

They no longer accepted, for example, that monarchies were the natural order of things. In this climate of critical evaluation, the two declarations were born. Both claimed the sanction of God. The Americans wrote in 1776 that men "are endowed by their Creator with certain unalienable rights."

The French in 1789 proclaimed the rights of man "under the auspices of the Supreme Being."

Both documents drew on the political ideas of John Locke, who had brilliantly defended the English Revolution of 1688. Locke had maintained that men are "by nature, all free, equal, and independent." Governments, he said, were established by people and could be changed by people—if necessary, by force.

There are two other striking parallels between the two declarations. First, each presented ideas in general terms; *all* mankind, in *all* societies, had the same rights the Americans and the French now claimed. Second, each carefully avoided a clear statement on the issue of slavery. Neither, however, explained how slavery could be reconciled with universal freedom.

There were also major differences between the two documents; they came out of different societies. The Declaration of Independence was the product of a country at war. The government in London refused to negotiate with the colonies. King George III declared the colonies in a state of rebellion. Bloody battles at Bunker Hill and Quebec resolved little except to strengthen the determination of the American freedom fighters. State assemblies were setting up governments to replace British officials who had fled or been thrown out. Many nations, including France, sympathized with the colonies.

Thus special features of the Declaration can be placed in perspective. Written largely by Thomas Jefferson, the document was carefully composed and elegantly written. It took pains to explain American actions to the outside world. It went from general principles to a lengthy set of charges against George III. The king, it said, had proved himself a tyrant "unfit to be the ruler of a free people." The Declaration vividly invited other oppressed peoples to follow the American lead. When governments become despotic, peoples must respond: "It is their right, it is their duty, to throw off such government."

In contrast, the Declaration of the Rights of Man came out of a country at relative—though uneasy—peace. The French had just overcome an unjust division into three estates: the clergy, the nobles, and the commoners. The commoners (the Third Estate) had chafed under the injustice of this division. They were the most numerous and the most heavily taxed. Why should they have little voice in government? They had rebelled and formed a national assembly. Now they prepared to write a constitution. The Declaration of the Rights of Man was composed to guide the constitution makers.

The Declaration of the Rights of Man lacked the organization and the brilliant force of its American counterpart, but its purpose was clear: to remind France's citizens of "the natural, inalienable, and sacred rights of man."

Starting with a statement of general principles, the Declaration followed with 17 specific claims. There was no direct attack on the king; no direct call for other peoples to follow the French in overturning an unjust government.

Instead, the Declaration took aim at specific abuses of the Old Regime. No one, it said, should be persecuted for religious beliefs. Taxation should depend on income. Public offices should be open to all.

While the American Declaration was a war cry for a society under attack, the French Declaration was intended to stabilize the new order. Yet it failed! The king balked at his diminished role. Some revolutionaries wanted to spread the new order beyond France's border, plunging the nation into war with its neighbors. Quarrels over the role of the Roman Catholic church led to civil war. France then fell under a dictatorship that ignored the very rights the Declaration of the Rights of Man so eloquently guaranteed.

Thus, the Declaration of the Rights of Man was overwhelmed by events, whereas the Declaration of Independence led Americans to victory and freedom.

Photos Page 372: Thomas Jefferson (top), signing the Declaration of Independence (bottom); Page 373: revolution in Paris (top), John Locke (middle), Declaration of the Rights of Man (bottom)

Young Woman with a Water Jug

What does this young lady see as she gazes through the window? The map on the wall behind her is of the far-flung Dutch provinces, and perhaps it has led her thoughts to faraway places.

The window lets light in on her starched linen headdress, and the sun sparkles on the metal pitcher and tray, defining the pattern on the Oriental rug. The rug is an example of the varied goods that overseas trade brought to the Dutch people after they had won their independence from Spain.

In the 1600s Dutch merchants grew rich enough to buy handsome silks and linens for their wives and to commission artists to paint for them. Artists flourished in the prosperous economy of the Netherlands, and Jan Vermeer, who painted this picture, was one of the finest. His painting gives us an accurate look at daily Dutch life.

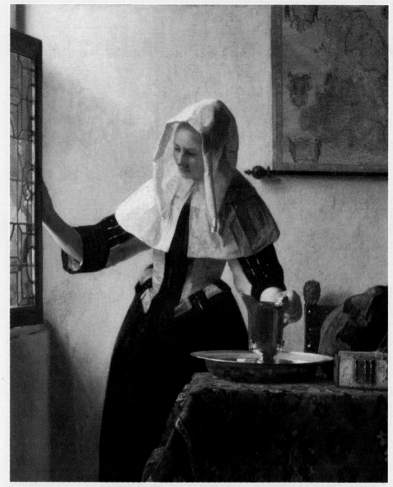

The Metropolitan Museum of Art, Gift of Henry G. Marquand, 1889. Marquand Collection, (89.15.21)

Netherlands' trade heavily to finance Spanish wars. Third, he persecuted the Calvinists.

Philip could not stop the revolt that erupted in 1568. The people of the Calvinist northern provinces lived on land that was below sea level, protected by large dikes. They simply opened the dikes, flooded the country, and left Philip's army helpless. William the Silent, prince of Orange, led the revolt of the northern provinces. He relied on quick strikes, raids by bands of his soldiers to keep the Spanish army off balance. Today we call this military technique **guerrilla warfare.**

In 1581, under William the Silent's leadership, the northern provinces declared their independence from Spain and became the Republic of the United Provinces. Today they are called simply the Netherlands.

William was assassinated in 1584, but his sons continued the struggle against Spain. Eventually, in 1609 the Spaniards agreed to a truce. By this time the Spaniards had won back the loyalty of the southern provinces of the Netherlands, partly because Philip promised the heavily Catholic southern provinces greater self-rule. The region remained under the rule of Spain and was known as the Spanish Netherlands (see map, page 378). In 1713 when the Austrian Hapsburgs took possession, it was called the Austrian Netherlands. Since 1830 it has been the independent kingdom of Belgium.

Dutch society. The people of the northern provinces of the Netherlands—the Dutch—created one of Europe's most remarkable societies. Primarily traders, they dominated European commerce throughout the 1600s. Their ships carried most of the world's trade. The city of Amsterdam became a world financial center. Dutch banks, trading companies, manufacturing enterprises—especially ship-building—and overseas colonies became models of efficiency.

The Dutch had an extraordinarily open society. Although only Calvinists could hold political offices, the government allowed all inhabitants freedom of religion. Victims of religious persecution elsewhere found tolerance in the Netherlands.

Amsterdam also became the liveliest cultural center in Europe. The philosopher René Descartes, Hugo Grotius (GROH • shee • uhs), the scholar of international law and freedom of the seas, and the painter Rembrandt thrived in this comfortable and inspiring setting.

The Dutch colonial empire. The Netherlands lay on the North Sea, and the Dutch, a seafaring people, built very efficient ships and became excellent sailors. In the age of exploration, Dutch merchants set up a number of companies to trade in various parts of the world. In 1602 the Dutch combined several of their trading companies into one powerful organization, the Dutch East India Company. The Dutch government gave this company the sole right to carry on trade between the Netherlands and Africa and the East Indies.

The Dutch established their first colony in Asia in 1619 at Batavia (now Jakarta) on the island of Java. From Java the Dutch expanded westward to take the island of Sumatra and eastward to seize the valuable Spice Islands from the Portuguese. Next came Malacca and the island of Ceylon, as well as Cochin on the southwest coast of India. In 1652 the Dutch founded a colony at the Cape of Good Hope, which helped them supply and protect their trade routes to Asia and along the African coast (see map, pages 368–69).

The Portuguese had held only strategic points along the coasts in order to control the sea lanes. The Dutch, however, realized that a successful empire required much more extensive control over both the land and the people. They did not stop with establishing a trading post at Batavia, for example, but took over the entire island of Java, with its large population and its sugar, tea, coffee, and spices.

The Dutch gained some commercial influence even in Japan. Since they had not come as missionaries, the shogun—the Japanese military ruler—allowed the Dutch to trade in Japan and to operate a trading post at Nagasaki.

In the New World, the Dutch founded colonies in the West Indies, South America, and North America. In 1626 they purchased Manhattan Island from the Indians. There they founded New Amsterdam, which later was called New York City.

The colonial empire that the Dutch established differed significantly from that of Spain. At no time did the Dutch try to convert the people they conquered to Christianity, nor did they force them to speak Dutch or to live under the laws of the Netherlands. The Dutch came as traders, to make money. In this sense the overseas empire of the Netherlands reflected the businesslike society of the home country.

Decline of the Spanish Empire

Spain's loss of the Netherlands in 1581 marked the beginning of the decline of the mighty Spanish Empire. The chief reason for this decline stemmed from the gold and silver that flowed into Spain from the colonies. Spanish rulers used the gold and silver to finance wars. Even with this wealth, they still needed to borrow money for their military campaigns. The government also minted new coins, driving up prices in Spain. And because it cost more to produce goods in Spain than in other countries, Spanish industries never developed.

An enterprising middle class might have helped Spanish industries develop despite these obstacles. Spanish nobles preferred military careers. In addition, by the early 1500s Ferdinand and Isabella had expelled first the Jews and the Moriscos—Moorish converts to Christianity who were suspected of secretly practicing Islam. Both the Jews and the Moriscos had once formed a vital part of Spain's middle class.

Spain thus developed an imbalance of trade. Much Spanish wealth simply passed through Spain on its way to buy goods from other nations. It was said that the treasure from the Americas was like rain on the roof—it poured down but drained away. With the gold and silver received for goods they sold to Spain, Spain's enemies—France, England, and the Netherlands—developed their own industries and grew strong at Spain's expense.

The Spanish government also adopted other unwise policies: building large warships instead of smaller commercial ships, selling monopolies that

Rembrandt Self-portrait

The successful Dutch revolt against the Spanish monarch created a new society, one that was dominated by Protestants rather than Catholics. In this new society, the middle class rose to power and made way for a new art, concerned more with daily life than with religion.

Dutch artists, no longer dependent upon the church or the aristocracy for patrons, could paint what they liked. Their new subjects consisted of wealthy merchants who, proud of their success, clamored to have their portraits painted.

In the mid-1600s, the Netherlands probably had more painters than any other country. About this time, in 1633, the 27-year-old Rembrandt van Rijn settled in Amster-

dam. He was brilliant in his ability to capture a person's spirit and personality on canvas, as is evident in this deeply moving self-portrait. It is one of 60 self-portraits that Rembrandt did during his lifetime. Here the artist, an aging and financially troubled man, lets us see inside his soul.

restricted trade, taxing wool exports, and setting up customs barriers that drove prices up. Economic discontent caused people to leave Spain.

Spain's inefficient government also contributed to the empire's decline. And in the colonies, shutting out all foreign trade encouraged attacks by England, France, and the Netherlands. Although the Spanish monarchy survived with its absolute powers intact, the country never regained its prominence in international affairs.

SECTION 3 REVIEW

1. **Define**   viceroy, guerrilla warfare
2. **Identify**   Charles V, Philip II, Ferdinand I
3. **Locate**   Vienna, Madrid
4. **Analyzing Ideas**   (a) How did Philip II's religious views affect government policy within Spain? (b) How did they affect Spain's relations with the rest of Europe?
5. **Contrasting Ideas**   How did the Dutch colonial empire differ from the Spanish colonial empire?
6. **Interpreting Ideas**   Why did Spanish power decline in the late 1500s?

4 France Emerged as a Great Power

Following Spain's slow decline, France emerged as the leading European power. It had recovered rapidly from the religious wars of the 1500s, thanks to the policies of King Henry IV, the first monarch of a new royal house in France, the Bourbons. Assisted by two cardinals of the Roman Catholic church, the Bourbons would make the monarchy absolute in France. Under Louis XIV, France became the dominant power in Europe.

Henry IV

Henry IV, who had lived in Navarre—a tiny kingdom that straddled the Pyrenees between France and Spain—was the first of the Bourbon family to be king of France. He had been a Huguenot, but he realized he could not rule France successfully as a member of a religious minority. He wanted a strong, united, and peaceful kingdom; therefore, he converted to Catholicism, reportedly remarking, "Paris is well worth a Mass." However, to protect his Huguenot friends, he issued a special order, the Edict of Nantes, guaranteeing freedom of worship and political rights. This edict defused the religious conflict and ended the civil wars.

Henry also attempted to resolve other major problems. Powerful nobles had undermined royal authority in the 1500s. Henry either persuaded them to join the central government or quieted them with large bribes, thus regaining real control over the whole country.

France's financial difficulties, however, defied easy solutions. The French system of taxation was inefficient, corrupt, and unjust. As in the Roman Empire, **tax farming,** selling the right to collect taxes to private individuals called tax farmers, was common. These tax farmers paid the government a fixed sum, collected all they could, and kept any surplus. Some estimates show that less than half of the taxes collected reached the French treasury. Only the tax farmers got rich. Also, since the nobles and clergy paid no taxes, the tax burden fell most heavily on the peasants.

Henry showed wisdom in choosing the Duke of Sully as minister in charge of finances. However, even he could not make the system fair. Nobles and clergy continued to be free from taxation. Nevertheless, Sully limited the expenditures of the royal household, fired dishonest tax collectors, and supervised the tax farmers more closely. The result was a sizable surplus in the treasury, which provided funds to build up trade and industry.

Cardinal Richelieu's Program for France

Henry's son and successor, Louis XIII, was only eight years old when a fanatic monk stabbed his father to death in 1610. The boy's scheming mother, Marie de Medici, became regent—the ruler of France until Louis came of age.

At the age of 16, Louis XIII took control of the government. He was not a strong ruler, but he quickly learned to select good advisers and to support them against all opposition. Louis XIII chose as his chief minister Cardinal Richelieu (RISH • uhl • oo), who ran the government of France from 1624 until 1642. It was Richelieu who created the system by which France was governed until the French Revolution nearly 150 years later.

Learning from Pictures *Cardinal Richelieu founded the French Academy to support literature. Today the Academy still awards literary prizes.*

A political genius, Richelieu had a keen understanding of the possibilities of politics and diplomacy. He wanted to make the king supreme in France, and France supreme in Europe. To accomplish the first aim, he set out to destroy the power of the nobles and the remaining political independence of the Huguenots that had been granted by the Edict of Nantes. In addition he wanted to strengthen France economically by continuing Sully's policy of encouraging trade and industry. To make France supreme in Europe, Richelieu planned to reduce the power of the Spanish and Austrian Hapsburgs.

Huguenots. Richelieu believed that the provisions of the Edict of Nantes that allowed the Huguenots to control fortified cities were politically dangerous. The Huguenot cities, which were like states within a state, made strong centralized government impossible. In 1627 Richelieu himself, temporarily trading his cardinal's hat for a military helmet, directed the attack on the Huguenot seaport of La Rochelle and other fortified towns.

EUROPE AFTER THE TREATY OF WESTPHALIA, 1648

- Possessions of the Spanish Hapsburgs
- Possessions of the Austrian Hapsburgs
- Possessions of the Hohenzollerns

RUSSIA

Moscow

KINGDOM OF DENMARK AND NORWAY

SWEDEN

Stockholm

Baltic Sea

EAST PRUSSIA

SCOTLAND

IRELAND

North Sea

POMERANIA

POLAND

Warsaw

ENGLAND

London

UNITED NETHERLANDS

Berlin

BRANDENBURG-PRUSSIA

SAXONY

ATLANTIC OCEAN

English Channel

SPANISH NETHERLANDS

Rhine R.

HOLY ROMAN EMPIRE

BOHEMIA

Prague

Paris

ALSACE

BAVARIA

Vienna

Buda Pest

HUNGARY

FRANCHE COMTÉ

SWITZERLAND

AUSTRIA

Bay of Biscay

FRANCE

SAVOY

PIEDMONT

MILAN

REPUBLIC OF VENICE

Danube River

Black Sea

Avignon

GENOA

TUSCANY

PAPAL STATES

Adriatic Sea

OTTOMAN

Constantinople

Corsica

Rome

EMPIRE

PORTUGAL

Madrid

SPAIN

NAPLES

Sardinia

Aegean Sea

N

BALEARIC ISLANDS

Mediterranean Sea

Sicily

Crete

AFRICA

0   150   300 Miles
0 150 300 Kilometers

AZIMUTHAL EQUAL AREA PROJECTION

Learning from Maps *France gained the territory of Alsace from the Holy Roman Empire after the Treaty of Westphalia. Who controlled land northwest of Alsace?*

After stubborn but futile resistance, the Huguenots asked for peace. Richelieu took away their special rights in fortified cities, but he allowed the Huguenots to continue to worship freely, hold public office, and attend schools and colleges.

Nobles. The cardinal next turned to the problem of the nobles, to finish the work that Henry IV had begun. It was a difficult and dangerous task. Moving first to crush the nobles' military power, he ordered that all fortified castles not necessary for the defense of France be leveled. The nobles complained in vain.

After Richelieu reduced the nobles' military power, he reduced their political power. With the king's consent, the cardinal appointed as governors of provinces only those who favored a strong monarchy. He also strengthened the power of the local administrators known as **intendants.** For these positions he chose middle-class people, who had no interest in advancing the power of the nobles. Richelieu gave the intendants strong administrative powers and made them directly responsible to the king, who appointed them and could remove them.

378

The Thirty Years' War

Richelieu's foreign policy was as determined and coldly calculating as his policy at home. He did not allow his position as a Catholic cardinal to interfere with his primary goal of strengthening France at the expense of the Hapsburgs. The Thirty Years' War offered a golden opportunity to achieve this purpose.

The Thirty Years' War actually consisted of a series of wars interrupted by intervals of peace. It began because the religious conflicts between Protestants and Catholics in Germany had never completely died down following the Peace of Augsburg in 1555. Constant rivalry continued among the more than 300 German princes, who also wanted to be independent of the Holy Roman Emperor. In addition, France, Denmark, and Sweden were all looking for opportunities to diminish the power of the Hapsburgs and the Holy Roman Empire.

When the Holy Roman Emperor suppressed a Protestant rebellion in Bohemia in 1620, Protestant German princes and Protestant Danes went to war against him. The emperor defeated the king of Denmark, who had to promise not to interfere in German affairs. Sweden then took up arms.

Cardinal Richelieu favored the Swedes over the Catholic Hapsburgs, but he believed that it was in France's interest to prolong the war without involving France directly. The other nations would become weak from fighting, while France remained strong. Most of the battles of the Thirty Years' War took place in Germany, which lost about one-third of its population to casualties, famine, and disease. In 1635, however, France actively joined the war against the Hapsburgs. By 1648 the French and their allies had claimed victory.

The participants in the Thirty Years' War signed the Treaty of Westphalia in 1648. This agreement was a landmark because it made changes that affected western Europe for centuries. Territorial changes outlined in the treaty greatly strengthened France, which received Alsace, a valuable territory along the Rhine River.

The Treaty of Westphalia also recognized the Netherlands and Switzerland as independent nations, which weakened the Hapsburgs. The Hapsburgs suffered further blows because the peace made the princes in Germany virtually independent of the Holy Roman Emperor.

Because the Austrian Hapsburgs no longer exercised any real authority in Germany, they began to look eastward rather than westward. They became more interested in their own possessions—Austria, Bohemia, and Hungary—and eventually created a new empire centered along the Danube River instead of in Germany.

The Sun King

Although France emerged powerful from the Peace of Westphalia, a series of rebellions erupted between 1648 and 1652. These rebellions are known as the Fronde, from the French word for "sling." The rebels—Frondeurs—were compared to mischievous schoolboys using slingshots when the teacher looked away. Nobles led the rebellions, but many peasants and the citizens of Paris also supported them. The Fronde threatened the centralized royal power that Richelieu and his successor Cardinal Mazarin had built up. The Frondeurs

Learning from Pictures Louis XIV was such a patron of the arts that the 1600s in French art is sometimes called the "Century of Louis XIV."

●READ
WRITE
INTERPRET
CONNECT
THINK

BUILDING HISTORY STUDY SKILLS

Reading About History: Making Inferences

As you study history, you often read a source in order to understand the facts of the event or events the author is explaining. For example, read the following description of Versailles:

> The palace of Versailles cost 5 million livres out of a total state budget of 120 million livres. . . . In 1682, 22,000 workers were laboring on it; the next year, there were 36,000. In 230 acres of gardens, 1,400 fountains were installed, and 25,000 full-grown trees were transplanted in one year so that Louis XIV would not have to wait for saplings to grow. 〞

The facts of the quotation are obvious. Thousands of people worked on the palace at Versailles (below) and the construction cost a great deal of money. By "reading between the lines," however, you can find information that is only implied—that Louis XIV possessed great power.

When you read between the lines, you are developing your reasoning ability to discover new meanings. In this way you can identify something that the writer does not actually state. Your identifications are called inferences.

How to Make Inferences

To make inferences, follow these steps.

1. Select the main idea or literal interpretation.
2. Look for clues that suggest additional meaning, such as key phrases or emotional words.
3. Add the clues to the original interpretation.
4. Create a revised meaning based on the connection between the stated idea and the implied ideas.

Developing the Skill

In the following selection from *A Description of the East India Company,* Peter Van Dam, an officer of the company, describes how the Dutch government stimulated and promoted trade by establishing the East India Company. What inferences can you make about the key to the company's success?

> The Company's charter authorized it to make alliances with princes and potentates east of the Cape of Good Hope and beyond the Straits of Magellan, to make contracts, build fortresses and strongholds, name governors, raise troops, appoint officers of justice, and perform other necessary services for the advancement of trade. . . . The Company after the date of this charter has made great progress in the Indies. It has captured a number of fortresses from the Spaniards and the Portuguese . . . and has established trading posts at several places. It was decided as a consequence that it was desirable to establish a formal government in the Indies. 〞

The selection states that the company could make treaties and set up governments. The key phrases "made great progress" and "as a consequence" are clues that can help you "read between the lines." These phrases indicate that although the company was set up for trade, it had many political successes. One inference that you can make is that the company owed its economic success to the political powers that it enjoyed. Control of certain political rights were linked to the development of trade. The Dutch East India Company was a political as well as an economic organization.

Practicing the skill. Read a political article in the daily paper or listen to a televised news program that focuses on a political issue. Then list 10 facts and any inferences you can make.

To apply this skill, see Applying History Study Skills on page 393.

wanted to revive the independence of local regions and the power of the nobility. Mazarin crushed the Fronde, but with some difficulty. No major attempts to restrict the royal power were made for more than 135 years.

Louis XIV—whose 72-year reign from 1643 to 1715 was the longest in French history—benefited from this strengthening of central authority. As a small boy, Louis had witnessed the rebellious nobles of the Fronde in Paris. He decided to remove himself from the dangers and humiliation he had faced, make his power absolute, and allow no opposition. To accomplish his goals, he built an enormous palace at Versailles (vur • SY), a few miles outside of Paris, where he established his court and moved the French government. The elaborate palace cost the equivalent of about 1 billion dollars in today's currency—an immense sum that strained the French economy.

The palace emphasized the grandeur and power of Louis XIV and France. Louis believed in the **divine right of kings**, meaning that God had ordained him to govern France. "L'état, c'est moi," ("I am the state,") Louis proclaimed.

To increase royal authority over the nobility, Louis insisted that the most important nobles of France live at Versailles. There they had to serve him at all times, helping him dress in the morning, joining him in the hunt—a passion with the Bourbons—performing the ceremonies of the court, and handing him his nightshirt when he went to bed. In this way Louis kept his eye on the nobles. Instead of trying to gain power by fighting the monarchy, the nobility now could advance only by getting royal favors and offices.

Versailles and its absolute king became the ideal of European royalty. Other monarchs built smaller copies of the palace. European nobility adopted French clothing, manners, cooking, and language. Louis XIV adopted as his personal emblem the sun, whose rays symbolized the extent of his power and influence. He looked like a king, lived like a king, and behaved like a king. He also took the business of being a king seriously.

Louis chose competent advisers, although he alone made the decisions. One of his most outstanding advisers was Jean Baptiste Colbert (kawl • BAIR), an expert in finance. Colbert, a member of the middle class, followed Sully's ideas in promoting economic development. He tried to build up French industry at home and French trade abroad. He granted government subsidies to private companies to build new industries or strengthen existing ones. He placed high tariffs on foreign imports, improved transportation, and replanted forests.

Like Sully, Colbert also tried to eliminate corruption and waste in the tax-farming system. His efforts resulted in the accumulation of enough money to finance all the economic improvements in France, maintain a large army, and support exploration abroad. Colbert encouraged French companies to establish colonies and carry on trade with Canada, the West Indies, and East Asia.

Louis XIV was concerned that the French were still not unified in their religious beliefs. The Huguenots, he believed, disturbed the unity of the country and weakened the central authority. Consequently, in 1685 he revoked the Edict of Nantes, ending the policy of toleration for Protestants. More than 100,000 productive citizens fled France rather than become Catholics. This action hurt the French economy, but Louis considered national unity and obedience to the crown more important.

The Wars of Louis XIV

Louis chose as his minister of war the Marquis de Louvois (loov • WAH), a military genius who completely reorganized the army. Soldiers were promoted on the basis of merit rather than commissions purchased for them. Louvois also created a quartermaster's department to furnish supplies to his troops so that they did not always have to live off the land. Officers and soldiers received extensive training and followed strict discipline. The officer responsible for this training, General Jean Martinet, furnished a word to the language: anyone who is a strict disciplinarian is called a *martinet*. By the early 1700s, the French had a force of 400,000 well-trained soldiers—an army larger and more powerful than Europe had ever seen.

Why did Louis XIV need such a large army? He had territorial ambitions and was convinced that French security depended on achieving France's natural frontiers. The Alps, the Mediterranean Sea, the Pyrenees, the Atlantic Ocean, and the English Channel already protected France on the southeast, south, west, and northwest. Like Richelieu, Louis wanted to make France even safer by reaching the Rhine River, its natural frontier to the northeast and east. To gain his ends, Louis XIV fought four wars between 1667 and 1713.

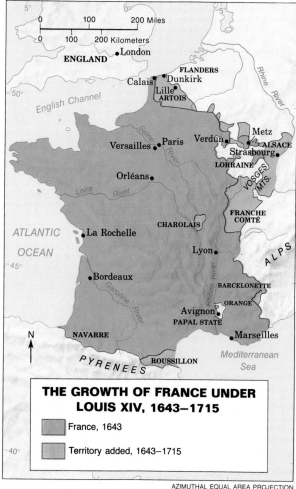

THE GROWTH OF FRANCE UNDER
LOUIS XIV, 1643–1715

France, 1643

Territory added, 1643–1715

AZIMUTHAL EQUAL AREA PROJECTION

Learning from Maps   Louis XIV extended French territory to the north, south, and east. What territory did he add to the south of France?

Louis XIV's goals alarmed the other European countries, which united to counteract the great power of France. At various times the Netherlands, England, Sweden, Spain, and Denmark, as well as Austria, Brandenburg, and other German states, formed alliances to amass enough power to equal or surpass that of France. Maintaining an equilibrium in international politics is known as the **balance of power.**

The wars took a tremendous toll on France's resources. By the end of Louis XIV's third war in 1697, the treasury was empty. Louis even melted down the royal silver to help pay for his wars.

War of the Spanish Succession. The War of the Spanish Succession was Louis XIV's last war. It was fought over the question of who should succeed to the throne of Spain. The last Spanish Hapsburg king had died in 1700, leaving the throne to a French prince, the grandson of Louis XIV.

The other European nations feared the prospect of Bourbon rulers in both Spain and France, particularly if the two thrones would ever merge under one monarch. Louis refused to promise that the two thrones would never be merged, so the nations of Europe declared war on France. Battles raged throughout Europe, on the high seas, and in America. French armies and fleets met defeat everywhere, and Louis finally submitted to a peace agreement in 1713.

The European settlement in 1713. The Treaty of Utrecht, which ended the War of the Spanish Succession, became important in the history of both Europe and America. It recognized Louis XIV's grandson as King Philip V of Spain, but provided that the French and Spanish crowns were never to be united. Great Britain had become France's chief enemy, since the treaty gave it lands in the New World at the expense of France.

The French Colonial Empire

The empire that France began to lose after the War of the Spanish Succession had begun in the early 1500s when French explorers such as Jacques Cartier (kahr·TYAY) made several voyages to North America. Cartier's voyage up the St. Lawrence River as far as Montreal gave the French a claim to much of eastern Canada. Not until 1608, however, did they make any permanent settlement. In that year Samuel de Champlain founded Quebec.

France then established several other settlements in the St. Lawrence Valley and in the Great Lakes region. The French developed a profitable fur trade with the Indians and engaged in fishing off Newfoundland and Nova Scotia.

Between 1679 and 1683, Robert de La Salle sailed down the Mississippi River to the Gulf of Mexico and claimed the entire inland region of North America for France. He named the region Louisiana in honor of King Louis XIV. French settlement in North America grew very slowly, however. Elsewhere in the New World, the French occupied Haiti and the sugar-producing islands of Guadeloupe and Martinique in the West Indies.

The French also expanded to the east. On the southeast coast of India, the French East India

Company, formed in 1664, established a trading post at Pondicherry and controlled part of India through the 1700s.

The Legacy of Louis XIV

Louis XIV died in 1715. The French people had tired of his endless wars in which so many lives were lost and so much money wasted. The long reign itself had exhausted the French. Nevertheless, despite his defeats, the Sun King had made France the most powerful nation in Europe. While Great Britain became the strongest colonial power within Europe, France remained the largest, the richest, and the most influential nation. Moreover, for more than 50 years after the king's death, the French government was remarkably stable. Louis XIV's great-grandson and successor, Louis XV, who reigned from 1715 to 1774, held unquestioned authority, though in fact a succession of ministers ran the country.

SECTION 4 REVIEW

1. **Define** tax farming, intendant, divine right of kings, balance of power
2. **Identify** Duke of Sully, Marie de Medici, Cardinal Richelieu, Cardinal Mazarin, Jean Baptiste Colbert, Marquis de Louvois, Jacques Cartier
3. **Locate** Navarre, La Rochelle, Alsace, Versailles, Alps, English Channel, Rhine River
4. **Understanding Ideas** What were the causes of the Thirty Years' War?
5. **Synthesizing Ideas** What goals did Cardinal Richelieu have for French domestic and foreign affairs?
6. **Summarizing Ideas** List some of the provisions of the Treaty of Westphalia.
7. **Interpreting Ideas** (a) How did the construction of Versailles contribute to the absolute power of Louis XIV? (b) Why did Louis XIV revoke the Edict of Nantes?

---

5 Monarchs in Eastern and Central Europe Expanded Their Power

While the countries of western Europe strengthened their national governments at the expense of local governments or class interests such as the nobility, the new empires of Russia, Prussia, and Austria grew up in eastern and central Europe.

Russian Isolation

After more than 200 years of Mongol rule, Russia became independent in 1480. By this time the rulers of Moscow had become the most important in Russia, and they continued to expand their power and their territory by conquests, marriages, and alliances. Moscow's rulers differed widely in their abilities, but a few had the qualities needed to build a large and powerful state.

Several factors—both physical and cultural—tended to separate Russia from western Europe. One was the Asian influence resulting from Mongol domination. Second, Western civilization had reached Russia from Constantinople and the Byzantine Empire, not from the West. Russia's religion was Eastern Orthodox rather than Roman Catholic or Protestant. Russia's use of the Cyrillic alphabet posed a barrier to communication with the rest of Europe, which used the Roman alphabet.

Most important, Russia's geography isolated the country from the rest of Europe. The country was almost entirely landlocked. The stronger kingdoms of Sweden and Poland blocked Russia from the Baltic Sea. To the south the Ottoman Turks held the Black Sea coast. To the west the vast plains of Poland and eastern Europe hindered commercial contacts. Russia's many navigable rivers did not flow into the great oceans and seas of commerce.

After the death of Ivan the Terrible in 1584, Russia underwent a long period of unrest. Nobles fought for power, false pretenders claimed the throne, and Russia's neighbors invaded. Finally, in 1613 a national assembly elected as czar Michael Romanov, the first of the Romanov dynasty that would rule Russia for 300 years.

In the mid-1600s, the Romanov monarchy faced a number of crises. It quieted rebellious townspeople by granting monopolies on trade and handicraft. It tried but failed to repress religious dissenters called "Old Believers," who broke away from the official church. The government succeeded, however, in crushing rebellious Cossacks, runaway peasants who had settled on Russia's southeastern frontier. Also, the Romanovs established serfdom more firmly during this time.

By dealing with these problems firmly, the czars thus created a Russian form of absolutism. In 1682 Peter I, a czar with remarkable vision, came to the throne. He would use this power to influence both Russia and Europe.

Peter the Great

Czar Peter I ruled Russia from 1682 to 1725. An energetic giant of a man—6 foot 9 inches tall—he had dark hair and eyes, a swarthy complexion, and a prominent nose, and he suffered from epilepsy. Peter also had a violent temper and was capable of great cruelty. It has been said that he murdered his son Alexis. This intemperate and ruthless czar decided that Russia's future lay toward Europe.

One of Peter's major goals was to break through Russia's landlocked position and acquire warmwater ports on the Sea of Azov and the Black Sea. However, the Ottoman Empire blocked those ambitions. It controlled all the land between the Black Sea and the Mediterranean Sea. Peter realized that to defeat the Turks he would need two things—help from western Europe and a stronger, more efficient Russia.

Peter's foreign mission. In 1697 Peter, who often disguised himself as a private citizen, went with a Russian delegation to several countries in western Europe to negotiate an alliance against the Turks. The mission failed in this purpose, but it was of great importance because the czar learned about the West. He met scientists and artisans and trained officers to return to Russia. He even worked as a carpenter in a Dutch East India Company shipyard to learn ship construction.

Westernization. Peter decided to remodel Russia along Western lines. He reorganized his army along French lines and equipped it with the best European weapons. He then tested this army in a long war (1700–1721) with Sweden, which resulted in Russia's gaining territory with access to the Baltic Sea. Peter also ended Sweden's short-lived role as a great power in Europe.

In this new territory at the eastern end of the Gulf of Finland (see map, this page), Peter built a completely new city, St. Petersburg (now Leningrad). In 1703 he moved the capital from Moscow to St. Petersburg, bringing the center of Russian government closer to the nations of western Europe. As Russia's "window to Europe," St. Petersburg symbolized the new Russian policy of Westernization.

Westernization meant that women abandon their isolation and take part in community life. The czar forced the nobles to give up their long robes—suitable for Russia's long, bitterly cold winters—and wear European-style short coats. Peter also ordered the men to shave off their long beards.

Much more important, however, were Peter's changes in Russian trade, finance, industry, and government. Armies and navies cost money, and to get it, Peter taxed nearly everything—from long beards to the birth of babies. He also encouraged the development of foreign trade and manufacturing.

In government Peter followed the absolutist ideas of Louis XIV of France. The czar had complete control of a highly centralized administration, and the nobles were merely his agents. The Orthodox church, too, fell under Peter's control. And, as in France, the monarchy also controlled local governments.

The nobility. Peter created a new service nobility, whose rank and privileges depended on the amount of government service performed rather than on family status. In return for government service, Peter granted the nobles large estates with thousands of serfs—many of them formerly free peasants. Peter's changes not only increased the number of serfs but also worsened their condition. At a time when serfdom was declining rapidly throughout western Europe, the czar began a policy of binding the Russian serfs to their lords as well as to the land. The serf's owners could buy and sell them much like slaves. Frequent uprisings occurred

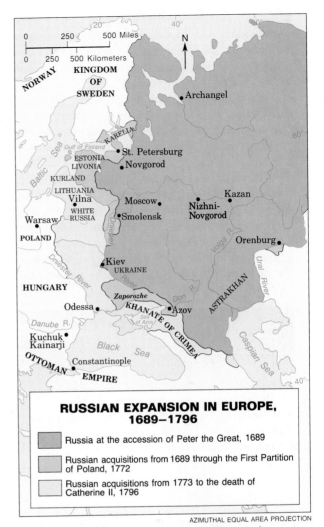

RUSSIAN EXPANSION IN EUROPE, 1689–1796

- Russia at the accession of Peter the Great, 1689
- Russian acquisitions from 1689 through the First Partition of Poland, 1772
- Russian acquisitions from 1773 to the death of Catherine II, 1796

AZIMUTHAL EQUAL AREA PROJECTION

Learning from Maps *Russia eventually won the ports it needed to increase trade. On which bodies of water are these ports located?*

as the peasants lashed out at their superiors who had inflicted this unhappy lot upon them. The government brutally crushed all such rebellions.

Although Peter the Great failed to westernize Russian society completely, under his leadership the nation rose to great power. He is called Peter the Great because he achieved astounding success in modernizing and centralizing the czarist monarchy and extending the nation's frontiers.

Catherine the Great

The male Romanovs who followed Peter the Great during the 1700s did not survive long. Three were

385

murdered and one died of smallpox. Peter's work was not carried forward until Catherine II, known as Catherine the Great, became empress.

A princess from a small German state, Catherine had married the heir to the Russian throne. Her unpopular husband, Peter III, preferred Germans and Germany to anything Russian. He ruled for only six months in 1762 and then was murdered by powerful nobles who supported Catherine. She ruled until 1796.

Domestic and foreign policy. Catherine II certainly did not earn her title "the Great" from her domestic policy. Catherine's support for the arts, science, literature, and the theater had little meaning or value to most Russians, who lived in deep ignorance and poverty. She extended serfdom into the new lands she acquired, and the masses—the

common people—lived much as they had before. Under Catherine II the nobility, however, became more westernized. They spoke French and lost touch with most of the Russian people. The vast differences between rulers and ruled help explain the undercurrent of discontent that finally exploded in revolution in the 1900s.

It was Catherine's foreign policy—a continuation of the expansionist policies of Peter the Great—that brought her fame. Russia still sought warm-water ports through the control of the Sea of Azov and the Black Sea. In a successful war against the Turks, Catherine won control of the Sea of Azov, most of the northern shore of the Black Sea, and a protectorate over the Crimea.

The Polish question. Catherine also made great territorial gains in the west. There the large

Learning from Pictures
Catherine the Great supported liberal ideas. She had schools and hospitals built, promoted education for women, and extended religious tolerance.

**THE PARTITIONS OF POLAND
1772–1795**

Poland	
—— Boundary of Poland before the partitions	
- - - - Partition boundary	
Territory acquired by Russia	
Territory acquired by Austria	
Territory acquired by Prussia	

0   150   300 Miles
0   150   300 Kilometers

AZIMUTHAL EQUAL AREA PROJECTION

Learning from Maps   *In less than 25 years Poland shrank to less than half its original size. Which country took most of Poland's land?*

kingdom of Poland had many weaknesses. The nobles elected its kings. The election campaigns to determine who would be king invited domestic and international troubles. Prussia, Austria, France, and Russia each repeatedly plotted to put its favorite on the Polish throne.

Only nobles were represented in Poland's legislature, the Diet. The Diet rarely accomplished anything because any one member could veto any legislation being considered.

Poland contained large minority groups of various nationalities and religions. The Roman Catholic Poles and their leaders often discriminated against and oppressed the minorities, and sometimes they appealed to Prussia, Austria, or Russia for help.

In 1772 these three powers decided to take advantage of Poland's weak condition and seize a slice of Polish territory. This action is known as the First Partition of Poland (see map, this page).

Unable to resist the partition, the Poles tried in 1791 to reform and strengthen their nation by adopting a new constitution. This new constitution would have established a hereditary monarchy and abolished the veto privileges in the Diet. However, in 1793 Russia and Prussia took a second helping of

Polish lands. The rebellion that broke out over this Second Partition was crushed, but it brought about the Third Partition in 1795 by Austria, Prussia, and Russia. With that, Poland disappeared from the map of Europe until 1919.

Catherine the Great had not only wrested control of the Black Sea from the Turks but also had acquired the largest share of Poland. She had added 200,000 square miles (520,000 square kilometers) of territory to her empire. Russia's borders now extended well into central Europe, and Russia became a force to consider in the European balance of power.

Russian Expansion

Russia's expansion differed from that of the western European countries. Instead of expanding overseas, Russia expanded overland. In addition to the political expansion south and west, Russian settlers, spearheaded by the freedom-loving Cossacks, moved eastward. In 1581 the Cossacks conquered the remnants of the Mongol Golden Horde and captured their capital city of Sibir. With that, the way lay open to the vast, sparsely populated region east of the Urals known as Siberia.

387

Learning from Pictures *Maria Theresa was one of Austria's most popular rulers. Among her 16 children was Marie Antoinette, future queen of France.*

This region's rich fur trade drew many people. Much like the pioneers of the American West, the early Russian settlers built small posts for trade and defense that grew into the towns and cities of Siberia. By the 1640s the Russians had reached the Pacific Ocean. At the Amur River they came in contact with the Chinese, who resisted Russian expansion into their country. In 1689 the Russians and Chinese signed a treaty that fixed the boundary between them north of the Amur River and provided for Chinese-Russian trade. Russia traded furs and raw materials with the Chinese in exchange for silk and tea. Also, by 1741 the Russians had crossed the Bering Strait to establish a colony in Alaska in North America.

Hapsburg Austria

The Austrian Hapsburgs lost much territory in the Thirty Years' War. In the 100 years after the war, however, Austria won new lands. These gains came in the form of lands won from the Turks in central Europe and the Balkans and territories received as a result of the Treaty of Utrecht, which ended the War of the Spanish Succession. The Hapsburgs now had an empire that extended to Hungary and the Italian Peninsula.

In 1740 Emperor Charles VI died, leaving no sons and only his 23-year-old daughter, Maria Theresa, to inherit Austria and the other Hapsburg lands. Charles had spent most of his reign trying to persuade other European rulers to sign an agreement called the Pragmatic Sanction. By this agreement the rulers of Europe promised to allow Maria Theresa to inherit the Hapsburg lands intact.

Although the laws of the Holy Roman Empire prevented Maria Theresa from being elected

What If?
Russian Expansion

Instead of expanding westward, Russia expanded overland to the east and colonized Alaska. If the Russians had colonized all of what is now Canada as well as Alaska, how might the history of the United States have been different?

empress, in 1745 she became Holy Roman Empress by making certain that her husband was elected emperor.

Maria Theresa inherited a patchwork of territories and peoples: Germans, Hungarians, Italians, Belgians, Romanians, Poles, Bohemians, Serbs, Croatians, and Slovenes. This great variety led to many conflicts of language, religion, and nationality within the empire.

Several German states envied Hapsburg power. Bavaria, in southern Germany, jealously guarded its lands and independence, sometimes by forming alliances with France against the Hapsburgs. In the north, Saxony and Hanover—whose rulers had been kings of England since 1714—also preferred to act independently of the Holy Roman Empire. Austria's chief rival, however, was Brandenburg-Prussia, a small north German state which in 1740 did not even have a common boundary with Austria.

The Rise of the Hohenzollerns

During the Middle Ages, the Hohenzollerns (HOH • uhn • zahl • uhrns) had ruled only a small territory in southern Germany. However, the ambitious family wanted to increase its power, influence, and landholdings. Near the end of the Middle Ages, one branch of the family settled in Brandenburg, in northern Germany. The ruler of Brandenburg eventually became an elector of the Holy Roman Empire.

During the Reformation the Calvinist Hohenzollerns seized lands belonging to the Catholic church in their territories. By the end of the Thirty Years' War in 1648, they ruled several widely scattered territories in Germany, including Prussia, which bordered the Baltic Sea.

One of the greatest of the Hohenzollerns, Frederick William, called the Great Elector, guided his state through the difficult last years of the Thirty Years' War. He then turned to the rebuilding and

Learning from Pictures Frederick the Great encouraged industry and agriculture. The German people considered him a strong king and a great military hero.

further strengthening of Brandenburg-Prussia. The Great Elector reorganized the armies of all his lands into one strong force. He also improved the tax collection system and encouraged agriculture, industry, and transportation.

Beginning with the reign of Frederick I, the Great Elector's successor and the first king of Prussia,* all the Hohenzollern possessions in northern Germany were called Prussia. The original duchy of Prussia became known as East Prussia.

Frederick William I. Frederick I, one of the many European rulers who tried to imitate Louis XIV of France, built a lavish palace in the style of Versailles. His son and successor, Frederick William I, disliked French ways intensely. He got rid of much of this luxury when he became king in 1713.

Frederick William I used the money he saved to strengthen Prussia. He doubled the size of the Prussian army and made it the best and most efficient

The Hohenzollerns	
1640–1688	Frederick William, the Great Elector
1688–1713	Frederick I
1713–1740	Frederick William I
1740–1786	Frederick II (the Great)

*As a reward for supporting the Hapsburgs in the War of the Spanish Succession, the Holy Roman Emperor granted Frederick I the title "King of Prussia" in 1701.

EUROPE IN 1763

Possessions of the Austrian Hapsburgs

Possessions of the Hohenzollerns

0   150   300 Miles

0   150   300 Kilometers

N

SWEDEN

St. Petersburg

Stockholm

Baltic Sea

RUSSIA

KINGDOM OF DENMARK AND NORWAY

EAST PRUSSIA

KINGDOM OF GREAT BRITAIN AND IRELAND

North Sea

P R U S S I A

Berlin

Warsaw

Vistula River

POLAND

ATLANTIC OCEAN

English Channel

London

UNITED NETHERLANDS

HANOVER

50°

AUSTRIAN NETHERLANDS

LESSER GERMAN STATES

SAXONY

SILESIA

Rhine River

Paris

BOHEMIA

LORRAINE

BAVARIA

Vienna

Bay of Biscay

FRANCE

SWITZERLAND

AUSTRIA

Buda • Pest

HUNGARY

Danube

River

Black Sea

SAVOY

MILAN

VENETIAN

30°

Avignon

PARMA

REPUBLIC

Adriatic

OTTOMAN

Constantinople

PORTUGAL

GENOA

TUSCANY

PAPAL STATES

MONTENEGRO

Sea

Madrid

KINGDOM OF SARDINIA

Corsica

Rome

40°

10°

SPAIN

Minorca (BR.)

Sardinia

KINGDOM OF NAPLES

EMPIRE

Aegean Sea

BALEARIC ISLANDS (SP.)

Gibraltar (BR.)

Mediterranean Sea

Sicily

Crete

AFRICA

0°

10°

20°

AZIMUTHAL EQUAL AREA PROJECTION

Learning from Maps   *Great Britain gained no new territories in Europe, according to the Peace of 1763. Who controlled Silesia?*

fighting force in Europe. A strict disciplinarian, Frederick William ran Prussia like a military barracks. At his palace, he treated his 14 children harshly. One of his few extravagances was recruiting, drafting, or even kidnapping tall soldiers to form his regiment of giants, the Potsdam Guards. Other European rulers knew the king of Prussia would owe them a great debt if they could furnish a soldier over six foot seven (2 meters) for this regiment.

In addition to strengthening the army, Frederick William I reorganized the civil service and encouraged trade and the development of new industries. Tax collecting and government spend-

ing were carefully planned to provide the Prussian treasury with a surplus for emergencies. And, convinced that all children should have a primary education, Frederick William I issued a decree requiring all parents to send their children to school.

Frederick the Great. Toward the end of his life, Frederick William I worried that his son Frederick had shown little interest in either military life or government service. Instead, the youth wrote poetry, played the flute, and read philosophy. The king used the harshest methods, even imprisonment, to force his heir to become the kind of son he desired. Frederick and a companion tried to escape the country, but they were caught. The king forced the son to watch as his friend was beheaded.

After this ordeal, the son seemed to have submitted to his father's wishes. Frederick William I need not have worried. Frederick II—or Frederick the Great—proved to be an even stronger ruler than his father. He became king in 1740, the same year that Maria Theresa became ruler of Austria.

Conflict Between Prussia and Austria

Though Frederick William I had signed the Pragmatic Sanction guaranteeing Maria Theresa her Hapsburg possessions, Frederick II argued that it did not apply to him. Almost immediately after becoming king, Frederick marched the strong army his father had created into Maria Theresa's richest province, Silesia. Prussia had no legal claim to Silesia. But it was a valuable region, populated largely by Germans, with rich farmlands and iron deposits, and its possession would greatly add to Frederick's own lands. Frederick did not declare war on Austria, and he took the Austrians by surprise. He said later that in seizing Silesia he lost only 20 men and 2 officers.

European and world war. The conquest of Silesia marked the beginning of two major European wars—the War of the Austrian Succession, which lasted from 1740 to 1748, and the Seven Years' War, from 1756 to 1763. Almost all of Europe became involved at one time or another. And, because European countries had colonies overseas, the fighting was not limited to Europe. Battles were also fought, notably between Great Britain and France, in India and North America. In America the Seven Years' War is known as the French and Indian War.

At one point Prussia, surrounded by enemies in Europe, was getting financial help only from Great Britain. Three times, enemy armies invaded the Prussian capital of Berlin. Fighting against great odds, Frederick dashed from one front to another to direct his troops in holding off the invaders. For all his great skill, he was spared only because Czar Peter III of Russia, who admired Frederick, made peace with Prussia. From then on the fighting decided nothing. Both sides agreed to the Treaty of Hubertusburg in 1763. Under its terms Prussia kept Silesia.

The years of peace. Frederick the Great spent the first 23 years of his reign at war. He spent the last 23 showing that he also had a genius for organization and administration. He expanded and further improved public education and the already excellent Prussian civil service system. He continued the Hohenzollern policy of religious freedom. For example, when the pope dissolved the Jesuit order in 1773, Frederick II invited its members to Protestant Prussia. He made legal and court reforms and encouraged trade and manufacturing. Through Frederick's hard work and wise direction, the expanded state of Prussia recovered the prosperity it had lost during the long years of war.

Prussia continued to make territorial gains. Frederick the Great helped to bring about the First Partition of Poland in 1772. By taking Polish territory along the Baltic coast, he linked Prussia and East Prussia. When he died in 1786, Frederick left a greatly enlarged and prosperous nation. Prussia had become a formidable rival of Austria for control of the German states and a first-class power in Europe.

The Diplomatic Revolution. Maria Theresa recognized that she could never recover Silesia, but she was determined not to lose any more of her possessions. To accomplish this, she gave up the old alliance with Great Britain—first formed in the long series of wars against Louis XIV—and made instead an alliance of Hapsburg Austria with its ancient enemy, Bourbon France. This was the Diplomatic Revolution, or reversal of alliances, made during the Seven Years' War. For many years afterward, France and Austria steadfastly opposed Great Britain and Prussia.

SECTION 5 REVIEW

1. **Identify** Peter the Great, Catherine the Great, Maria Theresa, Frederick William I, Frederick the Great
2. **Locate** Moscow, Black Sea, Sea of Azov, Gulf of Finland, St. Petersburg, Crimea, Siberia, Amur River, Bavaria, Silesia, Berlin
3. **Understanding Ideas** What factors separated Russia from western Europe?
4. **Interpreting Ideas** (a) Describe how Peter the Great tried to Westernize Russia both culturally and politically. (b) How did Catherine the Great continue Peter's foreign policy?
5. **Summarizing Ideas** What conditions in Poland made it easy for foreign powers to divide the country?
6. **Analyzing Ideas** (a) What were the reasons for the War of the Austrian Succession? (b) What were its results?

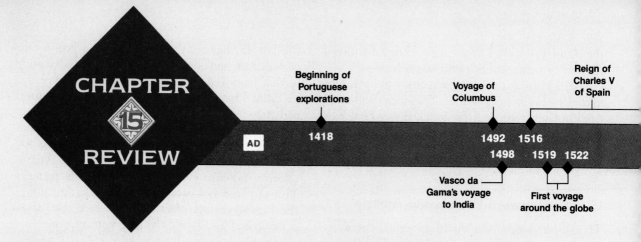

Beginning of Portuguese explorations 1418

Voyage of Columbus 1492

Reign of Charles V of Spain 1516

AD

1498   1519

1522

Vasco da Gama's voyage to India

First voyage around the globe

Chapter Summary

The following list contains the key concepts you have learned about European expansion and the formation of strong, centralized monarchies in Europe from about 1400 to about 1800.

1. Europeans were able to expand overseas because they developed or improved techniques in mapmaking, navigation, ship design, and weaponry.
2. The Commercial Revolution enabled Europeans to begin large-scale overseas expansion.
3. The development of new economic policies and methods also played an important part in carrying out exploration.
4. The political and economic changes associated with overseas expansion also contributed to a new economic theory called mercantilism.
5. Portuguese and Spanish explorers took the lead in discovering new lands and trade routes that paved the way for Europe's domination of the world.
6. The Portuguese developed the slave trade in Africa.
7. Spain established a vast colonial empire and became the greatest power on the European continent until the mid-1600s. It lost this superiority because it developed an imbalance of trade, squandered its resources in continuous wars, and neglected the national economy.
8. After the Dutch declared their independence from Spain, they created a large overseas empire. They dominated European commerce throughout the 1600s.
9. Cardinal Richelieu and Louis XIV humbled both the Spanish and Austrian Hapsburgs and made France an absolute monarchy. Their ambitions to achieve France's natural frontiers brought France into a series of wars.
10. During the 1700s Peter the Great and Catherine the Great extended both the powers of the central government and the boundaries of Russia.
11. War between the rising power of Hohenzollern Prussia and the Hapsburgs of Austria over the province of Silesia brought most of Europe into wars fought in Europe, North America, and India.

On a separate sheet of paper, complete the following review exercises.

Reviewing Important Terms

Supply the term that correctly completes each statement.

1. In an _____ _____ the ruler determines policy without consulting the people or their representatives and has complete power.
2. The captain of a ship at sea can determine latitude by means of an instrument called the _____ .
3. The changes in the European economy were so considerable that some historians have referred to the period from 1400 to 1750 as the _____ _____ .
4. A _____ _____ _____ raised money by selling shares in the company to investors.
5. An economic theory called _____ maintained that the world contained only a fixed amount of wealth and that to obtain a larger share, one country had to take some wealth away from another country.
6. By selling more goods in foreign countries than it buys, a country creates a _____ _____ _____ _____ .
7. A _____ is an import tax on foreign goods.
8. Government grants of money called _____ helped establish new industries and build ships.
9. _____ _____ was a term for selling the right to collect taxes to private individuals.
10. In France, Cardinal Richelieu strengthened the power of the local administrators known as _____ .
11. The _____ _____ was the shipment of slaves across the Atlantic Ocean to the West Indies or the southern colonies of British North America.
12. The principle of maintaining an equilibrium in international politics is known as the _____ _____ _____ .

Developing Critical Thinking Skills

1. **Interpreting Ideas** What changes in technology made it possible for Europeans to explore foreign lands?
2. **Summarizing Ideas** What social changes in Europe created a willingness to explore and settle overseas?
3. **Evaluating Ideas** Why was Dutch society considered one of Europe's most remarkable societies?
4. **Comparing Ideas** (a) How was Spanish colonization different from Portuguese colonization? (b) How

		Richelieu in power in France		1643–1715 Reign of Louis XIV in France			Reign of Frederick the Great in Prussia		1772 First Partition of Poland	

Election of Michael Romanov as czar

1556   1613   1624 1642   1740   1786
        1598 1618   1648   1682   1725   1762 1780 1796

Reign of Philip II of Spain

Thirty Years' War

Reign of Peter the Great in Russia

Reign of Maria Theresa in Austria

Reign of Catherine the Great in Russia

did Portuguese expansion affect the history of Africa?

5. **Understanding Ideas** **(a)** How did the Thirty Years' War weaken the Austrian Hapsburgs? **(b)** How did Austria benefit in the 100 years after the war? **(c)** Which country benefited most from this?

6. **Contrasting Ideas** **(a)** Compare the reigns of Peter the Great and Catherine the Great. **(b)** How were they similar? **(c)** What were the important accomplishments of each?

7. **Synthesizing Ideas** Explain how Cardinal Richelieu and Louis XIV strengthened the central government in France over local, religious, and class interests.

8. **Analyzing Ideas.** What factors enabled Prussia under the Hohenzollern family to create a strong, centralized government and become a great European power by the mid-1700s?

Relating Geography to History

During the Age of Exploration, certain geographical areas were important to navigation, exploration, and trade routes. Using the map on pages 360–61 and information in your textbook, explain the geographical importance of the following: **(a)** Cape of Good Hope, **(b)** Strait of Magellan, **(c)** African coast.

Relating Past to Present

1. It has been said that Louis XIV's control of a large and fine army gave him the desire to use it. Does the existence of great armies today lead to the same result? Explain your answer.

2. The 1600s are often called the "French century." What nation do you think the 1900s will be named after? Give reasons for your answer.

Applying History Study Skills

Before completing this activity, review Building History Study Skills on page 380.

Queen Elizabeth I addressed her troops on August 9, 1588, as they prepared to fight the Spanish Armada sent by Philip II. Read the selection. What inferences can you make about Queen Elizabeth?

❝ Let tyrants fear! I have always so behaved myself that, under God, I have placed my chiefest strength and safeguard in the loyal hearts and good will of my subjects; and therefore I am come amongst you, as you see, at this time, not for my recreation and disport, but being resolved, in the midst and heat of the battle, to live or die amongst you all, and to lay down for my God, for my kingdom, and for my people, my honour and my blood. . . .

I know I have the body of a weak and feeble woman, but I have the heart and stomach of a king, and of a king of England too, and think foul scorn that Parma or Spain, or any prince of Europe, should dare to invade the borders of my realm; to which, rather than my dishonour shall grow by me, I myself will take up arms. . . . ❞

1. Why is Elizabeth making the speech?

2. What does the speech tell you about Elizabeth's relationship to her people?

3. What does Elizabeth mean by "I have the body of a weak and feeble woman, but I have the heart and stomach of a king?"

4. What inferences can you make about Elizabeth's role as a ruler?

5. What inferences can be made about Elizabeth as a person?

Investigating Further

1. **Relating Literature to History** The novels of Alexander Dumas deal with France during the reign of Louis XIV. Read one of these novels to discover more about life in France during this period. *The Three Musketeers* would be especially appropriate.

2. **Conducting Research** St. Petersburg (now Leningrad), founded by Peter the Great, became a symbol of the new Russian policy of Westernization. Using books in your library, prepare a short report on St. Petersburg, concentrating mainly on its founding.

3. **Constructing a Chart** Use resources in your school or public library to find information on the Romanov czars. Then construct a family tree showing the imperial succession between Peter the Great and Catherine the Great.

16

The English-speaking World Took a New Political Course

Place The British Isles, North America, India

Time   1485—1800

3.7 mil. BC   4000 BC   AD 2100

Significance

England experienced much turmoil from the end of the 1400s to the beginning of the 1800s. The Tudor monarchs, who ruled from 1485 to 1603, had established Protestantism in England by naming the Anglican church the official church of England. However, other reformers called *Puritans* wanted to go further in reforming the church.

Continual clashes occurred between those who favored the Puritans and Parliament and those who favored the Anglican church and the monarchy. The struggle between these two factions erupted into a violent civil war.

In addition to the problems at home, rebellions in Ireland, Scotland, and later the North American colonies also troubled English rulers. Through all of this upheaval, however, England moved toward a parliamentary government and emerged as one of the strongest empires in the world.

Terms to Define

revolution	covenant	habeas corpus
gentry	constitution	cabinet
burgesses	natural rights	sea dogs

People to Identify

Elizabeth I	James II	Thomas
Charles I	Sir Francis Drake	Jefferson
Oliver Cromwell	Henry Hudson	Paul Revere

Places to Locate

English Channel	Jamestown
Ulster	Mississippi River
Bombay	Yorktown

Questions to Guide Your Reading

1 How did the Tudor monarchs and the Stuart monarchs differ in their relationship with Parliament?
2 What issues divided the English monarchy and Parliament?
3 Why did the King and the commons go to war in England?
4 How did England's colonial empire differ from those of other European powers?
5 What political arguments did the supporters of the Glorious Revolution and the American Revolution use to justify their actions?

Elizabeth I, the forceful queen who ruled England from 1558 to 1603, had a strong, sometimes contradictory personality. In the following passage, the author Lytton Strachey gives us a glimpse of this fascinating and vibrant queen.

> **❝W**hile the Spanish ambassador declared that ten thousand devils possessed her, the ordinary Englishman saw in King Hal's full-blooded daughter a Queen after his own heart. She swore; she spat; she struck with her fist when she was angry; she roared with laughter when she was amused. And she was often amused. A radiant atmosphere of humour coloured and softened the harsh lines of her destiny, and buoyed her up along the zigzags of her dreadful path. Her response to every stimulus was immediate and rich: to the folly of the moment, to the clash and horror of great events, her soul leapt out with a vivacity, an abandonment, a complete awareness of the situation, which made her, which makes her still, a fascinating spectacle. **❞**

Elizabeth I, one of England's strongest monarchs, led her country successfully through a very turbulent time in its history.

1 The Tudors and the Stuarts Clashed with Parliament

Chapter 15 described the struggle between central governments and local authorities for control in European countries. In these countries the central governments usually won, and the most extreme form of central government—absolute monarchy—became common. Of all the revolts in the mid-1600s, the most severe took place in England. The clash there led in the 1640s and 1650s to civil war and **revolution**—a radical attempt to change the very structure of a country's government. Although the English Revolution did not succeed, it influenced both English history and political ideas throughout Europe.

The Reign of Mary Tudor

In the late 1400s, a new royal family, the Tudors, became England's rulers. Following the turbulence

◀ *Elizabeth I knighting Francis Drake*

Learning from Pictures *This coin (both sides pictured) commemorates the wedding of Philip II of Spain to Mary I of England.*

of the Wars of the Roses, the first Tudor king, Henry VII, brought stability and prosperity to England. The Tudors made the same efforts to strengthen their powers as did the rulers of France and Spain. Of the five Tudor monarchs, Henry VIII, who reigned from 1509 to 1547, and his daughter Elizabeth I, who reigned from 1558 to 1603, had the greatest success. Henry VIII established a new official church in England, the Anglican church.

After the short reign of sickly Edward VI, Mary I, the oldest daughter of Henry VIII, ascended the throne at the age of 37 and became the first reigning queen of England. Her unhappiness and her devotion to Catholicism shaped her attitude. Though she did not lack courage or kindliness, she had a fierce determination to make England a Catholic nation again. Her unpopular marriage to Philip II of Spain, the leader of the Counter-Reformation, worried her Protestant subjects. Their worries proved to be well-founded. Mary, determined to rid England of those clergy who would not conform to the laws of the Catholic church, burned close to 300 people at the stake, including Thomas Cranmer, the archbishop of Canterbury. For this reason she was given the nickname "Bloody Mary." The queen's persecutions shocked the English, and Mary totally failed to destroy Protestantism.

The Reign of Elizabeth I

When Mary I died in 1558, her half-sister Elizabeth became queen. Elizabeth I used parliamentary acts to help make England Protestant. For example, people who did not attend the Anglican church had to pay a fine. The monarchy benefited from the break with the Catholic church because it took over church lands and consolidated its powers.

Mary Queen of Scots. Religion also entered into the question of who should succeed Elizabeth. In a monarchy the oldest child usually inherits the throne. But Elizabeth did not marry and had no children. Her closest relative and heir—Mary Stuart, queen of Scotland, or Mary Queen of Scots as she is more commonly known—was Catholic.

The prospect of Mary Queen of Scots becoming queen of England horrified English Protestants. However, it also delayed the plans of Philip II of Spain to invade England and force a Catholic ruler on the English people.

In 1568, to escape problems in Scotland, the headstrong Mary fled to England, only to be imprisoned by Elizabeth. Later, Mary foolishly plotted with Philip II's ambassadors in England to kill Elizabeth and seize the English throne. Reluctantly, Elizabeth signed the Scottish queen's death warrant, and in 1587 Mary was beheaded. With Mary dead, Philip II no longer had any reason to postpone his plans to invade England.

The Spanish Armada. In 1588 Philip sent a fleet of 130 ships, which he called the "Invincible Armada," north toward the English Channel. The English summoned all their ships to intercept the Spanish Armada. The swift, maneuverable English ships had the advantage. They also had guns that fired faster and had a longer range than the guns on the Spanish ships. The English managed to damage and sink a number of the lumbering Spanish vessels. The Spaniards ran low on ammunition and attempted to escape to the North Sea. A terrible storm—the "Protestant Wind"—began to blow, further battering the Spanish vessels. Some of the Spanish ships reached the open sea and attempted to limp home around Scotland and Ireland. Many of them foundered on the rocky, desolate coasts of these two countries. Only about 50 ships managed to return to Spain. The combination of bad weather and skilled English seafaring had proved deadly for Philip II's enormous Armada. With Spain no longer a threat and Elizabeth's throne and

Protestantism secure, England turned to exploring overseas. However, Elizabeth's government still faced two major problems.

The religious problem. The religious issue in England was unsettled. The monarchy had led the break with the pope and the establishment of Protestantism in England, but many people believed that the change had not gone far enough. They wanted to "purify" the English church even further. These people, called *Puritans*, objected to the continuation of many Catholic practices. Although the Anglican church had abolished the Mass, it still had bishops. Priests still dressed in elaborate robes for religious services, and the congregation still knelt during services. The Puritans thought these customs too Catholic and wanted to abolish them.

Like many monarchs of the time, the Protestant Tudors thought religious disunity threatened England's stability. They wanted all their subjects to be united in the Anglican faith. Therefore, they persecuted both the remaining Catholics and the Puritans. Not only did they fail to stamp out either group, they created a dangerous enemy in the Puritans.

The Puritans set very strict moral standards and became increasingly unhappy about the Anglican church and the quality of the clergy. Eventually, that unhappiness made the Puritans willing to revolt against their ruler. Queen Elizabeth, however, refused to allow any changes in the Anglican church. The Anglican church became a permanent institution largely through the force of her personality.

Elizabeth I and Parliament. In England, Parliament, the body of representatives from the whole country, had the right to approve all taxes and pass laws. Parliament gained power and prestige in the 1530s, when Henry VIII used it to pass the laws that made England a Protestant nation. Moreover, people looked to Parliament as a restraint on the monarchy because it represented the wishes of people outside the central government.

Parliament had two houses. The House of Lords consisted of nobles and higher clergy. The House of Commons represented two classes: gentry and burgesses. The **gentry** owned land and had social position. The younger sons of nobles, who could not inherit their fathers' titles or positions, sometimes moved into the gentry. Merchants and professional people from the towns and cities made up the **burgesses.**

Learning from Pictures The English built the tower of London as a fortress but later used it as a prison. Mary I briefly imprisoned Elizabeth I in the tower.

The gentry and burgesses mingled to a surprising extent in England. Class lines were blurred compared with those in continental Europe. Rich merchants who owned land might be considered gentry. Younger sons of nobles might enter professions and come to be regarded as burgesses. Together the two groups had considerable power that the monarch had to respect.

Elizabeth I summoned 10 Parliaments during her reign, and they met for a total of 140 weeks. She managed Parliament very cleverly, obtaining all the taxes she needed without letting the members influence her policy too directly. Although angered at their petitions urging her to marry, Elizabeth nevertheless always respected the members' freedom of speech in their meeting hall. Despite her skill at managing Parliament, Elizabeth found it increasingly difficult to prevent its members, particularly the Puritans, from questioning government policies. Under the reigns of her less clever successors, Parliament's questions became increasingly numerous and more challenging. Eventually, members of Parliament began a revolution when the monarchy refused to listen to their views.

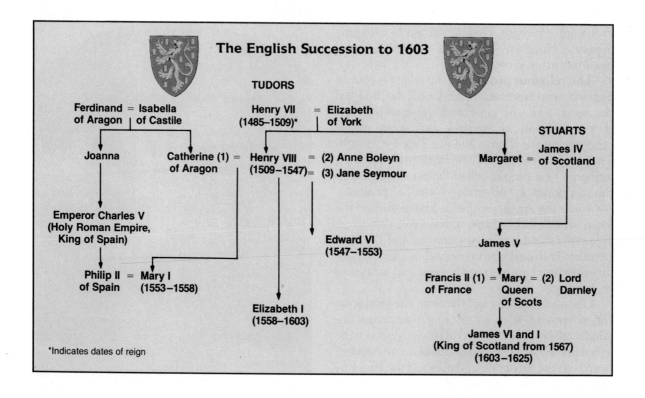

The English Succession to 1603

TUDORS

Ferdinand = Isabella
of Aragon | of Castile

Henry VII = Elizabeth
(1485–1509)* | of York

STUARTS

James IV
of Scotland

Joanna

Catherine (1) = Henry VIII = (2) Anne Boleyn
of Aragon | (1509–1547) = (3) Jane Seymour

Margaret = James IV
of Scotland

Emperor Charles V
(Holy Roman Empire,
King of Spain)

Edward VI
(1547–1553)

James V

Philip II = Mary I
of Spain | (1553–1558)

Francis II (1) = Mary = (2) Lord
of France | Queen | Darnley
of Scots

Elizabeth I
(1558–1603)

James VI and I
(King of Scotland from 1567)
(1603–1625)

*Indicates dates of reign

The Roots of the English Revolution

Between 1603, when Elizabeth died, and 1640, relations between the monarchy and its subjects deteriorated. The main stages in that deterioration suggest how and why it happened.

James I. The first problem arose almost immediately. King James VI of Scotland, a member of the Stuart family and the son of Mary Queen of Scots, succeeded Elizabeth to the English throne as James I of England.* He was tall and had blue eyes. At age 39, he had thin brown hair, a straggly beard, and spindly legs. The gangly king was also coarse in his habits. The French ambassador said that "where he wishes to assume the language of a king his tone is that of a tyrant, and where he condescends he is vulgar." But James had a taste for learning and was a man of considerable intelligence. Even so, he lacked common sense. According to Henry IV of France, he was "the wisest fool in Christendom."

James managed to rule in Scotland by pitting one faction against another and keeping the powerful church of Scotland under control. His English

subjects suspected that, as a foreigner, he did not really understand how their parliamentary system worked. At his first Parliament, some of its members drew up an Apology of the House of Commons, a document that arrogantly explained the way its authors thought England ought to be ruled. James, who strongly believed in the divine right of kings, openly ignored their advice.

Finance and foreign policy occupied the attention of James I during much of his reign. He left the Puritans alone and even pleased them by ordering a new translation of the Bible into English. This Bible, known as the Authorized Version, or King James Version, is still one of the most widely used English translations.

James I's troubles came not from the Puritans but from Parliament. The 1600s was a time of inflation and growing government activity. James could never collect enough money in taxes to finance his policies. When the taxes passed by Parliament proved insufficient, he raised money by selling titles of nobility, granting monopoly rights to private companies, and increasing customs duties. Parliament objected to these methods. It also objected to James's attempt to create an alliance with England's old enemy, Spain.

Charles I. At the time of his death in 1625, James I and his subjects had an uneasy relationship. The tension between the monarchy and the people increased during the reign of his son Charles I, who ruled from 1625 to 1649. Brave, arrogant, and tactless, Charles believed in the divine right of kings just as firmly as his father had. His high opinion of the role of the monarch kept him aloof even from his own advisers. Charles had few friends and had none of the common touch of his father. An unhappy marriage to the Catholic French princess Henrietta Maria completed his isolation.

When Charles I could not persuade Parliament to give him funds, he tried to force people to loan him the money he needed and imprisoned many who refused. The king's policies led to a terrible confrontation with Parliament during 1628 and 1629. The members presented Charles with a document known as the Petition of Right. Desperate for money, Charles signed the petition, promising not to levy taxes without the consent of Parliament, not to declare martial law or to quarter soldiers in private homes in peacetime, and not to imprison people without a specific charge. Although Charles had signed the petition, he continued to levy taxes.

When members of the House of Commons protested, he dissolved Parliament.

For the next 11 years, Charles refused to call Parliament into session, hoping never to have to do so again. During this time he used drastic methods to collect taxes and revived long-ignored dues and royal fees.

Charles I took his job as head of the Anglican church seriously. He favored a very formal and ritualistic Protestantism, which irritated the Puritans. They also despised the extravagant life of the royal family. Charles in turn increased the restrictions on Puritans. For example, he limited sermons to those that concerned the Ten Commandments and required government approval for the printing of any religious books. As a result of these restrictions, thousands of Puritans left the country for a new life in America during the 1630s. Those who stayed behind became determined opponents of the king's policies.

These Puritans were joined by some members of Parliament and many lawyers who thought the king's rule was tyrannical. Charles avoided the system of common law by offering cheap and rapid justice in the royal courts. In these courts decisions were made in secret by judges, not by juries.

Learning from Pictures *This patent of nobility, issued by Charles I in 1627, is considered a work of art. It shows Charles seated on the throne and the royal lion of England.*

Common-law lawyers resented these rivals to the circuit court system, especially because they believed the king controlled the judges. One royal court, the Court of Star Chamber—named for the wall and ceiling designs in the room where it met—was particularly efficient at prosecuting Puritans and critics of government policy. People bitterly hated the Star Chamber.

It seemed to many English people that Charles I was increasingly imposing his own absolute rule. Those who opposed the growing power of the central government waited for an opportunity to reverse this trend.

The Scots. When Charles tried to impose a standard prayer book on his Scottish subjects, the opportunity came. The Scots had accepted a branch of Puritanism known as Presbyterianism. Elders known as *presbyters,* rather than bishops, ruled the Presbyterian church. The Presbyterians had their own prayer book. In 1638 they responded to Charles's attempt to Anglicanize the Presbyterian service by signing a National Covenant. In this **covenant,** or solemn agreement, the Scots swore to the death that changes in the church in Scotland violated both their religion (modeled after Calvinism) and acts of the Scottish Parliament. Moreover, the king seemed to be reestablishing Catholic practices in Scotland. Though the Scottish Presbyterians did not question their loyalty to King Charles, loyalty to their church—the Kirk—came before loyalty to the king. Charles I insisted on being obeyed, so the Scots assembled an army to fight for their religious freedom. In desperate need of money to fight the Scots, Charles called Parliament into session in 1640.

SECTION 1 REVIEW

1. **Define** revolution, gentry, burgesses, covenant
2. **Identify** Mary I, Philip II, Elizabeth I, Mary Queen of Scots, James I, Charles I
3. **Locate** English Channel
4. **Summarizing Ideas** What religious problems plagued the royal succession when Elizabeth I came to the throne?
5. **Synthesizing Ideas** How did Elizabeth I control Parliament?
6. **Understanding Ideas** What difficulties arose between Parliament and each of the first two Stuart kings?
7. **Analyzing Ideas** (a) What issues divided Protestants in England? (b) How did those issues influence English politics?

---

2 The King and Commons Went to War

The Parliament of 1640—known as the *Long Parliament*—reconvened periodically for 20 years. The Puritans who controlled the House of Commons took a number of actions that limited absolute monarchy in England. For example, they abolished the king's power to dissolve Parliament and passed a law requiring that Parliament meet at least once every three years. They ended all forms of illegal taxation, abolished the Court of Star Chamber, and executed two of the most hated advisers of the king.

The Irish Problem

While the Long Parliament worked at reducing the king's authority, Charles also faced trouble in Ireland. England had ruled Ireland since the late 1100s, but it had never brought the Irish completely under control. The English conquerors seized land belonging to Irish owners and gave it to English settlers, who were mostly Anglicans. In time these landowning Anglo-Irish settlers became the upper class and controlled most of the wealth of Ireland. Later, Scottish Presbyterians settled in the northern region called Ulster. Mostly farmers and merchants, they became the middle class. The majority of the native Irish remained Roman Catholic, were tenant farmers, and formed the lower social and economic classes. In 1641, led primarily by the Irish Catholics, the Irish rebelled against England.

The rebellion in Ireland and the Scottish invasion of England forced Charles I at first to concede to Parliament and then to accept the changes that resulted. Later, however, the most radical Puritan group tried to pass an act that would abolish the appointment of bishops in the Anglican church. This group also issued a complete list of grievances against Charles I. As a staunch defender of the Anglican church, whose motto might have been "No bishop, no king," Charles I at that point led troops into the House of Commons and tried to arrest the leaders of the opposition. This hostile act led to the outbreak of a civil war in 1642 between supporters of the king and supporters of Parliament.

English Civil War

It was difficult to determine whether a citizen favored the king or Parliament. Generally, the king's supporters, called *royalists* or Cavaliers, after the king's cavalry, included Anglicans, Roman Catholics, nobles, and anyone who disagreed with the Puritans on political or religious issues. The Puritans supported Parliament. They were sometimes called Roundheads, after the Puritan soldiers who tucked their hair under their helmets. Anyone who believed that the powers of the king ought to be severely curbed joined the Puritan opposition.

Oliver Cromwell, leader of the Puritans, organized his forces into a New Model Army that the Cavaliers could not match. The New Model Army had well-drilled, disciplined, and zealous soldiers who charged into battle singing hymns. They easily outfought the royalists. After two defeats in battle, Charles I surrendered in 1646.

This surrender initiated a great maneuvering among various political and religious groups for control of the government. Chief among these groups were the Presbyterians, who held a majority in Parliament, and the Independents, led by Cromwell, who made up a majority of the army. Cromwell's Independents won the struggle. They used troops to keep all Anglican and Presbyterian members from entering the House of Commons, leaving only 60 members, all Independents. This remnant of the Long Parliament became known as the Rump Parliament, since it was the only part of the parliamentary body left sitting.

Death of the king. The Rump Parliament abolished both the monarchy and the House of Lords. It proclaimed England a *commonwealth*, a

Learning from Pictures
Oliver Cromwell was very modest. He is said to have told the artist not to make him look handsome, but to paint him "warts and all."

401

word used at that time to mean a republic, and appointed a special court to try Charles I for treason. The court condemned Charles and beheaded him in front of the palace at Whitehall in 1649. Charles I faced death courageously. This advanced the cause of the monarchy as many people now considered Charles a martyr. His courage enabled the English to overlook his faults and made it easier for Charles's son, who fled to France after his father's death, to return later as king. Meanwhile, Oliver Cromwell took control of England and became essentially a military dictator.

Cromwell's Commonwealth

Oliver Cromwell was a devout, honest, and upright Puritan who possessed the qualities of a powerful orator and skilled leader. However, he believed that only he could govern correctly. He suppressed all political and religious opposition with great severity. He even tried to control the country's social life by closing all theaters and limiting many other forms of popular entertainment.

Although Cromwell held considerable power, he was a reluctant dictator. He preferred a parliamentary, republican government and made several attempts to create one. He tried twice to establish a **constitution**—a document outlining the fundamental laws and principles that govern a nation. One such document, known as the Instrument of Government, was the first written constitution of a major European nation. It gave Cromwell the title of Lord Protector and provided that landowners would elect Parliament. Cromwell held the title of Lord Protector from 1653 until 1658, a period often called the *Protectorate.*

Cromwell's government might have been overthrown except for three factors: (1) It had enough money from taxes and the sale of confiscated royalist lands to support itself and its army. (2) Its enemies, the Irish and the royalists, had no organized army. Cromwell suppressed the Irish so mercilessly that his name inspires hate even today, and the royalists never posed a serious threat. (3) Its own army was disciplined and powerful.

Cromwell's domestic policy of developing manufacturing and trade related directly to his foreign policy. During the troubled times of the civil war in England, Dutch merchants and shipowners had built up a profitable trade. Cromwell challenged the Dutch by having Parliament pass the Navigation Act of 1651. This act required that all imports into England be shipped in English ships or the ships of the country producing the goods.

Cromwell's policies led to a commercial war with the Dutch from 1652 to 1654. Because the Dutch carried so much of the world's trade, they realized that the freedom of the seas was at stake. England seized the lucrative Portuguese slave trade away from the Dutch in 1654, but the war ended indecisively. During the war, however, the English navy gained prestige, and Cromwell demonstrated that the English government would use its might to strengthen English commerce.

The End of the Revolution

Cromwell's experiment with republican government failed. He quarreled almost as much with Parliament as had the Stuart kings, and parliamentary resentment of central power resurfaced. Shortly before his death in 1658, Cromwell dissolved Parliament and ruled alone. His son Richard, who succeeded him as Lord Protector, was a weak leader who could not win the necessary support of the army.

By 1660 the English people, too, had undergone a change in feelings. Though some had favored the execution of Charles I, Cromwell's rule had brought only confusion and resentment. After some hesitation, the new Parliament of 1660 invited Charles II, the son of Charles I, to return to England from exile. The English Revolution ended, and although the country seemed to have weathered its troubles, another 30 years would pass before anyone could be certain that any lessons—especially the need to give Parliament an important role in government—had been learned.

SECTION 2 REVIEW

1. **Define** constitution
2. **Identify** Long Parliament, Cavalier, Roundhead, Oliver Cromwell, New Model Army, Rump Parliament
3. **Interpreting Ideas** How did rebellions in Scotland and Ireland influence the civil war in England?
4. **Summarizing Ideas** (a) In what ways did the Long Parliament limit absolute monarchy in England? (b) How did the civil war begin?
5. **Synthesizing Ideas** Why was Oliver Cromwell unable to establish a permanent republic in England?

Learning from Pictures   *In 1660 Charles II returned to England where the people gave him an enthusiastic welcome.*

3 England Established a Constitutional Monarchy

The struggles between king and Parliament did not end in 1660. An echo of the crisis occurred in the 1680s. After that uncertainty passed, however, the English created a stable government that linked monarch and Parliament in a close, workable partnership.

Charles II and the Restoration

The revolution ended in 1660, when Charles II regained the throne. The period of his rule is called the Restoration, because monarchy had been restored in England.

Charles II was well over six feet tall. He had dark brown hair and eyes, and he resembled his Medici and Bourbon ancestors. Charles was quite dignified, but because he also loved entertainment and good times, people called him the "Merry Monarch." Charles removed the restrictions on the theater and other forms of entertainment that the stern Puritans of the Commonwealth had legislated. A lampoon of the time said of Charles II:

> **"W**e have a pretty witty king
>   Whose word no man relies on:
> He never said a foolish thing,
>   And never did a wise one. **"**

Despite this lampoon, Charles II had learned much from his years in exile. He said he had no desire "to go on his travels again." When his policies met opposition, he gave in, although he often used roundabout methods to gain his ends. Charles continued Cromwell's commercial policy, which eventually led to wars with the Dutch. During these wars England seized the Dutch settlement of New Amsterdam in North America and renamed it New York. Charles wanted an alliance with France, but English protests forced him to oppose France. This shift marked the beginning of 150 years of rivalry between England and France for mastery of the sea and for colonial power.

Charles II tolerated Roman Catholics and hoped to lift some of the legal restrictions on them in England. However, his attempt to do so met with such strong parliamentary opposition that he abandoned the effort.

Political Parties Develop

Because Charles II and his Portuguese queen, Catherine of Braganza, had no children, it seemed clear that Charles's younger brother James, a Roman Catholic, would succeed him. The issue of royal succession led to the development of England's first political parties.

Two groups of almost equal strength—*Tories* and *Whigs*—evolved in Parliament. Like Cavaliers and Roundheads, the terms Tories and Whigs were nicknames. The original Tories had been Irish Catholic guerrillas. The Whigs had been Presbyterian guerrillas in southwestern Scotland. The Tories wanted a strong hereditary monarch, but not an absolute one. They strongly supported the Anglican church but would willingly accept a Roman Catholic ruler provided that the heirs were Protestant. The Whigs favored a weak monarch and a strong Parliament. They vigorously opposed the idea of a Roman Catholic ruler.

James II and the Glorious Revolution

Charles II died in 1685 and his brother the Duke of York came to the throne as James II. The fair-haired, humorless, and stubborn James had learned less in exile than had Charles. As a Roman Catholic and an ardent believer in royal absolutism, like that of Louis XIV in France, he antagonized both Whigs and Tories.

Like Charles, one of James's main problems involved the succession to the throne. James's daughters, Mary and Anne, were both raised as Protestants, and both married Protestant princes.

Learning from Pictures William III and Mary II were the only monarchs in English history who ruled with equal power. Who invited them to become England's monarchs?

However, James's first wife died, and he was married again, this time to a Roman Catholic princess, Mary of Modena. In 1688 Mary gave birth to a son, who would by law succeed his father before his older half-sisters. Since the boy was a Catholic like his father and mother, English Protestants feared a whole line of Catholic rulers on the throne of mostly Protestant England.

Now all the groups who opposed James combined to bring about the event known as the Glorious Revolution. Whigs and Tories agreed that James must abdicate. A number of leading nobles invited James's daughter Mary and her Dutch husband William of Orange to take the throne of England. Although William landed in England with an army in 1688, armed force was hardly necessary. Unable to rally anyone to his support and fearful of assassination, James fled to France. Parliament gave the crown to William III and Mary II as joint rulers.

New Ideas About Government

The English civil war and the events that followed led not only to changes in government but also to new ideas about government. The English philosopher Thomas Hobbes lived through the civil war and was disturbed by the chaos it created. He set forth his political philosophy in a book called *Leviathan,* published in 1651.

Hobbes explained that groups of people first lived in anarchy, what he called a "state of nature." Life was violent and dangerous under these circumstances, so people chose a leader to rule them. In order to maintain a stable society, people made an unwritten "social contract." Hobbes argued that under this contract they had to give the monarch absolute power, or anarchy would again result. The people retained only the right to protect their own lives.

John Locke, another English philosopher, adopted many of Hobbes's ideas but interpreted them differently. Locke supported Parliament in the struggle that led to the overthrow of James II. Earlier, he established the principles on which the supporters of the Glorious Revolution acted in 1688, and in 1690 he published these principles in his *Two Treatises on Civil Government.*

Like Hobbes, Locke believed that people had first lived in a state of anarchy and then made a social contract. However, he believed that people had given up only some of their individual rights and had kept others. The rights they kept, called **natural rights,** included the right to live, the right to enjoy liberty, and especially the right to own property.

According to Locke, a ruler who violated these rights violated natural law and broke the unwritten social contract. The people had the right to overthrow such a ruler and replace him with another ruler who pledged to observe and protect their rights. Locke thus provided grounds for the people to force James II to leave the throne and for Parliament to offer the crown to William and Mary. Locke's ideas would influence later revolutions in America and France.

Safeguards Against Absolute Rule

Parliament passed safeguards against arbitrary rule as early as the reign of Charles II. In 1679 it passed an important measure, the *Habeas Corpus Act.* This act provided that anyone who was arrested could obtain a writ, or order, demanding to be brought before a judge within a specified period of time. The judge would decide whether the prisoner should be released or charged and tried for a crime. The writ itself was called **habeas corpus,** Latin for "you shall have the body." The Habeas Corpus Act protected individuals against illegal arrest and unlawful imprisonment.

Before granting the throne to William and Mary in 1689, Parliament required them to accept in advance certain fixed conditions named in a document known as the *Bill of Rights.* The Bill of Rights declared that Parliament would choose the ruler, who would be merely an official, subject to parliamentary laws. The ruler could not proclaim or suspend any law, impose any tax, or maintain an army in peacetime without Parliament's consent. Parliament had to meet frequently, and the monarch could not interfere in the elections of its members. The Bill of Rights guaranteed the right of the members of Parliament to express themselves freely.

The Bill of Rights also protected private citizens. All citizens had the right to petition the government for relief of any injustice. In addition, no one could be required to pay excessive bail or be subjected to cruel and unusual punishment.

In 1689 Parliament also passed the *Act of Toleration.* This act granted freedom of conscience and the right of public worship to those Protestants (now called Dissenters) who were not members of

Theaters

People have enjoyed going to see plays and entertainment since the earliest times. In ancient Greece and Rome, performances were given in great open-air arenas (right). In ancient Japan the *No* plays were popular entertainment.

During the Middle Ages, sacred stories and plays with Christian themes, called *morality plays,* were performed in or near churches. By the time of the Renaissance, special buildings were built for the performances. These buildings came to be known as *theaters.*

Perhaps the most famous theater in history was the Globe (below). This octagon-shaped theater was built in the late 1500s on the south bank of the Thames River, across from London. Most of William Shakespeare's plays had their earliest performances in the Globe.

Londoners flocked to see the latest comedies and tragedies of writers like Shakespeare, Christopher Marlowe, and Ben Jonson. These writers did not write morality plays. Imitating the models of classical Greece and Rome, they created dramas that were full of romance, humor, violence, and despair.

Plays had to be performed in the daytime, when there was enough natural light to illuminate the stage. The center of the theater was open to the sky. Ordinary tradespeople sat or stood in this open area, ready to be rained upon if the weather turned bad. Nobles and rich merchants sat in boxes around the sides of the theater. The stage itself was covered by an overhanging roof.

The human emotions explored by the plays of the Elizabethan and Restoration periods are so universal that many of the plays continue to be performed. Love, ambition, madness, and revenge were the themes of ancient Greek dramas. The same themes are still used by modern playwrights. Our enjoyment of the theater is one way in which we are linked with our ancestors.

the Anglican church. It did not, however, bring about complete religious freedom. For example, Roman Catholics still lived under heavy restrictions, and no Dissenters could hold public office.

In 1701 Parliament passed the Act of Settlement, designed to keep Roman Catholics off the English throne. The act provided that if William III should die with no children to succeed him, Mary's sister, Anne, would inherit the throne. If Anne had no children, the throne would go to another Protestant granddaughter of James I, the German Electress Sophia of Hanover.

Parliament Rules England

The Bill of Rights and the Act of Settlement marked the end of the long struggle between monarch and Parliament to determine who would rule the country. By 1700, although England remained a monarchy, Parliament held the power. However, Parliament did not represent all the people. Hereditary nobles and higher clergy made up the House of Lords. Even the House of Commons, which was gradually becoming the more powerful of the two houses, was not particularly representative. Only about 15 percent of the male population—the gentry who were landowners and the powerful commercial people—had the right to vote for members of the House of Commons.

In the 50 years following 1689, Parliament continued to gain importance as the real power in the government of England. During this time the organization and institutions characteristic of today's English government gradually emerged.

For centuries, English monarchs had met with advisers to discuss government problems. Beginning in the time of Charles II, a smaller group of advisers began to meet separately. Most of them were *ministers,* or heads of government departments. They made policy and dealt with issues effectively because they were leaders in Parliament. This group became known as the **cabinet.**

At first the cabinet included both Whigs and Tories. However, during the reign of William III, it became clear that the government ran more smoothly when most of the ministers of the cabinet belonged to the majority party in the House of Commons. Thus the monarch chose his or her ministers accordingly.

Several additional changes increased parliamentary control of the English government during and following the reign of William III. Parliament gained the right to declare war, and the monarch stopped vetoing acts of Parliament. Queen Anne, who reigned from 1702 to 1714, was the last monarch to veto an act of Parliament.

Act of Union

Before he died, William III urged the union of England and Scotland. He perhaps feared that Scottish resentment of rich England might lead the Scots to take sides with France again. In 1707 the Parliaments of England and Scotland passed the Act of Union. This act merged the two countries into one kingdom, known as Great Britain. The act abolished the Scottish Parliament and gave the Scots seats in the English House of Lords and House of Commons.

Learning from Maps *In 1707, Parliament united Scotland and England into the kingdom of Great Britain. What cities are outside the kingdom of Great Britain?*

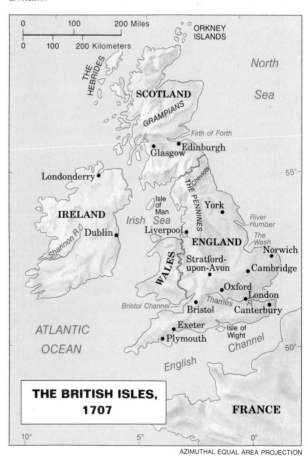

THE BRITISH ISLES, 1707

AZIMUTHAL EQUAL AREA PROJECTION

Learning from Pictures *George I founded the Knights of the Bath, shown here in a procession at Westminster. What language did George I speak?*

Some people opposed the union at first, particularly in Scotland, but the union proved beneficial. By removing trade barriers, it encouraged commerce and brought prosperity to both England and Scotland. The Scottish city of Glasgow grew from a fishing village into a great port. The universities of Edinburgh and Glasgow became major centers of learning in Europe during the 1700s.

Parliamentary control increased under the successors to Queen Anne. Queen Anne had 17 children, but none survived her. When she died in 1714, the elector of Hanover succeeded to the throne. Since Sophia of Hanover also died in 1714, her son George I became the first of the Hanoverian dynasty of Great Britain. Both he and his son George II were born in Germany and were unfamiliar with British government and customs. George I, who ruled until 1727, spoke no English. George II, who was king until 1760, spoke fluent English, but with a strong German accent. Although the details of British government interested both kings, neither understood the larger issues. As a result, the cabinet became increasingly important in the British system of government.

A Constitutional Monarchy

For over 20 years—from 1721 to 1742—the Whig party controlled the House of Commons. The recognized leader of the Whigs, Sir Robert Walpole, always became a minister. Walpole had strong leadership capabilities and came to be recognized as the **prime minister**, first minister, although the early prime ministers usually carried the title of "First Lord of the Treasury." Under the rule of the Hanoverians, the prime minister became the real head of the government and Great Britain became a **limited constitutional monarchy.** It was a monarchy in that a king or queen sat on the throne. It was limited and constitutional in that a constitution limited the monarch's powers, and the monarch had to consult Parliament.

The British constitution is not a single written document like that of the United States. It consists partly of great documents that include among others the Magna Carta, the Petition of Right, and the Bill of Rights. It also includes acts of Parliament, which any succeeding Parliament may change. Several features of the British governmental system have never been written down; for example, the powers of the prime minister and the functions of the cabinet are based largely on tradition. The prime minister rather than the monarch selects the other members of the cabinet. Together the prime minister and the cabinet plan and carry out government policy.

Great Britain is one of the oldest constitutional governments in the world today. Its limited monarchy became a model for governments of many other nations, and the British experience became a guide to those who wanted to abolish absolute monarchy elsewhere.

SECTION 3 REVIEW

1. **Define** natural rights, habeas corpus, cabinet, prime minister, limited constitutional monarchy
2. **Identify** Charles II, Tories, Whigs, James II, William III, Thomas Hobbes, "social contract," John Locke, Act of Toleration, Robert Walpole
3. **Understanding Ideas** What role did the issue of Roman Catholicism play in the Glorious Revolution?
4. **Comparing Ideas** Compare and contrast the political philosophies of Thomas Hobbes and John Locke.
5. **Interpreting Ideas** (a) How did the English Bill of Rights limit the powers of the monarch? (b) How did it protect private citizens?
6. **Analyzing Ideas** Why did the cabinet gain importance during the reigns of William and Mary, Anne, George I, and George II?

● READ
WRITE
INTERPRET
CONNECT
THINK

BUILDING HISTORY STUDY SKILLS

Reading About History: Identifying a Point of View

A point of view presents a person's outlook on a subject or an event. It is important to know the author's point of view in order to determine the accuracy of the information presented. By understanding the author's viewpoint, you can tell which data has been ignored or which data has been exaggerated. You can also evaluate how reliable the information is.

How to Identify a Point of View

Follow these guidelines to identify a point of view.

1. State the author's topic.
2. Identify the main idea.
3. Determine how and why emphasis has been placed on the main idea.
4. Select words and phrases that signal an opinion, emotion, or exaggeration.
5. Indicate ideas or facts about the subject that the author did not include.
6. State the author's point of view.

Developing the Skill

The issue of how and why government is organized was an integral part of the English Civil War and the Glorious Revolution. Thomas Hobbes in *Leviathan* and John Locke in *Two Treatises on Government* contributed their thoughts to the discussion. Read the selections from their works. What are their points of view? How are their ideas similar? How are they different?

❝ In the first place, I put for a general inclination of all mankind, a perpetual and restless desire of power after power, that ceaseth only in death. . . . during the time men live without a common power to keep them in all awe, they are in that condition which is called war; . . . as is of every man, against every man. . . . In such condition, there is no place for industry . . . and consequently no culture of the earth; no navigation . . . no commodious building; . . . no arts; no letters; no society; and which is worst of all, continual fear, and danger of violent death; and the life of man, solitary, poor, nasty, brutish, and short. . . .

The only way . . . they may nourish themselves and live contentedly; is, to confer all their power and strength upon one man, or upon one assembly of men, that may reduce all their wills, . . . unto one will. . . . This is more than consent, or concord; it is a real unity of them all, in one and the same person, made by covenant of every man with every man . . . This done, the multitude so united in one person, is called a COMMONWEALTH. ❞

(Thomas Hobbes, *Leviathan*)

❝ . . . *Political power* is that power, which every man having in the state of nature, has given up into the hands of the society . . . And this *power has its original only from compact,* . . . and the mutual consent of those who make up the community. . . .

The reason why men enter into society, is the preservation of their property; and the end why they chuse and authorize a legislative, is, that there may be laws made, and rules set, as guards and fences to the properties of all the members of the society, . . . whenever the *legislators endeavor to take away, and destroy the property of the people,* or to reduce them to slavery under arbitrary power, they put themselves into a state of war with the people, who are thereupon absolved from any farther obedience. ❞

(John Locke, *Second Treatise*)

Both men discussed how governments are formed. Hobbes's claimed that man in a state of nature was in constant disorder. He formed a government to insure protection, prosperity, and order for himself. Man gave up his individual will to a ruler. Revolution was never justified because the ruler protected the common good. The signal words are *fear, danger, brutish, concord, unity,* and *consent.*

Locke believed that man in a state of nature had political power and formed a society to protect property. Government was a contract between the ruler and the governed. The government's purpose was to protect individual rights. Locke said that the contract can be broken if the ruler does not protect property. The signal words are *arbitrary* and *slavery.*

Practicing the skill. Choose a current political article from a periodical and identify the point of view.

To apply this skill, see Applying History Study Skills on page 419.

The natural right of assembly

4 English Sea Power Helped Establish a Large Empire

Spain and Portugal established vast overseas empires during the 1500s, while England remained preoccupied with problems at home. Even though these problems persisted during the 1600s, English mariners began explorations that allowed England to claim lands in the Americas and Asia. English merchants founded companies to trade in these new lands, in addition to English companies that traded in the Baltic and Russia. By the mid-1600s English naval power had become a major force. By the 1700s Europe began to recognize British naval supremacy on the high seas. At the same time, the British merchant fleet began to overtake the Dutch fleet in the amount of goods carried. By the 1760s England's colonial empire had no serious competition in North America or India.

Explorers and Sea Dogs

Shortly after Columbus landed in the Western Hemisphere in 1492, King Henry VII commissioned an Italian captain named John Cabot to sail to North America. In 1497 and 1498 he explored the coasts of Newfoundland, Nova Scotia, and New England. Although Cabot's voyages gave the English a claim in the New World, almost a century passed before the English took steps to develop this territory.

During the reign of Queen Elizabeth I, in the second half of the 1500s, a hardy breed of sea captains appeared in England. The English called this group of traders and pirates **sea dogs.** These men—John Hawkins, Francis Drake, and Walter Raleigh, among others—challenged Portuguese and Spanish monopolies of overseas trade. They also made important voyages of exploration. Sir Francis Drake, for example, sailed westward from North America across the Pacific Ocean, around the southern tip of Africa, and north to England. In 1580 he became the first English sea captain to sail around the globe.

However, the English sea dogs were better known for plundering foreign shipping. They stole from Spanish ships not protected by convoys, and they seized slaves being shipped from Africa and sold them in Spanish colonies. The attacks by

Learning from Pictures *Francis Drake's ship, the* Golden Hind, *captured many Spanish treasure ships. Here it is seizing a load of gold from Peru.*

English sea dogs greatly angered King Philip II of Spain. He protested to Queen Elizabeth, but she claimed that she was helpless to control them. Secretly she supported the sea dogs and shared what they had stolen. Despite their involvement in piracy, the sea dogs played a part in England's defeat of the Spanish Armada in 1588, and they strengthened the seafaring tradition of the island nation.

The English in India

The defeat of the Spanish Armada encouraged the English to establish colonies overseas. In 1600 Queen Elizabeth I granted a charter to a trading company called the English East India Company.

This company set up trading posts at Bombay, Calcutta, and Madras in India. The company dealt mainly with local rulers because the Mogul Empire had declined in power. To gain the support of these rulers, the company helped those who were weak, used force without hesitation against those who opposed the company, and extended generous "gifts" to those who might be swayed by bribery.

The English East India Company eventually set up a few trading posts in Malaya and the East Indies, but India remained the company's headquarters and chief source of trade and wealth. The English East India Company rapidly became extremely wealthy and powerful, with a vast fleet of merchant ships and warships to protect its interests.

The English in the Americas

Because of its great interest in Asia, England was slow to establish colonies in North America. Initially, the English explored North America in hopes of finding a northwest passage to India—a water route around the Americas to the north and west. The Spanish dominated the southern route around Cape Horn in South America.

Henry Hudson searched unsuccessfully for the northwest passage, but in 1609, on a voyage for the Dutch, he charted much of the coast of eastern North America and explored the river which now carries his name. On a voyage for the English one year later, he explored Hudson Bay in northern Canada.

As the search for a northwest passage to India continued, the English began to establish colonies along North America's east coast. The first of these colonies were founded by private companies or individuals. The English established the first permanent settlement at Jamestown, Virginia, in 1607. In 1620 they founded the second settlement, Plymouth, in what is now the state of Massachusetts.

The English founded the settlements primarily for commercial purposes since they no longer wanted to be dependent on imports from Asia. Investors hoped that the settlers would raise products that would make the home country more self-sufficient. However, the North American colonies proved to be a disappointment. Few of the original investors made a profit or even got their money back. Many colonists had reasons other than profit for settling in the New World. These people hoped to find greater political and religious freedom and to make better lives for their families.

As in other colonial empires, the British used slavery in their colonies, especially those in southern North America and the West Indies. Settlements on the Caribbean islands, such as Barbados, were commercially successful largely because of slave labor.

Self-government set Britain's empire apart from other European colonial empires. Most English colonies had some form of representative assembly, or governing body, although official control remained firmly in the hands of the home country.

Learning from Pictures
Henry Hudson signs the contract with the Amsterdam Chamber of the Dutch East India Company to search for a northwest passage to China.

Mercantilism and the British Colonies

The British government, however, did intervene in colonial economies by following mercantilist principles. Mercantilism maintained that colonies existed for the benefit of the home country. Colonies supplied needed raw materials and furnished a market for Britain's manufactured products.

The British government passed a number of mercantilist regulations that affected its North American colonies, beginning with the Navigation Act of 1651. One regulation required that certain colonial products could be sold only in the home country, even though the colonists might have received higher prices for the products in another country. Other regulations discouraged colonists from manufacturing. For example, the British government forbade colonists to ship woolen cloth that they had manufactured to places outside their colony.

These trade regulations aroused resentment, and colonists found many ways to evade them. Colonists avoided paying taxes whenever and however they could. Smuggling became a respectable occupation, difficult to prevent because the long American coastline had many harbors and inlets. Until the mid-1700s, however, the English government only loosely enforced its trade restrictions.

SECTION 4 REVIEW

1. **Define** sea dogs
2. **Identify** John Cabot, Sir Francis Drake
3. **Locate** Bombay, Calcutta, Madras, Hudson Bay, Jamestown, Plymouth, Barbados
4. **Understanding Ideas** Why did England fail to develop a large colonial empire at the same time as Spain and Portugal?
5. **Explaining Ideas** What methods did the East India Company use to extend its influence throughout India?

5 The American Revolution Created a New Nation

Although the North American colonists of the 1700s resented British trade regulations, they disliked the French along their borders even more. After the defeat of the French, however, the North American colonists struggled with the British over many issues and finally declared their independence.

British-French Rivalry

While the British established colonies along the Atlantic coast of North America, the French developed settlements to the north and west in what was called New France. In the 1700s, American settlers moved westward across the Appalachian Mountains in search of new land. Conflict with the French was inevitable if this westward movement continued.

When Louis XIV threatened the balance of power in Europe during the reign of Charles II, the English opposed him. The wars in Europe had their counterparts in North America, mostly in frontier skirmishes. The colonies counted on British assistance for defense against the French and their Indian allies.

The decisive conflict that settled British-French rivalry in North America was the French and Indian War (1754–1763), known as the Seven Years' War in Europe. The Treaty of Paris in 1763 confirmed the sweeping British victories not only in North America but all over the world. The British now dominated the region from the Atlantic Ocean to the Mississippi River and from the Gulf of Mexico almost to the Arctic Ocean.

Increased Control over the Colonies

The worldwide conflicts between 1754 and 1763 had left the British with a large debt. The British fought in North America to protect the colonists. The British government, therefore, felt justified in asking the colonists to help pay the cost of this protection and relieve British taxpayers of some of their heavy burden.

However, British governments during the 1760s lacked a consistent policy toward their greatly expanded North American empire. The colonists nevertheless came to believe that the British intended to curb their liberties. In 1763, following an Indian uprising, the British forbade any colonists to settle in the land west of the Appalachian Mountains. Great Britain also attempted to bring its colonies under closer economic control by enforcing mercantilist trade regulations. The Sugar Act of 1764 imposed new taxes on sugar and many

METALWORKING

Engraved Sons of Liberty Bowl

Sons of Liberty Bowl. Paul Revere II U.S., 1735–1818 Silver H.: 5½ in. D.: 5 13/16 in. Gift by Subscription and Francis Bartlett Fund. The Museum of Fine Arts, Boston

Paul Revere is best known for the midnight ride he made to warn the Minutemen that the British were coming, before the battles at Lexington and Concord. Revere, however, was also a fine silversmith.

In the early American colonies, there were no banks to keep silver coins. Consequently, silver coins were often melted down and crafted into household objects. Teapots and serving trays were marked with the name or family crest of the owner and the initials of the silversmith.

In addition to being a silversmith, who crafted many lovely silver pieces before and after the American

Revolution, Paul Revere was also a patriot. Among his work was this exquisite bowl made in honor of the patriotic society called the Sons of Liberty. This organization was founded in 1765 to establish a communications network among the colonial leaders and to involve other colonists in violent protests against the British and British sympathizers.

The Sons of Liberty claimed that they were fighting for their rights as British subjects.

The engraved symbols of freedom—signatures, liberty bell, and flags representing the Magna Carta and the Bill of Rights—symbolize the colonists' fight, first for their rights as British subjects, then for their right to independence.

---

other items imported into North America from non-British colonies. The British were determined to collect these taxes.

In 1765 Parliament passed the Stamp Act. This law required that the colonists pay a tax—in the form of special stamps—on wills, mortgages, contracts, newspapers, pamphlets, calendars, playing cards, and almanacs. The colonists unified in opposition to the Stamp Act. They found a common ground in their opposition and began to think as a single people, not as people from 13 separate colonies. They began a trade boycott of British products. Their refusal to buy British goods brought economic pressure on British merchants, who complained to Parliament. As a result, the British repealed the Stamp Act in 1766.

Each time the British repealed one law, they devised another. And with each new law, the colonists increased their resistance. The colonists argued that they had no representatives in the British Parliament, and "taxation without representation" constituted tyranny. Between 1763 and 1775, relations between the British government and the American colonies grew steadily worse.

Intensified Conflict

King George III, who reigned from 1760 to 1820, was the first "thoroughly British" monarch of the House of Hanover. This meant that he was born in England and placed England's interests over those of his German possession of Hanover.

George also believed that Parliament had too much power in the constitutional system governing Great Britain. He determined to select his own ministers from the "King's Friends" in Parliament. Politics became extremely unsettled in Great Britain. Six prime ministers came to power during an eight-year period. Against this background of parliamentary confusion, the crises leading to the final break with the American colonies unfolded. As the colonists hardened their resistance to British policy, George III became equally determined to coerce them. By 1770 he found a prime minister who was willing to carry out this objective—Lord North.

The colonists were by no means united in wanting independence. However, as tensions increased, many colonists believed that their rights could be

413

Learning from Pictures *This engraving shows the British breaking ranks at the battle of Concord. Why did British troops march into Concord?*

guaranteed only if the colonies became completely independent.

About one-third of the colonists, called *loyalists* (also known as *Tories*), strongly opposed independence. Another one-third, called *patriots* actively favored independence. The remainder of the colonists did not take sides. In 1773 Lord North's British government allowed the English East India Company to ship tea directly to the colonies, in effect giving the company a monopoly on tea sales. Angry colonists, upset at the prospect of a monopoly, threw the tea into Boston harbor. The British responded to the "Boston Tea Party" by closing the port of Boston to all shipping. Colonists called this act and a series of other laws passed in 1774 the Intolerable Acts.

The patriots resented the Intolerable Acts and decided to take action. In the fall of 1774, delegates from 12 of the 13 colonies—Georgia did not attend—met in Philadelphia in the First Continental Congress. The delegates demanded that the colonists be granted the full rights of British people. The delegates also pledged to support each other in the future and agreed to meet the

following year if Great Britain did not repeal the Intolerable Acts.

In April 1775 British troops marched from Boston to seize guns and gunpowder that the colonists had stored nearby. At the towns of Lexington and Concord, the British met with armed resistance and retreated to Boston. The American Revolution had begun.

The Declaration of Independence

When delegates to a Second Continental Congress met in Philadelphia, the spirit of independence was stronger. The delegates voted to declare their freedom from Great Britain. On July 4, 1776, they adopted the Declaration of Independence, which established the United States of America as an independent nation. Thomas Jefferson, the declaration's principal author, expressed American sentiments with nobility and grandeur. The Americans wanted the whole world to read their declaration.

The Declaration of Independence shows the influence of political philosophers such as John Locke. It states that all people are created equal and are given by their Creator certain "unalienable rights" that cannot be taken from them. Among these rights are "life, liberty, and the pursuit of happiness." This idea—that every human being has the right to equal opportunity and must be treated with equal justice—is the foundation of the democratic ideal. Although the ideal was not stated to include women or slaves, the demand for equality created a new aim in politics.

The declaration also stated that all powers of government belong to the people. No government can exist without the consent of its citizens, because citizens create governments to protect individual rights. If a government fails to protect or attempts to destroy the people's rights, the people have the right "to alter or to abolish" the government and to set up a new government that will safeguard their rights.

These were extreme ideas, even for those who had rejected the unlimited authority of monarchs. Such ideas were especially bold when stated by a group of small, weak colonies against powerful Great Britain.

The War for Independence

Each side had advantages and weaknesses as the war began. The Americans were fighting to defend their own homes in territory they knew well. The British had to fight more than 3,000 miles (4,800 kilometers) from home, bringing with them most of their military supplies and equipment.

The American Revolutionary War was not popular in Great Britain. Many people did not support it, and some even sympathized with the Americans. The British had not favored large armies since the struggles of the 1600s between crown and Parliament. Therefore, King George III had to hire mercenaries, many of them foreign.

Nevertheless, Great Britain's strength lay in the organization of its army and navy. British troops were well trained, and the British fleet was the strongest in the world.

The lack of unity among the American states also helped the British. The states voluntarily sent representatives to the Continental Congress, but all of the Congress's proposals for action had to be sent back to the states for approval. In addition to the time required for the states to approve proposals, the colonial government faced other problems. To meet the immediate need of financing the war, the Continental Congress borrowed money and printed its own paper money. However, since it had no way of paying its debts, its credit was poor.

The weaknesses of the American government made it difficult to build a strong army. At first, American forces consisted mostly of poorly trained and undisciplined volunteers. The American troops

Learning from Maps   *The American victory at Saratoga helped the revolutionary forces secure French aid. What city outside the colonies did the Americans capture?*

MILITARY CAMPAIGNS OF THE AMERICAN REVOLUTION 1775–1783

← American campaign
← British campaign
★ American victory
✦ British victory
▲▲▲ Blockade

① Outbreak of revolution, April 19, 1775. British destroy military supplies.

② British defeat Americans, June 17, 1775.

③ Captured by Americans, Nov. 13, 1775.

④ Besieged by Americans; British leave, March 17, 1776.

⑤ First great American victory, Oct. 17, 1777. Turning point in revolution; France signs treaty of alliance with Americans.

⑥ Campaign of Sept. 1777 to June 1778. Instead of joining General Burgoyne to split the U.S. in two, British General Howe defeats General Washington at Brandywine and Germantown. Washington spends terrible winter at Valley Forge.

⑦ British General Clinton withdraws from Philadelphia to New York, 1778.

⑧ George Rogers Clark defeats British along Ohio River, 1778–1779.

⑨ Captured and controlled by British, 1778–1780.

⑩ Benedict Arnold plots with Major André to surrender West Point to British, 1780.

⑪ Occupied by British, May 12, 1780. Recaptured by American General Nathanael Greene, Dec. 14, 1782.

⑫ British fail to conquer North and South Carolina in 1781.

⑬ General Rochambeau's French forces join Washington's army and march to Yorktown, July 1781–Sept. 1781.

⑭ French blockade under Admiral de Grasse prevents British fleet from aiding General Cornwallis, Sept. 1781.

⑮ General Cornwallis surrenders to Washington, Oct. 19, 1781.

ALBERS EQUAL AREA PROJECTION

could seldom successfully oppose the well-trained British forces in a large-scale battle. But the Americans had good leaders, particularly General George Washington, who commanded the Continental Army. In addition, military officers from other nations came to help the Americans.

The fighting. Most of the fighting took place between 1776 and 1781, with neither side winning a clear victory (see map, page 415). After the Americans surrounded and defeated a British army under General John Burgoyne at Saratoga in October 1777, Lord North offered peace to the Americans. By the time the terms reached America, however, the colonies had signed an alliance with France. Spain and the Netherlands also joined the war against the British. In 1781 the Americans and their French allies won a decisive battle at Yorktown, Virginia (see map, this page).

Learning from Maps   During the siege of Yorktown, Virginia, the British were trapped with their backs to the sea. What country provided the Americans with sea power?

THE SIEGE OF YORKTOWN, SEPTEMBER 28–OCTOBER 19, 1781

——— American forces   ▪ Building

——— French forces   ——— Road

——— British forces   ⌐⌐⌐ Fortification

POLYCONIC PROJECTION

Ending the war. The British still had more troops in America than George Washington had in the Continental Army, and the British navy, after losing command of the sea at Yorktown, soon regained it. But the British people were tired of the costly American war.

In 1783 after two years of negotiation, with Benjamin Franklin as the shrewd and persuasive chief American negotiator, the British and the Americans and their allies signed the Treaty of Paris. The Americans won not only independence but also a territory much larger than the original 13 colonies (see map, page 417).

The Articles of Confederation

In 1781 the American states ratified, or accepted, the Articles of Confederation, a plan of government the Second Continental Congress had adopted in 1777. The Articles of Confederation provided for a central government, with a one-house Congress in which each state had a single vote. Congress had the power to declare war, make peace, conduct foreign relations, and settle disputes between the states.

The government under the Articles of Confederation lasted from 1781 to 1789, but because of its weaknesses, it lacked effectiveness. The government had no power to tax, to coin money, or to regulate trade with foreign countries or among the states. Laws required the approval of at least nine of the states. The Articles of Confederation provided for no chief executive officer, and the only courts were state courts, which tried all cases.

The Constitution

Americans soon realized that the Articles of Confederation provided inadequate government. In 1787 delegates from the states met again in Philadelphia to draw up a constitution to provide the framework for a new government. The delegates of the Constitutional Convention unanimously elected George Washington as its presiding officer. They then turned to the issue at hand—to create a central government strong enough to act on matters that concerned all of the states. At the same time, they wanted to leave the states some freedom to act for themselves. To solve this problem, the authors of the Constitution decided to adopt the **federal system of government.** The Constitution divided governmental powers between

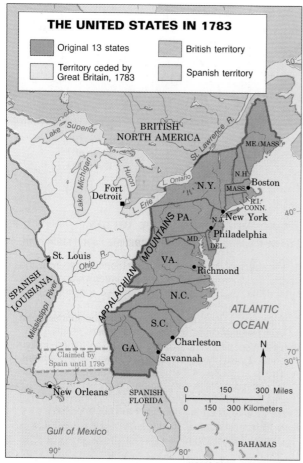

THE UNITED STATES IN 1783

- Original 13 states
- Territory ceded by Great Britain, 1783
- British territory
- Spanish territory

BRITISH NORTH AMERICA

Lake Superior
Lake Michigan
Huron
L. Ontario
L. Erie
St. Lawrence R.
ME. (MASS.)
N.H.
N.Y.
MASS.
R.I.
CONN.
Boston
N.J.
New York
PA.
MD.
DEL.
Philadelphia
Fort Detroit
Ohio R.
St. Louis
SPANISH LOUISIANA
Mississippi River
APPALACHIAN MOUNTAINS
VA.
Richmond
N.C.
S.C.
Charleston
GA.
Savannah
ATLANTIC OCEAN
Claimed by Spain until 1795
New Orleans
SPANISH FLORIDA
Gulf of Mexico
BAHAMAS

N

0   150   300 Miles
0   150   300 Kilometers

ALBERS EQUAL AREA PROJECTION

Learning from Maps   The Treaty of Paris gave the United States territory west of the Thirteen Colonies. What was the western border of the new nation?

the central, or federal, government and the individual states. It gave the federal government the power to declare war, make treaties, coin money, raise armies, and regulate trade with foreign countries. All other powers belonged to or were shared by the states and the people.

The framers of the Constitution created three branches of the federal government. The **executive branch** (the president) enforced the laws, the **legislative branch** (Congress) made the laws, and the **judicial branch** (the federal courts) interpreted and applied the laws. The framers gave each branch certain powers and specified in the Constitution how each branch of government acted as a check on the others.

The first 10 amendments of the Constitution, added in 1791, are known collectively as the Bill of Rights. They specifically guarantee the basic rights of every United States citizen. Among others, these rights include freedom of religion, speech, press, assembly, and petition. In addition, rights regarding search, seizure, and a public trial by a jury are listed. Many representatives to the Constitutional Convention insisted on spelling out these rights so that no question could arise as to what rights citizens did or did not have.

Effects of American Independence

The American Revolution put into practice the ideas of John Locke and other political philosophers. These ideas had previously existed only on paper. The Declaration of Independence contains two basic founding principles of democracy: that all people have certain unalienable rights and that all the powers of government belong to the people and are exercised only with the consent of the governed. The American experience gave encouragement to people everywhere who opposed domination by absolute monarchy and privileged classes.

The democracy that the Americans achieved in 1789, however, was very different from democracy today. The states restricted voting to adult, free males, who usually owned property. Women could not vote, and the large black slave population had no political rights at all.

Clearly, many liberties still had to be won. But from the American Revolution emerged a new kind of government and a new relationship among citizens. This may not have been what most Americans who opposed Great Britain intended when the Revolution began. However, their common beliefs and the economic and political needs of the new nation created a country that inspired loyalty.

SECTION 5 REVIEW

1. **Define** federal system of government, executive branch, legislative branch, judicial branch
2. **Identify** Lord North, loyalist, patriot, Bill of Rights
3. **Locate** Concord, Yorktown
4. **Interpreting Ideas** How did mercantilism affect the British colonies in North America?
5. **Evaluating Ideas** How did the Declaration of Independence show the influence of John Locke?
6. **Analyzing Ideas** Why were the Articles of Confederation ineffective?

CHAPTER
16
REVIEW

Reign of Tudor monarchs

Defeat of the Spanish Armada

AD 1485

1558

1588

Reign of Elizabeth I

Chapter Summary

The following list contains the key concepts you have learned about political developments and the revolutions in the English-speaking world.

1. Elizabeth I faced threats from Spain abroad, and from Catholics and Puritans at home. She established a strong central government while respecting the rights of members of Parliament.
2. The Stuarts believed in the divine right of kings. They got into endless quarrels with Parliament over taxation and a wide variety of other issues.
3. Oliver Cromwell and the Puritans defeated King Charles I and established a republic called the Commonwealth. Cromwell made England strong, but his experiment in republican government failed. After his death the English restored the monarchy under Charles II.
4. Under the later Stuarts, England always faced the issue of a Catholic succession to the throne. This issue led to the formation of political parties called Whigs and Tories. They finally created the permanent Protestant succession. In time Parliament passed the Settlement Act, which was designed to keep Catholics off the English throne.
5. Thomas Hobbes and John Locke each formed a theory of government based on a social contract between rulers and ruled. Locke's ideas that the people had the right to overthrow a ruler who violated the contract gave the English and the Americans justification for revolution.
6. By the 1760s Great Britain had an overseas empire in North America and India which was largely unchallenged.
7. Great Britain had been involved in worldwide conflicts from 1754 to 1763. This left the British heavily in debt, making it necessary for them to raise taxes. However, when they attempted to tax their North American colonies, they ran into opposition.
8. The American colonists disagreed with the way the British governed them. Unable to change British policy, the 13 colonies chose independence.

On a separate sheet of paper, complete the following review exercises.

Reviewing Important Terms

Supply the term that correctly completes each statement.

1. Members of the House of Commons came from the _____ , who represented the landowning classes, and the _____ , who represented the urban merchants and professional people.
2. A _____ is a document outlining the fundamental laws and principles that govern a nation.
3. The _____ _____ _____ protected individuals against illegal arrest and unlawful imprisonment.
4. The _____ was a small group of advisers or ministers who dealt with government policy and issues.
5. The economic theory called _____ maintains that colonies exist for the benefit of the home country.
6. A radical attempt to change the very structure of a country's government is called a _____ .

Developing Critical Thinking Skills

1. **Understanding Ideas** (a) Why did James I and Charles I quarrel with Parliament? (b) What issues precipitated the civil war in the 1640s?
2. **Evaluating Ideas** (a) Why did Catholicism cause fear among the majority of English people during the 1500s and 1600s? (b) What did the English Parliament do in 1701 to prevent Catholics from becoming kings and queens of England?
3. **Comparing Ideas** Compare the strengths and weaknesses of Parliament and monarchs during the reigns of Elizabeth I, Charles I, and William and Mary.
4. **Applying Ideas** (a) How did the English and French colonies in North America differ from one another? (b) In what other ways did the English and French differ as they struggled for leadership of the European world?
5. **Explaining Ideas** What works of English political philosophers helped the American authors of both the Declaration of Independence and the Constitution?

Relating Geography to History

Use the maps of the North American colonies on pages 415 and 416 to answer the following questions. (a) What advantages did the English

1688–1689
Glorious
Revolution and
Bill of Rights

English
Revolution

Petition
of Right

Hanoverian
dynasty
established

Act of
Settlement

French and
Indian War

Constitutional
Convention

1603   1628   1642   1701 1714   1754 1763   1787
        1625   1660
                1649   1679   1707   1775 1783

Stuart
dynasty
established

Reign of
Charles I

Restoration
of the
Stuarts

Habeas
Corpus Act

Union
of England
and Scotland

American
Revolutionary War

colonies along the Atlantic seaboard have over the French colonies in Canada and the west? **(b)** What geographical disadvantages did Great Britain have in fighting a war with the American colonies? What geographical advantages?

Relating Past to Present

1. The Petition of Right, the Habeas Corpus Act, the English Bill of Rights, and the Act of Toleration covered many important rights of individual citizens. List the rights protected by these measures. Use American civics or government books to find out how many of these rights are protected today by the United States Constitution.
2. The British monarchy today has little power, yet the monarchy as an institution is widely respected and supported in Great Britain. The monarch still serves certain functions in Great Britain and the nations of the Commonwealth. Examine textbooks that discuss comparative government or articles about British life today and list some important functions that the monarch still performs. You might want to compare the political role of Queen Elizabeth II with that of Elizabeth I, listing the powers that belonged to the earlier queen which do not belong to the current queen.

Applying History Study Skills

Before completing this activity, review Building History Study Skills on page 409.

Look again at the steps for identifying a point of view on page 409. Then complete the following exercise.

During the English Civil War, the victorious Parliamentarians and their generals sought to devise a new government for England. A small party of radicals, called the *Levelers*, demanded a radical change for the government of England. Their point of view is represented in the Putney Debates, from which the following selection is taken. Read the excerpt below and try to identify the point of view presented.

❝ I do hear nothing at all that can convince me why any man that is born in England ought not to have his voice in election of burgesses. It is said

that if a man have not a permanent interest, he can have no claim; and we must be no freer than the laws will let us to be . . . and I do think that the main cause why Almighty God gave men reason, it was that they should make use of that reason, and that they should improve it for that end and purpose that God gave it [to] them . . . I do not find anything in the law of God, that a lord shall choose twenty burgesses, and a gentleman but two, or a poor man shall choose none: I find no such thing in the law of nature, nor in the law of nations . . . and am still of the same opinion, that every man born in England cannot, ought not, neither by the law of God nor the law of nature, to be exempted from the choice of those who are to make laws and for him to live under, and for him (for aught I know) to lose his life under. ❞

1. **(a)** What is the main idea? **(b)** How is the main idea repeated and emphasized?
2. What are the signal words?
3. Which ideas has the speaker neglected to mention?
4. Why are the speaker's ideas considered radical?
5. What is the speaker's point of view about men and their relationship to his government?

Investigating Further

1. **Writing a Report** Prepare a report about the Spanish Armada. Discuss the following in your report: What was the background of the Spanish-English conflict? Why did Philip II want to conquer England? How was religion a factor? How was Elizabeth I regarded by other European monarchs? How was the Spanish fleet defeated? What was the significance of the English victory? You can use encyclopedias or Garrett Mattingly's *Armada* (Houghton Mifflin) as sources for your research.
2. **Presenting an Oral Report** Rulers such as Queen Isabella of Spain and Queen Elizabeth I of England supported voyages of exploration. Using books in your library, find out more about these rulers and why they supported these adventures. Include examples of voyages of exploration in your research. Present an oral report about your findings to the class.

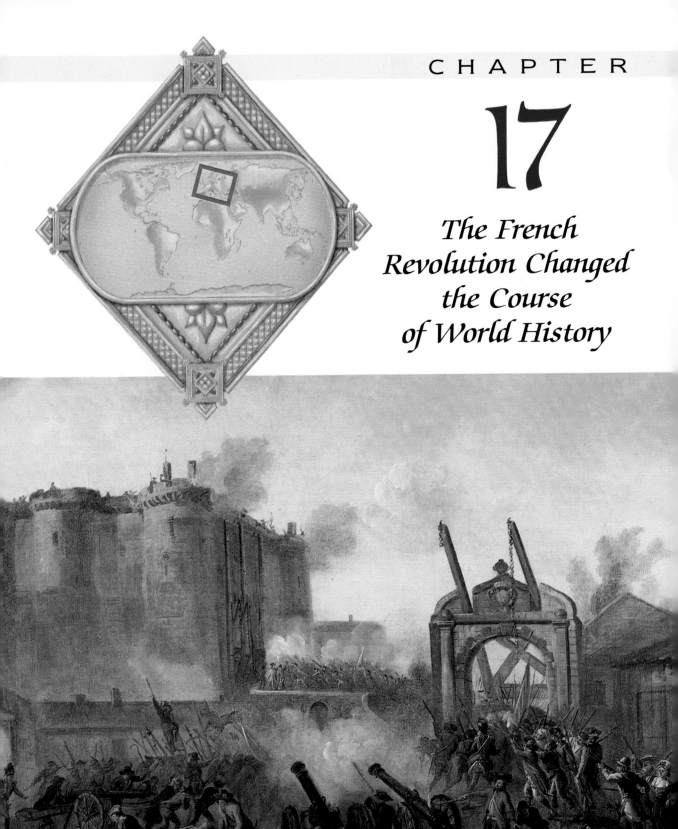

17

The French Revolution Changed the Course of World History

Place France and the rest of Europe

Time 1715–1829

3.7 mil. BC   4000 BC   AD 2100

Significance

The English ideal that people should have a voice in government greatly influenced French political writers of the 1700s. These writers spread this idea, paving the way for one of the greatest revolutions in history—the French Revolution. The American Revolution, with its central theme of the freedom and dignity of human beings, helped inspire the French people to overthrow the existing government and establish a government based on these ideals.

The beginning of this revolutionary tradition represents an important step in the development of the modern world. Our ancestors in the 1700s regarded change as dangerous and as something to be avoided. Our times differ markedly; now many people in the West regard change as useful. This totally new attitude about change permits us to accept the period of the French Revolution as a positive turning point in modern history.

Terms to Define

Enlightenment conscription
philosophe coup d'état
bourgeoisie legitimacy

People to Identify

Denis Diderot Maximilien Robespierre
Rousseau Napoleon
Louis XVI Metternich

Places to Locate

Paris Austerlitz
Corsica St. Helena

Questions to Guide Your Reading

1 How did the philosophy of the Enlightenment influence people's views on government in the 1700s?
2 How did the makeup of the three estates in France affect the outlook of each on the eve of the meeting of the Estates-General?
3 How did the National Assembly reorganize the French political system between 1789 and 1791?
4 Why did the French Revolution take a more extreme course in 1792?
5 How did Napoleon create an empire?
6 How did the Congress of Vienna try to restore absolutism?

Although Baroness Emmuska Orczy wrote the novel The Scarlet Pimpernel *years after the French Revolution, in it she captured the spirit of an age that transformed the social order. She wrote:*

❝*D**uring the greater part of the day the guillotine had been kept busy at its ghastly work: all that France had boasted of in the past centuries, of ancient names, and blue blood, had paid toll to her desire for liberty and for fraternity. . . . But this was as it should be: were not the people now the rulers of France? Every aristocrat was a traitor . . . for two hundred years now the people had sweated, and toiled, and starved, to keep a lustful court in lavish extravagance; now the descendants of those who had helped to make those courts brilliant had to hide for their lives—to fly, if they wished to avoid the tardy vengeance of the people.* **❞**

Like many revolutions, the French Revolution traced its roots to early political writers.

1 The Enlightenment Applied Scientific Ideas to Politics

The European people of the 1700s referred to their century as an "Age of Enlightenment." They believed themselves the first to have discovered the "light" of logical thinking revealed by science. Spurred by Descartes's methodology for understanding the truth and by Newton's explanation of the working of the universe, researchers had made great advances in the physical sciences. During the **Enlightenment** philosophers believed they could apply the scientific method and use reason to logically explain human nature.

Characteristics of the Enlightenment

During the 1700s an increasing number of people began to believe that every natural phenomenon had both a cause and an effect. The thinkers of the Enlightenment attempted to test everything by observation and to determine the cause-and-effect relationships between natural events.

Another characteristic of the Enlightenment was **rationalism,** the belief that truth can be

The taking of the Bastille

arrived at solely by reason, or rational, logical thinking. Because of this central belief, historians often refer to the Age of Enlightenment as the Age of Reason.

Thinkers during the Enlightenment also believed in natural law. The discoveries of Newton and other scientists seemed to support the idea of an orderly universe. Many individuals came to feel that natural law governed the universe and all of its creatures.

God, they believed, had created the world and made rules for all living things. Just as the law of gravity governed the physical movement of planets, so other laws governed human behavior. In order to live in harmony, people had to use reason to discover natural law. If they lived according to this natural law and made their government and other institutions conform to it, the world would become a perfect place. Thus the thinkers of the Enlightenment became convinced that progress would always take place.

Crusaders of the Enlightenment

Their contemporaries called the thinkers of the Enlightenment **philosophes** (fee•luh•ZAWFS); *philosophe* is the French word for "philosopher." The philosophes were not only philosophers, however, but also critics of society. They wrote to one another, and they published their ideas in books, plays, pamphlets, newspapers, and "encyclopedias." Before and during the Reformation, the humanists and religious reformers had used the printing press very effectively. Now the philosophes used the printed word to spread the ideas of the Enlightenment throughout Europe.

The *Encyclopedia*. Although England and its allies curbed Louis XIV's expansion of French rule and maintained the balance of power, France remained both the strongest political power and the dominant cultural influence in Europe. Educated people throughout Europe spoke and wrote French. They read the *Encyclopedia*, a handbook or reference book on the Enlightenment, which became the most famous publication of this period.

The philosophe Denis Diderot (dee•DROH) edited the *Encyclopedia*. Working 14 hours a day in a tiny attic, he and his assistant, Jean d'Alembert (dal•uhm•BAR), published the first edition of the *Encyclopedia* in 35 volumes between 1751 and 1780.

The leading philosophes all contributed articles to the *Encyclopedia*. Their writings criticized the church, the government, the slave trade, torture,

Learning from Pictures *Marie-Thérèse Geoffrin's salon provided the opportunity for authors to hear readings from other writers' works, like those of Voltaire.*

taxes, and war. They covered nearly every subject—many of them technical in nature—in the rational, questioning style of the Enlightenment.

The French authorities frowned on critical writings, however, and they imprisoned Diderot and several other philosophes. Nevertheless, people throughout Europe bought illegal editions of the *Encyclopedia,* read it, and adopted its ideas enthusiastically.

Salons. Philosophes gravitated to France, particularly to Paris. There famous hostesses set up **salons,** or gatherings of the social, political, and cultural elite, in their homes. One such hostess, Marie-Thérèse Geoffrin (zhaw • FRAN), had a chef who cooked superb meals for her gatherings. Amid lavish entertainment and witty and intelligent conversation, the philosophes could meet one another and discuss the important issues of the day.

Political Criticism

The philosophes critically examined the political and social institutions of their day. They tried to learn how these institutions had developed. They analyzed the power of kings, the special position of the church, and the privileges of clergy and nobles. Several philosophes attacked the idea of privileged classes. They thought that political and social institutions should be changed to benefit everyone instead of just certain groups.

Montesquieu. In the early 1700s, English political ideas and institutions became popular in France. A number of French philosophes adopted the ideas of John Locke, about whom you read in Chapter 16. In 1748 Baron de Montesquieu (mahn • tuhs • KYOO) published *The Spirit of the Laws,* in which he tried to describe what he considered a perfect government. After studying all existing governments, Montesquieu concluded that the English had the most nearly perfect form. He wrote that its greatest strength lay in the fact that power was divided equally among the three branches of government: the legislative, which made the laws; the executive, which administered them; and the judicial, which interpreted and applied them. Each branch balanced and checked the power of the others.

Montesquieu's high opinion of the English form of government was based on a misunderstanding of it. As you know from reading Chapter 16, the legislative and executive powers were largely combined in the House of Commons rather than separated

into the two branches of government. Nevertheless, Montesquieu's ideas carried great weight in the formation of limited monarchies in Europe. In the United States, his concept of checks and balances influenced the framers of the Constitution in 1787.

Voltaire. The French writer François-Marie Arouet, known as Voltaire, exemplified the spirit of the Enlightenment. After serving two sentences in the Paris prison called the Bastille (ba • STEEL), Voltaire fled for a time to England. He commented on the British political system and English customs in *Letters on England* (1734), which helped popularize English ideas in France.

When he returned to France, Voltaire savagely attacked everything he considered sham or superstition. He fought against intolerance and injustice, and he managed to reverse several legal decisions—unfortunately not always before the defendants had been unjustly punished. He did so by rallying public opinion and rousing people to oppose barbaric tortures and religious intolerance. Voltaire is credited with a famous statement on freedom of speech: "I do not agree with a word you say, but I will defend to the death your right to say it."

Rousseau. Jean-Jacques Rousseau (roo • SOH) first gained attention in 1749 by writing a prize-winning essay for the Academy of Dijon. The academy asked, "Has the reestablishment of the sciences and the arts tended to purify or corrupt social morality?" Rousseau responded that civilization had corrupted people. He said that history repeats itself in cycles of decay, and that we had only to look at Egypt, Greece, Rome, and Byzantium for examples.

In his most famous book, *The Social Contract,* published in 1762, Rousseau wrote that people are born good but that environment, education, and laws corrupt them. The free and good state into which people are born can be preserved only if they live under a government that they have chosen and can control. In other words, just laws and wise governments must be based upon **popular sovereignty**—that is, created by and subject to the will of the people. This idea of Rousseau's had enormous influence.

In some ways, Rousseau belongs outside the Enlightenment. In an age of reason, he distrusted reason, believing that it brought on corruption and misery, not progress. Rousseau preferred a kind of pastoral state, free of complicated institutions. By the 1780s many people who had tired of rationalism accepted Rousseau's philosophy of the "natural man." He had great influence in the later years of the Enlightenment.

Enlightened Despotism

The philosophes argued and worked to make a better world based on reason. They did not criticize religion and people's faith so much as they fought superstition, the institution of the church, and the ignorance of some of the clergy. They did not dislike monarchy itself so much as they disliked absolute monarchy. Most philosophes favored **enlightened despotism**—a system of government in which absolute monarchs ruled according to the principles of the Enlightenment.

In countries with absolute monarchies and strong censorship, the rulers and clergy fought the ideas of the philosophes. They prohibited the publishing of books by philosophes, or they severely censored the books, removing any material unflattering to public officials or the church. The public hangman symbolically burned many books. The clergy thundered from their pulpits against the philosophes, whom they accused of undermining the church.

Faced with this unfavorable attention, the philosophes became cautious. They wrote "Persians" when they meant "Parisians," as Montesquieu did with his *Persian Letters*. Voltaire, who did not wish to repeat his earlier imprisonment in France, moved to a residence near Geneva, Switzerland, out of reach of the French authorities.

Later, other people, not content to merely discuss such ideas, preferred instead to act upon them. By the late 1780s, France, the home of the Enlightenment, became the setting for a major political and social revolution.

SECTION 1 REVIEW

1. **Define** Enlightenment, rationalism, philosophes, salons, popular sovereignty, enlightened despotism
2. **Identify** Marie-Thérèse Geoffrin, Voltaire, Jean-Jacques Rousseau
3. **Relating Ideas** How did the *Encyclopedia* influence Europeans during the 1700s?
4. **Contrasting Ideas** How did Montesquieu's ideas of government differ from those of Rousseau?
5. **Analyzing Ideas** How did England and English ideas influence the French philosophes?

---

2 Revolution Swept Across France

When the French Revolution began in 1789, the rest of Europe watched in horrified astonishment. For more than 100 years, France had been the largest and most powerful European nation. Within a few months, however, the king lost his power to make laws, and eventually the people's elected representatives voted for his execution. These new rulers wrote a constitution and reformed many laws. The radical change made people feel that they were living in a new era. They began to refer to the period before 1789 as the Old Regime.

The Old Regime

How did the French Revolution happen? To answer that question, we must look first at the Old Regime. You will recall from earlier chapters that the French kings constructed an absolute monarchy in which the king's will was law. You will remember, too, that the French organized their society into three estates. Great inequality existed among these estates. The First and Second Estates had the fewest people, but they also had the most wealth, power, and privilege.

First Estate. The First Estate consisted of the clergy of the Roman Catholic church and totaled less than 1 percent of the population. The church retained many of the privileges it had held since the Middle Ages. Only church courts could try priests and bishops. The clergy did not have to pay taxes, but they agreed to make a "free gift" of money to the French king. The church owned about one-tenth of all French land and received enormous amounts of money from rents, taxes, and fees. The higher clergy—archbishops, bishops, and abbots—held most of this wealth. As a result, some of these people had become lazy, worldly, and neglectful of their spiritual duties.

In contrast, the lower clergy, made up of the parish priests, performed most of the work and received very low pay. In addition to giving religious guidance, they fed the poor and provided all education.

Second Estate. The nobility, the Second Estate, represented less than 2 percent of the population. They still had special privileges and customs that had originated in feudal times—the right to wear a sword; **primogeniture,** or the right of the eldest son to inherit titles and lands; and the right to function as "lord of the manor." The nobles paid few taxes, if any, and they still collected feudal dues from the peasants. Only nobles held the highest positions in the army and government. Although some cared about the welfare of France, as a class the nobility were thoughtless, irresponsible, and extravagant.

Third Estate. The rest of the people of France—approximately 97 percent—belonged to the Third Estate. This estate was itself subdivided into three groups.

At the top stood the **bourgeoisie** (boorzh • wah • ZEE)—the city-dwelling middle class—made up of merchants, manufacturers, and professional people such as doctors and lawyers. Many of them possessed wealth and education. Below the bourgeoisie came the laborers and artisans of the cities. The peasants ranked at the bottom of the Third Estate and often led miserable lives, mired in inescapable poverty. By the 1700s few peasants remained serfs, but most still owed feudal dues and services such as working on the roads. They paid rent for the land they worked, the heaviest taxes, and one-tenth of their income—the **tithe**—to the church. They worked long and hard, but they had no voice in making or changing the laws that kept them under the absolute and crushing control of their landlords and the king.

Growing Discontent

In the mid-1700s discontent in France began to grow. Several factors explain this discontent. The first resulted from the growth of the French population. Families had more children to support, and they needed more food and money.

Changing economic conditions in France also spurred discontent. In order to get more money, the nobles, clergy, and some of the bourgeoisie who owned land raised the rents they charged peasants. They hired lawyers to find old feudal dues that had fallen into disuse. Then they forced the peasants to pay these dues in addition to their already heavy taxes and other obligations. The nobles and clergy also tried to sell things they had once given away. For example, instead of letting peasants pick up twigs and branches in the woods for use as fuel, the landlords sold them firewood.

Learning from Pictures *Nobles dressed up as peasants to idealize peasant life. Peasant life though, was harsh, oppressive, and anything but idyllic.*

In the cities, laborers found food prices rising higher and higher, but wages were not going up as quickly. The artisans and peasants resented the rich, who collected their rents, lived in big houses, and had plenty to eat. The poor blamed the king for allowing prices to get so high. They loathed having to pay taxes when the nobles and clergy did not. Sometimes the poor took to the streets and rioted against these higher prices and taxes. Travelers' diaries of the period tell of the robbery and violent crime this widespread misery sparked. The poor economic conditions also reinforced the determination of the first two estates to protect their most important privilege: freedom from taxation.

Although the bourgeoisie prospered during the 1700s, they too became discontented. They wanted political power equal to their economic strength. Merchants and manufacturers resented paying taxes when the nobles and clergy did not. The bourgeoisie also wanted their sons to have important positions in the church, army, and government. However, only nobles could hold such positions.

The bourgeoisie wanted a say in government policy mainly because the government interfered with business. The bourgeoisie had at first welcomed mercantilism. By the mid-1700s, however, they disliked mercantilist regulations governing wages and prices. And they wanted freedom to trade with foreign countries without interference.

Discontent simmered among the First and Second Estates, too. Since the reign of Henry IV, the nobility and upper clergy had disliked the increasing concentration of power in the hands of French kings. France became larger and its kings more powerful, with larger armies at their disposal. The nobles did not profit from this trend; instead, they lost much of their influence.

Different Grievances, Similar Ideas

The various groups in French society had different kinds of grievances, but they shared the same ideas and used the same words to express them. They all talked of "liberty" and "equality" as their natural rights. For peasants and artisans, liberty and equality meant the right to eat and to have some reward for their labor. For the bourgeoisie, liberty and equality meant the freedom to trade without restrictions. It also meant the right to advance to the highest levels of society on merit alone. They called this "equality of opportunity." For the nobility, liberty and equality meant the liberty to enjoy their ancient privileges and to limit the authority of the king. Even though they meant different things to different people, these ideas of liberty and equality unified France's various groups in a major challenge to the king's power in 1789.

The Financial Crisis

The crisis that now paralyzed France stemmed from many years of conflict. The wars of Louis XIV had left France saddled with a huge debt. In 1715 a new king began his reign, and for 25 years France enjoyed peace. But the national debt continued to grow. Wise rulers might have averted this financial crisis, which ultimately toppled the monarchy, but the Bourbons lacked that wisdom.

Louis XV. King Louis XV's reign, the second longest in French history, lasted 59 years—from 1715 to 1774. Only five years old when he came to the throne, Louis XV began his reign backed by the goodwill of the French people, who called him "Louis the Well-Beloved." The intelligent Louis XV might have become a great king, but in later years his laziness, personal vices, intrigues, and uncaring attitude toward the French people exhausted their initial goodwill.

When taxes did not produce enough money to meet expenses, Louis XV borrowed more and more from the bankers. He turned his back on those people who summoned up enough courage to urge him to economize. Warned that his actions endangered France, Louis XV remarked, "It will survive for my time. After me, the deluge."

Louis XVI. In 1774 Louis XVI succeeded Louis XV as the ruler of France. Marie Antoinette, the daughter of the Austrian empress Maria Theresa and the wife of Louis XVI, seemed destined for tragedy. She served as the target for all people determined to undermine the monarchy. To begin with, her marriage to Louis XVI was part of an unpopular alliance between Austria and France. She had beauty, grace, and charm, but she chose her friends unwisely and meddled in politics. In time the French people came to hate her.

King at the age of 19, Louis XVI cared more for hunting than governing. But France's worsening debt, which had grown rapidly because of French assistance to the United States during the American Revolution, forced him to tackle his governmental tasks.

Louis XVI sought help from financial experts. They all gave him the same advice: tax the first two estates. Each time new taxes were proposed, however, the nobles protested and refused to cooperate. Sometimes they led riots that the king had difficulty putting down. By 1787 the country had exhausted its credit, and bankers refused to lend the government more money. France faced financial disaster.

Reluctantly Louis XVI decided to convene the Estates-General at Versailles in May 1789. He hoped that by calling together the representatives of all three estates, not just of the nobility, he could get approval for his plan to tax the wealthy.

The Meeting of the Estates-General

At the time the king called the meeting of the Estates-General, France was suffering from high unemployment and serious inflation in addition to the government's financial crisis. Moreover, the harvest of 1788 had been poor, and food prices had soared. Peasants and urban laborers were finding that they had to spend more than 60 percent of their income just for bread.

The planned meeting of the Estates-General created feelings of excitement and expectation among the people. The Abbé Sieyès (see • ay • YES), who became a leading revolutionary, published "What Is the Third Estate?"—a pamphlet that everyone in France talked about. In it Sieyès wrote:

> **"W**hat is the Third Estate? Everything. What has it been, till the present, in the political order? Nothing. What does it ask? To become something. **"**

The French people hoped the meeting of the Estates-General would solve their problems.

No one knew exactly what powers and rules the Estates-General had, because it had not met for 175 years. Many people felt that if it had power only to advise the king, and not to make and carry out laws, the meeting would be useless. They also argued about the rules. In the past the three estates had met separately, and each estate had cast one vote. This procedure had always allowed the clergy and nobles of the First and Second Estates to outvote the Third Estate.

Many representatives of the Third Estate were young lawyers acquainted with the ideas of Montesquieu and Voltaire. A few nobles, like the Count de Mirabeau, also consented to represent the Third Estate. As the representatives of the majority of the people, they insisted on having a real voice in decisions without being automatically outvoted by the other two estates. The Third Estate had as many representatives as the First Estate and Second Estate combined. Therefore, it wanted the three estates to meet together, with their representatives voting as individuals.

The Estates-General assembled first in a combined meeting on May 5, 1789. Louis XVI instructed the delegates to follow the old custom of each estate meeting separately and voting as one body. The representatives of the Third Estate refused. They claimed that the Estates-General represented the French people, not the three classes. Therefore, all the representatives should meet together and vote as individuals.

Always hesitant, Louis XVI failed to take action. As a result, on June 17, 1789, the Third Estate proclaimed itself the National Assembly. The rebellious representatives then invited the delegates of the other two estates to join them in working for the welfare of France. When the king had the representatives of the Third Estate locked out of their meeting place, they met at a nearby indoor tennis court. There, on June 20, they made a pledge called the Tennis Court Oath. The representatives declared that they would not adjourn until they had written a constitution for France and had seen it adopted. Finally the king gave in and ordered the three estates to meet together.

Learning from Pictures The Tennis Court Oath *was the decisive challenge to the absolute monarchy in France, established by Louis XIV.*

Independence Days

Most modern nations celebrate a day in honor of their nation each year. For many this takes the form of an independence day, marking the date when the nation became a distinct political unit.

The oldest such independence day is August 1 in Switzerland. It commemorates the day in 1291 when three Swiss cantons, or states, agreed to form a union. Switzerland has now grown to 21 cantons, and they all celebrate their independence on August 1.

After World War II, many colonies of European nations gained independence. Each year some hold festivals celebrating their freedom, such as the ones in India (below left) and in Mexico (below right).

Even nations so ancient that they cannot record an independence date have established a national festive day. For example, in England there are fireworks on Guy Fawkes Day, November 5, to commemorate the day in 1605 when the government uncovered and foiled a plot to blow up Parliament.

A number of nations consider themselves to be creations of revolutions. The French observe Bastille Day every July 14. It marks the day in 1789 on which a Paris mob stormed the dreaded royal prison, the Bastille. The French people regard this event

as the beginning of their freedom in modern times.

In the United States, Americans observe a holiday on July 4, the day in 1776 on which the Declaration of Independence was adopted. Americans celebrate the day with parades, speeches, and fireworks (above).

About the time of the American Revolution, Europeans first applied the techniques for making fireworks to the making of rockets for warfare. One of the earliest military uses of rockets occurred in the War of 1812

between the United States and Great Britain. After the British bombarded Fort McHenry, in Baltimore, Maryland, the American poet Francis Scott Key wrote a poem describing the battle, which he had watched. Later his poem, set to music, became the American national anthem. Today, as Americans watch "the rockets' red glare" during Independence Day fireworks displays, they are reminded of the link between the beauty of the celebration and the seriousness of battle.

The Spread of the Revolution

Now Louis XVI tried to do secretly what he dared not do openly. He began to bring troops to Paris and to Versailles, where the representatives were meeting. Fearing that he planned to drive out the National Assembly by force, the people of Paris took action. On July 14, 1789, they stormed and captured the Bastille, the hated prison-fortress, in search of weapons. They planned to use the weapons to defend the National Assembly against the royal troops.

This outbreak of violence in Paris led to the formation of a new government for the city. Under the leadership of General Lafayette, the French hero who had fought for American independence in the Revolutionary War, a people's army—the National Guard—was formed. The tricolor—a flag bearing vertical red, white, and blue stripes, which has remained the flag of France—replaced the white flag of the Bourbons with its *fleur de lis* (lily) symbols.

The events in Paris were repeated throughout France. In July and August, a "Great Fear" swept across the land. The peasants believed rumors that the nobles planned to send bandits into the countryside to crush them and the Revolution. They feared that the nobles would hoard grain and starve the peasants into submission. Eager to take revenge for old wrongs, the peasants attacked and often destroyed monasteries and manor houses. They burned the hated documents that recorded rents, feudal dues, and other obligations. They killed some of the nobles and their agents, as well as some government officials, especially tax farmers. These actions showed how widespread people's hatred of the social system of the Old Regime had become.

SECTION 2 REVIEW

1. **Define** primogeniture, bourgeoisie, tithe
2. **Identify** Louis XVI, Abbé Sieyès
3. **Explaining Ideas** Describe the social structure of France during the Old Regime.
4. **Interpreting Ideas** Why did discontent grow in France during the mid-1700s?
5. **Analyzing Ideas** (a) How were the terms "liberty" and "equality" interpreted by the peasants? (b) by the bourgeoisie?
6. **Understanding Ideas** (a) Why did Louis XVI call a meeting of the Estates-General? (b) Why did representatives of the Third Estate insist that all three groups of the Estates-General meet and vote together?

---

3 After a Period of Turmoil, the French Overthrew the Monarchy

Chaos engulfed France after the storming of the Bastille and the outbreaks of violence throughout the country. With the support of the people, the National Assembly assumed power.

The End of the Old Regime

Many members of the National Assembly felt that they could deal with revolutionary violence only by removing the oppression and injustice that produced it. In a little more than a month, they took several important steps in this direction.

As of August 4, 1789, the National Assembly abolished the last remnants of feudalism in France. Delegates repealed the tithe and canceled all feudal dues and services owed by the peasants. They also did away with the special privileges of the First and Second Estates.

Following these reforms, on August 27, 1789, the assembly adopted the Declaration of the Rights of Man. The English Bill of Rights, the writings of Rousseau and other philosophers, and the American Declaration of Independence strongly influenced this document.

The Declaration of the Rights of Man stated that men are born equal and remain equal before the law. It proclaimed freedom of speech, of the press, and of religion. It guaranteed men the right to take part in their government and to resist oppression and declared that all citizens had an equal right to hold public office. The Declaration of the Rights of Man also assured the right to personal liberty, which men could lose only after a fair trial and conviction. The Declaration stated and defined the principles that became the slogan of the French Revolution: "liberty, equality, fraternity."

These rights, however, were not extended to women. During the Revolution a group of women led by a Parisian housewife, Olympe de Gouges (duh • GOOZH), wrote a declaration of rights for women, but the National Assembly rejected it. The leaders of the Revolution were not ready to grant women legal rights or to share political participation with them. They believed in equality for men, but they did not believe that women were the equals of men.

Learning from Pictures This engraving depicts Parisian women marching to Versailles on October 5, 1789. For what did these women blame the king?

Although the National Assembly swept away the remains of feudalism in France, the Old Regime died hard. Many nobles fled to Great Britain, to Italy, and across the Rhine to Germany. There they plotted continuously to overturn the Revolution and set the clock back. These **émigrés** (EM • ee • gray)—French for "emigrants"—became a constant source of trouble for France for the next few years.

Some nobles remained at Versailles with the king. Their opposition to some of his policies had helped start the Revolution. Now, however, most nobles sided with the king against the National Assembly and others who insisted on change. The nobles urged the king to use force to restore the Old Regime. Taking their advice, Louis XVI again called troops to Versailles.

When news of this reached the people, a crowd led by women marched from Paris to Versailles. They believed that the king was trying to squelch the Revolution. They also blamed the king for food shortages and the high price of bread. The crowd stormed into the palace and forced Louis XVI, Marie Antoinette, and their family to return to Paris with them, away from the plotting and scheming royal advisers.

The National Assembly accompanied the royal family to Paris. There the Assembly held meetings in a public hall, where spectators often interrupted the debates with shouts or rose to give their own opinions from the gallery. This kind of open, democratic participation in government would have been unthinkable before 1789.

Reforms in Government

The abolition of feudalism and the issuing of the Declaration of the Rights of Man established the guiding principles of the French Revolution. The National Assembly then began to work out the details. Between 1789 and 1791, the Assembly passed more than 2,000 laws aimed at correcting abuses and setting up a new government.

The Assembly reformed France's administrative structure. It abolished the provinces and divided France into 83 districts called **departments.** It also called for the election of all local officials.

Because it had assumed responsibilities along with its new powers, the National Assembly also assumed the burden of the debt. In November 1789 the National Assembly seized land that belonged to the Catholic church and offered it for sale to the public. The proceeds from the sale could then be used to pay off the public debt. The wealthier peasants, who had been renting this land, bought a good portion of it.

430

In 1790 the Assembly issued the Civil Constitution of the Clergy. This law stated that people in the parishes and dioceses would elect their clergy. The government—as a compensation for seizing church lands—assumed church expenses and paid the salaries of priests and bishops. The pope refused to allow the clergy to accept this arrangement, and most obeyed him. Some clergy became émigrés, while others helped the remaining nobles stir up opposition to the Revolution.

The Constitution of 1791

In 1791 the National Assembly finally finished writing a constitution for France. This constitution limited the authority of the king and set up a government divided into three branches—executive, legislative, and judicial.

The constitution greatly reduced the powers of the king. He could not proclaim laws, nor could he block laws passed by the legislature. Taxpaying male voters elected the members of the one-house legislature—the Legislative Assembly. The National Assembly was dissolved, and no one who had been a member could run for election to the Legislative Assembly. Only men who owned considerable property could hold office. The Constitution of 1791 did not permit women to vote or run for office. Despite the guarantees of equal rights and powers by the Declaration of the Rights of Man, under France's new constitution wealthy men held most of the political power.

Louis XVI reluctantly consented to the limitations that the new constitution imposed on him. At the same time, he encouraged the émigrés to plot with foreign governments. The king hoped that such plots would lead to the overthrow of the new government and a return to the Old Regime.

Some of the king's advisers urged him to flee and seek help directly from nations friendly to the monarchy. On the night of June 21, 1791, Louis XVI, Marie Antoinette, their young son and daughter, and the king's sister slipped out of Paris and tried to escape to the Austrian Netherlands. Louis disguised himself as a coachman, but the military escort for his coach, as well as the enormous coach itself, aroused suspicion. Louis's profile was on every coin in the kingdom, and he was recognized and stopped at Varennes, a town near the border. The revolutionaries arrested Louis and his family and sent them back to Paris.

Despite Louis XVI's unsuccessful flight, the National Assembly decided to allow him to remain king. Louis pledged that he would abide by the new constitution. People hoped that under the new constitutional monarchy, France could recover without further revolutionary disturbances. Instead, the attempted escape marked a revolutionary turning point. People no longer trusted the king, and they publicly discussed creating a republic.

The Legislative Assembly and War

The new government provided for by the Constitution of 1791 went into effect in September 1791, but it lasted less than a year. The revolutionaries had been more skillful in overthrowing the Old Regime than in creating a sound government to replace it. They had set up a weak executive and a powerful but inexperienced legislature elected by a minority of the population.

Three factions, or groups of people with differing attitudes, sat in the Legislative Assembly. One group believed that the Revolution had gone far enough. They considered the ideal form of

Learning from Maps Revolutionaries forced Louis XVI and his family to move to the Tuileries palace. *What direction is Versailles from Paris?*

BUILDING HISTORY STUDY SKILLS

Thinking About History: Examining How Perspective Influences Viewpoints

A person's perspective often influences how he or she views events. Many factors, including education, social class, religion, age, sex, ethnic group, and personality, shape a person's perspective and influence his or her viewpoint. For example, a wealthy man might feel that only people who own property should be allowed to vote, because they have a stake in the society. In this case, the man's social class influences his viewpoint on voting rights. You can understand events in history more clearly if you can determine the way different groups of people interpret the meanings of these events.

How to Examine How Perspective Influences Viewpoints

To examine how perspective influences viewpoints, follow these steps.

1. Identify the goal or purpose of your analysis.
2. Determine what factors shape the person's perspective.
3. Identify how the person views specific events in history.
4. Determine how the person's perspective influences his or her viewpoint.

Developing the Skill

Olympe de Gouges was from the lower middle class in Paris at the time of the French Revolution. The following excerpt is from her "Declaration of the Rights of Women." Read the excerpt and determine how her perspective would influence her viewpoint on the Declaration of the Rights of Man and the Constitution of 1791.

    ❝ Woman is born free and her rights are the same as those of man. Social distinctions can be based only on the common good. . . . The law must be an expression of the general will; all

citizens, men and women alike, must be equally eligible for all public offices, positions, and jobs, according to their capacity and without any other criteria than those of their virtues and talents. [Women] . . . have the right to go to the scaffold; they must also have the right to go to parliament. . . . Women, wake up . . . recognize your rights. Man, the slave, has multiplied his strengths. . . . What advantages have you got from the Revolution? ❞

The goal is to determine if Olympe de Gouges would view the events of the Revolution as steps toward liberty. Her words show her concern for political justice and rights for women. She believes that if women can fight and die for the Revolution, they are entitled to its benefits. Her perspective as a woman influences her viewpoint.

    The Declaration of the Rights of Man made no mention of women. Olympe de Gouges wrote her declaration in response to this omission, asking, shouldn't the people who "go to the scaffold" also have the right "to go to parliament"?

    Olympe de Gouges would condemn the Constitution of 1791 as a denial of liberty. It reinforced property rights for upper-class men. People had to own property before they could have the right to vote. Women could not own property, so they could not vote. Olympe de Gouges's perspective would influence a point of view that the Revolution was not over because it had not gone far enough in guaranteeing liberty for all people.

    Practicing the skill. How might the perspective of a wealthy factory owner and that of an unemployed laborer influence their viewpoints on a new law lowering taxes and canceling unemployment insurance?

To apply this skill, see Applying History Study Skills on page 451.

A patriotic women's club at the time of the French Revolution

Learning from Pictures *During the Revolution, the food shortage was so severe that women in Paris stormed the Hôtel de Ville searching for food.*

government to be one in which the king had limited authority. They were the **conservatives**—that is, they did not want to change existing conditions. Another group called the **radicals** wanted to get rid of the king, set up a republic, and institute far-reaching changes. A third group, the **moderates,** had no extreme views. They sided with either conservatives or radicals depending on the issues.

In the hall where the Legislative Assembly met, conservatives sat on the right, moderates in the center, and radicals on the left. Since the French Revolution, the terms *right* (conservative), *center* (moderate), and *left* (radical) have meant different slants of political opinion.

The Legislative Assembly frequently deadlocked on domestic issues, but it united in facing a foreign threat. Before the Legislative Assembly first met, Marie Antoinette's brother, Emperor Leopold II of Austria, and King Frederick William II of Prussia had issued the Declaration of Pillnitz. This declaration invited European rulers to help Louis XVI restore the monarchy to its full power.

The fear of foreign invasion electrified the Legislative Assembly. Each group in the Assembly

hoped that a successful foreign war would increase its own influence. Louis XVI favored war because he hoped that foreign armies would defeat the French army and restore his authority. Only a few farsighted people feared that war would lead to dictatorship. With only seven members opposed, in April 1792 the Legislative Assembly voted to declare war on Austria. It hoped to keep Prussia and the other German states out of the war, but it failed in that objective. Soon afterward an army of Austrian and Prussian troops invaded France and headed toward Paris.

The End of the Monarchy

The invasion of France by Austrian and Prussian armies touched off mass uprisings in Paris. A group of radicals seized control of the city government and set up an organization called the Commune.*

When the Prussian commander, the Duke of Brunswick, vowed to destroy Paris and punish the revolutionaries if any harm came to the royal family, members of the Commune threatened the Legislative Assembly with violence unless it abolished the monarchy. The Commune accurately accused Louis XVI of plotting with foreign monarchs to overthrow the Constitution of 1791. Revolutionary troops arrived from Marseilles to help defend Paris, singing their marching song—the *Marseillaise*—which became France's national anthem.

On August 10, 1792, the Legislative Assembly, coerced by the Commune, voted to suspend the office of king. Troops marched on the Tuileries palace, massacred many of the king's guards, and imprisoned Louis XVI and his family in the Temple (see map, page 431). The Commune now ruled Paris, and the Legislative Assembly tried to govern France.

With the monarchy suspended, France needed a new constitution. The Legislative Assembly voted itself out of existence and set a date for the election of delegates to a National Convention to draw up a new constitution for France. In late 1792, in the

---

*People called *sans-culottes* (san-skyoo · LAHT) offered the greatest support to the Commune. The term *sans-culottes* means "without knee breeches"—the craftsworkers, artisans, apprentices, and small shopkeepers of Paris who belonged to the *sans-culottes* wore long pants, while the nobility and rich bourgeoisie wore knee breeches. It became unfashionable to dress like the nobles and the wealthy, so in this way, revolution and social class influenced fashion. In the 1800s and 1900s, all men in the West began wearing long pants.

midst of great danger, with a foreign war and political turmoil at home, France faced both a national election and a complete change of government.

SECTION 3 REVIEW

1. **Define** émigré, department, conservative, radical, moderate
2. **Identify** Olympe de Gouges, Duke of Brunswick
3. **Locate** Varennes
4. **Understanding Ideas** How did the National Assembly try to pay off the French government's enormous debt?
5. **Explaining Ideas** Describe the organization of the French government under the Constitution of 1791.
6. **Analyzing Ideas** (a) What three political groups made up the Legislative Assembly? (b) What were their political views?

4 The French Republic Faced Disorder at Home and War Abroad

The delegates to the National Convention were elected by **universal manhood suffrage**—every man could vote, regardless of whether he owned property. Although some 7 million qualified voters lived in France, only 10 percent cast their ballots.

The National Convention

The National Convention held its first meeting in September 1792. The delegates, like those in the Legislative Assembly, were divided into three main groups. This time, however, no one supported the king. On the right sat the Girondists (juh • RAHN • duhsts), so called because many of them came from the department of the Gironde in southwestern France. The Jacobins (JAK • uh • buhns), members of a radical political club of that name, sat on the left. Among the most powerful Jacobins were Georges-Jacques Danton and Maximilien Robespierre. The third group consisted of delegates that had no definite views. Later most of these delegates came to favor the Jacobins. The Convention also included some Jacobins who were extreme radicals and wanted reforms that would benefit all classes in society, including the *sans-culottes*. Jean-Paul Marat (muh • RAH), a doctor from Paris, led these radicals.

The National Convention governed France for three years. As soon as it met, it proclaimed the end of the monarchy and the beginning of a republic. Besides drawing up a new constitution, it had to assume many of the responsibilities of government. It had to suppress disorder and revolt at home and fight a war against foreign invaders.

The National Convention tried Louis XVI on charges of plotting against the security of the nation. Putting a king on trial was serious business. The Convention studied carefully the records of the Long Parliament, which had tried and executed Charles I in England 143 years earlier. The Convention declared Louis XVI guilty and by a margin of one vote sentenced him to death. On January 21, 1793, Louis was beheaded by the guillotine (GIL • uh • teen), a new device believed by its inventor to allow for quick and more humane executions.

Exporting the Revolution

Even before Louis's execution, the National Convention heard encouraging news. The French army had defeated the Austrian and Prussian forces and stopped the invasion. The French followed up their military victories by invading the Austrian Netherlands and capturing Brussels. Joyful over these victories, the National Convention declared that the French armies would liberate all the peoples of Europe from oppression.

The French decision to export the ideas of the Revolution by force of arms alarmed the monarchs of Europe. Great Britain, the Netherlands, Spain, and the kingdom of Sardinia joined Austria and Prussia to form an alliance against France called the First Coalition. For a time, the enemies of France succeeded in driving French troops out of the Austrian Netherlands, and they invaded France again.

In 1793 the National Convention took steps to meet these dangers. It set up the Committee

What If?
Louis XVI

Louis XVI was a weak monarch who was more interested in hunting than in governing France. How do you think world history would have been different if Louis XVI had been a strong king like Louis XIV?

Learning from Pictures
The beheading of Louis XVI shocked most of Europe. Even the United States, which a few years earlier had succeeded in its own revolution, condemned the execution.

of Public Safety to direct the army in crushing all foreign invaders. It also established a court called the Revolutionary Tribunal to try "enemies of the Revolution."

To meet the danger of invasion, the Committee of Public Safety adopted **conscription**—the draft. All men between 18 and 45 were liable for military service. As a force of loyal, patriotic young men, the French army took on a new spirit. Many of the nobles who had been professional officers had fled as émigrés, so now men of all classes who proved their ability and daring could serve as officers. For the first time, a country called upon the talents and abilities of its entire population to fight a war.

Despite the army's optimism, the war created many problems for France. In the cities, working people demanded that the government do something about food shortages and rising prices. In the countryside the clergy refused to take the oath of loyalty to the Revolution. Instead they organized small armies of peasants to fight against it. Some nobles joined them. In western France, particularly in the department of the Vendée (vahn • DAY), the "Royal and Catholic army" fought against the French revolutionary army. The term that describes their activities is **counterrevolution,** because it was aimed counter to, or against, the Revolution. In short, counterrevolutionaries supported the Old Regime.

Jacobins, including Danton and Robespierre, controlled the Convention. They arrested many Girondist delegates who opposed their policies.

Charlotte Corday, a woman from Normandy influenced by Girondist propaganda, journeyed to Paris and assassinated Marat. The Revolutionary Tribunal sent her to the guillotine for her crime.

The Reign of Terror

To meet the danger of opposition and revolt within France, the Convention started a systematic program to suppress all opposition. The Reign of Terror, as it became known, lasted from September 1793 to July 1794. According to one delegate, "What constitutes the Republic is the complete destruction of everything that is opposed to it."

The Revolutionary Tribunal conducted swift trials and handed down harsh sentences. It arrested, tried, and executed many people on mere suspicion. Marie Antoinette became an early victim of the Reign of Terror. The Jacobins directed the Reign of Terror not only against the nobility, however. The guillotine—the "national razor"—chopped off the heads of people of all classes suspected of disloyalty to the Revolution. The revolutionaries executed twice as many people from the bourgeoisie as nobles and clergy, and nearly three times as many peasants and laborers as people from all other classes. Danton and Robespierre sent their Girondist opponents and Olympe de Gouges to the scaffold. They also arrested the extreme radical followers of Marat. The Revolutionary Tribunal condemned Antoine Lavoisier, the famous chemist, because he had been involved in tax farming under the Old Regime. It sent him to death with the words, "The Republic has no need of genius."

In the spring of 1794, Danton felt that the Reign of Terror had accomplished its purpose and should be relaxed. But Robespierre became even more fanatical and accused Danton of disloyalty to the Revolution. He had Danton and his followers put to death.

For 100 days Robespierre carried out a policy of suppression that aroused fear even among his supporters. He was convinced that only he could protect the Revolution from its enemies. Finally, a few brave members of the National Convention called a halt. In July 1794 they arrested Robespierre and guillotined him. The Reign of Terror was over.

Work of the National Convention

Despite the dangers and difficulties of the time, the National Convention made many reforms in France. It began codifying French laws. It provided for a national system of public education, and it abolished slavery in the French colonies.

In addition, the Convention adopted the metric system of weights and measures. Today most parts of the world use the metric system. The Convention also adopted a new calendar with colorful names that reflected the seasons, such as *Thermidor* for the time of heat (roughly July) and *Ventôse* for the time of wind (roughly March). This calendar did not survive, however, perhaps because it also increased the number of days in a week from 7 to 10—an arrangement that met with little support among working people!

Meanwhile, the citizen army swept to victory. By 1795 the French had driven invaders from French soil and conquered territory as far as the Rhine River in Germany. Even more important, the First Coalition began to break up. However, the French paid a heavy price for victory. At home the spirit of militarism allowed the National Convention to use the army to quell any opposition. It crushed an uprising in Paris in October 1795, indicating that the new government did not welcome any opposition. In other countries, the French army behaved so harshly and with such arrogance that the people it supposedly "liberated" hated it.

Learning from Pictures The Reign of Terror ended with the execution of Robespierre and the closing of the Jacobin club.

The Death of Marat

It is hardly surprising that the art of France reflected the shattering changes brought about by the Revolution. In subject, in mood, and in technique, these changes are evident in this work by Jacques-Louis David. The Jacobin leader Jean-Paul Marat was stabbed to death by Charlotte Corday as he was bathing. She had been convinced by the Girondists that he was a cruel tyrant. (Marat suffered from a painful skin disease caught while he was hiding in the sewers, and he could find relief only by sitting in a warm bath.)

Because of its bizarre circumstances, Marat's assassination was not a conventional subject for a painting. But David—himself a revolutionary who at one time presided over the Convention—was a great artist and succeeded in creating a moving and forceful painting. In Marat's hand is a letter from his assassin. The knife that she plunged into his chest lies on the floor. The painting's stark drama is highlighted by David's simple inscription, "To Marat."

The Directory

In 1795 the National Convention drafted another constitution. Universal manhood suffrage disappeared and only property owners could vote. The wealthy controlled the government, as they had under the rule of the National Assembly. The new constitution established an executive branch of five men called *directors*. The directors gave their name to the government created by the Constitution of 1795: the Directory.

Although the Directory governed France for four years, it pleased neither the radicals nor the conservatives. Weak, corrupt, and selfish, the five directors constantly quarreled among themselves and could not agree on how to solve any of France's problems. Prices skyrocketed out of control, and the peasants, *sans-culottes*, and all the poor people in France suffered. But the directors made no effort to improve the desperate situation. They did not interfere with the activities of corrupt business leaders and speculators. As a result, the economic situation got worse. When crowds protested the government's inability to act, the directors called in the army to put down the unrest. A worker in Paris summed up his feelings this way:

> **"U**nder Robespierre blood was spilled and we had bread. Now blood is no longer spilled and we have no bread. Perhaps we must spill some blood in order to have bread. **"**

The Directory soon became as unpopular as the Old Regime. It repeated history by going bankrupt, and it prepared the way for military dictatorship.

Napoleon Bonaparte

The Directory did encourage good leadership in the French army. The continuing war with Great Britain, Austria, and Sardinia provided opportunities for able military leaders. During this period, from 1795 to 1799, a relatively unknown general named Napoleon Bonaparte caught the public's

Learning from Pictures *Although Napoleon was not the eldest son, at the age of 16 he became the head of his family after his father's death.*

attention. As a general at age 26, he had suppressed the uprising in Paris that attempted to prevent the establishment of the Directory.

Born in 1769 on the French island of Corsica, Napoleon Bonaparte attended military school in France and graduated as an artillery officer. He might have remained there had the Revolution not given him the opportunity to rise to the rank of general.

Bonaparte bundled extraordinary energy into a five-foot-two-inch (1.6-meter) frame. Requiring only two to three hours of sleep a night, he combined overwhelming ambition with a vain and domineering personality. Either despite or because of these traits, the general proved to be a superb organizer and administrator in both political and military affairs. Above all, he had military genius.

Napoleon Bonaparte ranks among the great generals of all time. Because of the dominant role Napoleon played beginning in 1796, the wars that

the French fought from then until 1815 are generally known as the Napoleonic Wars.

Napoleon's genius lay in his ability to rapidly move troops and to mass forces at critical points on the battlefield. These techniques gave him an advantage over his opponents' older, slower tactics.

In Italy Napoleon quickly showed his ability. He took a small, weak, and poorly equipped French army and, within weeks, so organized and inspired it that he forced the Sardinians to make peace. Napoleon defeated the Austrians twice, and in 1797 he forced them to sign a humiliating peace treaty that gave France control of all of northern Italy.

Napoleon's successes made him so popular in France that the Directory worried that he might seize power. Napoleon, on the other hand, continually sought new conquests to keep his name before the French people. He proposed to weaken the British in a military campaign that would cut off their trade with the Middle East and India. The Directory quickly agreed, since such a campaign would keep him out of Paris.

Napoleon's campaign met with disaster. The British destroyed the French fleet near Alexandria in Egypt, thus cutting off the French army's supply lines. Napoleon left his army to its fate and secretly returned to France. He concealed the true situation in Egypt and made exaggerated claims of victories.

Napoleon became the popular hero of the time. However, his popularity could not change the facts. France faced a truly dangerous situation. The British had organized a Second Coalition against France that included Austria and Russia. Coalition forces drove French armies out of Italy, and French control over the other conquered states slipped.

Napoleon's Seizure of Power

As conditions worsened, many people believed that only Napoleon could win victory abroad and restore order at home. People afraid that royalists might seize control organized a plot to overthrow the government and place Napoleon in power. The plotters wanted stability in France to insure that they could keep the nationalized property they had bought and the power they had acquired. Abbé Sieyès, one of the chief conspirators, said, "We had reached the point when it was a question of thinking of saving, not the principles of the Revolution, but the men who had made it." In 1799 three directors resigned and two were arrested, leaving the way open for change. Troops with bayonets surrounded the legislature and forced most of its members to leave. Those that remained turned the government over to Napoleon and his fellow plotters.

A seizure of power by force is called a **coup d'état** (kood • ay • TAH), meaning literally a "stroke of state." Napoleon himself said later, "I found the crown of France lying on the ground, and I picked it up with a sword."

SECTION 4 REVIEW

1. **Define** universal manhood suffrage, conscription, counterrevolution, coup d'état
2. **Identify** Georges-Jacques Danton, Maximilien Robespierre, Jean-Paul Marat
3. **Locate** Brussels, Vendée, Corsica
4. **Summarizing Ideas** Describe the three main groups that made up the National Convention.
5. **Analyzing Ideas** (a) What was the Reign of Terror? (b) What kinds of people were among its victims?
6. **Explaining Ideas** Explain the circumstances that made Napoleon's coup d'état possible.

5 Napoleon Built an Empire That Spread Across Europe

Although Napoleon's government kept the form of a republic, the coup d'état of 1799 had made him dictator of France. From 1799 until 1814, Napoleon influenced events in France and the rest of Europe to such a great extent that this period is known as the Napoleonic Era, or the Age of Napoleon.

The people of France accepted Napoleon's dictatorship. Some, weary of the long period of chaos, wanted stability. Others were afraid to protest because they feared arrest. Instead of trying to abolish the changes brought on by the Revolution, Napoleon supported them. He respected the ideals of the Declaration of the Rights of Man and did not restore serfdom and feudal privileges. He reassured the peasants that the land they owned would remain theirs.

However, liberty under Napoleon meant only freedom of opportunity. It was not liberty from control, because Napoleon believed that the people should obey orders given by a leader.

Napoleon and the Consulate

Napoleon reorganized and centralized the administration of France to give himself unlimited power. The executive branch, made up of three consuls, gave its name to the first five years of Napoleon's rule—the Consulate. In an attempt to appeal to popular admiration for the strength and virtues of ancient Rome, Napoleon took the title of First Consul—the title used in the Roman Republic.

As First Consul, Napoleon commanded the army and navy. He also had the right to appoint and dismiss all officials and to propose all new laws. None of the Consulate's legislative bodies had any real power; they merely rubber-stamped Napoleon's decrees.

Napoleon submitted the constitution of his new government to the people for a vote, a procedure known as a **plebiscite** (PLEB • uh • syt). People could vote only yes or no and could not make any changes. Nevertheless, a vast majority of French voters approved the new constitution.

People usually remember Napoleon for his military leadership. However, his work in government had more importance and a longer-lasting effect. Under Napoleon's direction, scholars completed the revision and organization of all French law begun by the National Convention. Many governments in Europe and elsewhere copied this system, called the Napoleonic Code.

Napoleon established the Bank of France because he wanted a central financial institution. Although the bank was privately owned, the government closely supervised it.

The government also established the public education system planned by the National Convention. This system included elementary schools, high schools, universities, and technical schools. A central agency called the University of France supervised and directed these schools.

The Civil Constitution of the Clergy of 1790 had ruptured relations between the Roman Catholic church and the French government. Napoleon ended the conflict by reaching an agreement called the *Concordat* with the pope in 1801. The Concordat acknowledged Catholicism as the religion of most French citizens, but it did not abolish the religious toleration guaranteed by the Declaration of the Rights of Man. Most important, the church gave up claims to the property the government had seized and sold during the Revolution.

439

In a display of shrewd and skillful diplomacy, Napoleon destroyed the Second Coalition against France. In 1799 he convinced Russia to desert the coalition. By 1801 Austria asked France for peace, and in 1802 Great Britain and France signed a peace treaty. For a time it looked as though Napoleon would keep his promises to the French people—peace won by military victory, firm and steady government, and economic prosperity.

Napoleon as Emperor

In France Napoleon moved to increase his power by making it permanent and hereditary. In another plebiscite in 1804, the French people voted to declare France an empire. First Consul Napoleon Bonaparte became Emperor Napoleon I.

The coronation of Napoleon in the Cathedral of Notre Dame in Paris inaugurated the empire, later known as the First Empire. One part of the elaborate ceremony was especially significant. The pope had come to Paris to crown the new emperor. However, when the time came for him to place the crown on Napoleon's head, Napoleon seized the crown and placed it on his head himself. Thus he demonstrated that the power and authority that he held were not given to him by anyone but himself.

The First Empire expanded far beyond France's old boundaries. But throughout Europe people wanted to destroy Napoleon's empire. The British became his most determined adversaries once they realized that his ambition threatened their commerce, their empire, and their control of the seas. Great Britain renewed the war against France and in 1805 organized the Third Coalition. Austria, Russia, and Sweden allied themselves with Great Britain; Spain was allied with France. Napoleon planned to defeat the British navy and then invade Great Britain.

However, in 1805 a British fleet led by Admiral Horatio Nelson defeated a combined French and Spanish fleet near Trafalgar off the southern coast of Spain. Nelson was killed in the battle, but not before he had almost destroyed the French and Spanish fleet. Napoleon succeeded spectacularly, however, in land battles against Austria and Russia.

The Continental System

Because they inflicted defeat upon him, Napoleon had nothing but contempt for the British, calling them "a nation of shopkeepers." He believed that if the British lost their foreign trade and its profits, they would be willing to make peace on his terms. Therefore, he ordered a blockade of the British Isles and forbade anyone in the French Empire or its allied states to trade with the British. This blockade was called the Continental System, because Napoleon controlled so much of the continent of Europe.

The British responded with a blockade of their own against the French. They ordered ships of neutral countries to stop at British ports to get a license before trading with France or its allies. Napoleon, in turn, ordered the French navy to seize any neutral ship that obeyed the British order.

This conflict placed neutral nations in an awkward position. If they disregarded the British order, the British might capture their ships. If they obeyed the British, the French might seize their ships. The Continental System and the British blockade hit especially hard at the United States, for it depended heavily on trade with both Great Britain and the continent of Europe. Both France and Great Britain stopped American ships, but British ships did the most damage to American trade. This conflict, in part, brought about the War of 1812 between Great Britain and the United States.

Although the British blockade hurt France, Napoleon continued to win battles against the powers in the Third Coalition. He struck his enemies before they could unite effectively. In December 1805 Napoleon smashed the combined forces of Russia and Austria at Austerlitz, a town north of Vienna. Shortly thereafter, the Third Coalition collapsed.

The Reorganization of Europe

By 1808 Napoleon completely dominated Europe (see map, page 442). He forced Austria and Prussia to sign humiliating peace treaties. Czar Alexander I allied Russia with France. Napoleon ruled the Austrian and Dutch Netherlands and Spain, and forced Denmark and the Papal States into alliances. To stop the possibility of any Russian gains, Napoleon formed the territory that Prussia had taken from Poland into the Grand Duchy of Warsaw, which he gave to his ally, the king of Saxony.

Since 1795 various treaties had given France the right to intervene in the affairs of the many small German states. Napoleon organized the most important of these states into the Confederation of the Rhine, with himself as protector. He abolished the Holy Roman Empire in 1806 and forced its emperor to take the lesser title of emperor of Austria. He unified all the small northern Italian states into the Kingdom of Italy and made them dependencies of France. He also placed members of his large family on the thrones of the countries he had conquered.

Napoleon did not limit the changes he made in Europe to enlarging his empire and reorganizing the conquered territories. On the contrary, he instituted far-reaching changes. Wherever the French army went, it put the Napoleonic Code into effect, abolished feudalism and serfdom, and introduced the modern methods of the French army.

Without intending to, the French also helped awaken in the people they conquered a spirit of **nationalism,** or love of one's country rather than of one's native region. In France the events of the Revolution and the stirring words of the Declaration of the Rights of Man had produced feelings of patriotism for the country as a whole, rather than just for local regions. People thought of themselves as French, with a country and ideals worth fighting for. Now these same feelings of loyalty and

patriotism for their homelands appeared among the conquered peoples, and they wanted to rid themselves of French rule.

In 1808 Napoleon ruled Europe, but time worked on the side of his enemies. The coalitions reformed and his opponents' armies grew stronger. The generals who opposed Napoleon in the field copied his methods of moving and massing troops rapidly. Other nations, especially Great Britain and Prussia, had learned how to train large bodies of troops. And, as you have read, nationalism strengthened Napoleon's opponents.

The Peninsular Campaign

To the south of France, on the Iberian Peninsula, lay Spain and Portugal. In 1807 Portugal refused to observe the Continental System because the nation's prosperity depended on trade with Great Britain. In retaliation the French army occupied Portugal and drove its king into exile.

Napoleon then decided to conquer Spain. After forcing the Spanish king to abdicate, Napoleon made his brother Joseph king of Spain. Resenting a foreign king, the Spanish people revolted in 1808. The British sent an army under Arthur Wellesley, the future Duke of Wellington, to help the Spanish and Portuguese drive out the French. In spite of everything Napoleon did, he failed to suppress the Spanish uprising and defeat the British.

The Peninsular Campaign, as this war was called, lasted from 1808 to 1814. Napoleon continued to control Spain's government, but the campaign drained French military resources when the emperor needed them elsewhere.

In 1814 the Spanish, with British help, captured Madrid and drove out Joseph Bonaparte. They then drew up a new constitution that provided for a limited monarchy. The Spanish revolt

and the new constitution illustrated the tremendous influence of the ideals of the French Revolution. It also showed the rising spirit of nationalism and opposition to Napoleon.

Catastrophe in Russia

Czar Alexander I of Russia, who reigned from 1801 to 1825, viewed Napoleon's domination of Europe with alarm and distrust. The French Continental System had disrupted a long-established exchange of Russian grain and raw materials for British manufactured goods. Gradually, the czar relaxed his

Learning from Maps Napoleon controlled the European coastline from the Mediterranean to the North Sea. On which other seas did he control some coastline?

AZIMUTHAL EQUAL AREA PROJECTION

442

enforcement of the Continental System in Russia, and in 1812 he announced the resumption of trade with Great Britain.

Inefficient as it was, the blockade remained Napoleon's only way of striking at the British. He found it intolerable for Russia, a French ally, to openly ignore it. Napoleon decided to invade Russia, and he exerted pressure on all parts of his empire to supply soldiers.

When finally assembled, Napoleon's Grand Army totaled 600,000 soldiers. However, this huge force differed greatly from the enthusiastic, loyal, and patriotic armies of the early French Empire. Fewer than half of the soldiers were French. The majority of the Grand Army consisted of soldiers from Napoleon's conquered states or from countries he forced to be his allies. The soldiers had little heart for this war.

In May 1812 Napoleon's army began its march eastward toward Russia (see map, page 442). Instead of battling the French on the vast plains of western Russia, the Russian army retreated slowly, drawing Napoleon's army deeper into the country. As they retreated, the Russians practiced a **scorched-earth policy,** burning or destroying crops and everything else that might be of value to the invaders.

In mid-September 1812 the French captured Moscow and Napoleon entered the Kremlin. But it was a hollow victory. As soon as the French entered the city, the Russians set it afire so that nothing would be left for their enemies. The fire destroyed so many buildings that the French troops had no housing. To make matters worse, the harsh Russian winter lay ahead, and Russian troops lurked in the countryside, endangering the Grand Army's long supply line from France. Napoleon had not expected the Russians to destroy the food supply that his troops and horses needed. Many soldiers in the Grand Army fell ill or starved. Faced with these horrible hardships, Napoleon decided to retreat to France.

Napoleon's retreat from Moscow ranks as one of the greatest military disasters of all time. The Russian winter struck with exceptional force. In addition to the snow and bitter cold, the French troops had to pass back through the devastated countryside, where the Russians attacked the bedraggled soldiers without mercy. Cossacks and peasants captured or killed stragglers. Discipline broke down, and many troops deserted. Napoleon abandoned

his army to fend for itself and hurried to France to raise new forces to defend his empire. When the Grand Army reached Prussia in December, it had lost four-fifths of its troops. The Russian army followed the retreating French and invaded Napoleon's empire.

Final Defeat

Everywhere in western Europe, monarchs broke their alliances with Napoleon and joined the invading Russians. Napoleon faced overwhelming odds. Prussia, Austria, Great Britain, and Sweden joined Russia in a new and final alliance to crush France.

Napoleon tried his old strategy of striking before his enemies could unite, but this time he was too late. In October 1813 Napoleon's forces and the army of the new alliance met at Leipzig, in Saxony. The allies beat the French decisively, and Napoleon retreated into France. A series of brilliant military maneuvers by Napoleon did not prevent the allies from capturing Paris in March 1814.

Napoleon tried to abdicate in favor of his son, but failing to get any support, he gave up all claims to the throne for himself and his family. The allies granted him a pension and allowed him to retire to the small island of Elba off the west coast of Italy.

The victorious allies now had to make peace with France. They wanted to make sure the country could never again disrupt European affairs. They agreed that France could keep the boundaries of 1792. They also restored the Bourbon monarchy to the throne in the person of Louis XVIII, brother of the executed Louis XVI.*

The Hundred Days

During 1814 and early 1815, the restored Bourbons made many enemies among the French people. Learning of the discontent in France, Napoleon plotted his return. He escaped from Elba and landed in France on March 1, 1815.

When Louis XVIII sent troops to capture Napoleon, the emperor faced them, saying, "If there is one among you who wishes to kill his emperor, he can do so: here I am!" Resistance quickly crumbled, and Napoleon led a triumphant

---

*Royalists referred to the young son of Louis XVI and Marie Antoinette as King Louis XVII. He is believed to have died in prison in 1795.

army into Paris on March 20, beginning a period called the Hundred Days. Since a frightened Louis XVIII had scurried across the frontier to Brussels, Napoleon once again ruled France. Acting immediately to avoid war, Napoleon renounced all claims to territories that had belonged to his empire.

The emperor hoped that disputes among his opponents over the division of territory in Europe would keep them from opposing his return, but he was mistaken. Under the command of the Duke of Wellington, the combined armies of Prussia, Great Britain, and the Netherlands moved toward France. Napoleon once more assembled a French army to battle them.

On June 18, 1815, the allied and the French armies met in battle at Waterloo, near Brussels, where the allies dealt Napoleon a humiliating defeat. Napoleon abdicated again, and the Bourbons again returned "in the baggage," it was said, of the allies.

Napoleon surrendered to the British, asking at first to be allowed to go to the United States. When denied that, he asked to take refuge in England. The British refused this request also. Instead they sent the defeated emperor to live under constant guard on the lonely, dismal island of St. Helena in the South Atlantic. There Napoleon died in 1821.

As the years passed, Napoleon's legend grew. People forgot the wars and Napoleon's failures and remembered only his glories and achievements. In people's minds, Napoleon was transformed from a vain and ambitious dictator into the "Little Corporal," the "Good Emperor," and the "true patriot of the Revolution." In 1840 the British allowed the French to take his body back to Paris, where it lies to this day under the dome of the Invalides, the magnificent home for old soldiers that Louis XIV had built.

SECTION 5 REVIEW

1. **Define** plebiscite, nationalism, scorched-earth policy
2. **Identify** Horatio Nelson, Duke of Wellington, Czar Alexander I, Louis XVIII
3. **Locate** Trafalgar, Austerlitz, Leipzig, Elba, Waterloo, St. Helena
4. **Interpreting Ideas** Why were the people of France willing to accept Napoleon's dictatorship?
5. **Analyzing Ideas** (a) Why did Napoleon declare war on Russia? (b) How did his Russian campaign end?
6. **Summarizing Ideas** (a) What nations were involved in the battle of Waterloo? (b) What happened to Napoleon afterward?
7. **Synthesizing Ideas** How did the conquests of the French under Napoleon influence other European peoples?

Government of France 1774–1814

1774	Louis XVI became king
1789	Third Estate, as National Assembly, assumed power
1791	Legislative Assembly, with Louis XVI as constitutional monarch, began rule
1792	Monarchy suspended and National Convention began governing
1795	Directory took control
1799	Consulate established, with Napoleon as First Consul
1804	Napoleon crowned emperor
1814	Napoleon overthrown and Bourbon monarchy restored

6 Peace Was Restored to Europe

With the final defeat of Napoleon in 1815, Europe reached an important turning point. For more than 25 years, the most powerful political influence on the continent had been the French Revolution. Even though Napoleon did not always uphold the ideals of the Revolution—liberty, equality, and fraternity—he did carry its influence throughout Europe.

As long as Napoleon ruled France, the governments of other nations feared that France would export political unrest or rebellion and challenge their authority. Once they defeated Napoleon, the major European powers were determined to restore order, keep peace, and squelch the ideas of the Revolution. After 1815 they followed policies designed

Learning from Pictures
Two of the most influential diplomats at the Congress of Vienna were Talleyrand (seated second from right) and Metternich (standing far left).

to maintain stability and to suppress any danger of political upheaval.

The Congress of Vienna

Stability could be achieved only by settling political and territorial questions arising from the Napoleonic Wars. The Congress of Vienna, a conference held in the Austrian capital, undertook the settling of these questions. The congress began in September 1814, while Napoleon was in exile on Elba. About 700 diplomats attended at one time or another. Napoleon's return from exile interrupted the congress in 1815, but after his final defeat at Waterloo, the congress resumed its work.

Despite the presence of many notable figures, only a few people made the real decisions at the Congress of Vienna. Great Britain, Austria, Russia, and Prussia had done the most to defeat Napoleon. Their four representatives were Lord Castlereagh (KAS • uhl • ray), foreign secretary of Great Britain; Prince Klemens von Metternich, chief minister of Austria and chairman of the conference; Czar Alexander I of Russia; and King Frederick William III of Prussia. Metternich, however, was the chief architect of the policies drawn up by the congress.

Surprisingly, the representative of defeated France, Charles Maurice de Talleyrand, played an important part at the Congress of Vienna. A shrewd negotiator, Talleyrand wielded great influence as the representative of Louis XVIII.

The Principles of the Congress of Vienna

Four principles guided the decisions of the Congress of Vienna. (1) **Legitimacy,** which meant that all former ruling families should be restored to their thrones, had to be upheld. (2) The balance of power had to be restored in Europe. This meant that the nations of Europe had to keep any one nation from becoming too powerful. (3) France had to be weakened. (4) The countries that suffered most at the hands of Napoleon, especially the four great powers—Great Britain, Austria, Russia, and Prussia—had to be compensated for their losses.

Legitimacy. At Talleyrand's urging, the Congress of Vienna made settlements based on the principle of legitimacy. The Bourbon monarchy, already restored in France, also returned to power in Spain and in the Kingdom of the Two Sicilies. Monarchies were also restored in Portugal and in the Kingdom of Sardinia.

Compensation and the balance of power. The winning powers soon quarreled over the division of spoils. The two most difficult problems concerned Poland and the German state of Saxony. From Prussia's Polish territory, Napoleon had created the Grand Duchy of Warsaw, which he had given to his faithful ally, the king of Saxony. Russia now demanded this territory. Prussia agreed to this, provided that the king of Saxony be deposed and Saxony be given to Prussia.

Both Great Britain and Austria opposed this arrangement. Great Britain did not want to see Russia become too strong. Austria feared that the addition of Saxony might make Prussia too powerful in German affairs. For a time the threat of war loomed. Then Talleyrand suggested a compromise that settled the argument. Most of what had been the Grand Duchy of Warsaw went to Russia. Prussia got the rest of it, along with part of Saxony (see map, this page).

The Netherlands, one of Napoleon's early conquests, received the Austrian Netherlands and became the single Kingdom of the Netherlands. As compensation for this loss, the Austrians gained the northern Italian states of Venetia and Lombardy. Austrian Hapsburgs also became rulers of the northern Italian states of Parma, Modena, and Tuscany.

In addition to gaining the largest share of the Grand Duchy of Warsaw, Russia had acquired Finland as a result of war with Sweden. Since Sweden had fought against Napoleon, it received Norway, formerly a Danish possession. This territorial adjustment punished Denmark for cooperating with Napoleon. Prussia, in addition to its share of

Learning from Maps *France was allowed to keep its pre-Napoleonic boundaries at the Congress of Vienna. What kingdoms gained territories to the north of France?*

AZIMUTHAL EQUAL AREA PROJECTION

Saxony and Poland, received an area along the lower Rhine River.

Although Great Britain did not receive any territory in continental Europe, it did gain possessions overseas. They included several islands in the French West Indies and the Mediterranean island of Malta. From the Danish the British gained Helgoland, an island in the North Sea. From the Dutch they took Cape Colony in Africa and what became British Guiana in South America.

France held in check. All of this territorial reshuffling set up a ring of strong states around France so that it could not again threaten the peace of Europe. The diplomats, however, did not consider the feelings of the people who lived in these regions that changed hands. They parceled out territories as if these lands were uninhabited deserts.

France was stripped of its conquests, and its boundaries were returned to what they had been in 1792. In addition, it had to pay a large **indemnity**—a compensation to other nations for damages it had inflicted on them. France also had to pay for forts that the victorious nations now maintained on the French borders.

Reaction, Absolutism, and Nationalism

A time of **reaction** followed the first few years after the Napoleonic Era. This means that those in authority wanted to return to the conditions of an earlier period. **Reactionaries** are extremists who not only oppose change, but generally would like to turn the clock back to the time before certain changes occurred. After 1815 the victors in Europe attempted to restore conditions to what they had been before the French Revolution.

In Spain, the Two Sicilies, and the states of northern Italy, the reinstated rulers abolished the constitutions that had been adopted during Napoleon's rule. They returned to absolutism as if nothing had ever happened. Switzerland alone retained its constitutional government but had to promise to remain neutral in European wars. The European powers guaranteed this neutrality.

Napoleon's conquests resulted in the spread of new political ideas and the rise of nationalism, which the reactionary powers considered dangerous and tried to stamp out. National feelings began to have such wide influence that they became accepted as a basic political ideal. Writers, artists, and politicians promoted nationalism by stressing

the people's shared history, common language, or cultural achievements.

The desire for national unity caused concern among the major powers of the time, and they tried to hold it back. For a while they succeeded, and the Congress of Vienna left nationalist groups disappointed. Some Italians, for example, had hoped for a united Italy. Their hope went unfulfilled. To make matters worse, many Italian states were placed under a hated foreign rule. The major powers also blocked the desire of the Polish people for national independence. Nor was self-government granted to national groups living within the Austrian Empire.

The German desire for national unity came closer to fulfillment. Napoleon had consolidated many of the German states into the 16-member Confederation of the Rhine. Now more states, including Prussia, formed the German Confederation, which had 39 members. Austria dominated this confederation, since an Austrian delegate always presided over the confederation's assembly.

Alliances Among the Great Powers

The idea of revolution still haunted the governments of Europe. As a result, they believed that a special watch had to be kept for the lurking dangers that might upset the peace they had so painstakingly created.

The Quadruple Alliance. The four allies that had finally defeated Napoleon—Great Britain, Austria, Russia, and Prussia—agreed in 1815 to continue their alliance. This became known as the Quadruple Alliance. The chief purpose of the alliance was "to guarantee Europe from dangers by which she may still be menaced"—that is, revolutionary movements. Members of the alliance agreed to make sure that France carried out the terms of the peace treaty. They planned to hold periodic conferences to keep the major powers in agreement on matters that concerned them all.

The Holy Alliance. Czar Alexander I of Russia doubted that alliances alone could maintain peace and prevent revolutions. He firmly believed in absolute monarchy. However, he believed just as firmly that Christian moral principles and a strong sense of duty should guide monarchs. Shortly before joining the Quadruple Alliance, he urged that all rulers pledge themselves to rule as Christian princes by signing an agreement called the Holy

Alliance. All the rulers of Europe signed it except the British king; the Turkish sultan, who was not a Christian; and the pope, who refused to be instructed in Christian principles by the Orthodox czar.

Those rulers who signed the Holy Alliance did so only to humor the czar and had little intention of following its principles. Castlereagh scoffingly called it "a piece of sublime mysticism and nonsense."

The Concert of Europe. Out of the more practical Quadruple Alliance grew what was called the Concert of Europe—a form of international government by concert, or agreement. It was aimed at maintaining peace and the *status quo* (a Latin phrase meaning roughly "the condition in which things exist"). In this case the status quo meant maintaining the balance of power established by the Congress of Vienna.

The first of the periodic conferences provided for by the Quadruple Alliance met in 1818. France, having fulfilled the terms of the peace settlements, returned to the European family of nations and was admitted to the Quadruple Alliance, making it a Quintuple Alliance. The Concert of Europe lasted until 1848.

The Age of Metternich

For 30 years after the Congress of Vienna, Prince Metternich influenced Europe so strongly that the period is sometimes known as the Age of Metternich. A reactionary, Metternich believed strongly in absolute monarchy. He looked with fear and horror at constitutions and liberalism. The movement known as **liberalism** extended the principles of the American and French revolutions with their ideals of individual rights and the rule of law. Metternich believed in suppressing completely such ideas as freedom of speech, religion, and the press.

Metternich aimed to prevent war or revolution and to preserve absolutism. He had little difficulty achieving these goals in Austria. He set up an efficient secret police system to spy on revolutionary organizations and individuals. Liberals were imprisoned, fined, or exiled.

Because Austria controlled the German Confederation, Metternich persuaded the rulers of most German states to adopt the same methods. Hapsburg rulers in northern Italy made sure that no revolutionary movements would succeed there. In France, King Louis XVIII moved cautiously in domestic affairs. However, he quite willingly joined in suppressing revolutions elsewhere.

Political Liberalism

The ideas of liberals greatly influenced politics during the 1800s. These ideas could be seen in the internal political conflicts of Great Britain, France, Italy, Germany, and the United States. Liberalism

Learning from Pictures
Political liberalism in Russia culminated with the Decemberist uprising. After the death of Alexander I, troops rebelled against the new czar in December 1825. The uprising failed to establish either a democratic republic or a constitutional monarchy.

took many different forms in these countries, but certain key ideas remained identical. These included a belief in the importance of individual liberty—freedom of thought, religion, and economic opportunity. Above all, liberals hated the tyranny of absolute rule. Thus they worked to secure constitutions and other legal safeguards to limit governmental authority and protect civil liberties. Most liberals did not believe that all people should have the right to vote. Instead, most believed that voting should be limited to men with property and education.

Reaction to Metternich

Liberals reacted strongly to the decisions of the Congress of Vienna and to Metternich's actions to check liberalism. A number of uprisings occurred in Europe, and Metternich turned the Concert of Europe into an instrument of suppression. Whenever a threat to the status quo appeared, representatives of the five powers gathered to discuss ways of handling it. Austria, Russia, and Prussia went further. They agreed to act in concert to put down any attempt at revolution anywhere.

Great Britain could not agree to this last step. It opposed interfering in the attempts of liberal popular movements to overthrow absolute rulers. Great Britain itself had a representative government. The British people as a whole sympathized with other peoples in their struggles to institute similar governments. More important, Great Britain depended on trade. Meddling in the internal affairs of other countries might hurt British commerce. Under the influence of George Canning, who became foreign secretary in 1822, Great Britain withdrew from the Quintuple Alliance.

The Metternich System in Operation

For a time the Metternich system operated successfully. When discontent flared up among German university students in 1819, Metternich called together the leaders of the larger states of the German Confederation at Carlsbad in Bohemia. At his insistence they adopted measures known as the Carlsbad Decrees. The decrees placed students and faculty members of the universities under strict watch. They censored newspapers and periodicals and formed an organization to search for secret revolutionary activities. These measures prohibited political reforms that conflicted with absolute monarchy.

Because of repression, several underground movements began that opposed the status quo. In 1820 a revolt in Spain forced King Ferdinand VII to restore the constitution he had abolished. This alarmed the four continental members of the Quintuple Alliance. Despite British protests they sent a French army to Spain. In 1823 they restored Ferdinand to full power, brutally crushing the revolt and its leaders.

The Spanish revolt inspired other uprisings in 1820. In the Kingdom of the Two Sicilies, revolutionaries forced the ruler to grant a constitution. An Austrian army put down this revolt. In Portugal, too, the people forced the ruler to accept a constitution. A few years later, however, he abolished it and assumed absolute power.

In 1821 nationalism upset the international order when the Greeks revolted against the Ottoman Turks. Influenced by Metternich, European rulers refused Greek pleas for aid. However, many individuals came to the support of the Greeks, either as volunteers or by sending arms. One of these volunteers was Lord Byron, the British poet, who died of a fever in Greece in 1824.

Finally Russia, Great Britain, and France brought pressure on the Ottoman sultan. By the Treaty of Adrianople in 1829, Greece became an independent state. The Serbs and Romanians, to the north on the Balkan Peninsula, received some rights of self-government within the Ottoman Empire.

Greek independence demonstrated the first real failure of the Metternich system in Europe. It showed that the sense of nationalism encouraged by the French Revolution could not be suppressed forever.

SECTION 6 REVIEW

1. **Define** legitimacy, indemnity, reaction, reactionary, liberalism
2. **Identify** Castlereagh, Talleyrand, Metternich
3. **Locate** Saxony, Kingdom of the Netherlands, Venetia, Lombardy, Malta
4. **Synthesizing Ideas** Give an example of the principle of legitimacy as it operated at the Congress of Vienna.
5. **Organizing Ideas** (a) What was the Quadruple Alliance? (b) the Holy Alliance? (c) the Concert of Europe?

Beginning of
reign of
Louis XV

Montesquieu's
*Spirit of
the Laws*

AD

1715

1734

1748

1751

Voltaire's
*Letters on
England*

First volume
of the
Encyclopedia

Chapter Summary

The following list contains the key concepts you have learned about the French Revolution and the Napoleonic Era.

1. During the Enlightenment thinkers began to criticize the established political institutions.
2. The philosophes included Diderot, Montesquieu, Voltaire, and Rousseau.
3. Discontent in France and Louis XVI's failure to solve the government's continuing financial crisis were the direct causes of the French Revolution.
4. In 1789 Louis XVI summoned a meeting of the Estates-General in an attempt to solve the financial crisis of the monarchy. When Louis XVI insisted on following the old voting procedures, the Third Estate met separately and proclaimed itself the National Assembly.
5. The National Assembly issued the Declaration of the Rights of Man and wrote the Constitution of 1791, creating a limited constitutional monarchy. Invasion by Austrian and Prussian troops to restore absolute power to the king touched off riots that led to the end of the monarchy in 1792.
6. The National Convention proclaimed a republic and executed the king. With France threatened by new invasions, it drafted an army to defend the nation and suppressed opposition at home with the Reign of Terror.
7. The inefficient and corrupt Directory followed the National Convention.
8. In 1799 Napoleon Bonaparte took over the government in a coup d'état. Napoleon ruled France as a military dictator and extended French control over much of Europe.
9. Napoleon became emperor and ruled Europe. French troops of the empire carried the ideals of the Revolution to other European nations. In response to French invasion, feelings of nationalism were ignited throughout Europe.
10. After several military defeats, Napoleon abdicated and went into exile on Elba in 1814. Napoleon soon escaped, only to be defeated again at Waterloo.
11. The Congress of Vienna and later alliances attempted to restore the status quo in Europe.

12. Despite the efforts of the reactionaries, the ideals of liberalism and nationalism could not be suppressed. In the 1820s several rebellions against reactionary policies broke out.

On a separate sheet of paper, complete the following review exercises.

Reviewing Important Terms

Match each of the following terms with the correct definition below.

a. Enlightenment
b. scorched-earth policy
c. moderate
d. popular sovereignty
e. department
f. conscription
g. coup d'état
h. conservative
i. bourgeoisie
j. enlightened despotism
k. reactionary
l. liberalism
m. émigré

___ 1. Movement stressing the use of reason to logically explain human nature
___ 2. City-dwelling middle class in France
___ 3. One of 83 administrative districts in France
___ 4. Person who does not want to change existing conditions
___ 5. Person with no extreme views
___ 6. Government policy requiring people to serve in the army
___ 7. Burning or destroying crops and everything else that might be of value to the enemy
___ 8. Seizure of power by force
___ 9. Government by free choice of the people
___ 10. System of government in which absolute monarchs ruled according to the principles of the Enlightenment
___ 11. A person who not only opposes change but generally would like to go back to the time before changes occurred
___ 12. Movement that extended the principles of the American and French revolutions with their ideals of individual rights and the rule of law
___ 13. French for "emigrant," person who fled France during the Revolution and plotted continuously to overturn the Revolution and set the clock back

Timeline:
- 1762 — Rousseau's *Social Contract*
- 1774 — Death of Louis XV
- 1789 — Beginning of French Revolution
- 1792 — National Convention Met
- 1793 — Execution of Louis XVI
- 1795–1799 — Rule of the Directory
- 1799 — Napoleon's coup d'état
- 1804 — Napoleon crowned emperor
- 1812 — Napoleon invaded Russia
- 1814–1815 — Congress of Vienna
- 1815 — Napoleon's defeat at Waterloo
- 1821 — Beginning of Greek revolt

Developing Critical Thinking Skills

1. **Understanding Ideas** (a) What were the major ideas of the Enlightenment? (b) How did Diderot help spread these ideas?
2. **Analyzing Ideas** (a) What did Louis XV mean when he said: "After me, the deluge"? (b) What do you think this statement shows about his attitude toward France?
3. **Understanding Chronology** In each of the following groups, place the items in the correct chronological order: (a) capture of the Bastille, calling of the Estates-General, Tennis Court Oath; (b) Constitution of 1791, Declaration of the Rights of Man, Reign of Terror; (c) flight to Varennes, Napoleon crowned emperor, Louis XVI becomes king; (d) First Coalition formed, Continental System, Napoleon invades Russia; (e) battle of Waterloo, Hundred Days, Peninsular Campaign; (f) Congress of Vienna, Greek independence, signing of Holy Alliance
4. **Summarizing Ideas** How was the French government organized under each of the following: (a) the Legislative Assembly; (b) the National Convention; (c) the Directory; (d) the Consulate.
5. **Synthesizing Ideas** (a) What were the lasting effects of the French Revolution? (b) In what ways did Napoleon both fulfill and destroy its ideals? (c) Did the Congress of Vienna fail to restore absolutism?

Relating Geography to History

Compare the map of Napoleonic Europe on page 442 with the map of Europe after the Congress of Vienna on page 446. Then write a paragraph describing the resulting boundary changes.

Relating Past to Present

1. The French Revolution completely altered the political structure of Europe. (a) What effects are revolutions having on life in today's world? (b) Where are revolutions currently taking place?
2. Spain used guerrilla warfare against Napoleon's forces. (a) How is guerrilla fighting conducted? (b) Describe how guerrilla fighting was used in a modern war.

(c) Why is this type of warfare often effective against modern armies?

Applying History Study Skills

Before completing this activity, review Building History Study Skills on page 432.

Edmund Burke was a British gentleman and a member of Parliament during the French Revolution. He published his *Reflections on the Revolution in France* in 1790. Read the excerpt below and explain how his perspective influences the way in which he views the events of the French Revolution.

> The fresh ruins of France, which shock our feelings wherever we turn our eyes, are not the devastation of civil war; they are the sad but instructive monuments of rash and ignorant counsel in time of profound peace. . . . Whilst they are possessed of these notions, it is vain to talk to them of the practice of their ancestors, the fundamental laws of their country, the fixed form of a constitution, whose merits are confirmed by the solid test of long experience. . . . They have the 'rights of men.' . . . But to form a free government; that is, to temper together these opposite elements of liberty and restraint in one consistent work, requires much thought, deep reflection, . . . a powerful and combining mind. This I do not find in those who take the lead in the National Assembly.

Investigating Further

1. **Determining Cause and Effect** Read *A Tale of Two Cities* by Charles Dickens. Describe how the French Revolution affected the lives of the main characters.
2. **Applying Ideas** The ideas of Montesquieu and Rousseau influenced political and social thought in the 1700s. Describe how their ideas were reflected in the Declaration of the Rights of Man and the constitutional monarchy set up by the National Assembly in 1791. A suggested resource for your research is J. Bronowski's and B. Mazlish's *Western Intellectual Tradition: From Leonardo to Hegel* (Harper & Row).

451

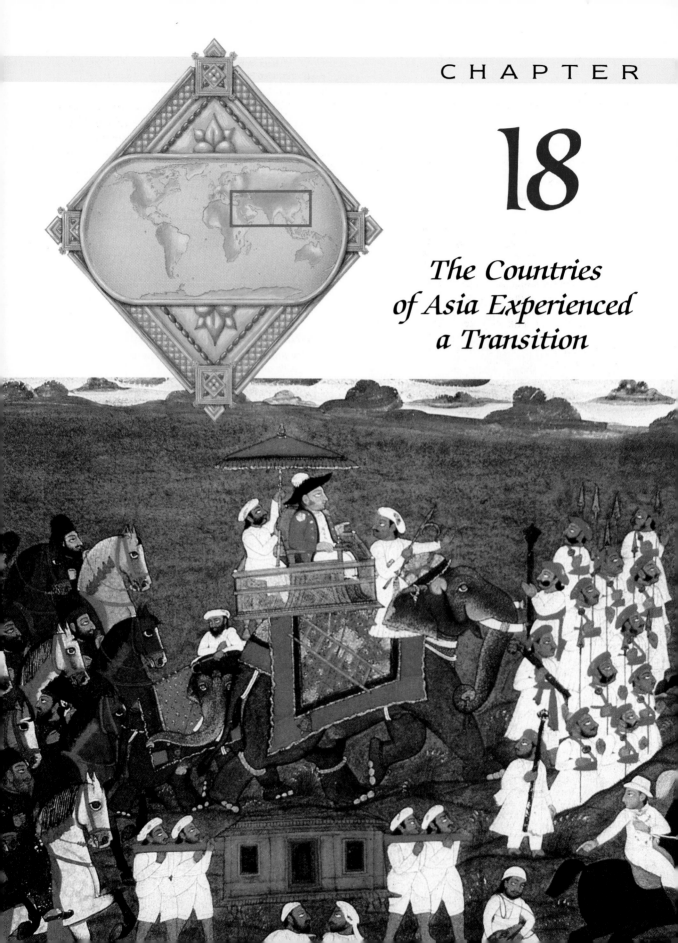

18

The Countries of Asia Experienced a Transition

Place China, Japan, the Middle East, and India

Time 1368—1868

3.7 mil. BC 4000 BC AD 2100

Significance

Between 1400 and the mid-1800s, many of the dominant countries in Asia reached a political and cultural peak and then began to decline. In China and Japan, following centuries of remarkable political and technological achievement, rulers attempted to keep their countries stable by opposing change and contact with the outside world. This stability, however, had a price. These civilizations stagnated. Although in 1500 China and Japan had civilizations at least as advanced as those in Europe, after 1500 these civilizations gradually fell behind.

The Ottoman, Persian, and Mogul empires reached the zenith of their political and cultural power in the 1500s and 1600s. However, decline also overtook these three empires.

As a result all these once splendid civilizations proved weak and ineffective when challenge came from the outside world. In some cases these empires were vulnerable not only to outside influence but also to colonization.

Terms to Define

junk

queue

philology

free trade

consulate

sepoy

People to Identify

Kangxi

Tokugawa Ieyasu

Matthew Perry

John Sobieski

Mahmud II

Nader Shah

Robert Clive

Lord Cornwallis

Places to Locate

Manchuria

Shanghai

Hong Kong

Nagasaki

Tehran

Delhi

Questions to Guide Your Reading

1 How did the Ming and Qing dynasties deal with the Europeans, and how did the Europeans finally gain a foothold in China?

2 By what means did the Tokugawa shoguns create a centralized, powerful government, and how were they able to keep Japan isolated?

3 How did Europeans gain control of trade in Asian nations and control of government in India?

◀ *A British parade in India*

One of the greatest contributions of the Japanese to the literary world is a form of poetry called haiku, which when translated means "comic," or "lighthearted." Known as the poetry of the common people, haiku consists of very short verses—17 syllables at most—that subtly convey ideas and achieve a desired effect. The following are some of these charming verses by the Japanese poet Matsuo Basho, who wrote in the 1600s.

> *"There goes my best hat*
> *as down comes rain on my bald*
> *pate, plop! plop! Oh well. . ."*

> *"Low clouds are shattered*
> *into small distant fragments*
> *of moonlit mountains."*

> *"Swallows, spare those bees*
> *humming westward at evening*
> *laden with honey."*

> *"Scattered on the sand*
> *like jewels, seashells tangled*
> *in kelp and rubbish. . ."*

> *"The best I have to*
> *offer you is the small size*
> *of the mosquitoes."*

> *"On a journey, ill,*
> *and over fields all withered, dreams*
> *go wandering still."*

From ancient times Asian civilizations had fascinated Europeans. However, Asian rulers did not always consider contact with Europeans desirable.

1 China Changed Gradually Under the Ming and Qing Dynasties

In 1368 Zhu Yuanzhang (JOO YOO•EN•JAHNG), a former Buddhist monk, overthrew the Yuan dynasty of the Mongols in China. At that time he established the Ming, or "brilliant," dynasty, which remained in power until 1644, when the Qing (CHING), or "untarnished," dynasty replaced it. Very little rebellion or warfare occurred in China during these two dynasties. This lengthy period of peace greatly contributed to China's stability and allowed it to maintain its culture.

Ming Policy Toward the Outside World

During the early Ming period, the Chinese were probably the most skillful sailors in the world. They built large, solid ships known as **junks,** some of which were over 400 feet (125 meters) long. Since the early 1100s, the Chinese had used the compass, which they probably invented, in navigation. They also drew detailed charts of Asian sea routes. In 1407 the emperor financed a Chinese fleet that sailed all the way around Southeast Asia to India. Another Chinese fleet crossed the Indian Ocean and reached Aden, at the southern tip of the Red Sea, in 1415.

These and other voyages occurred almost 100 years before Vasco da Gama sailed from Portugal to India by going around the tip of Africa. The Chinese clearly had the ability to become a great seafaring power, as both Portugal and England later did. However, the naval expeditions of the early Ming

Learning from Maps   After the beginnings of the Age of Exploration in the 1400s, many European traders visited Guangzhou (Canton). What is the name of the capital of the Ming Empire? Is it a seaport?

THE MING EMPIRE, 1424

⊛ Capital city

GOBI (DESERT)

MANCHURIA

Huang He

Great Wall

Beijing

KOREA

Yellow Sea

Wei He

(Yellow R.)

Grand Canal

Yalu R.

CHINA

Chang Jiang

Nanjing

Hangzhou

East China Sea

Chongqing

Guangzhou (Canton)

Xi Jiang

Taiwan

South China Sea

VIETNAM

Mekong R.

0   200   400 Miles

0   200   400 Kilometers

MODIFIED OBLIQUE CONIC CONFORMAL PROJECTION

period ended suddenly in the mid-1400s. The later Ming emperors—unlike Henry the Navigator in Portugal or Queen Elizabeth in England—had little interest in seapower or in overseas trade. They stopped financing naval expeditions and for a time outlawed overseas trade. Confucian attitudes toward trade and concern over protecting the land frontier between China and central Asia prompted this behavior.

Confucian Attitudes Toward Trade

After defeating the Mongol conquerors in 1368, the Ming emperors tried to rid China of all Mongol influences. They looked to the great ages of China's past for inspiration and tried to re-create the grandeur of the Han, Tang, and Sung dynasties. As part of that effort, the Ming emperors restored Confucianism—to which the Mongols had paid only lip service—as the official philosophy of the government.

Confucian philosophy divided society into four classes. First in order of importance were the scholar-officials, who governed the country for the emperor. Next came the peasants, who produced food and paid the taxes that supported the empire. Artisans, who made useful objects, came third. At the bottom of the social order were the merchants. The Chinese regarded them as "parasites" who made profits from selling things that the peasants and artisans had produced. The Chinese, then, regarded trade as a necessary evil, not as something desirable.

As followers of Confucius, the Ming emperors tried to keep trade with other countries to a minimum. Unlike European monarchs influenced by mercantilism, the emperors of China did not believe that foreign trade benefited the country. Instead, they received tribute from governments in Korea, Japan, and Tibet. In return the emperors gave the rulers of these nations lavish gifts. However, the emperors did not intend for these exchanges to increase China's wealth. Instead, they designed the tribute system to enhance China's prestige and security.

The Northern Frontier

After their victory over the Mongols, the Ming emperors wanted to make sure that no central Asian people ever again would conquer China. They therefore concentrated their efforts on securing the long northern land frontier rather than on venturing into overseas trade.

To protect that frontier, they strengthened the Great Wall and built new observation towers. They encouraged Chinese soldiers to move with their families into the frontier zone, offering the soldiers free land there in exchange for defending the strategic mountain passes.

In 1421 the Ming moved the imperial capital from Nanjing, in central China, to Beijing, in the north (see map, page 454). From there, only 40 miles (64 kilometers) south of the Great Wall, the emperors tried to prevent the nomadic tribes of the north from uniting into a powerful fighting force. Individual tribes that submitted to the Ming sent yearly tribute missions to Beijing and exchanged gifts. In return for their loyalty, the Ming emperors gave the chiefs of the nomadic tribes titles, money, and honors.

Defending the frontier required constant attention and cost a great deal of money. In addition, the emperors had to entertain and present lavish gifts to the hundreds of nomads who came to Beijing on the yearly tribute missions. The Ming emperors did not have the financial resources to encourage overseas expeditions as well. Therefore, primarily to save money for frontier defense, the Ming emperors ended the overseas expeditions of the early 1400s.

The Founding of the Qing Dynasty

Throughout most of the Ming period, the northern frontier remained secure. Occasionally, small bands of nomads seeking greater riches than they could obtain through the tribute system surged across the frontier, but the Chinese always succeeded in driving them away.

In the early 1600s, however, a new and very serious threat emerged in Manchuria, to the northeast of China. There a chieftain named Nurhachi (NOOHR • HAHCH • EE) unified the many tribes into a single people—the Manchus. After conquering Korea and Inner Mongolia in the 1630s, the Manchus captured Beijing in 1644 with the help of a Chinese general. The Manchus then established the Qing dynasty, which survived until 1911. Once again, despite all the efforts of the Ming, "barbarians" had conquered China and had established their own dynasty.

Even though the Qing dynasty was non-Chinese, it actually became one of the most "Chinese" in outlook. The Qing emperors adopted Chinese culture and used traditional Chinese techniques of government in their rule.

The adoption of the Chinese tradition was exemplified by the Emperor Kangxi (KAHNG • SHEE), who ruled from 1661 to 1722. Kangxi knew the Chinese classics well and sponsored many important literary projects. He presided over the examination system and appointed successful candidates to civil service positions. He supervised efforts to control flooding on China's major rivers and to establish storehouses throughout the land to hold grain for use in case of famine. The emperor urged both officials and the common people to behave virtuously. In short, Kangxi ruled in accordance with the teachings of Confucius, just as the Ming emperors had done.

At the same time, Kangxi and the other Qing emperors tried to preserve distinctions between the Manchus—who were a minority in the empire—and the Chinese people. All Manchus had to study the Manchu language and Manchu cultural traditions. The Qing forbade the Chinese people to marry Manchus or to settle in northern Manchuria. The dynasty maintained this region as a tribal homeland for the Manchus. Finally, the Qing required all Chinese men to wear their hair in a single braid, called a **queue** (KYOO). The queue distinguished the Chinese from the Manchus and signified Chinese submission to Manchu rule.

The Ming and Qing Economies

The Qing emperors, like those of the Ming dynasty, believed that agriculture was the basis of China's wealth. They maintained traditional political institutions, and they supported traditional Chinese ideas and values. Neither the Ming nor the Qing emperors showed any interest in change. Nevertheless, change occurred. For example, new patterns of commerce and trade began to appear.

The trend toward the growth of cities begun during the Song dynasty continued under the rule of the Ming and Qing emperors. Urban growth contributed to the expansion of trade within China. In theory the Chinese looked down on the merchants. In practice they needed them to supply the urban population with food, textiles for clothing, and other essential goods.

THE QING EMPIRE, 1760

ROBINSON PROJECTION

Learning from Maps   *The Qing dynasty's northern border extended beyond the Great Wall to the Amur River. In what region of China is the Amur River located?*

Certain regions of the country began specializing in the production of certain goods. For example, Guangzhou (GWAHNG•JOH), in the south, became a center for the manufacture of woks—the shallow iron cooking pans that the Chinese still use for cooking today. And the region near Shanghai in central China became a center for the weaving of cotton cloth.

Traders transported goods from these manufacturing centers by barges and junks along the rivers, canals, and coastal waters to Beijing, the new and rapidly growing capital city, and to other large urban centers such as Guangzhou and Shanghai.

An Italian missionary, Father Matteo Ricci, who traveled through China in 1583, gives a fascinating description of the Grand Canal and the hazards of traveling on it.

❝ So great is the number of boats that frequently many days are lost in transit by crowding each other, particularly when water is low in the canals. To prevent this, the water is held back at stated places by wooden locks, which also serve as bridges. . . . At times it happens that the rush of water is

so high and strong, at the exit from one lock or at the entrance to another, that the boats are capsized and the whole crew is drowned. The boats of the Magistrates and of other government dignitaries are drawn up the stream, against the current, by wooden devices on the shore, and the expense for such hauling is paid by the Government. . . . ❞

The Chinese shipped goods such as tea and silk by caravan to central Asia and as far away as Russia. In addition, Chinese ships continued to sail to Southeast Asia and India to trade, despite the government's disapproval of such voyages.

Despite the growth of cities, the vast majority of China's people continued to live in the countryside, where they increased the amount of land under cultivation. New crops such as sweet potatoes, peanuts, and tobacco were introduced from the Americas. The sweet potato became known as "the poor man's food" in south China because it thrived in soils unsuited to the growing of rice. It also provided more basic nutritional value than most other crops.

The Growth of Popular Culture

As in Europe the growth of cities and the increasing wealth of urban merchants and artisans in China encouraged the rise of popular culture. As early as the Yuan dynasty in the 1300s, city people read novels and watched plays written in the common, everyday language rather than in the literary language. During the Ming and Qing periods, these popular novels and plays increased in number. Old tales about bandits, corrupt officials, and beautiful women, which had once been recited by storytellers in the streets, now appeared in inexpensive books written by professional authors. The writings of this period realistically portrayed Chinese society and family life.

Scholarship also flourished under the rule of the Ming and Qing emperors. During the Ming dynasty, Chinese scholars wrote both long and detailed histories of earlier dynasties as well as essays on Confucian ethics. During the Qing dynasty, scholars studied the history of words, or **philology.** As the humanists had done in Europe during the Renaissance, Chinese scholars applied intensive study to ancient writings to determine their exact meaning.

A few scholars, mostly Daoists, compiled encyclopedias of plants and animals. In 1579 a scholar completed a huge book describing almost 2,000 animal, vegetable, and mineral drugs used in Chinese medicine. The book included information, for example, on how to inoculate people against smallpox. In contrast to Europe, however, pure science and the scientific method did not take hold in China.

City life contributed to the development of popular culture and scholarship, but it also contributed to a decline in the status of Chinese women. In rural China everyone, including women, had to work on the land so that families could survive. In the cities, however, women did not have such an important economic role. Officials and wealthy merchants grew very accustomed

Learning from Pictures
These Chinese silk weavers are working on a manual loom during the Qing dynasty. To what social class did textile workers belong?

457

Learning from Pictures *This picture scroll shows a street scene during the Ming dynasty. What Ming practice did the Qing rulers try to ban?*

to thinking of women as useless playthings. The practice of foot-binding illustrated this changing attitude toward women.

When a girl reached the age of five, her parents bound her feet tightly with strips of cloth, forcing each foot to bend into an upside-down U-shape. Gradually, over the course of several years, the arch of each foot would break. This created what the Chinese called a "golden lotus," a tiny foot half the normal size and curved under instead of straight. Foot-binding was extremely painful and made it very difficult for women to walk. It indicated that a woman's father or husband was rich enough that the woman did not need to work to help support the family. For this reason few peasant women had bound feet. This practice, which began among the upper classes in the Song period, spread throughout Chinese society and reached a peak under the Ming dynasty. The Qing rulers did not approve of foot-binding and tried unsuccessfully to ban it. The Chinese did not entirely give up the practice until the mid-1900s.

The Decline of the Qing Dynasty

By about 1800 the Qing dynasty had entered the stage of decline in the pattern of dynastic cycles.

After more than a century of peace, the soldiers of the Manchu army had lost much of their skill as warriors. They had grown used to peacetime life. Despite government policies to keep them separate from the Chinese people, the soldiers had developed closer ties to the Chinese and had become more and more like them in their behavior and values. Sensing that the Manchu army was weak, central Asian tribes began to threaten China's northern frontier.

Under the rule of the Qing, government services for the people also collapsed. China's population had doubled—from approximately 150 million in the late Ming period to 300 million by 1800. Peace and increases in agricultural output contributed significantly to this population growth. Chinese peasants raised more crops, making it possible to feed more people. However, increases in population were not matched by increases in either the number or the efficiency of government officials. During the late Ming period, the government had about 20,000 officials, or one for every 7,500 people. In 1800 the Qing government still consisted of only 20,000 officials—now only one for every 15,000 people.

As in the past, local officials relied on powerful local rural families, the gentry, to make the political system work. These local officials collected taxes from the peasants, sending the revenue to the government. They also supported local schools and supervised road repairs and other public works projects. In return the emperor permitted them to keep a small portion of the taxes they collected.

In normal times this system functioned very smoothly. A small number of government officials could administer the affairs of a large country. However, during the late Qing period, corruption among government officials caused serious problems. High-ranking bureaucrats began to use their positions in the emperor's service to acquire great personal fortunes. They pressured local officials throughout China to give them money and expensive gifts.

Those local officials, forced to pay bribes or lose their jobs, pressured the gentry for more tax revenues. The gentry in turn demanded more taxes from the peasants. Less and less of the money collected went to provide necessary services such as flood control and road repairs. Instead, the money ended up in the hands of high-ranking government officials.

Discontent and Rebellion

In 1796 discontent over increased taxes and decreased services erupted into a great peasant rebellion. Members of the White Lotus Society, a secret society that had risen up against the Mongols centuries earlier, led this revolt, called the White Lotus Rebellion. The government finally succeeded in restoring peace in 1804 after a long and expensive struggle. The emperor then tried to eliminate official corruption, but he lacked the financial resources to increase the number of officials and to create reforms in government at the local level. Thus the basic cause of discontent remained, and uprisings and rebellions occurred frequently.

The Qing dynasty seemed to be following in the footsteps of all previous Chinese dynasties. It had gained the Mandate of Heaven in battle and had achieved great heights. Now, however, a discontented people challenged the dynasty. If the pattern of past Chinese history had repeated itself, eventually a powerful rival to the Qing emperor would have emerged, defeated the Qing army in battle, and claimed the Mandate of Heaven for himself. The new emperor would then have established a new and more vigorous dynasty.

Chinese history did not follow that traditional pattern, however. Just as the Qing dynasty started its decline, new peoples appeared in China—Europeans.

The Portuguese in China

The first Portuguese ships reached the southeastern coast of China about 1514. After many years of negotiation, the Chinese allowed the Portuguese to establish a trading station at Macao (muh • KOW) in 1557. Portugal's impact, however, was not limited to trade.

The Jesuit missionaries who arrived on Portuguese ships enjoyed considerable success in China. They used their knowledge of advanced Western astronomy to gain admission to the emperor's circle. By helping to revise the Chinese calendar, they proved themselves useful to the emperor, whose duties still included predicting eclipses and the timing of the seasons. The emperor appointed the Jesuit missionaries to official positions in his palace, which gave them the opportunity to convert numerous high-ranking Chinese officials to Christianity.

In the 1700s, however, the Qing emperors turned against the Jesuits, claiming they had become too involved in politics. The emperors denounced Christianity as a subversive anti-Confucian sect. The number of converts to Christianity dwindled following this denouncement.

By this time troubles at home and competition from the Dutch had weakened Portugal's position in Asia. Portugal and the Roman Catholic church had to retreat from China. Thus Christianity never became an important religion in China.

Learning from Pictures
In the 1500s the Chinese allowed Europeans to establish trading stations. The opening of these stations boosted Chinese commerce.

The British in China

In the early 1700s, British ships began arriving frequently at Guangzhou, where the British had established a trading post in 1699. The British came to China to buy tea, which the Dutch had introduced to Europe in the 1600s. Great Britain was rapidly becoming "a nation of tea drinkers," and the British regarded Chinese teas as the best in the world.

The British East India Company monopolized the new trade in Chinese teas. The company agreed to accept Chinese restrictions on its activities in order to get adequate supplies of tea. The Chinese allowed company ships to dock only at Guangzhou and to trade only with a small number of officially licensed Chinese merchants. These merchants in turn paid large fees to the Chinese government. The government allowed only a few representatives of the British East India Company to stay in Guangzhou, where they lived in a special "foreign settlement" outside the city walls. They could not bring their families with them, and they had to abide by Chinese laws.

For a time the Chinese government succeeded in controlling the British with trading and housing restrictions. They kept contact between the British and the Chinese to a minimum. In the late 1700s, however, two new developments led to a deterioration in British-Chinese relations and eventually led to war between these two countries.

Free trade ideas. The first development that led to the crisis between China and Great Britain was the spread of **free trade** ideas from the West. Free trade, which developed as a reaction to mercantilism, illustrated the belief that government should not restrict or interfere in international trade. Not all British traders worked for the British East India Company. Those who tried to operate independently in Asia resented the monopolies enjoyed by the British company. Resentment also grew among American traders, who began sailing from New England to China in the 1780s.

The British government also expressed increasing concern about securing additional overseas markets for the products of British industry. It sent official missions to Beijing in 1793 and again in 1816 to request that the Chinese open several more ports to British ships. Both ended in dismal failure.

In 1834 the British government went a step further in initiating a free trade policy. It decided that the British East India Company had not been

Learning from Pictures *One of the Chinese products highly prized by Europeans for European markets was porcelain, like this finely crafted decorative plate.* †

aggressive enough in encouraging British exports. It therefore abolished the company's monopoly on trade with China. The British government sent an official to Guangzhou for trade talks, but the Chinese rebuffed this official's efforts.

The opium trade. The other development that resulted in war between China and Great Britain involved the steady expansion of the tea trade. The British East India Company had paid for its purchases of Chinese tea with cotton from India. Eventually, Chinese demand for this cotton, used to supply the many weavers in central China, reached its limit. The British demand for tea, however, continued to increase. The company had to find some new product to exchange for tea. The product they chose was opium, a habit-forming narcotic.

British India produced opium and exported it to China in increasing quantities from the late 1700s onward. Opium addiction spread among the Chinese people, and the Chinese government grew alarmed. It also expressed concern that so much of China's silver supply helped to pay for the growing volume of opium imports. Chinese authorities demanded that opium sales be stopped and that all opium cargoes be turned over to them.

†The Metropolitan Museum of Art, Purchase, The Lucille and Robert H. Gries Charity Fund, 1970.

Learning from Pictures
The British were victorious in this battle near Guangzhou. Why was the British navy so successful against the Chinese?

The Opium War in China. When the Chinese tried to suppress the opium traffic in South China and insisted on maintaining the traditional tribute system, a war broke out between China and Great Britain. This conflict—known as the Opium War or the First Anglo-Chinese War—lasted from 1839 to 1842.

During the Opium War, the Chinese army and naval forces proved no match against the better-armed and better-trained British. A small British naval force, which included iron-hulled steamships, moved up the coast from Guangzhou, defeating Chinese resistance with relative ease. In 1842 the British secured control of an important region near Nanjing (nahn•JING). At that point the Qing officials agreed to negotiate on British terms.

The treaty of 1842, which ended the Opium War, compelled China to give the island of Hong Kong to the British and to open the cities of Xiamen (Amoy) and Shanghai to foreign trade. These ports, together with Guangzhou, became the first Chinese treaty ports. No tariff of more than 5 percent could be charged on British goods entering these ports. A further provision stated that British subjects in these ports would be governed by British, not Chinese, laws and would be tried in British courts. This exemption of foreigners from the laws of the nation in which they live or do business is called **extraterritoriality.**

Great Britain could not hold its privileged trade monopoly in China for long. France and other Western powers, including the United States, soon demanded and received similar trade treaties with provisions for extraterritoriality. China did not negotiate these trade treaties but was forced to sign them. The Chinese called them "unequal treaties."

The Taiping Rebellion

An event that occurred in China itself made the intrusion of the Western powers easier. In the mid-1800s southern and central China were torn by a rebellion that threatened to overthrow the Qing. The leader of this revolt was a southern Chinese influenced by Christian teachings. He claimed to be the younger brother of Jesus, charged with the mission of establishing a new dynasty—the Taiping (ty•PING), or "Great Peace." His ideas attracted many followers among the Chinese.

When the government tried to suppress the Taiping movement, it turned into a political rebellion. The Taiping Rebellion lasted from 1850 to 1864 and caused great destruction in southern China and the Chang Jiang valley. The rebels were never able to establish the Mandate of Heaven. With the aid of some regional armies and foreign adventurers, the Qing finally suppressed the rebels.

READ
WRITE
INTERPRET
CONNECT
●THINK

BUILDING HISTORY STUDY SKILLS

Thinking About History: Analyzing Consequences

Every human action and decision produces a consequence or result. For example, if you stayed up until about 2:00 A.M. last night and had to get up at 6:00 A.M. this morning, the consequence would probably be that you are exhausted today. Or if you decided to study very hard for a test, the consequence would probably be that you received a good grade on the test. Since history deals with human actions, analyzing the consequences of these actions will help you gain new insights into historical events. Knowing the consequences helps you analyze the impact of change. Consequences can be immediate or long-range, positive or negative.

How to Analyze Consequences

To analyze consequences, follow these steps.

1. Identify the purpose or goal of the action or decision that you are studying. Ask: What did the person or persons hope to achieve?
2. State the positive and/or negative consequences of the decision or action.
3. Identify the immediate and the long-range consequences of the action or decision.
4. Form a conclusion by asking whether the action or decision helped to achieve the purpose or goal.

Developing the Skill

The statement below by H. G. Creel describes the civil service examinations in China. As you read the statement, consider what consequences the examinations had for the government of China.

> ❝ The civil service examination system . . . was competitive, objective, and open to practically everyone of ability. It broke down class distinctions, feudalism, and artificial barriers of race, tribe, religion and color. . . . It brought many of the ablest men of the country into government service. In so far as it was effective, it assured that officials were men of culture, not mere wasters who had inherited their position. ❞

The purpose of your study is to analyze the consequences that the civil service system had on Chinese government and society. Creel mentions the positive outcomes of the system. The examinations contributed to social mobility in that anyone could take them; the examinations had a performance requirement rather than a class requirement. People from different classes could be chosen for positions by scoring well. Therefore, the system provided for intelligent leadership by the ablest people. Other positive consequences included a common philosophy of rule, a commitment to ethical and moral beliefs as the foundation of leadership, and the stability of the system. The Chinese emperor might have changed, but the bureaucratic system remained intact, orderly, and continuous.

In the short term, the system promoted education. Long-term consequences of the system included stability and order.

What were the overall consequences of the civil service system on Chinese government and society? The civil service system promoted unity and the learning of new ideas.

Practicing the skill. In your local newspaper, read an article dealing with a government decision or policy. Then analyze the consequences that this decision or policy might have.

To apply this skill, see Applying History Study Skills on page 477.

Chinese scholars with scrolls

The Taiping Rebellion, however, weakened both the Qing dynasty and the country. To raise money, the government established a system of internal tariffs. These tariffs hurt trade without providing much help to the central treasury because tariff collectors stole most of the money. Then foreigners took over the collection of customs duties in Chinese ports, further weakening China's control over its revenues.

During the Taiping Rebellion, the Qing could not protect foreign citizens as Western governments had demanded. In 1856, war with Great Britain again broke out, and British forces, with French aid, again defeated the Chinese.

This forced the Chinese to sign another "unequal treaty," which opened additional treaty ports on the coast and along the Chang Jiang. The Chinese had to allow the British to open an embassy in Beijing, the Qing capital. Other foreign powers soon followed Great Britain's example by opening their own embassies in Beijing. In addition, Great Britain took possession of a small section of the Chinese mainland opposite Hong Kong. And the Chinese government pledged to protect Christian missionaries and their converts.

In separate treaties, Russia gained even more than trade privileges and extraterritoriality. It received territory north of the Amur River and east of the Ussuri River, bordering on the Sea of Japan. In the southern part of this newly gained territory, the Russians founded the port of Vladivostok.

SECTION 1 REVIEW

1. **Define** junk, queue, philology, free trade, extraterritoriality
2. **Identify** Nurhachi, Kangxi
3. **Locate** Beijing, Manchuria, Guangzhou, Shanghai, Macao, Hong Kong
4. **Interpreting Ideas** Why did foreign trade and overseas explorations experience a decline during the Ming dynasty?
5. **Summarizing Ideas** (a) What were the four classes of society, according to Confucianism? (b) How did the Ming emperors reinforce this philosophy?
6. **Evaluating Ideas** Why did the Qing dynasty decline?
7. **Understanding Ideas** (a) Why were the Jesuits successful at first in converting people in China to Christianity? (b) Why did they later lose favor with the Chinese emperor?
8. **Understanding Cause and Effect** (a) What were the causes of the Taiping Rebellion? (b) What was the result of this rebellion in China?

2 Japan Prospered Under the Rule of the Tokugawa Shoguns

China's culture influenced that of early Japan. However, until the late 1500s, feudal Japan followed a course of political development more like that of Europe than of China.

In the late 1400s, the Japanese daimyos began fighting among themselves for survival and supremacy. The struggle among the daimyos resulted in the creation of a political system that was a cross between feudalism and centralized monarchy. The Japanese established this hybrid system, known as the Tokugawa (TOH • KOOG • AH • WAH) shogunate, in 1603. It survived until 1868.

Founding of the Tokugawa Shogunate

In 1467 rival branches of the Ashikaga (AH • SHEE • KAH • GAH) family in Japan became involved in a dispute over the naming of the next shogun. This conflict marked the beginning of 100 years of almost constant warfare in Japan. Local daimyos, sensing the weakness of the Ashikaga, fought for control of the country. Three daimyos in turn emerged in the late 1500s as victors in this long struggle. They succeeded in establishing themselves as overlords to the other daimyos but not as absolute rulers of all Japan.

Oda Nobunaga. The first of these overlords, Oda Nobunaga (NOH • BOO • NAH • GAH), began his career as a minor daimyo. He succeeded, by means of conquest and alliances, in capturing the city of Kyoto in 1568. Nobunaga ended the Ashikaga shogunate in 1573 and then started to consolidate his power in central Japan. Before he could defeat his remaining rivals, however, one of his own vassals killed him.

Toyotomi Hideyoshi. Another vassal, Toyotomi Hideyoshi (TOH • YOH • TOH • MEE HEE • DAY • OH • SHEE), assumed Nobunaga's position as overlord. Born in 1537 to a humble peasant family, Hideyoshi had risen to a high position in Nobunaga's army, from warrior to general. In the 1580s Hideyoshi defeated several powerful daimyos in battle, and by threats and diplomacy, he forced the others to pledge their loyalty to him.

Hideyoshi thus did not destroy the powers of the defeated daimyos but weakened them by reduc-

Learning from Pictures *Japanese warriors regularly exercised and meditated to keep fit for battle. What country did Japan invade in 1592?*

ing the size of their territories so they could not threaten him again. He also carried out a "sword hunt" to disarm the peasants. Thereafter, peasants could no longer rise to become warriors. Only men born into warrior families could become warriors.

In 1592 the ambitious Hideyoshi sent an army to invade Korea. Hideyoshi took this action for two reasons. He wanted to build an extensive empire, and he also wanted to keep Japanese warriors busy with battles overseas while he increased his power at home. At first the Japanese invasion force succeeded. As the battles continued, however, the Korean navy began sinking Japanese ships carrying troop reinforcements, and a Chinese army aiding the Koreans pushed the invaders back to the coast. When Hideyoshi died in 1598, the Japanese withdrew to their homeland.

Tokugawa Ieyasu. Hideyoshi's most powerful vassal, Tokugawa Ieyasu (EE • AY • YAH • SOO), succeeded him as overlord. Ieyasu established his capital at Yedo (Tokyo). Other daimyos resisted Ieyasu, but he defeated them in 1600. Then in 1603 he forced the emperor to name him shogun. The Tokugawa family retained the title of shogun for the next 250 years—a period known as the Tokugawa shogunate.

Like Toyotomi Hideyoshi, Tokugawa Ieyasu did not destroy his defeated rivals. Instead Hideyoshi made them swear oaths of loyalty to him and his family. He allowed the daimyos, who then numbered about 250, to retain possession of their private domains. However, he reserved for himself the right to expand or reduce the size of their territories in the future.

Within his own domain, each daimyo governed almost as an absolute ruler. The local peasants paid taxes that the daimyo used to support both himself and those in his service, particularly the samurai. The Tokugawa family had its own very large domain, which included about one-fourth of the land area of Japan. Thus the Tokugawa did not rule the entire country directly, nor did they personally tax the entire population. In this way Japan maintained a degree of political and economic decentralization.

Tokugawa Power

As overlords the Tokugawa did have considerable influence over the behavior of the lesser daimyos. Behind this influence lay Tokugawa wealth and military power. The Tokugawa shoguns prohibited the less powerful daimyos from building new castles within their domains and from entering into alliances with other daimyos. The daimyos had to spend every other year in Yedo, the shogun's capital, and they left their families there as hostages when they returned to their own domains. In this manner the Tokugawa shoguns maintained control over the daimyos.

The expense of maintaining two grand residences—one in Yedo and one in the provinces—and of traveling to and from Yedo in elaborate processions drained the financial resources of most daimyos. The daimyos could no longer afford to engage in revolt. The threat that the Tokugawa shoguns might execute their sons and heirs if they did revolt provided another powerful restraint on the daimyos.

The Great Peace of the Tokugawa

The Tokugawa shoguns came to power in 1600 because of war, but they brought Japan a long era of peace. For more than 250 years, Japan did not experience rebellion or other violent upheavals. The period from 1600 to 1868—the end of the shogunate—is sometimes called the Great Peace of the Tokugawa.

The hostage system and other controls over the daimyos served to keep the peace. So did the disarming of the peasants, a policy that Hideyoshi began and the later Tokugawa shoguns continued. Japan also enjoyed peace because the Tokugawa adopted a policy of isolation. They had permitted overseas trade for only a brief period.

Foreign contacts. Even before the invasion of Korea under Hideyoshi, Japanese sailors and traders had traveled overseas. In the early 1400s, during the Ashikaga shogunate, Japanese ships had sailed to Korea and China seeking profitable trade. If refused, as often happened, the Japanese resorted to piracy, seizing whatever they could from the local inhabitants.

These Japanese traders sailed mostly from those ports in western Japan closest to the Asian mainland. The goods they brought back—whether paid for or stolen—contributed to the wealth of local daimyos in that part of the country.

The Portuguese in Japan. In the mid-1500s the daimyos found another source of wealth: trade with the Portuguese, whose ships began appearing in Japanese waters. Portuguese traders introduced two things to Japan that later Tokugawa shoguns considered undesirable: the musket and Christianity. The musket, a forerunner of the modern rifle, gave its possessor an enormous advantage over an opponent armed with only a sword. Christianity was undesirable because it taught loyalty to a power greater than the Tokugawa shogun.

Christian missionaries. In the wake of Portuguese traders came Christian missionaries, chief among them the Jesuits, who had achieved notable success during the Counter-Reformation in Europe. The Jesuits concentrated their efforts on converting the daimyos to Christianity. They had discovered that it was easier to first convert a daimyo and then build churches and seek converts throughout the domain that he controlled. By the early 1600s, the missionaries had converted almost 500,000 Japanese to Christianity.

Closing the country. The success of the Jesuits alarmed the Tokugawa shoguns. Fearing that Japanese Christians might revolt against their rulers, the shoguns outlawed Christianity. Then, in the early 1600s, the shoguns forced Portuguese traders and Christian missionaries to leave Japan.

By this time the Portuguese faced stiff competition from the Dutch in the spice trade in the islands off the coast of Southeast Asia as well as in Japan. The Dutch had accepted a strictly controlled trading relationship with the Tokugawa shogunate. The shoguns allowed only a few Dutch merchants to live in Nagasaki, a port city on the island of Kyushu. In addition, the shoguns themselves controlled the small amount of trade Japan conducted with the Dutch.

Even that limited trading was curtailed when the Tokugawa "closed the country" in the late 1630s. They prohibited the building of oceangoing ships and also banned travel abroad by Japanese.

Learning from Maps *Yedo was the capital of the Tokugawa shogunate. On what island is the city Yedo located?*

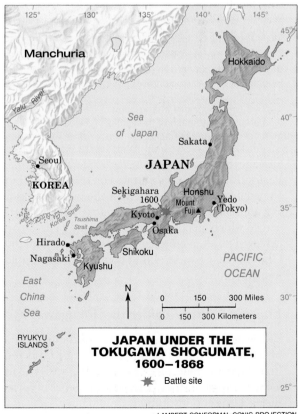

JAPAN UNDER THE
TOKUGAWA SHOGUNATE,
1600–1868

✴ Battle site

LAMBERT CONFORMAL CONIC PROJECTION

465

Evening Squall at Ohashi

The emergence of popular culture in Tokugawa Japan was reflected in the subjects of woodblock prints. Recreational and theatrical scenes as well as scenes of such commonplace activities as fishing and farming were captured by the gifted artists and printmakers of the 1700s and 1800s.

In this woodblock print by Ando Hiroshige, working people are opening umbrellas over their heads to protect themselves from the rain as they hurry over a wooden bridge. The artist shows a single moment caught in time. As we look at the picture, we can almost sense the suddenness of the storm and feel the sensation of the rain on our skin.

Prints such as this were the result of a collaboration of skilled artists and craftspeople. A publisher suggested the subject and directed the production of the print. The artist then made the first drawing, which the engraver cut into a series of woodblocks. Finally the printer chose the colors and applied one color to each block. Specially made paper was pressed onto each of the blocks in succession, and the accumulation

of color produced the total picture. Usually an edition of about 200 impressions was printed, to be sold in the publisher's shop.

The technique of printing by woodblock was first developed while the Tang dynasty held the Mandate of Heaven in China and was brought into Japan in the 700s. In the late 1700s and early 1800s, as the technique became more popular, it began to reflect the tastes of a people emerging from a feudal society into the modern world.

Japan, like China, concentrated on relations within the country and tried to ignore the outside world. As an island country without any land frontiers across which people might slip unnoticed, Japan achieved an even more complete isolation than did China. The Japanese almost completely eliminated foreign contacts.

Life and Culture Under the Tokugawa

The Tokugawa shoguns, like most of the emperors of China, did not value progress. They considered it more important to create a stable society. To achieve this goal, they borrowed a number of Confucian ideas and institutions from China.

First they adopted—with some modification—the Confucian structure of social classes. They ranked warriors, who performed roughly the same role as scholar-officials in China, first. Peasants, artisans, and merchants followed in descending order of importance.

In Japan people belonged to these classes by birth. Sons followed the occupations of their fathers, and the authorities allowed no one, male or female, to move freely about the country. For example, a person born into an artisan family in the city of Osaka remained a member of the artisan class in Osaka for life.

Second, the Tokugawa shoguns encouraged education in the Confucian classics for members of the warrior class. The shoguns established schools in every domain to prepare young warriors for their new peacetime role as government officials. However, the shoguns did not adopt the Chinese civil service examination system. In Japan warriors became officials by heredity alone. Males born into low-ranking warrior families worked as low-ranking officials in their domains. Those born into high-ranking families served as high-ranking officials.

As a further means of maintaining control, the shoguns required all warriors to live in the castle town of their daimyo. Instead of living off the income of their own estates in the countryside, they now received yearly payments from their daimyo. A warrior's rank determined the amount. This policy deprived warriors of the opportunity to develop independent sources of wealth or power. It also eliminated their opportunities to revolt against their lords.

Change in Tokugawa Japan

As in China, the rulers of Japan could not prevent social, economic, and political change. Much of the change that occurred resembled the change that occurred in China. Cities grew in both size and importance. Internal trade expanded, and various regions began to specialize in different crops and handicrafts. The growth of cities and the increasing wealth of merchants and artisans led to the rise of a popular culture. By the early 1700s, new forms of literature, theater, and art had taken root. All these new forms catered to the tastes and life styles of ordinary city residents.

The End of Japanese Isolation

As part of the Tokugawa plan for keeping Japan isolated, the Japanese government refused to give shelter to ships of other nations during storms. They treated shipwrecked sailors harshly. Such treatment of American whaling and merchant ships finally brought Japanese isolation to an end.

In 1853 United States President Millard Fillmore sent a naval force to Japan under Commodore Matthew Perry. Perry had orders to negotiate a commercial treaty that would open Japanese ports to American trade as well as guarantee the safety of American sailors. He presented a letter from President Fillmore that urged the Japanese to accept the

Learning from Pictures The Japanese enjoyed music and developed many musical instruments different from those in the West.

treaty, and he promised he would return for an answer the following year.

In Japan the American visit sparked controversy. Some powerful leaders favored military resistance and continued isolation. Others believed that Japan could not hold out, and their views prevailed. The shogun reluctantly agreed to negotiate when Perry returned in 1854.

Colorful ceremonies accompanied the negotiations, symbolic of the two contrasting cultures. The Japanese gave the Americans beautiful silk, lacquer ware, and other articles exquisitely made by hand. The Americans presented the Japanese with guns, a telegraph set, and a model railroad train on which dignified Japanese officials took rides.

The negotiations led to the Treaty of Kanagawa (kuh · NAHG · uh · wuh) in 1854, a turning point in Japanese history. The Japanese opened two ports to Americans for shelter and trade. Within two years Japan signed treaties with Great Britain, Russia, France, and the Netherlands. Several Japanese seaports were opened where representatives of foreign nations had the right to live, trade, purchase naval supplies, and establish **consulates**—diplomatic offices headed by consuls.

At first, conservative Japanese isolationists ignored foreign consuls and kept contacts with foreigners to a minimum. Nevertheless, in 1858 the Japanese and the United States governments agreed to exchange diplomatic representatives. The Japanese now admitted more American consuls and opened more treaty ports to the United States. Similar treaties with other nations soon followed.

The Decision to Modernize

The end of isolation brought Japan face to face with a great question. Should Japan resist Western influence, by force if necessary? Or should the nation try to become strong in the only way the imperial powers would respect—by Westernizing and industrializing?

The decision did not come about without a struggle. In the 1860s a civil war broke out between rival factions of the samurai warrior class. On one side were those who wanted to maintain the existing political system. On the other were progressive samurai who saw the need to modernize Japan, if only to keep Japan strong and independent. They pushed for the ouster of the shogun and the restoration of the emperor's powers. The pro-emperor forces won out in 1868. The last Tokugawa shogun resigned and turned his extensive domain over to the emperor. The daimyo soon followed suit. The emperor, a boy of 15, took the name Meiji (MAY · JEE), meaning "enlightened rule," for his reign.

Learning from Pictures
Encouraged by the Tokugawa shogunate, artists carved these miniature Japanese sculptures, called netsukes, in a variety of images. Many netsukes depict Westerners (left) as comical. Other netsukes relate to Japanese history, like this traditional dancer (right).

Learning from Pictures
This painting depicts Sultan Süleyman at the Battle of Mohács. What European capital did Süleyman almost capture?

SECTION 2 REVIEW

1. **Define** consulate
2. **Identify** Oda Nobunaga, Toyotomi Hideyoshi, Tokugawa Ieyasu, Matthew Perry
3. **Locate** Kyoto, Yedo, Nagasaki
4. **Interpreting Ideas** How were the Tokugawa shoguns able to control the daimyos?
5. **Understanding Ideas** Why did the Tokugawa shoguns decide to "close the country"?
6. **Summarizing Ideas** What Chinese ideas and institutions did the Tokugawa shoguns adopt?
7. **Contrasting Ideas** How did the way in which Japan ended its isolation differ from the way in which China did?

3 The Islamic Empires of Asia Declined

Followers of the Muslim faith spread the word of Allah from the Iberian Peninsula to the East Indies. By the 1500s three large Islamic empires existed in the central part of that vast stretch of land from Bengal in India to the Balkan Peninsula: the Ottoman Empire, Persia, and the Mogul Empire.

The rulers of these Muslim states set up strong central governments. They also faced deep religious divisions with lasting quarrels between Shiites and Sunnis.

The Ottoman Empire

After the Ottoman Turks conquered Constantinople in 1453, they continued to expand overland while Europe expanded overseas. Led by Süleyman (SOO • lay • mahn) the Magnificent, the Turks conquered Hungary and nearly captured the Hapsburg capital at Vienna in 1529. They may have failed in their capture of Vienna only because heavy rains prevented the sultan from bringing forward his heavy siege cannon.

Nearly a half century later, in 1571, Philip II of Spain inflicted a great naval defeat on the Turks at Lepanto. Later, the Turks surrendered control of Hungary, but in 1683 they again nearly captured Vienna. Troops led by the Polish king John Sobieski halted their attack.

Despite these defeats and great territorial losses, the Ottoman Empire still had considerable vitality in the late 1600s. Turks lived in the heart of the empire in Asia Minor. Christians inhabited the Balkans, and Muslim Arabs lived in the old Fertile Crescent and along the Mediterranean shore of North Africa. From the capital at Constantinople, the sultans and their grand viziers (vuh • ZIRZ)—who had duties similar to a prime minister's—ruled this diverse mass of people.

469

Decline begins. After Süleyman the Magnificent died in 1566, the empire began its slow decline. Food production could not keep pace with the growing population and the economy suffered because the empire lost control of both the silk and spice trades. The Turks also lost lands around the Black Sea and the Sea of Azov to the Russians. Corruption, rebellious Janissaries, and problems concerning the succession also weakened the empire.

Attempts at reform. Napoleon's army, which invaded the Ottoman possession of Egypt in 1798, spread the ideas of the French Revolution to the Ottoman Empire. These ideas greatly influenced Selim III, who ruled the empire from 1789 to 1807. He enacted enlightened reforms in administration, in taxation, and in the military. However, conservatives and Janissaries opposed to change overthrew him.

Selim's successor, Mahmud II, had more success with reform. Although Great Britain, France, and Russia forced him to recognize Greek independence in 1829, Mahmud destroyed the Janissaries—using their poor performance against the Greek rebels as an excuse—and introduced autocratic reforms. The Ottoman Empire continued under this reformed system of rule until the early 1900s. Although reduced in prestige and power, the Ottoman Empire continued to influence international affairs.

Persia

The peoples of Persia, the land lying between the Ottoman Empire and the Mogul Empire of India, had become part of the early Islamic empire. In 1501 a Turkic dynasty called the *Safavids* (say • FAH • vuhdz) established a very strong central

Learning from Maps At its zenith, the Ottoman Empire controlled eastern Europe and north Africa. What lands did the Turks lose to the Russians?

ROBINSON PROJECTION

470

government with its capital at Isfahan. The Safavids, under the rule of Shah Abbas I, brought Persian society to new heights in the late 1500s and early 1600s. Isfahan, with its brilliant royal court, was considered one of the great cities of the Muslim world. Shah Abbas's reign saw a flowering of literature—especially poetry—and of the arts—particularly calligraphy and textile and carpet design. During this same period, Persian was adopted as the language of diplomacy in much of the Islamic world.

In one respect Persia resembled the northern Europe of the 1500s. The Safavids followed the Shiite element of Islam, and they ruthlessly forced Shiism as the state religion upon the Persian population. Some historians have compared Shiite Islam to Protestantism because of its protest movement and the strength it gave to the central government. Most important to later history is the contribution the Shiite Muslims made to modern Iranian nationalism. Shiism gave the Persians—today's Iranians—a separate identity from the greater number of Sunnis—Turks and Arabs—who lived around them. This nationalism would have a strong effect on Iran in the 1900s.

The close ties between religion and government had both positive and negative aspects. The Shiite Safavids encouraged religious education, and many of the best students became members of the clergy or went into the law—professions that were closely related in strict Islamic societies. In time religious and legal leaders came to wield great power in the government. However, many of them opposed the government's efforts at change and modernization. Others became corrupt and supported only those government policies that would increase their power and wealth.

The rulers who succeeded Abbas proved increasingly inept, and in 1736 the Safavid dynasty fell. The Persian nobles then elected a brilliant military leader, Nader Shah, as their new ruler. Through numerous conquests Nader Shah extended Persia's boundaries to their greatest extent since the time of Darius and Xerxes. But after one of his own tribesmen assassinated Nader Shah in 1747, Persia lost these conquered lands. Persia then divided into a number of small states. At the end of the 1700s, the Qajar (kah • JAHR) dynasty—another Turkic people—established a Persian monarchy with its capital at Tehran.

Learning from Pictures   *Shah Abbas I, leader of the Safavids, leads a battalion against the Uzbeks. Why do historians compare the Shiite branch of Islam to Protestantism?*

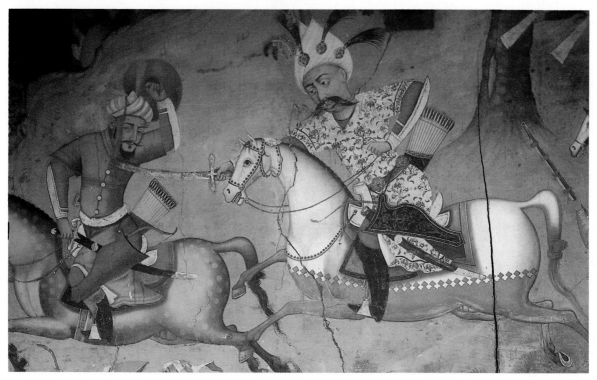

The Mercator Projection: A Map for Navigators

When people look at a map, they usually have no idea of which projection cartographers used to construct that map. However, almost everyone has heard of or seen the most frequently used projection—the Mercator—developed by Gerhard Mercator in 1569.

On his projection Mercator drew the lines of latitude and longitude as straight lines that crossed each other at right angles so that navigators could draw straight lines to plot courses. This meant that the distance between parallels, or lines of latitude, increased as latitude increased. If, however, Mercator had drawn the parallels with even spacing, as they are on a globe, straight

lines plotted on them would not be true compass bearings.

The actual mathematical computations that Mercator used to develop his projection were complex, but the idea behind his projection was quite simple. Picture a spherical balloon inside a hollow cylinder. Next, imagine that the balloon has lines of latitude and longitude marked on it and that the line marking the equator just touches the wall of the cylinder. Now imagine blowing up the balloon. As the balloon stretches, the lines of longitude lie as straight lines along the walls of the cylinder and the lines of latitude are stretched apart in proportion. As a result, the farther poleward you look the greater the distortion in scale.

And although land shapes appear correct, their areas are greatly distorted. Nevertheless, for every point on the map, the angles shown are correct in every direction. This allows a navigator to plot a straight line course, because a line connecting any two points follows an exact compass direction.

While the Mercator projection is a valuable navigational tool, it has been used far too frequently to depict the world on a flat surface. It seems convenient because the shapes of the continents are correct and are easily recognized. However, as a result of regularly seeing the Mercator projection, many people have no idea of the sizes of the continents in relation to one another.

On the Mercator projection, landmasses retain their true shape.

The Mogul Empire in India

The Mogul Empire had become the weakest of the three Muslim empires by the 1700s. Still, the wealth of India attracted traders. People believed the country had impressive supplies of jewels and gold. European travelers could see that India's rulers enjoyed luxurious life styles unmatched by those of any European monarchs. India's great cities, such as Agra and Delhi, seemed much larger than any city in Europe. Agriculture flourished on the subcontinent, where the monsoon season allowed more than one harvest a year.

Nevertheless, by the mid-1600s Mogul rulers faced financial difficulties that weakened the central government. The Moguls maintained huge and expensive armies supplied with enormous cannons. They believed they needed these forces to hold their empire together. In addition, the court became more luxurious and more expensive to support. To pay these costs, the Mogul emperors increased taxes. Sometimes as much as one-third of the peasants' income from the land went to pay these taxes. As a result, the peasants' levels of production and prosperity declined, further reducing the revenue base. Nevertheless, the Moguls expanded the size of the bureaucracy so that it could collect taxes more efficiently.

In 1739 Nader Shah, the powerful new Persian ruler, sacked Delhi and confiscated the jewel-encrusted Peacock Throne of the Moguls. The Moguls lost their wealth, their prestige, their army, and much of their territory. Nader Shah effectively destroyed Mogul power in India, although a shadow emperor remained on the throne in Delhi until the 1850s. During the remainder of the 1700s, the Marathas, Sikhs from the Punjab, and Afghan Muslim invaders fought for control of the country. With India torn by dissension, Europeans could more easily conquer it.

The British in India

The Mogul Empire had the least success of the major Muslim empires in confronting European power. To the east of India the Chinese and Japanese managed to keep Europeans out altogether for a long time. In India, however, the Mogul emperors could neither dislodge the Portuguese in the 1500s nor could they resist the English. By the

Learning from Pictures *Robert Clive laid the foundation for the expansion of Britain's Indian empire. Who did Clive defeat for control of India?*

1600s the English began to replace the Portuguese as the major European presence in India. Over the years this presence grew.

The British East India Company, founded in 1600, controlled England's trade with India. By the 1700s the company's chief rival was the French East India Company. Both the English and the French trading companies desired commercial profits, not Indian colonies. Very few English or French citizens lived in India.

Competition between the governments of Britain and France ultimately resulted in the Seven Years' War, which began in 1756. This occurred as the Mogul Empire was dissolving into hundreds of small states. Taking advantage of the chaos, the British and the French made alliances with rival Indian rulers.

The British trading post at Calcutta lay within the important Indian state of Bengal, whose ruler was allied with the French. In 1756 Bengali troops captured Calcutta and imprisoned 146 British citizens, locking them up overnight in a small jail cell that became known as the "Black Hole of Calcutta." By the next morning, 123 of the prisoners had died of suffocation.

The British East India Company, under its military leader Robert Clive, fought back with fury. In a series of decisive victories, Clive crushed the

473

70° HINDU KUSH 80° 90°

AFGHANISTAN KASHMIR

PLATEAU OF TIBET

PUNJAB Amritsar

Lahore

Sikhs TIBET

Brahmaputra R.

30°

THAR Delhi Meerut HIMALAYAS

RAJPUTANA OUDH NEPAL

DESERT Kanpur Lucknow ASSAM

Ganges R.

BENGAL BURMA

Calcutta

20°

DECCAN

Bombay

HYDERABAD

PLATEAU

Arabian Sea Bay of Bengal

Goa

(PORT.)

N

Calicut

Ceylon 10°

INDIAN OCEAN 0 600 Miles

0 600 Kilometers

INDIA, 1835–1857

------ Boundary of Ranjit Singh's territory, 1835

------ Boundary of area affected by Sepoy Rebellion, 1857

• Centers of rebellion, 1857

Territory under British rule, 1856

MODIFIED OBLIQUE CONIC CONFORMAL PROJECTION

Learning from Maps *The British eventually acquired control of the two largest river deltas in India. Which river delta did the British acquire first?*

French and their Indian allies. The Treaty of Paris in 1763 left the French with a few tiny footholds along the coast and gave the British a free hand in India.

Expansion of British Authority

After the Seven Years' War, the British government became uneasy at the thought of a commercial company controlling the lives of millions of Indian people. In the 1770s the government assumed the right to appoint the company's highest official, the governor general. However, the company remained free to earn profits and to use its officials and troops as it chose.

In the late 1780s, the British government named Lord Cornwallis—the same man who surrendered at Yorktown—to be governor general of India, an appointment that would have long-lasting

effects. One of Cornwallis's first actions was to clean up widespread corruption among company employees. For this purpose he created a civil service of company officials who were forbidden to have any part in the company's commercial activities. Blaming some of the corruption on Indian employees, Cornwallis ordered them excluded from all important company positions. Indian resentment over this discrimination lasted for years.

As time went on, the British were drawn deeper into the quicksands of Indian political rivalries. Several strong Indian states engaged in constant jealous rivalries and even warfare. The British took advantage of these rivalries and wars to win control of these regions. Religious hatred between Hindus and Muslims, and the caste system, which prevented Indians from uniting against the foreigners, helped the British. The British usually did not need to employ any of their own troops. Instead, when actual fighting was necessary, they made use of local troops called **sepoys** (SEE • poys), who were trained and led by British officers. In this way the British East India Company extended its power over the Indian subcontinent. By 1857 the British East India Company ruled about three-fifths of the subcontinent directly. It ruled most of the rest indirectly through its control over local princes. Great Britain also controlled the island of Ceylon, which it had seized from the Dutch during the time of the Napoleonic Wars.

Until about 1830 the British made no attempt to impose their way of life on India. In the 1830s, however, English became the language of instruction in Indian schools, and Indian pupils studied Western literature, history, and science.

The British also enforced several social reforms. They prohibited slavery and the killing of infant girls. They declared the ritual suicide known as suttee illegal. And the British suppressed Thuggee, a religious cult that required its members to commit ritual murder and robbery. It is from this cult that we get our word *thug*.

The Indian Revolt

India in the mid-1800s presented the strange spectacle of a huge land, with millions of people and an ancient civilization, controlled by a foreign commercial corporation. The British population in India had grown rapidly and by this time included British wives and families.

Indians resented the British and their increasing tendency to impose Western ways of life upon India. The sepoys were particularly dissatisfied because they had been forced to fight for the British in numerous campaigns in Afghanistan and Burma. In 1857 they revolted.

The immediate cause of the Indian Revolt, or Sepoy Rebellion, involved a new kind of rifle that the British East India Company issued in 1857. The cartridges for this rifle had been greased to make the bullets slide more easily through the barrel. In order to load his rifle, the sepoy had to bite off part of the cartridge. According to rumors, the cartridges were greased with the fat of cows and pigs. The Hindus regarded the cow as sacred. Muslims were forbidden to eat pork. India's forces included both Hindus and Muslims. Thus, biting the cartridge would violate the religious customs of both groups.

Agitators whipped up existing resentments by claiming that the company had purposely tried to insult the two religions. With help from the Indian people, the sepoy troops staged a widespread and violent mutiny against their British masters.

The Indian Revolt almost drove the British out of India, but troops sent from Great Britain finally suppressed the rebellion. To discourage future rebellions, the British executed leading sepoys by shooting them out of cannons. In 1858 the British Parliament dissolved the British East India Company and transferred the rule of India to the British government. In 1877 Queen Victoria was proclaimed Empress of India, and Great Britain filled the void left by the passing of the Moguls.

SECTION 3 REVIEW

1. **Define** sepoy
2. **Identify** John Sobieski, Mahmud II, Nader Shah, Robert Clive, Lord Cornwallis
3. **Locate** Lepanto, Black Sea, Sea of Azov, Isfahan, Tehran, Delhi, Bengal
4. **Contrasting Ideas** **(a)** In what ways were the three Islamic empires similar? **(b)** In what ways were they different?
5. **Synthesizing Ideas** How do you explain the rise of the European powers and the relative decline of the Islamic empires during the period from 1400 to 1800?
6. **Summarizing Ideas** What were the results of the Seven Years' War in India?
7. **Analyzing Ideas** **(a)** What led to the Indian Revolt? **(b)** How did this change the government in India?

Learning from Pictures
The massacre at Cawnpore during the Sepoy Rebellion left many women and children dead. This atrocity would affect Indian and British relations for a long time.

475

Ming dynasty
established
in China

1501–1763
Safavid
dynasty ruled
in Persia

AD   1368

1501

1514

First
Portuguese ships
reached China

Chapter Summary

The following list contains the key concepts you have learned about the non-European world in the era of European expansion.

1. The rulers of the Ming and Qing dynasties tried to isolate China by prohibiting Chinese merchants from trading overseas and by restricting foreign merchants to special settlements inside China.
2. The Ming and Qing emperors brought peace to China, but by the late 1700s, corruption among officials increased taxes, and decreased services led to discontent and rebellion. This made it difficult for the Chinese emperors to keep out the British. China's defeat in the Opium War with Great Britain forced China to deal with the outside world. Other rebellions in China allowed foreigners to make further inroads into China.
3. As the nations of Europe did in the 1500s and 1600s, the Japanese struggled over who was to be supreme—the central government run by the shoguns or the local lords called daimyos.
4. The Tokugawa shoguns established internal peace and in the 1630s closed Japan to foreign missionaries and merchants, except for a few Dutch traders. In 1853 the United States sent a naval force to Japan to negotiate a treaty for trading privileges and to guarantee the safety of American sailors. These negotiations led to the Treaty of Kanagawa in 1854. This opened up Japan to other foreign nations.
5. The Ottoman Empire remained a threat to central and eastern Europe until 1683, after which it began a gradual decline. Under Selim III some reforms, inspired by the French Revolution, were attempted. His successor, Mahmud II, introduced autocratic reforms, and the Ottoman Empire was ruled under this system until the early 1900s.
6. The Safavid dynasty brought Persia to great cultural and political heights, and it forced the Persian people to adopt the Shiite form of Islam as the official religion. After the Safavid dynasty fell, Nader Shah assumed power. He extended Persia's boundaries to their greatest extent since the time of Darius and Xerxes. After his assassination Persia lost these lands and divided into smaller states.

7. Unlike their counterparts in China and Japan, the Mogul emperors could not keep European traders out of India. The Seven Years' War between Great Britain and France resulted in British domination in India.
8. India was governed by the British East India Company, which managed to create resentment among the Indian troops trained by the British. In 1857 the Indians rebelled in what is known as the Indian Revolt, or Sepoy Rebellion. The British put down the rebellion and dissolved the British East India Company. They transferred the rule of India to the British government. Some years later Queen Victoria was proclaimed Empress of India.

On a separate sheet of paper, complete the following review exercises.

Reviewing Important Terms

Supply the term that correctly completes each statement.

1. Early Chinese ships were called _____ .
2. The Manchu emperors forced Chinese men to wear their hair in a long braid called a _____ to indicate their submission to them.
3. Like the humanists in Europe, Chinese scholars became interested in _____ , the history of words.
4. Under _____ _____ the government does not restrict or interfere in international trade.
5. Diplomatic offices headed by consuls are called _____ .
6. _____ were native Indian troops trained by British officers.

Developing Critical Thinking Skills

1. **Summarizing Ideas**   List the steps taken by the Ming dynasty to protect China's northern frontier.
2. **Explaining Ideas**   How was the Great Peace of the Tokugawa maintained?
3. **Interpreting Ideas**   In what ways were the decline of the Ottoman Empire and of the Persian Empire the same?
4. **Comparing Ideas**   Compare the way the British established trade in China with the way in which they established it in India.

Tokugawa shogunate in Japan

1566 — Death of Süleyman the Magnificent

1592 — Japan invaded Korea

1603 — Tokugawa shogunate in Japan

1644 — Qing dynasty established in China

1683 — John Sobieski turned back Turks at Vienna

1699 — British established trading post at Guangzhou

1763

1796 — White Lotus Rebellion in China

1808 — Reign of Mahmud II in Ottoman Empire

1839

1868

5. **Analyzing Ideas** **(a)** What issues concerned the Japanese in deciding whether to modernize their country? **(b)** What was the result of this decision?
6. **Understanding Relationships** Describe the results of European contact with each of the following: **(a)** China; **(b)** Japan; **(c)** India.

Relating Geography to History

Turn to the map on page 474 and answer the following questions: **(a)** Why did British control begin along the coast and move gradually inland? **(b)** Looking at British acquisitions from 1835 to 1857, what geographic pattern did they follow? **(c)** Why did the British have more difficulty controlling the interior than the areas along waterways?

Relating Past to Present

1. Review the military problems of the Ming and Qing dynasties along their land borders with central and northern Asia. Then use the *Readers' Guide to Periodical Literature* to find magazine articles that deal with the tensions between China and the Soviet Union in recent years. What are the reasons for the tensions between these two countries?
2. Europeans transmitted their culture to the areas of the world that came under their domination. Choose an area of the world today that is experiencing the influence of Western ideas and culture. Describe some of these influences. What impact might they have on the traditional way of life in the area?
3. The British excluded the Indians from any official positions in the British East India Company. Naturally the Indians developed a deep resentment over this policy of exclusion. How do you think this superior attitude that colonial rulers had over their subjected people has affected the relationship between the former colonial power and its former colony?

Applying History Study Skills

Before completing this activity, review Building History Study Skills on page 462.

Read the following selection from a 1636 Tokugawa edict banning contact with foreigners. Then answer the questions that follow.

“ No Japanese ships may leave for foreign countries. . . . No Japanese may go abroad secretly. If anyone tries to do this, he will be killed, and the ship and owner(s) will be placed under arrest while higher authority is informed. . . . No offspring of Southern Barbarians [Europeans] will be allowed to remain. Anyone violating this order will be killed and all his relatives punished according to the gravity of the offense. ”

1. What consequences did people who ignored the decree face?
2. What do you think were the positive and negative long-term consequences of the decree?

Investigating Further

1. **Writing a Report** As you read on page 466, the art form of woodblock prints became popular in Japan during the Tokugawa period. Use books in your library to write a report answering the following questions: Why was this art form so popular? What was its subject matter? How did Japanese woodblock prints change in the 1800s? One source for your research might be Seiichiro Takahashi's *Traditional Woodblock Prints of Japan* (Weatherhill).
2. **Presenting an Oral Report** Prepare an oral report describing how Indians reacted to British rule. The following selections are possible sources: "The Sepoy Rebellion" and "The Growth of National Feeling in India" in Sydney Eisen and Maurice Filler's *The Human Adventure*, Volume 2 (Harcourt Brace Jovanovich).
3. **Writing an Essay** The opium trade became a major problem between Great Britain and China. Write an essay describing the dilemma of the Chinese officials in attempting to stop the opium traffic. Also describe how the British used the Opium War to make demands on the Chinese. One possible source is "The Opening of China" in Sydney Eisen and Maurice Filler's *The Human Adventure*, Volume 2 (Harcourt Brace Jovanovich).

Unit Summary

The following list contains the key concepts you have learned about the emergence of modern nations.

1. In the late 1300s, a literary and artistic movement known as the Renaissance swept Europe.
2. In Germany, Martin Luther began the Protestant Reformation.
3. The Scientific Revolution of the 1500s and 1600s transformed the methods and understanding of astronomy, physics, and anatomy.
4. In the 1400s and 1500s, Europeans expanded overseas. Portuguese and Spanish explorers took the lead in discovering new lands and trade routes.
5. The rulers of Europe centralized government in their hands and established absolute monarchies in France, Russia, Prussia, and Austria.
6. In England monarchs and Parliament clashed throughout the 1600s.
7. In the 1700s the British colonists in what is today the United States revolted and set up their own government.
8. During the Enlightenment thinkers began to criticize the established political institutions.
9. Growing discontent in France and Louis XVI's failure to solve the government's continuing financial crisis led to the French Revolution in 1789.
10. Through a series of steps, France became first a republic and then an empire under Napoleon Bonaparte. When Napoleon was defeated in 1815, the European powers attempted to restore the Old Regime.
11. China and Japan tried to protect their cultures from outside influences.
12. The Ottoman, Persian, and Mogul empires declined in the 1700s. India then became a target for European colonialism as Great Britain began taking control in the late 1700s.

On a separate sheet of paper, complete the following review exercises.

Reviewing Concepts

Match each of the following people with the appropriate description from the list below:

a. Leonardo da Vinci   f. Michelangelo
b. Peter the Great   g. Maria Theresa
c. Prince Henry   h. Machiavelli
d. Louis XVI   i. Petrarch
e. Bartholomeu Dias   j. Charles V

___ 1. Built a new capital in Russia that would be a "window to Europe"
___ 2. Painted the *Mona Lisa*
___ 3. Hapsburg ruler protected by the Pragmatic Sanction
___ 4. Sailed around the southern tip of Africa
___ 5. Poet who is often called the founder of humanism
___ 6. Started a navigators' school in Portugal
___ 7. King who was executed during the French Revolution
___ 8. Painted the murals on the ceiling of the Sistine Chapel
___ 9. Italian Renaissance thinker who wrote about politics and government
___ 10. Hapsburg who was both king of Spain and Holy Roman Emperor

Applying Critical Thinking Skills

1. **Interpreting Ideas** In what ways did European art of the 1500s and 1600s reflect the new ideas and attitudes of the Renaissance?
2. **Analyzing Ideas** How did the ideas of humanism and the Scientific Revolution change Europe?
3. **Understanding Ideas** (a) According to the theory of mercantilism, what benefits did European nations hope to gain from colonial empires? (b) How did the building of empires affect the people of the colonial areas?
4. **Classifying Ideas** List the powers that Parliament gained at the expense of the English monarch between 1603 and 1714.
5. **Describing Ideas** (a) Describe the changes that occurred in China during the rule of the Ming and Qing dynasties. (b) How were they similar to the changes that took place under the Tokugawa shogunate in Japan?
6. **Comparing Ideas** Compare the goals and achievements of the French Revolution to those of the American Revolution.

Relating Geography to History

How did the relative locations of China and Japan make it easier for the governments in those countries to shun contact with foreigners, while the relative location of the Ottoman Empire made such isolation more difficult?

Writing About History

1. Find information on Japanese and Chinese painting in the 1700s and the 1800s. Then find sources that explain how Japanese and Chinese artists influenced European and American artists. Present your findings in a written report.
2. Develop a comparative essay explaining the unique features of Japanese, Chinese, European, Indian, and Ottoman cultures in the 1700s and the 1800s.

Further Readings

Bainton, Roland H. *Here I Stand: A Life of Martin Luther.* Nashville: Abingdon Press. Recounts major events of Luther's life.

Dickens, Charles. *A Tale of Two Cities.* New York: New English Library. A novel set in London and Paris at the time of the French Revolution.

Ferguson, Wallace K. *The Renaissance.* New York: Holt, Rinehart & Winston. Analyzes the causes of the Renaissance and compares the Italian Renaissance to the Northern Renaissance.

Turnbull, Stephen. *Samurai Warriors.* New York: Blandford Press. Provides an illustrated history of Japanese warriors.

Unit Four Chronology

Date	Political and Social Developments	Technological and Scientific Advances	Visual Arts and Literature	Religious and Philosophical Thought
1300–1450	Growth of Italian city-states 14* Ming dynasty 18	Prince Henry the Navigator 15 Printing press 14	Italian Renaissance 14	Humanism 14
1450–1550	Treaty of Tordesillas 15 Columbus 15 Da Gama 15 Henry VIII 14 Cortés 15 Magellan 15 Beginnings of Safavid dynasty 18	Copernicus 14 Vesalius 14	Northern Renaissance begins 14 *The Prince* 14 *Utopia* 14 *Institutes* 14 Da Vinci 14 Michelangelo 14 Fresco art 14 Dürer 14	Luther 14 Diet of Worms 14 Anglican church 15 Counter-Reformation 14 Council of Trent 14 *Institutes of the Christian Religion* 14
1550–1650	Peace of Augsburg 14 Edict of Nantes 14 Michael Romanov 15 Spanish Armada 15 Thirty Years' War 15 Tokugawa shogunate 18 Qing dynasty 18 Richelieu 15 Süleyman the Magnificent 18	Kepler 14 Galileo 14 Microscope 14 European shipbuilding 15	Rembrandt 15 Shakespeare 14	King James Version of the Bible 16
1650–1750	Louis XIV 15 Glorious Revolution 16 Peter the Great 15 Maria Theresa 15 Frederick the Great 15 Act of Union 16	Newton 14 Versailles 15	*Leviathan* 16 *Two Treatises on Civil Government* 16	Enlightenment 17 Voltaire 17 Rousseau 17 Jesuits banned from China 18
1750–1850	Catherine the Great 15 Partitioning of Poland 15 American Revolution 16 French Revolution 17 Napoleon 17 Congress of Vienna 17 Selim III 18		*Encyclopedia* 17 Japanese woodblock printing 18 Silverwork by Paul Revere 16 *The Social Contract* 17	French Commune 17 Declaration of the Rights of Man 17 U.S. Constitution 16

*Indicates chapter in which development is discussed

The Emergence of Modern Nations

14 The Renaissance, Reformation, and Scientific Revolution Changed Europe

A great burst of creativity began in Italy in the 1300s. Because this movement centered on a revival of interest in the classical learning of Greece and Rome, we call it the Renaissance (REN • uh • sahnts), a French word meaning "rebirth."

Renaissance Writers and Artists

Beginning about the mid-1300s, a number of Italian scholars, such as Francesco Petrarch (PEE • trahrk), developed a lively interest in classical literature, particularly that of the Romans. These Italian scholars stressed the study of grammar, rhetoric, history, and poetry, using classical texts. We call these studies the *humanities;* people who specialized in the humanities are called humanists.

Art as well as literature flourished during the Renaissance. The most noticeable characteristic of Renaissance painting, however, is its realism as shown in the works of artists such as Giotto (JAW • toh), Masaccio (mah • ZAH • choh), Leonardo da Vinci (duh VIN • chee), Michelangelo Buonarroti (my • kuh • LAN • juh • loh bwaw • nah • RAW • tee), Raphael, and Titian (TISH • uhn).

Over time the Renaissance spread beyond Italy. Trade, transportation, and the invention of printing helped this spread.

The Reformation

About 1500 several northern humanists suggested that the Roman Catholic church had lost sight of the spiritual mission proclaimed by Jesus. When the Catholic church ignored their concerns, reformers urged believers to form a new church.

This religious revolution, which split the church in western Europe and created several new churches, is called the Reformation.

The first break with the Roman Catholic church occurred in Germany, where some people opposed the church's policy of selling indulgences, or pardons from punishment for sin. The most vocal of these critics was Martin Luther, a German monk, who founded Lutheranism.

Calvin and the Counter-Reformation

In Switzerland, many rural areas remained Catholic, while the free cities developed a form of Protestantism significantly different from Luther's. The most prominent form of Protestantism was Calvinism, founded in Switzerland by John Calvin.

In response to the Reformation, the Catholic church launched a major reform movement known as the Counter-Reformation, or the Catholic Reformation, in the 1530s. Initially created to foster a more spiritual outlook in the Catholic church, the Counter-Reformation also clarified the doctrines of the church and pursued an aggressive campaign against Protestants.

The most striking result of the great religious struggle of the 1500s was the emergence of many different churches in western Europe. Another far-reaching result was a new interest in education. The Reformation also led to an increase in the power of national governments and a decrease in the power of the pope.

Popular Culture

At the time of the Renaissance and the Reformation, most Europeans lived in small villages and spent their entire lives raising food and combating nature to survive. Over time, however, changes did occur. Many people sought their fortunes in the growing towns and cities. Gradually, more

Florence, Italy

sophisticated attitudes began to take hold among the residents of towns and cities. In particular, people's understanding of how things happened in the world began to change. Demons and spirits no longer dominated views of daily life. People sought rational explanations for day-to-day events.

The Scientific Revolution

Science also changed as scientists worked to uncover the secrets of nature. These early investigators began to question traditional opinions and to observe and experiment for themselves. Most importantly, they described nature without any reference to previous beliefs. The foundation of this approach was the principle of doubt: nothing was to be believed unless it could be proved by experiment or mathematics. This approach became the new way of studying the world. The transformation in thinking that occurred during the 1500s and 1600s as a result of this new system of investigation is known as the Scientific Revolution.

15 Strong Monarchies Helped European States Expand

In 1400 Europe's monarchs lacked the wealth and power of the rulers of China, India, Africa, the Americas, and even Europe's close neighbor, the Ottoman Empire. Less than 400 years later, however, Europe had become the dominant civilization on earth.

Reasons for Exploration

Several factors encouraged the Europeans to explore the world. First, technological advances such as improved mapmaking, better navigation instruments, sturdier ships, and new weapons made long voyages possible. Second, newly powerful central governments encouraged exploration and colonization to enhance their prestige. Third, the development of new economic policies and methods played an important part in carrying out exploration. And finally, social changes such as overcrowding in Europe and the desire to seek religious freedom stimulated exploration.

Portugal and Spain

Explorers sailing for Portugal and Spain made the first European voyages into unknown waters. The Portuguese, encouraged by Prince Henry the Navigator, explored the coast of Africa and found a water route to India. The Spanish sent expeditions to the Americas to stake out an empire there.

One tragic aspect of this empire building was the slave trade. As Spain and Portugal established colonies, they imported African slaves to work the lands. This inhumane trade in human beings lasted until the 1800s.

Portugal rapidly acquired wealth and a vast empire, but its decline was almost as swift as its rise. Three main factors hastened this decline. First, the Portuguese government, neither strong nor well organized, had difficulty controlling its colonial officials. Second, many ships sank transporting products home from the colonies. The resulting loss of life drastically reduced Portugal's population. Third, Spain annexed Portugal in 1580, and Portugal did not regain its independence until 1640.

Taking advantage of these weaknesses, the Dutch and English captured much of the Asian trade from the Portuguese in the 1600s. Small Portuguese colonies survived in Africa, India, and China, but they no longer served as sources of great wealth. Only Brazil remained a major Portuguese colony.

The Spanish Empire

Spain turned most of its colonial energies to the Americas. By the 1530s it controlled almost all of Central and South America.

481

Spain also developed a centralized form of government for its colonies. Representatives of the monarch, called viceroys, reported to the Council of the Indies in Spain.

As Spanish explorers created a great empire outside Europe, Spanish kings expanded their authority in Spain itself. Perhaps one of the greatest of these kings was Charles V, who was Holy Roman Emperor as well as king of Spain. However, Charles's nearly continuous wars drained Spain's human and financial resources. In addition, Spain itself lacked industries and the government did little to encourage them. It also had difficulty feeding its people because so much land was devoted to raising sheep for wool. Finally, though tightly controlled by the king, the government could not operate efficiently over a territory that was scattered throughout Europe and the Americas.

Charles V realized that this scattered empire had become too large for any one monarch to rule alone. In 1556 he gave up his throne and divided his vast territory between his son, who became Philip II of Spain, and his brother, who became Holy Roman Emperor Ferdinand I.

France

In the mid-1600s, France emerged as a European power. It had recovered rapidly from the religious wars of the 1500s, thanks to the policies of King Henry IV, the first monarch of a new royal house in France, the Bourbons. Assisted by two able cardinals of the Roman Catholic church, the Bourbons would make the monarchy absolute in France. Under Louis XIV, France became the dominant power on the European continent.

Eastern and Central Europe

While the countries of western Europe strengthened their governments, new empires grew up farther east. In the 1600s the czars of Russia successfully dealt with many problems and created a Russian form of absolutism. Perhaps the greatest czar of this period was Peter the Great, who took power in 1682. Under his able rule, Russia claimed new territories and established closer ties with the West. Other rulers such as Catherine the Great further strengthened the monarchy. At the same time, the Hapsburgs of Austria and the Hohenzollerns of Prussia expanded their powers.

16 The English-speaking World Took a New Political Course

While nations on the continent of Europe were establishing absolute monarchies, England was developing a constitutional form of government.

The Tudors and the Stuarts

In the late 1400s, a new royal family, the Tudors, became England's rulers. The Tudor rulers brought stability and prosperity to England. When the throne passed to the Stuarts, however, relations between Parliament and the monarchs steadily deteriorated. Charles I even tried to rule without calling Parliament. Desperate for money, Charles finally assembled the legislative body in 1640.

Civil War

The Parliament of 1640, controlled by the Puritans, attempted to curb the powers of the monarch. Because of rebellions in both Ireland and Scotland, Charles I agreed to these limits. In 1642, however, the feisty monarch tried to arrest the leaders of Parliament. This action provoked a violent civil war that resulted in the king's execution and the establishment of a republican form of government under the Puritan Oliver Cromwell.

By 1660 the English people had undergone a change in feelings. Some had favored the execution of Charles I, but Cromwell's rule had brought only confusion and resentment. After some hesitation,

Queen Elizabeth I and Sir Francis Drake

482

the new Parliament of 1660 invited Charles II, the son of Charles I, to return to England from exile.

Constitutional Monarchy

Charles II had learned much from his years in exile and cooperated with Parliament. His brother, James II, however, clashed with the legislative body. Finally, when his Catholic wife gave birth to a son, the political parties of Whigs and Tories agreed that James must abdicate. A number of leading nobles invited James's daughter, Mary, and her husband William of Orange to take the throne of England. In 1689 William and Mary ascended the throne in what is known as the Glorious Revolution.

The English Revolution brought about safeguards against absolute monarchy in England. For example, in 1679 Parliament passed an important measure, the Habeas Corpus Act. This act provided that anyone who was arrested could obtain a writ, or order, demanding to be brought before a judge within a specified period of time. And before granting the throne to William and Mary, Parliament required them to accept certain fixed conditions named in a document known as the Bill of Rights. The Bill of Rights declared that Parliament would choose the ruler, who would be merely an official subject to parliamentary laws. The ruler could not proclaim or suspend any law, impose any tax, or maintain an army in peacetime without Parliament's consent. Parliament had to meet frequently, and the monarch could not interfere in the elections of its members. The Bill of Rights guaranteed the right of the members of Parliament to express themselves freely. By 1700, although England remained a monarchy, Parliament held the power. In the 50 years following 1689, Parliament continued to gain importance as the real power in the government of England. The organization and institutions characteristic of today's English government gradually emerged.

The English Empire

Spain and Portugal established vast overseas empires during the 1500s while England remained preoccupied with problems at home. Even though these problems persisted during the 1600s, English mariners began explorations that allowed England to claim lands in the Americas and Asia. Most notable were the Thirteen Colonies in North America and the commercial empire of the British East India Company in Asia.

The American Revolution

Although the North American colonists of the 1700s resented British trade regulations, they disliked the French along their borders even more. After the defeat of the French in 1763, however, relations between the colonists and the British steadily worsened. Finally, in 1776 the colonists declared their independence. After years of struggle, the British officially recognized the young nation—the United States of America—in 1783.

The new nation first attempted a loose union of states under the Articles of Confederation. When it became evident that the Articles did not give the central government enough power, the nation adopted the Constitution, which provided for a much stronger federal government. To guarantee the rights of the American people, the Constitution included the Bill of Rights—10 amendments specifying the basic rights of every United States citizen.

17 The French Revolution Changed the Course of World History

The English ideal that people should have a voice in government greatly influenced French political writers of the 1700s. These writers spread this idea, paving the way for one of the greatest revolutions in history—the French Revolution.

The Enlightenment

The people of the 1700s referred to their century as an "Age of Enlightenment." They believed themselves the first to have discovered the "light" of logical thinking revealed by science. During the Enlightenment philosophers believed they could apply the scientific method and use reason to logically explain human nature.

Their contemporaries called the thinkers of the Enlightenment philosophes (fee • luh • ZAWFS); philosophe is the French word for "philosopher." The philosophes were not only philosophers, however, but also critics who examined the political and social institutions of their day.

Storming the Bastille

The French Revolution

The French kings constructed an absolute monarchy based upon the division of society into three groups or estates. The First and Second Estates that included the clergy and the nobility had the fewest people, but they also had the most wealth, power, and privilege. The Third Estate, which included more than 90 percent of the people, had almost no power.

In the mid-1700s discontent in France began to grow. Several factors explain this discontent. The first resulted from the growth of the French population. Families had more children to support, and they needed more food and money. Second, the Third Estate chafed under a growing burden of taxation and spiraling prices, and the bourgeoisie clamored for a greater voice in government. Even the First and Second Estates were dissatisfied because they resented the absolute power of the monarch.

When a beleaguered Louis XVI called a meeting of the Estates-General in 1789, discontented groups throughout France hoped that the assembly would make necessary reforms. When the assembly finally met, the king proclaimed that each estate would meet separately and have equal power. In response, the delegates of the Third Estate boldly proclaimed themselves the National Assembly and proceeded to enact reforms.

Fearing that the king planned to close the National Assembly, the people of Paris took action. On July 14, 1789, they stormed and captured the Bastille, the hated prison-fortress, in search of weapons. They planned to use the weapons to defend the National Assembly against the royal troops. The French Revolution had begun.

The End of the Monarchy

Quite rapidly, the National Assembly became the real government of France and enacted reforms. As of August 4, 1789, the National Assembly abolished the last remnants of feudalism in France. Following these reforms, on August 27, 1789, the Assembly adopted the Declaration of the Rights of Man, guaranteeing basic human rights. Between 1789 and 1791, the Assembly passed more than 2,000 laws aimed at correcting abuses and setting up a new government. And in 1791 it finished writing a new constitution for France that established a constitutional monarchy.

When Austria and Prussia invaded France, a group of radicals seized control of the Paris government and established what they called the Commune. The Commune accurately accused Louis XVI of plotting with foreign monarchs to restore absolutism in France. On August 10, 1792, the Legislative Assembly, coerced by the Commune, voted to suspend the office of king.

The French Republic

A new legislative body, the National Convention, met in 1792. As soon as it met, it proclaimed the end of the monarchy and the beginning of a republic. The Convention also tried Louis XVI on charges of plotting against the security of the nation and ordered his execution. Fearful of counter-revolutionaries and foreign invasions, the Convention then instituted the Reign of Terror, during which thousands were executed.

In spite of the dangers and difficulties of the time, the National Convention brought about many reforms in France. It began organizing French laws into a single system, or code. It provided for a national system of public education, and it abolished slavery in the French colonies.

In 1795 the National Convention drafted another constitution under which the Directory controlled France. Although the Directory governed for four years, it pleased neither the radicals nor the conservatives. Finally, in 1799 Napoleon Bonaparte took over the government.

Napoleon

Though the government he set up kept the form of a republic, Napoleon became first dictator and then emperor of France. Under his rule, the French armies conquered most of Europe. In 1812, however, Great Britain, Austria, Sweden, and Russia united against the French. In March 1814 Paris fell to the allied armies, and Napoleon was exiled to the island of Elba. Although Napoleon returned to France in 1815, he was decisively defeated at the Battle of Waterloo in 1815.

Peace

After the final defeat of Napoleon in 1815, European leaders met at the Congress of Vienna to redraw the map of Europe. Four principles guided the decisions of the Congress of Vienna: (1) Legitimacy, which meant that all former ruling families should be restored to their thrones, had to be upheld. (2) The balance of power had to be restored in Europe. This meant that the nations of Europe had to keep any one nation from becoming too powerful. (3) France had to be weakened. (4) The four powers—Great Britain, Austria, Russia, and Prussia—had to be compensated for the losses they had suffered at the hands of Napoleon.

Although the delegates to the Congress of Vienna attempted to restore the old order, they ultimately failed. The national feelings that Napoleon had aroused throughout Europe became powerful forces in the years following the Congress of Vienna.

18 The Countries of Asia Experienced a Transition

Between 1400 and the mid-1800s, many of the countries in Asia reached a political and cultural peak and then began to decline.

China

Under the reign of the Ming and Qing dynasties, China enjoyed more than 400 years of peace. Except for the fighting that occurred when the Qing dynasty overthrew the Ming dynasty, very little rebellion or warfare occurred. This period of peace greatly contributed to China's stability.

Just as the Qing dynasty started its decline in the late 1700s, new peoples appeared in China—

Europeans. First the Portuguese, and then the British and the Russians claimed trading privileges in China—often with disastrous effects for the Chinese people.

Japan

In the late 1400s, the Japanese daimyos began fighting among themselves for survival and supremacy. The struggle among the daimyos resulted in the creation of a political system roughly halfway between feudalism and centralized monarchy. The Japanese established this hybrid system, known as the Tokugawa (TOH • KOOG • AH • WAH) shogunate, in 1603. It survived until 1868. Unlike in China, the Tokugawa shoguns successfully kept out the Europeans. Nevertheless, in 1858 the Japanese and the United States governments agreed to exchange diplomatic representatives. The Japanese now admitted more American consuls and opened more treaty ports to the United States. Similar treaties with other nations soon followed. With the establishment of contacts with the West came a decision to modernize Japan.

Islamic Empires

By the 1500s three large Islamic empires existed: the Ottoman Empire, Persia, and the Mogul Empire. The rulers of these three empires met with varying degrees of success in combatting European influences. Perhaps the least successful, however, were the Mogul leaders of India. There, the British steadily increased their powers until India became an official part of the British Empire in 1877.

SYNTHESIS REVIEW

1. **Understanding Ideas** Why did Martin Luther split with the Roman Catholic church?
2. **Classifying Ideas** What factors encouraged European explorations?
3. **Determining Cause and Effect** How did the English Revolution encourage the growth of constitutional government?
4. **Seeing Relationships** How did the discontent of the French people lead to the French Revolution?
5. **Summarizing Ideas** Which Islamic empire had the least success in combating the influence of the Europeans?
6. **Synthesizing Ideas** How did the English Revolution influence the French Revolution?

The Development of Industrial Society

◀ *Construction by Thomas Hart Benton*   **487**

CHAPTER

19

The Industrial Revolution Transformed the Modern World

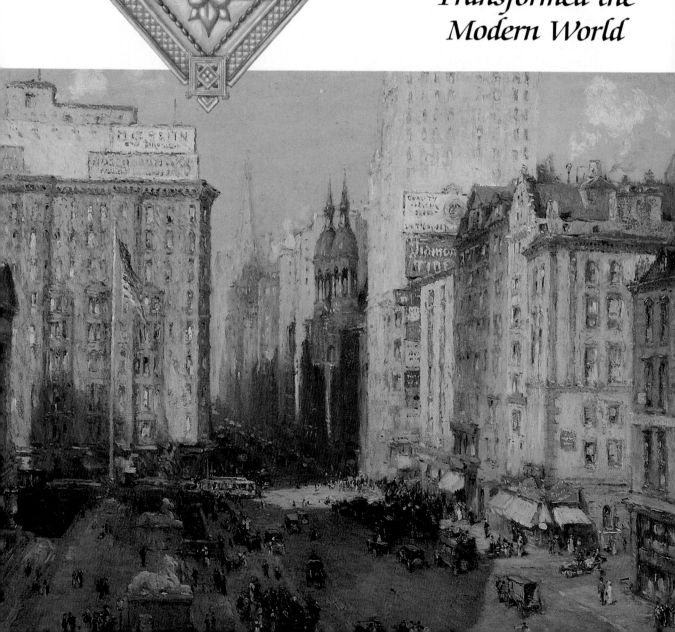

Place   Great Britain, the United States, France, and Germany

Time   1600–1900

```
┌──────────────╫───────────────────────────◆──┐
└──────────────╫──────────────────────────────┘
3.7 mil. BC   4000 BC                        AD 2100
```

Significance

The Scientific Revolution of the 1500s and 1600s expanded human understanding of the world through the work of scientists such as Isaac Newton. The struggles of people who fought for the right to be considered as individuals, to be equal before the law, and to have a voice in their own governments spawned great political revolutions. During the 1600s, 1700s, and 1800s, these revolutions changed Great Britain, North America, and France.

Now we will focus on a third kind of revolution, one that is neither scientific nor political. This revolution began in the 1700s, when power-driven machines began to perform much of the work that people had done before. The changes this industrial technology brought about affected manufacturing, or industry, so deeply that they are referred to as the **Industrial Revolution.** The Industrial Revolution led to such significant changes in the way goods were produced and in the way people lived that it completely transformed the world.

Terms to Define

factors of production   corporation
mechanization   business cycle
mass production   free enterprise

People to Identify

Eli Whitney   Charles Goodyear
James Watt   Samuel Morse
Henry Bessemer   Adam Smith

Places to Locate

London   Manchester
Liverpool   Silesia

Questions to Guide Your Reading

1 Why did the Industrial Revolution begin in Great Britain?
2 How did the factory system change working and living conditions?
3 What new methods and types of businesses produced an industrial economy?
4 What problems led workers to protest the effects of industrialization?
5 What political and economic changes did socialists seek?

The rhythmic grating of the rocking chair against the wooden planks of the front porch punctuated the still summer evening. An American farmer of English and German heritage peacefully scanned the land he and his ancestors had tilled for three generations. The farmer's granddaughter saw the pride in the old man's eyes and asked him to tell her about his life.

The old man thought for a moment and then began:

    ❝ *I think back to all the stories I heard the old folks tell when I was a boy in the 1890s—stories about how our ancestors had left the old country and migrated to America. They farmed and ranched, eking out a living from the land. They did not have tractors, planters, and harvesters. They could not drive a car on paved roads to buy frozen foods at supermarkets or frilly things at fancy stores. I think about how hard they worked, and about how different our lives are because of them.* **❞**

The old man's face crinkled with a smile as he continued:

    ❝ *I look back over my life and I realize that I have lived in one of the most exciting times in American history. As a boy I knew the old pioneers. As a young man at the turn of the century I saw more changes within a few years than generations of old folks had seen in a lifetime. And now, I look out onto this land and I see the promise of modern technology fulfilled, a better life for the generations to come, and new frontiers to explore.* **❞**

The conversation between the grandfather and his granddaughter took place during the early 1970s in Texas, but the rapid changes the old man witnessed were the product of the Industrial Revolution, which changed the way goods were produced and the way people lived.

1 The Industrial Revolution Began in Great Britain

A revolution in agriculture preceded and made possible the Industrial Revolution. Both the agricultural revolution and the Industrial Revolution began in Great Britain.

◀ *New York's Fifth Avenue 1913*

The Agricultural Revolution

Before the 1600s English villagers used common lands jointly for pastures and other agricultural endeavors. Then in the 1600s, English farmers began to fence off, or enclose, these common lands into individual holdings. The farmers combined scattered lands to form larger holdings that were efficient for large-scale farming. This **enclosure movement** continued into the 1700s. Finally, in the early 1800s, the increased demand for agricultural products in growing cities and the need for Great Britain to feed its own people during the Napoleonic Wars made large-scale farming a necessity.

The enclosure movement had two significant results. First, as large landowners added to their holdings, they forced owners of small plots to either become tenant farmers or give up farming and move to the cities. Second, since land did not have to be farmed in common, farmers could experiment with their new methods of farming without having to seek the consent of the other villagers.

Among the first who experimented in the early 1700s were the so-called "gentlemen farmers" such as Jethro Tull. Concerned about the wasteful practice of scattering seeds by hand over a wide area, Tull invented a seed drill, which made it possible to plant seeds in regular rows.

Experiments showed Tull that crops grew better if he periodically removed the weeds and broke up the soil between the rows of plants. Tull invented a horse-drawn cultivator to do this work.

Another English gentleman farmer, Viscount Charles "Turnip" Townshend, found a way to avoid another wasteful practice. Traditionally, farmers left some of their fields unplanted, or fallow, each year to allow nutrients to replenish the soil. By repeated experiments Townshend learned that alternating different kinds of crops would preserve soil fertility. For example, he would plant grain crops such as wheat and barley one year and root crops such as turnips the next. This system, called **crop rotation,** has become a basic principle of modern farming.

Additional improvements in machinery made farm labor easier and increased production. For example, iron plows replaced wooden ones. An American blacksmith, Robert Ransome, invented an iron plow in three parts so that a farmer could replace a broken part at low cost, rather than having to buy a whole new plow every time one part broke.

Some of the new agricultural techniques and machines were expensive. Farmers who could afford them made large profits, but many farmers with small holdings could not afford additional equipment.

By the 1800s improvements in agriculture had decreased the demand for farm laborers. Many unemployed farm workers moved to the cities, where they created a large labor force.

Factors of Production

The Industrial Revolution that followed the agricultural revolution began in Great Britain because a certain combination of conditions existed there. Great Britain had what economists call the **factors of production,** or the basic resources necessary for industrialization: land, capital, and labor.

When economists speak of *land,* they are referring to all natural resources, of which Great Britain had an abundant supply—particularly of coal and iron ore. Furthermore, Britain's excellent harbors facilitated trade, and its many rivers provided waterpower and inland transportation.

Great Britain also had access to capital. *Capital* includes money and goods such as tools, machinery, equipment, and inventory, which are used in the production process. Since the Commercial Revolution, many British people had grown wealthy from trade and could use this wealth to invest in new businesses.

In addition to land and capital, Great Britain had an abundant supply of industrial workers, primarily because the agricultural revolution had forced many farm laborers to seek jobs in cities. Furthermore, Great Britain could supply management to direct the development of industry. Traditionally, the British considered it honorable for young people from the upper and middle classes to go into business. Many became managers, and a few people of the lower class now had some opportunity to succeed in business.

Several other conditions help explain why the Industrial Revolution began in Great Britain. The British Isles and overseas colonies represented huge markets that created a large demand for British goods. Additional trade opportunities also existed in many other parts of the world, which could be reached by the British navy and merchant fleet, the best in the world. Equally important was the British government's concern for commercial interests. Parliament passed laws that protected businesses and helped them expand.

The Textile Industry

The cotton textile industry was the first industry in Great Britain to undergo **mechanization,** the use of automatic machinery to increase production. Although England had imported cotton cloth since the late Middle Ages, in the 1600s English businesses began importing raw cotton and employing spinners and weavers to make it into cloth. This industry was an example of the **domestic system,** a system in which men and women work in their homes. Although production increased, all the work was still done by hand, and England could not produce enough cotton cloth to meet the demand for it.

New inventions. The first step toward mechanization came with the improvement of the loom for weaving cloth. A loom is set up with a series of threads, called the warp, strung from top to bottom. The loom operator pushes a shuttle containing the woof, or the thread running crosswise to the warp, back and forth across the loom in a very time-consuming process. In 1733 a clockmaker named John Kay invented the flying shuttle, a cord mechanism that moved the woof thread more rapidly across the loom. Now the weavers could weave faster than the spinners could produce

thread on their simple spinning wheels. The demand for thread rose so dramatically that some people offered a prize for a better spinning machine.

James Hargreaves, a poor English worker, won the prize in 1764 with a machine that he named the spinning "jenny" in honor of his wife. This machine could produce eight times as much thread as a single spinning wheel. Five years later Richard Arkwright made further improvements with a machine called the water frame, a spinning machine driven by waterpower.

Workers could use the jenny and the small, hand-operated, and relatively inexpensive flying shuttle in their homes. However, most people who worked at home could not afford the expensive water frame, which required waterpower and more space. For this reason Arkwright opened a spinning mill, bringing workers and machines together in one place to make goods. Employees worked a set number of hours for a certain amount of money. By 1784 Arkwright employed several hundred workers. This mill marked the beginning of the modern **factory system.**

In 1784 Samuel Crompton combined the best features of the spinning jenny and the water frame in another machine, the spinning mule. Now weavers could get plenty of fine-quality thread. However, even with the flying shuttle, the weavers failed to meet the demand for cloth.

In 1785 an English minister, Edmund Cartwright, met the need for a faster weaving process

Learning from Pictures
Calico cotton cloth, once imported from India, is shown here being manufactured in a Lancashire, England, cotton mill.

491

with his invention of a loom powered by water. Using this power loom, one person could weave as much cloth as 200 hand-loom operators. About the same time, one of Kay's sons invented a way to print colored patterns on cotton cloth.

Effects of mechanization. With all these improvements, cotton cloth became cheaper to produce and sell. As the price went down, the demand increased, and so did the need for more raw cotton. In 1701 England imported 1 million pounds (450,000 kilograms) of cotton. In 1802 it imported 60 million pounds (27 million kilograms).

Most of the imported raw cotton came from the southern United States. At first, cotton cultivation had not been profitable there because it was difficult to remove the seeds to prepare the cotton for market. By hand, one person could clean only one pound (.45 kilogram) of cotton a day. In 1793 Eli Whitney invented the cotton gin, a machine that could do the work of 50 people. Equipped with Whitney's invention, the southern United States met the demands of the British textile manufacturers and became the cotton-producing center of the world.

Steam Engines

Waterpower drove the early machines of the Industrial Revolution. Although waterpower represented a great improvement over human, animal, and wind power, it did have drawbacks. A factory had to be located beside a stream or river, preferably near a natural waterfall or a place where a dam could be built. Often this location was not near transportation, raw materials, a labor supply, or markets. A second drawback was that the water flow could vary greatly with the seasons. People began to look for a continuous, dependable, and portable power source; they found it in steam.

People had observed the power contained in steam since ancient times. It was not until 1712, however, that Thomas Newcomen, an English engineer, produced the first successful steam engine. Initially, workers used Newcomen engines to pump water from mines. These crude machines were more powerful and dependable than water wheels, but they were slow and expensive to operate.

In the 1760s James Watt, a Scottish instrument maker and engineer, studied the Newcomen engine. He invented several improvements and in 1769

Learning from Pictures The Bessemer process shown here serves as part of the manufacturing process of railroad tracks.

produced the modern steam engine. Industry quickly adapted the Watt engine to drive the new spinning and weaving machines. As a result of Watt's invention, steam replaced water as industry's major power source.

Iron and Steel

The invention and availability of more and more machines produced a great demand for iron to make them. From early times people in the British Isles had produced iron, using wood or charcoal to fuel the forges needed to separate the element from its ore. Then someone discovered that coal worked even better than wood or charcoal. As the Industrial Revolution continued, iron and coal became the two major raw materials of modern industry. Great Britain had an enormous advantage over other countries, because it had large amounts of these two resources.

Many early steam engines exploded because the iron used to build them could not withstand the high pressure of steam. Industry needed a stronger, harder metal. Suppliers met this need with steel, which is iron with certain impurities removed. The early process for making steel was slow and expensive, however, and the metal remained rare until the 1850s. During that decade an American, William Kelly, and an Englishman, Henry Bessemer, discovered a new way of making steel. The **Bessemer process** involved forcing air through the molten iron to burn out carbon and other impurities. The process reduced the cost so much that steel became what it is today—the basic material of industrial civilization.

Industrialization in Other Fields

Using steam engines and iron and steel, British manufacturers quickly introduced power-driven machinery in many industries. The production of shoes, clothing, ammunition, and furniture became mechanized, as did printing and papermaking. People used machines to cut and finish lumber, to process foods, and to make other machines.

Some new inventions and innovative processes had important by-products. These by-products often developed into separate industries. For example, iron smelteries used coke, a by-product of coal, to improve the smelting process. Then someone discovered that the gases that coal released during the coke-making process could be burned to give light. During the 1830s London became one of the first cities to pipe in gas to burn in street lamps. By the 1850s hundreds of cities throughout the Western world used gas to light streets and homes.

The production of rubber created another new industry during the 1800s. Rubber was first used to make waterproof shoes and coats, but they became sticky in warm weather. In 1839, after years of experimenting, Charles Goodyear of the United States discovered a process of "curing" rubber to make it more elastic and usable. He mixed the raw rubber with sulfur and then heated the mixture. Goodyear's method, called *vulcanizing,* became the basis of the modern rubber industry.

The oil industry developed after 1850, when people discovered how to use crude oil, or petroleum, to produce paraffin for candles, lubricating oil for machinery, and kerosene for lighting and heating.

Transportation

The Industrial Revolution also transformed transportation. When the revolution first began, land transportation was almost the same as it had been during the Middle Ages. Roads, little more than trails blurred with thick dust in dry weather and buried in deep, slippery mud when it rained, made travel difficult.

A passenger in a stagecoach could travel 50 miles (80 kilometers) in one day, barring unforeseen delays. Packhorses and clumsy wagons carrying heavy goods made even less progress in a day's journey.

Roads and canals. Industrialization made improved transportation necessary. Factories required delivery of raw materials, and finished products had to be transported to markets as quickly as possible. A Scottish engineer, John McAdam, worked out a new way of building roads that improved travel conditions. Layers of carefully selected small stones topped a roadbed of large stones. These roads, called macadam roads, served as models for engineers in later times. Today road builders use asphalt to bind the smaller stones together.

Great Britain and other countries of western Europe also had extensive networks of rivers that served as water highways. Some canals connected them, but workers constructed many more canals after engineers began using locks—gates that regulate the level and flow of water. Many canals were built between 1760 and 1850. However, although canals provided a cheaper and slightly faster form of transportation than roads, new forms of transportation soon competed with them.

Railroads and steamboats. Watt's steam engine offered many possibilities for new means of transportation. In 1814 George Stephenson, an English engineer, perfected a steam-propelled moving engine, or locomotive, that ran on rails. In 1829 Stephenson's famous locomotive, the *Rocket,* pulled a line of cars from Liverpool to Manchester at an amazing speed for that time—29 miles (46 kilometers) per hour. Networks of railroads soon connected much of the Western world. Continuous improvements—steel rails, air brakes, more comfortable coaches, and special cars for different kinds of freight—made railroad transportation fast, safe, and affordable.

Many people tried adapting the steam engine to ships. Robert Fulton, an American who established the first regular inland steamboat service, received credit for accomplishing this task. His boat, the *Clermont,* was launched on the Hudson River in 1807, and immediately began regular trips between

Learning from Pictures *This scene of the Mississippi River is by Currier and Ives, publishers of hand-colored prints depicting United States social history.*

New York City and Albany. Steamboats soon appeared on many of the rivers and lakes of the world.

In 1838 the *Great Western*, a ship operated only by steam, crossed the Atlantic Ocean in 15 days, less than half the time it took a sailing ship. Samuel Cunard of Great Britain, who founded the Cunard Line shipping company, provided regular steamboat service across the Atlantic. Soon ships built of iron and steel instead of wood moved goods all over the world in less time and for less money than ever before.

The Communications Revolution

Science played only a small role in the invention of textile machinery, the steam engine, the locomotive, and the steamship. These inventions represented the work of amateur inventors and engineers and did not come from the scientist's laboratory. In communications, however, science played a significant role in the development of technology.

From early times people had observed electricity and its connection with magnetism, but they had put their knowledge to little practical use. For one thing, no one had found a way to provide a steady flow of electric current. About 1800 an Italian, Alessandro Volta, built the first battery, a device that provided a steady current of electricity. Soon afterward André Ampère of France worked

out principles governing the magnetic effect of an electric current.

Samuel Morse of the United States put the work of Volta and Ampère to practical use. Morse sent an electrical current over a wire to a machine at the other end of the wire. Each time the electricity passed along the wire, the machine clicked. Morse worked out a system of dots and dashes— the Morse code—by which these clicks could be translated into letters of the alphabet. By 1844 Morse's invention, the telegraph, had become a practical communication instrument. Soon telegraph wires, stretched across continents, transmitted ideas at the speed of electricity.

People also found a way to carry electricity under the sea by using cables—heavily insulated telegraph wires. Early in the 1850s, a cable across the English Channel connected Great Britain with the European continent. However, spanning the great distance of the Atlantic Ocean presented enormous difficulties. Not until 1866 did Cyrus Field and a group of Americans finally lay a cable across the Atlantic Ocean. Soon afterward cables connected all continents of the world.

The Spread of Industry

For various reasons the rapid changes in agriculture, industry, transportation, and communications had little effect on the European continent for several years. Many continental European countries did not have raw materials or large, accessible markets in which to sell their products. Great Britain, in order to keep its monopoly on new methods, prohibited the export of machines. It also refused to allow skilled workers to leave the country. In addition, the wars of the French Revolution and the Napoleonic Era slowed Europe's industrial development.

France, however, did develop some industry, especially textiles, iron, and mining. The French government helped this development in two ways. First, it imposed high tariffs to keep out foreign manufactured goods. Second, it encouraged the construction of railroads. However, in the 1800s France remained largely an agricultural country.

Industry grew slowly in the German states because Germany had no efficient central government to aid industrial growth. Although some factories were established in the middle 1800s, real industrialization had to await the unification of Germany in the 1870s.

The United States eagerly adopted British inventions and methods. The United States had everything that it needed for industrial development—national unity and a vast country with rich natural resources. It also had a rapidly increasing population, inventive genius, and a willingness to adopt, to adapt, and to take business risks.

A network of canals and railroads crept across the United States during the 1800s, and industry moved west as transportation developed. The steel industry grew in Pittsburgh and the Great Lakes region, and farm machinery was manufactured in Chicago. By 1869 a railroad connected the east and west coasts of the United States. By 1870 the United States was second only to Great Britain as a manufacturing nation.

Along with the growth of American industry came significant changes in farming. Eli Whitney's cotton gin enabled the southern states to supply cotton to the British textile industry. Another invention was a machine for harvesting grain, patented by Cyrus McCormick in 1834. The McCormick reaper, drawn by horses, freed many farmers from the slow, backbreaking work of cutting grain with a sickle or a scythe. Other inventions, such as the mechanical thresher for separating the grains of wheat from their stalks and hulls, followed.

SECTION 1 REVIEW

1. **Define** Industrial Revolution, enclosure movement, crop rotation, factors of production, mechanization, domestic system, factory system, Bessemer process
2. **Identify** agricultural revolution, James Hargreaves, Richard Arkwright, Eli Whitney, James Watt, Henry Bessemer, John McAdam, Robert Fulton, Samuel Morse, Cyrus Field
3. **Locate** London, Liverpool
4. **Determining Cause and Effect** **(a)** How did the enclosure movement lead to changes in agriculture? **(b)** What were the principal effects of the agricultural revolution?
5. **Analyzing Ideas** Why did the Industrial Revolution begin in Great Britain?
6. **Summarizing Ideas** Why was the Bessemer process so important to industry?
7. **Identifying Ideas** What were four important developments in transportation during the Industrial Revolution?

2 The Factory System Changed Working and Living Conditions

For centuries skilled artisans produced goods of all kinds in their homes or in small shops. The artisan controlled the training of apprentices, the quality and price of goods, and the pace of each workday. During the 1700s the opportunity for a higher standard of living lured thousands of English farm workers to the city to work in the factories spawned by the Industrial Revolution. The emergence of these factories was only one of the many changes the Industrial Revolution created.

The Effect of Machines on Work

The introduction of steam-powered machinery made work easier to do. Instead of spending several years as an apprentice learning a trade, a person could learn to work a machine in a few days.

Employers looked for people who could learn a few simple tasks and soon discovered that women and children could operate machines as efficiently as men. Employers preferred to hire young men and women rather than older, skilled people. Young people did not have set working methods and did not expect high wages. Women and children would work for lower wages than men. Consequently, the early textile factories employed mainly children and young adults under the age of 30.

As machines became more and more available, older skilled workers often found themselves unemployed. Factories no longer needed their abilities as weavers or spinners but would not hire them for simpler work. To make up for their loss of income, many of these people sent their children to work in textile factories while they looked for odd jobs in the cities or on nearby farms.

The Wage System

The factory system differed from the domestic system. Factories brought together large numbers of people. Instead of working on a product from beginning to end, each worker performed only a small part of the entire job. Instead of working in a shop with a few others, dozens of people worked in the same room, under the direction of a shop supervisor.

Under the domestic system a master served as both worker and employer. Under the factory system, a few masters became factory owners, but most became workers. Instead of owning a shop or some tools, artisans now worked for the people who owned the machines and the factories. Factory owners paid their workers wages based on the number of hours worked or the amount of goods produced.

Several factors determined factory workers' wages. First, employers wanted to produce goods as cheaply as possible. Thus, factory owners set wages in relation to other costs of production. For example, if the cost of land or capital increased, the owners lowered wages.

Second, competition for jobs lowered wages. But wages rose when there were not enough workers to do a particular job.

Third, wages often depended on what people could earn at other kinds of work. For example, early employers in textile factories wanted to attract young women as workers. So the employers paid young women more than they would have earned as household servants.

Fourth, wages took into account the needs of a worker and his or her family. Adult men earned higher wages than adult women because people thought men should support the family. Women were thought to be adding "a little something" to a man's wage, even if in reality a woman was the only one earning money for her family.

Workers who earned wages depended entirely on their earnings. Under the domestic system, artisans had owned their tools and the shops they worked in, and apprentices had eventually become masters. Now, someone else employed most workers throughout their lives.

Factory Rules and Regulations

Factory work changed people's work habits. Workers had many rules to follow. They had to arrive at work promptly. They could eat meals and take breaks only at set times, and they could leave only with permission. They worked whether it was hot or cold, winter or summer, day or night. Breaking the rules or missing work for any reason could result in heavy fines, pay cuts, or losing a job.

In the early factories, workers spent 14 hours a day, 6 days a week, on the job. Instead of the work being adjusted to the seasons, as it was under the domestic system or on farms, factory workers had to adjust their lives to the demands of machines, and the machines never needed to rest. Some workers even complained that people in authority expected them to become machines themselves.

Factories were uncomfortable places; they were noisy, dirty, and poorly ventilated. The air was hot and steamy in summer and cold and damp in winter. Sanitary facilities were primitive. Early machines had no safety devices, and serious injuries occurred frequently. Employers provided no accident insurance or other form of compensation for injury.

One of the worst features of early industrialization concerned child labor. Five-year-old children were commonly employed in cotton mills and mines. Conditions were particularly bad in coal mines, where women and children pulled carts through tunnels that were too low to allow a donkey or a grown man to pass through.

Abusive situations in factories soon scandalized Great Britain. In 1832 a parliamentary committee investigated working conditions of children in textile mills. The following exchange between the committee and 23-year-old Elizabeth Bently illustrates the committee's findings:

"*W*hat time did you begin work at the factory?—When I was six years old. . . .

What were your hours of labor in that mill?—From five in the morning till nine at night. . . .

Thonet Rocker

In the 1840s Michael Thonet, an Austrian cabinetmaker, invented a process that revolutionized furniture making. In 1860 he used this process to craft the bentwood rocker shown here. The chair may look familiar because similar chairs are still sold in stores today. Thonet's patent consisted of bending solid wood by steaming it and then clamping a thin strip of steel along one side. This process eliminated complex jointing and carving. It meant that Thonet could hire local people, rather than expensive artisans, for his European factories. Men did the cutting and bending; women and children did the sanding, polishing, and packing.

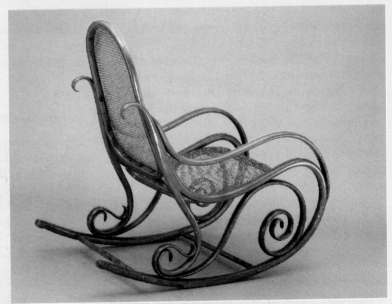

Rocking chair by Gebrüder Thonet. 1860. Bent beechwood; cane, 37 1/2" h. Collection, The Museum of Modern Art, New York. Gift of Cafe Nicholson.

Well before the Industrial Revolution affected the rest of the furniture industry, Thonet's chairs, hat stands, and other pieces were being produced in a factory and marketed to the new middle class. By the end of the 1800s, Thonet's company was making 4,000 pieces of furniture a day—more than 1 million a year—a triumph in mass production.

Were the children [beaten] . . . ?—Yes. . . . What was the reason for that?—[The overlooker] was angry.

Had the children committed any fault?—They were too slow. . . .

You are considerably deformed in your person in consequence of this labor?—Yes, I am.

At what time did it come on?—I was about thirteen years old when it began coming, and it has got worse since. **"**

Living Conditions of Workers

Life in the mines and factories was hard and monotonous, and life in the workers' homes was not much better. Working people lived in cramped and poorly maintained apartment houses called tenements. As many as a dozen people shared a room. As late as 1840, one out of every eight working-class families in Manchester, England, lived in cellars. Many children shared one bed in a sparsely furnished room. The illness, death, or unemployment of a working father or mother could drive a family to the brink of starvation.

Although the working classes suffered during the Industrial Revolution, their living standard improved considerably when cheap goods produced in the factories became available to them. During the 1800s real wages (wages measured in terms of what they will buy) increased rapidly.

Conditions in industrial cities during the Industrial Revolution were shocking compared to living and working conditions today. Compared to conditions in rural areas or nonindustrial cities at the same time, however, they were not so bad. The lower economic classes, whether peasants or artisans, had always worked long and hard. They had always suffered from periodic famines and epidemics. And women and children had always worked hard, especially in rural areas.

The Development of the Middle Class

During the Industrial Revolution, the balance of economic and political power shifted from agriculture to industry. As more jobs became available in cities, the middle class grew. This group consisted of many kinds of people—bankers, manufacturers,

497

merchants, lawyers, doctors, engineers, professors, and their families.

The life of the middle class contrasted sharply with that of the working class. The two groups lived apart—workers in crowded slums, middle-class people in larger houses in more spacious neighborhoods. The two groups dressed differently. Workers wore work shirts and trousers, while lawyers and merchants wore suits. Working-class women dressed in plain skirts and blouses, but the women of the middle class wore lace and frills.

Middle-class people benefited more than workers from the early Industrial Revolution. The laboring poor who worked on farms or in factories continued to suffer economically as had their parents and grandparents. But for the middle class, it was a time of increasing prestige and political recognition. Members of the middle class owned property and could afford to hire servants, to eat well, and to enjoy some comfort.

The members of the middle class were able to send their children to school to receive training for good jobs. Often the younger generation inherited money and social position from their parents.

Learning from Pictures *These young girls are working in a garment shop. How did industrialization affect the working-class women?*

Aristocratic government leaders sought the advice of middle-class economists. Soon government leaders became as concerned about the future of industry as they were about the future of agriculture.

Industrialization Affected Women's Lives

The Industrial Revolution affected women of different classes in different ways. In the past, in addition to working in the fields, women had made clothing at home, spun yarn, woven cloth, and prepared all meals. They manufactured goods for sale and assisted their husbands in craft shops or small family businesses. However, the Industrial Revolution moved most manufacturing into factories. Now all classes of people purchased food and clothing at large markets instead of making these products at home. As a result, important work that women previously had to do at home could now be done by others elsewhere.

Working-class women. The early textile mills hired women to tend machines that spun cotton into thread, a job that required little skill. Many women who had spun thread at home took jobs in the new factories. People referred to these jobs as "women's jobs," although a few men also performed them. Industrialization changed the location of work for working-class women, but it did not raise the status of their jobs.

While some working-class women took factory jobs, many others continued to work at a traditional job for women—domestic service. For centuries young, single women had been hired as maids, cooks, and nannies in other people's houses or businesses. And many men had worked as grooms, gardeners, footmen, coachmen, valets, and butlers. After industrialization more middle-class families could afford to hire servants. As a result, more jobs for servants became available.

As the number of farms declined during the Industrial Revolution, rural areas offered fewer jobs. Daughters of farm families now took jobs as servants in the city. For many country women, domestic service represented a first step into city life. Becoming a servant did not require special skills. In addition, servants lived with the families for whom they worked. Thus an employer guaranteed a young woman moving from the country a place to live and food to eat. After living for a while in the city as a servant, a young woman often took a job in a shop or factory.

Middle-class women. The Industrial Revolution brought new wealth and greater luxury to middle-class women, who could hire servants to cook, clean, and take care of their children. While their husbands left home to go to work each day, middle-class wives stayed home. Middle-class people placed increasing emphasis on the idea that women belonged at home and men belonged in the working world. According to some writers of the day, a woman's nature equipped her only for raising children and caring for the home. More and more people considered earning money, even by doing chores in the house, as a corruption of "true womanhood." Some women accepted and enjoyed this role, but others began to express a very different attitude.

This new attitude arose in Great Britain, where in the mid-1800s many middle-class women did not marry. Many came from families who could not support them throughout their lives. Therefore, they had to support themselves by going to work. Some women whose families could support them believed that women should have the opportunity to work if they wanted to. This idea gradually gained acceptance.

During the late 1800s, more jobs became available for women. The demand for public health care created a need for nurses and social workers, greatly increasing opportunities for women.

Demands also arose for improvements in education. College courses were opened to women, and special women's colleges were established. As public education spread in the 1870s and 1880s in France and Great Britain, the need for teachers increased. Women began to enter the teaching field in large numbers. By the end of the 1800s, elementary school teaching had become almost entirely a female profession.

SECTION 2 REVIEW

1. **Locate** Manchester
2. **Evaluating Ideas** How did machines change the way work was done?
3. **Interpreting Ideas** How were the wages of factory workers determined?
4. **Summarizing Ideas** Describe working conditions in factories and mines.
5. **Classifying Ideas** (a) What jobs were open to women in the late 1800s? (b) How did these jobs affect their lives?

3 New Methods and Giant Businesses Produced an Industrial Economy

Throughout the 1800s inventions, new sales methods, and new methods of production and distribution of goods transformed industry. The rapid growth caused by these developments brought many changes to the factory system and to the organization of businesses. Some of these changes date back to the early Industrial Revolution. Others came about after 1870 as a result of scientific contributions.

The factory system also introduced a new phase in the development of **capitalism**—the economic system in which individuals rather than the government control the factors of production. Before the Industrial Revolution, most capitalists were merchants who bought, sold, and exchanged goods. We call this type of capitalism **commercial capitalism.** However, because the capitalists of the Industrial Revolution became more involved in producing and manufacturing goods themselves, the capitalism of this period is often referred to as **industrial capitalism.**

Division of Labor

As we have seen, industrialization changed the methods of production. Instead of relying on a master and his apprentices, factory owners hired large numbers of unskilled laborers, divided the manufacturing process into a series of simple steps, and then assigned a step to each worker. This process was a form of **division of labor.** Because a large number of items could be produced in a given length of time, the cost of the items diminished. The use of machinery helped the division of labor, since machines performed many of the steps.

Interchangeable Parts

The American inventor Eli Whitney used division of labor to make muskets in the early 1800s. In Whitney's factory some people worked on musket barrels, others on trigger mechanisms, and still others on the wooden stocks or handles.

The use of interchangeable parts for his firearms became an essential part of Whitney's system. He designed machinery that unskilled workers

499

Learning from Pictures *In 1913, Henry Ford's main plant was located in the Detroit suburb of Highland Park.*

could operate. This machinery turned out identical, interchangeable parts. This development made division of labor possible in a product composed of several parts that had to fit together. Whitney's system resulted in the speedy production of a large number of inexpensive muskets that could be easily repaired. If part of a musket broke, repair involved inserting an identical replacement part. Other manufacturers, realizing the usefulness of interchangeable parts, quickly adopted Whitney's principle.

The Assembly Line

Division of labor and the system of interchangeable parts constituted two essential elements of **mass production.** Mass production is the system of manufacturing large numbers of identical items.

A third element of mass production is the assembly line. Until the late 1800s, separate parts were brought together and assembled into a final product at a central point—a slow and inefficient process. Then manufacturers devised the assembly line. A conveyor belt carried the unfinished products past each worker in turn. As each item passed, each worker performed a special task. The assembly line saved time and energy and increased the number of times per hour a worker could perform the assigned task.

Henry Ford saw great potential in the mass-production system. By applying it to the manufacture of automobiles, he founded one of the largest industries in the United States. A conveyor belt carried the frame of the automobile from one worker to the next. Each worker made a small contribution to the finished product by adding one or more of the 5,000 interchangeable parts that composed the Model T Ford. Mass production lowered the price of automobiles and made them available to most American families.

American and European industrialists began to mass-produce clothing, furniture, and machinery. Because mass production usually lowered the cost of an item, more people could buy more things and enjoy a higher standard of living.

Rise of the Corporation

Before the Industrial Revolution, most businesses were either sole proprietorships or partnerships. A business owned and controlled by one person is a **sole proprietorship,** while a **partnership** is a business owned and controlled by two or more people. Although both types of business organizations give their owners considerable freedom to make economic decisions, both types have disadvantages. For example, both sole proprietors and partners are responsible for all debts even if the debts exceed the original amount of investment. In addition, sole proprietorships and partnerships usually remain small. Small companies with few workers cannot use mass-production methods or afford to buy the machinery necessary for large-scale production.

As the scale of business grew during the 1800s, so too did the corporation. A **corporation** is a business organization in which individuals buy shares of stock, elect directors to decide policies and hire managers, and receive dividends according to the number of shares they own. In contrast to sole proprietors and partners, the shareholder's financial responsibility is limited to the amount that he or she invests. For this reason corporations attract greater numbers of investors.

In the late 1800s, corporations increased greatly both in the amount of capital invested and in the size of the manufacturing establishment or group of enterprises. In 1901 American financier J. P. Morgan and his associates formed the United States Steel Company, the first of many billion-dollar corporations. Banks and other financial institutions played an increasingly important role in forming and operating these large corporations.

Increasing the size of a corporation, however, did not solve all the corporation's problems. A large manufacturing enterprise could produce goods at a lower cost than a small one. To get lower costs, however, the factory had to operate at full capacity, turning out as many goods as possible. Sometimes the factory produced so many goods that selling them all became a problem.

If a number of corporations were producing the same products, competition became very keen. The smaller and less efficient businesses suffered if they tried to sell their products by cutting prices. Often these smaller firms had to sell out to larger firms.

As a result, although the size of individual corporations increased steadily, the number of corporations in some industries decreased. Sometimes a corporation would buy so many smaller companies that it would create a monopoly. A **monopoly** is the control of the total production or sale of a good or service by a single firm. In the United States, corporations such as Standard Oil and United States Steel created monopolies.

By 1900 many corporations in Germany had combined to control entire industries. These combinations of corporations were known as **cartels.** For example, a cartel might own coal and iron mines, steel mills, and factories that used steel to build machines, thus controlling all parts of an industry.

Business Cycles

As industrial production became more and more important, it influenced a country's entire economy. The Industrial Revolution brought alternating periods of prosperity and decline—a pattern known as the **business cycle.**

When one industry did well, other industries also prospered. If, for example, there was a great demand for machines, there would also be a demand for the coal and iron needed to make them. If, on the other hand, a large firm reduced its orders of iron and laid off workers, other companies would also be affected. The iron suppliers might have to cut down production and lay off workers. The workers then would have to find other jobs, because without wages they could not pay their rent or buy food. When the number of available workers exceeded the number of jobs available, employers could reduce wages. The effects would go on spreading to other industries, until the entire economy was in a **depression**—the lowest point of a business cycle.

These economic fluctuations affected the lives of all the people in an industrialized country, even those people who did not work in factories. In addition, events in one country could affect the economy of another country. During the American Civil War, for example, the United States could not ship cotton to Great Britain. The shortage of cotton set off a depression in the British textile industry.

SECTION 3 REVIEW

1. **Define** capitalism, commercial capitalism, industrial capitalism, division of labor, mass production, sole proprietorship, partnership, corporation, monopoly, cartel, business cycle, depression
2. **Identify** interchangeable parts, assembly line
3. **Evaluating Ideas** **(a)** What is the chief advantage of mass production? **(b)** What three elements are needed to make mass production possible?
4. **Comparing Ideas** What advantages did corporations have over sole proprietorships and partnerships?
5. **Analyzing Ideas** Why did corporations grow larger as the Industrial Revolution progressed?

4 Living and Working Conditions Gradually Improved

As the Industrial Revolution progressed, the interests of employers often conflicted with the interests of workers. Employers needed workers who would come to work on time, do their jobs quickly and well, follow the rules of the factory, and accept relatively low wages.

Workers, on the other hand, needed wages high enough to support their families even in time of illness or high prices. They wanted some control over their work hours, the conditions in the factories, and the conditions in the towns where they lived. Nevertheless, governments, influenced by certain economic theories that had become widespread as the Industrial Revolution progressed, at first refused to yield to workers' demands.

Adam Smith

During the Enlightenment of the 1700s, a group of economists attacked the ideas of mercantilism, the economic theory based on the belief that the world contained only a fixed amount of wealth and that in order to increase its wealth, a country had to take some wealth from another country. These economists believed that natural laws governed economic life. Any attempt to interfere with these natural economic laws was certain to bring disaster. Adam Smith, a Scot, best stated the views of these economists in his book *The Wealth of Nations*, published in 1776.

Smith reasoned that two natural laws—the law of supply and demand and the law of competition—regulate all business and economic activity. In any business, Smith believed, prices—and therefore profits—will be fixed by the relationship of supply to demand. If an article is scarce and in great demand, people will pay a high price for it. Thus profits from its sales will rise. People will then invest their money to produce more of the scarce article. Soon the supply of the article will exceed the demand for it.

Now each manufacturer will face competition. In order to get people to buy a product, the manufacturer will have to reduce the price or improve the quality, or both. If too many manufacturers produce the same article, the price of the item will go down so far that some manufacturers will not make enough money to cover their costs. The least efficient businesses—those that are so poorly organized and managed that their production costs are high—may be forced out of business. When such manufacturers quit producing the article, the supply of the article will decrease and the price will go up. Then the capable, efficient, and well-organized producers will make a reasonable profit.

Adam Smith wrote that every person should be free to go into any business and to operate it for the greatest advantage. The result, Smith said, would benefit everyone. Laborers would have jobs, investors and owners would make profits, and buyers would receive better goods at lower prices. Smith's system was one of complete **free enterprise.**

Smith's ideas appealed to industrialists because the forces he outlined supposedly worked automatically. Smith argued that if anything interfered with the absolutely free working of supply and demand and competition, the system could not work well. Laws and regulations, such as those imposed under mercantilism, were thought of as interfering with the workings of natural law.

Learning from Pictures Adam Smith asserted that if business or government undermined the laws of a free competitive market, economic life would break down.

READ
WRITE
●INTERPRET
CONNECT
THINK

BUILDING HISTORY STUDY SKILLS

Interpreting Visuals: Determining Cause and Effect

Understanding history requires that you identify the causes of historical events and determine their effect on history. A *cause* is the reason that something happened. An *effect* is the result or consequence of an action or a situation. Usually an event, an idea, or a situation results from several causes. Causes can be divided into two types. Underlying causes are long-term. Immediate causes lead directly to an event. For example, practicing a sport may lead to a championship. The immediate cause of that victory, however, is the winning game.

How to Determine Cause and Effect

To determine cause and effect, follow these steps.

1. Identify the focal point of your study.
2. Determine the underlying causes. For example, did new ideas cause people to act in a certain way?
3. Identify the immediate cause. For example, did a political candidate win or lose an election because bad weather resulted in a low voter turnout?
4. Formulate a conclusion about the significance of the causes and effects of a historical event.

Developing the Skill

Economists often wonder why industrialization suddenly "takes off" at a certain time in a particular place. Walter Rostow, a twentieth-century economic historian, has advanced the theory that every society develops according to a dynamic production pattern that consists of five stages. The chart below explains the five stages of Rostow's theory.

The chart shows that in stage one, the economy is based on agriculture. Traditional values prevail. The underlying causes for the Industrial Revolution are economic, political, social, and intellectual. Economically, there needs to be an agricultural surplus that generates capital. The traditional social structure declines with the rise of a commercial class. A centralized national government encourages economic modernization. Ideas about the benefits of profit are praised rather than degraded. The immediate cause of the production pattern originates from a surge of production and the rapid expansion in one industry, which serves as the basis for modernization. The significance of the process is that in order for the Industrial Revolution to occur, a social, political, and intellectual change must take place. The economic system is intertwined with the culture and the value system.

Practicing the skill. Use the characteristics of society on the chart as the basis for constructing your own chart on the development of the space industry.

To apply this skill, see Applying History Study Skills on page 513.

Rostow's Theory of Industrial Development					
Characteristics	Stage One: *Traditional Society*	Stage Two: *Pre-Conditions for Take-Off*	Stage Three: *Take-Off*	Stage Four: *Drive to Maturity*	Stage Five: *Age of Mass Consumption*
Economy	• agricultural • limited production	• agricultural surplus • surplus capital • expansion of trade	• surge of technology • rapid expansion of industry	• technology extended to all sectors	• increased production and use of durable goods
Society	• hierarchical social structure	• beginning of a commercial class	• Entrepreneurial class more dominant	• urbanization • skilled and professional workers increase	• rise of a new middle class • shift to suburbs
Political Power	• regionally based power in the hands of landowners	• centralized national government	• groups in power encourage economic modernization	• industrial leaders highly influential	• social welfare • more resources for military
Values	• belief that change will not occur	• spirit of progress	• investment of capital for profit becomes important	• emphasis on technology • expectation of progress	• acquisition of consumer goods important

*"Rostow's Theory of Industrial Development" (chart) is based on information from *The Stages of Economic Growth* by W. W. Rostow. Published by Cambridge University Press (England), 1971.

Thomas Malthus and David Ricardo

Smith's ideas received strong support from Thomas Malthus and David Ricardo. Malthus was an Anglican clergyman who became a professor of economics. In his book *An Essay on the Principle of Population,* published in 1798, he wrote that population increases present the greatest obstacle to human progress. People, he said, multiply more rapidly than the food supply increases, despite such checks as famines, epidemics, and wars. He believed that human misery and poverty are inevitable.

David Ricardo was an English businessman who built up a large fortune early in life and then was elected to the House of Commons. He, too, wrote that working-class poverty was inevitable. In his book *Principles of Political Economy and Taxation,* published in 1817, Ricardo stated that supply and demand determined wages. When labor was plentiful, wages remained low. When it was scarce, wages soared. As population grew, Ricardo wrote, more and more workers would become available and wages would inevitably drop. Ricardo's idea became known as the "iron law of wages."

Malthus and Ricardo painted a grim picture of the worker, condemned to inevitable poverty and suffering by unchangeable laws. Understandably, the new social science of economics became known as the "dismal science."

Laissez-faire

The writings of economists supported early industrialists who wanted to buy labor, like any other commodity, as cheaply as possible. Economic theories also indicated that governments should not interfere with the operations of business. This attitude was summed up in the French phrase **laissez-faire** (le • say-FAYR), meaning "let do" or leave things alone.

The British put the theory of laissez-faire into practice during the 1800s. Formerly either the government or the guilds had regulated the quantity and quality of goods produced, the hours and wages of workers, and the qualifications of apprentices and masters. In the middle 1800s, most regulations were discontinued. Tariffs, which had been used to regulate foreign trade, were abolished. Free trade became the rule. Other European countries and the United States adopted many features of laissez-faire economics, although not as completely as Britain.

Growing Interest in Reform

As time went on, more and more people realized that things could not be left entirely alone. Humanitarians—people who work to improve the conditions of others—urged reforms. Ministers preached against what they considered the unchristian selfishness of businesspeople.

Influential writers made people aware of the terrible conditions in mines and factories. The great English writer Charles Dickens used his novels *Dombey and Son* and *Hard Times* to attack selfish business leaders. In *David Copperfield* Dickens described his own wretched boyhood experiences as a worker in a warehouse. Essayists and critics such as Thomas Carlyle and John Ruskin denounced the materialism—the obsession with money and the neglect of spiritual values—of their times.

Many people began to feel that government needed to regulate work hours and set minimal standards for wages and working conditions. These people argued that such laws would not interfere with the natural workings of the economy.

In Great Britain some reformers adopted Jeremy Bentham's ideas. Bentham strongly believed that every act of a society should be judged in terms of its utility, or usefulness. His theory was thus known as **utilitarianism.** A law was useful, and therefore good, said Bentham, if it led to "the greatest good for the greatest number" of people. The "greatest good" meant whatever brought happiness to the most people. Bentham believed that people needed education so they could determine what things were good for them.

Bentham and his followers advocated reform of the prison system and education as well as legal reform. They thought government should create conditions to enable as many people as possible to find happiness.

John Stuart Mill

Philosopher John Stuart Mill, although a believer in laissez-faire, criticized the economic injustices and inequalities of British society. Mill worked to correct the problems associated with industrialization. He thought government should intervene to protect working children and improve housing and factory conditions. Mill's father had been associated with Bentham and had taught his son the principles of utilitarianism.

Hard Times

English novelist Charles Dickens (1812–1870) achieved lasting fame for his portrayal of British society during the early Industrial Revolution. The following excerpt describes Coketown, a town spawned by the Industrial Revolution.*

66 It was a town of red brick, or of brick that would have been red if the smoke and ashes had allowed it; but as matters stood it was a town of unnatural red and black like the painted face of a savage. It was a town of machinery and tall chimneys, out of which interminable serpents of smoke trailed themselves for ever and ever, and never got uncoiled. It had a black canal in it, and a river that ran purple with ill-smelling dye, and vast piles of buildings full of windows where there was a rattling and a trembling all day long, and where the piston of the steam-engine worked monotonously up and down like the head of an elephant in a state of melancholy madness. It contained several large streets all very like one another, and many small streets still more like one another, inhabited by people equally like one another, who all went in and out at the same hours, with the same sound upon the same pavements, to do the same work, and to whom every day was the same as yesterday and tomorrow, and every year the counterpart of the last and the next. . . .

Seen from a distance . . . Coketown lay shrouded in a haze of its own, which appeared impervious to the sun's rays. You only knew the town was there, because you knew there could have been no such sulky blotch upon the prospect without a town. A blur of soot and smoke, now confusedly tending this way, now that way, now aspiring to the vault of Heaven, now murkily creeping along the earth, as the wind rose and fell, or changed its quarter: a dense formless jumble, with sheets of cross light in it, that showed nothing but masses of darkness:—Coketown in the distance was suggestive of itself, though not a brick of it could be seen. . . .

The streets were hot and dusty on the summer day. . . . Stokers emerged from low underground doorways into factory yards, and sat on steps, and posts, and palings, wiping their swarthy visages, and contemplating coals. The whole town seemed to be frying in oil. There was a stifling smell of hot oil everywhere. The steam-engines shone with it, the dresses of the Hands were soiled with it, the mills throughout their many stories oozed and trickled it. 99

---

*Coke is the residue left after distillation of coal or other materials such as petroleum. Coke was often used as fuel.

Mill believed government should work for the well-being of all its citizens. Governments would pass good laws, he said, only if the laws met the interests of all individuals and groups. People would obey laws if they felt they had a part in making the laws. Mills wrote that because governments must represent all citizens, everyone of a certain age, including women, should be allowed to vote. "All human beings have the same interest in good government," he wrote in 1861. "The welfare of all is alike affected by it, and they have equal need of a voice in it to secure their share of its benefits."

In Mill's view individual liberty, which included the liberty to think as one pleased and to express one's views, was a basic human right. Mill believed governments should guarantee that liberty.

Early Reform Laws

Great Britain made the first attempts to improve working conditions through legislation. The earliest laws dealt with the employment of women and children. Working conditions for these two groups, in particular, scandalized many people.

The Factory Act of 1819 illustrates how bad working conditions had become. The act prohibited the employment of children under nine years of age in cotton mills. Children between the ages of 9 and 18 could work no more than 12 hours a day. In 1833 this law was applied to all textile factories. Children between the ages of 9 and 13 could work no more than 9 hours daily, and those between ages 13 and 18 could work no more than 12 hours a day.

Nine years later another law prohibited the employment in mines of all women and girls and of boys under 10. A great advance came in 1847 with the passage of the Ten Hours Act. This law established a 10-hour working day for women and for children under the age of 18 in textile factories. Since it was not profitable to keep the factories running when the women and children were gone, textile factories adopted the 10-hour workday for all workers.

Despite these reform laws, the conditions under which many workers labored remained harsh. Laws often were not strictly enforced, and they did not solve all of the workers' problems. For example, the factory reform laws did not deal with wages. Eventually, workers would achieve improved working conditions through more organization and government legislation.

Worker Strikes

One way that workers could protest poor working conditions and low wages was for a group of them to refuse to work. A group of miners, for example, who believed they were being paid too little for their work would refuse to enter the mines. When an entire group of workers refused to work, they were said to be on **strike.** Workers often made a list of their demands and told the employer they would not work until these demands were met. Employers sometimes agreed to give the strikers what they wanted. At other times the employers either fired all the strikers and hired new workers, or waited until the workers returned to work.

Hundreds of strikes took place in industrial countries during the first half of the 1800s. The strikers usually made two kinds of demands—higher wages for workers and more control over working conditions.

Strikes were usually local events. But in some cases, the strikes spread from one town to another. In the 1830s, for example, shoemakers in one French town after another went out on strike demanding higher wages. Tailors and carpenters went on similar waves of strikes.

Learning from Pictures These young textile workers in Philadelphia are on strike. In the early 1900s, 1.7 million children under 16 were employed.

Sometimes strikes began as demands for higher wages but became protests against general working and living conditions of the working class. Strike leaders demanded a reorganization of society to end the differences between rich and poor, employers and workers.

Large protest movements occurred in northern England in 1811 and 1812; in the silk-weaving city of Lyons, France, in 1831 and 1834; and in Silesia, in eastern Europe, in 1844. The protests ended when the governments sent troops to arrest protesting workers.

The Union Movement

In order to strengthen their position, workers sought ways to organize permanently. They felt their efforts would be more successful if they belonged to associations of workers. These associations would collect dues and use the money to pay workers while they were on strike. The associations could plan actions and coordinate the demands of different types of workers in the same factory. These associations came to be called **unions.**

Organizing unions was not easy. English, French, and German law, for instance, regarded workers' associations as illegal. When English workers tried to unite anyway, employers persuaded Parliament to pass laws against them. The Combination Acts of 1799 stated that persons who united with others to demand higher wages, shorter hours, or better working conditions could be imprisoned.

Eventually, however, the workers began to make some progress. In 1825 Parliament passed a law that permitted laborers to meet in order to agree on wages and hours. Finally, in the 1870s Parliament passed laws legalizing strikes. The French government legalized unions in 1884, and the German government followed suit in 1890.

Now that workers had gained the legal rights to form unions and to strike, they had more power to deal with employers. Gradually, factory owners granted unions recognition; they agreed that union representatives could speak and bargain for all the members. Union and management representatives met to negotiate wages, hours, and working conditions. If the bargainers could agree, they wrote their agreements into a contract that would last for a fixed period of time. This process of negotiation, called **collective bargaining,** became accepted only during the 1900s.

SECTION 4 REVIEW

1. **Define** free enterprise, laissez-faire, utilitarianism, strike, union, collective bargaining
2. **Identify** Adam Smith, Thomas Malthus, David Ricardo, Charles Dickens, Jeremy Bentham, John Stuart Mill
3. **Locate** Lyons, Silesia
4. **Evaluating Ideas** (a) According to Adam Smith, how did the law of supply and demand and the law of competition work? (b) What conclusion did Smith draw from these laws?
5. **Interpreting Ideas** How was the theory of utilitarianism applied to social reform?
6. **Summarizing Ideas** What were the two kinds of demands usually made by strikers?
7. **Analyzing Ideas** Why were unions created?

5 Socialists Proposed Radical Changes

In the economy that resulted from the Industrial Revolution, a few people became enormously rich, but most remained poor. The uneven distribution of wealth disturbed many people. Some reformers became convinced that laissez-faire capitalism was not the best economic system. They argued that laws could not do enough to remedy inequalities. The only way to distribute wealth more evenly, they thought, was to change the ownership and operation of the means of production. The means of production include the capital and equipment used to produce and exchange goods—for example, land, mines, railroads, factories, stores, banks, and machines.

Socialism

Some reformers of the 1800s advocated a political and economic system called **socialism.** In this system the government owns the means of production and operates them for the welfare of all the people.

Socialists wanted to establish an economic system that would abolish the profit motive and competition. They believed that everyone, not just capitalists and owners, had a right to share in the profits of industry.

The early socialists believed that people could live at peace with each other if they lived in small cooperative settlements, owning all the means of

Text continues on page 510.

Historians consider the Industrial Revolution one of the two most important changes that have taken place in the history of the world. Just as the start of agriculture did 10,000 years ago, the Industrial Revolution marks a turning point in history.

The Industrial Revolution is, of course, a more recent change. Just 200 years ago, people could produce goods only by using their own muscles, the muscles of animals, or unreliable sources of power such as wind (in windmills) or water (in watermills). As a result, production was limited.

The Industrial Revolution made it possible to produce goods in abundance. Now people could use machines driven by fuels such as coal and oil. And the supply of these fuels seemed unlimited.

This remarkable change began at a particular time, the late 1700s, and in a particular country, Great Britain. Why then and why there?

For one thing, after the mid-1700s, the demand for manufactured goods such as cloth grew rapidly and outran the capacity of small, rural clothmakers, who often worked in their own homes. The population grew faster than the supply of goods. Moreover, European countries had established empires in other parts of the world: North and South America, Asia, and Africa. A European country that could produce goods quickly and cheaply had existing markets—both at home and overseas. The demand was there. The problem was how to satisfy it. Here, Britain had an advantage over its European neighbors. Because of advances in agriculture, Britain had better farm machinery and more scientific methods of cultivation than the rest of Europe. This paved the way for industry because fewer farm workers were needed, and more workers were available for other jobs.

BE UNITED AND INDUSTRIOUS

In contrast, Britain was a country with limited government, enthusiasm for change, and a stimulating contact with the outside world. By the 1780s the Industrial Revolution had begun to transform the textile industry, and in 1785 Richard Arkwright applied the technology of the steam engine to textile production.

More than any other invention, the steam engine drove the Industrial Revolution forward by providing a source of power that did not depend upon human muscle or the power of the wind or moving water. The growth in power now available to produce goods was remarkable. An average worker using only muscle can provide one-tenth of one horsepower. Most 18th-century watermills reached five horsepower. But the steam engines of 1800 could produce between 6 and 20 horsepower.

Already wealthy because of trade with the outside world, Britain could afford to invest in new ventures. In addition, the British government safeguarded property against seizure by the government. Both these facts provided a perfect climate for individual and industrial innovation. Thus, a talented inventor like James Watt, who devised an efficient steam engine, found himself richly rewarded for his work—in a country where such wealth was secure.

Even the other wealthy countries of western Europe could not match Britain's advantages. By 1763 France had lost much of its empire to Britain, and in 1789 a revolution toppled the Bourbon monarchy. The Netherlands, another rich nation, had a small population and lacked Britain's manufacturing experience.

Industrial change was even less probable in non-Western nations such as China. There, society valued stability and continuity over change. The Chinese saw themselves as members of an advanced and self-contained society, one that did not need contact with the outside world. Chinese were even prevented from settling overseas.

Industrial change spread in two important ways. First, new industries sprang up as people applied the steam engine to new uses. Second, the Industrial Revolution crossed from Britain to other countries. Between 1815 and the 1850s, steam engines, factories, and railroads began to appear in parts of France, Belgium, Holland, Germany, and northern Italy.

After 1870 the Industrial Revolution entered still another phase. It is the period that extends to the present, and some historians call it the "Second Industrial Revolution." Electric power and the internal combustion engine now joined the steam engine. Many of the latest products of industry—the telephone, the automobile, radio, and television—became available to almost all citizens of industrialized countries.

The great industrial transformation that had begun in the special conditions of Great Britain soon encircled the globe.

Photos Page 508: emblem of an early labor union (top), ironworks in Wales (bottom); Page 509: Paris Exhibition of 1878 (top), steam harvester in California (bottom left), a schematic view of Watt's steam engine (bottom right)

Learning from Pictures *Robert Owen's cooperative community of New Harmony, located in southern Indiana, lasted only two years.*

production in common and sharing the products. The socialists tried to work out detailed schemes for model communities and then tried to persuade people to set up the communities. Thomas More, an English humanist, described such a model community in 1516 in his *Utopia*. Thus these early socialists were sometimes called **utopian socialists.**

In Great Britain the most influential utopian socialist was Robert Owen, who lived from 1771 to 1858. As a boy Owen quit school and went to work. By the age of 19 he managed a large cotton mill. Eventually, he became both owner and manager of a large mill in New Lanark, Scotland.

Owen believed in the natural goodness of people. If they lived in a good environment, he thought, they would cease to act selfishly. As a factory owner, Owen felt responsible for his workers and devoted much time and money to making their lives happier and more secure. He built nice homes for them, paid them decent wages, established a store where they could buy inexpensive food, and set up schools for their children.

Owen believed, however, that workers should not be completely dependent on their employers. He encouraged workers to form unions. He also established cooperative communities in both Great Britain and the United States.

The Theories of Karl Marx

Some thinkers grew impatient with early socialism, which they regarded as impractical. Their primary objections, however, concerned capitalism and the Industrial Revolution. Karl Marx, a journalist and the most important of these critics, was born in Prussia in 1818. Marx's radical political views made him unpopular in his own country. Forced to leave, he eventually settled in London, where he lived until his death in 1883.

Marx believed that all the great changes in history came from changes in economic conditions. In 1848, with a fellow German, Friedrich Engels, Marx published the *Communist Manifesto*, a pamphlet outlining his ideas.

Marx wrote that human history had moved through several stages. First, people had shared property and worked together in small communities or tribes. Then slavery arose. Some people owned all the property as well as people who were forced to work for them. Feudalism followed slavery, according to Marx. Under feudalism, landowners controlled the lives of serfs, who depended on them for land and food. Capitalism emerged from feudalism and brought with it industrial development. Capitalists owned machinery and tools and employed workers in their factories.

Marx stated that each stage of history involved inequality, and therefore struggle, between those who owned property and those who did not. In the capitalist stage, for example, the struggle existed between the owners, or **bourgeoisie** (boorzh • wah • ZEE), and the working class, or **proletariat** (proh • luh • TAYR • ee • uht).

Marx argued that all wealth is created by labor. Under capitalism, he said, labor receives only a small fraction of the wealth it creates. Most of the wealth goes to the owners in the form of profits, which Marx called surplus value. As a result of this unequal distribution of wealth, the capitalist system necessarily suffered from increasingly severe depressions because working people lacked money to buy the products manufactured in the factories. He thought the time would soon come when capitalist society would divide into two classes—a few capitalists and a vast mass of workers, or proletarians. The proletarians, concentrated in cities, would suffer poverty and unemployment.

In these circumstances the proletarians in the most advanced and industrialized nations would unite, seize power by force in a revolution, and establish socialism. Since many people would not readily accept socialism, initially the workers would have to control the government. Marx referred to this phase as the "dictatorship of the proletariat." After a period of education, people would become experienced in working together cooperatively. Force would no longer be needed, and the state would "wither away." This last stage, characterized by a truly classless society, Marx called *pure communism.*

Marx believed that pure communism was the inevitable outcome of human history. Each person would contribute what he or she could and would receive what he or she needed. Marx said, "From each according to his abilities, to each according to his needs."

In Marx's time the terms *communism* and *socialism* were used in many different ways. To Marx and Engels, a communist was one who believed that people could live cooperatively without being forced to do so.

Marx called his variety of socialism "scientific socialism" because he thought he was describing objective laws of historical development—laws that would work inevitably. Marx published many of his ideas in *Das Kapital* (German for "capital"), a book that analyzed capitalism in detail.

Variations of Marxist Socialism

In the mid-1800s socialists began forming political parties to put their ideas into practice. The ideas of Marx and Engels influenced many of these parties. Marxist, or radical, socialists generally believed in the necessity of revolution to overthrow the capitalist system. They wanted to establish a system in which the government owns almost all the means of production and controls economic planning. Today we call this economic and political system— which ignores basic human rights—**authoritarian socialism,** or **communism.**

Another group of socialists, though influenced by Marx, believed that socialism could develop gradually through education and democratic forms of government. These moderate socialists believed that when enough people became educated about socialism, they would elect socialist representatives to their government. Then the government would take over the means of production peacefully. The owners would be paid for their property, and the

Learning from Pictures *Karl Marx did not foresee how collective bargaining would better working conditions, avoiding the dictatorship of the proletariat.*

government would operate the means of production in the interest of all the people. Today we call this type of socialism **democratic socialism.** Under democratic socialism, unlike under authoritarian socialism, the people retain basic human rights and partial control over economic planning through the election of government officials. Individuals may own private property, but the government controls at least some of the means of production.

Marx believed that workers had to unite in order to fight capitalism successfully. In 1864 he helped found the International Workingmen's Association, called the First International. This organization disbanded in 1876. A Second International was formed in 1889, after Marx's death. Torn by disagreements between moderate and radical socialists, it survived only into the early 1900s. Elsewhere, particularly in Russia, Marx's ideas would have profound effects.

SECTION 5 REVIEW

1. **Define** socialism, utopian socialist, bourgeoisie, proletariat, authoritarian socialism, communism, democratic socialism
2. **Identify** Thomas More, Robert Owen, Karl Marx
3. **Sequencing Ideas** Describe the stages of history, according to Marx, that would lead to pure communism.
4. **Contrasting Ideas** How do authoritarian socialism and democratic socialism differ?

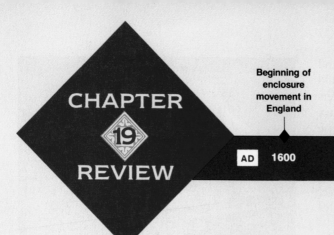

CHAPTER 19 REVIEW

Chapter Summary

The following list contains the key concepts you have learned about the Industrial Revolution and the resulting changes in political and economic thought.

1. The Industrial Revolution—changes brought about by the introduction of power-driven machinery—began in Great Britain. In time the Industrial Revolution transformed the world.
2. The Industrial Revolution was preceded by an agricultural revolution.
3. The replacement of waterpower by steam power was basic to the Industrial Revolution. Almost as important was the development of the Bessemer process, a new method of making steel, that made steel readily available to the newly founded industries.
4. Transportation improved with better roads, networks of canals and railroads, and the use of steam power in ships. The wireless telegraph made rapid communication possible.
5. By gathering workers together in factories, the Industrial Revolution brought an end to the traditional practices of artisans who had worked in their homes or in small shops.
6. Factory workers became dependent on wages and no longer controlled the pace of their work because they had to do what they were told.
7. Living and working conditions were often poor during the early Industrial Revolution.
8. A series of innovations in business practices accompanied the Industrial Revolution. Mass production—based on the division of labor, interchangeable parts, and the assembly line—transformed several industries and permitted the growth of enormous corporations.
9. Workers began to protest harsh working conditions and low wages. The first labor unions were organized to seek improvements in working conditions and to obtain higher wages.
10. Socialists like Karl Marx believed that a more fundamental transformation of politics and society was necessary.

On a separate sheet of paper, complete the following review exercises.

Reviewing Important Terms

Supply the term that correctly completes each sentence.

1. The changes industrial technology brought about affected manufacturing so deeply that they are referred to as the _____ _____ .
2. The basic resources necessary for industrialization (land, labor, and capital) are called the _____ ____ _____ .
3. Alternating crops to replenish nutrients in the soil is called _____ _____ .
4. _____ is the use of automatic machinery to increase production.
5. The _____ _____ involved burning impurities such as carbon out of iron with a blast of air forced through molten metal.
6. A _____ occurs at the lowest point in the business cycle.
7. A _____ occurs when a group of workers refuses to work.
8. The idea that government should not interfere with the operations of business is called _____ .
9. _____ is an economic system in which individuals control the factors of production.
10. A _____ is the control of the total production or sale of a good or service by a single firm.
11. A _____ is a business organization in which individuals buy shares of stock, elect directors to decide policies and hire managers, and receive dividends according to the number of shares they own.

Developing Critical Thinking Skills

1. **Determining Cause and Effect** How did the Industrial Revolution change the relationship between workers and employers that had existed during the Middle Ages?
2. **Using Primary Sources** Laws regulating child labor did not exist in the 1700s. For example, during the early years of the Industrial Revolution, it was common for five-year-old children to work in damp, dark coal mines or poorly ventilated textile mills for as long as 14 hours a day. The lines below, from a poem by Elizabeth Barrett Browning, describe the life of working-class children.

Invention of the steam engine by Thomas Newcomen — 1712

Invention of the spinning "jenny" by James Hargreaves — 1733

Beginning of the factory system — 1764

1774

Invention of the spinning mule by James Crompton — 1784

1793 Invention of the cotton gin by Eli Whitney

Invention of the locomotive by George Stephenson — 1814

Invention of a rubber-curing process by Charles Goodyear

Installation of transatlantic cable — 1866

1769 · 1785 · 1807 · 1839 · 1848

Invention of the flying shuttle by John Kay

Production of James Watt's modern steam engine

1776 Publication of Adam Smith's *Wealth of Nations*

Invention of the power loom by Edmund Cartwright

Beginning of Robert Fulton's inland steam service

Publication of Karl Marx's *Communist Manifesto*

" 'For oh,' say the children, 'We are weary, and we cannot run or leap;
For all day, we drag our burden tiring
Through the coal-dark underground;
Or all day, we drive the wheels of iron
In the factories, round and round.' "

(a) How did Browning view working conditions in Great Britain? **(b)** What evidence in the poem supports your answer? **(c)** Based on information in this chapter, how were working conditions gradually improved?

3. **Relating Ideas** Why might each of the following be considered a result of advances in technology? **(a)** corporations **(b)** unions
4. **Analyzing Ideas** How did industrialization affect the lives of women?
5. **Summarizing Ideas** **(a)** What problems did workers face during the Industrial Revolution? **(b)** What problems did employers encounter?
6. **Understanding Ideas** **(a)** Why did Adam Smith's ideas appeal to industrialists? **(b)** Why did industrialists oppose the ideas of Karl Marx?

Relating Geography to History

Using information in this chapter, write a short essay on the relationship between geography and the Industrial Revolution. For example, how might working conditions have been different if the geography of Great Britain and the United States had not been suited to growing cotton or producing coal?

Relating Past to Present

1. During the Industrial Revolution, many countries held exhibitions to showcase the latest technological developments. Investigate some of the important technological achievements of the 1980s. Use this information to design a poster for a similar exposition in the near future.
2. Use resources in your school or public library to construct a chart showing how long it took to travel from New York to California in 1850, 1900, 1930, and today. Your chart should include what form of transportation people used in each of the years listed.

Applying History Study Skills

Before completing this activity, review Building History Study Skills on page 503.

In the following excerpt from *The Stages of Economic Growth*, W. W. Rostow suggests why the Industrial Revolution began in England. Read the excerpt. Then answer the questions that follow.

" Now why Britain? Why not France? . . .
The French . . . were too rough with their Protestants. They were politically and socially too inflexible, caught up . . . in . . . a caste society. The best minds and spirits of eighteenth-century France . . . had to think about political, social and religious revolution rather than economic revolution. Moreover the French were committed heavily to ground warfare in Europe; and they cheated on shipping and naval strength . . . when ships mattered greatly. . . .
Britain alone was in a position to weave together cotton manufacture, coal and iron technology, the steam-engine, and ample foreign trade to pull it off. "

1. What question is Rostow posing?
2. What are the underlying causes for France's inability to industrialize?
3. What are the underlying causes for Britain's industrializing first?

Investigating Further

1. **Practicing Map Skills** By the 1850s iron and coal had become the two major raw materials of modern industry. Using an atlas, draw an outline map of the world showing the global distribution of these resources today.
2. **Relating Literature to History** Read the chapter entitled "No Way Out" in *Hard Times* by Charles Dickens. As you read, consider the differences between the worker (or "hand") and the owner of the factory. **(a)** How did Dickens portray industrial society in the 1800s? **(b)** What aspects of that society did he seem to be criticizing? **(c)** Why would Dickens be accurate in his description?

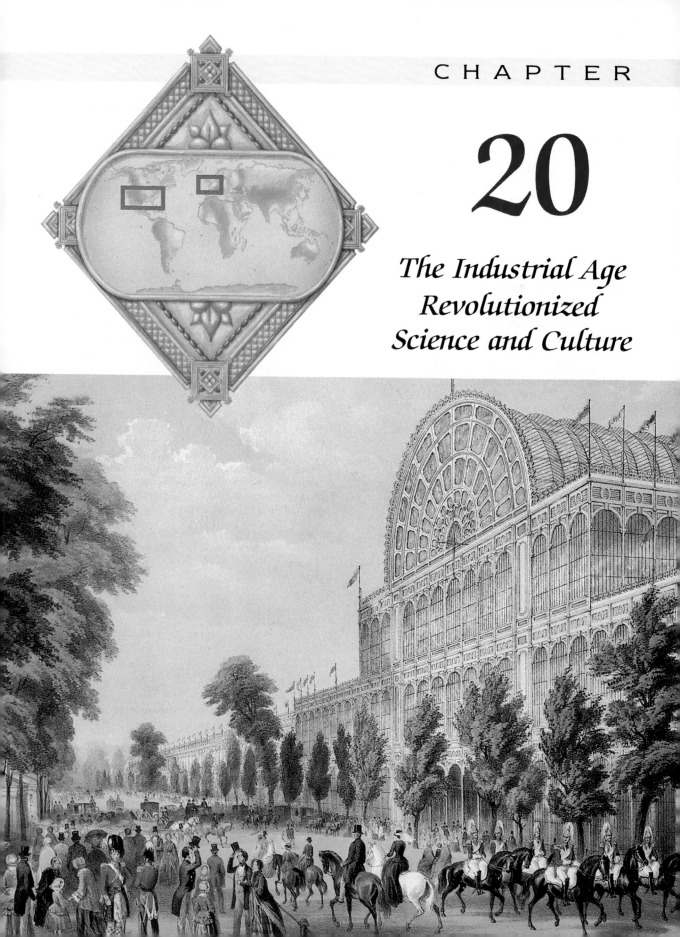

20

The Industrial Age Revolutionized Science and Culture

Place   The United States and Europe

Time   1800–1928

3.7 mil. BC   4000 BC   AD 2100

Significance

In addition to changing the economy and society, the Industrial Revolution had a profound effect on science, art, music, and literature. Improved technology brought about sweeping changes in transportation and communication. Scientists developed new theories to explain the physical world. Advances in medicine greatly improved people's lives. Some people began to apply scientific methods to the study of people, both as individuals and as members of social groups.

In the 1800s compulsory education laws in many countries led to the creation of public schools. As more and more people were educated, a larger audience for intellectual and cultural activities developed.

Some writers and artists glorified progress, science, and change. Others, however, disagreed with this view. They looked to the past and insisted that no scientific theory could ever describe the true spiritual nature of human beings. In music, sculpture, and painting, styles changed frequently and rapidly, responding to the impact of industrialization on people's lives.

Terms to Define

physical science   pasteurization
radioactivity   social science
genetics   romantic movement

People to Identify

Alexander Graham Bell   Charles Darwin
Thomas Edison   Sigmund Freud
Pierre and Marie Curie   Emily Davies

Places to Locate

Kitty Hawk   Paris

Questions to Guide Your Reading

1 What advances were made in technology and communication?
2 What advances were made in science and medicine?
3 What factors helped spur population growth?
4 When did interest in the social sciences and educational institutions develop?
5 How did literature, music, and art reflect the spirit of the times?

Stories of "the good old days" transcend both time and generations. In the following excerpt from Sparks from the Anvil, *Carl Schmidgall, an American inventor and a pioneer in mechanical engineering, recounts boyhood memories of conversations among visitors to his father's blacksmith shop in the early 1900s.*

> *"During the winter months, I have seen and heard many a good political discussion while they sat and stood around our cannon stove. [The upright portion of the stove was shaped like the barrel of a cannon.] There were some hot arguments sometimes over subjects ranging from religion and politics to the welfare of the country. It was here where such men from the crossroads of life met, and during these periods of my entering the shop as a small boy, until I grew to manhood, the information I gained from their talks and arguments gave me much to think about. I learned the philosophy of a better life.*
>
> *There was at times much humor connected with their talks, but there was also present many times the reverence of religion and the ways of mankind. To me all of these things meant that there was room for study—to venture out into the world and to help make it a better place to live in. All through my later years away from the old blacksmith shop, little recollections of it have kindled a spark within my heart which has inspired me."*

Vivid memories of the blacksmith shop and the people he met there inspired Schmidgall as he grew up. By 1916 he was president of his own manufacturing company. Several of his inventions—all of them based on the technology of the Industrial Revolution—are still used today.

1 Advances Continued in Technology and Communication

Beginning about 1870, manufacturers increasingly applied the findings of pure science to their businesses, generating a new wave of industrial growth. The application of scientific solutions to industrial problems resulted in: (1) inventions that provided rapid communication over long distances; (2) the

◀ *The Great Exhibition of London, 1851*

Paris Exposition Poster

In 1889 the French held a spectacular exposition in Paris to celebrate the one hundredth anniversary of the French Revolution. In its many buildings, the exposition featured examples of the tremendous industrial progress that had been made during the nineteenth century. To celebrate the exposition, the French newspaper *Le Figaro* published a special supplement using this poster as its cover. In the foreground is the Seine River; the famous Eiffel Tower soars

in the background. At the time the tower was the tallest structure in the world. It stands as a monument to the engineering skills and achievements of the 1800s.

The 1889 exposition was the first to use electricity extensively. At night the lower part of the Eiffel Tower and the surrounding fountains were lit, creating a spectacular show. People from all over the world traveled to Paris to view the unique exhibits and the splendor of the exposition.

Thousands of exhibits such as advanced machinery, military aircraft, glass, and applied arts were displayed. From a high-moving platform in the Gallery of Machines, under the arch of the Eiffel tower, visitors viewed the inventions developed during the Industrial Revolution. The exposition demonstrated to the world that the 1800s had indeed been technically dynamic. It also provided a preview of technology that would characterize everyday life in the 1900s.

Today, people flock to World's Fairs, which, like the 1889 exposition, showcase technological advances.

---

development and use of new sources of power; and (3) the creation of new products and materials and the improvement of old ones.

By 1900 most people thought of technology and progress as the same thing. Many individuals viewed science as an endless source of new ideas and inventions. Machines seemed capable of constantly improving the quality of life. There appeared to be no end to the progress made possible by industrialization. People thought that science and technology could solve any problems that the Industrial Revolution might create.

Communications

An important development in the communications field occurred in the 1870s when Alexander Graham Bell sent the human voice over a long distance by means of an electrical circuit. Bell, an American, patented his telephone in 1876. Then in 1895 an Italian inventor, Guglielmo Marconi, developed a way to send messages through space without wires.

Marconi's invention was based on the work of two earlier scientists, James Clerk Maxwell of Great Britain and Heinrich Hertz of Germany. Maxwell had made a mathematical study of electricity and magnetism. In 1864 he asserted the existence of invisible electromagnetic waves that travel through

space at the speed of light. In the 1880s Hertz not only proved that such waves did exist, by transmitting and receiving them, but also measured their length and speed.

Marconi invented instruments for sending and receiving these radio waves, as they came to be called. His wireless telegraph soon proved itself valuable for ship-to-ship and ship-to-shore communication. In 1901 he sent the first wireless message across the Atlantic Ocean.

Electricity

As industry grew during the 1800s, manufacturers continued to search for new and better power sources. In the 1870s a tremendous new power source—electricity—was developed.

An English scientist, Michael Faraday, discovered the scientific key to the problem in 1831. From the work of Ampère and other scientists, Faraday knew that electricity could produce magnetism. He wanted to find out whether magnetism could produce electricity. He found that by moving a magnet through a coil of wire he could generate an electric current in the wire.

Faraday concentrated primarily on exploring the nature of electricity. Others used his discovery to develop the dynamo, or electric generator. Driven either by a steam engine or by waterpower, the dynamo transformed mechanical power into electrical energy. This energy in turn could generate power to run machinery in factories.

English and American inventors kept trying to make practical use of another scientific discovery about electricity—that a current passing through certain kinds of wire caused the wire to glow. Here was a possible source of light for city streets, homes, and factories. Electric light bulbs were first produced in 1845, but they burned out in a matter of minutes. In 1879 Thomas Edison, an American, made a bulb that glowed for two days before burning out. In a few years, after further improvements, electric lighting replaced gas lighting.

To make electricity practical, it had to be transmitted from the place it was generated to the place it would be used. After much work on the problem, Edison developed a successful central powerhouse and transmission system that began operating in 1882 in New York City, London, and Milan.

The electrical industry grew rapidly. Waterfalls, such as Niagara Falls, were tapped to run huge dynamos, whose hydroelectric power was sent long distances through wires. Tremendous dams were built in many countries to provide artificial sources of waterpower.

As large-scale production and transmission of electricity became available in the late 1800s, electric motors replaced steam engines in factories. Where hydroelectric power was either unavailable or too expensive, steam engines turned the generators at central powerhouses.

The Internal-combustion Engine

The electric motor had one significant limitation—it had to be connected to its power supply. Therefore, it was not very useful as a means of moving vehicles.

Automobiles. In the late 1800s, several European inventors worked on engines that would use a portable fuel supply of oil or gasoline to propel individual vehicles. The device was called the internal-combustion engine because the combustion, or burning, of fuel took place inside a closed cylinder. (In the steam engine, combustion takes place outside the cylinder.) Pioneers in this field included Gottlieb Daimler and Karl Benz of Germany and Louis Renault of France. In 1893 Charles and Frank Duryea (duhr • ee • AY) built the first successful gasoline-driven automobile in the United

States. Three years later the American inventor Henry Ford produced his first automobile.

Airplanes. Since the 1700s people had used balloons filled with gases lighter than air to float above the ground. Beginning in the 1800s, inventors tried to devise a heavier-than-air machine that would actually fly. Many early airplanes were not designed to carry people. The first people to succeed in flying an airplane in powered, sustained, controlled flight were Wilbur and Orville Wright of the United States. They achieved this feat at Kitty Hawk, North Carolina, in 1903. The flight lasted 12 seconds and covered 120 feet (37 meters).

The Wright brothers' achievement was another example of the combination of science and technology. The Wrights succeeded where others had failed because they had studied aerodynamics—the principles governing the movement of air around objects—and had used the internal-combustion engine to propel their plane through the air. From this modest beginning, today's multi-billion dollar airplane industry developed.

Learning from Pictures In 1909 Louis Bleriot was the first pilot to fly across the English Channel. Where did the first successful airplane flight take place?

1. **Identify** Alexander Graham Bell, Guglielmo Marconi, Thomas Edison, Wilbur and Orville Wright, internal-combustion engine, aerodynamics
2. **Classifying Ideas** What three developments resulted from applying scientific solutions to industrial problems?
3. **Evaluating Ideas** What ideas of earlier scientists did Marconi use?
4. **Summarizing Ideas** What developments made electricity a new source of power?
5. **Interpreting Ideas** How was the internal-combustion engine first used?

2 Advances in Science and Medicine Helped Improve Human Life

The **physical sciences** are those sciences that deal with the inanimate, or nonliving, aspects of nature. They include astronomy, geology, physics, and chemistry. The most significant developments in the physical sciences during the 1800s and early 1900s centered on the atomic theory.

The Atomic Theory

According to modern atomic theory, all matter in the universe consists of very small particles called atoms. The arrangement and structure of these atoms and their chemical combinations with each other account for the different characteristics of the materials that make up our world.

We can trace the beginnings of the atomic theory, as we can many other scientific ideas, back to the Greek philosophers, such as Democritus. For many centuries, however, atomism was only one of several philosophical theories about physical reality. During the Scientific Revolution of the 1500s and 1600s, people began to accept the atomic theory as part of science, although neither experimental proof nor mathematical demonstration yet supported it.

John Dalton, an English chemist and schoolteacher, became the first scientist to obtain convincing experimental data about the atom. In 1803 he outlined a method for "weighing" atoms. After studying the ratios of elements in various gases, Dalton assigned an arbitrary weight of one to the lightest element, hydrogen. Dalton then expressed the weights of all of the other known elements in relation to it.

During the 1800s many scientists explored the paths opened up by Dalton, learning much about the atom. In 1869 a Russian chemist, Dmitri Mendeleyev (men • duh • LAY • uhf), produced the first workable classification of the elements. Although somewhat modified, Mendeleyev's *Periodic Table* is a familiar feature of modern chemistry textbooks.

Modern atomic theory originated in the study of chemistry. However, it soon became part of physics—the science of matter and energy. This began to occur when scientists studying heat and gases explained their findings with a new theory of atoms in motion.

In the 1800s some scientists began to think of heat as the result of the motion of a body's atomic particles. In a cold substance—ice, for example—the atoms move relatively slowly. In a hot substance—such as scalding water—the atoms move much more vigorously, even colliding with one another. When water boils, the atoms move extremely fast and the water turns into a gas—water vapor. These discoveries established the atomic theory as a part of physics.

The Structure of the Atom

In 1895 a German physicist, Wilhelm K. Roentgen (RENT • guhn), was sending electricity through a vacuum inside a glass tube. He noticed that a fluorescent substance on a table nearby glowed brightly when the electric current was switched on in the tube. Roentgen immediately concluded that the tube was sending out a new form of ray. Soon he discovered that the rays penetrated many substances, including human skin and tissue, and would leave an image on a photographic plate. Because he did not know what caused this powerful penetrating radiation, Roentgen named the rays X rays. X rays became an important diagnostic tool in medicine, and their existence raised new questions about the physical world.

An English physicist, J. J. Thomson, probed further into the nature of matter. In 1897 he discovered the electron, a tiny particle that had a negative electrical charge. Thomson announced that an electron was more than 1,000 times lighter than

Science Fiction

Storytellers since the time of the ancient Greeks have enjoyed imagining that people are capable of breaking the laws of nature and gaining fantastic strength or powers. They have also invented amazing machines (right) and mythical figures with magical abilities.

Since the time of the Scientific Revolution, these fantasies have often taken a special form, inspired by the achievements of science. They are usually referred to as science fiction.

A favorite subject of science fiction has been travel in space. In fact, one of the earliest works of science fiction was written by Johannes Kepler, who played a major part in the revolution in astronomy during the 1600s. Kepler wrote a book called *The Dream,* in which he imagined his mother flying to the moon on a broomstick. This book created problems for his mother, for it was used as evidence that she was a

witch. However, it is one of the most imaginative descriptions of life in space ever written.

Science fiction was particularly popular in the 1700s and 1800s. The French philosopher Voltaire imagined a visit to earth by an enormous native of the star Sirius. An English novelist, Mary Wollstonecraft Shelley, invented a medical student called Victor Frankenstein, who created a monster out of a corpse. In the late 1800s, a French writer, Jules Verne, wrote a series of stories about incredible journeys—in a balloon, on a rocket, and even on a submarine. The English novelist H.G. Wells imagined a machine that could stop time and Martians who invaded Earth (bottom right).

In more recent times, much of science fiction—in films as well as books—has dealt with outer space (bottom left). But the basic theme has remained the same: fantastic people or creatures who can do things that normally are impossible. By showing us the impossible, science fiction tries to teach us something about the limits under which we live.

Learning from Pictures *The German-born Albert Einstein emigrated to the United States before Hitler came to power.*

the smallest known atom, and he theorized that all atoms contained electrons. Therefore, he said, subatomic particles (that is, particles inside atoms), rather than the atoms themselves, must be the true building blocks of all matter in the universe.

While most physicists reluctantly accepted the electron's existence, a French husband-and-wife team of chemists, Pierre and Marie Curie, provided new evidence that atoms were not the simple, indivisible particles pictured by earlier scientists. The Curies experimented with uranium and radium. They found that the atoms of these elements constantly disintegrated and released energy on their own. This process is called **radioactivity.** Elements that disintegrate and release this energy are called radioactive elements.

Ernest Rutherford of Great Britain combined Thomson's ideas about electrons and the Curies' discovery of disintegrating atoms in a new theory of the atom. Rutherford maintained that at the center of the atom lay an extremely small and heavy core, or nucleus. Electrons whirled in circular orbits around the nucleus. When Rutherford bombarded the nucleus with heavy particles from radioactive elements, he found that it held even smaller particles, which he called protons. With this discovery

scientists no longer thought of the atom as a solid piece of matter.

Later scientists modified Rutherford's description of the atom. He had thought in terms of two subatomic particles—electrons and protons. However, his successors discovered another, the neutron, and eventually more than 30 elementary atomic particles.

Planck and Einstein

In 1900 the German physicist Max Planck disproved the then-common belief that energy was continuous and that it could be divided into any number of smaller units. Planck proved that energy could be released only in definite "packages," which he called *quanta* (the plural of *quantum,* the Latin word for "how much"). Planck's **quantum theory** formed the basis for a completely new approach to the study of matter and energy.

In 1905 an extraordinary young German scientist, Albert Einstein, wrote four papers that revolutionized physics. In his first paper, Einstein examined some of the basic concepts of mechanics and tried to prove the existence of atoms. Einstein realized that if large grains of pollen were put into a gas or liquid, movement of the grains could be observed under a microscope. An earlier scientist had also made this observation but could not explain why the grains of pollen moved. In his paper Einstein maintained that the movement of pollen resulted from atoms hitting the grains.

In his second paper, Einstein extended Planck's quantum theory to describe the nature of light. Planck believed that light was a continuous wavelike phenomenon. Einstein used mathematics to show that light can also consist of a cascade of minute particles of energy. Einstein's theories were not confirmed by other scientists until the mid-1920s, but in time they led to the development of improvements such as the electric eye that triggers automatic door openers.

In his third paper, Einstein developed the **special theory of relativity.** He concluded the following: (1) No particles of matter can move faster than the speed of light. (2) Motion can be measured only relative to some particular observer. Thus it does not make sense to speak of absolute motion, space, or time.

A brief fourth paper developed Einstein's equation $E = mc^2$. According to this equation,

E (energy) equals m (mass) multiplied by c^2 (the speed of light squared). This formula states that a small amount of mass can be transformed into a tremendous amount of energy.

Einstein's theories overturned long-held ideas. Isaac Newton and the scientists who followed him had thought of the universe in terms of three dimensions: length, breadth, and depth. They claimed that gravity forces all particles of matter to move toward one another. Einstein declared that all events occur not only in the three dimensions of space but also in a fourth dimension—time. This four-dimensional system he called the *space-time continuum*. Gravity, he said, is not a property of matter, but rather a property of the space-time continuum.

By 1912 the theories of Max Planck and Albert Einstein paved the way for more advanced scientific discoveries. Niels Bohr, a student of J. J. Thomson, became intensely interested in atomic structure. Dispensing with traditional scientific approaches, Bohr applied the quantum theory to the challenging problem. He discovered that the behavior of atoms reveals atomic structure.

Cell Theory in Biology

Scientists of the 1800s were as interested in explaining the nature of life as they were in exploring the nature of nonliving matter. However, matter is extremely complex in the **biological sciences**—those sciences dealing with living organisms.

Biologists had long been familiar with the idea of cells, the tiny units of living matter. Various scientists of the 1600s examined living matter under their microscopes, seeing what we now know to be plant and animal cells. The cells of different species were of different shapes and sizes, but these early observers did not draw any general conclusions about them.

In 1858 the work of the German scientist Rudolf Virchow expanded the cell theory. Virchow showed that the destruction or change of cells by some outside force or agent caused disease in living organisms. From his study of cells, Virchow also concluded that every new cell must come from some older cell and that only living matter can produce new living matter. Thus by the late 1800s, scientists generally accepted the cell as the basic unit of living matter.

Lamarck's Theory of Inheritance

The cell theory, however, could not account for the rich variety of plants and animals on the earth. Until the mid-1800s most people explained the variety of living things by the concept of "special creation." They believed that all the different kinds of plants and animals had been created at one time.

One group of scientists, however, offered a different theory. They argued that the thousands of kinds of modern plants and animals had evolved, or developed, from common ancestors of long ago. This kind of development through change is called **evolution.**

In science new theories often raise new questions. Those who believed in evolution now had to explain how plants and animals had evolved. In the early 1800s, a French biologist, Jean Baptiste Lamarck, suggested that living beings changed their form in response to their environment. A giraffe, for example, acquired a long neck because it always had to stretch to eat leaves high up in trees. Such changes were then passed on by inheritance to its descendants. Conversely, other characteristics might gradually disappear if they were not used at all. Lamarck maintained that changes of this sort, continuing from generation to generation for millions of years, could have produced present-day plants and animals out of the first bits of living matter.

Lamarck's theory did not become a part of modern biology because it was later disproved. However, it influenced other scientists, among them a British biologist named Charles Darwin.

Darwin's Theory of Evolution

Charles Darwin had spent 25 years studying plant and animal life. In 1859 he published his theory of evolution in a book called *On the Origin of Species by Means of Natural Selection.*

Darwin began with a well-known biological fact—no two creatures are exactly alike, and offspring are not exactly like their parents. He combined this fact with the ideas of Thomas Malthus. Malthus believed that there were always more creatures born than could survive, because of natural dangers and restrictions, including the limited food supply. Therefore, Darwin said, in any generation some creatures would survive and some would perish. Those who survived would, in general, be those whose characteristics were best adapted to the existing environment. This idea is often called the "survival of the fittest." The strongest survivors would live to produce offspring, who would then repeat the process. Thus, Darwin claimed, one could explain the evolution of all forms of life.

According to Darwin's theory, the ancestors of the giraffe may not have had long necks, but they gave birth to offspring that were not exactly like their parents. Some had necks slightly longer than their parents had. Others had shorter necks. In an environment where leaves were found on tall trees, the offspring with the longer necks had an advantage. They could eat the leaves on the higher branches. Therefore, Darwin believed that nature "selected" the longer-necked offspring. These offspring lived and gave birth to another generation. The short-necked giraffes starved. Once again natural selection was repeated, and the longer-necked individuals survived.

Darwin's theory had a great impact on other scientists. It inspired them to gather evidence that would either prove or disprove it—evidence they looked for in the records of fossils as well as in the study of living organisms. However, the theory of

Learning from Pictures Darwin gathered most of the material for his theory of evolution during a surveying expedition off the coast of South America.

natural selection stirred up controversy because (1) it placed human beings in the animal kingdom, an idea many believed incorrect, and (2) many people believed that it contradicted the story of Creation in the Bible.

Genetics

Darwin left an important question unanswered: why were the offspring not exactly like their parents? Unknown to Darwin, a monk in Austria, Gregor Mendel, had been gathering evidence that would answer this question. Mendel founded **genetics**—the study of the ways in which inborn characteristics of plants and animals are inherited by their descendants. He did much of his research in the 1860s and 1870s, although other scientists did not know about it until later.

Mendel worked in a quiet monastery garden, where he bred pea plants. He mated tall plants with short plants, which produced not medium-sized pea plants, but all tall plants. Then Mendel fertilized these tall offspring with their own pollen and was surprised to find that they produced a mixed generation of both short and tall plants. In some way the characteristic of shortness had been hidden in the tall plants.

From these experiments Mendel concluded that inborn characteristics were not necessarily blended or mixed together. Instead, he believed, they were all inherited as if they were separate particles. For example, tall plants could carry and pass on to the next generation the particles that would cause shortness.

The Fight Against Disease

Remarkable breakthroughs in medicine accompanied the advances in science and helped prolong human life. Until the late 1800s, two out of every three children died while very young. Epidemics killed more people than did wars, famines, or natural disasters. Little was known about the causes of diseases. Scientists had seen bacteria under the microscope as early as the 1600s but had not suspected their connection with disease.

Smallpox, one dreaded disease common among children, swept through cities in periodic epidemics. A well-known saying of the time was that mothers did not count their children until they had had smallpox and lived through it.

Edward Jenner. An English physician of the late 1700s, Edward Jenner, made a thorough investigation of smallpox in the hope of finding a way to prevent it. He learned that milkmaids who had once had cowpox (a mild disease similar to smallpox) did not get the dreaded disease even during an epidemic. After years of experimenting, Jenner developed the principle of *inoculation,* which had been known in India 1,300 years earlier. In 1796 Jenner made a *vaccine* from the fluid in cowpox sores and scratched it into the skin of a boy's arm. The boy had a mild case of cowpox but quickly recovered. When the boy was later exposed to smallpox, he did not contract it.

Louis Pasteur. Jenner had developed a method of preventing smallpox through inoculation, but he did not know the scientific principle that made it work. This principle came to light in the late 1800s through the work of the French chemist Louis Pasteur. Until Pasteur's time scientists believed that certain living things, including bacteria, sprang to life out of nonliving matter. This process was called *spontaneous generation.* Pasteur's experiments showed that bacteria reproduced like other living things and traveled from place to place in the air, on people's hands, and in other ways.

Pasteur learned that bacteria are responsible for many phenomena. For example, some cause fermentation, turning grape juice into wine or making milk sour. In the 1860s Pasteur developed a process of heating liquids to kill bacteria and prevent fermentation—a process that was named **pasteurization** in his honor. He also determined that some bacteria cause diseases in animals and humans. These harmful bacteria are called *germs* or *microbes.*

During the 1870s Pasteur experimented with the germ that caused anthrax, a disease often fatal to both animals and humans. He produced a vaccine containing weakened anthrax germs, which he injected into animals. This prevented them from catching the disease. He determined that when weakened germs enter the body, the system builds up substances called antibodies to fight them. These antibodies remain in the body and are strong enough to kill the more deadly germs if exposure occurs. Thus Pasteur showed why Jenner's smallpox inoculations had been effective.

Pasteur used this same technique in fighting rabies, a fatal disease communicated to humans by

Learning from Pictures *Louis Pasteur never profited monetarily from his discoveries, but humankind benefited immeasurably from his experiments with bacteria.*

dogs or other animals infected with a certain virus (a minute organism smaller than bacteria). In the 1880s Pasteur found a way to weaken the rabies virus. He injected the vaccine he produced into a boy who had been bitten by a rabid dog, and the boy survived.

The Development of Surgery

Through the centuries surgery had been a desperate measure, always painful and often fatal. Surgeons dared to attempt only those operations that could be completed in a few minutes, such as tooth extractions and limb amputations. Patients had to be forcibly held down, or their senses dulled with liquor or opium.

In the 1840s it was discovered that ether and chloroform would cause unconsciousness or deaden sensation and thus eliminate pain. Such anesthetics not only relieved the patients' suffering but also made longer operations possible.

Even after anesthetics came into use, however, many patients survived the surgeon's knife only to die from infection soon afterward. Pasteur's discoveries about germs helped to resolve this dilemma.

Learning from Pictures *The discovery of anesthetics led to new surgical techniques. Why were anesthetics better than liquor and opium for deadening pain?*

An English surgeon, Joseph Lister, studied Pasteur's work and developed antisepsis—the process of killing disease-causing germs. Lister used carbolic acid as an antiseptic; milder chemicals later came into use for this purpose. The use of antiseptics helped reduce bacterial infection not only in surgery but also in childbirth and in the treatment of battle wounds. Hospitals, once houses of death, became houses of healing.

Other Medical Advances

A German physician, Robert Koch, made discoveries that reinforced those of Pasteur. In 1882 he isolated the germ that causes tuberculosis. He also identified the germ responsible for Asiatic cholera and developed sanitary measures, such as water filtration, to prevent disease.

The discoveries of Pasteur, Lister, and Koch were the starting point of an international fight against disease. Knowing the nature and role of germs and viruses, scientists could now isolate the causes of many diseases and develop vaccines for inoculation.

Scientists traced some epidemic diseases, including malaria and yellow fever, to germs carried in the bodies of mosquitoes and transmitted by

their bite. Thus the battle against disease was extended to the mosquitoes that carried it. Bubonic plague, found to be carried by fleas on rats, was brought under control in Western countries through rat-extermination campaigns.

Scientists developed and tested many new medicines. Aspirin, which became available in the 1890s, reduced pain and fever. Insulin, developed in the 1920s, saved diabetics from certain death and enabled them to lead normal lives. Other medicines were used to treat bacterial infections. For example, Alexander Fleming of Great Britain discovered penicillin in 1928. The sulfonamides, or sulfa drugs, were developed in Germany in the 1930s. However, neither penicillin nor the sulfas came into wide use until the 1940s.

SECTION 2 REVIEW

1. **Define** physical science, radioactivity, quantum theory, special theory of relativity, biological science, evolution, genetics, pasteurization
2. **Identify** John Dalton, Dmitri Mendeleyev, Wilhelm Roentgen, Pierre and Marie Curie, Max Planck, Albert Einstein, Gregor Mendel, Edward Jenner
3. **Classifying Ideas** **(a)** What contributions to atomic theory were made by Dalton? **(b)** Thomson? **(c)** Rutherford?
4. **Summarizing Ideas** What were Albert Einstein's major contributions to physics?
5. **Contrasting Ideas** **(a)** Explain how Lamarck's theory of evolution differed from that proposed by Darwin. **(b)** What differences of opinion did Darwin's theory cause?
6. **Evaluating Ideas** In what ways did Gregor Mendel's ideas build upon Darwin's theory?
7. **Identifying Ideas** What were four great contributions made by Louis Pasteur?

3 The Population Grew and Became More Mobile

From about 1600 to 1750, the population of Europe grew very little. When the Industrial Revolution began, 140 million people lived in Europe. By 1850, only 100 years later, the population had increased to 266 million. The rate of population growth during most of the period was highest in Europe and the United States, the areas in which industrialization advanced most rapidly. The progress made possible by science and technology helped produce this rapid population growth.

Improvements in Diet and Food Storage

Another reason that life expectancy increased after 1850 was that more food became available, and more was known about the relationship of food to health. In the early 1900s, biologists discovered the importance of vitamins and minerals in the diet. Diseases resulting from vitamin deficiencies, such as beriberi and rickets, were wiped out in advanced regions of the world.

Science and technology combined to produce better methods of preserving and transporting food. Pasteurization was one important step. So was refrigeration, which also retards the growth of bacteria. Refrigerators appeared in the late 1800s. They later became an indispensable household feature in many industrialized countries. Refrigerated railroad cars were first used around 1850 to transport meats, fruits, and vegetables. All these developments made a balanced diet available year-round.

Emigration

As the population grew in industrialized countries, it also became more mobile. Large numbers of people moved across national boundaries and oceans to foreign lands. The great movement shifted away from Europe to North and South America, Africa, Australia, and New Zealand.

Like so many other changes, this movement to other lands, or **emigration,** intensified after 1870. Between 1870 and 1900, more than 10 million people left Europe for the United States alone. This mass movement of people has no equal in human history.

Many people fled from countries with poor economic conditions, such as Ireland and Italy. Other people, such as Jews, Armenians, and Slavs, fled oppression and discrimination. The general trend of movement was toward the more sparsely populated nations in northern and western Europe, where rapid industrialization had created a great demand for factory labor. Higher wages in these countries attracted people, and steamships and trains made travel faster, safer, and affordable.

Learning from Pictures
Tiny Ellis Island in New York Harbor symbolized hope for immigrants, who traveled from Europe on overcrowded ships. More than 16 million people passed through the island on their way into the United States between 1892 and 1943.

The Shift to the Cities

As the population increased, changes in agriculture, industry, and transportation produced another striking result—the rapid growth of cities. As employment opportunities on farms declined, the developing industries located in or near cities offered new jobs. The factory system became the greatest spur to city growth.

Many early factories were located in already established cities, which then grew tremendously. The population of Manchester, England, for example, expanded from 25,000 in 1772 to 455,000 in 1851. When factories were built in rural areas, cities grew up around them. City living became the way of life for more and more people.

Before the Industrial Revolution, the vast majority of people lived in rural areas or in small villages. By 1900, however, in many nations more people lived in or near cities than in the countryside. In Great Britain about 10 percent of the population lived in cities in 1800. By 1921 that figure had grown to 80 percent. Similar changes took place in other countries. In 1800 not a single city in the Western world had a population of 1 million. Yet only 100 years later, cities such as New York, London, Paris, and Berlin each had more than 1 million inhabitants.

Sanitation and Public Order

Until very late in the century, cities did not have sewers. European and American cities of the 1800s differed significantly from cities today. People got their daily water supply from public fountains because houses did not have running water inside. The water in fountains came from polluted rivers, and no one knew how to purify it.

Neither public nor private garbage collection companies existed, so people dumped garbage on the streets. In cities smoke from the factories added to the smells from sewage and garbage. Thus people thought of cities as foul-smelling places.

After the 1870s the situation began to change. Technological advances made possible many improvements such as iron pipes, toilets, and water systems. Cities installed closed public sewers and piped water into houses. City governments passed laws requiring better heating systems and better construction of buildings. Governments also installed street lights and paved roads.

The governments of the growing cities also found they needed a new kind of police force. Law enforcement officers had to patrol streets to prevent robberies, direct crowds safely, and protect the lives and property of city dwellers.

In 1829 Sir Robert Peel, a leader of the House of Commons, organized a permanent police force for the city of London. This force was responsible for maintaining order and making sure that people obeyed the law. The London police were nicknamed "bobbies" after Peel's first name, Robert, and are still called that today. Other major cities soon followed London's lead and established police forces.

The Development of Suburbs

As cities grew and became more crowded, their boundaries expanded to include surrounding areas. In addition, people moved outside cities to new areas called suburbs—residential areas on the outskirts of cities. Suburbs first began to develop in the late 1800s. Families lived in the suburbs, where there was less crowding, noise, and dirt, but their working members journeyed each day to jobs in the city.

Railroad and bus lines made this daily travel possible. During the late 1800s, more and more cities established public transportation systems so that people could travel between home and work. At first ordinary working people could not afford the fares of trains and horse-drawn buses. Only employers, managers, merchants, and professionals enjoyed these transportation luxuries. They could afford to live fairly long distances from work, in the new suburbs, while factory workers had to live within walking distance of their jobs. By the end of the 1800s, however, lower fares made it possible for most city dwellers to ride trolleys or horse-drawn buses to work.

Leisure and Cultural Activities

Many currently popular forms of entertainment first developed during the 1800s. Before that time, of course, people enjoyed concerts, plays, games, and sports. As the populations of cities grew during the industrial age, the numbers and variety of these activities increased. Large audiences now paid to hear professional musicians perform or to watch professional athletes compete.

Learning from Pictures   *This football match, played around 1900, was sponsored by a British ladies' football club. Who is known as the "Father of Football"?*

Sports. People had participated in athletic events for many centuries. The rich hunted and played a form of tennis. The poor organized informal games on the village common. In fact, we can trace the origins of soccer, rugby, and football to a game played by villagers using an inflated pig's bladder as a ball.

During the 1800s, however, many games became more organized. In Great Britain, "football" (known as soccer in the United States) was among the first games to change from an informal community activity to a professional spectator sport. Rugby and the American game of football then evolved from this early kicking game.

According to legend, in 1823 a young student at Rugby School in England caught a kicked ball during a "football" game. Instead of dropping it on the ground to kick toward the opponents' goal, he held it and ran toward the goal. Although the boy's teammates and the spectators admonished him for violating the rules of the game, the idea of running with the ball eventually won favor and in time led to the organization of a game called *rugby*.

"Football" clubs for working-class people were created in the 1850s. By that time laws granted factory workers Saturday afternoon and Sunday as rest days. Groups of players gathered each week to compete, and the rest of the community came to watch.

Soon certain clubs had reputations for their skill, and they attracted large crowds. Many people who did not play football themselves knew the rules of the game and enjoyed watching it. In the 1860s the London Football Association drew up official rules for games called *soccer* and *rugby*, and in 1871 the association established a national competition among football clubs.

Americans played soccer before rugby was introduced in England. Then in 1880 an American named Walter Camp, known as the "Father of Football," adapted rugby, and the game we know as football evolved. Although professional football leagues were not established in the United States until 1920, by the mid-1880s many soccer and rugby players were full-time athletes. "Football" had evolved into three sports played by amateurs and professionals and watched by paying spectators.

527

Concert halls, museums, and libraries. Before the 1800s individuals and private groups sponsored most cultural activities. Musicians performed concerts in the homes of the rich or as part of religious services. Wealthy individuals who wanted to commemorate a family or personal event commissioned paintings. Individual families and religious or civic groups also commissioned paintings and sculpture for display in homes, churches, or clubs.

During the 1800s art and music became available to many people. City governments built concert halls and opera houses, and theaters presenting a wide variety of plays opened in both large and small towns. Music halls offered popular entertainment and vaudeville*, generally to working-class audiences, while middle-class people usually preferred classical drama.

---

*Vaudeville, named after a town in France where popular songs were composed, consisted of light, often comical theatrical performances that frequently combined dialogue, dancing, pantomime, and singing.

Cities began to support symphony orchestras, bands, and choral groups. Performances took place in large concert halls. Bands played on Sunday afternoons in parks, where people picnicked, fished, or strolled.

During the 1800s art collections originally displayed in private homes and churches were moved to public museums. The Louvre (LOOV) museum in Paris had contained the art collections of the kings of France. Now it became a public museum. Paintings were organized and displayed by historical period and by the country of the artist. The museum received money from the French government, which wanted to educate its citizens in matters of art.

Great libraries were opened, among them the Bibliothèque Nationale in Paris and the British Museum (now called the British Library) in London. These libraries contained large book collections and were open to public use in the 1840s. In some cities, too, lending libraries with small collections offered books to subscribers for a small fee.

Learning from Pictures *La Scala opera house was opened in Milan, Italy, in 1778. Early operas centered around scenery, song, and pastoral themes.*

Learning from Pictures
This painting of a croquet game in the park was done by Winslow Homer in 1866. This great American painter began his career as a magazine illustrator.

Public parks and urban planning. Crowded cities had few places for outdoor recreation. When railroads were built, people often rode trains to the countryside. They could spend the day there, away from the congestion, noise, and dirt of city streets. Some people demanded, in addition, that city governments provide parks within cities for recreation.

By the end of the 1800s, many cities had playgrounds for children. Private lands were donated or purchased by city governments and given to the people as public parks. Large areas inside city limits—for example, the Bois de Boulogne (BWA duh boo • LOHN) in Paris and Central Park in New York City—were set aside as public parks.

During the late 1800s, amusement parks appeared in some cities. To entertain the crowds who visited them, the amusement parks offered games and rides, circuslike shows, and food. One famous amusement park, Coney Island, opened in 1895 in Brooklyn, New York, and is still in operation today.

SECTION 3 REVIEW

1. **Define** emigration
2. **Identify** Sir Robert Peel, "bobbies," Walter Camp
3. **Locate** New York, Paris, Berlin
4. **Interpreting Ideas** Describe how the preservation of food was improved after 1850.
5. **Summarizing Ideas** What improvements in the cities were made possible by new technology?
6. **Classifying Ideas** What new forms of leisure activities developed in the 1800s?

4 Interest in the Social Sciences and Education Increased

In 1800 illiteracy was widespread, even in those countries of the world that were becoming industrialized. In European countries schools were private. Religious groups ran the majority of these schools. Only wealthy or middle-class people could afford to educate their children. Most children either did not go to school at all or went for only a few years.

During the 1800s interest in education and in a new field of study, the **social sciences,** grew rapidly. The social sciences consist of those branches of knowledge that study people as members of society. This group of studies deals with many subjects—economic development, political institutions, history, and relations among people. The idea of making the study of these subjects objective and factual—of treating them like sciences—was new in the 1800s.

Political Science and Economics

The study of politics dates back to the Greek philosophers Plato and Aristotle. Later it was the subject of such thinkers as Machiavelli, Locke, and Rousseau. In the 1800s the study of politics became known as *political science,* and writers tried to study law and government in the scientific manner of physicists and biologists.

Another social science, *economics*, was already well developed in the work of Adam Smith. However, not until the later 1800s did economists begin to imitate scientists by collecting and arranging statistics in order to test their theories.

History

Like political science, the study of history dates back to the Greeks. History, too, underwent change in the 1800s. Influenced by nationalism, many scholars wrote histories detailing the accomplishments and glories of their native countries. In addition, historical writing became based more and more on the systematic study of original materials and the careful organization of facts. Historians began a massive search for evidence of the past in documents, diaries, letters, and other sources. New interpretations of history began to emerge.

Another way historians encouraged nationalism was by observing and including in their studies all the people in a society. Here a writer of the 1700s proved influential—the French philosopher Voltaire, who was noted for his attention to social and intellectual history. His works inspired many historians to concentrate less on wars and great leaders and more on the study of ordinary people and how they lived. Later historians, influenced by Darwin, also tried to interpret historical events in terms of evolution.

Anthropology

It was in the 1800s that scientists realized how old the earth was and how long humans had lived on it. They found prehistoric cave paintings, discovered Egyptian, Sumerian, and Assyrian remains, and excavated such ancient cities as Troy and Mycenae.

Anthropologists also began to explore the continuity in the attitudes of human societies and in the way people relate to one another. An English anthropologist, E. B. Tylor, adopted the German term *kultur* to describe the set of beliefs and behaviors that a society shares. He discussed this concept in his book *Primitive Culture* (1871). In it he looked at one particular subject, religion, as it evolved in all human cultures.

Another English anthropologist, James George Frazer, took this approach further in his book *The Golden Bough* (1890). Frazer compared the customs of different societies and tried to show

Learning from Pictures   *In 1923 Howard Carter (left) and A. R. Callender crated artifacts from the tomb of Tutankhamen for shipment to England.*

links between those societies through magical beliefs, religion, and attitudes toward authority. The study of similarities and differences among various societies has remained a major interest of anthropologists.

Sociology

Sociology—the study of human relationships in society—also first appeared in the 1800s. The writings of the French philosopher Auguste Comte greatly influenced this branch of the social sciences. He argued that the study of society should follow scientific methods by using objective facts and avoiding personal interpretations.

In the late 1800s, sociologists became particularly interested in adopting the theories of the biological sciences. Herbert Spencer, for example, used Darwin's theory of evolution as the basis for studying human communities. As you have read, Darwin claimed that nature "selected" certain individuals—those most fit to survive—and allowed others to die. In his *Principles of Sociology*, published between 1877 and 1896, Spencer applied this theory of natural selection to society. A society, he said, includes superior people who are well adapted to it. In exercising their "natural rights," these people also contribute to the progress of civilization. At the same time, a society will contain inferior types—

the poor, the lazy, the ignorant, the criminal—who contribute nothing.

Spencer wrote that human society, like the plant and animal worlds, had evolved from lower to higher forms through natural selection. If so-called inferior types were permitted to die out, then society would ultimately consist exclusively of superior people. This application of Darwin's theory came to be known as **social Darwinism.** However, as social problems grew more severe and society became more complex during the 1800s, sociologists rejected social Darwinism.

Psychology

Psychology, another new science of the 1800s, studied the human mind—how it works and how it affects behavior. Psychology's origins trace back to the works of Greek thinkers, and since it did not involve experimentation, most people considered it a branch of philosophy. However, in the mid-1800s a number of scientists decided to make psychology an experimental science like biology.

Pavlov. Darwin's theory of evolution had a strong impact on the new science of psychology. Among other things, it influenced psychologists to study animal behavior and to apply their findings to humans. The most famous of these early experimenters was a Russian biologist, Ivan Pavlov.

In the 1890s Pavlov discovered the conditioned reflex. Psychologists had long known that certain behavior was automatic. A child does not have to be taught to pull his or her hand away from fire, but removes it automatically. In the same way, a dog does not have to be taught to salivate, or water at the mouth, when eating food. Psychologists call this kind of involuntary response a *reflex action.*

By experimenting with dogs, Pavlov proved that an animal could be conditioned, or taught, to have certain reflex actions. First, he offered food to a dog. The dog salivated. Second, he rang a bell each time the food was presented to the dog. The animal salivated and also began associating the sound of the bell with food. Finally, Pavlov offered no food to the dog but rang the bell. The dog salivated. It had been conditioned to salivate when it heard the bell. As a result of his research, Pavlov believed that all habits, even mental activity, constitute a series of connected conditioned reflexes.

Freud. In the early 1900s, the Austrian physician Sigmund Freud (FROID) developed another explanation of human behavior. Freud introduced the revolutionary concept of the unconscious—the mental processes of which a person is unaware—as a determining factor in behavior.

Freud had hypnotized certain mentally disturbed patients. He had found that under hypnosis they could remember past experiences that they could not otherwise recall. Freud believed that these early experiences had led to their illness. He treated his patients by gradually bringing the disturbing memories, fears, and conflicts back to the level of consciousness. To do this he studied their dreams and encouraged them to talk about whatever came into their minds. Then he interpreted these dreams and thoughts to show what lay beneath them in the unconscious mind.

Freud believed that troubled patients had unknowingly forced unpleasant experiences into the unconscious. To cure such people, it was necessary to make them aware of these experiences again.

Learning from Pictures Sigmund Freud's pioneering work in psychoanalysis had a great influence on art, literature, and education.

Alice's Adventures in Wonderland

The modern era witnessed a new attitude toward children—that of treating them as children and not as small adults. One reflection of this change was the publication of books for young people that would amuse rather than instruct them. A landmark children's story was Lewis Carroll's *Alice's Adventures in Wonderland*, a fantasy both humorous and menacing. The drawings that accompanied it, by John Tenniel, were a high point in the art of illustration, perfectly capturing the story's whimsy and lack of logic. Here Alice is shown with the ill-tempered Duchess. Alice in Wonderland continues to entertain children of all ages in many countries of the world.

Freud called this process of revealing and analyzing the unconscious **psychoanalysis.** He discussed his theory fully in a book titled *A General Introduction to Psychoanalysis*, published in 1920.

Later, some psychologists challenged details of Freud's theories. However, much of his basic theory and method forms the foundation of psychiatry—the study and treatment of mental illness.

Growth of Public Education

The American and French revolutions, with their ideas of liberty, equality, and representative government, made it seem important to provide education for all citizens. In the years following the revolutions, both France and the United States took steps to establish public school systems. Many people opposed the idea, however. They feared that education would encourage revolutionary ideas and make people less willing to do farm and factory work. They also believed that the cost of education would result in increased taxes.

As the years went by, many other factors encouraged the development of free public education—schooling free of charge for all, regardless of social class. Schools were easier to establish in larger towns and cities than in rural areas. Industrialists wanted literate workers as well as more engineers, scientists, and skilled technicians. Other people believed that schools other than government-established schools would not develop patriotic citizens. Military leaders wanted educated soldiers for their armies. As more people gained the right to vote, they voted for more education. They believed that education would improve their children's chances for a better life.

After 1870 governments in western Europe and the United States began to pass laws making some form of education both universal and compulsory. In a number of countries, the government provided only elementary education. In others the government also funded secondary, or high school, public education. In the United States, many public school systems were expanded to include kindergarten for young children and state universities for advanced study. Many new subjects, especially the sciences, were added to the curricula, and vocational and technical training were introduced.

Teachers had to take special courses that prepared them to teach new subjects.

In European nations the central governments established and controlled schools. In the United States, where local governments were stronger, the individual states established schools and set standards. Local school districts administered schools and levied taxes to support them.

For the most part, children of the lower classes attended school only as long as the law required. Then they went to work to earn money to help support their families. Middle-class children, however, went on to secondary school and often to college.

Education for Women

During the 1800s a great deal of debate focused on education for women. Some people argued that most educational courses were either unsuitable or unnecessary for women. Other people insisted that education was important because it made women better wives and mothers. Still others said that women should have equal opportunity in every aspect of society, including education and the opportunity to have careers outside the home.

Toward the end of the 1800s, when many countries passed laws guaranteeing education for all, elementary education for girls was included. However, opportunities for secondary education remained limited. In the United States, as in Great Britain and France, high schools for girls offered different courses than did schools for boys. Girls' schools emphasized foreign languages, literature, history, and home economics. Boys, on the other hand, studied sciences, mathematics, and philosophy, as well as classics, history, and literature.

Many people objected to the practice of having different courses for boys and girls. For example, Emily Davies, an Englishwoman, urged her government to improve women's education sufficiently to allow women to attend the universities. In 1865 she said:

66*W*e are not encumbered [burdened] by theories about equality and inequality of mental power in the sexes. All we claim is that the intelligence of women, be it great or small, shall have full and free development. And we claim it not especially in the interests of women, but as essential to the growth of the human race. 99

Learning from Pictures These women are studying subjects traditionally studied only by males. What are these subjects?

Few colleges admitted women as students during the 1800s. Therefore, those people who believed that women should have the opportunity to receive university educations opened colleges for women. In the United States, Mary Lyon founded the Mount Holyoke Female Seminary in 1837. This school later became Mount Holyoke College. In Great Britain, Girton College opened in 1874 and Newnham College opened in 1875. Today these colleges are part of Cambridge University.

The Effects of Education

The spread of education had many positive results. People became better informed about current issues and took an active interest in a variety of government activities. Since more people could read, massive quantities of newspapers, magazines, and books were published and distributed to people of all ages.

Newspapers, which were not widely read before 1800, became especially popular and important. During the 1800s newspapers expanded their coverage to include politics, foreign affairs, and art and science. To attract readers the editors also included weekly stories by famous authors such as Zola and Dickens.

Newspapers often advocated a particular political position. They either supported or criticized the policies of one government figure or another and often featured humorous political cartoons. France, for example, had republican newspapers and monarchist newspapers as well as Catholic newspapers.

As more and more people bought newspapers, the prices decreased. Publishers also used advertising as a way of increasing income, attracting readers, and keeping prices low. In addition, new technology, such as the linotype, which set type by machine instead of by hand, and the electric-powered rotary press, improved printing processes. The invention of the telegraph made it possible for reporters to transmit the news quickly. Reporters could now extend their coverage to distant places and transmit news to their hometown newpapers.

As newspapers grew, so did the number of job opportunities for journalists and editors. In the past, writing had been something that people did in addition to their other work. It was not a full-time profession. In the 1800s, however, journalism became an accepted and respected occupation. Consequently, more people viewed journalism as an exciting career.

5 Literature, Music, and Art Reflected the Spirit of the Times

Literature, music, and art reflected the dramatic social and economic developments of the industrial age. Even in their most personal statements, artists portrayed in their works a sense of the rapidly changing times and of the influences of revolutionary scientific ideas.

Romanticism

Many writers of the early 1800s belonged to what is known as the **romantic movement,** or **romanticism.** Their work appealed to sentiment and imagination and dealt with the "romance" of life—life as it used to be, or as they thought it ought to be, rather than as it actually was. The romantic movement was partly a reaction to the Enlightenment, the movement in the 1700s that had emphasized reason and progress. Romantics glorified feeling, emotion, and instinct. They idealized nature and the golden past.

The romantic movement was also a product of the revolutions of the 1700s and 1800s. Political revolution in France had overturned the old order of society and released the spirit of liberty and equality. So, too, romanticism overturned the formal structures that literature and art had possessed in the 1700s and released a spirit of creativity, enthusiasm, and individuality.

Learning from Pictures *Edgar Degas sculpted this small bronze statue entitled* Little Fourteen-Year-Old Dancer. *His ballet paintings have long had worldwide popularity.* †

In Great Britain the most famous romantics were a group of young, intense poets whose works were filled with emotion and a strong love for beauty and nature. The works of romantic poets such as William Wordsworth, Percy Bysshe Shelley, John Keats, Lord Byron, and Samuel Taylor Coleridge are among the classics of literature.

Many romantic writers glorified the past, especially the Middle Ages with its chivalrous knights, ladies, and castles. For example, in *Ivanhoe*, the Scottish novelist Sir Walter Scott wrote about the days of knighthood. *The Hunchback of Notre Dame*, by the French author Victor Hugo, was also set in medieval times. Alexandre Dumas told the tale of

†The Metropolitan Museum of Art, Bequest of Mrs. H. O. Havemeyer, 1929. The H. O. Havemeyer Collection.

The Three Musketeers, who roamed France in the days of Cardinal Richelieu.

Interest in the past was related to the growing nationalism of the times. Many writers turned to folklore, songs, and the history of their own countries for their subject matter. Germany was not yet a unified nation in the early 1800s, but a national literature arose there. The Grimm brothers collected the famous fairy tales that bear their name. This collection remains a favorite of children even today. Friedrich von Schiller wrote of liberty in *William Tell,* a drama about a Swiss hero. Johann Wolfgang von Goethe (GUHR • tuh), a master of poetry, drama, and the novel, also wrote during this period of rising national feeling. The drama *Faust,* the story of a man's bargain with the devil, is the most famous of Goethe's works.

Romanticism also influenced American writers of the early 1800s. James Fenimore Cooper wrote adventure stories that idealized the Indian and the frontier. Washington Irving produced romantic stories set in New York's Hudson River valley.

Romantic Music

In music, as in literature, the 1800s began with a shift to romanticism. One of the leaders of this transition was the German composer Ludwig van Beethoven (BAY • toh • vuhn). Beethoven brought to music the same interests and aims that the British poets of his time brought to literature. He expressed his love of nature in a symphony (known as the *Pastoral Symphony*) devoted entirely to evoking the atmosphere of the countryside. His call for liberty and freedom dominated the one opera he wrote, *Fidelio,* as well as the final movement of his last symphony. Beethoven wrote his music to arouse powerful and passionate emotion. Like all the other romantics, he praised human heroism and achievement and thought that people should express their feelings strongly.

The romantic movement led to a great outpouring of music, especially in Austria and Germany. Johannes Brahms composed powerful symphonies and concertos. Although they were classical in form, they surged with rich, intensely emotional music. Franz Schubert, Robert Schumann, and Felix Mendelssohn brought to their music the lyric quality of romantic poetry. Schubert and Schumann are especially remembered for their great songs, or *lieder.*

Learning from Pictures *Frédéric Chopin was a self-taught pianist, whose musical genius began to show early in his childhood.*

Frédéric Chopin (SHOH•pan), a Polish-born composer who lived in France, wrote graceful yet dynamic piano pieces. Franz Liszt of Hungary used native folk songs and dances in some of his compositions. He also developed the tone poem, a symphonic piece based on a literary or philosophical theme, often taken from romantic literature.

In Russia, Peter Ilich Tchaikovsky (chy•KAHF•skee) wrote highly emotional and melodic symphonies, operas, ballet music, and orchestral works. Often his compositions were built around stories, such as the fairy tale of *The Nutcracker*, the romance of *Romeo and Juliet*, and Napoleon's defeat at Moscow in the *1812 Overture*. He and other Russian composers, especially Modest Mussorgsky—known for his opera *Boris Godunov*—developed nationalistic music that emphasized Russian folk themes. As in literature, strong national feeling was an essential part of the romantic movement in music.

The greatest Italian operatic composer of the 1800s was Giuseppe Verdi. His best-known works, such as *Otello* and *Aïda*, contain some of the most beautiful and dramatic music ever written for the human voice. In keeping with the spirit of his times, the stories and themes of many of his early operas were highly nationalistic. Verdi's operas inspired a generation of Italians who were not yet politically united.

In Germany the greatest operatic composer of the 1800s was Richard Wagner (VAHG•nuhr). He called his operas "music dramas," and in them he combined singing, music, dancing, costumes, and scenery to create a spectacular theatrical effect. Like his contemporaries, Wagner was an intense nationalist. He based many of his operatic plots on German myths.

Several composers of the late 1800s followed in the general tradition of romantic music. They are sometimes called *post-romantics.* Gustav Mahler of Austria, for example, used huge orchestras and choruses to perform his lengthy symphonies. Another trend, however, was to break away from older styles. Claude Debussy (deb•yoo•SEE) of France developed unusual harmonies and rhythms in trying to create delicate musical impressions of clouds, sea, or moonlight.

Romantic Painting and Architecture

Although Germans, Austrians, Russians, and Italians dominated the music world in the 1800s, the outstanding painters and sculptors were French.

In the 1820s and 1830s, romantic painters, like romantic writers, chose subjects from the past and depicted scenes bursting with action and drama. Such a painter was Eugène Delacroix (del•uh•KRWAH) of France. Landscape painters John Constable and J. M. W. Turner of Great Britain reflected the romantic interest in nature. Their work had intense color and vitality, partly because they often painted outdoors instead of working in their studios.

Romanticism in architecture expressed itself first in the so-called Gothic revival of the mid-1800s. This was an attempt to re-create a great period of the past. The British Houses of Parliament as well as many American churches, college buildings, and other public structures of the time were designed in the Gothic style.

The Rise of Realism

The rich imagination as well as the ornate style of the romantics produced a type of literature and art of little relevance to the lives of most people. In the mid-1800s writers and artists began to abandon this approach and turn to **realism,** the realities of everyday life. One of the most important realists was Gustave Flaubert (floh•BAIR) of France. His novel *Madame Bovary* described with extraordinary attention to detail the life of an ordinary woman. In Great Britain, Mary Ann Evans wrote realistic novels under the name George Eliot. In one of

READ
WRITE
●INTERPRET
CONNECT
THINK

BUILDING HISTORY STUDY SKILLS

Interpreting Visuals: Using Art as a Historical Document

Works of art are not isolated from society but are created as part of human activity. Works of art often reflect the values of the artist as well as those of his or her society. The artist may be criticizing social conventions or political practices or reflecting the values of the historical period. By paying attention to the details and themes that the artist depicts, you can gain a better understanding of the historical period. Asking questions, such as the ones below, is an important part of viewing a work of art and helps you to understand its significance.

- What is the painting telling you about politics, society, or the people of the historical period?
- To what extent is the artist reflecting or criticizing the society?
- To what extent is the painting a document?

How to Use Art as a Historical Document

To use art as a historical document, follow these steps.
1. Identify the historical period of the work of art.
2. Explain the theme of the painting.
3. Connect the theme to the historical period.
4. Indicate whether the artwork reflects or criticizes the society and explain how it does so.

Developing the Skill

Study Honoré Daumier's painting *The Washerwoman* (right). What is it saying about working class people? How is it connected to the life style of the working class?

Daumier rebelled against the romantic tradition in art and sympathized with the working class. Instead of aristocracy and nature, Daumier's art reflects social realities. The Industrial Revolution created an urban working class with laboring chores. The theme of *The Washerwoman* focuses on the dignity and humanity of the working people. The artwork sensitively portrays poor, working people as having strength and dignity; harsh working or living conditions do not prevent the humanity of the individual from being revealed.

Is there a message in this particular painting? Daumier is realistically portraying the hardship and struggles by showing the heavy bundle the woman carries and the posture of both figures. These are not people to pity, however. Instead, the artist portrays the humanity of his subjects.

Daumier's painting is telling us about the social effects of the Industrial Revolution. Although members of the working class led difficult lives, they retained both their humanity and their individuality.

Practicing the skill. Visit a local art museum or look in an art history book to find a modern painting. Study the painting carefully so that you may interpret what the artist is saying. Using the steps above, try to determine how this work of art could be used as a historical document.

To apply this skill, see Applying History Study Skills on page 541.

Learning from Pictures *The American impressionist Mary Cassatt lived in France. Her favorite theme was motherhood as shown in this painting titled* The Bath.

Toward the end of the 1800s, a number of writers called **naturalists** carried realism even further. They described the ugly and sordid aspects of everyday life, carefully screening emotion and opinion from their writings. The French novelist Émile Zola was a leader of this approach. He wrote as if he were a scientist objectively studying and carefully recording all human activities. Though people objected to his frankness, his exposure of shocking conditions in industries helped bring reform. Another realist was the English novelist Charles Dickens, who often wrote about the poor people of London.

In painting, the kind of realism that portrayed people and everyday life in the industrial age characterized the works of the French artists Gustave Courbet (koor • BAY) and Honoré Daumier (doh • MYAY). Another kind of realism was attempted by a group of French painters who are known as **impressionists.**

Impressionist painting flourished during the 1860s and 1870s. Impressionist painters tried to give vivid impressions of people and places as they might appear in a brief glance. To do this, the impressionists studied light and color. They experimented with small patches of different colors placed side by side to create shimmering effects. Claude Monet (moh • NAY) and Pierre-Auguste Renoir (REN • wahr) were leading impressionist painters.

Experiments in Art Forms

In painting and sculpture, romanticism and realism were brief movements, followed quickly by intensely individualistic experimentation. There was less nationalism in art than in literature or music, and more "art for art's sake." Like writers and musicians, painters and sculptors often rebelled against the materialism and mechanization of an industrial world.

In the late 1800s, painters abandoned tradition in favor of experimentation. Form, color, and emotion became more important than subject matter. Realism was left to the newly invented camera, and painting styles became highly individualistic.

Paul Cézanne's landscapes and still lifes emphasized the forms and shapes of his subjects. He began to move beyond surface appearances to explore the abstract qualities of color and design. This shift away from showing recognizable, real scenes influenced other artists.

her novels, *Middlemarch,* she focused on country life of the Victorian period.

Often the realists made social and economic conditions their theme. The Russian Leo Tolstoy, in his monumental novel *War and Peace* (published in 1868–69), portrayed war not as a romantic adventure but as a vast confusion of misery and death. The Norwegian dramatist Henrik Ibsen brought human problems onto the theater stage. His play *A Doll's House* (1879) advocated the equality of husband and wife in marriage.

In the United States, realism took the form of **regionalism**—the portrayal of everyday life in different parts of the huge country. Examples are Mark Twain's novels *Tom Sawyer* (1876) and *Huckleberry Finn* (1884), with their earthy and humorous depiction of life along the Mississippi River.

Learning from Pictures *The French impressionist Pierre-Auguste Renoir's painting,* Le Moulin de la Galette, *depicts a cafe in Paris.*

Also influential was Paul Gauguin (goh • GAN). Gauguin, who left Europe to live in Tahiti, stressed color and simple, flat shapes in his paintings. Henri Matisse painted many decorative scenes of southern France. He, too, emphasized design at the expense of realism. The Dutch painter Vincent van Gogh (van GOH) expressed intense emotions in his work. He used thick blobs of pure color, swirling brush strokes, and distorted perspectives and made no pretense at realism. Edgar Degas, Henri de Toulouse-Lautrec (too • LOOZ • luh • TREK), and Édouard Manet (ma • NAY) all painted scenes of Parisian life in their own personal style.

The French sculptor Auguste Rodin (roh • DAN) also broke with tradition. Some of his statues included unworked portions of the marble from which they were carved, giving his work a deliberately unfinished quality. Rodin rejected the traditional demands that art should show people, objects, and scenes as they appeared in real life.

The growing interest in abstract forms marked the end of the emotional strivings of romanticism and pointed the way toward the new artistic interests of the 1900s.

CHAPTER 20 REVIEW

Method of "weighing" atoms outlined by John Dalton

Production of electric current in wire by Michael Faraday

AD   1803   1831

Chapter Summary

The following list contains the key concepts you have learned about advances in technology, science, education, and the arts between 1800 and 1928.

1. After 1870 new inventions such as the telephone and wireless telegraph made rapid communication possible. The use of electricity became widespread, and the development of the internal-combustion engine improved transportation.
2. Science developed rapidly during this period. In the physical sciences, the atomic theory became the basis for understanding matter. The brilliant work of Einstein revolutionized the study of energy and matter.
3. Significant progress also was made in the biological sciences. Knowledge about the cell, the basic unit of living matter, increased. The theory of evolution proposed by Darwin had an enormous impact. And the new science of genetics, founded by Mendel, answered many questions about biological inheritance.
4. Jenner, Pasteur, Lister, and Koch made advances in medicine. New drugs and medical techniques, such as surgery with anesthesia, were developed.
5. Improvements in diet and food storage changed people's lives, while immigration to the cities changed population patterns.
6. Those who studied the behavior of people as members of societies began to use scientific methods. Their fields of study came to be known as the social sciences and included new techniques for understanding history, politics, and economics. These new social sciences also included anthropology, sociology, and psychology.
7. Compulsory education won gradual acceptance in western Europe and the United States in the late 1800s. More and more people learned to read and write. This educated audience made possible the publication of books, magazines, and newspapers that presented a wide range of opinions and ideas.
8. The arts reflected the social and economic changes of the industrial age. In the early 1800s, many writers, musicians, and artists were caught up in the romantic movement, which emphasized emotion, nature, and nationalism.

9. In the late 1800s, romanticism gradually gave way to realism. In painting and sculpture, romanticism and realism were followed by an intensely individualistic period.

On a separate sheet of paper, complete the following review exercises.

Reviewing Important Terms

Match each of the following terms with the correct definition below.

a. physical science
b. special theory of relativity
c. social science
d. romantic movement
e. genetics
f. biological science
g. realism
h. regionalism
i. impressionists

_____ 1. the portrayal of everyday life in different parts of the country
_____ 2. artists who painted people and places as they might appear in a brief glance
_____ 3. deals with the realities of everyday life
_____ 4. deals with living organisms
_____ 5. studies people as members of society
_____ 6. deals with the "romance" of life
_____ 7. $E = mc^2$
_____ 8. deals with nonliving aspects of nature
_____ 9. studies the ways in which inborn characteristics of plants and animals are inherited by their descendants

Developing Critical Thinking Skills

1. **Summarizing Ideas** What were four of the technological advances during the period from 1870 to 1900 that made life easier?
2. **Understanding Ideas** What medical advances saved lives in the late 1800s and early 1900s?
3. **Classifying Ideas** Identify the name of the author or composer of each of the following literary or musical works: **(a)** *Madame Bovary,* **(b)** *Middlemarch,* **(c)** *A Doll's House,* **(d)** *Tom Sawyer,* **(e)** *Fidelio,* **(f)** *The Nutcracker,* **(g)** *War and Peace,* **(h)** *Aïda.*
4. **Determining Cause and Effect** How did advances in

Publication of Charles Darwin's *On the Origin of Species by Means of Natural Selection* — **1859**

Development of first workable classification of the elements by Dmitri Mendeleyev — **1868 1869**

Publication of Mark Twain's *Tom Sawyer* — **1876**

Invention of the telephone by Alexander Graham Bell

Publication of Mark Twain's *Huckleberry Finn* — **1884**

Invention of the first successful gasoline-driven automobile in the United States — **1893**

1895 Discovery of X rays by Wilhelm Roentgen

1897 Discovery of the electron by J. J. Thomson

1900 Development of quantum theory by Max Planck

1903

First successful airplane flight by the Wright brothers — **1905**

Development of special theory of relativity by Albert Einstein

Discovery of penicillin by Alexander Fleming — **1928**

the physical and biological sciences affect the development of other branches of knowledge?

5. **Analyzing Ideas** Why might each of the following be considered a response to industrialization: **(a)** romanticism; **(b)** realism; **(c)** compulsory education.

✦ Relating Geography to History

Select a particular author, composer, or artist discussed in this chapter. Use encyclopedias or other references to find out if he or she traveled extensively. Then write a short summary explaining how that person's environment and the extent of his or her travel may have affected his or her contributions to literature, music, or art.

Relating Past to Present

1. To investigate medical progress during the 1900s, interview a physician, nurse, pharmacist, or public health official in your community. You may wish to include the following questions: **(a)** How have medical advances made during the 1800s been improved upon? **(b)** What has been the most significant medical breakthrough in recent years? Record the responses to such questions for use in a general discussion of current medical technology.

2. Newspapers and news magazines became very popular during the late 1800s. What newspapers and news magazines can you find on the newsstands in your town or city? Select two or three of these and find out the year in which they were first published. Did any of the publications originate in the 1800s or early 1900s? If so, ask your librarian about the availability of early issues. Notice the kinds of articles and advertisements that ran when the magazine or newspaper first appeared. How do they compare with those printed today? What do the advertisements suggest about changes in society over a period of time?

Applying History Study Skills

Before completing this activity, review Building History Study Skills on page 537.

Several historical themes of the first half of the 1800s are combined in *Le Moulin de la Galette* by French painter Pierre-Auguste Renoir, shown on page 539. The painting is part of the impressionist school and shows people in a common meeting place in a French city. Study the painting and answer the following questions.

1. **(a)** How would you define *impressionism*? **(b)** How is it portrayed in *Le Moulin de la Galette*?
2. How does the setting of the painting show the middle class?
3. **(a)** What is the theme of the painting? **(b)** How do you know?
4. **(a)** Are the people portrayed in the painting different from the traditional ideal of men and women? **(b)** If so, in what ways?
5. Compare *Le Moulin de la Galette* to Daumier's *The Washerwoman*. What similarities or differences can you identify?

Investigating Further

1. **Writing a Report** Using books on the history of art, research Honoré Daumier's paintings on political themes. You might use Helen Gardner's *Art Through the Ages* (Harcourt Brace Jovanovich) or H. W. Janson's *History of Art* (Prentice-Hall) as sources. What is the subject of each painting? What techniques did Daumier use to influence public opinion? Why might a painting or other work of art sometimes have a greater impact than a written commentary?

2. **Preparing a Book Report** Writers of the early 1800s sought to appeal to the emotions and sentiments of their readers. They turned to nature and the past for inspiration, and their stories were often filled with adventure, romance, and personal heroics. Read one of the following novels and explain how it reflected the ideas of the romantic movement: Sir Walter Scott's *Ivanhoe* (Pocket Books); Rafael Sabatini's *Scaramouche* (Houghton Mifflin); Baroness Emmuska Orczy's *The Scarlet Pimpernel* (Macmillan).

3. **Preparing a collage** Using posterboard and a variety of magazines that may be discarded, make a collage of products that might be displayed in a 1980s exposition.

541

Reforms Swept Through Many Areas of the World in the 1800s

3.7 mil. BC   4000 BC   AD 2100

Significance

As the Industrial Revolution swept through Europe and the United States, people clamored for social and political reforms. An upper-middle class who profited from the Industrial Revolution emerged. Many members of this class believed in the political philosophy of **liberalism,** which advocated representative government, the protection of individual rights by law, and the ability of people to think and work as they please.* In many countries these reforms came through new laws. In others, however, it took revolutions and wars to win more rights.

The British Parliament passed laws extending rights to many citizens and granting its colonies self-government. In the United States, sectional tensions erupted in a bloody civil war before constitutional amendments extended citizens' rights. In France people endured riots, revolution, unstable governments, and wars before securing a democratic government. And leaders of revolutions set up republics throughout Latin America.

Terms to Define

liberalism   anarchist
sectionalism   mestizo

People to Identify

Benjamin Disraeli   Alfred Dreyfus
Louis Napoleon   Simón Bolívar

Places to Locate

Quebec   Florida
New South Wales   Texas
New Zealand   Mexico

Questions to Guide Your Reading

1 In what ways did liberal theories affect Great Britain and its empire?
2 How did social change affect the United States?
3 What effect did revolutions and changes of government have in France?
4 How did the Latin American nations gain independence from European powers?

---

*Liberalism in the 1800s differed greatly from liberalism today. For example, the liberals of the 1800s wanted to restrict voting to educated male property owners.

Florence Nightingale was a heroic Englishwoman who fought long-standing prejudices to make nursing a respectable profession. During the Crimean War, under terrible circumstances, she reorganized the inept military hospitals into efficient, sanitary places for saving lives. The following excerpt from Cecil Woodham Smith's biography, Florence Nightingale, describes the admiration and respect she earned from the doctors and fighting men who observed her during the war.

❝ *I*n January, 1855 there were 12,000 men in hospital and only 11,000 in the camp before Sebastopol; and still the shiploads came pouring down. It was, Miss Nightingale wrote, 'calamity unparalleled in the history of calamity.'

In this emergency she became supreme. She was the rock to which everyone clung.

Her calmness, her resource, her power to take action raised her to the position of a goddess. The men adored her. . . . The doctors came to be absolutely dependent on her. ❞

The voices of women struggling for recognition of their rights through political reform were beginning to be heard in the 1800s.

1 Liberal Theories Affected Great Britain and Its Empire

Those who believed in liberalism were often active in politics during the 1800s. In Great Britain and in parts of the British Empire, for example, liberals helped enact a number of reforms aimed at protecting political and civil liberties. Some reforms extended the right to vote to working men and to women. Another abolished slavery, which had denied human and civil rights to black people.

British Reforms of the 1800s

Great Britain was one of the first European nations to abolish divine-right monarchy. The Glorious Revolution of 1688 (see Chapter 16) made Parliament the real ruler of the country. Great Britain became a limited constitutional monarchy with executive power vested in a cabinet headed by the prime minister.

◀ *William Gladstone in the House of Commons*

Voting restrictions. Theoretically the House of Commons represented all the British people. The voters of each district elected the members of Commons. The government, however, was not a complete democracy because not all the people had a chance to participate in it. The rights to vote and to hold public office were severely restricted in several ways: (1) Only property owners and a few other privileged people could vote. (2) Catholics, Jews, and Dissenters (non-Anglican Protestants) could not hold political office. (3) People voted in the open rather than in private. Unscrupulous people could ensure "cooperation" of bribed or intimidated voters. (4) The boundaries of election districts, or boroughs, had not been changed since 1664, even though the distribution of population had changed dramatically. (5) In some boroughs nobles who were members of the House of Lords controlled the choosing of a representative. (6) Only men who owned considerable property could be elected to the House of Commons.

The Reform Bill of 1832. As time went on, the middle class and the workers began to demand reforms. At first the upper classes resisted reforms because they feared a political change might bring about a reign of terror just as it had in the French Revolution. Then, from 1793 to 1815, British involvement in wars with France provided a convenient excuse for delaying action.

After Napoleon's defeat, Britain, like continental Europe, experienced a period of reaction that threatened even long-established civil liberties such as the right of *habeas corpus.* Reformers who once might have tried to gain the king's support could find no help because of George III's insanity and George IV's incompetency. However, in 1829, near the end of George IV's reign, one piece of reform legislation passed. The Catholic Emancipation Act permitted the election of Roman Catholics to Parliament if they recognized the Protestant monarch as the legitimate ruler of Great Britain.

As time went on, the middle class and the laboring class demanded more extensive reforms. Several times the House of Commons passed bills that gave more people the right to vote and reapportioned election districts more fairly. Each time, the House of Lords refused to pass the bill. When the Whigs came to power in 1830, the cabinet forced the new king, William IV, to announce that he would create as many new lords as necessary to give the bill a majority in the House of Lords. To avoid this move, the lords grudgingly gave in and passed the bill in 1832.

The Reform Bill of 1832 took seats in the House of Commons away from the less populated boroughs and gave the seats to the new industrial cities. It also lowered property qualifications for voting. Now about 1 out of every 30 Englishmen could vote. As a result, people made wealthy by the Industrial Revolution gained parliamentary power, and this new class now had a voice in government.

The Whig Party, which had forced the passage of the Reform Bill of 1832, had the support of the new voters. Since many voters favored even more liberal reforms, the party changed its name and became the Liberal Party. The Tory Party of the large landowners, who had opposed the reforms and hesitated to go any further, became known as the Conservative Party.

Social and economic change. Vital social and economic developments took place after 1832. In 1833 Parliament passed an act that provided for the gradual abolition of slavery throughout the British colonies. The act gave freedom to all children under the age of six; all children six and older were to be free within seven years.

The Liberal Party soon forced the adoption of other reforms. The government took a timid first step toward free public education by giving financial support to private and church schools. Another reform abolished imprisonment for debt.

The Liberal Party also helped repeal the unpopular Corn Laws. For many years Britain's Corn Laws had set high tariffs on imported grain. By raising prices on imports, the Corn Laws protected expensive British grain against competition from cheaper foreign crops. British landowners benefited because they could sell their grain at high prices; however, the high prices created a hardship for workers who had to buy grain products or starve. In 1846, after a bitter fight, Parliament repealed the Corn Laws. Grain could now be imported into Britain free of tax. The repeal of the Corn Laws represented Britain's first step toward free trade.

Chartism. Beginning in the 1830s, a group known as the Workingman's Association petitioned Parliament to adopt reforms such as universal manhood **suffrage,** or voting rights, and the secret ballot. These proposals were made in a document called *A People's Charter,* and those who advocated them became known as *Chartists.* They proposed complete democracy for Great Britain.

The Chartists held conventions in 1839, 1842, and 1848. Although the Chartists made relatively mild proposals, many people believed they threatened the very foundations of society. In 1848 the British authorities worried that revolution might occur in Great Britain. But the Chartists were not unified in their aims, and the movement died out.

Despite the failure of the Chartist movement, Parliament eventually adopted most of the reforms its members advocated. Workers continued to demand voting rights, and many others who favored more democratic government joined them. Leaders of both the Conservative and Liberal parties came to realize that reforms might gain the gratitude and the votes of the new voters.

In 1867 Parliament passed a second Reform Bill with more sweeping reforms than the first. It almost doubled the number of those who could vote. By lowering property qualifications, the second Reform Bill extended the vote to most city industrial workers. However, household servants, members of the armed forces, agricultural workers, and women did not gain voting rights.

Disraeli and Gladstone

William IV died in 1837. Since he had no male heirs, the throne went to his 18-year-old niece,

Learning from Pictures   Disraeli was Queen Victoria's favorite prime minister. What did he achieve in foreign policy between 1874 and 1880?

Learning from Pictures   Thomas Sully portrayed Queen Victoria shortly after she became queen. Her reign was the longest in British history.

Victoria. She interfered very little in the government and allowed her prime ministers a free hand. Victoria reigned from 1837 until 1901, a 64-year period so outstanding in British history that it became known as the *Victorian Era*.

Two outstanding prime ministers—Benjamin Disraeli and William Gladstone—dominated the political arena between 1866 and 1894. Benjamin Disraeli led the Conservative Party and served twice as prime minister. In addition to his wit and shrewdness, Disraeli had an intense interest in foreign affairs and the expansion of the British Empire.

Disraeli's first term as prime minister lasted only a few months. He first became prime minister when Lord Derby resigned in February of 1868, but he was defeated by Gladstone and the Liberals in the general election held later that year. During his second ministry, from 1874 to 1880, Britain gained control of the Suez Canal and Queen Victoria became Empress of India.

William Gladstone led the Liberal Party and served four terms as prime minister. He was devout, cautious, and formal. His formality even bothered

545

The Victorians and King Arthur

Waving farewell to the magical sword Excalibur, Sir Bedivere watches as the mysterious Lady of the Lake takes back the weapon that had served his beloved King Arthur for so many years.

This ancient legend of Arthur, the ideal king, and his Knights of the Round Table dates back to the 600s. Stories about the good and powerful leader were spread by word of mouth throughout England, Wales, and France for centuries. Then, in the 1400s, the English writer Sir Thomas Malory adapted these tales, and William Caxton, one of England's first printers, published them. Children and adults have loved reading them ever since.

King Arthur was a special favorite during the Victorian Era. This scene was drawn in 1893 by Aubrey Beardsley, who was only 21 when he was commissioned to illustrate the King Arthur stories. Beardsley established a personal form of art, blending the ornate curves of art nouveau (new art) with the feeling and pattern of Japanese prints. He quickly became

the leading illustrator of his day. But Beardsley did not live to enjoy his fame. He died of tuberculosis when he was only 25. Although often imitated, his exquisite, flat black-and-white style has remained unique.

Queen Victoria, who complained, "Mr. Gladstone addresses me as if I were a public meeting." Gladstone concerned himself with British domestic and financial matters. Under his leadership, Parliament attempted additional reforms, many of which went into effect.

Gladstone first became prime minister in 1868. One of his finest achievements as prime minister was the passage of the Education Act of 1870, which created a national elementary education system. The passing of this act meant that the children of the working classes could now receive an elementary education for a small fee. Elementary education became free in England in 1891.

In 1872, under Gladstone's leadership, Britain adopted the secret ballot. Now a man could vote as he chose, without fearing that he might suffer because someone disapproved of his politics. The secret ballot also reduced bribery, which had been common, and protected the workers in the cities from intimidation by their bosses.

In 1884 Gladstone and the Liberals pushed through Parliament the third Reform Bill, which gave the vote to most agricultural workers. In the following year, 1885, the Redistribution Bill divided Britain into electoral districts approximately equal in population. Although this bill did not achieve complete equality in representation, it was an important step in this direction.

The Irish Question

One area in which the Liberals proved unsuccessful was the "Irish Question." In 1801 the Act of Union had joined Ireland and Great Britain to form the United Kingdom of Great Britain and Ireland. The Act of Union disbanded Ireland's Parliament, leaving the Irish with little representation in the British Parliament. In addition to resenting the poor parliamentary representation, the Irish people—mostly Roman Catholics—resented having to pay taxes to help support the Anglican church.

The Irish hated British rule, especially the absentee landlords who owned much of the land. Several times in the mid-1800s, the potato crop failed, and famine swept Ireland. The worst famine came in 1848, causing many Irish people to abandon their homes and flee to the United States. Those who remained wanted new land laws and **home rule,** or self-government. Gladstone tried unsuccessfully to get home-rule bills passed. Finally, the Conservatives made concessions to the Irish during the 1890s, and the "Irish Question" ceased to be troublesome for the next few decades.

British Reforms of the Early 1900s

Social reform accompanied political reform. During the late 1800s and early 1900s, the labor union movement grew stronger in Great Britain. Socialism, too, attracted many followers.

Social reforms. In 1884 a group of intellectuals founded the Fabian Society, a socialist organization aimed at "reconstructing society in accordance with the highest moral possibilities." At first the Fabians worked through the established political parties. In 1906 they helped workers, frustrated over the policies of the Liberal and Conservative parties, to found a new organization, the British Labour Party.

In 1905 the Liberal Party came to power. Under Herbert Asquith, prime minister from 1908 to 1916, the Liberals adopted extensive social welfare legislation. Laws provided for child care, old-age pensions, better housing, and health and unemployment insurance. In order to pay for all of these welfare benefits, Parliament raised taxes.

Changes within Parliament. The budget of 1909 increased taxes for the wealthy. Because the House of Lords opposed the budget, the Liberals took steps to decrease the power of the lords. The Parliament Bill of 1911 took away the lords' powers to veto tax and appropriation bills and allowed them only to delay passage of other bills. The lords bitterly opposed the act and passed it only after George V, who had become king in 1910, threatened to create enough new Liberal lords to pass it.

Within a month after the passage of the Parliament Bill, Liberals and workers achieved another vital goal. Parliament passed a law giving members of the House of Commons a salary of 400 pounds ($2,000) a year. Although by today's standards the amount seems small, it was a good salary for that time. It meant that a person without an independent income could afford to serve in Parliament.

Women's voting rights. Since the late 1880s, many women in Great Britain had demanded the right to vote. Led by energetic and outspoken women like Christabel Pankhurst and her mother, Emmeline, they were known as **suffragettes** because they wanted suffrage for all women. Suffragettes petitioned Parliament and marched. Many expected that women would receive the right to vote in 1910, but this did not happen. *

Reforming the Parliamentary System	
1829	Catholic Emancipation Act permitted Roman Catholics to be elected to Parliament
1832	First Reform Bill redistributed seats in Parliament and lowered property qualifications for voting
1867	Second Reform Bill further lowered property qualifications, almost doubling electorate
1872	Secret ballot adopted
1884	Third Reform Bill gave vote to most farm workers
1885	Redistribution Bill divided Britain into approximately equal electoral districts
1911	Parliament Bill took away power of lords except to delay passage of bills
1928	All British women over the age of 21 were granted voting rights

*In 1919, a bill gave the right to vote to women over the age of 30 if they or their husbands owned property. In 1928 another bill granted all British women over the age of 21 the right to vote.

● READ
WRITE
INTERPRET
CONNECT
THINK

BUILDING HISTORY STUDY SKILLS

Reading About History: Understanding Ideology

An ideology is a body of ideas on which a particular system is based. In the 1800s in Europe, the two conflicting ideologies were liberalism and conservatism. Liberalism was based on the political philosophy of the French Revolution and the Enlightenment. Those who followed the ideology of political liberalism believed in a constitution that protected individual rights. The role of the government was to protect these rights. An economic liberal believed in the freedom of the individual to pursue economic gain without government interference.

On the other hand, conservatism was the ideology of the old order that was hostile to the French Revolution and the Enlightenment. Those who followed the ideology of political conservatism believed in a traditional government system that upheld the privileges of the upper classes. Economic conservatives believed in the government's role to manage the economy so that the state would prosper.

Understanding an ideology helps you determine the extent to which a person's position is based on his or her belief in an ideology rather than the facts. For example, to what extent is a newspaper's support for a presidential candidate determined by ideology?

How to Understand Ideology

To understand an ideology, follow these steps.

1. Define the ideology. Find out what a person's ideology is by determining how he or she views change and the role of government.
2. Make connections. How does the ideology affect the author's viewpoint or the development of the author's argument?
3. Categorize the ideology. Is it economic or political?

Developing the Skill

The cartoons on the right were printed during the debate over the extension of suffrage to the workingman in 1867 in Great Britain. The argument sharply divided the liberals and the conservatives. Study the cartoons to determine the ideology of each of the cartoonists.

The political cartoon on the top expressed the liberal ideology. The cartoonist depicted the workingman as an angel carrying his tools, while drinking holy water from a font in a church. The cartoonist must have favored change and supported the government's extension of the right to vote, because he drew the worker in such a positive way.

The political cartoon on the bottom expressed the conservative ideology. In this cartoon the workingman is portrayed as a slovenly drunkard. This cartoonist's sympathy with the conservative ideology was apparent by

the negative way in which he depicted the workingman. The cartoonist opposed change because he would not want the government to extend voting rights to the undeserving worker.

Practicing the skill. Find a political cartoon in your local newspaper. By using the skills listed above, attempt to determine the political ideology of the cartoonist.

To apply this skill, see Applying History Study Skills on page 571.

Changes Within the British Empire

As Great Britain instituted social and political reforms, other changes occurred within the British Empire. Settlers in the British colonies of Canada, Australia, and New Zealand benefited from the liberal policies being enacted in Great Britain.

Canada

The French Canadians in Lower Canada (part of what is now Quebec) and British settlers in Upper Canada (part of what is now Ontario) had long been discontented with British rule. The problem arose primarily because the British Canadians wanted even more self-government, and the French-Canadians resented British rule.

During the 1830s a business depression, unemployment, and crop failures led to uprisings in both Lower and Upper Canada. The French Canadians tried to establish an independent French republic, while the British Canadians sought greater freedom from British officials. Neither revolt met with success.

The Durham Report. In 1838 the British government sent a new governor general, Lord Durham, to Canada to try to settle disagreements between the English- and French-speaking Canadians. A leader of the Liberal Party, Durham had helped write the Reform Bill of 1832. He was given broad powers to reform Canada's government.

In 1839 Lord Durham submitted a report to Parliament with a basic recommendation that became a guide for all later British colonial policy.

Learning from Maps In Canada the British avoided the mistakes they had made in the 13 American colonies. What is Canada's smallest province?

Learning from Pictures *This picture of Victoria, the capital of British Columbia, was taken in 1890. Victoria is among the most "British" of Canada's cities.*

Lord Durham suggested that if Great Britain granted self-government to colonies like Canada, it would keep these colonies in the empire.

The Durham Report also recommended that the British government aid immigration to Canada, build a railroad to help unite and develop the country, reform the tax and the court systems, and expand education. In 1840 the British Parliament passed laws to carry out the recommendations of the Durham Report. Known collectively as the Acts of Union, these laws joined Upper Canada and Lower Canada. It created a Parliament in which each region had equal representation. Between 1846 and 1848, the British enlarged the powers of the Canadian Parliament and granted self-government to the Canadian people.

The British North America Act. The union of Upper and Lower Canada did not work well in every respect. Each region was suspicious of the other, and their equal strength in Parliament resulted in many deadlocks. A solution came in 1864, however, when the eastern colonies of New Brunswick, Nova Scotia, and Prince Edward Island considered forming a federal union. Delegates from Canada and the colonies met in the city of Quebec.

They recommended a plan of federation, which the British Parliament approved as the British North America Act of 1867. The act created the Dominion of Canada with the provinces of Ontario, Quebec, Nova Scotia, and New Brunswick.

By the terms of the British North America Act, each province kept its own legislature to deal with local affairs. The federal Parliament, which dealt with national problems, met in Ontario at the Dominion capital, Ottawa. Dominion government was a parliamentary democracy with a cabinet based on the British model. The Liberal and Conservative political parties in Canada resembled those in Great Britain. The party in power appointed the premier, who had much the same influence as the British prime minister.

The Canadian provinces did not become completely independent through the British North America Act. Instead, Canada remained part of the British Empire and recognized the British king or queen, whose representative, the governor general, had the power of veto. (This power, however, would be rarely used.) The British government greatly influenced Canada's foreign relations.

Learning from Pictures *Great transcontinental railroads traversed the vast distances of Canada just as they did in the United States.*

Territorial growth. In 1869 Canada purchased a huge area, including the present Northwest Territories, from the Hudson's Bay Company, a private trading company in Canada. Because the Canadians feared that the United States would try to annex all or part of this vast area, they quickly created the province of Manitoba in the southeast portion of the area. British Columbia and Prince Edward Island became provinces during the 1870s, bringing the number of provinces in the Dominion to seven.

The completion in 1885 of the Canadian Pacific Railway (see map, page 549) opened western Canada to immigration. As a result, two more provinces—Alberta and Saskatchewan—joined the Dominion of Canada in 1905. *

The discovery of gold in the Klondike region led to the development of northwestern Canada. During the late 1890s, thousands of prospectors rushed to the area searching for gold. The Klondike gold rush brought so many people that the area was organized as the Yukon Territory in 1898.

Australia

Australia is a huge island, a continent in itself. Yet for centuries it remained unknown to the rest of the world. The European explorers who sailed into the Pacific Ocean in the 1500s missed it entirely. The Dutch sighted the continent in the early 1600s and named it New Holland, but considered it too poor to colonize. Captain James Cook, an English sailor on a scientific expedition for the navy, sailed along Australia's eastern shore in 1770. He named the region New South Wales, because of its resemblance to southern Wales, and claimed it for Great Britain.

Before the American Revolution, Great Britain sent many convicted prisoners to North America. After the British lost their 13 American colonies, they decided to send convicts to Australia. The first shiploads arrived in New South Wales in 1788, and soon the convicts founded the town of Sydney on the southeast coast. Free settlers arrived shortly afterward with land grants. Convicts who served their time and gained their freedom were allowed to remain in Australia and own land. However, these two groups did not always get along.

*In 1949 Newfoundland and its dependency, Labrador, became the tenth province of the Dominion of Canada.

AUSTRALIA AND NEW ZEALAND
First British Settlement, 1788–1834

1830 Date of first settlement   —— Present-day state boundary

LAMBERT CONFORMAL CONIC PROJECTION

Learning from Maps   *Australia is the world's only nation that occupies an entire continent. What city is the westernmost state capital?*

Australia experienced a lawless period in the early 1800s. Clashes among immigrants, exconvicts, and gangs of escaped convicts called bushrangers occurred frequently. Uncaring people hunted down and almost exterminated many of the aborigines (ab•uh•RIJ•uh•neez), the original inhabitants of Australia, as if they were animals.

In 1829 the British claimed the entire continent of Australia. By 1836 the colonies of Tasmania, Western Australia, and South Australia had been organized. The colony of Victoria was formed in 1851, and Queensland in 1859 (see map, this page).

The discovery of gold in 1851 in the new colony of Victoria brought a flood of immigrants to Australia. Soon the colonial legislatures began to pass acts that allowed only white people to immigrate. This "White Australia" policy antagonized many nations, particularly in the Orient. The Australian government strictly enforced the policy, however, and admitted only a few immigrants from countries other than Great Britain.

The Australian colonies developed independently for many years. They modeled their legislatures after the British Parliament, except that both upper and lower houses were elected. (In New South Wales, the members of the upper house were appointed for life.) In the 1890s the Australian colonies began to consider forming a federal union as protection against European nations seeking to expand their territories. Finally, in 1901, the colonies united to create the Commonwealth of Australia—a self-governing part of the British Empire.

Australian trade unions and the Labor Party influenced Parliament to adopt a great deal of social legislation. Parliament passed bills establishing old-age pensions, compulsory arbitration of labor disputes, and wage-fixing boards, among others.

New Zealand

Dutch sailors, and later Captain Cook, sighted the islands of New Zealand, southeast of Australia. Private companies developed the islands in the 1820s and 1830s. A treaty with the Maori (MOW • uhr • ee) chieftains, the native rulers of the islands, established British control in 1840. A few years later, the British Parliament gave New Zealand a constitution, and the islands became a self-governing colony.

Disputes over land brought the British settlers into conflict with the native inhabitants, and several Maori wars took place in the 1840s and 1860s. In other respects the development of New Zealand resembled that of Australia. The discovery of gold and the establishment of restricted immigration occurred in 1861. In 1893 New Zealand became the first country in the world to adopt voting rights for women. In 1907 New Zealand joined the British Empire as a dominion.

SECTION 1 REVIEW

1. **Define** liberalism, suffrage, home rule, suffragette
2. **Identify** Chartists, Queen Victoria, Benjamin Disraeli, William Gladstone, Fabian Society, Christabel Pankhurst, Lord Durham, Maori
3. **Locate** Ontario, Quebec, Ottawa, Australia, New Zealand
4. **Understanding Cause and Effect** (a) Why was the Reform Bill of 1832 necessary in Great Britain? (b) How did the bill affect the British government?
5. **Summarizing Ideas** What important political reforms were made in Great Britain between 1832 and 1867?
6. **Analyzing Ideas** Explain the terms of the British North America Act of 1867.
7. **Organizing Ideas** Name two social reforms passed by the British Parliament in the 1800s.

---

2 The United States Expanded and Changed

When the United States ratified its Constitution in 1788, the new nation consisted of 13 states along the Atlantic coast and additional territories that stretched westward to the Mississippi River. The country's population totaled about 4 million people, most of whom lived in farming communities in the eastern states.

The young nation was born during a time of European turmoil, and most Americans wanted to stay out of European affairs and develop their nation in peace. They did this so successfully that, during the next 100 years, the territory of the United States grew to almost 4 times its original size and its population increased to 60 million. By 1900 the United States took its place among the great nations of the world.

Territorial Growth

Many European powers expanded overseas and set up colonies. The United States, in contrast, expanded overland, within the continent of North America. Unlike European countries, the new nation expanded without acquiring any colonies.

The Northwest Territory. The land bounded by the Appalachian Mountains, the Ohio and Mississippi rivers, and the Great Lakes was known as the Northwest Territory. States that had originally claimed this area turned the land over to the United States when they ratified the Articles of Confederation. Once the country had gained independence, hundreds of settlers pushed across the mountains into the Northwest Territory. In 1787 Congress passed the Northwest Ordinance to provide some form of government for the settlers.

The Northwest Ordinance of 1787 guaranteed that people who lived in territories would have rights equal to those who lived in the original 13 states. It provided that the Northwest Territory would be divided into states and admitted into the Union on an equal basis with existing states. When a territory had 5,000 adult males, it could form a legislature to govern the territory. Then, when a territory had 60,000 inhabitants, it could adopt a constitution and apply for statehood. The ordinance, therefore, ensured orderly expansion.

Many people left their homes on the Atlantic seaboard to settle the Northwest Territory. These settlers knew that their territories would be admitted to the Union as equal states. As a result, 10 new states joined the United States between 1791 and 1820.

Completing the expansion. Most of the principles of the Northwest Ordinance were applied to all new lands as the country continued to expand. In 1803 Napoleon sold the vast territory of Louisiana (which Spain had ceded to France) to the United States for $15 million. Extending westward from the Mississippi River roughly to the Rocky Mountains, the so-called Louisiana Purchase almost doubled the size of the United States. The United States also purchased Florida from Spain in 1819 (see map, this page).

In 1836 American settlers in Mexican territory south of the Louisiana Purchase declared themselves independent and established the Republic of Texas. The United States annexed Texas by treaty in 1845, and war with Mexico resulted. The United States won the Mexican War and gained the Mexican Cession, a huge region that became the states of Utah, Nevada, California, and parts of Arizona, Colorado, New Mexico, and Wyoming.

In 1846 a treaty with Great Britain gave the United States the Oregon Country. The states of

Learning from Maps In its westward expansion, the United States encountered little opposition. How long did it take the nation to stretch from coast to coast?

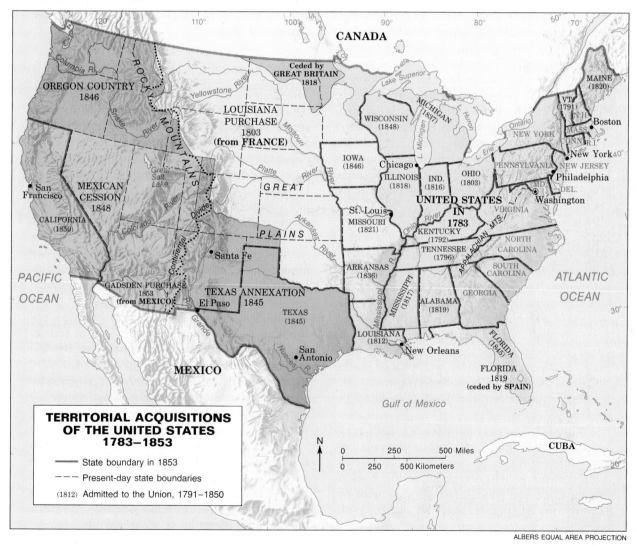

ALBERS EQUAL AREA PROJECTION

553

Oregon, Washington, Idaho, and parts of Montana and Wyoming were created from this land.

Finally, in 1853 the United States bought a small strip of land known as the Gadsden Purchase, in what is now southern New Mexico and Arizona, from Mexico for $10 million.

Thus, by the 1850s, the relatively new nation stretched from coast to coast and from Mexico to Canada. During the next 50 years, settlement caught up with territorial acquisitions. The discovery of gold in California in 1848 led to the California gold rush. Cattle ranchers, farmers, and miners settled in the plains and mountains of the western United States.

Political Growth

In the early days of the United States, some states had allowed only white male property owners to vote. The new states farther west imposed no such property qualifications. In time eastern states dropped property qualifications for male voters.

During the presidency of Andrew Jackson in the early 1830s, many changes occurred. Public education became widespread. An increasing number of political offices became elective instead of appointive. Political candidates came to be chosen by party conventions rather than by small groups of legislators. Foreign visitors spoke frequently of the "great democratic revolution" taking place in the United States.

The Slavery Question

Although the United States had a unified federal government, **sectionalism**—a rivalry among the various sections of the country—plagued the young nation. During the early 1800s, three major sections emerged: the Northeast, a region of growing cities and industry; the South, an area of many large farms, especially cotton and tobacco plantations; and the West, a frontier region of small, independent farms between the Appalachians and the Mississippi.

With such different ways of life, it is not surprising that people from each of these sections held very different views on such issues as internal improvements at federal expense, tariffs, banking and currency, and public lands. As time went on, however, the question of slavery became the greatest issue dividing the country.

Black slavery existed in the American colonies almost from the beginning. The Constitution accepted slavery but left its regulation up to the states. In states where slavery existed, only the state government could abolish it.

People in the southern states believed they needed slaves to harvest their crops of cotton and tobacco. Therefore, slavery increased in the South, especially after the invention of the cotton gin made cotton a profitable crop.

Both cotton and tobacco crops exhausted the soil. Southerners needed new lands and moved to the unsettled lands of the territories, bringing with them the institution of slavery. The question soon arose: Should slavery be permitted in the new territories? Southerners argued that Congress did not have the power to prohibit slavery in the territories; Northerners and Westerners argued that it did. A growing number of people came to advocate the abolition of slavery.

Secession and Civil War

The slavery question, as well as the issue of states' rights versus the federal government, led to bitter sectional quarrels throughout much of the 1800s. Southern states threatened many times to **secede,** or withdraw from the Union. Each time, compromises staved off secession. Then in 1860 Abraham Lincoln was elected president. Lincoln headed the newly formed Republican Party, which had pledged to prevent the spread of slavery into the territories.

Shortly after the election, South Carolina seceded and other southern states followed. They formed the Confederate States of America, with Jefferson Davis as president. Eventually 11 southern states joined the Confederacy.

President Lincoln and Congress said the Constitution did not give a state the right to secede. They declared that the Southerners had rebelled and that the United States government had a duty to suppress the rebellion. Efforts to compromise proved useless. By 1861 the Union and Confederate States of America were engaged in a bloody civil war that would last four years.

The Civil War was the most costly conflict in which the United States had been involved up to that time. It has been called the first modern war because it introduced new and lethal devices such as explosive shells, ironclad warships, and the Gatling gun, a forerunner of the machine gun.

MAJOR CIVIL WAR BATTLES 1861–1865

← Union forces
← Confederate forces
✴ Union victory
✴ Confederate victory
Union free states
Confederate states
Union slave states
⊛ Capital city

ALBERS EQUAL AREA PROJECTION

Learning from Maps   President Lincoln led the North in the fight to save the Union. What major battle was fought in the North?

Many European nations favored the Confederacy. Industrial and commercial interests hoped the war would weaken their business competitors in the Northeast. The British needed Southern cotton and frequently aided Confederate ships by letting them use British ports. Napoleon III of France took advantage of the conflict to intervene in Mexico.

As time went on, it became clear that the agricultural South lacked the industries and railroads necessary to supply its armies. The end finally came in April 1865, when the Confederacy surrendered. The Union was preserved.

In January 1863 President Lincoln had issued the Emancipation Proclamation, freeing slaves in

555

those parts of the country "still in rebellion against the United States." However, many plantation owners in the South did not honor the proclamation, and many slaves did not know about it. Following the Civil War, Congress passed three amendments to the Constitution: The Thirteenth Amendment abolished slavery, the Fourteenth Amendment gave former slaves citizenship and equal protection under the law, and the Fifteenth Amendment granted them the right to vote. Although in some areas of the country these laws were not strictly enforced, the amendments strengthened the principle of equality before the law.

The cost of preserving the Union had a tragically high price. The North and South together had lost nearly 600,000 people. Families had been torn apart as brother fought against brother. Freedom did not solve all the problems of the former slaves. The war left deep scars on the nation that remained well into the 1900s.

A Changing Nation

The United States experienced phenomenal growth from 1865 to 1900 primarily as a result of industrialization. Cities doubled and tripled in size, and a network of railroads crisscrossed the nation to link the cities together.

Immigration. Another important factor in this growth was immigration. For many decades people had come to the United States from England and Scotland. In the mid-1800s, a heavy wave of immigration came from two other regions—Ireland, which suffered severe potato famines, and Germany, where many people fled from revolutions in 1848.

In the late 1800s, immigration increased from southern and eastern Europe, especially Italy, Russia, and Austria-Hungary. The United States absorbed more immigrants than any other country in the world and soon became known as a "melting pot."

Woman suffrage. Many women had campaigned for the abolition of slavery. Some of these abolitionists, such as the sisters Sarah Moore Grimké and Angelina Emily Grimké, had begun publicly to address the status of women. They insisted that equality be extended to women as well as men.

In 1848 a women's rights conference, organized by Elizabeth Cady Stanton and Lucretia Mott, was

Learning from Pictures
Wyoming was the first state in the United States to grant woman suffrage. And some other states soon followed. Here Boston women vote in a municipal election.

556

held in Seneca Falls, New York. The delegates drew up a list of demands, including suffrage for women.

In the 1890s and early 1900s, many women continued the campaign for the right to vote. Finally in 1920, with the ratification of the Nineteenth Amendment to the Constitution, women won the right to vote.

SECTION 2 REVIEW

1. **Define** sectionalism, secede
2. **Identify** Northwest Ordinance, Grimké sisters, Elizabeth Cady Stanton, Lucretia Mott
3. **Locate** Louisiana Purchase, Mexican Cession, Oregon Country, Gadsden Purchase
4. **Organizing Ideas** List the steps in the territorial expansion of the United States from 1787 to 1853.
5. **Analyzing Ideas** In what ways did the United States become more democratic during the 1800s?
6. **Interpreting Ideas** How did the issue of slavery lead to the Civil War in the United States?

3 France Underwent Revolutions and Changes of Government

The Congress of Vienna restored the Bourbon monarch, King Louis XVIII, to the throne of France following Napoleon's exile in 1814. Louis, glad to be king and unwilling to upset the situation, carried on many of the reforms established between 1789 and 1815. He retained the Bank of France, the state-supported schools, and the Napoleonic Code. He accepted a constitution that limited his power and established a legislature to assist in governing the country. The constitution gave only the wealthy people the right to vote.

Charles X

When Louis XVIII died in 1824, his brother, Charles X—an ardent believer in absolute monarchy—succeeded him. As soon as he became king, Charles antagonized his subjects. First, he pledged that the government would reimburse the *émigrés* whose estates had been seized and sold to the peasants. This unpopular policy meant taxing all the people for the benefit of the emigrant nobles, who had opposed any progress or democracy in France. Second, Charles abolished most of the liberal provisions of the weak constitution his brother had accepted and tried to restore many features of the Old Regime.

Charles's actions caused trouble in France. Since 1789 the nation had learned too much about throwing off autocratic rule to accept these changes peacefully. In July 1830 a revolt spread throughout the country. Faced with growing hostility, Charles X abdicated.

The successful revolt in France inspired revolutions elsewhere. Two months after Charles's abdication in 1830, for example, the Belgians declared independence from their Dutch rulers.

Louis Philippe, the "Citizen King"

The leaders of the French revolt of 1830 wanted to be rid of Charles X, but they could not agree on the kind of government they wanted after his departure. Those favoring a republic lacked the strength to win. Finally, they reached a compromise and all groups agreed on the choice of another king. They selected Louis Philippe, Duke of Orléans, who belonged to a branch of the Bourbon family but had a record of liberal beliefs.

Louis Philippe was in a delicate position. He was a king, but an elected king. From the experience of Charles X, Louis Philippe knew that he could be deposed if he did not have the support of the majority of the French people. Therefore, he tried hard to please the people and called himself the "Citizen King."

The upper-middle class benefited more than any other class during the reign of Louis Philippe. After the revolt of 1830, the right to vote was extended to 200,000 of the wealthiest citizens, which included many newly rich manufacturers. Under Louis Philippe workers could not organize, and the government outlawed labor unions. High tariffs placed on imported goods benefited the owners of industries because they kept foreign-made goods out of France. However, the tariffs resulted in higher prices for domestic goods.

While the middle class generally favored Louis Philippe, he faced opposition from both monarchists and republicans. One group of monarchists wanted a direct descendant of Charles X to be king, while another group, the Bonapartists, wanted to revive Napoleon's empire.

The republicans stood at the other extreme from the monarchists. They believed that France should become a republic and should grant political rights and social changes to benefit all the people. Most French workers agreed. They disliked Louis Philippe's anti-labor measures and the high prices that resulted from his tariff policy. Food shortages and widespread unemployment increased discontent between 1846 and 1848.

The Roman Catholics, especially the higher clergy, also disliked Louis Philippe. They opposed the separation of church and state, a policy begun during the French Revolution and continued by Napoleon and Louis Philippe.

The Revolutions of 1848

In 1848 opposition to the regime of Louis Philippe erupted into violence. Trouble began over the principle of free speech. In February opponents of the government organized meetings where they criticized official policy. Louis Philippe issued a decree prohibiting the final meeting.

The publication of the decree sparked riots in Paris. The disorders did not seem serious until the National Guard, summoned to restore order, joined the rioters. The disturbances forced Louis Philippe to abdicate and flee to England.

The people of Paris established a temporary government and proclaimed the Second French Republic in 1848. (The First Republic had lasted from 1792 until 1804, when Napoleon became emperor.) The most active group in the new government consisted of the urban working classes, whose leaders believed in socialism. Because economic depression and widespread unemployment had paralyzed France, the socialist members of the government established "national workshops" to give people work. This action marked the first appearance in modern times of the idea that the government has a responsibility to remedy chronic unemployment.

Adopting universal manhood suffrage, the Second Republic held elections in April to choose a National Assembly to write a constitution for a permanent government. When the new National Assembly met in June, conservative members in the majority voted to stop the program of national workshops.

This action led to violent rioting in Paris. Fearing a widespread revolution, the Assembly allowed army officers to assume power. For three days Paris became a battlefield. Finally, the army crushed the rebellion and imprisoned, exiled, or executed its socialist leaders. Karl Marx, the founder of modern socialism, was expelled from France.

Louis Napoleon

The new constitution written by the National Assembly provided for a republican form of government, with an elected president. The president would serve a four-year term and would not be eligible for a second term. The National Assembly would be a single legislative body, consisting of representatives elected by universal manhood suffrage.

In December 1848 the Republic held its first elections. Instead of electing as president someone who had helped to create the Second Republic, however, the voters overwhelmingly chose Louis Napoleon Bonaparte, the nephew of Napoleon.

Louis Napoleon wanted to be more than a president. He began to work for the support of various influential groups in France. Like his uncle, he did everything he could to gain the backing of the army. To win support from French Catholics, he helped the pope suppress an attempt by Italian patriots to set up a republic in Rome. He also repealed certain laws so that the Catholic church could have more control over French education.

Economically, Louis Napoleon favored the middle class by encouraging the development of manufacturing and railroads. At the same time, however, he tried to keep the favor of the workers through actions such as setting up a program of public works that gave jobs to many. To the peasants, who owned their land, the newly elected president spoke of his devotion to the principle of private property. He reminded the peasants of the prosperity he had brought them through better transportation and larger markets. He also established a new bank that provided funds for agricultural improvements.

In addition, Louis Napoleon posed as a champion of democratic rights. Meanwhile, however, he limited criticism of his actions through strict censorship and by driving his critics out of France.

Louis Napoleon now employed the plebiscite, a device his uncle had used so successfully. He asked the French people to permit him to draft a new constitution for the Second French Republic. Most people believed that he was defending law and order. They voted almost 12 to 1 in his favor.

History Through the Arts

PAINTING

© Musées Nationaux

The Gleaners

"This art offends me and disgusts me," said the French director of fine arts about the work of Jean-François Millet. Millet not only rejected the popular romanticized style of his day—the 1850s and 1860s—but also used peasants and workers as his subjects.

Millet, a peasant himself, worked on the land until the age of 19 when he began studying with another artist. Understandably, then, he identified heavily with the peasant class.

Gleaners are the poorest peasants, who gather the leavings from a field after reaping. In this painting Millet makes them appear noble and dignified. That *The Gleaners* seems sentimental and idealized today is evidence of constantly changing tastes and values in art.

The Second French Empire

The new constitution extended Louis Napoleon's term as president to 10 years. Although it gave him greater power, he remained dissatisfied. He wanted to follow in the footsteps of his uncle, Napoleon I— and Napoleon I had been an emperor.

In 1852 Louis Napoleon held another plebiscite for another constitution. By cleverly manipulating the votes, Louis Napoleon won consent to take the title Emperor Napoleon III. (He called himself the "third" Napoleon because Napoleon I had had a son. "Napoleon II" had never reigned and died in 1832.)

On the surface the Second French Empire looked like a democracy. It allowed for a constitution and a legislature elected by universal manhood suffrage. In reality, however, France came under a new style of absolutism. The legislature could pass only those laws proposed by the emperor. The legislature had no power over spending and could not question the emperor's ministers.

People suspected of opposing the government could be imprisoned or exiled without trial. Newspapers were strictly censored. The government warned that any paper criticizing the emperor or his government would be warned twice, then shut down. Freedom of speech did not exist. Liberal professors in the universities lost their jobs. With all these restrictions, it became impossible to organize opposition to the government of Louis Napoleon.

Problems in the Crimea and Mexico

In order to quiet discontent at home, Napoleon III tried to win glory abroad. The weakening Ottoman Empire gave him his chance.

Because of earlier agreements, Russia claimed the right to protect all Orthodox Christians living under the rule of the Ottoman Turks. Similarly, France protected the Roman Catholics. In the 1850s both Russia and France claimed jurisdiction over certain holy places in Palestine, which was part of the Ottoman Empire. The Ottomans granted privileges to the Roman Catholics but did not do the same for the Orthodox Christians. The czar demanded these same privileges for the Orthodox Christians. Napoleon III took a firm stand against these Russian demands and formed an alliance with Great Britain, which feared Russian expansion toward the eastern Mediterranean.

The Ottoman Turks, backed by France and Great Britain, resisted Russian claims in the Palestine dispute. The three allies declared

559

Learning from Pictures Known as the Lady with the Lamp, Florence Nightingale tended to the wounded with her nursing corps during the Crimean War.

war in March 1854, and full-scale fighting began six months later. The fighting took place mostly in the Crimea, in southern Russia.

The Crimean War has been called "the most unnecessary war in history." The hostilities were conducted with inefficiency and wastefulness. The famous poem "The Charge of the Light Brigade," by Alfred, Lord Tennyson, described one tragic event of the war. A brigade of 600 horsemen charged across a valley and were cut to pieces by enemy fire. The following are two verses from the poem.

> **❝**Half a league, half a league,
> Half a league onward,
> All in the valley of Death
>   Rode the six hundred.
> 'Forward the Light Brigade!
> Charge for the guns!' he said.
> Into the valley of Death
>   Rode the six hundred. . . .
>
> Cannon to right of them,
> Cannon to left of them,
> Cannon in front of them
>   Volley'd and thunder'd;
> Storm'd at with shot and shell,
> Boldly they rode and well,
> Into the jaws of Death,
> Into the mouth of hell,
>   Rode the six hundred. **❞**

Despite the carnage of the war, the conflict did have two constructive results. First, modern field hospitals to care for the wounded came into use.

Second, Florence Nightingale established professional nursing of the wounded.

It took two years of fighting, with huge losses on both sides from battle and disease, for the allies to defeat Russia. France won glory but little else.

Napoleon III now turned to building the French colonial empire. In North Africa he took advantage of a native revolt to strengthen French rule over Algeria, which had begun in 1830. In 1859 French engineers began constructing the Suez Canal in Egypt. In Asia, Napoleon established French control over Cambodia, thus beginning a move into Indochina. He also tried, although unsuccessfully, to intervene in Mexico. From 1863 until 1867, French troops protected the Archduke Maximilian, the brother of the emperor of Austria, who had become ruler of Mexico with Napoleon's help. The Mexicans hated Maximilian and finally overthrew and executed him in 1867.

Napoleon now faced mounting pressures in France. The elections held in 1869 showed strong opposition by both liberals and conservatives.

The Franco-Prussian War

Napoleon III decided to try another bold and risky venture, hoping to regain the support of all groups in France. At this time Prussia was working to unite all the German states under its leadership (see Chapter 22). By opposing this unification, Napoleon could gain the support of almost all French people because they distrusted Prussia.

Napoleon really hoped that Prussia would back down and that war would not be necessary. However, Otto von Bismarck, the head of the Prussian government, had decided that war with France would help to achieve German unification. Bismarck made a series of clever maneuvers that angered the French, and in July 1870 the French legislature declared war on Prussia.

French defeat. From the start of the Franco-Prussian War, the French suffered disastrous defeats. Napoleon III went to the front to take command of the army, and at the battle of Sedan, he fell into the enemy's hands.

Immediately after the capture of Napoleon III, the Legislative Assembly proclaimed the fall of the Second French Empire and the establishment of a Third Republic. The new government tried to defend the nation, but Paris fell to the Prussians in January 1871, signifying the end of the war.

France Under German Domination

Bismarck drew up the Treaty of Frankfort, which dictated harsh terms to France. France had to give up the territories of Alsace and the eastern part of Lorraine on the French-German border. It also had to pay a huge indemnity to Germany within three years. German troops were to occupy northern France until they paid the indemnity.

In February 1871 Bismarck permitted the election of a National Assembly to decide whether France wanted to sign the peace treaty or to resume the war. The republicans urged renewal of the war. The monarchists took the position that France had already suffered defeat and should negotiate with the conquerors. About 70 percent of the elected delegates were monarchists—not because the French people favored monarchy, but because they wanted peace.

As in the revolutions of 1848, the people of Paris were strongly republican. They had fought almost alone to defend the city against the Prussians and were angered by the peace terms.

In March the socialists and radical republicans of Paris, supported by the National Guard, set up a municipal council to govern the city. It was called the Commune, like the Paris government established in 1792 during the French Revolution. The Communards, members of the Commune, proposed a program to reform France. Their pro-gram included decentralization—the redistribution of power from the central government to regional and local governments—separation of church and state, and replacement of the army by a national guard.

Disagreement between the Communards and the National Assembly resulted in a violent revolutionary uprising in Paris. Troops sent by the National Assembly entered Paris and fought several bitter and bloody battles against the Communards, defeating them in May 1871. The National Assembly immediately approved the Treaty of Frankfort.

The government borrowed money to pay the Germans the indemnity, and German soldiers left France in September 1873.

The Third Republic

After the fall of Napoleon III, quarreling factions in the National Assembly were unable to agree on a constitution until 1875. Finally, the assembly passed a group of laws known as the Constitution of 1875, which officially made France a republic.

The Third Republic included a president, elected by the legislature for a term of seven years. The cabinet of ministers had to approve the president's actions and was responsible for government policy. Although the constitution did not specifically provide for a premier, or prime minister, the position soon became established.

Learning from Pictures
Many famous buildings such as the Tuileries, the old royal palace, were burned during the fighting of 1871 in Paris.

During the late 1800s, France faced many problems, created mostly by groups represented in the legislature. One group wanted to make war on Germany in revenge for the Franco-Prussian War. Another group was hostile to the Catholics. Still another backed French expansion overseas, along the lines begun by Napoleon III. The conservative republicans managed to steer a course that avoided extremes; their legislation encouraged education and legalized trade unions. But the nation lacked financial stability, and unemployment soared.

In the 1890s a financial scandal rocked France. The crisis stemmed from the failure of the Panama Company, which had been formed to build a canal across the Isthmus of Panama. Ferdinand de Lesseps, the man responsible for building the Suez Canal, had been president of the company, and thousands of French people had invested in it. It failed because of dishonesty, mismanagement, and malaria, which killed many of the French working on the canal in the jungles of Panama. Accusations of bribery against a number of legislators endangered the government.

Another threat to the republic came from extremists of the labor movement; clashes occurred between workers and troops. **Anarchists,** who believed in the abolition of all governments by force, set off bombs and attempted to assassinate public figures, including the president.

The Dreyfus case. The most serious danger to the Third Republic arose in 1894. An attempt to betray French military secrets to Germany was uncovered. A court accused and convicted Captain Alfred Dreyfus, a Jewish officer, and sentenced him to life imprisonment. However, evidence soon came to light indicating that Dreyfus had been falsely convicted. Even so, the French army command would permit no criticism of its actions. Monarchists, many Catholics, and anti-Semites—people who dislike Jews—supported the army.

The real traitor was discovered, but the army cleared him. Émile Zola, a famous French novelist, wrote an open letter, *"J'Accuse"* ("I Accuse"), in which he placed blame on the army command and its supporters for this scandal. Although many responsible for the false charges against Dreyfus confessed, his name was not cleared until 1906.

The Dreyfus case led to a clash between the two major groups in France—those who had condemned Dreyfus and supported the army, and those who supported his cause.

Reform and political instability. After the Dreyfus case, French republicans planned several reforms. They took steps to end the favored position that Napoleon I had given the Roman Catholic church in France in 1801. The church and the state were officially separated in 1905, and France had complete religious freedom.

The existence of many different political parties caused political instability in France in the early 1900s. The parties ranged from the monarchists on the far right to radical socialists on the far left. Major parties contained a number of "splinter groups," or smaller divisions. No one party ever completely controlled the French government. In order to get anything done, parties temporarily united to form **coalitions,** or political groups organized in support of a common cause.

SECTION 3 REVIEW

1. **Define**   anarchist, coalition
2. **Identify**   Louis XVIII, Charles X, the "Citizen King," Florence Nightingale, Archduke Maximilian, Alfred Dreyfus
3. **Interpreting Ideas**   **(a)** Which class benefited most during the rule of Louis Philippe? **(b)** What groups opposed Louis Philippe?
4. **Analyzing Ideas**   How did Louis Napoleon become emperor?
5. **Evaluating Ideas**   How did the results of the Franco-Prussian War affect France?
6. **Explaining Ideas**   Describe France's internal political problems in the late 1800s and early 1900s.

4 The Nations of Latin America Gained Independence

By the early 1800s, the ideologies behind the French Revolution and Napoleonic Wars had strongly affected the political and social thinking of many Europeans. The people in Spain and Portugal's Latin American colonies also felt some of the effects. In time strong independence movements swept the region extending from the northern border of Mexico southward to the tip of South America. These independence movements traced their roots to the structure of colonial economies and societies, and once started, they spread rapidly.

Colonial Economy

Both the Spanish and Portuguese followed mercantilist principles in organizing their colonies. They wanted to provide as much income as possible for the rulers of the home country, for merchants engaged in overseas trade, and for the white colonists. In the Latin American colonial system, silver, gold, and plantation crops such as sugar provided the profits.

Large, self-sufficient farming estates called **haciendas** (hahs • ee • EN • duhz) and smaller farms of various sizes became the major economic units of colonial Latin America. Monarchs granted some enormous estates to conquistadors, or conquerors, and to court favorites. Huge land grants dotted California during the Spanish period, for example, and many of the grants survived under United States rule.

Many people who received these grants eventually sold them to rich merchants and mining entrepreneurs who wanted to diversify their investments. Landowners who did not live on their haciendas hired overseers to manage them.

In parts of Latin America, such as the Caribbean, much of the Indian population died as a result of disease and forced labor on the land or in the mines. Although the Indians later became free subjects under Portuguese and Spanish law, many worked for wages and became bound to their occupations because of debt. The demand for labor, however, became so great that the Spanish and Portuguese then imported black African slaves to relieve the labor shortage.

In the 1690s the Portuguese discovered gold in the Minas Gerais (MEE • nuhs zhuh • RYS) region of Brazil. The city of Rio de Janeiro, which became the colonial capital in 1763, grew because of its location near the mines. The gold discovery also brought on a labor shortage in other regions of Brazil. The Portuguese answered the shortage by importing more black slaves.

The wealth of the Spanish and Portuguese colonies impressed visiting Europeans. Mexico City, Lima, and other cities had large populations and imposing cathedrals and government palaces. The colonial governments built immense fortresses, like the one guarding the port of San Juan in Puerto Rico, to protect the water approaches to the cities from pirates and sea dogs.

Learning from Pictures *Many West Indian economies depended on slave labor. The slaves shown here are working on an indigo plantation in the 1700s.*

Colonial Society

Social classes based on privilege divided colonial society. The highest ranks of society consisted of the royal bureaucrats, the owners of large estates, and the great merchants. An enormous social gap opened between these classes and the town workers, peasants, and slaves.

Racial discrimination made the situation in Latin America worse than in Europe. White people, called **peninsulars** because they were born in Spain or Portugal, ruled colonial society. Whites born in the colonies—called **creoles**—suffered social snobbery and job discrimination at the hands of the peninsulars.

Indians and blacks shared the bottom of the social pyramid. Many of them did not speak the language of the ruling class. Furthermore, laws upheld racial distinctions.

By the 1700s people of mixed race became the majority in Latin American society: **Mestizos** were of Indian and white background, and **mulattoes** were of black and white ancestry. Distribution of mestizos and mulattoes varied considerably. For example, mestizos became prominent in Mexico, but in Brazil mulattoes became the largest group. Mestizos and mulattoes usually faced social and racial barriers constructed by the peninsulars and creoles. In the Andes, southern Mexico, and parts of Central America, Indians remained the largest group.

563

Learning from Pictures *Toussaint-Louverture was the leader of Haitian independence. He struggled to free slaves and resisted Napoleonic rule.*

Catholic church. The Roman Catholic church wielded great power and an enormous influence in the Spanish and Portuguese colonies. Missionaries who accompanied the explorers and conquistadors immediately began converting the Indians to Catholicism. The missionaries not only took an interest in Indian culture, but in many cases they also tried to prevent the government and colonists from abusing the Indians.

By the 1700s the Jesuits had become extremely powerful and rich, through the ownership of haciendas, town property, mines, and thousands of slaves. During the mid-1700s Spanish and Portuguese kings dissolved the Jesuit order in their kingdoms and seized all their colonial property.

Social life. Spain and Portugal greatly influenced social customs in the colonies. The male-dominated society of the Iberian Peninsula carried over into Latin America. For example, men had a rigid conception of family honor, and they believed in restricting the younger women of the household. A man could kill an unfaithful wife and go unpunished.

At lower levels of society, women, by necessity, participated more actively in economic life. Often they headed the households and their families lived on their earnings. Many women in the towns ran small businesses.

Growing Discontent

By the late 1700s, the Spanish and Portuguese colonies underwent administrative reform and economic growth, inspired in part by the Enlightenment (see Chapter 17). Nevertheless, the revolutionary events in British North America and France in the late 1700s aroused interest, particularly among discontented creoles. Although the creoles had begun to fill many upper-level positions in the colonial government, King Charles III of Spain sent peninsulars to take over the top jobs.

Not only did the creoles suffer discrimination in the colonial bureaucracy, but Spain's economic policy also angered them. Charles III began to relax some of the stiff mercantilist restrictions, and creole merchants feared they might lose their monopolies.

The Spanish and Portuguese colonists fared even worse than the British colonists. Spain and Portugal had little industry, so their merchants supplied the colonies with goods from Great Britain and France, after taking a substantial profit for themselves. Widespread smuggling resulted. The Spanish colonists also resented having to pay taxes to finance Spain's wars.

The colonists in Latin America believed they had good reason to rebel. In 1815 the creole revolutionary Simón Bolívar (see • MOHN boh • LEE • vahr) stated, "The hatred that the Peninsular has inspired in us is greater than the ocean which separates us."

Haiti's Slave Revolution

By the early 1800s, Spain's American colonies were ripe for revolution. The first successful revolt, however, took place in the French colony of Haiti, on the island of Hispaniola in the West Indies.

In Haiti a small number of French planters grew sugarcane and coffee trees on plantations tended by African slaves. When the French Revolution broke out, the free mulattoes demanded the same rights as French settlers. In 1794 the black slave population rebelled. Mulattoes and blacks united under the leadership of François-Dominique Toussaint-Louverture (too • SAN loo • ver • TOOR), a freed slave, and won control of the island.

Napoleon sent an army to try to reestablish French authority. The French captured Louverture, and he died a prisoner in France in 1803. Later, a

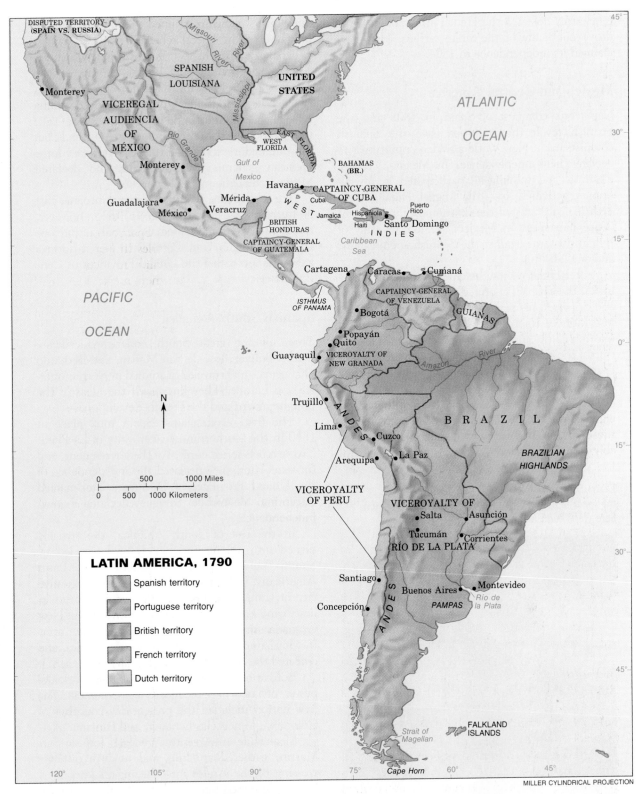

LATIN AMERICA, 1790

- Spanish territory
- Portuguese territory
- British territory
- French territory
- Dutch territory

DISPUTED TERRITORY
(SPAIN VS. RUSSIA)

• Monterey

SPANISH
LOUISIANA

UNITED
STATES

VICEREGAL
AUDIENCIA
OF
MÉXICO

ATLANTIC

OCEAN

Rio Grande

Missouri River

Mississippi

• Monterey

EAST FLORIDA
WEST
FLORIDA

Gulf of
Mexico

BAHAMAS
(BR.)

Guadalajara •

Mérida •

• México
• Veracruz

Havana •

CAPTAINCY-GENERAL
OF CUBA

Cuba

Jamaica

Puerto
Rico

Hispaniola

Haiti

Santo Domingo

W E S T

I N D I E S

BRITISH
HONDURAS

CAPTAINCY-GENERAL
OF GUATEMALA

Caribbean
Sea

PACIFIC

OCEAN

Cartagena •

• Caracas

• Cumaná

CAPTAINCY-GENERAL
OF VENEZUELA

ISTHMUS
OF PANAMA

• Bogotá

GUIANAS

• Popayán
• Quito

Guayaquil •

VICEROYALTY OF
NEW GRANADA

Amazon River

B R A Z I L

• Trujillo

A
N
D
E
S

• Lima

• Cuzco

BRAZILIAN
HIGHLANDS

• Arequipa

• La Paz

VICEROYALTY
OF PERU

VICEROYALTY OF

• Salta

• Asunción

• Tucumán

• Corrientes

RÍO DE LA PLATA

N

0   500   1000 Miles

0   500   1000 Kilometers

• Santiago

• Buenos Aires

• Montevideo

PAMPAS

Río de
la Plata

• Concepción

A
N
D
E
S

FALKLAND
ISLANDS

Strait of
Magellan

Cape Horn

120°   105°   90°   75°   60°   45°

45°

30°

15°

0°

15°

30°

45°

MILLER CYLINDRICAL PROJECTION

Learning from Maps *Spain allowed little colonial participation in governing its New World colonies. What six cities are located in the Viceroyalty of Peru?*

rebel army defeated the French army and killed or drove out many of the white settlers. Haiti proclaimed its independence in 1804.

Mexico and Central America

Napoleon's conquest of Spain in 1808 and the Spanish revolt that followed gave the Spanish colonists in the New World a golden opportunity to declare their independence. In Mexico, creoles, mestizos, and Indians all participated in revolutionary activities. In 1810 Miguel Hidalgo (ee·THAHL·goh) started the first important independence movement in Mexico. He led an army of Indian peasants against the Spanish, peninsulars, and creoles.

After Hidalgo's forces achieved some early victories, the Spanish captured and executed Hidalgo and dispersed his peasant army in 1811. A priest, José Morelos (moh·RAY·lohs), who wanted land reform and the abolition of slavery, assumed leadership of the rebels. Upper-class Mexican creoles preferred things the way they were, and in 1815 they captured and shot Morelos.

In 1814 the very conservative Ferdinand VII regained the throne of Spain. The Mexican creoles, who had been frightened by Hidalgo, looked favorably upon Ferdinand. However, in 1820 liberal

Learning from Pictures *José de San Martín, the great hero of Argentine independence, is shown here (left) with his military staff.*

army rebels in Spain stripped the king of some of his powers. The liberal rebellion in Spain caused upper-class Mexicans to fear that the new Spanish government would apply liberal reforms in the colonies. Therefore, in 1821 they carried out an independence movement of their own. A militia general named Agustín de Iturbide (ee·toor·BEE·thay) proclaimed himself Emperor Agustín I, but his unpopular dictatorial rule did not last long. Mexican generals overthrew him and declared Mexico a republic in 1824.

For a brief time, Central America became part of Iturbide's Mexican empire. In 1823, however, representatives from Guatemala, El Salvador, Honduras, Nicaragua, and Costa Rica met to form a federal union called the United Provinces of Central America.

Spanish South America

Three of the great South American leaders—Simón Bolívar, José de San Martín, and Bernardo O'Higgins—had traveled or studied in North America and Europe. They knew well the ideas of the Enlightenment and the French Revolution.

The first revolt against Spain took place in 1810 in the southernmost viceroyalty of La Plata. Creole rebels seized control of the government, and six years later, they declared the independence of the United Provinces of La Plata, later named Argentina. Meanwhile, Paraguay declared its own independence.

In the rest of South America, the struggle turned into a long and bloody civil war led by Simón Bolívar, called "the Liberator" by Latin Americans. Bolívar started the revolt in his native city of Caracas in 1810. He did not succeed in destroying Spain's power in the viceroyalty of New Granada until 1819. Then he raised another army in what is now Venezuela, crossed the Andes, and defeated the Spanish at Boyacá (bah·yuh·CHAY).

Bolívar became president, with almost absolute power, of a new nation called Great Colombia. The new nation included the present-day countries of Colombia, Venezuela, Ecuador, and Panama.

Meanwhile an Argentine general, José de San Martín, gathered an army and made a difficult crossing of the Andes into the region known as Chile. He joined forces with the Chileans, led by Bernardo O'Higgins, and overcame Spanish resistance there in 1818.

From Chile, San Martín's forces sailed north to capture the city of Lima in Peru. The Spanish viceroy fled, and San Martín declared the independence of Peru in 1821. Royalist forces, however, remained in parts of Peru. Internal squabbling among the independence leaders led some Peruvians to invite Bolívar to help them defeat the Spanish. San Martín then withdrew, turning leadership over to the ambitious Bolívar.

In August 1824 Bolívar won a major victory over the forces led by the Spanish viceroy at Junín (hoo•NEEN) in Peru. By December of that year, the revolutionaries achieved total victory over the forces loyal to Spain at Ayacucho (eye•uh•KOO•choh). Peru was free. In 1825 the northern territory of Upper Peru became a separate republic, named Bolivia in honor of Bolívar.

Brazil

When Napoleon's army invaded Portugal in 1808, King John VI and his family fled to Brazil. Once there, John elevated Brazil to a realm equal to Portugal and opened its ports to foreign trade. Even after the overthrow of Napoleon, King John stayed in Brazil. In 1820, however, a revolt broke out in Portugal, and the Portuguese persuaded King John to return home.

The Portuguese then tried to return Brazil to the status of a colony. Angered Brazilian creoles persuaded Pedro, King John's son who had stayed in Brazil, to become ruler of an independent Brazil. Brazil declared its independence as a constitutional monarchy in 1822, and Pedro I ruled as its emperor until 1831.

The new nations of Brazil and Argentina struggled over territory that lay between them. Patriots in this disputed territory gained independence in 1825, calling their new country Uruguay.

Almost all of Latin America had thus become independent by 1825. Portugal lost its entire New World empire. The Spanish lost all their colonies except Cuba and Puerto Rico. Elsewhere in Latin America, only Jamaica, the Guianas, British Honduras, and a few smaller islands in the Caribbean remained under colonial rule.

Foreign Reactions to Independence

The British hoped to benefit from Latin American independence. They were eager to increase their

Learning from Pictures *Influenced by the Enlightenment, the creole Simón Bolívar led the independence movement in northern South America.*

trade with the region, which they imagined to be richer than it really was. Also, the British viewed the Latin Americans as potential allies against continental Europe, which was growing more conservative. For this reason, the British had provided the rebels with small amounts of arms, primarily in South America.

The War of 1812 with Great Britain had distracted the United States. In addition, the United States did little to help the Latin American revolutionaries, because it did not wish to anger Spain while trying to get that country to give up Florida. Even after Spain ceded Florida in 1819, the United States had no Latin American policy until late in the administration of President James Monroe. Like the British, however, Americans saw the region as a vast new market and became alarmed when the Spanish tried to regain their colonies in the 1820s.

In 1823 President James Monroe sent a message to Congress that came to be known as the Monroe Doctrine. It declared that the United States would not intervene in Europe's affairs or interfere in any of Europe's remaining colonies in the Western Hemisphere. At the same time, the United States would oppose any attempt by European nations to reestablish lost colonies, to form new colonies, or to interfere with any of the American governments in the Western Hemisphere.

567

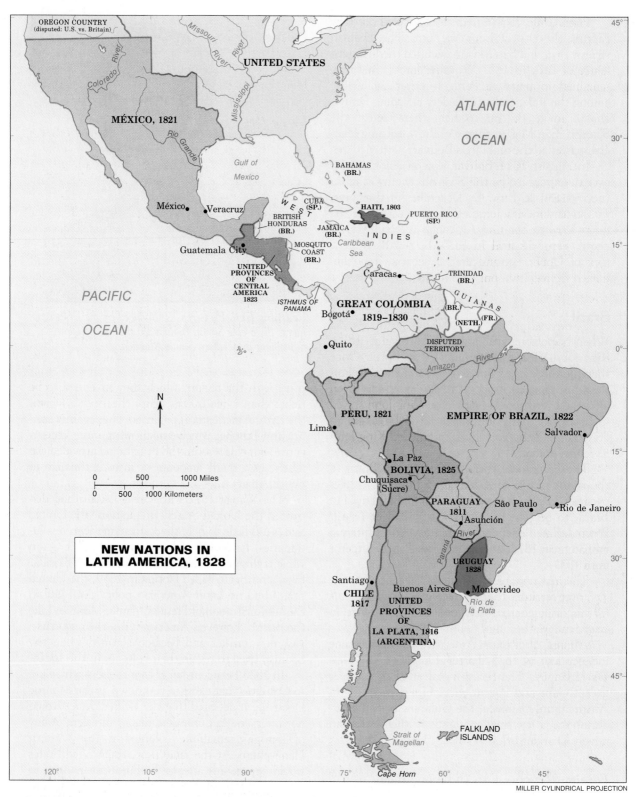

OREGON COUNTRY
(disputed: U.S. vs. Britain)

UNITED STATES

Missouri River

Colorado River

MÉXICO, 1821

Rio Grande

México

Veracruz

Gulf of
Mexico

ATLANTIC

OCEAN

45°

30°

BAHAMAS
(BR.)

W E S T
CUBA
(SP.)

HAITI, 1803

PUERTO RICO
(SP.)

BRITISH
HONDURAS
(BR.)

JAMAICA
(BR.)

I N D I E S

Guatemala City

MOSQUITO
COAST
(BR.)

Caribbean
Sea

15°

UNITED
PROVINCES
OF
CENTRAL
AMERICA
1823

Caracas

TRINIDAD
(BR.)

G U I A N A S

(BR.)

ISTHMUS OF
PANAMA

GREAT COLOMBIA
1819–1830

Bogotá

(FR.)

(NETH.)

PACIFIC

OCEAN

Quito

DISPUTED
TERRITORY

Amazon
River

0°

N

PERU, 1821

EMPIRE OF BRAZIL, 1822

Lima

Salvador

15°

La Paz

BOLIVIA, 1825

Chuquisaca
(Sucre)

PARAGUAY
1811

São Paulo

Rio de Janeiro

0   500   1000 Miles

0   500   1000 Kilometers

Asunción

Paraná
River

NEW NATIONS IN
LATIN AMERICA, 1828

URUGUAY
1828

30°

Santiago

Buenos Aires

Montevideo

CHILE
1817

UNITED
PROVINCES
OF
LA PLATA, 1816
(ARGENTINA)

Rio de
la Plata

45°

Strait of
Magellan

FALKLAND
ISLANDS

120°   105°   90°   75°   60°   45°

Cape Horn

MILLER CYLINDRICAL PROJECTION

Learning from Maps   *Within a short span of years, the huge Spanish and Portuguese*
empires became independent nations. What regions remained Spanish colonies?

Although European leaders denounced the Monroe Doctrine, no nation of Europe tried to defy it or test it. The combination of British and United States power discouraged other European countries from meddling in Latin American affairs.

Latin American Unity

Enormous distances, geographical barriers, and regional rivalries prevented unity among the new Latin American countries. Of the former Spanish and Portuguese territories, only Brazil managed to maintain national unity. Ecuador and Venezuela broke away from Great Colombia. The United Provinces of Central America crumbled into five separate countries, and Argentina was threatened with internal divisions. By 1840 Latin America contained 17 independent nations.

In 1826 Bolívar called a congress of the Latin American nations to meet at Panama to promote unification. Only Colombia, Peru, Central America, and Mexico attended. Although the Panama Congress failed, many Latin Americans cherished the ideal of unity.

Internal Problems

Independence gave the creole upper classes in Latin America the benefits they had hoped for. They sold more goods abroad at higher prices than ever before, and they could buy manufactured goods more cheaply. However, the creoles rarely built lasting political institutions. Latin American governments came to power as often by rebellion as by elections.

Political instability stemmed in part from the failure to establish strong central governments. The conflict between liberals and conservatives also kept some countries in a state of turmoil. Conservatism thrived in part because the colonial governments never prepared local people for political leadership. During colonial times, the figure of the king bonded together different interests within colonial society. After gaining independence, Brazil had an emperor, but nations with republican institutions had no substitute for a king. In some countries, dictators filled this gap. Dictatorial government provided political stability but no freedom. Conservatism worked against social change and for the preservation of the status quo.

The new governments of Latin America did little to promote social justice. The creole upper classes had little interest in eliminating the inequalities inherited from colonial society. Conservatives believed that reforms had gone too far. In addition, the new Latin American nations lacked the economic resources to finance welfare.

The creoles abolished slavery in every country—though in some not until the 1850s, and in Brazil not until 1888. For the most part, creoles sought to take over the positions of privilege. They also battled to take over communal lands that belonged to the Indian population, claiming that such lands slowed economic progress. The haciendas continued to grow during the next 100 years.

The position of the Roman Catholic church also became a tremendous issue in the new nations. Liberals proposed changes in the powers of the church. They wanted the government to take over functions that the church had performed in colonial times. For example, they thought the government, rather than the church, had the exclusive right to run schools. In some countries, liberals proposed that the government take over the church's extensive landholdings. Conservatives, on the other hand, opposed the loss of church rights.

With all these conflicts, the first 50 or 60 years of independence proved difficult in many Latin American countries. However, in the latter part of the 1800s, trade and government tax revenues increased, and many controversies were concluded successfully. Latin American countries began to achieve some stability and economic growth.

SECTION 4 REVIEW

1. **Define** hacienda, peninsular, creole, mestizo, mulatto
2. **Identify** Simón Bolívar, Toussaint-Louverture, Miguel Hidalgo, Agustín de Iturbide, José de San Martín, Bernardo O'Higgins, Monroe Doctrine
3. **Locate** Rio de Janeiro, Lima, Haiti, Caracas, Boyacá, Great Colombia, Junín
4. **Explaining Ideas** What was the outcome of the revolution in Haiti?
5. **Summarizing Ideas** (a) What were the goals of the revolutions that took place in Mexico and Central America? (b) What were the results?
6. **Synthesizing Ideas** Why did unification of large regions in South America ultimately fail?
7. **Relating Ideas** (a) What were the economic and social problems facing the creoles in Latin America on the eve of independence? (b) What problems were evident after independence?

CHAPTER 21 REVIEW

AD | 1794 | 1801 | 1804 | 1810 | 1819 | 1824
1818 | 1823

Revolt in Haiti

Haitian independence proclaimed

Independence movement began in Mexico

Bolivar became president of Great Colombia

Mexican republic declared

Act of Union in Great Britain

First revolt in United Provinces of La Plata (Argentina)

Chileans overcame Spanish rule in Chile

Monroe Doctrine proclaimed

Chapter Summary

The following list contains the key concepts you have learned about political changes in the British Empire, the United States, France, and Latin America during the 1800s and early 1900s.

1. Many reforms occurred in Great Britain in the 1800s and early 1900s. With the Reform Bill of 1832 and agitation from people such as the Chartists, voting rights were greatly broadened in England. In the early 1900s, women finally gained the right to vote.
2. Queen Victoria gave her prime ministers a great deal of power. Two dominant prime ministers of the Victorian Era were Benjamin Disraeli, leader of the Conservative Party, and William Gladstone, leader of the Liberal Party. Under these two prime ministers, many political changes occurred in Great Britain.
3. The labor union movement and socialism grew in Great Britain in the late 1800s and early 1900s. This movement led to the rise of the Labour Party. When the Liberal Party came to power in 1905, Great Britain adopted extensive welfare legislation.
4. Britain's social and political reforms extended to colonies within the British Empire. Canada, Australia, and New Zealand were allowed self-government while remaining within the British Empire.
5. Territorial growth and sectionalism in the United States led to conflict over the issue of slavery. Eventually, the North and South fought a bitter civil war.
6. Following the Civil War, Congress passed the Thirteenth, Fourteenth, and Fifteenth Amendments to the Constitution. These Amendments abolished slavery, made former slaves citizens, and gave black men the right to vote. Women in the United States were given the right to vote in 1920, when the Nineteenth Amendment was ratified.
7. France experienced a series of upheavals in 1830, 1848, and 1871 that rekindled the revolutionary spirit of the 1790s. Each time, politics soon returned to more stable forms. The monarchy was eventually abolished, as was the position of emperor that Napoleon III created for himself. By the early 1900s, France was a republic, governed by coalitions of parties that represented monarchist, liberal, and socialist beliefs.

8. In the early part of the 1800s, revolutions took place throughout Latin America. Following their independence from Spain, most Latin American countries set up democratic governments.
9. The peoples of Latin America had many regional, economic, racial, and social differences. For these reasons, they did not unite but split into many nations after their wars for independence in the early 1800s. Only Brazil managed to maintain national unity.

On a separate sheet of paper, complete the following review exercises.

Reviewing Important Terms

Supply the term that correctly completes each statement.

1. _____ was a movement whose followers believed that people ought to be free to think and work as they please.
2. _____ _____ is a term for self-government.
3. _____ were women who wanted voting rights for all women.
4. _____ is a rivalry among the various sections of a country.
5. An _____ believes in the abolition of all government.
6. A _____ is formed by political groups organized in support of a common cause.
7. People called _____, who were whites born in the Latin American colonies, led the revolutions in South America.
8. _____ are people of mixed Indian and white ancestry.

Developing Critical Thinking Skills

1. **Analyzing Ideas** (a) What were the aims of the Chartists? (b) How did they contribute to the growth of democracy in Great Britain?
2. **Interpreting Ideas** Louis Napoleon Bonaparte once said, "I believe that from time to time men are created . . . in whose hands the destinies of their countries are placed. I believe myself to be one of those men." (a) How did Louis Napoleon attempt to fulfill this

1832

First Reform Bill in Great Britain

1852

Second French Empire founded by Napoleon III

1854–1856 Crimean War

1861 1863 1865

President Lincoln's Emancipation Proclamation

Civil War in the United States

1867
- Dominion of Canada created
- Second Reform Bill in Great Britain

1870
Third French Republic established

1872
Secret ballot adopted in Great Britain

1870–1871
Franco-Prussian War

1884
Third Reform Bill in Great Britain

1894
Dreyfus case in France

1901
Commonwealth of Australia created

1906

1907
Dominion of New Zealand formed

1911
Parliament Bill in Great Britain

---

prophecy? **(b)** Would you describe his actions as liberal or reactionary? **(c)** Explain.

3. **Understanding Ideas** What conditions favored revolutions in Latin America during the 1800s?

4. **Summarizing Ideas** **(a)** What was the Monroe Doctrine? **(b)** Why was it issued?

5. **Explaining Ideas** How did the geography of Latin America prevent unity among these countries?

Relating Geography to History

Turn to the map on page 553 and answer the following questions. **(a)** After 1783, how did the United States acquire most of its territory? **(b)** Was the land in your state part of the United States before the 1800s? **(c)** If not, when was it acquired? **(d)** How long did it take for the United States to expand its borders from the Mississippi River to the Pacific Ocean? **(e)** Why might such rapid growth encourage the development of liberalism and nationalism?

Relating Past to Present

1. Before taking office, William Gladstone pledged, "My mission is to pacify Ireland." Review the events that prompted Gladstone to make this remark. Then investigate the situation in Ireland today. Which of the problems faced in the 1880s have lingered into the present? How has the British government dealt with the problems in the 1980s?

2. How did the spread of liberalism inspire the start of the women's suffrage movement in Great Britain and the United States? Even though women now have the vote, some people are still working to extend the rights of women. What are some of the reforms that women have called for during the last decade?

Applying History Study Skills

Before completing this activity, review Building History Study Skills on page 548.

Read the following selection from William Gladstone's speech to Parliament on April 8, 1886, supporting home rule for Ireland.

66 . . . Our intention is, Sir, to propose to the House of Commons that which, as we think . . . will liberate Parliament from the restraints under which of late years it has ineffectually struggled to perform the Business of the country; . . . obtain an answer . . . to the question whether it is or is not possible to establish good and harmonious relations between Great Britain and Ireland on the footing of those free institutions to which Englishmen, Scotchmen, and Irishmen are alike unalterably attached. . . . In point of fact, law is discredited . . . in Ireland upon this ground especially—that it comes to the people of that country with a foreign aspect, and in a foreign garb. These Coercion Bills of ours . . . are stiffly resisted by the Members who represent Ireland in Parliament. The English mind . . . is estranged from the Irish people and the Irish mind is estranged from the people of England and Scotland. 99

1. How does Gladstone defend his view of home rule for Ireland?

2. Does Gladstone's position represent a liberal or conservative ideology? How do you know?

3. Is Gladstone's ideology economic or political? Write a response to Gladstone from another ideology. How did you determine what would be included in your response?

Investigating Further

1. **Presenting an Oral Report** Use encyclopedias to learn more about the ministries of Benjamin Disraeli and William Gladstone. Give an oral report on the types of programs each supported and how they influenced the direction of Great Britain's domestic and foreign policy.

2. **Writing a Report** During the revolutions of 1848, the people of Paris set up a provisional government and proclaimed the Second French Republic. Prepare a report explaining the form that this republic was to take. One source you may use is the "Proclamations of the French Provisional Government, February–March, 1848" in Louis Snyder's *Fifty Major Documents of the Nineteenth Century* (Van Nostrand Reinhold).

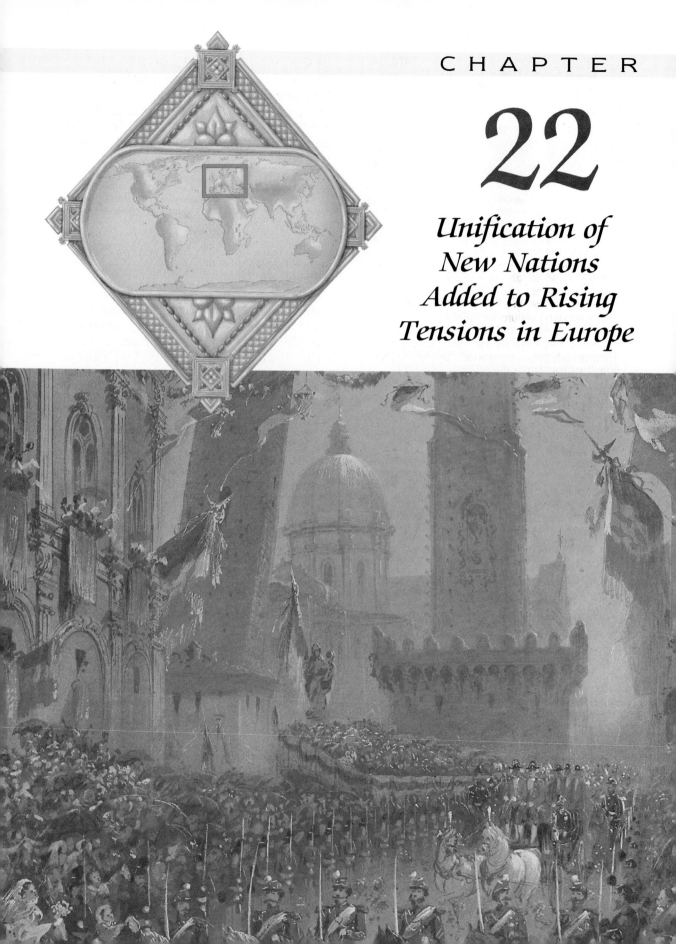

CHAPTER

22

Unification of New Nations Added to Rising Tensions in Europe

Place Europe

Time 1806–1913

3.7 mil. BC   4000 BC   AD 2100

Significance

For about 100 years, from the mid-1700s to the mid-1800s, relations among the major nations of Europe had remained the same. However, a new force—nationalism—would disrupt and permanently alter those relationships.

Nationalism, which linked people through ties of history, language, culture, and territory, caused much upheaval in Europe in the mid-1800s. In divided Italy and Germany, nationalistic feelings fueled successful efforts to unify these two nations. Feelings of nationalism also resulted in the emergence on the European continent of two strong economic and political powers—the kingdom of Italy and the German Empire.

During the second half of the 1800s, therefore, political life in Europe changed significantly. In eastern Europe, for example, nationalism became an increasingly important political influence as various nationalist groups began to agitate continually for self-government. After more than a century of relative stability, the European situation was becoming more and more unsettled as well as more complex.

Terms to Define

Risorgimento   terrorism
kaiser   pogrom
autocrat

People to Identify

Cavour   Alexander II
Iron Chancellor   Francis Joseph I

Places to Locate

Venetia   Bavaria
Papal States   Bulgaria
Saxony   Cyprus

Questions to Guide Your Reading

1 How, after years of struggle, did Italy finally become a unified nation?
2 How did Prussia create a unified and powerful German Empire?
3 In what ways did socialism create opposition to Bismarck?
4 Why did Russia remain a rigid autocracy?
5 Why did Austria-Hungary's interest focus on the Balkans?

◀ *Celebrating Italian unification*

Giuseppe Mazzini, who lived from 1805 to 1872, was one of the three rulers of the republic set up in Rome during the ill-fated revolution of 1848–1849. He expresses his anger and sadness at losing the struggle in the following excerpt from a letter he wrote to the French woman novelist George Sand on June 28, 1849, as French forces overwhelmed Rome.

> **❝** *I am looking on at the agony of a great city, and my soul is sharing her agony. Since the 20th (in consequence of the treachery of an officer), the soldiers of General Oudinot are in the breach. Rome is not a fortress; it is a town eighteen miles in circumference. . . . (The French) proceed, an inch a day, with the help of covered passages. They killed our brave officers singly. They try to crush our batteries with large cannon. . . . They cut off our water-supplies. They seize our provisions and our cattle, which come from the country. They throw bombs night and day. They do not even respect the hospitals. . . . The war which they make upon us is base and cowardly. Oudinot will not face our barricades; but by tiring the population out, harassing our soldiers, killing people with his bombs, and cutting off our provisions, he will end by exciting those elements of fear and local egoism which always exist in a town, however heroic it may be.* **❞**

The upheaval in Rome was only one of many that erupted in Europe in the mid-1800s.

1 After Years of Struggle, Italy Became a Unified Nation

The conquests of Napoleon I had given the Italian Peninsula something resembling unity for a few years. The Italians, inspired by the liberal and nationalistic ideals of the French Revolution, had overthrown several rulers of the Italian states. However, after the Congress of Vienna in 1815, Italy was again divided. Austria annexed Lombardy and Venetia. The rest of Italy was fragmented into several large and small states. These states were either dominated by Austria or ruled by reactionary monarchs who tried to wipe out any advances made during Napoleon's time (see map, page 577).

Early Movements Toward Unification

Italian nationalism became a strong force in the early 1800s when many thinkers and writers tried to revive interest in Italy's traditions. This nationalistic movement, with its goals of liberation and unification, became known as the **Risorgimento** (ree • sor • jee • MEN • toh)—the Italian word for "resurgence." Because nationalists could not support their cause openly, they formed secret societies. An early group of this sort was the Carbonari (kahr • buh • NAH • ree). One of its most famous members, Giuseppe Mazzini, greatly influenced later Italian history.

Mazzini, born in 1805, envisioned a united Italy, and he devoted his entire life to this goal. Mazzini spent time both imprisoned and exiled for his part in an unsuccessful uprising against Sardinia in 1830. In 1831 he called for all Italian patriots to join a new movement, known as Young Italy, to spread the ideals of the Risorgimento. Mazzini described Young Italy as "a brotherhood of Italians who believe in Progress and Duty."

In 1848 liberals and nationalists led rebellions in several of the Italian states. These rebellions forced the rulers of Sardinia, the Kingdom of the Two Sicilies, and Tuscany to grant constitutions to their subjects, and overthrew Austrian rule in Lombardy and Venetia. Revolutionaries seized Rome in 1849 and set up a republic that Mazzini and two other leaders governed. All but one of these revolutionary movements soon failed. The Austrian army succeeded in recapturing some of its former possessions in northern Italy during the summer of 1849. Former rulers returned to power, revoking the constitutions. The revolt succeeded only in Sardinia, which remained independent.

Despite the failure of the revolts of 1848 and 1849, Italian patriots continued their efforts. They now agreed on their principal aim—a united Italy. However, they could not agree on how to achieve unity or what the ideal form of government would be after unification had succeeded.

Many Italians, especially the Catholic clergy, wanted a federation of Italian states headed by the pope. Liberals, however, wanted an Italian republic. They opposed federation, partly because the papacy had turned against liberalism after 1849. Still others wanted a constitutional monarchy under King Victor Emmanuel II of Sardinia, who sympathized with liberal aims.

Learning from Pictures *Count Cavour sought an alliance with Napoleon III to evict the Austrians and unify Italy under Sardinia's leadership.*

Cavour in Sardinia

The chief minister or premier, Count Camillo Benso di Cavour (kahv • OOHR), and not the king of Sardinia, actually governed the nation. Born in 1810, Cavour was a well-educated and widely traveled aristocrat. He edited a nationalist newspaper in 1847, took part in the revolutions of 1848, and in 1852 became premier of Sardinia.

Cavour disliked absolutism and admired the British system of parliamentary government. He wanted Italy to be both united and industrialized under Sardinia's leadership.

Cavour reorganized and strengthened the Sardinian army. He helped to establish banks, factories, and railroads, encouraged shipbuilding, and negotiated treaties with other countries to increase trade. Under the slogan "A free church in a free state," he tried to reduce the political influence of the Roman Catholic church. He expelled the politically powerful Jesuit order from the country. He also brought Sardinia to prominence through its participation on the side of France and Great Britain in the Crimean War and in the peace conference at Paris in 1856 that ended that war.

Napoleon III and War with Austria

Since Austrian control of part of northern Italy presented the greatest obstacle to Italian unity, Cavour searched for allies against that nation. He proposed an alliance of France and Sardinia against Austria. Although Napoleon III always sought ways to increase French prestige, he hesitated at first to take this step because he feared antagonizing the pope and French Catholics. However, he hoped that with Austria driven out of Italy, France could dominate a weak confederation of Italian states. Cavour, on the other hand, believed that with Austria out of Italy, the other Italian states would join Sardinia to form a strong alliance against both France and Austria.

In 1858 Cavour and Napoleon met secretly to plan a war against Austria. Napoleon agreed that if Austria could be provoked into declaring war on Sardinia, France would send troops to help drive the Austrians out of Lombardy and Venetia. In return for this help, Cavour promised to give the French-speaking regions of Nice and Savoy that then belonged to Sardinia to France. In 1859 Cavour began his preparations for war. Austria played right into Cavour's hands by demanding that the military buildup in Sardinia be stopped in three days. When Cavour rejected Austria's "attempt to interfere in the affairs of Sardinia," Austria, as Cavour had hoped, declared war.

At first the war went according to Cavour's plans. The combined Sardinian-French forces quickly drove the Austrians out of Lombardy and marched on into Venetia. Italian patriots in Tuscany, Modena, and Parma overthrew their Austrian rulers and asked to be annexed to Sardinia.

Napoleon III had not planned on this happening, however. He did not want a strong, united Italy any more than he wanted a united Germany. He feared that if the war lasted a long time, Prussia, for its own ends, might help Austria. Napoleon had no desire to get involved in a war against both Austria and Prussia. In July 1859, only three months after the war began, Napoleon signed a secret armistice with Austria. According to its terms, Sardinia received Lombardy, but Austria kept Venetia. The agreement also returned Austrian rulers to Tuscany, Modena, and Parma.

This armistice marked a severe setback for Cavour and the Italian nationalists. Napoleon III had delivered only half of his side of the bargain—control of Lombardy to Sardinia. However, he insisted on collecting his full price—Nice and Savoy. Afraid of losing even the partial victory, King Victor Emmanuel II agreed to the French terms.

The Italian people, however, refused to give up their goals. Popular feeling ran far ahead of governmental caution. Rebellions in Parma, Modena, and Tuscany again expelled the Austrian rulers and set up popular temporary governments. The people of Romagna, a province in the Papal States, also revolted. When all of these areas held elections, the voters overwhelmingly favored joining Sardinia.

Garibaldi's Red Shirts

The southern half of the Italian Peninsula, together with the large island of Sicily, made up the Kingdom of the Two Sicilies. A harsh Bourbon king ruled this kingdom. Earlier revolts there had failed, but it now became the target of the Italian nationalists. Giuseppe Garibaldi, a man devoted to Italian freedom, led the way.

Garibaldi was born in Nice in 1807. As a youth, he joined Mazzini's Young Italy movement. In 1834, after being involved in a revolutionary plot in Piedmont, Garibaldi had to flee for his life to Latin America. Returning to Italy, he fought in the revolutions of 1848. Forced to flee again, he lived in the United States for a few years, returning once more to Italy in 1854.

With financial assistance secretly furnished by Cavour, Garibaldi recruited an army of 1,100 soldiers. They called themselves Red Shirts because of the uniform they wore into battle. In the spring of 1860, Garibaldi and his Red Shirts invaded Sicily, where the people welcomed them. Crossing to the Italian mainland, Garibaldi and his forces seized Naples, the capital city, and drove Francis II and his forces north to the border of the Papal States.

Garibaldi planned to continue his march north to capture Rome and then Venetia. But Cavour, afraid that Garibaldi might try to set up a republic, sent an army south to stop Garibaldi's advance. In the process Sardinia annexed most of the territory of the Papal States.

In the fall of 1860, Garibaldi and Cavour met in Naples where Garibaldi reluctantly agreed to abandon his plan to conquer the entire Italian Peninsula. For the sake of Italian unification, Cavour persuaded Garibaldi to support the establishment of the kingdom of Italy, with Victor Emmanuel II of Sardinia as its ruler.

Final Unification

In 1860 elections were held everywhere in Italy except in Venetia and Rome. The people voted overwhelmingly for national unity under the king of Sardinia. Representatives of the various states met at a parliament in the Sardinian capital of Turin in February 1861, where they confirmed Victor Emmanuel II as king of Italy "by grace of God and the will of the nation."

The new kingdom included all of Italy except Venetia, which still belonged to Austria, and the western part of the Papal States around the city of Rome, which the pope ruled (see map, page 577). European governments were left primarily with two choices—either to recognize the new state or to fight it. The embarrassed Napoleon III stopped short of making war on the new country but did send French troops to Rome to prevent the Italian nationalists from seizing it.

Unification was completed when Italy gained Venetia in the Seven Weeks' War of 1866. When the Franco-Prussian War broke out in 1870, Napoleon III had to recall his troops from Rome. The Italians entered the city, and the citizens of Rome voted overwhelmingly for union with Italy. Later that year Rome was proclaimed the capital of the kingdom of Italy.

Problems of a United Italy

Although now politically united, Italy still had many problems. Few Italians had experience with self-government, and scandals frequently rocked the young nation. The various regions of the country remained divided by their own traditions and independence. Tensions arose between the industrialized north and the agricultural south. In Sicily

Learning from Pictures
The aspirations of Italian nationalism were strengthened by Garibaldi's liberation of Sicily, where the Red Shirts defeated an army 20 times its size.

UNIFICATION OF ITALY
1858–1870

- Kingdom of Sardinia, 1858
- Austrian territory annexed by Sardinia, 1859
- Territory annexed by Sardinia to form Kingdom of Italy, 1860
- Austrian territory annexed by Italy, 1866
- Territory annexed by Italy, 1870

FRANCE

SWITZERLAND

AUSTRO-HUNGARIAN EMPIRE

SAVOY (to FRANCE in 1860)

SOUTH TIROL

LOMBARDY

VENETIA

Turin

Milan

Venice

NICE (to FRANCE in 1860)

PARMA

MODENA

Genoa

MONACO

LUCCA

SAN MARINO

Florence

TUSCANY

PAPAL STATES

Adriatic Sea

OTTOMAN EMPIRE

KINGDOM OF SARDINIA

Corsica (FRANCE)

Rome

KINGDOM

Naples

OF

Tyrrhenian Sea

THE

Sardinia

N

TWO

Mediterranean Sea

SICILIES

Sicily

0   100   200 Miles

0   100   200 Kilometers

10°   15°

AZIMUTHAL EQUAL AREA PROJECTION

Learning from Maps *By agreeing to help Sardinia against the Austrians, France received Nice and Savoy. What year did France receive these territories?*

local leaders organized a secret society known as the Mafia. The society formed a kind of state within the state, which the central government was powerless to control.

Italy's leaders admired the military strength of Germany and hoped to follow a similar course in their own country. Within a few years, Italy had the world's third largest navy and the third largest merchant marine.

Italy paid for this military buildup by taxing its people heavily, a policy that sparked strikes, riots, and peasant uprisings, particularly in Sicily, in the 1890s. Looking for victories that would build the country's prestige, Italy engaged in expensive colonial ventures in Africa. A brief war against the Ottoman Empire in 1911 cost a great deal of money and brought Italy little in return. Although unified, Italy had not achieved stability.

SECTION 1 REVIEW

1. **Define**   Risorgimento
2. **Identify**   Carbonari, Young Italy, Victor Emmanuel II, Cavour, Garibaldi, Red Shirts, Francis II
3. **Locate**   Lombardy, Venetia, Sardinia, Kingdom of the Two Sicilies, Tuscany, Modena, Parma, Romagna, Papal States, Turin
4. **Analyzing Ideas**   Who was Mazzini and what was his place in Italian history?
5. **Organizing Ideas**   Trace the steps toward Italian unification as they occurred in the following years: 1848–49, 1852, 1858, 1859, 1860, 1866, and 1870.
6. **Explaining Ideas**   Describe the problems that Italy faced following its unification in 1870.
7. **Understanding Ideas**   Why did France and Sardinia form an alliance against Austria?

2 Prussia Created a Unified and Powerful German Empire

The inability of the German people to form an enduring union before the late 1800s appears as a great historical mystery. The Germans shared a common language and history. Several times, vigorous, intelligent rulers came close to achieving a strong central government, but all of them failed. In the mid-1800s Germany remained what it had been for centuries—a patchwork of independent states. Each has its own laws, currency, and rulers. By the late 1800s, Prussia took the lead in uniting these states.

Prussia as Leader

The Prussians built a strong and prosperous state in the 1700s during the reigns of Frederick William I and his son Frederick the Great. A new situation arose when Napoleon I dominated Prussia from 1806 until 1812. He seized Prussian lands, formed new states from them, and gave them to his relatives and allies. To prevent Prussia from becoming a military threat, he limited the size of the Prussian army and levied a large indemnity. He also forced Prussia to support an occupation army within its territory and contribute soldiers to the French armies.

577

The Prussians found ways around Napoleon's restrictions, however. For example, the strength of Prussia had long rested on its army, which the French had now restricted in size. But the Prussians craftily drafted all able-bodied men and required them to serve short army terms, during which time they received intensive military training. They then went into the reserves, and a new group of men was drafted into the regular army. Thus trained men, not really part of the regular army, could be called into active service when needed. Technically Prussia observed the limits placed on its standing army by the French and at the same time kept available a large force of trained soldiers.

Napoleon's territorial changes in Germany also worked in Prussia's favor. Austria had been Prussia's strongest rival for leadership of the German states. An Austrian Hapsburg had held the position of Holy Roman Emperor since the 1400s, thus giving Austria a vague claim over the German states. Napoleon abolished the Holy Roman Empire and reorganized and consolidated many German states into the Confederation of the Rhine.

In addition, Napoleon's rule stimulated nationalism in the German states as it had throughout Europe. Some of Germany's greatest thinkers and writers were active during the period of the French Revolution and Napoleon. Frederick the Great himself had despised the German language and usually wrote and spoke French. Now Germans began to appreciate their language, their past, and their traditions.

German nationalism favored Prussia more than Austria. The population of Prussia was mostly German. In Austria, although the Germans ruled, many other nationalities, including Hungarians, Romanians, Italians, and Slavs, held the majority. Most of them wanted independence from Austria so that they could establish their own national governments.

The revived Prussian state played a major part in the final struggle against Napoleon. Prussian armies fought at Waterloo, and Prussia earned the right to be one of the four great powers represented at the Congress of Vienna. It also joined the Quadruple Alliance.

In 1815 the Congress of Vienna turned Napoleon's Confederation of the Rhine into the German Confederation with additional members that included Prussia. The Congress gave Prussia much important territory, including two-thirds of Saxony and an area along the lower Rhine River. Prussian lands now stretched almost unbroken from Russia to the Rhine and beyond. Prussia had a well-organized and efficient government and a strong economy.

The Zollverein

The first major step toward German unity after the Congress of Vienna concerned the economy. The tariffs that each state levied made movement of goods from one German state to another extremely difficult. The Prussians even placed tariffs on items shipped from one Prussian possession to another. The tariffs increased the prices of goods while reducing the amount sold.

The drive for freer movement of goods was begun by the Junkers (YOOHN • kuhrz)—the aristocratic landowners of Prussia—who wanted to sell their farm products. In 1818 they persuaded the king of Prussia to abolish all tariffs within his territories. Beginning the next year, Prussia and other German states made a number of treaties that set up a customs union called the Zollverein (TSAWL • fer • yn). By 1844 it included almost all of the German states except Austria.

The Zollverein benefited its members by making prices both lower and more uniform. It also led to the spread of industrialization in the German states by providing a wide, free market for German goods and by offering tariff protection against foreign competition. The German states adopted uniform systems of weights, measures, and currency. Manufacturers produced and sold more goods, and business leaders became strong supporters of German unification.

The establishment of the Zollverein had no immediate political effects, and each of the various states in the German Confederation continued to act independently. However, by making its members economically dependent on one another the Zollverein paved the way for later political unification.

In the years after the Congress of Vienna, strong nationalistic and democratic movements emerged within the states of the German Confederation. In 1848 uprisings in France touched off demands for liberal reforms throughout Germany. Agitation was intense for a while, and elections were held for representatives to a National Assembly in Frankfurt to try to unify Germany. Eventually, however, the demands of liberals for representative government were defeated. German unification was to be accomplished by the policies of a king and his powerful chancellor.

Bismarck and Prussian Strength

William I became king of Prussia in 1861. In 1862 he appointed Otto von Bismarck, a conservative Junker politician, to head the Prussian cabinet.

Bismarck opposed democracy and the idea of a parliament. He also believed in Prussian destiny to lead the German people to unification. He was willing to use trickery, bribery, or military force to help Prussia fulfill this destiny. Bismarck had great contempt for idealists, regarding them as mere talkers, not people of action. He once said of German policy that it could not be carried out by "speeches and majorities . . . but by iron and blood."

For years Bismarck really ruled Prussia. He had the full cooperation of the king and the generals in charge of the army. They agreed with Bismarck on the necessity of reorganizing and further strengthening the Prussian army. First, however, the government had to increase taxes.

When the Prussian parliament refused to approve the money for a military expansion program, Bismarck simply dismissed it and collected the taxes without parliamentary authorization. In so doing, he ignored the protests of the liberals. He planned to quiet critics with military victories.

Bismarck and his generals proceeded to build the Prussian army into a great war machine. Prussian military strategists tried to plan for every possible situation that their army might encounter in the field.

Learning from Pictures
Bismarck's diplomatic abilities led to his appointment as head of the Prussian cabinet. His military policy brought about German unification under the leadership of Prussia.

Unification Through War

To increase the power and size of Prussia, Bismarck had to overcome two major obstacles: First, he had to drive Austria out of its position of leadership in the German Confederation. Second, he had to overcome Austria's influence over the southern German states, which he considered the major opponents to Prussian leadership. He accomplished these objectives in three wars—the Danish War, the Seven Weeks' War, and the Franco-Prussian War.

The Danish War. On the border between Denmark and Germany lay two small states—the duchies of Schleswig and Holstein (see map, page 582). The population of Holstein, which had been part of the German Confederation since 1815, was entirely German. Schleswig's population included a mixture of Germans and Danes. The Danish king ruled the two duchies under a constitution that provided separation from Denmark. In 1863 King Christian IX came to the Danish throne. At the insistence of many Danes, he proclaimed a new constitution under which he tried to annex Schleswig to Denmark.

Both Prussia and Austria protested the new Danish constitution. Together they demanded that it be revoked. When Denmark refused, Prussia and Austria declared war on Denmark. Denmark had hoped for help from France and Great Britain, but neither acted. In 1864, after three months of fighting, Denmark surrendered.

The peace treaty gave the two duchies to Prussia and Austria jointly. That arrangement caused problems, however. Austria demanded that the two duchies form a single state within the German Confederation. Prussia opposed this settlement. After bitter quarreling, Prussian and Austrian leaders agreed that Prussia would administer Schleswig, and Austria would administer Holstein.

The Seven Weeks' War. As Prussian influence expanded, Bismarck moved to drive Austria out of the German Confederation. He prepared the way with a series of skillful diplomatic actions ensuring that no one would aid Austria. First, he persuaded Napoleon III of France to remain neutral if war broke out between Prussia and Austria. In return for its neutrality, France demanded certain territory then held by the southern German states. Bismarck persuaded Napoleon III to put these demands in writing, but the clever Prussian never did the same with his vague promises to Napoleon.

Bismarck next formed an alliance with the new nation of Italy. In return for fighting against Austria, Italy would receive the Austrian territory of Venetia. Then, by various complicated moves, Bismarck provoked Austria into declaring war on Prussia in 1866.

Austria had not counted on the superb training and preparation of the Prussian army. In fact, Prussia's conduct of the war came as a surprise to the whole world. Prussian forces took advantage of modern technology, moving by train and communicating via the telegraph. Prussia defeated the Austrians in only seven weeks.

The Treaty of Prague ended the so-called Seven Weeks' War in the summer of 1866. Under its lenient terms Austria approved the dissolution of the German Confederation and surrendered Holstein to Prussia. The Italians gained Venetia.

In 1867 several northern German states united with Prussia to form the North German Confederation. Each state had self-government, but the king of Prussia was hereditary president of the Confederation. As the largest state, with the most powerful industry and army, and with the greatest number of representatives, Prussia dominated the legislature of the new confederation.

Only the three southern states of Bavaria, Baden, and Württemberg and the southern part of Hesse-Darmstadt remained outside Prussia's influence. If they could be persuaded to join Prussia, German unity would be complete.

The Franco-Prussian War. Bismarck decided that the way to unite the southern states with the rest of Germany was to provoke a war with France. His opportunity came in 1870 when Spain was looking for a new ruler. The Spaniards offered the throne to Prince Leopold, a cousin of the king of Prussia. Napoleon III took a strong stand against this development because it meant that both Prussia and Spain would be ruled by the Hohenzollern family. He dispatched notes to Prussia and Spain asking that Leopold turn down the offer.

Leopold did withdraw, but the French ambassador gambled further. He insisted that King William I of Prussia pledge publicly that no member of the Hohenzollern family would ever be a candidate for the Spanish throne.

The French ambassador delivered the French demand to King William at a resort known as Ems. The king's vague reply made the ambassador request another meeting to discuss the subject. The king told the ambassador that he would not be able to meet with him again at Ems.

Bismarck received a dispatch from the king at Ems summarizing his meeting with the French ambassador. Bismarck decided to use it to trick Napoleon III into declaring war on Prussia. He altered the dispatch slightly and made it sound as though the king had dismissed the ambassador offensively and contemptuously. Then Bismarck released the so-called Ems dispatch to the newspapers.

Outraged at the humiliation of the Ems dispatch, France declared war on Prussia. Bismarck then showed the leaders of the southern German states the 1865 document in which Napoleon III had demanded their territory for France. He persuaded them that France posed a greater danger than Prussia. Bismarck thus converted the states from rivals into allies against France and secured their help in winning a Prussian victory.

The Franco-Prussian War was short but decisive. No outside nation made any move to help France. Superbly trained, well equipped, and ably led, the Prussian army totally defeated the French within only a few months.

Bismarck had been lenient with Austria following its defeat because he did not want as enemies its large German population. He had no such feeling about France, however. France was occupied by German troops, lost Alsace and part of Lorraine, and had to pay a huge indemnity.

Formation of the German Empire

For Germany the peace was not as important as an event that took place before the signing of the treaty. On January 18, 1871, representatives of the allied German states met in the Hall of Mirrors of the palace of Versailles near Paris. There they

Learning from Pictures   *This painting depicts the ceremony proclaiming the German Empire. Where did the ceremony take place?*

**UNIFICATION OF GERMANY
1865–1871**

Kingdom of Prussia, 1865

States annexed by Prussia, 1866

States joining Prussia to form the
North German Confederation, 1867

States joining the German Empire, 1871

Prussian forces in Seven Weeks'
War, 1866

German forces in the Franco-Prussian
War, 1870–1871

Boundary of the German Empire, 1871

Prussian/German victories

LAMBERT CONFORMAL CONIC PROJECTION

Learning from Maps   *The liberal southern German states hesitated to join conservative
Prussia. What were the names of these states?*

issued an official proclamation declaring the formation of the German Empire, which included all of
the German states except Austria (see map, this
page). Berlin, the Prussian capital, also became the
capital of the new empire.

King William I of Prussia was proclaimed German emperor. Bismarck became the chancellor—or
chief minister—of the German Empire, with the
nickname of the "Iron Chancellor" because of his
policy of "iron and blood."

Much as he disliked constitutions, Bismarck
accepted one that united the 25 German states in a
federal form of government. Each state had its own

ruler as well as the right to handle its own domestic
matters, including public health, education, law
enforcement, and local taxation.

The federal government controlled all common
matters, such as national defense, foreign affairs,
and commerce. The emperor, called the **kaiser**
(KY•zuhr), headed the German government. He
was not an absolute monarch, but he did have
tremendous power. He could appoint the chancellor, and he commanded the army and navy. The
kaiser could declare a defensive war on his own,
and he could order an offensive war with the agreement of the upper house of the legislature.

The legislative branch of the government contained two houses. The Bundesrat (BOON • duhs • raht), or upper house, was a federal council, with 58 appointed members.

The Reichstag (RYKS • tahg), or legislative assembly, made up the legislature's lower house. Its nearly 400 members were elected by universal manhood suffrage. The Bundesrat drew up all the bills for consideration by the Reichstag and could veto its actions. The Bundesrat and the kaiser acting together could dismiss the Reichstag. This combination thus made it almost impossible for the Reichstag to pass any liberal democratic laws that the Bundesrat or kaiser might oppose.

The German constitution strongly favored Prussian interests. The king of Prussia had become kaiser of Germany. Prussia had the greatest number of delegates in the Bundesrat. As the most populous state, it also had the largest number of delegates in the Reichstag.

SECTION 2 REVIEW

1. **Define**   kaiser
2. **Identify**   Junkers, William I, Treaty of Prague, Iron Chancellor, Bundesrat, Reichstag
3. **Locate**   Saxony, Schleswig, Holstein, Bavaria, Württemberg
4. **Analyzing Ideas**   **(a)** What was the Zollverein? **(b)** Did it serve the purpose for which it was founded?
5. **Organizing Ideas**   Prussia fought three wars to unite Germany.   **(a)** Name each war.   **(b)** List what territory was acquired as a result of each.
6. **Explaining Ideas**   How did Bismarck persuade the southern German states to accept Prussian leadership of Germany?
7. **Summarizing Ideas**   Name the powers held by the kaiser.

---

3 Industrialization and Socialism Created Opposition to Bismarck

Because the constitution did not give Bismarck the absolute monarchy he wanted, he tried to achieve it in other ways. However, in the years after the formation of the German Empire, he had to accept many compromises to make the political system work. Even though the constitution did not give the people much voice in their own affairs, the government had to take their demands into account.

Opposition to Bismarck

In spite of rigid control by the aristocratic Prussians, the new German federal government soon ran into difficult problems. Dissatisfied groups formed political parties that opposed Bismarck's policies. Some wanted the government to be more liberal and democratic and to enact social reforms. Others feared Bismarck's military policy and the ever-growing army and navy.

Representatives in the legislative assembly from the southern German states, especially those from Bavaria, resented the interference of the federal government in what they considered to be their local affairs. They thought their own state governments should deal with such matters.

Relations with the Roman Catholic church presented special problems for Bismarck. The pope's long-standing claim of the right to administer church property seemed to Bismarck like foreign interference in German domestic affairs. He came to see the Catholic church as a threat to the German Empire. The fact that the southern German states were mostly Catholic strengthened this feeling.

In 1872 Germany and the papacy broke diplomatic relations. Bismarck then initiated the anti-Catholic *Kulturkampf*—German for "war of civilization"—in which Germany passed strict laws to control the Catholic clergy and Catholic schools. The laws expelled the Jesuits and stated that all the Catholic clergy had to be Germans who had been educated in German schools.

This religious policy stirred up opposition among the German people. The Catholics formed a political party to oppose the *Kulturkampf* and to work for other changes. Many non-Catholic liberals also joined the opposition. By 1880 Bismarck began to modify the *Kulturkampf* because he needed the support of the Catholic Party. Bismarck reestablished diplomatic relations with the papacy and repealed the laws against Catholics. By 1887 the *Kulturkampf* had ended.

Industrial Development Under Bismarck

Bismarck wanted to transform Prussia into an industrial giant. Germany contained a rich store

Two Men Looking at the Moon

Many artists were inspired by the nationalistic spirit that flooded Europe during and after the Napoleonic Era. Art, literature, and music were all affected by this movement. Caspar David Friedrich, a German landscape artist, painted the work at the right. He was a patriotic German, who admired German art of the Middle Ages. He deliberately included in his paintings some of its common motifs. Among these were gnarled and twisted trees, like the one shown in this painting entitled *Two Men Looking at the Moon*. This brooding nighttime scene, with its air of melancholy, is typical of the romantic movement. Romanticism emphasized the

Staatliche Kunstsammlungen Desden, DDR

past and thus was especially appealing to Germans, who, in the early 1800s, were taking a new interest in their national traditions and customs.

Romanticism inspired nationalism which, by the mid-1800s, had become a major movement in Germany.

of natural resources, including the great coal and iron deposits in the Ruhr valley, where a huge steel industry developed. The German government owned the railroads, and it managed them in order to promote industrial development. In addition, a system of canals provided cheaper, though slower, transportation.

The fact that industrialization came later in Germany than in Great Britain and France proved to be an advantage for Germany. German industries could use the best methods and most advanced machinery that had been developed elsewhere. German scientists then worked out further changes and improvements.

Under Bismarck's leadership, the government helped industry in many ways. It standardized money and banking laws throughout the empire. Postal and telegraph services—the means of communication by which so much business was conducted—were centralized. The government encouraged German industrialists to form cartels. In addition, Germany adopted a high-tariff policy to protect its industries from foreign competition. Germany rapidly became an industrial nation, and soon rivaled Great Britain and France.

Socialism in Germany

With the growth of German industry, cities grew rapidly, and a class of factory workers appeared. German laborers, like those in other nations, wanted decent working conditions. Some people believed that the action of the cartels led to lower wages for workers and higher prices for consumers. Many thought that these various problems needed government action. They wanted the government to pass laws that would benefit workers and regulate industry.

Just as in other European nations, socialist reformers in Germany went even further, advocating government ownership of all major industries. German socialists banded together in 1869 to form the Social Democratic Party. The party grew quickly, with most of its members coming from the ranks of the city workers. In 1871 it elected two members to the Reichstag. By 1877 that representation had increased to 12.

Even if the Social Democrats had had a much greater representation, they could have done very little. The Reichstag could not pass any laws that the Bundesrat opposed. Since the Bundesrat represented the hereditary rulers, there was little chance that it would propose or pass the laws that the socialists wanted. The Reichstag, however, served as a good public forum in which socialist members could express their grievances and make promises of what they would do if given the power.

Bismarck's Antisocialist Campaign

Every gain in socialist voting strength—and every new demand for reform—alarmed Bismarck. When the Social Democrats won 500,000 votes in the election of 1877, the chancellor decided to use all of his power to fight them. His opportunity came in 1878, when two attempts to assassinate the emperor occurred. Neither of the would-be assassins had any connection with socialism, and Bismarck knew this. However, he took advantage of the public concern to accuse the Social Democrats of plotting the attempts. The emperor and the Bundesrat dissolved the Reichstag and called for new elections. A widespread campaign against socialists and their ideas followed.

The election did not change the strength of the Social Democrats in the Reichstag. Bismarck, however, pushed through laws aimed at repressing the socialists. The new laws prohibited newspapers, books, or pamphlets from spreading socialist ideas and banned public meetings of socialists.

Despite such restrictive laws, the socialists continued their efforts, and by 1884 Social Democratic representation in the Reichstag had increased to 24. As he did in the *Kulturkampf*, Bismarck had to re-examine his tactics in order to see how to achieve his aims against a growing opposition.

Since repression had failed, the Iron Chancellor was forced to try another tactic. He decided to grant many of the reforms the socialists had proposed. If the government granted reforms, Bismarck believed, people would have less reason to join the socialists, and their support would collapse.

Bismarck's new policy was called "stealing the socialists' thunder." He said that he wanted to pass laws to help workers so that the Social Democrats would "sound their bird call in vain." Beginning in 1883, he put through several far-reaching reforms. First came insurance against sickness, then insurance against accidents—both paid for by employers. Other laws limited working hours, provided for certain holidays from work, and guaranteed pensions for disabled and retired workers.

Germany thus adopted a pioneering program of government-directed social reforms. The reforms did not wipe out socialism in Germany, but they did eliminate many of the workers' grievances. Many other industrial nations later copied this program of social legislation.

Learning from Pictures
As capital of the German Empire, Berlin became a thriving cultural and political center. This picture shows the center of Berlin and the Spree River in 1890.

READ
● WRITE
INTERPRET
CONNECT
THINK

BUILDING HISTORY STUDY SKILLS

Writing About History: Writing a Comparison Essay

To make comparisons is to identify both similarities and differences. Writing a comparison essay helps us to see relationships, make connections between conflicting ideas, and analyze the similarities and differences between these ideas.

How to Write a Comparison Essay

To write a comparison essay, follow these steps.

1. State the topic for comparison.
2. On a separate sheet of paper, write the categories for comparison. The categories should be broad points under which similarities and differences on the topic can be listed.
3. List the similarities and differences under each category, then begin writing the essay, further explaining these similarities and differences.
4. In the last paragraph, form a conclusion that synthesizes the information in your essay. The conclusion should be more than a summary. It should be an analytical statement of comparison, using the categories that you developed.

Developing the Skill

If you were to write an essay comparing Italian and German unification, you could establish the categories of comparison as leadership, methods, and results. Study the following essay and identify the categories.

❝ A renewed spirit of nationalism marked the late 1800s in Europe. Nationalism triumphed in both Italy and Germany. The unification of these nations was accomplished because of the leadership of Cavour and Garibaldi in Italy, and of Bismarck in Germany.

Cavour's skill lay in his ability to direct political events to his own grand scheme. After he started a war with Austria in 1859, France entered on the side of Italy. Cavour also succeeded in getting Lombardy and some of the central states annexed to Italy.

Garibaldi led his republican army in rebellion in the Kingdom of the Two Sicilies and, in a compromise with Cavour, made them part of the kingdom of Italy.

German unification did not have the multiple leadership and republican elements that existed in Italian unification. However, the manipulation of Austria and the provoking of war were similar characteristics. Bismarck manipulated events and took advantage of opportunities. He united the southern part of Germany with the rest of the country when he stirred up nationalistic and emotional feelings against France after provoking a war with that nation. Republicanism and liberalism were not part of German unification.

Italian unification, although it did involve war, incorporated the ideals of republicanism and nationalism and had two leaders, Cavour and Garibaldi. The unification of Germany included nationalism but came about through Bismarck's policies of "iron and blood." ❞

Notice that the first paragraph identified the topic and stated the categories. The second, third, and fourth paragraphs developed the categories of leadership, methods, and results. The concluding paragraph synthesized the categories by showing the different methods of unification.

Practicing the skill. After reading current newspaper or magazine articles, write a comparison essay on the views of any two political candidates.

To apply this skill, see Applying History Study Skills on page 597.

A caricature of Bismarck

The Resignation of Bismarck

Emperor William I died in 1888. His son, Frederick III, reigned for only a few months before he, too, died and was succeeded by his son, William II. The young monarch and the old chancellor soon disagreed violently. William II felt that Bismarck was too powerful. Bismarck resented the way that the young emperor took away the powers the chancellor had used wisely for years. He also feared that William was too rash and undisciplined to use his considerable authority wisely.

For a long time, Bismarck had thought himself indispensable to Germany. However, in 1890 William forced him to resign, which he did with a great deal of bitterness. Although he and William II later reconciled, Bismarck never again served Germany in an official role.

With Bismarck gone, William II set out to expand Germany's colonial empire. He increased the size and strength of the German army and began to build up the German navy. This move brought Germany into competition with Great Britain, which was at that time the world's strongest naval power. William signed new agreements with neighboring nations, and by the early 1900s, Germany emerged stronger than ever before.

SECTION 3 REVIEW

1. **Identify** *Kulturkampf*, Social Democratic Party, William II
2. **Organizing Ideas** What were three problems faced by the German Empire in the 1870s and 1880s?
3. **Analyzing Ideas** What were the major factors responsible for Germany's rapid industrial development?
4. **Explaining Ideas** (a) Describe the most important social reforms adopted under Bismarck. (b) Why did he favor these reforms?
5. **Interpreting Ideas** How did Bismarck attempt to destroy socialism?

---

4 Despite Reforms, Russia Remained a Rigid Autocracy

By the mid-1800s Russia had the largest territory and population of any European nation. Yet it remained weak. Industrial development, which so strengthened the West, lagged in Russia. Most of the country's extensive natural resources lay undeveloped. Ports blocked by ice for much of the year, or exits from the seas controlled by other countries, made Russia almost entirely landlocked. This situation led to continuous Russian attempts to win access to the Mediterranean, past Constantinople and the Dardanelles. These efforts led to conflicts with the Ottoman Empire, which controlled the Dardanelles.

Russia had another problem. Unlike Great Britain or France, it lacked unity. The huge Russian Empire included a great variety of peoples and national groups. Most people in the European part of Russia belonged to one of three related groups: (1) the Great Russians, in central and northern Russia, (2) the Ukrainians, in the south, and (3) the White Russians, in the west. Most of them belonged to the Orthodox church. Scattered throughout the empire were smaller racial, national, and religious groups speaking a variety of languages. Many of these groups, such as the Poles and Finns, had been conquered by the Russians and disliked Russian rule.

Russian Domestic and Foreign Policies

The liberal movement that influenced other European nations so strongly in the 1800s made little headway in Russia. The czar ruled the huge Russian Empire as an **autocrat**—meaning, one who holds absolute power. Although the czars tried to maintain autocracy, liberal political developments in western Europe affected the country.

Russia had felt the influence of the West from before the time of Peter the Great. Improved transportation and communication made this influence stronger still. Nationalistic ideas appealed to the Russian minorities, especially to the strongly patriotic Poles and Finns. By the early 1800s, liberalism began to attract some of the educated members of the Russian aristocracy.

Faced with problems caused by liberal ideas and restless nationalities, the czars took harsh measures. To counteract liberalism the government strictly censored speech and the press and rejected all demands for a constitution. To lessen the nationalities' tensions, in the 1830s Czar Nicholas I began a program of "Russification." This program forced non-Russian peoples in the empire to use the

Russian language, accept the Orthodox religion, and adopt Russian customs.

The Russian rulers had two goals for their foreign policy: (1) In the Balkans they backed Pan-Slavism—the union of all Slavic peoples under Russian leadership. (2) Elsewhere the Russian rulers followed the program of expansion, begun under the first czars, east into Asia and south toward the Ottoman Empire. Russian expansion, however, suffered a setback with the empire's defeat in the Crimean War when it lost territory.

Alexander II and Reforms

Alexander II became czar in 1855. Although he was basically conservative and autocratic, public opinion strongly influenced him, and he heeded the liberals' demand for freedom for all serfs.

Serfdom had taken a different form in Russia than it had in the rest of Europe. After the time of Peter the Great, serfs were bound to persons and not to the land. They could not leave their villages or masters' homes unless so ordered by government officials or permitted to do so by their owners. Although unable to move freely from the land, and largely under the control of their masters, serfs still retained a few civil rights such as the right to sue in court.

Toward the middle of the 1800s, nobles who, under pressure from radical intellectuals, felt guilty about owning serfs began to support the campaign against serfdom. Also, factory owners began to urge that the serfs be freed. The industrialists did not believe in liberal ideas, however; they simply needed workers for their factories. Another group, the "enlightened state bureaucrats," or government employees, also urged freedom for the serfs and convinced Alexander II to consider abolishing this institution.

In response to these urgings, Alexander II appointed committees to study the problem of the serfs. In 1861 he issued the Emancipation Edict that freed all the serfs. The terms of the edict also provided that the government would give the nobles bonds for their land and that peasants or former serfs could buy small tracts of land from the government.

Emancipation did not really improve conditions for the former serfs. Some of the land they had previously farmed was sold to them in small plots and at high prices. Most freed serfs could not afford to buy enough land to earn the payments for the land, pay the taxes, and still make a living. Therefore, they had to rent additional land from their former owners—and rents were high. Some former serfs, unable to either buy or rent land, moved to the growing towns and cities, where they became a source of cheap labor for the factories.

Alexander II attempted other liberal reforms. Beginning in 1864 he allowed each province of European Russia to have an assembly of nobles and of delegates elected by townspeople and peasants. These assemblies decided local taxes and controlled public health, schools, assistance for the poor, and some public works programs.

Alexander also reformed the courts. Civil and criminal cases, formerly tried in secret by administrative officials, were now tried by juries in open courts. However, trials for political offenders accused of plotting against the government were held in secret.

Alexander's policies did not please everyone. People with extremely conservative views opposed them and tried to convince the czar that such actions endangered the position and privileges of the ruler and the nobles. Liberals considered Alexander's reforms as only modest first steps and pointed out the need for further changes. Radicals criticized Alexander even more strongly.

Radicals and Government Reaction

Several groups carried on radical political activity in Russia. The Nihilists (NY•uh•luhsts)—whose name comes from the Latin word *nihil*, meaning "nothing"—were active in the 1860s. They wanted to abolish the whole political and social structure and build a completely new Russia. They rebelled against the traditions of family, school, and society. They believed in keeping nothing of the old values and standards.

In the 1870s another group, the Populists, urged its followers to live among peasants as teachers and doctors. Some believed that all the large estates of the nobles should be seized and the land divided among the peasants. After the government arrested many Populists, some Russian radicals turned to violent action, joining a movement known as the People's Will. These radicals favored the use of **terrorism**—bombings and assassinations of high officials by political groups—to force the government to grant their demands.

Fabergé Egg

This unusual piece of art is an enameled gold egg containing a completely accurate model of the Gatchina Palace near St. Petersburg. Only five inches (13 centimeters) high, it even includes a tiny flag flying from the palace tower. It is decorated with pearls and diamonds. Historians think this egg was given to the mother of Czar Nicholas II on Easter morning, 1902. It was customary for the Russian royal family to exchange eggs like this one every Easter. An egg symbolized the resurrection of Jesus as well as the ancient concepts of fertility and the earth's rebirth in spring.

The Gatchina egg, as it is called, was created in the jewelry firm of Carl Fabergé, in St. Petersburg. Founded in 1842, this company employed the finest jewelers and goldsmiths in all of Europe. These artisans also designed magnificent boxes, clocks, tableware, and jewelry. It was the series of eggs, however, that made Fabergé's reputation. Most of the eggs were signed by

Michael Perchin, who was one of the few native Russians employed by Fabergé.

The famed House of Fabergé was closed in 1918 by officials of the new government. In order to raise money, the government sold all but 10 of the eggs. Today, many of these priceless eggs are housed in private collections and museums.

Radical activity frightened Alexander II, and in the late 1860s, he turned to repressive measures. Gradually, however, he became convinced that additional reforms were necessary. Ironically, a terrorist assassinated him in 1881.

The assassination of Alexander II ended liberal reforms and led to another intensive campaign of repression. Alexander III and his successor, Nicholas II, used every available means to stamp out liberalism—censorship, control of the church and of education, spies and informers, even imprisonment and exile. They intensified "Russification." They severely persecuted Jews in massacres called **pogroms** (POH • gruhmz). Under the slogan "One Czar, One Church, One Language," other minorities felt the heavy hand of oppression.

The attempt to preserve the old order met with much opposition both open and underground. The development of industry in Russia had produced a class of city workers who wanted the right to form unions and to strike. Middle-class industrialists wanted a voice in the government. Liberals and radicals became more determined than ever to gain reforms.

The attempts of the Russian government to suppress all of these varied aims produced an explosive situation. Terrorism increased. Socialists, who in 1898 had founded the Social Democratic Labor Party in imitation of the German Social Democratic Party, grew increasingly radical in their demands. Clearly the government's reaction had backfired.

The Revolution of 1905

In 1904 and 1905, Russia fought a war with Japan in East Asia. To the surprise of the world, the Japanese dealt the Russians a humiliating defeat. Russia's defeat exposed a government that was corrupt and inefficient, as well as autocratic, reactionary, and oppressive. The defeat in turn spurred almost all of the discontented groups in the country to action.

On January 22, 1905, "Bloody Sunday," the czar's troops shot at a group of unarmed strikers on their way to deliver a petition to the czar. The incident triggered the Revolution of 1905. Workers struck and held demonstrations. Merchants closed their stores, and industrialists shut down their factories. Lawyers refused to plead cases, and servants deserted their employers. Czar Nicholas II faced a crisis. Russian autocracy had to yield or perish. He reluctantly decided to yield.

The czar issued a decree called the October Manifesto, which guaranteed individual liberties and provided for the election of a parliament called the Duma. These measures ended the strikes and the revolution.

After the end of the Russo-Japanese War in 1905, the czar's government could better deal with its critics at home. The czar dismissed two sessions of the Duma because its members insisted that the czar's ministers be responsible to the Duma. Then in 1907 the czar changed the qualifications for voting so that only large landowners could vote. This resulted in a more conservative Duma, and one more cooperative with the czar.

The revolutionary movement of 1905 failed to achieve more widespread results for three main reasons: (1) The army remained loyal to the czar and thus would not overthrow the regime. (2) The French, bound to Russia by a military alliance, lent money to support the government. (3) The various

Learning from Pictures
After shooting into the crowd of protestors on Bloody Sunday, Russian Cossacks dispersed the crowd with whips.

Learning from Pictures *In 1906 the first national assembly in Russian history was elected.*

revolutionary groups remained divided in their goals. Moderates feared radical demands. Radicals disagreed among themselves. Workers lost heart and deserted their leaders.

The reactionaries learned nothing from the Revolution of 1905. The government hunted down, imprisoned, exiled, or executed revolutionary leaders. Using all the repressive measures just as before, the government tried to remain as it had been—an autocracy.

SECTION 4 REVIEW

1. **Define** autocrat, terrorism, pogrom
2. **Identify** "Russification," Pan-Slavism, Emancipation Edict, Nihilists, People's Will, Social Democratic Labor Party, Duma
3. **Interpreting Ideas** What were the most important aims of Russian foreign policy?
4. **Summarizing Ideas** (a) What groups favored the abolition of serfdom in Russia? (b) Did emancipation improve the condition of the serfs? (c) Why or why not?
5. **Organizing Ideas** (a) List the liberal reforms that Alexander II accomplished in Russia. (b) What did he do with regard to the serfs?
6. **Analyzing Ideas** (a) Why did the Revolution of 1905 fail to achieve its goals? (b) How did Nicholas II respond to the Revolution of 1905?

5 Austria-Hungary's Interest Focused on the Balkans

"When France sneezes, all Europe catches cold," the Austrian leader Metternich said in 1848. He was referring to the fact that uprisings in France had set off revolts in almost every other European nation. The Austrian Empire proved no exception.

In Vienna demonstrators and the army clashed. A frightened Emperor Ferdinand ordered Metternich, his chief minister, to resign. After having dominated European affairs for well over 30 years, Metternich now fled the country. In 1848 Ferdinand himself abdicated, and the throne went to the 18-year-old Francis Joseph I.

Uprisings occurred in Hungary, too. The people of this region—one of the largest parts of the Austrian Empire—chafed under Austrian rule. Most of them were Magyars—descendants of the nomadic warrior group that had migrated to Hungary from Russia and Romania in the 900s. The Magyars spoke a language unlike other European languages and maintained a distinctive culture. A strong nationalist movement centered on making

RUSSIAN EMPIRE

GERMANY

Prague •
BOHEMIA
Czechs
MORAVIA
•Brno

Kraków •
GALICIA

Slovaks

Salzburg •
AUSTRIA

Vienna •

Buda •Pest

HUNGARY

Innsbruck •
TIROL

CARNIOLA

TRANSYLVANIA

Trieste •
Croats
CROATIA-SLAVONIA

VOJVODINA BANAT
Belgrade •

ROMANIA

ITALY

Serbs
SERBIA

BOSNIA
Sarajevo •
HERZEGOVINA

DALMATIA

Adriatic Sea

N

0   50   100 Miles
0   50   100 Kilometers

**ETHNIC GROUPS IN
AUSTRIA-HUNGARY, 1867**

SLAVS

Croats and Serbs

Czechs and Slovaks

Poles

Slovenes

Ukrainians

OTHER

Germans

Magyars

Romanians

Italians

LAMBERT CONFORMAL CONIC PROJECTION

Learning from Maps   *The Germans of Austria and the Magyars of Hungary were equals
under the Dual Monarchy. What other non-Slavic peoples lived in Austria-Hungary?*

the Magyars dominant in Hungary and freeing the region from Austrian domination.

The Hungarian patriot Louis Kossuth led the revolt in 1848. For a time it looked as though Hungary would gain its independence, and in 1849 Kossuth was elected "responsible governor president" by the Hungarian Diet. However, Austria, with Russia's assistance, soon defeated the revolutionaries. Czar Nicholas I offered his help because he feared that the revolt might spread to Russian Poland. Kossuth fled the country. This ended, for a time, any further Hungarian attempts at independence.

Formation of the Dual Monarchy

For almost 20 years after the Revolution of 1848, Austria managed to keep liberalism and nationalism from becoming major issues. However, after Austria's defeat by Prussia in 1866, Hungarians demanded more freedom. Austria solved this problem in 1867 by forming the Dual Monarchy—also called Austria-Hungary—in which the Hungarians shared power with the Austrians.

The Dual Monarchy had a common ruler, Francis Joseph I, whose title was Emperor of

Austria and King of Hungary. Although three ministries—war, finance, and foreign affairs—conducted government business for the whole empire, Austria and Hungary each had its own parliament. The Austrian parliament met in Vienna; the Hungarian met in Budapest.

From an economic standpoint, the Dual Monarchy proved a practical arrangement. The various parts of the empire fitted together into one economic unit. Hungary, chiefly agricultural, furnished raw materials and food. Austria, strongly industrial, produced manufactured goods. Each provided a market for the other.

Many problems existed, however. Because of its manufacturing interests, Austria wanted high protective tariffs. As a farming region, Hungary favored low tariffs and freer trade.

Nor did the formation of the Dual Monarchy solve the problem of nationalities. The Austrian Germans and the Hungarian Magyars dominated the population in each of their separate national states. National minorities—the Czechs, Serbs, Croats, Romanians, Poles, and Italians—existed in both Austria and Hungary. These people benefited very little from the Dual Monarchy and continued to agitate for self-government.

Other problems arose over command and language in the common army. The Austrians spoke German. The Hungarians spoke Magyar, or Hungarian, which had been declared the official language of Hungary. Some soldiers also spoke the various Slavic languages.

Bismarck, to strengthen Prussia and form a united Germany, declared war on Austria in 1866. Its defeat in the Seven Weeks' War forced Austria out of positions of power in Germany and Italy. To compensate for this setback, and hoping to gain influence and territory, the Dual Monarchy turned toward the Balkans, a region to the southeast controlled chiefly by the Ottoman Empire.

The Ottoman Empire

By the 1800s the Ottoman Empire had declined dramatically. The completely autocratic government had a sultan, or commander-in-chief, who controlled both governmental and religious affairs. Early sultans had been responsible rulers, but later sultans turned to the pleasures of palace life and left government business to lesser officials. These government officials acted as both administrators and military commanders, since the army and the government were one and the same. Favoritism, bribery, and corruption existed everywhere.

Economic and social weaknesses. The Ottoman rulers did little to improve agriculture, maintain irrigation systems, or build public works projects such as roads, hospitals, and schools. The tax system discouraged both agriculture and industry, and production declined. Most peasants planted only enough land to produce a crop that they could harvest quickly and hide from the tax collector. The subject peoples of the Ottoman Turks did not regard their rulers favorably. Many of the people living in the empire were Christians or Jews. In strictly religious matters, the Turks granted toleration to non-Muslims under their own religious leaders. However, when Jews or Christians planned rebellions or plotted with enemy powers, the Turks slaughtered them mercilessly.

Discontent in the Balkans

In the early 1800s, the rise of nationalism increased discontent in the Balkan area of the Ottoman Empire. The Balkan region contained several different peoples—Serbs, Bulgarians, Romanians, and Slavs, for example—all of whom wanted to govern themselves.

The Turks tried to suppress nationalistic movements. During the 1820s the Greeks and Serbs revolted. Aided by outside powers, Greece gained independence in 1829, and Serbia achieved a degree of self-rule. Encouraged by these successes and by the evident weakness of the Turks, Serbia and Greece tried to gain more territory.

Foreign countries intervened for their own ends in the struggles between the Turks and these nationalist groups. Russia supported Balkan nationalists for several reasons. The Russians were Slavs like the Bulgarians and Serbs. In addition, like many of the discontented Balkan groups, the Russians were Orthodox Christians. More importantly, if the Ottoman Empire collapsed, Russia hoped it might be able to gain control of the water route from the Black Sea to the Mediterranean.

The Russian drive toward the eastern Mediterranean caused the British to support the crumbling Ottoman Empire. Great Britain did not want the Russians in the Mediterranean, where they might challenge British sea power.

THE DECLINE OF THE OTTOMAN EMPIRE
1699–1913

- Territory lost, 1699–1913
- Ottoman Empire in 1913
- ⊛ National capital
- • Other city

Dates on map indicate independence or acquisition by another country

SINUSOIDAL PROJECTION

Learning from Maps *Greek independence sparked nationalism in the Balkans. What other countries in the Balkans became independent?*

It was a curious alignment of nations. The autocratic Russian government promoted the freedom and independence of the Balkan peoples. Democratic Great Britain supported the autocratic Turks in suppressing freedom.

The Congress of Berlin and the Balkans

In 1875 revolts broke out in several Turkish provinces in the Balkans. Two years later Russia decided to support the rebels and declared war on the Ottoman Empire. The Turks were defeated and forced to sign the Treaty of San Stefano in 1878. The treaty granted independence to Romania, Montenegro, and Serbia. It also created an enlarged Bulgaria, which Russian troops then occupied for some years. The new boundaries of

Bulgaria extended to the Aegean Sea in the eastern Mediterranean.

The sudden increase of Russian influence in the Balkans alarmed other European powers. Before the Treaty of San Stefano could go into effect, a group of nations led by Great Britain and Austria forced the Russians to consent to an international conference at Berlin.

All the major European powers met at the Congress of Berlin in 1878. The Congress approved several terms. Serbia, Montenegro, and Romania retained their independence. Bulgaria was granted self-government, but its area was reduced in size, and it was kept within the Ottoman Empire—thus removing Russia's access to the Aegean Sea. Austria continued to govern Bosnia and Herzegovina but was not permitted to annex them.

594

The British were given the right to occupy and administer the island of Cyprus, long held by the Turks. The Turkish sultan still officially ruled the island, but Great Britain actually took it over. The use of Cyprus as a naval base increased Great Britain's power in the eastern Mediterranean and kept Russia out of this region.

Other nations continued to reduce both the size and the power of the Ottoman Empire. France, Great Britain, and Italy each seized parts of its African territory. In 1908 Bulgaria became completely independent. In the same year, Austria broke the agreement of the Congress of Berlin by annexing Bosnia and Herzegovina outright. In 1912 Italy seized several islands in the southeastern Aegean Sea, including Rhodes. The island of Crete revolted in 1896 and 1905, which resulted in a degree of self-government and, finally, annexation by Greece in 1913.

In 1912 and 1913, two wars between independent Balkan nations and the Ottomans further altered national boundaries and increased international tensions. Bulgaria, Serbia, Greece, and Montenegro, known as the Balkan League, declared war on the Ottoman Empire and quickly defeated it. The Balkan League wanted to take and divide among themselves the Balkan territories of the Ottoman Empire. However, they could not agree on the partition of the Turkish territories and hostilities broke out again in 1913. This time, Serbia, Greece, Montenegro, Romania, and the Ottoman Empire fought against and defeated Bulgaria.

As a result of the first war, Serbia gained a seaport on the Adriatic, and Albania became independent. Bulgaria claimed considerable territory in the central Balkans and along the Aegean Sea. As a result of the second war, however, Bulgaria suffered humiliating territorial losses to Serbia and Greece and was left with only a small outlet on the Aegean.

By the end of 1913, the territory of the Ottoman Empire in Europe had shrunk dramatically. It included only the city of Constantinople and a small region that gave it control of the vital water route from the Black Sea to the Mediterranean (see map, page 594). The stage was set for a showdown of the major European powers.

Everywhere in Europe, therefore, aggression and expansion marked the behavior of nations both new and old in the early 1900s. Tension and hostility

Learning from Pictures *This cartoon shows the European powers as vultures waiting for the independence of the Balkans and the fall of the Ottoman Empire.*

began to rise to dangerous levels. Overseas rivalries, the result of a new force—imperialism—only made matters worse.

SECTION 5 REVIEW

1. **Identify**   Magyars, Louis Kossuth, Francis Joseph I, Treaty of San Stefano, Balkan League
2. **Locate**   Romania, Budapest, Serbia, Montenegro, Bulgaria, Bosnia, Herzegovina, Cyprus, Rhodes
3. **Summarizing Ideas**   **(a)** When was the Dual Monarchy formed?   **(b)** What were its strengths and weaknesses?
4. **Organizing Ideas**   How was the Ottoman Empire reduced in size between 1878 and 1913?
5. **Interpreting Ideas**   **(a)** Why did the Western nations fear Russian influence in the Balkans? **(b)** What prompted the Congress of Berlin?

Chapter Summary

The following list contains the key concepts you have learned about the unification of Italy and Germany as well as about problems that arose in other European nations in the late 1800s and early 1900s.

1. Major new forces entered the European scene with the formation of a united Italy and a united Germany.
2. Italy was unified in 1870 due to the efforts of Mazzini, Garibaldi, and Cavour. A kingdom was established with Rome as its capital.
3. The kingdom of Prussia led the German unification under the leadership of Otto von Bismarck.
4. In both cases, but especially that of Germany, aggressive behavior accompanied the new unity. The Italians militarized rapidly, until their navy was the third largest in the world. The Germans went further, using three victorious wars to crush rivals and strengthen German national feeling.
5. Bismarck clashed with the new emperor, William II, and was forced to resign in 1890. However, Germany remained both prosperous and aggressive.
6. In Russia the czar maintained autocratic control over the country, despite such reforms as the freeing of the serfs.
7. Discontent and rebellion continued in the Austrian Empire even after Austria-Hungary, the Dual Monarchy, was created. Holding its various nationalities together was a major problem of the Dual Monarchy.
8. As the Ottoman Empire declined, discontent in its Balkan territories led to two Balkan wars in 1912 and 1913, with the result that international tensions increased. This would eventually lead to a greater show of hostility.

On a separate sheet of paper, complete the following review exercises.

Reviewing Important Terms

Supply the term that correctly completes each statement.

1. The nationalistic movement in Italy, with its goals of liberation and unification, was called _____ .
2. The emperor or king of Prussia was called the _____ .
3. An _____ is someone who holds absolute power.
4. Bombings and assassinations of high officials by political groups are called _____ .
5. The massacres of the Jews in czarist Russia were called _____ .

Developing Critical Thinking Skills

1. **Comparing Ideas** (a) What were the similarities and differences between the processes of unification in Italy and Germany? (b) What generalizations can you make about how these two nations came into existence?
2. **Analyzing Ideas** Otto von Bismarck once remarked, "Politics is the art of the possible, the art of the attainable." How did Bismarck's actions in forming the German Empire demonstrate his belief in this statement?
3. **Interpreting Ideas** (a) Why did the liberal movement make little progress in Russia during the 1800s? (b) How did Russian radicals attempt to bring about change?
4. **Understanding Relationships** Why might each of the following events be considered a response to the rise of nationalism? (a) Unification of Italy and Germany; (b) Start of the "Russification" program (c) Establishment of the Dual Monarchy; (d) Further decline of the Ottoman Empire.

Relating Geography to History

You read in Chapter 15 about the rivalry between Prussia and Austria to dominate central Europe. To study the outcome of this struggle, compare the two maps on pages 390 and 582. How did the balance of power change during the period from 1763 to 1871? Using the information in this chapter and in Chapter 15, briefly explain how Prussia came to rule the German Empire.

Relating Past to Present

1. The Zollverein was a major step toward German unity. (a) Who belonged to this customs union? (b) How did the various member states benefit from economic

Timeline:
- 1848 — Revolts in Italy, Germany, and Austrian Empire
- 1861 — Formation of Dual Monarchy
- 1861 — Emancipation of serfs in Russia
- 1862 — 1862–1890 Bismarck as chancellor of Prussia
- 1867
- 1870 — Final unification of Italy
- 1861–1888 Rule of William I in Prussia
- 1878 — Congress of Berlin
- 1888
- 1890
- 1905 — Revolution in Russia
- 1912 1913 — Balkan wars

cooperation? **(c)** Using American history or civics books, find out about the laws regulating trade among the states in this nation. Can the states impose or collect tariffs? **(d)** Can the federal government grant special trade concessions to any one state or region? **(e)** What evidence of trade among the states can you find in your home?

2. Review the objectives of Russia's foreign policy during the 1800s. Then clip newspaper and magazine articles that illustrate foreign-policy objectives of the Soviet Union today. Compare the objectives of the 1800s with those of the present day. What seem to be the similarities and differences?

Applying History Study Skills

Before completing this activity, review Building History Study Skills on page 586.

Read the following statements. The first is from a speech by Otto von Bismarck on his view of the unification of Germany. The other is from a letter by Giuseppe Garibaldi on his conquest of Naples. How are their views of unification different? How are they similar?

66 Germany does not look to Prussia's liberalism, but to her power. The south German states . . . would like to indulge in liberalism, and because of that no one will assign Prussia's role to them! Prussia must collect her forces and hold them in reserve for an opportune moment, which has already come and gone several times. . . . Not by speeches and majorities will the great questions of the day be decided—that was the mistake of 1848 and 1849—but by iron and blood. 99

(Otto von Bismarck. Speech to the Reichstag on September 30, 1862)

66 Having reached the strait, it became necessary to cross it. To have reinstated Sicily in the great Italian family was certainly a glorious achievement. But what then? Were we, in compliance with diplomacy, to leave our country incomplete and maimed? What of the two Calabrias, and Naples, awaiting us with open arms?

And the rest of Italy still enslaved by the foreigner and the priest?. . .

I entered Naples with the whole of the southern army as yet a long way off in the direction of the Straits of Messina, the King of Naples having, on the previous day, quitted his palace to retire to Capua.

At Naples, as in all places we had passed through since crossing the strait, the populace were sublime in their enthusiastic patriotism, and the resolute tone assumed by them certainly had no small share in the brilliant results obtained. 99

(Garibaldi's Report on the Conquest of Naples)

1. How did Bismarck feel about liberalism?
2. **(a)** How did Garibaldi feel about the role of the people in uniting Italy? **(b)** How did his opinion differ from Bismarck's?
3. What does Bismarck mean by the expression "iron and blood"?
4. **(a)** How was Garibaldi greeted in Naples? **(b)** What might Bismarck have said about this greeting?
5. What was the primary difference between Garibaldi's and Bismarck's approaches to unification?

Investigating Further

1. **Presenting an Oral Report** Read Garibaldi's entire "Proclamation to the Italians," and Bismarck's entire "iron and blood" speech in a source such as Louis Snyder's *Fifty Major Documents of the Nineteenth Century* (Van Nostrand Reinhold). Give an oral report explaining why each of these documents might be considered an expression of nationalism. Discuss which one is more idealistic and why.
2. **Writing a Report** Garibaldi and his comparatively small army succeeded in conquering the Kingdom of the Two Sicilies, which later became part of a united Italy. Prepare a written report on Garibaldi's exploits in Sicily. One source for your report is "Garibaldi and His Thousand Redshirts Win Palermo" in Louis Snyder and Richard Morris's *A Treasury of Great Reporting* (Pocket Books).

597

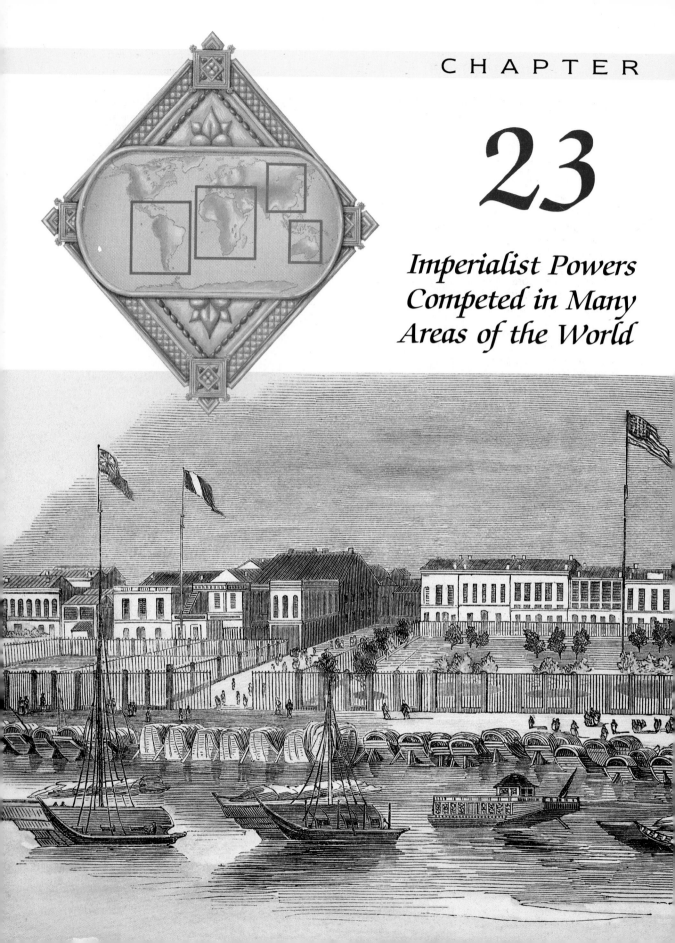

Imperialist Powers Competed in Many Areas of the World

Place   Africa, Asia, the Pacific, and Latin America

Time   1798–1914

```
  3.7 mil. BC   4000 BC              AD 2100
```

Significance

Beginning in the late 1400s and continuing into the 1700s, European nations extended their power to Asia and the Americas. By the late 1700s, however, this interest declined. Great Britain and France had lost colonies in North America. Also, the French Revolution and Napoleonic Wars had prompted Europeans to focus more attention on European affairs.

Beginning about 1870 several factors rekindled interest in establishing colonies. During the next 40 years, many nations became involved in a new kind of empire building called **imperialism**—the domination by a powerful nation over the political, economic, and cultural affairs of another nation or region. Imperialism differed from the colonization of the 1500s and 1600s. Colonies established after 1870 were both more heavily populated and more thoroughly dominated. By the early 1900s, European nations, the United States, and Japan had brought most of the world under their control.

Terms to Define

imperialism	direct rule
colony	paternalism
protectorate	assimilation
concession	indirect rule

People to Identify

Rudyard Kipling	Boers
Ashanti	Cecil Rhodes

Places to Locate

Suez Canal	Singapore
Brazzaville	Panama Canal

Questions to Guide Your Reading

1 What forces stimulated imperialism?
2 How did Europeans win control of North Africa?
3 What colonies did Europeans carve out of Sub-Saharan Africa?
4 How did imperialism in South and East Asia differ from imperialism in Africa?
5 Why did imperialist powers claim colonies in the Pacific?
6 How did the United States become an imperialist power?

▲ *European trading centers in Guangzhou, China*

In 1869 the New York Herald *hired journalist Henry Stanley to locate Dr. David Livingstone, who had disappeared in Africa. In 1871 Stanley finally located Livingstone and wrote of their meeting.*

❝ ***S****o I did that which I thought was most dignified. I pushed back the crowds, and, passing from the rear, walked down a living avenue of people until I came in front of the semicircle of Arabs, in front of which stood the white man with the gray beard. As I advanced slowly toward him I noticed he was pale, looked wearied. . . . I would have run to him, only I was a coward in the presence of such a mob. . . . So I did what cowardice and false pride suggested was the best thing—walked deliberately to him, took off my hat, and said, 'Dr. Livingstone, I presume?'*

'Yes,' said he, with a kind smile, lifting his cap slightly. **❞**

Stanley's highly publicized trip did much to spark European interest in Africa.

1 Several Forces Stimulated Imperialism

Imperialism arose out of a complex mixture of political, economic, and social forces, although historians do not agree on which influences were most dominant.

Desire for Self-sufficiency

After 1850 the Industrial Revolution accelerated as new sources of power, new machinery, and new industries were developed. Increased industrial production spurred the demand for traditional raw materials such as iron and coal. In addition, the new factories needed other raw materials such as manganese and tungsten for making steel alloys, copper for the electrical industry, and rubber for a variety of uses. Industrialization also brought rising standards of living in Europe and the United States and increased demands for products such as coffee, tea, and spices.

Although none of the industrialized nations produced all of these products, none of the leaders of these nations wanted to depend on other nations for raw materials. Government leaders feared that in the event of war their countries would be at the mercy of an enemy. Thus the leaders of the industrial nations concluded that the best solution was to become self-sufficient by gaining control of the sources of the raw materials they needed.

Need for New Markets

After 1870 new technology made it possible to produce goods in enormous quantities. Indeed, manufacturers had to produce large quantities of goods in order to realize a profit. Only when the new and expensive machinery was used to full capacity could it pay for itself and generate profits for its owners.

Even with their rising standards of living, people in Europe and the United States could not buy all the goods on the market. In order to sell all of the goods they produced, industrialists began to look for new markets in nonindustrialized regions, especially in Asia, Africa, and Latin America.

Imperialists believed that if people in non-industrialized areas were aware of manufactured goods and if the goods were available, they would buy them. Imperialists even argued that the customs of these people might be remolded to create new markets. Advocates of imperialism wrote articles describing how busy European and American factories would be, and how much profit they would earn, if only the people of central Africa could be persuaded to wear shirts and ties.

Many people argued that industrialized nations should control their new markets abroad, just as they controlled the colonial sources of their raw materials. Industrialists wanted their governments to guarantee them exclusive rights to sell in these markets. At the same time, they demanded protective tariffs to assure their exclusive markets at home.

Nationalism

Nationalism, a strong force throughout the 1800s, became particularly powerful between 1870 and 1914. Many nationalists now argued that having colonies added to their nations' strength and prestige. The recently unified nations of Germany and Italy felt that they had to build up colonial empires in order to compete with longtime colonial powers such as Great Britain, France, and the Netherlands. However, it is notable that the British, who

already had a large empire, entered the imperialistic race for colonies as enthusiastically as did the Germans or Italians. National "honor" would not allow the British to watch territorial prizes go to rival nations.

Imperialists also viewed colonies as sources of troops for the rapidly growing armies of the day. Gurkhas and Pathans, the fighters of Nepal and Afghanistan, joined Australians and New Zealanders to build up British armies. Senegalese troops from West Africa fought for the French.

A large navy was even more important than a large army to protect widely scattered colonies and far-ranging merchant ships. For many years steam-powered ships burned coal, and the range of a steamship was "from coal to coal." Thus the coaling station, a place where warships and merchant ships could refuel, became strategically important for military and commercial purposes. Tiny islands with nothing to offer except their strategic location became coaling stations or naval bases. Often these stations became objects of fierce competition among naval powers.

Outlets for Population

Rapid population growth accompanied industrialization. Industrial development created many jobs, but in Europe there was not enough work to employ all the new job seekers. As a result, people left Europe in great numbers and immigrated to the United States, Latin America, and Australia.

Nationalists regretted seeing these people leave because the emigrants often became naturalized citizens of the countries in which they settled, breaking all ties with their former homelands. How much better, the nationalists thought, if emigrants would instead settle in one of the colonies. There they would remain loyal subjects under the political control of their home country. Although many new colonies were already heavily populated or were so remote that they attracted few European settlers, these drawbacks did not trouble the nationalists.

Missionary Motives

The urge to spread the Christian religion influenced colonial expansion during the 1500s and 1600s. Although Roman Catholic missionaries had continued their work since that time, they increased their activities during the period of

Learning from Pictures *This missionary classroom was in the Philippines. What types of knowledge did missionaries spread?*

imperialism. Growing numbers of Protestant missionaries also attempted to convert people in the colonies to Christianity.

Missionaries did other important work as well. Education became a regular missionary activity. Trained medical missionaries went out from Europe and the United States. Consequently, knowledge of medicine, hygiene, and sanitation spread with Christianity.

The "White Man's Burden"

Closely related to the missionary motive was the idea that the people of advanced Western nations had a duty to transmit Western ideas and techniques to more "backward" people. People were considered backward if their religion or their culture differed from those of the West.

The British poet Rudyard Kipling wrote a poem that urged members of his race to "take up the white man's burden."

> Take up the white man's burden—
> Send forth the best ye breed—
> Go bind your sons to exile
> To serve your captives' need;
> To wait in heavy harness,
> On fluttered folk and wild—
> Your new-caught, sullen peoples,
> Half-devil and half-child.

Kipling was referring to the obligation to carry Western civilization to those he considered less fortunate. The French spoke of their "civilizing mission." The people of each industrial nation considered its civilization and culture to be the highest and, therefore, the one most suited for enlightening the "backward" peoples of the earth.

Opponents of imperialism claimed that the only burden the white man wanted to take up was the burden of colonial wealth, which he wanted to carry back home as fast as possible. Such opponents, however, formed a minority with little influence in their countries.

The Nature of Imperialism

Imperialism created bitter rivalries among the imperial powers and hatred among the colonized peoples. Rivalries led to the building of larger armies and navies and eventually to world conflict.

In the beginning, European governments did not actively plan imperialism. Usually it began with the work of individuals such as merchants, explorers, scientists, or missionaries. Sometimes the Europeans met with resistance and violence from the local inhabitants. Then European soldiers appeared, followed by government officials to protect the interests of their citizens. Builders, engineers, and technicians who opened mines and built roads, railroads, bridges, and dams usually followed the soldiers and officials. Then the region would be developed for the benefit of the developers. The local population had very little, if any, say in this process.

Loans to local rulers often provided the initial wedges of imperialism. If the local rulers spent the money recklessly, they found themselves heavily in debt and were forced to grant economic privileges. Economic privileges often led to political control. Europeans often used this means of gaining control of an area or region.

Several terms used in connection with imperialism need explanation. Originally a colony was a settlement established in another region by citizens of a country. Early examples of colonies include the ancient Greek colonies throughout the Mediterranean and the British colonies in North America. During the imperialistic era, however, a **colony** was an area in which a foreign nation gained total control over a given region and its local population. A colony was first gained by settlement or conquest and then annexed, becoming a part of the empire.

In a **protectorate,** the local ruler kept his title, but officials of the foreign power actually controlled the region. The "protecting" power kept out other foreign nations. In a **condominium,** two nations ruled a region as partners. A **concession** was the grant of economic rights and privileges in a given area. Concessions were given to foreign merchants or capitalists who wanted to trade, to build railroads, or to develop mineral deposits and other natural resources. Concessions held exclusively by one foreign power were called monopoly concessions. A **sphere of influence** was a region in which one nation had special, sometimes exclusive, economic and political privileges that were recognized by other nations.

SECTION 1 REVIEW

1. **Define** imperialism, colony, protectorate, condominium, concession, sphere of influence
2. **Identify** "white man's burden"
3. **Determining Cause and Effect** (a) Why did European interest in colonies decline between the late 1700s and the late 1800s? (b) Why was interest in colonies rekindled in the late 1800s?
4. **Summarizing Ideas** Describe four motives behind imperialism that were related to the Industrial Revolution.

2 Europeans Made Claims in North Africa and the Sudan

Throughout history many conquerors, including the Romans, the Byzantines, and the Arabs, imposed their rule on North Africa. In the 1800s most of the region belonged to the Ottoman Empire, although Turkish control was weak.

The French in North Africa

For a long time, expert Muslim seafarers known as the Barbary pirates operated off the coast of North Africa, taking a heavy toll on Mediterranean shipping. The term *Barbary* means "of the Berbers"—a people of North Africa who had converted to Islam during the 600s. Four Muslim states—Morocco, Algiers, Tunis, and Tripoli—made up the so-called Barbary States. (These countries are now called Morocco, Algeria, Tunisia, and Libya.)

The operations of the Barbary pirates gave the French, who wanted to compensate for the loss of French prestige after the defeat of Napoleon in 1815, an excuse to intervene in North Africa. The French complained about the Barbary pirates to the Algerian ruler and received what they considered an insulting reply. In 1830 a French force occupied Algeria, arrested the ruler, and settled down to stay. For more than 40 years, the French had to fight against almost continuous local rebellions and violence.

Economically, however, the struggle for Algeria proved worth the price. Many French people and other Europeans moved to Algeria, taking over the best land and running the nation's businesses. Algeria soon became an exporter of farm products, wine, and meat, playing an important role in French economic life.

Seizure of Tunisia. East of Algeria lies Tunisia, a small country with a long history. Its capital, Tunis, grew up near once-formidable Carthage, the rival of ancient Rome. A poor and underdeveloped country, Tunisia belonged to the Ottoman Empire. Its Turkish ruler, the bey of Tunis, spent money lavishly and cared little about financial management. He borrowed heavily from European bankers until they refused him further loans. The French government, seeing a chance to gain influence, lent him more money.

When the French loan was due, the bey raised the already high taxes, inciting rebellion. In 1869 a commission of the bey's creditors was established to restore order and reorganize Tunisia's finances. The commission included representatives of the British, French, and Italian governments.

All three of these nations wanted Tunisia. Italy, in the process of becoming united and eager to gain colonies, had encouraged many Italians to emigrate to Tunisia. In a complicated series of negotiations, France and Great Britain reached an agreement, which was announced in 1878 at the Congress of Berlin. The French were to have a free hand in Tunisia, and the British could occupy the island of Cyprus. Italy—new, poor, and inexperienced at the diplomatic game—was ignored.

In 1881 the French declared Tunisia a protectorate. The bey remained ruler in name, but the senior French official in Tunis wielded the power. French rule brought certain improvements to Tunisia—public order, roads, schools, industries, and sound finances. However, religious differences, local pride, and a rising spirit of nationalism inspired many Tunisians to work for independence.

Rivalry over Morocco. After acquiring Algeria and Tunisia, France felt it needed Morocco in order to protect its interests in North Africa. Morocco's strategic location along the narrow Strait of Gibraltar made it a tempting prize for imperialist nations. However, so many European countries wanted Morocco that each one was afraid to take it because doing so might trigger a war.

By the early 1900s, France was willing to take the necessary risks to acquire Morocco. As a result, France and Germany became entangled in a bitter dispute over Morocco. A compromise was eventually reached in 1911. France was given a free hand in Morocco, while Germany received territory in West Africa. Spain acquired the small northern strip of Spanish Morocco, and the city of Tangier came under international control. The rest of rich Morocco became a French protectorate.

The British in Egypt

Egypt had been part of the Ottoman Empire for centuries. However, by the mid-1800s, the empire was crumbling. The Turkish viceroy in Egypt, called the khedive (kuh•DEEV), had become almost entirely independent. The khedive still paid some tribute to the Ottoman sultan but ruled Egypt with absolute authority.

Learning from Pictures
French cavalry crushed resistance in Tunisia in order to forestall Italian ambitions in North Africa.

603

READ
WRITE
INTERPRET
CONNECT
●THINK

BUILDING HISTORY STUDY SKILLS

Thinking About History: Determining Relevancy

As you do research in history, you often must sift through mountains of information to find what you need. As you do so, you need to be able to distinguish between relevant and irrelevant information. Relevant information includes the data that applies to your topic or purpose. For example, if you are researching the topic of how the Japanese resisted European imperialism, the shogun's response to Commodore Perry's ultimatum would be relevant information. A description of the beauty of Kyoto, the emperor's residence, would not be relevant because it would not help you explain the resistance to imperialism.

How to Determine Relevancy

To determine relevancy, follow these steps.

1. State the topic that you are researching.
2. Identify categories that will help you to organize the topic.
3. Look for definitions, descriptions, details, and evidence on your topic.
4. Examine each piece of information and relate it to the topic. Use the categories that you have devised and discard all the information that has no bearing on them.

Developing the Skill

If you were researching the impact that imperialism had on European economies, you might use two categories—*costs* and *benefits*. Read the following two selections and determine whether either would be relevant in your research. The first excerpt is from a speech by the British imperialist Joseph Chamberlain. The second is from the writings of Marco Polo.

❝ We have suffered much in this country from depression of trade. We know how many of our fellow-subjects are at this moment unemployed. Is there any man in his senses who believes that the crowded populations of these islands [the British Isles] could exist for a single day if we were to cut adrift from us the great dependencies which now look to us for protection and assistance, and which are the natural markets for our trade? . . . If tomorrow it were possible, as some people apparently desire, to reduce by a stroke of the pen the British Empire to the dimensions of the United Kingdom, half at least of our population would be starved. ❞

❝ On the interior side of the palace are large buildings with halls and chambers, where the Emperor's private property is placed, such as his treasures of gold, silver, gems, pearls and gold plate, and in which reside the ladies and secondary wives. These rooms are only for him and no one else has access to them. ❞

In the first excerpt, Chamberlain discusses one of the major benefits of imperialism. It provides trade outlets and also helps to feed the many people of Great Britain. It would be relevant in your research of the costs and benefits of imperialism.

The second excerpt, however, would not be relevant to your topic. It merely discusses Marco Polo's impression of the emperor's palace. In addition, Marco Polo lived centuries before the imperialism of the 1800s that you are researching.

Practicing the skill. Read the excerpt from Rudyard Kipling on page 601. Then determine whether it would provide relevant information about the costs and benefits of imperialism.

To apply this skill, see Applying History Study Skills on page 627.

Morocco's reception of the French ambassador

604

In 1854 a French company headed by Ferdinand de Lesseps gained a concession to build a canal through the Isthmus of Suez. The Egyptian government bought almost half of the stock in the company. Individual French citizens bought most of the remaining shares.

Ismail Pasha, the khedive when the canal was completed in 1869, had very expensive habits and little concern with financial management. Between 1869 and 1879, he increased the foreign debt of his government by more than 20 times. Finally, foreign banks refused to lend him more money.

Ismail's solution to his financial problem was to sell Egypt's stock in the Suez Canal. This action provided an opportunity for the British, who wanted to control the canal because it was a vital link in the trade route between Great Britain and India, Australia, and New Zealand. In 1875 the British government bought the Egyptian stock and became the largest single stockholder. Because the British owned so much of the stock and because the rest was so widely scattered among private investors, the British gained virtual control of the canal.

After an Egyptian rebellion in 1882, a British fleet bombarded Alexandria, landed troops, and soon occupied the entire country. There they remained, claiming that they had to safeguard the Suez Canal, their main route to India. The Egyptian government remained outwardly independent, but the British actually ruled.

Anglo-Egyptian Sudan

The Sudan, a vast geographic region of savannas south of the Sahara, stretches from the Atlantic Ocean to the Nile River valley and beyond. In the imperialistic era, the term *Sudan* also referred to a specific eastern part of this region south of Egypt. Arabs and various local tribes inhabited this region, which Egypt claimed.

After Great Britain established control over Egypt in 1882, the Sudan became important to the British. Since the upper Nile River flows through the Sudan, control of the region would afford a chance to build dams to store water for irrigation and to control the flow of water in the lower Nile. France also wanted the Sudan, both because of its possessions farther west and because it already had a toehold on the Red Sea (French Somaliland) and wanted to extend its territory inland.

In 1881 Muhammad Ahmad, taking the title Mahdi, or Islamic savior, organized a revolt in the Sudan. Mahdi's troops captured Khartoum and established a government that ruled until 1898. In that year, Great Britain ordered a military force to move into the Sudan. Under General Herbert Kitchener, these troops defeated a Sudanese army at Omdurman and then moved farther south.

Meanwhile the French sent an expedition from the French Congo, under Major J. B. Marchand. Marchand and his small force of Senegalese soldiers made a daring two-year journey through some 3,000 miles (5,000 kilometers) of tropical rain forest. In July 1898 Marchand reached Fashoda, on the upper Nile River, and raised the French flag.

The British force reached Fashoda in September, and Kitchener insisted that the French flag be lowered and the British and Egyptian flags be raised. Tension was relieved only when both officers decided to ask their governments for further instructions.

Since neither government really wanted war, they negotiated a settlement of what became known as the Fashoda Incident. The French recognized the British as masters of the Sudan, in return for recognition of all their possessions in French West Africa. Great Britain and Egypt established a condominium in the Sudan, known as the Anglo-Egyptian Sudan. In this way Great Britain established political dominance of this area.

The Italians in Libya

Desert covered most of Tripoli, a region lying to the west of Egypt. Like Tunisia, it belonged to the Ottoman Empire, but Turkish control was weak. Italy was interested in joining the other European powers by establishing an empire. The region had almost no economic value, but, as one diplomat put it, when Italy came to the table, only the crumbs were left. So Italy decided to eat the crumbs.

First, Italy secured guarantees of neutrality from several European powers. Then in 1911 Italy declared war on the Ottoman Empire. Although the Turks showed surprisingly strong resistance, the Italians finally defeated them.

Italy took Tripoli as a colony and renamed it Libya. It was a profitless victory. Except for a narrow strip along the coast, the land was barren. The small population violently opposed Italian rule. As a result, the expense of maintaining troops in Libya drained the Italian economy.

3 Several European Nations Carved up SubSaharan Africa

In the 1500s and the 1600s, the first great period of European colonization, several nations established trading posts on the east and west coasts of Sub-Saharan Africa. The imperialism of the late 1800s increased interest in this vast portion of Africa.

Competition for West Africa

West Africa had been a major center of the slave trade. First the Portuguese and the Dutch, and later the British and the French, had established trading posts along the coast. When most European countries abolished the slave trade in the early 1800s, these former slaving centers turned increasingly to other types of commerce. They traded in palm oil, hides and feathers, ivory, rubber, and other natural products from the interior. Eager to control this trade, the Europeans began to push inland.

By pushing into the interior, European countries sought to link their coastal possessions. In the "bulge" of western Africa, the French pushed inland and claimed the ancient city of Tombouctou. They also increased the number of commercial settlements in the coastal areas of French Guinea, the Ivory Coast, and Dahomey. By 1900 France had claimed a vast area called French West Africa (see map, page 607).

In many cases the French as well as other Europeans met with fierce resistance in their drive to colonize Africa. In what is today Senegal, for example, the ruler Samari Touré signed an agreement with the French in the late 1800s. When the French broke their part of the bargain Touré led his people in revolt. For seven years the French were unable to subdue the fiesty Touré and his forces. Finally in 1898, the superior fire power of the French troops paid off, and Touré was captured. In another instance of heroic resistance, the king of Dahomey resisted the French until 1894.

The British competed with the French throughout West Africa. They too sought to connect their coastal settlements and expand into the interior. The Gold Coast (modern Ghana) particularly interested them. From their coastal bases there, the British thrust inland, coming up against the powerful African kingdom of Ashanti. By 1901, however, Great Britain had annexed all the territory of Ashanti and made the Gold Coast a colony.

The British also expanded into Nigeria, a territory to the east of the Gold Coast that took its name from the Niger, one of the great rivers of Africa. Control of the Niger River assured control of a huge region rich in resources. In 1861 the British annexed the port city of Lagos and then pushed steadily inland. African merchants and Muslim states resisted the British. But British military forces crushed all African resistance and made Nigeria a protectorate.

By the early 1900s, France, Britain, Germany Spain, and Portugal had claimed all of West Africa except Liberia (see map, page 607). Settled by freed slaves from the United States, Liberia had become an independent republic in 1847.

Although economically and militarily weak, Liberia maintained its independence. It no doubt would have become the protectorate of an ambitious European power if not for its special relationship to the United States. American diplomatic pressure discouraged European attempts to take over the small republic.

Competition for Central Africa

Henry Stanley's successful search for Dr. David Livingstone did much to publicize the possibilities for imperialistic development in Africa. Stanley tried but failed to interest the British government in the vast area he had explored. He then turned to King Leopold II of Belgium, who did want the region. After much national and international maneuvering, Leopold, acting as a private citizen, carved out a personal empire of 900,000 square miles (2.3 million square kilometers).

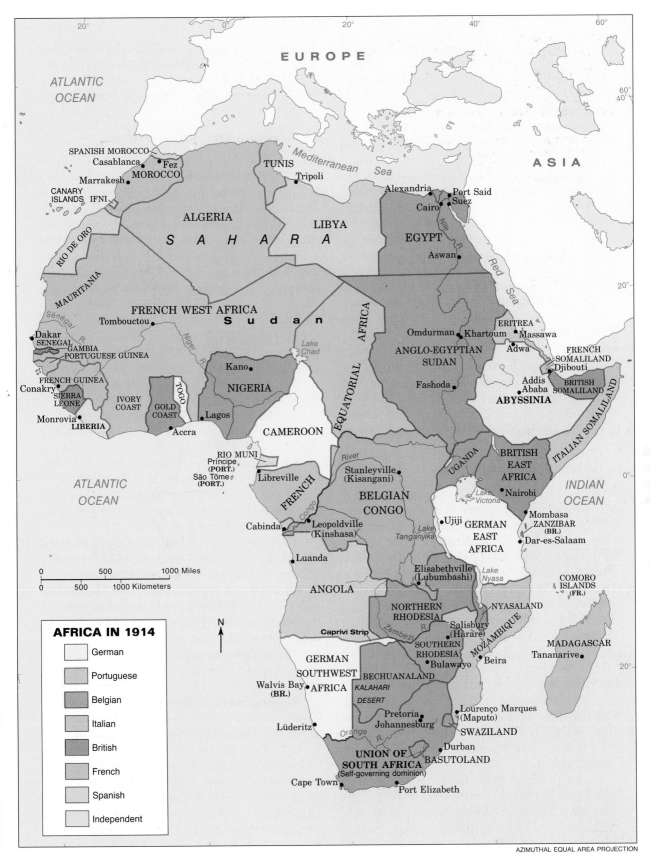

ATLANTIC
OCEAN

EUROPE

ASIA

Mediterranean Sea

SPANISH MOROCCO
Casablanca • Fez
Marrakesh • MOROCCO
CANARY ISLANDS IFNI

TUNIS
Tripoli •

Alexandria •
Cairo
Port Said
Suez

ALGERIA

LIBYA

EGYPT

RIO DE ORO

S A H A R A

Aswan •

Nile R.

Red Sea

MAURITANIA

FRENCH WEST AFRICA
S u d a n

Sénégal R.

Tombouctou •

Niger R.

Lake Chad

EQUATORIAL AFRICA

ERITREA
Omdurman • Khartoum • Massawa
Adwa •
ANGLO-EGYPTIAN SUDAN
FRENCH SOMALILAND
Djibouti
Fashoda •
BRITISH SOMALILAND
Addis Ababa •
ABYSSINIA

Dakar •
SENEGAL
GAMBIA
PORTUGUESE GUINEA
FRENCH GUINEA
Conakry •
SIERRA LEONE
Monrovia •
LIBERIA

Kano •
NIGERIA
IVORY COAST
GOLD COAST
TOGO
Lagos •
Accra •

CAMEROON

RIO MUNI
Príncipe (PORT.)
São Tomé (PORT.)

Libreville •

FRENCH

Cabinda •

ITALIAN SOMALILAND

UGANDA

BRITISH EAST AFRICA
Nairobi •

Stanleyville (Kisangani) •
BELGIAN CONGO
Leopoldville (Kinshasa) •

River

Lake Victoria

ATLANTIC OCEAN

Ujiji •
GERMAN EAST AFRICA

INDIAN OCEAN

Mombasa •
ZANZIBAR (BR.)
Dar-es-Salaam •

Lake Tanganyika

Luanda •

Elisabethville (Lubumbashi) •

Lake Nyasa

COMORO ISLANDS (FR.)

ANGOLA

NORTHERN RHODESIA

NYASALAND

Zambezi R.

Salisbury (Harare) •
SOUTHERN RHODESIA
Bulawayo •

MOZAMBIQUE

MADAGASCAR
Tananarive •

Beira •

Caprivi Strip

GERMAN SOUTHWEST AFRICA

Walvis Bay (BR.) •

BECHUANALAND
KALAHARI DESERT

Lüderitz •

Orange R.

Pretoria •
Johannesburg •

Lourenço Marques (Maputo) •
SWAZILAND

Durban •
BASUTOLAND
UNION OF SOUTH AFRICA
(Self-governing dominion)

Cape Town •

Port Elizabeth •

N

0 ——— 500 ——— 1000 Miles
0 —— 500 —— 1000 Kilometers

AFRICA IN 1914

- German
- Portuguese
- Belgian
- Italian
- British
- French
- Spanish
- Independent

AZIMUTHAL EQUAL AREA PROJECTION

607

Leopold's rule of the Congo provides an example of the worst aspects of imperialism. His only interest was in extracting as much wealth as possible from the colony. Forming a corporation, he sold concessions to speculators who shared his interest in a fast profit. Their exploitation of the Congo's supply of natural rubber became an international scandal. Leopold set aside whole regions as monopolies and uprooted Africans from their homes and forced them to collect rubber. Large areas of rubber trees and vines were destroyed without any thought of replanting for the future. Finally, faced with international criticism of conditions in the Congo, falling world rubber prices, and dwindling rubber supplies in the Congo, Leopold transferred ownership to the Belgian government in 1908.

North of Leopold's Congo, Pierre de Brazza founded the city of Brazzaville on the lower Zaire (Congo) River in 1880, thus laying the basis for French claims to an area known as the French Congo. The French extended their claims to the northeast, gaining control of a large region north of the Congo and adjoining French West Africa. Combined with the French Congo, this region formed French Equatorial Africa (see map, page 607).

Competition for East Africa

On the east coast of Africa, Portugal strengthened and extended its control over Mozambique. To the north of Mozambique, Great Britain and Germany competed for territorial domination. Slave raiding had taken place in the 1700s and 1800s in East Africa. These slave raids disrupted political relations among African peoples and made penetration of the interior easier. At the same time, the efforts of missionaries to end the slave trade focused public attention on the area and helped to justify European intervention.

The European nations rapidly carved the rest of East Africa into colonies (see map, page 607). The only exception was the ancient empire of Ethiopia. Although Italy invaded Ethiopia, the Ethiopian army defeated the Italians at Adwa (AHD•wuh) in 1896, thus ensuring their country's freedom from foreign domination.

Another factor that made it easier for Europeans to colonize East Africa was an ecological disaster in the 1880s and 1890s. Scholars think the Italians in Eritrea or the Russians in the Sudan brought cattle carrying a fatal disease known as rinderpest. Whatever its origins, rinderpest killed as many as 80 percent of the cattle, leading to widespread starvation. The weakened people often lacked the ability to resist European colonization.

Competition for Southern Africa

European settlement in South Africa began in 1652, when Dutch settlers founded Cape Town as a resupplying station for ships sailing to the East Indies. The Dutch settlement grew into a large colony called Cape Colony. During the Napoleonic Wars of the early 1800s, the British seized Cape Colony, which then became a British possession.

As British administration became established, many people left the colony and moved to the north and east. These people were Boers (BOHRZ)—descendants of the original Dutch settlers, who had their own language, known as Afrikaans. In the new territories the Boers carved out three colonies—Natal (nuh•TAL), on the southeast coast, the Orange Free State to the west, and the Transvaal (trans•VAHL) to the north.

As the Boers moved into the new territories, they came into contact with the Zulu people, a Bantu people who lived in the region. Under the great leader Shaka, the Zulu had created a thriving empire with a strong army. For years this army fought the Boers for control of the region. In 1879 the British joined in the war, defeating the Zulu and destroying their empire.

The discovery of vast reserves of gold and diamonds in the Transvaal soon intensified the competition in southern Africa. Germany, hoping to find rich mineral reserves, declared a protectorate over the territory of Southwest Africa in 1884. In the same year, Great Britain began moving into the interior from the south, greatly increasing its holdings. Closely associated with these territorial acquisitions was one individual, Cecil Rhodes, a British speculator.

Rhodes and his influence. Rhodes arrived in Cape Colony in 1870, a sickly young man who hoped the climate would improve his health. Moving to the diamond fields in northern Cape Colony, he soon demonstrated a talent for business and a genius for organization. Within 20 years he completely controlled South African diamond production.

Rhodes later organized the colonization of a huge territory farther north. This territory was named Rhodesia after him. In 1890 Rhodes sent several hundred adventurers into Rhodesia in search of gold. He staked his reputation and much of his fortune on this hope. When little gold was found, it became essential for Rhodes to make up his losses by increasing production and profits in the Transvaal mines.

In 1895 a colleague of Rhodes tried to topple the Transvaal government, which had restricted mining operations. The attempt failed, but Great Britain's apparent support of the attempt made relations between the Boers and the British openly hostile. In 1899 war broke out. After three years of costly fighting, the British defeated the Boers and imposed a settlement that favored mining interests.

To ensure Boer support of the peace, the British allowed the Boers to continue using the Afrikaans language in their schools and courts. The British also provided funds for Boers—though not for Africans—to rebuild their destroyed farms. In 1910 a federal constitution united the Cape Colony, Natal, the Transvaal, and the Orange Free State into the Union of South Africa, a British dominion. The constitution made it virtually impossible for nonwhites to be given voting rights. The settlement of the South African War, or the Boer War, thus laid the basis for the later development of a system of complete racial segregation.

European Government in Africa

The European powers that established empires in Africa generally used one of two forms of government in their territories. France, Germany, Belgium, and Portugal practiced direct rule. Great Britain practiced indirect rule.

Direct rule. In colonies with **direct rule,** the imperialist power controlled all levels of government and appointed its own officials to govern. The Europeans based this type of government on their belief that the Africans could not rule themselves. As a result of this belief, the Europeans practiced **paternalism,** the system of governing colonies in much the way that parents guide their children.

The European nations practiced various forms of direct rule. For example, the French encouraged **assimilation,** in which the people of the colonies abandoned their local cultures and adopted all aspects of French culture. When the French judged that most of the people of a colony had been assim-

ilated, the territory would be made a department of France.

Indirect rule. Under the British system of **indirect rule,** a British governor and a council of advisers made colonial laws, but local rulers exerted some authority. The British chose indirect rule largely because they lacked enough workers to staff all the governments of their vast empire, which by then covered almost one-fourth of the earth's land surface.

Costs and Benefits of Imperialism

Imperialism was a harsh experience for all of Africa. However, the costs and the benefits resulting from European expansion were unevenly distributed across the continent.

The Europeans constructed roads and railroads. These means of transportation were used mostly to connect areas of European settlement with the coast. They also served to make African products available for the world market. The Europeans built cities, but crowded and unsanitary slums grew up around them. Europeans introduced medicines to help people live longer and healthier lives. However, development reduced the amount of land available for crop cultivation, contributing to malnutrition among the African people. One of

Learning from Pictures This battle during the Boer War took place in the Transvaal. What other regions were united into the Union of South Africa?

the great tragedies of imperialism was the economic effect it had on the people. Europeans paid Africans the lowest possible wages, thus forcing them to become migrant workers. As such, imperialism changed the very fabric of African society—the family—because migrant workers would move to cities and leave their families at home to eke out meager existences.

Despite the hardships, some individuals and groups in African society did benefit. In West Africa, profits that Africans earned from the rubber trade helped to finance the cultivation of cocoa plants. The spread of cocoa farming, in turn, brought prosperity and raised living standards. In Uganda, British support of cotton cultivation gave rise to a large class of wealthy peasant producers. Even in South Africa, the gold discoveries brought prosperity for African farmers for a brief period, who sold more food to the growing population.

The introduction of Western laws and courts often benefited the unprotected members of society, especially women. Africans adapted to foreign cultures that missionary and government schools introduced. From the experience came a new group of African leaders in the 1900s.

SECTION 3 REVIEW

1. **Define**   direct rule, paternalism, assimilation, indirect rule
2. **Identify**   Ashanti, Henry Stanley, Leopold II, Pierre de Brazza, Boers, Afrikaans, Cecil Rhodes
3. **Interpreting Ideas**   Why did the Europeans want territorial possessions in the interior of Africa?
4. **Determining Cause and Effect**   **(a)** What were the reasons for British and Boer competition? **(b)** What were the results of the Boer War?
5. **Evaluating Ideas**   What were some of the costs and benefits of imperialism in Africa?

4 Europeans Expanded Their Influence in South and East Asia

The strong forces of imperialism that swept Africa in the 1800s brought important and fateful changes to South and East Asia. In these regions, however, the changes were not as abrupt as they were in so many parts of Africa.

British Imperialism in India

As you read in Chapter 18, the British government ruled India directly after the Sepoy Rebellion in 1858. But British control of the subcontinent remained essentially the same as it had been under the British East India Company. British India still made up about three-fifths of the subcontinent. The rest consisted of over 550 states, headed by local princes. The British government, through its viceroy, controlled the local princes' right to make treaties and declare war, either with foreign countries or with one another. Great Britain also regulated Indian internal affairs when it seemed necessary.

To control both British India and Indian states, the British government used the old Roman method of "divide and rule." It granted favors to those princes who cooperated with British rule and dealt harshly with those who did not. It treated Hindus and Muslims equally but did little to ease religious hatred between them.

The British were interested chiefly in profitable trade in India. To achieve it, they maintained public order by ending the many local wars and massacres. They set up an efficient governmental administration that built roads, bridges, railroads, factories, hospitals, and schools. They tried to improve agricultural methods, public health, and sanitation.

Many of these improvements helped the Indians, but other effects of British rule were harmful. The Indian handicraft industry almost disappeared. British cotton mills made cloth so cheaply that it could be transported to India and sold for less than handwoven Indian products. Local artisans had to search for work in the cities or eke out a meager living from farming small plots of land.

During the late 1800s and early 1900s, British rule in India had created a situation in which the peoples of two very different cultures lived side by side with almost no contact. The British had imposed themselves above Indian society as a superior race, a sort of super-caste. The British formed exclusive social circles, open to any European but closed to any Indian, no matter how distinguished. Posted everywhere—in railway carriages and waiting rooms and even on park benches—were signs reading "for Europeans only." For generations all Indians were subjected to contemptuous treatment by the British.

The Rise of Indian Nationalism

Although the British did not mingle socially with the Indians, Western civilization had a powerful impact on India. For one thing, it led to a serious conflict of values.

Both Hinduism and Islam stressed age-old customs and respect for tradition. Western culture, on the other hand, emphasized material progress and political change. Indians, especially educated Indians, regarded Europeans as materialists who cared little for the higher values of mind, soul, and spirit.

British education had a profound effect on India. Before British rule, only Brahmans were educated. Indian merchants might be schooled only in reading, writing, and mathematics. Men of other castes and all women went uneducated. During the 1800s the British East India Company, the British government, missionaries, and private individuals started schools and colleges in India. They educated only a small percentage of the people, but among other things, they taught them about nationalism and the ideals of democracy. Indian scholars could, and did, use quotations from British writers to condemn British imperialism. Many Indians also came to learn about and believe in the ideas of socialism.

A movement for Indian self-rule began in the late 1800s. Not all Indian nationalists supported the same approach. Some, especially those who had been educated in British schools and universities, wanted to advance toward independence gradually and by democratic methods. They also wanted to keep certain aspects of Western culture and industry that they thought could benefit India. The Indian National Congress, a political party founded in 1885, advocated this moderate approach.

Other people wanted to break all ties with Great Britain in an effort to sweep away all Western influence. The Hindus, particularly, wished to revolt not only against Western culture but also against Islam. The views of this second group alarmed Indian Muslims. They were a minority in the land, and British rule protected them from discrimination and violence. They feared that if British rule were removed, their future might be in danger. The Muslims were therefore much less enthusiastic about driving out the British than were the Hindus. In 1906 Muslims formed the Muslim League to protect their interests. The independence movement in India gathered strength very slowly, and the British kept the country under a tight rein.

Learning from Pictures
In 1875 the Prince of Wales, later to become Emperor of India, took a tour of India. Here the city of Bombay welcomes him.

The Meiji Restoration in Japan

While imperialism remained firmly entrenched in India, it took a different course in Japan. Although European influence in Japan became strong after the overthrow of the Tokugawa shogunate in 1868, Europeans did not dominate Japan as they did India. Rather, the Japanese under the rule of the Meiji emperors controlled their own affairs and began to industrialize.

Real power in the Meiji government was exercised not by the emperor but by samurai from several domains in western Japan. These samurai had grown impatient under the strict, hereditary system of the Tokugawa period, in which birth, not ability, counted. They persuaded the emperor that Japan must take the road toward modernization. Even though the samurai were members of Japan's traditional ruling class, they advocated and carried out radical changes in Japan.

The Meiji Restoration, as the change from the Tokugawa shogunate to imperial government is called, was really a social, political, and economic revolution. It corresponded in its scope to the revolutions in the Western nations during the 1700s.

The old system of social classes was abolished, and all Japanese became free to choose the occupations they wished. The government established universal compulsory education and almost wiped out illiteracy. For nearly 300 years Japanese commoners had been denied the right even to own swords. Only samurai, as members of the warrior class, had been allowed to bear arms. Now this restriction was removed, and a new, highly centralized and modernized military, in which all Japanese men had to serve, was created.

A centralized government replaced the political system of the Tokugawa period. The city of Yedo, renamed Tokyo, became the new imperial capital, and the domains fell under the control of government officials. The central government imposed taxes on the Japanese people as a whole, and it established laws that applied to the entire population.

During the 1880s an appointed commission wrote a constitution, which the emperor accepted

Learning from Pictures
The Meiji empress inspects the rice fields of the Imperial Palace. Notice the Western-style military uniforms worn by her escorts.

612

The Influence of Japanese Art

Although she wears a kimono and is studying Japanese woodblock prints, the woman in this painting is not Oriental. Rather she is a model used by the American painter James McNeill Whistler (1834–1903). Many years later Whistler would paint a picture of his mother in a similar pose but with more restrained colors.

Like many artists of his time, Whistler studied in Paris. There he discovered the enchantments of Oriental art, particularly Japanese prints, which became increasingly popular in Europe during the period. Though his paintings reflected the

Courtesy of the Freer Gallery of Art, Smithsonian Institution, Washington, D. C. # 04.75

influence of Europe, Whistler eventually adapted the use of both Oriental subjects and techniques.

Whistler was a leader of the new attitude of "art for art's sake." A flamboyant figure for his time, Whistler sued an art critic in 1878 who criticized him for "flinging a pot of paint in the public's face." Although Whistler won the libel suit, the horrendous court costs eventually forced him into bankruptcy.

---

and proclaimed in 1889. The constitution had two major purposes—to impress Western governments with Japan's progress and to provide the Japanese people a limited voice in national affairs.

The leaders of the Meiji government were monarchists who did not believe in democracy. However, they knew from their study of Western history that political absolutism led to popular discontent. Although the new constitution gave the emperor supreme power, it established a two-house national assembly, called the Diet, one house of which was elected. Initially, only those Japanese who owned a substantial amount of property had the right to vote, and the elected house of the Diet had very limited powers.

The new constitution and the Diet satisfied most Japanese. The government did not have to deal with the problems of political instability that afflicted so many other nations that were struggling to modernize. It could concentrate its energies and its resources on promoting industrialization and economic development. Japanese leaders believed that their nation had to either catch up with the Western nations in technology and wealth or face the humiliation of foreign domination.

Industrialization

Fortunately, Japan was in a position to make rapid economic and industrial progress. Its traditional agricultural economy had created surpluses that could be used to finance industrialization. The government invited foreign experts to Japan to help modernize transportation and communications. The government also used factory machinery purchased from several Western countries and enacted a new commercial code to encourage private investment in industrial enterprises.

By 1900 Japan had acquired the foundations of an industrial economy. Railroads, the telegraph, and telephones linked Japanese cities. Banks existed throughout the country. Light manufacturing, especially of textiles, was well developed, and Japan had begun exporting machine-made cotton cloth and silk to other countries. The money that these exports earned helped to pay for imports of industrial raw materials such as iron and petroleum, which Japan lacked. The Japanese then used these raw materials in steel production and shipbuilding. Although Japan's economy remained smaller and weaker than the economies of the Western nations, the gap gradually narrowed. In fact, Japan was the first country in Asia to industrialize.

Nevertheless, Japan's leaders continued to feel threatened by imperialist expansion in Asia. This fear motivated the Japanese to embark on a course of imperialist expansion themselves.

The Sino-Japanese War

The territory that most interested Japan was the nearby Korean Peninsula, long a dependency of China. Korean authorities had to refer all matters involving foreign relations to the Chinese emperor. No foreigners were allowed into the country. However, Russia, France, and the United States were all interested in gaining trade privileges there. Fearing that a Western-controlled Korea might threaten its safety, Japan began to demand privileges in the Korean Peninsula.

Japan maintained that Korea was independent, while China still claimed Korea as a dependency. In 1876, out of this confusion, Japan secured a treaty

Learning from Pictures This was the scene at Yokohama in 1871, as Prince Iwakura left for the United States on Japan's first foreign mission.

that opened three Korean ports to Japanese trade. China then allowed the Koreans to make similar treaties with six Western nations.

In 1894 a rebellion broke out in Korea. Both Japan and China sent armed forces to end it. It was a turbulent situation that exploded into the brief Sino-Japanese War, in which Japan defeated China. (*Sino* means "Chinese.")

In addition to trade privileges, the Japanese wanted territory. The Treaty of Shimonoseki (shim • uh • noh • SEK • ee) in 1895 forced China to recognize the complete independence of Korea. China also had to give to Japan the island of Formosa and the nearby islands, the Pescadores. In another provision of the treaty, China gave Japan the strategic Liaodong (LEE • AYOOH • DOOHNG) Peninsula on the southern coast of Manchuria. At the tip of the Liaodong Peninsula, which juts into the Yellow Sea, lay the excellent harbor of Port Arthur (see map, page 615). Finally, China also had to pay Japan an indemnity equivalent to $150 million.

Russia and the East Asian Mainland

The Treaty of Shimonoseki displeased the Russians, who did not want a strong power in Korea close to their naval base at Vladivostok. In addition, Russia wanted to build a railroad across Manchuria and the Liaodong Peninsula to Port Arthur.

With these plans afoot, Russia was more than willing to help China keep Japan away from the Asian mainland. France, which had recently signed an alliance with Russia, was also willing to help. Germany, eager to be on better terms with Russia and perhaps to weaken the alliance between France and Russia, also offered its services. In a joint note, Russia, France, and Germany advised the Japanese government to withdraw from the Liaodong Peninsula.

The Japanese were furious, but they were not able to resist such powerful forces. They gave the Liaodong Peninsula back to China in return for a larger indemnity. France and Russia gave China loans to help pay the indemnity to Japan.

The Price of European Assistance

China had to pay a price for this financial help, however. China had to pledge that no foreign power would receive any special rights in Chinese

IMPERIALISM IN EAST ASIA TO 1914

TERRITORY CLAIMED BY:

- France
- Germany
- Great Britain
- Japan
- Netherlands
- United States
- ⊙ Chinese treaty port
- • Other city

MILLER CYLINDRICAL PROJECTION

Learning from Maps *The Portuguese empire in East Asia had dwindled by 1914. What two trading centers did Portugal still control?*

financial affairs unless France and Russia received them too. Great Britain and Germany quickly made similar loans with similar provisions.

Beginning in 1896, the Europeans placed still more demands on China. France demanded and received special trading privileges and the right to develop mineral resources in southern China. It also received a 99-year lease to the territory of Zhanjiang and the right to build a railroad linking southern China with the French protectorate in Indochina.

Germany received a 99-year lease to the port of Qingdao (CHING·DOW) and surrounding territory on the south shore of the Shandong Peninsula. Germany also received mining rights and permission to build a railway in Shandong.

Great Britain would not be left out. It negotiated for more trading privileges in the Chang Jiang valley and the right to build a naval base at Weihai on the north shore of the Shandong Peninsula to balance the German base at Qingdao.

Russia demanded and received the right to lease a tax-free right-of-way for its railroad across Manchuria—to be called the Chinese Eastern Railway. It also received permission to police the Manchurian route as well as certain other extraterritorial privileges. In effect, northern Manchuria would be under Russian economic and military domination. In a further and secret treaty, Russia and China formed an alliance pledging mutual assistance in case either should become involved in war with Japan.

Learning from Pictures
This Chinese porcelain punch bowl was imported for European markets. The bowl depicts the European trading centers at Canton.

© 1980, The Metropolitan Museum of Art, Winfield Foundation Gift, 1958; The Helena Woolworth McCaan Collection.

These territorial privileges greatly angered the Japanese. Western powers had forced them to give up the spoils of their victory. Both China and Japan recalled these humiliations over the next 50 years when they strove for power in East Asia.

SECTION 4 REVIEW

1. **Identify**   Indian National Congress, Muslim League, Treaty of Shimonoseki, Chinese Eastern Railway
2. **Locate**   Formosa, Liaodong Peninsula, Vladivostok
3. **Evaluating Ideas**   What were the beneficial and harmful effects of British rule in India?
4. **Analyzing Ideas**   **(a)** In what sense can the Meiji Restoration be considered a revolution? **(b)** What were its results?
5. **Determining Cause and Effect**   Describe the causes and results of the Sino-Japanese War.

5 Foreign Influence in Southeast Asia and the Pacific Increased

The tide of imperialism did not stop in South Asia and East Asia. It also affected Southeast Asia and the islands of the Pacific.

Imperialism in Southeast Asia

In the late 1400s and early 1500s, European traders explored the East Indies. In the seaports of these islands and on the nearby mainland, Portuguese and Dutch merchants enjoyed a rich and active trade until the early 1800s.

In the 1800s and early 1900s, European imperialism came to Southeast Asia as it did to nearby India and China. The area became an important source not only of spices but also of the world's tea and coffee and later of such valuable products as tin and oil.

British successes. It was natural that the British should take an interest in the kingdom of Burma, on the eastern border of India. By 1886 all of Burma had come under British control.

The island of Singapore, on the tip of the Malay Peninsula, guarded the entrance to the Strait of Malacca—one of the most vital trade routes in the world. The British first moved onto Singapore, then uninhabited, in 1819. Throughout the 1800s they gradually extended their influence northward to include large parts of the peninsula up to the southern border of Siam (today known as Thailand). They created a city at Singapore, which became an important naval base in the empire.

French gains. The eastern part of the mainland of Southeast Asia contained several small, weak nations that were under Chinese influence. Beginning in the late 1700s, French merchants gained trading rights at seaports on the South China Sea. In the late 1800s, French imperialists forced China to give up its claim to the area, and the French became the dominant power in what became known as French Indochina.

Siam. The kingdom of Siam was better organized than were other parts of Southeast Asia. The British on the Malay Peninsula and the French in Indochina nibbled at the borders of Siam. To maintain their independence, Siamese rulers skillfully maneuvered British interests against French interests. The British and French finally agreed that an independent Siam was a useful buffer state between their possessions. A **buffer state,** located between two hostile powers, is a small country that often lessens the possibility of conflict between them.

The Dutch East Indies. The Dutch East India Company, formed in 1602 to exploit the island possessions of the Netherlands, succeeded in doing so for many years. By the late 1700s, however, it had become corrupt and inefficient. In 1798 the government of the Netherlands revoked the company's charter and took over the administration of the Netherlands East Indies.

The Dutch East India Company had used a system of forced labor in the East Indies. The Dutch government somewhat improved working conditions for the locals. By the late 1800s, however, several local revolts convinced the government of the Netherlands to make basic reforms in the administration of its richest imperial possession.

Interest in the Pacific Islands

Only a few of the islands and island groups in the Pacific were economically attractive to the imperialist powers. These few areas had large local populations that, it was hoped, could be persuaded to want and buy manufactured goods. Some of the areas had fertile soil that could support rich plantations. Other islands had minerals to be mined. Imperialism in most of the Pacific islands, however, was based on another motive—the need for coaling stations and naval bases. Since the imperialist powers competed in the Pacific, as elsewhere, none was willing to trust the others for its coal supplies and naval repairs. Each of the powers, therefore, sought out its own Pacific islands. By 1900 imperialist nations controlled almost all the islands (see map, page 618).

The Samoan Islands. In the late 1800s, the most serious rivalry over territory in the Pacific involved the Samoan Islands. Here the United States played a major role. American interests in Samoa had been developing for a number of years. In 1878 Americans gained the right to use the harbor city of Pago Pago (PAHNG • oh PAHNG • oh), on the island of Tutuila (toot • uh • WEE • luh), as a trading post, coaling station, and naval base. Great Britain and Germany secured similar rights in other parts of the Samoan Islands.

For a number of years, rivalry among the three foreign nations for control of the Samoan Islands simmered until they teetered on the brink of war. To prevent further trouble, the three nations set up a system of joint control in 1889, but it soon failed.

In 1899 the rivals signed a treaty ending the dispute. Great Britain, preoccupied with the South African War, withdrew its interests. The United States established firm control over Tutuila and six other small islands whose combined area was only about 75 square miles (195 square kilometers). Together, these possessions became known as American Samoa. Germany gained control of all the other islands in the Samoan group, which eventually became known as Western Samoa.

The Hawaiian Islands. Far more important to the United States than its Samoan possessions were the Hawaiian Islands (see map, page 618). This group of islands had fertile soil, plentiful rainfall, and a mild climate. Foreign traders and missionaries, including Americans, had begun settling there in the 1820s but interfered little with the government and economy of the locals. After 1865, however, businesses from the United States and other foreign nations began to develop sugarcane and pineapple plantations on the islands.

The local rulers of the Hawaiian Islands resented foreign influence and announced that they intended to bring it to an end. American planters then asked the United States representative in the islands to call for a force of American marines. Hawaiian troops, ill-prepared to match this show of force, refused to fight. By 1893 foreign business leaders, supported by American marines, were in control of the islands, and in 1898 the United States annexed the islands.

The Philippines, Guam, and Wake Island. Since the 1500s and 1600s, the Philippine Islands and Guam in the western Pacific Ocean had been parts of Spain's far-flung empire. In 1898 the United States declared war on Spain. Most of the fighting occurred in Cuba and Puerto Rico, but the

What If?

Imperialism

In the late 1800s and early 1900s, European countries carved out empires in Africa, Asia, and the Pacific. How do you think world history would have been different if the Europeans had not established these empires?

first United States military action against Spain took place in the Pacific.

When war erupted, United States naval forces were in peak condition. Under orders from Assistant Secretary of the Navy Theodore Roosevelt, four cruisers and two gunboats under the command of Commodore George Dewey steamed from the British port of Hong Kong and moved quickly into the harbor of Manila, the capital of the Philippine Islands. Early on the morning of May 1, Dewey's forces attacked the decrepit Spanish fleet. By noon the Spanish ships were sunk or in flames and the city of Manila was at Dewey's mercy. Within a few months, American land forces, supported by local revolutionaries, defeated the Spanish forces in Manila. With the collapse of Spanish power at Manila, the entire Philippine Islands came under the control of the United States. At about this time, American forces also occupied Guam, a small, Spanish-held island east of the Philippines (see map, this page).

Some Filipinos welcomed the Americans and even fought with them against the Spaniards. Most of the local population, however, had suffered under Spanish rule for centuries and saw little advantage in changing one foreign master for another. Led by Emilio Aguinaldo (ahg•ee•NAHL•doh), Filipino locals fought for independence for three years against thousands of American troops. The Filipinos used guerrilla warfare against the better-equipped United States army, but were finally defeated in 1902.

Besides acquiring the Philippine Islands and Guam, the United States also took possession of Wake Island in the central Pacific. Thus the United States acquired yet another link in a strategic chain of island possessions running from its west coast across the vast distances of the Pacific Ocean all the way to East Asia.

Learning from Maps Spain's empire in the Pacific Ocean crumbled after the Spanish-American War. What islands does the United States possess under the terms of the peace treaty?

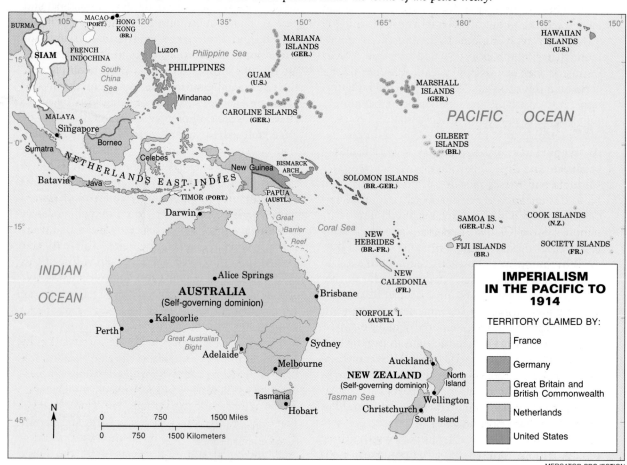

MERCATOR PROJECTION

6 Latin America Became Involved with Imperialist Powers

Imperialism in Latin America differed from that in the Pacific. Although the Latin American countries were weak, the Monroe Doctrine of the United States, along with Great Britain's navy and its commercial policy, prevented them from being turned into colonies again. Nevertheless, the countries of Latin America experienced economic interference as they increasingly attracted European and American investment.

New Opportunities for Trade

As the pace of the Industrial Revolution increased in Europe and the United States, more agricultural products and raw materials were purchased from Latin American countries. Americans, for example, acquired a taste for bananas, which they imported from Central America, and for coffee, which came mostly from Brazil. They bought sugar made from sugarcane grown in Cuba, and they smoked cigars made from Cuban tobacco.

The British purchased large quantities of wool, which their factories needed, as well as wheat, beef, and mutton from Argentina and Uruguay. Chile mined nitrates from natural deposits in its northern deserts and sold them to the industrial countries to make fertilizers and explosives. Brazil exported natural rubber from its vast Amazon forests.

Railroads were built to bring these goods to Latin American port cities. The ports were also improved to ease the loading of the newly perfected steamships. All these developments brought prosperity to those countries of Latin America that had the opportunity to engage in trade. Argentina especially benefited from these developments. However, other Latin American countries such as Bolivia and Paraguay hardly participated in trade at all. In these countries, nearly all trade benefits were concentrated in the capital cities and the ports.

As had occurred in the United States, a few of the Latin American countries—most notably Argentina, Brazil, Uruguay, and later Cuba—attracted a large number of immigrants from Europe. In those Latin American countries with the greatest export trade, industries also began to develop. Imperialists built factories such as sugar mills to process export goods. Other new factories—textile mills, flour mills, and metalworking shops—produced consumer goods for local markets.

Economic Imperialism

Foreign investors owned many of the new railroads, ranches, plantations, and mines in Latin America. Central governments granted these investors many special favors—for example, monopoly privileges, free land, and exemption from taxes—in the hope that the foreigners would develop the economy by establishing new businesses there. However, the investors usually sent the profits from these businesses and the interest payments from loans back to their own countries.

The central governments in Latin America now had more tax revenues. As a result, foreign banks willingly lent them funds for public improvements. Central governments spent some of this money on strengthening their armies and navies, which made it easier to suppress internal rebellions. However, a revolution often toppled the government that had borrowed the money, and the new government would refuse to pay the old debts. In addition, although Latin Americans spent some money to install electricity and streetcars in the capital cities, much money was wasted on payments to powerful politicians.

Unpaid loans frequently led to intervention by the foreign powers. European banking and business leaders would persuade their governments to pressure the Latin American governments for payment. Sometimes warships and troops were sent to compel payment. A typical method involved taking over the collection of the customs—the principal tax—and holding back enough money to pay the debts.

619

Learning from Pictures *This railroad funded by the United States runs through a banana plantation in Costa Rica.*

American Intervention

As the United States became an industrial power, it began to challenge Great Britain, its main rival for dominance of the Western Hemisphere. In the early 1800s, the Americans had not enforced the Monroe Doctrine in any region farther away than Central America when the offender was Great Britain. For example, the British had occupied the Falkland Islands, near the tip of South America, in 1837. Although Argentina protested, the United States did not support the Argentinians.

In 1895, however, the United States did intervene in a dispute between Great Britain and Venezuela. Early in the 1800s, Great Britain had acquired British Guiana (gy·AN·uh), on the northern coast of South America. On a number of occasions, Great Britain had tried to extend the boundary of British Guiana westward into territory claimed by Venezuela.

Venezuela had asked the United States for support in its demand that the border dispute be submitted to **arbitration**—negotiation for a settlement of the dispute by a party agreed upon by all sides. When Great Britain refused to arbitrate, President Grover Cleveland insisted that they do so. Finally, Great Britain, preoccupied with the

South African War, submitted, and the dispute with Venezuela was settled. The United States had championed the cause of a weak Latin American nation against powerful European interests. Beyond this, however, the United States had its own motives for helping Venezuela. The gold thought to be in the region was now more accessible to American investors.

The Spanish-American War

In 1898 the United States became even more deeply involved in Latin American affairs. Its involvement grew out of disputes with Spain.

The main cause of tension between Spain and the United States was Cuba (see map, page 624), a Spanish colony in the West Indies. For many years the Cubans had been unhappy under Spanish rule. Several rebellions flared, which the Spanish government suppressed with great difficulty. These rebellions alarmed United States citizens and corporations that had invested money in Cuba, especially in its railroads and its sugar plantations and mills.

Concern for American-owned property was only one reason for the tense relations between the United States and Spain. Many Americans felt sympathetic toward Cuba's desire for independence and indignant over Spanish treatment of the Cuban rebels. Anti-Spanish speeches and writings by Cubans who had settled in the United States and sensational stories in American newspapers telling of Spanish atrocities in Cuba stirred these sentiments.

More anger arose in 1898 when an American battleship, the *Maine*, exploded in Havana harbor, and 260 Americans perished. The *Maine* had been sent to Cuba to protect American citizens and their property. No one knew the cause of the explosion, but many in the United States assumed that the Spaniards were to blame. American newspapers played on this assumption, encouraging a rising popular demand in the United States for war with Spain.

Spain showed some willingness to come to terms with the United States regarding the difficulties in Cuba. President McKinley and his cabinet did not want war. However, American leaders felt unable to resist the popular demand for aggressive measures and declared war in April 1898. To pacify its members who opposed rising

American imperialism, Congress declared that the United States was fighting only on behalf of Cuban independence and had no intention of taking the island for itself.

Cuban leaders had not wanted United States intervention, which they feared as much as Spanish rule. Judging themselves capable of winning the war on their own, Cubans regarded American intervention as interference.

The war lasted only a few months, and after being defeated both on land and on the sea, Spain asked for peace. The Treaty of Paris was signed in December 1898.

The United States government did not invite the Cubans to the peace conference. Instead it dealt only with Spain. By the terms of the peace treaty, Spain surrendered its claim to Cuba. It also ceded Puerto Rico, in the Caribbean, and the Pacific island of Guam to the United States. In addition, Spain sold the Philippines to the United States for $20 million.

Following the war, United States troops occupied Cuba. Americans established schools, built roads, provided sanitation, and eradicated yellow fever. The United States government also recognized Cuba's independence. However, Cuba was not turned over to its own leaders but to a provisional military government. Although the United States government permitted a Cuban assembly to draw up a constitution, it insisted that the Cuban constitution include the so-called Platt Amendment. This amendment gave the United States the right to intervene in Cuba whenever it thought orderly government was endangered. The United States also insisted on having four naval bases in Cuba but later agreed to only one—Guantánamo Bay.

The Panama Canal

In addition to governing its new and far-flung possessions, the United States now had to defend them. The major problem of defense came to light during the Spanish-American War.

Before the war the American battleship *Oregon* had been stationed on the Pacific coast of the United States. When war became likely, this battleship was summoned to strengthen American forces in the Caribbean Sea. It had to race around the entire South American continent, a distance of over 11,000 miles (17,600 kilometers), to reach the Caribbean. The United States realized at this point that it would either have to build two complete navies to protect its empire or find an easier and quicker way to route warships between the Atlantic and Pacific oceans.

A canal across the Isthmus of Panama had long been considered. The same French company that built the Suez Canal tried unsuccessfully to build a canal across Panama. In the late 1800s, the United States government began negotiating for

Learning from Pictures
On July 1, 1898, Theodore Roosevelt, along with Cuban troops called Mambís, led American troops in the Battle of Santiago. They captured this high ground overlooking the city of Santiago and the fort El Viso.

permission and a right-of-way to build a canal. It asked Colombia for a lease to a strip of land across the isthmus in Panama, at that time a province of Colombia (see map, page 624).

After a treaty had been negotiated, the Colombian senate adjourned without ratifying it, a move that angered people in the United States and in the province of Panama. The people of the province wanted the canal because it would create great benefits for them. When negotiations seemed to break down, certain Panamanian business leaders and some American residents of Panama began a revolution to gain independence from Colombia.

American warships stationed at Panama prevented Colombian troops from moving in to suppress the revolt, and the revolution succeeded. The United States then quickly recognized the independence of Panama. In 1903 the new government of Panama gave the United States all the rights necessary to build a canal across Panama.

The Panama Canal, one of the world's greatest achievements in engineering, opened in 1914. It would probably have been impossible to build without recently invented power shovels and other new machines. Medical science, too, played a vital part. Cuban and American scientists had discovered that mosquitoes carry yellow fever, a disease that contributed to France's inability to build a canal across

Learning from Pictures The two doors being installed at the Gatun Locks are actually floatable metal structures 65 feet wide (about 20 meters) and 7 feet thick (about 2 meters).

Panama. By destroying the mosquitoes, scientists controlled the spread of the disease, thus enabling the construction crews to work in the jungles of Panama.

The new canal shortened the sea route from New York to San Francisco by over 5,000 miles (8,000 kilometers) and the sea route from New York to the new territory of Hawaii by 4,400 miles (7,100 kilometers). Fleets in the Atlantic and Pacific oceans could now be quickly shifted when necessary. Merchant ships of all nations paid a toll to use the canal. The toll was well worth the price because the shortened route lowered the operating cost of a ship, far outweighing the amount of the toll itself.

The Panama Canal also had an important effect on the countries of Central and South America that bordered the Caribbean Sea. Formerly this region had been a sleepy backwater of the world, a dead end of commerce. The canal made it a thriving worldwide trading center.

The Roosevelt Corollary

Long before the completion of the Panama Canal, the United States recognized that any strong European power with a foothold in the Caribbean region could threaten the canal or the sea lanes leading to it. Therefore the United States adopted a new policy regarding foreign influence in Latin America.

In 1904 President Theodore Roosevelt's State of the Union address included a section on Latin America. Roosevelt said that if any situation threatened the independence of any country in the Western Hemisphere, the United States would act as an "international police power" to prevent a foreign country from stepping in. This statement became known as the Roosevelt Corollary to the Monroe Doctrine. It was regarded as a natural consequence of the earlier policy, and it would be called into use several times in the coming years.

Although European and American investors supported the Roosevelt Corollary, Latin Americans were enraged at the implication that they could not manage their own affairs. Thus Latin American nations supported a statement made by Luis Drago, foreign minister of Argentina. He had vehemently denied the European or American right to collect foreign debts—a declaration known as the Drago Doctrine.

The Berlin Conference: Making a New Map of Africa

The continent of Africa has a distinctive location. It sits directly on the equator and reaches almost as far north as it does south of the earth's midline. In addition, Africa occupies an amazingly central position in relation to the other landmasses of the world. The Americas lie to the west, Eurasia to the north and east, Australia to the southeast, and Antarctica to the south. Africa's central location, along with its huge size and vast stores of mineral wealth, made it a prime target for colonization by European nations during the 1800s. As you have read in this chapter, each of the European colonial powers created spheres of influence in Africa. Among the most significant of these powers was Germany. Otto von Bismarck, the German imperial chancellor, planned not only to expand Germany's control in Africa but also to play his country's European rivals one against the other, thereby weakening their influence. By the 1880s Germany had begun to carry out these plans by establishing colonies in locations designed to obstruct the imperial designs of other European powers. For example, the Germans had taken Cameroon which lay between French colonies, and German East Africa separated two huge British colonies. Then in 1884 Bismarck called for a meeting in Berlin to complete the division of Africa among all interested parties.

At the time of the Berlin Conference many Africans still lived under their own government. With absolutely no regard for local boundaries, the representatives carved up the continent among themselves. These representatives argued over, drew, erased, and redrew the boundary lines of their new colonies. Huge parcels of land changed hands, sometimes simply at the whim of one representative. Often, people from the same ethnic group found themselves separated and ruled by differ-

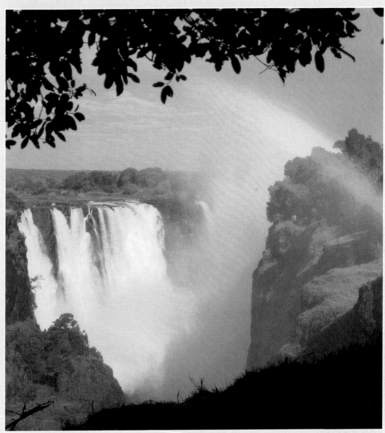

Victoria Falls, on the Zambia-Zimbabwe border

ent colonial powers. Conversely, the new boundaries frequently threw together ethnic groups hostile to one another. Also, in drawing boundary lines the representatives ignored such natural boundaries as rivers and mountain ranges. Ignorant of the continent's geography, the representatives had no idea of the location of such natural dividing lines.

Probably no meeting in history has had the lasting impact on a continent that the Berlin Conference had on Africa. In many ways the decisions made at the Berlin Conference still plague Africa today. Much of Africa secured independence after

1950, but the colonial boundaries established by the Berlin Conference had acquired the legitimacy of time. Even though many of these boundaries were arbitrary and a possible cause for future trouble, the leaders of the new African nations feared that drawing new boundaries might result in complete chaos. Yet at the same time these leaders found they could not make the old boundary lines function. For many Africans, loyalty to their ethnic group still had far greater meaning than national identity. Conflicting loyalties had disastrous consequences in many countries.

623

Further United States Expansion

Because of political disturbances and defaults on loans, the United States continued to expand its influence in the Caribbean. It created military governments in Nicaragua from 1912 to 1933, in Haiti from 1915 to 1934, and in the Dominican Republic from 1916 to 1924. Cuba was again subjected to an occupation government from 1906 to 1909, and United States marines were stationed there from 1917 to 1922.

The United States intervened in these countries for several reasons. During the early 1900s, world tensions increased and the economies of the Caribbean nations almost collapsed. The United States feared that governments might fall into anarchy or into the hands of leaders who would refuse to pay the debts owed to foreign banks. European nations might have used this refusal to pay debts as an excuse to intervene in the Caribbean region.

In 1917 the United States purchased from Denmark three of the Virgin Islands east of Puerto Rico. With this purchase the United States added another base to assure its control over the Caribbean. At the same time, Puerto Ricans became United States citizens and received a few more rights of self-government in order to guarantee their loyalty in dangerous times.

Mexico's Revolution

The greatest upheaval in Latin America during the age of imperialism was the Mexican Revolution. For 34 years one dictator, Porfirio Díaz (DEE • ahs), had dominated Mexico. He had permitted foreign companies to develop many of Mexico's natural resources and had allowed the major landowners to buy up much of the country's land from poor peasants. In 1910, although Mexico appeared outwardly stable, Díaz's regime suddenly collapsed.

Learning from Maps Imperialism in the Caribbean Sea was checked by the Roosevelt Corollary. Which island is part of the United States?

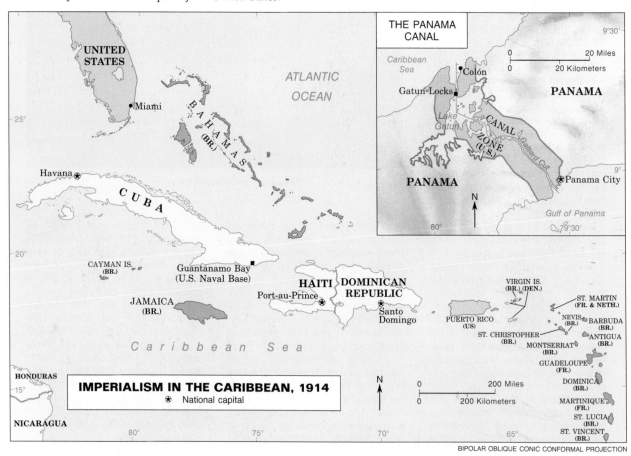

BIPOLAR OBLIQUE CONIC CONFORMAL PROJECTION

Learning from Pictures *The Mexican revolutionary Pancho Villa is shown here sitting in the Presidential Chair. Why was the United States pursuing Villa?*

A rebellion against the aging dictator put Francisco Madero in power in 1911. He was assassinated in 1913, and Victoriano Huerta (WERT • uh), one of Díaz's former generals, seized control of the government. A rebellion led by constitutionalist Venustiano Carranza against Huerta then began and later deepened into intensive civil warfare among various factions. The war dragged on for 10 years and cost perhaps 1 million lives. Underlying these struggles were widespread demands for rights to the land. The peasant leader Emiliano Zapata (sah • PAH • tah) voiced these demands.

The violence and unrest in Mexico frightened American investors who had billions of dollars invested there. President Woodrow Wilson refused to recognize Huerta's government and tried to force Huerta's overthrow. President Wilson opposed the Huerta regime because it was imposed upon the Mexican people without their consent. Wilson also ignored requests to send troops into Mexico to protect American lives and property, instead choosing a policy known as "watchful waiting." However, in 1914, after the arrest of some American soldiers, United States marines were sent to occupy Veracruz. President Wilson also allowed shipment of arms to Carranza and persuaded England to withdraw its support of the Huerta regime.

Two years later, United States troops were sent into Mexico to capture Pancho Villa (VEE • yuh), a revolutionary leader who had raided a border town in New Mexico, killing several Americans. Tensions between the two countries mounted, and for a time there was a threat of war. Tensions eased in 1917, when the United States withdrew troops from Mexico and focused its attentions on the world war in Europe.

SECTION 6 REVIEW

1. **Define** arbitration
2. **Identify** *Maine,* Platt Amendment, Roosevelt Corollary, Porfirio Díaz, Victoriano Huerta, Venustiano Carranza, Emiliano Zapata, Pancho Villa
3. **Locate** Cuba, British Guiana, Puerto Rico, Panama Canal, Nicaragua, Virgin Islands
4. **Summarizing Ideas** Give examples of economic imperialism in Latin America.
5. **Understanding Ideas** Explain how the United States exerted its influence **(a)** in Venezuela's dispute with Great Britain, and **(b)** in Cuba.
6. **Understanding Ideas** What were the results of the Spanish-American War?
7. **Interpreting Ideas** **(a)** Why was the United States interested in building the Panama Canal? **(b)** What were the results?

3:12 to 6:40

CHAPTER
23
REVIEW

French occupation
of Algeria

Liberian
independence

AD 1830

1847

Chapter Summary

The following list contains the key concepts you have learned about imperialism in the late 1800s and early 1900s.

1. In the late 1800s, European nations became involved in a new kind of empire building—imperialism—that arose from the need for self-sufficiency, new markets, and places in which an ever-growing population could settle.
2. European nations divided up almost all of Africa in the late 1800s. Communication and transportation improved, slavery was abolished, and some Africans profited from the many economic investments foreigners made. For the most part, however, Africa was mercilessly exploited, and tensions developed that would lead to further struggles later in the 1900s.
3. In India the British government assumed direct control. However, the British set themselves up as a caste superior to the local population.
4. After a civil war in Japan, the emperor was restored to power in 1868. The Japanese then began a remarkably quick and successful process of industrialization.
5. Although foreign powers helped China resist the Japanese, the Chinese had to make concessions for receiving this assistance.
6. Imperialism was also a strong force in Southeast Asia and in the Pacific. By the late 1800s, the kingdom of Siam was the only area of Southeast Asia that remained free.
7. The Pacific islands became valuable as coaling stations and naval bases.
8. The countries of Latin America were weak and vulnerable to economic imperialism. The United States sought to extend its influence and to protect Latin America from powerful European interests.
9. The relatively easy American victory in the Spanish-American War dramatized the growing strength of the United States. In the early 1900s, the United States became increasingly involved in Latin American affairs, often invoking the Roosevelt Corollary to the Monroe Doctrine.

On a separate sheet of paper, complete the following review exercises.

Reviewing Important Terms

Match each of the following terms with the correct definition below.

a. paternalism g. sphere of influence
b. assimilation h. buffer state
c. imperialism i. colony
d. arbitration j. concession
e. direct rule k. indirect rule
f. protectorate l. condominium

_____ 1. System of government in which the local ruler kept his title but officials of the foreign power actually controlled the region
_____ 2. System in which the people of the colonies abandoned their local cultures and adopted all aspects of the colonial power's culture
_____ 3. Settlement of a dispute by a party agreed upon by all sides
_____ 4. The domination by a powerful nation over the political, economic, and cultural affairs of another nation or region
_____ 5. A small country that is located between two hostile powers and that often lessens the possibility of conflict between them
_____ 6. System of colonial government in which the imperialist power controlled all levels of government and appointed its own officials to govern the colony
_____ 7. A region in which one nation had special, sometimes exclusive, economic and political privileges that were recognized by other nations
_____ 8. System of governing the colonies just as parents guide their children
_____ 9. System of government under which the governor and a council of advisers made colonial laws, but local rulers exerted some authority
_____ 10. A grant of economic rights and privileges in a given area usually given to foreign merchants or capitalists
_____ 11. System whereby two nations ruled a region as partners
_____ 12. An area in which a foreign nation gained total control over a given region and its local population

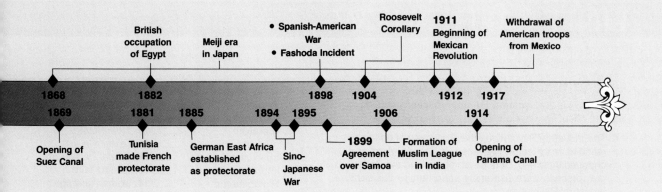

British
occupation
of Egypt

Meiji era
in Japan

• Spanish-American
  War
• Fashoda Incident

Roosevelt
Corollary

1911
Beginning of
Mexican
Revolution

Withdrawal of
American troops
from Mexico

1868   1882   1898 1904   1912 1917

1869   1881   1885   1894 1895   1906   1914

Opening of
Suez Canal

Tunisia
made French
protectorate

German East Africa
established
as protectorate

Sino-
Japanese
War

1899
Agreement
over Samoa

Formation of
Muslim League
in India

Opening of
Panama Canal

Developing Critical Thinking Skills

1. **Classifying Ideas** Name the imperialist nation that claimed each of the following territories: **(a)** Libya, **(b)** Togo, **(c)** Algeria, **(d)** Gold Coast, **(e)** Río de Oro,   **(f)** Sudan.
2. **Contrasting Ideas** **(a)** How does economic imperialism differ from political imperialism? **(b)** Why did one often lead to the other during the late 1800s?
3. **Seeing Relationships** How did European imperialism encourage the growth of nationalism in other parts of the world?
4. **Summarizing Ideas** How were each of the following nations able to preserve their independence: **(a)** Liberia, **(b)** Ethiopia, **(c)** Japan, **(d)** Siam.
5. **Contrasting Ideas** In what ways did the colonial policy of the United States differ from that of other nations?
6. **Evaluating Ideas** What were the positive and negative effects of imperialism in Africa and in India?
7. **Analyzing Primary Sources** Reread the lines from the Rudyard Kipling poem "The White Man's Burden" on page 601. **(a)** What does Kipling mean by the phrase "white man's burden"? **(b)** How does he characterize the people who must be "served"? **(c)** Based on what you have learned about early African, Asian, and Indian civilizations, what arguments might you use to prove Kipling wrong?

Relating Geography to History

Use the world map on pages R4–R5 of the Atlas section to answer the following questions: **(a)** If the Suez Canal did not exist, what would be the shortest water route between London and Bombay? **(b)** If the Panama Canal did not exist, what would be the shortest water route between New York and Hawaii?

Relating Past to Present

1. Using a world atlas, prepare a map showing the distribution of natural resources in Africa. Compare this map with the map on page 607. **(a)** What resources did each imperialist nation stand to gain through its possession of African colonies? **(b)** Which of these resources are most important to industrial nations today?
2. Review the reasons for the United States government's decision to build a canal across the Isthmus of Panama. Then investigate the debate surrounding the 1978 decision to turn ownership of the canal over to Panama by the year 2000.

Applying History Study Skills

Before completing this activity, review Building History Study Skills on page 604.

Your topic is: "How did the Meiji Restoration speed the industrialization of Japan?" Which of the following items would be relevant to your topic?

1. Yedo was renamed Tokyo when it became the new imperial capital.
2. A system of universal education was set up in Japan.
3. Compulsory military service was established.
4. European nations began to set up trading barriers such as tariffs on Japanese goods.
5. The divinity of the emperor was stressed during the Meiji Restoration.
6. The special stipend for samurai was abolished during the Meiji Restoration.
7. Government policy was mainly decided by a group of able samurai from the daimyo domains of Satsuma and Choshu.
8. Political parties formed protest movements.

Investigating Further

1. **Conducting a Debate** Work with several of your classmates to find information on European imperialism in Africa. Prepare a debate on the following topic: *Resolved:* The Europeans exploited Africa and severely damaged the local cultures.
2. **Writing a Report** Imperialism arose out of a complex mixture of political, economic, and social forces. One of these was the missionary motive. Using books in your library, prepare a report on missionary activities in colonial areas.

627

UNIT 5 REVIEW

Unit Summary

The following list contains the key concepts you have learned about the development of industrial society.

1. The Industrial Revolution—the production of goods by machinery in factories—began in Great Britain and changed the world. Both steam power and the Bessemer process were extremely important to the early Industrial Revolution.
2. Workers began to protest harsh working conditions and low wages. The first labor unions were organized to seek improvements in working conditions.
3. Socialists like Karl Marx believed that a more fundamental transformation of politics and society was necessary and would resolve human problems.
4. After 1870 new inventions, scientific discoveries, compulsory public education, and a lively interest in the arts helped improve the quality of life.
5. Many social and political reforms occurred in Great Britain and the British Empire in the 1800s and early 1900s.
6. Territorial growth and sectionalism in the United States led to conflict over the issue of slavery. Eventually the North and South fought a bitter civil war.
7. France experienced political instability in the 1800s. By the early 1900s, France was a republic governed by coalitions of parties that represented monarchist, liberal, and socialist beliefs.
8. The peoples of Latin America gained their independence in the 1800s but did not unite.
9. Due to the efforts of Mazzini, Garibaldi, and Cavour, Italy was unified by 1870. In Germany, Prussia led the movement toward unification.
10. In Russia the czar maintained autocratic control over the country, while rebellion in the Austrian Empire led to the formation of the Dual Monarchy.
11. In the late 1800s, European nations became involved in a new kind of empire building—imperialism. Europeans established colonies in Africa, Asia, and the Pacific. In most of Latin America, imperialism was economic rather than political.

On a separate sheet of paper, complete the following review exercises.

Reviewing Concepts

Match each of the following individuals with the correct concept in column two.

a. Mazzini
b. Bismarck
c. Spencer
d. Smith
e. Marx
f. Daumier
g. Beethoven

h. Pankhurst
i. Mill
j. Monet
k. Einstein
l. Metternich
m. Kipling
n. Freud

____ 1. romanticism in music
____ 2. psychoanalysis
____ 3. liberalism
____ 4. relativity
____ 5. absolutism
____ 6. impressionism
____ 7. Risorgimento
____ 8. "white man's burden"
____ 9. pure communism
____ 10. *Kulturkampf*
____ 11. realism in art
____ 12. Social Darwinism
____ 13. laissez faire
____ 14. woman suffrage

Applying Critical Thinking Skills

1. **Interpreting Ideas** **(a)** How did the agricultural revolution help to create a large labor force in the cities? **(b)** Why was this necessary for the development of an industrial economy?
2. **Determining Cause and Effect** What effect did the Industrial Revolution have on each of the following: **(a)** living conditions, **(b)** women's lives, **(c)** family size, **(d)** use of leisure time.
3. **Understanding Ideas** During the 1800s liberalism emerged as a vital force in Europe. **(a)** What were some of the political ideas associated with liberalism? **(b)** In what nations did liberalism make the greatest progress? **(c)** the least progress?
4. **Analyzing Primary Sources** Metternich once commented, "When France sneezes, all Europe catches cold." **(a)** What do you think he meant by this remark? **(b)** In light of the actions taken by Napoleon III, would you agree or disagree with Metternich? Why or why not?
5. **Classifying Ideas** Identify the major accomplishments of each of the following scientists: **(a)** John Dalton, **(b)** Marie Curie, **(c)** Albert Einstein, **(d)** Charles Darwin, **(e)** Edward Jenner, **(f)** Louis Pasteur, **(g)** Joseph Lister, **(h)** Sigmund Freud
6. **Evaluating Ideas** **(a)** What conditions encouraged the growth of nationalism in Europe? **(b)** How did the spirit of nationalism affect the development of Italy? **(c)** of Germany? **(d)** of Austria-Hungary? **(e)** of Russia?
7. **Synthesizing Ideas** **(a)** How did the Industrial Revolution and the rise of nationalism rekindle the desire for colonies? **(b)** What other factors promoted the renewed interest in empire building? **(c)** How did the imperialism of the late 1800s differ from the colonization of the 1500s and 1600s?

Relating Geography to History

Turn to the map of Africa on page R16. **(a)** How many independent nations exist in present-day Africa? **(b)** How does this number compare with the number of nations shown on the map on page 607? **(c)** Which imperialist power gave up the most territory? **(d)** the least territory?

Writing About History

1. Choose one of the scientists discussed in Chapter 20. Then use resources in your school or public library to find what recent discoveries have advanced the work of this scientist. Write a report detailing your findings.
2. Write a newspaper article dated October 25, 1876, that tries to convince your readers that European countries should establish colonies.

Further Readings

Fieldhouse, D. K. *The Colonial Empires*. New York: Dell. Compares European and North American empire building from the 1500s to the 1900s.

Hibbert, Christopher. *Africa Explored: Europeans in the Dark Continent, 1769–1889*. New York: Penguin Books. Description of European exploration of Africa and the growing competition to carve spheres of influence throughout the world.

Mosse, Werner. *Alexander II and the Modernization of Russia*. New York: Collier. Comprehensive biography of Alexander II of Russia that analyzes his impact on Russian society, particularly the peasant classes.

Sinclair, Upton. *The Jungle*. New York: Signet Classics. Social critique of the Industrial Revolution in the United States. Graphic descriptions of abuses of workers.

Twain, Mark. *The Adventures of Huckleberry Finn*. New York: Signet Classics. One of many reprintings of the most famous (and probably the first) American novel about life on the Mississippi during the early nineteenth century.

Unit Five Chronology

Date	Political and Social Developments	Technological and Scientific Advances	Visual Arts and Literature	Religious and Philosophical Thought
1750–1800	Enclosure continues 19* French and British anti-union activity 21	Watt's steam engine 19 Cartwright's power loom 19 Cotton 19 Jenner and smallpox 20 Factory system 19	*Wealth of Nations* 19 Beethoven 20 Shift to romanticism 20 Malthus's *Essay . . . Population* 19	Commercial capitalism 19 Adam Smith 19 Robert Owen 19
1800–1850	British industrial reform 19 Decline of Ottoman Empire 22 Zollverein 22 Revolutions of 1848 21, 22 Latin American independence 21 Imperialism in China 23	Fulton's *Clermont* 19 Stephenson's locomotive 19 McCormick's reaper 19 Goodyear's vulcanized rubber 19 Morse's telegraph 19	Tchaikovsky, Wagner, and Verdi 20 Brothers Grimm 20 Goethe 20 *Communist Manifesto* 19 Victorian Age 21 Cooper and Irving 20	Chartism 21 Utopians 19 David Ricardo 19 John Stuart Mill 19
1850–1920	2nd and 3rd French Republics 21 European imperialism 23 Meiji Restoration 23 Spanish-American War 23 U.S. Civil War 21 Franco-Prussian War 21 Woman suffrage 21 Russo-Japanese War 22 Boer War 23 Establishment of Germany, Italy, Dual Monarchy 22 Reform Bills in Great Britain 21	Mendeleyev's periodic table of elements 20 Darwin 20 Bessemer steel process 19 Transatlantic cable 19 Bell's telephone 19 Edison's light bulb 20 Suez Canal 21, 23 Pasteur 20 Wireless 20 Wright brothers 20 Panama Canal 23 Planck and Einstein 20	*Das Kapital* 19 Dickens 19 *Principles of Sociology* 20 Realism 20 Impressionists 20	*Kulturkampf* 22 Socialism 19 Nationalism 22 Social Darwinism 20 Liberalism 21 Universal education 21 Nihilism 22 Freud 20 "White Man's Burden" 23

*Indicates chapter in which development is discussed

The Development of Industrial Society

19 The Industrial Revolution Transformed the Modern World

A revolution quite different from the Scientific Revolution of the 1500s or the political revolutions of the 1600s and the 1700s began in Great Britain in the 1700s. This revolution—the Industrial Revolution—transformed the ways goods were produced and profoundly affected the world.

The Early Industrial Revolution

The Industrial Revolution began in Great Britain because of a certain combination of conditions. Great Britain had what economists call the factors of production, or the basic resources necessary for industrialization: land, capital, and labor.

But even before the Industrial Revolution had begun, Great Britain experienced a revolution in agriculture. This revolution had started when British farmers began to fence off, or enclose, common lands into individual holdings efficient for large-scale farming.

By the 1800s, because of improvements in agriculture, farmers needed fewer farm laborers. Many unemployed farm workers moved to the cities, where they created a large labor force. Many of these workers found jobs in the cotton textile industry, which was the first industry in Great Britain to undergo mechanization—the use of automatic machinery to increase production.

The Factory System

Soon, inventors perfected the steam engine, which could be used to power machinery. This introduction of steam-powered machinery made work easier to do and made it possible to produce a wide array of products in a relatively short time. Most of these goods were manufactured in factories rather than in people's homes.

Life in the mines and factories of the early Industrial Revolution was hard and monotonous, and life in the workers' homes was not much better. Working people lived in cramped and poorly maintained apartment houses called tenements. At the same time, the middle class grew and enjoyed many luxuries unknown before the Industrial Age.

New Business Methods

The factory system introduced a new phase in the development of capitalism—the economic system in which individuals rather than the government control the factors of production. Before the Industrial Revolution, most capitalists were merchants who bought, sold, and exchanged goods. We call this type of capitalism commercial capitalism. However, because the capitalists of the Industrial Revolution became more involved in producing and manufacturing goods themselves, the capitalism of this period is often referred to as industrial capitalism.

Industrialization changed the methods of production and depended on division of labor, interchangeable parts, and the assembly line. It also gave rise to a new form of business organization—the corporation.

Improving Living Conditions

During the Enlightenment of the 1700s, a group of economists attacked the ideas of mercantilism. These economists believed that natural laws governed economic life, and that any attempt to interfere with these natural economic laws was certain to bring disaster. Adam Smith, a Scot, best stated the views of these economists. Smith wrote that every person should be free to go into any business and to operate it for the greatest advantage. The result, Smith said, would benefit everyone. We call this system of complete free enterprise *laissez-faire*.

As time went on, more people realized that things could not be left entirely alone. Many people, such as John Stuart Mill, felt that government needed to regulate work hours and set minimum standards for wages and working conditions. These people argued that such laws would not interfere with the natural workings of the economy. Over time, governments began to agree with these reformers.

Many workers, however, felt that governments were not moving fast enough. Sometimes these workers took matters into their own hands and refused to work until demands were met. We call such a work stoppage a strike.

In order to strengthen their position, workers sought ways to organize permanently into associations called labor unions. Although these organizations were at first outlawed, they later became legal.

Socialism

Some reformers of the 1800s advocated a political and economic system called socialism. In this system the government owns the means of production and operates them for the welfare of all the people.

Some thinkers grew impatient with early socialism, which advocated peaceful methods to attain goals. Karl Marx, the most important of these critics, believed that all the great changes in history came from changes in economic conditions. Under capitalism, he said, labor receives only a small fraction of the wealth it creates. Most of the wealth goes to the owners in the form of profits. As a result of this unequal distribution of wealth, the capitalist system necessarily suffered from increasingly severe depressions that would ultimately lead to a revolution led by the workers, or proletarians.

Marxist, or radical, socialists generally believed in the necessity of revolution to overthrow the capitalist system. They wanted to establish a system in which the government owns almost all the means of production and controls economic planning. Today we call this economic and political system authoritarian socialism, or communism.

Another group of socialists, though influenced by Marx, believed that socialism could develop gradually through education and democratic forms of government. Today we call this type of socialism democratic socialism. Under democratic socialism, the people retain basic human rights and partial control over economic planning through the election of government officials.

The Great Exhibition of London, 1851

20 The Industrial Age Revolutionized Science and Culture

In addition to changing the economy and society, the Industrial Revolution had a profound effect on science, art, music, and literature.

Technology and Communication

Beginning about 1870 manufacturers increasingly applied the findings of pure science to their businesses, generating a new wave of industrial growth. The application of scientific solutions to industrial problems resulted in: (1) inventions that provided rapid communications over long distances; (2) the development and use of new sources of power; and (3) the creation of new products and materials and the improvement of old ones.

Advances in Science and Medicine

The most significant developments in the physical sciences—those that deal with the inanimate, or nonliving, aspects of nature—during the 1800s and early 1900s centered on the atomic theory. This theory states that all matter in the universe consists of very small particles called atoms. The arrangement and structure of these atoms and their chemical combinations with each other account for the different characteristics of the materials that make up our world.

Scientists also investigated the biological sciences—those dealing with living organisms. Many

631

explored the structure of cells, the tiny units of living matter, in an attempt to better understand organic matter and thereby improve human life.

Population

The progress made possible by science and technology helped produce rapid population growth in industrialized countries. As the population grew, it also became more mobile. Large numbers of people moved across national boundaries and oceans to foreign lands. Others moved to cities to find jobs in the new factories.

Social Sciences and Education

During the 1800s interest in education and in the social sciences grew rapidly. The social sciences are disciplines that study people as members of society. These subjects include political science, economics, history, anthropology, sociology, and psychology.

Literature, Music, and Art

Literature, music, and art reflected the social and economic developments of the Industrial Age. Even in their most personal statements, the artists portrayed in their works a sense of the times and of the influences of scientific ideas and rapid change.

Many writers of the early 1800s belonged to what is known as the romantic movement. Their work appealed to sentiment and imagination and dealt with the "romance" of life—life as it used to be, or as they thought it ought to be, rather than as it actually was. In the mid-1800s writers and artists began to abandon romanticism and turn to realism, which emphasized the realities of everyday life.

21 Reforms Swept Through Many Areas of the World in the 1800s

During the late 1800s, people throughout the world clamored for reform. Their appeals met with varying degrees of success.

British Reforms

Although Great Britain was a limited constitutional monarchy with executive power vested in a cabinet headed by the prime minister, not everyone had a voice in government. In the 1800s, however, a series of reforms extended rights to the entire population. At the same time, vital social and economic reforms took place. Two outstanding prime ministers—Benjamin Disraeli and William Gladstone—helped push through many of these reforms.

As Great Britain instituted social and political reforms, other changes occurred within the British Empire. The British colonies of Canada, Australia, and New Zealand won self-government. Nevertheless, each maintained close ties with Great Britain.

The United States

Unlike European governments, the United States expanded without acquiring any colonies. Instead, it expanded across North America and gave new territories the opportunity to become states on an equal basis with the original 13 states.

Despite phenomenal growth, the United States had one significant problem—the unresolved issue of slavery. This issue, along with the issue of states' rights, led to a brutal civil war that raged between 1861 and 1865 and left much of the nation—particularly the South—in ruins. Nevertheless, the Union was preserved.

After the Civil War, the United States experienced phenomenal growth primarily as a result of industrialization and immigration.

France

For many years after the Congress of Vienna, the Bourbons continued to rule France. Then in 1830 a revolt forced King Charles X to abdicate. The leaders of the French revolt then chose Louis Philippe, Duke of Orléans, who belonged to a branch of the Bourbon family but who had a record of liberal beliefs, as king.

But in 1848 opposition to the regime of Louis Philippe erupted in violence. A new government—a republic—under the leadership of Louis Napoleon was soon proclaimed. Napoleon, however, had imperial ambitions similar to those of his illustrious uncle and soon proclaimed the Second Empire.

The Second Empire lasted until a humiliating defeat by Prussia toppled it in 1871. France once again proclaimed a republic.

Latin America

By the late 1700s, the Spanish and Portuguese colonies underwent administrative reform and economic growth, inspired in part by the Enlightenment. Nevertheless, the revolutionary events in British North America and France in the late 1700s aroused interest, particularly among discontented creoles, as upper-class Latin Americans were known. By the mid-1800s this discontent had become full-scale revolution, and the nations of Latin America had won their independence.

22 Unification of New Nations Added to Rising Tensions in Europe

In the late 1800s, the political situation in Europe changed significantly. Italy and Germany each became unified nations. Russia remained a rigid autocracy, and Austria and Hungary formed the Dual Monarchy.

Italy

Italian nationalism became a strong force in the early 1800s. Under the leadership of fiery patriots such as Giuseppe Mazzini, people in many parts of Italy clamored for national unity. Although the nationalists made some gains, they could not agree on what type of government the united Italy should have.

One group favored union under the leadership of Sardinia. There, the chief minister or premier, Count Camillo Benso di Cavour (kahv • OOHR), provided the major impetus for Italian unification. Throughout the 1850s and the 1860s, Cavour used diplomacy, war, and persuasion to achieve unity. Finally, in 1870 unification was completed when the Italians claimed Rome.

Prussia

Like Italy, Germany remained fragmented in the early 1800s. But during the 1860s and 1870s, the

Celebrating Italian Unification

long-delayed process of centralization and consolidation under the leadership of Prussia began to pick up great speed.

Perhaps the person most responsible for German unification was the Prussian chancellor Otto von Bismarck, who used clever diplomacy and war against Denmark, Austria, and France to achieve unification in 1871.

The new German Empire was a federal union under the leadership of the Prussian kaiser, or emperor. The federal government controlled all common matters, such as national defense, foreign affairs, and commerce.

Opposition to Bismarck

In spite of rigid control by the aristocratic Prussians, the new German federal government soon ran into difficult problems. Dissatisfied groups formed political parties that opposed Bismarck's policies. Relations with the Roman Catholic church proved troublesome, and socialists clamored for government ownership of businesses. Through delicate diplomacy, however, Bismarck was able to deal with these problems and transform Germany into an industrial power.

In foreign policy Bismarck worked to build up Germany's military strength and develop a system of alliances to prevent Russia and France from becoming allies.

Russia

Ruled by an autocratic czar, Russia steadfastly opposed reform. Nevertheless, liberal ideals became popular among discontented Russians—particularly

633

among intellectuals. Faced with problems caused by liberal ideas and restless nationalities, the czars took harsh measures.

Although the late 1800s witnessed reforms such as the freeing of the serfs during the reign of Alexander II, most reform efforts failed. And the czars continued to use repression to combat any erosion of their powers. Then in 1904 and 1905 the Russians fought a disastrous war with Japan. Defeat at the hands of the Japanese spurred all the discontented groups in the country to action and led to revolution. Although the beleaguered Czar Nicholas II granted a few reforms, he later reneged on his promises and resumed his policies of repression. This repression would have disastrous consequences for the Romanovs.

Austria-Hungary

The Hapsburgs in Austria also had to deal with the rising tide of liberalism in the late 1800s. And to combat nationalist demands in the empire, the Austrians formed the Dual Monarchy in which both Hungarians and Austrians played a vital role in government.

The formation of the Dual Monarchy failed to solve the problem of nationalities. The Austrian Germans and the Hungarian Magyars dominated the population in each of their separate national states. National minorities—the Czechs, Serbs, Croats, Romanians, Poles, and Italians—existed in both Austria and Hungary. These people benefited very little from the Dual Monarchy and continued to agitate for self-government.

The Dual Monarchy also faced problems abroad. In the late 1800s, the Hapsburgs clashed with the autocratic government of the Ottoman Empire over the Balkans. Although the Ottomans had ruled the Balkans for centuries, their influence steadily weakened as their empire declined.

23 Imperialist Powers Competed in Many Areas of the World

Beginning about 1870 several factors rekindled interest in establishing colonies. During the next 40 years, many nations became involved in imperialism—the domination by a powerful nation over the political, economic, and cultural affairs of another nation or region.

Background of Imperialism

Imperialism arose out of a complex mixture of political, economic, and social forces. These forces included a desire for self-sufficiency, the need for new markets, the search for national pride and prestige, the need for places where people could settle and still remain loyal to the home country, and the desire to convert people to Christianity.

Imperialism created bitter rivalries among the imperial powers and hatred among the colonized peoples. As European powers took over more and more of the world, these rivalries and hatreds intensified.

North Africa and the Sudan

In the 1800s most of North Africa and the Sudan belonged to the Ottoman Empire. Because Turkish control in many areas was weak, the Europeans scrambled to claim new colonies. The French claimed Algeria, Tunisia, and Morocco. The British established dominance in Egypt and the Sudan, and the Italians took Libya.

SubSaharan Africa

The Europeans repeated their colonial ambitions in SubSaharan Africa. During the empire building of the 1500s and the 1600s, the Europeans had established settlements on the coasts. In the late 1800s, however, the Europeans moved inland. By 1900 Europeans claimed all land in SubSaharan Africa except Liberia and Ethiopia.

Imperialism was a harsh experience for all of Africa. However, the costs and the benefits resulting from European expansion were unevenly distributed across the continent.

South and East Asia

The strong forces of imperialism that swept Africa in the 1800s brought important and fateful changes to South and East Asia although the changes were not as abrupt as they were in so many parts of Africa. In India, for example, the British had long played an important role. In the mid-1800s, they increased this role and made India a part of their vast empire.

European trading centers in Guangzhou, China

Although European influence in Japan became strong after the overthrow of the Tokugawa shogunate in 1868, Europeans did not dominate Japan as they did India. Rather, the Japanese under the rule of the Meiji emperors controlled their own affairs and industrialized. At the same time, China came increasingly under European domination even though it remained nominally independent.

Southeast Asia and the Pacific

The tide of imperialism did not stop in South and East Asia. It affected Southeast Asia and the islands of the Pacific as well. The British, the French, and the Dutch claimed parts of Southeast Asia and several islands in the Pacific. The United States claimed the Philippines, Hawaii, Guam, and Wake Island.

Latin America

Imperialism in Latin America differed from that in the Pacific. Although the Latin American countries were weak, the Monroe Doctrine of the United States, along with Great Britain's navy and its commercial policy, prevented them from being turned into colonies again. Nevertheless, the countries of Latin America experienced economic interference as they increasingly became a field for investment from Europe and the United States. We call this type of imperialism economic imperialism because the colonial power controls the subject area's economy rather than its government.

In two areas, Cuba and Puerto Rico, however, a foreign government did take political control. These islands had been a part of the Spanish Empire for centuries. But in 1898 the United States defeated Spain in the Spanish-American War and claimed the islands. Cuba later became independent, while Puerto Rico became a commonwealth of the United States. And in Panama, the United States built a canal and ruled the territory known as the Canal Zone.

SYNTHESIS REVIEW

1. **Interpreting Ideas** Why did the Industrial Revolution begin in Great Britain?
2. **Determining Cause and Effect** How did the Industrial Revolution alter population patterns?
3. **Comparing Ideas** How did political developments in France and Great Britain differ in the late 1800s?
4. **Understanding Ideas** How did Bismarck deal with the socialists?
5. **Analyzing Ideas** What factors led Europeans to found colonies in the late 1800s?
6. **Synthesizing Ideas** Why do you think democracy triumphed in Great Britain and the United States but failed in Russia?

635

World War in the Twentieth Century

◀ *The British Rescue at Dunkirk*

World War I and the Russian Revolution Altered the Course of History

Place   Europe, Africa, and the Middle East

Time   1882–1920

```
   3.7 mil. BC   4000 BC              AD 2100
```

Significance

During the late 1800s, world leaders had striven to promote cooperation among nations. Philanthropists—people interested in the welfare of the human race—gave time and money to encourage cooperation between nations. For example, Andrew Carnegie, an American financier, built the Palace of Peace at The Hague, in the Netherlands, where diplomats could hold international conferences designed to reduce world tensions.

Representatives of several nations met at The Hague in 1899 and again in 1907 in an effort to limit armaments. Even as nations met to discuss peace, however, they prepared for war. The war that began in the summer of 1914 resembled no previous war. For the first time in history, industrial technology played a major role.

Because of the devastation that the war caused, the people of the time rightly called it the Great War. We know the Great War as World War I.

Terms to Define

militarism	belligerent
mobilize	propaganda
entente	contraband
ultimatum	Fourteen Points

People to Identify

Andrew Carnegie	Alfred Zimmermann
Archduke Francis Ferdinand	Ferdinand Foch
Woodrow Wilson	Big Four

Places to Locate

Sarajevo	Polish Corridor
western front	Czechoslovakia

Questions to Guide Your Reading

1 What conflicting national interests set the stage for war?
2 In what ways did the nations of the world fight a new kind of war?
3 How did the war bring about the Russian Revolution and the end of the czarist regime?
4 After defeating the Central Powers, what peace terms did the Allies draft?
5 How did the peace treaties create a "new Europe" after World War I?

◀ *American soldiers in trenches east of Paris, 1918*

As in all other wars, the soldiers of World War I came to realize that terror and death stalk both sides. The following excerpt from All Quiet on the Western Front describes a German soldier's feelings upon the death of an enemy.

    "The rattle of machine-guns becomes an unbroken chain. Just as I am about to turn around a little, something heavy stumbles, and with a crash a body falls over me into the shell-hole, slips down, and lies across me— . . .

    The silence spreads. I talk and must talk. So I speak to him and say to him: 'Comrade, I did not want to kill you. . . . You were only an idea to me before. . . . But now, for the first time, I see you are a man like me. . . . Forgive me, comrade. We always see too late. . . . Why do they never tell us that you are . . . like us, that your mothers are just as anxious as ours, and that we have the same fear of death, and the same dying and the same agony—Forgive me, comrade; how could you be my enemy? If we threw away these rifles and this uniform you could be my brother.'

The events that culminated in the horror soldiers experienced on battlefields during World War I began with conflicting national interests among European nations during the late 1800s and the early 1900s.

1 Conflicting National Interests Set the Stage for War

Some historians have referred to the decades before 1914 as a period of "international anarchy." Each nation in Europe pursued policies without regard for the wishes or interests of its neighbors. These conflicting interests set the stage for war.

Since the Congress of Vienna in 1815, relations among European powers had been more or less harmonious. Beginning in the late 1800s, however, cooperation among nations broke down as intense rivalries increased. These rivalries grew both within Europe as new nations were formed, and overseas as a result of imperialism.

In *The Guns of August*, Barbara Tuchman describes an event in England that temporarily brought the European nations together and marked the transition between the old and the new.

"So gorgeous was the spectacle on the May morning of 1910 when nine kings rode in the funeral of Edward VII of England that the crowd, waiting in hushed and black-clad awe, could not keep back gasps of admiration. In scarlet and blue and green and purple, three by three the sovereigns rode through the palace gates, with plumed helmets, gold braid, crimson sashes, and jeweled orders [military decorations] flashing in the sun. After them came . . . heirs, . . . queens . . . and a scattering of special ambassadors from uncrowned countries. Together they represented seventy nations in the greatest assemblage of royalty and rank ever gathered in one place and, of its kind, the last. The muffled tongue of Big Ben tolled nine by the clock as the cortege left the palace, but on history's clock it was sunset, and the sun of the old world was setting in a dying blaze of splendor never to be seen again. **"**

As rivalries intensified in the early 1900s, the great powers plunged toward war, pressed forward by four factors: nationalism, imperialism, militarism, and the system of alliances.

Nationalism and Imperialism

Spurred by the nationalism that developed after the French Revolution and the Napoleonic Wars, national groups throughout the 1800s tried to unite under governments controlled by their own people. This desire to unite all the people of a nation under a single government, however, had explosive possibilities in a Europe where a single government often ruled many nationalities.

In the early 1900s, the imperialist nations came to the brink of war several times as they scrambled to partition Africa among themselves. Germany and France, for example, narrowly avoided war over their rival claims to Morocco on two occasions between 1905 and 1911. They managed to settle each incident with makeshift compromises that usually left one of the participants dissatisfied.

Militarism

The glorification of armed strength, or **militarism,** dominated the thinking of many European leaders before World War I. These leaders believed that only the use of force could solve problems among nations.

According to these leaders, a militarily strong nation usually got what it wanted, as Prussia had proved in its wars with Denmark, Austria, and France. Weaker nations lost out, as Italy had learned from its imperialistic ventures in Africa.

In the late 1800s, European nations built reserve armies of soldiers who were drafted, given military training, and then returned to civilian life. These soldiers could be called into service at any time. If one nation **mobilized,** or organized its resources for combat, other nations would mobilize for their own protection. It was a cyclical process that was difficult to stop once it had begun.

As international rivalries intensified, each European nation believed it necessary to keep its armed forces stronger than those of any potential enemy. Armies grew larger as spending for new weapons and for the fortification of national boundaries multiplied. In the 1890s Germany began to build a large and modern navy to rival that of Great Britain. France, the United States, Japan, and Italy followed Germany's example. Great Britain responded by expanding its navy even more.

The System of Alliances

During the late 1800s, the unification of Germany and of Italy shifted the balance of power in Europe. Germany, more than Italy, created an entirely new situation. In place of a group of relatively weak states, a powerful German Empire, under the leadership of Prussia, emerged. Otto von Bismarck, the skillful and ruthless German chancellor, shaped its ambitious foreign policy.

The Triple Alliance. Bismarck feared that France would seek revenge for its 1871 defeat in the Franco-Prussian War by trying to regain Alsace-Lorraine, which it had lost to Germany. He therefore dedicated his foreign policy to keeping France isolated and without allies. Bismarck particularly wanted to prevent a Franco-Russian alliance because it would serve to isolate Germany diplomatically and—at worst—mean that Germany would have to fight on both its eastern and western borders in the event of war.

In 1879 Bismarck formed the Dual Alliance, a mutual defense pact between Germany and Austria-Hungary. Then in 1881 the chancellor set up the Three Emperors' League, a secret agreement among the emperors of Germany, Russia, and Austria-Hungary.

Learning from Pictures In 1906 the British Navy launched a new type of battleship called the dreadnought that featured heavy armor plating and batteries of big guns.

In 1882 Bismarck agreed to Italy's request for the Triple Alliance, a pact among Germany, Austria-Hungary, and Italy. Bismarck considered Italy a weak link in the Triple Alliance; however, the forging of the alliance isolated France and therefore enabled Bismarck to accomplish his primary foreign policy goal.

The formation of the Triple Alliance completely upset the balance of power in Europe. For a while, Bismarck's skillful diplomacy kept France isolated. France, however, became uneasy and began to seek allies.

The Reinsurance Treaty. In 1885 a Balkan crisis, sparked by Bulgarian nationalism in Eastern Rumelia (a Turkish province in the Balkan region), resulted in the dissolution of the Three Emperors' League. Russian nationalists, who resented Germany's support of Austria-Hungary in the Balkans, demanded that the Russian government make an alliance with France. However, the Russian government hesitated to sever diplomatic relations with Germany and suggested instead that Germany enter into a new treaty that would exclude Austria-Hungary. The Reinsurance Treaty of 1887 provided for neutrality in case either Russia or Germany became involved in a defensive war.

In 1888 William II became kaiser and soon dismissed Bismarck. Bismarck's careful plans collapsed as William II abandoned Bismarck's policies.

The Triple Entente. France, meanwhile, had been trying to gain allies. The opportunity arose after William II allowed the Reinsurance Treaty to collapse. An economic crisis shook Russia, and the czar sought a loan. The French hurried to lend the money and took other steps to win Russia's friendship. In 1894 France and Russia formed an alliance, making Bismarck's fear of facing potential enemies on two sides a reality.

After 1888 Germany entered the race for colonies with full force, demanding its "place in the sun." William II also began a great naval buildup. The rapid growth of the German navy troubled the British. Germany also began to interfere with some of Great Britain's imperial schemes, as goods from German industries competed with British goods in world markets.

Great Britain, too, began to look for allies. In 1904 the British and the French reached an agreement over the control of Morocco and Egypt. The agreement was an **entente** (ahn • TAHNT)—a friendly understanding or agreement between nations—rather than an alliance. Still, in order to

641

counterbalance the Triple Alliance, Great Britain and Russia had to come to an agreement as well. Reaching such an agreement proved difficult, however, because of the two nations' rivalry in the Middle East. But with French help they finally arrived at an understanding in 1907. The resulting alignment of France, Russia, and Great Britain was called the Triple Entente. Both France and Russia also had secret understandings with Italy, which meant that the Italians had a foot in both camps.

Dangers of the alliance system. By 1907 the alliance system threatened world peace because it divided Europe into two armed camps. Should hostilities develop between any two rival powers, all six nations would become involved in the fighting, whether or not the original dispute concerned all of them. A minor quarrel could lead to serious consequences, as events in 1914 would prove.

The Balkan Powder Keg

The many conflicts that plagued the Balkans gave rise to the region's nickname—"powder keg of Europe." Amid the growing system of alliances, the powder keg threatened to explode.

Nationalists in Serbia, which had become independent in 1878, hoped to make their country the center of a large Slavic state. They wanted Slavic territories still under Ottoman and Austro-Hungarian rule to become part of this state. The Serbian nationalists especially wanted the provinces of Bosnia and Herzegovina (hert • suh • goh • VEE • nuh) because Serbia was landlocked and these two provinces would provide an outlet on the Adriatic Sea.

The decision of the Congress of Berlin in 1878 to make the two provinces protectorates of Austria-Hungary (see Chapter 22) severely disappointed the Serbs. After Austria-Hungary annexed Bosnia and Herzegovina in 1908, infuriated Serbian nationalists distributed propaganda against Austria-Hungary to win sympathy for their cause. The rivalry between the two groups intensified.

Hoping to assume leadership of a Slavic league, Russia supported Serbia's nationalistic goals. Great Britain, however, opposed Pan-Slavism, the nationalist movement that pressed for the political and cultural unity of all Slavs under Russian leadership. The British distrusted Russian influence in the Balkans. They also feared for the safety of the Suez Canal, their main route to India and Britain's most important colonial possession.

These rivalries heightened tensions in the Balkans. Another factor made the situation even more explosive. To strengthen the Triple Alliance and make up for the weakness of Italy, the young, arrogant William II of Germany sought new allies. He began negotiating to bring the Ottoman Empire into the Triple Alliance and thereby extend German influence into the Balkans.

Germany also planned to build a railroad from Berlin through the Balkans to Constantinople and on to Baghdad, near the Persian Gulf. This plan aroused many fears. The British regarded the proposed railroad as a threat to the sea route through the Suez Canal, their Mediterranean-Red Sea "lifeline" to India. They feared that such a railroad would provide a better route to India. The Russians feared that Germany would become a strong protector of the Ottoman Empire. This would diminish Russia's age-old hope of gaining Constantinople, the Dardanelles, and the Bosporus.

Germany's actions in the Balkans complicated an already confused situation and resulted in what Bismarck had carefully avoided—the strengthening of ties between Great Britain and Russia. Both countries wanted to resist German expansion in the Balkans. Austria-Hungary, on the other hand, feared Pan-Slavism and won Germany's support in its opposition to Slavic nationalism.

Assassination at Sarajevo

The spark that touched off the explosion of the Balkan "powder keg" and led to war came on June 28, 1914. The heir to the Austro-Hungarian throne, Archduke Francis Ferdinand, and his wife were visiting Sarajevo (sahr • uh • YE • voh), the capital of Bosnia and Herzegovina, on a mission of goodwill. As they rode in an open automobile, a young man fired a revolver, killing both the archduke and his wife.

The assassin, Gavrilo Princip, belonged to the Black Hand, one of the many secret societies of Serbian nationalists opposed to Austro-Hungarian rule. Although Princip had acted without the authority of the Serbian government, certain Serbian leaders were aware of his plans and had furnished arms and ammunition.

The assassination brought to a head the long struggle between Serbia and Austria-Hungary. The Austro-Hungarian government was determined to punish the Serbs. But before Austria-Hungary

Learning from Pictures *Gavrilo Princip fires the fatal shots at Archduke Francis Ferdinand and his wife. Why was the Archduke in Sarajevo?*

acted, it wanted to make sure of German support in case the Russians tried to help Serbia. Germany promised to back Austria-Hungary in anything Austria-Hungary did. Encouraged by this so-called blank check, the Austro-Hungarians presented an **ultimatum** to the Serbian government. An ultimatum puts forth the final terms offered for a settlement. It states that if the ultimatum is rejected, negotiations will end and the country that issued the ultimatum will use force.

War Between Austria-Hungary and Serbia

In its ultimatum Austria-Hungary made the following demands: (1) The Serbian government would condemn all propaganda against Austria-Hungary and suppress publications and societies that opposed Austria-Hungary. (2) Serbia would ban from its schools books and teachers who did not favor Austria-Hungary. (3) Serbia would dismiss any officials who had promoted propaganda against Austria-Hungary. (4) Austro-Hungarian judges would conduct the trial of those accused of the crime at Sarajevo. (5) Serbia had to accept all of these terms within 48 hours or Austria-Hungary would declare war.

The Serbian government returned a mild and conciliatory reply. Serbia accepted all the terms except the last two, but offered to submit the entire dispute to the international court at The Hague. However, assuming that Austria-Hungary would not accept this offer, the Serbian government ordered mobilization.

In spite of the Serbian reply, Austria-Hungary declared war on Serbia on July 28, after the time limit on the ultimatum had elapsed.

Mobilization of Europe

All attempts to persuade Austria-Hungary to continue negotiations proved futile, especially since Germany continued to support Austria-Hungary. Russia prepared to defend Serbia by mobilizing troops along the Russian–Austro-Hungarian border. Expecting Germany to join Austria-Hungary, Russia also sent troops to the German border.

Germany immediately demanded that Russia cancel mobilization within 12 hours or face war. Russia ignored this ultimatum, and on August 1, 1914, Germany declared war on Russia. Convinced that France was prepared to side with Russia and hoping to gain a military advantage by swift action, Germany declared war on France two days later.

Great Britain Enters the War

The great powers had guaranteed Belgian neutrality in 1839, shortly after Belgium gained its independence. Under the terms of this guarantee, Belgium agreed to stay out of any European war and not to help any **belligerents,** or warring nations. In turn, the other powers agreed not to attack Belgium. However, Belgium's location was of great importance to Germany's military plans. The German General Staff counted on the German army to mobilize, strike, and knock France out of the war before the Russians could attack from the east. Because the Franco-German border was hilly, the Germans planned to launch their first attack through Belgium on the extremely flat coastal plain between France and Germany (see map, page 644).

After the German government declared war on France, it sent an ultimatum to Belgium, demanding that German troops be allowed to cross Belgian territory. The British protested, insisting that Germany observe Belgian neutrality. The German foreign minister replied that surely Great Britain would not fight over "a scrap of paper."

EUROPE ON THE EVE OF WORLD WAR I, 1914

- Triple Alliance
- Triple Entente
- National boundary
- ⊛ National capital

ARCTIC OCEAN

FINLAND

NORWAY

SWEDEN

⊛St. Petersburg

Volga River

RUSSIAN EMPIRE

60°

60°

North Sea

Baltic Sea

DENMARK

GREAT BRITAIN

NETHERLANDS

ATLANTIC OCEAN

London⊛

BELGIUM

•Berlin

GERMAN EMPIRE

Rhine R.

LUX.
ALSACE-LORRAINE

Vistula R.

Dnieper R.

Volga River

Paris⊛

Danube R.

Caspian Sea

40°

FRANCE

SWITZERLAND

•Vienna

AUSTRIA-HUNGARY

PORTUGAL

SPAIN

Corsica

ITALY

Adriatic Sea

BOSNIA

Sarajevo•

MONTENEGRO

SERBIA

ROMANIA

Danube R.

Black Sea

Rome⊛

Sardinia

ALBANIA

BULGARIA

BALKAN PENINSULA

OTTOMAN EMPIRE

Tigris R.

BALEARIC ISLANDS

Sicily

GREECE

Baghdad•

Euphrates R.

AFRICA

Mediterranean Sea

Suez Canal

0 300 600 Miles
0 300 600 Kilometers

N

0° 20° 40°

AZIMUTHAL EQUAL AREA PROJECTION

Learning from Maps *Defensive alliances polarized Europe into two armed camps. What great powers belonged to the Triple Entente?*

German soldiers marched into Belgium on August 4, 1914, secure in the kaiser's message—"You will be home before the leaves have fallen from the trees." Great Britain declared war on Germany later that day.

Expansion of the War

Within six weeks after Gavrilo Princip had assassinated Archduke Francis Ferdinand and his wife at Sarajevo, the rapidly modernizing nation of Japan had entered the war on the side of Great Britain and France. In addition, all the nations of the Triple Alliance and the Triple Entente except Italy were at war. The Italian government took the position that the Austro-Hungarians and Germans had acted as aggressors when they marched through neutral Belgium. Thus the Triple Alliance, a defensive treaty, did not require Italy to help them.

Italy remained neutral for nine months, while each side pleaded desperately for its help. Finally, Italy signed secret treaties with Great Britain, France, and Russia that guaranteed Italy a share of the spoils of war in case of victory over Germany and Austria-Hungary. In May 1915 Italy entered the war against Germany and Austria-Hungary, its former allies.

In the meantime, Germany had been negotiating to win other allies. In November 1914 the Ottoman Empire had plunged into the war on the side of Germany and Austria-Hungary. The Turks, although not a strong military power, occupied a strategic position. Their control of Constantinople and the Dardanelles bottled up Russia's Black Sea fleet. It also prevented Russia's allies from sending supplies through the Mediterranean and Black seas. Germany also persuaded Bulgaria to enter the war in October 1915.

SECTION 1 REVIEW

1. **Define** militarism, mobilize, entente, ultimatum, belligerent
2. **Identify** Triple Alliance, Triple Entente, "powder keg of Europe," Pan-Slavism, Archduke Francis Ferdinand
3. **Locate** Serbia, Bosnia, Adriatic Sea, Sarajevo
4. **Identifying Ideas** (a) Describe the chief aims in the Balkans of the following nations: Serbia, Russia, Great Britain, and Germany. (b) Why was the alliance system dangerous?
5. **Summarizing Ideas** What event can be said to have "lit the fuse" in 1914?
6. **Evaluating Ideas** How did Belgium play a strategic role in the outbreak of World War I?

2 The Nations of the World Fought a New Kind of War

The soldiers who marched enthusiastically off to war in the summer of 1914 thought they would win a quick and decisive victory and come home as heroes in time to celebrate the New Year. They were wrong—tragically wrong.

The Belligerents

Germany, Austria-Hungary, Bulgaria, and the Ottoman Empire became known as the Central

EUROPE IN 1916

Central Powers | Battle site
Allied Powers | British blockade
Neutral Nations | German U-boat blockade

AZIMUTHAL EQUAL AREA PROJECTION

Learning from Maps *The British set up a naval blockade in the North Sea to cut off Germany's sea routes. What battle was fought to break the blockade?*

Powers. Notice on the map on this page that they formed an almost solid block of territory from the North Sea to the Persian Gulf. This geographical proximity gave them an advantage for easy communication and rapid troop movements. Another advantage was Germany's well-organized, well-trained, and well-equipped army.

Great Britain, France, Russia, and their partners in the war became known as the Allied Powers, or the Allies. Although they did not have the geographic advantages of the Central Powers, they had more soldiers and a greater industrial potential. They also controlled the seas. Therefore, they could obtain food and raw materials more easily and could blockade and attempt to starve the Central Powers.

As a result of diplomatic maneuvers, Greece and Romania joined the Allies in 1916. Eventually 32 countries made up the Allied side. Many of

Text continues on page 648.

645

Armies have fought each other throughout history. What has determined the outcome of these wars?

One answer is the bravery—or cowardice—of the individual soldier. Another answer is the skill of the commander.

Most battles and wars, however, have been decided by weapons. In some eras, armed forces have used offensive weapons against which the enemy could find no successful defense. More commonly, the advantage has rested with the defensive side. Today we have the ultimate defensive weapon—nuclear arms. Their power is so awesome that their mere presence discourages attack.

In the early eras of warfare, most weapons were muscle-powered: swords in the hands of Roman legionnaires, lances and longbows in the hands of medieval knights and archers. Innovative generals added mechanical devices. The ancient Assyrians and Egyptians put sharp blades on the wheels of their chariots, and Alexander the Great used huge catapults.

Animal power augmented human power. In 217 B.C. Hannibal

invaded Italy with elephants only to be defeated by Roman foot soldiers. But the Romans learned the value of cavalry when fierce Goth invaders on horseback crushed the Roman infantry at Adrianople in A.D. 378. From then to the Middle Ages, the battlefield was ruled by soldiers on horseback. But horses were effective only in the open field. They were useless against the last line of defense—the wall. Cities became self-contained fortresses when surrounded by high walls. Ramparts allowed defenders to fight from above. The Byzantines, for example, sprayed "Greek fire"—an early form of the flame thrower—on attackers from the walls of Constantinople. The balance of power in warfare swung to the offense with the advent of gunpowder. Invented in China, it was first used in the West about 1320. By 1500 any army worth its salt had rifles and cannon. At first, cannon seemed to be the ideal offensive weapon. King Louis IX of France, the "Spider King," used cannon to destroy the castles of upstart nobles—and to create a powerful and artillery barrages to soften the enemy, followed by mass infantry charges. But now a new weapon had come to the fore—the machine gun. In the hands of determined defenders in trenches or behind fortifications, machine guns made a quick Napoleonic victory impossible. World War I ended, as had the American Civil War, with one side collapsing from exhaustion.

World War II brought a shift to the offense, based on fast-striking weapons such as the tank and the airplane. Hitler's war machine quickly crushed Poland (September 1939) and France (May–June 1940).

The tide of the war against Germany turned not because of new defenses against the tank and the plane. It turned when the Allies were able to produce more offensive firepower than the Germans. Against such force, Hitler's last stand in "Fortress Berlin" was doomed.

World War II in the Pacific was ended by the most fearsome offensive weapon ever developed—the atomic bomb. But it was an offensive weapon only as long as it

was possessed by one side alone. As other nations learned to build it, it became the final defense. In a war between nuclear powers there can be no winners.

You have heard of homicide (the killing of a person) and genocide (the killing of a race). "Nuclear war," an opponent of nuclear weapons said, "is omnicide (the destruction of all)."

Photos   Page 646: Trojan horse (top), medieval catapult (bottom left), English knights fighting invaders (bottom right); Page 647: tank in World War I (top), atomic explosion (middle), American aircraft carrier (bottom left), F–16 fighters (bottom right)

centralized French monarchy. But it was not long before the cannon was put to defensive use—it could destroy attacking armies as easily as it destroyed fortifications.

At the start of the 1800s, Napoleon Bonaparte used combinations of attacking artillery, infantry, and cavalry with dazzling success. He battered the enemy lines with heavy guns, sent his infantry charging in to break the foe, then crushed the retreating troops with his cavalry. This type of offense seemed unstoppable. It was, but only for a while. Defense caught up in the form of transportation. In the American Civil War, railroads made it possible for reinforcements to reach retreating armies quickly. The Battle of Bull Run (July 1861) provided a clear example of this strategy.

The Civil War was one of the first great conflicts fought with firearms. It was won only when one side had been worn down after years of fighting—not destroyed quickly in Napoleonic fashion.

World War I was directed by generals who tried to imitate Napoleon. There were long them, however, joined late in the war and made only token contributions to the war effort.

Innovations in Warfare

World War I was an industrialized war. Industry produced weapons with the same efficient mass production methods that it had applied to other items.

One of the most important weapons of World War I was the machine gun. Its sweeping, rapid-fire spray of bullets made it so deadly that armies often found any advance difficult and costly. To protect themselves from the machine gun's raking fire and from artillery bombardments, soldiers dug elaborate systems of trenches.

Both sides used weapons that had never been tried before. In 1916 the British introduced the tank, an armored vehicle on which guns were mounted. Tanks enabled troops to tear through barbed wire and break through enemy lines.

Another untried weapon was the recently invented airplane. Although these first airplanes were not very maneuverable or fast, they sometimes engaged in air battles called dogfights. However, the airplanes were primarily used for observing troop movements and for dropping explosives.

Germany became the first nation to make extensive use of submarines. Its U-boats (from the German word *unterwasser*, meaning "underwater") damaged Allied shipping. The Germans also introduced poison gas, which the Allies later employed.

Except for the wars of the French Revolution, most previous European wars had been fought by professional soldiers whose only source of income was their military pay and rations. In contrast, armies of drafted civilians fought the battles of World War I. Those who could not fight worked at home to help the war effort. Many women participated by working in factories. This type of war became known as total war. To stir the patriotism of the people, governments made wide use of **propaganda**—ideas, facts, or rumors spread deliberately to further one's cause or to damage an opposing cause. Newspapers and popular magazines portrayed the enemy as brutal and subhuman, while praising national aims and achievements.

The War from 1914 to 1916

Germany's attack on France, launched through neutral Belgium, nearly succeeded. By September,

German troops had reached the Marne River near Paris. But the French army stood fast and Paris was saved.

The Battle of the Marne changed the entire nature of the war. Germany's hope of swift victory ended. Both armies dug trenches on the western front, which stretched from the Swiss border to the shores of the North Sea.

On the eastern front, the Russians completed mobilization much more quickly than the Germans had expected. One Russian army moved westward toward Budapest, the capital of Hungary. A second army moved through East Prussia, threatening the important Baltic seaport of Danzig.

In late August this second Russian army met a German force in a fierce battle at Tannenberg, in East Prussia (see map, this page). The Russians

Learning from Maps The Central Powers controlled most of Russia's land around the Baltic Sea. What port city did the Russians control?

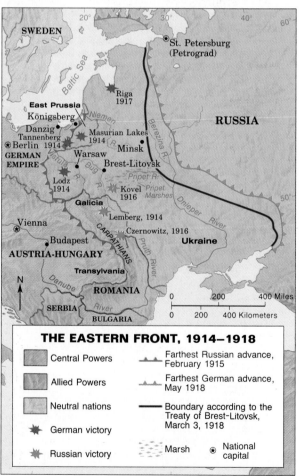

AZIMUTHAL EQUAL AREA PROJECTION

648

Codes and Ciphers

Codes have been used as secret ways of communicating for thousands of years. The ancient Egyptians flew code flags on their ships, and in medieval Europe the Beggars' Association marked houses with signs meaning "food" or "vicious dog." Anyone who knows the key to a code, whether the code consists of flags, signs, or smoke signals, can understand the message.

Most often we think of codes as involving secret messages, danger, and spying activities in wartime (above). The most common way to devise codes for secret messages is by the use of ciphers. A cipher is a letter, number, or symbol that replaces the normal alphabet in a coded message. Since the Japanese and the Chinese languages do not use alphabets, they cannot be used to create ciphers. But all other languages have found this the best method of sending secret, coded messages.

By the time of World War I, coded communication had become so important that the British decided to create a special department of crypt-analysts or cryptographers. These were people who studied ways of solving codes and ciphers. The department operated in the Office of Naval Intelligence and helped the war effort significantly. For example, the British captured the keys to two German codes: the book of naval codes and the official diplomatic cipher system. These keys enabled the British to read a number of vital secret messages and helped them figure out how other German codes worked.

Today computers (above) and satellite dishes (top) have become the main tools for cryptographers. Although they are now much more complicated, codes and ciphers remain an essential form of communication.

retreated after suffering a humiliating defeat. Soon afterward the Germans launched an offensive in the east and drove the Russians completely out of Germany and eastward into Russian Poland.

The Gallipoli campaign. Russia had a large army, but it lacked enough guns and ammunition to properly equip its soldiers. In 1915 Great Britain and France decided on a daring venture to try to help Russia. They would attempt to force their way through the Dardanelles and capture Constantinople on the Bosporus and Sea of Marmara.

At first the British and French thought that bombardment from their heavily armed battleships would force the Ottomans to surrender Constantinople. After five days of Allied bombardment, troops landed on the Gallipoli (guh • LIP • uh • lee) Peninsula in an effort to establish a foothold on the beach. The Turks, supervised by German officers, resisted stubbornly. After eight months of fighting and the loss of 145,000 men killed or wounded, the Allies abandoned the attempt.

Naval warfare. Since the British had not achieved quick victory on land, they decided to blockade the North Sea to keep merchant ships from reaching Germany. Originally the British set up the blockade to prevent the Germans from getting raw materials to manufacture war equipment. Gradually, however, the blockade became an attempt to starve the German people and ruin their economy.

Germany also set up a naval blockade. Employing its fleet of U-boats, Germany attempted to force Great Britain to surrender by sinking ships carrying food and munitions to the British.

In May 1915, without warning, a German submarine sank the British passenger liner *Lusitania* off the coast of Ireland. The sinking of the *Lusitania*, which carried a cargo of war materials to England, killed 1,200 people, including 128 Americans. Woodrow Wilson, the American president, warned Germany that the United States would not tolerate another such incident. For the next two years, Germany used submarine warfare only sparingly. It did not wish to provoke the neutral Americans into entering the war on the side of the Allies.

In May 1916 the only large naval battle of the war was fought by Germany and Britain off the coast of Jutland in the North Sea. Neither side could claim total victory, but the German navy retired into the Baltic Sea, where it remained until the end of the war.

LAMBERT CONFORMAL CONIC PROJECTION

Learning from Maps The Germans never captured the city of Paris. What French cities fell to the Germans?

The War of Stalemate

By 1916 the war had reached a stalemate on land as well as at sea. Each side realized that it could not break through the other's line of trenches. A small area of land on the western front changed hands again and again, costing each side thousands of lives. The conflict had become a **war of attrition**— a slow wearing-down process in which each side tries to outlast the other.

The most famous example of such warfare occurred at Verdun, in northeastern France (see map, this page). The Germans attacked Verdun in February 1916, hoping to use the Verdun offensive to bleed the French army to death. However, after six months of fighting, the Germans gave up. At Verdun, Germany lost 330,000 soldiers; French losses were 350,000.

The Role of the United States

When World War I began in 1914, the United States declared its neutrality. Most Americans viewed the war as a European affair in which the United States should not become involved.

Trade with the belligerents. Nevertheless, the war soon affected the United States. As the strongest industrialized neutral nation, the United States became a supplier of food, raw materials, and munitions. The government insisted on the right of American citizens and business firms to trade freely with either side. However, if an American ship carried **contraband**—war materials supplied by a neutral to a belligerent nation—the goods could be seized. The United States also insisted on the right of its citizens to travel in safety on ships of any nation, neutral or belligerent.

Because of the United States' neutrality, its government could not lend money to either side. Yet the government made no effort to stop banks, corporations, or private citizens from buying bonds of foreign governments or selling goods on credit.

At the beginning of the war, American investors and businesspeople dealt with both sides. However, as the British blockade of Germany tightened, American trade became more and more one-sided. Soon the United States traded only with the Allies, who paid for most of the goods with money borrowed from American interests.

American entry into the war. Britain's propaganda impressed Americans far more than did Germany's. Graphic stories of German **atrocities**—brutal crimes of war, often committed against defenseless civilians—angered Americans. Many of these stories were untrue, but many Americans believed them because the United States got most of its war news from British sources.

In 1917 the issue of American involvement was settled. In January the German foreign minister, Alfred Zimmermann, sent a secret telegram to the German ambassador in Mexico. It instructed him to draw Mexico into the war on Germany's side. In exchange, Germany promised Mexico the return of parts of the southwestern United States that Mexico had lost in 1848. The British intercepted the telegram, decoded it, and sent it to Washington. Publication of the Zimmermann telegram in American newspapers enraged the public.

At the same time, Germany, faced with extreme food and munitions shortages, decided that the war must end before all hope of victory vanished. Germany decided to resume unrestricted submarine warfare, taking the chance that the United States would not enter the war or, if it did, that Germany could defeat Britain before the United States had time to mobilize. German submarines attacked any naval vessel, enemy or neutral, found in what Germany determined to be a "war zone."

Meanwhile, in March 1917, revolutionaries overthrew the autocratic czarist government of Russia. The leaders of the revolution promised to establish a constitutional government. After the czar's government fell, all the major Allied powers had democratic governments. Americans would more readily accept a war in which the lines were drawn between democratic and nondemocratic countries.

On April 2, 1917, President Woodrow Wilson appeared before Congress. Announcing that "the world must be made safe for democracy," he asked for a declaration of war. On April 6 Congress voted to declare war on Germany and to enter the war on the side of the Allies.

SECTION 2 REVIEW

1. **Define** propaganda, war of attrition, contraband, atrocity
2. **Identify** Central Powers, Allied Powers, U-boats, *Lusitania,* Woodrow Wilson, Alfred Zimmermann
3. **Locate** Marne River, western front, Danzig, Tannenberg, Gallipoli Peninsula, Jutland, Verdun
4. **Summarizing Ideas** **(a)** As the war began, what advantages did the Central Powers have? **(b)** the Allied Powers?
5. **Classifying Ideas** Name some important new weapons and military techniques introduced in World War I.
6. **Analyzing Ideas** **(a)** How was the United States as a neutral power affected by World War I? **(b)** What factors led to its entry into the war?

---

3 The Russian Revolution Ended the Czarist Regime

Russia, torn by revolutionary disturbances throughout the 1800s, faced continuing problems in the early 1900s. The Revolution of 1905 brought about

Learning from Pictures *Czar Nicholas II and his family were the last absolute monarchs of Europe. What was the last order the czar gave the Duma? What was the Duma's response?*

no real changes. The elected legislative body, the Duma, had little power. The czar, Nicholas II, did not trust the Duma and remained an almost absolute ruler. Many of the Russian people, long denied the democratic rights and civil liberties that they had been promised, joined secret societies that often committed violent acts to express their members' frustration.

Grave economic problems also confronted Russia, which lagged far behind western European countries in its industrial development and agricultural methods. For example, in 1914 industrial workers made up only 1.5 percent of Russia's population, compared with 40 percent of Great Britain's population. Debts, taxes, and rents kept most Russian peasants in poverty despite their 1861 emancipation.

Russia in World War I

World War I exposed Russia's weaknesses. The country lacked enough railroads and good roads, and its industry could not adequately equip or supply its army. The Ottoman Empire's entrance into the war on the side of the Central Powers cut Russia off from outside supplies.

The Allies had counted heavily on the Russian "steamroller"—the great masses of soldiers in the Russian army. When war came, however, Russian troops proved to be poorly equipped and badly led.

The courage of the Russian soldiers could not hide an inefficient and corrupt government, which was completely unfit to deal with the problems of modern warfare. Nevertheless, for more than three years, Russian troops held back more than half the troops of the Central Powers. During this period more than 2 million Russians were killed, approximately 5 million were wounded or crippled, and more than 2 million were taken prisoner. If the Russians had not fought so well, the Allies might have lost the war.

The spring of 1917 found the Russian people weary of hardships and disheartened by the appalling casualties they had suffered in the war. The people had lost all faith in their government and in Czar Nicholas II. Strikes and street demonstrations broke out in Petrograd, as St. Petersburg had been called since 1914. The czar ordered his troops to crush the demonstrations. When the Duma demanded reforms in the government, Nicholas dissolved the legislative body.

In the past the government had always been able to use the army against disturbances such as those in Petrograd. Now, however, the soldiers joined the rioters. The Duma, encouraged by the army's disobedience, refused the czar's order to disband.

On March 15, 1917, unable to control either his subjects or his army, Nicholas II abdicated. He and his family were executed the following year. The Romanov dynasty that had maintained Russian autocracy for 300 years was finished.

Lenin and the Bolsheviks

A liberal provisional government was set up to rule Russia until a constitutional assembly could be elected to choose a permanent system of government. While the provisional government tried to restore order, a rival force worked for change in Russia.

Known as the Petrograd Soviet of Workers' and Soldiers' Deputies (*soviet* is the Russian word for council), the rival force had been quickly organized when disorders began in Russia. The leaders modeled the Petrograd Soviet on similar organizations that had participated in the Revolution of 1905. Most members of the Petrograd Soviet were moderate socialists called Mensheviks. The organization also included a small number of radical socialists, known as Bolsheviks.

Other soviets similar to the one in Petrograd sprang up. Many people throughout Russia supported their program, which was more attractive than that of the provisional government. The program called for immediate peace, land reform, and the turning over of factories to the workers.

The leader of the Bolsheviks, Nikolai Lenin, was born Vladimir Ilyich Ulyanov, but he assumed the name Nikolai Lenin as a young man. An intelligent and forceful person, Lenin came from the middle class and had studied law. After his older brother was executed by the czarist police as a revolutionary, Lenin became a revolutionary himself.

On April 16, 1917, Lenin returned to Russia from exile in Switzerland. His first act was to insist that all governing power be turned over to the soviets.

Lenin was a radical socialist, but he favored a modified Marxism, partly because of the conditions that existed in Russia. Lenin believed that because Russia had comparatively little industry and only a small working class, the forces of history there might not move in the direction Marx had predicted. Therefore, he advocated the establishment of a small group of dedicated Marxists. This group would train the workers to become a revolutionary force. Lenin's adaptation of Marxism formed the basis of what we now know as Russian communism. His slogan, "Land, Peace, and Bread," reached the hearts of the masses.

On November 7, 1917, the Bolsheviks overthrew the provisional government and seized control of Russia. This revolution is often called the Second Russian Revolution (the first having been in March), or the Bolshevik Revolution. In the spring of 1918, the Bolsheviks renamed themselves the Communist Party.

Civil War

The Communists signed peace treaties with each of the Central Powers early in 1918 at Brest-Litovsk. Russia anxiously made peace on any terms, since its army was exhausted from three years of bitter fighting. The harsh treaties forced Russia to give up a sizable amount of territory.

The new regime then turned its attention to internal problems. The Communists faced much opposition within Russia, not only from former aristocrats and other reactionaries, but also from middle-class liberals and the Mensheviks. In

Learning from Pictures Germany allowed Lenin to pass through its territory on his way back to Russia from Switzerland. German leaders hoped that the fiery Bolshevik would take Russia out of the war.

scattered groups, opposition forces tried to overthrow the Communists in a civil war.

The Communists had adopted red, the symbolic color of European revolutionary socialism, as their color. For this reason they became known as the Reds. Those who opposed the Communists were called the Whites. The civil war, which began in early 1918, lasted almost three years, adding to the devastation begun by World War I. The Red Army—as the forces of the new government were called—fought many battles with the White armies, leaving an appalling trail of destruction.

The Allies had been angered by the new Russian government's signing of separate peace treaties with the Central Powers. They also feared that if the Communists gained control of Russia, the revolution would spread. Therefore, the Allies aided the White forces with arms and money. Several nations, including the United States, even sent small forces of troops to help overthrow the Communist government. The Allies helped prolong the civil war, but they could not change the result. By 1921 the Communists had completely defeated the White forces.

1. **Identify** Petrograd Soviet, Mensheviks, Bolsheviks, Nikolai Lenin, Reds
2. **Locate** Brest-Litovsk
3. **Understanding Cause and Effect** **(a)** What were the causes of the Russian Revolution in March 1917? **(b)** What were the immediate effects of the Revolution? **(c)** What were the far-reaching effects?
4. **Organizing Ideas** What kind of program did the Petrograd Soviet propose for Russia?
5. **Explaining Ideas** Explain the type of Marxism that Lenin advocated for Russia.
6. **Analyzing Ideas** How did the signing of the peace treaty by the Communists in 1918 help the new regime establish power?

4 After Achieving Victory, the Allies Drafted Peace Terms

President Wilson's statement of America's aim in entering the war—to make the world "safe for democracy"—held a lofty and idealistic theme. However, the November 1917 Russian Revolution and Russia's signing of a separate peace treaty with Germany at Brest-Litovsk dampened Allied morale. Meanwhile, the Russians published the terms of the secret treaties signed by the Allies when Italy entered the war.

The Fourteen Points

The revelation that their governments were fighting for bits of land made the war seem shoddy to many people on the Allied side. British Prime Minister David Lloyd George tried to undo the bad impression these revelations left. He stated more idealistic aims in a speech to Parliament. However, it was President Wilson who best expressed what many people thought the Allied aims should be. In a speech to Congress in January 1918, Wilson announced his **Fourteen Points.** Six of the points contained plans of a general nature (points 1–5 and 14). The eight remaining points dealt with specific countries and regions, such as Russia, Belgium, Alsace-Lorraine, and the Balkans.

The six general proposals may be summarized as follows: (1) No secret treaties. (2) Freedom of the seas for all nations. (3) Removal of all economic barriers or tariffs. (4) Reduction of national armaments. (5) Fair adjustment of all colonial claims, with equal consideration given to the people of a region and the nation. (14) Establishment of "a general association of nations," which would guarantee political independence and protection to large and small states alike.

The Fourteen Points caught the imagination of people everywhere and raised the morale of Allied troops. Copies dropped behind the German lines made the German people willing to surrender. Some historians believe, however, that Wilson made one serious mistake. During the war, when his influence was the greatest, he did not make the Allies promise to accept the Fourteen Points.

Defeat of the Central Powers

The Treaty of Brest-Litovsk with Russia allowed the Germans to withdraw troops from the eastern front and concentrate their efforts on a huge offensive in the west during the spring and summer of 1918. This offensive represented a last desperate gamble to break through the Allied lines, capture Paris, and end the war before the Americans could arrive in strength and turn the tide.

The German offensive lasted until mid-July. It almost succeeded. In May the Germans reached the Marne River, only 37 miles (59 kilometers) from Paris. By this time, however, more than 250,000 Americans were landing in France every month.

Under a newly organized joint command, headed by the French general Ferdinand Foch (FAWSH), the Allied forces stopped the Germans in June at Château-Thierry (shah•toh-tye•REE). In July the Allies began to counterattack. A final Allied push in September at St. Mihiel (san mee•YEL) and in the Argonne Forest forced the German armies back to the borders of Germany (see map, page 650).

At the same time, conditions worsened for the Central Powers in the Middle East and the Balkans. Bulgaria, seeing little hope for victory or for help from its allies, surrendered first, in September 1918. The Turks soon asked for peace also. By November a revolution in Austria-Hungary had brought the old Hapsburg Empire to an end. Austria and Hungary then formed separate governments.

In Germany the government of Kaiser William II soon collapsed. Woodrow Wilson had said he

Learning from Pictures *These victorious American soldiers march through the Arch of Triumph, France's equivalent of our Tomb of the Unknown Soldier.*

would deal only with a government that truly represented the German people. Many Germans, wishing to end the war, looked upon the kaiser as an obstacle to peace. On November 9 the kaiser abdicated and the German Republic was proclaimed.

On November 11, 1918, the chancellor of the new German Republic signed an **armistice,** an agreement to stop fighting until a treaty can be drawn up. The armistice provided that at the eleventh hour on the eleventh day of the eleventh month of 1918, all fighting would cease. The Germans grimly signed the armistice in a railroad car in the forest of Compiègne (kohmp • YAYN) in France.

According to the severe terms of the armistice, Germany had to cancel the Treaty of Brest-Litovsk that it had forced the Russians to sign. Germany also had to surrender all its submarines and a large part of its surface fleet. In addition, it had to release all war prisoners and turn over munitions that might make additional fighting possible. The Allies reserved the right to occupy all German territory west of the Rhine River and a narrow strip of land along the east bank of the Rhine.

Costs of the War

The costs of World War I stagger the imagination. Each of the belligerent nations suffered enormous and lasting consequences. Reliable estimates indicate that the war left more than 10 million soldiers dead and over 20 million more wounded—many of them crippled for life.

Militarily, Russia suffered the most severely, losing more than 2 million people. Germany lost almost that many, and France and its colonies lost nearly 1.5 million. Austria and Hungary counted 1.25 million dead after the war, Great Britain almost 1 million. American lives lost numbered 115,000.

For the first time in history, civilian casualties numbered almost as many as those among the armed forces. Naval blockades, artillery and aerial bombardments, famine, disease, and political violence all took their toll. The destruction of property was appalling. One historian has estimated that the total cost was $400 billion.

The Peace Conference at Paris

After the armistice in November 1918, the Allies faced the task of arranging peace terms. President Wilson had written and spoken of a peace conference in which both sides would write a treaty that was fair to all. However, the war had caused so much bitterness and had cost so much in terms of human lives and property that the Allies were determined to dictate the terms of peace.

Delegates of the victorious nations met in Paris in January 1919. Almost all the Allied Powers sent representatives. Russia, in the midst of a civil war, was the only Allied power not invited.

The Allies agreed to call in representatives of the defeated powers only to accept the terms of the treaties. They decided that a separate treaty should be written for each of the defeated Central Powers. Since Austria and Hungary now had separate governments, five treaties had to be drawn up. In

History Through the Arts

PAINTED GLASS

Duchamp and the Dadaists

World War I raged violently for four years. When it ended, more than 20 million soldiers and civilians had lost their lives. Such devastation did not go unnoticed in the art world. Artists expressed their anger and bitterness over the war by producing anti-art, works that mocked the values of a society that could have supported the war. This school of art was called *Dada.* * Some critics refer to Dadaistic works as non-art.

Buenos Aires, 1918. Oil paint, silver leaf, lead wire, and magnifying lens on glass (cracked), 19½ × 15⅝" (49.5 × 39.7 cm), mounted between two panes of glass in a standing metal frame, 20⅛ × 16¼ × 1½" (51 × 41.2 × 3.7 cm), on painted wood base 1⅞ × 17⅞ × 4½" (4.8 × 45.3 × 11.4 cm); overall height 22' (55.8 cm). Collection, The Museum of Modern Art, New York. Katherine S. Dreier Bequest.

Marcel Duchamp's painted glass (1918) is an example of Dada art. Its seemingly meaningless design served to criticize the war-mad world. Even its title is Dadaistic, or nonsensical: "To be looked at (from the other side of the glass) with one eye close to, for almost an hour." When this piece and others by Duchamp were accidentally cracked, the artist seemed not to care. He said the fracture lines enhanced his initial design. Perhaps Duchamp, like other Dadaists, believed the war had cracked the world beyond repair.

Dada is a French word for wooden horse. A sculptor and a German writer accidently discovered the word in a dictionary. They liked the sound and brevity of the word and because a wooden horse is useless, as they believed the violence of World War I was, they applied it to the art form.

theory, the representatives of all the victorious nations had a hand in writing the treaties. In fact, the work had been done in advance, behind the scenes, by the leaders of the four most powerful Allies—Great Britain, France, the United States, and Italy. Known as the Big Four, the leaders were Prime Minister David Lloyd George of Great Britain, Premier Georges Clemenceau (klem • uhn • SOH) of France, President Woodrow Wilson of the United States, and Premier Vittorio Orlando of Italy.

Problems Facing the Peacemakers

By 1919 Europe faced a confusing political situation. Republics replaced hereditary monarchies in the three great empires of Germany, Austria-Hungary, and Russia. A fourth empire, that of the Ottoman Turks, tottered on the brink of collapse. Nationalist groups pressed their claims in Russia and the defeated empires. Each group wanted independence, self-government, and unity within the borders of a single nation. Nationalism took hold in colonial possessions as well.

Territorial claims. The victorious nations had many conflicting territorial demands that they found difficult to reconcile. France wanted, above all, security from another German attack. It insisted on the return of the former provinces of Alsace and Lorraine, which had been guaranteed

in the Fourteen Points. In addition, it demanded that the French boundary be extended to the Rhine River so that France would possess the Rhineland, a territory located on the west bank of the Rhine in Germany. France also demanded the Saar River valley, with its valuable deposits of coal.

Italy claimed the Tirol region and the city of Trieste in accordance with the secret treaties it had made in 1915. It also claimed Fiume (FYOO • may), although this port city had not been promised in the secret treaties. Lloyd George, Wilson, and Clemenceau gave in willingly on the Tirol region. However, Wilson steadfastly opposed giving Fiume to Italy. The controversy became so bitter that Orlando left the conference and went home in disgust. The Big Four then became the Big Three.

Belgium, which had suffered under wartime German occupation, requested two small portions of German territory along the border. Great Britain wanted Germany's African colonies. It also insisted that the German navy be destroyed and that Germany be prohibited from building warships.

During the war Japan had occupied the previously German-held Marshall, Caroline, and Mariana islands, as well as Qingdao and most of the Shandong Peninsula. Japan now demanded permanent ownership of all these regions. It also asked that the powers recognize its "special position" in China. This meant, in effect, that in any further

BUILDING HISTORY STUDY SKILLS

Interpreting Visuals: Using a Map as a Historical Document

The Congress of Vienna in 1815 resulted in border changes in Europe (see maps entitled "Napoleonic Europe, 1805–1815," Chapter 17, page 442 and "Europe After the Congress of Vienna, 1815," Chapter 17, page 446). Studying changes in the map of Europe before and after the Congress of Vienna helps you to understand the political and historical development of Europe before World War I.

A major goal of the participants at the Congress of Vienna was keeping France in check to prevent the aggression that Napoleon had engaged in. Consequently, the Austrian Netherlands (Belgium) united with Holland (Dutch Netherlands) to act as a buffer state. The Rhineland became the border of Prussia. Savoy and Genoa were added to Sardinia to make Sardinia a larger state along the border of France. Lombardy and Venetia in northern Italy were given to Austria to lessen the temptation to invade France. The changes at the Congress of Vienna did not allow for self-determination; the overall principle focused on the balance of power. Do you notice any other balance-of-power provisions based on the changes in the two maps? What consequences did this have for the historical development of Europe?

How to Use a Map as a Historical Document

To use a map as a historical document, follow these steps.

1. Identify the topic of the map.
2. Identify the historical context of the map.
3. Explain what information about the topic is included on the map.
4. Connect the information on the map to the historical context of the topic.
5. Make comparisons with other maps.

Developing the Skill

World War I created new borders on the map of Europe. The Treaty of Versailles changed the nature of Europe's geography, economy, and politics. Studying a map of Europe before and after the Treaty of Versailles, just as you have studied a map of Europe before and after the Congress of Vienna, also helps you to understand the political and historical development of Europe. Now look at the maps entitled "Europe on the Eve of World War I, 1914" on page 644 and "Europe After the Paris Peace Settlements, 1919–1920" on page 659. How did Europe change? How did these changes affect European history?

The historical context involves the impact of World War I on Europe. The maps illustrate many ways in which Europe changed after World War I. Germany lost Alsace-Lorraine to France; Serbia became part of Yugoslavia; Austria-Hungary was divided into Austria, Hungary, Czechoslovakia, and Yugoslavia. Poland reappeared, and the Soviet Union became the Union of Soviet Socialist Republics. The Polish Corridor was created out of part of Germany, and Germany lost part of its access to the Baltic Sea. The maps give clues as to the impact on European history. The large empires could no longer serve as a balancing force, and Europe was divided into many small countries. An attempt was made to prevent German aggression (as at the Congress of Vienna there was an attempt to prevent French aggression). Alsace-Lorraine and the Polish Corridor, for example, were two limits on Germany. However, the changes also contained the seeds of a future war because of the political aspects of German antagonism and national security interests.

Practicing the skill. Look at a map of Europe showing non-Communist nations at the end of World War II. Then look at a recent map showing the Soviet Union and that country's satellite nations. What can you conclude about the spread of communism since 1945?

To apply this skill, see Applying History Study Skills on page 663.

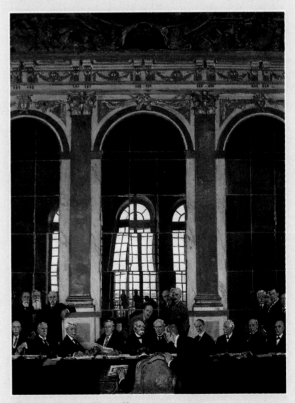

The Big Four at Versailles

657

seizure of Chinese territory, Japan was to have the first choice and the largest share. A bitter fight and Japan's threat to leave the conference caused Wilson to give in on the Shandong Peninsula.

Reparations and peacekeeping. The destruction caused by the war brought up the problem of **reparations**—payment for war damages. Who should pay for restoring the land? Did war damages include damage to property only? Or should reparations also include pensions to wounded veterans and to widows and orphans?

Finally, the conference had to consider the issue of a world organization to maintain peace. The formation of a League of Nations had widespread appeal, but many European leaders doubted its chances for success.

The Peace: Justice or Vengeance?

Early in the conference, two conflicting viewpoints surfaced. The British, French, and Italian governments had appeared to support the Fourteen Points. Yet they had never really given up the aims stated in the secret treaties—to divide the territories taken from the Central Powers among themselves after the war. The Fourteen Points represented a "peace of justice," whereas the terms of the secret treaties represented a "peace of vengeance."

Wilson believed that the conference must write a "peace of justice." Many people disagreed. The war had left bitterness, hatred, and a longing for revenge. Many of the victors believed that the defeated must be taught a lesson. Only harsh treatment could teach Germany and Austria the consequences of starting a war.

SECTION 4 REVIEW

1. **Define** Fourteen Points, armistice, reparations
2. **Identify** Ferdinand Foch, Paris Peace Conference, Big Four, Big Three, League of Nations
3. **Locate** Château-Thierry, St. Mihiel, Rhineland, Saar River valley, Tirol, Trieste, Fiume
4. **Summarizing Ideas** (a) What were the six general proposals of Wilson's Fourteen Points? (b) What effect did the Fourteen Points have?
5. **Interpreting Ideas** Describe the territorial demands the following nations made after World War I: (a) France; (b) Italy; (c) Great Britain; (d) Belgium; (e) Japan.
6. **Evaluating Ideas** (a) Why did Wilson believe in a "peace of justice"? (b) Why did others oppose this belief?

5 The Peace Treaties Created a "New Europe"

The victors made separate treaties with each of the five Central Powers. The most famous was the Versailles Treaty with Germany.

The Versailles Treaty

In May 1919 leaders of the new German Republic were called in, presented with a peace treaty, and told to sign it. The Germans complained bitterly that the treaty did not follow the Fourteen Points. They objected especially to two features. First, the treaty made Germany admit that it alone was guilty of starting the war and therefore must pay reparations. Second, the treaty did not specify the amount of reparations. In spite of their protest, the Germans had no choice but to sign.

Under the Versailles Treaty, Germany agreed to pay $5 billion in reparations within two years and an unspecified sum later. In 1921 the Allies set the total amount at $33 billion. The treaty also provided for the formation of the League of Nations and for numerous territorial adjustments.

Germany lost considerable territory along its northern, western, and eastern borders (see map, page 659) as well as its overseas colonies. Germany agreed not to fortify the Rhineland, which Allied troops would occupy for an unspecified period of time. The Saar Valley would fall under the administration of the League of Nations for 15 years. During that time all of the coal mined in the area would go to France in partial payment of reparations. At the end of 15 years, the people of the region were to vote on whether to continue under the League, to become part of France, or to rejoin Germany.

The restored nation of Poland received a large area of German land. This region included the Polish Corridor, which cut off East Prussia from the rest of Germany and gave Poland an outlet to the Baltic Sea. Danzig became a free city administered by the League of Nations.

Germany had to abolish conscription and could not maintain a reserve army. It was not allowed to manufacture heavy artillery, tanks, military airplanes, or poison gas. In addition, Germany could have no submarines and no battleships larger

**EUROPE AFTER THE
PARIS PEACE SETTLEMENTS
1919–1920**

— Former boundary
⊛ National capital
• Other city

AZIMUTHAL EQUAL AREA PROJECTION

Learning from Maps *After World War I nine new countries were added to the continent
of Europe. Which of these countries now had a coastline on the Mediterranean Sea?*

than 10,000 tons. The authors of the treaties imposed these measures to ensure that Germany would be a peacekeeping nation. However, although the Allies made strict rules for Germany, they had weak means of enforcing them.

Austria-Hungary

The Dual Monarchy split in two as the war ended. Therefore, the victors arranged one treaty with Austria in September 1919 and a separate treaty with Hungary in June 1920. Austria, now recognized as an independent republic, lost the southern Tirol and the city of Trieste to Italy. The new republic could not grow enough food for its people or supply its industries with adequate raw materials. Austria rapidly sank into financial crisis and poverty.

Hungary lost a great deal of the territory it had governed under the Dual Monarchy to the new nation of Czechoslovakia that included Czechs, Slovaks, and Ruthenians. In the western Balkans, the new nation of Yugoslavia united the former independent kingdoms of Serbia and Montenegro, the former Hapsburg provinces of Bosnia and Herzegovina, and a section of the Adriatic coast.

Bulgaria and the Ottoman Empire

The victors also penalized Bulgaria. According to the terms of its peace treaty, signed in 1919, Bulgaria lost territory, including its outlet to the Aegean Sea, which went to Greece.

The Ottoman Empire paid an even higher price for being on the losing side. Its treaty, signed in 1920, resulted in a great loss of territory. Although Constantinople and the Dardanelles and Bosporus remained in Turkish hands, they had to be unfortified and controlled by an international commission.

Several new nations—Palestine, Trans-Jordan, and Syria (including present-day Lebanon)—eventually emerged from former Turkish territory along the eastern Mediterranean Sea. Turkish territory farther east became the country of Iraq. Only the kingdom of Hejaz in Arabia, however, gained immediate independence. The others were administered by Great Britain or France under the supervision of the League of Nations.

New Problems After the War

By altering political boundaries and territories, the peace settlements created some serious problems. Four new nations—Finland, Estonia, Latvia, and Lithuania—had formed along the Baltic Sea, in territory previously held by Russia. In 1918 these nations had declared their independence from Russia, and the victorious powers recognized their sovereignty at the end of the war. Much of the territory of restored Poland also came from Russia. In addition, Russia lost the province of Bessarabia, in the southwest, to a greatly enlarged Romania.

Another problem grew out of the attempt to solve the problem of national self-determination by uniting people of each nationality under their own government. This did not always succeed. For example, there were 250,000 German-speaking Austrians in the Tirol, which came partly under Italian rule. Germans lived in Danzig and the Polish Corridor. Almost 3 million former Austrian subjects—a German-speaking group called Sudeten Germans—lived in Czechoslovakia.

These national minorities, people of one nationality living under a government controlled by another nationality, presented a problem. Therefore, all five treaties contained clauses in which each government pledged to treat fairly any minority group within its borders. Each minority group was guaranteed certain rights, to be protected by the League of Nations.

Dissatisfied minorities. President Wilson held out the promise of independent nationhood for all national groups, most of whom had belonged to one of the great empires that vanished at the end of the war. But peoples such as the Armenians and Kurds, who lived in the Ottoman Empire, never saw this promise fulfilled. They suffered greatly at the hands of the larger national groups under which they were placed. During World War I, the Ottoman government had carried out terrible atrocities against the Armenians, whom the Ottomans believed to be disloyal. Today some Armenians live in one of the republics constituting the Soviet Union. Others continue to live in Turkey. Today Kurds hold out a forlorn hope of a Kurdistan that they can call home.

The League of Nations

In helping to draft the peace settlements, President Wilson made several compromises with the ideals of his Fourteen Points. He realized that the treaties failed in many respects to provide a "peace of justice." He consoled himself, however, with the thought that the new League of Nations would be able to remedy the injustices inflicted by the treaties.

While diplomats hammered out the treaty settlements, a special commission, which included Wilson, wrote the covenant of the League of Nations. This covenant, adopted by the Paris conference, became part of the Versailles Treaty.

Organization. According to the covenant, the League of Nations had two main aims: (1) to promote international cooperation, and (2) to maintain peace by settling disputes peacefully and by reducing armaments. The League was to include all independent sovereign nations. Three main agencies—an assembly, a council, and a secretariat—would conduct League business. The League was to work closely with a related but independent body, the Permanent Court of International Justice, or World Court, located at The Hague.

The Assembly was to be a sort of lower house composed of representatives of all member nations. Regardless of size, each nation was to have one vote. The Council, an upper house, was to be composed of 9 member nations (later increased to 15). It was to consist of 5 permanent members—Great

Learning from Pictures *The lack of support by the United States did not discourage the League of Nations. It held its first public meeting in Madrid, Spain, in 1920.*

Britain, France, Italy, Japan, and the United States—the victorious powers of the war. The remaining seats on the Council were to be filled by rotation from among the other nations.

Peacekeeping measures. The League of Nations provided a way to deal with the many problems created by imperialism in so-called "backward" regions of the world. Until the people of an area were considered ready for independence, the League took the area in trust and assumed responsibility for it. The League assigned the area as a **mandate** to be administered by the government of an advanced nation. The administering nation had to pledge that it would prepare the people of the area for self-government and would make annual reports to the League about the area's progress.

The members of the League of Nations agreed not to resort to war, promising to submit any disputes to the World Court or specially convened commissions for arbitration. The League of Nations covenant provided that if a member nation broke this agreement, the League could impose penalties. Possible penalties included breaking diplomatic relations, imposing **economic sanctions**—the refusal to trade with the offending member nation—or blockades. Military force would be considered only as a last resort.

Although the League of Nations had been Wilson's idea, the United States never became a member of the organization. Some senators disapproved of the League itself, while others wanted changes in the Versailles Treaty, which included the League covenant, and refused to ratify the treaty. President Wilson prophetically stated that if the United States did not join, another war would be fought.

Despite the absence of the United States, the 42 member nations represented at the League's first meeting at Geneva in November 1920 held an optimistic view of the future. Germany could not join the League until 1926, and Russia did not become a member until 1934. By 1935 membership in the League included 62 nations.

SECTION 5 REVIEW

1. **Define** mandate, economic sanction
2. **Identify** Treaty of Versailles, World Court
3. **Locate** Polish Corridor, Czechoslovakia, Yugoslavia, Finland, Estonia, Latvia, Lithuania
4. **Summarizing Ideas** Summarize the provisions of the Versailles Treaty concerning: **(a)** reparations, **(b)** Germany's colonies, **(c)** German military power.
5. **Using Maps** **(a)** Name six nations that lost territory and six nations that gained territory as a result of the peace treaties. **(b)** What new nations were created in Europe?
6. **Evaluating Ideas** How did the peace settlements create problems with regard to Russia and national minorities?
7. **Interpreting Ideas** **(a)** What were the aims of the League of Nations? **(b)** What were its main agencies? **(c)** What provisions did it make for peacekeeping?

661

CHAPTER 24 REVIEW

AD   Formation of Triple Alliance 1882   Accession of William II in Germany 1888

Chapter Summary

The following list contains the key concepts you have learned about World War I and the Russian Revolution.

1. Suspicions among European nations intensified in the early 1900s. These suspicions were caused by strong national feelings, the spread of imperialism, growing militaristic buildups, and a system of rival alliances.
2. The 1914 assassination of Archduke Francis Ferdinand in Sarajevo sparked World War I.
3. Within a few months, almost all the nations of Europe, plus Japan, were at war.
4. Everyone expected the conflict to be over quickly and decisively. Instead, the struggle dragged on for four long years of trench warfare.
5. In Russia a revolution toppled the 300-year-long rule of the Romanov dynasty and abolished the monarchy.
6. Germany tried and failed in a final drive to break the military deadlock. In early 1918 Russia and Germany signed a peace treaty that put Russia out of the war. The Americans provided the fresh troops and new resources that helped defeat the Central Powers.
7. Although the war ended in 1918, the problems it caused continued to plague governments for years. Many lives had been lost, much property had been destroyed, and many problems remained unresolved.
8. After the war national groups demanded recognition, especially in eastern Europe. The victors wanted to punish the losers. Violence erupted in Germany, Russia, and the former Austro-Hungarian and Ottoman territories.
9. Woodrow Wilson's Fourteen Points offered idealistic goals that might have created a peaceful and lasting framework among nations after the war. At the Paris Peace Conference, however, many of these goals were forgotten as the Allies sought to collect reparations for their wartime losses and to gain additional territory.
10. Many hoped the League of Nations would help keep the peace and settle disputes among countries. However, the United States did not join, and the League's efforts were thus crippled from the start.

On a separate sheet of paper, complete the following review exercises.

Reviewing Important Terms

Match each of the following terms with the correct definition below.

a. entente   e. mandate
b. contraband   f. reparations
c. militarism   g. armistice
d. belligerent   h. ultimatum

____ 1. Territory being prepared for independence
____ 2. Payment for war damages
____ 3. Friendly agreement between nations
____ 4. Final terms offered for a settlement
____ 5. Agreement to stop a war
____ 6. War materials supplied by a neutral to a belligerent nation
____ 7. Glorification of armed strength
____ 8. Warring nation

Developing Critical Thinking Skills

1. **Classifying Ideas** **(a)** What was the immediate cause of World War I? **(b)** What were four underlying causes?
2. **Contrasting Ideas** President Wilson believed World War I would be the "war to end all wars." **(a)** What ideals in the Fourteen Points worked toward this goal? **(b)** What obstacles blocked Wilson's efforts to carry out his plan?
3. **Interpreting Ideas** How did the Allies view the Russian Revolution and civil war?
4. **Evaluating Ideas** **(a)** How did peace negotiations readjust the balance of power in the world? **(b)** Did these changes correct the causes of World War I or ignore them? **(c)** Explain.
5. **Using Maps** Study the map on page 659. **(a)** Which of the Central Powers lost the most territory as a result of World War I? **(b)** Which of the Central Powers lost the least? **(c)** Which Allied Power lost territory? **(d)** Based on evidence in this map, what new problems might have been created by changing the political boundaries of Europe?
6. **Using Pictures** As you learned in this chapter, governments used propaganda to encourage citizens to support the war effort. Locate a copy of a propaganda poster from the era. **(a)** What techniques or symbols used in the

662

Disarmament talks held at The Hague

1899

• Disarmament talks held at The Hague
• Formation of Triple Entente

1907
1908

Annexation of Bosnia and Herzegovina by Austria-Hungary

Assassination of Archduke Francis Ferdinand

• Entrance of Italy into World War I
• Sinking of *Lusitania*

1914 1915

Beginning of World War I

• Entrance of the United States into the war
• Russian Revolution

• Defeat of the Central Powers
• Signing of the armistice

1917 1918

First meeting of the League of Nations

1920
1919

• Paris Peace Conference
• Signing of Versailles Treaty

poster might arouse a sense of patriotism? **(b)** To what other emotions does this poster seem to appeal?

7. **Analyzing Information** In assessing World War I, Prime Minister Lloyd George once commented that "no one at the head of affairs quite meant war. It was something into which they glided, or rather staggered and stumbled." **(a)** Do you agree with this interpretation of the war? **(b)** What evidence in the chapter supports your answer?

Relating Geography to History

Using information from this chapter, draw a map showing the reorganization of European nations after World War I. Then use encyclopedias or other library references to show the reorganization of European nations immediately following World War II and the later realignment of Communist nations.

Relating Past to Present

1. Review the following causes of World War I: nationalism, militarism, imperialism, and international alliances. Which of these forces are still present in the world? Clip newspaper or magazine articles that support your answer.

2. Before World War I, the Balkan region was known as the "powder keg of Europe." **(a)** Why was it given this name? **(b)** Are there any similar trouble spots in the world today? **(c)** If so, what actions might be taken to keep them defused? **(d)** What can be done to prevent another Balkan situation from occurring?

3. In 1899 and again in 1907, several nations participated in disarmament conferences held at The Hague. Using the *Readers' Guide to Periodical Literature,* locate articles about recent disarmament talks between the United States and the Soviet Union. Are any of the obstacles to disarmament the same as those faced in the late 1800s and early 1900s? Are any unique to the present? Explain.

Applying History Study Skills

Before completing this activity, review Building History Study Skills on page 657.

Study the maps entitled "Europe in 1916" on page 645 and "The Eastern Front 1914–1918" on page 648. Then answer the following questions to help you use the maps as historical documents.

1. Why would the Central Powers be more successful in the east than in the west?

2. Why was the Brest-Litovsk line important to the Central Powers?

3. Which side do you think had the greater strategic advantage? Why?

4. Why do you think Switzerland was neutral?

5. What military strategy enabled the Allied Powers to win? Why?

6. What strategy could the Central Powers have followed that might have enabled them to succeed? Why?

7. Why can these maps be described as historical documents?

Investigating Further

1. **Writing a Report** While troops bogged down in the muddy trenches of Europe, other battles were taking place in the skies. Write a short report on developments in air warfare during World War I. Also investigate the pilots who flew these missions, such as Baron von Richthofen (the "Red Baron"), Eddie Rickenbacker, or members of the Lafayette Escadrille. One source for your report is Quentin Reynolds's *They Fought for the Sky: The Dramatic Story of the First War in the Air* (Holt, Rinehart and Winston).

2. **Preparing a Book Report** Read one of the following novels and present a book report to the class: Ernest Hemingway's *A Farewell to Arms* (Scribner); Erich Maria Remarque's *All Quiet on the Western Front* (Fawcett); Willa Cather's *One of Ours* (Random House). Note the author's point of view on war. How does it compare with the idealism expressed by President Wilson at the start of World War I?

3. **Conducting Research** Using a variety of references from your library, conduct research on one of the following World War I topics: **(a)** the role of blacks, **(b)** the role of women, **(c)** music and literature of the period, **(d)** military technology. Report your findings to the class.

25

The Great Depression Helped the Rise of Totalitarian Dictators

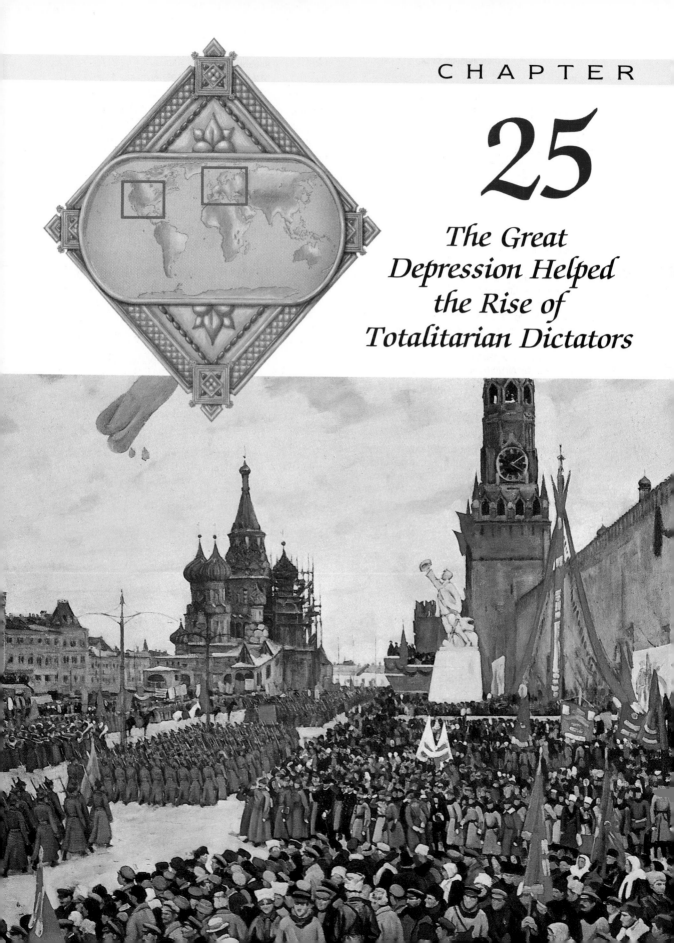

Place Europe and the United States

Time 1919–1936

3.7 mil. BC   4000 BC   AD 2100

Significance

World War I, according to Woodrow Wilson, was fought to make the world "safe for democracy." For a time immediately following the war, it seemed as if this aim had been achieved.

However, the war dramatically changed how people viewed the world. Disgusted by the death and destruction of World War I, writers and painters began reacting against traditional forms of literature and art.

The tremendous economic prosperity that appeared immediately after the war soon crumbled into a terrible economic depression. This caused a cynical view of life to prevail.

Postwar tensions extended into politics as many democratic nations struggled to survive, particularly in Europe. **Totalitarian regimes**—highly centralized governments that allowed no opposition and held total control—seemed to offer Europeans security amid the instability and uncertainty of the period. Tragically, this era served only as a prelude to an even more devastating war.

Terms to Define

cubism	fascism
functionalism	corporate state
market speculation	collective farm
nationalize	purge

People to Identify

Pablo Picasso	Adolf Hitler
Benito Mussolini	Joseph Stalin

Places to Locate

Ural Mountains	Vladivostok

Questions to Guide Your Reading

1 How did the uneasiness of the postwar era affect the arts and the development of new ideas?
2 How did postwar prosperity eventually crumble into a worldwide depression?
3 What political tensions developed in postwar Europe?
4 How were totalitarian dictatorships established in postwar Italy and Germany?
5 How did Stalin firmly establish communism in the Soviet Union?

During the 1930s a natural disaster overtook the American farmer as an 18-month drought destroyed farmland from Texas to the Dakotas. As the drought continued, wind blew the dry topsoil into swirling dustclouds, turning the region into what became known as the Dust Bowl. These conditions forced many farm families to leave their homes. In his novel, The Grapes of Wrath, John Steinbeck describes the hardships of Dust Bowl families as they prepare to leave Oklahoma for the fields of California.

❝ *I*n the little houses the tenant people sifted their belongings and the belongings of their fathers and of their grandfathers. Picked over their possessions for the journey to the west. The men were ruthless because the past had been spoiled, but the women knew how the past would cry to them in the coming days. . . . How can we live without our lives? How will we know it's us without our past? No. Leave it. Burn it. . . . And they piled up the goods in the yards and set fire to them. They stood and watched them burning, and then frantically they loaded up the cars and drove away, drove in the dust. The dust hung in the air for a long time after the loaded cars had passed. ❞

Just as these families experienced hardships, so, too, did many millions struggle during the years between the two world wars.

1 An Uneasy Postwar Era Affected the Arts and Ideas

World War I disrupted people's lives. Everything seemed unsettled, and all traditional values seemed under attack. A journalist writing in 1938 offered an impression of these times:

❝ *S*piritually and morally, civilization collapsed on August 1, 1914—the civilization . . . which with all its shortcomings did give more satisfaction to more people than any other yet evolved. Young people cannot realize how the world has been coarsened and barbarized since 1914. They may feel the loss of security . . . but they cannot appreciate how much else has been lost. ❞

◀ *A Red Army parade in Moscow*

The work of the leading thinkers, writers, and artists of the time heightened this sense of disquiet and uncertainty.

The Effects of New Scientific Ideas

Following World War I, many people rejected the beliefs of reason and progress first expressed during the Enlightenment. Instead they felt a sense of helplessness and cynicism. Scientists, who since the 1600s had been proving that human beings could solve almost any problem, had begun to suggest something else in the early 1900s. During this period some people interpreted the ideas of psychologist Sigmund Freud, for example, to mean that people could no longer be quite so confident about the powers of rational thought.

Freudian psychology. Sigmund Freud had developed theories of the unconscious (see Chapter 20). He believed that the unconscious mind governed human behavior. In Freud's opinion people were generally unaware of the mental processes of the unconscious. Freud had begun writing in the early 1900s, but his ideas about the unconscious mind and irrationality did not gain popularity until after World War I. If people believed that they could not rationally control their actions, then much that seemed bewildering could be explained. These ideas seemed to help people understand why the dreadful devastation of World War I had taken place, why things had not turned out as they had hoped, and why the uneasiness was continuing.

Einstein's physics. The theory of relativity made Albert Einstein famous (see Chapter 20). In this theory he had argued that even such seemingly absolute and definite concepts as space, motion, and time had to be seen as relative, or dependent on one another. This concept gave comfort to those who denied that any standard, whether of morality or of artistic taste, was absolute. Believers in this concept argued that attitudes depended on the individual—that they were relative to each person. They claimed that Einstein's physics supported their view.

Certainty in basic scientific measurements no longer seemed possible. As a result, people believed that science no longer provided indisputable knowledge. This change in attitude destroyed the assumption that constant progress would unlock the secrets of nature. It also added to a sense of unease and a lack of confidence in the future. The

scientists intensified, rather than relieved, the uncertainty and the doubts about traditional attitudes that marked the postwar world.

New Directions in Literature

The major writings of World War I and the postwar years revealed a dissatisfaction not only with the times but with the way books and poems had been written in the past. Writers experimented with form and, influenced by Freud, began to probe unconscious motivations. The German historian and philosopher, Oswald Spengler, set the mood for the era with *The Decline of the West.* Spengler believed that all civilizations pass from youth to maturity, and from maturity to old age and eventually death. In his book Spengler predicted that European civilization would disintegrate. World War I had been only the first step in the process.

Novels. The French novelist Marcel Proust suggested that people could not make realistic or proper judgments by reasoning and thinking. Proust believed that the only reality is sensation, or what is felt through the senses. In exhaustive detail, Proust vividly brought to life the sensations of taste, touch, and smell. His main work, *Remembrance of Things Past,* is a multivolume novel. The first part appeared in 1913, but most of it was published after World War I. In the 1920s his work became famous and was widely read.

Thomas Mann, Proust's German contemporary, used as his themes the constant presence of death amid life and the alienation of the writer from society. A constant atmosphere of decadence and sadness prevails in his novels—reflecting the moods of the 1920s and 1930s. The somber atmosphere is most notable in *The Magic Mountain* (1927). This book, set in a tuberculosis sanitarium, deals symbolically with the moral sickness of Europe.

After the war the works of Franz Kafka, the Czech writer, were particularly influential in Germany—even though Kafka spent all but the last year of his life in Prague. In his works, most of which became popular after his death, Kafka used a technique known as **surrealism**—an attempt to portray and interpret life as if it took place in a dream. In *The Trial* (1925), the main character is being tried in a hostile atmosphere for a crime he knows nothing about. In *The Castle* (1926), a man is looking for someone, but despite searching through endless

History Through the Arts

PAINTING

The City by Fernand Léger

During World War I many soldiers suffered from the effects of poison gas. One of these was the French artist Fernand Léger. Before he entered the army, Léger painted glorified machines and technology. While recovering in a hospital, he realized that individuals were more important than things. When he began painting again, Léger included people in his canvases. In this painting of city life, human figures descend the staircases, walk on the streets, and appear in the posters.

Léger's interest was not only in painting but in set design as well. He conceived, directed, and produced sets for ballets and motion pictures.

Philadelphia Museum of Art: A. E. Gallatin Collection

Léger was part of the cubist movement in art that started in Paris about 1907. Cubists portrayed objects broken down into their basic geometric forms. In theory a cubist painter stepped into the picture and then walked around the subject, trying to show all the sides at once. Thus the artist could expand what the human eye could see.

---

corridors and seeing many other people in the castle, he can never accomplish his goal. Kafka's writings later influenced the work of many writers.

The Irish writer James Joyce caused a great stir during this period. In his sometimes bewildering masterpiece, *Ulysses* (1922), Joyce tried to convey everything that happened to a man and everything the man thought, both consciously and unconsciously, in a single day. Joyce used a technique called stream of consciousness. Influenced by psychoanalysis, the technique demands that everything that comes into a character's mind be recorded or noted on paper. *Ulysses* is difficult to understand because it lacks normal punctuation and skips about at random. *Ulysses* was a revolutionary work that broke away from many of the traditions of the novel. It revealed both the dissatisfaction with the past and the restlessness of the people of the postwar era.

The American writer Ernest Hemingway wrote in clear, simple prose. His aim, especially in *A Farewell to Arms* (1929), was to express the disillusionment over human behavior that was so common in the years after World War I.

Poetry. The American-born poet T. S. Eliot, who spent most of his life in England, best expressed through his poetry the break with traditional forms and the deep pessimism of the postwar years. In his most famous poem *The Waste Land* (1922), Eliot gave a despairing description of a world without faith, incapable of restoring its spiritual and moral values. Many other poets of this period also abandoned traditional rhyme and meter. Instead they wrote poetry without rhyme that had lines of varying lengths. They also experimented with punctuation and even with the physical appearance of their poems.

New Directions in Music and Painting

Musicians and painters rejected traditional forms and styles with the same determination as did the writers of this period. Some of the new ideas of musicians and painters began before World War I, but they did not take hold until the unsettled postwar years.

Music. One of the pioneers of the new direction in music was Igor Stravinsky. Born in Russia,

667

Charlie Chaplin in *Modern Times*

Mechanization created feelings of uneasiness in many people. One of these people was the brilliant comedian Charlie Chaplin. Characterizing the human spirit in its loneliness and humor, he used the new invention, the movie, as the vehicle for his satire. One of his most famous films was *Modern Times,* which was released in 1936. The movie depicts him, in his usual role as a gentle tramp, at work in a huge factory. Here he is shown tightening bolts on an endless assembly line. In pursuit of one neglected bolt, he knocks other workers over, upsets the entire factory routine, and ends as a captive of the machinery.

he lived most of his life in western Europe and the United States. Stravinsky's *The Rite of Spring* (1913) caused a disturbance at its first performance because it broke so completely with traditional music composition. Stravinsky directed different instruments to be played in different keys at the same time, creating a sound that many people found disturbing.

Three Austrians, Arnold Schoenberg and his students Alban Berg and Anton von Webern, were even more revolutionary. They wrote what is called atonal music. In Schoenberg's atonal compositions, he completely abandoned the conventional eight-tone musical scale and used instead a twelve-tone scale. Schoenberg and his followers avoided such traditional forms as the sonata, the symphony, and the concerto. They wrote pieces for unusual collaborations of instruments, such as Webern's *Quartet for Violin, Clarinet, Saxophone, and Piano.* Their melodies were not developed in the traditional way, and their music often sounded strange and unfamiliar. This discordant music is controversial even today.

Painting. The same rejection of traditional forms and styles occurred in the field of painting. Artists of the early 1900s overturned the standards of beauty and the recognizable portrayal of nature taken for granted since the Renaissance.

The first pioneers of this new style of art were the Spaniard Pablo Picasso and the French artist Georges Braque, who worked in Paris. They created a new art style called **cubism,** which emphasized geometric forms, shapes, and designs. Using shapes such as cones, cylinders, spheres, flat planes, and especially cubes, they showed the abstract structures of the objects they painted, not their surface appearance. In fact, Picasso and Braque often depicted the objects from several different perspectives at the same time. Thus, for example, one would see half a face in profile and the other half from the front.

Picasso justified the severe distortions of reality in his artwork by saying that "nature and art, being two different things, cannot be the same thing. Through art we express our concept of what nature is not." Like the composers of the time, Picasso knew that his work disturbed many people, but that was part of his purpose. He was protesting the easy acceptance of old forms.

Other painters turned away from traditional art in various ways. Surrealistic painters attempted to symbolize the unconscious. Their works featured perfectly painted objects that did not seem to relate to one another. The Spanish surrealist Salvador Dali painted *The Persistence of Memory* (1931), which depicts a dreamlike landscape with what looks like liquid clocks draped over a tree branch and the edge of a shelf. Other artists, notably the Russian, Wassily Kandinsky, and the Dutchman, Piet Mondrian, painted purely abstract designs.

Like the writers of the period, the musicians and the painters of the post-World War I era broke dramatically with the attitudes and styles of the past. They created works that reflected the pessimism and doubts of the people in the late 1920s and the 1930s.

Popular Culture

Novelists such as Franz Kafka and musicians such as Arnold Schoenberg appealed only to a small audience. Most people found escape from the disillusionment of troubled times in other new forms of entertainment.

Popular music. One favorite diversion was listening to music on phonograph records or on the radio. More and more households had radios in the 1920s and 1930s, and music aimed at a mass audience filled the air waves. This was the start of the era of the "Big Bands." These bands played dance music with catchy melodies written by composers such as Irving Berlin and Cole Porter. In addition, the musical, a type of play featuring song and dance, became a major attraction in the theater.

The most innovative popular musicians played a distinctive form of music known as jazz. Jazz began in the southern United States in the late 1800s. Performed primarily by black musicians, its style developed particularly in New Orleans. Using African as well as American music as inspiration, jazz emphasized individual experimentation. One of its major forms, the blues, concentrated on sad, pessimistic themes. The work of jazz musicians did not differ from the experimental and untraditional writing and painting of the day.

Film. The chief entertainment for popular audiences of the 1920s and 1930s came from another new art form, the film, or motion picture. Invented around the year 1900, motion pictures swept through Europe and the United States. Thousands of movie houses, or theaters, opened in the 1920s and 1930s. The first public showings occurred around 1910, and by the 1920s millions of moviegoers routinely waited in long lines to see their favorite films.

Film, too, reflected the pessimism of the postwar era. Although early movies were often simple dramas or hilarious comedies, they also carried disturbing messages. The greatest film directors—D. W. Griffith in the United States and Sergei Eisenstein in the Soviet Union—made powerful films about human intolerance and cruelty. Most movies, however, offered viewers an escape from the problems of a difficult world.

Learning from Pictures
The internationally known American jazz trumpet player Louis Armstrong (fourth from left), played with the King Oliver band during the early 1920s in Chicago.

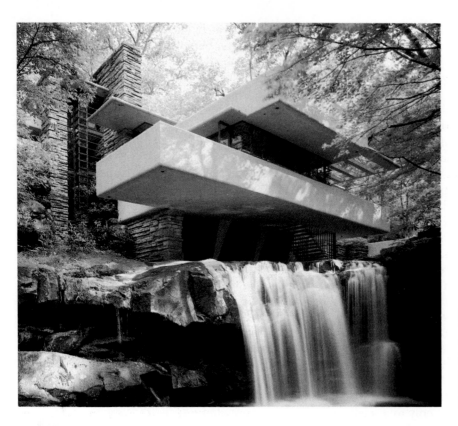

Learning from Pictures
This house named "Fallingwater" was designed by Frank Lloyd Wright in the 1930s. The house is built over a waterfall near Uniontown, Pennsylvania.

Architecture

Architecture also underwent great change during the postwar years. New technical advances, such as the use of structural steel, made a remarkable transformation possible.

The American Louis Sullivan pioneered the new architecture. Not only did he help to develop the skyscraper, but he also developed a style called **functionalism.** The fundamental principle of functionalism is that a building should be designed for its specific use rather than according to popular style.

Louis Sullivan's pupil Frank Lloyd Wright adopted Sullivan's ideas and added his own. One of Wright's major theories stressed that buildings should be appropriate to their environment. For example, Wright's prairie houses in the Middle West were low buildings with long horizontal lines. In the 1920s Wright built the Imperial Hotel in Tokyo. Adapting the hotel to its location, he floated it on a cushion of mud instead of anchoring it rigidly to rock. Because of this adaptive construction, it was the only large structure in Tokyo to survive the severe earthquake of 1923.

European architects developed a new style of architecture. Influenced by Sullivan and Wright, a group including the Frenchman Le Corbusier and the German Walter Gropius developed a functional architecture called the **international style.** This style used uninterrupted expanses of steel and glass.

The new art forms all showed a radical change —a break as dramatic as the one between medieval and Renaissance styles. It was as if nothing—neither music, books, paintings, nor architecture— could be the same again after World War I.

SECTION 1 REVIEW

1. **Define** totalitarian regime, surrealism, cubism, functionalism, international style
2. **Identify** Thomas Mann, James Joyce, Ernest Hemingway, *The Waste Land,* Igor Stravinsky, Pablo Picasso, Frank Lloyd Wright
3. **Analyzing Ideas** What was the main function of popular culture during the 1930s?
4. **Interpreting Ideas** The 1920s and 1930s witnessed much experimentation in art forms. Give an example of this experimentation in each of the following categories: **(a)** literature, **(b)** music, **(c)** painting, **(d)** film, and **(e)** architecture.

2 Postwar Prosperity Crumbled into a Worldwide Depression

Like France and Great Britain, the United States had fought on the victorious Allied side in World War I. Unlike the Europeans, however, the Americans had fought in the war for less than a year. The Atlantic Ocean had separated the United States from the battlefields, and therefore no American land had been devastated. The United States emerged much stronger economically at the end of the war. By 1918 both industry and agriculture had expanded tremendously, resulting in an **economic boom,** or sudden increase in prosperity.

Postwar Prosperity

The United States emerged from the war as the apparent successor to Great Britain in world leadership. The American involvement in the war had contributed greatly to the Allied victory, and the United States had also taken a strong role in drawing up the peace settlement.

The United States' new financial status most dramatically indicated its leadership role in the world. In 1914 the United States had owed about $4 billion to foreign governments and businesses. By 1919 these conditions had reversed, with foreign governments owing the United States government about $10 billion. Much more was owed to United States citizens who had bought foreign bonds.

However, the refusal of the United States to join the League of Nations indicated that the United States did not want the responsibility of world leadership. Americans seemed to want to sit back and enjoy their newfound prosperity and avoid any further entanglement in European affairs.

The Roaring Twenties

Historians have dubbed the 1920s the Roaring Twenties because of the fast pace of life and sometimes frantic pursuit of pleasure that marked the era. Some have attributed that atmosphere to the American exposure to European attitudes during World War I. However, other factors also contributed to this social change.

During the 1920s many changes affected people's lives. Automobiles became a popular means of transportation. Commercial airlines began carrying mail (passenger service did not begin until the 1930s). Telephones linked millions of homes, and movies became a favorite form of entertainment. During this era jazz became popular, new fast dances like the Charleston gained acceptance, and movie stars became public idols. Charles Lindbergh gained fame overnight for his solo flight across the Atlantic Ocean, a feat that had never before been accomplished.

This era of enormous confidence also prompted a revolt against traditional morality and standards. Changes brought more freedom for women as they won the right to vote and joined the work force in greater numbers than ever before. Another sign of changing morality came with the widespread evasion of **Prohibition**—the law forbidding the manufacture, sale, and transportation of alcoholic beverages. Smuggling and bootlegging—the illegal manufacture and sale of liquor—made Prohibition ineffective.

The Economy

Although the United States was prosperous, some flaws did exist. For example, wages paid to laborers did not keep pace with increased productivity. In other words, not enough money ended up in the hands of consumers to buy the goods being produced. Instead, profits went either to wealthy stockholders or toward reinvestment in new machinery and additional factories. Increased use of labor-saving machinery not only stimulated production but also increased unemployment.

Agriculture suffered as well. Farmers had greatly increased production during the war to help feed the Allies. But now that market had dried up. The use of modern machinery and methods led to a serious overproduction of food, and prices fell. In the wheat market especially, production far outweighed consumption in the 1920s.

Another flaw in the system occurred through **economic nationalism.** This is the policy a nation uses to improve its economic well-being by establishing protective tariffs and similar restrictions on the import and export of goods. A healthy world market depends on a free flow of goods from one country to another. In the 1920s, however, many countries set up tariffs to protect their own expanding industries from foreign competition. Each country's home market could not consume all that was being produced, and high tariffs made it difficult for foreign buyers to absorb the surplus.

During the 1920s the United States raised its tariffs to the highest level in its history. The United States insisted upon American dollars in exchange for goods sold abroad. High tariffs now made it hard for European countries to sell their goods in the United States. If they could not sell goods *to* the United States, then they could not acquire dollars to purchase goods *from* the United States. As a result, banks and businesspeople in the United States willingly lent money to Europeans so that they could buy American goods. But this practice merely created more indebtedness, and European nations already had heavy war debts.

Speculation, Panic, and Crash

Throughout the 1920s millions of Americans made **market speculations,** or risky investments, in the stock market in the hope of quick, high profits. The stock market is the organization through which a company's stock certificates are bought and sold. A company issues shares of stock to raise money for expansion. Investors buy these shares to make a profit or earn an income from the company's earnings known as dividends. During the 1920s prices of stocks sold on the New York Stock Exchange soared, and many investors did make large profits. Trouble rose, however, because much of the money invested in the stock market had been borrowed. Frequently, the only security the borrower had to offer to the lender was the hope of future profits from stock investments. Everyone had expected the prices of stocks to rise indefinitely.

However, on October 29, 1929, a wave of panic swept investors in the New York Stock Exchange. On this day prices sank to an all-time low when more than 16 million shares of stock were suddenly dumped on the market. No one would buy stocks while prices declined. As a result, many of the stocks on the exchange became virtually worthless. Vast fortunes vanished. Hundreds of banks, factories, mining companies, and business firms in the United States declared bankruptcy.

The Great Depression

The collapse of the New York Stock Exchange marked the beginning of a worldwide depression called the **Great Depression.** Some of the reasons for this economic crisis included the slowdown of business activity, the high rate of unemployment, and falling wages and prices. Many of the most reliable European banks closed their doors. By 1932 more than 30 million workers in countries throughout the world could not find jobs. Germany stopped paying reparations, and the Allied nations ceased the payments of war debts to the United States.

The strange thing about poverty during the Depression was that it occurred in the midst of abundant productivity. The prices of goods fell very low, but the goods could not be sold because people simply did not have the money to buy them. Manufactured products piled up in warehouses, and crops rotted. Some countries tried to force prices to rise by destroying surpluses. Canada burned part of its wheat crop. Brazil dumped coffee into the sea. European exports and imports declined more than 60 percent in three years, and United States trade abroad decreased by 68 percent.

Responses to the Great Depression

The United States responded to the Great Depression by continuing its policy of economic nationalism. It raised tariffs even higher and cut off American loans to Europe. Germany and Austria had wanted to establish a customs union to aid their economies. However, several European nations opposed the project, and the World Court banned it. In every case, it appeared, the immediate response to the Great Depression made recovery more difficult.

In 1933 an International Monetary and Economic Conference met in London, but it failed to promote greater financial cooperation among the industrial nations. Most of these countries had already decided upon economic nationalism as the proper answer to the Great Depression.

Great Britain tried to induce full employment and stimulate production by granting low-interest loans to its industries. In addition to raising its tariffs against foreign goods, in 1931 Great Britain formed a system for economic cooperation within its empire. In 1932 at a conference in Ottawa, Canada, Great Britain devised a system of "imperial preferences." Through this system the dominions and possessions within the British Empire agreed to levy low tariffs on one another's products. In a period of international economic uncertainty, they were attempting to become economically self-sufficient.

France, less industrialized than Great Britain, did not suffer as much during the Great Depression. However, French trade declined, unemployment increased, and industrial production dropped sharply. The uncertainty of the Depression years caused even greater political instability in France than the troubles following the war had created. In 1933 alone there were four changes of government.

Elsewhere in the world, the Great Depression caused unrest and violence. In Germany it helped destroy the Weimar Republic established at the end of the war. The representative governments that did survive the severe shock of the Great Depression had strong democratic traditions.

The New Deal

The United States had fallen behind most other industrial nations in creating social legislation. Unemployment insurance and government relief programs did not exist. As a result, when the Great Depression occurred, American workers had to rely on their savings, if any, and on charity provided by private organizations. People stood in breadlines to receive a bowl of soup or a plate of stew. Some earned money by selling apples in the streets.

Under President Herbert Hoover, the federal government tried to remedy these severe conditions, but the measures adopted were not extensive. Hoover believed that prosperity was "just around the corner."

Elections brought a new President, Franklin D. Roosevelt, to office in 1933. He immediately embarked upon a program of relief and reform called the New Deal. Under the provisions of the New Deal, the government granted money to each state for food, shelter, and clothing for the needy. The government also began a program of public works to provide employment.

Following Roosevelt's emergency relief program, Congress enacted a sweeping reform of America's economic system. Banks and stock exchanges were placed under strict regulation. The Social Security Act of 1935 provided for unemployment and old-age benefits. A 40-hour work week and minimum wage levels were established. The federal government had previously remained neutral or sided with the industrialists in labor disputes. Now it guaranteed workers the right to establish unions.

The federal government also tried to relieve the desperate situation of farmers by paying them to take land out of production and to plant crops that would revitalize the soil. Later the government adopted a program of buying and storing surplus

Learning from Pictures   *In this scene from the Great Depression, women and children receive food from the New Hope Mission in New York City.*

Learning from Pictures *President Roosevelt dedicated many public works. Here he is at the opening of a bridge that crosses the Choptank River in Maryland.*

before in the welfare of the individual citizen. It attempted in many ways to restore prosperity. However, the causes of the Great Depression remained too deeply rooted to be cured completely even by a program as ambitious as the New Deal. Only when the United States mobilized for war did the hardships caused by the Great Depression finally end.

SECTION 2 REVIEW

1. **Define** economic boom, Prohibition, economic nationalism, market speculation, Great Depression
2. **Identify** Roaring Twenties, Herbert Hoover, Social Security Act, Tennessee Valley Authority, Trade Agreements Act
3. **Summarizing Ideas** Why was the United States considered a world leader in the years following World War I?
4. **Analyzing Ideas** How did American economic policies during the 1920s and 1930s affect economic conditions in Europe?
5. **Organizing Ideas** What conditions helped to bring about the Great Depression?
6. **Understanding Ideas** What measures did Great Britain take to cope with the effects of the Great Depression?
7. **Explaining Ideas** (a) What was the New Deal? (b) Give some specific examples of its provisions.

farm crops. This program helped prevent the prices of farm goods from plunging.

Another federal program of far-reaching economic and social significance involved the establishment of the Tennessee Valley Authority, or TVA. Having established the TVA in the valley of the Tennessee River and its tributaries, the government built a series of multipurpose dams there, intending to generate cheap electricity, to help prevent floods and soil erosion, and to improve navigation.

The Roosevelt administration also tried to revive world trade. The Trade Agreements Act of 1934 allowed the president to make special agreements with foreign countries. If a foreign nation lowered its tariff rates on some American products, the president was empowered to lower American tariff rates on some of that foreign country's products. As a result of this and other measures, United States foreign trade began to recover.

Under the New Deal, the United States government became more deeply involved than ever

3 Europe Experienced Political Tensions After World War I

The events of the postwar years put a strain on the older and more experienced European democracies, such as France and Great Britain. Demobilization of the armed forces led to widespread unemployment and intense competition for jobs. Many people could not find jobs because production by farms and factories had expanded to fill wartime needs, and now an overabundance existed.

Many Europeans believed that governments needed to take a more active role in economic matters to solve the unemployment problem. Before World War I, many people had believed that governments should not interfere in business matters. However, wartime needs had led several nations to adopt a **planned economy**—an economy in which governmental regulation and direction of national

674

resources was established to achieve economic stability. Since the system had worked well in wartime, why not use it to solve peacetime economic problems?

In the new European nations, such as Poland, different problems arose. Many of these new countries set up their governments more in imitation of Western systems than because of any deep devotion to democratic principles. Most of the people who administered them had no experience in democratic government. As a result, social and economic troubles increased, and serious signs of weakness began to appear.

France's Postwar Difficulties

During the four years of World War I, northern France had been a major battleground. At war's end, farmhouses and even entire cities lay in ruins, and trenches and shell holes scarred the land. Wharves needed replacing. Railroads and roads needed restoration. Most tragic of all, a high percentage of the young men of France had been killed.

Thus France emerged from World War I victorious but unstable. It still owed money that it had borrowed from its citizens and from the United States during and after the war. Inflation also took its toll. The burden of higher prices fell mostly on industrial workers and the lower middle class—those least able to pay.

The expenses of the French government soared for several reasons. The number of civil servants increased during and after the war. The government had to repair war-damaged areas and to pay interest on its heavy debt. But most important, perhaps, it had to pay for military security.

The Maginot Line. Twice in less than 50 years, the Germans had invaded France. To prevent this from happening again, the French rebuilt their army. They also constructed a series of steel and concrete fortifications that stretched nearly 200 miles (320 kilometers) along the borders of Germany and Luxembourg. This extensive line of fortifications was named the Maginot (MAZH • uh • noh) Line, after the minister of war who planned it.

Construction of the Maginot Line cost enormous sums of money. Since trench warfare had been a major feature of World War I, the French planned to make their defenses so strong that the country could never again be invaded overland from the east.

International affairs. In July 1922 Germany had informed the Allies that it could not continue to pay reparations on schedule. Despite British objections, France and Belgium therefore marched troops into Germany's coal- and iron-rich Ruhr Valley in January 1923. France intended to occupy the area and operate the steel mills there until it collected the money Germany owed. The German workers refused to cooperate, and the attempt ended in failure. The French then withdrew their troops.

By 1925 the political situation in Europe seemed to be improving. In that year, representatives from Great Britain, France, Germany, Belgium, Italy, Czechoslovakia, and Poland met at Locarno, Switzerland. There they signed a number of treaties known together as the Locarno Pact. The delegates to the conference pledged that their countries would settle peacefully all future disputes, guaranteed the existing Franco-German boundaries, and invited Germany to join the League of Nations. In addition, France signed mutual assistance treaties with both Poland and Czechoslovakia.

However, France's protective alliances began to show serious weaknesses. By the mid-1930s Belgium canceled its defensive alliance with France and declared itself neutral in any future war. France formed a shaky alliance with its prewar ally Russia, now under a Communist government. France's wartime ally Italy, now under the rule of a dictatorship, resumed its old opposition to France. In keeping with its aim of encircling Germany, France developed postwar alliances with Yugoslavia and Romania as well as with Poland and Czechoslovakia. However, these relatively weak nations, although they shared France's mistrust of Germany, were undependable allies.

Political unrest. In early 1934 a scandal in the French government touched off riots in Paris. Rioters demanded an end to the republican form of government. They called for a military dictatorship to "discipline" the country and to reunite the opposing parties.

The trade unions responded to the threat from the right-wing conservatives by calling a **general strike**—a refusal by workers in various industries to continue working until their demands are met. Shortly thereafter the parties of the left-wing organized a coalition government called the Popular Front. Its leader, Léon Blum, a socialist, became premier of France in 1936. United for the moment against the threat of a coup d'état, Blum's government carried out many reforms.

The Popular Front first persuaded the leaders of industry to grant an immediate pay raise to all workers. The government then established a 40-hour work week and granted every worker the right to a paid vacation. It also promised to protect labor union organizers, and it set up a system for the arbitration of labor disputes. The Bank of France came under public control and the armaments industry was partially **nationalized**—put under government control or ownership.

Prices, however, continued to rise to such levels that the increased wages did little to help. In addition, industrialists proved uncooperative. Blum's ministry lasted only one year. Through his leadership in this brief period, however, France's government developed great power and determination and enacted many important reforms.

After the fall of the Popular Front, the French working classes suffered severe setbacks. The 40-hour work week was abolished in 1938. Workers protested by organizing general sit-down strikes during which they stayed at their jobs but refused to work. Severe antilabor legislation followed.

France remained a democracy, but bitter divisions existed among the French people. They also feared German military power, which began regaining strength at an alarming rate.

Great Britain After World War I

Like France, Great Britain faced grave economic difficulties after World War I. A huge war debt owed both to people at home and to the United States made taxes extremely high.

British industry and trade suffered. The coal mines, on which industry depended, were beginning to give out. During the war the United States and Japan had taken over many of Great Britain's world markets. After the war Britain's run-down factories and worn-out machinery made competition with newer American or Japanese machines impossible.

In addition, the high tariffs of economic nationalism damaged British trade because Great Britain needed to sell abroad in order to pay for needed imports of food and raw materials.

Labor troubles. By 1921 the British government had to support about 2 million unemployed

Learning from Pictures *World War I left psychological as well as physical scars on people throughout Europe. Here a cafe in postwar Paris bustles, as the French people try to regain a sense of normalcy in their everyday lives.*

Learning from Pictures
The British attacked Liberty Hall, the headquarters of the Irish nationalists during the Easter Rebellion.

workers. This high unemployment rate meant labor unrest. Labor unions fought hard to maintain the high wages and full employment rate of the war years. Industrialists fought just as hard to resist the unions' demands.

In 1926 the coal miners called a strike, and their action led to a general strike. Soon almost half of Great Britain's 6 million unionized workers had left their jobs. The British government declared a state of emergency and ordered soldiers and sailors to replace the striking workers. The general strike failed, and the miners returned to work. Later the government passed the Trades Disputes and Trade Unions Act of 1927, which controlled unions and made general strikes illegal.

Discontented workers found a spokesman in Ramsay MacDonald, leader of the Labour Party. Although the Labour Party grew stronger, it did not have a majority in the House of Commons. Therefore, MacDonald formed a coalition with the Liberal Party, which had declined in strength because it could not attract working-class members. MacDonald was elected prime minister in 1924 and again in 1929. His government brought about moderate reforms, such as the extension of unemployment benefits and old-age insurance. Thus Great Britain avoided the social unrest that toppled democratic institutions elsewhere in Europe during the postwar years.

Ireland. In the 1920s Great Britain faced a major problem in a country it had ruled for centuries. During the 1800s the British government and Irish nationalists struggled over the issue of home rule for Ireland. The matter of limited self-government was unresolved by 1914, and most Irish people continued to yearn for complete independence for their country.

During World War I, with Great Britain's attention focused elsewhere, Irish nationalists revolted in the Easter Rebellion of 1916. The British suppressed the rebellion, but fighting broke out again in 1918. For years the Irish Republican Army fought British troops in a series of violent and bitter struggles.

In 1921 the British submitted to Ireland's demands and signed a treaty dividing Ireland into two parts. The following year the southern part of Ireland became the Irish Free State, a self-governing dominion with loose ties to Great Britain. Six counties in the northern region of Ireland chose to remain in the United Kingdom, with representatives in the British Parliament. This region became known as Northern Ireland.

In 1937 the Irish Free State adopted a new constitution and the name Eire (AR • uh). Eamon De Valera (dev • uh • LER • uh) was elected its first prime minister. (In 1949 Eire became completely independent, calling itself the Republic of Ireland.)

Both religion and politics divided the island. Most people in the Republic of Ireland were Roman Catholic, while the majority in Northern Ireland were Protestant. These same problems continue to trouble relations between Great Britain and Ireland today.

Eastern Europe

While the countries of western Europe attempted to recover economically, the new nations of eastern Europe began to create their own economies. However, the eastern European nations lagged far behind the western democracies in industrial development. For centuries the economy of eastern Europe had focused on the manor, and serfdom existed in some areas until the mid-1800s. As late as World War I, the economy was still mainly agricultural, with a few wealthy aristocrats owning most of the land.

Immediately after the war, the governments of Czechoslovakia, Romania, Bulgaria, and the Baltic countries (Estonia, Latvia, and Lithuania) divided the large estates and gave the land to the peasants. Yet most peasants lacked the funds to buy the farm equipment, fertilizers, and seeds necessary to make their farms productive.

The breakup of the Russian and Austro-Hungarian empires disrupted old patterns of trade. Most of the new eastern European countries tried to industrialize and turned to economic nationalism to protect their industries. As a result, trade among the countries proved difficult. Goods produced by the new industries could not be sold to neighboring countries at a reasonable profit.

The push toward economic development created a period of instability in the new nations of eastern Europe. Finland, Czechoslovakia, and the Baltic countries managed to sustain democratic regimes, but few other nations in eastern Europe succeeded in doing so. Three examples help illustrate what happened.

Austria. The Austria created after the war was a small country. Many Austrians wanted *Anschluss* (union) with Germany, but the peace treaties forbade it. Austria's economic weakness—one-third of the country's people lived in Vienna, the former capital of a large empire—and a continuing struggle between socialists and conservatives weakened the democratic system. Each faction set up private armies in the streets. The country became less democratic, and the Catholic church played an important role in the battle for control of the Austrian government.

Hungary. Hungary was declared a republic in November 1918. In March 1919, Béla Kun, a Hungarian Communist who had participated in the Russian Revolution, overthrew the republic and tried to establish a Communist system modeled on Russia's new government. He planned to break up the large estates and distribute the land to the peasants. However, the aristocrats who owned the land bitterly opposed Kun and with outside help overthrew his government in August of the same year.

By 1920 Hungarian Admiral Nicholas Horthy, a reactionary representative of the military class, ruled Hungary. Under Admiral Horthy's rule, landlocked Hungary was called "a kingdom without a king, ruled by an admiral without a fleet." In 1921 the emperor Charles I tried to restore the Hapsburg monarchy. However, the Allies would not permit the Hapsburgs to return to power, and for the next 10 years, Hungary was ruled by the nobility.

Poland. Soon after the war, a constitutional assembly met in Poland. It adopted a democratic constitution closely modeled on that of France's Third Republic (see Chapter 21). However, bitter opposition from both the conservatives and liberals prevented the new government from operating effectively. In 1926 Poland followed the example of Hungary and turned to military dictatorship. Dictator Marshal Józef Pilsudski (peel • SOOT • skee) represented the aristocracy and the military.

SECTION 3 REVIEW

1. **Define** planned economy, general strike, nationalize
2. **Identify** Maginot Line, Locarno Pact, Popular Front, Ramsay MacDonald, Easter Rebellion, Eamon De Valera, Józef Pilsudski.
3. **Organizing Ideas** What internal problems did France experience after World War I?
4. **Summarizing Ideas** What were the causes of the economic problems faced by the British after World War I?
5. **Analyzing Ideas** Why was Great Britain able to avoid the social unrest that troubled other nations after World War I?
6. **Understanding Ideas** What prevented Austria from achieving *Anschluss*?
7. **Explaining Ideas** How did eastern European countries try to improve their economies after World War I?

4 Fascist Dictatorships Were Established in Italy and Germany

As it did elsewhere, the war and its aftermath took their toll in Italy and Germany. Heavy losses of life, a crushing burden of debt, unemployment, and inflation plagued these countries. In Italy labor troubles resulted in many violent strikes. The Italian government, a constitutional monarchy, seemed helpless to meet the pressing needs of this situation.

The Rise of Fascism in Italy

One person who did offer a positive plan was Benito Mussolini. The son of a blacksmith, he had been a socialist as a young man and had edited a socialist newspaper. His writings had brought him a term in jail and a period in exile. During World War I his views changed. Mussolini became an extreme nationalist, and the Italian Socialist Party expelled him. After Italy joined the Allies, he enlisted in the army and was wounded in battle.

When Mussolini returned from the war, he began to organize his own political party. He called it the Fascist Party and called its doctrine **fascism** (FASH • iz • uhm). The words *fascist* and *fascism* come from the Latin word *fasces.* In ancient Rome a *fasces* was a bundle of rods bound tightly around an ax. It symbolized governmental authority. The various groups of the nation, Mussolini said, should be bound together like the rods of the fasces. He defined fascism as "the dictatorship of the state over many classes cooperating."

In his book *Delivered from Evil,* Robert Leckie described Benito Mussolini's physical features and the imposing personality that brought him and the Fascist Party to power in Italy in the 1920s:

> "*A*t . . . his full height. . . [he was] . . . remarkable for his commanding head and his broad low brow, piercing black eyes, wide mouth and jutting square jaw. Because of his great head, he gave the impression of physical strength. Yet, if he were to remove his outer garments, it would be seen that his shoulders were thin, his arching chest a pouting pigeon's breast and his arms and legs spindly. However, like Napoleon, he could strike fear into men twice his size with a direct glance from those astonishing eyes."

Fascism, like communism, relies on dictatorial rule and a totalitarian regime, in which the state

Learning from Pictures *Mussolini ordered military training for all males ages 6 to 83. These young soldiers, called "sons of the wolf," parade in Rome.*

679

maintains rigid control of the people through force and censorship. All authority belongs to the state, with individuals completely subordinate to it. However, important differences exist between communism and fascism. Communism, which is based on a socialist economy, seeks international revolution. It appeals to workers and promises a classless society. Fascism, on the other hand, is extremely nationalistic, appeals to the middle class, while promising to preserve all existing social classes, and defends the ownership of private property. Both systems violently oppose the other.

Mussolini Gained Power

Mussolini found his first followers among demobilized soldiers and discontented nationalists. Gradually, the Fascists attracted professionals, wealthy landowners, and businesspeople, especially large manufacturers interested in the anticommunist program. These new supporters gave the Fascists much financial assistance. Fascists also found strong support among the lower middle classes, who had been severely hurt by inflation, and among the unemployed.

Recognizing that strong anticommunism appealed to the people, Mussolini emphasized this in his program. Fascism began to stand for the protection of private property and of the middle class. Mussolini promised to prevent a proletarian revolution. At the same time, he offered the industrial working class full employment and social security. He also stressed national prestige, pledging that Italy would gain all its war aims and return to the glories of the Roman Empire.

The Fascist Party began a violent campaign against its opponents, especially socialists and communists. Rowdy groups broke up strikes and political meetings and drove properly elected socialist officials from office. The Fascists adopted the black shirt as their uniform and became known as the Black Shirts.

In October 1922 Black Shirt groups from all over Italy converged on Rome, claiming they were coming to defend Italy against a communist revolution. Liberal members of the Italian parliament insisted that the king declare martial law. When he refused, the cabinet resigned. Conservative advisers then persuaded the king to appoint Mussolini as the premier and to ask him to head a coalition government.

Mussolini had often criticized democracy as a weak and ineffective form of government. Once in office, he began to destroy democracy in Italy and set up a dictatorship. He appointed Fascists to all official positions both in the central government and in the provinces. He pushed through parliament a new election law providing that the party receiving the most votes would automatically gain two-thirds of the seats in the Chamber of Deputies, the lower house of parliament. After the Fascists won the election in 1924, the Chamber of Deputies voted to give Mussolini "decree powers"—which meant that his decrees would have the force of law. He took the title *il Duce* (DOO • chay), Italian for "the leader."

Italy as a Police State

Now all of the outward signs of a dictatorship began to appear. Opposition parties ceased to exist. The government suspended freedom of speech, freedom of the press, and freedom of assembly, as well as trial by jury. Labor unions came under government control, and strikes were outlawed. Uniformed police, as well as secret police, spied on everyone.

Mussolini became commander-in-chief of the army, navy, and air force and head of the police. Although he allowed the king to reign as a figurehead, real power lay in the hands of the Grand Council of the Fascist Party. Mussolini headed the Council.

The Corporate State

Mussolini argued that in a modern industrial society, representation according to geographic location was outmoded. Instead, he introduced a new and complicated system of government in which representation was according to profession or occupation. The country's major economic activities, such as agriculture, transportation, manufacturing, and commerce, were formed into syndicates that resembled corporations. Thus Italy became known as a **corporate state.**

By the 1930s, Italy had 22 of these syndicates. In each syndicate representatives of government, management, and labor met to establish wages and prices and to agree upon working conditions. Labor unions and capitalists alike had to submit to the will of Mussolini's government. Private property remained in the hands of its owners, and profits were allowed. All parts of the society had to cooperate with one another for the welfare of the nation.

The Fascist dictator, Mussolini, sat at the top of the entire system. In addition to the changes in the government, he strengthened the army and navy and increased armaments. These two additional changes in Italy had a double purpose: unemployment was reduced, and military strength increased. Mussolini promoted war as a glorious, patriotic adventure.

The Weimar Republic

As with Italy, difficulties in postwar Germany gave rise to political change following World War I. In November 1918 Germany was declared a republic. The following year, an assembly met in the city of Weimar (VY • mahr) and drafted a constitution that made Germany a federal republic, known as the Weimar Republic.

Germany's new government had a president and a two-house parliament elected by universal suffrage. The parliament included the Reichsrat (RYKS • raht) and the Reichstag. The president appointed the chancellor, Germany's prime minister.

The Weimar Republic was not popular with the German people. The republic had been created in response to Woodrow Wilson's announcement that he would deal only with a government elected by the German people. Many Germans opposed a republican government, and because Weimar representatives had signed the humiliating Versailles Treaty, the German people viewed the republic as a traitorous government.

Many of the difficulties of the Weimar Republic reflected the economic, social, and political problems that faced all of Europe after the war. Unemployment was high, and inflation soared. For example, in 1913 a German mark was worth about 25 cents. In 1923 it took 1 trillion marks to equal 25 cents.

Within its first year, two attempted revolutions threatened the Weimar Republic. A Communist government took over Munich, the capital of the state of Bavaria, and attempted to withdraw the state from the federal union. Later in Berlin, a right-wing group tried to overthrow the republic and to elevate to power men of its own choosing. The republic was powerless to defend itself and in

Learning from Pictures *The value of the German mark fell so low that people baled it and sold it for fuel.*

both cases had to rely on temporary alliances with anti-republican groups.

The Bavarian Communist revolt was crushed by the "free corps"—private right-wing armies made up of demobilized soldiers loyal only to their generals. The attempted overthrow in Berlin was defeated when members of the legal government, fleeing the city, called for a general strike. The workers of Berlin left their jobs, paralyzing the city and making it impossible for the right-wing rebels to set up their own government.

The Nazis and Hitler

One of the many political parties that formed in Germany after World War I was the German Workers' Party. In 1920 the party, attempting to broaden its appeal, changed its name to the National Socialist German Workers' Party, or Nazi Party. The party did not represent the working class, as its name might indicate, but was extremely nationalistic and violently anticommunist. Promising to protect Germany from communism, the party in time attracted the support of wealthy business leaders and landowners.

One of the first Nazi recruits, an ex-soldier named Adolf Hitler, was born in Austria in 1889, the son of a minor government official. As a young

681

Learning from Pictures *Hitler (left) and Mussolini (right) review German troops in Berlin on one of Mussolini's many state visits.*

man, he had gone to Vienna, where he failed as an artist and worked at various odd jobs. In Vienna, where Jews contributed to the city's rich cultural life and had risen to respected positions, Hitler became resentful and violently anti-Semitic.

Hitler served in the German army in World War I and later moved to the city of Munich, where he joined the Nazi Party. In 1923 Hitler took part in a Nazi uprising in Munich in the state of Bavaria. The uprising failed, and Hitler was sentenced to prison. While there, he wrote *Mein Kampf* (My Struggle), a rambling book that expressed the spirit of the Nazi movement. In this writing, Hitler left no room for doubt about his goals for the German nation. He wrote:

> **"***I***f** the National Socialist [Nazi] movement really wants to be consecrated [honored] by history with a great mission for our nation . . . it must find the courage to gather our people and their strength for an advance along the road that will lead this people from its present restricted living space to new land and soil. **"**

After his release from prison, Hitler became the leader of the Nazis and wanted to implement his

ideas. He possessed a hypnotic talent as an orator. In the confusion of the postwar years, his emotional speeches attracted enthusiastic listeners. The frustration, self-pity, and hatred Hitler expressed reflected the feelings of many Germans who believed that they had suffered a great humiliation in the Versailles Treaty. The war reparations and loss of territory made them eager to follow a leader they hoped would restore Germany's lost glory.

Hitler's program found appeal with almost every element in the German population. To farmers he promised land reforms. To the workers he offered better working conditions, social legislation, nationalization of big business, and the abolition of unearned profits. To nationalists Hitler promised to repeal the Versailles Treaty, especially the "warguilt" clause. He said that he would restore Germany to equality in armaments and also regain all its lost territory and colonies to build a "Greater Germany." Like Mussolini, he promised protection against communism.

To these promises Hitler added his garbled racial doctrine. According to this doctrine, the Germans, as "Aryans" (a misapplied use of the word), were the "master race." All other races were inferior. As Hitler's power increased, his personal traits of intolerance, hatred, and contempt for non-Germanic people became the policies of the government.

Hitler's Rise to Power

The Nazis had few followers[*] until the Great Depression. In the election of 1930, however, many middle-class voters turned to the Nazi Party. These voters had experienced economic hardships and had lost their savings. In addition, many of them feared a Communist revolution. Two years later the Nazi Party won 230 seats in the Reichstag. Although the largest single party there, the Nazis did not have enough votes to form a government.

In January 1933, when it appeared that no other party could successfully form a government, the president of the republic, Paul von Hindenburg, appointed Hitler as chancellor.

Since the Nazis still lacked a majority, Hitler used the Nazis' private army—the storm troopers, or Brown Shirts—to intimidate the Reichstag.

---

[*]In 1921 the Nazi Party had 6,000 members; by 1932 it had 50,000 members.

READ
WRITE
INTERPRET
CONNECT
●THINK

BUILDING HISTORY STUDY SKILLS

Thinking About History: Analyzing Documents

Documents are basic sources for historians. They are used to answer a question, to develop a theory, or to support a view of a historical event. Documents can be any information written on a particular subject and may consist of essays, books, charts, and graphs, to name a few. Reading and analyzing documents helps you to formulate your own view of events based on the evidence and your analysis. Using documents helps you to integrate information and form conclusions.

How to Analyze Documents

To analyze documents, follow these steps.

1. Explain the question, theory, or point of view being researched in the documents.
2. Classify the documents. Determine whether they deal with political, economic, or social issues.
3. Identify the source of the documents.
4. Determine the validity and bias of the documents.
5. Connect the documents to each other.
6. Formulate a thesis statement based on the connection found in the documents.

Developing the Skill

The following documents deal with Hitler's rise to power in Germany. The question the documents focus on is, "How did Hitler destroy parliamentary democracy in Germany?"

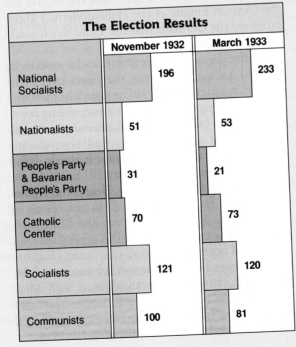

The Election Results

	November 1932	March 1933
National Socialists	196	233
Nationalists	51	53
People's Party & Bavarian People's Party	31	21
Catholic Center	70	73
Socialists	121	120
Communists	100	81

❝ On February 27, a week before the election, the Parliament building was set on fire. The event was described by the Nazis as the first move in a vast Communist conspiracy, and on the following day the President issued an Emergency Decree 'for the protection of the People and the State' and as 'a defensive measure against the Communist acts of violence': 'Articles 114, 117, 118, 123, 124 and 153 of the constitution . . . are suspended until further notice. Consequently, restrictions on personal liberty, on the right of free expression of opinion, including freedom of the Press, on the right of assembly and association . . . and warrants for house searches . . . are permissable beyond the legal limits normally laid down.' ❞

The documents should be classified as political since the subject of both is government. The source of the documents is Tony Edward's *History Broadsheets, Hitler & Germany 1919–1939*. The documents are unbiased since they merely state facts.

The chart of the election results tells us that there was a multiparty system in Germany's Weimar Republic after World War I. The parties are listed from extreme right-wing National Socialists (Nazis) to extreme left-wing Communists. In order to rule, a party had to have most of the seats, or a majority, in the Reichstag. No party was ever strong enough to have a majority without combining their votes with those of at least one other party. As the chart indicates, the Nazis won the most seats in the Reichstag in the election of November 1932 but did not have a majority. Their major competitors were the Communists and the Socialists at the other end of the political spectrum. However, following the election of 1933 the Nationalists formed a coalition with the Nazis giving them a majority in the Reichstag.

The second document helps explain how the Nazis were able to consolidate their power by destroying the opposition. The Emergency Decree was based on the burning of the Reichstag, which the Nazis unjustly blamed on the Communists. This played on the fear of disorder and revolution that people believed was caused by the Communists. The Emergency Decree also put restrictions on the Communists who were the Nazis' biggest rivals and to whom they lost seats in the Reichstag in the election of 1933.

Practicing the skill. Read the excerpt from *Mein Kampf* on page 682. What bias does the document show? What can you learn about Hitler's plans for Germany by studying the document?

To apply this skill, see Applying History Study Skills on page 689.

Learning from Pictures *Stalin won the power struggle after Lenin's death even though Lenin had opposed him.*

A plan for economic growth, the first Five-Year Plan, was published in 1928. It set industrial, agricultural, and social goals for the next five years. It also laid plans for expanding the educational system and for building more hospitals and housing.

The Five-Year Plan stretched the resources of the Soviet Union to the breaking point in an attempt to turn the country into a modern, industrialized society. The expansion of heavy industries occurred at the expense of industries producing consumer goods.

The planners hoped that collective farming would produce enough food for the Soviet people as well as a surplus for export. Money received from farm exports would help pay for modern machinery, which would in turn advance the drive toward industrialization. Therefore, the future of the Soviet Union as an industrial nation depended on a rapid increase in farm production. All farms were to be merged into collectives. Peasants had to join or suffer severe consequences. The wealthier peasants who attempted to retain their lands faced execution, imprisonment, or exile.

The first Five-Year Plan succeeded in most industries. The government turned about 70 percent of the productive farmland into collective farms. A second Five-Year Plan, even more comprehensive than the first, began in 1933. This sec-

ond program called for production increases in heavy industries. As a reward for the hard work and sacrifices, people could expect an increase in the production of consumer goods such as food and clothing. However, what actually happened was a decrease in consumer goods as the Soviet government placed all of its efforts on the expansion of heavy industry. Rather than receiving any reward for their hard work, the Soviet people faced higher prices as consumer goods became more scarce.

Stalin's Dictatorship

As the years passed, Soviet leaders admitted that it would take time for a classless society of pure communism to develop. In the meantime the Communist Party would rule.

A police state. The czars had used secret police and spies to maintain their absolute rule. Now Stalin used similar tactics. Under Stalin the Soviet people still experienced rule by fear. People had to conform to the "party line," the policy of the Communist Party, or face repression.

The Soviets had disestablished the Orthodox church and seized its property. They ridiculed religious worship and taught children atheism. Artists, writers, and musicians were ordered to produce "socialist realism" in the service of the state, with works subject to rigid control and censorship.

Government under Stalin. In 1936 Stalin proclaimed a new constitution for the Soviet Union. The Stalin Constitution, as it was called, preserved the essential framework that had existed under Lenin. The parliamentary body, called the Supreme Soviet, met twice a year. While in recess, its authority was assumed by the Presidium, a small committee elected by the Supreme Soviet. The Council of People's Commissars, later renamed the Council of Ministers, held executive and administrative authority.

On paper the Soviet government appeared to be democratic. In reality, however, most power lay in the hands of the Politburo (Political Bureau) of the Communist Party. As head of the party, Stalin controlled the Politburo. In other words, he held dictatorial powers, with virtually complete authority over the people.

The Soviet Union's totalitarian dictatorship under Stalin gradually grew harsher. In 1934, following the assassination of a high party official, Stalin began a **purge** of party members supposedly disloyal to him. Through intimidation, brutality,

ICELAND (DEN.)

GREENLAND (DEN.)

ALASKA (U.S.)

GREAT BRITAIN

NORWAY

SWEDEN

SVALBARD (NOR.)

North Pole

Bering Strait

ARCTIC OCEAN

Murmansk

KAMCHATKA PENINSULA

GERMANY

Baltic Sea

FINLAND

Leningrad

Archangel

Siberia

Sea of Okhotsk

PACIFIC OCEAN

LITHUANIA

ESTONIA

LATVIA

GER.

POLAND

BELORUSSIAN S.S.R.

Minsk

Moscow

Gorki

RUSSIAN SOVIET FEDERATED SOCIALIST REPUBLIC

Sakhalin Island

ROMANIA

Kiev

Kazan

UKRAINIAN S.S.R.

Kharkov

MOLDAVIAN S.S.R.

Odessa

Rostov

Volga

Sverdlovsk

Tobolsk

Ob River

Yenisei River

Lena River

Sevastopol

Black Sea

Don R.

Stalingrad

Samara

URAL MOUNTAINS

Omsk

Novosibirsk

Lake Baikal

Amur R.

TURKEY

Magnitogorsk

GEORGIAN S.S.R.

Irkutsk

MANCHURIA

Vladivostok

ARMENIAN S.S.R.

Caspian Sea

KAZAKH S.S.R.

Aral Sea

TANNU TUVA

AZERBAIJAN S.S.R.

Lake Balkhash

MONGOLIA

JAPAN

KOREA

Baku

Tashkent

TURKMEN S.S.R.

Ashkhabad

UZBEK S.S.R.

KIRGHIZ S.S.R.

IRAN

Stalinabad

TADZHIK S.S.R.

CHINA

AFGHANISTAN

N

INDIA

0   400   800 Miles

0   400   800 Kilometers

THE SOVIET UNION IN 1936

–+–+– Trans-Siberian Railroad

MODIFIED OBLIQUE CONIC CONFORMAL PROJECTION

Learning from Maps *People Stalin deported were sent to labor camps in Siberia via the Trans-Siberian Railroad. What city is located at the eastern end of the railroad line?*

and public trials staged only for show, Stalin began to rid the party of all members who would not submit to his will. Scholars estimate that by 1939 nearly 8 million people had been arrested. Following arrest usually came deportation, imprisonment in forced labor camps, or execution.

The Comintern

Soviet foreign policy during the 1920s and 1930s contained contradictions. On the one hand, the new Communist government wanted to be accepted by the established nations of the world. On the other hand, its support of the Third International, also called the Communist International or the Comintern, alienated many countries. Lenin founded this organization in 1919 to help spread the revolution throughout the world. The Comintern continued to agitate for the overthrow

of the governments of the capitalist democracies.

Communist parties existed in many countries outside Russia. The Comintern worked through these parties to incite workers and urge rebellion. Such open calls for revolution caused fear, suspicion, and hostility in the outside world.

SECTION 5 REVIEW

1. **Define** collective farm, command economy, purge
2. **Identify** Union of Soviet Socialist Republics, Trotsky, Presidium, Politburo, Comintern
3. **Explaining Ideas** Describe the New Economic Policy of Russia.
4. **Comparing Ideas** What was the main political difference between Trotsky and Stalin?
5. **Analyzing Ideas** (a) What economic policies did Stalin initiate? (b) What were the consequences for those who resisted Stalin's policies?

687

CHAPTER 25 REVIEW

AD

Weimar Republic established
1919
Cominterm founded

Mussolini began rule in Italy
1922
Irish Free State

Chapter Summary

The following list contains the key concepts you have learned about political, social, and economic conditions in the United States and Europe following World War I.

1. The period following World War I was a time of major stresses and uncertainties.
2. The literature, music, art, and science of the time reflected the new outlook and the uncertainties of the period. James Joyce and Pablo Picasso abandoned traditional forms and created works that had disturbing implications. Even new popular art forms, film and jazz, had pessimistic overtones. The Western world had entered an unsettled and less optimistic era.
3. Following the victory in World War I, people in the United States realized that their country was the richest nation in the world. A sense of optimism and the influence of European contact brought about rapid change. The pace of life quickened during the decade appropriately called the Roaring Twenties.
4. The economic bubble burst with the stock market crash and the beginning of the Great Depression in 1929. President Franklin Roosevelt enacted policies for recovery known as the New Deal.
5. In Europe instability was widespread. The British and the French maintained their democratic traditions despite labor unrest and the problems of unemployment caused by the Great Depression. In eastern Europe, a number of the new nations abandoned democracy for rule by dictators.
6. In Italy and Germany, dissatisfaction with the weakness and hesitations of democratic governments led to an extreme form of dictatorship, fascism. Mussolini in Italy and Hitler in Germany established totalitarian regimes, and both had expansionist foreign ambitions that further undermined Europe's stability.
7. Following the civil war, Russia became the Soviet Union, with a government based on the principles of Marx and communism. However, when its first leader Lenin died, his successor Stalin maintained control only by brutally crushing his opponents and setting up a totalitarian dictatorship.

On a separate sheet of paper, complete the following review exercises.

Reviewing Important Terms

Supply the term that correctly completes each statement.

1. _____ _____ are formed when land is pooled into large farms on which people can work together.
2. Governmental regulation and direction of national resources to achieve economic stability occurs in a _____ _____ .
3. A _____ _____ occurs when workers refuse to continue working until their demands are met.
4. When a country tries to improve its own economic well-being through protective tariffs and similar restrictions, it is adopting the policy of _____ .
5. _____ was the doctrine of Mussolini.
6. A sudden increase in prosperity is called an _____ _____ .
7. When people make _____ _____ , they are investing in stocks in the hope of attaining quick, huge profits.
8. A technique used by artists to interpret or portray life as if it took place in a dream is called _____ .
9. The painting style created by Pablo Picasso and Georges Braque, which emphasizes form, shape, and design, is called _____ .
10. The plain and severe style of architecture that uses uninterrupted expanses of steel and glass is called _____ .

Developing Critical Thinking Skills

1. **Summarizing Ideas** (a) What was War Communism? (b) What was the New Economic Policy? (c) How did each program attempt to stimulate the Soviet economy?
2. **Analyzing Ideas** (a) Why did the demobilization of troops put economic pressures on the nations of Europe? (b) Why were Great Britain and France better able to deal with these problems than the new nations of eastern Europe?
3. **Explaining Ideas** Explain the similarities and differences between fascism and communism.
4. **Organizing Ideas** How did each of the following contribute to the rise of nazism in Germany? (a) creation of the Weimar Republic, (b) signing of the Versailles Treaty, (c) high unemployment and soaring inflation

688

French occupation of Ruhr Valley — 1923

Locarno Pact — 1925

Stalin assumed full power in Soviet Union — 1928

First Soviet Five-Year Plan — 1928

Beginning of Great Depression — 1929

Hitler appointed chancellor of Germany — 1933

Germans reoccupied Rhineland — 1936

Blum's Popular Front government — 1936

5. **Comparing Ideas** **(a)** How did the economic situation in the United States compare with the economic situation in Europe during the postwar years? **(b)** What brought the boom years to an end?

6. **Interpreting Ideas** **(a)** How did the arts reflect the disillusionment of the postwar era? **(b)** How did popular culture reflect this disillusionment?

Relating Geography to History

Turn to the map titled "The Soviet Union in 1936" in this chapter, page 687, and to the one titled "Europe After the Congress of Vienna, 1815" Chapter 17, page 446. Then complete the following. **(a)** List the republics in the Soviet Union. **(b)** List the countries bordering the Soviet Union that were part of Russia in 1815. **(c)** Why had the Soviet Union lost a sizable amount of its territory after pulling out of World War I?

Relating Past to Present

1. **(a)** What did the leaders of the 1917 Russian Revolution hope to accomplish? **(b)** Based on what you know about conditions in the Soviet Union today, which of these goals have been achieved? **(c)** Which of these goals have not?

2. **(a)** List the programs that President Roosevelt instituted during the New Deal. **(b)** Which of these programs are still in existence? **(c)** Choose one of these and find out why this program has continued. **(d)** What is its main purpose? **(e)** Do any groups of people think the program should be discontinued? If so, why?

Applying History Study Skills

Before completing this activity, review Building History Study Skills on page 683.

Study the following documents. The first document is Stalin's justification of his methods in industrializing the Soviet Union. The second document is a chart summarizing the results of the Five-Year Plans. Decide how each document helps to answer the question "How was Stalin able to industrialize the Soviet Union?"

66 It is sometimes asked whether it is not possible to slow down the tempo a bit, to put a check on the movement. No, comrades, it is not possible! The tempo must not be reduced! On the contrary, we must increase it as much as is within our powers and possibilities. . . .

To slacken the tempo would mean falling behind. And those who fall behind get beaten. . . . No, we refuse to be beaten! One feature of the history of old Russia was the continual beatings she suffered for falling behind, for her backwardness. She was beaten by the Mongol Khans. She was beaten by the Turkish beys. She was beaten by the Swedish feudal lords. She was beaten by the Polish and Lithuanian gentry. She was beaten by the British and French capitalists. . . . All beat her—for her backwardness: . . . 99

The Five-Year Plans			
	First 5-Year Plan		Second 5-Year Plan
	1928	1932	1937
Industrial production (million rubles)	18.3	43.3	95.5
Electricity (million kilowatts)	5.05	13.4	36.2
Steel (million tons)	4.0	5.9	17.7
Grain harvest (million tons)	73.3	69.6	75.0
Cattle (million head)	70.5	40.7	63.2

Investigating Further

1. **Writing a Report** Using encyclopedias and books, prepare a brief biographical sketch of Benito Mussolini.

2. **Presenting an Oral Report** Prepare a report on the response of the United States and European nations to the Great Depression, explaining why the policy of economic nationalism created more problems than it solved.

689

26

New Political Forces Emerged in Africa, Asia, and Latin America

Place Africa, Asia, and Latin America

Time 1900–1938

3.7 mil. BC   4000 BC   AD 2100

Significance

As you have read, Europe and the United States faced many social, political, and economic challenges during the early decades of the 1900s. In other parts of the world, however, people's main concern was with political change. Among the countries of the British Empire, India started on the path toward independence and others developed new relationships with Great Britain. The major independent countries of the Middle East—Turkey and Persia—also began rapid political transformation, and new political forces stirred throughout Africa.

At the same time, profound changes transformed the great civilizations of China and Japan. In China the dynastic cycle was finally broken, and the long and difficult process of creating new political structures began. Neighboring Japan set its course for economic growth and foreign expansion.

The countries of Latin America faced economic and social change as well as an uncertain relationship with the United States. Many Latin American governments, like others in the 1920s and 1930s, decided that strong centralized power provided the best answer to their problems.

Terms to Define

Zionism   passive resistance

People to Identify

Mahatma Gandhi   Chiang Kai-shek
Jomo Kenyatta   Fulgencio Batista

Places to Locate

Trans-Jordan   Haifa
Palestine   Shaanxi

Questions to Guide Your Reading

1 How did the British Empire adjust to the changes that World War I brought?
2 What forms of government developed in Turkey, Persia, and Africa?
3 On what principles was the Chinese republic based?
4 How did the military come to play a major role in the Japanese government?
5 Why did authoritarian governments come to power in many Latin American countries?

◀ *Chinese poster art honoring Mao Zedong*

In 1930 thousands of Indians peacefully demonstrated against the British salt tax. As the reporter Webb Miller wrote in the New Freeman, however, the demonstration met with a violent and tragic end.

> **"** *uddenly, at a word of command, scores of native police rushed upon the advancing marchers and rained blows on their heads. . . . Not one of the marchers even raised an arm to fend off the blows. They went down like tenpins. From where I stood I heard the sickening whacks of the clubs on unprotected skulls. . . .*
>
> *Those struck down fell sprawling, unconscious or writhing in pain with fractured skulls or broken shoulders. In two or three minutes the ground was quilted with bodies. Great patches of blood widened on their white clothes. The survivors without breaking ranks silently and doggedly marched on until struck down.* **"**

India was only one area of the world convulsed in change after World War I.

1 The British Empire Adjusted to the Postwar Era

Although the British Empire had grown larger as a result of the Paris Peace Conference, its continued existence was threatened from within. People in all parts of this vast empire voiced demands for more freedom, for self-government, and even for complete independence.

Independence for Egypt

Technically, the Turks ruled Egypt, but since 1882 the British had been in control. In 1914, when the Ottoman Empire joined the Central Powers, Great Britain declared Egypt a protectorate. This protectorate formally ended in 1922. Great Britain continued to influence the Egyptian government, however, because of British interests in the Suez Canal.

During the 1920s and early 1930s, a strong independence movement grew in Egypt. In 1936 the British and Egyptian governments reached an agreement on the independence issue. In the previous year, Italy had invaded Egypt's neighbor,

Ethiopia. The British needed Egyptian support to prevent further Italian aggression. Thus they agreed to help Egypt become a member of the League of Nations. The two nations also pledged mutual assistance in time of war. In addition, Egypt gave Great Britain military control of the Suez Canal for 20 years. With this agreement Egypt became completely independent, and it joined the League in 1937.

The Palestine Issue

The peace settlements after World War I gave Great Britain the mandates for Trans-Jordan, Iraq, and Palestine. These lands were all formerly part of the Ottoman Empire.

The spirit of nationalism had arisen among Arabs during the final years of the Ottoman Empire. It grew stronger after the British assumed control in the Middle East. Unable to extinguish this spirit, the British recognized the independence of Trans-Jordan in 1923. However, they maintained some control in the area through the presence of military advisers. By 1930 the British had also recognized the kingdom of Iraq as an independent nation. Again Great Britain retained some control, especially in military and financial matters.

Of the three Middle Eastern mandates, only Palestine now remained completely under British control. Palestine was important to the British because of its strategic location and because a vital oil pipeline from Iraq ended at the Palestinian port of Haifa. The British found themselves in a difficult position in Palestine, however.

Since the late 1800s, Jews from Europe had been establishing small colonies in Palestine. These colonists supported a nationalist movement called **Zionism,** which aimed to build a Palestinian homeland for the Jews.* In 1917 the British foreign secretary, Arthur Balfour, eager to secure Jewish support for the Allied war effort, told Zionist leaders that the British would "view with favor" the creation of a Jewish "national home" in Palestine. This Balfour Declaration, as it came to be called, also stated that the establishment of such a homeland should not threaten the civil and religious rights of non-Jews, who made up 98 percent of Palestine's population.

The British also had promised to aid the formation of an independent Arab state that might include parts of Palestine. Therefore, the Balfour Declaration had to be cautiously worded, since the British wanted Arab support against the Turks who had joined the Central Powers.

After the war, with the British holding mandates in the Middle East, both the Jews and the Arabs wanted Great Britain to fulfill its promises. While Britain sought an equitable solution to the problem, tensions between Arabs and Jews intensified. The Arabs viewed the number of Jews settling in Palestine as especially alarming.

During the 1930s many Jews fled Europe to avoid Nazi persecution. Hoping to calm the fears of the Arabs, the British placed strict limitations on the number of Jews allowed to immigrate to Palestine. Jewish settlers bitterly resented this policy, especially when Nazi persecution of European Jews increased. Thus, by trying to please everyone, the British had succeeded only in making the situation worse. The Palestine question continued to plague the British throughout the 1940s.

Independence Movements in India

As the largest of the British colonies, India posed even greater difficulties than did the Middle Eastern mandates. India had taken part in World War I on the side of the Allies, contributing both troops and money. In return, Great Britain had promised India a greater degree of self-government.

Any settlement for India had to recognize the tensions and hostilities present in Indian society. For example, an uneasy truce marked the relationship between Hindus and Muslims, and wide gulfs existed between upper-caste and lower-caste Hindus. Such a settlement also had to satisfy many conflicting demands. British conservatives completely opposed giving up this important part of the British Empire. Indian princes, many of whom were almost absolute rulers in their domains, also favored the existing state of affairs. Indian nationalists, on the other hand, wanted to rid India of British rule.

The chief advocate of Indian nationalism was Mohandas K. Gandhi, who in 1920 became leader of the Indian National Congress—India's most important political party. Many Indians looked

---

*Theodor Herzl, an Austrian Jew, is considered the founder of this Zionist movement. *Zion* is another name for Israel, the Jewish homeland.

READ
● WRITE
INTERPRET
CONNECT
THINK

BUILDING HISTORY STUDY SKILLS

Writing About History: Writing a Problem-solution Essay

Writing a problem-solution essay includes analyzing a problem in order to provide a solution to the problem. For example, assume that a city's crime rates are increasing. Consequently, a problem can be identified—it is not safe to walk alone on city streets at night. The problem also has a logical solution—the mayor of the city and the city council could approve more funds so that the police could patrol the high crime areas more frequently at night.

How to Write a Problem-solution Essay

To write a problem-solution essay, follow these steps.

1. Identify the problem.
2. Describe the problem.
3. State a solution and relate it to the problem.

Developing the Skill

Mohandas Gandhi lived for a time in South Africa where he formulated many of his theories about nonviolence. Gandhi believed that practicing "satyagraha" would help end the injustice he witnessed in South Africa. *Satya* means truth and is the equivalent of love. Gandhi believed truth and love to be characteristics of the soul. *Agraha* means firmness or force. Satyagraha is therefore translated as "soul force." If you were to write an essay on the problem of injustice that Gandhi first faced in South Africa and the solution that he formulated, it might appear as follows.

> On August 22, 1906, the *Transvaal Government Gazette* of South Africa published the draft of the Asiatic Registration Act, a law requiring all Indian people above the age of eight to submit to official registration and fingerprinting. People who did not have a certificate of registration would be fined and imprisoned. Gandhi, speaking to a large crowd in Johannesburg, told the people to pledge defiance of the ordinance and go to jail if necessary. Gandhi believed the people should protest rather than forfeit their right to free movement.
>
> Gandhi's solution to the problem was to develop the idea of satyagraha, which he said is 'the vindication of truth not by infliction of suffering on the opponent, but on one's self.' According to Gandhi, 'the opponent must be weaned from error by patience and sympathy.' Satyagraha reverses the 'eye for an eye' policy, which ends in making everyone blind. It returns good for evil until the evildoer tires of evil. This was Gandhi's plan for dealing with South African injustice.

The first paragraph identifies and defines the problem—the injustice of the South African government which requires the Indian people to carry registration certificates that monitor their movement and create racial distinctions. The solution that Gandhi develops is "satyagraha," or soul force. If you resist the law nonviolently and are willing to suffer the consequences, ultimately you will change the opposition. Gandhi's method, not to allow the protestor to adopt the methods of the oppressor, was designed to appeal to the conscience of the opposition.

Practicing the skill. Research the effects of Gandhi's solution and explain how they might be incorporated into the model problem-solution essay.

To apply this skill, see Applying History Study Skills on page 709.

Mohandas Gandhi with followers

693

on Gandhi as more than a political leader. They also revered him as a spiritual force, calling him *Mahatma* (muh•HAHT•muh), or "Great Soul." Gandhi wanted nothing short of complete self-government for India. He also urged Indians to give up Western ways and return to their ancient culture and religions.

Gandhi opposed all use of force and violence. As early as 1909, he expounded his reasons for favoring nonviolence over violence as a means of achieving Indian independence.

❝ *I*t is perfectly true that [the English] used brute force and that it is possible for us to do likewise, but by using similar means we can get only the same thing that they got. . . . [It is like] saying we can get a rose through planting a noxious weed. . . . We reap exactly as we sow. . . . [F]air means alone can produce fair results. . . . **❞**

Drawing on ideas in Hindu scriptures and in the New Testament, Gandhi developed a political approach known as *nonviolent noncooperation.* This technique, a form of **passive resistance,** or civil disobedience, called for citizens to peacefully refuse to cooperate with their government in order to win concessions from it.

Among other things Gandhi's program of nonviolent noncooperation included refusing to buy British goods or to pay taxes. Such actions often resulted in imprisonment for Gandhi and many of his followers. In an attempt to control the nationalist movement, the British authorities issued orders restricting the civil liberties of many of its leaders. In addition, British soldiers often used force to break up nationalist political gatherings.

In 1935, after many committee reports and conferences, Great Britain granted India a new constitution that provided for home rule. However, the British viceroy still controlled India's national defense and foreign affairs. Committed to total self-government, the nationalists rejected the new constitution. During the next few years, discontent continued to simmer in India.

The Statute of Westminster

Even in those parts of the British Empire that already had a degree of self-government, people demanded greater independence. In Canada, New Zealand, Australia, and the Union of South Africa, Great Britain still appointed a governor-general. This official had a veto power over laws, although it was rarely used. Great Britain also controlled the foreign policy of these areas.

After World War I these dominions demanded complete self-government. Showing a remarkable readiness to accommodate, adjust, and accept the political realities, the British gave in without a struggle.

In 1931, by an act of Parliament called the Statute of Westminster, Britain recognized Canada, Australia, New Zealand, and South Africa as completely independent. The four nations joined with Great Britain as equal partners in a very loose organization called the British Commonwealth of Nations. The British Parliament had no power either to make laws for Great Britain's Commonwealth partners or to interfere in their affairs. However, each member agreed to declare its loyalty to the British monarch and to recognize its cultural ties with Great Britain.

Over the years several other British colonies became independent and joined the Commonwealth. Favorable trade arrangements with Great Britain made membership especially attractive. Like other major nations, Britain faced an economic depression after World War I and needed increased trade to stimulate its economy. As you have read, British trade abroad had been hurt by economic nationalism. Thus the Commonwealth's economic arrangement worked remarkably well for both Great Britain and the regions that had formerly been British colonies.

Politically, however, Great Britain's vast empire proved burdensome. In the Middle East and India especially, the empire became more a source of problems than one of support.

2 Varied Political Forms Developed in Turkey, Persia, and Africa

The nationalist feelings that swept the Middle East after World War I also affected the southwest Asian countries of Turkey and Persia and the whole of Africa. As a result new political forces began to stir.

Turkey Under Mustafa Kemal

The Treaty of Sèvres stripped the Ottoman Empire of all its territories except Turkey. Then in 1919 the Greeks invaded and seized part of Turkey. Inept and weak, the sultan could not even organize resistance to the invasion.

For some time a group of nationalists, called the Young Turks, had been trying to reform the corrupt Ottoman government. Discontent over the terms of the Treaty of Sèvres and shock at the sultan's inability to resist the Greeks finally forced the Young Turks into action. Under their able and energetic leader, Mustafa Kemal (kay • MAHL), they drove the Greeks out of Turkey and in 1922 overthrew the sultan.

With their revolution the Young Turks put an end to the Ottoman Empire and established the Republic of Turkey. They moved the capital from Constantinople to Ankara. For the republic's system of government, they selected a Western-style parliamentary democracy with a strong executive. In 1922 Mustafa Kemal became the republic's first president.

Kemal wanted Turkey to become a modern, progressive nation like the industrialized powers of the West. He therefore ordered the Turkish people to adopt Western ways. He prohibited the wearing of traditional clothing such as the fez, the traditional Turkish hat. In addition, he insisted that all Turks adopt family surnames, as Europeans had. He himself took the Muslim name *Atatürk*, meaning "father of the Turks." He also passed laws that gave women the right to vote and hold office, and he abolished polygamy—the practice of having more than one wife.

Atatürk drew up a new constitution that severed the long-lived relationship between the Muslim religion and the Turkish government. He abolished the position of caliph and tried to lessen Islam's influence over the Turkish people.

In a further effort to modernize, Atatürk introduced the Western calendar, the metric system of weights and measures, and the Roman alphabet. He also adopted a westernized program of economic development, paying subsidies to farmers and providing aid for new industries.

Modernizing Persia

Turkey's neighbor, Persia, had never come under Ottoman control. Rather, since the late 1700s, it had been ruled by shahs of the Qajar dynasty. In the early 1900s, however, both Great Britain and Russia established spheres of influence in Persia. Until the 1920s these two countries practically ran the Persian government.

In 1921 Reza Khan, a Persian army officer with strong nationalist sentiments, seized control of the government in a coup d'état. Some four years later, he deposed the ruling shah and assumed the throne, taking the title Reza Shah Pahlavi. Like Kemal Atatürk, Reza Shah wanted to modernize his country and free it from foreign domination. Therefore, he embarked on a massive reform program. He stripped the Muslim religious leaders of much of their power, reorganized and strengthened the army, built schools and hospitals, and gave

Learning from Pictures *The Shah of Persia (right) and Kemal Atatürk (left) met in 1934 in the city of Ankara, Turkey.*

women more rights. Reza Shah also introduced an ambitious economic development plan that improved the nation's transportation system and established many new industries. And in 1935 he announced that the country would be officially called by the name its own people called it—Iran.

Although Iran's constitution specified a limited monarchy, most of the power remained in Reza Shah's hands. The new leader soon began to use this power in an authoritarian manner, strictly controlling the press and suppressing political parties. His private police force ruthlessly put down any opposition to his government. Later in his reign, Reza Shah came to believe that he was divinely ordained, and he took the title "Shadow of God."

Africa After World War I

The many Africans who fought on the side of Great Britain and France during World War I expected to be rewarded with greater political freedom after the war. Like the Indians, they were disappointed.

Increased political activity. The years after World War I saw an increase in political activity among Africans. The war itself had served as a broadening experience for many. Military service took them away from their homes. For the first time, they became aware of the world beyond their immediate family and village. When these ex-soldiers returned home, they brought with them new ideas about freedom and nationalism. In time they put these ideas to work organizing anticolonial protest movements.

Colonial education also influenced many Africans to become politically involved. Missionary and government schools taught their African students the Western ideals of equality and self-improvement. Yet colonial governments denied these same Africans the opportunity for self-determination and economic advancement. As more and more Africans personally experienced this contradiction between Western teaching and the reality of colonialism, they realized that change had to come. Racism and political repression awakened in many Africans a desire to work for reform and even independence.

New political associations. Alarmed at the growing spirit of dissent among Africans, many colonial governments moved to close off all avenues of protest. However, Africans still found ways to organize. In Tanganyika, a former German colony

whose mandate had been assigned to Great Britain, Africans from the lower ranks of the civil service formed a civil servants' association. Since the association was open to all Africans, it overcame traditional ethnic barriers. It soon became a center of anticolonial protest in Tanganyika. Similarly, railroad and dockworkers in both Nigeria and South Africa organized trade unions. These also became important forums for the expression of African grievances.

In response to the formation of these new political associations, colonial governments strengthened the authority of tribal chiefs who favored colonial rule. They rewarded these chiefs with pensions or positions of local power—judgeships, for example. At the same time, the colonial authorities agreed to institute some reforms. For instance, colonial governments placed restrictions on forced labor, the method by which most mining and construction companies obtained their workers. But a few cooperative chiefs and piecemeal reform could not stem the rising tide of African opposition to colonialism.

New leaders. By the 1930s Africans increasingly were calling for independence rather than reform. The loudest of these calls came from the group of young, Western-educated men—among them Nnamdi Azikiwe (ah • ZEEK • way) of Nigeria, Jomo Kenyatta (ken • YAHT • uh) of Kenya, and Léopold Senghor of Senegal—who had assumed the leadership of the anticolonial movement. Following Gandhi's example they organized demonstrations, strikes, and boycotts against their colonial rulers. They also employed Western methods of political organization to attract more people to their cause. By the end of the decade, these men led a growing movement dedicated to ending colonial rule.

SECTION 2 REVIEW

1. **Identify** Young Turks, Reza Shah Pahlavi, Nnamdi Azikiwe, Jomo Kenyatta, Léopold Senghor
2. **Locate** Ankara, Iran
3. **Comparing Ideas** (a) How were the reform programs of Kemal Atatürk and Reza Shah alike? (b) How were they different?
4. **Understanding Ideas** Why did many Africans become more involved in politics after World War I?
5. **Analyzing Ideas** How did colonial governments respond to the formation of African political associations?

3 China Struggled to Become a Modern Nation

Many historians believe that in order to understand the changes that occurred in China during the 1920s, it is necessary to go back to events that took place around 1900. Until that time the imperialist powers of France, Germany, Great Britain, Japan, and Russia had maintained their spheres of influence mainly along the Chinese coast and up the Chang Jiang. At the turn of the century, however, they began to move into China's interior, carving out spheres of influence there as well.

The United States watched this new development with some concern. It did not want American merchants excluded from Chinese trade. In 1899, therefore, the American government appealed to the nations with interests in China to recognize what it called the Open Door policy. Under this policy all nations would have equal rights to trade anywhere in China. The nations contacted by the United States agreed to the policy, but in practice, they continued as before. None of these nations wanted to openly refuse to support the policy. Yet none truly intended to observe it.

Learning from Pictures *Sun Yat-sen, pictured with his wife, plotted the overthrow of the Qing dynasty from Japan during the Boxer Rebellion.*

The Boxer Rebellion

By the end of the 1800s, China's fate as a subservient nation seemed sealed. Foreign powers had won numerous grants of special privileges from the Chinese. Traders and missionaries traveled about the country's interior at will. And foreign governments all but ran China's largest cities.

In 1898, hoping to stem foreign interference by revitalizing his government, the young Qing emperor instituted a series of reforms to change the examination and governmental administration and to promote industry. The drastic nature of these reforms shocked China's conservative leaders. They called on the emperor's aunt, the aging empress dowager (widow of an earlier ruler) Cuxi (TSOO·SHEE), to take action. She quickly had the emperor imprisoned, and for the next 10 years she ruled China in his place.

The empress dowager chose to fight outside interference by doing everything she could to stir up hatred for foreigners, especially the missionaries. Her efforts strongly influenced the members of a patriotic movement called the Society of Righteous and Harmonious Fists. In English they became known simply as "Boxers." In what became known as the Boxer Rebellion, the Boxers roamed throughout China, attacking foreigners at every opportunity. Seeking protection, many foreigners fled to their embassies in Beijing. There they came under siege by an army of angry Boxers.

Despite their rivalries the imperialist nations were determined to protect their common interests in China. They decided to act jointly against the Boxers, sending to Beijing an army comprised of soldiers from Great Britain, France, Germany, Russia, Japan, and the United States. This army relieved the besieged embassies and put down the rebellion in 1901. The foreign powers then imposed heavy penalties on the Chinese, including a demand for payment of a large indemnity. In addition, the foreign powers claimed the right to maintain troops at Beijing and along the Chinese Eastern Railway to the coast.

697

Chinese Painting

For many centuries Chinese painters saw only works of art that had been created within their own country. With the formation of the Chinese republic in 1912, however, painters began to study in Japan and Europe, bringing back new ideas and art forms.

Qi Huang (1863–1957), one of China's most famous poets and painters, lived through both of these periods. As a young man, he worked in the fields by day and learned to

paint by night. By the age of 30, he had achieved recognition as a professional artist, had acquired a clas-

sical education, and had founded a poetry society.

Chinese painters as well as calligraphers considered the mastery of brushstrokes very important. The artists wanted to be quick enough to paint or to write their impressions while they were still fresh in their minds. The blending of calligraphy and art, of poetry and painting, was accomplished most elegantly by Qi Huang. This painting, done in 1935, was strongly influenced by Japanese art. It illustrates the artist's respect for learning and shows how he pursued knowledge by candlelight at night. The inscription reads: "Returning home one night, I find mice perusing the pages of a book. Why are you awake when everyone else is sleeping?"

1980.98 *Browsing by Candlelight* Ch'i Huang. Ink and light color on paper. Gift of Madame fan Tchum-pi Courtesy Museum of Fine Arts, Boston

The crushing of the Boxer Rebellion brought China completely under foreign domination. Had it not been for China's neighbors, Russia and Japan, the other imperialist powers might have divided China into colonies. However, these other powers realized that, because of location, Russia and Japan would benefit most from any division of China. As it was, Russia had used the Boxer Rebellion as an excuse to move 100,000 troops to the northern Chinese province of Manchuria.

Overthrow of the Qing Dynasty

The Boxer Rebellion failed to fulfill its major aim—to drive all foreigners from Chinese soil. But it did foster a nationalistic sentiment among the Chinese people, especially the young and well-educated. Instead of attacking foreigners as the Boxers had done, these young nationalists advocated the reform of China itself. A new political party, the Kuomintang (KWOH·MIN·TANG), or Nationalist People's Party, grew out of this reform movement. Many members of the Kuomintang had studied in Europe or the United States. For example, the party's founder and leader, Sun Yat-sen, had spent most of his life in the United States, attended school in Hawaii, and studied medicine at a British college in Hong Kong.

Influenced by Western democratic ideas, these young nationalists wanted a constitutional government, with civil liberties guaranteed by a bill of rights. They also wanted China to industrialize, so that it could defend itself economically against the imperialist powers. In the nationalists' view, China would be able to protect itself against foreign domination only if it became a modern nation.

The Qing rulers, under pressure from nationalists, tried to carry out reforms. But for many Chinese, their efforts came too late. These people called for a complete break with the "Old China" and an end to the corrupt Qing dynasty.

In 1911 a series of revolts, led mostly by young army officers who supported Sun Yat-sen, spread throughout southern China. In a last, desperate gesture to preserve their dynasty, the Qing proclaimed a constitutional monarchy. The rebels, however, would accept nothing but a republic.

Forming the Chinese Republic

In February 1912 the Kuomintang forced the last Qing emperor, a young child, to abdicate. The Kuomintang then proclaimed China a republic. Sun Yat-sen described the republic's ruling philosophy as "The Three Principles of the People," or people's government, people's rights, and people's livelihood. These principles called for: (1) political unification and the ending of foreign influence; (2) a gradual change to democratic government, with full personal liberties and rights for all Chinese people; and (3) economic improvements, including industrializing and providing for a more equitable distribution of land.

Problems with the warlords. Proclaiming revolutionary change proved to be easier than accomplishing it. At first the Republic of China existed mainly on paper. The Kuomintang controlled only a small region around Guangzhou (GWAHNJ·JOH), in southern China. Warlords, who had acquired power during the last years of the Qing dynasty, ruled the rest of the country. These warlords refused to surrender their power to the Kuomintang without a fight. Some even hoped to defeat their rival warlords and start a new imperial dynasty.

The Nationalists—as members of the Kuomintang called themselves—hoped to defeat the warlords and establish the Republic of China as a strong central government. To fulfill this aim, they asked for help from foreign powers. Only the Soviet Union responded. In the early 1920s, the Soviets sent technical, political, and military advisers to help reorganize the Kuomintang and build up a modern Chinese army.

A split in the Kuomintang. When Sun Yatsen died in 1925, Chiang Kai-shek (CHANG KY·SHEK), a military commander who had trained with the Red Army in the Soviet Union, assumed leadership of the Nationalists. Under Chiang's command the Nationalist army grew stronger. In 1926 Chiang began a military campaign—called the Northern Expedition—against the warlords of the north. Warlord resistance collapsed when confronted by the efficient, highly motivated Nationalist troops. In quick succession the Nationalists seized Wuhan and Nanjing on the Chang Jiang. Two years later they occupied Beijing.

At the same time that the Kuomintang was expanding the area under its control, disagreements began to divide its membership. The left wing of the party, composed of socialists and Communists, wanted to put more power into the hands of peasants and workers. The conservative right wing opposed such radical change, especially any reforms designed to redistribute land and give it to the peasants. Chiang Kai-shek became the leader of this right wing.

In 1927, before the Kuomintang completed the Northern Expedition, Chiang expelled all Soviet advisers from the country and moved against the party's left-wing members. Troops loyal to Chiang attacked the Communist stronghold of Shanghai, arresting thousands of Communists and executing them on the spot. Those few who survived this onslaught went into hiding. Secure in the knowledge that the left-wingers no longer posed a threat to his leadership, Chiang established a Nationalist government in Nanjing.

The Nanjing Government

Chiang and his followers wanted a strong, efficient government, but not a democratic one. Eventually, they set up a one-party system with Chiang as virtual dictator.

Chiang tried to promote economic development, but lack of capital hindered his efforts to industrialize. Defense expenditures took much government revenue that could have been used for industrialization. Foreign control of many of China's natural resources also held back economic development.

Even so, by 1937 the area of China under Nationalist control had made notable progress. The Nationalists had begun a massive road construction program and had started to repair, rebuild, and extend the railroad system. In addition, they strengthened the financial system by establishing a national bank. They also improved all levels of the educational system.

However, the Nationalists failed to deal with two crucial problems. Because they needed the support of landowners and merchants, they made no changes in the oppressive, age-old system of land ownership or in the method of collecting taxes in the countryside. In short, they did nothing to eliminate the causes of suffering and discontent among Chinese peasants.

The Growth of Chinese Communism

In July 1921 a small group of Chinese intellectuals met in Shanghai and founded the Chinese Communist Party. Inspired by the example of the Russian Revolution and by the ideologies of Marx and Lenin, the founders of Chinese communism hoped to free their country from foreign domination and economic backwardness. They first set about

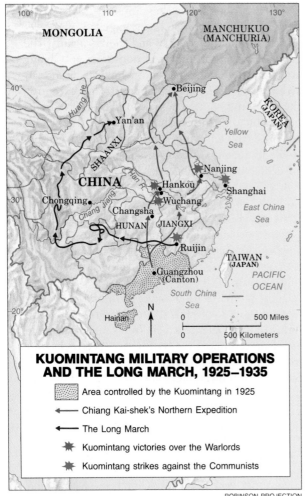

**KUOMINTANG MILITARY OPERATIONS
AND THE LONG MARCH, 1925–1935**

▒ Area controlled by the Kuomintang in 1925

← Chiang Kai-shek's Northern Expedition

← The Long March

✶ Kuomintang victories over the Warlords

✶ Kuomintang strikes against the Communists

Learning from Maps *The Communists' Long March
ended in military defeat. What city is at the end of the
Long March?*

The Long March. Those Communists who
escaped the purge of 1927 fled first to Jiangxi
province, in southeastern China. There they set up
their own government—modeled after the Russian
Communist regime—called the Chinese Soviet
Republic. In late 1933, after repeatedly attacking
the soviet, the Nationalist forces besieged it. Some
months later the Communists broke through the
Nationalist siege lines and evacuated Jiangxi.

In the famous Long March, lasting for more
than a year, about 100,000 Communists made
their way on foot to Shaanxi province in northwestern China. Under incredibly arduous conditions, they crossed 18 mountain ranges and 24
rivers, a distance of about 6,000 miles (10,000 kilometers). A few deserted on the march, but many
more perished on the difficult journey. The 10,000
who did complete the march, along with 10,000
Communists already in Shaanxi, established their
headquarters in the isolated mountain town of
Yan'an. They chose a charismatic young man
named Mao Zedong (MAOH ZEE·DAWNG) as their
leader.

Mao Zedong. Born in the countryside of southeastern Hunan province, Mao had long argued that
Chinese peasants, not the urban proletariat, could
provide the best basis for a Communist revolution
in China. Now, in a rural province far from the
major cities of China, he had a chance to prove his
arguments.

Mao and his followers introduced a program of
land and tax reforms in Shaanxi province. To
ensure the program's success, they met with the
peasants and listened to their problems. The Communists also explained China's problems to the
peasants and urged them to support the revolution.

Since the peasants of Shaanxi were suspicious of outsiders, at first they did not trust the
Communists. However, when they found that the
Communists were trying to understand and help
them solve their problems, the peasants rallied to
the Communist cause. Many volunteered to serve
in the Communist army, called the Red Army.
Others provided the Communists with useful information about the location and movement of
Nationalist troops.

With the support of the local peasant population, the Communists managed to rebuild their
strength and resist the efforts of the Nationalists to
destroy them. In time they would take the offensive
against the Nationalists.

building strong party organizations and labor
unions in the cities. They also cooperated with
the Kuomintang in efforts to defeat the regional
warlords.

At first, when the Kuomintang was weak and
in need of all the help it could get, the Nationalists welcomed Communist support. As the Communist Party grew stronger, however, conservative
Nationalists became alarmed. Chiang Kai-shek
purged the Communists from the Kuomintang
in 1927, and executed many of them. In the early
1930s, when he realized that he had failed
to destroy the Communist Party, Chiang undertook several large-scale military campaigns to
"annihilate" communism once and for all.

Learning from Pictures   *On the Long March, Mao Zedong (on horseback) waged battle against Chiang Kai-shek's pursuing army and against regional warlords.*

SECTION 3 REVIEW

1. **Identify**   Open Door policy, Kuomintang, Sun Yat-sen, warlords, Chiang Kai-shek, Long March, Mao Zedong
2. **Locate**   Nanjing, Shanghai, Jiangxi, Shaanxi
3. **Analyzing Ideas**   (a) What was the Boxer Rebellion?   (b) What were its results?
4. **Classifying Ideas**   Describe Sun Yat-sen's three goals for the Chinese republic.
5. **Understanding Ideas**   What successes did the Nationalists have in modernizing China?
6. **Evaluating Ideas**   Why was Mao Zedong able to involve the peasants of Shaanxi in the Communist revolution?

4   Japan Underwent Change and Increased Its Military Strength

Japan had begun to modernize in the late 1800s. However, the economic, social, and political reforms achieved during that time had created problems. Japan's desire to expand on the Asian continent only exaggerated these problems.

Japanese Expansion

The reforms introduced by the leaders of the Meiji Restoration transformed Japan into a modern industrial and military power. This newly acquired status enabled Japan to embark on a policy of expansionism in the late 1800s. Gaining overseas possessions would serve two purposes. First, it would provide both new sources of raw materials for their country's growing industries and new markets for the products of those industries. Second, it would show the nations of the West just how far Japan had progressed. Other parts of Asia, especially China, seemed to provide the best opportunities for expansion.

Korea.   Korea had long interested Japan. The Treaty of Shimonoseki that ended the Sino-Japanese War provided for Korean independence and forced China to cede Taiwan and the Pescadores to Japan. Very soon, however, Japan dominated the Korean government.

China indirectly caused another Japanese conflict, this one with Russia. After the Boxer Rebellion, most foreign powers withdrew their troops from China. However, a force of 100,000 Russian soldiers lingered on in Manchuria. Despite several protests by the Japanese government, Russia continued to drag its feet. Finally, the Japanese, who looked on Manchuria as a future sphere of influence, prepared to force out the Russians.

In 1902 Japan signed an alliance with Great Britain. Each nation agreed that the other had the right to defend its special interests in China, Manchuria, and Korea against any third power. The two powers agreed that if either one became involved in a war with a single power, the other would remain neutral. They would aid each other, however, if a third power joined the conflict. Although neither country openly admitted it, the alliance targeted Russia as a potential enemy.

The Anglo-Japanese alliance meant great prestige for Japan. The nation no longer stood alone but now had the support of the most powerful country in the world. The alliance also increased pressure on Russia to withdraw its troops from Manchuria. The Russians agreed to negotiate the issue with Japan, but they made little effort to actually begin talks.

The Russo-Japanese War.   Early in 1904, without any declaration of war, the Japanese attacked and badly damaged the Russian fleet at Port Arthur

Learning from Pictures After a five-month bombing siege, Port Arthur surrendered to Japanese forces. What treaty ended the Russo-Japanese War?

in Manchuria. In retaliation the Russians sent part of their Baltic fleet to Asia. The Japanese navy, however, annihilated this Russian force of 32 ships at the Battle of Tsushima in 1905. Earlier, during the summer of 1904, Japanese troops had marched northward through Korea into Manchuria and defeated the Russians in a series of battles. Another Japanese force landed on the Liaodong Peninsula in Manchuria and, with the help of the navy, placed Port Arthur under siege.

Shorter supply lines, a better-prepared military, and greater support from its people helped Japan in the war against Russia. However, the Japanese army suffered heavy casualties, and the cost of the war strained the Japanese economy. As a result, the Japanese asked Theodore Roosevelt, president of the United States, to mediate the conflict. Roosevelt reluctantly agreed, and in 1905 he invited representatives from Japan and Russia to take part in negotiations at Portsmouth, New Hampshire. Later that year these representatives signed an agreement ending the Russo-Japanese War.

The Treaty of Portsmouth. Under this agreement, called the Treaty of Portsmouth, Russia ceded to Japan its lease on the Liaodong Peninsula, including Port Arthur, and control of the southern branch of the Chinese Eastern Railway. In addition, Russia agreed to withdraw all its troops, except for railway guards, from Manchuria. Also, instead of paying an indemnity, Russia turned over

to Japan the southern half of the Russian island of Sakhalin, north of Japan. Finally, Russia gave the Japanese special fishing rights along its Siberian coast.

The Treaty of Portsmouth essentially gave Japan complete control of Manchuria. More importantly, it signaled that other countries recognized and respected Japan's position as a great power. A further indication of this recognition and respect came in 1910. When Japan proclaimed the annexation of Korea—renaming it Chosen (choh • SEN)—none of the other imperialist powers protested.

Problems of Modernization

In less than 50 years, Japan had advanced from a feudal agrarian nation to one of the world's leading industrial powers. Its victories over China and Russia had established it as a military power. However, these considerable achievements also created new problems for the island nation.

Industrialization and scientific development brought higher standards of living and improved medical care to Japan, spurring population growth. Cities grew rapidly, and every inch of suitable land was placed under cultivation. Even so, the increase in the food supply could not match the rapid population growth. And although the economy grew rapidly, it could not provide jobs for all those who wanted them. As a result Japanese people began to emigrate to Korea and Taiwan, as well as to Hawaii and other islands of the Pacific. Thousands more left for the United States.

In time the United States prohibited the immigration of Asians, while still permitting the immigration of Europeans. As proud people, the Japanese deeply resented such discrimination.

Japanese industrialization created yet another problem. Japan had to import raw materials, since it lacked almost all those needed in modern industry. To pay for these raw materials, it had to sell its own goods abroad. Since Japan also needed to import food, it had to export or face economic collapse.

In exporting goods, Japan met with restrictions, just as it did in its "export" of people. Many countries passed tariff laws to protect their home markets against Japanese competition. These countries argued that Japanese manufactured goods had an unfair advantage, since cheap Japanese labor enabled Japanese companies to charge lower prices for their goods.

Social Tensions in the 1920s

Social and political stability marked the Meiji era. During this time the Japanese people were content with the rights their leaders were willing to give them. By the 1920s, however, the situation had changed. Economic development, universal education, and new ideas from the West had all contributed to a change in attitude among the Japanese people. The time had come, many Japanese said, for the people to benefit from the nation's economic advances.

Industrial workers organized labor unions and went out on strike for higher wages and better working conditions. Tenant farmers organized unions, too, and demanded lower agricultural rents. Urban intellectuals and university students, inspired by the victory of the Western democracies over Germany in World War I, argued that democracy was the wave of the future. They organized a movement for universal manhood suffrage, which they saw as an essential first step toward promoting democracy in Japan. Other Japanese became interested in socialism and communism. These people protested the government's expansionist policies and tried to organize a revolutionary political movement in Japan.

Also, some young Japanese began to question the traditional values of their society. These values required that young people obey and respect their parents, especially their fathers. When making decisions—taking a job or choosing a husband or wife, for example—young people had to accept their parents' choice. And military training taught young soldiers and sailors to follow orders without question or hesitation, even if following those orders might lead to their deaths. Japanese military leaders considered it an honor to die in battle for the emperor.

Few young Japanese rejected these values openly. In their private lives, however, they tried to escape, at least temporarily, and experience greater freedom. They listened to jazz and played baseball. Young women in the cities cut their hair short like "flappers" in the United States and refused to wear the traditional female attire of a long kimono. Eager to learn about other societies, young people cleared the bookstores of every Western novel. Japanese novels that dealt with the loneliness and frustration of individuals in Japanese society also enjoyed great popularity among the young.

Growing Influence of the Military

Japanese political leaders of the 1920s had difficulty finding answers to all the demands of the Japanese people. They granted universal manhood suffrage in 1925, yet they could not agree on what to do

Learning from Pictures Japanese melodramatic theater, featuring colorful costumes and makeup and portraying historical or domestic events, is called Kabuki.

about other demands. In addition, they seemed to have no solutions to the country's growing economic problems. In this atmosphere of discord and dissatisfaction, the influence of the Japanese military grew steadily stronger.

The constitution of 1889 had granted special powers to the military. Top-ranking officers recommended to the emperor who should serve as the government's minister of war and minister of the navy. If the ministers of war and of the navy disapproved of a government policy, they could resign and force all the other ministers to resign as well. And since only members of the military could hold these two posts, the civilian authorities had almost no control over military affairs.

Until the late 1920s, military ministers generally cooperated with civilian members of the government. Then, however, the military ministers began to assert their special powers in order to influence government policy. In many ways their knowledge of World War I helped them expand their role in government. They saw the recent conflict as a new kind of war in which victory depended on total mobilization, not only of troops but also of the entire spiritual and material resources of the nation. Believing that victory in any future war would require the same kind of mobilization, they saw the discontent in Japan as a serious problem. It indicated weakness in Japanese society and constituted a threat to the nation's security in the event of war. To preserve the nation, the military ministers felt they must do everything in their power to eliminate this discontent.

The economic problems that Japan faced in the late 1920s also influenced military leaders to take a more active role in government. Officers in the army and navy believed that Western nations would never treat Japan as an equal. As proof of this, they pointed to the restrictions many Western nations had imposed on Japanese immigration and exports. They concluded, therefore, that the government's policy of cooperation with the Western powers was unproductive. In the future, they argued, Japan should pursue a more independent course, especially in Asia.

In time the military leaders began to insist that the Japanese people pay greater attention to traditional values. These leaders also called for a larger army and a stronger navy. In addition, they advocated a Japanese "Monroe Doctrine" that would give Japan special powers in East Asia similar to those exercised by the United States in the Western Hemisphere. In particular, the military leaders saw Manchuria as a target for future expansion. The growing influence of the military ultimately would have far-reaching consequences for all of Japanese society and for the rest of the world as well.

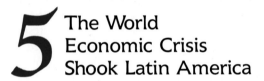

SECTION 4 REVIEW

1. **Identify** Treaty of Portsmouth
2. **Locate** Port Arthur, Sakhalin
3. **Understanding Ideas** Why was the Anglo-Japanese alliance so important for Japan?
4. **Determining Cause and Effect** Why were the Japanese able to defeat Russia in the Russo-Japanese War?
5. **Summarizing Ideas** What new problems were created by Japanese modernization?
6. **Analyzing Ideas** Why did the Japanese military begin to exert more influence over government policy in the late 1920s?

5 The World Economic Crisis Shook Latin America

As the 1920s began, Latin America appeared to be headed for prosperity. However, the region soon would suffer the effects of the worldwide economic crisis of the 1930s.

Economic Developments

Agricultural products, such as beef, wheat, sugar, coffee, and fruits continued to dominate the economy of Latin America. However, during the early 1900s, Mexico became a leading exporter of oil. Oil was also discovered in Venezuela, Peru, Bolivia, and Colombia. The mining of other resources, such as copper in Chile and Peru, tin in Bolivia, and bauxite in Guiana, also developed rapidly during this period. For the most part, British and American companies owned these oil and mining operations.

In addition, the 1920s saw a great expansion in the generation of electric and hydroelectric power, financed mainly by foreign investors. The energy that was produced enabled many Latin American countries to industrialize during the 1920s. For example, the larger countries in the region began

Rivera's *Fruits of Labor*

After World War I, life in Mexico changed dramatically. Diego Rivera, one of Mexico's greatest artists, recorded these changes. As a youth Rivera studied in Spain and France. After World War I, he joined the Cubist school in Paris and later traveled extensively throughout Europe. In Italy Rivera studied fresco painting.

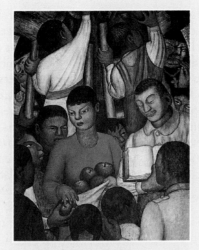

He returned to Mexico in 1921, where the clamor for social reform

changed the direction of his work.

As a member of the art movement known as Social Realism, Rivera produced many paintings that dealt with current problems. Of particular interest are his works that show the plight of the peasants of Mexico. Another frequent subject in his paintings are children. The Mexican government liked Rivera's art and commissioned him to paint murals for many schools and government buildings. On the left is a detail from his mural *Fruits of Labor*—commissioned by the Ministry of Education in Mexico City—in which he honors working people and their children. This impressive fresco took Rivera and a crew of assistants from 1923 to 1929 to complete.

to produce textiles, construction materials, machinery, and automobiles. Oil refining and food processing became important industries at this time also.

Changes in Society

Industrialization contributed to the growth of cities. By 1935 Mexico City, Rio de Janeiro, São Paulo, and Buenos Aires all had 1 million or more inhabitants. These and other major cities in the region extended their transportation, sewer, and utilities systems to accommodate the influx of people and industries.

Industrialization also contributed to a change in Latin America's social structure. To provide labor for their growing industries, many countries—particularly Argentina, Brazil, and Chile—encouraged immigration from Europe. The new arrivals from across the Atlantic swelled the ranks of Latin America's working classes.

This growth, in turn, led to an increase in labor union activity. Although Latin American workers had first begun to organize in the late 1800s, the 1920s saw a surge in labor union membership. The Latin American unions, which were largely anarchist or socialist in outlook, employed the strike as the primary way to achieve their ends. As a result, by the late 1920s, practically every major city in Latin America had been hit by general strikes. Many governments mobilized police and troops to put down these strikes violently. Some

governments went so far as to outlaw strikes and labor unions.

The middle class also began to grow as new jobs opened up in the professions, government service, and commerce. The increasing numbers of merchants, shopkeepers, and small-business owners added to this growth. Soon the sons of middle-class people took most of the places in the military academies. And changes in university programs created opportunities for middle-class youth in engineering, business, and public administration. Such developments gave the middle class potential access to greater power.

Political Changes

Political life in Latin America underwent sweeping change in the early 1900s. In Chile, Argentina, Peru, and Brazil, for example, political parties backed by the middle class emerged. Mexico, wracked by regional factionalism, opted for a single-party political system. Mexico's leaders hoped such a system would encourage a feeling of nationalism among the people and unify them behind the revolution that shook the country in the early 1900s. And in Uruguay reformers led by President José Batlle y Ordóñez (BAHT • yay ee or • THOWN • yas) enacted a broad reform program that included free elections, a social security system, and nationalization of the railroads and public utilities.

Even with these changes, democracy eluded most Latin American governments. Although many countries had passed laws granting universal manhood suffrage, throughout the region voting was largely restricted to literate males. In most countries this group accounted for less than 25 percent of the population. Furthermore, dishonesty and corruption marked many elections. In rural areas, for example, large landowners manipulated elections, controlling the way their tenants voted. And in some countries, forcible overthrow remained the typical way of changing governments.

The Effects of the Great Depression

As the 1920s drew to a close, prices for Latin America's major agricultural exports, such as sugar and coffee, began to fall. Chile's export economy suffered a particularly crippling blow. German scientists had perfected a process for making synthetic nitrates, used in fertilizers and explosives. As a result the bottom dropped out of the market for Chile's major export, nitrates.

The worldwide economic depression caused the prices of Latin America's exports to fall even further. Since they got such a small return on their exports, many Latin American nations found it impossible to import any but the most essential goods. Some countries stopped making payments on their foreign debt. As the region's economies continued to falter, unemployment became widespread, causing worker unrest.

Authoritarian Regimes

Economic crisis soon led to political crisis. Coups d'état overthrew most Latin American governments in the 1930s. In many cases these coups toppled constitutional systems that had worked for 30 to 40 years. Only Uruguay, which experienced a minor crisis between 1933 and 1935, and Mexico, which had undergone a revolution from 1911 to 1917, avoided major political upheaval.

The planters and exporters, whose fortunes had been wiped out during the Depression, no longer held power. Instead the military strongly influenced or controlled these new governments. In some countries American-trained military leaders came to power. The result was that the military became the best equipped to take power. In Nicaragua, for example, General Anastasio Somoza seized power in 1936, two years after assassinating his chief rival, nationalist guerrilla leader

Augusto César Sandino. And in the Dominican Republic, General Rafael Trujillo (troo • HEE • yoh) began a 31-year dictatorship in 1930.

The new military officers considered the upper-class landowners and exporters corrupt, accusing them of having conducted dishonest elections and of allowing foreigners to take control of national resources. Consequently, the military leaders limited the landowners' political influence. At the same time, the new military governments broke the power of labor unions and other worker and peasant organizations. Many governments simply abolished these groups and jailed their leaders. Sometimes the military governments reacted more violently. In El Salvador, for example, the army massacred more than 10,000 peasants in an effort to destroy a popular movement led by Agustín Faribundo Martí, a one-time follower of Sandino in Nicaragua. And in Brazil, President Getúlio Vargas used arrests, mock trials, and torture in his crackdown on the National Liberation Alliance, a left-wing popular movement.

Some military leaders, however, saw that they could curb popular movements through persuasion rather than terror. A number of governments controlled the labor movements by recognizing and giving favors only to those unions loyal to the military. At the same time, many military governments tried to limit the appeal of left-wing movements by

Learning from Pictures In 1933 police opened fire on Cubans in Havana who were celebrating the rumor that President Machado had resigned.

responding to some of the needs of ordinary people. These governments enacted some land reforms and passed laws giving workers benefits such as paid vacations and accident compensation.

Relations with the United States

In its relations with Latin America, President Franklin D. Roosevelt's administration tried to undo the ill will and suspicion created by the earlier United States policy of intervention. Roosevelt fostered a program, begun in the 1920s, called the Good Neighbor policy. This policy stressed mutual cooperation among the American nations and noninterference by the United States in Latin American affairs.

Then in 1933 the United States joined with other American nations in an agreement called the Montevideo (mahnt • uh • vuh • DAY • oh) Pact. This pact declared that "No state has the right to intervene in the internal or external affairs of another state." As proof of its intentions, the United States recalled the army units that had occupied Haiti since 1915. It also surrendered its right to interfere in the affairs of Panama.

A situation in Cuba, however, sorely tested the Roosevelt administration's commitment to the Montevideo Pact. In 1933 a group of radical reformers overthrew the Cuban dictator, Gerardo Machado. The new government immediately declared a socialist revolution and nationalized a number of companies owned by investors from the United States. In response the Roosevelt administration refused to grant diplomatic recognition to the new government. Once again it appeared that the United States would intervene, as was its right under the Platt Amendment (see page 621).

The United States did not directly interfere, but when a Cuban army sergeant, Fulgencio Batista, decided to overthrow the reformers, Roosevelt's envoy to Cuba encouraged him. Once in power, Batista received economic and military assistance from the United States. In order to strengthen Batista's regime, the United States signed a treaty with Cuba in 1934, canceling the Platt Amendment.

Economic Nationalism

Most Latin American governments during the 1930s followed a policy of economic nationalism.

They reacted to the decline in markets for their exports by encouraging industry. In this way they hoped to become more self-sufficient. The Vargas regime in Brazil achieved the most success in this effort. By the time the army ousted Vargas in 1945, Brazil was producing many of its own consumer goods.

Foreign nations responded in a number of ways to this new Latin American initiative. On the whole the United States and Great Britain tried to discourage the Latin American effort to industrialize, since it constituted a threat to their investments and export markets in the region. The German government under Hitler, however, cleverly promoted exports of its own machinery to equip Latin American factories. In this way it hoped to undermine the financial and political influence of the United States and Great Britain.

The most significant act of economic nationalism occurred in Mexico in 1938. American- and British-owned oil companies operating in Mexico became involved in a wage dispute with their workers. When the Mexican Supreme Court ruled in favor of the workers, the foreign-owned oil companies refused to accept its decision. As a result, President Lázaro Cárdenas intervened and nationalized the oil industry.

At first the Roosevelt administration made angry threats and demands. However, supporters of the Good Neighbor policy soon prevailed, insisting on a more subtle approach. The administration then applied various indirect pressures, trying to force the Mexican government to pay the oil companies what they claimed their holdings were worth. Finally the two governments reached a compromise. With the threat of war in Europe growing, the United States thought it necessary to maintain good relations with Mexico.

SECTION 5 REVIEW

1. **Identify**   Good Neighbor policy
2. **Locate**   Mexico City, Buenos Aires
3. **Understanding Ideas**   How did Latin American society change during the 1920s and 1930s?
4. **Analyzing Ideas**   (a) What economic problems did Latin America experience in the late 1920s and the 1930s?   (b) What impact did these problems have on political life in Latin America?
5. **Evaluating Ideas**   How did the Good Neighbor policy affect relations between the United States and Latin America?

Suppression
of Boxer
Rebellion

Russo-
Japanese War

Japanese
annexation
of Korea

AD

1901
1902

1904 1905

1910 1912

Anglo-Japanese
Alliance

Formation
of Chinese
republic

Chapter Summary

The following list contains the key concepts you have learned about the political forces that emerged in Africa, Asia, and Latin America in the early 1900s.

1. During the 1920s and 1930s, Egypt became completely independent, and Trans-Jordan and Iraq gained limited self-government. At the same time, Palestine's future remained in doubt, and India took its first steps toward independence.

2. Great Britain and its former colonies organized the Commonwealth of Nations.

3. Political and social reforms were attempted in Turkey and in Persia. Africa witnessed the stirrings of political activity that were to lead to major transformations in the years ahead.

4. The Chinese began the long and difficult process of adjusting to the modern world. Revolution brought imperial rule to an end, but the Kuomintang had trouble establishing its power in the new republic.

5. Dramatic change took place in Japan, which defeated first China and then Russia at the turn of the century. The Japanese also faced economic and social pressures after World War I.

6. Developments in Latin America reflected the worldwide economic crisis. The 1920s and 1930s were also a time of rapid social change, and in a number of countries, governments became more authoritarian.

7. Latin American relations with the United States improved as a result of the Good Neighbor policy, but economic nationalism led to a certain degree of tension.

On a separate sheet of paper, complete the following review exercises.

Reviewing Important Terms

Supply the term that correctly completes each sentence.

1. Many Jews supported _____ , which aimed to build a Palestinian homeland for the Jews.

2. Gandhi's technique of _____ _____ called for citizens to peacefully refuse to cooperate with their government in order to win concessions from it.

Developing Critical Thinking Skills

1. **Classifying Ideas**   Name the country in which each of the following people played vital leadership roles: **(a)** Anastasio Somoza,   **(b)** Kemal Atatürk,   **(c)** Chiang Kai-shek,   **(d)** Mohandas Gandhi,   **(e)** Fulgencio Batista,   **(f)** Reza Shah Pahlavi.

2. **Comparing Ideas**   After World War I, many colonies wanted independence. Compare the British reaction to demands for Indian independence with the reaction to similar demands from Canada, Australia, New Zealand, and the Union of South Africa.

3. **Interpreting Ideas**   **(a)** How did Sun Yat-sen hope to bring democracy to China?   **(b)** What obstacles prevented him from succeeding?

4. **Summarizing Ideas**   **(a)** What changes did the Nationalists begin in China?   **(b)** What problems did they fail to solve?

5. **Determining Cause and Effect**   What economic and social problems did Japan face as a result of its rapid modernization and industrialization?

6. **Analyzing Ideas**   Why did President Roosevelt support a continuation of the Good Neighbor policy during his administration?

7. **Analyzing a Primary Source**   The lines below are from a poem entitled "Reproach" by Muhammad Iqbal, an Indian poet and a fervent nationalist who wanted independence for India. Read these lines, and answer the questions that follow.

> Your fate, poor hapless India, there's
>   no telling—
> Always the brightest jewel in someone's
>   crown;
> Mortgaged to the alien, soul and body too,
> Alas—the dweller vanished with the
>   dwelling—,
> Enslaved to Britain you have kissed the
>   rod:
> It is not Britain I reproach, but you.

(a) What does Iqbal think India's fate will be? **(b)** Whom does he blame for this situation? **(c)** Why? **(d)** What actions do you think Iqbal might want the Indian people to take?

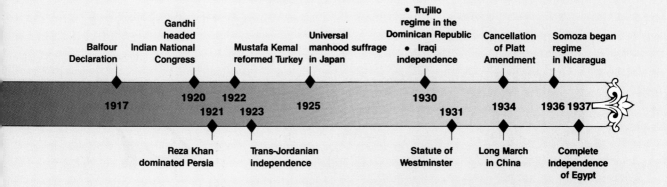

Balfour Declaration — 1917
Gandhi headed Indian National Congress — 1920
1921 — Reza Khan dominated Persia
Mustafa Kemal reformed Turkey — 1922
1923 — Trans-Jordanian independence
Universal manhood suffrage in Japan — 1925
Trujillo regime in the Dominican Republic • Iraqi independence — 1930
1931 — Statute of Westminster
Cancellation of Platt Amendment — 1934 — Long March in China
Somoza began regime in Nicaragua — 1936 1937 — Complete independence of Egypt

Relating Geography to History

Study the map of the Kuomintang military operations on page 700. **(a)** Where did Kuomintang victories over the warlords take place? **(b)** Where did Kuomintang strikes against the Communists take place?

Relating Past to Present

1. Examine a historical atlas containing a map of the Middle East in the 1930s. **(a)** What nations existed as mandates or protectorates? **(b)** What nations were independent? **(c)** How does this map compare with a map of the Middle East today? **(d)** What nations hold the land that once made up Palestine?
2. **(a)** What issue strained relations between the United States and Mexico in the 1930s? **(b)** Does this issue still cause difficulties between these two nations? Explain.
3. Review the information in this chapter on the importance of the military in Japan, Persia (Iran), and Latin America. Choose one of these areas. Use newspapers and magazines to determine what role the military plays in these areas today. Is the military stronger or weaker than it was in the 1920s and 1930s?

Applying History Study Skills

Before completing this activity, review Building History Study Skills on page 693.

Mohandas Gandhi organized the "Salt March" in India in 1930 to protest the British tax on salt. Read the following excerpt on the "Salt March" from *Gandhi* by Daniel R. Birch, D. Ian Allen, John U. Michaelis, and Robin J. McKeown. Then answer the questions that follow.

❝ The salt deposits were surrounded by ditches filled with water and guarded by four hundred native Surat police. . . . Half a dozen British officials commanded them. The police carried *lathis*—five-foot clubs tipped with steel. Inside the stockade twenty-five native riflemen were drawn up.

In complete silence the Gandhi men drew up and halted a hundred yards from the stockade. A picked column advanced from the crowd, waded the ditches, and approached the barbed wire stockade, which the Surat police surrounded, holding their clubs at the ready. Police officials ordered the marchers to disperse under a recently imposed regulation which prohibited gatherings of more than five persons in any one place. The column silently ignored the warning and slowly walked forward. . . .

Suddenly, at a word of command, scores of native police rushed upon the advancing marchers and rained blows on their heads with their steel-shod *lathis*. Not one of the marchers even raised an arm to fend off the blows. They went down like tenpins. . . .

Then another column formed while the leaders pleaded with them to retain their self-control. ❞

1. What problem does the excerpt describe?
2. What is the solution to the problem?
3. How is the solution related to satyagraha?
4. **(a)** How would you evaluate the method? **(b)** Can nonviolence triumph over violence? **(c)** Why or why not?
5. Write a conclusion analyzing the method of nonviolence in response to the Salt Tax. Use your answers for question 4 to support your conclusion.

Investigating Further

1. **Writing a Report** Prepare a report on the rise of nationalism in Turkey. Your report should focus on the efforts of the Young Turks and the role of Mustafa Kemal. One possible source for your report is Desmond Stewart's *Turkey* (Time-Life Books).
2. **Preparing an Oral Presentation** Empress Cuxi—the empress dowager—held power in China from 1861 until her death in 1908. Using encyclopedias and books in your library, prepare a brief report on the life of the empress. In your report note reasons why her policies might have helped to bring about the end of the Qing dynasty.
3. **Constructing a Chart** Make a list of the major changes that took place in Latin America during the 1920s and 1930s. Then prepare a chart in which you classify each of the items on your list under one of the following headings: economic, social, or political.

27

Local Aggressions Brought About World War II

Place   Asia, Africa, and Europe

Time   1921–1945

3.7 mil. BC   4000 BC   AD 2100

Significance

By the 1930s most European nations once more claimed loyalty to one of two opposing camps. One group included those nations generally satisfied with the World War I peace settlement. The other group consisted of dissatisfied nations. With each passing year, international relations between the two groups grew more strained.

Despite its serious weaknesses, the League of Nations tried valiantly to preserve the peace. Since the United States had never joined, however, and the Soviet Union was not admitted until 1934, the League's membership was incomplete. In addition, the League could not make laws for its members, but could only make recommendations that it had no means of enforcing. Peace became increasingly difficult to preserve, and in 1939 Japanese aggression in Asia and German aggression in Europe erupted in World War II.

Terms to Define

appeasement	collaborator
blitzkrieg	Holocaust

People to Identify

Benito Mussolini	Winston Churchill
Francisco Franco	Franklin Roosevelt
Adolf Hitler	Hideki Tojo
Neville Chamberlain	Bernard Montgomery
Joseph Stalin	Dwight Eisenhower

Places to Locate

Manchuria	Polish Corridor	Leningrad
Sudetenland	Danzig	Pearl Harbor
Maginot Line	Dunkirk	Philippine Islands
Munich	El Alamein	Yalta

Questions to Guide Your Reading

1 How did local conflicts threaten world peace?
2 How did Hitler's aggressions in Europe bring about World War II?
3 What significant gains did the Axis achieve in the early years of the war?
4 Why did the Soviet Union and the United States enter the war?
5 What Allied victories over Germany and Japan ended the war?

In the early morning hours of August 6, 1945, an American army sergeant sat resolutely at the wheel of a battered, mud-encrusted jeep. Propping a small pad of paper awkwardly against his knee, he wrote a loving note to his fiancée in the United States. A portion of the letter read:

> 66 *I*'ve never doubted that we would win the war. After four years much of Europe is in ruins. During these last few weeks of occupation the guns have remained silent. Today men in my unit are preparing to board troopships for Japan. We're tired of war, but we're ready to do whatever it takes to win it. 99

The young sergeant had no way of knowing that as he wrote, a B-29 bomber named Enola Gay was en route to Japan, carrying the world's first atomic bomb. Before the soldier's fiancée received the letter, Japan had surrendered unconditionally, and World War II was over. The Allied victory came nearly six years after the beginning of World War II, but concern about world peace actually arose in the 1920s.

1 Local Conflicts Threatened World Peace

Because of the political weakness of the League of Nations, the major powers held diplomatic conferences outside the organization. The first of these conferences was held in 1921 and 1922 in Washington, D.C. Nine of the powers having interests in East Asia (excluding the Soviet Union, which was not invited to the meeting) attended this Washington Conference.

Several treaties resulted from the conference. The Five-Power Treaty provided for a 10-year "naval holiday," during which no warships would be built. The participating nations also signed the Nine-Power Treaty, agreeing to take no additional territory from China and to maintain the existing Open Door policy. As a result of the Washington Naval Conference and other diplomatic settlements, peace was preserved throughout the 1920s.

The most optimistic of the international conferences took place in 1928 in Paris. The American secretary of state, Frank B. Kellogg, and the French foreign minister, Aristide Briand, drafted a treaty

◀ *Pearl Harbor after Japan's surprise attack*

condemning war. Eventually, more than 60 nations signed the Kellogg-Briand Pact, which made war "illegal," but no one had yet found a way to prevent war. In the 1930s, it became clear that such makeshift arrangements would no longer be effective.

Japanese Aggression in Asia

Beginning in the late 1920s, the military gained increasing power in Japan. In 1930 Japan's liberal prime minister, Yuko Hamaguchi (HAH·MAH·GOO·CHEE), was fatally shot. Political disorder followed, and within two years militarists controlled the Japanese government.

Attack on Manchuria. In September 1931 a mysterious explosion near the city of Mukden, Manchuria, damaged a Japanese-controlled railroad. Without warning and without the consent of China, Japanese troops occupied Mukden. The Republic of China appealed to the League of Nations for help. The Japanese delegate to the League stated that the occupation of Mukden was purely a local matter and warned the League not to interfere. This incident sparked a conflict between Japan and China that was to continue, intermittently, until 1945.

The League of Nations sent an investigating commission, headed by Lord Lytton of Great Britain, to Manchuria. At the same time, Japan continued its conquest. In 1932 Japan declared Manchuria to be an independent nation, under the name Manchukuo (MAN·CHOO·KWOH).

The Lytton Commission advised the League not to recognize Manchukuo's independence and recommended that the region be restored to China. When the League voted on this recommendation, only Japan opposed it. As a result of its diplomatic defeat, Japan withdrew from the League of Nations. Some historians regard Japan's successful aggression against China as the actual beginning of World War II.

The League's inability to restrain Japan's territorial ambitions showed that although the major nations joined in condemning aggression, they were unwilling to take drastic measures to stop it. Japanese aggression started a chain reaction that led to the collapse of peace in the West as well as in the East.

War in China. Confidently Japan pressed further demands on China. It announced its intention to extend its influence to all of China, not merely to outlying regions. In July 1937 Japanese and Chinese troops clashed near Beijing. Japanese armies captured the city and at once began to move southward. China resisted the invasion, but its armies proved inferior to those of Japan.

By 1939 the Japanese occupied about one-fourth of China (see map, page 713), including all its seaports, the Chang Jiang Valley as far as Hankou, and many cities in the interior. Still the Chinese stubbornly resisted. This resistance proved an enormous strain, not only on their own resources, but also on those of Japan. By 1939 Japan had lost nearly 500,000 troops in China and had spent $10 billion. Chinese losses were uncountable.

Italy's Conquest of Ethiopia

The Fascist Party in Italy, like the Communist Party in Russia, considered itself a ruling elite. Premier Benito Mussolini, the party's leader, focused his policy on improving the nation's economy through increased taxation, reduced government spending, and suppression of strikes.

Mussolini also sought to solve his country's economic problems by overseas expansion. Ethiopia, one of the few independent nations in Africa, became the object of his ambitions.

A border incident provided the pretext for aggression. In December 1934 an Italian border patrol in Italian Somaliland (so·MAHL·ee·land) clashed with an Ethiopian border patrol. Mussolini at once sent Italian forces from Eritrea (er·uh·TREE·uh) and Italian Somaliland to invade Ethiopia and "restore order."

Ethiopia, poorly prepared to resist such an invasion, asked the League of Nations for protection. The League maintained no armed forces and made only a minimal effort to bring the dispute to arbitration. In October 1935 Mussolini waged an all-out campaign to conquer and colonize the independent nation of Ethiopia.

The League then declared Italy an aggressor and applied economic sanctions—the stoppage of trade and other economic relations with an offending nation. The sanctions, although sweeping enough, generated only half-hearted observance. In a long war, the effects of the sanctions might have weakened Italy and forced it to give in to the League's demands. However, the poorly equipped Ethiopian army was not prepared to engage in a long war. The Italians triumphantly entered the

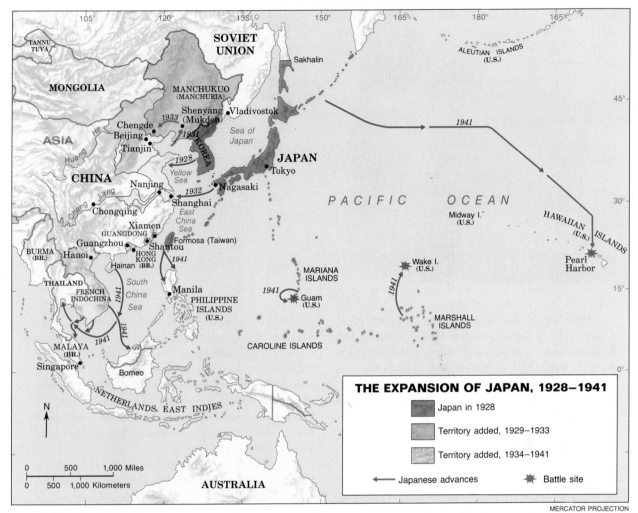

THE EXPANSION OF JAPAN, 1928–1941

- Japan in 1928
- Territory added, 1929–1933
- Territory added, 1934–1941
- ← Japanese advances
- ✶ Battle site

MERCATOR PROJECTION

Learning from Maps *Militarism was the driving force behind Japanese expansion. What groups of islands did the Japanese attack in 1941?*

Ethiopian capital, Addis Ababa (ad•uh SAB•uh•buh), in the spring of 1936. Mussolini declared Ethiopia a part of the Italian Empire and proclaimed the Italian king, Victor Emmanuel III, emperor of Ethiopia.

By this time the League of Nations' ineffectiveness had become apparent. During the summer of 1936, the League called off its sanctions on Italy. However, in 1937 Italy withdrew from the organization anyway. Thereafter, the League failed to command international respect. Its inability to prevent aggression, despite almost universal disapproval of Italy's actions, caused deep concern throughout the world. Meanwhile, Japan and Italy had learned that the democracies were apparently unwilling to go to war to prevent aggression.

Civil War in Spain

Economically Spain lagged far behind the rest of western Europe during the 1800s. Although some industry existed, the economy remained primarily agricultural. The nobility owned large estates that included much of the nation's land. The wealthy and powerful Catholic church controlled the educational system.

By the early 1900s, the Spanish government had become a constitutional monarchy. An elected parliament called the *Cortes* limited the king's power. Politically the country was unstable. Throughout the early 1900s, violent strikes, political assassinations, military plots, and separatist movements in the provinces plagued the nation.

713

After World War I, the chaos in Spain grew worse. In 1923 General Miguel Primo de Rivera led a revolt and established a military dictatorship. King Alfonso XIII remained as a figurehead, but Primo de Rivera, backed by the army, held the power. However, after Rivera lost the support of the army in 1930, he resigned. In 1931 King Alfonso abdicated, and Spain became a republic.

The Spanish Republic. Spain's new leaders planned to establish freedom of religion, separate church and state issues, and place the government in control of education. The government took land from the Catholic church and the nobility and gave it to landless peasants. The government barred members of the clergy from teaching in schools, and the Catholic church now had to pay its clergy. Workers received many benefits—shorter hours, better wages, the right to organize, and a voice in the management of business.

These sweeping reforms antagonized Spanish conservatives, who quickly organized a fascist party called the Falange (FAY•lanj)*. The Falange was determined to preserve the power of the army, the landowners, and the church, regardless of whom the voters might elect to office.

Nationalists versus Loyalists. In February 1936 a Popular Front government that included Socialists and Communists won a major election. The Spanish Popular Front, like the Popular Front

in France, represented a coalition of left-wing working-class parties united in their opposition to fascism. Prominent rightists were jailed, and the Falange responded with terrorist acts. In July a Falange leader was assassinated. Following his murder, army uprisings, led by Falangists, erupted in Spanish Morocco, the Canary Islands, and Spain itself. The bitter civil war that followed lasted for almost three years.

The Falangist rebels, led by General Francisco Franco, called themselves Nationalists. Those who supported the republic were known as Loyalists, or Republicans. By the end of 1936, the Nationalists held most of northern and western Spain. The Loyalists controlled the east and southeast, most of the northern coastline, and the capital city of Madrid.

Foreign Assistance to Spain

The Spanish civil war soon became a small European war. Germany and Italy saw a fascist Spain as a part of their plan to surround France with unfriendly powers and threaten Great Britain. They sent fully equipped military units to bolster the Nationalist forces.

Sympathetic to the republican government, the Soviet Union sent planes, technicians, and military advisers. Soviet help to the Loyalists, however, was not nearly as extensive as that which Franco received from his fascist allies.

Volunteers from France, Great Britain, the United States, and other nations also clamored to

---

Falange is the Spanish word for "phalanx."

Guernica by Pablo Picasso

Although he lived in France, Pablo Picasso had been born in Spain and was keenly sympathetic to the Loyalist cause during the Spanish civil war. This painting expressed his outrage over the bombing of the town of Guernica, which had no strategic value. Using only blacks, grays, and whites, Picasso evoked anguish and horror with his distorted figures writhing in agony under a stark electric light. The painting was on tour in New York City in 1939 when World War II began. Picasso suggested that it stay in the United States until "the reestablishment of public liberties" in Spain. *Guernica* was returned to Spain in 1981 and was placed in the Prado museum in Madrid.

---

help the Spanish Republic. These antifascist volunteers became known as the International Brigade. The International Brigade, however, numbered only about 40,000, while Italy alone sent more than 50,000 trained troops to assist the Fascists.

The Spanish civil war brought into the open the seething struggle between fascism and socialism in Europe during the 1930s. It also became a testing ground for new weapons and tactics such as improved aircraft and strategic bombing missions.

The French and the British feared that the Spanish civil war might spread to the rest of Europe and involve them. In September 1936, at the suggestion of the French government, a nonintervention committee representing 27 nations was established. These nations unanimously agreed to a policy of nonintervention in Spain that included a blockade intended to halt the flow of volunteers and supplies to both sides. The blockade cut off most help to the Loyalists, but not German and Italian assistance to Franco. To Hitler and Mussolini, this constituted one more proof that Great Britain and France would do nothing to stop aggression unless it involved their own territory.

Spain Under Franco

By the spring of 1938, the Nationalist forces in Spain had grown strong enough for a large-scale offensive. They defeated the weakened Loyalist troops in March 1939, with the capture of Barcelona and Madrid. During the campaign to seize Madrid, one of Franco's generals announced that he had four columns—long narrow lines of troops—marching on the city and a fifth column within Madrid that would rise against the defenders at the appropriate time. The expression *fifth column* has come to mean traitors within a country who assist its enemies.

Franco then set up a fascist government modeled on Mussolini's dictatorship in Italy and became head of the state with unlimited power. He assumed the title *el Caudillo* (cow • DEE • yoh)—Spanish for "the leader." He was responsible, as one decree said, "only to God and history." Franco's political party, the Falange, was the only one permitted. Its national council, chosen by Franco, "advised" him on legislation.

The economic organization of Spain resembled that of fascist Italy, with syndicates, or corporations, organized according to occupations and economic activities. The government abolished free elections and most civil rights. Under Franco's regime, the old ruling groups—the army, the landowners, and the Roman Catholic church—continued to hold positions of power.

Although Spain had become a fascist dictatorship, Franco did not join the Rome-Berlin Axis (see below). The civil war had devastated the country, and many years were to pass before economic recovery took place and hatred among Spaniards waned.

2 Hitler's Aggressions in Europe Sparked World War II

As Germany grew stronger, Hitler's foreign policy became more aggressive. In 1933 he had taken Germany out of the League of Nations and announced his intention to rearm the country. In March 1936 German troops marched into the Rhineland, violating the Treaty of Versailles. In October 1936, following the outbreak of the Spanish civil war, Hitler and Mussolini formed a military alliance called the Rome-Berlin Axis and began referring to themselves as the Axis Powers.*

Shortly afterward, Japan and Germany pledged to work together to prevent the spread of Russian communism. The two countries signed an agreement called the Anti-Comintern Treaty, which Italy soon endorsed. Thus by the end of 1936, the nations that would eventually enter World War II as the Axis Powers—Germany, Italy, and Japan—had camouflaged their aggressive intentions under the pretense of resisting communism. Hitler became convinced that he could do as he pleased, and for a

---

*Mussolini originated the term *Axis Powers*. He claimed that an imaginary line drawn from Rome to Berlin formed the "axis" on which the world would turn from that time forward.

time he seemed right. The democratic nations had done very little to halt the spread of fascism in Ethiopia and Spain.

Annexing Austria

A Nazi party had been formed in Austria in the late 1920s. By the early 1930s, the extremely conservative Austrian government was doing little to resist Nazi inroads. By 1938 threats from both Hitler and Mussolini forced the Austrian government to include Nazi members in its cabinet.

When the Austrian chancellor offered to take a vote of the Austrian people on the question of *Anschluss* (union) with Germany, Hitler refused to permit it. The chancellor resigned, and a German army marched into Austria unopposed. In March 1938 Hitler proclaimed Austria a part of the Third Reich. The League of Nations took no action. Great Britain and France sent protests to Hitler, which he ignored. Once again, no stronger steps were taken. The democracies seemed to prefer inaction to the danger of war.

The addition of Austria enlarged Germany's population, territory, and resources. It also increased Hitler's influence in Europe. Strategically, Germany had now penetrated the heart of central Europe and reached a common border with its ally, Italy. A glance at the map on page 717 will show what the annexation of Austria did to Czechoslovakia, which Hitler had designated as the next objective in his expansion program. Germany now almost completely encircled the Czech republic. Nazi propaganda, however, claimed that Czechoslovakia had become "a dagger aimed at the heart of Germany."

Czechoslovakia and the Sudeten Crisis

Around the western rim of Czechoslovakia, in a region known as the Sudetenland (soo•DAYT•uhn•land), lived more than 3 million Germans. This territory, once part of the huge Hapsburg Empire, had been included in Czechoslovakia after World War I. A chain of mountains, which gave the new state a natural and defensible frontier, separated the Sudetenland from Germany and Austria. Czechoslovakia had fortified these mountains heavily. Now they had become a defensive line—second in importance in Europe only to France's Maginot Line.

AXIS AGGRESSION IN EUROPE 1935–1939

- ✪ National capital
- • Other city
- Germany in 1934
- To Germany by plebiscite, 1935
- Reoccupied by Germany, 1936
- Occupied by Germany, 1938
- Occupied by Germany, March 1939
- Italy in 1938
- Occupied by Italy, April 1939

AZIMUTHAL EQUAL AREA PROJECTION

Learning from Maps Axis aggression was directed at poorly defended eastern Europe and Africa. What country in Africa did the Axis Powers invade?

The Czech government tried to protect the rights of the Sudeten Germans. It allowed them to use the German language in their schools and to be represented fairly, according to population, in the parliament, the civil service, and the army. Still, many Sudeten Germans wanted union with Germany, and with the Nazi victory in Germany, a strong Nazi party grew in the Sudetenland.

After Germany's annexation of Austria, Sudeten Nazis demanded a completely self-governing Sudetenland. Hitler took up their cause, ranting against the Czech "oppression" of Germans. Nazi propagandists spread many fictitious stories of Czech discrimination and atrocities against the Sudetens. Riots broke out, and in September 1938 the situation became so critical that the Czech government placed the country under martial law.

Hitler said that the German army would invade the Sudetenland to "protect" Germany's "Sudetenland brothers." He also decreed that Germany

717

with France and Great Britain. Stalin apparently hoped that Hitler would find himself bogged down in the West. This would give the Soviet Union adequate time to prepare for its eventual, inevitable encounter with Germany.

Publicly the Nazi-Soviet Pact pledged that Germany and the Soviet Union would never attack each other. Each would remain neutral if the other became involved in war. Secretly, however, the two dictators agreed to divide eastern Europe into spheres of influence. Germany was to take western Poland. The Soviet Union was to have a free hand in the Baltic countries, in eastern Poland, and in the province of Bessarabia, which it had lost to Romania in 1918.

Little doubt existed as to the meaning of the pact. The Western nations had lost a possible ally in the East, and Germany had secured a pledge of the Soviet Union's neutrality. It was a tremendous military advantage, which Hitler was quick to use.

Danzig and the Polish Corridor

The crisis that finally touched off World War II began in Poland. Hitler's dispute with that country involved the Polish Corridor, the strip of territory cut through Germany to allow Poland access to the seaport of Danzig (see map, page 717). Danzig, a free city protected by the League of Nations, was a port for both Germany and Poland.

Because Danzig had a large German population, Hitler claimed that the city had been "torn from the fatherland." He attacked the commissioner appointed by the League as a "foreigner."

A strong Nazi party, encouraged by propaganda and financial help from Berlin, developed in Danzig. By 1937 it controlled the city government. It took actions and issued demands that made relations with Poland increasingly difficult. The League commissioner was powerless to do anything.

After securing Austria and Czechoslovakia, Hitler intensified his campaign against Poland. The Nazis demanded the return of Danzig to the fatherland. A propaganda campaign claimed Polish mistreatment of the Germans in the Polish Corridor. Within a week after signing the nonaggression pact with the Soviet Union, Hitler demanded a "German Solution" to the "Polish Question": Danzig must be returned to Germany, and the Germans must be allowed to occupy a strip running through the Corridor.

On the morning of September 1, 1939, Hitler declared the annexation of Danzig to the Reich. At the same time, without warning, his air force made a massive attack on Poland. Nazi troops, led by tank columns, penetrated the border. Two days later Great Britain and France decided that they would not tolerate any further Nazi aggression. They kept their promises to Poland and declared war on Germany. Within 48 hours the unannounced attack on Poland had become the beginning of World War II.

SECTION 2 REVIEW

1. **Define** appeasement
2. **Identify** Axis Powers, Anti-Comintern Treaty, Neville Chamberlain, Edouard Daladier, Munich Conference, Nazi-Soviet Pact
3. **Locate** Sudetenland, Munich, Memel, Albania, Polish Corridor, Danzig
4. **Evaluating Ideas** How did Hitler's annexation of Austria benefit Germany?
5. **Sequencing Ideas** Describe the steps by which Hitler took over Czechoslovakia.
6. **Understanding Ideas** How did France and Great Britain prepare for war in 1939?
7. **Summarizing Ideas** (a) What was the significance of the Nazi-Soviet Pact? (b) What may have been Hitler's and Stalin's reasons for signing it?

3 The Axis Made Significant Gains

Hitler's invasion of Poland introduced the world to a new kind of warfare. The German attack was called a **blitzkrieg**—German for a "lightning war" conducted with great speed and force. Dive bombers screamed down from the skies, dropping explosives on cities below. Panzer* units—tanks and armored trucks—advanced swiftly. On September 27, 1939, after a brief but devastating war, the Poles surrendered to Hitler.

The "Phony" War

While Germany launched its attack on Poland, France moved its army up to the Maginot Line, the

---

*Panzer is from the German word for armor.

chain of fortifications guarding France's eastern frontier. British forces crossed the English Channel and landed on the northern coast of France. The British navy blockaded Germany's ports. The Germans massed troops behind the Siegfried Line, the system of fortifications they had built in the Rhineland. Although German submarines had begun to sink merchant ships—both enemy and neutral—there was little action on the western front. Despite the escalation of mobilization and arms production, newspapers began to speak of the "phony" war in western Europe. Many people referred to the "phony" war as a "sitzkrieg," or sitting war, instead of a blitzkrieg. However, they still hoped that an all-out war could be avoided.

As the Germans marched into Poland, the Soviet army massed on the Soviet-Polish border. Then, in accordance with the secret provisions of the Nazi-Soviet Pact, the Soviets moved into eastern Poland. Once again, Poland disappeared from the map of Europe. The Soviets also seized control of Estonia, Latvia, and Lithuania.

On November 30, 1939, the Soviet Union attacked Finland. The Finns appealed to the League of Nations, which expelled the Soviet Union for its aggression against a fellow member nation. Although the Finns fought bravely for three months, their resistance crumbled in March 1940.

Scandinavia and the Low Countries

On April 9, 1940, the "phony" war ended with a sudden German invasion of Denmark and Norway. Hitler had prepared the way in these Scandinavian countries by sending Germans there as workers. These Germans were to secure the services of native **collaborators,** people who were willing to assist their country's enemies. In a single day, German troops seized several of Norway's strategic North Sea ports. Both Denmark and Norway fell under German control.

The reasons for Hitler's invasion of these countries soon became clear. By seizing them, Germany had secured an outlet to the Atlantic. Thus Hitler made certain that his country's navy would not be bottled up in the Baltic Sea as it had in World War I. The long, irregular Scandinavian coastline gave Germany excellent submarine bases. The terrain also provided many good sites for airfields. Thus sea lanes to France and Great Britain were put in grave danger.

The British soon realized that Hitler posed an immediate threat to their safety. Neville Chamberlain, who symbolized the policy of appeasement, was forced to resign as prime minister in May 1940. He was succeeded by Winston Churchill, one of the few prominent politicians in the 1930s to attack appeasement and to warn against the Nazi menace.

Hitler, meanwhile, continued to attack. He intended to take as much territory as possible before his opponents could mount an offensive against him. On May 10, 1940, German armored units invaded the Low Countries—the Netherlands, Belgium, and Luxembourg. Luxembourg fell in one day, the Netherlands in five. When the Dutch city of Rotterdam resisted the German army, Hitler ordered his air force to attack it. Even while a surrender was being negotiated, Nazi bombers leveled the heart of the city. At the end of May, Belgium also surrendered.

Hitler's forces were now in a position to outflank France's Maginot Line. The German panzers drove westward toward the English Channel. At Dunkirk, a seaport in northern France, they cut off the British, Belgian, and French troops from the major French force to the south. Outnumbered and with no room to maneuver, the encircled Allied troops withdrew.

Evacuation of Dunkirk. At this point, the British air force was able to gain momentary

Learning from Pictures The defeated Allies evacuate the beach at Dunkirk. What allowed the evacuation to succeed?

control of the air to defend the trapped forces at Dunkirk from bombing attacks. Every available ship and boat in England, including fishing craft and rowboats, was ordered to Dunkirk. Between May 27 and June 4, some 340,000 men were safely transported across the channel to England.

For unknown reasons, Hitler decided not to attack the retreating allies. For three days he held back his tanks—a decision that later would be considered a costly Axis mistake because it allowed Britain to rally. Hitler's panzer leaders bombarded their superior officers with protests but received only a message that holding the tanks back was "the Führer's personal order."

Although the evacuation of Dunkirk was a military defeat for the Allies, the success of the astounding rescue operation helped raise British morale considerably. On June 4 Prime Minister Churchill addressed the British people in one of his most stirring speeches. His forceful and engaging voice boomed over the airwaves:

> **"W**e shall go on to the end. We shall fight in France, we shall fight in the seas and oceans, we shall fight with growing confidence and growing strength in the air, we shall defend our Island, whatever the cost may be. We shall fight on the beaches, we shall fight on the landing-grounds, we shall fight in the fields and in the streets, we shall fight in the hills; we shall never surrender; and even if, which I do not for a moment believe, this island or a large part of it were subjugated and starving, then our Empire beyond the seas, armed and guarded by the British Fleet, would carry on the struggle, until, in God's time, the New World, with all its power and might, steps forth to the rescue and the liberation of the Old. **"**

The Fall of France

After the evacuation of Dunkirk, the French were left to fight alone on the European continent. The Maginot Line was useless. Having taken Belgium, the Germans were in a position to attack France from the north, where few fortifications existed.

Germany began its offensive against France early in June 1940. The French fought a desperate, losing battle. Their army was neither trained nor equipped for this new kind of war. Northern France was a scene of utter confusion. Civilians, carrying whatever possessions they could save, blocked roads in their attempts to flee southward. German planes bombed and machine-gunned the helpless refugees, causing panic and disorder.

Mussolini, taking advantage of France's weakness, declared war on France and Great Britain on June 10, and Italian forces invaded southern France. On June 14 the Germans entered Paris, and French armed resistance collapsed. Rather than surrender, the French cabinet resigned.

Some of the French leaders, however, were willing to surrender. The aged Marshal Philippe Pétain (pay • TAN), a hero of World War I, formed a government and assumed dictatorial powers. Late in June Hitler forced the Pétain government to sign an armistice with Germany and Italy. Ironically, it was signed in the same railroad car where the Germans had signed the armistice to end World War I in November 1918.

The terms of the armistice were severe. German troops were to occupy northern France, including Paris, and a strip of territory along the Atlantic coast southward to Spain. France had to pay the costs of this occupation. The French navy was to be disarmed and confined to French ports. Pétain's government moved to the city of Vichy (VISH • shee), in the south. Thus France was divided into Occupied France, administered by the Germans, and Vichy France, which collaborated with the Germans. The Vichy government also controlled most French possessions in North Africa and the Middle East. This government became another symbol of appeasement and surrender to fascism.

The French resistance. Some of the French who wanted to continue to fight against Germany escaped to Africa or to England. Under the leadership of General Charles de Gaulle (duh GOHL), they formed the Free French government, with its headquarters in London.

Within France itself an underground movement, the resistance, flourished. Its members worked secretly to oppose the German occupation forces. Similar resistance movements developed in most of the other countries occupied by Germany. Members of some of these resistance groups were called *maquis* (mah • KEE)—a French term for scrubby undergrowth, common in the areas where resistance fighters hid. To cripple the Germans, the

722

Learning from Pictures *Members of the French resistance, shown here after the liberation of Paris, helped Allied forces undermine German authority in occupied France.*

maquis engaged in sabotage. They blew up bridges, wrecked trains, and cut telephone and telegraph lines.

The Battle of Britain

After France fell, French generals predicted that Great Britain, which they considered a weaker country, would "have her neck wrung like a chicken's in three weeks." (Churchill later commented: "Some chicken! Some neck!")

Hitler began scattered bombing raids on Great Britain, gradually increasing them in intensity. He then offered to negotiate a peace settlement, but the feisty British leaders rebuffed him.

At the end of June 1940, Churchill braced the British people for the treacherous battle that he was certain would soon come:

> ❝*H*itler knows that he will have to break us in this island or lose the war. If we can stand up to him, all Europe may be free and the life of the world may move forward into broad, sunlit uplands. But if we fail, then the whole world, including the United States, including all that we have known and cared for, will sink into the abyss of a new Dark Age. . . . Let us therefore

brace ourselves of our duties, and so bear ourselves that, if the British Empire and its Commonwealth last for a thousand years, men will say, 'This was their finest hour.' ❞

Hitler ordered his air force, the *Luftwaffe* (LOOFT • wahf • uh), to soften Great Britain for invasion. He shifted the Luftwaffe squadrons to airfields in occupied France and Belgium near England. Germany stepped up its devastating air attacks on Great Britain, striking civilian population centers, railroads, and industrial targets. The period of the heaviest attacks, from August through November 1940, is known as the Battle of Britain.

German bombers blasted British cities with explosives and firebombs. The Luftwaffe bombed London continually during September and October. In November the city of Coventry burned almost to the ground. The Germans wanted to lower morale and destroy the people's will to fight, but the undaunted British resolutely dug out of the ruins and fought on. Essential to their resistance was the highly successful defense by fighter planes of the Royal Air Force—the R.A.F.

British planes, though fewer in number, were of better quality than the German planes. Daring and superbly trained British pilots courageously flew combat missions day after day, night after night.

●READ
WRITE
INTERPRET
CONNECT
THINK

BUILDING HISTORY STUDY SKILLS

Reading About History: Understanding a Biographical Account

History is more than the factual study of events and the analysis of important issues. People, and the decisions they make, have a significant impact on history. One way to understand the role of people from a historical perspective is to study biographical accounts—secondary sources that are based on primary sources. Biographical accounts help to establish a person's place and significance in regard to a historical event.

How to Understand a Biographical Account

To understand a biographical account, follow these steps.

1. Explain the historical context of the account. For example, what events led up to the events of the person's life?
2. List the major events of the person's life.
3. Identify the person's beliefs.
4. Explain the person's responses to historical events.
5. Identify how other people have viewed the person.
6. Assess the historical significance of the individual. For example, what role did he or she play in the causes or the effects of the event?

Developing the Skill

Prime Minister Winston Churchill's leadership abilities in government and his influence as the author of books such as *The Second World War* and *A History of the English-speaking Peoples* affected not only British history, but world history as well.

The following excerpt from the prime minister's speech to the House of Commons in May 1940 and the wartime conferences listed below illustrate Churchill's place in world history. What information do the excerpt and the list suggest about Churchill's ideas and actions? How did other people view him?

> 66 I have nothing to offer . . . but blood, toil, tears, and sweat. You ask, what is our policy? I will say: it is to wage war by sea, land and air, with all our might and with all the strength that God can give us; to wage war against a monstrous tyranny, never surpassed in the dark, lamentable catalogue of human crime. That is our policy.
>
> You ask, what is our aim? I answer in one word. It is *victory*: victory at all costs, victory in spite of all terror, victory however long and hard the road may be, for without victory there is 99 no survival.

The following list contains several of the wartime conferences Churchill attended during World War II.
- August 1941: Churchill and Roosevelt meet on a battleship off the coast of Newfoundland to issue the Atlantic Charter on postwar aims.

- December 1941: Churchill and Roosevelt meet in Washington, D.C., to confirm that the defeat of Germany will take precedence over the defeat of Japan.
- August 1942: Churchill confers with Stalin in Moscow and informs the Soviet leader that there can be no second front in Europe in 1942.
- August 1943: Churchill and Roosevelt meet in Quebec to confirm the Allied landings at Normandy and agree to landings in southern France.
- September 1944: Churchill and Roosevelt meet in Quebec to discuss victory plans.
- October 1944: Churchill and Stalin meet in Moscow to discuss eastern Europe's future.
- July-August 1945: Churchill, Truman, and Stalin meet at Potsdam to hammer out peace treaties.

Churchill became prime minister at a moment of disaster. The German armies occupied Holland, the Belgian king surrendered, and the French army was driven back to Paris. Although the outlook for Europe appeared dim, the inspiring words of Churchill's "blood, sweat, and tears" speech rallied the British people and encouraged them to persevere. His unwavering leadership at the wartime conferences contributed to the Allied victory, thus impacting world history.

Practicing the skill. Find excerpts from two of Roosevelt's speeches to Americans during World War II. How do these excerpts help you to determine Roosevelt's significance in world history?

To apply this skill, see Applying History Study Skills on page 739.

Winston Churchill amidst bombing damage

British planes also had the advantage of radar, a new electronic tracking device that could detect the number, speed, and direction of enemy aircraft or ships, even in darkness, fog, or clouds.

The R.A.F. challenged German control of the air and prevented German invasion across the channel. Of these British fighter pilots, Churchill said, "Never in the field of human conflict was so much owed by so many to so few."

The Germans continued their night bombing raids for almost two years. At the same time, British bombers made increasingly heavy raids on German cities. By the middle of 1941, air warfare had reached a stalemate. However, because of Germany's effective blockade of British shipping from European ports, there was a chance that Great Britain could be starved into surrendering. This might have happened had it not been for the United States.

United States Involvement

In the Neutrality Act of 1937, the United States expressed its determination to remain neutral in future wars. This legislation forbade Americans to sell war equipment to belligerent nations, prohibited loans to belligerents, prohibited Americans from sailing on ships of belligerents, and restricted the entry of American ships into war zones.

When war in Europe broke out in 1939, public opinion in the United States was divided. Many people believed that Nazi Germany threatened not only Europe but civilization itself. Other people believed that Europe's wars were of no concern to the United States. These **isolationists,** as they were called, had risen to power at the end of World War I, when they had succeeded in keeping the United States out of the League of Nations. Now, however, their power faded as the fear of a Nazi conquest of the world increased.

As the war progressed, the United States gradually became more involved. In 1939 a revised Neutrality Act allowed American firms to sell munitions to belligerent nations, but only on a cash-and-carry basis. In spite of German submarine attacks, the British still controlled the sea routes between the United States and Great Britain. Thus, in effect, this law permitted the sale of arms only to Great Britain.

After the disaster at Dunkirk and the fall of France, Americans' sympathies for the British increased. In September 1940 President Franklin D. Roosevelt, by executive agreement, transferred 50 old American naval destroyers to Great Britain. In exchange, Great Britain gave the United States long-term leases on British naval and air bases in Newfoundland, the British West Indies, and British Guiana. In that same month, Congress passed the first national draft law ever adopted by the United States during peacetime.

Early in 1941 Churchill appealed to the United States: "Give us the tools, and we will finish the job." In March, Congress passed the Lend-Lease Act, authorizing the president to supply war materials to Great Britain on credit. Now the direction of America's involvement became clear.

The Atlantic Charter

Because they wanted to avoid the criticism that the secret treaties of World War I had raised, President Roosevelt and Prime Minister Churchill announced the war aims of the two democracies. In August 1941 they met on board a British battleship off the coast of Newfoundland and drew up a statement that became known as the Atlantic Charter.

Among its provisions and in the spirit of Wilson's Fourteen Points, the charter stated that Britain and the United States: (1) sought no territorial gain, (2) would allow no territorial changes without the consent of the people concerned, (3) respected the right of all people to choose their own form of government, (4) believed that all nations should have equal rights to trade and to raw materials, (5) wanted nations to cooperate on economic matters to ensure everyone a decent standard of living, (6) believed people everywhere should have the right to security and "freedom from want and fear," (7) believed freedom of the seas should be guaranteed, and (8) believed that nations must abolish the use of force and establish a "system of general security," implying the formation of an international organization.

By the fall of 1941, the United States Navy was waging an undeclared war on German submarines. The nation had moved far away from its neutrality of 1937. The only remaining restrictions prohibited American merchant ships from being armed or entering war zones. In November 1941 Congress abolished even these restrictions. The United States, as a nonbelligerent ally, now gave the British "all aid short of war."

1. **Define** blitzkrieg, collaborator, isolationist
2. **Identify** "phony" war, Winston Churchill, Philippe Pétain, Charles de Gaulle, maquis, Battle of Britain, Luftwaffe, Neutrality Act of 1937, Franklin D. Roosevelt, Lend-Lease Act, Atlantic Charter
3. **Locate** Maginot Line, Siegfried Line, Rotterdam, Dunkirk, Occupied France, Vichy France, Coventry
4. **Summarizing Ideas** What advantages did Germany gain by seizing Norway and Denmark?
5. **Evaluating Ideas** Why was the Maginot Line useless in June 1940?
6. **Sequencing Ideas.** Describe the progression of United States involvement in World War II, from the Neutrality Act of 1937 to giving Great Britain "all assistance short of war."

4 The Soviet Union and the United States Entered the War

In the fall of 1940, Germany held almost all of western Europe. It controlled the Atlantic coastline from the tip of Norway to Spain, and its submarines were allowed to use Spanish ports. Spain did not join in the fighting, but neither was it neutral. Franco called his country a "nonneutral nonbelligerent." Germany and Italy also controlled much of the western Mediterranean coastline, an important advantage for their side.

Great Britain still held Gibraltar, on the southern coast of Spain; the islands of Malta and Cyprus, in the Mediterranean; and Alexandria, in Egypt. British troops were stationed in Palestine and in Egypt, protecting the Suez Canal. In September the Japanese government joined the Rome-Berlin Axis as an ally of Hitler and Mussolini.

Eastern Europe and the Mediterranean

Mussolini, hoping to build a Mediterranean empire for Italy, sent his troops into Egypt and Greece in the fall of 1940. The decision proved to be unwise. The Greeks routed the invading Italian army, and the British stopped the advance into Egypt. In their counterattack the British took Tobruk, a port city of Libya (see map, page 727). The Italian invasion of British Somaliland at the same time also failed,

and a counterattack by the British drove the Italians out of Ethiopia as well.

When Hitler turned his attention to the Balkans, Axis fortunes in eastern Europe improved. Germany seized Romania, which it needed for the rich oil fields there. In March 1941 pressure on Bulgaria resulted in the German occupation of that country. By November, Romania, Bulgaria, and Hungary had allied themselves with Germany.

In April 1941 Hitler invaded Yugoslavia, having failed to persuade its government to allow German troops to march through the country to Greece. In less than two weeks, the Germans had crushed Yugoslav resistance.

Next came Greece. Despite stubborn resistance by the Greeks, the German panzers prevailed. The British withdrew to the island of Crete, where the Germans used a new tactic. German troops parachuted onto Crete, and by the end of May the British had abandoned the island and fled to Egypt. Thus Germany controlled the entire Balkan Peninsula except for European Turkey, the city of Istanbul, the Dardanelles, and the Bosporus (see map, page 727). In June, Germany and Turkey signed a treaty assuring Turkish neutrality.

The German victories in Greece and Crete enabled Hitler to launch the next move in his giant strategy—a huge pincers movement aimed at the Suez Canal. One part of the Axis force was to come by way of North Africa, the other through Syria, Iraq, Trans-Jordan, and Palestine.

The rich oil fields of the Middle East would give Hitler a considerable advantage in the war because vital war equipment such as airplanes, tanks, and trucks needed fuel to operate. But Hitler failed to conquer the region. He had hoped that neutral Turkey would allow German troops to pass through its territory to British and French possessions in the Middle East. However, Turkey refused. Consequently, the British and Free French held Iraq and, in July 1941, drove the Vichy French out of Syria. One month later, Allied forces also occupied Iran.

Meanwhile, German forces had moved across the Mediterranean to North Africa. Throughout 1941 Italian and German troops led by General Erwin Rommel—known as the "Desert Fox"—fought the British in Libya. In the summer of 1942, Rommel's forces drove the British out of Libya and back into Egypt. At El Alamein, only 70 miles (112 kilometers) from Alexandria (see map, page 727), the German offensive began to falter for lack of

MAJOR BATTLES

1—Britain, Aug.–Oct. 1940
2—Leningrad, Sept. 1941–Jan. 1944
3—El Alamein, Oct.–Nov. 1942
4—Stalingrad, Nov. 1942–Feb. 1943
5—Anzio, Jan.–Mar. 1944
6—D-Day, June 6, 1944
7—Minsk, June–Aug. 1944
8—Battle of the Bulge, Dec. 1944
9—Warsaw, Aug. 1944–Jan. 1945
10—Berlin, Apr.–May, 1945

WORLD WAR II IN EUROPE AND NORTH AFRICA, 1939–1945

Allied countries
Axis countries
Axis-controlled territory at its greatest extent, 1942
Neutral countries
★ Major battle
⊛ National capital
← Allied advance
← Axis advance
• Other city

AZIMUTHAL EQUAL AREA PROJECTION

Learning from Maps *World War II transformed Europe and North Africa into one huge battlefield. In which country did the Battle of the Bulge take place?*

supplies. The British made a stand, and Rommel remained stalled at El Alamein.

Germany's Attack on the Soviet Union

The Soviet Union regarded the German victories in the Balkans with alarm and anger. It considered the Balkans, especially Romania and Bulgaria, to be within its own sphere of influence.

At a Soviet-German conference in Berlin in November 1940, the Soviets demanded that Bulgaria, Istanbul, the Dardanelles, and the Bosporus be included in their sphere of influence. Hitler suggested instead that Germany should have Europe, and that the Soviet Union should establish a sphere in Asia. The Soviets rejected these suggestions.

On June 22, 1941, the war entered a new phase. Without a declaration of war, German

The World Ocean: Earth's Largest Region

The historical events discussed in this book all took place in specific areas, or regions, of the world. In fact, many of the chapters of the book are organized around the various regions of the world. However, largely because no humans live there, the greatest region on earth—the world ocean—receives little mention. Yet a sense of the geography of the world ocean is necessary for a full understanding of historical processes. The world ocean's size alone staggers the imagination. While geographers give names to four major oceans—the Arctic, Atlantic, Indian, and Pacific—in reality a series of narrow waterways and other sea passages connect all four to form just one great world ocean. Further, around the margins of this world ocean lie the seas, gulfs, and bays that extend its waters.

To gain a sense of the size of the world ocean, look at a globe. With your finger, trace a line on the globe through the four oceans, noting the waterways that connect them. As you can see, the name *Earth* is actually a misnomer. For the early Greek geographers, however, the world consisted of just one comparatively small body of water, the Mediterranean Sea, surrounded by large amounts of land. Hence, calling this planet Earth seemed appropriate to them. Had they known that more than 70 percent of the planet's surface was covered by water, they might have named it *Ocean*.

Actually, some Greek geographers did suggest that a world ocean existed. However, they located it incorrectly. To them the ocean consisted of an endless, boundless stream that flowed around the margins of the world. They believed that if people ventured far out upon this ocean, they would pass through a region of dense fog and ultimately arrive in an even more dreaded region where water and sky met.

There they would find themselves cast into a world of darkness from which they would never return.

The voyages of exploration and discovery during the 1500s provided people with an understanding of the vastness of the world ocean. However, 400 years passed before people developed a similar understanding of the ocean floor. During these years most people assumed the floor of the ocean consisted of a vast level plain. However, exploration conducted in the second half of the 1900s showed clearly that the ocean bottom is as varied and broken as the earth's surface. In fact, some of the world's most spectacular scenery lies beneath the ocean's waters. The ocean floor's towering mountain ranges, enormous canyons, and expansive plains make their counterparts on land appear miniscule by comparison.

For example, one huge mountain range—the Mid-Atlantic Ridge—runs down the middle of the Atlantic Ocean for more than 10,000 miles (16,000 kilometers). Also, many long, narrow valleys cut into the floor of the Pacific Ocean. One of these valleys, the Mariana Trench, is so deep that if the world's highest mountain, Mount Everest, were dropped into it, more than one mile (1.6 kilometers) of ocean water would lie above the mountain's summit. While the ridges and trenches represent the most dramatic landforms of the ocean floor, in terms of area, plains dominate the ocean world. Like plains on land, these undersea plains are mostly smooth and flat.

Research also has shown that the ocean contains many minerals. In addition, some scientists have suggested that the abundant marine life of the world ocean may offer a solution to the problem of food shortages. In the years to come the world ocean may play a much greater role in history than it has in the past.

Big Sur, on the Pacific Coast of California

armies invaded the Soviet Union. Hitler had opened a new front in the east, 2,000 miles (3,200 kilometers) long. Churchill declared that, although he did not admire communism, any nation that fought the Nazis was an ally and should receive help. The United States also declared its willingness to assist the Soviet Union.

As in World War I, sending aid to the Soviet Union became extremely difficult. Ships sailing the route across the Mediterranean and through the Dardanelles, the Bosporus, and the Black Sea risked submarine and air attacks from bases in Italy and the Balkans. The route through the Baltic Sea was impossible. Convoys to two Soviet ports, Murmansk and Archangel in the Arctic, had to pass the long, German-held coast of Norway. To avoid these dangers, the Allies developed a new route from the Persian Gulf across Iran by train and truck to the southern part of the Soviet Union.

The Soviet Defense

The initial thrust of the Nazi armies into the Soviet Union was tremendous. Everywhere the Soviet armies were driven back. Within a very short time, Moscow and Leningrad were under siege. There, however, the attack bogged down.

The Soviet defenders used the same scorched-earth tactics against Hitler that their ancestors had used against Napoleon. The retreating armies and civilians carried away what they could and destroyed everything else. Thus the territory the Germans gained was more a hindrance than a help. In addition, many Soviet soldiers remained, hiding out in swamps and forests and making daring guerrilla attacks on railroads, bridges and trains.

Hitler had expected the Soviet Union to surrender quickly. But the Soviet stand at Leningrad and Moscow disrupted his timetable. When the short Russian autumn came, Hitler faced the same decision Napoleon had had to make: Should he retreat or should he stand? Hitler chose to stand.

Soon the Germans had to face a new enemy—the bitterly cold Russian winter. The Soviets chose the winter for a counterattack, which was intended primarily to relieve pressure on Moscow. For the first time in World War II, the Germans retreated.

The year 1941 ended with the Germans deep inside the Soviet Union. In the spring of 1942, they struck southward, aiming to cut the Soviet supply line from Iran. One German spearhead drove toward the city of Stalingrad (see map, page 727). The southern part of the German army drove deep into the Caucasus. Fighting fiercely, the Soviets stopped the Germans before they reached their goal, the port of Baku on the Caspian Sea. North of the Caucasus, however, the Germans forced the Soviets all the way back to Stalingrad.

"New Order" and "Final Solution"

The invasion of the Soviet Union was part of Hitler's master plan for the creation of a "New Order" for Europe. Hitler wanted to organize the continent into a single political and economic system ruled from Berlin and dominated by the "Aryan race." According to this plan, the Soviet Union would supply Germany with food and raw materials. An official economic plan issued by the German government stated: "There is no doubt that . . . many millions of people will be starved to death if we take out of the country the things we need." Causing the Russians to starve did not concern Hitler. According to Nazi ideology, all Slavs were "racially inferior."

Another aspect of Hitler's "New Order" went into effect as the Germans continued their offensives. In 1941 Hitler ordered the annihilation of the entire Jewish population of Europe. The Nazis referred to this program as the "Final Solution" of the "Jewish Problem." This unbelievably barbaric goal was possible in Hitler's Germany because so many people had accepted as fact the Nazi theories about the racial superiority of the Aryans.

Jews by the hundreds of thousands were transported to eastern Germany and Poland. There they were held in "protective custody" in concentration camps. Among the most infamous were Dachau and Buchenwald in Germany, and Treblinka and Auschwitz in Poland. The captors used some inmates as slave laborers. Most, however, were murdered by poison gas or were shot.

In his book *Never to Forget*, Milton Meltzer quotes an SS* officer sent to a Polish death camp to deliver poison gas. There he witnessed the mass extermination of Polish Jews. The following excerpt is from the officer's handwritten account:

---

*Hitler's SS (*Schutzstaffel*) was an elite corps of officers sworn to absolute obedience. They served as Hitler's bodyguards and later took charge of intelligence, central security, and extermination of people in concentration camps.

"They walked along the path, . . . and entered the death chambers. A sturdy SS man stood in the corner and told the wretched people in a clerical tone of voice: 'Nothing at all is going to happen to you! You must take a deep breath in the chambers. That expands the lungs. This inhalation is necessary because of illness and infection.' . . .

This gave some of these poor people a glimmer of hope that lasted long enough for them to take the few steps into the chambers without resisting. The majority realized—the smell told them—what their fate was to be. So they climbed the steps and then they saw everything. . . . They hesitated, but they went into the gas chambers, pushed on by those behind them, or driven by the leather whips of the SS. . . . Many people were praying. . . .

The SS forced as many in together as was physically possible. The doors closed. . . . After 28 minutes only a few were still alive. At last, after 32 minutes everyone was dead.

Men of the work squad opened the wooden doors from the other side. . . . The dead were standing upright . . . pressed together in the chambers. . . . One could see the families even in death. They were still holding hands. . . . Two dozen dentists opened the mouths with hooks and looked for gold. . . . The . . . corpses were carried in wooden barrows just a few meters away to the pits."

During the war, people in some western European countries, especially Denmark, tried to protect Jewish citizens. In eastern Europe, however, a long tradition of anti-Semitism made the Nazi program easier to carry out and its results more devastating.

By the time the Nazi government fell, its leaders and its followers had murdered an estimated 6 million European Jews. This systematic Nazi destruction of almost an entire race is referred to as the **Holocaust.** The Nazis also murdered nearly as many non-Jews—mainly Slavs, Gypsies, and members of the resistance.

Japanese Aggressions in the Pacific

The struggle against the Axis Powers received a major boost in December 1941, when expanding conflict and events in the Pacific area drew the United States into the war. Japanese militarism and aggression had increased throughout the 1930s. Early in 1939, with the situation in Europe growing increasingly tense, Japan saw a long-awaited chance to extend its control over East Asia. Japan's first move was to capture the island of Hainan (HI • nahn) and several small islands off the coast of French Indochina (see map, page 713). Thus Japan severed the British sea route from Hong Kong to Singapore. Neither France nor Great Britain could prevent this move.

After both the Netherlands and France fell, Japan made further aggressive moves in East Asia. The Japanese government declared the Netherlands East Indies to be under Japanese "protective custody." Japanese pressure forced the Vichy government to allow French Indochina to become a Japanese protectorate.

In September 1940 Japan formed an alliance with Germany and Italy. The United States responded to this action in three ways: by protesting violations of the Nine-Power Treaty, providing assistance to Chiang Kai-shek, and placing an embargo on the sale of oil and scrap iron to Japan. Japan thus became even more intent on removing any rivals that might jeopardize its oil reserves in the Netherlands East Indies. Now only the American-held Philippines and the Hawaiian Islands threatened Japanese supremacy in the Pacific. The United States, meanwhile, had already moved a large part of its Pacific Fleet to Hawaii.

During 1941 relations between the United States and Japan steadily deteriorated. Japan and the Soviet Union signed a five-year nonaggression treaty. An even more militaristic government came to power in Japan under Premier Hideki Tojo. By the middle of 1941, the Japanese government had begun to plan an attack upon the United States. However, in November the Japanese government also sent special "peace" mission representatives to Washington, D.C.

American Entry into the War

On December 7, 1941, while Tojo's representatives were still in Washington, the Japanese launched a surprise attack on the American naval base at Pearl Harbor, Hawaii. They intended to strike such a severe blow that the United States would not rival the Japanese in the Pacific. Several American ships

Learning from Pictures *In the United States, posters like this one encouraged civilians to take part in the war effort.*

were sunk; others were badly damaged. American dead totaled more than 2,300.

In an excerpt from his book *At Dawn We Slept*, historian Gordon Prange relates an eyewitness account of the attack on Pearl Harbor:

66 *W*hen the attack began, . . . the explosion of bombs, the whine of bullets, the roar of planes, the belching guns of aroused defenders, the acrid smell of fire and smoke—all blended into a nerve-racking [sound] of chaos. . . . Bombardiers still dropped their torpedoes, while dive bombers pounced like hawks. . . . Far above, high-level bombers rained their deadly missiles as fighters shuttled in and out, weaving together the fearful tapestry of destruction. 99

On December 8, 1941, Congress declared war on Japan, as did the British Parliament. Three days later, Germany and Italy declared war on the United States, and Congress replied with its own declaration of war. The United States became a full-fledged belligerent in World War II.

The Japanese quickly took advantage of American unreadiness. On the same day as the attack on Pearl Harbor, Japan began aerial attacks on the Philippines. Soon afterward the Japanese landed on Luzon. Within a month they captured the American island outposts of Guam and Wake. In less than three months, mainland areas of Burma, Thailand, and Malaya, including the British fortress of Singapore, fell to Japan (see map, page 733).

Japan went on to conquer a vast island empire: most of the Netherlands East Indies (Indonesia), the Philippines, and the Gilbert Islands. Australia remained the last stronghold of resistance in the southwest Pacific. It could be supplied only over a long route from Hawaii. Japanese landings on New Guinea and the Solomon Islands threatened this critically important supply line.

SECTION 4 REVIEW

1. **Define**   Holocaust
2. **Identify**   Erwin Rommel, "New Order," "Final Solution," Auschwitz, Hideki Tojo
3. **Locate**   El Alamein, Murmansk, Stalingrad, Pearl Harbor, Gilbert Islands, Solomon Islands
4. **Summarizing Ideas**   What gains did the Germans make in southeastern Europe in 1941?
5. **Interpreting Ideas**   **(a)** What was Hitler's strategy concerning the Middle East?   **(b)** How well did it succeed?
6. **Understanding Ideas**   What event sparked the entry of the United States into World War II?

5 Allied Victories over Germany and Japan Ended the War

Representatives of 26 nations met in Washington, D.C., in January 1942 to unite in the common purpose of defeating the Axis. Chief among these Allies were Great Britain, the Soviet Union, and the United States. Other nations in Europe, Asia, and the Americas contributed what they could. Each nation pledged to use all its resources to defeat the Axis, not to sign a separate peace treaty, and to abide by the provisions of the Atlantic Charter.

Important Offensives

The German offensive in the summer of 1942 pushed the Soviets back to Stalingrad (see map, page 727). There a tremendous battle, the most spectacular of the war, was fought for six months. The Germans penetrated the city, suffering terrible losses in the process. Instead of retreating, the determined Soviets defended their city—street by street and house by house.

In November 1942 the Soviets began a counterattack, encircling the German troops in Stalingrad. Although Hitler ordered his trapped forces to fight to the death, what was left of his army in the city surrendered in January 1943. The heroic and successful defense of Stalingrad was a crucial turning point in the war. The Germans never completely recovered from this defeat.

North Africa. The Allies also made progress in North Africa during 1942. Late in the summer, Allied reinforcements were rushed to El Alamein, where British troops were under German attack. In a decisive battle in October, troops under General Bernard Montgomery of Great Britain routed Rommel's force. They pushed the Germans westward across Libya into Tunisia.

In November 1942 American and British forces under General Dwight Eisenhower of the United States landed in Morocco and Algeria. They pushed eastward into Tunisia as Montgomery's army moved westward. Rommel's army was thus trapped between the two Allied forces. By the middle of May 1943, the Axis Powers in North Africa were forced to surrender.

As a result of Rommel's defeat, the Allies gained a stronghold in North Africa. Italy's African empire disappeared, and control of the French colonies in Africa passed to the Free French. The Allies had maintained control of the Suez Canal and had made the Mediterranean more secure for Allied naval operations.

The Invasion of Italy

Throughout 1942 Stalin demanded that the British and Americans open a second front in Europe to relieve the German pressure on the Soviet Union. The Allies argued that an attack before they were fully prepared would be too risky. Stalin suspected the Allies of hoping that Germany and the Soviet Union would destroy each other.

When the Allies secured North Africa, Stalin renewed his demands for a landing in Europe. Churchill insisted upon an attack on what he called the "soft underbelly of the Axis"—through Italy and the Balkans. In July 1943 Allied armies that had been fighting in North Africa landed on the strategic island of Sicily. Resistance was strong, but the Allies took the island in little more than a month. Then they bombed the Italian mainland in preparation for a landing.

In Italy, Mussolini was forced to resign, and Marshal Pietro Badoglio (buh • DOHL • yo) became premier. His first act was to dissolve the Fascist Party. When the Allied army landed on the southwestern Italian mainland in September 1943, the Italians surrendered unconditionally. They then declared war on Germany. German troops in Italy quickly filled the void left by the Italian Fascists. They skillfully resisted the Allied advance.

The War at Sea and in the Air

Meanwhile, the Allies were winning the Battle of the Atlantic. This conflict between German and Allied ships had begun in the spring of 1940. Although German submarines sank an enormous number of Allied ships, by the fall of 1943, destroyers and other armed ships escorted convoys of troop and supply ships sailing from the United States. Planes based both on land and on aircraft carriers also protected the convoys. New technological devices, such as sonar, located submarines.

Allied air attacks against Germany and the occupied countries intensified. At first the Allies, operating from bases in the British Isles, concentrated on strategic military sites. Later they attacked civilian areas as well. The Allies bombed almost every German city, severely damaging some.

The War in the Pacific

The Japanese advance in the Pacific suffered its first setback in May 1942. In the Battle of the Coral Sea, American and Australian air and naval forces defeated a Japanese fleet steaming toward Australia. Soon afterward an American fleet met a larger Japanese fleet pushing eastward to try to capture the Midway Islands, northwest of Hawaii (see map, page 733). The Americans defeated the Japanese in the crucial Battle of Midway, fought in June by ships and carrier-based planes. With these

Learning from Maps *The dropping of atomic bombs on two Japanese cities ended the war in the Pacific. Which Japanese cities were hit by atomic bombs?*

two victories, the United States Navy began to turn the tide in the war against Japan.

Early in August 1942, to protect the Australian supply line, American marines landed on the Solomon Islands, seizing the airfield on Guadalcanal. This was the first invasion of Japanese-held territory and an important morale-booster for the United States. Four times in the next three months the Japanese launched savage attacks on the

American forces. All were repulsed, with horrendous losses on both sides.

In 1943 the Allied nations took the offensive in the Pacific. Forces from Australia and New Zealand assisted sea, air, and land forces of the United States. Together, they waged a long series of battles aimed at driving the Japanese entirely out of the Solomon Islands. The Allies then adopted a strategy called "island hopping." Certain Japanese-held

Learning from Pictures *After suffering heavy casualties in fierce fighting to capture the island, American marines unload supplies on Iwo Jima.*

islands were captured, while others were bypassed and left helpless for lack of supplies.

During 1944 the Americans cleared the Japanese from the Marshall Islands, New Guinea, and the Marianas. Saipan and Tinian, in the Marianas, became bases for long-range bombing attacks on Japan. In October 1944 an American army under General Douglas MacArthur landed at Leyte (LAYT • ee) in the central Philippines. Shortly after the landing, the Japanese fleet suffered a crushing defeat in a great air and sea fight, the Battle of Leyte Gulf. After six months of heavy fighting, the Allies recovered the Philippine Islands.

Victory in Europe

As the Allies fought their way through Italy in late 1943, plans were being made for another, larger invasion of Europe—Operation Overlord—aimed at the heart of Germany. The landing was to be made on the beaches of the narrow, heavily wooded French peninsula of Normandy (see map, page 727).

The long-awaited landing came on June 6, 1944—D-Day as the military called it. Soldiers and supplies were transported across the English Channel in one of the most daring invasion operations in military history. Within a month, more than 1 million troops had landed in France. The Germans

had expected a landing in France but were unable to discover the exact location of the assault. When they did find out, German forces rushed to meet the Allied invasion but were outnumbered.

After heavy fighting, Allied troops broke out of Normandy and into northern France. At the same time, Allied forces landed on the Mediterranean coast of France and fought their way northward. On August 25, 1944, Allied troops entered Paris. By September they faced the strongly fortified Siegfried Line along Germany's western frontier.

The drive from the east. In June 1944 the Soviets began a major drive against Germany from the east. By the end of 1944, the Red Army had taken Finland, Estonia, Lithuania, Latvia, Romania, and Bulgaria. The British assisted in driving the Germans out of Greece. Yugoslavia had been liberated earlier with the help of resistance fighters under Marshal Tito. By far the heaviest Soviet fighting, however, was in Poland. By July 1944 Soviet troops were approaching the eastern outskirts of Warsaw.

The drive from the west. The Americans pierced the "unconquerable" Siegfried Line in October after five weeks of fighting. The Allies captured port cities in France and Belgium, easing supply problems. The Allies also cleared Alsace and Lorraine of German troops.

The Germans still had enough strength for one desperate counterattack. Just before Christmas in 1944, they drove a 50-mile (80-kilometer) wedge into Allied lines in Belgium. After a costly 10-day battle—the Battle of the Bulge—the Allies turned back the German drive. Finally, in early spring 1945, German defenses collapsed. At the end of April, the German army in Italy surrendered unconditionally. Italian guerrillas pursued and captured Mussolini. He was shot, and his body was hung upside down and displayed to jeering crowds.

The Soviet and American armies made their first contact at Torgau, in eastern Germany, on April 25, 1945. It was agreed that the Soviets would take Berlin. On April 30, as the Soviets neared their objective, Hitler committed suicide.

Learning from Pictures This Japanese war poster features a giant samurai fighting for the Axis Powers. Which countries belonged to the Axis Powers?

Two days later the Soviets captured the battered and devastated city. Within a week the German high command surrendered unconditionally. May 8, 1945, was V-E Day—the day of victory in Europe.

Attacks on Japan

Though the war had ended in Europe, it continued in the Pacific. Long-range bombers from Saipan could now reach the main islands of Japan. Raids on Japanese industrial cities began early in 1945. However, the Allies needed still closer islands to use as fighter bases and emergency landing fields.

The first move was into a group of islands about 750 miles (1,200 kilometers) directly south of Tokyo. American marines landed on the volcanic island of Iwo Jima (see map, page 733) and captured it after a month of the most bitter fighting of the war. The Japanese resisted even more strongly as their home islands were approached. Okinawa, the largest of the Ryukyu Islands, was taken after more desperate fighting. At Okinawa, nearly 250 Allied ships were damaged by suicide attacks of Japanese pilots who crashed their planes into the ships. These suicide missions were called kamikaze attacks, meaning "Divine Wind." The Japanese believed that pilots who pledged to die for the emperor would save the empire, just as the Divine Wind had saved Japan from Chinese-Mongol attack in 1281. The kamikaze pilots were usually very young, most of them in their teens or early twenties. According to some historians, these pilots often had only about 12 hours of flight training. Their only mission was to select an appropriate target and die for the emperor while destroying it. An excerpt from a diary kept by a sailor includes a kamikaze pilot's last letter to his girlfriend:

> *"D*o not weep because I am about to die. If I were to live and one of my dear ones to die, I would do all in my power to cheer those who remain behind. I would try to be brave. . . .
>
> I pray for the happiness of you all, and I beg your forgiveness for my lack of piety.
>
> I leave for the attack with a smile on my face. The moon will be full tonight. As I fly over the open sea off Okinawa I will choose the enemy ship that is to be my target.
>
> I will show you that I know how to die bravely. *"*

Despite such determined resistance, the Allies continued their intensive bombing of Japan. Japanese ports were effectively blockaded, and the Japanese navy was immobilized. Nevertheless, the Japanese government still refused to surrender.

Yalta and Potsdam

Roosevelt and Churchill had long hoped to persuade Stalin to enter the war in the Pacific. Before the defeat of Germany, however, the Soviet Union had been completely occupied in defending itself. Moreover, it considered the war against Japan the business of the United States.

In February 1945 Roosevelt and Churchill met with Stalin at Yalta, in the Soviet Union. The Big Three, as these Allied leaders were called, agreed that Germany should be temporarily divided and occupied by Allied troops including those of France. The liberated areas of Europe were to have democratically elected governments. The Soviet Union was to enter the war against Japan. As compensation it was to receive several Japanese territories.

Another conference began on July 17, 1945, at Potsdam, near Berlin. Roosevelt had died in April,

Learning from Pictures On the grounds of Livadio Palace located in Yalta in the Soviet Union, the Big Three decide the fate of postwar Europe.

and Harry Truman was now president of the United States. He scheduled a meeting with the other members of the Big Three—Churchill and Stalin. However, before the conference ended on August 2, Clement Attlee of the Labour Party had become Britain's prime minister and replaced Churchill at the conference. The three leaders planned for the control and occupation of Germany and issued an ultimatum to Japan, demanding its unconditional surrender. Japan rejected the ultimatum.

However, the Allies now had a secret weapon—a workable atomic bomb. Scientists from many nations, including refugees from fascist-controlled countries, had worked to harness the enormous energy released by splitting atoms. They had succeeded in creating the most destructive weapon yet known. By using this weapon, the Allies would not need to invade Japan.

Japanese Surrender

When the Japanese government refused to surrender, President Truman made an important decision—to use the atomic bomb against Japan. Accordingly, on August 6, 1945, an American B-29 bomber dropped the deadly weapon on Hiroshima.

Exploding with a force equal to 20,000 tons (18,144 metric tons) of TNT, the bomb killed some 80,000 of the 320,000 people in the city and leveled more than half of the buildings. Two days later the Soviet Union declared war on Japan. Soviet armies swept into Manchuria, where they met little resistance. On August 9 an American plane dropped a second and even more powerful atomic bomb on the city of Nagasaki.

What If?
The Atomic Bomb

The atomic bomb had been tested earlier in the war, but in August 1945 only two atomic bombs existed. One bomb was dropped on Hiroshima, and a few days later the second bomb was dropped on Nagasaki. How do you think world history might have been different if the bombs had not detonated, or if the Japanese had known that the Allies had no more atomic bombs? Since Germany was also developing atomic weapons near the end of the war, how might history have been different if Germany had actually produced the atomic bomb first?

Learning from Pictures *These sailors, veterans of the Iwo Jima and Okinawa landings, celebrate V–J Day on board their ship.*

On August 14 the Japanese surrendered unconditionally, asking only that the emperor be allowed to retain his title and authority as emperor. The Allies agreed, on the condition that he accept the orders of the supreme allied commander in the Pacific, General Douglas MacArthur. On September 2, 1945 (known as V-J Day), representatives of both sides signed the official Japanese surrender documents in a ceremony aboard the American battleship *U.S.S. Missouri* anchored in Tokyo Bay.

Costs of the War

World War II, to a much greater extent than World War I, was a war of movement and of machines. Military casualties were enormous. The war was the most destructive in history. More than 22 million people died, and more than 34 million were wounded. Battle losses of the Soviet Union alone have been estimated at 7 million lives, although an accurate count has never been made. Germany lost more than 2 million people in battle. Japan's total loss—civilian and military—was nearly 2 million. Great Britain, France, and the United States each lost hundreds of thousands in battle. Six million Jews died in German concentration camps and gas chambers. Millions of civilians were uprooted by the war or killed or injured by bombs.

As the war progressed, weapons and tactics became more devastating. More shocking, people grew accustomed to this increased destructiveness. By 1943 Allied air attacks on Axis civilian centers were accepted simply as part of modern warfare. The destruction of Hamburg and the atomic bombings of Japan did not immediately bring any great public protest. By 1945 the killing of civilians was accepted as a normal practice of war.

SECTION 5 REVIEW

1. **Identify** Dwight Eisenhower, "soft underbelly of the Axis," "island hopping," Douglas MacArthur, Operation Overlord, V-E Day, V-J Day
2. **Locate** Stalingrad, Guadalcanal, Saipan, Tinian, Normandy, Iwo Jima, Okinawa, Hiroshima
3. **Analyzing Ideas** **(a)** Why did Stalin want a second front? **(b)** How was it launched?
4. **Summarizing Ideas** What were the fates of Mussolini and Hitler?
5. **Classifying Ideas** List the chief decisions made at Yalta and Potsdam.
6. **Understanding Ideas** What action did the United States finally take against Japan to end the war?

CHAPTER 27 REVIEW

Japanese attack
on Manchuria

Beginning
of Spanish
civil war

AD   1931   1936

Chapter Summary

The following list contains the key concepts you have learned about World War II.

1. In the 1930s a series of aggressions by the Japanese and the Fascists brought about World War II. At first the democracies were reluctant to resist these aggressions, preferring a policy of appeasement.
2. The Japanese made gains in Manchuria and China. Italy captured Ethiopia, Fascists took over Spain following the country's civil war, and the Germans seized Austria and Czechoslovakia. The League of Nations proved incapable of halting these advances.
3. Only when Hitler invaded Poland in September 1939 did his principal opponents, Great Britain and France, decide at last to stand firm. They were at a severe disadvantage, because their obvious ally, the Soviet Union, had signed a nonaggression pact with Germany. Nevertheless, Great Britain and France declared war on Germany in 1939.
4. By the fall of 1940, the Axis Powers had conquered most of Scandinavia, defeated France, and forced British troops off the continent of Europe. They also had formed an alliance with Japan. During the next year, their success in battle reached its highest level and then began to decline.
5. Despite some isolationist opposition, the United States began to send supplies to Great Britain in 1940. During this same year, Great Britain's air force turned back German air attacks and prevented an invasion of England.
6. In 1941, after considerable successes in the Balkans, Germany suddenly attacked the Soviet Union. In that same year, the Japanese attacked the American fleet at Pearl Harbor, in Hawaii. This assault brought the United States into the war.
7. Within Germany, a vicious and barbaric policy of exterminating all the Jews of Europe was put into effect. The Holocaust diverted essential German efforts away from the front line. The Soviets counterattacked, and the German army was forced to engage in heavy fighting on the eastern front.
8. In 1943 the Allies invaded Sicily from North Africa. At the same time, they began an offensive to drive the Japanese out of the Pacific islands.

9. In 1944 the Allies invaded France. Finally, in 1945, they conquered Germany.
10. The atomic bombing of Hiroshima and Nagasaki forced Japan to surrender.
11. The cost of the war, in suffering and death, was worse by far than that of any other war in history.
12. The end of the war brought hope that the aims proclaimed in the Atlantic Charter of 1941—including an end to wars and self-determination and decent living conditions for all people—might now be realized.

On a separate sheet of paper, complete the following review exercises.

Reviewing Important Terms

Match each of the following terms with the correct definition below.

a. appeasement   d. maquis
b. Holocaust   e. isolationists
c. blitzkrieg   f. collaborators

_____ 1. Members of resistance movements
_____ 2. Those who oppose involvement in the affairs of other nations
_____ 3. Systematic destruction of Jews by the Nazis
_____ 4. People who cooperate with their country's enemies
_____ 5. Lightning war
_____ 6. Attempt to preserve peace by giving in to aggressor's demands

Developing Critical Thinking Skills

1. **Analyzing Ideas** (a) Many historians regard the Japanese conquest of Manchuria as the start of World War II. Why? (b) At what point do you think world war became inevitable? Explain.
2. **Evaluating Ideas** (a) In certain respects, the Spanish civil war was a preview of the global war to come. Why? (b) What role did Spain play once World War II started?
3. **Classifying Ideas** (a) Which nations participated in the conference at Munich? (b) What did each of these nations hope to achieve? (c) How did the decisions reached at Munich affect the future of Czechoslovakia?

Evacuation from Dunkirk
Fall of France
Battle of Britain

Battle of the Coral Sea
Battle of Midway

Invasion of Normandy
Battle of the Bulge

Munich Conference

German invasion of the Sudetenland

1938   1939   1940   1941   1942   1943   1944   1945

German invasion of Poland

Invasion of the Soviet Union
Attack on Pearl Harbor

Allied victory in North Africa
Fall of Italy

Surrender of Germany and Japan

4. **Sequencing Ideas** **(a)** List the major events that occurred in the war during 1942. **(b)** Why might this year be considered a turning point in the war?

5. **Summarizing Ideas** What new weapons and military tactics were employed during World War II?

Relating Geography to History

Turn to the map on page 727. **(a)** What nations did the Axis Powers hold at the height of their power? **(b)** What nations remained neutral or nonaligned? **(c)** Based on information in this map, why might Churchill have considered Italy the "soft underbelly of the Axis"?

Relating Past to Present

1. "The next war," declared Albert Einstein after the bombing of Japan, "will be fought with stones." **(a)** What might he have meant by this comment? **(b)** What efforts are being made today to limit the production and sale of nuclear weapons?

2. Prior to American entry into the war, President Roosevelt called the United States the "arsenal of democracy." **(a)** What did he mean by this statement? **(b)** Does the United States still play this role in world affairs? **(c)** Why or why not? If possible, clip current articles that illustrate your answer.

3. Review the failure of the League of Nations to end Italian aggression in Ethiopia during the 1930s. Then find information on Soviet intervention in Afghanistan and Poland during the 1980s. **(a)** What actions did the United Nations take? **(b)** Were any of the problems faced by the United Nations similar to those experienced by the League? Explain.

Applying History Study Skills

Before completing this activity, review Building History Study Skills on page 724.

Read Mussolini's description of the nature of fascism. Then answer the questions below.

“   The foundation of Fascism is the idea of the state—its character, its duty, and its aims. The state guarantees the people's security, both within the nation and abroad. It represents the spirit of the nation. It is the state which educates its citizens. It makes them aware of their purpose in life and unites them. It leads men from primitive tribal life to the highest expression of human power, which is empire.

But building an empire demands discipline . . . This fact explains the severe measures we must take against those who oppose this movement in Italy in the twentieth century. Never before has the nation stood more in need of authority, direction, and justice.   ”

1. How did Mussolini define fascism?

2. What do you think Mussolini meant by the phrase "authority, direction, and justice"?

3. Use information in the chapter to determine if Mussolini's ideas coincided with his actions.

4. **(a)** What was Mussolini's place in Italian history? **(b)** In world history?

Investigating Further

1. **Researching Ideas** Review the information on codes in the Connections feature on page 649. Then use books in your library to investigate the use of codes during World War II.

2. **Writing a Report** Prepare a report on one of the following books about the Holocaust: Anne Frank's *Diary of a Young Girl* (Doubleday); John Hersey's *The Wall* (Pocket Books); Ilse Koehn's *Mischling, Second Degree* (Greenwillow); Arnost Lustig's *Night and Hope* (Avon); Elie Wiesel's *Night* (Avon). In your report, note whether the story is fiction or nonfiction. Also briefly discuss the background of the author. Then describe the way in which each of the central characters responded to Nazi persecution.

3. **Conducting an Interview** Interview a friend or relative who remembers the war years. Ask this person to explain the meaning of the following words or phrases: *victory garden, ration books, blackouts, dog tags, Rosie the Riveter, war bonds, C-rations, black market.* Try to discover other World War II terms that might be added to the list.

Unit Summary

The following list contains the key concepts you have learned about world war in the twentieth century.

1. The rivalries among European nations intensified in the early 1900s.
2. The 1914 assassination of Archduke Ferdinand in Sarajevo sparked World War I and within a few months, almost all the nations of Europe, plus Japan, were at war.
3. A dramatic upheaval took place in Russia, where in 1917 a revolution abolished the monarchy. Following the civil war in Russia, a government based on the principles of Marx and communism was created.
4. Although World War I ended in 1918, the problems it caused continued to plague governments.
5. Woodrow Wilson's Fourteen Points offered idealistic goals, but as the Allies sought to collect reparations for their wartime losses and to gain additional territory, many of Wilson's goals were forgotten.
6. In 1920, 42 nations founded the League of Nations. However, the United States did not join, and the League's efforts were thus crippled from the start.
7. The new outlook and the uncertainties of the stressful period following World War I were reflected by the science, literature, music, and art of the time.
8. In the United States, a sense of optimism and the influence of European contact brought about rapid change during the decade called the Roaring Twenties.
9. The stock market crash marked the beginning of the Great Depression in 1929, and in Europe instability due to the depression was widespread.
10. In Italy and Germany, dissatisfaction with the weakness and hesitations of democratic governments led to an extreme form of dictatorship, fascism.
11. In territories controlled by Great Britain, major political changes took place during the 1920s and 1930s. Political and social reforms were also attempted in Turkey, Persia, China, Japan, and Africa.
12. Developments in Latin America reflected the worldwide economic crisis.
13. In the 1930s the League of Nations failed to halt aggressions by the imperial government of Japan and the Fascists, which brought about World War II. In 1945 the Allies conquered Germany and Japan.

On a separate sheet of paper, complete the following review exercises.

Reviewing Concepts

Match each of the following items with the correct description in column 2.

a. Kellogg-Briand Pact
b. Balfour Declaration
f. Fourteen Points
g. Yalta Conference

c. Nazi-Soviet Pact
d. Atlantic Charter
e. Zimmerman telegram
h. *Mein Kampf*
i. Treaty of Portsmouth
j. Versailles Treaty

_____ 1. Called for "peace with justice"
_____ 2. Stated principles underlying Nazi movement
_____ 3. Settled Russo-Japanese War
_____ 4. Levied heavy reparations on Germany
_____ 5. Outlawed war
_____ 6. Announced war aims of the democracies
_____ 7. Pledged Soviet Union's neutrality
_____ 8. Temporarily divided Germany
_____ 9. Favored creation of Jewish "national home"
_____ 10. Invited Mexico to join the Central Powers

Applying Critical Thinking Skills

1. **Summarizing Ideas** (a) How did World War I help bring about a boom period in the United States? (b) What conditions brought this period to an end?
2. **Classifying Ideas** Choose two of the following and discuss how they reflected the uncertainties of the period following World War I: (a) literature, (b) music, (c) painting, (d) architecture, (e) film.
3. **Contrasting Ideas** How did Sun Yat-sen, Chiang Kai-shek, and Mao Zedong differ in their plans for China's future? Include the following topics in your answer: (a) the role of the people; (b) foreign interference in China; (c) economic reforms; (d) constitutional government; (e) the need for modernization.
4. **Evaluating Ideas** (a) What were the foreign policy objectives of Italy, Germany, and Japan in the 1930s? (b) How did these nations achieve their objectives?
5. **Determining Cause and Effect** (a) Compare the causes of World War I with the causes of World War II. (b) Why might the Versailles Treaty be considered a cause of World War II?
6. **Comparing Ideas** (a) Compare the principles expressed in the Atlantic Charter with those listed in the Fourteen Points. (b) How did each of these documents seek to establish "peace with justice"?
7. **Analyzing Ideas** (a) How did the United States assist the Allies before December 1941? (b) Why did the United States move away from its neutral status?
8. **Determining Cause and Effect** (a) How did the bombings of Hiroshima and Nagasaki change the nature of warfare? (b) What other technological developments grew out of World War II?

Relating Geography to History

Refer to maps in Chapter 24 and Chapter 27. How did the map of Europe change after the Versailles Peace Conference? How did it change after the end of World War II?

Writing About History

President Truman once declared, "Men make history and not the other way around." Use three of the following leaders as examples to explain Truman's statement: **(a)** Woodrow Wilson, **(b)** Sun Yat-sen, **(c)** Mustafa Kemal, **(d)** Mohandas Gandhi, **(e)** Winston Churchill.

Further Reading

Archer, Jules. *African Firebrand: Kenyatta of Kenya.* Julian Messner, New York. Tells the story of Kenya's struggle for independence during the turbulent 1950s and 1960s.

Feuerlicht, Roberta. *Desperate Act: The Assassination of Franz Ferdinand at Sarajevo.* McGraw-Hill, New York. Describes the events leading to war and the assassination of the archduke.

Marshall, S. L. A. *World War I.* McGraw-Hill, New York. Summarizes the war and its effects.

Richter, Hans Peter. *I Was There.* Dell, New York. Gives an eyewitness account of a boy who participated in German Youth.

Robertson, John R. *China: From Manchu to Mao.* Atheneum, New York. Chronicles twentieth-century China.

Sulzberger, C. L. *World War II.* McGraw-Hill, New York. Covers campaigns of World War II.

Unit Six Chronology

Date	Political and Social Developments	Technological and Scientific Advances	Visual Arts and Literature	Religious and Philosophical Thought
1880– 1910	Triple Alliance and Triple Entente **24*** Boxer Rebellion **26** Russo-Japanese War **26**	Industrial Revolution continues **24** Einsteinian physics **25** Louis Sullivan **25**	Picasso, cubism **25** Motion pictures **25**	Freudian psychology **25** Zionism **26**
1910– 1920	Chinese Republic **26** Assassination of Francis Ferdinand **24** World War I **24** *Lusitania* sunk **24** Russian Revolution **24** Treaties of Brest-Litovsk and Versailles **24**	U-boats **24** Machine guns **24** Poison gas **24** Tanks **24**	Proust **25** Stravinsky, Schoenberg, Berg, Webern **25**	Gandhi **26**
1920– 1930	Weimar Republic **25** Chiang Kai-shek **26**, Mussolini **25**, Stalin **25**, Atatürk **26** Lenin's NEP **25** African and Asian nationalism **26** Fascism **25**	Frank Lloyd Wright **25** Auto, phone, radio **25** Industrialization **24–26**	Mann **25** Kafka and surrealism **25** Joyce's *Ulysses* **25** T. S. Eliot **25** Jazz **25**	Gandhi **26** Spengler's *The Decline of the West* **25**
1930– 1939	Rise of Hitler **25** Great Depression **25** FDR's New Deal **25** Soviet purges **25** Kenyatta, Azikiwe **26** Long March **26**	TVA **25**	*The Grapes of Wrath* **25** Dali **25** Big Band Era **25**	
1939– 1945	Germany invades Poland **27** Pearl Harbor **27** Yalta and Potsdam **27** Hiroshima **27**	Blitzkrieg **27** Nuclear power **27** Panzer units **27** Radar **27**		Meltzer's *Never to Forget* **27**

*Indicates chapter in which development is discussed.

World War in the Twentieth Century

24

World War I and the Russian Revolution Altered the Course of History

The war that began in the summer of 1914 resembled no previous war. For the first time in history, industrial technology, especially the mass production of armaments, played a major role. This horrifying war dragged on for more than four years, taking a terrible toll in lives and property.

Conflicting National Interests

Beginning in the late 1800s, cooperation among European nations broke down as intense rivalries increased. As rivalries intensified in the early 1900s, the great powers built up their military strength and formed secret alliances to protect themselves. Soon they were plunging toward war, pressed forward by four factors: nationalism, imperialism, militarism, and the system of alliances. In 1914 Europe was divided into two armed camps, and even a minor disagreement would threaten global devastation.

The minor incident that plunged Europe into war came in the Balkans on June 28, 1914, when the heir to the Austro-Hungarian throne, Archduke Francis Ferdinand, and his wife were assassinated. The assassin belonged to a secret society of Serbian nationalists who opposed Austria-Hungary.

The assassination brought to a head the long struggle between Serbia and Austria-Hungary. When Serbia did not accept all of the terms of an ultimatum issued by Austria-Hungary, Austria-Hungary declared war. Then on August 1, 1914, Germany declared war on Russia. Convinced that France was prepared to side with Russia and hoping to gain a military advantage by swift action, Germany declared war on France two days later. When German troops passed through neutral Belgium on their way to France, Great Britain declared war on Germany. Many other nations soon entered the war.

A New Kind of War

Germany, Austria-Hungary, Bulgaria, and the Ottoman Empire became known as the Central Powers. They fought the Allied Powers that included Great Britain, France, Russia, and their partners in the war. Eventually 32 countries made up the Allied side. Many of them, however, joined late in the war and made only symbolic contributions to the war effort.

Except for the wars of the French Revolution, most previous European wars had been fought by professional soldiers whose only source of income was their military pay and rations. In contrast, armies of drafted civilians fought the battles of World War I. Those who could not fight worked at home to help the war effort. Many women participated in the war effort by working in factories. This type of war became known as *total war*.

The war soon became a stalemate. Both sides dug long lines of trenches on the western front, which stretched from the Swiss border through Germany, France, and Belgium to the shores of the North Sea. On the eastern front, the Germans forced the Russians back into Poland. Only a few sea battles took place.

As the strongest industrialized neutral nation, the United States became a supplier of food, raw materials, and munitions. Then in 1917, when the Germans began attacking merchant ships, the United States entered the war on the side of the Allies.

The Russian Revolution

The spring of 1917 found the Russians weary of hardships and disheartened by the appalling casualties they had suffered. They had lost all faith in their government and Czar Nicholas II. Strikes and

American soldiers in trenches east of Paris, 1918

street demonstrations broke out in Petrograd, as St. Petersburg had been called since 1914. On March 15, 1917, unable to control his subjects or his army, Nicholas II abdicated. He and his family were executed the following year.

A liberal provisional government was set up to rule Russia until a constitutional assembly could be elected to choose a permanent system of government. While the provisional government tried to restore order, a rival force—the Marxist Bolsheviks—worked for change in Russia. By November the Bolsheviks, or Communists, under the leadership of Nikolai Lenin, had taken over the Russian government.

The Communists signed separate peace treaties with each of the Central Powers in the spring of 1918. The new regime then turned its attention to quelling a civil war that had erupted. By 1921 the Communists had completely defeated their opponents.

Peace Terms

President Wilson of the United States wanted the Allies to work out a just peace. But when the Central Powers finally surrendered in November 1918, the victorious Allies sought revenge. In a series of peace treaties, the Allies redrew the boundaries of Europe. They also humiliated Germany and declared the end of the Dual Monarchy.

The League of Nations

In helping to draft the peace settlements, President Wilson made several compromises with his ideals. He realized that the treaties failed in many respects to provide a "peace of justice." He consoled himself, however, with the thought that the new League of Nations would be able to remedy the injustices inflicted by the treaties.

However, the League of Nations had no real powers to help it maintain peace. In addition, the United States never joined the League.

25 The Great Depression Helped the Rise of Totalitarian Dictators

For a time after World War I, it appeared that the world had indeed been made "safe for democracy." Within a few short decades, however, events proved this assumption false.

Uneasiness in the Postwar Era

Following World War I, many people rejected the beliefs of reason and progress expressed during the Enlightenment. Instead, scientists, writers, and artists expressed a sense of helplessness and cynicism.

These intellectuals, however, appealed only to a small audience. Most people found escape from the disillusionment of troubled times in other new forms of entertainment that "Big Bands," jazz, and films provided.

Architecture also underwent great change during the postwar years. New technical advances, such as the use of structural steel, made skyscrapers and bold new architectural designs possible.

Worldwide Depression

The United States emerged from the war as the apparent successor to Great Britain in world leadership. But the refusal of the United States to join the League of Nations indicated that the United States did not want the responsibility of world leadership. Americans seemed to want to sit back and enjoy their newfound prosperity during what historians have named the Roaring Twenties.

Prosperity, however, was short-lived. The collapse of the American stock market plunged the United States and the rest of the industrial world into a severe economic depression known simply as the Great Depression.

A Red Army parade in Moscow

In response to the hardships of the Great Depression, voters in the United States elected Franklin D. Roosevelt president. Roosevelt quickly set up a series of measures, known as the New Deal, to combat the Depression. Only when the United States mobilized for war once more in the late 1930s, however, did the hardships caused by the Great Depression finally end.

Political Tensions

The events of the postwar years put a strain on the older and more experienced European democracies, such as France and Great Britain. France still owed money that it had borrowed from its citizens and from the United States during and after the war. And inflation soared.

Although conditions improved in the 1920s, the Great Depression brought havoc to France. Riots in 1934 almost toppled the government. In 1936 a socialist government took power, but it lasted only a year. Although France remained a democracy, bitter divisions still existed.

Like France, Great Britain faced grave economic difficulties after World War I. While Great Britain retained its democratic government, military dictatorships took power in the nations of eastern Europe.

Fascist Dictatorships

As it did elsewhere, the war and its aftermath took their toll in Italy and Germany. Heavy loss of life, a crushing burden of debt, unemployment, and inflation plagued these countries. In Italy the problems led to the rise of Benito Mussolini, whose Fascist Party set up a military dictatorship. In Germany Adolf Hitler and the Nazi Party came to power in the 1930s. In both countries the new leaders established totalitarian regimes that stripped the citizens of all human rights.

The Soviet Union

Similar developments occurred in the Soviet Union. Although Lenin had allowed some freedoms

744

as well as free enterprise to exist under his New Economic Policy, his successor, Joesph Stalin, announced the end of the NEP and the return to a completely controlled economy. Through a series of bold Five-Year Plans, the Soviets tried to industrialize. This industrialization, however, concentrated on heavy industry and defense at the expense of consumer goods, creating shortages of the basic necessities of life. Just like the Fascists in Italy and the Nazis in Germany, Stalin created a totalitarian regime that deprived the people of basic human rights. In addition, the Soviets began to export communism to other parts of the world.

Chinese poster art honoring Mao Zedong

26 New Political Forces Emerged in Africa, Asia, and Latin America

The postwar years also witnessed profound changes outside Europe.

The British Empire

Although the British Empire had grown larger as a result of the Versailles peace agreements, its existence was threatened from within. People in all parts of the empire voiced demands for more self-government, and even for complete independence.

In the Middle East in 1923, the British recognized the independence of Trans-Jordan. By 1930 the British had also recognized the kingdom of Iraq as an independent nation. Then in 1936 the British and Egyptian governments agreed that Egypt would be independent but that Great Britain would control the Suez Canal for 20 years. Only Palestine remained under British control.

As the largest British colony, India posed even greater difficulties than did the Middle Eastern mandates. Indian nationalists clamored for complete independence. Finally, in 1935, after many committee reports and conferences, Great Britain granted India a new constitution that provided for home rule. However, the British viceroy still controlled India's national defense and foreign affairs. Committed to total self-government, the nationalists rejected the new constitution. During the next few years, discontent continued to simmer in India.

Even in those parts of the British Empire that already had a degree of self-government, people demanded greater independence. After World War I these dominions demanded complete self-government. Showing a remarkable readiness to accommodate, adjust, and accept the political realities, the British gave in without a struggle.

Turkey, Persia, and Africa

The nationalist feelings that swept the Middle East after World War I also affected the Southwest Asian countries of Turkey and Persia and the whole of Africa. In Turkey an able and energetic leader, Mustafa Kemal (kay·MAHL), emerged as the republic's first president and worked to modernize the nation. In 1921 in Persia an army officer with strong nationalist sentiments seized control of the government in a coup d'état. Some four years later, he deposed the ruling shah and assumed the throne, taking the title Reza Shah Pahlavi. Like Kemal, Reza Shah wanted to modernize his country and free it from foreign domination. In Africa many leaders worked for independence; however, their success was limited.

China

In the 1800s the Western powers carved out spheres of influence in China. When the Chinese attempted to oust the foreigners during the Boxer Rebellion, the Westerners crushed the revolt and imposed heavy penalties on the Chinese. The humiliation of this defeat brought on a revolution against the Qing dynasty. In 1911 a series of

745

revolts, led mostly by young army officers who supported Sun Yat-sen, spread throughout southern China. In a last desperate gesture to preserve their dynasty, the Qing proclaimed a constitutional monarchy. The rebels, however, would accept nothing but a republic. In 1912 the emperor abdicated and the republic was proclaimed.

But China's problems were far from over. The ruling political party, the Kuomintang, soon split into rival factions. On one side were the Nationalists, led by Chiang Kai-shek. Opposing them were the Communists, led by Mao Zedong. The two sides never resolved their differences, and until the late 1940s, continued to wage war.

Japan

By 1920 Japan had advanced from a feudal agrarian nation to one of the world's leading industrial and military powers. However, this rapid change brought a deterioration of traditional values. Although the economy grew rapidly, it could not provide jobs for all those who wanted them. As a result, Japanese people began to emigrate to Korea, Taiwan, and Hawaii, as well as other islands of the Pacific. Thousands more left for the United States.

In addition, Japan had to export goods in order to buy needed raw materials from other countries. Many countries, however, levied high tariffs on Japanese goods. The Japanese resented these tariffs. This resentment led many Japanese to accept the arguments of military leaders that Japan needed to become an imperialist power in order to survive.

Latin America

The 1920s brought prosperity to Latin America as it did to much of the world, and for a time the region seemed destined for stability. But the Great Depression dashed these prospects. Demand for the region's products shrank, and the United States and Europe halted investment in Latin America.

Economic crisis soon led to political crisis. Coups d'état overthrew most Latin American governments in the 1930s. In many cases these coups toppled constitutional systems that had worked for 30 to 40 years. Only Uruguay, which experienced a minor crisis between 1933 and 1935, and Mexico, which had undergone a revolution from 1911 to 1917, avoided major political upheaval.

27 Local Aggressions Brought About World War II

By the 1930s most European nations once more claimed loyalty to one of two opposing camps. One group included those nations generally satisfied with the World War I peace settlement. The other group consisted of dissatisfied nations that wanted change.

Threats to World Peace

Although many international conferences in the 1920s worked to maintain peace, several local conflicts erupted. In Asia, Japan, under the influence of its militaristic leaders, invaded Manchuria, set up the puppet state of Manchukuo, and invaded China itself. In Africa, Mussolini invaded and conquered Ethiopia. And in Spain a bitter civil war resulted in the establishment of a fascist government under the leadership of Francisco Franco.

Nazi Aggressions

Germany also embarked on a program of conquest in the 1930s. In March 1936 German troops marched into the Rhineland, violating the Treaty of Versailles. Then in October 1936, following the outbreak of the Spanish civil war, Hitler and Mussolini formed a military alliance called the Rome-Berlin Axis and began referring to themselves as the Axis Powers. Shortly afterward, Japan and Germany pledged to work together to prevent the spread of Russian communism.

Perhaps emboldened by the inability of the League of Nations to act, Hitler continued his conquests. In March 1938 his troops marched unopposed into Austria, and later that year he occupied the Sudetenland in Czechoslovakia. The next year he occupied all of Czechoslovakia. Even though the Czechs had alliances with Great Britain and France, the Western democracies were unwilling to defend their ally.

Wanting still more territory, Hitler took part of Lithuania in early 1939. About the same time, Mussolini conquered Albania.

Faced with all of this Fascist aggression, Great Britain and France prepared for war. Although the two countries tried to forge an alliance with Joseph Stalin of the Soviet Union, their negotiations failed. Instead, Stalin shocked the world by announcing that he had concluded a nonaggression pact with Germany. Publicly the Nazi-Soviet Pact pledged that Germany and the Soviet Union would never attack each other. Each would remain neutral if the other became involved in war. Secretly, the two dictators agreed to divide eastern Europe into spheres of influence.

Emboldened by the pact with Stalin, Hitler launched his next act of aggression with an attack on Poland on September 1, 1939. This time Great Britain and France stood by their ally and declared war. World War II had begun.

Axis Gains

On September 27, 1939, after a brief but devastating war, the Poles surrendered to Hitler. Then after several months of inaction, Hitler invaded Scandinavia, the Netherlands, Belgium, and France. By June 14, 1940, the Nazis were marching through Paris. Hitler tried to conquer Great Britain as well, but the British held their own, assisted by the United States. Although the United States remained officially neutral, it gave assistance to Great Britain in the form of war supplies.

Soviet and American Involvement

By late 1941 it appeared that the Axis Powers were winning the war, conquering much of eastern Europe and pushing into North Africa. Hitler failed, however, in his attempt to conquer the Middle East and its rich oil fields. By 1942 the British had stalled Nazi advances in North Africa.

On June 22, 1941, the war entered a new phase. Without a declaration of war, German armies invaded the Soviet Union. British Prime Minister Churchill declared that, although he did not admire communism, any nation that fought the Nazis was an ally and should receive help. The United States also declared its willingness to assist the Soviet Union. This assistance helped the Soviets stall the Nazi offensive.

The invasion of the Soviet Union was part of Hitler's master plan for the creation of a "New Order" for Europe. To build this New Order, the Nazis mercilessly slaughtered millions of Jews, Gypsies, and other groups whom they considered inferior races.

Pearl Harbor after Japan's surprise attack

The struggle against the Axis Powers received a major boost in December 1941, when Japan attacked the United States naval base at Pearl Harbor, Hawaii, and the United States declared war on the Axis Powers.

Allied Victory

Throughout 1942 the Axis Powers faced defeats on every front. Then with the Allied invasion of France in 1944, the war reached its final phase. By 1945 Germany surrendered. Japan soon followed suit after the United States unleashed the power of the first atomic bombs on Hiroshima and Nagasaki.

Even before the end of the war, Allied leaders Franklin Roosevelt of the United States, Winston Churchill of Great Britain, and Joseph Stalin of the Soviet Union had met at Yalta in the Soviet Union. The Big Three, as these Allied leaders were called, agreed that Germany should be temporarily divided and occupied by troops of the victorious powers, including France. Another conference began on July 17, 1945, at Potsdam, near Berlin. At this conference the leaders planned for the control and occupation of Germany.

SYNTHESIS REVIEW

1. **Comparing Ideas** How did World War I differ from earlier wars?
2. **Interpreting Ideas** Why did the Great Depression lead to political instability in Europe?
3. **Evaluating Ideas** What factors led many Japanese to favor the militarists?
4. **Understanding Ideas** What event precipitated Japan's surrender?
5. **Synthesizing Ideas** How did disillusionment with the World War I peace settlements lead to World War II?

◀ *Singapore, an example of modern Asia*   **749**

28

Challenges Faced Europe and North America in the Postwar Years

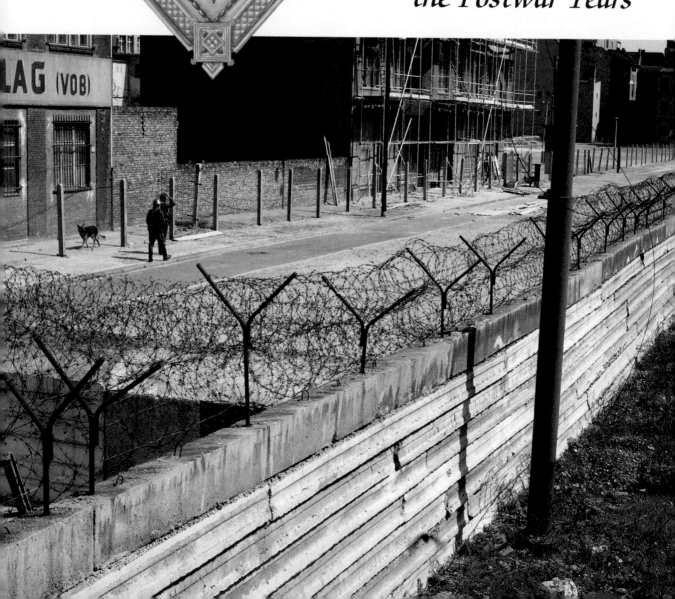

Place Europe, the United States, and Canada

Time 1945–1968

3.7 mil. BC   4000 BC   AD 2100

Significance

The Allies met several times before the end of World War II and mutually agreed to terms for the restructuring of postwar Europe. However, with the need to maintain an alliance against a common enemy removed, old antagonisms between the United States and the Soviet Union soon revived. The split that developed among the former Allies placed the democratic nations and other non-Communist countries, led by the United States, Great Britain, and France, on one side and the Communist nations, led by the Soviet Union, on the other side.

Suspicion and hostility between the Communist and Western nations led to the so-called **cold war**—waged by political and economic means rather than with weapons. The cold war shaped the foreign policies of the East and West, established the United States and the Soviet Union as "superpowers," and had a profound effect on world events after the end of World War II.

Terms to Define

veto power	containment
satellite	recession
iron curtain	lobbying

People to Identify

George C. Marshall	Ludwig Erhard
Marshal Tito	Alexander Dubcek
Nikita Khrushchev	Joseph McCarthy
Konrad Adenauer	Martin Luther King, Jr.

Places to Locate

Stettin	Oder-Neisse line
Trieste	East Prussia
Berlin	Nuremberg

Questions to Guide Your Reading

1 How did the victors attempt to settle Europe's postwar problems?
2 How did the cold war influence events in Europe?
3 What cooperative ventures contributed to the economic recovery of Western Europe?
4 How did the Communist bloc develop during the postwar era?
5 What challenges faced the United States and Canada in the postwar world?

In 1946 Sir Winston Churchill, the former prime minister of Great Britain, visited Westminster College in Fulton, Missouri. His address to an audience of students, faculty, and their distinguished guest, President Harry Truman, became one of the most memorable speeches of his career.

The recent takeovers by Soviet-backed Communist regimes in Eastern Europe had deeply disturbed the Western nations. The following excerpt from Churchill's speech describes the shadow of uncertainty that darkened postwar Europe—and the world.

❝*A* shadow has fallen upon the scene so lately lighted by the Allied victory. . . . *From Stettin in the Baltic to Trieste in the Adriatic, an iron curtain has descended across the Continent. Behind that line lie all the capitals of the ancient states of central and eastern Europe. . . . All these famous cities and the populations around them lie in what I must call the Soviet sphere, and all are subject in one form or another, not only to Soviet influence, but to a very high and, in many cases, increasing measure of control from Moscow. . . . I have felt bound to portray the shadow which, alike in the west and in the east, falls upon the world.*❞

This standoff between East and West colored world events during the postwar era.

1 Europe Attempted to Regain Stability

Throughout the war Allied leaders met to plan strategy and postwar policy. Many of their discussions centered on the proposed fate of postwar Germany. At the Yalta Conference in 1945, Churchill, Roosevelt, and Stalin agreed to divide both Germany and Austria into four zones. The United States, the Soviet Union, Great Britain, and France would each be responsible for administering one zone in each country. The four Allies would also divide Berlin and Vienna into four zones. The Allied Control Council, composed of military leaders of the occupying armies, would supervise the occupied regions. Decisions of this council had to be unanimous.

At the Potsdam Conference, later in 1945, Joseph Stalin, Clement Attlee (the new British

◀ *The Berlin Wall*

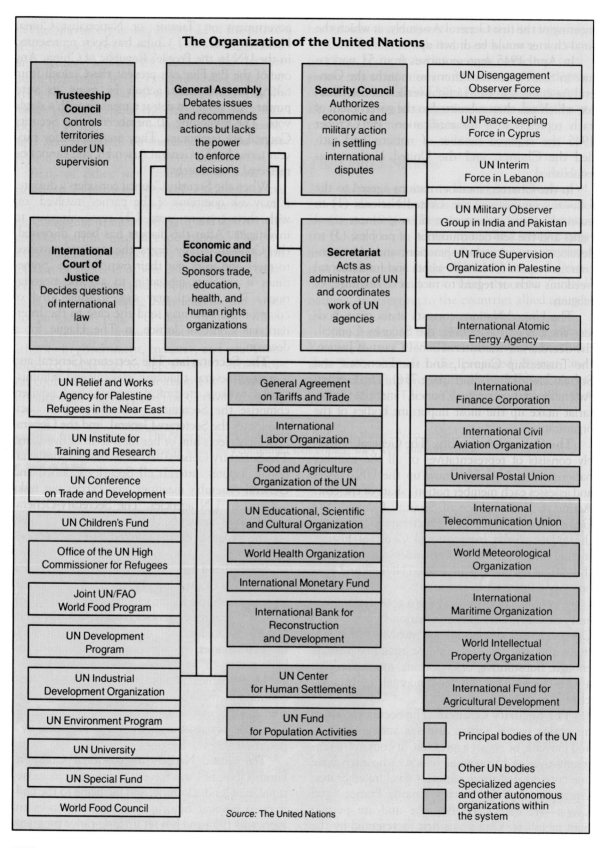

The Organization of the United Nations

Trusteeship Council
Controls territories under UN supervision

General Assembly
Debates issues and recommends actions but lacks the power to enforce decisions

Security Council
Authorizes economic and military action in settling international disputes

UN Disengagement Observer Force

UN Peace-keeping Force in Cyprus

UN Interim Force in Lebanon

UN Military Observer Group in India and Pakistan

UN Truce Supervision Organization in Palestine

International Court of Justice
Decides questions of international law

Economic and Social Council
Sponsors trade, education, health, and human rights organizations

Secretariat
Acts as administrator of UN and coordinates work of UN agencies

International Atomic Energy Agency

UN Relief and Works Agency for Palestine Refugees in the Near East

UN Institute for Training and Research

UN Conference on Trade and Development

UN Children's Fund

Office of the UN High Commissioner for Refugees

Joint UN/FAO World Food Program

UN Development Program

UN Industrial Development Organization

UN Environment Program

UN University

UN Special Fund

World Food Council

General Agreement on Tariffs and Trade

International Labor Organization

Food and Agriculture Organization of the UN

UN Educational, Scientific and Cultural Organization

World Health Organization

International Monetary Fund

International Bank for Reconstruction and Development

UN Center for Human Settlements

UN Fund for Population Activities

International Finance Corporation

International Civil Aviation Organization

Universal Postal Union

International Telecommunication Union

World Meteorological Organization

International Maritime Organization

World Intellectual Property Organization

International Fund for Agricultural Development

Principal bodies of the UN

Other UN bodies

Specialized agencies and other autonomous organizations within the system

Source: The United Nations

to combat disease, illiteracy, and malnutrition among the children of the world. UNICEF works primarily in developing nations,* helping establish community-based services in the areas of applied nutrition, child and maternal health, education, social-welfare services, and sanitation. UNICEF also directs emergency relief operations when natural disasters strike.

The World Health Organization (WHO) directs and coordinates international health programs. Its goal is for all peoples to enjoy good health. WHO provides governments with advice and assistance on expanding health services; trains doctors and health workers; controls and attempts to eradicate major diseases such as leprosy, malaria, tuberculosis, and smallpox; protects the health of mothers and children; improves sanitation and water supplies; and promotes mental health.

The United Nations Educational, Scientific, and Cultural Organization (UNESCO) was established to promote international collaboration in the fields of science, education, culture, and communication. Its major aims are to promote universal respect for justice, the rule of law, human rights, and fundamental freedoms for all. The major emphasis of this agency has been on stamping out illiteracy and on improving basic skills by establishing teacher-education programs, designing inexpensive school facilities, advising governments on curriculum reform and educational planning, and overseeing the production of textbooks and other educational materials.

The International Bank for Reconstruction and Development, or World Bank, helps to finance the rebuilding of devastated areas and developing regions. The World Bank encourages economic progress through such projects as railroads and power plants.

Another agency, the International Atomic Energy Agency (IAEA), works directly with the General Assembly and the Security Council to promote peaceful uses of atomic energy. The IAEA holds scientific meetings and establishes safety regulations.

---

*Economists often classify the nations of the world as developing or developed. **Developing nations** are characterized by limited resources, a rapid population growth rate, and agricultural economies with traditional life styles. In contrast, the **developed nations** have a high degree of economic sophistication. Of the more than 160 nations in the world today, only about 30 of them are considered developed.

Learning from Pictures *During the 1960s UNICEF provided needed medical services and supplies to children in Egypt.*

What If?
The United Nations

One of the main purposes of the United Nations is to maintain world peace. How might peace have been maintained in the postwar world if the UN General Assembly had the power to enforce decisions and the Big Five did not have veto power?

SECTION 1 REVIEW

1. **Define** cold war, veto power, developing nation, developed nation
2. **Identify** Allied Control Council, Council of Foreign Ministers, Charles de Gaulle, Nuremberg trials, denazification, General Assembly, Security Council, Big Five, Secretariat
3. **Locate** Trieste, Berlin, Oder-Neisse line, East Prussia
4. **Explaining Ideas** Describe the principal terms of the Austrian peace treaty.
5. **Analyzing Ideas** What problems arose after the Allied Control Council limited German industry?
6. **Classifying Ideas** How have the specialized agencies of the UN helped people of the world?

2 The Cold War Divided Europe

Difficulties over the writing of the treaties and over the governing of occupied Germany grew increasingly severe during the early postwar years. Many people in the West feared that Communist nations, led by the Soviet Union, planned to take over all of Europe.

Soviet Advances

The Soviets fought their way toward Germany at the end of World War II, liberating and occupying Poland and Germany's eastern allies—Romania, Bulgaria, and Hungary. The Soviets then set up Communist-controlled governments in these countries. In Albania and Yugoslavia, local Communists who had led resistance groups during the war established governments.

Learning from Pictures Winston Churchill gave his "iron curtain" speech at Westminster College in Fulton, Missouri.

These nations came to be known as Soviet **satellites** because, like planets circling the sun, they depended upon the Soviet Union. The Soviet Union justified this ring of Communist countries surrounding its western borders as a badly needed buffer zone against the possibility of future German expansion.

In matters of both domestic and foreign policy, the satellite countries were subordinate to the Soviet Union. Following Winston Churchill's speech in 1946, in which he referred to the Communist takeover in Eastern Europe as the "iron curtain," the Soviet Union and its satellites were often referred to as **iron-curtain countries.**

The Soviet Union soon made known its intentions to foster communism throughout Europe. In 1947 a Soviet-sponsored agency, the Communist Information Bureau (Cominform),* began to publish propaganda about the supposed unity of European Communist parties. This campaign continued until the dissolution of Cominform in 1956.

The Truman Doctrine

Early in 1947 the United States emerged as the Western leader against Soviet expansion. In March 1947 President Truman, speaking before Congress, announced what came to be called the Truman Doctrine. The United States, Truman said, considered the continued spread of communism to be a threat to democracy. The United States would not try to stamp out communism in countries where it already existed, or in any country that freely chose communism. The United States would, however, use its money, materials, technical knowledge, and influence to help countries threatened by communism if they asked for help. This policy, referred to as **containment,** aimed at "containing," or restricting the spread of communism; it constitutes the Truman Doctrine.

Truman further declared that the United States would "support free peoples who are resisting attempted subjugation by armed minorities or by outside pressures." He asked Congress to appropriate $400 million to help defend Greece and Turkey from Communist aggression. His request was granted after a United Nations investigating committee reported that neighboring Communist

---

*Cominform was the successor to Comintern, which was dissolved in 1943.

countries were helping the Greek rebels try to overthrow the Greek government. With American financial and technical assistance, the Greek government put down the rebellion. Thus the United States demonstrated to the Communists its determination to enforce the policy of containment as outlined in the Truman Doctrine.

The Marshall Plan

The United Nations Relief and Rehabilitation Administration (UNRRA), formed in November 1943, provided emergency assistance for war-torn countries. Nations that had escaped invasion were asked to contribute one percent of their 1943 national income to the relief project. The United States, Great Britain, and Canada made the largest contributions. However, by 1947 Europe's most pressing need was for more economic assistance. For this help to be effective, distributing the funds would require a coordinated effort.

In 1947 United States Secretary of State George C. Marshall suggested a new policy that formed the basis for legislation adopted by Congress the following year. The European Recovery Program, often called the Marshall Plan, stipulated that the United States was prepared to assist Europe on certain terms. The European countries were to: (1) confer and determine their needs on a continental basis; (2) show what resources they could put into a common pool for economic rebuilding; (3) stabilize their currencies; and (4) try to remove trade barriers so that goods could flow freely throughout the continent. In this way prosperity was to be restored.

Eventually, 17 European nations participated in the European Recovery Program. Congress appropriated about $13 billion for the first four years of the program. Thus the United States economy shared its benefits with war-ravaged Europe. The United States also offered assistance to the Soviet Union and its satellites, but they rejected it.

The Cold War in Central Europe

Prewar Czechoslovakia had been the most democratic of all the Central European countries. The democratic postwar government, however, included many Communist officials.

In February 1948 national elections in Czechoslovakia showed a decline in the Communist vote.

A few weeks later, shortly after the death (some thought murder) of the Czech foreign minister, the Communists held a new election. They presented a single list of party-approved candidates and wrote a new constitution, which the president of Czechoslovakia refused to sign. In June the president resigned and a Communist, who approved the constitution, succeeded him. Thus Czechoslovakia became a member of the Soviet-dominated Communist bloc* of Eastern Europe.

Only one break appeared in the iron curtain that divided East and West. During the spring of 1948, a disagreement arose between Joseph Stalin and Marshal Tito of Yugoslavia. Tito objected to Soviet domination and announced that Yugoslavia would follow an independent course. By June 1948 the split had become definite, and Yugoslavia was expelled from the Cominform.

The Division of Germany

By 1948 joint government in Germany by the four former Allies had become impossible. As a result, the country experienced great economic difficulty. The three Western occupying powers began discussions aimed at uniting their zones. In response, in June 1948 the Soviets blockaded all land and water traffic into Berlin from the West. They refused to allow trucks, barges, and trains to pass the checkpoints at the borders, thus threatening the people of West Berlin with starvation.

The Western nations acted swiftly during the Berlin blockade. The United States and Great Britain organized an airlift to supply West Berlin. They flew daily supplies of food and coal to the 2 million inhabitants of the Western sectors of the city. The airlift operated so efficiently that raw materials were supplied to West Berlin factories. In May 1949 the Soviet Union lifted its blockade of the city.

Meanwhile, the three Western occupying powers announced that if no peace treaty with Germany were written, they would unite their zones and allow the Germans to write a constitution and set up a democratic government. A constitutional assembly held on May 23, 1949, proclaimed the Federal Republic of Germany, known as West Germany.

*The Communist bloc consists of all satellite nations of the Soviet Union.

● READ
WRITE
INTERPRET
CONNECT
THINK

BUILDING HISTORY STUDY SKILLS

Reading About History: Identifying an Argument

When we hear the word *argument,* we often think of a dis-agreement or a dispute. However, when historians use the word argument, they are speaking of a thesis or main point supported by reasons and examples. Identifying the argument is the first step in determining its validity.

How to Identify an Argument

To identify an argument, follow these steps.
1. Explain the author's thesis or main point. Ask what the author is attempting to prove. You can look for key words and phrases such as *therefore, in conclusion, consequently,* or *I support.*
2. Identify the reasons supporting the main thesis. How does each reason elaborate on the main point?
3. Determine the examples that support the reasons.
4. Connect the thesis of the argument to the reasons and examples.

Developing the Skill

Read the following selection from Thomas G. Paterson's *On Every Front: The Making of the Cold War.*

❝ The Cold War derived from three closely intertwined sources: the conflict ridden *international system,* the divergent *fundamental needs* and *ideas* of the major antagonists, America and Russia, and the diplomatic conduct or *tactics* of American and Soviet leaders. . . . Officials in Washington and Moscow abandoned any quest for a community of nations and instead built competing spheres of influence. They thereby expanded and protected what they respectfully [sic] perceived to be their interests, divided the world, and stimulated more conflict. . . . Two nations emerged from the rubble of World War II to claim first rank. The competitive interaction between the United States and the Soviet Union . . . contributed to the bipolarism of the immediate postwar years. . . . The major powers, in short, intervened abroad to exploit the political opportunities created by the destructive scythe of World War II. The stakes seemed high. A change in a nation's political orientation might presage [predict] a change in its international alignment. The great powers tended to ignore local conditions which might mitigate against alignment with an outside power. Americans feared that a . . . Communist Greece would look to the East and permit menacing Soviet bases on Greek territory or open the door to a Soviet naval presence in the Mediterranean. The Russians dreaded a conservative anti-Soviet Polish government . . . for it might prove so weak and so hostile to Moscow as to permit a revived Germany to send stormtroopers once again through the Polish corridor into the heart of Russia. A Communist China . . . might align with Russia; a Nationalist China would remain in the American camp. All in all, the rearranging of political structures *within* nations drew the major powers into competition, accentuating the conflict inherent in the postwar international system. ❞

President Truman

The author's main point or thesis is that the origin of the cold war lies in the goals of the United States and the Soviet Union. Both nations, in their efforts to protect their big-power status and their national security, engaged in tactics that reinforced mutual suspicion. The competing ideologies were a basis for mutual mistrust.

The writer supports his thesis with details about the political situation at the end of World War II. He contends that the Soviet Union and the United States interfered in local conflicts because they saw their own power interests at stake. The examples that Paterson cites are in Greece, Poland, and China.

The author's argument is based upon his thesis that both powers, the United States and the Soviet Union, share responsibility for the development of the cold war.

Practicing the skill. Read a recent newspaper or mag-azine article that states a thesis or argument on a political point. Identify the argument using the skill you have just learned.

To apply this skill, see Applying History Study Skills on page 773.

In October 1949 a provisional Communist government, the German Democratic Republic, was established in the Soviet zone of Germany. This region became known as East Germany (see map, this page).

Political Alliances

With the Soviet takeover of satellite nations in Eastern Europe, many people feared a Soviet push to the West. Indeed, Churchill later said that only the fear of American atomic bombs had prevented the Soviet Union from overrunning Western Europe. Increasingly the Western nations felt a need to deter any Soviet drive.

The North Atlantic Treaty Organization. In April 1949 a mutual defense pact provided for creation of the North Atlantic Treaty Organization (NATO). Twelve nations originally signed the North Atlantic Treaty: the United States, Great Britain, France, Italy, Portugal, Norway, Denmark, Iceland, Canada, Belgium, the Netherlands, and Luxembourg. Greece and Turkey joined NATO in 1952, and West Germany followed in 1955 (see map, page 763). The signers agreed that if one member nation was attacked, all members would take united action against the aggressor.

In 1954 the NATO members drew up a detailed defense plan, calling for each nation to contribute to a standing NATO force of about 750,000 troops. The plan also asked for extensive commitments of ships and aircraft.

Not all the goals set in 1954 were reached. Consequently, NATO members came to rely more and more on American nuclear weapons rather than on the proposed force of ground troops.

The Warsaw Pact. The Soviet Union responded immediately to the strengthening of the North Atlantic Treaty Organization. In May 1955, in Warsaw, Poland, the Soviet government held a meeting of representatives of the European Communist bloc—the Soviet Union, Poland, East Germany, Czechoslovakia, Hungary, Romania, Bulgaria, and Albania (see map, page 763). Yugoslavia did not participate.

These nations adopted a 20-year agreement called the Warsaw Pact. The nations pledged, in the event of war, to furnish about 1.5 million troops. Adding these figures to the number of Soviet troops, the Warsaw Pact provided the Communist bloc with a potentially formidable force.

Learning from Maps Today West Berlin is still divided into occupied sectors. In which sector is the Free University located?

Summit Conferences

After Stalin's death in 1953, many people in the West hoped that the world's leaders could meet to discuss problems and reach general agreements on various issues. Begun in the 1950s, these meetings, or **summit conferences,** involved the highest officials of the participating countries.

Summit conferences, which have occurred at irregular intervals during the last 30 years, have rarely produced substantive results. The May 1960

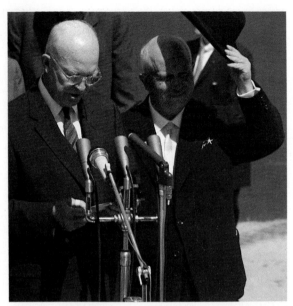

Learning from Pictures *President Eisenhower welcomes Nikita Khrushchev to the United States in 1959. The two leaders discussed many of the problems of the cold war.*

summit meeting between Premier Nikita Khrushchev (kroosh • CHAHWF) of the Soviet Union and President Dwight Eisenhower of the United States, for example, was canceled when news that an American spy plane had been shot down over the Soviet Union came to light. The plane had been photographing Soviet military operations. Still, most Americans agreed that it was important to keep lines of communication open with the Soviets.

Weakening Alliances

During the late 1950s, many NATO members became discontented with the organization for several reasons. First, the alliance had grown increasingly dependent for its defense on nuclear weapons, which could be used only when the president of the United States gave permission. This meant, in effect, that the United States controlled the defense of Europe. Second, because of the growing strength of Western Europe, and problems of the Soviet Union in its own sphere, Western leaders felt that the Soviets would not risk a military push in Europe. Third, with the development of long-range missiles Europeans feared that the Soviet Union could conquer Europe and threaten to destroy cities in the United States. In this case, they thought,

the United States might not risk its own destruction in order to defend Western Europe from Soviet domination.

The chief challenge to NATO, however, came from the president of France, Charles de Gaulle. Wishing to take a more independent course, he withdrew some of the French troops from NATO in 1966 and asked the United States to give up its NATO bases in France. De Gaulle's successors supported the Western alliance. Nevertheless, they acted independently from NATO in dealing with the Communist bloc.

SECTION 2 REVIEW

1. **Define** satellite, iron-curtain countries, containment, summit conference
2. **Identify** Cominform
3. **Understanding Ideas** What was the purpose of the Truman Doctrine?
4. **Summarizing Ideas** What were the basic features of the Marshall Plan?
5. **Explaining Ideas** Briefly describe the East-West struggle over the city of Berlin.
6. **Analyzing Ideas** (a) What were the functions of NATO and the Warsaw Pact? (b) Why were these alliances formed?

3 Western Europe Experienced Progress and Setbacks

Thanks to the Marshall Plan and the resolve of the European people, postwar Western Europe experienced a remarkable economic and political recovery. Most of the nations of Western Europe were **market economies** in which private businesses and individuals answer three economic questions: (1) what goods and services should be produced; (2) how these goods and services should be produced; and (3) for whom these goods and services should be produced. In contrast, the Communist bloc nations had **command economies** in which the government made the economic decisions. The market economies of Western Europe helped those nations achieve a higher standard of living than that in Eastern Europe. In a relatively short time, Western Europeans cleared away the rubble of bombed cities and rebuilt roads, rail lines and bridges. Industries rapidly returned to full production.

EUROPEAN ALLIANCES, 1955

- NATO nations
- Warsaw Pact nations
- Other Communist nation
- Neutral nations
- —— Iron Curtain
- ⊛ National capital
- • Other city

Learning from Maps *Not all Western European nations belong to NATO. Which NATO nations border Warsaw Pact nations?*

The West German "Miracle"

The reconstruction and industrial development of West Germany progressed at such a remarkable rate that many people referred to it as the "German miracle." West Germany developed a capitalist economy, and by the 1950s its industrial production had more than doubled, making it the leading industrial nation in Western Europe.

During the postwar years, the West German government managed to provide housing and jobs for the many refugees from East Germany and other Eastern European nations. The labor of these refugees contributed to West Germany's rapidly

763

growing economy. German industry flourished, thanks to technological innovation, a commitment to quality, and the absence of strikes and other labor troubles. The German automobile industry, for example, made impressive advances and became a strong competitor of its American counterpart. The West German currency, the mark, became one of the most stable in the world.

In his book, *Germany and the East-West Crisis,* William S. Schlamm describes how one West German built a successful business after the war.

> **"** . . . a young friend of mine, a former Sudeten-German, in 1948—when he was thirty-two—crossed the border of the German Soviet Zone and started to manufacture nylon stockings in West Germany. At the end of 1957, nine years later . . . his plant would be the pride of any United States chamber of commerce. Beautifully remodeled in 1957, it is an authentic example of shrewd rationalization techniques, of mechanical perfection, of tidiness and profitability. **"**

Two political parties, the Christian Democrats and the Social Democrats, dominated politics in the Federal Republic of Germany in the 1950s and 1960s. The first West German chancellor, Konrad Adenauer, was a Christian Democrat. Under Adenauer, West Germany established a strong alliance with the Western nations, and it joined NATO in 1955.

In 1963 Adenauer retired without having realized his dream of German reunification. Ludwig Erhard, a Christian Democrat, became chancellor, but by the late 1960s the Christian Democrats were losing ground to the Social Democrats.

Throughout the postwar period, Berlin remained a major trouble spot in the East-West struggle. With American assistance, West Berlin made an astonishing recovery from the devastation of war. In East Berlin, however, recovery stagnated. More and more people in East Berlin, discontented with the totalitarian Communist rule there, fled to West Berlin. Political refugees also streamed into West Berlin from East Germany and other satellite countries.

In 1961 the East German government tried to stop the flow of refugees to the West by building walls and fences along the boundary between the Allied and Soviet sectors of Berlin. They guarded crossing points at all times. East and West Berliners could move through these points only with authorization. This restriction stemmed the flow of refugees. East German guards shot at anyone trying to escape to West Berlin. The concrete portion of the Berlin Wall, topped by barbed wire, became a symbol of world tensions.

Great Britain After the War

In 1945 Clement Attlee, head of the Labour Party, defeated Winston Churchill and the Conservative Party and became prime minister of Great Britain. The Labour Party, a moderate socialist party, made many changes in the British economic and social systems. The government nationalized railroads, utilities, coal mines, and the Bank of England. Many welfare measures were passed, including free medical care for everyone. Great Britain became a **welfare state**—or one in which the government undertakes primary responsibility for the social welfare of its citizens.

Great Britain also faced many severe economic problems after the war. Its industrial equipment was outdated and inefficient. Many workers had been killed in the war. In addition, the country had lost, and continued to lose, scientists and managers. Many emigrated to Canada, Australia, and the United States.

Great Britain lost valuable colonies and possessions, and the cost of the nation's remaining overseas commitments created a heavy burden. British problems in Northern Ireland also flared.

Despite its many problems, Great Britain began to experience favorable economic development in the 1950s. The government reduced unemployment, stabilized its currency, improved housing conditions, and raised the general standard of living.

However, limited economic freedom and incentives resulted in a decline in these favorable trends. Great Britain's industrial productivity fell to one of the lowest levels in the industrialized world in the 1960s. Some of its principal industries, such as auto manufacturing, experienced hard times.

The Fifth French Republic

Postwar France also faced severe problems. In spite of assistance provided through the Marshall Plan, economic recovery came slowly. The French Empire crumbled in Southeast Asia and in North Africa, where bitter and costly struggles drained

Learning from Pictures
An example of West German technological innovation in the automobile industry was the Volkswagen plant in Wolfsburg, Germany. In the United States, this popular car, created by Dr. Ferdinand Porsche, was referred to as a "beetle."

the nation's treasury. France's political parties bickered among themselves so much that they could not form a coalition long enough to run a stable government.

Finally, in 1958, the French legislature, under pressure from army leaders, authorized General Charles de Gaulle to write a new constitution and to rule by decree until its ratification. Thus, the Fourth French Republic ended without a struggle.

The new constitution, approved by French voters in October 1958, created the Fifth French Republic. The constitution concentrated much power in the hands of the president. The president appointed the prime minister and could dissolve the legislature and assume dictatorial powers in a national emergency. Through the prime minister, the president could enact laws unless a majority of the National Assembly opposed them.

General de Gaulle became the first president of the Fifth Republic. He ended France's colonial warfare and established stability at home. This stability was attained, however, at a high cost to the French taxpayer.

In foreign policy, de Gaulle was a nationalist, believing that Europe could prosper only under a system of national states. De Gaulle opposed British and American influence in Europe and wanted to keep Germany weak. He hoped to maintain close relations with the Soviet Union and Poland as a check on possible German aggression.

In the late 1960s political conditions within France became unstable. Violent riots shook the nation in 1968. Militant students demanded reforms in the educational system, and strikes for higher wages and better working conditions spread rapidly throughout industrial areas. To meet the crisis, de Gaulle dissolved the National Assembly and called for a general election.

To win a favorable vote, de Gaulle acknowledged the need for social improvements in France. When reelected, he approved a 15 percent increase in workers' wages. This concession strained the finances of the nation without increasing industrial production and led to spiraling inflation. De Gaulle's popularity declined. In April 1969, in a direct vote, the French people rejected his proposals for reform. The 79-year-old president resigned.

Other Western European Nations

Recovery in the other nations of Western Europe took many different paths. Denmark, Norway, and Sweden, for example, adopted democratic socialistic systems and established welfare states. Although these systems provided many social benefits, they resulted in very high taxes.

In Italy the Christian Democrat Party dominated the political arena during the 1950s and 1960s. Under Alcide de Gasperi, the prime

Chapel by Le Corbusier

World War II, so devastating for people in Europe and elsewhere, also had among its casualties many great works of art. Numerous old and beautiful churches were damaged or destroyed. It was with great joy, then, that Europeans hailed the construction of this new place of worship. Built between 1951 and 1955 by the great architect Le Corbusier, the chapel stands proudly in the green fields of Ronchamp, in France.

Called Notre Dame du Haut, this was one of Le Corbusier's most famous works. The idea for its dramatic roof line came to the architect when he saw a large crab shell on a beach in Long Island, New York. The chapel, which almost resembles sculpture, was one of the first buildings completed by the architect after the war. It is unique both in design and overall effect.

Le Corbusier also developed the modular, or unit, system of design. In it all the architectural elements are similar, though not identical. They can be individually arranged, yet are well suited to mass production.

minister from 1948 to 1953, Italy established a capitalist economy and the country experienced industrial and agricultural growth.

By the 1960s the Socialist and Communist parties had gained considerable strength as labor unrest increased. At the end of the decade Italy's economic growth declined sharply. This decline contributed to the undermining of political stability.

Economic programs in Greece, Spain, and Portugal met with varying degrees of success. All three nations, however, were able to develop free-enterprise systems.

European Economic Cooperation

In the 1950s the French proposed that the nations that produced most of Western Europe's steel and coal unite their facilities and production. In 1952 France, West Germany, Italy, and the Benelux countries (Belgium, the Netherlands, and Luxembourg) formed the European Coal and Steel Community (ECSC). A central authority regulated production and prices, and members did not charge each other tariffs on coal or steel. A remarkable feature of the ECSC was its freedom from national control.

The Common Market

In 1957 the same six nations took another important step toward economic union by establishing the European Economic Community (EEC)—usually called the Common Market. The treaty provided for the gradual abolition of tariffs and import quotas among the six member nations. A common tariff would be placed on goods coming into the Common Market from nonmember nations. The member nations established the European Investment Bank with capital contributed by member governments. The bank's purposes included financing projects beyond the means of individual nations and investing in developing industries in poor areas of member nations.

The Common Market made steady progress toward European economic unity in the 1960s. In 1967 it adopted a five-year plan to provide greater price and wage stability and more uniform tax levels among member countries. Also in 1967 the EEC merged with the European Coal and Steel Community and the Atomic Energy Community, which the six nations had created to share information on the peaceful uses of atomic energy, to form the European Community, or EC. The European Community set up a single European commission with headquarters in Belgium.

The founding members of the Common Market had dreamed of political as well as economic unity for Europe. Although many unresolved issues stood in the way, the nations did seek ways to achieve political unification.

4 The Communist Bloc Faced Challenges in the Postwar Period

The death of Joseph Stalin, the Soviet dictator, in 1953 created a power struggle within the Soviet government. Eventually, Nikita Khrushchev emerged as Communist Party leader and in 1955 became Soviet premier.

The Soviet Union Under Khrushchev

Soon after he came to power, Khrushchev gave a speech in which he ridiculed Stalin for the political purges during the 1930s. By condemning Stalin for the imprisonment and death of many Communist Party members, Khrushchev hoped to win favor with the discontented Soviet people.

Khrushchev initiated a program called de-Stalinization in which he lifted restrictions on intellectuals and artists, freed many political prisoners, and ended some of the terrorism of the secret police. Stalin was publicly denounced. The city of Stalingrad became Volgograd. However, in spite of

this public change in attitude, the government still tightly controlled Soviet society.

Khrushchev loosened the central government's tight grip on the economy. Incentives were given to increase agricultural production. Factory and farm managers were given more control in order to meet production quotas.

One major problem that continued under Khrushchev involved heavy investment in the defense industry rather than in agriculture or industries that produced consumer goods. Khrushchev's inability to deal with this problem eventually led to his forced resignation in 1964.

Soviet foreign policy under Khrushchev seemed less threatening than it had under Stalin as Khrushchev adopted a policy known as "peaceful coexistence." However, this temporary thaw in East-West relations lasted only until 1960, when an American U-2 spy airplane was shot down, leading to the cancellation of the planned summit talks. Diplomatic relations further deteriorated with the building of the Berlin Wall in 1961. Khrushchev's successors, Communist Party Secretary Leonid Brezhnev and Prime Minister Aleksei Kosygin, reversed many of Khrushchev's domestic and foreign policies.

East Germany

The history of East Germany differed greatly from that of West Germany after 1948. The German Democratic Republic faced harsh political and economic measures at the hands of the Soviet Union. As war reparations the Soviets seized $8 billion worth of industrial plants and transported the machines and equipment to the Soviet Union. The Soviets also forced 200 large industrial enterprises to produce goods for the Soviet Union. Until the mid-1950s the output of these industries amounted to about one-fourth of East Germany's total production. In addition, the division of Germany cut off East Germany from most of its natural resources, making economic recovery a slow and painful process.

Even though the East German standard of living remained low compared to that of West Germany, by the 1960s the East Germans had begun to make impressive economic progress. Within a decade East Germany had become highly industrialized and was one of the most technologically advanced members of the Communist bloc.

Upheavals in Eastern Europe

During the early postwar years, the Communist bloc seemed a solid, firmly knit group of nations united by common beliefs, policies, and goals. However, the satellite countries had once been independent nations, some with long-standing antagonisms toward the Soviet Union.

Yugoslavia's growing independence from the Soviet Union after 1948 aroused envy among the satellites. This independence, called "Titoism" after the leader of Yugoslavia, became a kind of goal for some people in the satellite countries. In 1953 Soviet tanks and troops put down a revolt by East German workers. In 1956 Poland threatened to revolt and, as a result, gained a small amount of independence in domestic policy-making.

In 1956 Hungary revolted against Soviet domination. At first Soviet troops withdrew, but they later returned and bloodily suppressed the revolt.

In 1968 Czechoslovakia, under Alexander Dubcek (DOOB • chek), began a program of reforms. Dubcek promised civil liberties, democratic political reforms, and a more independent political system. This short-lived period of freedom became

Learning from Pictures *When the people of Czechoslovakia tried to institute reforms in 1968, the Soviet Union invaded the country.*

known as the "Prague Spring." Within six months, Warsaw Pact troops, chiefly from the Soviet Union, invaded Czechoslovakia. They seized the reform leaders and replaced them with pro-Soviet people.

These upheavals pointed to several changes that seemed to be taking place between the Soviet Union and its satellites. First, many people in the satellites seemed less willing to accept continued Soviet domination. Second, the troops from satellite countries, promised in the Warsaw Pact, might prove of little help to the Soviet Union in the event of war.

COMECON

In 1949 several Communist nations joined to form their own common market, the Council for Mutual Economic Assistance (COMECON). Its members included the Soviet Union, Poland, East Germany, Czechoslovakia, Hungary, Romania, Bulgaria, Albania,[*] and Mongolia. Over the years, China, North Vietnam, North Korea, and Yugoslavia have sometimes attended COMECON meetings.

The main purpose of COMECON was to coordinate industrial development and trade within the Soviet bloc. The organization tried to integrate the economies of its members and to expand trade with the capitalist countries.

COMECON was far less successful than its counterpart, the EEC, chiefly because COMECON lacked trading flexibility. Members conducted trade on a balanced nation-to-nation basis. Bulgaria, for example, would sign an agreement with Poland, providing for an exchange of a certain amount of Bulgarian products for products of about the same value received from Poland. No money would change hands in the trade. Deliveries from one country would be checked off against deliveries from the other.

COMECON members found this system cumbersome and unsatisfactory. Some members also objected to plans under which they supplied raw materials while other members—especially the Soviet Union—did the manufacturing.

For the first decade after the establishment of COMECON, the Soviet Union profited from its trading relationships with the Communist bloc countries. However, since the 1960s the Soviet Union has had to subsidize these bloc nations.

*Albania was expelled in 1961.

5 The United States and Canada Entered a New Era After 1945

Despite flourishing economies and powerful roles in world affairs, the United States and Canada faced a number of problems in the postwar years. These difficulties included internal conflicts, political problems, and a gradual realization that economic growth has limits. Both nations, however, remained committed to maintaining positions of great influence.

Challenges Facing the United States

Between 1945 and 1968, three Democratic presidential administrations and two Republican presidential administrations represented the American people. Although these five presidents often had similar goals, they just as often differed on policies for carrying out their goals. Some of the problems that arose during this period proved extremely trying for the men who held the highest office in the land. Their decisions set precedents and shaped the way the American people viewed both the world and themselves during a critical period in their country's history.

Foreign policy. For the most part, United States foreign policy during the postwar period revolved around the containment of communism. As discussed earlier in this chapter, President Harry Truman successfully blocked a Communist attempt to take over the government of Greece. He also implemented the Marshall Plan, which helped European nations recover from World War II. During his administration the United States took part in the Berlin airlift and helped establish NATO. Both the Berlin airlift and the establishment of NATO were bold attempts to contain Soviet aggression in Europe. In Asia, the United States sent troops to South Korea in a police action to stop the Soviets and the Chinese from taking over the country (see Chapter 29).

Truman's successor, Dwight D. Eisenhower, brought the Korean War to an end and created the Southeast Asia Treaty Organization (SEATO) in an attempt to halt further Communist advances in that region. He also announced the Eisenhower Doctrine, which provided economic and military assistance to anti-Communist countries in the Middle East. During the administrations of John F. Kennedy and Lyndon B. Johnson, the war in Vietnam was the major focus of American foreign policy.

All of these undertakings were part of the cold war between Western and Communist nations. The United States, however, also had other concerns during this period. It provided economic assistance to developing nations in Latin America, Asia, and Africa. It also made major efforts to reduce tensions in troubled regions.

Domestic policy. At home, the United States presidents consistently aimed to resolve social and political problems and maintain a flourishing economy. Following the example of the New Deal, later presidents created new programs to address social problems. Social programs were launched during the Kennedy and Johnson administrations. President John F. Kennedy introduced a broad program of domestic reforms, highlighted by legislation to reduce social inequalities. His tragic assassination in November 1963 occurred before Congress had passed much of his proposed legislation.

Vice President Lyndon B. Johnson succeeded Kennedy and attempted to create what he called the Great Society. His program included much of Kennedy's domestic reform legislation, along with important new civil rights programs.

The economy. After World War II the American economy reached new peaks of productivity, with huge new industries and rapid growth of new construction. Nevertheless, during the 1940s and 1950s, several **recessions**—periods of temporary business slowdown and increased unemployment—occurred. The 1960s had no recession, but toward the end of the decade inflation soared.

769

Learning from Pictures *In an unusual occurrence, captured in this 1961 photograph, four American presidents appear together. From left to right they are: John F. Kennedy, Lyndon B. Johnson, Dwight D. Eisenhower, and Harry S Truman.*

Political unrest. Many of the American successes of the postwar world lasted for a relatively long period of time. However, the discouraging results of many of the defeats and setbacks surfaced almost immediately. For example, some Americans did not understand why the United States had allowed the Soviet Union to spread its sphere of influence throughout Eastern Europe and other parts of the world. A number of people tried to explain these setbacks by a "conspiracy theory." They believed that Soviet gains had occurred because certain people in the United States government were "soft on communism."

Senator Joseph McCarthy of Wisconsin became the most dramatic spokesman for the "conspiracy theory." Between 1950 and 1954 he questioned the loyalty of many government officials and built up a large following. In the process he damaged the reputations of many Americans.

In 1954 a Senate committee investigated McCarthy's conduct and found his charges groundless. The Senate then censured, or reprimanded, him for "conduct unbecoming to a Senator," and his influence collapsed.

Civil rights. Black Americans had been freed from slavery during the Civil War and had officially been granted their rights as citizens but, in fact, still lived under many social, political, and economic restrictions. In many regions, in both the North and the South, black people were prevented from voting and from obtaining decent educations, jobs, and housing. Dissatisfaction grew, especially after World War II. Organizations such as the Urban League and the National Association for the Advancement of Colored People (NAACP) worked to find employment and to secure civil rights for black Americans. These organizations achieved gains through legal action and **lobbying**—trying to persuade legislators to vote for or against a measure.

A turning point in the black civil rights movement came in 1954. In the landmark case of *Brown v. Board of Education of Topeka*, the United States Supreme Court unanimously declared that state laws requiring black children to attend separate schools were unconstitutional. States having such laws were ordered to integrate their schools "with all deliberate speed."

This important decision encouraged the growing civil rights movement of the late 1950s and 1960s. The most prominent civil rights leader was Dr. Martin Luther King, Jr., a Baptist minister. He advocated the use of nonviolent methods such as

770

boycotts, marches, and sit-ins to bring about change. Blacks attempted to hold peaceful demonstrations and mass protests against discrimination. For his efforts in furthering the cause of civil rights through nonviolent means, Dr. King was awarded the Nobel Peace Prize in 1964. However, in spite of Dr. King's efforts, many of these protests resulted in violence. From 1964 to 1967, more than 100 people died in 329 riots across the nation.

Ironically, Dr. King died violently at the hands of an assassin. His murder in 1968 dealt a severe blow to the civil rights movement and sparked another wave of violence in cities across the country.

In the 1960s Congress passed several civil-rights and voting-rights acts that guaranteed political equality for blacks and other minorities.

Antiwar protest. A military issue that developed into a major social issue by the late 1960s was the continued involvement of American troops in Vietnam. Many antiwar protesters, particularly college students and civil rights supporters, expressed their discontent by staging demonstrations on university campuses. The protesters argued that United States involvement in Vietnam caused needless loss of life.

Antiwar protests sometimes ended in violence. At the 1968 Democratic National Convention in Chicago, a confrontation between antiwar protesters and the police interrupted the proceedings.

Antiwar protests later reached an all-time high and did not all end until the withdrawal of all American troops from Vietnam was completed in 1975.

Canadian Challenges

Active participation in two world wars ended the isolation policy Canada had maintained for many years. After World War II, Canada became a vigorous supporter of the United Nations and an important member of NATO, loaned almost $4 billion to other countries, and welcomed thousands of refugees from Europe.

Economic growth. Canada experienced considerable economic development after World War II. Much of the country remained basically agricultural. Production of crops such as wheat, barley, flax, and feed grains provided a surplus for export. During the 1960s, world food shortages forced China and the Soviet Union to purchase large quantities of Canadian grain. Most of the surplus disappeared.

Canada's industries also grew after World War II. The large Canadian forest areas provided many wood products. The wood pulp and paper industries expanded, with most of the paper sold to the United States. Development of electric power and improvement of transportation stimulated the mining of iron, coal, and uranium, and greater production of oil and gas. Aircraft, electrical, textile, and automobile industries developed in the provinces of Quebec and Ontario. The United States furnished much of the capital for this industrial development.

Relations with the United States. For more than a century Canada has had a close relationship with the United States. During and after World War II this relationship strengthened, especially with regard to military and economic affairs.

Canadian national defense relied heavily on the United States. Together the two nations built a line of radar installations, called the Distant Early Warning (DEW) Line, across the Arctic, to furnish early warnings of air attacks. They also established the North American Air Defense Command.

In 1959 close economic cooperation between Canada and the United States produced the St. Lawrence Seaway, a 2,400-mile (3,840-kilometer) waterway linking the Great Lakes and the Atlantic Ocean. The Seaway enables oceangoing ships to reach every port on the Great Lakes. Another important cooperative venture was the development of the Columbia River basin. This project doubled the water-storage capacity of the Pacific Northwest.

SECTION 5 REVIEW

1. **Define** recession, lobbying
2. **Identify** SEATO, Great Society, Joseph McCarthy, NAACP, Martin Luther King, DEW Line, St. Lawrence Seaway, Columbia River basin
3. **Explaining Ideas** Describe the foreign policy concerns of United States presidents from 1945 to 1968.
4. **Analyzing Ideas** (a) What was the "conspiracy theory"? (b) How did this theory develop?
5. **Interpreting Ideas** Why did political issues cause social dissent during the 1960s?
6. **Understanding Cause and Effect** (a) What effect did world shortages of food have on the Canadian economy? (b) Why?

CHAPTER 28 REVIEW

UN established · Truman Doctrine announced · Berlin blockade · Brown v. Board of Education of Topeka

AD 1945 1946 1947 1948 1949 1954

Nuremberg trials · Marshall Plan adopted · Creation of NATO · Berlin airlift

Chapter Summary

The following list contains the key concepts you have learned about Europe, the United States, and Canada.

1. After World War II, disagreements between the Soviet Union and the United States resulted in the cold war. Germany was divided into four zones and occupied by France, Great Britain, the United States, and the Soviet Union. Many Nazi leaders were brought to trial.
2. Following World War II, the United Nations was established to help maintain world peace. The UN also assumed an important humanitarian role in the promotion of human rights and world health.
3. The creation of satellite nations and establishment of the Cominform revealed Soviet plans to spread communism throughout the world. The Truman Doctrine and the Marshall Plan were attempts by the United States to contain communism.
4. The Soviet threat in Europe resulted in the formation of the North American Treaty Organization, which most Western European nations joined. The Soviet Union responded with the Warsaw Pact.
5. West Germany recovered quickly after the war. Great Britain faced difficult economic conditions while maintaining political stability. France experienced economic prosperity, despite the political uncertainties of the postwar period.
6. A major source of the growing wealth of Western Europe was the European Economic Community, which was founded in 1957. The organization attempted to eliminate trade barriers between nations.
7. The Communist bloc nations experienced economic and political discontent throughout the 1950s and 1960s. In 1956 the Hungarians revolted, and in 1968 Czechoslovakia attempted reforms. In 1961 they formed their own economic community, the Council for Mutual Economic Assistance (COMECON).
8. Demands for civil rights and opposition to the war in Vietnam confronted the United States during the Johnson administration.
9. Canada enjoyed a manufacturing and mining boom after 1945.

On a separate sheet of paper, complete the following review exercises.

Reviewing Important Terms

Supply the term that correctly completes each statement.

1. The _____ _____ was waged by political and economic means rather than with weapons.
2. _____ _____ is a name given to the Eastern European nations that depend directly on the Soviet Union.
3. The United States policy that attempted to restrict the spread of communism during the postwar era was called _____.
4. A state in which the government undertakes the primary responsibility for the social welfare of its citizens is called a _____ _____.
5. A period of temporary slowdown and increased unemployment is called a _____.
6. Trying to persuade legislators to vote either for or against a measure is called _____.

Developing Critical Thinking Skills

1. **Analyzing Ideas** (a) How are decisions made in the UN General Assembly? (b) How are decisions made in the Security Council?
2. **Summarizing Ideas** What developments in the occupation of Eastern Europe and Germany increased tensions between the Soviet Union and the Western nations?
3. **Explaining Ideas** (a) Why did the cold war develop? (b) How did it affect the postwar foreign policies of the major world powers?
4. **Interpreting Ideas** How were the Marshall Plan and the Truman Doctrine designed to carry out the containment policy?
5. **Organizing Ideas** What was the purpose of the alliance systems set up by the Western nations and by the Communist bloc after 1945?
6. **Understanding Ideas** (a) Why did the countries of Western Europe establish the Common Market? (b) Why did the countries of the Communist bloc establish COMECON?
7. **Synthesizing Ideas** How did the work of civil rights leaders such as Dr. Martin Luther King lead to changes in the United States' policy toward equal rights for all of its citizens?

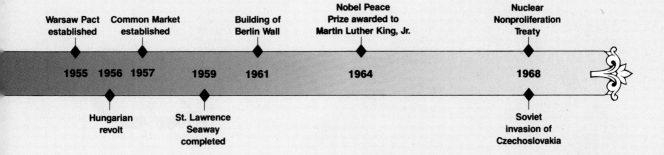

Warsaw Pact established

Common Market established

Building of Berlin Wall

Nobel Peace Prize awarded to Martin Luther King, Jr.

Nuclear Nonproliferation Treaty

1955 1956 1957 1959 1961 1964 1968

Hungarian revolt

St. Lawrence Seaway completed

Soviet invasion of Czechoslovakia

Relating Geography to History

Turn to the map on page 763. **(a)** Which European nations belong to NATO? **(b)** Which nations belong to the Warsaw Pact? **(c)** Which nations have remained neutral? **(d)** How has the system of alliances changed since World War II? **(e)** What factors account for this realignment?

Relating Past to Present

1. The policies of containment and economic aid were used after World War II to stem the spread of communism. **(a)** Does the United States still try to prevent the spread of communism? **(b)** Has the United States been successful in containing communism? **(c)** What method does it use today?
2. In the 1950s several satellite nations tried to free themselves from Soviet control. **(a)** Are there any instances today of satellite nations in Eastern Europe trying to lessen Soviet control? **(b)** To what extent have these nations been successful?
3. Cooperation between the United States and Canada has continued since 1945. Using information in the textbook and recent articles in the news, identify some of the ways in which Canada and the United States work together today. What actions might be taken to strengthen our ties with Canada?

Applying History Study Skills

Before completing this activity, review Building History Study Skills on page 760.

On March 12, 1947, President Truman addressed the Congress of the United States with a justification for containment as a basis for American foreign policy. Read the following excerpt from his speech and then answer the questions to help you identify his argument.

66 At the present moment in world history nearly every nation must choose between alternative ways of life. The choice is too often not a free one. . . . One way of life is based upon the will of the majority, and is distinguished by free institutions, representative government, free elections . . . and freedom from political oppression. . . . The second way of life is based upon the will of a minority forcibly imposed upon the majority. It relies upon terror and oppression, a controlled press . . . and the suppression of personal freedoms. . . . I believe that it must be the policy of the United States to support free peoples who are resisting attempted subjugation . . . I believe that our help should be primarily through economic and financial aid which is essential to economic stability and orderly political processes. 99

1. How is containment illustrated in President Truman's speech?
2. What reasons does President Truman use to support his main point?
3. How does the president feel about the Soviet Union? Are there examples to support his position? Explain your answer.
4. How would you define the Truman Doctrine?

Investigating Further

1. **Presenting an Oral Report** After Franklin Roosevelt's death, his widow, Eleanor Roosevelt, became the United States ambassador to the United Nations in New York City. Using the *Dictionary of American Biography* or the most recent edition of *Notable American Women,* research Eleanor Roosevelt's public life beginning with the years as first lady and ending with her career as a diplomat of the United States. Present your findings to the class.
2. **Writing a Report** The position of secretary-general of the United Nations is a demanding and sometimes controversial job. Prepare a written report by using the encyclopedias and books in your library to find out more about each of the following secretaries-general: Trygve Lie, Dag Hammarskjöld, U Thant, and Javier Pérez de Cuéllar.
3. Use resource materials in your library to research the satellite upheavals discussed in the chapter (Yugoslavia, 1945–48; Hungary, 1956; Czechoslovakia, 1968). Why did each nation try to free itself from Soviet control? Evaluate to what extent each of these nations was successful in its objectives.

773

29

Asian Nations Struggled to Gain Stability

Place Asia

Time 1945 – the present

3.7 mil. BC 4000 BC AD 2100

Significance

The years after World War II saw major political, economic, and social changes in Asia. In China, for example, a Communist government came to power in 1949 after many years of internal struggle. Japan rose out of the ashes of war to become a leading economic power whose influence has extended far beyond Asia.

The movements for self-rule in Asia that had begun decades earlier came to fulfillment in the postwar period. However, this transition from domination to independence was not achieved peacefully. A number of newly independent Asian nations became the focus of armed conflicts arising out of the cold war. Both Korea and Vietnam, for example, saw serious confrontations between Communist and Western nations.

As the 1900s drew to a close, other Asian nations attempted to imitate Japan's "economic miracle." In time, all of these nations began to take an independent, active role in world economic and political affairs.

Terms to Define

non-alignment   mixed economy

People to Identify

Deng Xiaoping   Indira Gandhi
Park Chung Hee   Benazir Bhutto
Yasuhiro Nakasone   Corazon Aquino

Places to Locate

38th parallel   17th parallel

Questions to Guide Your Reading

1 How did the Communists take control and create a new society in China?
2 How did Japan become a leading economic power in the postwar years?
3 By what means did India, Pakistan, and Bangladesh achieve independence?
4 How did the countries of Southeast Asia achieve independence?
5 What impact did the conflict in Vietnam have on other countries in Southeast Asia?
6 In what ways did Asian nations seek security and economic growth?

◀ *Fireworks over Hong Kong's harbor*

The hopes and aspirations of all peoples seeking freedom from colonial rulers were eloquently summed up by Jawaharlal Nehru in a speech made on August 14, 1947, announcing Indian independence.

❝*L*ong years ago we made a tryst [appointment] with destiny, and now the time comes when we shall redeem our pledge, not wholly or in full measure, but very substantially. At the stroke of the midnight hour, when the world sleeps, India will awake to life and freedom. A moment comes, which comes but rarely in history, when we step out from the old to the new, when an age ends, and when the soul of the nation, long suppressed, finds utterance. . . .

At the dawn of history India started on her unending quest, and trackless centuries are filled with her striving and the grandeur of her successes and her failures. Through good and ill fortune alike she has never lost sight of that quest or forgotten the ideals which gave her strength. We end today a period of ill fortune and India discovers herself again. The achievement we celebrate today is but a step, an opening of opportunity, to the greater triumphs and achievements that await us. . . .❞

Within 20 years of Nehru's speech, almost every Asian nation had, like India, redeemed the pledge of self-determination.

1 Communists Took Control in China and Created a New Society

During World War II, the Nationalist and Communist Chinese agreed to halt their civil war and form a united front against their common enemy, the Japanese. However, this alliance soon broke down, and the two parties returned to warring with each other. After World War II, the Communists increased their military strength and expanded the territory under their direct control. In time the Communists gained the upper hand in the civil war, and by 1949 they had driven the Nationalists from power.

In 1949 Chiang Kai-shek, the Nationalist leader, fled with his supporters to the island of Taiwan and established a government there (see map,

SPREAD OF COMMUNISM IN CHINA, 1934–1949

AREAS OCCUPIED BY COMMUNISTS

1934–1945
1945–June 1946
July 1946–June 1948
July 1948–June 1949
July–Sept. 1949
After October 1949

—— National boundary
⊛ National capital since 1949
◉ Communist capital until 1949
★ Nationalist capital(s)
• Other city

The People's Republic of China is proclaimed on October 1, 1949

In late 1949, Chiang Kai-shek's Nationalist government flees to Taiwan, where it re-establishes the Republic of China.

0   250   500 Miles
0   250   500 Kilometers

N

MERCATOR PROJECTION

Learning from Maps *In order to protect Taiwan and attack the mainland, the Nationalists fortified small offshore islands. What is the capital of Taiwan?*

this page). On the Chinese mainland, the Communists, led by Mao Zedong, established the People's Republic of China. The United States, which had aided the Nationalists, refused to recognize this new Communist government on the mainland.

The Chinese Economy

The Communists wanted to create a modern, industrialized nation dominated by the Communist Party. To achieve this goal, the Communists first took a political step. Through either election or appointment, they placed Communist Party members in all of the key government and military offices. The new constitution gave executive power to the party's Central Committee and its Politburo, both headed by Mao Zedong.

An overwhelming task faced this new Communist government. China had been devastated by more than 30 years of war. Farms lay destroyed, and industry and transportation had almost ceased to function. The Chinese people had fared little better than their country. Miserably poor, they had been decimated by periodic epidemics and famines.

In 1953 the Communists began the process of rebuilding China by issuing their first Five-Year Plan for economic growth. Although this plan stressed the rapid buildup of heavy industry, it also focused on land reform. Peasants received some land, which they organized into collective farms, while the government operated state farms on much of what remained. The Soviet Union provided part of the capital for the plan, but most of the financing came from China itself.

Despite natural disasters such as droughts and floods, peasant opposition to land reform, and inefficient planning by government officials, the first Five-Year Plan achieved considerable success. Agricultural production increased, and output more than doubled in such heavy industries as coal and steel.

The Great Leap Forward. In 1958 the government announced a second Five-Year Plan, the Great Leap Forward. More ambitious than the first Five-Year Plan, it aimed to speed up economic development while simultaneously developing a completely socialist society.

The Great Leap Forward established huge collective communities, called people's communes, that incorporated agricultural activities and small industries. The largest of these communes had populations in excess of 25,000. Life on a commune bore a strong resemblance to life in the military. Men, women, and children lived in separate dormitories and ate in communal dining halls. People worked long hours in the fields or factories under strict supervision, and everyone received the same pay, regardless of how much he or she produced.

Under the Great Leap Forward, the Chinese government hoped to increase industrial output to the point where it matched that of many Western European countries. To reach this goal, China

Learning from Pictures   *These music students are wearing the red bandanna of the Young Pioneers, a young people's organization open to boys and girls.*

purchased modern machinery and even complete steel mills, first from the Soviet Union and then from the countries of Western Europe. The government even encouraged the Chinese people to make their own iron and steel in small backyard blast furnaces.

The Great Leap Forward failed dismally. Poor planning by government officials and factory managers brought industry practically to a standstill. In addition, three successive crop failures left millions of people facing severe food shortages. Further, the Chinese people resented the ideas behind the plan. Industrial workers complained bitterly about the long hours they had to work, and the peasants hated communal living. Faced with falling productivity and constant criticism from workers and peasants, the government abandoned the Great Leap Forward in the early 1960s. New policies modified the communes, allowing families to live in their own homes. People still had to work on the communal farmland, but they also had small plots of land on which they could raise their own crops. During the 1960s, under these modified communal arrangements, Chinese agriculture recovered and became moderately successful.

The Four Modernizations. In the late 1970s, the government instituted a new economic development plan, the Four Modernizations, that aimed at improving and updating four important areas of the economy—agriculture, industry, science and technology, and military defense. The plan introduced incentives to increase production. For

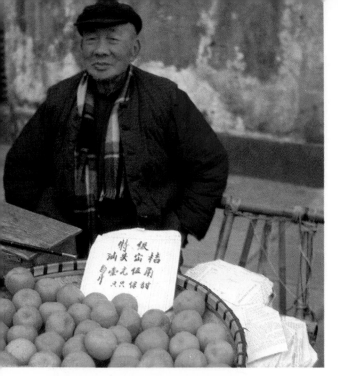

Learning from Pictures *Limited free enterprise is now legal in China. This Chinese merchant sells fruit from his own government-allotted farm plot.*

example, although central planners set production quotas for workers, anything produced above the quotas could be sold for profit. In addition, the Four Modernizations reduced government control of factories and farms and encouraged the import of technology from the West. This new approach certainly helped China become a major industrial power. By the mid-1980s it led the world in coal production, stood second in the production of cement, third in steel, and sixth in petroleum.

The seventh Five-Year Plan (1986–1990) continued this more open approach to the economy. It focused less on industrial growth and more on economic reforms, particularly in the banking and agricultural sectors. In addition, it encouraged a degree of free enterprise. This new direction in Chinese economic policy has resulted in a rising standard of living for the Chinese people. Per capita income, for example, increased more than 14 percent from 1982 to 1983.

Leadership Struggles

Since 1949 officials of the Chinese Communist Party have remained in agreement about the two goals of their revolution: (1) economic develop-

ment and (2) creation of a classless society. They have often disagreed, however, about the way to achieve these goals. One group believed that economic development had to come first; if necessary, wage incentives should be used to increase production. The other group believed that both goals should be pursued at the same time; if a conflict arose between these goals, social change should take priority over economic issues. This group also believed wage incentives were dangerous, claiming they created inequality and rivalry among workers.

In the early years of Communist rule in China, Liu Shaoqi (LEE·OO SHOW·CHEE) led the advocates of the first point of view. Mao Zedong and his followers advocated the second point of view. In the early 1960s, after the failure of the Great Leap Forward, Liu successfully put his economic development policies into effect. Accusing him of leading China down the "capitalist road," Mao began a concerted effort to destroy Liu's work.

The Cultural Revolution. To this end, in 1966 Mao launched the Great Proletarian Cultural Revolution, a violent attempt at social change. Mao aimed to rid China of the "Four Olds"—old customs, habits, thoughts, and culture—replacing them with a new socialist culture. Mao chose China's young people to lead this revolution. These high school and college students, whom Mao called his "little generals," soon became known as the Red Guard. They went on a rampage throughout China, vandalizing historic buildings, ruining ancient works of art, burning books, and destroying anything they considered part of the "old way." However, they saved their greatest zeal for those people who did not totally comply with Mao's teachings. The Red Guard denounced these people, publicly humiliated them, and sometimes beat, tortured, or even killed them. Those people who survived the Red Guard lost their jobs and their Communist Party membership. Liu himself suffered denunciation and died while in jail.

The Cultural Revolution had a disastrous effect on the Chinese economy. Agricultural and industrial production fell dramatically, and the country's economic development plans suffered a severe setback. In 1969, with the country in a state of chaos, Mao finally called a halt to his experiment in social change.

Moderates in control. Upon Mao's death in 1976, a struggle began between Communist moderates and a radical group led by Mao's widow, Qiang

Jing (JEE·AHNG JING). The moderates wanted to return to the policies of Liu Shaoqi, whereas Qiang Jing's group—known as the Gang of Four—wanted to continue the Cultural Revolution and rid China of all vestiges of the past.

In time, the moderates won control of the major party and government offices, and in an attempt to crush the threat posed by the radicals, they placed the Gang of Four on trial for treason. Found guilty, Qiang Jing and her three compatriots received life sentences. The moderates then began to reinstate many of those who had been purged from government offices and the Communist Party during the Cultural Revolution. They even made a reassessment of Mao's ideas and policies, noting that he had made mistakes, specifically in starting the Cultural Revolution. However, the moderates concluded that "his merits are primary and his errors secondary."

By the late 1970s, Deng Xiaoping (DUNG SHOU·PING) had emerged as the leader of the moderates. Although Deng had helped to found the Chinese Communist Party, during the Cultural Revolution he had been denounced as one of the worst "capitalist roaders." As the basis for his Four Modernizations, Deng now used the same ideas that had earned him so much criticism. He also fostered greater openness in social life by encouraging cultural and scientific exchanges with Western countries. In the late 1980s, Deng gave up his government and Communist Party positions, leaving the country in the hands of a younger generation of leaders. Then in the spring of 1989 the government faced a severe challenge as students occupied Tienanmen Square in Beijing to demand democratic reforms. Fearing for the survival of their regime, Chinese leaders declared martial law and ordered the brutal suppression of the demonstrations. Almost 3,000 people were massacred, and 10,000 more were wounded in the crackdown. At the same time, thousands of suspected "counter-revolutionaries" were arrested and executed throughout China. Although martial law was lifted in 1990, the Communist regime continued to suppress human and civil rights.

Foreign Relations

In the early 1950s, the Soviet Union and the People's Republic of China were allies, united by political ideology and common economic interests.

However, they soon disagreed, first about the interpretation of Marxism and then over economic policy.

Soviet leaders believed that world communism could be achieved through scientific and economic successes rather than by military conquests. Therefore, they felt that they could live in peaceful coexistence with the West. In the economic realm, the Soviets thought that each Communist country should specialize in those economic activities it did best. Further, the Soviet leaders felt that the Communist nations should integrate their economies under the direction of the most prominent Communist power. Naturally, the Soviet leaders believed that only the Soviet Union was capable of providing such leadership.

Chinese leaders, on the other hand, claimed that Communist nations had an obligation to support "national wars of liberation." In addition, they argued that nations could never live in peaceful coexistence while capitalism existed. In rejecting revolution as the means of social change, the Soviets had abandoned true Marxism, the Chinese said. The Chinese also held that each Communist country should develop its own economy, and that no one country of the Communist bloc should dominate the other countries. They argued that the Soviet model of economic development, which stressed heavy industry, would not work in China with its large agricultural population. The Chinese were not ready to accept the point of view of another government, not even that of the Soviet Union.

At first, the Chinese and the Soviets confined their differences to bitter public speeches and to a struggle for leadership in the Communist bloc and in the developing regions of the world. However, during the 1960s both countries began to station troops along their common border. As a result, a number of clashes occurred on the border, especially in Xinjiang (SHIN·JEE·AHNG), where the Chinese had nuclear facilities.

These border skirmishes helped to bring about a change in Chinese foreign policy. In the past, Mao Zedong and his advisers had made foreign-policy decisions based on which nation they believed represented the greatest threat to China's security. For 20 years, no one doubted that the United States, with military bases in Japan, Taiwan, the Philippines, and Vietnam, posed the most danger to China.

779

As Chinese-Soviet relations worsened, however, China grew more willing to come to terms with the United States. The first major sign of change came in 1972, when President Richard Nixon visited China. Soon after, the two nations began to permit the exchange of sports teams, journalists, educators, artists, and business leaders. By the mid-1970s, China had opened its doors to American tourists. Finally, in 1979 the United States gave full diplomatic recognition to the People's Republic of China. At the same time, the United States withdrew its recognition of the Nationalist government in Taiwan.

The Nationalists in Taiwan

After the Communists took control of China in 1949, the Chinese Nationalists established themselves on the island of Taiwan, about 100 miles (160 kilometers) from the Chinese mainland. Their government, called the Republic of China, appeared to be democratic. In reality, however, it operated more like a one-party system, with Chiang Kai-shek and other Kuomintang officials having all of the power. The Taiwanese people, who had inhabited the island long before the Nationalists arrived, did not participate much in the government. Nevertheless, the Republic's free enterprise system boosted productivity, and the people enjoyed a relatively high standard of living.

The Republic of China, or Nationalist China, occupied China's permanent seat on the United Nations Security Council for many years. Then, in 1971, the UN expelled the Nationalists and admitted the People's Republic. However, the Nationalists, in anticipation of the UN's move, had already decided to withdraw from the organization.

The United States had given aid to Chiang Kai-shek for many years and had maintained army and navy bases on Taiwan. In agreements reached during President Nixon's visit to the People's Republic, however, the United States promised to withdraw its troops from Taiwan "as soon as tension in the area was reduced."

The renewal of diplomatic ties between the United States and the People's Republic of China dismayed the Taiwanese government. The United States, however, continued to maintain its commercial relations with Taiwan, though it ended diplomatic and military ties.

Diplomatic isolation did not prevent Taiwan from developing into a leading economic power in Asia. Even though it had few natural resources, Taiwan became one of the world's major producers and exporters of manufactured goods. In the 1980s Taiwan's volume of international trade, for example, equaled that of mainland China.

In the political sphere, fundamental changes took place during the 1980s. A native Taiwanese held the presidency and the leadership of the Kuomintang. And Taiwan's leaders encouraged the formation of opposition political parties, promising that future elections would be completely open.

The Korean War

Much of the tension between the People's Republic of China and the United States during the 1950s and 1960s grew out of events that took place in Korea after World War II. Agreements made at the end of the war divided Korea at the 38th parallel. The Soviet Union occupied Korea north of this line, while the United States moved troops into the southern part of Korea. The two occupying powers agreed that elections should be held to form a government that would rule the entire country. However, in 1948 the Soviet Union prevented the United Nations commission sent to supervise these elections from entering the north.

Elections held in the south resulted in the creation of the Republic of Korea, known as South Korea, with Syngman Rhee as its president, and the city of Seoul (SOHL) as its capital. At the same time, the Democratic People's Republic, or North Korea, led by Kim Il Sung, was created in the north. The United Nations recognized South Korea as the legal government, while Communist countries recognized only North Korea.

In June 1950 the North Korean army invaded South Korea, quickly taking Seoul. The United Nations Security Council, meeting in emergency session, declared the invasion an unwarranted

aggression. It called on UN members to furnish troops and supplies for an army to resist the invasion.

Chinese intervention. Most of the UN troops, as well as their commander, General Douglas MacArthur, came from the United States. In September 1950 MacArthur launched an attack at

Learning from Maps North Korea's farthest advance almost left it in control of the whole peninsula. Which cities did the South control at this time?

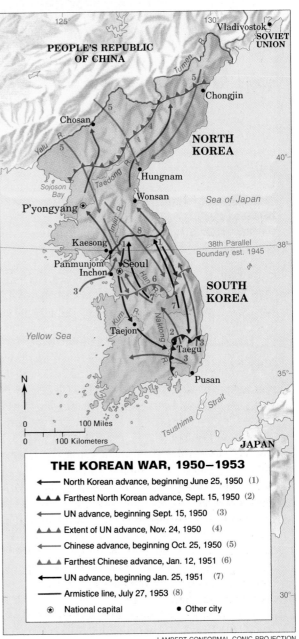

THE KOREAN WAR, 1950–1953

⟵ North Korean advance, beginning June 25, 1950 (1)

▲▲▲ Farthest North Korean advance, Sept. 15, 1950 (2)

⟵ UN advance, beginning Sept. 15, 1950 (3)

▲▲▲ Extent of UN advance, Nov. 24, 1950 (4)

⟵ Chinese advance, beginning Oct. 25, 1950 (5)

▲▲▲ Farthest Chinese advance, Jan. 12, 1951 (6)

⟵ UN advance, beginning Jan. 25, 1951 (7)

⟶ Armistice line, July 27, 1953 (8)

⊛ National capital   ● Other city

LAMBERT CONFORMAL CONIC PROJECTION

Learning from Pictures Taiwan has developed industries such as shipbuilding. What has contributed to Taiwan's success as a leading economic power in Asia?

781

Learning from Pictures *Supporters of Roh Tae Woo gather in Seoul for a campaign rally. According to opposition leaders, how did Roh win the election?*

Inchon, on the coast near Seoul. The North Koreans fell back behind their border, with the UN forces in hot pursuit. As the UN troops approached the Yalu River, the border between Korea and China, close to 200,000 Chinese soldiers joined those of North Korea. This combined force quickly drove MacArthur and his army south of the 38th parallel.

A controversy then arose over MacArthur's desire to bomb China's supply bases in Manchuria and to blockade the Chinese coast. President Truman and the UN General Assembly opposed these actions, fearing that they might cause the Soviet Union to come to China's assistance. When MacArthur continued to urge bombing attacks on China, Truman removed him from his post.

Under MacArthur's successor, General Matthew B. Ridgway, the UN forces pushed the Chinese and North Koreans back across the 38th parallel. In July 1951, with the situation at a stalemate, talks to end the hostilities began.

The armistice. After two years of negotiations, the two sides signed an armistice in July 1953 at Panmunjom. It fixed the boundary line between the two Koreas near the 38th parallel. It also established a demilitarized zone of 1.25 miles (2 kilometers) on either side of the boundary. The armistice also called for a peace conference to be held within three months. This conference never took place, however, and no peace treaty was ever signed.

South Korea in the 1980s

Despite South Korea's small size—it is only slightly larger than Indiana—various antagonisms divided the country. These antagonisms—between provinces, between Buddhists and Christians, and between rural and urban people—had existed for years. However, despite those differences, one issue—fear of North Korea—united South Koreans.

After 1953 President Syngman Rhee used this fear to justify moves to increase his power and to curb criticism of his policies. Therefore, although it was established as a democracy in 1948, South Korea virtually became a dictatorship.

Violent protests followed Rhee's election to a fourth term as president in March 1960. He resigned a few weeks later, and for a brief time Korea had a truly democratic government. Then, in 1961 about 250 army officers, led by General Park Chung Hee, staged a coup. For the next 18 years, Park ruled with an iron fist. He introduced a new constitution that reduced the power of the legislature and guaranteed his reelection as president every six years. In addition, he imposed strict censorship on the press and created a powerful secret police force to suppress political opposition. The secret police performed this task by arresting hundreds of dissident political leaders, students, members of the clergy, writers, and labor organizers.

However, President Park also used his power to promote economic development. South Korea's economy, which had grown little during Syngman Rhee's presidency, expanded very rapidly under Park. The most notable developments came in the production of steel and textiles, and the nation's exports of these two products increased dramatically. Because South Korean companies kept wages relatively low and the government held labor unions in check, the country's manufactured goods could be priced to compete successfully in world markets. Today South Korea's economy, based on the free enterprise system, continues to be among the fastest-growing in the world.

Political differences between Park and members of his government led to his assassination in 1979. For a time it appeared that democracy might return to South Korea under a civilian government. But almost immediately a military strongman, Chun Doo Hwan, took control. Chun pledged to end political corruption and to foster real democracy in South Korea. His actions, however, did not match his words. First, he had himself named president. Then he imposed martial law and press censorship and began a campaign of repression against his opponents. The United States, which had maintained a strong military presence in South Korea since the Korean War, strongly objected to Chun's dictatorial policies. He finally ended martial law in 1981 but continued to rule South Korea with an iron hand.

Throughout the 1980s, Chun's opponents continually called for greater political and civil rights. In 1987 a series of particularly violent demonstrations against Chun's government resulted in his resignation. Roh Tae Woo, Chun's hand-picked successor, won the election that followed, largely because the opposition could not unite behind a single candidate. Opposition leaders, however, suggested that Roh's election had more to do with ballot-rigging than with their lack of unity.

Like Chun before him, Roh promised democratic reforms. But with the almost constant student demonstrations and the growing calls for reunification with the North, the future of Roh's government and of South Korea itself seem somewhat unclear.

SECTION 1 REVIEW

1. **Identify**   Great Leap Forward, Four Modernizations, Liu Shaoqi, Great Proletarian Cultural Revolution, Gang of Four, Deng Xiaoping, Syngman Rhee, Park Chung Hee, Chun Doo Hwan
2. **Locate**   Taiwan, Xinjiang, 38th parallel, Seoul, Yalu River, Panmunjom
3. **Determining Cause and Effect**   **(a)** What was the reason for the Great Proletarian Cultural Revolution?   **(b)** What impact did it have on life in China?
4. **Analyzing Ideas**   Why did Chinese foreign policy change in the early 1970s?
5. **Making Comparisons**   How do the political changes that took place in Taiwan during the 1980s compare to those that took place in South Korea during the same period?

---

2 Japan Became an Economic Giant in the Postwar World

After World War II, Japan lost all the territory it had gained during its period of expansion. Its population, now confined to the home islands, faced incredible shortages of food and other necessities. The country desperately needed to increase imports to satisfy the people's needs. But most of the industries that had produced export goods to pay for imports had been damaged or destroyed during the war.

The Occupation of Japan

After the war American troops under the command of General Douglas MacArthur occupied Japan. As supreme commander of the Allied Powers in Japan, MacArthur became the country's virtual ruler. His first task involved the demilitarization of Japan. To this end, he planned to confiscate as reparations the war industries that remained in Japan. But taking factories for reparations would have created the same difficulties in Japan as in Germany. Unless the Allied Powers wished to support them indefinitely, the Japanese had to be given the opportunity to provide for themselves. To do this, however, the Japanese needed to keep their factories and convert them to peacetime activities. The United States, therefore, suggested that the payment of reparations be postponed indefinitely.

MacArthur's second task involved the creation of a non-military and democratic government. Under his supervision the Japanese adopted a new constitution in 1947. The "MacArthur constitution" established Japan as a parliamentary democracy. It called for direct election of the Diet, or parliament, with all adults having the right to vote. The emperor, having renounced his divine status, remained only as a symbol of state. He had little power. Finally, the constitution ended Japan's militarism and limited the country's armed forces to those needed for police purposes.

Postwar Developments

Before World War II, Japan had been the most industrialized of the Asian nations. Although the destruction of many factories and the loss of its

Asian possessions had hurt its economy, Japan made a rapid and impressive recovery after the war.

Economic development. Mechanization and the introduction of new types of seeds and fertilizers had a major impact on Japanese agriculture. Farm output increased dramatically, even though the number of people in the agricultural work force fell. Within a few years, Japan had become practically self-supporting in the production of food.

In the postwar years, Japan also developed efficient industries that made products of high quality. Before the war Japanese goods had been known for their low price and poor quality. Postwar products—photographic, optical, and electronics materials and automobiles—could compete with any in the world in quality as well as price.

Japan entered the 1980s as Asia's leading economic power. Surpassing all others in shipbuilding and electronics manufacturing, it stood as the world's third-ranking industrial nation. However, the country's economic leaders faced a growing problem—where to find markets for a rapidly expanding volume of production.

For many years the United States had been Japan's best customer and principal supplier of raw materials and agricultural products. In this trade relationship, Japan bought more from the United States than the United States purchased from the Japanese. Thus the trade balance favored the United States for many years.

Beginning in the late 1960s, however, the balance of trade swung heavily in favor of Japan. In response, many American politicians pressured their government to limit Japanese imports. They also wanted Japan to remove controls that restricted the number of American imports into Japan. By the late 1980s, the trade imbalance between the two countries had become a major political issue that heightened tensions between the two nations.

Economic and social changes. Postwar economic growth did not benefit everyone in Japan, but it did bring prosperity to a large part of the population. This prosperity led to an increase in consumerism. For example, many families who had lived simply before the war acquired labor-saving household appliances and new automobiles. These better times also brought a better diet and, consequently, a healthier population.

Economic growth, however, did not necessarily lead to an improvement in the quality of life. Rapid industrialization and population growth put land for building at a premium, and prices for land and housing soared. By the mid-1980s many young married couples had no choice but to live with their parents or in tiny apartments in drab high-rise buildings. Industrialization also created another serious problem—environmental pollution. As the decade drew to a close, many Japanese called on their government to pay more attention to improving the quality of life and less to promoting further industrial development.

Postwar economic developments brought about two far-reaching social changes. As more and more women joined the work force, their status in Japanese society began to change. In time they won greater legal, political, and social freedoms. Changing roles within the family and different housing arrangements helped to cause a decline in the emphasis on the family, traditionally the center of all Japanese life. As a result, young people began to make decisions and choices for themselves—on marriage partners and work, for example—that their parents had once made for them.

Political Life and Foreign Relations

The cold war between the Soviet Union and the West led to a reversal of Japan's international position. The MacArthur constitution had limited Japanese armed forces and military production. In addition, the Japanese had signed a treaty agreeing to renounce war as a method of resolving international differences. The Communist victory in China and the stalemate in Korea changed Western policy toward Japan. The Western nations now felt that Japan should be able to defend itself and to aid them in case of war in Asia. These nations, therefore, urged Japan to increase its armed forces.

Fearing a return of the militaristic governments of prewar days, the Japanese had little desire to rearm. They preferred to spend their money building peacetime industries, expanding exports, and raising living standards. As a result, Japan's military expenditures remained at about 1 percent of the GNP. In response to continued pressure from the United States, however, Japan did begin to develop a small, but increasingly powerful, self-defense force.

Japanese political life continued to reflect disagreements over the nation's domestic and foreign policies. The conservative Liberal Democratic

ARCHITECTURE

Japanese Ceremonial Gate

Although Japan today is a leading modern nation, traditional customs are still very much in evidence. Here we see a ceremonial gate, or *torii*, that has been carefully preserved. Standing in the waters of the Inland Sea, southwest of Hiroshima, the torii greets visitors to the sacred Shinto shrine of Itsukushima. Records of the shrine go back to the year 811, when it was dedicated to the three daughters of the Shinto god Susano. At one time it also enshrined the Japanese god who protected those who fished. In the 1300s the shrine was carefully restored, at great cost, by a samurai ruler and his family.

Today the buildings form a unique architectural complex extending into the sea. The shrine itself is made up of several structures joined together by covered pathways and bridges. One of these buildings, a five-story pagoda built in 1407, contains beautiful treasures of the past. An impressive hall was added by Toyotomi Hideyoshi (see page 463) in the 1600s, and in 1875 this huge torii was completed.

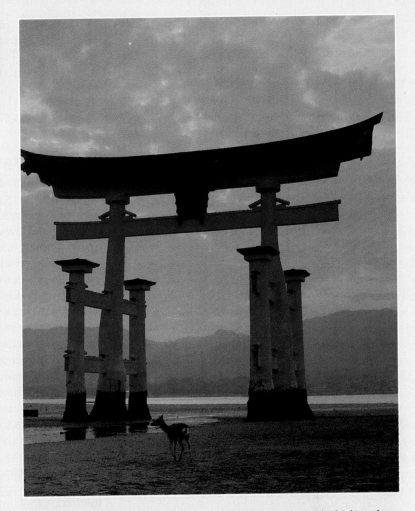

Once each year a favorite Japanese tradition is re-created in front of the torii. On the seventeenth day of the sixth month of the lunar calendar, a colorful water festival takes place, reproducing some of the customs of ancient times through music and dance.

Party controlled the Diet and, therefore, the government. But the Socialist and other opposition parties voiced strong criticism of its policies. These parties also condemned the signing of the security pact with the United States, which was renewed in 1970 and again in 1980. Critics of the government denounced the presence of American military bases on Japanese soil. And they protested the visits of American nuclear-powered vessels to Japanese ports.

Although Japan and the United States continued on friendly terms, United States-Japanese relations came under some stress during the Nixon administration. The reestablishment of contacts between the United States and the People's Republic of China in 1972 dismayed the Japanese because they had not been informed beforehand. The Japanese also resented the new economic pressures put upon them by the United States and other nations during the 1970s.

Since the late 1940s, Japan had been a staunch and unquestioning ally of the United States. By the mid-1980s, however, disagreements over trade and defense policies had complicated United States-Japanese relationships. Many Americans felt apprehensive about the growing trade deficit with Japan, which reached almost $60 billion in 1987. At the same time, many Japanese thought that the time had come for Japan to pursue a more independent course in international affairs. However, no serious rift developed between the two countries, due largely to the efforts of Yasuhiro Nakasone (yah • soo • HEE • roh nahk • uh • SOH • neh), Japanese prime minister from 1982 to 1987. Throughout his time in office, Nakasone stressed the benefits both countries could gain from continued close relations.

SECTION 2 REVIEW

1. **Identify** MacArthur constitution, Diet, Yasuhiro Nakasone
2. **Analyzing Ideas** What difficulties would have arisen if Japanese war industries had been taken as reparations?
3. **Classifying Ideas** What two far-reaching social changes were brought about by economic growth after World War II?
4. **Evaluating Ideas** How did the cold war change Japan's international position?
5. **Determining Cause and Effect** What caused strains in Japanese-American relations after 1970?

3 India, Pakistan, and Bangladesh Became Independent Nations

A movement for independence from Great Britain had developed in India after World War I. Indian nationalists continued to make strong demands for immediate independence throughout World War II. Finally, the British Labour Party government, elected in 1945, agreed that India should become independent no later than 1948.

During the independence negotiations, longstanding differences between Hindus and Muslims surfaced. The Muslim League, led by Mohammed Ali Jinnah, felt that its people would be secure only if they had their own state. After much discussion the two sides decided to partition the Indian subcontinent along religious lines (see map, page 787).

The process of partition caused tremendous upheaval and resulted in violence and bloodshed. As the day of independence approached, millions of Hindus and Muslims rushed to cross the borders into their own areas. Violent riots erupted, in which more than 500,000 people died.

The stroke of midnight on August 15, 1947, marked the official birth of the two nations of India and Pakistan. Their first task involved the integration of the princely states. Over the next two years, these states decided which nation to join. Only Kashmir, which had a Hindu ruler and a predominantly Muslim population, joined neither.

India's Government and Leaders

In 1950, India adopted a new constitution that established its government as a federal republic with an elected president and parliament. Although the president was the official head of state, the prime minister and cabinet wielded the power.

Jawaharlal Nehru (NAY • roo), India's first prime minister, served from 1950 until his death in 1964. A wealthy Brahman, Nehru had been educated at Cambridge University in England. On his return to India, he became a lawyer. But after meeting Mahatma Gandhi in 1916, Nehru devoted himself entirely to the independence movement.

Unlike Gandhi, who wanted independent India to return to its traditional way of life, Nehru emphasized modernization. As prime minister, he had five main goals. First, he wanted to unify India by overcoming the dividing forces of religion, language, caste, and regional interests. Next, having seen the religious passions stirred by partition, he wanted India's government to be free of religious interference. Third, he hoped to strengthen and protect democracy in India. With regard to the economy, Nehru intended to follow the example of the Communist countries and develop five-year plans. Finally, in foreign affairs he wanted to follow a policy of **non-alignment,** refusing to ally India with either the United States or the Soviet Union. Nehru's views on this last matter significantly influenced the leaders of other developing nations. In time they, too, adopted a policy of non-alignment.

After Nehru's death, his daughter, Indira Gandhi, became prime minister in 1966 and attempted to carry out his policies. A controversial figure, Indira Gandhi dominated Indian politics for nearly two decades.

In 1971, after Indira Gandhi's reelection as prime minister, her opponents charged that she had rigged the voting. In 1975, when the courts found her guilty, opposition leaders called for her immediate resignation. Gandhi then declared a constitutional state of emergency. The state of

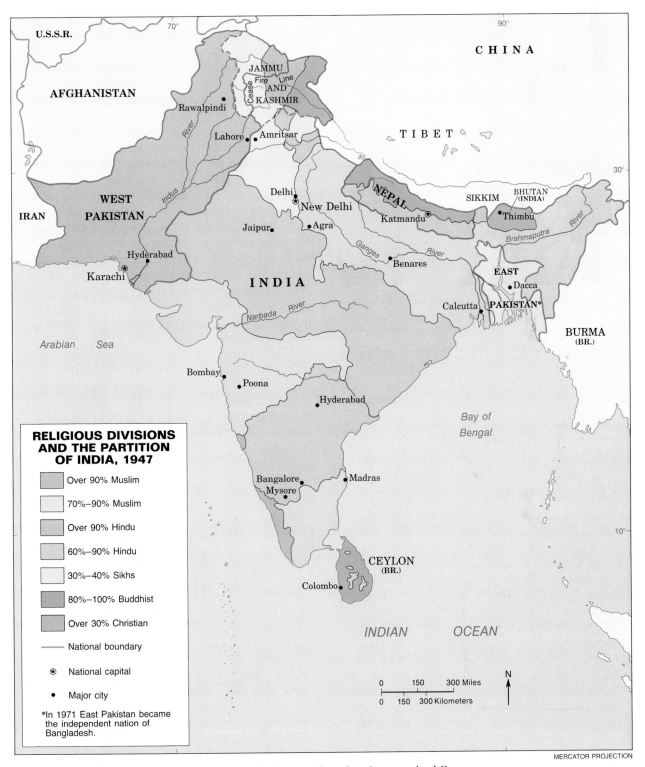

RELIGIOUS DIVISIONS AND THE PARTITION OF INDIA, 1947

- Over 90% Muslim
- 70%–90% Muslim
- Over 90% Hindu
- 60%–90% Hindu
- 30%–40% Sikhs
- 80%–100% Buddhist
- Over 30% Christian
- —— National boundary
- ⊛ National capital
- • Major city

*In 1971 East Pakistan became the independent nation of Bangladesh.

MERCATOR PROJECTION

Learning from Maps *The partitioning of India created conflicts between the different religious groups in India. The multi-religious ancient state of Kashmir, which did not want to join India or Pakistan, continues to be a scene of conflict and is a divided state. What two religious groups are fighting for control of Kashmir?*

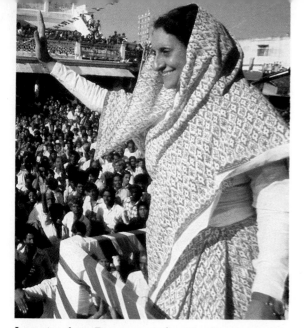

Learning from Pictures *Indira Gandhi campaigns for prime minister of India. What did opponents accuse her of doing to win the elections?*

emergency gave her the power to arrest anyone she thought might threaten internal security.

During the state of emergency, which lasted two years, Gandhi enacted a number of harsh laws. This turned many Indians against her, and in 1977 they voted her out of office. However, she came back as prime minister in 1980.

The most pressing problem that she faced on her return involved a religious minority, the Sikhs. A group of Sikh extremists, in a campaign to win independence for the province of Punjab, had attacked a number of government officials. In 1984 Gandhi ordered the Indian army to storm the extremists' base, the Golden Temple—the Sikhs' holiest shrine—in Amritsar. About 1,000 people died in the attack. The Sikhs, incensed by this act of sacrilege, vowed revenge. A few months later, two of Gandhi's bodyguards—both Sikhs—assassinated her. Her son, Rajiv Gandhi, succeeded her. But rumors of financial scandals as well as continuing protests from Sikhs rocked his administration. When Gandhi's party lost the national elections of November 1989, V. P. Singh became the new prime minister.

Social and Economic Problems

Indians speak with great pride of the social and cultural diversity of their country. But this very diversity, by hindering attempts at unification, has created problems. India's great variety of languages provides but one example of this. The country has 15 major languages, 300 minor languages, and some 3,000 dialects. In newly independent India, government officials from different regions often found that they could not understand one another. As a result, in 1950 the government adopted English as the country's administrative and business language. An attempt some years later to make Hindi—spoken by only 40 percent of the population—the official language met with violent resistance. To this day English remains the only linguistic link among many of the regions of India.

By the end of the 1980s, India also faced major economic problems, even though its economy had made considerable progress. Under Nehru, the country had developed a **mixed economy,** in which private companies owned some industries and the government owned the rest. Through a series of five-year plans, the government charted the way in which it wanted the economy to grow.

These plans proved quite successful, for by the end of the 1980s, India had become self-sufficient in agricultural production and was even exporting crops to other countries in Asia. The country's textile and steel industries also experienced considerable growth. And exports of related manufactured products, such as shirts and bicycles, showed a marked increase.

India's economic problems, in large part, stemmed from its ever-growing population. At the time of independence, the population stood at 350 million. In a little over 40 years it had increased to about 800 million. By the mid-1980s, India had 15 percent of the world's population but only 2 percent of the world's land area.

India's economy failed to grow as rapidly as its population. Consequently, by the late 1980s annual per capita income averaged below $300, and the unemployment rate stood well above 10 percent. Millions of Indians subsisted at the poverty level, and the country's large cities teemed with thousands of homeless people living in the streets.

Foreign Relations

Partition left India and Pakistan with a difficult problem in the northern state of Kashmir (see map, page 787). Kashmir's ruling prince, a Hindu, chose to join India. However, Pakistan claimed Kashmir because 85 percent of its people were Muslim.

Sporadic fighting between the two countries continued until 1949, when the United Nations established a cease-fire line. At this point India occupied two-thirds of Kashmir. The cease-fire agreement called for an election in Kashmir to determine the political wishes of the population. However, India prevented that election from ever taking place.

In 1957 India officially annexed part of Kashmir. Pakistan protested, and after sporadic fighting a full-scale war erupted between the two countries in 1965. A year later, the prime ministers of India and Pakistan agreed to withdraw their troops behind the cease-fire line and to negotiate a settlement at a later date. Since that time an uneasy peace has existed between India and Pakistan, but the issue of Kashmir remains unsettled.

In world affairs India tried to cultivate friendships with both the Communist bloc and the West. As a result it soon assumed a leadership role in the non-aligned movement among African and Asian nations. However, India's commitment to non-alignment was strained by tensions with China. In 1959 the Chinese moved into Tibet to put down a revolt. For a long time India had supported the Dalai Lama (dah • LY LAH • muh), Tibet's religious and political leader. After the Chinese attack, the Dalai Lama and some of his followers fled to India, forming a government in exile.

Indian relations with China became even more strained in 1960 with the discovery of a Chinese military base in territory claimed by India. The Indian government declared that the Chinese had unlawfully occupied Indian territory, but the Chinese refused to withdraw. Then, in 1962, the Chinese invaded northeastern India, winning easy victories on their advance toward the Indo-Gangetic Plain. With the Indian army in full retreat, Prime Minister Nehru called on the United States for military assistance. Almost immediately the Chinese declared a cease-fire and withdrew.

During the 1970s India moved further from its non-aligned stance, forging close ties with the Soviet Union. And once again it went to war with Pakistan, this time over independence for Bangladesh.

The Division of Pakistan

At the time of independence, Pakistan consisted of two parts—West Pakistan and East Pakistan—separated by a huge wedge of Indian territory some

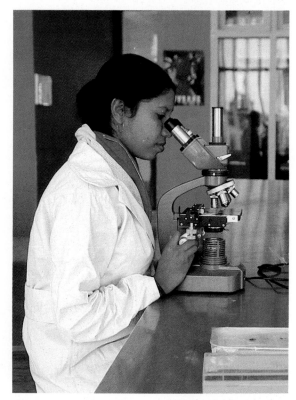

Learning from Pictures *In Bangladesh a research technician works to increase agricultural output.*

1,000 miles (1,600 kilometers) wide. The divided nation faced problems similar to those that plagued India—a rapidly growing population, poverty, illiteracy, and cultural and linguistic differences. In addition, a lack of natural resources and its peculiar geographic situation hindered Pakistan's economic development. Defense expenditures further slowed Pakistan's economic growth.

At first a dominion of the British Commonwealth, Pakistan became a parliamentary republic in 1956. Soon, however, a succession of military leaders took control of the government. General Muhammad Ayub Khan, the first of these, came to power in 1958, vowing to eliminate political corruption and improve the economy. However, opposition to Ayub's government grew as he failed to respond to increasing demands for economic reforms, direct elections, democratic government, and greater autonomy for East Pakistan.

Independence for Bangladesh

Finally, a political scandal forced Ayub Khan to resign in 1969. In the elections held in December

Learning from Pictures
On December 2, 1988, Benazir Bhutto was sworn in as the prime minister of Pakistan, becoming the first woman to govern a Muslim country.

1970, the Awami League—a political party dedicated to independence for East Pakistan—won many seats in the national assembly. When the central government, fearful of being outvoted, refused to convene the assembly, riots erupted in East Pakistan. The new president, General Agha Muhammad Yahya Khan, sent troops to quell the riots and to arrest the leaders of the Awami League. The situation soon developed into a civil war in which more than 1 million people lost their lives. Another 10 million East Pakistanis fled to safety in India. During the war India came to the aid of the East Pakistani rebels first by sending arms and then by providing troops. Late in 1971 the Pakistani troops surrendered, and a cease-fire was arranged. East Pakistan then became the new nation of Bangladesh.

In 1973 India, Pakistan, and Bangladesh signed a peace settlement. They agreed to an exchange of prisoners of war and the repatriation of people who chose to live either in Bangladesh or in Pakistan. In addition, Pakistan pledged to recognize the independence of Bangladesh.

Bangladesh and Pakistan in the 1980s. Both Bangladesh and Pakistan faced major problems after the division. Bangladesh, ravaged by war, also suffered recurrent famines, epidemics, floods, and devastating tropical storms. The new government proved unequal to the huge task of rebuilding the country, and in the mid-1970s it was toppled by a military coup. Since 1982 General Hussain Muhammad Ershad has ruled the country with an iron fist. Regular batterings from the elements, economic instability, and political unrest make the future of this desperately poor country very uncertain.

For the first half of the 1970s, a civilian government led by Zulfikar Ali Bhutto ruled Pakistan. However, General Muhammad Zia ul-Haq seized control of the government in 1977 and, two years later, had Bhutto executed. Zia imposed martial law, banned political parties, and reformed the legal system so that it more closely followed Islamic teachings. In foreign affairs, although claiming to follow a course of non-alignment, Zia forged strong ties with the United States. And after the Soviet invasion of Afghanistan in 1979, Zia provided refuge and assistance to the Afghan rebel forces.

Zia answered a growing clamor for a return to democratic rule by promising to hold free elections late in 1988. However, in August of that year, Zia was killed when his plane exploded in midair. The elections still took place, with Benazir Bhutto, the daughter of Ali Bhutto, emerging as the winner. She became the first woman to serve as head of state of a Muslim nation.

SECTION 3 REVIEW

1. **Define** non-alignment, mixed economy
2. **Identify** Jawaharlal Nehru, Indira Gandhi, Muhammad Ayub Khan, Awami League, Muhammad Zia ul-Haq, Benazir Bhutto
3. **Locate** Pakistan, Kashmir, Tibet, Bangladesh
4. **Understanding Ideas** What were Nehru's five main goals for India?
5. **Classifying Ideas** List the major social and economic problems faced by India.
6. **Analyzing Ideas** What led to the hostility between East and West Pakistan?
7. **Comparing Ideas** How did the foreign policies of India and Pakistan differ during the 1970s?

4 The Countries of Southeast Asia Achieved Independence

Southeast Asia consists of 10 countries: the Philippines, Indonesia, Malaysia, Singapore, Brunei, Vietnam, Cambodia (Kampuchea), Laos, Burma, and Thailand. With the exception of Thailand, all were at one time colonies. After World War II, these countries gained independence. Some did so peacefully, while others resorted to violent means. After achieving independence each began the long and difficult process of political and economic development.

The Philippines

When Spain ceded the Philippines to the United States in 1898, many Filipinos resisted American rule. After a three-year struggle, the United States finally crushed this resistance. However, the American government promised to grant the Filipinos their independence at a later date.

Fulfilling this promise, the United States Congress passed an act granting independence to the Philippines in 1934. But World War II and the Japanese occupation delayed the enactment of independence. Then, on July 4, 1946, the Filipinos proclaimed their country the independent Republic of the Philippines.

After independence the United States maintained military bases in the Philippines. In return it contributed large sums of money to repair war damage and rebuild the Philippine economy. These close ties to the United States led the Philippine government to adopt a strongly pro-Western foreign policy.

In the 1970s Marxist guerrillas began to threaten the peace in the Philippines. A revolt by Muslims, who represented 5 percent of the population, further strained the country's stability. To deal with this internal disorder, President Ferdinand Marcos declared martial law and arrested hundreds of his political opponents. In 1973 Marcos further extended his power by proclaiming a new constitution that gave him an almost unlimited term in office.

Marcos described his government as "constitutional authoritarianism" and promised to "make democracy real." He ended martial law in 1981 and released hundreds of political prisoners. However, the country made little progress toward democracy, and random acts of repression continued. Meanwhile, although Marcos made some reforms, economic conditions in the Philippines worsened.

Opposition to the Marcos regime slowly began to grow. Then, the assassination of opposition leader Benigno Aquino (ah•KEE•noh) in 1983 sparked widespread rioting. Three years later, in 1986, Corazon Aquino, the widow of Benigno Aquino, ran against Marcos in a specially called presidential election. Marcos claimed victory, but when it become obvious that he had rigged the election, the people took to the streets in protest. After a number of army officers shifted their support to Aquino, Marcos fled the country.

On taking office Aquino pledged to recover the billions of dollars that she said Marcos and his family had embezzled from the treasury. She also promised to bring an end to the Marxist and Muslim insurrections in the country. But a number of coup attempts and the withdrawal of support by some key politicians have hindered her efforts to attain these goals.

Indonesia

During World War II, the Japanese occupied the East Indies, a group of some 3,000 islands including Sumatra and Java. When the war ended, the

WEAVING

Ikat Cloth

During the last 30 years, in an effort to reduce the tremendous poverty in their countries, Asian governments began to encourage industrialization and economic growth. Many started exporting both manufactured items and handcrafted goods to other areas of the world. Often these goods were sold in stores throughout the United States and Europe.

The woven cloth shown here, from Java, was made by an ancient method of dyeing and weaving known as *ikat*. This technique, more than 1,000 years old, is particularly common in Indonesia and Japan.

The process involves winding the yarn over a frame and then tying the strands at certain points. When the yarn is dyed, the places where the strands are tied together do not absorb color, thus creating a pattern. After the yarn is dyed, it is woven on a loom. The entire process of producing the ikat cloth—from growing the cotton to dyeing the cloth to designing and executing the weaving—is done completely by women.

Decorated textiles such as these have been an important part of Indonesian culture for centuries. Ikat cloths were used to wrap around newborn babies, given as wedding gifts between families, worn as ceremonial costumes, and used as wrappings for the bodies of the dead. Because of the long time needed to produce them and the high quality of the weaving, the cloths became a symbol of wealth.

Dutch, who had administered the East Indies since the 1600s, expected to regain control. However, Achmed Sukarno, a Dutch-trained engineer, led an independence movement against the Dutch. After a year of bitter fighting, the United Nations intervened to secure a cease-fire. Then in 1949, the Netherlands granted independence to the East Indies. The East Indies became the Republic of Indonesia, with Sukarno as its first president.

Indonesia faced problems similar to those of many other newly independent countries. It had few trained civil servants or competent administrators, a high rate of illiteracy, and a chaotic political system. However, the country made some significant gains, especially education and health care. Sukarno also worked to develop a sense of national identity among the Indonesian people.

In the early 1960s, Sukarno became much more authoritarian. In a move that established what he called a "guided democracy," Sukarno dissolved the elected parliament and appointed a new one. This appointed legislature proclaimed him "President for Life" in 1963. During this time Indonesia's problems multiplied. The economy slowed almost to a standstill, and reckless government spending brought the nation close to bankruptcy.

In 1966, taking advantage of a Communist insurrection, General Suharto seized control of the government. As president, Suharto emphasized economic reforms and worked to build closer ties with the West. Using Western aid he began an ambitious industrial development program. He carried this program further with revenues from the state-owned oil industry.

The slump in oil prices in the early 1980s had a devastating effect on the Indonesian economy. Also, a large share of the small amount of oil revenue the government did receive had to be used to pay off foreign debts. As a result, the pace of industrial development in Indonesia again slowed.

In the late 1980s, Suharto's government came under criticism from people both within and outside the country. Many Indonesians complained about the lack of economic progress and the continued mismanagement and corruption of many government officials. And a number of Western countries voiced concern over human rights abuses allegedly committed by the Indonesian military and police forces.

Malaysia, Singapore, and Brunei

In 1963 Malaya, Singapore, Sarawak, and Sabah (North Borneo), which had all become independent from Great Britain, united to form the Federation of Malaysia. The new nation faced difficult problems both externally and internally. To begin with, the Philippines claimed part of Sabah. Also, President Sukarno of Indonesia accused the newly formed Federation of being nothing more than a move by the British to encircle his country. In addition, Sarawak and Sabah had come under heavy attack from Indonesian Communist guerrillas.

Internally, a clash of cultures threatened the Federation. The nation's population consisted of Malays, Chinese, and a small percentage of Indians and other ethnic groups. The majority of the population were Malays; however, Singapore had a large majority of Chinese. Most Malays were uneducated farmers, whereas the Chinese were mainly city dwellers, technically trained and experienced in commerce. Malays controlled the government of the Federation, but the Chinese controlled most of the business and the wealth.

Fearing that the Chinese might increase their political influence, the Malays forced Singapore to secede from the Federation in 1965. Tensions continued to grow between the Malays and the Chinese remaining in Malaysia. Then, in 1969, the tensions exploded in racial riots. Hundreds of people lost their lives before the government declared a state of emergency.

Following these riots, the government began to promote rural development as a means of raising the living standard of Malays. It also increased educational opportunities for Malays and required that the Malay language be used in government-run schools and universities. Thus, by improving the status of the Malay majority, the government hoped to eliminate the educational and economic differences between Malays and other ethnic groups.

Racial tensions erupted once again in the late 1970s with the arrival of thousands of Vietnamese refugees. Since many of these refugees were ethnic Chinese, the Malays feared that the Chinese faction would gain power. As a result, the Malaysian government denied entry to the refugees. Racial friction continued to be Malaysia's major problem as the 1980s drew to a close.

The Republic of Singapore. Singapore, a cluster of one major island and 54 smaller islands, measures less than 240 square miles (620 square kilometers) in area. Since its founding in 1965, Singapore's government has been dominated by one political party—Prime Minister Lee Kwan Yew's People's Action Party. Throughout his time in office, Lee has kept a tight rein on the country, imposing strict controls on labor unions, political activity, and the media.

Singapore prospered as an independent country after it seceded from the Federation of Malaysia. This prosperity grew out of a program of industrial

Learning from Pictures This view of Singapore shows the city's modern setting. Notice in the foreground the athletic fields showing Western influences.

development that emphasized petroleum refining, textiles, and electronics. By the mid-1980s, Singapore's per capita income, the highest in Southeast Asia, exceeded $6,600. The country's mixed economy of free enterprise and state participation in business helped raise the standard of living for most of its 2.5 million people.

Brunei. The small sultanate of Brunei on the northern coast of Malaysian Borneo decided against joining the Federation of Malaysia. Its leaders feared that it would be overwhelmed by the larger states of Malaya and Singapore. This oil-rich land remained a protectorate of Great Britain until it achieved full independence in 1984.

Burma

Since before World War II, British-held Burma had been strategically important as the starting point of the Burma Road, over which supplies moved to China. Japanese armies invaded Burma in 1942 and held it until 1945. After the war the Burmese did not want the British back, nor did the British try to return. In 1948 Great Britain recognized Burma's independence.

The new nation faced difficulties that included the lack of a strong central government, a scarcity of trained civil servants, tribal and political dissension, and Communist attempts to seize the country. The first premier, U Nu, headed a coalition government that brought the nation some degree of order. This government introduced reforms in land distribution, agriculture, education, and public health.

However, the coalition soon broke into rival factions. As a result, the government—and democracy—did not last long. In 1962 the army, led by General Ne Win, seized control of the government. Ne Win promised to end political dissension, eliminate corruption, and reduce living costs.

In foreign affairs Burma tried to remain neutral. To this end the government accepted help from both Communist and Western nations and refused to take sides in the ongoing East-West conflict. In 1974 a new constitution proclaimed Burma a socialist democratic republic. Under this constitution the country remained neutral and was to seek what it called "the Burmese Way" to socialism.

However, this way led to state-sanctioned brutality and economic ruin. In 1988 student-led violent demonstrations forced Ne Win to resign. But his successors remained unwilling to share power with any other political party. Meanwhile, public order continued to deteriorate. As the 1980s drew to a close, the future of Burma—renamed Myanmar by its new leaders in 1989—looked very unclear.

5 Conflict in Vietnam Affected Other Countries in Southeast Asia

After World War II, some Southeast Asian countries won independence with little or no violence. However, independence movements in Vietnam, Laos, and Cambodia resulted in years of conflict.

The French in Indochina

In the early 1900s, the French became the dominant power in the eastern part of the Indochina Peninsula—an area roughly equivalent to the present-day countries of Vietnam, Laos, and Cambodia (Kampuchea). However, in 1940 after France fell to Germany, the Japanese took control of the area. When the French tried to return after the war, the League for the Independence of Vietnam, a largely Communist group better known as the Viet Minh, resisted them. In order to make a complete break with the French, the League's leader, Ho Chi Minh, declared the country independent on September 2, 1945. But no major governments recognized Ho's declaration, and by the end of 1945 the French had regained control of much of Vietnam.

Ho hoped to negotiate a quick settlement to the independence question. However, the French

INDEPENDENT NATIONS IN SOUTHEAST ASIA, 1946–1984

⊛ National capital

• Other city

— National boundary

✦ Battle site

1945 Date of independence

Continuously independent

0 250 500 Miles

0 250 500 Kilometers

MERCATOR PROJECTION

Learning from Maps *Nationalism in Southeast Asia contributed to the formation of dynamic modern countries. Which country is next to the island of Singapore?*

would agree only to recognize Vietnam as a free state within the French Union, or empire. Ho reluctantly accepted this arrangement. But the situation soon deteriorated, and in 1946 fighting broke out between the French and the Viet Minh in the northern cities of Hanoi and Haiphong.

Against the French the Viet Minh fought what Ho called the "war of the flea." No matter how many "fleas"—Viet Minh soldiers—the French killed, he said, others would take their place and eventually force the French into submission. By the 1950s the French people had grown tired of this

costly conflict, which they called "the dirty war." It took a major defeat, the siege of Dien Bien Phu (DYEN BYEN FOO) in May 1954, before the French government agreed. French leaders then quickly indicated their willingness to negotiate an end to the war.

The Geneva Accords, signed in 1954, called for the withdrawal of all foreign troops from the area. They also recognized the independence of Laos and Cambodia and divided Vietnam into two zones at the 17th parallel (see map, page 797). For the time being, Ho Chi Minh would remain in control of the

795

north. But an election, set for 1956, would allow the Vietnamese to select a government to reunite the country.

The Geneva Accords left the Viet Minh in a better situation than that of the government in the south. The north had most of Vietnam's raw materials and industries, and it had enough good farmland to become almost self-sufficient in food production. With Chinese and Soviet assistance, the Viet Minh began to consolidate their economic and political strength, building a Communist state in the north.

In contrast, chaos ruled in the south. A war-torn economy, a flood of refugees from the north, and fighting among political and religious groups all posed problems for the newly-formed government of Ngo Dinh Diem (NOH DIN deh • EHM).

Guerrilla War in Vietnam

Under Diem, South Vietnam returned to some semblance of order. But this restoration of order came at a price. Diem outlawed a number of political parties, including the Communists, and tried to suppress all other opposition to his government. He also showed little interest in social or economic reforms and refused to take part in the proposed election of 1956.

During the late 1950s, Diem's government became increasingly repressive. As a result opposition to Diem grew in the south. In 1960 the Viet Minh took advantage of this, forming the National Liberation Front (NLF) with the goal of overthrowing Diem and reuniting Vietnam. The NLF, a mixture of Viet Minh members and dissidents from the south, soon became known as the *Viet Cong,* or Vietnamese Communists.

After undergoing guerrilla training in the north, the Viet Cong infiltrated the rural areas of South Vietnam and began a program of assassinating government officials. And, through a combination of persuasion and terror, they worked to gain either the support or passive acceptance of the South Vietnamese peasants.

Ngo Dinh Diem responded to both internal dissent and Viet Cong guerrilla activity by becoming even more repressive. With conditions in the south growing more and more chaotic, a group of army officers assassinated Diem and took control of the government in 1963. Over the next three years, nine different military groups ruled South Vietnam.

American Involvement

United States involvement in Vietnam began almost unnoticed. It grew slowly, without either a declaration of war by Congress or an announcement by the government to the American people. President Eisenhower sent military and economic aid to South Vietnam and allowed the CIA to assist the Diem government in gathering information on opposition groups. President Kennedy continued this policy and also sent American military advisers to help the South Vietnamese army. As the guerrilla war increased in intensity, so did the American commitment. In time American soldiers began to go into battle along with South Vietnamese troops.

American troop strength began to reach significant numbers in the mid-1960s under President Lyndon Johnson. The Johnson administration explained the increased American military presence in a number of ways. First, communism had to be contained. Second, the administration cited the **domino theory,** or the belief that if South Vietnam fell to communism, all of Southeast Asia would follow. Third, the North Vietnamese were aggressors in the conflict and had to be stopped.

In January 1965 President Johnson expanded the war by ordering air attacks on North Vietnam, and the country came under heavy bombing. James Cameron, a British reporter, described the impact of this bombing on everyday life in North Vietnam.

❝ Through the daylight hours nothing moves on the roads of North Vietnam, not a car nor a truck. It must look from the air as though the country had no wheeled transport at all. That, of course, is the idea, it is the roads and bridges that are being bombed; it is no longer safe after sunrise to be anywhere near either. . . .

Then the sun goes down and everything starts to move.

At dusk the roads become alive. The engines are started and the convoys grind away through the darkness behind the pinpoints of masked headlamps. There are miles of them, heavy Russian-built trucks, antiaircraft batteries, all deeply buried under piles of branches and leaves; processions of huge green haystacks. North Vietnam by day is abandoned; by night it thuds and grinds with movement. ❞

At the beginning of 1968, North Vietnamese troops and the Viet Cong launched a major offensive. They overthrew some village governments in South Vietnam and threatened a number of large cities, including Saigon, the capital (see map, this page). However, American and South Vietnamese forces drove back the attackers, inflicting heavy casualties. Even so, the Viet Cong considered this Tet Offensive—named for the Vietnamese New Year celebration—a psychological victory, for many Americans, after seeing television pictures of their embassy in Saigon under direct attack, openly questioned United States involvement in the war.

In March of 1968, President Johnson announced a temporary halt to the bombing of North Vietnam. An agreement with North Vietnam to begin negotiating an end to the war soon followed. However, these peace negotiations, held in Paris, France, quickly became deadlocked.

During 1969, the first year of President Richard Nixon's administration, the number of American troops involved in the Vietnam conflict reached a high of 543,400. But promising to end the war "with honor," President Nixon introduced a policy of "Vietnamization"—preparing the South Vietnamese to take over fighting the war. As a first step in this process, he announced the gradual withdrawal of American troops. Yet, at the same time, he escalated the war. In 1970 he ordered an invasion of neutral Cambodia, long-used by the Viet Cong as a refuge and a supply base. And in 1972 he resumed the bombing of North Vietnam.

Ending the War

In 1973 the major parties in the Vietnam War reached an agreement on a cease-fire. Under this agreement, known as the Paris Accords, the United States withdrew its remaining troops from South Vietnam. In return the North Vietnamese released American prisoners of war. But in violation of the accords, fighting continued in Vietnam. The South Vietnamese army, without American support, could not hold back the enemy advance, and in April 1975 North Vietnamese troops entered Saigon. Within hours the South Vietnamese government surrendered.

The Vietnam War caused widespread devastation. Civilian and military casualties for both North and South Vietnam numbered more than 5 million. American combat casualties stood at about

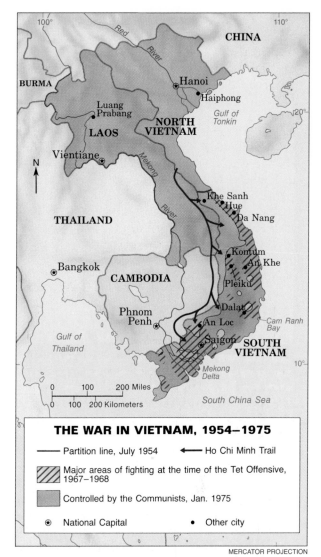

THE WAR IN VIETNAM, 1954–1975

——— Partition line, July 1954   ◄——— Ho Chi Minh Trail

▨ Major areas of fighting at the time of the Tet Offensive, 1967–1968

▦ Controlled by the Communists, Jan. 1975

⊛ National Capital   • Other city

MERCATOR PROJECTION

Learning from Maps *The Tet Offensive reached into the heart of South Vietnam. How did President Nixon combat North Vietnam's continued psychological victories?*

58,000 killed and approximately 300,000 wounded. The neighboring countries of Laos and Cambodia did not escape the death and destruction either. Long-standing rivalries among these two countries and Vietnam complicated efforts to recover and rebuild after the war.

A Reunited Vietnam

After the war North Vietnamese officials immediately began to administer all of South Vietnam.

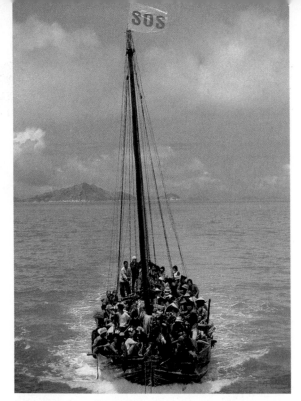

Learning from Pictures *These South Vietnamese boat people are being towed from the South China Sea, where they fled after the unification of Vietnam.*

food shortages. By and large, however, most people left because they did not want to live under a Communist government.

Usually these refugees had to pay bribes to government officials just to leave Vietnam. Then they faced a dangerous sea voyage to Malaysia, Thailand, or some other Southeast Asian country. Many of these "boat people," as the refugees became known, died at sea. Those who survived spent long months in crowded camps waiting to obtain permission to settle permanently in another country. Over the years the United States accepted more than 700,000 of these boat people as immigrants.

Cambodia

Cambodia, which had gained independence from France in 1953, attempted to remain neutral in the Vietnam War. The country's leader, Prince Norodom Sihanouk (SEE • hah • nook), found neutrality a difficult path to follow, however. North Vietnamese and Viet Cong troops frequently fled into Cambodia to escape capture, and their chief supply route—the Ho Chi Minh Trail—ran through the eastern part of the country.

In 1970 Lon Nol, a pro-American army general, overthrew Sihanouk in a military coup. Lon Nol promised to take a firmer stand against the Vietnamese Communists who used Cambodia as a refuge.

The Khmer Rouge. While in hiding in Cambodia, the Vietnamese Communists had helped to arm and train a group of Cambodian insurgents called the *Khmer Rouge*. With this assistance, the Khmer Rouge rapidly grew in strength. Sihanouk, who had gone into exile in China, voiced his support for them. In 1975, just a few days before Saigon fell, the Khmer Rouge seized the Cambodian capital, Phnom Penh. They then established a new Communist regime under the leadership of Pol Pot.

This new government evacuated all of Cambodia's cities, sending most residents into the countryside to create new agricultural villages. Lacking tools and farming experience, and without food to tide them over until their first harvest, many of these city people died of starvation. The Khmer Rouge also undertook a program to systematically eliminate almost all Cambodia's government officials, army officers, doctors, lawyers, teachers, and

Then, in July 1976 the two Vietnams united as one country—the Socialist Republic of Vietnam—with Hanoi, in the north, as the capital. The former southern capital, Saigon, was renamed Ho Chi Minh City.

Even before unification the North Vietnamese had begun to reform the south along northern lines. Economically, this reform involved replacing the South Vietnamese currency with a new national currency, rationing certain consumer goods, and imposing controls on private enterprise. Socially, major educational reforms took place. All schools in the south closed while textbooks underwent revisions and teachers received training in Communist ideology from North Vietnamese advisers. Other changes limited university education to the children of workers and peasant farmers. All students had to spend part of every school year working on farms or in factories.

After the fall of Saigon, more than 6 million South Vietnamese fled their country and became refugees. Some fled because they had worked in the South Vietnamese government or served in the army, and they feared they would be punished by the North Vietnamese. Others left because of the

● READ
WRITE
INTERPRET
CONNECT
THINK

BUILDING HISTORY STUDY SKILLS

Reading About History: Identifying Fallacies in Reasoning

In order to prove a point, an author uses logic, or reasoning. Logic is the process of reaching a conclusion based on the available evidence. We have learned how to identify an author's thesis and evaluate the evidence. One way of determining the strength of an argument is to identify fallacies in the reasoning. A fallacy is an error in the logic. One category of fallacies involves cause and effect. The author has committed a fallacy in reasoning if the conclusion focuses on only one cause or mistakes coincidence for a cause.

Events in history usually have many causes. Thus a conclusion that an event has only one cause oversimplifies history. For example, the statement, "Poverty caused the French Revolution," would be a fallacy in reasoning because it ignores the many other causes.

Another example of a fallacy in reasoning would be the substitution of coincidence as a cause. For example, a Republican president negotiated an end to both the Korean War and the Vietnam War. It is a coincidence and not a cause-and-effect relationship that Republican presidents negotiate successful peace treaties. Some connection must be proven for it to be a cause rather than a coincidence.

How to Identify Fallacies in Reasoning

To identify a fallacy in reasoning, follow these steps.

1. Identify the author's conclusion.
2. Explain the author's reasoning in supporting the conclusion.
3. Identify whether cause-and-effect is involved in the reasoning.
4. Evaluate the use of cause-and-effect. Is only one cause being identified? Is the one cause being used as the sole cause or as the main cause? Is a connection between the cause and the effect being proven?

Developing the Skill

Read the following description of the domino theory in Southeast Asia. Are there any fallacies in the reasoning?

❝ You have a row of dominoes set up, you knock over the first one, and what will happen to the last one is that it will go over very quickly. So you have a beginning of a disintegration that would have the most profound influences. . . . If Indochina fell to Communism the Malay Peninsula 'would be scarcely defensible.' ❞

The main point or conclusion of the domino theory is that if one country falls to the Communists in Southeast Asia, the others will easily fall under their control. It will be an escalating effect because of the country's weaknesses and the Communist buildup of power. The domino theory involves fallacies in reasoning, however. It attributes the ultimate cause of Communist success to only one factor—its success in a neighboring country. It ignores other factors that contribute to the spread of communism. Some of these factors include the economic weaknesses of the country, the political stability, and the extent of nationalism.

Practicing the skill. Reread the steps to identify fallacies in reasoning. Then state how the case of Thailand has provided further evidence that the domino theory involved fallacies in reasoning.

To apply this skill, see Applying History Study Skills on page 805.

United States soldiers in Vietnam

intellectuals. More than 2 million people met their deaths by execution or starvation in the first three years of Pol Pot's regime. Thousands more fled to makeshift refugee camps in the neighboring country of Thailand.

The Vietnamese invasion. Border disputes and centuries-old rivalries soon brought the Khmer Rouge into conflict with their Vietnamese neighbors. To settle certain territorial questions once and for all, the Vietnamese invaded Cambodia (Kampuchea) in 1978. As the Vietnamese advanced toward Phnom Penh, the Chinese threw their support to the Khmer Rouge. Even so, by early 1979 the Vietnamese had overthrown Pol Pot and had established a pro-Vietnamese government in Phnom Penh.

In the late 1980s, under pressure from the UN, Vietnam withdrew its troops from Cambodia, and China halted military aid to the Khmer Rouge. The UN sponsored talks on the future of Cambodia to which all affected parties—the Vietnamese-sponsored government, the Khmer Rouge, and Sihanouk and his followers—were invited.

Laos

Like Cambodia, Laos gained independence from France in 1954. Almost immediately, civil war broke out among the country's political factions. This turmoil continued for the next 20 years.

In the meantime, Laos, although neutral, became increasingly involved in the Vietnam War. The Ho Chi Minh Trail, the Viet Cong's major supply route, wound through the mountain valleys of eastern Laos into Cambodia and South Vietnam. To break this supply line, the United States began bombing the Laotian countryside, causing heavy damage and many civilian casualties.

By 1975 the internal strife in Laos had ended. The Communist faction, the *Pathet Lao,* had set up a Communist regime—the Lao People's Democratic Republic. This new government followed a non-aligned course in the complicated politics of Asia. It accepted aid from both China and the Soviet Union. In addition, it avoided taking sides in the dispute between Vietnam and Cambodia.

Ultimately, however, a nonaligned course proved impossible. Laos had to call on the Vietnamese for help in controlling anti-Communist forces in its northern provinces. In return it allowed Vietnam to station 30,000 troops on Laotian soil.

In fact, Vietnam used Laos as the staging area for its invasion of Cambodia. Because of such incidents, relations between Laos and its neighbors continued to be tense throughout the 1980s.

Thailand

Thailand, formerly called Siam, had never been a European colony. During World War II, however, Japan occupied the country. Under Japanese pressure Thailand joined the Axis and declared war on Great Britain and the United States. Later it renounced this alliance and became the first Axis partner admitted to the United Nations.

In the late 1950s, the Thai army took control of the government, establishing a military dictatorship. Strongly pro-Western, this government received military and economic aid from the United States. During the Vietnam War, this close relationship continued. The United States used bases in Thailand as a staging area for bombing raids on North Vietnam, Laos, and Cambodia. In addition, Thai troops fought beside American and South Vietnamese soldiers in Cambodia. When American troops withdrew from Vietnam, many of them were reassigned to bases in Thailand.

Communist victories in Vietnam, Laos, and Cambodia during the mid-1970s forced Thailand to reconsider its relationship with the United States. The Thai government persuaded the Americans to close their military bases in Thailand. It then established diplomatic relationships with China and sought accommodation with the Soviet Union and Vietnam.

SECTION 5 REVIEW

1. **Define** domino theory
2. **Identify** Viet Minh, Ho Chi Minh, Ngo Dinh Diem, Viet Cong, Tet Offensive, Vietnamization, Paris Accords, boat people, Norodom Sihanouk, Lon Nol, Khmer Rouge
3. **Locate** Hanoi, Haiphong, Dien Bien Phu, 17th parallel, Saigon, Ho Chi Minh Trail, Phnom Penh
4. **Analyzing Ideas** Why were the provisions of the Geneva Accords a victory for the Viet Minh?
5. **Classifying Ideas** What changes took place in Vietnam after the war?
6. **Interpreting Ideas** What impact did the Pol Pot regime have on Cambodia (Kampuchea)?
7. **Determining Cause and Effect** How did the Vietnamese invasion of Cambodia affect Thailand's diplomatic relations?

6 Asian Nations Sought Security and Economic Growth

Asia is a region of great diversity containing many nations that differ significantly from one another. However, a closer look at these nations reveals a number of experiences they all have shared.

Political Development

Most of the countries of Asia at one time had been colonies. After independence, most new Asian nations set up representative governments and attempted to build democratic societies. With the passage of time, however, democracy faded in most of Asia. Violent revolutions established Communist governments in China, Vietnam, Cambodia, and Laos. Elsewhere—in the Philippines, Indonesia, and Burma, for example—civil rights came under attack, and authoritarian rule emerged.

By and large, three factors gave rise to this trend toward authoritarianism in Asia. The first factor involved the ethnic and cultural diversity within Asian nations. In India, Malaysia, and the Philippines, for example, age-old antagonisms existed among groups with different heritages or religions. From time to time, these antagonisms erupted into violence. In such cases, government leaders often relied on their military and police forces to maintain domestic peace. To make their work easier, these forces frequently argued for the imposition of strict controls on civil rights. Occasionally, the military forces themselves took over the government when civilian leaders seemed reluctant to impose such controls.

The second factor that helped the development of authoritarianism involved fears about national security. For example, because of the Communist movements on the Indochina Peninsula, leaders in the Philippines, Indonesia, and Thailand feared the spread of revolutionary ideas to their own countries. As a result, these leaders cracked down on leftist groups and granted sweeping powers to the military whenever the slightest signs of Communist influence arose. Similarly, Communist countries feared the anti-Communist policies of the free world. They also feared each other's intentions. For these Communist countries too, fear led to a desire for strong central government and a lack of tolerance for debate and dissent.

The third factor concerned the desire for economic growth. Many Asian leaders perceived

Learning from Pictures
Newly elected Philippine President Corazon Aquino salutes the country's military after a successful revolt against the dictator Ferdinand Marcos.

democratic government as wasteful and inefficient and a hindrance to the speedy development of industrialization policies and programs. Therefore, the desire of these leaders for rapid economic growth contributed to the emergence of authoritarian regimes. To understand this development, it is necessary to examine the issue of economic growth in Asia.

Economic Development

In the late 1980s, roughly 3 billion people, more than half of the total population of the world, lived in Asia. A significant number of Asia's people lived in poverty and suffered its consequences—malnutrition, illiteracy, and sharply reduced life expectancy.

Attempts at economic development. To help create more prosperous and stable societies, in the 1950s most Asian governments began to foster economic development. The approaches of these governments varied. Some used capitalist means, encouraging private enterprise. Others followed socialist principles, with the central government taking control of the economy. Still others pursued a middle course, combining government planning with private enterprise. Whatever the approach, most governments experienced the same result. With a few exceptions, economic development proceeded slowly, if at all.

By and large, most Asian countries experienced slow economic growth because they had little wealth in the first place. Industrialization required huge investments of money in machinery, factories, and distribution networks. Also, the later a country began the process of industrialization, the greater the investment needed to bring that country up to the level of the more developed nations.

In order to get the investment funds they needed, Asian countries depended either on loans or on the export of agricultural goods or natural resources: cocoa, tea, spices, timber, rubber, and copper and other minerals. Throughout most of the 1950s and 1960s, however, the prices of these items in world markets remained relatively low. In addition, periodic economic recessions in the West reduced the demand for the export goods of the Asian nations.

A shortage of experienced managers and trained workers also slowed economic development in much of Asia. To combat this problem, many Asian governments reformed their educational systems and established vocational schools and industrial training programs. But time was needed for these changes to take effect.

Cooperating for development. In the 1970s Asian countries began to find ways of dealing with these and other economic problems. For example, to ensure higher and more stable prices for their exports, many countries combined to form loose economic associations. In addition, Asian countries joined with other developing nations to work for greater concessions from such international loan agencies as the World Bank and the International Monetary Fund (IMF).

Also, Asian countries followed the example of such bodies as the European Community (EC), cooperating to develop common trade and economic policies. For example, the Association of Southeast Asian Nations (ASEAN), although organized in 1967 to combat communism in the region, has concerned itself since the 1970s almost solely with economic matters. Member nations—Brunei, Indonesia, Malaysia, the Philippines, Singapore, and Thailand—have held regular meetings to discuss ways to encourage trade and to handle the problems associated with economic development. Communist nations in Asia have sought similar cooperative agreements by joining the Council for Mutual Economic Assistance, or CMEA (formerly known as COMECON).

Many Asian nations, however, have attempted to spur economic growth through greater government control. Some Asian governments have nationalized certain key industries—oil in Indonesia, for example. By such actions they hoped to ensure the reinvestment of profits in the country's development. Many governments, to prevent interruptions in production, have passed laws limiting the organization of labor unions or prohibiting strikes and other industrial actions. Such authoritarian measures, in some cases, have led to more rapid economic growth but at the expense of individual rights and freedoms.

By the end of the 1980s, economic development in Asia remained a mixed picture. Some countries, such as Japan, South Korea, Singapore, and Taiwan, all strong supporters of free enterprise, have enjoyed remarkable success. However, the economies of the majority of Asian countries are burdened by huge foreign debts. These countries have yet to make any major advances toward significant economic development.

Learning from Pictures
An example of Western cultural diffusion is this popular American food franchise found in many Japanese shopping centers. What Asian-made products have dominated world markets?

Asian Cultural Diffusion

For hundreds of years, Asia has influenced the West. The ancient religions, philosophies, and martial arts of China and Japan have long fascinated many Westerners. Exhibits of Asian porcelain, carpets, manuscripts, and other arts and crafts have frequently appeared in prominent Western art galleries. More recently Asia has strongly influenced the buying habits of Western consumers. For example, Asian-made radios, cameras, video equipment, and automobiles, by and large, have dominated world markets over the last decade.

This economic competition from Asia has both alarmed and intrigued Western business leaders. Since the late 1970s, Western economists have traveled throughout Japan trying to discover why Japanese goods compete so well in world markets. Many economists have suggested that the answer lies in the cooperative relationship between management and workers. Others have noted the availability of low-interest business-development loans that enable Japanese companies to buy the latest machinery.

Asian thought also has influenced the West, especially since the end of World War II. For example, Mahatma Gandhi's ideas on nonviolent resistance had a powerful impact on the leaders of the civil rights movement in the United States during the 1960s.

In the late 1800s, the English author Rudyard Kipling wrote, "East is East, and West is West, and never the twain shall meet." He meant that because of the great cultural differences between the two areas, their peoples could never understand one another. For a long time, Kipling's observation appeared correct. Since the early 1970s, however, a greater understanding seems to have developed. As the role played by the Pacific Rim countries—Hong Kong, Japan, South Korea, Singapore, and Taiwan—in the world economy increases, this understanding almost certainly will continue to improve.

SECTION 6 REVIEW

1. **Identify**   ASEAN, Pacific Rim countries
2. **Classifying Ideas**   List three factors that contributed to the development of authoritarian governments in Asia.
3. **Analyzing Ideas**   What problems have Asian nations faced in bringing about industrial development?
4. **Understanding Ideas**   How have some Asian nations cooperated to overcome economic problems?
5. **Summarizing Ideas**   How have Asian ideas influenced life in the West?

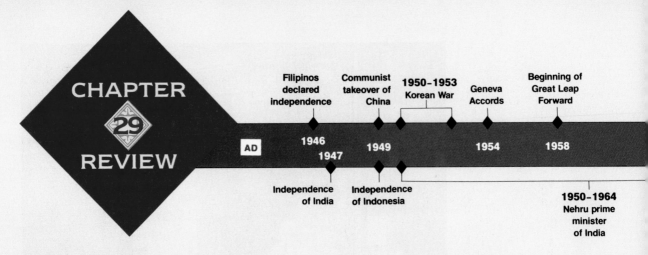

Filipinos declared independence

Communist takeover of China

1950–1953 Korean War

Geneva Accords

Beginning of Great Leap Forward

AD

1946

1947

1949

1954

1958

Independence of India

Independence of Indonesia

1950–1964 Nehru prime minister of India

Chapter Summary

The following list contains the key concepts you have learned about the nations of Asia between the end of World War II and the present.

1. The period following World War II was a time of conflict and tension for many Asian nations.
2. The victory of Mao Zedong in 1949 brought the Communist Party to power in China. The Chinese Nationalists, led by Chiang Kai-shek, fled to the island of Taiwan off the coast of China.
3. The Communists implemented several plans to modernize their vast nation, while the Nationalists on Taiwan achieved rapid industrialization.
4. Korea was divided after World War II. When Communist North Korea invaded South Korea in 1950, it was repulsed by UN forces, and an armistice was eventually signed.
5. Japan achieved extraordinary economic success in the postwar period and became the most advanced industrial nation in Asia.
6. Japanese society also changed, as women gained recognition of their rights and the family lost its dominant role in daily life.
7. India, under Nehru, adopted a mixed economy but could make few gains because of its constantly growing population.
8. Pakistan faced problems similar to those of India. In addition, Pakistan was separated into two parts. After a civil war, East Pakistan became Bangladesh.
9. In the Philippines, Indonesia, Malaysia, Singapore, and Burma, economic development was fostered by strong central governments. Despite experiencing social problems, these nations began a very gradual process of industrialization.
10. In Southeast Asia, the United States became heavily involved in fighting in Vietnam. North Vietnam conquered South Vietnam and united the nation in the mid-1970s.
11. Vietnam dominated its neighbors, Cambodia and Laos. It also had considerable influence on Thailand. All of these nations struggled with the problems caused by war.
12. The difficulties of economic development led many Asian nations to rely on strong central governments.

On the other hand, the Asian nations attempted to promote greater international cooperation.

On a separate sheet of paper, complete the following review exercises.

Reviewing Important Terms

Supply the term that correctly completes each sentence.

1. A _____ _____ is an economic system in which private companies own some industries and the government owns the rest.
2. India followed a policy of _____, refusing to ally itself with either the United States or the Soviet Union.
3. According to the _____ _____ , if South Vietnam fell to communism, other nations of Southeast Asia would follow.

Developing Critical Thinking Skills

1. **Summarizing Ideas** What political and economic changes did the Communists bring about in China after they took over the government?
2. **Interpreting Ideas** (a) How did President Truman and General MacArthur disagree over the conduct of the Korean War? (b) Why did Truman replace MacArthur as commander of the UN forces?
3. **Evaluating Ideas** (a) Explain how Japan became the third largest industrial nation in the world. (b) What problems and benefits accompanied this rapid growth? (c) Do you think the benefits outweighed the problems? Why or why not?
4. **Understanding Ideas** (a) What economic problems did India face after achieving independence? (b) How did it attempt to solve these problems?
5. **Determining Cause and Effect** (a) What were the causes of the Vietnam War? (b) How did the United States become involved?
6. **Classifying Ideas** List reasons for past hostilities between the following countries: (a) the Soviet Union and China, (b) India and Pakistan, (c) Pakistan and Bangladesh, (d) Singapore and the Federation of Malaysia.
7. **Comparing Ideas** (a) How did the Korean War differ from the Vietnam War in terms of causes and results?

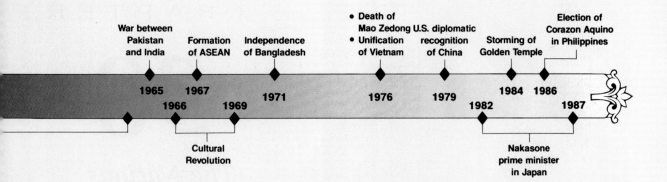

War between Pakistan and India — 1965

Formation of ASEAN — 1967

1966

Independence of Bangladesh — 1971

1969

Cultural Revolution

Death of Mao Zedong
Unification of Vietnam — 1976

U.S. diplomatic recognition of China — 1979

Storming of Golden Temple — 1984

1982

Nakasone prime minister in Japan

Election of Corazon Aquino in Philippines — 1986

1987

(b) How were the two conflicts similar? **(c)** What roles did the United States and the People's Republic of China play in each of these wars?

8. **Analyzing Primary Sources** Below is the preamble to the Indian constitution. Read this selection and answer the questions that follow.

> We, the people of India, having solemnly resolved to constitute India into a sovereign democratic republic and to secure to all its citizens: *justice*—social, economic, and political; *liberty* of thought, expression, belief, faith and worship; *equality* of status and of opportunity; and to promote . . . *fraternity* assuring the dignity of the individual and the unity of the nation . . . do hereby adopt, enact, and give to ourselves this Constitution. 〃

(a) What type of government does the constitution promise to the Indian people? **(b)** What ideals does it swear to uphold? **(c)** How do these ideals compare with those stated in the preamble to the United States Constitution?

Relating Geography to History

Turn to the map of Asia on page 776. **(a)** How many miles separate Taiwan and the People's Republic of China? **(b)** How many kilometers? **(c)** Why is Japan in a strategic location for defense of American interests in the Pacific? **(d)** Based on your knowledge of current events, what Asian nations might be most concerned with protecting their borders today? Explain.

Relating Past to Present

1. On a sheet of paper, list evidence that your community has contact with the nations of Asia. For example, observe the cars on a busy street. How many of them are Japanese? Can you buy a shirt made of Indian cotton or a book of Chinese or Japanese poetry? Based on this information, write a short essay discussing Asia's influence on the Western world.
2. Use the *Readers' Guide to Periodical Literature* to find articles on China today. Then prepare a report on how the Communists have changed traditional Chinese society, what economic problems still exist in China, and what life in China is like.

Applying History Study Skills

Before completing this activity, review Building History Study Skills on page 799.

Read the following statement and identify any fallacies in reasoning.

> Japan's economic growth since World War II took place because the United States helped rebuild the nation's wartorn factories. 〃

Investigating Further

1. **Writing a Report** Use books in your library to gather information on the Vietnam War. One source for your research might be Frances Fitzgerald's *Fire in the Lake* (Little, Brown). Use the information you have found to answer the following questions: **(a)** What were the goals of Ho Chi Minh between 1945 and 1954? **(b)** Why did the peasants support the Viet Cong? **(c)** How did American involvement end? **(d)** What was the final outcome of the war?
2. **Analyzing Literature** One way to gain insight into a culture is to read its literature. Present a short report to the class on one of the following Japanese novels: Yukio Mishima's *Sound of Waves* (Knopf) and *Spring Snow* (Knopf); Junichiro Tanizaki's *Some Prefer Nettles* (Knopf).
3. **Preparing an Oral Report** Unlike most other Asian nations, Japan, Singapore, and Taiwan experienced rapid economic growth after 1945. Using reference materials in your school or public library, gather information on the economic policies that made such development possible. Present your findings to the class in the form of a five minute oral report.
4. **Creating a Chart** Use atlases and encyclopedias in your school or public library to construct a chart comparing the major urban centers of Southeast Asia. Include information on population, places of interest, and major economic activities.

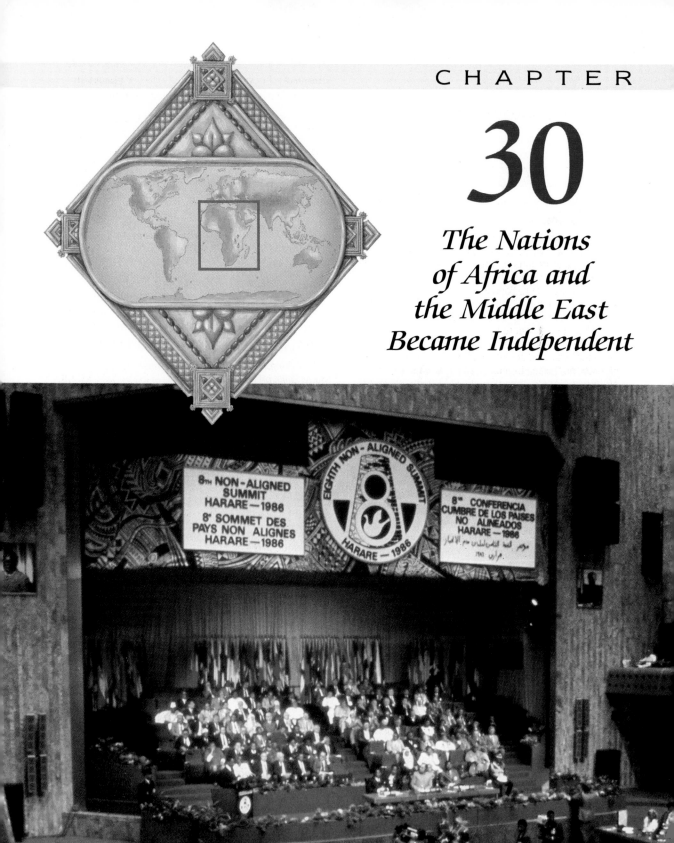

8ᵀᴴ NON - ALIGNED
SUMMIT
HARARE — 1986

8ᵉ SOMMET DES
PAYS NON ALIGNES
HARARE — 1986

EIGHTH NON - ALIGNED SUMMIT
HARARE — 1986

8ᴿᴬ CONFERENCIA
CUMBRE DE LOS PAISES
NO ALINEADOS
HARARE — 1986

Time   **1945—the present**

3.7 mil. BC   4000 BC   AD 2100

Significance

One of the most important long-term consequences of World War II was the destruction of the empires of the European nations. In the four decades after the war, more than 1.5 billion people won independence, and the number of nations in the world tripled, mainly as a result of the dissolving of the old European empires. Most of the new nations were located in Africa and the Middle East.

The newly independent nations faced many political, economic, and social problems in their first years of freedom. Politics in these nations usually revolved around one central question: Could the government win the authority it needed to rule? These nations often lacked the proper balance of industry and agriculture necessary for successful economic growth. In addition, many nations lacked an educational base as well as adequate supplies of physicians, teachers, and skilled workers. The ways in which the new nations attacked these problems are as diverse as the nations themselves.

Terms to Define

apartheid   desertification
ujamaa   kibbutz

People to Identify

Jomo Kenyatta   Haile Selassie
Nelson Mandela   Gamal Abdel Nasser
Helen Suzman   Ayatollah Khomeini

Places to Locate

Katanga   Gulf of Aqaba
Biafra   Tehran
Aswan Dam   Beirut

Questions to Guide Your Reading

1 How did African nations achieve independence after 1945?
2 What problems did African nations face after independence?
3 How did the nations of the Middle East secure their independence?
4 How did wars, oil, and revolution transform the Middle East?
5 What conflicts arose between old and new ways in the Middle East?

In 1960 Chief Obafemi Awolowo, a political leader from western Nigeria, reflected on how his newly independent homeland should view human rights.

> *I believe that every citizen, however humble and lowly his station in life, has a right to demand from his government the creation of those conditions which will enable him progressively to enjoy, according to civilized standards, the basic necessities of life as well as reasonable comfort and a measure of luxury. In other words, every citizen, regardless of his birth or religion, should be free and reasonably contented. . . .*
>
> *All men and women should be treated as equal, both as political and economic beings. For this reason all laws, measures, and programs introduced by government must be framed so as to give equal treatment and opportunity to all. . . .*

Awolowo was only one of many African and Middle Eastern leaders who worked to help the people in newly independent nations after 1945.

1 African Nations Achieved Independence After World War II

Momentous changes took place in SubSaharan Africa after World War II. In a relatively short time, from 1946 to 1980, all the African colonies except Namibia (Southwest Africa) achieved independence.

African Nationalism

Although nationalism became a popular force in the postwar world, its roots went back many years. In the British colonies of West Africa, the families of African merchants, along with chiefs from the interior, formed an elite, or select, group. These Africans engaged in trade and other business relationships with Europeans. Many received an education in Great Britain. Some worked as missionaries, spreading Christianity in Africa. Others became civil servants.

The members of this elite group became influential representatives of the African point of view. They petitioned the British government in London for constitutional reform. In addition, they started

◀ *The Non-Aligned Nations Conference in Zimbabwe*

newspapers and organized political associations in their homelands. They accepted the European point of view, however, that it would be many years before Africans were ready for independence.

These nationalists found themselves in a difficult position. As members of a privileged group, they did not feel at ease with their own people and in fact did not seek broad popular support. At the same time, because of their African heritage, they were excluded from European society. Nonetheless, the reforms for which these nationalists fought helped pave the way for nationalism in the postwar era.

A new generation of nationalists gained power after World War II. They were less patient and more determined to obtain equality in the world community. Leaders such as Kwame Nkrumah (en • KROO • mah) in the Gold Coast, Jomo Kenyatta (ken • YAH • tuh) in Kenya, and Nnamdi Azikiwe (ah • zih • KEE • wee) in Nigeria typified this new generation. Unlike earlier leaders, they appealed to the whole population and demanded immediate independence.

The March to Independence

The struggle for national independence in Africa took many forms. Some colonies followed a constitutional process, with popular elections and a peaceful transfer of power. Others, such as Angola, Mozambique, and Zimbabwe (formerly Rhodesia), suffered lengthy wars of national liberation. In each case the specific form of the independence effort depended on the particular experience of imperialism in that part of Africa. The following examples demonstrate the various roads to independence.

Ghana. The first SubSaharan colony to achieve independence was in West Africa. In 1957 the British Gold Coast colony became the independent nation of Ghana (see map, page 809). Ghana's leader, Kwame Nkrumah, chose this name to commemorate the ancient African kingdom of Ghana.

Nkrumah had been educated in the United States, where he led the African Students Association. In 1946, when he returned to the Gold Coast colony, the United Gold Coast Convention, a political party of the Westernized elite, invited him to be party secretary. From this post, Nkrumah began to build up a national following based on the slogan "Self-government now." In 1948 he started a newspaper that criticized the British administration and called for civil disobedience.

In 1949 Nkrumah started his own Convention People's Party (CPP). It became the first African political party supported by a large part of the population. The CPP's activities forced the British government to make concessions, and in 1951 it agreed to a national election in the Gold Coast colony. Nkrumah's party won a huge victory, and he formed a government with limited powers under British direction. Nkrumah continued to pressure the British for complete independence, and in 1957 it was finally granted.

Rebellion in Kenya. National parties, inspired by Nkrumah's success, began to appear in other British colonies about the same time. Often, however, they had to face problems very different from Ghana's. For example, in Kenya in East Africa (see map, page 809), white settlers held large tracts of fertile land in the central highlands. Africans were prohibited from owning land in this area. As the African population grew and land shortages became critical after World War II, the exclusion of Africans from the highlands became a source of tension. The Kikuyu (ki • KOO • yoo), Kenya's largest ethnic group, considered this area to be their ancestral homeland.

In the early 1950s, the question of landownership exploded into violence that lasted for several

Learning from Pictures Although the British jailed Jomo Kenyatta for subversive activities, he later became the first prime minister of an independent Kenya.

Learning from Maps *The nations of Africa won their independence from European rulers after 1945. What African nations were never colonies?*

years and took thousands of lives. The British finally succeeded in suppressing the terrorist movement, known as the Mau Mau, that the Kikuyu had formed. Jomo Kenyatta, a Kikuyu leader, was arrested and jailed until 1961. However, the British failed to suppress the demand for independence.

809

Kenyatta emerged as the natural leader of the Kenyan independence movement. His popular leadership helped overcome ethnic rivalries and brought about a shared sense of Kenyan nationalism. In 1963 Kenya became independent, and Kenyatta served as president from 1964 until his death in 1978.

The French Colonies

Developments in the French-controlled territories of Africa reflected a different political experience. During World War II, France's African colonies had contributed to the Free French forces led by General de Gaulle. Following the Allied victory, the French sought to improve political conditions in French Africa through a system of political federation. Africans elected representatives who sat in the French Assembly in Paris and served in the French government. Although this system provided many Africans with political experience, it fell short of real independence. And many Africans resented that their economic and political interests remained subordinate to those of France.

Political parties with broad-based popular support, similar to Nkrumah's CPP in Ghana, soon emerged in French Africa. Led by Africans educated in France such as Léopold Senghor of Senegal, Félix Houphouët-Boigny (oof • WAY-BWAH • nyee) of the Ivory Coast (Côte d'Ivoire), and Sékou Touré (too • RAY) of Guinea, these parties demanded complete independence.

In 1958 Charles de Gaulle, the French president, offered the African colonies a choice. They could remain independent within the French community, subject to French control of their foreign affairs, or they could become totally independent. Only Guinea chose complete independence.

Those nations that chose to remain within a French-style commonwealth received aid from the French government and from private investors. Guinea, on the other hand, was politically and economically isolated. Although later granted full independence, the French-speaking nations of Africa continued to coordinate their economic and foreign policies with France.

The Belgian Congo

Zaire (zah • EER), formerly the Belgian Congo, experienced one of the most difficult transitions to independence. Belgium, which opposed independence because of the colony's great wealth in timber and mineral resources, provided few opportunities for Africans to develop their skills in government.

As in the British and French colonies, a strong independence movement sprang up in the Belgian Congo after World War II. In the 1950s nationalists demanded the right to choose their own government. Finally, in 1960, when the Belgians arrested nationalist leaders and rioting broke out, Belgium gave in and allowed general elections to be held. The nationalist leader, Patrice Lumumba (luh • MUHM • buh), was elected premier of the independent Democratic Republic of the Congo. His rival, Joseph Kasavubu (kah • sah • VOO • boo), became president.

In addition to his political activities, Lumumba was a poet. In his poem "Dawn in the Heart of Africa," he expressed his hopes for independence:

> ❝The dawn is here, my brother! Dawn!
>   Look in our faces,
> A new morning breaks in our old Africa.
> Ours alone will now be the land, the water,
>   mighty rivers
> Poor Africa surrendered for a thousand years.
> The moment when you break the chains, the
>   heavy fetters,
> The evil, cruel times will go never to come
>   again.
> A free and gallant Congo will arise from
>   black soil,
> A free and gallant Congo—black blossom
>   from black seed! ❞

Although independent, the Congo still faced serious problems. In July 1960, Congolese soldiers mutinied against their Belgian officers. A period of bloodshed followed, during which many people lost their lives.

The turmoil increased and threatened Belgian interests in the mining province of Katanga (see map, page 809). To protect its interests, the Belgian government supported the secession of Katanga under a local leader, Moise Tshombe (SHOM • bay).

The Congo moved rapidly toward complete anarchy. Tshombe's forces in Katanga imprisoned Lumumba. There he was murdered following an alleged escape attempt.

In an attempt to end the bloodshed, the UN Security Council called on Belgium to withdraw its troops from Katanga. It also authorized a UN force to restore order in the Congo. This force, composed mainly of troops from other African nations, was sent into the Congo in the summer of 1960. By the beginning of 1963, Tshombe's army was defeated, and he went into exile.

When UN troops were withdrawn from the Congo in mid-1964, revolts broke out in several provinces. Kasavubu invited Tshombe to return from exile and become premier in a "government of national reconciliation." Although Tshombe accepted, instability continued to plague the young nation, and in 1965 President Kasavubu removed Tshombe from office. Kasavubu himself was then overthrown in a military coup led by Joseph Mobutu, an army general. Mobutu later took the African name Mobutu Sese Seko (SAY • say SAY • koh).

Leadership of the Congo was not clearly established for several years. In 1970 Mobutu was elected president of what became, in the following year, the Republic of Zaire. Zaire gradually began to recover from the political chaos and civil wars of the 1960s.

The Portuguese Colonies

While many African nations were winning their independence, the Portuguese government opposed

Learning from Pictures *United Nations troops arrive in the Congo in 1960. What colonial power controlled Zaire?*

independence for its colonies. In desperation, African leaders in Angola, Portuguese Guinea, and Mozambique organized "liberation armies" to fight for freedom. In a series of long, bloody wars, they gained control of much of the countryside. However, they failed to dislodge the Portuguese from the major urban centers.

This bloody stalemate continued until 1974, when the military staged a coup in Portugal and announced that Portugal would withdraw from Africa. Within months of the announcement, Portuguese Guinea, Mozambique, and Angola became independent. Only Southern Rhodesia, South Africa, and the trust territory of Namibia remained under minority rule.

Rhodesia

Developments in the British colony of Rhodesia represented an unusual example of both guerrilla warfare and constitutional change. Rhodesia had a large white population that controlled colonial politics. As in their other colonies, the British supported a policy that gradually would allow the African population to gain the right to vote and that eventually would lead to African majority rule. Within the colony, however, the white government, led by Ian Smith, refused to submit to the British policies.

In 1965 the colony declared its independence — a status that Great Britain and the rest of the world, except for South Africa, refused to recognize. Although the Smith government was isolated internationally, it still refused to meet with African leaders or initiate needed reforms. Consequently, as happened in the neighboring Portuguese colonies, a war of national liberation began. Little success was achieved in the early years of fighting. However, when Angola and Mozambique became independent in 1975, the liberation forces gained a military advantage. They now had countries friendly to their cause in southern Africa.

Under the leadership of Robert Mugabe (moo • GAH • bee) and Joshua Nkomo (en • KOH • moh), the African forces intensified their attacks and succeeded in disrupting the economy of Rhodesia. As the war became increasingly unpopular among the white population, Smith was forced to seek a solution. An arrangement was worked out with moderate African leaders to form a new government under African leadership that would continue to guarantee the privileged economic and social status of whites.

In 1978 Bishop Abel Muzorewa (moo • zuh • RAY • wah) became the new prime minister. However, his new government, which included Ian Smith, did not receive international recognition, and the guerrilla war continued. In 1979 the Muzorewa-Smith government was finally forced to accept a cease-fire and to agree to hold free elections. The elections were to be open to all parties, including the liberation leaders. According to the agreement, the British government would supervise both the cease-fire and the elections. In the elections, held in 1979, Robert Mugabe, considered the most radical of the candidates, won an absolute majority.

In April 1980 Rhodesia became the new nation of Zimbabwe. After years of civil war, Zimbabwe's needs were clear and the government turned its energies to economic recovery. The advance of independence had now reached the borders of the nation of South Africa.

South Africa

South Africa's experience differed from that of any other African nation. It gained independence from Great Britain in 1910 as a white-ruled nation with dominion status. Although linked to Great Britain in foreign affairs, the dominion ruled itself internally as it saw fit. Relying on its resources of gold, diamonds, and cheap labor, South Africa experienced an industrial revolution in the early 1900s. Although industrialization was based on their labor, blacks, who vastly outnumbered whites, were excluded almost totally from the benefits of South Africa's economic success.

Apartheid. Before World War II, English-speaking whites had dominated the government. By custom, non-whites were kept out of better jobs and were segregated socially. In 1948 the Afrikaans-speaking whites, descendants of the original Dutch settlers, came to power in South Africa and passed a series of laws designed to ensure that these customs would not change. This policy, based on the principle of racial separation, became known as **apartheid** (uh • PART • hyt), the Afrikaans word for apartness.

South Africa also extended apartheid to Namibia (Southwest Africa), which it had acquired as a mandate from the League of Nations after World War I. Although the United Nations voted in 1966

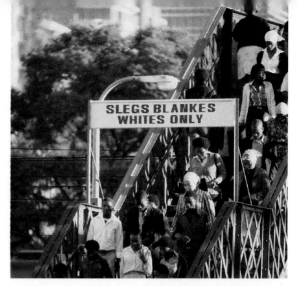

Learning from Pictures *Although the South African government has integrated some facilities, opposition by white extremist political groups has created increasing tensions within the government.*

to end South Africa's control of Namibia, South Africa ignored the ruling. South Africa's harsh policies led to an increasingly militant nationalist movement in Namibia. Finally, in 1990, South Africa granted Namibia its independence.

Within its own territory, South Africa formed separate "tribal states," known as "homelands" or "Bantustans," for Africans. These homelands had no economic resources of their own and were completely dependent on the South African government.

Protests against apartheid. Blacks have protested apartheid since the South African government first adopted the racial policy. One vocal organization is the African National Congress (ANC), which the government banned in 1960. Despite the ban, the ANC has continued to operate from bases in neighboring countries. Although Nelson Mandela, the ANC's leader, was sentenced to life in prison in 1962, other ANC members—particularly Mandela's wife Winnie—have continued to fight apartheid. In addition, black leaders such as Desmond Tutu and Zulu Chief Gatsha Buthelezi (boo • tuh • LAY • zee), as well as an increasing number of white South Africans including Helen Suzman, a member of Parliament, have opposed the government.

In 1976 the South African police brutally crushed a peaceful demonstration by black schoolchildren at Soweto, a black township near Johannesburg. After the Soweto incident, which triggered massive uprisings around the country, many people in South Africa were no longer willing to wait peacefully for change. Thousands of South Africans have since died during the civil unrest.

Faced with growing protests, the South African government relaxed some regulations of apartheid. The government, for example, allowed black unions and interracial marriages. And in 1984 a new constitution went into effect, granting coloreds (people of mixed race) and Asians the right to be represented in the previously all-white Parliament. Blacks, however, were still denied any political participation, and civil strife continued.

In July 1985 the South African government under President P. W. Botha (BOH • tah), faced with the prospect of urban guerrilla warfare, substantially increased its own military and police powers by declaring a state of emergency. As a result the police arrested black union leaders and black nationalists.

In response, many Western nations condemned apartheid and urged Western firms to withdraw investment funds from South Africa. As international pressures increased, the South African government relaxed a few more of apartheid's strict regulations. Then with the election of F. W. de Klerk as state president in September 1989, the pace of change quickened. De Klerk lifted a 30-year ban on antiapartheid rallies and legalized the African National Congress. He also released Nelson Mandela in February 1990 and agreed to meet with him to discuss further reforms. Although de Klerk's actions did not immediately end international economic sanctions, world leaders applauded de Klerk and urged the South Africans to pass further reforms.

SECTION 1 REVIEW

1. **Define** apartheid
2. **Identify** Jomo Kenyatta, CPP, Mau Mau, Sékou Touré, Joseph Kasavubu, Robert Mugabe, Bantustans, Nelson Mandela, Helen Suzman
3. **Locate** Zimbabwe, Ghana, Kenya, Zaire, Katanga, South Africa
4. **Interpreting Ideas** How did France deal with its African colonies that wished to be independent?
5. **Summarizing Ideas** What problems did the Belgian Congo experience after achieving independence?
6. **Analyzing Ideas** Why was independence so difficult to achieve in Rhodesia?
7. **Determining Cause and Effect** How has apartheid deprived black South Africans of basic human rights?

2 The New African Nations Faced Various Problems

Having achieved independence, the new nations of Africa still faced many serious problems. Each new nation had to create a sense of national unity among people often divided by differences of language and culture. Many of them had to overcome economic underdevelopment. Finally, a sense of pride in Africa's history and its cultural achievements had to be restored.

National Unity

The most pressing need for each of the new African nations involved developing a sense of national identity among its citizens. This proved to be a difficult task because the boundaries of the new nations were often artificial, drawn by the imperialist powers in the 1800s for their own convenience. In some cases, people of similar racial or cultural backgrounds were separated, while people of different heritages were grouped together.

In addition, colonial administrations had encouraged regional and ethnic differences. In this way they had hoped to discourage the development of national political parties. These ethnic rivalries continued after independence and on occasion led to civil war, as happened in Nigeria.

Nigeria's Civil War

The former British colony of Nigeria gained independence in 1960. The new constitution created a federation of four regions, each of which retained a large degree of local independence. Strong ethnic and regional differences existed in Nigeria, and the government hoped that this loose plan would prevent warfare among the various tribes. The plan, however, did not work.

In 1966 the military took over the government, but it could not overcome the tensions created by ethnic and regional distrust. In 1967 the Eastern Region, home of the Ibo-speaking people, seceded from the federation and declared itself the independent Republic of Biafra.

Nigeria plunged into civil war. Throughout the fighting, Nigerian officials maintained that the war with Biafra was a purely domestic problem. They regarded any aid to the Biafrans as interference in Nigeria's internal affairs. For this reason most African nations refused to recognize Biafra. After 4 years of war and the deaths of about 2 million Biafrans from starvation and disease, Biafra surrendered.

Gradually the Nigerian government restored stability at home and regained a position of leadership in Africa. Nigeria became a respected voice for African interests in the United Nations. Ethnicity and regionalism, however, continued to be sensitive issues in Nigeria.

A democratically elected civilian government returned to Nigeria in 1970. At the same time, the country's oil wealth provided Nigerians with the opportunity to escape the poverty that threatened most other African nations. It also appeared that Nigeria might be the first African nation other than South Africa to achieve a high degree of industrialization.

In the 1980s, however, a drop in the international demand for oil caused Nigeria's oil revenues to fall, and Nigeria's economy suddenly faltered. In late 1983 military officers overthrew the civilian government and boldly introduced new economic measures. As of the late 1980s, however, the Nigerian economy had not recovered, and Nigeria had to borrow from other countries.

Angola and the Horn of Africa

Superpower rivalry complicated the efforts of new African nations to achieve national unity. The problems of the new nations, which included the need for financial and technical assistance, created opportunities for the United States and the Soviet Union to establish their influence in Africa.

When civil war broke out in Angola after independence in 1975, the United States and the Soviet Union rushed arms and support to the rival factions. A Marxist faction aided by Soviet and Cuban troops finally came to power. Cuban troops remained in Angola to ensure the continuation of the regime. Even though the Angolan government continued to rely on Cuban troops in the mid-1980s, it actively sought Western investment in the country.

Soviet-American rivalries were even more complex in the Horn of Africa, a strategic area that includes Ethiopia and Somalia (see map, page 809). The Horn overlooks the Red Sea as well as the Indian Ocean sea lanes to the oil-rich Persian

Gulf. It is also an area of relative instability, characterized by frequent border disputes and local independence movements.

When the Ethiopian emperor, Haile Selassie, was overthrown in 1974, a socialist regime came to power. To support the socialist governments in Ethiopia and in nearby Somalia, the Soviet Union provided military aid and advisers. Cuban and East German troops were stationed in Ethiopia. In exchange, Somalia and Ethiopia granted the Soviets rights to local air and naval bases.

Although the Soviet Union gained a temporary advantage, it had provided arms to two traditionally hostile neighbors. When Somalia invaded Ethiopia in 1977, the Soviets supported Ethiopia. Somalia then expelled all Soviet diplomats and advisers and granted rights to a navy base to the United States in exchange for military assistance. This topsy-turvy situation demonstrated that African nations often preferred practical assistance to ideological commitments. This was even more true by the 1980s, when a devastating famine threatened millions of Africans with starvation.

Economic Difficulties

In addition to political challenges, the new African nations faced economic uncertainty. As colonies, they had been part of the economic system of imperialism. In most cases, upon receiving their independence, the new nations lacked the balance between agriculture and industry required for economic growth. Many of them depended on a single crop or mineral resource for most of their income. These products, such as cocoa in Ghana, copper in Zambia and Zaire, or cotton in the Sudan, were subject to large price swings in world markets.

Overcoming dependence on a single resource continued to be one of the greatest challenges facing the nations of Africa in the 1980s. Nations with few resources were unable to escape the cycle of poverty. Zaire, for example, borrowed heavily from international banks to finance its economic expansion. It became the largest debtor nation in SubSaharan Africa.

Tanzania tried a different approach, based on a traditional African social system. It organized local, cooperative villages, known as **ujamaa** (family), to increase productivity and improve standards of living. Unfortunately, most of these villages failed, and economic conditions worsened.

Learning from Pictures *This copper mine is in Lubumbashi, Zaire. Zaire ranks as one of the top producers and exporters of copper and copper products.*

Tanzania was a vivid reminder of the economic problems that African nations still had to overcome.

Among these problems was a constant threat of famine. As the population of Africa continued to expand, many farmers overused the land. To grow more food, farmers planted crops in dry areas or on hills, where fierce winds often stripped away the topsoil. In addition, people in many parts of Africa cut down trees for firewood. As a result of these practices, **desertification,** or the spread of the desert, became common. From 1984 to 1989, for example, the Sahara took over an estimated 250,000 square miles (647,500 square kilometers) of the Sahel, the semiarid plain that stretches across the southern Sahara.

Desertification has created untold miseries for the people of Africa. Only international aid in the form of food supplies has helped people survive widespread famines.

Revival of African Culture

Despite the economic and political disappointments that followed independence, the people of Africa made great strides in one very important area. They experienced a rebirth of cultural self-confidence.

During the colonial era, many Africans lost faith in their own culture as they adopted European attitudes toward Africa. African art and music were considered primitive and crude. Magnificent constructions like Great Zimbabwe, which you read about in Chapter 13, or exquisite artifacts like the bronze masks of Benin, were wrongly attributed to foreign influences. They were thought to be works of ancient Greeks or other people who had been shipwrecked on Africa's shores and had wandered into the interior. The literature of Africa—a treasury of oral traditions including myths, proverbs, and folk tales—was largely unknown to Europeans. Seeing the attitudes of Europeans, most Africans themselves turned away from their history and their cultural heritage.

Not all Africans, however, followed the European example. In East Africa, Swahili poetry and tales continued to be studied as they had been for hundreds of years. The traditions of Swahili were kept alive in the Islamic mosque schools of coastal towns. The written records of this Bantu language go back to the 1600s. The language itself has continued to evolve. James Mbotela's novel, *Uhuru wa Watumwa* (*Freedom for the Slaves*) (1934), helped give Swahili the modern form from which it continued to grow. Many plays and novels have been written in Swahili, the national language of Tanzania and Kenya.

In West Africa, a new literary tradition developed, using the colonial languages of English and French. Many African authors, especially those from French-speaking areas, first achieved international recognition through works of protest against colonial oppression. In a very intense and personal style, the poems of Léopold Senghor, who later became president of independent Senegal, described the hardships of colonialism. Senghor's works, and the novels of Camara Laye of Cameroon, proudly pointed to the deep, spiritual traditions of Africa and its sense of social community.

In 1986 the Nigerian playwright and poet Wole Soyinka won the Nobel Prize in Literature, becoming the the first African to win the coveted award. Soyinka accepted the award saying: "I don't for a minute consider that the prize is just for me. It's for what I represent. I'm a part of the whole literary tradition of Africa."

These African writers created a new artistic tradition. The result was a remarkable and varied

815

Learning from Pictures *Miriam Makeba, a South African singer and composer, sings at a concert dedicated to Nelson Mandela. Her music reaches out to people's sense of human dignity.*

artistic outpouring. Similar achievements were made in reawakening an interest in African music. In addition, a film industry was begun.

In South Africa, themes protesting racial oppression continued to be important. *The Rhythm of Violence*, a play by Lewis Nkosi, and *Down Second Avenue*, an autobiographical novel by Ezekiel Mphalele, were major cultural contributions. They revealed very vividly the difficulty and bitterness of life in South Africa for the black majority.

The creativity of Africa's contemporary literature, music, and films was also seen in sculpture. At workshops in Nigeria, Zimbabwe, and elsewhere, African artists employed age-old techniques to give shape to wood and copper. Others were more clearly influenced by Western art. Throughout Africa, this willingness to mix African and outside influences gave an unusual vitality to the arts. More and more Westerners began to appreciate the achievements of African art. At the same time, Africans themselves found a new pride in their ancient heritage and in Africa's unique contribution to world culture.

3 The Nations of the Middle East Won Their Independence

The Middle East, as it is often defined today, contains the nations of Iran, Israel, Turkey, and the entire Arabic-speaking world. From 1945 to 1962, the nations of the Middle East made great advances in securing independence. Many gained their independence from Western imperial rule. Others, such as Egypt and Iran, were officially independent but were dominated by outsiders. They, too, achieved greater freedom from foreign influence during this period and sought to increase their power within the Middle East.

Iran

At the end of World War II, Great Britain and the Soviet Union still occupied Iran. Although technically a sovereign ruler, the young Shah Muhammad Reza Pahlavi held no power. Iranian leaders wanted to free their country from both Soviet and British influence. With United States support, Iran halted Soviet attempts to gain greater control over the country.

In the early 1950s, Iran acted to reduce British influence. The popular Iranian prime minister, Muhammad Mussadegh (MOO • sah • daig), nationalized the British-owned Anglo-Iranian Oil Company in 1951. Mussadegh also led a nationalist struggle against Iranian conservatives who supported the shah and the monarchy.

816

The struggle within Iran between Mussadegh and the shah reached a showdown in 1953. For a brief time, the shah had to flee Iran. He returned in triumph after the military, supported by the United States, overthrew Mussadegh.

Thereafter, the shah worked to establish his power and to impose rapid modernization upon his country. He relied on close ties with the United States and on his army. By the early 1960s, the shah appeared to be firmly in control.

Turkey

After World War II, Turkey faced Soviet pressure and turned to the West for support. After 1947 Turkey increasingly relied on military and economic aid from the United States, and in 1952 Turkey became a full member of NATO.

At the same time, Turkey moved toward democratic rule. In late 1945 the successor to Kemal Atatürk announced the end of one-party government. The more authoritarian aspects of Atatürk's government were abolished. Free elections were held in May 1950, and the opposition party under Prime Minister Adnan Menderes came to power.

In the late 1950s, the Menderes government lost popularity and began to impose restrictions on its opposition. The Turkish army intervened in 1960, fearing Menderes would eventually destroy some of the reforms Atatürk had instituted. Menderes and many others were arrested, and the former prime minister was later executed. Although the army restored civilian government, the precedent of military intervention in Turkish politics had been established.

Egypt

After 1945 Egyptians were concerned with two foreign issues, both involving Great Britain. The Egyptians wanted to remove the British military base at Suez; they also wanted to eliminate British control over Sudan and to unite that country with Egypt.

The Egyptian ruler, King Farouk, had lost favor with ordinary Egyptians, most of whom lived in extreme poverty and resented the king's extravagance. In addition, Egyptians wanted to speed economic reforms. Egypt was therefore ripe for revolution, and in July 1952, a group of young military officers overthrew the government of King Farouk.

Learning from Pictures *Aswan, Egypt, is one of the most important commercial, mining, and resort cities in the Nile Valley.*

After a power struggle, Gamal Abdel Nasser emerged as Egypt's new leader. From 1954 until his death in 1970, Nasser enjoyed almost complete control in Egypt. He was careful, however, to observe the formalities of democratic rule.

Nasser and his fellow officers represented Egyptians of modest means in revolt against corrupt rulers. The former ruling class had been allied, both commercially and politically, with Great Britain and the West. Thus Nasser's revolution also was characterized as a revolt against the West.

The Nasser government emphasized land reform, industrialization, greater government control over the economy, and the expansion of education. By 1954 Great Britain had agreed to evacuate the Suez base and to allow free elections in Sudan. Sudan, however, chose independence rather than union with Egypt.

Nasser still feared Western influence in the Middle East. He launched Egypt on an assertive foreign policy aimed at dominating the Arabic-speaking world.

Israel and the Arabs

After the Holocaust, which you read about in Chapter 27, the Zionists became more determined to have Palestine as a Jewish homeland. Palestinian Arabs continued to resist what they saw as an

817

invasion of their homeland. Neighboring Arabs supported the Palestinians.

Great Britain, which held the mandate for Palestine, was never able to obtain an agreement between Zionists and Palestinians. After World War II, Great Britain referred the problem to the UN. In November 1947 the UN voted to partition Palestine into separate Jewish and Arab states with Jerusalem as an international city. When the last British troops left Palestine in May 1948, Zionist leaders proclaimed the Republic of Israel. Chaim Weizmann became its first president and David Ben-Gurion its first prime minister.

The establishment of a Jewish nation infuriated the Palestinian Arabs. As soon as British troops withdrew from the area, armies from neighboring Arab countries moved against Israel.

Although outnumbered by the Arabs, the determined Israelis triumphed. When the war ended in early 1949, Israel had won more territory than it had been allotted in the UN partition plan. The Arab nations accepted a cease-fire, but UN-sponsored efforts to negotiate permanent peace failed. Moreover, some 750,000 Palestinians had been uprooted by the conflict and were living as refugees in neighboring Arab lands. Attempts to work out either the return or resettlement of these Palestinian refugees also failed.

Learning from Pictures Golda Meir was a Jewish immigrant who came to the United States from Russia. After working for Israeli independence, she moved to the Jewish state, where she later became prime minister.

From 1949 to 1952, Israel absorbed nearly 600,000 immigrants, almost doubling the Jewish population of the new country. Impressive social and economic programs were also developed. Collective farms (the best-known form of which is called the **kibbutz**) proved successful in turning former desert areas into productive land.

Among the Arab nations, only one emerged from the 1948 war with territorial gains. What remained of the proposed Palestinian state was absorbed into Trans-Jordan in 1949. (Trans-Jordan then changed its name to Jordan.) Other Arabs, including many Palestinians, bitterly opposed this action.

Algeria

Most nations of the Middle East had gained independence through limited violence. In Algeria, however, independence came only after a long war.

Algeria was not just a colony but had been legally absorbed into France. In addition, Algeria contained about 1 million French citizens, many from families that had lived in Algeria for several generations. Some families had been there since France had taken over the country in 1830.

There were also French settlers in the neighboring countries of Morocco and Tunisia, although not as many as in Algeria. Moreover, these countries were only French protectorates, not parts of France. France finally gave in to persistent Moroccan and Tunisian nationalist movements and granted independence to both countries in 1956.

In Algeria, however, the French wanted to keep control. An Algerian group called the National Liberation Front (FLN, the initials for its name in French) launched a guerrilla war in 1954. France kept sending in more troops, but the determined FLN could not be crushed. Although bottled up by the strong French army, the FLN won increasing support from all classes of Algerians.

In 1958, as you have read, General de Gaulle became head of the French government. The French in Algeria thought he would push the war there to a successful finish for France. They were disappointed. Slowly, de Gaulle prepared the French to accept Algerian independence.

Talks between the French and the Algerians began in 1961, but the negotiations were long and difficult. Finally, the two sides reached a settlement, and Algeria became independent in July 1962.

The Middle East in World Politics

Soon after the end of World War II, Soviet pressures on Iran, Greece, and Turkey provoked an American-led Western response. American resistance to Soviet efforts in the Middle East, formalized in the Truman Doctrine (see Chapter 28), proved successful in the late 1940s and early 1950s. In general, the West wanted to maintain a strong presence in the Middle East through economic agreements and military bases.

The Soviet Union challenged Western influence in the area by entering into an arms deal with Egypt in 1955. Nasser willingly accepted Soviet arms because he feared continued Western domination more than the possibility of Soviet control. He also had ambitions for Egypt to play a larger role in the Middle East.

The United States and its allies responded to the Soviet-Egyptian arms deal by offering to help finance a major development project—a dam at Aswan on the Nile River. The dam would irrigate new lands for agricultural expansion and also would produce hydroelectric power. It was hoped this would keep Egypt from slipping further into the sphere of Soviet influence. When Nasser later displeased the West, the Aswan Dam offer was abruptly withdrawn. Nasser retaliated by nationalizing the Suez Canal in July 1956.

The Suez Crisis

The nationalization of the Suez Canal posed many problems, including a threat to Europe's oil supply. The industrialized nations of the West depended heavily on oil shipped through the canal from oil fields in the Middle East. In addition, as more Soviet arms poured into Egypt, the West feared increased Soviet influence in the Middle East.

The Egyptian actions especially alarmed Israel. Relations between Israel and the neighboring Arab nations, especially Egypt, had been most unfriendly. Egypt had refused to allow Israeli ships or ships of other countries with cargoes bound for Israel to pass through the Suez Canal.

Egypt's seizure of the canal in 1956 brought tensions to a head. Israel, in a lightning invasion, seized the Gaza Strip—an Egyptian-administered coastal district adjoining Israel's southern border. The Israelis then defeated the Egyptians in the Sinai Peninsula and advanced toward the canal.

Great Britain and France, in a secret agreement with Israel, sent an ultimatum to Egypt. The ultimatum demanded a cease-fire and insisted on temporary British-French occupation of the canal. When Egypt refused, Great Britain and France seized the Mediterranean end of the canal, driving back the Egyptian army. Both sides sank ships in the canal to block it.

The matter was brought before the United Nations. The General Assembly demanded a cease-fire and withdrawal of the invading forces. It also authorized UN forces to patrol the cease-fire line. Great Britain and France, facing pressure from hostile world opinion, withdrew their troops. The Israelis tried to gain Egypt's agreement to their use of the canal, but failed. Then they too withdrew.

In the short war over the Suez Canal, Israel had crippled Nasser's growing military power. Arab fear and distrust of Israel intensified, and a negotiated Arab-Israeli peace became even more remote.

Aftermath of the Suez Crisis

The years 1956 to 1958 brought Soviet influence in the Middle East and Egypt's influence among the Arab nations to a peak. American efforts to rally Middle Eastern nations against further Soviet moves in the Middle East failed. The Soviet Union then agreed to help build the Aswan Dam and developed close ties with other Middle Eastern nations.

Nasser's influence in the Middle East grew to such an extent that an Egyptian-led Arab unity movement, Pan-Arabism, appeared possible. In 1958, partly to coordinate efforts against Israel, Egypt and Syria merged to form the United Arab Republic. Later that year a military coup toppled the pro-Western monarchy in Iraq, the strongest Arab opponent to Nasser's leadership. This event strengthened Nasser even further.

After 1958, however, Nasser's Pan-Arabism policies achieved no more gains. Syria broke away from the United Arab Republic in 1961. In addition, Israel remained strong, despite its isolation.

International politics now settled into a fragile balance. The Middle East was no longer solidly in the Western camp, but the Soviet Union had no major diplomatic triumphs after the 1950s. Indeed, by the end of 1962, no outside power dominated the Middle East, nor was any power within the Middle East likely to do so. The region seemed destined for instability.

SECTION 3 REVIEW

1. **Define** kibbutz
2. **Identify** Adnan Menderes, Farouk, Gamal Abdel Nasser, Chaim Weizmann, David Ben-Gurion, FLN, Pan-Arabism
3. **Locate** Aswan Dam
4. **Summarizing Ideas** What changes did Nasser's government bring to Egypt?
5. **Interpreting Ideas** Why was Algerian independence difficult for the French to accept?
6. **Determining Cause and Effect** (a) What factors led to the Suez crisis of 1956? (b) How was it resolved?

4 Wars, Oil, and Revolution Changed the Middle East

By 1962 most of the countries of the Middle East had achieved independence. The remaining British colonies in the Persian Gulf area gained their independence without conflict in the early 1970s. Great power rivalries in the Middle East continued, however, especially between the Soviet Union and the United States. Yet these rivalries were not as intense as they had been between 1945 and 1962. The major issues during the final decades of the 1900s concerned adjustments within the Middle East itself.

The Arab-Israeli Confrontation

After the breakup of the union between Egypt and Syria in 1961, Nasser became more cautious about Pan-Arabism. Yet Egypt's president did not want to forfeit his country's leadership role in the Arabic-speaking world. He therefore faced a difficult choice when tension rose along Israel's border with Syria and Jordan in late 1966. Nasser could support his Arab neighbors at the risk of war with a militarily strong Israel, or he could hold back at the risk of losing his standing as leader of the Arabic-speaking world. Nasser decided to act.

In May 1967 Nasser demanded the withdrawal of UN troops who had been policing the border between Egypt and Israel since the end of the Suez crisis in 1956. Nasser also announced the closing of the Gulf of Aqaba to block Israel's direct sea route to Africa and Asia (see map, this page).

ISRAEL, 1947–1988

- Jewish state under 1947 UN partition plan for Palestine
- Acquired by Israel in 1948 War of Independence
- Israeli-retained conquests of the Six-Day War of 1967
- Israeli conquests of 1967 and 1973 returned to Egypt
- Israeli conquests returned Apr. 1979–Jan. 1980
- Israeli conquests returned Jan. 1980–Apr. 1982
- Buffer Zone since Apr. 1982
- ——— National boundary ⊛ National capital
- - - - Disputed boundary • Other city

LAMBERT CONFORMAL CONIC PROJECTION

Learning from Maps *Israel has fought many wars to safeguard and expand its borders. What territories did the Israelis win in the Six-Day War?*

The Six-Day War. Seeing the danger of delay, Israel entered into a lightning war on June 5, 1967. In six days of fighting, Israel captured the Sinai Peninsula and the Gaza Strip from Egypt, seized the Golan Heights from Syria, and took from Jordan the entire west bank of the Jordan River. The so-called "West Bank," part of the original Palestine mandate, had remained in Arab hands after the Arab-Israeli war of 1948. Israel also captured the

Windows in Jerusalem

At the beginning of World War II, almost 16 million Jews lived scattered throughout the world. Then, during the Nazi terrorism that engulfed Europe, as many as 6 million Jews lost their lives. In 1948, when the state of Israel was proclaimed, many Jews went to live there, to join earlier settlers in developing the land.

During the early years when Israel experienced tremendous growth, the

Israelis constructed houses, schools, and other facilities for the growing population. One of these was a hospital in the capital, Jerusalem. This

brilliantly colored stained-glass window from the hospital's chapel, or synagogue, is called "The Tribe of Joseph." It is one of a series of 12 windows, each devoted to one of Jacob's 12 sons, the founders of the tribes of ancient Israel.

The windows were designed by Marc Chagall, a Russian Jewish artist who fled to France in the 1920s in search of religious and political freedom. There are no figures of human beings in any of these windows because, by Jewish law, images of people are not permitted to appear in synagogues. The artist cleverly used symbols and abstractions of animals, birds, plants, and fish to tell the stories of the Old Testament. An intensely devout man, Chagall conveyed his love for his faith as well as his sense of history in these beautiful windows.

Jordanian section of Jerusalem. Israel then annexed Jerusalem, despite a UN ruling making it an international city.

The Six-Day War, as it came to be called, radically changed Middle Eastern politics. Israel's military superiority over its neighbors was confirmed, but peace remained elusive. The displaced Palestinians no longer expected help from Arab governments to restore them to what had been Palestine. They now relied more on their own guerrilla organization, the Palestine Liberation Organization (PLO) led by Yasir Arafat.

Realizing that they might be drawn into an Arab-Israeli war, the United States and the Soviet Union became interested in arranging a permanent peace settlement in the area. Egypt, Jordan, and Syria wished to regain lost territory. All parties involved had reason to seek a compromise settlement after 1967. However, mutual suspicions and fears doomed many efforts to work out a peace over the next six years.

Egypt Under Sadat

Nasser died in September 1970 and was succeeded by Anwar el-Sadat. Under Sadat's leadership Egypt and Syria secretly planned a war against Israel that began on October 6, 1973. Although the Arabs fought hard, Israeli troops pushed them back and crossed the Suez Canal to occupy Egyptian land.

However, the Israelis suffered severe losses during their drive into Egypt.

As had been true after the Six-Day War, all sides had reason to seek a compromise settlement. The United States Secretary of State, Henry Kissinger, began an intensive campaign of **shuttle diplomacy**—moving back and forth from Israel to Egypt to Syria to try to reach an agreement. He eventually achieved two settlements between Israel and Egypt and one between Israel and Syria. Thereafter, the peace initiative ran out of steam. In November 1977, however, Sadat surprised the world. He went to Israel to speak in person to the Israeli Parliament and to Israeli Prime Minister Menachem Begin (BAY • guhn). This was the first time that an Arab leader had visited Israel or even dealt directly with the young nation.

Sadat's action opened a new path of negotiations between Egypt and Israel, which the United States openly supported. Many more months of delicate negotiations were required, aided by the direct intervention of President Jimmy Carter. In September 1978 Carter invited the two leaders to the presidential retreat Camp David, in Maryland. After meetings and negotiations there, Sadat and Begin agreed upon the framework for a peace settlement. The Camp David Accords were followed by a peace treaty that was signed by Israel and Egypt in March 1979.

Sadat's actions divided the Arab world. His opponents claimed he had sold out the Palestinians to regain Egyptian territory. His supporters argued that he had started a process that could lead to peace for all, including the Palestinians. Most Israelis supported the peace with Egypt but resisted the idea of a process that might lead to a Palestinian state.

Egypt and Israel had achieved a great breakthrough. Many people doubted, however, whether it would lead to an eventual agreement between the Israelis and the Palestinians—and thus end the Arab-Israeli confrontation. The assassination of Sadat in October 1981 darkened the hopes for peace, and hopes further darkened in 1988 when Egypt's President Hosni Mubarak announced his support for an independent Palestinian state.

Oil and World Energy Needs

The Middle East and the West have dealt with each other over oil since 1901. In that year the shah of Iran (then Persia) granted a concession to a British prospector. Seven years later oil was discovered. Other foreign companies, mainly British and American, later obtained oil concessions from Middle Eastern countries.

With the rising tide of nationalism following World War II, many of the oil-producing countries began to demand more of the profits. Often the companies were willing to grant these demands. In Iran, however, the Anglo-Iranian Oil Company and the government were unable to reach agreement. As a result, the Iranian government nationalized the oil industry. This was a political victory for Iran, but the economic gains it received were less favorable. Because oil glutted the world market, Iran had little economic bargaining power; neither did the other Middle Eastern oil producers.

The Formation of OPEC

Quite rapidly the situation in the oil industry began to change. In 1960 the Latin American nation of Venezuela and the oil-producing nations in the Middle East created the Organization of Petroleum Exporting Countries (OPEC).

As the bargaining agent between the oil companies and oil-consuming industrial nations, OPEC's important advances began in the 1970s. A world oil shortage was by then apparent to everyone.

Learning from Pictures *Throughout the Middle East today, traditional and modern ways exist side by side, as this picture of a camel near an oil rig illustrates.*

During the war with Israel in October 1973, the Arab members of OPEC used their oil as an economic weapon. They drastically cut back production as a means of pressuring Israel and its Western supporters. OPEC's oil embargo caused world oil prices to skyrocket. Although production cutbacks were later eased, it became clear that OPEC had the economic power to fix oil prices.

This power, however, eventually created difficulties as well as benefits for the oil-producing nations of the Middle East. The increases in oil revenues led to rapid and unpredictable social change. Furthermore, the international oil surplus of the 1980s caused many OPEC nations to go into debt.

The Iranian Revolution

Throughout the 1960s the Iranian government carried out ambitious modernization programs. These included land distribution to the peasants, a campaign against illiteracy, increased industrialization, and women's liberation. These efforts continued into the 1970s.

BUILDING HISTORY STUDY SKILLS

Interpreting Visuals: Reading a Special-Purpose Map

Historians use many different types of special-purpose maps. A special-purpose map relates data to the geographic setting shown on the map.

How to Read a Special-Purpose Map

To read a special-purpose map, follow these steps.
1. Determine the purpose of the map. Is it designed to give you information on troop movements? resources? land use?
2. Formulate conclusions about the information presented on the map. For example, if the map shows troop movements, can you learn why the troops took the particular routes they did?

Developing the Skill

Study the map of Oil Resources of the Middle East below. The map shows the major oil and natural gas pipelines as well as the major oil and natural gas fields of the countries of the Middle East. The purpose of the map, then, is to show which countries of the Middle East contain major deposits of natural gas and oil. The map also shows how the oil and natural gas are transported to seaports for shipment throughout the world. One conclusion that you can draw from the map is that the Persian Gulf is a vital link in the transport of oil and natural gas throughout the world. Another conclusion you can draw is that P.D.R. Yemen is poorer than its neighbors because it has no oil or natural gas.

Practicing the skill. What other conclusions can you formulate from the information shown on the map of oil resources below?

To apply this skill, see Applying History Study Skills on page 829.

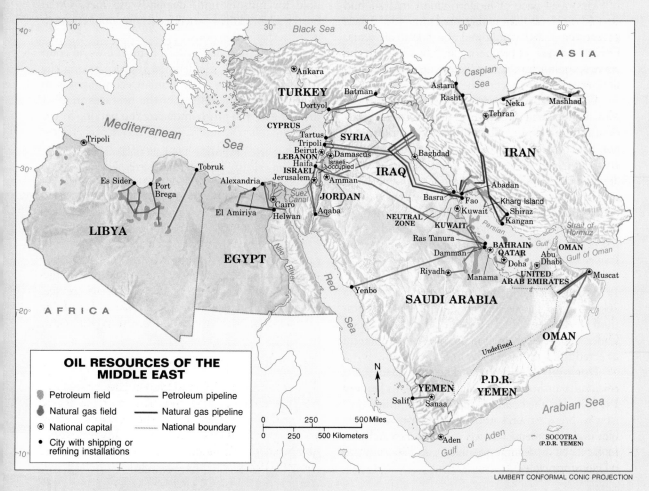

LAMBERT CONFORMAL CONIC PROJECTION

823

Iran's increasing oil revenues, combined with political changes in surrounding nations, gave Shah Muhammad Reza Pahlavi an opportunity to play a major role in the Middle East. In 1968 Great Britain announced plans to withdraw from the Persian Gulf and to grant independence to Qatar (GUHT·tar), Bahrain, Oman, and the Trucial Sheikdoms (later called the United Arab Emirates). All of these former British colonies were independent nations by 1971. Iran thereafter was the major military power in the Persian Gulf area.

Ties between the shah and the United States were especially close during this period. In addition, since the mid-1960s Iran had enjoyed good relations with the Soviet Union. As a result, the shah's regime appeared strong and stable in the late 1970s. Many Iranians, however, opposed the shah. Some were extremists seeking to establish a Communist state. Others were traditionalists eager to rid the country of Western influences and create a government ruled by religious leaders.

The rapid pace of modernization in Iran had created problems. These increased after 1973 when an economic slump followed the boom oil years. During the years of prosperity, millions had left the countryside for Iran's cities. These uprooted masses were now ready to accept the call for revolution.

The shah failed to win loyalty even from those Iranians who had directly benefited from the modernization programs. Thousands of young Iranians had been sent abroad for higher education at government expense. Yet most of them feared and detested the shah's rule. They felt it was symbolized by the Savak, the hated secret police who were believed responsible for many atrocities. Moreover, the shah tried to keep all power in his hands. As a result, not even his own ministers developed strong loyalty to him.

Riots and mass demonstrations throughout 1978 set the stage for revolution. By this time the 76-year-old religious leader Ayatollah Khomeini (hoh·MAY·nee) had become the revolution's leader. Banished from Iran since 1964, Khomeini directed the fight from exile in France.

Downfall of the shah. The shah made concessions, but they came too late. Finally, in January 1979, he left the country, appointing a prime minister to preside over a gradual transition of power. However, Khomeini insisted that the monarchy be replaced by an Islamic republic, run according to religious principles.

Khomeini returned to Iran in February 1979. Support for the government quickly faded. Leadership within the army was divided, and by mid-February Khomeini's revolution had triumphed. Iranians overwhelmingly voted to establish an Islamic republic, and they elected a president in January 1980. Real power, however, remained with Khomeini.

The hostage crisis. On November 4, 1979, Iranian militants captured the American Embassy in Tehran and seized more than 50 American hostages. The militants were protesting the American decision to let the ailing shah enter the United States for medical treatment. They demanded that the shah be returned to Iran to stand trial. The shah left the United States in December 1979. He died in Egypt in July 1980.

The hostage crisis points out a problem that plagued much of the world in the 1970s and 1980s. Revolutionaries—often frustrated because their demands had not been met—relied on terrorism. **Terrorism** is the kidnapping of innocent people to hold for ransom until demands are met. Often hostages are killed when governments refuse to grant terrorist demands.

As with most acts of terrorism, the world community of nations condemned Iran for taking the American hostages. The Iranian economy was in disarray. Even the release of the hostages in 1981 did not ease the problems facing the nation. In the

Learning from Pictures Iranian militants turned the American embassy compound into a revolutionary headquarters.

meantime, Iraq had launched an attack against Iran in September 1980 because of a dispute involving a waterway that divides the two countries. The Iran-Iraq War raged until 1988, with both sides suffering heavy casualties.

SECTION 4 REVIEW

1. **Define** shuttle diplomacy, terrorism
2. **Identify** PLO, Anwar el-Sadat, Henry Kissinger, Menachem Begin, Camp David Accords, Savak, Ayatollah Khomeini
3. **Locate** Gulf of Aqaba, Qatar, Bahrain, Oman, United Arab Emirates, Tehran
4. **Summarizing Ideas** Describe the efforts to attain peace in the Middle East after the Arab-Israeli war of October 1973.
5. **Analyzing Ideas** (a) How has OPEC demonstrated its power in world affairs? (b) Has it succeeded? Explain.
6. **Interpreting Ideas** (a) What factors led to the Iranian revolution of 1979? (b) Why did Iranian militants seize American hostages in 1979?

5 A Struggle Between Old and New Ways Plagued the Middle East

After 1945 the Middle East changed rapidly. The political and economic transformation of the region brought about great social change as well, resulting in a clash between old and new that still continues.

People and Politics

The Middle East is a vast territory, twice the size of the United States. In the 1980s nearly 270 million people lived in the region, and more than 90 percent were Muslims. Population densities varied widely. Saudi Arabia, for example, more than three times the size of Texas, had only 12 million inhabitants, or only 13.9 persons per square mile. Egypt's Nile Valley, by contrast, averaged almost 3,000 persons per square mile. (A square mile equals 2.59 square kilometers.)

The countries of the Middle East vary in size and importance. Qatar, the size of Delaware, had only about 370,000 inhabitants in 1986. Turkey, somewhat larger than Texas, had about 50 million inhabitants. In fact, just two countries, Egypt and

Turkey, contained one-third of the total population of the entire Middle East.

It was not just the size of their populations that made some of the Middle Eastern countries important. The four Persian Gulf states of Kuwait, Qatar, Bahrain, and the United Arab Emirates, for example, contained less than one percent of the Middle East's population. However, they possessed enormous oil wealth and thus had considerable influence.

For centuries, three major languages—Arabic, Persian, and Turkish—have been used throughout the region. With the creation of the state of Israel, Hebrew also has become an important language in the Middle East.

Until modern times the Middle East was not so politically divided. The Ottoman Empire, which lasted until after World War I, controlled most of the Middle East for some 400 years. Only Morocco in the west and Iran in the east escaped Ottoman rule.

The political breakup of the region into separate countries began with Western imperialism. The Middle East, as you have read, was colonized by four different European powers. Great Britain and France divided up most of the area between

Learning from Pictures Iran's mining of the Persian Gulf and its attacks on neutral shipping forced the United States Navy to escort ships out of the gulf.

them. Italy ruled Libya, and Spain controlled part of Morocco. Turkey, Iran, and most of the Arabian Peninsula were never directly colonized. However, they were subjected to persistent economic and military pressures from Europe.

After World War II, there were a number of attempts to create a new political unity in the Middle East. The creation of the Arab League in 1945 was the most important. Egypt, Saudi Arabia, Yemen, Syria, Lebanon, Trans-Jordan, and Iraq formed the league to promote economic and cultural ties among the member nations. Fourteen other Arab nations joined the league after 1945. Nevertheless, in the 1980s the Arab nations remained politically divided, especially on foreign policy.

Unequal Distribution of Resources

Great differences also exist in the distribution of natural resources in the region. As you have read, most of the oil-rich Middle Eastern countries are thinly populated. Only Iran, Iraq, and Algeria have both large populations and large oil resources. By contrast, heavily populated areas such as Turkey, Egypt, Sudan, and Morocco have little oil.

Egypt's great agricultural wealth does not meet the needs of its enormous population. Sudan cannot exploit its agricultural potential because of limited transportation facilities. Other countries, such as Morocco, have a good mix of agricultural and mineral resources. For the entire Middle East, however, oil is a source of imposing wealth.

Thus, the unequal distribution of natural resources and of population produces difficult economic conditions. The national wealth (what economists call the **gross national product,** or **GNP,** and define as the dollar value of all new, final products produced in a nation each year) in Kuwait, Qatar, and the United Arab Emirates is almost as high as that of the United States. In 1986 the GNP in the United States was more than $16,500 per person per year. In those three tiny Persian Gulf states, the average GNP per person was $16,450. At the other end of the scale, the GNP per person was less than $1,000 in Egypt, Sudan, and Yemen.

Cities and Population Growth

Cities have existed in the Middle East since the dawn of history. Damascus is believed to be the world's oldest continuously occupied city. In 1945 the Middle East already had a significant proportion of its population living in cities. The increase since then has been dramatic.

The population of Cairo, Egypt, was less than 2 million in 1945. It was at least 7 million in 1985. Tehran, the capital of Iran, expanded tenfold in the same period, from 500,000 to 5 million. Baghdad, in Iraq, with a population in 1945 of about 440,000, had more than 3 million inhabitants 40 years later.

In the 1980s nearly half of Lebanon's total population lived in the capital city of Beirut. Israel, often thought of as a land of agricultural pioneers, had a population that was 90 percent urban.

Traditional Middle Eastern cities had narrow, winding streets, bazaars—market streets with rows of tiny shops—and city walls with handsome gates. Although much of this older style has remained, urban growth in recent years has taken the form of high-rise buildings and wide streets.

Before modern times most city dwellers lived in one- or two-story houses hidden behind windowless walls. The few outside windows were heavily shuttered with ornate patterns of metal or wood. Rooms of such city homes opened onto an interior patio. All this assured greater family privacy. In the 1980s more and more people lived in apartment buildings. Also, as industrialization intensified, increasing numbers of people worked in factories and offices.

Much of the growth of Middle Eastern cities was due to migration from the countryside. Much also stemmed from high population growth rates. The population increase was caused both by declining death rates and high birth rates, and the result was a very young population. For example, about one half of Iran's population in 1985 was under the age of 15, while two-thirds was under the age of 30.

Education and Women's Status

The large percentage of young people in the population increased the need for schools and teachers. Middle Eastern countries made great progress in education after 1945. At that time probably fewer than 15 percent of the primary-school-age children were actually in school. In 1980, despite the vast population increase, the average was closer to 65 percent. Several countries, such as Israel, Lebanon, and Tunisia, had almost all primary-school-age children in school.

Learning from Pictures *While many women in the Middle East wear traditional clothing, others, as in this scene in Kuwait, have adopted Western style clothing.*

The years since 1945 also brought significant expansion in secondary and higher education. Turkey, for example, had more than 240,000 students in colleges and universities in the 1980s. The figure for Egypt was more than 500,000.

The students spent their time on subjects similar to those studied in the West. Many of them trained to become government officials. With the coming of industrialization, there was also a growing need for people with technical skills. Many became mechanics, electricians, and business managers.

Women, too, achieved gains. Only a fraction of the female population received schooling before 1945. After that time the percentage of females in school increased even more rapidly than that of males. Each year more women finished school and took jobs in factories, offices, and in such professions as medicine. A few women entered politics. In general, Middle Eastern societies continued to be male dominated, but improvements in women's status after 1945 were striking.

Religious Nationalism

Many Muslims in the Middle East reacted to the rapid changes by turning to Islamic fundamentalism. This was an attempt to revive the stability and values of the past and was a form of religious nationalism. It was a way for Muslim nations to reject Western influences.

Followers of Islamic fundamentalism differed on leadership and policy, but they agreed in rejecting foreign influences. They wanted to return to traditional Muslim ways. They wished to create religious nations that would apply Islamic law strictly. They opposed such modern trends as women's emancipation.

Ayatollah Khomeini, leader of the Iranian revolution against the shah, was the best-known spokesman of Islamic fundamentalism until his death in 1989. Colonel Muammar al-Qaddafi (kah • DAH • fee), who overthrew the Libyan monarchy in 1969, claimed as well to represent traditional Islamic political values. The religious conservatives of Saudi Arabia were also Muslim fundamentalists, but they opposed both Khomeini and Qaddafi. In the 1970s and 1980s, Muslim and Christian factions in Lebanon engaged in bloody guerrilla warfare. The Lebanese civil war killed thousands of people and destroyed the nation's economy.

Many young people in these countries disliked traditional ways. They rejected outside political influence, but they sought education and were eager to modernize their societies. There was often tension between them and the religious nationalists.

Thus, after 1945 the nations of the Middle East became more industrialized, more urbanized, and better educated. However, the struggle between continuity and change, between old and new, seemed destined to continue.

SECTION 5 REVIEW

1. **Define**   gross national product, GNP
2. **Identify**   Arab League, bazaars, Muammar al-Qaddafi
3. **Locate**   Kuwait, Yemen, Lebanon, Damascus
4. **Summarizing Ideas**   **(a)** What changes in education were made in the Middle East after 1945?   **(b)** What gains did women in the Middle East achieve?
5. **Determining Cause and Effect**   **(a)** Define Islamic fundamentalism.   **(b)** Give two examples in the Middle East.   **(c)** How has fundamentalism affected relations with the West?

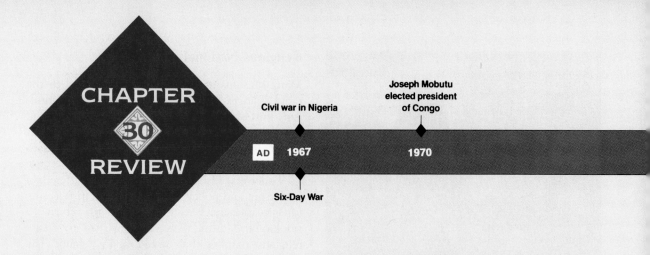

CHAPTER 30 REVIEW

Civil war in Nigeria

Joseph Mobutu elected president of Congo

AD 1967

1970

Six-Day War

Chapter Summary

The following list contains the key concepts you have learned about Africa and the Middle East since 1945.

1. Independence came rapidly to the African nations after World War II. Most African nations achieved independence peacefully, but a few resorted to violence.
2. Only South Africa resisted any efforts to give the black majority of the population a real voice in their own government. There, the Afrikaans government instituted the apartheid system that separated the races.
3. Africa's new nations faced a number of difficulties. There was often hostility among the groups within a country. This led to a bitter civil war in Nigeria. In Angola the superpowers intervened, as they did in the conflict between Ethiopia and Somalia in the Horn of Africa.
4. Africans also faced economic difficulties and, in the early years of independence, a sense of inferiority about their culture.
5. African cultural achievements gradually gained wide recognition and admiration.
6. Many nations in the Middle East also gained independence after 1945. In addition, nations that were already officially independent were able to reduce foreign influences.
7. A revolution in Iran resulted in the overthrow of the shah and the establishment of an Islamic republic.
8. A continuing problem in the Middle East was the relationship between Israel and its Arab neighbors. Four Arab-Israeli wars were fought between 1948 and 1973. An offer of peace by Egypt led to the signing of a peace treaty in 1979, but the other Arab nations rejected the pact.
9. The nations of the Middle East vary enormously in size, population, and wealth. A number of them gained considerable power as a result of the rise in oil prices in the 1970s.
10. The rapid changes of the period after World War II led to upheaval and a revival of Islamic fundamentalism. The region faced continuing uncertainties and tension in the 1980s.

On a separate sheet of paper, complete the following review exercises.

Reviewing Important Terms

Supply the term that correctly completes each statement

1. The South African policy based on the principle of racial separation became known as _____ , the Afrikaans word for apartness.
2. The Tanzanian local, cooperative villages are known as _____ .
3. Unwise land use patterns have led to _____ , or the spread of the desert in Africa.
4. A collective farm in Israel is known as a _____ .
5. In the 1970s Secretary of State Henry Kissinger began an intensive campaign of _____ _____ , in which he moved back and forth from Israel to Egypt to Syria to try to reach a peace agreement.

Developing Critical Thinking Skills

1. **Classifying Ideas** Name the country of each of the following political and cultural leaders: **(a)** Robert Mugabe, **(b)** Kwame Nkrumah, **(c)** Chaim Weizmann, **(d)** Anwar el-Sadat, **(e)** Muammar al-Qaddafi, **(f)** Jomo Kenyatta, **(g)** Gamal Abdel Nasser, **(h)** Ayatollah Khomeini, **(i)** Sékou Touré, **(j)** Menachem Begin, **(k)** Nnamdi Azikiwe.
2. **Comparing Ideas** **(a)** How did nationalists after 1945 differ from earlier African leaders? How did each of the following contribute to the rise of nationalism in Africa: **(b)** Kwame Nkrumah; **(c)** Jomo Kenyatta; **(d)** Robert Mugabe.
3. **Analyzing Ideas** **(a)** Which African nations achieved independence with relatively little opposition? **(b)** Which did not? **(c)** What reasons might account for these different experiences?
4. **Interpreting Ideas** How did economic problems and ethnic rivalries threaten the stability of many newly independent African nations?
5. **Determining Cause and Effect** **(a)** What were the causes of the Arab-Israeli war of 1948–1949? **(b)** What were the results?
6. **Listing Ideas** What changes occurred in the nations of the Middle East in the years after 1945?
7. **Analyzing a Primary Source** Reread the poem by Patrice Lumumba on page 810. **(a)** What did

- Civil war in Angola
- Independence of Angola and Mozambique

Camp David Accords

Independence of Zimbabwe

Military coup in Nigeria

Imposition of martial law in South Africa

Wole Solyinka awarded Nobel Prize in literature

1975 1976   1978 1979 1980 1981   1983 1984 1985 1986   1988

Violence in Soweto

- Revolution in Iran
- Hostage crisis in Iran

Assassination of Anwar Sadat

New South African constitution

Iran-Iraq War

Withdrawal of Cuban troops from Angola

Lumumba mean by the phrase "the dawn is here"? **(b)** To what "evil, cruel times" was he referring? **(c)** Why might this poem appeal to an emerging sense of African nationalism?

Relating Geography to History

Study the map on page 823. **(a)** What nation or nations of the Middle East have no oil or natural gas reserves? **(b)** What problems might the lack of oil and natural gas reserves have for that nation or nations?

Relating Past to Present

1. In the 1980s the situation in the Middle East remained unsettled. In some cases, affairs changed on almost a weekly basis. Using the *Readers' Guide to Periodical Literature,* locate recent articles on events in one of the following nations: Egypt, Israel, Saudi Arabia, Iran, Iraq, Syria, Jordan, or Lebanon. **(a)** How have conditions in this country changed since the printing of this book? **(b)** How have the United States and the Soviet Union responded to these changing conditions in the Middle East?
2. Examine the pictures of African art on pages 296, 300, 301, and 302. Then find examples of present African art in sources such as *National Geographic* or general histories of Africa. Based on evidence in these pictures, support or challenge the following statement: "Modern African art reflects a pride in the cultural achievements of earlier African civilizations."

Applying History Study Skills

Before completing this activity, review Building History Study Skills on page 823.

Study the map entitled "The World: Land Use and Economic Activity" on page R8–R9 and answer the following questions.

1. In what countries outside the Middle East is drilling for oil a major economic activity?
2. How is most of the land on Madagascar used?

Investigating Further

1. **Writing a Report** Prepare a report on the policy of apartheid practiced in the Republic of South Africa. You may consult the *Readers' Guide to Periodical Literature* for articles on this topic. Include in your report answers to the following questions: **(a)** What is the origin and racial makeup of the population in the Republic of South Africa? **(b)** How does the government defend apartheid? **(c)** By what means does the government enforce apartheid? **(d)** How do other African nations react to this racial policy? **(e)** How does the rest of the world react?
2. **Preparing an Oral Report** The novels of Chinua Achebe give Westerners a glimpse into Nigerian society and a changing Africa. Read one of these novels and prepare an oral report on the effects of modernization and the struggle to save or adapt old ways. Possible titles include *Man of the People* (Doubleday), *No Longer at Ease* (Fawcett), and *Things Fall Apart* (Fawcett).
3. **Preparing a Panel Discussion** Prepare a report on the capture of the American Embassy in Tehran and the seizure of more than 50 American hostages by Iranian militants on November 4, 1979. In your report describe the effects of the incident on the Iranians, the hostages, the United States, and the world. Conclude your report by stating the terms of the hostages' release.
4. **Dramatizing History** In recent years the Organization of Petroleum Exporting Countries (OPEC) has become increasingly prominent in world affairs. Work with several of your classmates to find out how OPEC conducts its meetings. Then conduct a mock OPEC meeting in which the ministers discuss how to raise the price of oil and how to enforce their decisions.
5. **Conducting a Debate** Work with several classmates to prepare a debate on the following topic to present to the class:
   Resolved: The world community of nations should agree never to meet any terrorist demands.
   As you prepare your debate, you might find it useful to research some of the terrorist kidnappings that have taken place in the world in recent years. Possible choices include kidnappings in Lebanon in the late 1980s.

CHAPTER

31

Latin America Became the Focus of World Attention

Place Latin America

Time 1945–present

3.7 mil. BC   4000 BC   AD 2100

Significance

Sometimes referred to as the "slumbering giant" because of its wealth in human and natural resources, Latin America stands on the threshold of dynamic change and development. Wracked by revolutions and military upheavals, the countries of this region continue to suffer political and economic instability. Nevertheless, the people of this dynamic area of the world persist in working for political, economic, and social progress.

For many years Latin America was overshadowed by the colossus to the north—the United States. The governments and economies of this region, particularly those bordering the Caribbean, depended on the United States. However, this situation is fast changing as the 1900s draw to a close. These developing nations have begun to steer their own courses, often quite different from that which the United States envisions for them. In so doing, the Latin American nations face ever changing challenges.

Terms to Define

multinational corporation   campesino
import substitution   covert
geopolitical region   dissident

People to Identify

Daniel Ortega   Oscar Arias
Manuel Noriega   Fidel Castro

Places to Locate

Guatemala   Panama
Grenada   Cuba
Nicaragua   Dominican Republic
El Salvador   Haiti

Questions to Guide Your Reading

1 What conflicts have plagued Latin America since 1945?
2 What major changes occurred in Mexico, Central America, and the Caribbean islands in recent decades?
3 What type of political and economic system did Castro set up in Cuba?
4 What were some of the upheavals experienced by many of the nations of South America in recent decades?

The death in 1952 of Eva [Evita] Perón, first lady of Argentina, sparked an outpouring of national grief. In Evita, the former actress and radio star, the working class believed they had found their champion. Whether she truly had their interest at heart remains a matter for conjecture. The following is a description of the flamboyant Evita as she declined the nomination for vice president in 1951.

❝ *The woman who mounted the steps and looked out upon the frenzied crowd was a far cry from the fledgling first lady of 1946, or the glamour queen of the Rainbow Tour. The blonde curls and gaudy attire had long since given way to what one scholar has called 'the streamlined, eternally classic style which was to be hers—and uniquely hers at that time—until her death.' Her hair was pulled back severely, accentuating the growing gauntness of her features. Tears flooded her eyes. She raised her arms in response to the delirium, and a look of uncertainty clouded her expression.* ❞

Like Argentina, other nations of Latin America have witnessed dramatic changes in governments during the recent chapters of their histories.

1 Political Conflicts Shook Many Latin American Nations

The countries of Latin America underwent enormous changes after World War II. Once relatively unimportant in world affairs and economically backward, Latin America became a focus of world attention. Its growing population, the discovery of vast petroleum deposits and other resources, and its rapid industrialization increased its importance to the rest of the world.

Since achieving independence in the early 1800s, most Latin American societies had followed traditional social and economic patterns. After 1945, however, Latin America seemed to be not merely catching up with the industrialized world, but creating its own patterns.

Rapid Population Growth

The most important change in Latin America after World War II was the sudden surge in population.

◀ *The Panama Canal Zone*

In 1940 the population of Latin America totaled about 126 million. By the 1980s its population was estimated to be 398 million.

A decline in the death rate spurred this population explosion. Public health measures, such as insecticides against malaria-carrying mosquitoes, reduced the number of deaths from malaria each year. Most significantly, improved medical care led to a decline in the death rate of children and infants. More children survived their first years of life and went on to adulthood and to parenthood.

Rapid population growth had enormous consequences for Latin America. Birth rates were highest in rural regions, where unequal distribution of land, and in some areas a short supply of it, forced more and more people into the cities.

The Growth of Cities

Cities exercised a powerful attraction of their own because they contained a concentration of social services, schools, and popular entertainments. For example, hospitals, universities, and secondary schools were often found only in cities.

The populations of cities grew twice as fast as the general population. In 1940, approximately 16 million Latin Americans lived in various cities of more than 100,000 inhabitants. By 1980, the number had risen to 150 million. Rio de Janeiro, for example, grew from 4.2 million in 1970 to 5.8 million in 1987.

City and national governments had to deal with complex administrative problems. For example, sewer lines, water mains, and electric lines had to be built. Large investments had to be made in road building, public buses, and even subway systems. The heavy machinery and other equipment for all of these building projects could not be found in most Latin American countries. The need to import these items often created a financial burden on the economy.

Many other problems arose in connection with the growth of cities. Most cities faced severe housing shortages. The governments, with so many other new expenses, could not afford to build public housing for the expanded city population. In addition, most of the rural migrants received wages too low to afford any housing. They therefore "squatted" on steep hillsides, tidal flats, and even publicly owned garbage dumps. In the poorest cities of Latin America, as many as half the inhabitants became squatters.

Learning from Pictures *Rio de Janeiro, one of South America's most beautiful cities, constantly struggles to house its growing population.*

The expanded urban population also required a reliable food supply. Until the 1940s commercial agriculture had been designed to supply overseas markets. The supply of food for the cities came from those small farmers who had surpluses to sell. With the growth of cities, however, many Latin American countries needed to import food.

New Political Forces

Most of the constitutions of Latin American countries allowed only literate persons to vote. As they moved to the cities, people were more likely to gain some schooling or learn to read. Thus, the lower class, able to read and therefore to vote, suddenly acquired political importance.

The votes of rural workers had always been controlled by the large landowners, through the bonds of loyalty or fear. These pressures did not exist in the cities. Now, for the first time, politicians had to appeal to a large mass of people to gain votes.

Women had gained the right to vote in a few Latin American countries in the 1930s. However, it was not until the mid-1950s that women were given the right to vote throughout the region. Their votes also increased the electorate.

Labor became another force of political power in postwar Latin America. As employment in factories increased, labor organizing spread and the union movement grew stronger. Governments sensed a danger in allowing unions to grow on their own. Therefore, government leaders followed the policy, begun in the 1930s, of attempting to control the unions. The unions continued to gain strength, however, especially through political parties that supported their interests.

Religion represented another active political force. More than 90 percent of Latin Americans were Catholics. In the past, the Catholic church had espoused conservative ideas in Latin American society and politics. At the same time, the church's concern for the poor and uneducated was an important tradition in many countries. However, following a meeting of the Catholic bishops of the region in 1968, the church's leaders began to take liberal stands on the political issues of welfare and human rights.

The church's strong position on such issues placed it in opposition to government and military leaders and to members of the upper and middle classes. These dominant elements of Latin American society thought of the growing urban class as a danger. They resisted social reforms and the labor movement because they saw them as threats to order and the existing political system.

Learning from Pictures *During Pope John Paul's visit to Chile in 1987, he asked the people to preserve peace but to demand their human rights.*

Problems of Economic Development

During World War II, Latin America had provided vast quantities of raw materials and food to the Allies. After the war Latin American nations found it difficult to stabilize their economies. They continued to supply a few unfinished goods to the industrialized countries. However, demand for their agricultural products and raw materials did not rise fast enough to supply Latin Americans with the income necessary to fund economic growth. Meanwhile the list of goods that Latin America needed to import grew longer.

Most political leaders in Latin America saw economic development as the key to resolving the region's problems. Economic development would provide jobs for the increased population. Industrialization would lessen the country's dependence on foreign sources for vital manufactured goods and would provide consumer goods for everyone. In every country the drive for economic development became a major government project.

Latin American nations invited foreign corporations and manufacturers to establish businesses in their countries in the hope that their investments and technology would help spur industrialization. Since foreign participation would bring in machinery and capital, it seemed to be the cheapest and most rapid way to promote economic development.

Relations between foreign-owned businesses, known as **multinational corporations,** and their host countries developed into a major political issue. Many Latin Americans resented the foreign ownership of important factories. In addition, factory owners often took their profits out of the country rather than reinvesting the funds. Any attempts by the governments to control the flow of profits out of the country proved futile.

Industrialization to Reduce Imports

Between 1956 and 1960, Brazilian leaders continued the economic policy known as **import substitution.** This policy became one of the few political programs on which most Latin Americans could agree. Under import substitution, government officials examined the list of goods that their country imported to find those items that could be produced inside the country. The government would then grant various kinds of favors to encourage manufacturers to produce these items. Tariffs or

◆ READ
WRITE
INTERPRET
● CONNECT
THINK

BUILDING HISTORY STUDY SKILLS

Making Connections with History: Linking Economics to History

All societies have access to a limited amount of resources that can be used to produce the goods and services needed to satisfy people's wants. Specifically, at any one time, each society has a given amount of labor, capital, and natural resources. In every society people's wants seem to be greater than all that can possibly be produced. This condition is called "scarcity," and it forms a basic economic problem. Because we cannot have everything we want, we make choices. Much of economics involves how and why institutions, people, and societies make the choices that they do.

"Opportunity cost," another key economic concept, deals with the economic choices that are made in relation to the sacrifices involved. For example, if you are given a choice between going to a play or a rock concert, and you choose the play, the rock concert becomes your opportunity cost since you sacrificed it when you chose the play.

Economic systems determine the manner in which people decide what to produce, how to produce it, and for whom to produce it. These are the basic economic decisions every society must make. They are based upon scarcity and opportunity cost. The economic system of a society affects people's relationships with one another, the kind of government they create, and the history of the society.

How to Link Economics to History

To link economics to history, follow these steps.
1. Identify and define the economic concept being discussed. It is either scarcity, opportunity cost, or an economic system.
2. Describe the effects of the economic concept on government or society.

Developing the Skill

Read the following selection. How does the description of a hacienda in Latin America help us to understand the development of the society there?

❞ The hacienda as a society may be described by saying that it was—and is—an economic and social system that seeks to achieve self-sufficiency . . . on a local scale. . . . Each unit expands until it has within its own borders all that it needs—salt from the sea, *panela* (black, unrefined sugar) from its own cane fields, corn, barley, wheat, coconuts, bananas, apples, and pears. All of this depends upon where the hacienda is located. . . . it can run from the seacoast to the mountain top . . . Not all haciendas . . . satisfy this ideal completely, but that is the aim of hacienda organization: to buy nothing; to raise and make everything within the

limits of its own boundaries. The big house is built from the timbers found on the land . . . the furniture is made at home. The cloth is woven there from wool shorn off home-grown sheep. The llamas that graze in the hills, the oxen and the horses are raised and broken where they were born. . . . The wooden plow, the wagon, the windmill for the grinding of the corn, or the water mill for the grinding of the cane are all fabricated [made] locally. ❞❞

The passage is describing an economic system. The decisions about what to produce, how to produce it, and for whom to produce it are made by the owner of the hacienda. The goal of the owner is to make and keep this economic unit self-sufficient and self-governing. The problem of scarcity is solved by the planned use of natural resources. The opportunity cost comes in when the owner makes the choice of what is to be produced on the hacienda.

Practicing the skill. In the free enterprise system of the United States, who answers the three basic economic questions?

To apply this skill, see Applying History Study Skills on page 849.

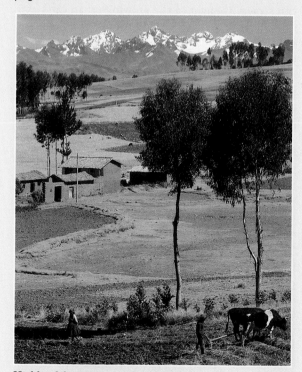

Highland farming near the Andes

Learning from Pictures *During the 1980s Mexico's major source of income was crude oil. What products was Mexico producing in the early 1960s?*

quotas would be set to discourage or prevent importation of similar goods, giving the local industries a chance to develop.

Import substitution worked fairly well in the largest countries—Brazil, Mexico, and Argentina—which had large markets and enough resources to accomplish the task. By the early 1960s, these countries produced steel, heavy machinery, automobiles, pharmaceuticals, and many other consumer goods. These manufactures represented 20 percent of the national output of all goods and services. Some other countries of Latin America, such as Venezuela, Chile, Colombia, Peru, and Uruguay, experienced lesser but significant rates of development.

By the mid-1980s, all the easier substitutions of imports had been made. Many other problems could not be resolved quickly, however. For example, only wealthy people could afford refrigerators, washing machines, and other expensive consumer products. Meanwhile, many people could barely afford to buy enough food or "luxuries" such as toothbrushes and shoes. As a result, in some cases the new factories producing these products ran at half capacity because there was so little demand for their output.

Recent Economic Developments

In the postwar years, Latin American countries attempted new forms of economic association in an effort to lessen dependence on industrialized countries and to cooperate in areas of production, tariffs, and trade. The Andean Pact, enacted in 1969, had some success in meeting these goals. It restricted foreign investment and encouraged both lower tariffs and economic cooperation within Latin America.

Latin American influence also grew in other parts of the world. Trade with the newly independent nations of Africa and Asia increased. The countries of Latin America took leading roles in political and economic world forums, expressing positions closer to those of African and Asian countries than to those of the United States.

Alliances in the Western Hemisphere

During and just after World War II, the nations of the Western Hemisphere entered into several mutual defense pacts. Many leaders viewed such pacts as necessary steps to prevent the spread of communism.

The Organization of American States. Inter-American cooperation went a step further in 1948, when delegates from 21 Western Hemisphere countries met at Bogotá, Colombia, and founded the Organization of American States (OAS). Each member nation sent a representative to a policy-making council. The OAS met regularly at five-year intervals and also in special sessions from time to time. Each member nation agreed to consult the OAS before taking action against another member.

The founding of the OAS represented a continuation of the Good Neighbor policy, through which the United States sought cooperation with its southern neighbors. This ideal, however, proved difficult to achieve.

The Alliance for Progress. In 1961 President John F. Kennedy of the United States announced a 10-year program aimed at improving the quality of life in Latin American nations. The "Alliance for Progress" focused on housing, education, sanitation, public services, and tax and land reforms. The United States and 20 Latin American countries participated in the program. The United States alone contributed about $10 billion to the Alliance in the 1960s.

Despite the large amount of financial assistance provided through the Alliance for Progress, the program failed to achieve most of its goals. Much of the money fell into the hands of corrupt leaders and never reached the poor people for whom it was intended. By the early 1970s, the Alliance for Progress came to an end, mainly because of funding cuts.

SECTION 1 REVIEW

1. **Define** multinational corporation, import substitution
2. **Identify** OAS, Alliance for Progress
3. **Analyzing Ideas** What problems arose as a result of the growth of Latin American cities?
4. **Evaluating Ideas** (a) Briefly describe three new political forces that emerged in Latin America in the postwar years. (b) Explain the impact of each on this region.
5. **Interpreting Ideas** (a) Why were foreign corporations encouraged to establish businesses in Latin America? (b) Why did their participation become a political issue?

2 Mexico and Central America Set a Different Political Course

Mexico, Central America, the Caribbean islands, and the countries of South America bordering the Caribbean are called the Caribbean Basin (see map, page 837). This area forms a single **geopolitical region,** one whose members share similar political and geographic features.

The importance of the Caribbean Basin lies in its location as a commercial and military crossroads. The region connects the north-south routes of the hemisphere as well as the routes between the Atlantic and Pacific oceans via the Panama Canal. Although modern aircraft carriers and supertankers cannot pass through the canal, most commercial vessels have no difficulty traversing it. Such heavy traffic in the waterway results in the continued strategic and commercial importance of the canal.

As political instability has rocked the Caribbean Basin in recent years, world attention, particularly that of the United States, has focused on this region.

United States Involvement

In the early 1950s, the United States became heavily involved in Latin American politics. In Guatemala in 1954, for example, the United States intervened to help overthrow a leftist government. The Guatemalan government had passed a land-reform law permitting it to take over and redistribute unused land, much of which was American-owned. Despite international criticism the United States assisted a rebel group that overthrew the Guatemalan president, Jacobo Arbenz.

The United States became even more involved in Latin America in the 1960s, particularly in Cuba (see pages 841–42). Then in 1983 President Reagan, after being asked by neighboring Caribbean countries, sent marines to the island of Grenada to overthrow a Communist regime and replace it with a pro-Western one. The United States also played a complex and controversial role in the internal affairs of Nicaragua and El Salvador.

Mexico

Immediately after World War II, Mexico appeared to be one of the most stable countries in Latin

Learning from Pictures At the Miraflores locks, these ships are raised and lowered from one sea level to another on their way through the Panama Canal.

836

Label on map	Text
Castro seizes power, Jan. 1, 1959	Castro seizes power, Jan. 1, 1959
Cuban missile crisis, Oct. 22–28, 1962	Cuban missile crisis, Oct. 22–28, 1962
Bay of Pigs, Apr. 17–20, 1961	Bay of Pigs, Apr. 17–20, 1961
Arbenz overthrown June 27, 1954	Arbenz overthrown June 27, 1954

UNITED STATES

Miami

Gulf of Mexico

24°

80°

88°

Straits of Florida

Nassau

BAHAMAS
7-10-1973

ATLANTIC OCEAN

72°

64°

Havana

CUBA
5-20-1902

TURKS AND CAICOS ISLANDS (U.K.)

HAITI
1-1-1804

DOMINICAN REPUBLIC
2-27-1844

MEXICO

CAYMAN IS.
(U.K.)

GUANTÁNAMO BAY
(U.S. Naval Station)

Windward Passage

Port-au-Prince

San Juan

ANGUILLA

Belmopan
BELIZE
9-21-1981

JAMAICA
8-6-1962

Kingstown

Santo
Domingo

PUERTO RICO
(U.S.)

ST. CHRISTOPHER-NEVIS

ANTIGUA AND
BARBUDA

16°

GUATEMALA
9-15-1821

Guatemala

HONDURAS
9-15-1821

Tegucigalpa

MONTSERRAT

GUADELOUPE

DOMINICA

San Salvador
EL SALVADOR
9-15-1821

Caribbean Sea

MARTINIQUE

ST. LUCIA

NICARAGUA
9-28-1821

Managua

| Jean-Claude Duvalier flees to France, Feb. 7, 1986 |
| Assassination of Trujillo, May 30, 1961 |
| U.S. intervention, April 27, 1965 |

ARUBA
(NETH.)

NETHERLANDS
ANTILLES
(NETH.)

ST. VINCENT AND
THE GRENADINES

BARBADOS

GRENADA

Area of map below

| Somoza flees to Paraguay, July 17, 1979; Sandinistas seize power. |
| Assassination of Archbishop Romero, March 24, 1980 |

Maracaibo

Caracas

Port of Spain

TRINIDAD
AND
TOBAGO
8-31-1962

San José

Panama
Canal

Panama

VENEZUELA

COSTA RICA
9-15-1821

8°

PACIFIC OCEAN

PANAMA
11-3-1903

| United States agrees to turn over control of Canal Zone to Panama, Oct. 1979 |

BRITISH VIRGIN IS.
(U.K.)

ANGUILLA
(U.K.)

| Independent, Feb. 1967–Dec. 1980, when it became a British dependency again. |

Charlotte Amalie

ST. MARTIN
(FR.-NETH.)

0   200   400 Miles

0   200   400 Kilometers

N

U.S. VIRGIN
ISLANDS

SABA
(NETH.)

ANTIGUA AND BARBUDA
11-1-1981

COLOMBIA

Basseterre

ST. CHRISTOPHER-NEVIS
9-19-1983

St. Johns

MONTSERRAT
(U.K.)

GUADELOUPE
(FR.)

ATLANTIC
OCEAN

16°

**NATIONS OF CENTRAL AMERICA
AND THE CARIBBEAN TODAY**

Independent nation

Caribbean Sea

DOMINICA
11-3-1978

Roseau

CUBA Communist or Left-leaning nation

ECUADOR

MARTINIQUE
(FR.)

1-1-1804 Date of independence

Dependency

ST. LUCIA
2-22-1979

Castries

National boundary

0   50   100 Miles

0   50   100 Kilometers

BARBADOS
11-30-1966

National capital

Guerrilla activity

PERU

Kingstown

Bridgetown

ST. VINCENT AND THE GRENADINES
10-27-1979

| U.S. invasion to eject Cubans, Oct. 25, 1983 |

GRENADA
2-7-1974

St. George's

64°

BIPOLAR OBLIQUE CONIC CONFORMAL PROJECTION

Learning from Maps *Countries of Central America and the Caribbean have confronted many political upheavals. Which countries in the region are Communist?*

America, functioning smoothly under a presidential system of government. The government swiftly squelched occasional political dissent. At the same time, the government took steps toward establish-

ing a foreign policy that did not necessarily agree with that of the United States. For example, it was the only Latin American country that refused to break relations with Cuba in the early 1960s.

Learning from Pictures *Mexico and Central America are under constant threat of earthquakes, like the one that struck Mexico City in 1985.*

The nation also went heavily into debt, further damaging its economy. A tremendous earthquake ravaged Mexico City in late 1985, putting even more strain on the nation's economy. The government now faced rebuilding the shattered capital and providing for the 50,000 persons left homeless by the earthquake.

The growing population also strained Mexico's resources and led to widespread unemployment. To escape this unemployment, tens of thousands of Mexicans slipped illegally into the United States each year to look for work. The issue of illegal immigrants troubled United States-Mexican relations. An attempt to reduce the tension between the two countries occurred in 1986 when the United States Congress passed a new immigration law. The following are major points included in this law: (1) Those who entered the country illegally before January 1, 1982, and had been residing in the United States continuously since then, would be provided temporary residence status and could become permanent residents after 18 months. (2) Persons who were permanent residents for five years would become eligible for citizenship. (3) Employers were required to check job applicants for documents proving citizenship or immigrant status. (4) Those who hired illegal aliens would be subject to civil penalties ranging from $280 to $10,000 for each alien.

Revolution in Central America

Historically the countries of Central America have quarreled with one another and have been susceptible to outside influences. Often one nation would call on a major power, particularly the United States, to intervene in the affairs of a neighboring country.

Following World War II, Central America experienced rapid economic growth. Between 1950 and the late 1970s, the annual gross domestic product of Central America increased at a rate of 5 percent. As exports increased, per capita income doubled. Employment rose as manufacturing doubled. People moved to the cities, and the urban population grew from 15 percent to 43 percent. World prices for major exports such as sugar, coffee, bananas, and cotton soared. Telephone lines, electricity, fertilizers, and pesticides all came into use.

However, while this prosperity continued, only a certain sector of the population benefited. The

In the late 1960s, student protests racked Mexico, just as they had done in many other nations. This led to numerous confrontations between protesters and police, the largest of which occurred on October 2, 1968, at Tlateloco (tlahl • TEEL • koh). When the protesters refused to disperse, the troops shot into the crowd, killing hundreds. By 1971 guerrilla activity began against the government, further undermining its stability.

Throughout the three decades following World War II, Mexico faced economic problems caused by inflation and a negative trade balance. To remedy these difficulties, the government lowered the value of the currency several times and cut back its spending.

Mexico's economic picture improved greatly with the discovery of huge oil reserves in the 1970s, and it looked as though the country might finally overcome its economic difficulties. However, by the 1980s the worldwide slump in oil prices had ended the dream of a bright economic future.

peasants, known as the **campesinos,** did not share in this prosperity. During the 1960s the price of land nearly quadrupled as available arable land decreased. As rents rose, more peasants joined the ranks of a growing class of landless farm workers. These people could not even afford land for subsistence farming.

In addition, earthquakes in Guatemala and Nicaragua in 1972, and killer hurricanes in Honduras in 1974 and Nicaragua in 1988, left many of the poor homeless. Throughout the 1970s and the 1980s, the countries of Central America remained some of the poorest in the world, owing in part to inequality in the distribution of wealth.

A lack of sufficient medical help,* sanitation facilities, and educational services** plagued the countries of Central America. The population increased at an annual rate of 3 percent. In the late 1970s and early 1980s, skyrocketing inflation slowed the economies of the region to a standstill. Faced with these problems, people in El Salvador, Nicaragua, Honduras, and Guatemala began to demand reforms.

The Nicaraguan Revolution

Following the meeting held by the Catholic bishops of Latin America in 1968, the clergy blamed the wealthy for the misery of the poor and no longer supported the military dictatorships so prevalent in this region. Some of the lower-level clergy even joined guerrilla bands fighting the governments. For the first time, the church sided with the peasants against their oppressive rulers.

In addition, a growing class of educated people joined the ranks of those opposing the corrupt dictators. Both of these factors bolstered the revolutionary movement against the corrupt and oppressive dictator Anastasio Somoza in Nicaragua. Almost the entire population rose up against this regime in 1979.

A Marxist-inspired revolutionary organization, the Sandinistas, gained control of the anti-Somoza revolution by promising a mixed economy, nonaligned foreign policy, and pluralism. The Sandinistas took their name from the Nicaraguan guerrilla leader of the 1920s, Augusto Sandino.

---

*Life expectancy was about 55 years and 1 in 10 infants died.
**Only half the population learned to read.

After taking over the government of Nicaragua, the Sandinistas established close military ties with the Communist governments in Cuba and the Soviet Union. A guerrilla group, called the Contras, attempted to overthrow the Sandinista government with monetary and military aid from the United States. However, fearing a situation similar to that which had occurred in Vietnam in the 1960s and 1970s, the United States Congress voted to stop all aid to the Contras. This led to **covert** or undercover military and financial aid being given to the Contras by men close to President Reagan. Known as the Iran-Contra Scandal, this became a political embarrassment to the president when a few of the people involved were questioned by a congressional investigating committee in 1987 and brought to trial in 1989.

Plunged into a civil war and faced with severe economic problems, the Sandinista leader and Nicaraguan president, Daniel Ortega, looked for ways to come to terms with the Contra rebels. Despite his efforts, however, solving this problem proved impossible to achieve throughout the 1980s.

El Salvador

The Central American country of El Salvador, located adjacent to Nicaragua (see map, page 837), was ruled either by wealthy civilians or military dictatorships from the 1940s to the late 1970s. Guerrilla groups began to form in the 1970s in order to fight the inequities imposed by the government. These organizations managed to mobilize tens of thousands of people into antigovernment demonstrations. At first the military government then in power attempted reforms.

José Napoleón Duarte led the reformist challenge and was president through most of the 1980s. But violent collisions between leftist guerrillas and government-backed right-wing groups continued to plague the country. This violence led to the murder in 1980 of Oscar Romero, the Catholic archbishop of El Salvador, while he was saying mass, and, three months later, the unprovoked deaths of three American nuns and an American volunteer.

A stable government and economy seemed to be impossible to obtain in El Salvador. A permanent peace appeared to be the only way of bringing stability to the region. But no one seemed to know how to accomplish this task.

Learning from Pictures *Oscar Arias informally addresses a crowd of supporters in Costa Rica. Why did he win the 1987 Nobel Peace Prize?*

Panama

The country of Panama shared the same political and economic fate as its Central American neighbors. The only major difference was that the United States controlled the Panama Canal and 10 miles (16 kilometers) of territory on either side known as the Canal Zone, once part of Panama. American-Panamanian negotiations over control of the canal continued throughout the postwar period. The two nations finally negotiated a treaty, ratified by the United States Senate in 1979, which would gradually turn the canal over to Panama by the year 2000. This treaty caused much controversy in the United States, because many people believed that United States security would be jeopardized when it lost control of the canal.

In the late 1980s, relations between Panama and the United States deteriorated. United States officials accused the Panamanian dictator, General Manuel Noriega, of helping South American narcotics dealers send illegal drugs into the United States. President Reagan attempted to pressure Noriega into resigning and when this failed, cut off all United States military and economic aid to Panama. Then in December 1989, after Panamanian forces killed one American soldier and

detained and severely beat another one, President Bush sent a force of 10,000 soldiers to Panama to restore order and capture Noriega. Finally, in January 1990, Noriega, who had gone into hiding, surrendered and was transported to the United States to face trial on drug trafficking charges.

A Peace Proposal for Central America

In August 1987, representatives from throughout Central America met in Guatemala City, Guatemala, for a regional summit conference. At this conference Oscar Arias, the president of Costa Rica, a country with relative economic and political stability, proposed a peace plan for Central America. He desperately hoped to seek a solution to the conflicts and violence shaking this region. For this proposal, Arias was given the Nobel Prize for Peace in 1987. The following is an excerpt from a speech given by Arias on the subject of peace in Central America.

> *"The democracy in which many American nations live today cannot be consolidated without economic development and social justice. Before any political or economic conditions can be imposed on the democracies of the Americas, there must be a commitment from the Western world to strengthen democracy in all our nations. In the Americas, peace must be democratic, pluralistic, tolerant, and free. While dogmatism and intransigence persist and there is no dialogue, peace will be impossible. Working together for democracy, freedom, and development is working together for peace."*

SECTION 2 REVIEW

1. **Define** geopolitical region, campesino, covert
2. **Identify** Tlateloco, Daniel Ortega, José Napoleón Duarte, Manuel Noriega, Oscar Arias
3. **Locate** Grenada, Mexico, Nicaragua, El Salvador, Panama, Costa Rica
4. **Understanding Cause and Effect** **(a)** What caused economic prosperity in Central America in the 1950s and 1960s? **(b)** How did this lead to the establishment of a class of landless poor?
5. **Organizing Ideas** What were two factors that greatly contributed to the revolutionary uprising in Nicaragua?
6. **Analyzing Ideas** Why did the United States Congress vote to discontinue aid to the Contras?

3 Revolution Shook the Islands of the Caribbean

In 1959 a revolution in Cuba overthrew Fulgencio Batista, the dictator who had held power since 1934. Led by Fidel Castro, the Cuban Revolution was the greatest political upheaval Latin Americans had experienced since the Mexican Revolution of the early 1900s.

Revolution in Cuba

Fidel Castro and his brother Raúl began their campaign to overthrow the Cuban government on July 26, 1953, when they led an assault on an army barracks at Moncada. Although they failed and were captured by Batista's forces, the Castro brothers only spent 11 months in prison. The Castros spent the next few years in exile in Mexico where they trained a group of revolutionaries. They returned to Cuba with a band of 82 men in 1956, and for the next three years the Castro brothers, along with a 27-year-old revolutionary, Ernesto ("Ché") Guevara, conducted guerrilla operations against the Batista government.

By late 1958 Batista lost both public support as well as support from the United States government. He fled to exile in the Dominican Republic on New Year's Eve, and the revolutionaries under Fidel Castro took over the Cuban government.

Cuba under Castro. At first the nations of the world had difficulty determining whether Castro's regime would favor the West or the Communist bloc. However, in a relatively short time the new Cuban government began its swing toward the Soviet bloc, and by the end of 1960, Cuba clearly stood on the path toward communism.

Under Castro's now openly Communist regime, the government proclaimed land reform. The government took over large holdings and nationalized all major firms, seizing United States-owned oil, electric, and telephone companies, and sugar mills and nickel mines.

Castro's Marxist policies led to social unrest in Cuba. The lower class, which made up the majority of the population, supported Castro because his policies guaranteed jobs. Before the revolution unemployment had exceeded 20 percent, and most workers had frequently been unemployed. In addition, Castro's government showed a strong commitment to racial equality in a country where blacks and mulattoes accounted for more than 25 percent of the population. Improvements in welfare, education, and medical care also benefited the lower class.

On the other hand, many of these reforms angered the upper class. The government took over businesses and buildings. Employees ran newspapers that private industry had owned. People formerly associated with the Batista dictatorship fled the island. Increasing numbers of business leaders, landowners, professionals, and technicians also fled.

Learning from Pictures
Many of Castro's revolutionary ideals were challenged by responsible Cuban leaders who wanted a democracy in Cuba. Most of these people became political prisoners or exiles. Those left to enforce Castro's plans were his loyal revolutionary followers.

The Bay of Pigs. In 1961 the Cuban government ordered the two American-owned oil refineries on the island to process fuel supplied by the Soviet Union. When the refineries refused, Cuba intervened in their operations. The United States responded by refusing to import sugar from Cuba. Left without a customer for its main product, Cuba offered to supply sugar to the Soviet Union in exchange for arms.

The United States government viewed the relationship between Castro and the Soviets as a threat to American national security. President John Kennedy, elected in 1960, continued President Eisenhower's policy of providing secret assistance to anti-Castro rebels. Accordingly, in 1961 Kennedy approved a landing in Cuba of rebels who had been secretly trained and equipped in the United States. The invasion, which took place at the Bay of Pigs, did not succeed, in part because the expected local uprising did not materialize, in part because the promised United States air cover did not occur, and in part because Castro's forces mounted a strong defense.

The Cuban missile crisis. Fidel Castro feared that the United States would attempt another invasion of Cuba. In 1962 American intelligence services learned that the Soviet Union was sending nuclear missiles to Cuba and building missile sites there. After a tense confrontation, which included the possibility of a nuclear war, Soviet leaders agreed to dismantle the bases and remove the missiles. In return, the United States agreed not to invade Cuba. This agreement allowed Castro's government to continue without further direct interference from the United States

The United States persuaded the Organization of American States to expel Cuba and to join in an economic boycott of the island nation. Cuba thus began a long period of political and economic isolation from its hemispheric neighbors.

Despite his country's isolation, Castro launched a program of exporting Communist revolution to other developing nations, particularly in Latin America and Africa. The Cuban government exported arms, troops, and military advisers to Nicaragua, Angola, and Ethiopia. Ché Guevara instituted as well as implemented this plan. A former Argentine physician, Guevara became a revolutionary when he witnessed the overthrow of President Arbenz of Guatemala in 1954. Ever the revolutionary, Guevara personally led a band of guerrillas in the mountains of Bolivia in 1967, where he was killed by a troop of American-trained Bolivian Rangers.

Economic and social difficulties. Castro's lack of success, first in industrializing Cuba and then in attempting to return the economy to dependence on the sugar crop, led to more economic dependence on the Soviet Union by the 1970s. The failure of Cuba's centrally planned command economy and the lack of consumer goods created social unrest in Cuba. In 1980 this dissatisfaction with the government led many Cubans to seek political asylum in other countries. These people first sought refuge at the Peruvian embassy in Havana. When the Castro government realized how many **dissidents,** or people dissatisfied with the government, were among its citizens, it allowed anyone to emigrate provided he or she informed the authorities. The total reached 125,000, and most left Cuba from the port of Mariel in boats provided by Cuban exiles in Miami. However, not only did Castro rid Cuba of the dissidents but he also opened the gates of prisons and mental hospitals forcing criminals and mentally ill people onto boats that carried other refugees to the United States.

By the late 1980s, Cuba continued Ché Guevara's policy of exporting revolution. Close political and economic ties with the Soviet Union also continued, making it as dependent on the Soviets as it had once been on the United States.

Learning from Pictures During the Mariel boatlift, Cuban refugees are towed to safety by a United States Coast Guard vessel.

Puerto Rico

Puerto Rico had been administered since 1898 from Washington, D.C. (see Chapter 23). In the early 1930s, Puerto Ricans under the leadership of Luis Muñoz Marín (mah·REEN) began to lobby for increased autonomy from the United States. In the 1940s, under pressure from Marín and the United Nations, the United States permitted Puerto Rico to draft a new constitution.

Puerto Rican voters and the United States Congress approved Puerto Rico's new status as a commonwealth in 1952. The Commonwealth of Puerto Rico has enjoyed certain tax advantages. As a result, the Puerto Rican economy developed very quickly over the next two decades. This growth depended on capital from the United States and on access to American markets.

Puerto Rico, however, did not have real self-government. During the 1970s, as economic growth slowed, many Puerto Ricans went to the United States to find jobs. Beginning in the 1980s, those Puerto Ricans who remained at home demanded a new political status—either independence, commonwealth, or statehood.

Other Nations of the Caribbean

Cuba was not the only troubled island nation in Latin America in the 1960s. Many countries experienced a shift toward the left and were disrupted by a series of coups and assassinations.

The Dominican Republic. The Dominican dictator Rafael Trujillo, assassinated in 1961, was succeeded by Juan Bosch, the first president to be democratically elected in that country in 38 years. After a coup toppled Bosch in 1965, his followers, some of whom were Communists, started an uprising to return him to power. To prevent a Communist takeover, President Lyndon Johnson of the United States sent 400 marines to support the Dominican Republic's military regime.

Since 1965 the Dominican Republic has made many economic and political strides. The democratic government established there appeared fairly stable by the late 1980s as did its economy, which relied more on light industry and tourism rather than on sugar alone. A strong middle class and a free press and media emerged, making the Dominican Republic one of the most stable countries in the Caribbean.

Learning from Pictures *Armed troops in the streets of Port-au-Prince, Haiti, patrol the city during the elections of 1987.*

Haiti. In 1986, following 30 years of the harsh and corrupt military rule of the Duvalier family, the impoverished country of Haiti attempted a democratic government. The military regime that first took over the reins of government reluctantly allowed an election to be held in November 1987. However, this election was canceled because of the violence that erupted among the rival political parties. Another election held in January 1988 brought a civilian government to power, but this government lasted less than 6 months. By the late 1980s, the future of democracy in Haiti did not look bright.

SECTION 3 REVIEW

1. **Define**   dissident
2. **Identify**   Fidel Castro, Ché Guevara
3. **Locate**   Cuba, Dominican Republic, Haiti
4. **Understanding Cause and Effect**   **(a)** What steps did Castro take to reform the economic structure of Cuba?   **(b)** What effect did this have on the upper classes?   **(c)** What effect did this have on the lower classes?
5. **Interpreting Ideas**   **(a)** Why did the United States get involved in the Bay of Pigs invasion? **(b)** What were the reasons for the failure of the Bay of Pigs invasion?
6. **Summarizing Ideas**   What were the results of the Cuban missile crisis?

4 South American Nations Faced New Challenges

Many of the nations of South America experienced turbulent political development in the decades following World War II. Revolutions swept the continent, leaving very few governments and individuals untouched.

Argentina

General Juan Perón came to power in Argentina in the 1940s claiming to be a defender against foreign interference and a supporter of the labor movement. Elected president by a huge majority in 1946, Perón depended greatly on the advice and assistance of his wife, Eva, also known as Evita, a former film and radio star. Eva Perón had a keen understanding of the political uses of the mass media. By appealing particularly to the working class, the Peróns won the support of the people and created an authoritarian regime that suppressed all political opposition.

During World War II, Argentina had profited from selling beef and wheat to the Allies. The Peróns used these profits to nationalize British-owned railways and utilities. Although the Perón regime controlled inflation, other attempted reforms did not improve the economy. By the early 1950s, Argentina had many economic troubles.

When Eva Perón died of cancer in 1952, her husband's popularity suffered. Trouble between Perón and the Catholic church as well as a bankrupt economy brought an end to his dictatorship. Argentina remained politically divided for the next 18 years.

In 1972 Perón returned from exile and was again elected president. His new wife, Isabel Perón, won election as vice president. When Juan Perón died, his widow became the first woman to be president in the Americas.

Political and economic conditions in Argentina continued to deteriorate in the 1970s. Isabel Perón was overthrown in 1976. The military regime that succeeded her led the country into a costly and disastrous war with Great Britain over claims to the Falkland (or Malvina) Islands in 1982. The British succeeded in winning a decisive victory, which proved humiliating to the Argentines.

Learning from Pictures *Isabel Perón carries out her duties as the president of Argentina. What position did Isabel have before she became president?*

The defeat of Argentina in the Falklands War led to the downfall of the military government, and free elections were held in 1983. The civilian government put military and government officials on trial to bring to justice those who had tortured and murdered so many political dissenters during the years of military rule. However, this succeeded in undermining its stability because some members of the military attempted mutinies against military officials siding with the government.

Brazil

Political unrest and economic chaos have marked Brazil from the postwar period to the present. Too often the overthrow of governments took place in an effort to save the economy. An example of this

Sunken Ships

Ships have been an important form of transportation since the earliest times. Unfortunately, as long as there have been ships, there have been shipwrecks. One expert estimates that 40,000 ships had sunk in the Mediterranean even before the birth of Jesus.

Since early times, too, people have tried to recover sunken ships and the objects that went down with them. As early as the 200s B.C., the Greeks were diving for sunken treasure. And today divers in the Caribbean use sophisticated equipment to locate gold from Spanish shipwrecks.

Treasure is not the only object of underwater exploration. Archaeologists are interested in recovering sunken ships and the objects they carried. One of the first expeditions recovered artifacts from a ship that sank off the coast of Turkey around 1200 B.C.

Sunken ships are seldom found intact. Sometimes, however, the hulls have been buried in the sand and preserved. The sunken Roman ships from the naval battle of Actium, fought in 31 B.C., have been found intact. More complete ships are being raised to the surface as special equipment is developed for the work.

Because fresh water preserves better than salt, many sunken ships in lakes are still in prime condition. Two warships that sank in Lake Ontario in 1812 are still intact with their guns on deck.

problem occurred in the early 1960s when João Goulart (GOO • lahr), with the support of a growing labor movement, became president of Brazil. Goulart's policies increased the income of the lower class at the expense of the upper class. As a result, wealthy Brazilians and foreign companies converted their profits into American dollars and deposited them in banks outside the country.

In an effort to prevent what they thought was a threat to the economy, the army overthrew Goulart in 1964. The military government forced wages down by setting a low minimum wage and by pressuring the labor unions. These policies increased the income of business owners. To encourage productivity, the government also made low-cost loans available to businesses. Foreign corporations were also urged to invest in Brazil.

The economy grew so fast that it was widely hailed as the "Brazilian Miracle." The gains from this miracle, however, went mostly to the rich. In fact, most of the population found themselves somewhat poorer than before, even though they worked longer hours and more family members took jobs. In order to maintain its economic program, the government had to control elections, forbid strikes, and censor television and newspapers. The government also went heavily into debt. By the late 1980s Brazil had a total foreign debt of $100 billion, the highest in the world.

Chile's Elected Revolutionaries

Chile, once the oldest continuing democracy in Latin America, underwent important governmental changes in the 1970s and 1980s. In 1970 an alliance of the Socialist and Communist parties resulted in the election of Salvador Allende (ah • YEN • day). With Allende as president, a Marxist government had come to power through peaceful means, the first to do so in the Western Hemisphere.

Allende's administration nationalized all American-owned copper mines, paying low prices for these valuable assets. The government then implemented an across-the-board wage increase, which raised incomes for people in the lower class. For a time the demand for goods increased, producing a business boom. The upper class, however, feared the changes taking place and stopped investing in the economy. Foreign banks also hesitated to make loans to the government.

Hard-pressed for funds, Allende's treasury printed more money to meet its needs. By 1972 staggering inflation had created hardships for all segments of the population. As the economy worsened, unrest and disillusionment spread.

In September 1973 a revolt backed by the United States broke out. Allende was killed and the army took power. Once in power, the military swiftly eliminated all forms of opposition.

The new military government executed thousands of people. Fearing for their lives, thousands of others fled into exile. The government under the leadership of Augustin Pinochet tightly controlled the press and media and curtailed many civil liberties. However, civil unrest continued to plague the country, and a free election was finally held in 1988. The military lost the election to a civilian government, but because of the way in which the constitution was written, the military actually held power in Chile after the election.

Peru

In the decades following World War II, the government of Peru was run by either military dictators or conservative civilians. However, Peru, like so many other Latin American nations, faced economic crises that included inflation, unemployment, and mounting debt.

Although the Peruvian people took great pride in the election of Javier Pérez de Cuéllar of Peru as Secretary-General of the United Nations in 1982, domestic conditions worsened in Peru in the 1980s. In that decade Peru suffered the worst economic depression of the century. This further weakened democracy as successive governments lost popularity in their attempts to grapple with this economic crisis. In addition, the Communist-inspired guerrillas continued to gain strength, making them one of the strongest revolutionary organizations in Latin America.

The Tragedy of Colombia

The years immediately following World War II were ones of severe civil and political upheaval for the people of Colombia. Rioting followed the assassination of a popular leftist leader, Jorge Eliécer Gaitán, in 1948, leaving thousands dead. The years from 1946 to 1958 saw both military and civilian dictators come to power amid civil and economic strife.

Learning from Pictures *Supporters of a civilian government in Chile rally in preelection demonstrations against further military rule.*

However, by the 1960s Colombia's future appeared brighter under a democratic regime. The economy stabilized, and Colombia became known as one of the models of democracy in Latin America.

Unfortunately, a desire for illegal narcotics increased in Europe and the United States during the late 1960s and early 1970s. The fertile land of Colombia became one of the prime regions for growing the marijuana and coca plants used in making narcotics. The lucrative profits brought by trade in these illegal products led to an increase in their production. Crime soared, as those wishing to control this trade jockeyed for power and position. Medellín, once a flourishing industrial city in Colombia, became headquarters for the Medellín cartel that ran the Colombian drug trade.

The Medellín cartel used assassinations as well as other means of intimidation to gain control of law enforcement agencies. Government officials at higher levels often remained uncorrupted and desperately sought ways to end the stranglehold which the cartel held on the government and the economy. However, officials at lower levels, either bribed or threatened by the drug kings, cooperated with the cartel. By the early 1990s, efforts to curtail this destructive trade continued with varying degrees of success.

SECTION 4 REVIEW

1. **Identify**   Juan Perón, Eva Perón, Isabel Perón, Salvador Allende, Medellín cartel
2. **Summarizing Ideas**   What was the result of the Falkland War in Argentina?
3. **Analyzing Ideas**   (a) What was the "Brazilian Miracle"?   (b) How was it achieved?
4. **Synthesizing Ideas**   (a) What reforms did Allende attempt to make in Chile?   (b) Why did the United States aid in the overthrow of the Allende government?
5. **Understanding Cause and Effect**   (a) What caused the growth of the drug trade in Colombia?   (b) How did this affect the government and economy of Colombia?

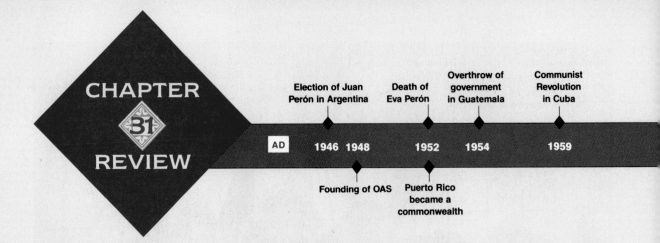

CHAPTER
31
REVIEW

AD   1946 1948   1952   1954   1959

Election of Juan
Perón in Argentina

Death of
Eva Perón

Overthrow of
government
in Guatemala

Communist
Revolution
in Cuba

Founding of OAS   Puerto Rico
became a
commonwealth

Chapter Summary

The following list contains the key concepts you have learned about the countries of Latin America from the postwar period to the present.

1. The rapid increase in population and growth of the cities changed traditional Latin American society.
2. The lower classes in the cities, women, and labor all emerged as new political forces.
3. The role of foreign-owned corporations in Latin America became a major political issue.
4. Attempts to reduce imports and efforts at economic cooperation were among the steps taken to reduce Latin America's dependence on more developed countries.
5. Organizations such as the OAS and the Alliance for Progress were founded in order to set up security for the Western Hemisphere and to promote better understanding between the United States and Latin America.
6. Revolution in Nicaragua in 1979 brought a Marxist regime to power. A civil war broke out in that country between the Marxist government, run by the Sandinistas, and the antigovernment guerrillas called Contras. The United States aided the Contras until Congress voted against this aid in 1983.
7. Revolution in Cuba in 1959 brought a Communist dictatorship to that country under Fidel Castro. Confrontations with the United States occurred with the Bay of Pigs invasion in 1961 and the Cuban missile crisis in 1962.
8. Both the Dominican Republic and Haiti overthrew dictators. While the Dominican Republic later established a democratic government, Haiti teetered between dictatorship and democracy.
9. In Argentina, Juan Perón established a dictatorship but was ousted in 1952. Although he later returned to power, in 1976 a military regime overthrew the government led by Perón's widow, Isabel.
10. Political unrest and economic chaos have marked Brazil from the postwar period to the present. By the 1990s the country faced a massive foreign debt.
11. Peru faced many problems in the 1980s, while Colombia had to deal with the illegal narcotics trade.

On a separate sheet of paper, complete the following review exercises.

Reviewing Important Terms

Supply the term that correctly completes each statement.

1. A foreign-owned business is called a _____ _____ .
2. _____ _____ is an economic policy in which a country encourages the production of goods that the country had been importing.
3. An area with common geographical and political features is called a _____ _____ .
4. _____ are peasants in Central America.
5. _____ operations are secret or undercover.

Developing Critical Thinking Skills

1. **Understanding Cause and Effect** (a) What were the causes of the population increase in Latin America? (b) What were the consequences?
2. **Interpreting Ideas** (a) Why did Latin American nations feel that economic development was necessary? (b) What efforts did they make to achieve it?
3. **Synthesizing Ideas** How would economic prosperity in Latin America help to establish more political stability?
4. **Understanding Relationships** What were the results of the United States involvement in each of the following: (a) Guatemala, (b) Nicaragua, (c) Cuba, (d) Dominican Republic.
5. **Analyzing Ideas** How did the change in the position of the Catholic church after the bishops' conference in 1968 affect the attitude of the peasants with regard to their governments?
6. **Comparing Ideas** (a) How were the revolutions in Cuba and Nicaragua different? (b) How were they the same?

Relating Geography to History

Turn to the map of Central America and the Caribbean on page 837. (a) How many of these nations have Communist governments? (b) How

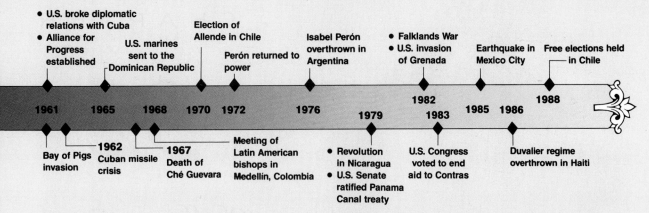

many miles are they from the United States? **(c)** How many kilometers? **(d)** What effect might the presence of Communist governments throughout this region have on United States security?

Relating Past to Present

1. Political affairs in many Latin American countries remained unsettled. Choose one of the Latin American countries and use the *Readers' Guide to Periodical Literature* to find articles on recent developments there. How have changes in Central America affected American foreign policy?
2. For decades many Latin American governments came to power through revolution or coups. Find out how many governments in Latin America today came to power by either a coup or a revolution. Are these governments secure? How many are dictatorships?

Applying History Study Skills

Before completing this activity, review Building History Study Skills on page 834.

Read the following paragraph on what takes place on a hacienda during a revolution. Then answer the questions that follow.

“ What we call social revolutions have all occurred in agricultural countries where the mass of the people lived on what they themselves raised from the soil. In such a society, a revolution is a simple thing. First, you cut off the head of the *hacendado,* then you divide the wheat, corn, and barley stored in the barn and the hacendado's cows, horses, sheep, and chickens. Similarly the plows, digging sticks, and other tools are distributed. The land is taken by the peasants and the revolution is over. What really happens is that the stored consumer goods are divided up among the surrounding peasants, and the limited producers' goods, in the form of seed, animals, tools, and the land itself, fall into the hands of those who have used the tools and animals and worked the land. ”

1. What economic questions are raised by the passage?
2. How is the problem of scarcity dealt with after a revolution?
3. What does the passage imply might be some of the causes of the revolution?

Investigating Further

1. **Presenting an Oral Report** Although the Brazilian economy grew rapidly in the 1960s and 1970s, many Brazilians still lived in poverty in large slums at the edges of cities. Find out about living conditions in the slums and present an oral report to the class. You might read Carolina de Jesus's *Child of the Dark* (New American Library). Why don't the people of the slums trust the government? How is Carolina different from most people in the slums?
2. **Writing a Report** Select a country in Latin America and prepare a written report on the positive and negative effects of foreign-owned corporations there. You may use the *Readers' Guide to Periodical Literature* to locate articles on this topic. You may wish to select one corporation that operates in a specific Latin American country and prepare a case study detailing the impact that the corporation has had on the citizens of the host country.
3. **Preparing a Chart** Use resources in your school or public library to find the per capita gross national product, the major exports, and the major imports of the following countries: Mexico, Guatemala, El Salvador, Honduras, Belize, Nicaragua, Costa Rica, Panama, Cuba, the Dominican Republic, Haiti, Colombia, Venezuela, Bolivia, Peru, Chile, Brazil, Paraguay, Uruguay, and Argentina. Then assemble the information you have gathered into a chart to display in class.
4. **Preparing a Panel Discussion** The nations of Latin America face many problems typical of developing nations in the world today. Work with a group of your classmates to find more information on how these nations are dealing with the problems of low rates of economic growth, high rates of unemployment and population growth, and burgeoning foreign debts. Then use the information you have collected to prepare a panel discussion detailing possible solutions to the problems.

CHAPTER

32

Challenges Faced the Superpowers in the Modern Era

Place North America and Europe

Time   1968—the present

3.7 mil. BC   4000 BC   AD 2100

Significance

An economic recession gripped much of the world during the early 1970s and caused major problems for most of the Western nations. After a 10-year struggle, the economies of most of these nations recovered.

During this period the United States worked to maintain its position as a leading nation on the world scene, cementing its already strong ties with Canada and Western Europe and attempting to improve relations with Eastern Europe. Meanwhile, the nations of Western Europe moved toward economic and political unity.

The Soviet Union and Eastern Europe faced major economic and political challenges in the 1970s and 1980s. However, a new Soviet leader attempted to restructure the political and economic organization of his country. Mikhail Gorbachev's new policies and the easing of tensions between East and West seemed to offer new hope for the future.

Terms to Define

stagflation   Ostpolitik
trade deficit   glasnost
détente   perestroika

People to Identify

Gerald Ford   Margaret Thatcher
Jimmy Carter   Willy Brandt
Ronald Reagan   Mikhail Gorbachev
Brian Mulroney   Lech Walesa

Places to Locate

Afghanistan   Armenia
Reykjavik   Latvia
Quebec   Estonia
Azerbaijan   Gdansk

Questions to Guide Your Reading

1 How did the United States maintain its leadership role in world affairs in the 1970s and 1980s?
2 What signs of political and economic stability were evident in Western Europe in the 1970s and 1980s?
3 What political and economic challenges did the Soviet Union and Eastern Europe face as the twentieth century drew to a close?

◀ *A United States-Soviet summit in New York*

On August 1, 1975, in Helsinki, Finland, representatives from 35 nations signed the Final Act of the Conference on Security and Cooperation in Europe. The following excerpt from this document, better known as the Helsinki Accords, describes the participating nations' view of human rights.

> **"** *The participating States will respect human rights and fundamental freedoms, including the freedom of thought, conscience, religion or belief, for all without distinction as to race, sex, language or religion.*
>
> *They will promote and encourage the effective exercise of civil, political, economic, social, cultural and other rights and freedoms all of which derive from the inherent dignity of the human person and are essential for his free and full development.*
>
> *. . . [T]he participating States will recognize and respect the freedom of the individual to profess and practice, alone or in community with others, religion or belief acting in accordance with the dictates of his own conscience.*
>
> *The participating States on whose territory national minorities exist will respect the right of persons belonging to such minorities to equality before the law, [and] will afford them the full opportunity for the actual enjoyment of human rights and fundamental freedoms.* **"**

In time the human-rights aspect of the Helsinki Accords became a factor in diplomatic relations among nations. As you will read, Soviet violations of the Helsinki Accords led to tensions between the United States and the Soviet Union.

1 The United States Tried to Maintain Its World Leadership

During the 1970s and 1980s, the United States faced a number of problems, including internal political conflicts and several economic reversals. Despite such problems, the country's commitment to its leadership role in world affairs remained strong. Meanwhile, Canada, also confronted with internal political and economic problems, somewhat reluctantly moved toward closer relations with its neighbor to the south.

Learning from Pictures *United States naval vessels helped evacuate American and South Vietnamese people when North Vietnam unified the country.*

Ending the Vietnam War

During the presidential campaign of 1968, Richard M. Nixon vowed to end American involvement in the Vietnam War "with honor." As a new decade dawned, the public clamored for the newly elected president to keep this promise.

Antiwar protest. The antiwar movement had begun during the mid-1960s, several years before President Nixon took office. However, its strength grew tremendously during his administration. College students, the movement's most vocal members, regularly staged huge demonstrations against Nixon's war policies on university campuses.

The most violent demonstrations occurred after Nixon's announcement of the American invasion of Cambodia in 1970. In early May four students were shot and killed when the National Guard attempted to break up a protest at Kent State University in Ohio. A few days later, a clash between students

and police at Jackson State University in Mississippi led to the deaths of two more students. Almost immediately hundreds of universities across the country closed as students took to the streets to protest these campus shootings. Close to 100,000 people took part in one protest march on Washington, D.C. Such antiwar protests continued unabated almost until the final withdrawal of American troops from Vietnam. Although most American forces left Vietnam by 1973, some remained until the fall of Saigon in 1975.

The impact of the war. The Paris Accords, signed in 1973, finally ended American involvement in the Vietnam War. However, the impact of the war proved long-lasting for the United States. American casualties numbered about 58,000 dead and 150,000 wounded. About 2,500 Americans were listed as missing in action (MIA), and many of them have not been accounted for. In addition to the human toll, the monetary cost of the war, some $160 billion, placed a heavy burden on the American economy. One of the most devastating consequences of the war was the damage it inflicted on the American national identity. Such was the extent of the damage that many Americans, after considering the monetary and human cost of the war, began to doubt the wisdom of the United States playing a major role in world affairs.

The Watergate Scandal

American national identity took another blow from a scandal that brought down the Nixon administration. During the 1972 presidential campaign, burglars had broken into the Democratic Party offices in the Watergate building in Washington, D.C. The burglars had tried to photograph campaign documents and install listening devices in the offices.

In 1973 a Washington newspaper charged that officials of President Nixon's reelection campaign had planned the break-in. The Senate set up a special committee to investigate this charge. During the investigation, evidence verified that members of the White House staff had secretly used illegal funds to conceal the nature of the burglary. Finally, it became clear that President Nixon had known about this cover-up. Impeachment proceedings began in the House of Representatives, but Nixon resigned the presidency before the question of his guilt came to a vote.

Despite Nixon's resignation and his subsequent pardon by President Gerald R. Ford, the Watergate scandal shook the faith of many people in the American political system. Many people began to feel that politicians generally lacked integrity. For them the name *Washington, D.C.,* soon became synonymous with the words "dishonesty" and "corruption." Jimmy Carter, elected in 1976, and Ronald Reagan, elected in 1980, both campaigned for the presidency as outsiders, with no ties to Washington. They vowed to clean up the corruption that had crept into the political system and to restore the faith of Americans in their country's government.

The Economy

During the late 1960s, government spending had skyrocketed as President Johnson tried to finance both his Great Society programs and the Vietnam War. This escalation in government spending, in turn, led to a general increase in prices and a decline in the buying power of the dollar. In the early 1970s, the stability of the American economy became an issue of some concern.

Attempts to stabilize the economy. President Nixon tried to fight the inflation that resulted from the escalation in government spending by cutting federal expenditures and encouraging an increase in interest rates—the cost of borrowing money. However, these measures had little effect on inflation and triggered a recession. Economists gave the name **stagflation** to this unusual combination of decreased economic activity (stagnation) and continued price increases (inflation).

Stagflation plagued the administrations of presidents Ford and Carter. Regardless of the programs they introduced—tight controls on federal spending, tax cuts, and voluntary price and wage freezes—the economic situation showed little improvement.

Then, in 1981 President Ronald Reagan took office, promising to bring the unruly economy under control. A conservative, President Reagan planned to cut many social programs and drastically reduce both government spending and tax rates. With the assistance of Congress, he carried out most of his programs. As a result, by the mid-1980s the rate of inflation had dropped from 13 percent to 4 percent and unemployment from 7 percent to less than 6 percent. Even so, government spending, especially on defense, continued to increase. To cover this increase, the government had to borrow large amounts of money. Consequently, the United States government assumed a huge national debt.

Changes in the American economy. For much of the 1900s, the United States had led the world in heavy industry and manufacturing. During the 1970s and 1980s, however, the United States began to lose ground in these areas. American steel companies, shipbuilders, and automakers found it increasingly difficult to compete with their counterparts in Japan, South Korea, and Taiwan, who had more modern factories and much lower labor costs.

As a result, during the 1980s many American steel mills, shipyards, and automobile plants closed, throwing hundreds of thousands of people out of work. This greatly added to the country's unemployment problems and marked a major change in the nature of the American economy. For years manufacturing had dominated economic life in the United States. In the 1980s, however, service-oriented businesses such as financial institutions, retail stores, and restaurants generated the most important economic activity. Some economists worried that the change from a manufacturing economy to a service economy might create problems in the future. They pointed out that although many service jobs commanded high salaries, the majority were low paying. Such jobs, these economists argued, could not support continued economic growth.

In addition to these changes in the American economy, Americans began to buy more and more foreign goods. At the same time, many American businesses found it increasingly difficult to sell their products abroad. This created a **trade deficit**—a situation in which a country imports more than it exports. By the time President George Bush took office in 1989, the trade deficit stood at about $110 billion.

Energy Concerns

One factor that contributed greatly to American economic woes—the OPEC oil embargo of 1973—also caused concern about future energy supplies. The embargo highlighted American dependence on imported oil. This dependence, coupled with the fact that oil, once used, cannot be replaced, forced many Americans to consider alternative energy sources.

Georgia O'Keeffe

Georgia O'Keeffe, who lived from 1887 to 1986, an American artist, painted this stark and powerful image of a skull set against a blue sky. O'Keeffe lived in New York with her husband, photographer Alfred Stieglitz. Like millions of other Americans, O'Keeffe found the endless variety of the American landscape fascinating and exciting. Each summer she traveled to the desert in the Southwest to paint. It was here that O'Keeffe derived a great source of inspiration for many of her paintings. She wrote,"I brought home the bleached bones as my symbols of the desert. To me they are as beautiful as anything I know."

O'Keeffe's confident style made a clear statement that American artists no longer depended on European influences. She commented about her work, "As I painted along on my cow's skull I thought to myself, I'll make it an American painting. They will not think it great with the

© 1984/5 The Metropolitan Museum of Art, the Alfred Stieglitz Collection, 1952. (52.203)

red stripes down the sides— Red, White, and Blue—but they will notice it."

Today the painting hangs in the Metropolitan Museum of Art in New York—for all the world to notice.

Some Americans ruled out the alternative of using other fossil fuels, such as coal and natural gas. Like oil, coal and natural gas are nonrenewable. In addition, the use of coal and natural gas causes major pollution problems. Many people considered nuclear energy to be an economical alternative to fossil fuels. During the 1970s, however, concerns about the safety of nuclear energy began to surface. These concerns peaked in 1979, when an accident at the Three Mile Island nuclear power plant in Pennsylvania released dangerous levels of radioactivity into the air.

In the early 1980s, many people began to protest the use of nuclear power. They advocated the development and use of such renewable energy sources as solar power and wind power. These protesters won few victories against supporters of nuclear power, but their concerns had

important effects on American society. In particular, Americans became more aware of the relationship between sensible energy use and a healthy environment.

Changes in Foreign Policy

The United States adopted new approaches to foreign affairs during the 1970s. Intent on easing some of the tension created by the cold war, President Nixon called for better relations with Communist countries. To this end, in 1972 he visited the People's Republic of China. This visit began a period of diplomatic activity that culminated in American recognition of the People's Republic of China in 1979.

Relations with the Soviet Union. President Nixon also made efforts to improve relations with the Soviet Union, and in 1972 he became the first American president to visit that country. During the visit President Nixon and Soviet leader Leonid Brezhnev signed agreements known as the Strategic Arms Limitation Treaties (SALT I). These agreements limited each country's production and deployment of certain missiles. Nixon and Brezhnev also signed several accords relating to environmental, health, and technological cooperation. This improvement in United States–Soviet relations became known as **détente** (day • TAHNT), a French word meaning "an easing of strain."

Presidents Ford and Carter continued the policy of détente throughout much of the 1970s. However, by the end of the decade, strains between the two nations began to show. President Carter, insisting that human rights be made a factor in relations between nations, began to speak out against the way the Soviet government treated **dissidents**— people who opposed Soviet policies. He also criticized Soviet and Cuban intervention in Africa, specifically in the Angolan and Ethiopian civil wars. In response, the Soviets characterized Carter's efforts at peacemaking in the Middle East as interference in other nations' affairs.

The most serious break in the relationship, however, came in 1979, when the Soviet Union invaded Afghanistan to give added support to the Communist regime there. The United States retaliated by rejecting the Strategic Arms Limitation Treaty (SALT II), cutting trade ties with the Soviet Union, and boycotting the 1980 Olympic Games in Moscow.

By the 1980s détente had come to an end. President Reagan, who accused the Soviet Union of encouraging revolution throughout the world, greatly increased defense spending. During the Reagan administration, the United States built up its arsenal of nuclear weapons and provided economic and military assistance to anti-Communist governments. In the next few years, relations between the United States and the Soviet Union deteriorated to such an extent that people began to talk of a new cold war.

In the mid-1980s, however, tension between the two nations eased once again. President Reagan and the new Soviet leader, Mikhail Gorbachev (gawr • bah • CHAWF), held summit meetings in Geneva, Switzerland, in 1985 and in Reykjavik (RAY • kyah • veek), Iceland, in 1986. The two leaders made little, if any, progress on substantive issues at these two meetings. However, when Gorbachev visited Washington, D.C., in 1987, the two countries signed an agreement limiting the deployment of long-range missiles. Although much distrust still remained between the two countries, as the 1980s drew to a close a return to the détente of the 1970s seemed possible.

Learning from Pictures
The greatest foreign policy achievement for President Carter was the Camp David Accords. Here Anwar el-Sadat (left), President Carter (center), and Menachem Begin (right), sign the agreements.

855

Terrorism and American foreign policy.
In 1979 international terrorism became a major influence on American foreign affairs when the Iranians seized the American embassy in Tehran (see Chapter 30). The hostages gained freedom on the day that Ronald Reagan took office in 1981.

Calling the hostage-taking an act of terrorism, Reagan vowed he would never negotiate with terrorists. Rather, he promised to seek them out and make military strikes against them. To this end, in 1986 United States Air Force jets bombed the headquarters of Libyan leader Muammar al-Qaddafi, long suspected by the Reagan administration of financing terrorist acts throughout the world.

Frustration over his government's inability to win freedom for a number of Americans held hostage in Lebanon caused President Reagan to adjust his antiterrorist policy. The hostage-takers, militant Muslims, had strong ties to the Iranian government. An arrangement that would send weapons to Iran—for use in its war with Iraq—in exchange for the release of the hostages was authorized. When this arrangement came to public attention in late 1987, many foreign governments condemned it. Later, after it became known that the proceeds of the arrangement had been secretly diverted to help the cause of the Nicaraguan Contras, some Americans also began to question the wisdom of the Reagan administration's approach to foreign affairs.

An increased role in the world. During President Reagan's administration, the United States began to play a greater part in world affairs. The government sponsored rebel groups fighting against the Communist governments of Angola, Afghanistan, and Nicaragua. Then, in 1983, American troops played an active role in the overthrow of the Marxist government of Grenada, a small island-nation in the Caribbean.

In the Middle East, Reagan sent troops to Lebanon to oversee a cease-fire in that country's long and bloody civil war. He also dispatched a fleet to the Persian Gulf to protect neutral merchant ships from becoming targets in the Iran-Iraq War. But these two moves ended in tragedy. A terrorist attack in Lebanon in 1983 resulted in the deaths of more than 200 American marines. Then in 1988 about 300 Iranian civilians lost their lives when the United States Navy accidentally shot down an Iranian passenger jet.

President Reagan's efforts at diplomacy, however, achieved marked success. His endeavors, in part, helped the peaceful transition from dictatorship to democracy in the Philippines. And, late in his administration, new diplomatic approaches led to better relations with the Soviet Union and other Communist-bloc countries.

Canada

The second largest country in the world, Canada possesses a vast wealth of raw materials. Yet much of its land—especially in the north—is completely unsuitable for habitation. As a result nearly all Canadians live within 200 miles (322 kilometers) of the United States border.

Government and culture. Although Canada's 10 provinces and 2 territories form a federal system much like that of the United States, Canada's provinces have more power than the American

Learning from Pictures Quebec City is often called the "cradle of French civilization in North America." Notice the signs in the French language.

states. For example, the Canadian constitution does not require any of the provinces to abide by future amendments passed by the federal government.

People of two very different cultural backgrounds—those of French descent and those of English descent—make Canada their home. French Canadians, because of their distinct language, Roman Catholic religion, and French-based traditions, have remained culturally separate from the majority of Canadian people. Although a minority in the country as a whole, French Canadians predominate in the province of Quebec, where more than 80 percent of the people speak French as their first language.

Separatism. During the 1960s a French-Canadian separatist movement gathered strength in Quebec. French Canadians sought special recognition of their language and heritage. They also demanded a greater role in both provincial and national governments and protection from discrimination. After Pierre Trudeau (tru • DOH), himself a French Canadian, became prime minister, many of the French Canadians' demands were met. Perhaps their greatest victory came with the passage of the Official Languages Act in 1969. This act made both French and English the official languages of Canada.

In 1976 the Quebec Party, which favored the complete separation of Quebec from Canada, gained control of the provincial government. Four years later, in 1980, the party put the separatism issue to the test by holding a referendum.* By a 60-percent majority, the people of Quebec voted to remain part of Canada.

Even so, French Canadians continued to demand special status for Quebec. And Quebec's leaders refused to ratify the 1982 constitution until the federal government offered such recognition. An amended constitution, which accepted Quebec as a "distinct society," finally won the province's support in 1987.

Relations with the United States. For the most part, relations between Canada and the United States have been friendly and productive. The two countries share the longest unguarded border in the world, and they tend to agree on most

major international issues. Their closest ties, however, come in the area of trade. For many years each nation has been the other's biggest trading partner. In 1987 alone the value of trade transactions between the two totaled about $150 billion.

The relationship between the two countries has come under intermittent strain, however. For example, the two countries have engaged in bitter disputes about fishing rights in the waters of the Pacific Northwest. But by far the greatest strains have resulted from Canadian uneasiness over American involvement in the Canadian economy. Since World War II, Americans have dominated many Canadian companies, either by absorbing them into multinational corporations or by controlling them through large stockholdings.

Canadian uneasiness turned to resentment after the announcement of the United States–Canada Free Trade Agreement in 1988. This agreement proposed the elimination of almost all tariff barriers between the two countries by 1999. Many Canadians characterized the arrangement as a betrayal that would make their country a mere economic colony of the United States. Free trade, they said, would give the United States the opportunity to drain Canada of all its natural resources. Stunned by the furor over the agreement, Prime Minister Brian Mulroney called for a general election. This election, Mulroney said, would serve as a referendum on the free trade issue.

After a bitter campaign, Mulroney's Progressive Conservative Party won a majority of seats in Parliament. However, it received only 44 percent of the popular vote. The election, then, reflected the Canadian uneasiness about the free trade issue.

SECTION 1 REVIEW

1. **Define** stagflation, trade deficit, détente, dissidents
2. **Identify** Gerald Ford, Jimmy Carter, Ronald Reagan, SALT I, SALT II, Mikhail Gorbachev, Official Languages Act, Brian Mulroney
3. **Analyzing Ideas** How did the nature of the American economy change in the 1980s?
4. **Understanding Ideas** What changes took place in American foreign policy during the 1970s and 1980s?
5. **Evaluating Ideas** What successes were achieved by the French-Canadian separatist movement?
6. **Classifying Ideas** List the causes of strains in Canadian-American relations.

---

*A *referendum* is the process in which a measure passed by a legislative body is submitted to the voters for final approval or rejection.

2 Western Europe Searched for Stability

During the 1970s and 1980s, many countries in Western Europe tried to consolidate the economic gains they had made in the early postwar period. Other countries made political advances, turning from dictatorship to democracy. Although the progress was far from smooth, Western Europe made great strides toward political and economic union.

Great Britain

The period of prosperity that had begun in Great Britain during the 1950s began to fade in the mid-1960s. By the end of the decade, the country faced severe economic problems. Outdated and inefficient factories, low productivity, and worker apathy

Learning from Pictures   Margaret Thatcher waves outside the official residence of Great Britain's prime minister at 10 Downing Street.

made it difficult for Great Britain to compete with other industrial nations. As a result, the country's imports soon far outweighed its exports. To help pay for this growth in imports and to finance the expanding number of social programs in its welfare state, the government raised taxes and increased borrowing. These actions, however, put the economy under greater stress. Even the discovery of huge oil deposits in the North Sea off the coast of Great Britain failed to bring relief. By the end of the 1970s, Great Britain, like the United States, staggered under the burden of stagflation.

Changes under Margaret Thatcher. In 1979, after a decisive victory in a general election, the Conservative Party took control of the British government. The Conservative leader, Margaret Thatcher, became prime minister—the first woman to hold that office. Thatcher charged that Great Britain's government spent too much money on social programs, regulated business and industry too closely, and taxed the people too heavily. She promised to return the country to prosperity by reversing the government's role in the economy.

Over the next few years, Thatcher made huge cuts in social programs. These cuts were so deep that some programs were eliminated. Her opponents argued that her real intention was to completely dismantle the welfare state. Thatcher also passed laws that eased government regulation of business, and she drastically reduced taxes. In addition, she began a program to return most government-owned industries to the private sector.

These policies helped to slash the rate of inflation and to revitalize the economy, especially in southern England. At the same time, however, unemployment grew rapidly in the country's predominantly industrial northern areas, partly as a result of a shift in Great Britain's economy from manufacturing to services. In some older industrial cities, more than 25 percent of the workers were without jobs. Unemployment among young people, unskilled workers, and minority groups ran closer to 50 percent. As the 1980s drew to a close, unemployment in the north began to ease. Even so, critics of Thatcher's government charged that her economic policies had created two societies in Great Britain—one in the prosperous south and another in the economically depressed north.

An old conflict. Ireland and the Irish had perplexed successive governments in London practically since the English invasion of Ireland in the

1100s. Most people assumed that the partition of the country in 1922—which created an independent Republic of Ireland in the South and Northern Ireland, which remained part of Great Britain—had solved all problems. Instead, it brought forth new problems. Over the years the Protestant majority in Northern Ireland had gained control of the government and of most of the country's businesses. In contrast, Northern Ireland's Catholic minority had little power and limited political and economic opportunities.

In the late 1960s, Catholics in Northern Ireland began to demonstrate to end discrimination in voting, employment and housing. At first peaceful, these demonstrations soon turned violent. To restore order and to protect the Catholic population from a Protestant backlash, the British government sent troops to Northern Ireland in 1969. Announced as a short-term measure, this stationing of soldiers in Northern Ireland quickly became a permanent policy. By the late 1980s large numbers of British troops remain garrisoned there.

Throughout the 1970s the violence in Northern Ireland escalated as extremists on both sides took advantage of the situation. Assassinations, car bombings, and attacks on British troops became an almost daily occurrence. The most active extremist group was the Irish Republican Army (IRA). Almost entirely Catholic, the IRA wanted to drive the British out of the north and reunite the two Irelands. The IRA took its "war of liberation" far beyond the Irish borders, bombing stores in a number of British cities and attacking British soldiers in other parts of Europe.

Characterizing the activities of both Catholic and Protestant extremists as terrorism, the British government gave the police and the courts in Ireland special powers. The police could detain suspected terrorists without charging them with any offense, and the courts could try without a jury any person charged with terrorist activities. In the late 1980s, the Thatcher administration extended these powers by ending the defendant's right to remain silent in trials in Northern Ireland's courts. Also, Thatcher banned direct radio and television statements by supporters of terrorist organizations. This, she said, would cut off the terrorists' "life-blood"—publicity.

The British government also tried to end the violence in Northern Ireland through political means. The most promising attempt came in 1985 with the Hillsborough Agreement. This gave the Republic of Ireland some participation in the governing of Northern Ireland. In time, however, both Catholics and Protestants denounced the agreement.

By the end of the 1980s, the death toll in what the Northern Irish simply called "the Troubles" stood at more than 2,500. With a peaceful settlement apparently further away than ever and with violence once again beginning to escalate, it seemed likely that this figure would increase.

France

After Charles de Gaulle resigned in 1969, his prime minister, Georges Pompidou (PAHM • pih • doo), replaced him as president. Although the two men had worked together for many years, they viewed France's interests differently. Charles de Gaulle saw France as a major player on the world scene. In contrast, Pompidou felt that France should limit its involvement in foreign affairs and focus instead on domestic issues.

A more realistic approach. Georges Pompidou felt that changes on the international scene had rendered de Gaulle's nationalist approach to foreign affairs impractical. A more realistic strategy, Pompidou believed, would be to seek close, cooperative relations with traditional allies. Therefore, he sought stronger ties with the United States and ended French opposition to British membership in the European Community (EC). Within the EC, Pompidou tried to cooperate with other members rather than to lead them. The one area where Pompidou did take a lead was in arms sales. During his administration France became one of the world's leading weapons dealers.

Pompidou focused on domestic issues for much of his time in office. He introduced a number of social programs that he hoped would ease the problems that had given rise to the political upheavals of the late 1960s. He also embarked on an ambitious plan to renovate much of Paris, France's capital and major tourist attraction. However, an economic crisis, largely brought on by the OPEC oil embargo and price increases in 1973, curtailed many of his plans.

On Pompidou's sudden death in 1974, Valéry Giscard d'Estaing (zhee • SKAHR des • TANG) became president. Like President John F. Kennedy of the

United States, Giscard wanted to take a strong stand in international affairs and encourage social change at home. Giscard continued Pompidou's foreign policies and, in addition, strengthened ties with the Soviet Union, China, and other Communist-bloc countries. On the domestic front, he introduced programs that increased unemployment benefits and health benefits and raised retirement pensions. But economic problems drastically undermined Giscard's plans for social change, making it virtually impossible for him to carry out his programs.

A socialist president. The French electorate, disappointed at Giscard's failure to fulfill his promise of prosperity and social change, chose socialist François Mitterrand (MEE·tehr·ahn) as president in 1981. Mitterrand inherited a country with severe economic problems. For much of the 1970s, France's rate of inflation had averaged above 10 percent. At the same time, budget and trade deficits had grown steadily. And unemployment levels had risen dramatically in the late 1970s.

Mitterrand tried to bolster the fragile economy by nationalizing a number of industries and banks and by increasing taxes on the highest incomes. He also established job-training programs for young people and the unemployed. In addition, he introduced programs to give tax breaks and other assistance to businesses that made special efforts to find work for the long-term unemployed and school dropouts. However, after a major economic reversal in the mid-1980s, Mitterrand dropped most of these policies and adopted a more conservative approach.

Under Mitterrand, France once again took a very active role in foreign affairs. Mitterrand sent French troops to help supervise the cease-fire in the Lebanese civil war. In addition, he provided military assistance to the African nation of Chad—a former French colony—in its border war with Libya. Such actions generally won the approval of the world community. However, not all of Mitterrand's foreign policy measures received such support. His decision to continue nuclear weapons tests in the South Pacific was condemned by Australia, New Zealand, and other South Pacific nations. Many nations denounced Mitterrand's readiness to negotiate and make deals with terrorists. However, such negative world opinion did not seem to lessen Mitterrand's popularity among the French people. In 1988 he easily won election to a second term as president.

Learning from Pictures *Connected to West Germany by only one highway and three air corridors, West Berlin stands as a symbol of free enterprise inside East Germany.*

West Germany

By the late 1960s, West Germany had become an economic power in Western Europe. However, it still faced major political problems. Access to West Berlin and relations with East Germany, the Soviet Union, and other Communist countries posed difficult foreign policy challenges. Social Democrat Willy Brandt, who became chancellor in 1969, met these challenges with a new approach.

Ostpolitik. Chancellor Brandt believed that West Germany had to remain firmly allied with Western Europe and the United States. At the same time, however, he felt that tensions between his country and the Eastern bloc had to be reduced. Brandt's efforts at creating better relations between East and West, known as *Ostpolitik* (German for "Eastern Policy"), resulted in West German treaties with the Soviet Union and Poland in 1972. *Ostpolitik* eventually led to mutual recognition of East and West Germany in 1973.

In 1974, when it became known that one of his staff members had been spying for East Germany, Brandt resigned. Brandt's finance minister, Helmut Schmidt, replaced him as chancellor. Chancellor Schmidt tried to develop a greater spirit of

Looking Beyond Planet Earth

The successful mission of the space shuttle *Discovery* in October 1988 reaffirmed the American commitment to space exploration that had faltered some two years before with the loss of the *Challenger* and its crew of seven. President Ronald Reagan underscored this rekindled commitment when he declared that the United States fully intended to "expand human presence and activity beyond Earth into the solar system."

The National Aeronautics and Space Administration (NASA) has already begun planning journeys to the farthest reaches of the galaxy. The first step involves the construction of a space station named *Freedom* some 220 miles (354 kilometers) above the surface of the earth.

Between 1995 and 1998, 20 shuttle flights are scheduled to carry the parts of the half-million pound station into earth orbit. There astronauts will assemble the space station, which will consist of three laboratories and a housing unit. Once the station is ready for occupancy, crews of 8 astronauts will come aboard for 90-day tours of duty. During these missions, the astronauts will conduct experiments and make observations of the solar system.

All these operations, and many others, constitute the preparation for NASA's ultimate goal—an expedition to our closest planetary neighbor, Mars. This expedition will begin with the assemblying of a huge unmanned cargo ship at the space station *Freedom*. According to NASA's schedule, the cargo ship should depart in 2006 for a nine-month, 34-million mile (54-million kilometer) journey to Mars. About a year later, a second space craft, also assembled at *Freedom* and more than two times larger than the cargo ship, will carry 8 astronauts and embark on a more direct six-month flight to Mars. The two ships will rendezvous in orbit around Mars.

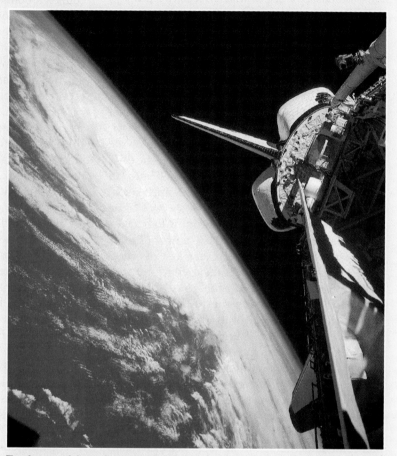

Earth viewed from the space shuttle

Once the docking is completed, 4 astronauts will fly to the surface of Mars for 10 to 20 days of exploration. After collecting rock samples and making scientific observations, the astronauts will return to their spacecraft. They then will begin the long voyage back to earth by way of the space station *Freedom*.

If the Martian mission proves too complex or too expensive, NASA has planned an equally exciting and ambitious voyage to Phobos, one of Mars' two tiny, mysterious moons. A Phobos mission would be similar to the voyage to Mars. It would require two vessels, one a cargo ship, the other a crewed spacecraft. However, the Phobos mission would cost much less. Since the ships would not enter Martian gravity, less fuel would be needed for the return journey. And the ships could be constructed on earth, a far less costly operation than working from *Freedom*.

In the past, historical events and the personalities engaged in them were confined to the surface of the earth. However, NASA's plans ensure that a new history will soon unfold in a new geography—that of the planets that lie in the vastness of space far beyond our own world.

861

economic and political cooperation among the Western European nations. He also continued Brandt's *Ostpolitik*. However, Schmidt's administration of this policy strained diplomatic relations with the United States.

During much of Schmidt's time in office, West Germany experienced remarkable economic growth, and the West German people enjoyed one of the highest standards of living in the world. In the early 1980s, however, West Germany plunged into an economic recession. For the first time since World War II, West Germans faced the prospect of rising unemployment coupled with rampant inflation.

Christian Democrats regain power. In late 1982, after more than a dozen years out of office, the Christian Democrats regained control of the government. Helmut Kohl, the new chancellor, charged that Schmidt and the Social Democrats had spent West Germany into a recession. Chancellor Kohl promised to return the country to prosperity through policies similar to those followed by Prime Minister Margaret Thatcher in Great Britain and President Ronald Reagan in the United States.

The chancellor also made changes in West German foreign policy. He strongly reaffirmed his government's support for the NATO alliance, which had come under attack from many West Germans in the early 1980s. For example, he backed NATO deployment of American nuclear missiles in West Germany, even though this position sparked huge demonstrations across the country. He also worked to improve relations with the United States. To this end, he supported President Reagan's proposed antimissile program, the Strategic Defense Initiative (SDI). Kohl continued to support the Reagan administration throughout the 1980s.

The Nations of Southern Europe

During the 1970s the four nations of Southern Europe underwent major political changes. Italy, once one of the more stable European nations, experienced almost constant political turmoil. At the same time, Spain, Portugal, and Greece returned to democratic forms of government.

Italy. The world economic recession of the early 1970s hit Italy especially hard. For much of the decade, unemployment levels soared and inflation was rampant. During the same period, the country's political system experienced a great deal of turmoil. No single political party could gain a majority in the Italian parliament, so governments had to be formed through coalitions. Since few of these coalitions lasted very long, little could be done to alleviate the country's severe political and economic problems.

In the late 1970s, a wave of political violence threw the country into a state of chaos. The Red Brigades, a terrorist group, began a series of kidnappings, assassinations, and bombings that continued into the 1980s. Perhaps their bloodiest act was the kidnapping and murder of Aldo Moro, a former prime minister, in 1978.

By the mid-1980s, the police had managed to break the power of the Red Brigades and other terrorist groups, and peace returned to Italy. However, the specter of economic and political turmoil continued to plague the country.

Spain. In 1969 Francisco Franco named Prince Juan Carlos as his successor. On Franco's death in 1975, Juan Carlos became king and immediately set about the task of returning the country to democracy. About 18 months later, in 1977, Spain held its first free elections in more than 40 years. In those elections, moderate political parties led by socialists won the majority of seats in the Cortes, or parliament.

Spain's young democracy faced its first real challenge in 1981. In February of that year, a group of army officers seized the lower house of the Cortes in an attempt to take control of the government. However, their coup failed when the army remained loyal to the king.

By far the greatest challenges that faced the Spanish government in the 1980s concerned the economy and the question of Basque separatism. The Basque region, in the western Pyrenees, has a distinct language and culture, and its people have long sought independence from Spain. In 1980, after the Basque people overwhelmingly voted for home rule, Spain granted the region self-government. However, an extremist Basque separatist group has continued its campaign of violence to win complete independence for the region.

Learning from Pictures *High in the Pyrennes Mountains, Basque villagers maintain their traditional way of life. What did they gain from Spain in 1980?*

Spain's economic problems included a very high rate of unemployment, which in 1985 stood at 22 percent, the highest in Europe. Spanish leaders hoped that membership in the EC, which Spain joined in 1986, would spur economic activity.

Portugal. Ironically, Portugal's return to democracy came about after a military coup. In 1974 army officers led by General Antonio de Spinoza overthrew the dictator Marcello Caetano. Spinoza drew up agreements giving independence to Portugal's remaining colonies and then, after calling for democratic elections, resigned. In those elections moderate parties won more than 60 percent of the seats in the parliament. However, the Communist Party also gained in influence.

Throughout the 1970s and 1980s, Portugal's political situation became increasingly volatile, harming the country's economy, the least developed in Western Europe. Portugal's leaders hoped that the economy would improve as a result of the country's acceptance into the EC in 1986.

Greece. "The colonels," the military junta (HOON • tuh) that seized control of the Greek government in 1967, continued their repressive rule until 1974. Discovery of their involvement in an attempted military coup on the island of Cyprus in that year led to their downfall.

Constantine Karamanlis, a former prime minister, took over, named a civilian cabinet, released all political prisoners, and ordered free elections for November 1974. He also called for a referendum on whether to allow the return of King Constantine II.

In this election the Greek people rejected the king's return, voting instead to make the country a republic.

Conservatives held power in Greece until 1981, when the Socialist Party, led by Andreas Papandreou (pop • uhn • DRAY • ooh), took control of the government. Papandreou introduced socialist economic policies and moved toward closer ties with Communist-bloc countries. These policy changes caused strains in relations between Greece and the United States in the mid-1980s. The two countries also had major differences of opinion on NATO policies. As the 1980s drew to a close, relations between the two countries remained tense.

Continuing Cooperation

The spirit of cooperation among the nations of Western Europe that had developed in the years after World War II continued to grow in the 1970s and 1980s. Formal institutions such as NATO and the EC grew in both strength and numbers, and new steps were taken to ensure the economic, political, and military security of the region. Even though individual nations still had differences of opinion, by the end of the 1980s a real union of European states seemed possible.

The Helsinki Accords. In 1975 representatives of 35 nations, including the United States and the Soviet Union, met in Helsinki, Finland, to discuss the topics of security and cooperation in Europe. These representatives signed an agreement, known as the Helsinki Accords, that specified ways of improving economic and technological cooperation between East and West. The agreement also endorsed the use of peaceful means rather than force in settling differences between nations. Perhaps the most important part of the Helsinki Accords, however, concerned the protection of human rights such as freedom of speech and freedom of worship. All nations, the Accords said, should respect their citizens' basic human rights.

The Helsinki Accords did bring about some improvement in cooperation between East and West. But the Soviet Union and other Eastern-bloc countries largely ignored the human rights aspects of the Accords. This drew strong criticism from the United States and other Western nations. In part, the disagreement over human rights brought about the end of détente between the United States and the Soviet Union in the late 1970s.

863

EUROPEAN TRADE ASSOCIATIONS

- EC countries
- CMEA countries*
- EFTA countries
- ⊛ National capital

*Non-European countries are also members of CMEA

AZIMUTHAL EQUAL AREA PROJECTION

Learning from Maps *The CMEA does not include all the Communist nations of Eastern Europe. Which Communist nations do not belong to the Warsaw Pact?*

The North Atlantic Treaty Organization. The purpose and policies of the North Atlantic Treaty Organization (NATO) came under close scrutiny during the 1970s, and a number of nations reevaluated their own roles within the alliance. In 1974, in response to the Turkish invasion of Cyprus, Greece withdrew its armed forces from NATO.

Although Greece rejoined the alliance in 1980, it continued to question NATO policies.

During the 1980s the alliance came under the heaviest criticism it had experienced since its establishment in 1949. The placement of American nuclear missiles in a number of European countries touched off protests throughout the continent. The

Greek government continued to oppose the presence of American troops in Greece. And Spain agreed to remain in the alliance only so long as no American nuclear weapons were placed on Spanish soil. Then the United States Congress threatened to reduce American contributions to NATO unless other members agreed to share the burden of maintaining the alliance.

By the late 1980s, European alliance members readily agreed that they had to share defense costs with the United States. They also discovered that the Warsaw Pact conventional forces far outnumbered those of NATO.

The European Community The 1970s and 1980s saw the European Community, or EC, grow from 6 members to 12. After lengthy negotiations Great Britain finally became a member in 1973. Ireland and Denmark also joined that year. Greece became a full member of the EC in 1981, and five years later Spain and Portugal joined the organization. Six other European nations—Austria, Finland, Iceland, Switzerland, Sweden, and Norway —have formed a separate organization called the European Free Trade Association, or EFTA (see map, page 864).

While the EC grew, it made headway toward setting common practices for its members in taxation, credit, and benefits for workers. It also introduced the European Monetary System, hoping that its members would eventually share one currency. In 1986 the EC predicted that its members would achieve full economic integration by 1992. However, these hopes received a blow in 1988 when British prime minister Margaret Thatcher stated that the dream of a single European market should not be at the expense of individual nations.

Politically, European unity also seemed somewhat elusive. Even so, the EC made important steps toward that goal with the creation of such political structures as the European Parliament and the Council of Ministers. At first, the national parliaments of the various members of the EC selected representatives for the European Parliament. In 1979, however, members of the European Parliament were elected directly by the voters.

For the most part, the parliament served an advisory purpose, but during the 1980s it played a greater role in EC decisions on finance and legislation. The Council of Ministers—consisting of representatives from the 12 member states—made most of the important decisions. By the end of the

1980s, these decisions went beyond EC internal matters. For example, the EC strongly denounced South Africa's policy of apartheid and offered its help in the restructuring process underway in Eastern Europe.

SECTION 2 REVIEW

1. **Define** *Ostpolitik*
2. **Identify** Hillsborough Agreement, François Mitterrand, Helmut Schmidt, Helmut Kohl, King Juan Carlos, Andreas Papandreou, Helsinki Accords, European Free Trade Association
3. **Analyzing Ideas** How did Margaret Thatcher change the British government's role in the economy?
4. **Determining Cause and Effect** What caused the reduction of social programs in France under presidents Pompidou and Giscard d'Estaing?
5. **Contrasting Ideas** What were the differences between the foreign policies of the Social Democrats and those of the Christian Democrats of West Germany?
6. **Classifying Ideas** What major political changes took place in Southern Europe during the 1970s and 1980s?
7. **Evaluating Ideas** What progress did the EC make toward economic unity during the 1970s and 1980s?

3 Political Challenges Faced the Soviet Union and Eastern Europe

During the 1950s and 1960s, the Soviet Union crushed challenges to its authority in a number of satellite nations. However, groups within these satellite nations continued to call for greater freedom and autonomy. Then, in the mid-1980s, a new leader undertook the restructuring and liberalization of the Soviet Union itself.

The Soviet Union in the Late 1900s

As the Soviet Union entered the 1970s, it took a firmer grasp on the satellite nations. At the same time, it tried to improve relations with the West.

The Brezhnev years. With the 1968 invasion of Czechoslovakia, Soviet leader Leonid Brezhnev forcefully demonstrated that he tolerated no dissent in the satellite nations. He indicated that nations that strayed from the Soviet line would be dealt with according to the Brezhnev Doctrine. This doctrine gave the Soviet Union the right to intervene in any satellite nation that appeared to be moving away from communism. The Brezhnev Doctrine brought the satellite nations under Soviet control. Although some people continued to call for change, no satellite government attempted reforms as far-reaching as those made during the Prague Spring.

Brezhnev also clamped down on dissent at home. The basic human rights—freedom of speech, of worship, and of movement—were virtually nonexistent. Dissidents, people who criticized the government, usually suffered severe punishment. Some had their union memberships revoked and were thus prevented from working at their chosen careers. Other dissidents, such as the physicist and human rights activist Andrei Sakharov, were sent into internal exile. Still others received harsh prison sentences or were classified as "social misfits" and sent to mental hospitals. In some cases the Soviet government forced them to leave the country. Conversely, it refused to give exit permits to many dissidents, such as Soviet Jews, who wanted to leave the Soviet Union.

While crushing all opposition in both the Soviet Union and the satellite nations, Brezhnev also sought closer ties with the West. He played an active role in détente, or the improvement of Soviet-American relations. He also worked to slow down the arms race. As you have read, he and President Nixon signed SALT I in 1972. In 1979 Brezhnev and President Carter continued this process by signing SALT II. Later that year, however, arms limitation talks and détente came to an abrupt halt with the Soviet invasion of Afghanistan.

Gorbachev takes charge. After Brezhnev's death in 1982, a struggle for leadership began between the "old guard"—people born before the revolution of 1917—and a younger generation of Communist Party members. At first the old guard won control. Yuri Andropov (an • DRO • paf), a former head of the KGB—the Soviet secret police—became the country's leader. In poor health, Andropov held office for less than two years. On Andropov's death Konstantin Chernenko (chur • NEEN • koh), a close associate of Brezhnev, took control. However, Chernenko died just a few months later. The younger generation finally won

the struggle in 1985, when Mikhail Gorbachev became leader of the Soviet Union.

A stagnant economy, a costly and bloody war in Afghanistan, and tensions with the West because of a poor human rights record presented the new leader with major problems. Early in 1986 these problems were compounded by an explosion at a nuclear power plant in Chernobyl, near Kiev. Fears about the safety of other nuclear plants undermined the whole of the Soviet Union's energy policy.

To revitalize the Soviet economy and to combat other problems, Gorbachev introduced two new policies. The first, *glasnost,* or openness, loosened the reins of censorship and eased the repression of the Brezhnev years. Under *glasnost,* the media had more latitude to report sensitive stories. For example, Soviet journalists gave coverage to the disaster at Chernobyl—a story that in the past the Soviet government would have hidden from its people and the world at large. Also, social scientists began to write studies critical of past leaders, such as Stalin and Brezhnev. Artists and writers were allowed greater freedom of expression, and publishers started to circulate the works of long-banned authors. In addition, many dissidents were freed from exile or prison and allowed to leave or travel outside the Soviet Union. And although the Soviet government still frowned on the practicing of religion, in 1988 it allowed celebrations marking 1,000 years of Christianity in Russia.

With the second new policy, *perestroika,* or restructuring, Gorbachev planned to completely overhaul the Soviet political and economic systems. Reforms pushed through by Gorbachev limited the power of the Communist Party, created the new and powerful position of state president, and established a new state legislative body that had broad authority. Gorbachev's political restructuring also limited top government officials' terms of office and called for open and competitive elections.

Gorbachev's economic *perestroika* followed the reforms implemented in Czechoslovakia during the Prague Spring. He shifted many production decisions to on-site farm and factory managers. He also allowed the introduction of free enterprise practices in some areas of the economy. In addition, he tried to create new incentives for increased worker productivity, and he worked to remove corrupt officials from all government economic agencies. Finally, Gorbachev made efforts to shift the emphasis of the Soviet economy from heavy industry to the production of consumer goods.

The following statistics illustrate the challenge facing Gorbachev. In 1988 the population of the Soviet Union was about 284 million. Only about 90 million television sets were in use throughout the country. In addition, only about 50,000 personal computers existed in the Soviet Union. Conversely, the population of the United States reached about 248 million in 1988. Most Americans had at least one television set in their homes, and about 30 million Americans owned personal computers.

A reduction in defense spending. Gorbachev realized that this economic shift could be achieved, in part, by cutting back on defense expenditures. For example, in 1987 Gorbachev joined with President Reagan in signing arms treaties that

Learning from Pictures In Moscow clergy from around the world joined the Russian Orthodox church in celebrating the 1,000th anniversary of Christianity.

eliminated certain types of nuclear weapons and strictly limited the production of others. Then, in a speech before the United Nations in 1988, Gorbachev announced a plan to reduce Soviet conventional forces. By 1990, he said, the number of troops in the Soviet army would be cut by 500,000 soldiers. The vast majority of Soviet troops and tanks deployed in the satellite nations would return to the Soviet Union. And many troops stationed in Soviet border regions would be pulled back. Most NATO and Warsaw Pact countries applauded this step toward disarmament, although some Western leaders expressed reservations as to its effectiveness.

In addition, Gorbachev acted to end Soviet involvement in Afghanistan, which constituted an incredible drain on the economy. Also, with the Soviet death toll standing at more than 13,000, Gorbachev had begun to doubt the wisdom of continuing the war. Therefore, in 1988 he announced his plan to withdraw the more than 125,000 Soviet troops from Afghanistan. By mid-1989 all Soviet troops had been withdrawn.

Challenges to *glasnost* and *perestroika*. Gorbachev's new policies faced challenges both at home and from abroad.

A direct challenge came from the restlessness among national and ethnic minorities. In part, *glasnost* had helped to bring about this restiveness. The new openness prompted people to express opinions that in the past they would have kept to themselves. For example, in 1988 Christian Armenians, who had lived peacefully in a region of the predominantly Muslim Republic of Azerbaijan (az•uhr•by•JAHN), suddenly demanded that the Republic of Armenia annex their region. Ethnic rioting, which claimed the lives of dozens of people, soon followed. Fearful of further violence, close to 100,000 Armenians fled Azerbaijan. Thousands of these refugees were killed in a massive earthquake that struck Armenia in December 1988.

Throughout 1989 an uneasy truce prevailed between the Azerbaijanis and the Armenians who had remained in Azerbaijan. Then in 1990 ethnic rioting erupted yet again in the beleaguered republic. Hundreds of Armenians were killed. Thousands more fled. Soviet leaders declared a state of emergency and sent in troops. Although the troops restored order, fierce resistance by the Azerbaijanis left many dead. At the same time, Azerbaijani leaders called for secession from the Soviet Union. The

Soviets, however, rejected such a possibility, and the troops maintained a strained peace in the republic.

Meanwhile, in the Soviet Baltic republics—Latvia, Lithuania, and Estonia—many people called for greater autonomy. This, they hoped, would come with Gorbachev's political restructuring. However, perestroika centralized power in the office of state president. The Baltic peoples felt that perestroika had not progressed quickly enough. For them, Gorbachev's pledge of political freedoms and a more open economy seemed little more than empty promises. In an attempt to hasten reform, both Lithuania and Latvia legalized noncommunist political parties and actively called for secession from the Soviet Union in 1990. Although Mikhail Gorbachev admitted that secession might be possible, the Soviets worked to keep them in the U.S.S.R.

The movement to hasten reforms and make the Soviet Union more democratic spread to the capital of Moscow in early 1990. There, Russians took part in demonstrations and demanded democracy. Only a few short years earlier, the army would have crushed such outpourings of discontent. Now, however, the Soviet leaders allowed the demonstrations. Then in February 1990, Mikhail Gorbachev bowed to public pressure and announced that the Soviet Union would allow opposition political parties and would work toward becoming a democracy. Although many Western leaders remained skeptical of such promises, people throughout the world looked for signs that the Soviets would live up to their promises. For their part, the Soviet people themselves remained skeptical. Despite reforms, consumer goods remained in short supply, and few people believed that the Communists would give up either their economic or political power.

The Nations of Eastern Europe

The threat of the Brezhnev Doctrine had prevented any real liberalization in Eastern Europe. However, people throughout the region continued to call for reform.

Continued dissent. During the 1970s the governments of the Eastern European nations followed the Soviet line and imposed harsh, repressive measures to end internal dissent. Even so, many Eastern Europeans continued to voice their opposition to totalitarian rule. Writers skirted government censors by issuing **samizdat**—a Russian word

meaning "self-published"—editions of their work. Exchanging manuscripts, the writers typed about a dozen copies of each, which they then passed on to friends. These friends made more copies and passed those on. In time these samizdat editions reached a wide audience.

After the signing of the Helsinki Accords, human rights became a major issue for Eastern European opposition groups. In 1977 a group of about 250 Czechoslovakian artists and intellectuals signed a charter calling on their government to abide by the human rights articles of the Accords. The government quickly branded Charter 77—as the group became known—as a subversive organization and arrested many of its members. Such repression failed to break the spirit of the opposition groups. During the 1980s groups from various countries even began to cooperate in their opposition activities. In 1986, for example, dissidents from Hungary, Czechoslovakia, East Germany, Poland, and Romania jointly issued a statement proclaiming their support for such values as self-government and democracy.

A long period of unrest in Poland that began in 1970 probably posed the greatest threat to communism in Eastern Europe. A few days before Christmas 1970, the Polish government announced huge price increases for food and fuel. About 300 people were killed in the demonstrations and riots that followed.

The atmosphere remained tense in Poland throughout the 1970s. Then, in 1980, a further round of huge price increases was met by a series of strikes. Led by Lech Walesa (vah • WEHN • sah), an unemployed electrician, and a number of shipyard workers, the strikers called for political and economic reforms. In the Gdansk Agreements—named for the Baltic port where the strikes began—the Polish government met many of the strikers' demands, including the right to organize labor unions free of Communist Party control.

The federation of independent trade unions, known as Solidarity, that grew out of the Gdansk Agreements increased in strength during 1981. By the end of the year, membership numbered more than 10 million. Seemingly in a position of power, the leaders of Solidarity called for more concessions from the government. However, in December 1981, under threat of a Soviet invasion, the Polish government imposed martial law, banned Solidarity, and arrested Walesa and other union leaders.

READ
WRITE
INTERPRET
CONNECT
•THINK

BUILDING HISTORY STUDY SKILLS

Thinking About History: Conducting a Debate

A debate is a formal competition between two teams to determine which team has greater skill in speaking and reasoning. The two sides publicly dispute an issue in a systematic way, appealing to logic and reason rather than emotion.

How to Conduct a Debate

To conduct a debate, follow these steps.

1. Select the teams. Select two teams, each composed of two or three members, although the size of the team may vary depending on the debate topic or the format used.
2. State the proposition. A proposition is a thesis statement or conclusion that the teams research and then discuss in the debate. The proposition is most often stated as a resolution. For example:
   Resolved: The United States government should cut back on further developing the space program.
   Resolved: The United States government should raise import quotas to correct the trade deficit.
3. Prepare for the debate. Assign the team members research on the proposition. Team members should organize the information into an orderly and logical outline called a brief. Organize the brief on index cards that may be used during the debate.
4. Conduct the debate. The debate itself should consist of two parts separated by an intermission. In the first part—the constructive speeches—each team presents its arguments. Members of each team speak alternately, beginning with the affirmative team. Each constructive speech is limited to eight minutes. Intermission follows. After the intermission, each team refutes the arguments of the opposing team in four-minute speeches called rebuttals.

Developing the Skill

Read the following proposition as well as the constructive speech of the affirmative side and the rebuttal of the negative side.

Resolved: Soviet leader Mikhail Gorbachev's policy of *perestroika,* or moving the Soviet economy away from a command economy and toward a market economy, will have a positive effect on the Soviet Union as well as on world peace.

Affirmative Constructive Speech: Communism, with its strict command economy, was clearly failing in the Soviet Union. The government's plan of putting capital into defense, rather than into the production of consumer goods, led to scarcity of consumer goods and long lines in stores. By introducing the concept of *perestroika,* Gorbachev has taken a revolutionary step toward improving the Soviet economy.

Laws passed in 1987 allow some free enterprise to exist in the Soviet Union. Soviet citizens are now allowed to own small family businesses. New economic incentives have been given to both managers and workers. There is more reliance on the free market mechanism.

The results of all of this will mean that the Soviet people will have an abundance of high-quality consumer goods. As factory managers and workers are paid according to output, the rate of production will rise. As the free market mechanism begins to regulate the economy, competition will develop, further increasing productivity.

Negative Rebuttal: The idea that *perestroika* will benefit the economy of the Soviet Union and thus the world is unrealistic. It is unreasonable to think that the centralized Soviet economy can be converted to a free market economy. The disruption of Soviet life caused by this restructuring will almost certainly be doomed.

So far the cost of restructuring the Soviet economy into one based on consumerism is squeezing the finances of the average person. Prices in the privately owned shops are much higher than they are in the state-owned stores.

Workers are being asked to work harder while seeing little of the promised incentives. Unemployment is looming as factory managers are now allowed to fire employees.

Finally, even if *perestroika* were to succeed, an economically strong Soviet Union would hardly bode well for world peace. On the contrary, if the Soviets had a thriving economy, they might be inclined to once again invest in military defense.

Practicing the skill. From a recent copy of your local newspaper or a news magazine, find an article dealing with a controversial issue. Use this issue to write a proposition and from this, develop and conduct a debate.

To apply this skill, see Applying History Study Skills on page 873.

Perestroika *at work in a farmer's market*

In 1982, however, Polish leader General Wojciech Jaruzelski (jahr • uhl • ZEHL • skee) lifted martial law and later released Walesa and other union leaders from jail. Demonstrations in support of Solidarity continued through much of the 1980s. After a series of strikes during the summer of 1988, the Polish government once again agreed to discuss political and economic reform with union representatives. The authorities even allowed Walesa to present his case in a debate on national television.

Economic problems. During the late 1970s and 1980s, the economies of the Eastern European nations, in general, began to show signs of fragility. Outdated factories and machinery, products of poor quality, low levels of worker productivity, the imbalanced trade arrangements of CMEA (formerly called COMECON), and a huge foreign debt all contributed to this economic weakness.

Even the "economic miracle" countries of East Germany, Hungary, and Yugoslavia exhibited signs of failure. For example, in Yugoslavia, once one of Eastern Europe's most vigorous economies, industrial output increased only marginally in 1987, and farm output actually fell. The annual rate of inflation reached 150 percent, and unemployment pushed toward 10 percent. Debts owed to other countries proved to be Yugoslavia's most crushing economic problem, however. In 1987, the government had to ask its creditors to reschedule repayment requirements for $19 billion. To combat these growing economic problems, Yugoslavia chose to follow the path taken by most other Eastern European nations. It imposed austerity measures that included huge price increases for food, fuel, and clothing, and tight wage controls.

Responses to *glasnost* and *perestroika*. Most of the Eastern European governments have expressed doubts about *glasnost*. Some have even blamed the policy for problems in their countries. Yugoslavian leaders, for example, have suggested that the resurgence of ethnic and nationalist feelings in their country has resulted from the new openness. However, even though few governments have officially adopted *glasnost*, signs of a new, more open atmosphere have appeared. In 1988 the East German government supported the reopening of a Jewish synagogue in East Berlin that had been closed since the 1930s. The government also relaxed some of its restrictions on other religions. And some observers have suggested that the Polish

government's readiness to negotiate with union leaders in 1988 had more to do with *glasnost* than with political need.

It would seem that since the Eastern European nations had so many economic problems, they would have willingly embraced the new policies of Mikhail Gorbachev. However, the response has been mixed at best. The East Germans, who have had a small private sector since World War II and who experimented with *perestroika* in the 1970s, seemed unimpressed. Czechoslovakian leaders, on the other hand, appeared uninterested in economic reform. One reason for this lack of interest was that after the Prague Spring, reform leaders were ousted from the Communist Party. Some governments, however, expressed concern. Most complaints centered on Gorbachev's wish to integrate the economies of the Communist-bloc countries, which would require the Eastern Europeans to adopt all the economic changes the Soviet Union introduced. A number of Eastern Europeans had other problems with *perestroika*. For example, Karoly Grosz, Hungary's leader, felt that the restructuring did not go far enough. Grosz believed that a capitalist approach—if it proved more effective—should be adopted.

Response among dissidents to the new policies also has been mixed. Some have expressed outright disbelief, while others have voiced skepticism. Still others have proclaimed disgust that these policies—essentially their greatest hope of freedom—have come from the Soviet Union, the country that made their dissent necessary. A number of dissidents, however, have thrown their support to the

Learning from Pictures *During Pope John Paul II's visit to Gdansk, Solidarity mounted a huge demonstration.*

new policies, stating that these changes represent an important step toward democracy in Eastern Europe.

In 1987 Alexander Dubcek, the leader of Czechoslovakia during the Prague Spring of 1968, summed up the feelings of these dissidents.

66 *P*erestroika is indispensable and I support it because I find in it a profound connection with what presented itself to us 20 years ago. Had there been a political leadership in the U.S.S.R. at that time similar to the one today, the military intervention . . . in Czechoslovakia would have been unthinkable. 99

Effects of *glasnost* and *perestroika*. Throughout 1988 and 1989, Eastern Europeans cited *perestroika* and *glasnost* as they urged more and more government reforms. Poland, the birthplace of Solidarity, led the way by allowing noncommunist political parties to participate in the elections in June 1989. The result was that the Communists shared power with several political parties, particularly Solidarity. In August, the newly elected legislature proclaimed Tadeusz Mazoweiki (maz • oh • VEHT • skee) the first noncommunist prime minister in more than 40 years.

Other Communist regimes soon followed Poland's example. All of these nations followed the same pattern. First, the people took to the streets demanding democratic reforms. Party leaders ignored demands and attempted to crush the fledgling reform movements. In country after country, however, the people refused to be suppressed, and Communist party leaders, desperate to retain some of their powers, agreed to reforms. By early 1990, Hungary, Czechoslovakia, Bulgaria, East Germany, and Romania had promised to allow noncommunist political parties and had set elections for mid-1990.

East Germany and Romania proved two of the most dramatic examples of reform. Before 1989 these two nations had perhaps the most repressive Communist regimes in Europe.

In East Germany, Communist party chief Erich Honecker tried to maintain control. Frustrated by the lack of reform, almost 50,000 East Germans obtained permission to visit Czechoslovakia or Hungary and then fled to West Germany during 1989. Citing ill health, Honecker resigned only to be replaced by Egon Krenz—another Communist. On November 9, 1989, amidst growing protest, Krenz informed the world that East Germany would open its borders at midnight. That night thousands of Berliners gathered at the infamous Berlin Wall. At midnight, people raced to break holes in the wall or to climb over it. In the days that followed, the East German Communists—like those of the rest of Eastern Europe—renounced their monopoly on power, and the two Germanies worked on plans to reunify their nation.

The last nation of the Soviet Bloc to grant reforms was Romania where dictator Nicolae Ceausescu (chow • CHES • koo) ruled ruthlessly. Even there, however, the government could not suppress the will of the people. And by the end of 1989 Ceausescu had been driven from power and executed for treason. The new leaders promptly promised free elections.

By 1990 Western observers had become cautiously optimistic about developments in Eastern Europe. Throughout the region governments had caved in to the demands of citizens who had been deprived of basic human and civil rights for years. Democracy appeared attainable. Troop reductions seemed probable. Although few experts believed that the cold war was indeed over, most hoped that the "Iron Curtain" that had sliced through Europe for more than 40 years was disintegrating.

SECTION 3 REVIEW

1. **Define** *glasnost, perestroika, samizdat*
2. **Identify** Andrei Sakharov, Charter 77, Lech Walesa, Gdansk Agreements, Wojciech Jaruzelski, Karoly Grosz
3. **Locate** Azerbaijan, Armenia, Latvia, Lithuania, Estonia
4. **Analyzing Ideas** What impact did *glasnost* have on Soviet society?
5. **Summarizing Ideas** How did *perestroika* change the political system of the Soviet Union?
6. **Determining Cause and Effect** What factors helped to bring about economic failures in Eastern Europe?
7. **Evaluating Ideas** How did Eastern European governments respond to Mikhail Gorbachev's new policies?

Soviet invasion
of Czechoslovakia

Watergate
break-in

OPEC
oil embargo

Helsinki
Accords

AD   1968   1969   1972   1973   1974   1975

Beginnings
of *Ostpolitik*

Withdrawal of
American troops
from Vietnam

Giscard d'Estaing
president of France

Chapter Summary

The following list contains the key concepts you have learned about North America, Europe, and the Soviet Union from 1968 to the present.

1. The Vietnam War had a long-lasting impact on the United States.
2. Many Americans lost faith in their government when the Watergate scandal became public in 1973.
3. Inflation and unemployment were among the economic problems that plagued the United States throughout the 1970s and into the mid-1980s. During President Reagan's administration these problems were reduced.
4. The nature of the American economy changed significantly during the 1970s and 1980s.
5. Efforts were made to ease tensions between the United States and the Soviet Union during the 1970s. The invasion of Afghanistan by the Soviet Union ended these efforts. However, by the mid-1980s, the two countries once again sought better relations.
6. A separatist movement in Quebec threatened Canadian unity during the 1970s.
7. Canadians were uneasy about their economic relations with the United States.
8. During the 1970s many Western European nations turned to conservative governments to solve their economic problems.
9. A number of nations in southern Europe moved from dictatorships to democracies.
10. The purpose and policies of NATO came under close scrutiny from member nations during the 1970s and 1980s.
11. The EC grew in membership during the 1970s and 1980s and made headway toward organizing Europe into an integrated economic unit.
12. During the 1970s the Soviet Union repressed dissent both at home and in its satellite nations. At the same time, it tried to improve its relations with the West.
13. Mikhail Gorbachev introduced a number of changes in the Soviet Union through the policies of *glasnost* and *perestroika*.
14. The nations of Eastern Europe faced such problems as internal dissent and failing economies during the 1970s and 1980s.

On a separate sheet of paper, complete the following review exercises.

Reviewing Important Terms

Supply the term that correctly completes each statement.

1. _____ is the name given to the improvement in relations between the United States and the Soviet Union during the 1970s.
2. West German chancellor Willy Brandt's efforts to create better relations between East and West became known as _____ .
3. Mikhail Gorbachev's policy of _____ loosened the reins of censorship and eased the repression of the Brezhnev years.
4. Through _____ , or restructuring, Mikhail Gorbachev planned to overhaul the political and economic systems of the Soviet Union.
5. Eastern European writers skirted government censors by publishing _____ editions of their works.

Developing Critical Thinking Skills

1. **Analyzing Ideas** **(a)** What economic problems faced the United States in the 1970s and 1980s? **(b)** What policies did presidents Ford, Carter, and Reagan use to try to solve these problems?
2. **Explaining Ideas** Some observers have said that American foreign policy has come full circle since the early 1970s. What did they mean by this statement?
3. **Interpreting Ideas** Why do you think many Canadians have expressed concerns about their country's economic relationship with the United States?
4. **Comparing Ideas** What similarities and differences are there between the political changes that took place in Great Britain and those that took place in West Germany during the late 1970s and 1980s?
5. **Understanding Ideas** Why did some members of NATO begin to question that alliance's purpose and policies during the 1970s and 1980s?
6. **Summarizing Ideas** What progress has the EC made toward political unity in Western Europe?
7. **Organizing Ideas** How did *glasnost* and *perestroika* change life in the Soviet Union?

Jimmy Carter president of the United States

• **Recognition of People's Republic of China by U.S.**
• **Soviet invasion of Afghanistan**

Defeat of separatist referendum in Canada

François Mitterrand president of France

Mikhail Gorbachev leader of Soviet Union

• **Reykjavik summit**
• **Disaster at Chernobyl**

President Mubarek announced support of Palestinian state

1976 1977 1979 1980 1981 1982 1985 1986 1988

Free elections held in Spain

Margaret Thatcher prime minister of Great Britain

• **Election of Ronald Reagan**
• **Gdansk Agreements**

Helmut Kohl chancellor of West Germany

Geneva summit

Earthquake in Armenia

8. **Evaluating Ideas** The Nissan plant in Kentucky below is an example of Japan's economic expansion. Why has it become increasingly difficult for the United States to compete economically with Japan?

Relating Geography to History

Turn to the map on page 864. **(a)** How many nations belong to the EC? **(b)** Where are the majority of EFTA nations located? **(c)** According to the map, how do the EC and CMEA differ? **(d)** In your opinion, what problems does the EC face in building an integrated economy in Europe?

Relating Past to Present

1. Canada's uneasiness about its relationship with the United States is not new. Using information in this textbook and in encyclopedias, trace the development of this feeling among Canadians, describing when these feelings have surfaced in the past.
2. Many political scientists have noted the similarities between the reforms introduced in Czechoslovakia during the Prague Spring and Mikhail Gorbachev's policies of *glasnost* and *perestroika.* **(a)** What similarities do you see between the two? **(b)** Explain your answer.

Applying History Study Skills

Before completing this activity, review Building History Study Skills on page 869.

Conduct a debate by using the following steps and proposition or thesis statement.

Resolved: The nations of Western Europe should achieve political as well as economic unity.

1. Select teams.
2. State the proposition.
3. Prepare for the debate.
4. Conduct the debate.

Investigating Further

1. **Presenting an Oral Report** Relations between Canadians who speak English and Canadians who speak French have occasionally been tense. Prepare a report on the differences between these two cultural groups. Your report should also include a discussion of recent trends toward separatism and away from it. Consult the *Readers' Guide to Periodical Literature* for articles on these topics. Present your report to the rest of the class.
2. **Constructing a Diagram** Use resources in the library to gather information on the relative troop and weapon strengths of the NATO and Warsaw Pact alliances. Then construct a diagram comparing these strengths. Display your diagram on the bulletin board.

873

The Modern World Faced the Challenge of Rapid Change

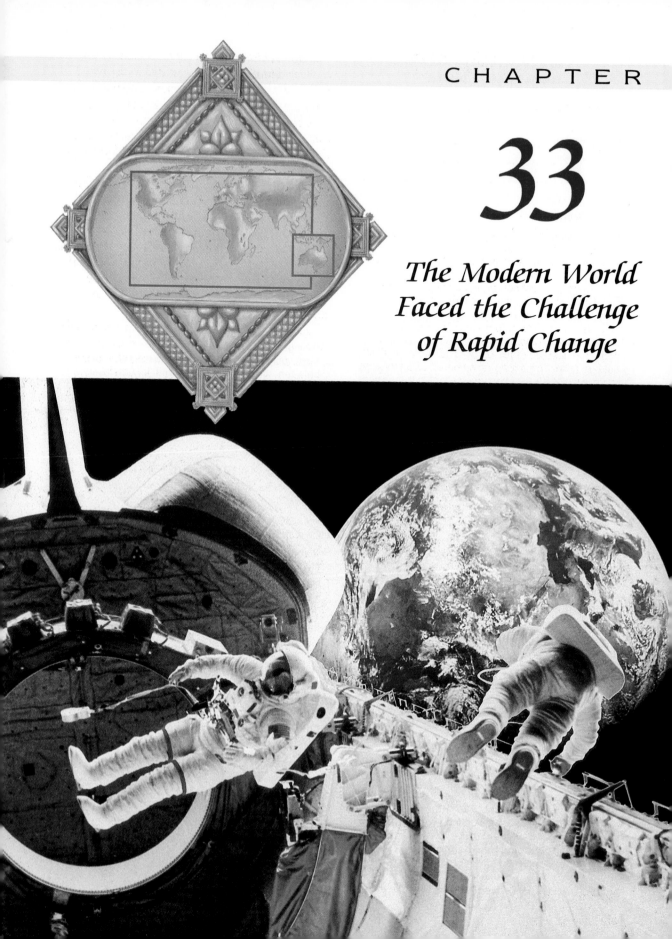

Place The world and beyond

Time 1945 to the present

3.7 mil. BC   4000 BC   AD 2100

Significance

Vast changes in people's life styles and attitudes about the world marked the years following 1945. The emotional scars of World War II remained, but people rebuilt their lives.

Advances in technology and communication unified the world community. Satellites made it possible for millions of television viewers, otherwise separated by distance and ideas, to witness historic events as they occurred. Although it was an American spacecraft that first achieved a manned lunar landing, astronaut Neil Armstrong represented all people on earth when in 1969 he became the first human being to set foot on the moon.

In the 1970s and 1980s the United States embarked upon an ambitious space exploration program. Television coverage of successful launches became almost routine. Then on January 28, 1986, millions of horrified television viewers watched in disbelief as the space shuttle *Challenger* exploded shortly after lift-off. The crew of seven American astronauts perished, and people all over the world shared the tragedy.

Though people remain separated by geography, cultures, and governments, we are all members of the world community. We laugh and cry. We share some victories and some defeats—we are human beings journeying together on the spaceship *Earth*.

Terms to Define

miniaturization	pop art
antibiotics	op art
abstract expressionism	process art

People to Identify

Neil Armstrong	Ralph Ellison
Steven Spielberg	James Baldwin

Places to Locate

Ethiopia	Marseilles

Questions to Guide Your Reading

1 How did technological change affect ideas and behavior after World War II?
2 What direction did the arts and literature follow after World War II?
3 Why did patterns of living take new forms?

Throughout history the lure of the unknown has challenged people's courage, tested their ingenuity, and inspired them to embark upon dangerous quests. Over time many individuals and groups of people have blazed the trail of human progress. Many have come before our time, and many will come after our time. But each era of history has provided unique challenges to the people of the world.

We live in an era of rapid change. Many ideas that existed only in dreams and science fiction 40 years ago have become a reality in the 1980s. Children of the 1940s could only imagine what it would be like to travel in space. Today children can hear the giant engines of the space shuttle roar to life and then watch the massive white spacecraft slice through the clouds in search of new information about the universe beyond.

Other frontiers remain on earth—in science labs where new treatments for disease are discovered; in computerized industries and businesses that bring changes to our lives; and in classrooms, where traditional knowledge and current ideas spark creativity in a new generation that will discover new frontiers and enhance the quality of human life.

1 Technological Change Affected Ideas and Behavior

Dramatic advances in technology after World War II affected all the nations of the world. Although industrialized societies felt the effects most directly, inventions and new devices also brought changes to developing nations.

It would be impossible to list all the discoveries and applications of new ideas that affected the way people thought or lived after 1945. However, a look at some of the most spectacular will illustrate the broad range and sweeping significance of the advances that have taken place in these decades of rapid change.

Air Travel

Improvements in airplanes transformed travel throughout the world. Passenger airliners became larger and faster. In the 1970s the jumbo jet became a common means of transportation. These giant airplanes could easily carry more than 350

◀ *Shuttle astronauts outside the cargo bay*

passengers. One jumbo jet could carry more cargo in a year than could all the airliners in the world in 1939.

The jumbo jet could also fly much farther and faster than earlier airliners. In 1945 a flight from London to New York took at least 15 hours. This trip had to include a stop because the plane could not fly more than 2,000 miles (3,200 kilometers) without refueling. In 1988 a regular jet airliner could complete the trip in less than six hours. The Concorde, a sleek airliner developed by the British and the French, cuts travel time for the same trip to three hours. New technologies may soon make it possible to fly from Washington, D.C., to Tokyo, Japan, in two hours. Today the world's busiest airports serve millions of passengers each year. Although other means of transportation have also advanced rapidly, air travel has become the most popular and convenient way to reach distant places.

Space Exploration

Although Canada, Japan, and several Western European nations have developed space exploration programs, the United States and the Soviet Union have dominated the "space race." In the 1930s and 1940s, engineers experimented with rockets that could fly at incredible speeds. Both the Soviet and the United States space programs achieved several early successes.

Early successes. The "Space Age" began on October 4, 1957, when the Soviet Union launched *Sputnik 1*, the world's first space satellite, into orbit around the earth. Then in 1961 the Soviets built a rocket with enough power to put a person into orbit around the earth, and Soviet astronaut Yuri Gagarin became the first person to travel in space. The United States responded with its own ambitious program for space exploration.

The United States space program expanded rapidly. In 1957 the United States successfully launched an unmanned rocket into space, and in 1961 Alan Shepard became the first American to travel in space. In 1965 the United States promptly responded to the first Soviet space walk with the first American space walk.

Lunar landing. On July 20, 1969, the United States won the intense race to put the first person on the moon. The Apollo 11 mission transported three American astronauts—Neil Armstrong, Edwin Aldrin, Jr., and Michael Collins—to the moon aboard the spaceship *Columbia*. While Collins stayed behind on the *Columbia* to help coordinate the mission, Armstrong and Aldrin descended to the surface of the moon aboard the lunar module, the *Eagle*. The following excerpt from the transmission between *Eagle* at Tranquillity Base on the moon, the orbiting spacecraft *Columbia*, and two control teams—Apollo 11 Control and Mission Control—at the Johnson Space Center in Houston, Texas, illustrates the triumph of this historic event.

"*E*AGLE: Houston, Tranquillity Base here. The Eagle has landed. . . .

HOUSTON: Roger, Tranquillity. Be advised there are lots of smiling faces in this room and all over the world. . . .

HOUSTON (10:37): Neil, this is Houston, what's your status on hatch opening?

TRANQUILLITY BASE: Everything is go here. . . . We're going to try it. The hatch is coming open (Aldrin). . . .

ARMSTRONG: Okay, Houston, I'm on the porch. . . .

HOUSTON: We're getting a picture on TV. . . .

ARMSTRONG: I'm at the foot of the ladder. . . . The surface appears to be very, very fine-grained. . . . I'm going to step off the LM [lunar module] now.

That's one small step for a man, one giant leap for mankind. "

Edwin Aldrin joined Neil Armstrong on the moon's surface and for the next two hours the astronauts took photographs, collected lunar soil and rocks, posted a United States flag, and conducted experiments. About 22 hours after the *Eagle* had landed, the astronauts left the moon and returned to the command module. On July 24, 1969, they returned to earth.

The world watched, listened, and followed the quest for knowledge about space into the 1970s, when the main results of space exploration came from unmanned spacecraft.

Unmanned spacecraft. Following a series of manned moon landings from 1969 to 1972, America's space program shifted its emphasis to unmanned spacecraft that explored farther into our solar system. *Pioneer 10* became the first spacecraft to fly by Jupiter. Then in 1977 and 1978, *Voyager 1* and *Voyager 2* explored the outer planets and provided new information about their makeup. These "flybys" produced spectacular photographs that led researchers to describe Jupiter's mysterious red spot as a giant hurricane in the planet's atmosphere. Other voyages of unmanned spacecraft produced dramatic photographs of Mercury and Venus and of Saturn's majestic rings. Spacecraft also mapped the volcanic peaks and treacherous canyons of Mars. They even landed on the "red planet" in a futile search for life.

Both the United States and the Soviet Union have launched satellites into orbit around the earth. These satellites are divided into three classifications—communications, earth survey, and navigation.

Communication satellites have made 24-hour-a-day global communications possible. Earth survey satellites monitor the weather. Orbiting cameras enable meteorologists to more accurately predict and track life-threatening storm systems. These satellites also offer new ways to improve maps of the world. Navigation satellites enhance ocean and aircraft navigation systems.

New frontiers in space. The 1980s brought even greater American and Soviet successes in space. A new phase of space exploration began in 1981 with the launch of the first American space shuttle, *Columbia*. By 1986 these reusable shuttles, which contained elements of both the traditional space capsule and the airplane, had completed two dozen successful missions. Everyone thought that the launch of the *Challenger* and its crew of seven on January 28, 1986, would be another routine success. However, 73 seconds after lift-off the shuttle exploded in a huge ball of flame. The expected single vapor trail separated into two erratic paths in a crystal-clear sky as the rocket boosters broke away. People watching the launch at the space center or on television gasped in horror. The *Challenger* and its crew were lost. The disaster halted America's manned exploration of space for 32 months.

Learning from Pictures The voyage of Columbia *paved the way for astronauts to conduct medical experiments in the weightless environment of space.*

Then in September 1988 Americans returned to space. Again the world watched—and waited. An excerpt from the cover story in the October 10, 1988, issue of *Time* magazine describes the event.

"*A*s the countdown clock flashed out the number of seconds until lift-off, the eyes of an entire nation focused on Launch Pad 39-B and the gleaming white shuttle *Discovery*, flanked by its two solid rocket boosters and clinging to the side of the giant, rust-colored external fuel tank. . . .

Finally, spectators joined in the last 15 seconds of countdown, the engines ignited and the shuttle rose majestically from the pad, carrying its crew of five veteran astronauts. Over the space center's loudspeakers came the triumphant announcement: 'Americans return to space, as *Discovery* clears the tower.' But the cheers were muted as the crowd— many with clenched fists, gritted teeth and teary eyes—nervously watched the spacecraft rise on its pillar of flame, then begin its roll out over the Atlantic. . . . *Discovery* passed the 73-second mark. . . . A smattering of applause and cheers grew into a chorus near the two-minute mark, when the spacecraft successfully jettisoned its two spent solid rocket boosters. But experienced space observers did not relax until *Discovery* shut down its three main engines 6 1/2 minutes later, shucked off its external fuel tank, then slipped safely into orbit 180 miles [290 kilometers] above the earth. "

In November 1988 the Soviet Union successfully launched an unmanned space shuttle. Manned flights of the Soviet shuttle followed shortly thereafter. The Soviet shuttle appears to be very similar to the American version. However, the Soviet orbiter is powered by a huge disposable rocket rather than the three reusable main engines that propel the United States shuttle.

The successful exploration of space has been hindered by sporadic failures. But the triumphant successes and the benefits of those accomplishments will have far-reaching effects upon the people of the earth. For example, *Spacelab*, a joint venture of the United States and several Western European nations, was launched from a space shuttle in 1983. The laboratory includes facilities for scientists to perform experiments in industry, medicine, astronomy, and many other fields of study. The shuttle carries *Spacelab* and the scientists into space and then returns them to earth, where the lab is readied for its next mission.

The exploration and the conquest of space have already produced significant opportunities and remarkable products for people on earth. The future holds promises for greater opportunities and even more extensive benefits for humankind.

Miniaturization

Rockets can lift only limited amounts of weight. Therefore, to be sent into space, equipment had to be made as light and as compact as possible. An important consequence of space exploration was the invention of ways of making machines, especially electrical equipment, smaller. This process is called **miniaturization.**

The most significant device that resulted from the process of miniaturization is the transistor. This tiny electronic device, invented in 1948, can do the work done previously by a much larger vacuum tube. Entire electronic circuits, consisting of numerous transistors, can fit into smaller spaces and use less electricity than a single vacuum tube.

Miniaturization made possible dozens of new products that affect the lives and leisure activities of people throughout the world. Portable radios, pocket calculators, digital watches, compact tape recorders, and automatic cameras were developed. Initially, these products were expensive and not widely available. However, costs decreased as technology became more advanced and the demand for such products increased. Today many types of electronic products have become common household items. The manufacture of these products has created huge industries and thousands of jobs.

Computers

The most remarkable product of miniaturization was the modern computer. In the 1600s the French scientist Blaise Pascal invented a machine that could perform arithmetical calculations. The idea intrigued scientists and engineers over the next 300 years. However, the necessary machinery was too large and cumbersome to have many practical applications.

In the 1950s scientists developed smaller machines capable of storing and processing information

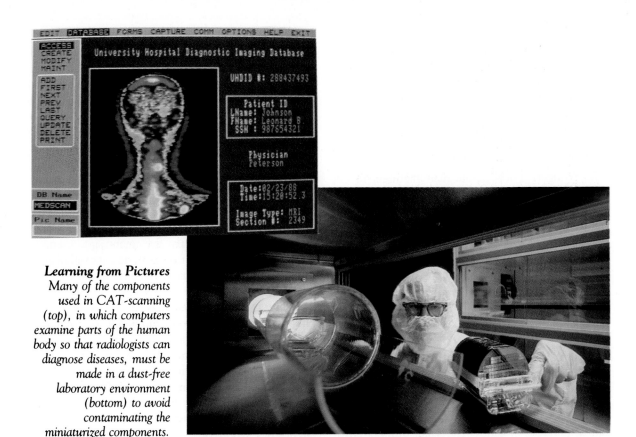

Learning from Pictures
Many of the components used in CAT-scanning (top), in which computers examine parts of the human body so that radiologists can diagnose diseases, must be made in a dust-free laboratory environment (bottom) to avoid contaminating the miniaturized components.

quickly. These computers rapidly made an impact on society and were improved from year to year. They operated more and more quickly and efficiently, while requiring a smaller and smaller amount of space to store gigantic amounts of information.

By the mid-1980s computers performed a multitude of functions. They guided the flights of spacecraft and recorded every airline reservation in the world. Computers also created significant changes in medicine, enabling doctors to diagnose diseases and treat patients more effectively than ever before. A complex machine called the CAT scanner now allows doctors and technicians to view cross sections of all parts of the human body. As a result, many medical problems that would have required extensive exploratory surgery even a few years ago can now be diagnosed with little or no discomfort to the patient. Other computers can detect a broad range of diseases in their earliest and most treatable stages.

In other fields computers draw maps, keep accounts, and print newspapers. Computers also control the flow of fuel to a car's engine and solve complex mathematical questions. Machines with artificial intelligence can now resolve problems in every field that would have been considered impossible 40 years ago.

Computers affect the everyday lives of people in their homes, schools and businesses. Personal computers that play games as well as help families with educational tasks have become as popular as videocassette recorders and compact discs. Businesses use computers to control all types of financial and administrative activities. Computers can even be hooked up to an automobile engine to diagnose specific malfunctions. The range of computer-controlled activities is almost unlimited.

Lasers

In 1960 scientists invented a device called a laser. The laser can store energy and release it all at once in an intense beam of light. This beam remains straight, narrow, and very concentrated, even after it has traveled millions of miles. The laser's uses are extraordinarily varied—a perfect example of the combination of scientific discovery and engineering applications. Surgeons use lasers to weld damaged tissue in the eye, to burn away skin growths, and to repair decayed parts of teeth. A laser procedure that produces no heat allows doctors to clear clogged arteries from the heart by cutting through blockages and vaporizing them without damaging the artery walls. For many people, this procedure has become an alternative to heart bypass surgery.

Lasers help engineers make tunnels and pipelines straight. They enable manufacturers to cut precisely into hard substances, such as diamonds. Lasers also transmit radio, television, and telephone signals. They make it possible to show three-dimensional pictures on a television or film screen. Thus one invention has significantly affected dozens of activities and people from many walks of life.

Genetic Research

In 1962 the Nobel Prize for medicine, the most prestigious scientific award in the world, was given to an American, James D. Watson, and two British scientists, Maurice Wilkins and Francis Crick, who had discovered the structure of DNA (deoxyribonucleic acid) during the 1950s. DNA is an essential component of genes—the small units of chromosomes that convey characteristics, such as color of hair and eyes, from parent to child. By understanding DNA, one can understand how a gene is structured—what scientists call the "genetic code."

By unraveling the genetic code, the DNA experimenters came closer to explaining how different life forms are created. This breakthrough made possible new research into viruses, bacteria, human cells, and diseases such as cancer. Scientists could now reproduce life forms in the laboratory and achieve major advances in treating illness.

Recently scientists have deciphered a second genetic code that directs the synthesis of proteins inside cells. This new discovery will also shed light on some inherited disorders caused by malfunctions in the second code. It completely changes our understanding of the nature of what the molecule does within the cell and allows developments thought impossible only five years ago. Genetic engineers can now alter the genetic material of cells to make specific proteins used to treat diabetes and heart disease.

The genetic engineers' work carries significant implications for future diagnosis and treatment of other diseases. Rapid progress is being made in the treatment of cancer. Scientists have also successfully transplanted the major elements of the human immune defense system into mice. This technique may lead to important breakthroughs in the study of AIDS, the common name for acquired immune deficiency syndrome.

AIDS erupted in the United States in the late 1970s and early 1980s. Since that time it has claimed the lives of approximately 75,000 Americans and is expected to claim millions of lives worldwide over the next few years. Unfortunately, there are no known medicines to cure the disease

Learning from Pictures In order to study atoms, this engineer is operating a particle accelerator that smashes them.

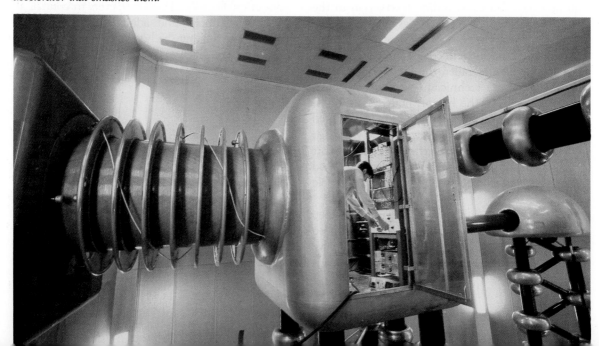

and no vaccines to prevent it. However, treatments have been developed and their effectiveness is being studied over a period of time.

AIDS is not inherited genetically. It is acquired through sexual contact and contaminated needles, usually associated with intravenous drug use. Babies can acquire the AIDS virus before birth from infected mothers. Ultimately the breakthrough in genetic engineering may lead to a cure for AIDS. Until that time local and national education programs continue to teach and warn people of all ages about the causes and effects of the disease.

The Atom

Just as biologists were able to probe inside the cell, physical scientists became more knowledgeable about the smallest of nature's building blocks, the atom. With increasingly powerful instruments, scientists could examine the tiny particles within the atom. They soon learned how to use the energy released when the structure of the atom is altered.

Atomic energy was first used to build more powerful bombs. Later it was used to develop efficient generators to produce electricity for a burgeoning population. Whenever atomic energy is tapped, dangerous radiation, known as radioactivity, is released. When carefully controlled, radioactivity can have extremely beneficial medical uses—for example, in the treatment of cancer. Even peaceful uses, however, have their dangers. Extensive uncontrolled exposure to radioactivity can alter genes and kill life forms. Thus the advances in understanding the atom offered both benefits and dangers.

Plastics

The first synthetic substances—substances that do not occur in nature—were developed by chemists in laboratories in the 1800s. A few of these substances began to have wide applications. For example, celluloid was used to make movie films, and Bakelite was used for electrical equipment. It was not until after 1945, however, that these substances, called plastics, began to appear in every area of life. By the mid-1960s, for example, there was more synthetic rubber than natural rubber in the world.

Plastics became an essential part of daily existence. They completely altered the appearance as well as the manufacture of most of the things people use every day, from toothbrushes to telephones.

Synthetic fibers were woven into easy-care fabrics for clothing and upholstery.

Many plastics are made from petroleum products. The availability—and price—of plastics, therefore, depends on the unpredictable nature of international oil prices.

Antibiotics

In 1928 Alexander Fleming discovered penicillin, noting that it stopped the growth of many types of disease-carrying bacteria. Thus it could help cure illnesses caused by those bacteria. In the years after Fleming's discovery, other substances were found to have similar effects. Streptomycin, which was discovered in 1944, attacked bacteria that could resist penicillin. Substances that kill bacteria are called **antibiotics,** and after 1945 they transformed the fight against disease. They cured certain illnesses, such as tuberculosis, that previously had no cure, and they lessened the risk of infection following surgery. The use of antibiotics also improved the health of animals used for food. Although some bacteria came to resist antibiotics, these medicines became essential in reducing sicknesses and preventing contamination of food.

The "Green Revolution"

Through intensive research, scientists in the 1960s developed seeds that yielded much more rice and wheat than ever before. The use of better fertilizers and advances in irrigation techniques further improved the new seeds.

The ability to feed large numbers of people became increasingly critical as the world's population grew to about 5 billion by 1988. Unfortunately, most of the fastest-growing countries are also the poorest and the least able to provide food both for their own people and for export. In the 1980s, for example, Ethiopia, a mountainous nation in northeastern Africa, was unable to cope with a long period of drought and famine that plagued the country. Millions of people starved to death.

Ethiopia's plight concerned people from many other nations of the world. Food supplies eventually became available; but for many Ethiopians, especially children, the help came too late. Ethiopian leaders are now directing their efforts toward long-range agricultural development that will help replenish the soil and produce more food.
Text continues on page 884.

The history of fortifications began with prehistoric people. Cowering in caves or behind rocks or trees, early people hid from their enemies. Their two purposes were to protect themselves from attack and position themselves to strike back against the enemy. Throughout history, fortresses have met such needs.

Of course, different circumstances produced different kinds of fortresses. Wealthy societies such as the Roman Empire and modern France built very elaborate walls. Poor societies such as those of northern Europe in the early Middle Ages dug ditches around their towns.

As societies grew stronger, so did their fortifications. Earthen walls or wooden stockades were replaced by masonry. The Egyptians, the Assyrians, and the early Greeks all built walled cities. Some walls were built across open country to protect farmlands. A wall 50 miles (80 kilometers) long was built about 800 B.C. to safeguard the ancient city of Babylon and its surrounding territory against the hostile Medes.

The Roman Empire protected its frontiers with walls. Hadrian's Wall stretched for 73 miles (117 km) across northern England to shelter Roman territory from the "savages" of Scotland. Another Roman wall system (the *Limes*) stretched from the Rhine to the Danube. About 250 B.C. the Chinese, another wealthy society, built the largest wall of all, the Great Wall of China, to keep out the Huns.

After the western half of the Roman Empire crumbled and western Europe became a poor, rural land, there were no more great nations to build great walls. When raiders—such as the Vikings—threatened, everyone had to fend for themselves. Small castles began to spring up everywhere. They often began as little more than a ditch and a wooden stockade.

In eastern Europe, however, the Roman Empire remained strong, and so did the fortresses. Constantinople was surrounded by a massive system of walls. Attacking Arabs found it impossible to penetrate such mighty defenses.

The invention of gunpowder and siege cannon seemed to spell the end of walled cities. By 1350 attackers were using cannons with success against the castles of French nobles. In 1453 Constantinople's walls,

The 1900s also brought the greatest failure in fortifications—the Maginot Line. This was an "impregnable" defense system built by the French in the 1930s along the German border. The Maginot Line consisted of gun emplacements, underground fortresses, and miles of tunnels. The Germans, instead of attacking this formidable bulwark, simply went around it through Belgium. There they captured the fort at Eban Emael, the strongest fortress in Europe and the key to the Belgian defenses, with glider troops in a few hours. Thus the two strongest fortifications in the world, believed to be impenetrable, were overcome as though they hardly existed.

Some fortified cities in World War II held out for months, even years. But at the war's conclusion, atomic bombs on Hiroshima and Nagasaki showed that today no wall is strong enough or trench deep enough.

Great fortifications are relics of the past.

Photos Page 882: Alcazar castle (top), Walled City of Carcassone (bottom); Page 883: Walls of Jericho (top left), Gibraltar (center); Masada (bottom)

which had stood against attack for 1,000 years, tumbled under the fire of Turkish artillery.

But fortresses did not vanish. The 1500s and 1600s brought a new kind of walled city. Bastions were built jutting from the main wall. From them defenders could fire on attackers from several directions.

In the 1800s and 1900s, reinforced concrete made fortifications stronger than ever before in history. Many cities were now protected by rings of steel and concrete forts armed with heavy artillery. But the attackers soon learned how to cope with these new defenses. In the attack on Russia's Pacific stronghold of Port Arthur, Japan's General Nogi wasted 15,000 lives in futile infantry assaults before he found the key to success in his 280-millimeter howitzers. These giant guns could fire shells upward so that they descended on Port Arthur's defenders at a steep and deadly angle.

In 1914 the Germans opened their way through Belgium in the same way. They crushed the massive defenses at the city of Liege with huge howitzers. This was in World War I—the same war that saw a return to the most basic fortification, the ditch. The killing power of modern weapons—especially the machine gun—forced soldiers to dig trenches. By Christmas of 1914, an unbroken line of trenches extended on both sides of the French-German front from the English Channel to Switzerland. In the end, the deadly stalemate of trench warfare broke only when Germany's forces cracked from exhaustion.

Commercial Applications of Technology

Since 1945 technological advances have virtually transformed the world. Devices such as telephones, radios, refrigerators, and cameras had been known before 1945. However, only after 1945 were they manufactured cheaply enough to be bought by millions of people. These products are more common in the industrialized nations, but they have also had an enormous impact on the developing nations of the world.

What was so remarkable in the period after 1945 was the widespread application of these modern products. Entire new industries, such as television and computer manufacturing, sprang up. Millions of people were employed in new kinds of jobs, and world markets flourished as nations imported and exported the products of the new technological age. What appears to be almost unbelievable advancement of such technology may be only the beginning of future technological developments.

2 The Arts and Literature Followed New Directions

Two trends became particularly noticeable in the arts and in literature after 1945. One was the commitment to experimentation, which had been evident since the early 1900s. The other was the enormous popular interest in artistic and intellectual developments.

Painting and Sculpture

After 1945 New York City became one of the liveliest centers of new ideas and painting styles. The dominant style of painting was **abstract expressionism.**

The leading abstract expressionist was an American, Jackson Pollock. Pollock believed that the form, colors, and shapes of a painting constituted its most important features. A painting did not have to show recognizable objects; therefore, it was abstract. At the same time, it had to reflect the nature of the artist who was expressing feelings or ideas in paint.

Pollock chose to express himself by randomly dripping different colors of paint onto the surface of a canvas spread out on the floor. When the paint dried, his painting was finished.

Other abstract expressionists used different techniques. Mark Rothko, also an American, created large areas of rich colors. The colors blurred into one another, creating a dazzling effect.

In the 1950s painters moved away from abstract expressionism to experiment in other ways. It was no longer possible to speak of one dominant style. In Great Britain and the United States, a number of artists returned to showing reality—but a special kind of reality. Developing a style called **pop art,** these artists chose as their subjects popular objects such as soup cans, pictures from comic books, or flags.

Experimentation could also be seen in the sculpture of the period. The American sculptor Louise Nevelson, for example, created monumental designs out of "found" objects, such as wooden boxes.

New styles of painting arose in the 1960s. One small group concentrated on **op art**—the use of optical effects. These artists rejected reality as the subject of paintings, instead using brilliant colors and shapes. Another group, the "hard-edge" school, produced bright stripes and slabs of color with well-defined edges.

The 1970s and 1980s saw a return to realism in paintings of scenes, objects, and people. Experiments continued, however, and all styles seemed acceptable in the art world.

Although the earlier art styles remained popular and many classic works of art increased in value, during the 1970s and 1980s many people also came to appreciate folk art, the work of talented but not necessarily professionally trained painters, sculptors, and craftspeople. Folk art has been popular in many nations of the world for centuries. Because it reflects everyday life and often portrays social, political, or religious views of people who live in a particular place, it is a source of information as well as enjoyment.

The modern age has led artists to incorporate views from outer space and futuristic technology into their work. In the 1980s the title "artist" has come to include photographers, filmmakers, ceramists, glassblowers, and electricians. The artist's materials range from the traditional canvas, paint, marble and bronze to materials such as plastic and scrap metal. Modern art forms may be welded, wired, glued, sewn, or lighted. Today some artists even construct and paint images from sand or create artistic patterns in plowed fields. Skywriting has also become increasingly popular, especially in urban areas.

Current art trends also include **process art** and **conceptual art.** Both of these art trends reduce the emphasis on isolated art objects and focus instead on the arrangement of "environments" composed of both objects and people. Process artists believe that the process of creating the art is more important than the actual art object. Conceptual art carries this idea one step further with the claim that creative thought is more important than either the process or the product created.

Architecture

The search for new ideas and techniques dominated architecture, as it had since the invention of the skyscraper in the early 1900s. Since 1945 materials have changed almost yearly.

One popular new material was rough-cast concrete. This mixture contains pebbles and creates a grainy, rough finish. A pioneer in the use of this technique was French architect Charles-Édouard Jeanneret, known as Le Corbusier (luh kor • BUEZ • yay), one of the most influential architects of the century. Between 1946 and 1952, Le Corbusier built an enormous apartment complex in Marseilles, France, using rough-cast concrete.

The opposite effect, smoothness and polish, also interested architects. They created this smoother look mainly by using huge walls of glass. Le Corbusier himself took this approach when he designed the headquarters of the United Nations in New York City. One of the UN buildings has two enormous walls of glass, with narrow walls of solid concrete at each end. The Lever House in New York City, completed in 1952, set the pattern for a

Learning from Pictures *The skylines of the world's cities, such as Dallas, have changed dramatically with modern architectural innovations.*

READ
WRITE
INTERPRET
● CONNECT
THINK

BUILDING HISTORY STUDY SKILLS

Making Connections with History: Linking Architecture to History

Architecture often reflects the values of a culture. The skyscraper is both the triumphant symbol of, and at the same time, an unwelcome intruder into, the city. It shatters scale and steals light, yet it suggests the personality of the city of which it is a part. It has also made the city's character a reflection of its own quality. For example, the Sears Tower in Chicago and the Empire State Building in New York City are the symbols of these metropolitan areas just as the Cathedral of Notre Dame is a symbol of Paris. Linking architecture to history helps historians explain how the environment affects a society, determine the individual's reaction to the environment, and visualize the society's values.

How to Link Architecture to History

To link architecture to history, follow these steps.
1. Establish the historical context of the architecture.
2. Identify the society that built the structure.
3. Identify the major characteristics of the architecture.
4. Describe characteristics of the environment.
5. Relate the environmental characteristics to the historical context.
6. Identify the values expressed by linking the historical context and the environmental characteristics.

Developing the Skill

Analyzing the skyscraper's architecture helps you link architecture to modern history. The skyscraper has become the symbol of the twentieth-century American city. It defines life in the metropolis.

Skyscrapers began to rise above 40 stories by 1910. These towering symbols of urbanization housed more than offices—they also included stores and restaurants. Their lobbies became so large that they became gathering places. The massive arcades became a city within a city.

One example of the skyscraper is the Woolworth Building in New York City. Completed in 1913, it gracefully extends 792 feet (241 meters) above the ground. Although the building is perceived as a sheer tower, its base consists of a 29-story U-shaped mass. Rising from the center front of the structure is a square tower that culminates in an ornate crown at the top. The vertical lines of the base shoot up into the tower, melding the upper and lower masses together.

The architecture of a particular society also reveals more than cultural values—it reveals information about the economic characteristics of a society. For example, an impressive building is a symbol of a successful corporation. The visual effect of massive buildings suggests corporate glory and represents human ability and technical achievement. In the modern age, skyscrapers have become the cathedrals of commerce.

Practicing the skill. Select several books from the library that include photographs of buildings in foreign cities. Then write a brief explanation of the architecture's correlation to the culture and history of that country.

To apply this skill, see Applying History Study Skills on page 895.

Woolworth Building

ARCHITECTURE

Sydney Opera House

Like a ship with its sails set for the future, the Opera House dominates the harbor in Sydney, Australia. Built on a peninsula, the building consists of a series of concrete shells that house a center for the performing arts.

Despite its geographical isolation from continental Europe, Australia has maintained a strong British heritage. After World War II, however, many European refugees settled in the island continent. They have helped to make the nation's culture more international.

Thus, when the Australian government decided to build a center to celebrate the arts, it sponsored a worldwide competition to choose an architect. Joern Utzon, a Dane,

was the winner. His building rests on a high platform, and the shells rise more than 200 feet (60 meters) above ground level. Utzon's structure contains four theaters—a concert hall, an opera theater, a drama theater, and a chamber music and

film hall—each acoustically perfect for the type of performance it holds. Completed in 1973, the Sydney Opera House is among the most recognizable buildings in the world and is considered to be a masterpiece of modern architecture.

---

wave of skyscrapers sheathed in glass and supported on the inside by steel and reinforced concrete.

Architects also experimented with new ways of building houses. Some houses were cast in concrete in standard units and then shipped to the building site. Others made use of new plastic materials.

New shapes appeared in architectural designs. Notable among these unusually shaped buildings is the group of concrete shells that make up the Sydney Opera House in Australia. The spiral-shaped form of the Guggenheim Museum in New York City was designed by the American architect Frank Lloyd Wright, a leader in the use of unconventional shapes.

In the 1970s and 1980s, architectural designs assumed more contemporary lines. The rapid development of new engineering techniques prompted the construction of domed stadiums such as the Astrodome in Houston, Texas. Graceful contemporary lines also appeared in buildings erected for the Summer Olympic Games in Los Angeles, California, in 1984, and in Seoul, South Korea, in 1988. Other distinctive buildings were constructed

for the winter Olympic Games in Sarajevo, Yugoslavia, in 1984 and in Calgary, Canada, in 1988.

Architectural designs of the 1980s emphasized spaciousness and employed innovative features. Some modern homes combined attractive and practical design with solar energy or other devices to save fuel. Many cities had buildings with unique designs, large expanses of glass, or gleaming mirrored tiles that reflected light.

Amid all these new ideas and techniques, no single design or method of building has dominated architecture in the years after 1945. Experimentation has led to a wide variety in architectural styles since World War II.

Music and Dance

Experimentation has been equally apparent in the world of music. New uses of instruments, rhythm, harmony, and melody were introduced. Some composers, however, did write traditional types of music. The British composer Benjamin Britten, for example, wrote operas. The Russian composer

Learning from Pictures *Even before Mikhail Gorbachev initiated* glasnost, *Soviet youths jammed rock and roll concerts.*

Dmitry Shostakovich (shahs•tuh•KOH•vich) wrote symphonies divided into four distinct movements, which had been the standard form since the late 1700s.

After 1945 new kinds of sound entered the world of serious music. Experimenters found that computers could produce sounds. Innovative composers wrote pieces for special machines known as synthesizers or for combinations of traditional instruments and synthesizers.

Composers also began to write music that gave performers a major role in determining how a piece would sound. The composer might provide a few notes and some instructions. Then the performer could decide the order, length, and mood of a composition. The pioneer of this method was an American composer, John Cage.

The determination to break new ground, to leave the past behind, was especially obvious in popular music. During the 1950s a form of music known as rock and roll was created in the United States. It had a heavy, accented beat and a simple, repetitive melody. A number of different styles, with such names as folk rock, hard rock, punk rock, and disco, soon developed.

Another form of popular music, country and western music, usually consisted of sentimental ballads. Black* musicians developed such styles as soul music and rhythm and blues.

These musical forms spread rapidly throughout the world, especially among teenagers. A new song quickly became as familiar to the young in Indonesia as in Indiana. The most successful performers became world famous. These individuals and groups toured extensively, and their concerts were sometimes broadcast throughout the world by satellites.

The world of dance also followed new directions after 1945. Artists who had left Russia after its revolution were especially influential in ballet. The greatest of these artists was George Balanchine. He continued in the United States the traditions that had made Russia such an influential center of ballet in the 1800s and 1900s. In the 1960s and 1970s, young ballet stars who came from the Soviet Union to make their careers in the West joined Balanchine.

After 1945 the freer and looser forms of modern dance influenced ballet. An American, Martha Graham, was the most influential teacher of modern dance. She collaborated with ballet dancers in trying to combine the two forms. The use of more modern music to accompany the dancers forced performance changes. As in all the performing arts, the tendency was to leave uniformity

---

*In the mid-1980s, there was a growing movement to use the name African Americans instead of Black Americans.

behind, to experiment, and to allow more individual expression.

Film

Traditional subjects—adventure stories, comedies, and social dramas—dominated most filmmaking after 1945. Spectacular productions, costing millions of dollars, continued to be popular. Other films, however, made efforts to break free of traditional restrictions. In the 1940s and 1950s, a group of Italian directors produced shattering attacks on social and political injustice. French filmmakers known as the "New Wave" created experimental movies in the 1950s and 1960s. They rejected traditional storytelling techniques and created instead a mysterious and powerful atmosphere in their films. Japanese director Akira Kurosawa's films used violence and psychological insight to create startling new effects.

Technical mastery was particularly evident in American films. A number of directors turned their attention to themes about ordinary people or how outside influences affected the pattern of family life. For example, Steven Spielberg became famous for producing films such as *E. T. —The Extraterrestrial* and *Back to the Future*. By the 1980s filmmaking had become a major art form around the world.

Drama

In the theater, too, important new techniques developed. In East Germany the company founded by playwright Bertolt Brecht staged plays with an emphasis on artificiality. The members of the audience were not to be drawn in but were to be constantly reminded that they were watching a play. In Great Britain traditional forms of Asian drama influenced theatrical productions. Greater emphasis was placed on the actors' spontaneous reactions. Performers were encouraged to improvise, and thus to create something new each night. In South Africa a black theater group emerged from the black-liberation movement. In a presentation called *Asinamali,* which in Zulu means "We have no money," black actors portrayed prisoners of the South African apartheid regime.

Perhaps the most powerful new vision of the modern age was the biting social commentary of the playwrights of the so-called theater of the absurd. Its leaders were Samuel Beckett and Eugène Ionesco, an Irishman and a Romanian, respectively, who lived in France.

Beckett's most famous play, *Waiting for Godot* (1956), is a long, apparently aimless dialogue between two tramps. It portrays a bleak world in which human beings have great difficulty communicating. The play has no real plot and makes no attempt to bring out the character of the two tramps. Bewilderment and absurdity run throughout Beckett's works. These qualities are apparent also in the plays of Ionesco, such as *Rhinoceros* and *The Bald Soprano.*

More realistic but no less biting attacks on modern society were apparent in the works of other playwrights of this period. The most notable of these dramatists were John Osborne, an Englishman, and Arthur Miller, an American. Miller's powerful dramas explored human weaknesses and the tensions in families. Another American, Tennessee Williams, looked at similar themes in the society of the American South.

Social analysis and comment even entered the boisterous world of American musical theater. To some, the most remarkable musical of the post-1945 period was *West Side Story.* It recounted the struggles between rival gangs of New York teenagers. Leonard Bernstein, the noted composer and conductor, wrote the score.

In 1988 Andrew Lloyd Webber directed *The Phantom of the Opera,* a mystery about a ghost's love for a lady singer at the Paris Opera. The plot develops as a young nobleman rekindles his boyhood interest in the singer but notices that she is under a strange influence. As the story unfolds, the nobleman discovers the presence of the phantom in the opera, and the audience learns the phantom's identity.

Poetry and Novels

The aim of these playwrights was to take a stand against the comfortable assumptions of an ever more complicated world. Society's most prosperous citizens and their values were the target of another group of writers, the so-called Beat Generation. These poets and novelists, most of them living in San Francisco and New York City, began writing in the 1950s. They attacked the commercialism they saw in America. They thought writing should be completely spontaneous, and they rejected the traditional forms of the novel and the poem.

Protest was a major theme of the leading writers of the postwar years. The most powerful black American writers were Ralph Ellison and James Baldwin. Each explored, with dismay and anger, the life of a black person in the United States. Nigerian novelist Chinua Achebe examined the effects of colonial rule on his native land. The leading German novelists, Günter Grass and Heinrich Böll, explored Hitler's impact on Germany. Boris Pasternak and Alexander Solzhenitsyn wrote savage descriptions of the repressions of the Soviet system.

Another major theme of postwar literature was escape from an increasingly hostile and confusing world. Writers like the American Kurt Vonnegut, Jr., created fantasies about imaginary worlds. They used these fantasies to suggest alternatives to what they saw as the brutality and uncaring behavior of the times.

Prominent Latin American writers chose a similar approach. Octavio Paz, a Mexican poet, contrasted the savagery and the civilized grace of his country's history in surrealistic, dreamlike poems. The Colombian Gabriel García Márquez and the Mexican Carlos Castaneda wrote mystical novels that move puzzlingly through time. Castaneda implied that ordinary people cannot achieve profound levels of wisdom.

Not all writers and poets emphasized protest or disturbing uncertainties. Some, like the American poet Wallace Stevens, enjoyed the traditional poetic function of celebrating nature. Many of his poems try to capture the lushness of the tropics. Another American poet, Marianne Moore, urged poets to be genuine and useful, and to write about topics ordinary people could understand. Attacking snobbery, she cited business documents and school books as acceptable subjects for her poetry. She liked to quote from magazines in her poems, and she wrote one poem to celebrate her favorite baseball team, the Brooklyn Dodgers.

The variety of the interests and styles of poets and novelists was astonishing. Never before had so many books been published. During 1987 in the United States alone, more than 7,500 titles in fiction, poetry, and drama were published.

The Audience for the Arts

The excitement of postwar artistic and literary activity generated enormous public appeal,

Learning from Pictures   *This audience in Buenos Aires, Argentina, enjoys an opera at the Colón Theater.*

particularly in the United States. Between 1950 and 1988, Americans spent more than half a billion dollars to construct new museums and art centers. More Americans paid to go to museums, concerts, operas, ballets, or theaters each year than those who paid to attend sporting events.

Throughout the world, more people are completing the equivalent of a high school education, and more people are going to college. People have more time for leisure activities, particularly in industrialized countries. Television exposes more people to more kinds of cultural activities. TV brings music, dramatizations of books, plays, and movies to millions of people at home. Many people continue to seek similar entertainment outside the home. Thus education, extra leisure time, and a new awareness have combined to give the arts and literature greater support than they have ever enjoyed before.

3 Patterns of Living Took New Forms

As opportunities multiplied and the pace of life speeded up in industrialized nations, the way people spent their lives changed drastically. Change in developing nations was less dramatic, but there, too, the quickening pace was narrowing the gap between old and new ways of life.

Life Styles

In the decades that followed World War II, women entered the work force as never before. In the 1980s women have had more occupational opportunities than at any other time in history. Today busy families juggle work schedules and responsibilities at home in order to enjoy the rewards of careers and a higher standard of living than their parents and grandparents experienced.

Another feature of life after 1945 that set it apart from life in earlier periods was the speed with which things happened. Illnesses that once would have required months of recovery were cured in a few days with new medicines of the 1980s. A worker might live many miles away from a job, but because of expressways and other improvements related to transportation, he or she could travel from home to work in less than an hour. After

work, people could relax at home and watch live coverage of sports events on television. If a person wanted a quick meal, he or she could go to a so-called fast-food restaurant and get almost any kind of food in less than a minute.

An important result of these changes, especially in developed nations, was a greater amount of leisure time. However, people sometimes experienced a restlessness and uncertainty about the best way to spend their time. The use of drugs, the number of crimes committed, and the rate of divorce all increased markedly. Despite these problems, additional leisure time also made possible the pursuit of new interests and opportunities.

Another factor that increased leisure time in developed nations was the shortening of the working year as machines took over more work. Families took vacation trips for granted, especially as travel became cheaper and easier. Even in developing nations, television and movies brought news and entertainment to remote villages.

As a result of rapidly changing life styles after 1945, attitudes and behavior changed rapidly. But it was far from clear what the long-term consequences of advanced technology and more leisure time would be.

The Search for Stability

Amid rapid changes, people looked for anchors of stability. Many renewed their commitment to religion.

In the developing nations, a major response to technological progress was a return to traditional beliefs. For example, the 1970s saw a strengthening of Islam in the Middle East accompanied in many cases by a rejection of non-Muslim ideas and developments.

In Western countries, Christian revivalism had an impact, perhaps for similar reasons. The religious renewal among Christians took a number of forms. In 1962 Pope John XXIII, then head of the Catholic church, called a special council to the Vatican. The effects of the council, which came to be known as Vatican II, were wide reaching. The council modernized the Roman Catholic religious service. It also condemned anti-Semitism and called for reconciliation among all Christian churches.

The worldwide movement, which sought unity among Christians, made some progress after the

891

1960s and remains a vital concern among Christians today.

Social Concerns

Another feature of the world after 1945 was the heightened sense of social concern. In earlier ages, one nation cared little about the rights and freedoms of the people in another nation. One country might help a revolution in another country, but the oppression of citizens was usually considered to be an internal problem.

Harsh conditions became more widely noticed after 1945. The Red Cross, founded in 1863, had long been devoted to relief work after disasters, especially war. Now the United Nations established agencies to deal with refugees and hungry children, and to provide medical care. In addition, other new organizations were formed. Amnesty International tried to help political prisoners and mistreated prisoners all over the world. Oxfam devoted itself to relieving famine. After the civil war in Nigeria in the 1960s and the destruction of Cambodia in the 1970s, Oxfam and other organizations fed millions of starving people.

Repressive governments were pressured to ease conditions for their citizens. The Soviet Union, for instance, was urged to give its citizens certain rights—such as the right to emigrate. As a result of these efforts, thousands of Jews, many of whom had been severely treated, were permitted to leave the Soviet Union. Similar pressures were applied to harsh governments in Africa and the Middle East. For example, South Africa was expelled from the United Nations because of its apartheid policy.

In Latin America the criticism was less consistent. The Catholic church became the main force for social change. Priests were often the main critics of governments and the most prominent activists seeking reforms and helping the distressed.

Some concerns went beyond the policies of specific governments. The continuing growth of the world's population, especially in poorer countries, caused worries about food shortages. Another concern was the growing awareness that the world's resources are limited. Oil and such vital metals as copper and chromium appear likely to become more scarce.

Perhaps the most crucial endangered resource was the environment itself. As industries grew, and as developing countries struggled to create their own industries, the air, the oceans, and the earth became polluted by industrial waste products. New international organizations arose to tackle these

Learning from Pictures
Religion continues to be a strong social force in the modern world, as this worship service indicates.

Learning from Pictures *Protesters march to show their opposition to nuclear energy, an issue that requires the serious attention of world leaders.*

problems. They found it difficult to persuade countries to cooperate with one another. However, they were able to make some progress. Nuclear tests in the atmosphere were prohibited, and regulations to protect the seas were set up.

The Lessons of History

The search for answers and the attempt to understand ourselves and the world we live in brings us back to the question with which this book began: Why does anyone bother to study history? Some of the answers that others have come up with over the centuries may have occurred to you by now. For example, history teaches us why some nations gain power while other nations lose it. We learn how decisions made by world leaders and other individuals change history and set precedents for future decisions.

You may have come to realize how and why certain kinds of change take place. Or you may have become able to better understand something that you do or believe, or something that you have observed in current events.

You may have enjoyed studying some periods of history more than others. A story or a primary source reading may have sparked your interest and clarified your understanding of a particular subject.

You may have found yourself rooting for the side of justice and visualizing the broad scope of events over time.

To the extent that you have come to better understand the world in which we live and the events that have shaped its vibrant history, you have acted as a historian. You have not just read history; you have become part of it and have discovered why it is important. This insight, more than any of the specific facts or ideas that you may have read about for the first time, has been an essential addition to your education. It has taught you a new way of thinking. In the end, the most vital reason for studying history is that it teaches us how to understand people, events, ideas, particular eras, ourselves, and our place on the time line of history.

SECTION 3 REVIEW

1. **Identify**   Vatican II, Red Cross, Amnesty International, Oxfam.
2. **Evaluating Ideas**   How did increased leisure time affect life styles in the postwar period?
3. **Summarizing Ideas**   Discuss religious revivalism in the 1960s, 1970s, and 1980s.
4. **Interpreting Ideas**   What progress was made after 1945 in each of the following areas of social concern? **(a)** health? **(b)** human rights? **(c)** the environment?

893

- • Development of computers
- • Development of pop art

AD 1950s

Launch of *Sputnik 1*

1957

Invention of lasers

1960

1961

First person traveled in space

Chapter Summary

The following list contains the key concepts you have learned about the challenges of the modern age.

1. Major technological advances brought about changes in ideas and behavior after 1945. Advances in air travel, space exploration, miniaturization, computers, lasers, knowledge of heredity and genes, understanding of the atom, plastics, antibiotics, and the Green Revolution transformed communications, the understanding of the universe, the processing of information, the products people used every day, economic activities, medicine, and food production.

2. The arts and literature continued the experimentation that had marked their development since the early 1900s. New forms of painting, notably abstract expressionism, pop art, and op art, transformed art.

3. New materials and shapes were created in architecture. Musicians experimented with new kinds of sounds, both in serious compositions and in popular forms. New styles of creativity were also evident in dance and filmmaking. Drama moved in new directions as traditional plays were transformed by the theater of the absurd.

4. Writers all over the world expressed new ideas of protest and escape.

5. All of these cultural activities enjoyed large and growing audiences. More people than ever before went to museums, attended concerts and plays, and bought books.

6. Better education and increased leisure time created more viewers, listeners, and readers than had existed in any previous period.

7. The effects of all these changes on the life styles of ordinary people can be summed up by the word *speed*. Events happened more quickly, and people expected rapid developments. People sought stability amid this rapid change. Some made a renewed commitment to religious beliefs. People of all nations became concerned about political repression and the dwindling of the world's resources.

On a separate sheet of paper, complete the following review exercises.

Reviewing Important Terms

Supply the term that correctly completes each sentence.

1. The process of making machines smaller is called _____ .

2. Substances that do not occur in nature are called _____ .

3. _____ are medicines used to treat bacterial infections.

4. A painting that does not show recognizable objects is an example of an art style called _____ .

5. Paintings of popular objects such as soup cans are examples of an art style called _____ _____ .

Developing Critical Thinking Skills

1. **Comparing Ideas** (a) How were the early successes of the space exploration programs of the United States and the Soviet Union similar? (b) What have the two superpowers accomplished in the space race in the 1980s?

2. **Analyzing Ideas** How did changes in the arts during the modern age reflect changes in society as a whole?

3. **Debating Ideas** (a) What are some of the benefits of atomic power? (b) What are some of the dangers?

4. **Summarizing Ideas** (a) Give evidence to show that more people participate in cultural activities today than ever before. (b) What are some of the reasons for this increased participation?

5. **Determining Cause and Effect** (a) How did life styles change after World War II? (b) What factors account for these changes? (c) How did many people come to terms with the new pace of life?

6. **Interpreting Ideas** (a) What are some of the many reasons that people study history? (b) How can a knowledge of the past help people understand the present?

Relating Geography to History

Select a writer, a composer, or an artist from the United States or a foreign country. Write a short biographical essay; then describe how that person's environment influenced his or her contribution to the arts.

Apollo 11 landed
on the moon

Launch of
American
space shuttle

Explosion of
the *Challenger*

1969

1981

1986
1988

● Americans return
to space
● Launch of a
Soviet shuttle

Relating Past to Present

1. **(a)** Turn to the pictures on pages 877 and 879. What technological advances does each photograph illustrate? **(b)** What new industries have developed as a result of these discoveries? **(c)** How have such changes affected your own life?

2. In 1970 Alvin Toffler wrote a book about the effect of rapid change, about people facing the future too soon. Read the passage below from Toffler's *Future Shock,* and then answer the questions that follow.

   66 The high velocity [rapid rate] of change can be traced to many factors. Population growth, urbanization, the shifting proportions of young and old—all play their part. Yet technological advance is clearly a critical node [force] in that network of causes; indeed, it may be the node [force] that activates the entire net. 99

   a. According to Toffler, what factors bring about rapid change?
   b. Which of these factors is most important?
   c. **(1)** Based on what you learned in this chapter and on your knowledge of current events, do you agree with Toffler? **(2)** Why or why not?

3. **(a)** Using a tape recorder, prepare a program of popular music of the 1980s. Then prepare a similar tape for a previous decade. Be sure to have all of the music approved by your teacher. Possible sources of recordings include friends, relatives, and your school or local library. **(b)** What do the tapes reveal about each period? **(c)** How have popular tastes changed? **(d)** How might musical recordings contribute to an understanding of history?

Applying History Study Skills

Before completing this activity, review Building History Study Skills on page 886.

Compare photographs of the medieval cathedral at Salisbury in England and the Trump Tower building in New York City. Then answer the following questions.

1. **(a)** What characteristics of Gothic architecture can you find in the photographs? **(b)** How are these characteristics similar? **(c)** How are they different?

2. Which of the following values do Gothic architecture and medieval society reflect? **(a)** materialism **(b)** human achievement **(c)** God's glory **(d)** power
3. Which values listed in the previous question do skyscraper architecture and modern society reflect?
4. Write a brief essay that compares the cathedral to the skyscraper.

Investigating Further

1. **Preparing a Book Report** Read Aldous Huxley's *Brave New World* (Harper & Row), George Orwell's *Nineteen Eighty-four* (New American Library), or some other book dealing with science fiction or predictions about the future. **(a)** Prepare a book report in which you consider the author's vision of the future. **(b)** What events or changes did Huxley or Orwell fear might take place in the late 1900s? **(c)** Have any of these predictions come true? Explain. **(d)** Using information in this chapter and your knowledge of world affairs, describe how you think the world will look in the year 2020.

2. **Researching Ideas** Use the *Readers' Guide to Periodical Literature* to find articles on the *Voyager* spacecraft. **(a)** What planets did this satellite explore? **(b)** What new moons of other planets did it discover? **(c)** What other new information about the planets did *Voyager* provide? **(d)** You might also want to investigate the plans that the United States has for future space exploration programs.

3. **Writing a Report** The Space Age began in 1957 with the launching of the Soviet satellite *Sputnik.* Using reference materials in your library, prepare a report on why the United States has emerged as the world leader in space exploration. Based on your research, what are some reasons for the success of the United States space program?

4. **Preparing an Oral Presentation** Technological advances have had an impact not only on developed nations but also on developing nations. Select one area of scientific or technological progress, and present information to the class on how advances in this area have changed life in the developing nations of Asia, Africa, and Latin America.

UNIT 7 REVIEW

Unit Summary

The following list contains the key concepts you have learned about the challenges that faced the postwar world from 1945 to the present.

1. After World War II, conflicts between the Soviet Union and the United States resulted in the cold war that threatened world peace.
2. When Communist North Korea invaded South Korea in 1950, its troops were repulsed by UN forces, and an armistice was eventually signed.
3. In Southeast Asia, the United States became heavily involved in fighting in Vietnam.
4. Independence came rapidly to the African nations after World War II. Only South Africa resisted any efforts to give the black majority of the population a real voice in their own government.
5. A continuing problem in the Middle East was the hostility between Israel and its Arab neighbors. Four Arab-Israeli wars were fought between 1948 and 1973.
6. A civil war broke out in Nicaragua between the Marxist government, run by the Sandinistas, and the anti-government guerrillas called Contras. The United States assisted the Contras until 1983.
7. Although the Soviet Union's invasion of Afghanistan brought an end to efforts to ease tensions between the Soviet Union and the United States, by the mid-1980s the two countries once again sought better relations.
8. The purpose and policies of NATO came under close scrutiny from member nations during the 1970s and 1980s.
9. After 1945 technological changes transformed communications, the understanding of the universe, the processing of information, the products people used every day, economic activities, medicine, and food production.

On a separate sheet of paper, complete the following review exercises.

Reviewing Concepts

Supply the term that correctly completes each statement.

1. _____ is a term used to describe the Eastern European nations that depend on the Soviet Union.
2. The South African policy based on the principle of racial separation became known as _____, the Afrikaans word for "apartness."
3. _____ is the name given to the improvement in relations between the United States and the Soviet Union during the 1970s.
4. Through _____, or restructuring, Mikhail Gorbachev planned to overhaul the political and economic systems of the Soviet Union.

Applying Critical Thinking Skills

1. **Organizing Ideas** What was the purpose of the alliance systems set up by the Western nations and by the Communist bloc after 1945?
2. **Synthesizing Ideas** How did the work of civil rights leaders such as Dr. Martin Luther King lead to changes in the United States government's policy toward equal rights for all of its citizens?
3. **Comparing Ideas** How did the Korean War and the war in Vietnam differ in terms of causes and results?
4. **Comparing Ideas** How did each of the following contribute to the rise of nationalism in Africa? **(a)** Nkrumah? **(b)** Jomo Kenyatta? **(c)** Mugabe?
5. **Identifying Ideas** What changes occurred in the nations of the Middle East after 1945?
6. **Synthesizing Ideas** How would economic prosperity in Latin America help to establish greater political stability?
7. **Understanding Relationships** What were the results of the United States involvement in each of the following: **(a)** Guatemala, **(b)** Nicaragua, **(c)** Cuba, **(d)** Dominican Republic.
8. **Understanding Ideas** Why did some members of NATO begin to question that alliance's purpose and policies during the 1970s and 1980s?
9. **Interpreting Ideas** **(a)** What are some of the many reasons that people study history? **(b)** How can a knowledge of the past help people understand the present?

Relating Geography to History

Refer to maps in Chapter 27 and Chapter 28. How did the spread of communism affect the map of Europe after the end of World War II?

Writing About History

Write a report that summarizes three major areas of disagreement between the United States and the Soviet Union after 1945. Which was most threatening to world peace? Why?

Further Readings

Fitzgerald, Frances, *Fire in the Lake: The Vietnamese and Americans in Vietnam.* New York: Little, Brown. Describes the Vietnam War.

Gunther, John, *Inside South America.* New York: Harper and Row. Describes South American society and industrial change during the postwar era.

Lee, Harper, *To Kill A Mockingbird.* New York: Harper and Row. Describes the tragedy of prejudice in a small, isolated southern town in the United States after World War II.

Unit Seven Chronology

Date	Political and Social Developments	Technological and Scientific Advances	Visual Arts and Literature	Religious and Philosophical Thought
1945–1955	Formation of UN 28,* OAS 31, NATO 28, Warsaw Pact 28 Egyptian 30, Chinese 29, and Viet Minh 29 revolutions Filipino 29, Indian 29, and Israeli 30 independence Nuremburg trials 28 Truman Doctrine and Marshall Plan 28 Berlin blockade 28 Korean conflict 29 *Brown v. Bd. of Ed.* 28 Peróns in Argentina 31	Nuclear power 32 Transistor 33 Computer revolution 33 DNA research 33 Television 33 "Fast food" 33 Increase in leisure time 33	Education of lower classes 33 Abstract expressionism 33 Britten and Shostakovich 33 Baldwin and Ellison 33 "Beat Generation" 33 Le Corbusier 33 Mark Rothko 33 John Cage 33	Social analysis and comment by art on society 33
1956–1965	Suez Crisis 30, Hungarian revolution 28 Common Market 28, 32 US in Vietnam 29 Berlin Wall 28, Cuban revolution and missile crisis 31 OPEC 29 Alliance for Progress 31 Martin Luther King and civil rights 28	St. Lawrence Seaway 28 *Sputnik* 33 Laser technology 33 "Green Revolution" 33 Satellite communication 33 Synthetics and plastics 33	Black Nationalist prose and poetry 30 Pop and op art 33 Martha Graham 33 French "New Wave" movies 33 Beckett and Ionesco 33 Arthur Miller and Tennessee Williams 33 *West Side Story* 33 Pasternak and Solzhenitsyn 33	Vatican II 33 Ecumenical movement 33
1966–1975	SALT 32, Détente 32, Soviet invasion of Czechoslovakia 28 Six-Day war 30, Arab-Israeli War of 1973 30, PLO 30 OPEC embargo 32 Watergate 32 Helsinki Accords 32	Lunar landing 33 Jumbo jets 33 Japanese industrialization 29 Ecology 33	Chinese Cultural Rev. 29 Leopold Senghor 30 Camara Laye 30 Realism in art 33 George Balanchine 33 Vonnegut and Castaneda 33 *Samizdat* 32	Islamic fundamentalism 30 Objection to Vietnam War 28, 32 Roman Catholicism as conscience of Latin America 31
1976–1988	SALT II 32, Camp David Accords 30 *Perestroika, glasnost* 32 Gorbachev and Reagan summit 32 Assassinations of Sadat 30, Indira Gandhi 28 Soviets in Afghanistan 30 Southeast Asian independence 29 Solidarity 32	Three Mile Island 32 Chernobyl 32 *Columbia, Challenger* shuttles 33 Asian economic revolution 29	Pol Pot executes intellectuals 29 Lewis Nkosi and Ezekiel Mphalele 30 Reassertion of folk art forms 33 Steven Spielberg 33 *Asinamali* 33	Christian fundamentalism 33 Protests against apartheid 30

*Indicates chapter in which concept is discussed.

The World Since 1945

28 Challenges Faced Europe and North America in the Postwar Years

Although the Soviet Union had been part of the Allied Powers in World War II, tensions between the Soviet Union on one side and Western Europe and the United States on the other side mounted after the war. This mutual suspicion and hostility between the Communist and Western nations led to the so-called cold war, which they waged by political and economic means rather than with weapons.

The Postwar Settlement

At the end of the war in Europe, Allied occupation zones were set up in Germany and Austria. Practical arrangements lasted as long as the Allies remained on friendly terms. As the postwar hostility grew, however, decisions by the Allies became more and more difficult to reach. For example, it took 10 years to reach an agreement over Austria, and no final agreement was ever reached on Germany. Instead, the country remained occupied by American, British, French, and Soviet troops. Despite these disagreements, however, the United Nations was founded as an international body dedicated to preserving peace.

The Influence of the Cold War

The problems of the cold war intensified in the late 1940s. Soon after the German surrender, the Soviets set up Communist-controlled governments in Poland, Romania, Bulgaria, and Hungary—known as satellite nations—and made known their intentions to foster communism throughout Europe.

Early in 1947 the United States acted to fight the spread of communism. In March 1947 President Truman, announcing what came to be called the Truman Doctrine, dedicated the United States to helping countries threatened by communism. This policy, referred to as containment, was aimed at "containing," or restricting, the spread of communism.

The United States also instituted the European Recovery Program, often called the Marshall Plan, to help Europe recover from the war. According to the plan, the United States would furnish supplies and funds to help nations rebuild.

Because the nations of Western Europe feared that the Soviets would launch an invasion, they founded the North Atlantic Treaty Organization (NATO), a mutual defense pact. The Soviets responded by founding the Warsaw Pact.

Progress

One of the most outstanding characteristics of postwar Western Europe was its economic and political recovery. In a comparatively short time, Western Europeans had cleared away the rubble of bombed cities, rebuilt roads, rail lines and bridges, and returned their industries to full production.

The nations also made attempts at economic cooperation. In 1957, for example, the European Economic Community (EEC)—usually called the Common Market—was founded.

The Communist Bloc

As the years wore on, people in the satellite nations chafed under Communist rule. In 1956 the Hungarians revolted, and in 1968 the Czechs tried to institute reforms. The Soviets crushed rebels in both countries.

Even though the Communist nations joined to form their own common market, the Council for Mutual Economic Assistance (COMECON or CMEA), living standards in these nations lagged far behind those in the West.

The United States and Canada

For the most part, United States foreign policy during the postwar period revolved around containment. At home, the government consistently aimed to resolve social and political problems and to maintain a flourishing economy.

After World War II, Canada became a vigorous supporter of the United Nations and an important member of NATO. It loaned almost $4 billion to other countries and welcomed thousands of refugees from Europe. Canada also experienced rapid economic growth.

Fireworks over Hong Kong

29 Asian Nations Struggled to Gain Stability

The years after World War II saw major political, economic, and social changes in Asia.

China

After World War II the battles between the Nationalists and the Communists in China continued. By 1949 the Communists had forced the Nationalists to set up a government in Taiwan and had taken control of the mainland.

Once in power the Communists worked to set up a Marxist state. Although the Communists did achieve some economic growth, they began to allow some elements of free enterprise into their economy in the 1980s to speed this growth.

Since 1949 officials of the Chinese Communist Party have often disagreed. To combat these arguments, Mao Zedong launched the Great Proletarian Cultural Revolution, a violent attempt at social changes, in 1966. In time, the moderates won control of the major party and government offices and began to reinstate many of those who had been purged from government offices and the Communist Party during the Cultural Revolution.

China's foreign affairs also underwent change. China was first closely aligned with the Soviet Union, but tensions soon cooled this relationship. As Chinese-Soviet relations worsened, China grew more willing to come to terms with the United States, and in 1979 the two nations established diplomatic relations.

Much of the tension that had separated the People's Republic of China and the United States during the 1950s and 1960s grew out of the Korean War in the 1950s. During that war the Communists had openly aided North Korea's attempts to conquer South Korea. Thanks to intervention by the United Nations, however, the South Koreans remained independent. Today South Korea with its free enterprise system is highly industrialized.

Japan

Although defeated in World War II, Japan has become one of the most industrialized and prosperous nations in the world today. Japan entered the 1980s as Asia's leading economic power. Surpassing all other nations in shipbuilding and electronics manufacturing, it stood as the world's third-ranking industrial nation. However, the country's economic leaders faced a growing problem—where to find markets for a rapidly expanding volume of production. This problem intensified as many nations, including the United States, protested the flooding of their markets with Japanese goods.

India, Pakistan, and Bangladesh

The movement for independence from Great Britain that had begun in India after World War I intensified after World War II. Finally, in 1947, the vast subcontinent was granted independence. However, in doing so the British created fragmented nations by establishing India and East and West Pakistan based upon the Muslim and Hindu populations of each region.

India became the leader of the non-aligned nations—those that steered a middle course between the Communist bloc and the Western powers—and worked to industrialize. By the end of the 1980s, India faced major economic problems even though its economy had made considerable progress. The country's mixed economy, in which private companies owned some industries and the government owed the rest, charted the way in which it wanted the economy to grow in a series of five-year plans.

The nations of Pakistan, divided into two parts separated by a huge wedge of Indian territory some 1,000 miles (1,600 kilometers) wide, proved unworkable. In 1971 the nation divided into Pakistan (formerly West Pakistan) and Bangladesh (formerly East Pakistan).

Both Pakistan and Bangladesh faced daunting problems after the division. Bangladesh, ravaged by war, also suffered recurrent famines, epidemics, floods, and devastating tropical storms. And in Pakistan a military dictatorship ruled until 1988.

Southeast Asia

The Southeast Asian countries of the Philippines, Indonesia, Malaysia, Singapore, Brunei, Vietnam, Cambodia (Kampuchea), Laos, and Burma also won independence after World War II. These nations have all faced varying problems since independence.

Conflict in Vietnam

One of the most troubled countries of the region has been Vietnam which was racked by civil war after its independence. North Vietnam had a Communist government, while South Vietnam had a pro-Western government. After more than 20 years of war, which included direct intervention by the United States, the Communists prevailed and united the country in 1975.

Although reunited, Vietnam faces many problems. The years of war had drained the nation's resources. In addition, many people fled the country.

Vietnam's neighbors also faced problems. When the Communist *Khmer Rouge* captured the government of Cambodia, for example, they tried to impose a Marxist state on the people. In so doing, they murdered thousands of civilians and drained

the country of a nation's most important resources—its citizens.

Security and Economic Growth

Most of the countries of Asia at one time had been colonies. After independence, most new Asian nations set up representative governments and attempted to build democratic societies. With the passage of time, however, democracy faded in most of Asia.

In the late 1980s, roughly 3 billion people lived in Asia, more than half of the total population of the world. A significant number of Asia's people lived in poverty and suffered its consequences—malnutrition, illiteracy, and reduced life expectancy.

By and large, most Asian countries experienced slow economic growth because they had little wealth. Industrialization required huge investments of money in machinery for factories and distribution networks. Also, the later a country began the process of industrialization, the greater the investment needed to bring that country up to the level of the more developed nations.

30 The Nations of Africa and the Middle East Became Independent

In the four decades after World War II, more than 1.5 billion people won independence, and the number of nations in the world tripled, mainly because of successful independence movements in old European empires. Most of the new nations were located in Africa and the Middle East.

African Independence

After World War II, a generation of determined nationalists began to work for African independence. Leaders such as Kwame Nkrumah (en • KROO • mah) in the Gold Coast, Jomo Kenyatta in Kenya, and Nnamdi Azikiwe in Nigeria typified this generation. By 1980 all of Africa except Namibia (Southwest Africa) had gained its independence.

All of these new nations except South Africa had black African leaders. In South Africa, however,

Non-aligned summit

the white minority continued to rule and to segregate the races through its policy of apartheid.

The New African Nations

Having achieved independence, the nations of Africa still faced many serious problems. Each new nation had to create a sense of national unity among peoples often divided by differences of language and culture. Many of them had to overcome economic underdevelopment. Finally, a sense of pride in Africa's history and its cultural achievements had to be restored. Throughout the postwar era, the new nations struggled to achieve these goals, meeting with varying degrees of success.

Independence in the Middle East

Between 1945 and 1962, the nations of the Middle East made great advances in securing independence. Many gained their independence from Western imperial rule. Others, such as Egypt and Iran, were officially independent but were dominated by outsiders. They too achieved greater freedom from foreign influence during this period and also sought to increase their power within the Middle East.

One of the most troublesome problems of the Middle East concerned the creation of the independent nation of Israel in 1948. The Arabs violently opposed the new state, and warfare plagued the region.

Wars, Oil, and Revolution

After 1962 the struggle against colonialism was no longer an issue in the Middle East. Nevertheless, tensions continued to rack the region. The Arab-Israeli confrontation continued despite the signing of the Camp David Accords between Egypt and Israel. Although oil provided income for many Middle Eastern nations, the world oil glut of the 1980s created financial problems. And in Iran a violent revolution toppled the shah and created a government based on Islamic fundamentalism.

Old Versus New

Today political and social fragmentation marks the Middle East. Many nations with different forms of government occupy the region. The unequal distribution of natural resources as well as varying population densities produce difficult economic conditions. Although the nations of this dynamic region are making strides to improve education and to give women more rights, these moves to modernize often conflict with traditional values. And many Muslims in the Middle East have reacted to the rapid changes of the times by turning to Islamic fundamentalism.

31 Latin America Became the Focus of World Attention

The countries of Latin America underwent enormous changes after World War II. Once relatively unimportant in world affairs and economically undeveloped, Latin America became a focus of world attention.

Political Conflicts

The most important change in Latin America after World War II was the sudden surge in population. The governments of Latin America had to provide new services to meet the demands of this growing population. Often economic instability as well as political tensions interfered with the governments' abilities to meet the needs of the populations.

Mexico and Central America

Mexico, Central America, the Caribbean Islands, and the countries of South America bordering the

Caribbean are considered part of the Caribbean Basin. The importance of the countries in this region is their location. The Caribbean Basin is considered a commercial and military crossroads in the Western hemisphere. Ships from throughout the world carry goods between the Atlantic and Pacific oceans via the strategic Panama Canal.

As political instability continues to rock the Caribbean Basin, world attention, particularly that of the United States, has focused on this region. Since the early 1950s, the United States has been heavily involved in several countries of the region, including Guatemala, Cuba, Grenada, Nicaragua, and El Salvador.

Mexico, long one of the most stable countries of the region, faced increasing economic and political problems after the 1950s. Although Mexico's economic picture improved greatly with the discovery of huge oil reserves in the 1970s, by the 1980s the worldwide slump in oil prices had burst the dream of a bright economic future.

Communist Revolution

The island nation of Cuba was the site of one of the greatest upheavals in the region. There, in 1959, Fidel Castro led a Communist revolution that toppled long-time dictator Fulgencio Batista. The presence of a Communist government so close to the United States alarmed American leaders. And throughout the postwar era, an uneasy peace typified relations between the two countries.

Cuba was not the only troubled nation in Latin America in the 1960s. Many countries experienced a shift toward the left, being disrupted by a series of coups and assassinations. In the Dominican Republic, the people toppled a dictator and made the first steps toward democracy. The people of Haiti, however, were less successful in their quest for democratic rule. In 1986, an uprising forced the ruling Duvalier family out of the country, but attempts at democratic civilian rule failed.

South America

Revolutions also swept South America after 1945. Argentina, Brazil, Chile, and Peru teetered between dictatorship and democracy, and in Colombia, the growing cocaine traffic threatened to rip the nation apart.

32 Challenges Faced the Superpowers in the Modern Era

After 1968 the struggles between the Western nations and those of the Communist bloc continued as each group encountered new challenges.

The United States

During the 1970s and 1980s, the United States faced a number of problems, including internal political conflicts and several economic reversals. Discontent spurned by United States involvement in Vietnam ended with the withdrawal of American troops in 1973. At the same time, the news that President Richard Nixon had known of plans to break into the Democratic Party offices during the presidential election of 1972 shocked the nation. As the Watergate scandal unfolded, President Nixon resigned.

High inflation rates and unemployment plagued the nation in the 1970s. Both, however, had been brought under control by the 1980s.

Foreign policy also underwent changes, as relations with the Soviet Union deteriorated in the 1970s and then appeared to grow friendlier in the late 1980s. And in the late 1970s, the United States established ties with Communist China.

Challenges also faced Canada in this period. The nation successfully withstood a French-Canadian separatist movement and maintained close, although at times strained, relations with the United States.

U.S.-Soviet summit

Western Europe

Western Europe was plagued by many of the same problems that plagued the United States in the 1970s and the 1980s. The strengthening of the European Community, or EC, and the North Atlantic Treaty Organization, or NATO, encouraged a spirit of cooperation among the various member nations. In 1975 representatives of 35 nations, including the United States and the Soviet Union, signed the Helsinki Accords that set down ways of improving economic and technological cooperation between East and West.

The Soviet Union and Eastern Europe

In the 1970s and early 1980s, the Soviet Union attempted to take a firmer hold on the Eastern-bloc nations, particularly Czechoslovakia and Poland where opposition to the Soviets was widespread. At the same time, Soviet leaders acted to clamp down on dissent at home. When a new leader, Mikhail Gorbachev, took power in 1985, however, Soviet policy changed. Gorbachev instituted the programs of *glasnost* and *perestroika* to lessen political repression and to provide a certain amount of free enterprise in the Communist nation. In foreign policy Gorbachev sought closer ties with the West.

33 The Modern World Faced the Challenge of Rapid Change

Vast changes in how people lived and how they viewed the world marked the years following 1945.

Technological Change

Dramatic advances in technology affected all the nations of the world. Passenger jets transformed travel, and the United States, the Soviet Union, and other nations launched voyages of space exploration. An important consequence of space exploration was the invention of ways of making machines, especially electrical equipment, smaller in a process called miniaturization. The most remarkable product of miniaturization was the modern computer.

During the postwar era, atomic energy was used to build more powerful bombs. It was also used to develop efficient power for generators to produce electricity for a burgeoning population, although the question of safety at nuclear power plants became an issue of deep public concern after accidents at Three Mile Island and Chernobyl.

The Arts and Literature

After 1945 New York became one of the liveliest centers of new ideas and painting styles based upon experimentation. New styles included abstract expressionism, pop art, op art, process art, and conceptual art. Many people also came to appreciate folk art, the work of talented, but not necessarily professionally trained painters, sculptors, and craftspeople. The same search for new ideas and techniques dominated architecture, music, literature, film, and drama.

Patterns of Living

Just as with science and the arts, the postwar period was a time of rapid social change, particularly in Western nations. Women, for example, joined the work force in increasing numbers.

Amid rapid changes, people looked for ways to create anchors of stability. One way was to renew their commitment to religion. At the same time, people throughout the world became increasingly concerned with social issues such as human rights and the environment.

SYNTHESIS REVIEW

1. **Understanding Ideas**   How did the United States react to Soviet attempts to spread communism?
2. **Comparing Ideas**   How do the economies of Japan and China differ?
3. **Interpreting Ideas**   How did oil resources prove to be both advantages and disadvantages for the countries of the Middle East?
4. **Summarizing Ideas**   What were the results of the revolution in Cuba?
5. **Analyzing Ideas**   Why did Mikhail Gorbachev institute the policies of *glasnost* and *perestroika*?
6. **Seeing Relationships**   Why did many people protest nuclear power?
7. **Synthesizing Ideas**   How did tensions between the Soviet Union and the United States affect the entire world?

REFERENCE SECTION

150°   120°   90°   60°   30°

Meridian

Greenland

West

Baffin
Bay

Arctic   Circle

Prime

BRITISH
ISLES

Bering
Sea

Hudson
Bay

N O R T H

ATLANTIC

OCEAN

Nort
Sea

English
Channel

R
O
C
K
Y

A M E R I C A

PYRENEE

Strait of
Gibraltar

ATLAS MTS.

M
T
S.

APPALACHIAN MTS.

Mississippi R.

30°

Sargasso
Sea

Disputed

S A H

HAWAIIAN
ISLANDS

Tropic of Cancer

Gulf of
Mexico

W E S T   I N D I E S

SAHEL

PACIFIC

Central
America

Caribbean Sea

Cape
Verde

OCEAN

0°   Equator

A

S O U T H

Amazon   R.

A M E R I C A

ATLANTIC

N
D
E
S

OCEAN

Tropic of Capricorn

30°

ATACAMA
DESSRA

N

Meridian

THE WORLD: Physical

——— National boundary

MILLER CYLINDRICAL PROJECTION

0   1000   2000 Miles

0   1000   2000 Kilometers

Prime

Cape Horn

60°

150°   120°   90°   60°   30°   0°

Antarctic Circle

R2

ARCTIC OCEAN

EUROPE

CARPATHIAN MTS.

Black Sea

CAUCASUS MTS.

Mediterranean Sea

Caspian Sea

URAL MTS.

ASIA

Disputed

HIMALAYAS

Ganges R.

GOBI DESERT

He

Huang

Chang Jiang

Sea of Okhotsk

Bering Strait

Bering Sea

East China Sea

60°

30°

AFRICA

Red Sea

NUBIAN DESERT

Arabian Peninsula

Persian G.

Undefined

Arabian Sea

Bay of Bengal

South China Sea

PACIFIC OCEAN

(Congo) R.

KALAHARI DESERT

Madagascar

INDIAN OCEAN

Strait of Malacca

INDONESIA

Equator

AUSTRALIA

Cape of Good Hope

0°

30°

ANTARCTICA

30° 60° 90° 120° 150° 180°

60°

R3

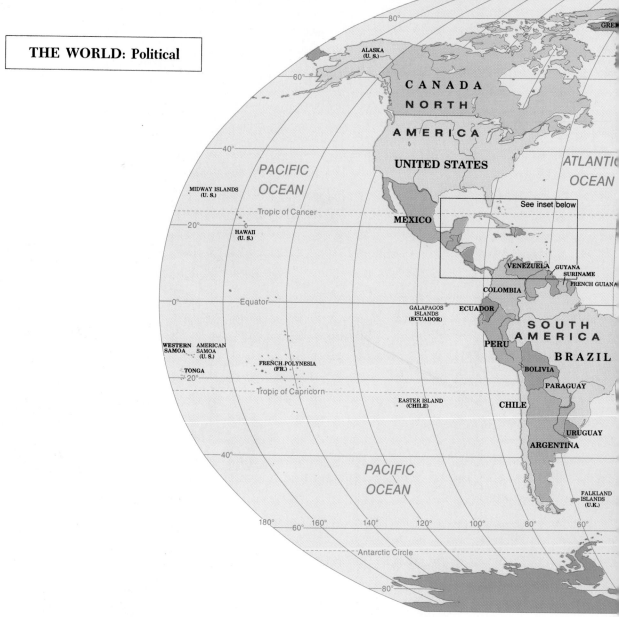

THE WORLD: Political

ALASKA (U.S.)

C A N A D A

N O R T H

A M E R I C A

UNITED STATES

PACIFIC OCEAN

MIDWAY ISLANDS (U.S.)

ATLANTIC OCEAN

See inset below

Tropic of Cancer

MEXICO

HAWAII (U.S.)

VENEZUELA   GUYANA
SURINAME
FRENCH GUIANA

COLOMBIA

GALAPAGOS ISLANDS (ECUADOR)   ECUADOR

Equator

WESTERN SAMOA   AMERICAN SAMOA (U.S.)

PERU

S O U T H
A M E R I C A

B R A Z I L

TONGA

FRENCH POLYNESIA (FR.)

BOLIVIA

PARAGUAY

Tropic of Capricorn

EASTER ISLAND (CHILE)

CHILE

URUGUAY

ARGENTINA

PACIFIC
OCEAN

FALKLAND ISLANDS (U.K.)

180°   160°   140°   120°   100°   80°   60°

Antarctic Circle

GRE

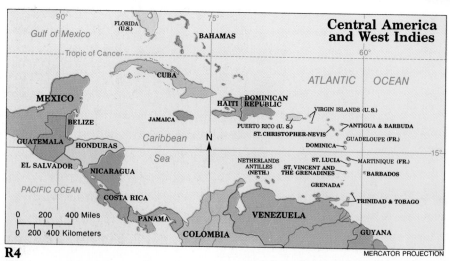

Gulf of Mexico

FLORIDA (U.S.)

BAHAMAS

**Central America
and West Indies**

Tropic of Cancer

60°

CUBA

ATLANTIC   OCEAN

MEXICO

JAMAICA

HAITI   DOMINICAN
REPUBLIC

VIRGIN ISLANDS (U.S.)

PUERTO RICO (U.S.)
ST. CHRISTOPHER-NEVIS

ANTIGUA & BARBUDA

GUADELOUPE (FR.)

BELIZE

GUATEMALA   HONDURAS

Caribbean

N

DOMINICA

Sea

EL SALVADOR   NICARAGUA

NETHERLANDS ANTILLES (NETH.)

ST. LUCIA   MARTINIQUE (FR.)
ST. VINCENT AND
THE GRENADINES   BARBADOS

15°

PACIFIC OCEAN

COSTA RICA

GRENADA

PANAMA

VENEZUELA

TRINIDAD & TOBAGO

0   200   400 Miles
0   200   400 Kilometers

COLOMBIA

GUYANA

R4

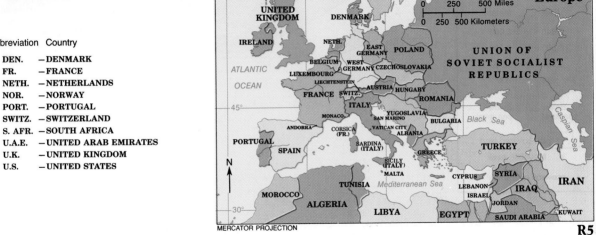

ROBINSON PROJECTION

Abbreviation	Country
DEN.	— DENMARK
FR.	— FRANCE
NETH.	— NETHERLANDS
NOR.	— NORWAY
PORT.	— PORTUGAL
SWITZ.	— SWITZERLAND
S. AFR.	— SOUTH AFRICA
U.A.E.	— UNITED ARAB EMIRATES
U.K.	— UNITED KINGDOM
U.S.	— UNITED STATES

MERCATOR PROJECTION

R5

THE WORLD: Land Use and Economic Activity

Manufacturing

Woodlands

Farming

Grazing

Limited economic use

$ Tourism

Drilling

Mining

Fishing

Forestry

Greenland

ATLANTIC OCEAN

NORTH AMERICA

PACIFIC OCEAN

Gulf of Mexico

Caribbean Sea

SOUTH AMERICA

ATLANTIC OCEAN

BRITISH ISLES

Arctic Circle

Tropic of Cancer

Equator

Tropic of Capricorn

Antarctic Circle

N

| 0 | 1000 | 2000 Miles |
| 0 | 1000 | 2000 Kilometers |

R8

150° 120° 90° 60° 30°

60°

30°

0°

30°

ARCTIC   OCEAN

ASIA

EUROPE

Baltic Sea

Black Sea

Mediterranean Sea

AFRICA

INDIAN
OCEAN

Madagascar

INDONESIA

AUSTRALIA

NEW
ZEALAND

PACIFIC

OCEAN

Tropic of Cancer

Equator

Tropic of Capricorn

ANTARCTICA

30°   60°   90°   120°   150°   180°

60°

30°

0°

30°

60°

Antarctic Circle

R9

NORTH POLE

SOVIET UNION

ARCTIC OCEAN

EUROPE

180° 170° 160° 80° 70° 60°

ICELAND

ALEUTIAN ISLANDS

Beaufort Sea

Yukon R.

GREENLAND (DEN.)

Arctic Circle

Anchorage

Gulf of Alaska

Mackenzie R.

Great Bear Lake

Baffin Bay

PACIFIC OCEAN

Great Slave Lake

Peace R.

Athabasca R.

Saskatchewan R.

CANADA

Hudson Bay

Calgary

Vancouver

Lake Winnipeg

Gulf of St. Lawrence

Seattle

Portland

Nelson R.

Quebec

Halifax

ROCKY MOUNTAINS

Missouri R.

Lake Superior

Montreal

Ottawa

St. Lawrence R.

Boston

Snake R.

CASCADE RANGE

Minneapolis

Lake Huron

Toronto

Lake Ontario

Hudson R.

New York

Great Salt Lake

SIERRA NEVADA

Milwaukee

Detroit

Lake Michigan

Lake Erie

Philadelphia

San Francisco

COASTAL RANGE

Chicago

Cleveland

Pittsburgh

Baltimore

UNITED STATES

Omaha

Denver

Cincinnati

Washington

Colorado River

Kansas City

St. Louis

Ohio R.

ATLANTIC OCEAN

Los Angeles

San Diego

STATES

Memphis

APPALACHIAN MTS.

Atlanta

Charleston

BERMUDA (U.K.)

Phoenix

Red River

Dallas

Mississippi R.

Savannah

BAJA CALIFORNIA

El Paso

San Antonio

Houston

Jacksonville

New Orleans

Rio Grande

Tampa

SIERRA MADRE

MEXICO

Miami

Tropic of Cancer

Monterrey

Gulf of Mexico

Nassau

BAHAMAS

TURKS AND CAICOS IS. (U.K.)

ST. MARTIN (NETH. & FR.)

ST. BARTHÉLE (FR.)

SIERRA MADRE

Havana

CUBA

PUERTO RICO (U.S.)

VIRGIN IS. (U.S.)

ST. CHRISTOPHER NEVIS

ANTIGUA

Guadalajara

Santiago de Cuba

HAITI

DOMINICAN REPUBLIC

MONTSERRAT DOMIN

YUCATÁN PENINSULA

CAYMAN ISLANDS (U.K.)

Port-au-Prince

Santo Domingo

GUADELOUPE (FR.)

Mexico City

Veracruz

Kingston

JAMAICA

MARTINIQUE (FR.)

ST. LUCIA

Cuernavaca

ST. VINCENT AND THE GRENADINES

BARBADOS

Oaxaca

BELIZE

Belmopan

Caribbean Sea

GRENADA

TRINIDAD AND TOBAGO

CURAÇAO (NETH.)

GUATEMALA

HONDURAS

ARUBA (NETH.)

BONAIRE (NETH.)

Guatemala

Tegucigalpa

San Salvador

NICARAGUA

EL SALVADOR

Managua

COSTA RICA

San José

Panama

PANAMA

N

SOUTH AMERICA

NORTH AMERICA

⊛ National capital

• Other city

— National boundary

AZIMUTHAL EQUAL AREA PROJECTION

R10

0 250 500 750 Miles

0 250 500 750 Kilometers

CARIBBEAN SEA

Barranquilla
Maracaibo
Caracas
VENEZUELA
Orinoco River
Medellín
Bogotá
COLOMBIA
GUYANA
Georgetown
Paramaribo
Cayenne
SURINAME
FRENCH GUIANA (FR.)

Magdalena River

ATLANTIC OCEAN

Equator

Quito
ECUADOR
Guayaquil
Iquitos
Manaus
Amazon River
Fortaleza

PERU
A N D E S
Lima

B R A Z I L

Recife

Lake Titicaca
La Paz
BOLIVIA
Sucre
São Francisco River
Salvador

Brasília

Belo Horizonte

PARAGUAY
Paraná River
Rio de Janeiro
São Paulo

Tropic of Capricorn

Asunción
Paraguay River
Uruguay River
Pôrto Alegre

PACIFIC OCEAN

CHILE

Córdoba
Rosario
URUGUAY
Montevideo

Valparaíso
Santiago
Buenos Aires
Rio de la Plata
ARGENTINA
PAMPAS

ATLANTIC OCEAN

A N D E S

N

SOUTH AMERICA

⊛ National capital
• Other city
— National boundary

AZIMUTHAL EQUAL AREA PROJECTION

0 250 500 Miles
0 250 500 Kilometers

TIERRA DEL FUEGO

Stanley
FALKLAND ISLANDS (U.K.)

SOUTH GEORGIA (U.K.)

R11

Cape Horn

EUROPE

⊛ National capital

● Other city

⊹⊹⊹ Canal

—— National boundary

AZIMUTHAL EQUAL AREA PROJECTION

Reykjavík
ICELAND

FAROE IS.
(DEN.)

SHETLAND IS.
(U.K.)

Arctic Circle

• Trondheim

SWEDEN

NORWAY

• Bergen

⊛ Oslo

Uppsala •

• Stavanger

Stockholm ⊛

• Göteborg

Glasgow • Edinburgh

Belfast •

DENMARK

**UNITED
KINGDOM**

Copenhagen ⊛

Baltic Se

North

Bornholm
(DEN.)

Dublin ⊛

IRELAND

• Liverpool

Sea

Kalining

Gdansk •

Cardiff •

Manchester •

Hamburg •

• Birmingham

NETHERLANDS

Bremen •

EAST

Bristol •

London •

Thames R.

Berlin ⊛

Vistul

Dover •

Amsterdam •

The Hague ⊛

Oder

GERMANY

POLA

Calais •

Rotterdam •

English Channel

BELGIUM

WEST

Leipzig •

Elbe

River

Le Havre •

Brussels ⊛

GERMANY

⊛ Bonn

Prague ⊛

Kraků

Seine

LUXEMBOURG

• Frankfurt

R.

⊛ Paris

Luxembourg ⊛

R.

Strasbourg •

Stuttgart •

R.

CZECHOSLOVAKI

Loire

River

FRANCE

Dijon •

Rhine R.

Danube

Munich •

Vienna •

La Rochelle •

Zürich •

LIECHTENSTEIN

AUSTRIA

Budapest •

Geneva • Bern ⊛

SWITZERLAND

HUNGA

Bordeaux •

Lyon •

A L P S

Zagreb •

Garonne

Milan •

Venice •

Trieste •

R.

Rhône R.

Turin •

Po River

Genoa •

Belgr

PYRENEES

Nice •

SAN

Ebro River

Marseilles •

MONACO

Florence •

MARINO

YUGOSLAV

Porto •

ANDORRA

Corsica
(FR.)

APENNINES

Sarajevo •

Tagus

⊛ Madrid

Adriatic

Lisbon ⊛

R.

• Barcelona

Tiber

Rome ⊛

Sea

PORTUGAL

SPAIN

ITALY

Tira

• Valencia

Sardinia
(IT.)

ALBA

• Seville

**BALEARIC ISLANDS
(SP.)**

Naples •

Tyrrhenian

Cádiz •

Strait of

Sea

Gibraltar

M e d i t e r r a n e a n   S e a

Ionian
Sea

Palermo •

Sicily

A F R I C A

R12

• **MALTA**

ATLANTIC

OCEAN

Bay of
Biscay

Gulf

60°

30°

20°

10°

10°

40°

30°

50°

20°

40°

30°

10°

0°

10°

ARCTIC
OCEAN

30°   40°   50°   60°   70°   60°   80°

White Sea

● Arkhangelsk

North Dvina River

U R A L   M O U N T A I N S

NLAND

70°

Lake
Ladoga

● Helsinki   ● Leningrad

Gulf of Finland

● Tallinn

● Gor'kiy

50°

● Riga

S O V I E T   U N I O N

● Moscow

● Kuibyshev   River

Ural River

● Vilnius

● Minsk

saw

● Kiev   ● Kharkov

Volgograd ● Volga   River

Dniester   River

Don River

R

Dnieper

● Odessa

Sea of Azov

CAUCASUS   MTS.

60°

PATHIAN

MTS.

Caspian

40°

ROMANIA

● Sevastopol

Sea

● Bucharest ⊛

Sea

Danube River

Black

BALKAN   MTS.

⊛ Sofia

BULGARIA   TURKEY

● Istanbul

N

A S I A

ECE

Aegean
Sea

● Athens ⊛

Crete

30°   40°   50°   30°

0   100   200   300 Miles

0 100 200 300
Kilometers

R13

EUROPE

Arctic Circle

Ural Mountains

70°

60°

50°

40°

Sverdlovsk
Chelyabinsk

Ob

River

Irtysh

Omsk

Novosibirsk

Yenisei

River

Lake Balkhash

Aral Sea

Alma-Ata

Tashkent
Samarkand

Black Sea

CAUCASUS

Caspian Sea

Baku

Ankara
TURKEY

Nicosia
CYPRUS

Mediterranean Sea

Beirut
Jerusalem

ISRAEL

SYRIA
LEBANON
Damascus

Amman

JORDAN

Euphrates R.
Tigris R.

Baghdad

IRAQ

Tehran

IRAN

Kabul
AFGHANISTAN

Islamabad

Lahore

PAKISTAN

Disputed

HIMALAYAS

NEPAL

Brahmaputra R.

Kuwait
Neutral Zone
KUWAIT

Persian Gulf

OMAN

New Delhi

Indus R.

Ganges R.

Katmandu

BANGLADESH
D.

SAUDI

Manama
BAHRAIN
Doha
QATAR

Abu
Dhabi

UNITED ARAB
EMIRATES

Muscat

Karachi

Calcutta

Riyadh

Tropic of Cancer

Red Sea

Jiddah
Mecca

ARABIA

Undefined
OMAN

INDIA

Bombay

Arabian Sea

Bay of Beng

30°

20°

Sanaa
YEMEN

AFRICA

Aden
Gulf of Aden

Undefined

PEOPLE'S DEMOCRATIC
REPUBLIC OF YEMEN

Socotra I.
(P.D.R. YEMEN)

LACCADIVE
ISLANDS
(INDIA)

Madras

ANDAMA
ISLAND
(INDIA

10°

N

Equator

Colombo

SRI LANKA

Male

MALDIVES

NICOB
ISLAN
(IND

INDIAN

OCEAN

0   500   1000 Miles

0   500   1000 Kilometers

R14

ARCTIC OCEAN

110° 120° 130° 140° 150° 160° 170° 180° 170° 160° 150° 80°

Arctic Circle

70°

Lena River

OVIET   UNION

Lena   River

60°

Bering Sea

Lake Baikal

Sea of Okhotsk

KAMCHATKA PENINSULA

50°

Amur   River

Ulaanbaatar

MONGOLIA

•Harbin

KURIL ISLANDS (U.S.S.R. & JAPAN)

GOBI (DESERT)

Vladivostok

Yalu R.

Sea of Japan

40°

Beijing

N. KOREA

Pyongyang

JAPAN

Tianjin

Truce Line

Seoul

Tokyo

CHINA

Huang He

S. KOREA

Kobe

Yokohama

Yellow Sea

Osaka

PACIFIC

30°

Chang Jiang

•Shanghai

Chongqing

East China Sea

OCEAN

RYUKYU IS. (JAPAN)

Taipei

River

Guangzhou

TAIWAN

Tropic of Cancer

MA

Hanoi

MACAO (PORT.)

HONG KONG (U.K.)

20°

LAOS

entiane

South China Sea

Philippine Sea

ngoon

Mekong R.

THAILAND

PHILIPPINES

ASIA

Bangkok

Manila

⊛ National capital

CAMBODIA (KAMPUCHEA)

VIETNAM

• Other city

Phnom Penh

Ho Chi Minh City

—— National boundary

ROBINSON PROJECTION

10°

BRUNEI

MALAYSIA

Bandar Seri Begawan

Kuala Lumpur

Singapore

SINGAPORE

Equator

0°

Java Sea

Jakarta

INDONESIA

R15

10°

100° 110° 120° 130° 140° 150° 160°

AUSTRALIA, NEW ZEALAND, AND THE SOUTH PACIFIC

⊛ National capital
• Other city
— National boundary

MERCATOR PROJECTION

120° 135° 150° 165° 180° 165° 150° 135°

15° N. MARIANA IS. (U.S.) Wake Island (U.S.) HAWAII (U.S.)

Philippine Sea

Guam (U.S.)

MARSHALL ISLANDS

PACIFIC OCEAN

CAROLINE IS. Kolonia ⊛ Majuro ⊛ MARSHALL IS.

TRUST TERR. OF THE PACIFIC ISLANDS (U.S.)

FEDERATED STATES OF MICRONESIA

Equator 0°

Tarawa

Yaren ⊛

NAURU

KIRIBATI

Arafura Sea

PAPUA NEW GUINEA

SOLOMON ISLANDS

TUVALU

Port Moresby ⊛ Honiara • Funafuti

TOKELAU IS. (N.Z.)

MARQUESAS IS.

Darwin •

Timor Sea

Gulf of Carpentaria

Great Barrier Reef

Coral Sea

VANUATU

W.SAMOA AMERICAN SAMOA (U.S.)

Apia ⊛

TUAMOTU ARCH.

15°

Alice Springs •

AUSTRALIA

Port-Vila • Suva •

NEW CALEDONIA (FR.)

FIJI

LOYALTY IS.(FR.)

TONGA

Nuku'alofa ⊛

NIUE I. (N.Z.)

COOK IS. (N.Z.)

SOCIETY IS.

Tahiti •

FRENCH POLYNESIA (FR.)

Tropic of Capricorn

Perth •

Great Australian Bight

Broken Hill •

Adelaide •

Brisbane •

Port Macquarie •

Sydney •

Canberra ⊛

NORFOLK ISLAND (AUST.)

International Date Line Monday Sunday

N

INDIAN OCEAN

Geelong • Melbourne •

Tasman Sea

Auckland •

NEW ZEALAND

North Island

500 1000 Miles

Bass Strait

Tasmania

Hobart •

Wellington ⊛

500 1000 Kilometers

South Island

Christchurch •

Dunedin •

CHATHAM IS. (N.Z.)

45°

120° 135° 150° 165° 180° 165° 150° 135°

ANTARCTICA

■ Stations
▢ Ice shelf

POLAR AZIMUTHAL EQUIDISTANT PROJECTION

180° 160° 140° 120° 100° 80°

PACIFIC OCEAN

Antarctic Circle

60°

Amundsen Sea

Bellingshausen Sea

SOUTH AMERICA

Presidente Frei (CHILE) ■

70°

Ellsworth Land

ANTARCTIC PENINSULA

Ross Sea

Marie Byrd Land

Ronne Ice Shelf

Weddell Sea

40°

Victoria Land

Ross Ice Shelf

McMurdo (U.S.) ■

+ SOUTH POLE

■ Amundsen-Scott (U.S.)

Gen. Belgrano (ARGENTINA) ■

ANTARCTICA

Halley (U.K.) ■

SOUTH MAGNETIC POLE

Dumont d'Urville (FR.) ■

Queen Maud Land

ATLANTIC OCEAN

20°

140°

Wilkes Land

Vostok (U.S.S.R.) ■

250 500 750 Miles

250 500 750 Kilometers

INDIAN OCEAN

Davis Sea

Mawson (AUSTRALIA) ■

Syoma (JAPAN) ■

Enderby Land

60°

120° 100° 40° 20°

R17

120° 50° 110° 100°

Seattle
Olympia
WASHINGTON

River

R

Portland
Columbia
Salem

CASCADE RANGE

OREGON

IDAHO

Helena

MONTANA

NORTH DAKOT

Bismarck

Boise

O

Billings

Snake *River*

C

WYOMING

BLACK
HILLS

SOUTH DAKOT

Pierre

Sioux

K

Carson City

SIERRA NEVADA

Great
Salt
Lake

Salt Lake
City

Y

Cheyenne

NEBRASKA

COASTAL RANGE

Sacramento
San Francisco

NEVADA

UTAH

M
O
U
N

Denver

KANSAS

Lin

CALIFORNIA

Las
Vegas

River

COLORADO

T
A

Wichit

Los Angeles

ARIZONA

Colorado

Santa Fe

Albuquerque

I
N
S

Amarillo

OKLAHO

Oklaho
C

San Diego

Phoenix

NEW MEXICO

Lubbock

PACIFIC
OCEAN

30°

Tucson

El Paso

TEXAS

D

120° 110°

160°
Kauai
Nihau
Oahu
Honolulu
HAWAII
Molokai
Lanai
Maui
PACIFIC
OCEAN
Hawaii

0   100 Miles
0   100 Kilometers

160°

ARCTIC
OCEAN

70°
30°
Arctic Circle

ALASKA

Yukon River

Fairbanks

Austin

20°

20°

Mt. McKinley
20,320 ft.
6,194 m

San Antonio

60°

Rio Grande

50°   0   250   500 Miles
170° 0   250   500 Kilometers

Bering
Sea

Anchorage

60°

R18

PACIFIC
OCEAN

ALEUTIAN   ISLANDS

Juneau

Gulf of
Alaska

50°

170°

150°

100°

130°

90°
80°
50°
70°

Lake Superior

MICHIGAN

Lake Huron

Duluth
NESOTA
neapolis
St. Paul
Minneapolis
WISCONSIN
Mississippi River

Lake Michigan

Milwaukee
Madison
Lansing

Detroit

IOWA
Des Moines
aha

Chicago
Gary

INDIANA

Indianapolis

ILLINOIS
Springfield

Kansas City
ka

St. Louis

Jefferson City
MISSOURI

tsa

ARKANSAS

Little Rock

Memphis

MISSISSIPPI

Red River

LOUISIANA
Baton Rouge
New Orleans
Houston

Mobile

Jackson

ALABAMA
Montgomery

Birmingham

TENNESSEE
Nashville

Tennessee River

KENTUCKY

Ohio River
Louisville
Frankfort

OHIO
Columbus

Cincinnati

WEST VIRGINIA
Charleston

Pittsburgh

Cleveland

PENNSYLVANIA
Harrisburg
Philadelphia

Washington
Annapolis
MARYLAND
Baltimore
Wilmington
Dover
DELAWARE

NEW JERSEY
Trenton

New York

Lake Erie

Lake Ontario

NEW YORK
Rochester
Buffalo
Albany

Hudson River

St. Lawrence River

MAINE
Augusta

VERMONT
Montpelier
GREEN MTS.
NEW HAMPSHIRE
Concord

Boston
MASSACHUSETTS
Providence
Hartford
RHODE ISLAND
CONNECTICUT

APPALACHIAN MTS.

VIRGINIA
Richmond
Norfolk
Chesapeake Bay

ATLANTIC OCEAN

NORTH CAROLINA
Raleigh
Charlotte

SOUTH CAROLINA
Columbia
Charleston

GEORGIA
Atlanta
Savannah

Jacksonville

Tallahassee

FLORIDA
Orlando
Tampa
Miami

Gulf of Mexico

N

40°

70°

30°

90°

80°

THE UNITED STATES

⊛   National capital
★   State capital
•   Other city
—— National boundary
—— State boundary

ALBERS EQUAL AREA PROJECTION

0   250   500 Miles
0   250   500 Kilometers

R19

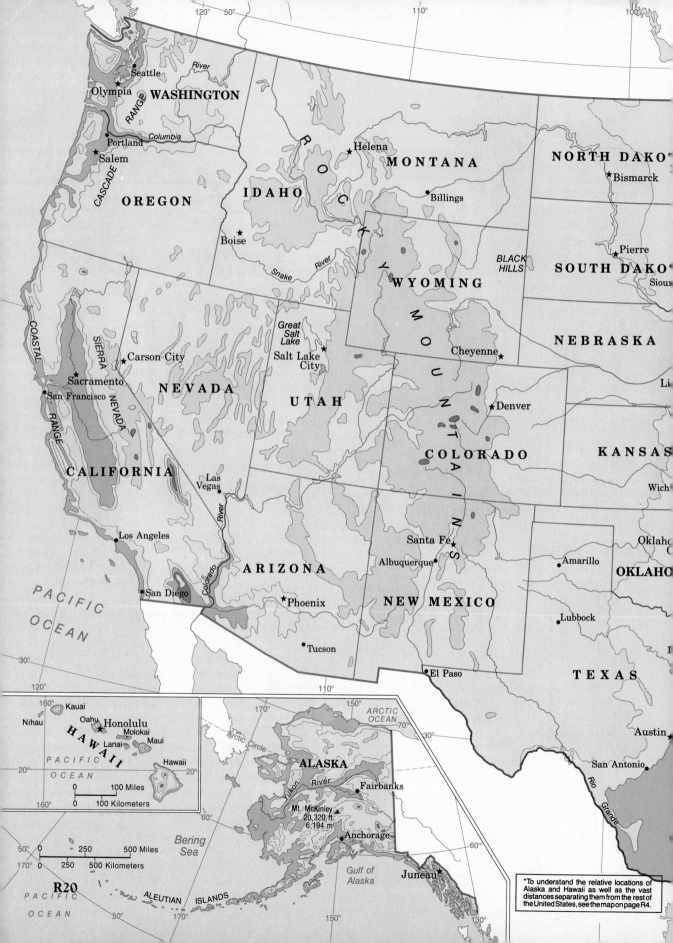

Seattle
Olympia
WASHINGTON
River
R A N G E
Portland
Salem
Columbia
OREGON
CASCADE
Helena
MONTANA
Billings
NORTH DAKO
Bismarck
IDAHO
R O C K Y
Boise
Snake
River
WYOMING
BLACK
HILLS
SOUTH DAKO
Pierre
Sioux
COASTAL
SIERRA NEVADA
Carson City
Great
Salt
Lake
Salt Lake
City
M O U N
Cheyenne
NEBRASKA
Sacramento
San Francisco
NEVADA
UTAH
T
Denver
KANSAS
RANGE
CALIFORNIA
Las
Vegas
River
Colorado
N
Santa Fe
Albuquerque
I
N
S
Amarillo
Wich
Li
Los Angeles
ARIZONA
Phoenix
NEW MEXICO
Lubbock
OKLAHO
Oklaho
C
San Diego
Colorado
PACIFIC
OCEAN
Tucson
El Paso
TEXAS
30°
120°
110°

HAWAII
160°
Kauai
Nihau
Oahu
Honolulu
Molokai
Lanai
Maui
PACIFIC
OCEAN
Hawaii
20°
20°
0   100 Miles
0   100 Kilometers
160°

170°
ARCTIC
OCEAN
70°
Arctic Circle
30°
ALASKA
Yukon
River
Fairbanks
Mt. McKinley
20,320 ft;
6,194 m
60°
Anchorage
60°
Bering
Sea
Gulf of
Alaska
Juneau
ALEUTIAN   ISLANDS
50°
150°
130°

Austin

San Antonio
Rio
Grande

50°   0   250   500 Miles
170° 0   250   500 Kilometers
R20
PACIFIC
OCEAN

*To understand the relative locations of
Alaska and Hawaii as well as the vast
distances separating them from the rest of
the United States, see the map on page R4.

90°   80°   50°   70°

Duluth

MINNESOTA

Minneapolis ★ *St. Paul*

WISCONSIN

Milwaukee ★
★ *Madison*

I O W A

★ *Des Moines*

maha

ILLINOIS

Springfield ★

Lake Superior

M I C H I G A N

Lake Huron

Lake Michigan

Lansing ★

★ *Detroit*

Lake Erie

Chicago ★
Gary

INDIANA

★ *Indianapolis*

O H I O

★ *Columbus*

Cincinnati

Lake Ontario

Rochester   *Albany* ★

NEW YORK

Buffalo ●

PENNSYLVANIA

Harrisburg ★

Pittsburgh ●

St. Lawrence River

MAINE

★ *Augusta*

VERMONT
Montpelier ★

NEW HAMPSHIRE
★ *Concord*

GREEN MTS.

Boston ★

MASSACHUSETTS

Hartford ★   ★ *Providence*

RHODE ISLAND

CONNECTICUT

★ *New York*

NEW JERSEY

★ *Trenton*

Philadelphia ★

Wilmington ●

★ *Dover*

DELAWARE

Hudson River

MISSOURI

Kansas City

eka

★ *Jefferson City*

★ *St. Louis*

KENTUCKY

★ *Frankfort*
Louisville ●

Ohio River

WEST VIRGINIA

★ *Charleston*

Washington ⊛

Baltimore ●

★ *Annapolis*

MARYLAND

Chesapeake Bay

Richmond ★

Norfolk ●

VIRGINIA

APPALACHIAN MTS.

NORTH CAROLINA

Raleigh ★

ATLANTIC OCEAN

ARKANSAS

ulsa

Little Rock ★

Memphis ●

TENNESSEE

★ *Nashville*

Tennessee River

Mississippi River

Charlotte ●

SOUTH CAROLINA

★ *Columbia*

Atlanta ●

Charleston ●

ALABAMA

Jackson ★

★ *Montgomery*
Birmingham ●

GEORGIA

Savannah ●

MISSISSIPPI

Mobile ●

Red River

LOUISIANA

Baton Rouge ★
New Orleans ●

Houston ●

Jacksonville ●

★ *Tallahassee*

FLORIDA

Orlando ●

Tampa ●

Miami ●

Gulf of Mexico

UNITED STATES*
Elevation

Feet	Meters
13,120	4,000
6,560	2,000
1,640	500
656	200
0	0
Below sea level	Below sea level

⊛ National capital
★ State capital
● Other city
─ National boundary
─ State boundary

ALBERS EQUAL AREA PROJECTION

N ↑

0   250   500 Miles

0   250   500 Kilometers

R21

40°

70°

30°

80°

90°

PHONETIC RESPELLING
AND PRONUNCIATION GUIDE

Many of the key terms in this textbook have been respelled to help you pronounce them. The following Phonetic Respelling and Pronunciation Guide offers the simplest form of usage and is adapted from *Webster's Ninth New Collegiate* *Dictionary, Webster's New Geographical Dictionary,* and *Webster's New Biographical Dictionary.* The letter combinations used in the respellings are explained below.

MARK	AS IN	RESPELLING	EXAMPLE
a	alphabet	a	*AL • fuh • bet
ā	Asia	ay	AY • zhuh
ä	cart, top	ah	KAHRT, TAHP
e	let, ten	e	LET, TEN
ē	even, leaf	ee	EE • vuhn, LEEF
i	it, tip, British	i	IT, TIP, BRIT • ish
ī	site, buy, Ohio	y	SYT, BY, oh • HY • oh
	iris	eye	EYE • ris
k	card	k	KARD
ō	over, rainbow	oh	oh • vuhr, RAYN • boh
u̇	book, wood	ooh	BOOHK, WOOHD
ȯ	all, orchid	aw	AWL, AWR • kid
ȯi	foil, coin	oy	FOYL, KOYN
au̇	out	ow	OWT
ə	cup, butter	uh	KUHP, BUHT • uhr
ü	rule, food	oo	ROOL, FOOD
yü	few	yoo	FYOO
zh	vision	zh	VIZH • uhn

*A syllable printed in small capital letters receives heavier emphasis than the other syllables in a word.

PINYIN

Most of the names of Chinese people and Chinese geographical names in this textbook use the Roman alphabet and pronunciation system introduced by the Chinese in the 1950s and in general use since the 1970s. This system, called Pinyin, most accurately reflects the sounds of the Chinese language. The United States government and many newspapers, magazines, and atlases accept and use Pinyin. Both the maps and narrative in this textbook consistently use Pinyin. Some exceptions occur where the names are so well known by their older spellings—using the Wade-Giles system—that the use of Pinyin would confuse rather than help you. Exceptions include Chiang Kai-shek, Kuomintang, Sun Yat-sen, Tibet, Hong Kong, Mongolia, and the word "China" itself.

G·L·O·S·S·A·R·Y

This GLOSSARY contains many of the terms you need to understand as you study world history. After each term there is a brief definition or explanation of the meaning of the term as it is used in world history. The page number in parentheses after each definition refers to the page on which the term is boldfaced in the textbook. A phonetic respelling is provided to help you pronounce many of the terms. (Please refer to the Phonetic Respelling and Pronunciation Guide on page R22.)

The brief definitions in this GLOSSARY do not always provide all the information that you may need to know about these terms. You may find it useful to refer to the page listed in parentheses to read more about the terms.

A

abbot: elected head of a monastery (*p. 234*)

absolute monarchy: system of government in which the ruler determines policy without consulting either the people or their representatives (*p. 355*)

abstract expressionism: painting style characterized by forms, colors, and shapes rather than recognizable objects (*p. 884*)

acropolis: hill or mountain in Greece, together with temples and other public buildings on it (*p. 106*)

acupuncture: Chinese medicinal practice that involves insertion of needles into designated parts of the body to release energy for healing (*p. 87*)

adobe: sun-dried brick used to build houses (*p. 305*)

agora: public meeting place in Greece where all citizens could gather (*p. 106*)

agriculture: raising crops and livestock for food (*p. 8*)

almanac: book that predicts the weather and the prospects for growing crops (*p. 344*)

anarchist: person who believes in the abolition of all governments by force (*p. 562*)

anarchy: absence of any government at all (*p. 168*)

animism: ancient religion characterized by belief that spirits inhabited all things (*p. 52*)

anthropologist: (an • thruh • PAHL • uh • jist) scientist who studies the skeletal remains of early humanlike creatures and people to determine how they looked, how long they lived, and other physical characteristics (*p. 3*)

antibiotic: substance that stops the growth of bacteria (*p. 881*)

apartheid: (uh • PART • hyt) official policy of racial separation followed by the South African government after 1948 (*p. 812*)

appeasement: policy of attempting to preserve peace by yielding to the demands of the aggressor (*p. 718*)

apprentice: person who went through stages of training and was a candidate for membership in a craft guild (*p. 257*)

aqueduct: bridgelike structure that carried water from the mountains to the city (*p. 156*)

arbitration: negotiation for the settlement of a dispute by a party agreed upon by all sides (*p. 620*)

arch: curved structure over an opening (*p. 30*)

archaeologist: (ahr • kee • AHL • uh • jist) scientist who excavates ancient settlements and studies artifacts (*p. 3*)

archon: elected ruler in the early government of Athens (*p. 114*)

aristocracy: city-state in ancient Greece governed by nobles; today, means a privileged social class (*p. 110*)

armistice: agreement to stop fighting until a treaty can be drawn up (*p. 655*)

artifact: human-made material object, for example, a tool, a weapon, or a coin (*p. 3*)

artisan: skilled craftworker (*p. 10*)

assimilation: situation in which people of a colony abandoned their local culture and adopted all aspects of another culture (*p. 609*)

astrolabe: instrument used to calculate latitude (*p. 356*)

atrocity: brutal crime of war (*p. 651*)

authoritarian socialism: economic and political system in which the government owns almost all the means of production; communism (*p. 511*)

autocracy: form of government in which the ruler holds total power (*p. 78*)

autocrat: one who holds absolute power (*p. 587*)

B

balance of power: principle of maintaining equilibrium in international politics (*p. 382*)

barter: exchange of one good or service for another good or service (*p. 39*)

barter economy: economic system in which goods are exchanged for goods without the use of money (*p. 255*)

belligerent: warring nation *(p. 643)*

Bessemer process: way to make steel involving forcing air through molten iron to burn out impurities *(p. 493)*

biological science: science that deals with living organisms *(p. 521)*

blitzkrieg: German word for "lightning war" *(p. 720)*

bourgeoisie: (boorzh • wah • ZEE) city-dwelling middle class in France *(pp. 425, 510)*

boyar: noble in Kievan society *(p. 196)*

Brahman: priest in the Vedic religion *(p. 55)*

broadside: single printed sheet often making fun of a favorite object of humor, such as monks *(p. 344)*

buffer state: small country located between two hostile powers that often lessens the possibility of conflict between them *(p. 617)*

burgesses: merchants and professional people from towns and cities in early England *(p. 397)*

Bushido: (BOOH • shee • doh) samurai code that stressed bravery, loyalty, and honor *(p. 286)*

business cycle: pattern consisting of alternating periods of prosperity and decline *(p. 501)*

C

cabinet: leaders of the House of Commons who advised the English monarch *(p. 407)*

caliph: Islamic word meaning "successor to the prophet" *(p. 208)*

caliphate: one of three divisions of the Muslim Empire *(p. 210)*

calligraphy: (kuh • LIG • ruh • fee) artful form of writing originated by the Chinese *(p. 75)*

campesino: name given to a Central American peasant *(p. 839)*

canon law: church code of law *(p. 236)*

capital: wealth earned, saved, or invested in order to produce profits *(p. 256)*

capitalism: economic system in which private individuals use money that is earned, saved, or invested to produce profits *(p. 499)*

caravan: group of people traveling over long distances together for safety *(p. 24)*

cartel: combination of corporations that control an entire industry *(p. 501)*

caste system: Indian social organization composed of four classes *(p. 58)*

cavalry: military unit of soldiers on horses *(p. 34)*

censor: person who registered citizens according to their wealth to determine how much they should pay in taxes *(p. 146)*

checks and balances: system that prevents any one part of a government from becoming too powerful *(p. 146)*

chinampa: floating artificial island farmed by Aztecs *(p. 310)*

chivalry: code of conduct for knights *(p. 231)*

chora: land outside walls of Greek city-states *(p. 105)*

citadel: strong central fortress *(p. 52)*

city-state: form of government developed by the Sumerians; it consisted of a town or city and the surrounding land it controlled *(p. 29)*

civil service: system that administers the government on a day-to-day basis whose members are usually appointed on the basis of competitive examinations *(p. 79)*

civilization: highly organized society with complex institutions and attitudes that link a large number of people together *(p. 3)*

coalition: political groups organized in support of a common cause *(p. 562)*

cold war: hostility between the Communist and Western nations waged by political and economic means rather than with weapons *(p. 751)*

collaborator: person willing to assist his or her country's enemies *(p. 721)*

collective bargaining: process of negotiation between union members and management *(p. 507)*

collective farm: land pooled into a large farm where people can work together as a group *(p. 685)*

collegia: (kuh • LEE • jee • uh) workers' trade associations in ancient Rome *(p. 167)*

colonus: Roman tenant farmer who replaced slaves on large estates *(p. 157)*

colony: area in which a foreign nation gained total control over another region and its local population *(p. 602)*

comedy: Greek play mocking ideas and people *(p. 132)*

command economy: economic system in which government planners make all economic decisions *(pp. 685, 762)*

commercial capitalism: early phase of capitalism involving merchants who bought, sold, and exchanged goods *(p. 499)*

Commercial Revolution: changes and developments in the European economy from about 1500 to about 1750 *(p. 357)*

common law: law based on judges' decisions rather than on a code of statutes *(p. 242)*

communism: authoritarian socialism *(p. 511)*

compass: instrument used for navigational purposes showing direction *(p. 356)*

conceptual art: art trend that claims that creative thought is more important than either the process or the product created *(p. 885)*

concession: grant of economic rights and privileges in a given area *(p. 602)*

condominium: situation occurring when two nations rule a third nation as partners *(p. 602)*

conscription: draft adopted in France that made men from 18 to 45 years of age liable for military service *(p. 435)*

conservative: person who does not want to change existing conditions *(p. 433)*

constitution: document outlining the fundamental laws and principles that govern a nation *(p. 402)*

consul: chief executive in early Rome who ran the government and served as an army commander *(p. 145)*

consulate: diplomatic office headed by a consul *(p. 468)*

containment: policy aimed at restricting the spread of communism *(p. 758)*

contraband: war materials supplied to a belligerent nation by a neutral nation *(p. 651)*

corporate state: nation in which the major economic activities are organized into syndicates that resemble corporations *(p. 680)*

corporation: business organization involving the sale of stock to investors but limiting the shareholders' financial responsibility to the amount invested *(p. 501)*

Counter-Reformation: major effort in the 1530s to create a new, more spiritual outlook in the Catholic church *(p. 337)*

counterrevolution: fight against the regular French army and the Revolution in the western part of France *(p. 435)*

coup d'état: (kood•ay•TAH) seizure of power by force *(p. 439)*

covenant: solemn agreement or promise *(p. 400)*

covert: term describing undercover military and financial aid to a nation *(p. 839)*

craft guild: organization of skilled workers engaged in one particular craft *(p. 257)*

creole: native-born white person who lived in a Latin American colony *(p. 563)*

crop rotation: alternating crops of different kinds to preserve soil fertility *(p. 490)*

crucifixion: common Roman method of execution in which the accused was placed on a cross and left to die a slow death from suffocation *(p. 151)*

Crusade: expedition to regain the Holy Land *(p. 250)*

cubism: art style that emphasized forms, shapes, and designs *(p. 668)*

cultural diffusion: spread of culture from one area of the world to another *(p. 11)*

culture: what humans acquire by living together—language, knowledge, skills, art, literature, and life styles *(p. 4)*

cuneiform: (kyoo•NEE•uh•fawrm) Sumerian method of writing using a stylus to make combinations of wedge shapes *(p. 29)*

czar: Russian word for "caesar" or emperor *(p. 200)*

D

daimyo: (DY•mee•oh) samurai leader who gained the loyalty of the lesser samurai *(p. 286)*

democracy: government in which all citizens take part and limit the power of rulers *(p. 110)*

democratic socialism: political system in which the government takes over the means of production peacefully; people retain basic human rights and partial control over economic planning *(p. 511)*

department: administrative district of France *(p. 430)*

depression: lowest point of a business cycle *(p. 501)*

desertification: spread of the desert *(p. 815)*

détente: (day•TAHNT) era of improved Soviet-American relations *(p. 855)*

developed nation: nation with a high degree of economic sophistication *(p. 757)*

developing nation: nation with limited resources and rapid population growth *(p. 757)*

dharma: Hindu belief in fulfillment of moral duty so that the soul can progress toward deliverance from punishment in the next life *(p. 58)*

dictator: leader with absolute power *(p. 146)*

direct democracy: form of government in which all citizens participate directly in making decisions rather than through elected representatives *(p. 115)*

direct rule: situation that occurs when the imperialist power controls all levels of government and appoints its own officials to govern *(p. 609)*

dissident: person dissatisfied with the government *(pp. 842, 855)*

divine right of kings: belief that God ordained certain individuals to govern *(p. 381)*

division of labor: characteristic of early civilization or later manufacturing process in which different people perform different tasks *(pp. 9, 499)*

domain: manor land the lord kept for himself; consisted of about one-third of the manor *(p. 230)*

domestic system: method of production in which work is done in homes rather than in a shop or factory *(pp. 255, 491)*

domesticate: to tame animals, such as the goat *(p. 8)*

domino theory: belief that if one nation in a region falls to communism, other nations in the region will also fall to communism *(p. 796)*

dower: groom's marriage gift to his bride *(p. 211)*

dowry: money or goods a wife brings to a marriage *(p. 188)*

drama: play containing action or dialogue and usually involving conflict and emotion *(p. 131)*

dynasty: family of rulers whose right to rule is hereditary *(p. 20)*

E

economic boom: sudden increase in prosperity *(p. 671)*

economic nationalism: policy nations use to try to improve their own economic well-being through protective tariffs and similar restrictions without consideration for other countries *(p. 671)*

economic sanction: refusal to trade with an offending nation *(p. 661)*

emigration: movement of people to other lands *(p. 525)*

émigré: noble who fled France during the Revolution *(p. 430)*

empire: form of government that unites different territories and peoples under one ruler *(p. 22)*

enclosure movement: practice of fencing or enclosing common lands into individual holdings *(p. 490)*

enlightened despotism: system of government in which absolute monarchs ruled according to the principles of the Enlightenment *(p. 424)*

Enlightenment: belief that people could apply the scientific method and use reason to logically explain human nature *(p. 421)*

entente: (ahn • TAHNT) friendly understanding or agreement between nations *(p. 641)*

ephor: one of five rulers or overseers elected by the Assembly in Sparta *(p. 112)*

epic: long poem describing heroes and great events *(pp. 58, 106)*

Epic Age: period in the history of India from 1000 B.C. to 500 B.C. *(p. 57)*

equites: (EK • wuh • teez) class of Roman business people who had great wealth but little political power *(p. 150)*

ethical monotheism: Jewish form of monotheism that emphasizes proper conduct *(p. 45)*

evolution: belief that plants and animals developed from common ancestors long ago *(p. 521)*

excommunication: official act that bars a person from church membership and from taking part in any church ceremonies *(p. 191)*

executive branch: branch of government that enforces the laws *(p. 417)*

export: good or service that is sold to another country *(p. 110)*

extraterritoriality: exemption of foreigners from the laws of the nation where they live or do business *(p. 461)*

F

factors of production: basic resources necessary for industrialization *(p. 490)*

factory system: production of goods through use of machines and many workers *(p. 491)*

fascism: governmental doctrine that relies on dictatorial rule and a totalitarian regime, in which rigid control is maintained by the government through force and censorship *(p. 679)*

favorable balance of trade: situation that exists when a country sells more goods than it buys from a foreign country *(p. 359)*

federal system of government: system of government with powers divided between a central, or federal, government and individual states *(p. 416)*

feudalism: political and military system of local government based on the granting of land in return for loyalty, military assistance, and services *(p. 228)*

fief: grant of land given by a feudal lord to a vassal *(p. 228)*

Fourteen Points: President Woodrow Wilson's plan based on the Allies' aims to end World War I *(p. 654)*

free enterprise: Adam Smith's economic system based on supply, demand, and competition *(p. 502)*

free trade: practice based on the belief that government should not restrict or interfere in international trade *(p. 460)*

fresco: wall painting made on wet plaster *(p. 104)*

functionalism: architectural principle that a building's design should reflect its specific use rather than reflect popular styles *(p. 670)*

G

galley: type of early European trade ship *(p. 356)*

general strike: bargaining method in which workers in various industries refuse to work until their demands are met *(p. 675)*

genetics: study of the ways in which inborn characteristics of plants and animals are inherited by their descendants *(p. 522)*

gentry: class of Englishmen who owned land and had social position **(p. 397)**

geocentric theory: theory that earth is at the center of the universe **(p. 348)**

geopolitical region: area that shares similar political and geographic features **(p. 836)**

glacier: large, slowly moving mass of snow and ice **(p. 5)**

glasnost: Soviet policy that loosened censorship and eased the repression of the Brezhnev years **(p. 866)**

Great Depression: worldwide depression beginning in 1929 **(p. 672)**

gross national product (GNP): dollar value of all new, finished products produced in a nation in one year **(p. 826)**

guerrilla warfare: military technique relying on raids by small bands of soldiers **(p. 374)**

H

habeas corpus: legal right protecting individuals against illegal arrest and imprisonment **(p. 405)**

hacienda: (hahs • ee • EN • duh) large, self-sufficient farming estate **(p. 563)**

hegira: (hih • JY • ruh) flight of Muhammad and his followers to Medina in 622; marks the first year of the Muslim calendar **(p. 206)**

heliocentric theory: theory that the sun is at the center of the universe **(p. 348)**

Hellenistic culture: culture founded on Greek ideas blended with features from other cultures of the Mediterranean region **(p. 125)**

helot: (HEL • uht) agricultural worker of Peloponnesus forced to work for the Spartans after the area was conquered **(p. 111)**

heresy: opinion that conflicts with church doctrine **(p. 191)**

hieroglyphics: (hy • uhr • GLIF • iks) method of Egyptian writing that uses pictures or symbols to indicate words or sounds **(p. 19)**

history: record of events since people first developed writing about 5,000 years ago **(p. 3)**

Holocaust: systematic destruction of European Jews by the Nazis **(p. 730)**

home rule: self-government **(p. 547)**

hubris: (HYOO • bruhs) arrogance that doomed character in a Greek play to a tragic fate **(p. 132)**

humanist: person who stressed dignity of human nature and had appreciation for the arts and for public life **(p. 326)**

I

Ice Age: time when the Earth had extremely cold weather **(p. 5)**

icon: Byzantine picture of Jesus, the Virgin Mary, or the saints **(p. 190)**

iconoclast: Byzantine who believed that the presence of icons constituted idol worship **(p. 191)**

iconoclastic controversy: argument between the supporters and the opponents of icons **(p. 191)**

imam: Shiite leader believed to be a direct descendant of Muhammad **(p. 210)**

imperialism: domination of a powerful nation over the political, economic, and cultural affairs of another nation or region **(p. 599)**

import: good or service that is bought from another country **(p. 110)**

import substitution: economic policy in which officials examine the list of goods that a country imports to find those items that could be produced inside the country **(p. 833)**

impressionist: French artist who painted vivid impressions of people and places as they might appear in a brief glance **(p. 538)**

indemnity: money for war damages **(pp. 148, 447)**

indirect rule: British system in which a governor and a council of advisers made colonial laws, but local rulers exerted some authority **(p. 609)**

indulgence: pardon given in return for repentance or donations to the church **(p. 333)**

industrial capitalism: phase of the Industrial Revolution in which capitalists were directly involved in producing and manufacturing goods **(p. 499)**

Industrial Revolution: introduction of industrial technology that changed the way goods were produced **(p. 489)**

infantry: soldiers trained and equipped to fight on foot **(p. 133)**

inflation: rise in prices caused by a decrease in the value of the exchange medium **(pp. 166, 345)**

Inquisition: the search for heretics begun during the mid-1200s **(p. 237)**

intendant: local administrator of a French province **(p. 378)**

interdict: church's punishment of an entire region; it involved withholding sacraments **(p. 236)**

international style: style of architecture that was functional, plain, and severe, using uninterrupted expanses of steel and glass **(p. 670)**

iron-curtain country: Soviet satellite nation **(p. 758)**

irrigation: method of supplying water for crops based on using ditches and canals **(p. 10)**

isolationist: person who believed that Europe's wars were no affair of the United States *(p. 725)*

J

joint-stock company: business organization that raised money by selling stock, or shares, in the company to investors *(p. 358)*

journeyman: skilled artisan who worked for a master for wages *(p. 258)*

judicial branch: branch of government that interprets and applies the laws *(p. 417)*

jungle: thick growth of plants found on the forest floor in a tropical rain forest *(p. 294)*

junk: large Chinese ship first built during the Ming period *(p. 454)*

K

kaiser: (KY•zuhr) title of the German emperor *(p. 582)*

karma: Hindu belief that the present condition of a person's life reflects what a person did during a previous life *(p. 58)*

kibbutz: collective farm in Israel *(p. 818)*

kingdom: term for *monarchy,* an early form of government headed by a king or queen *(p. 20)*

L

laissez-faire: (le•say-FAYR) belief that government should leave business alone *(p. 504)*

latifundia: (lat•uh•FUHN•dee•uh) large Roman estates *(p. 150)*

latitude: distance north or south of the equator *(p. 356)*

legion: most important military unit of the Roman army; consisted of 4,500 to 6,000 soldiers *(p. 146)*

legislative branch: branch of government that makes the laws *(p. 417)*

legitimacy: policy stating that all former ruling families should be restored to their thrones *(p. 445)*

liberalism: movement that extended the principles of the American and French revolutions; stressed individual rights and the rule of law rather than rule of a monarch *(pp. 448, 543)*

limited constitutional monarchy: government led by a monarch whose powers were limited by a constitution *(p. 408)*

linguist: scholar who studies languages *(p. 295)*

lobbying: policy of trying to get legislators to vote for or against a measure *(p. 770)*

loess: (LES) extraordinarily fertile soil *(p. 71)*

M

Magna Carta: English document intended to protect the liberties of nobles *(p. 240)*

mandate: area to be administered by the government of an advanced nation *(p. 661)*

Mandate of Heaven: orders ancient Chinese rulers were believed to have received through communication with the spirits *(p. 73)*

manor: economic unit of the Middle Ages; an estate that included a village *(p. 229)*

market economy: an economy in which land, labor, and capital are controlled by individuals *(pp. 256, 762)*

market speculation: risky investment in the stock market in the hope of quick, high profits *(p. 672)*

martyr: person put to death because he or she refused to renounce certain beliefs *(p. 164)*

mass production: system of manufacturing large numbers of items that are exactly alike *(p. 500)*

matrilineal: (ma•truh•LIN•ee•uhl) describes a society in which people trace their ancestry through their mothers rather than through their fathers *(p. 296)*

mechanization: use of automatic machinery to increase production *(p. 491)*

medieval: term that describes the period known as the Middle Ages *(p. 223)*

mercantilism: economic theory stating that there is a fixed amount of wealth in the world and that in order to receive a larger share, one country has to take some wealth away from another country *(p. 358)*

mercenary: professional soldier paid to serve in a foreign army *(p. 35)*

merchant guild: organization of merchants *(p. 257)*

mestizo: person of American Indian and white background *(p. 563)*

metic: alien or person who was not an Athenian *(p. 114)*

metropolitan: chief bishop of the Kievan church *(p. 198)*

Middle Ages: medieval period between ancient times and the modern period *(p. 223)*

Middle Passage: second stage of the triangular trade system *(p. 365)*

migrate: to move from place to place *(p. 5)*

militarism: glorification of armed strength *(p. 640)*

millet: community of religious minorities within the Ottoman Empire *(p. 214)*

miniaturization: process of making electronic equipment smaller *(p. 878)*

miracle play: mystery play; a biblical drama performed in marketplaces **(p. 260)**

mixed economy: economy characterized by the private ownership of some industries and government ownership of others **(p. 788)**

mobilize: to organize a nation's resources for combat **(p. 640)**

moderate: a person who had no extreme views and sided with conservatives or radicals depending on the situation **(p. 433)**

monarchy: term for *kingdom*, an early form of government headed by a king or queen **(p. 20)**

monasticism: system of monasteries and convents in which Christians withdrew from the world to lead a life of prayer, fasting, and self-denial **(p. 234)**

money economy: economic system based on the use of money rather than on barter **(p. 39)**

monism: Hindu belief that God and human beings are one **(p. 58)**

monopoly: control of the total production or sale of a good or service by a single firm **(p. 501)**

monotheism: (MAHN • uh • thee • iz • uhm) belief in one god **(p. 22)**

monsoon: seasonal wind named for the direction in which it blows or the season in which it occurs **(p. 51)**

mosaic: picture or design formed by inlaid pieces of stone, glass, or enamel **(p. 193)**

mosque: Muslim temple **(p. 207)**

mulatto: person of black and white ancestry **(p. 563)**

mullah: person learned in Islamic faith and law **(p. 207)**

multinational corporation: foreign-owned business in a host country **(p. 833)**

mummification: Egyptian preservation process that involved treating a corpse with various substances **(p. 27)**

myth: traditional story about the deeds and misdeeds of gods, goddesses, and heroes **(p. 108)**

N

nationalism: love of one's country rather than love of a native region **(p. 441)**

nationalize: to put industry under government control or ownership **(p. 676)**

natural rights: rights to life, liberty, and property **(p. 405)**

naturalist: person who writes of the ugly and sordid in life, carefully screening emotion and opinion from his or her writings **(p. 538)**

Neolithic Revolution: shift from food hunting to food production in prehistoric times **(p. 8)**

95 theses: Luther's protests against indulgences, which he posted on the church door at Wittenberg **(p. 334)**

nirvana: Buddhist belief of attaining perfect peace by freeing the soul from the endless cycle of reincarnation **(p. 60)**

nomad: wanderer who travels from place to place in search of food **(p. 8)**

non-alignment: nation's policy of refusing to ally with either the United States or the Soviet Union **(p. 786)**

O

oasis: place in the desert where there is irrigation or an underground spring **(p. 17)**

op art: art style characterized by the use of optical effects **(p. 884)**

oracle bones: bones used by Chinese priests, who wrote questions on the shoulder bones of cattle or the bottom of tortoise shells and then interpreted answers to the questions from patterns or cracks that developed when the bones were heated **(p. 75)**

oral tradition: passing of poems, songs, and stories by word of mouth from one generation to another **(p. 295)**

orator: public speaker **(p. 134)**

Ostpolitik: German chancellor Brandt's efforts to create better relations between East and West **(p. 860)**

P

papyrus: reed plant the Egyptians used to make a smooth material to write on **(p. 19)**

partnership: business owned and controlled by two or more people **(p. 500)**

passive resistance: civil disobedience; peaceful refusal of citizens to cooperate with their government in order to win concessions from it **(p. 694)**

pasteurization: process of heating liquids to kill bacteria and prevent fermentation **(p. 523)**

paterfamilias: (pat • uhr • fuh • MIL • ee • uhs) father of a Roman family; had absolute authority **(p. 147)**

paternalism: system of governing colonies in much the same way as parents guide their children **(p. 609)**

patriarch: bishop of administrative centers for the church in the last years of the Roman Empire **(p. 166)**

patrician: citizen in the ancient Roman aristocracy **(p. 146)**

patriotism: feeling of loyalty to a country **(p. 265)**

Pax Romana: period of Roman peace from 27 B.C. to A.D. 180: from the beginning of Augustus' reign until the death of Marcus Aurelius **(p. 155)**

pedagogue: male slave who taught a young boy manners and went everywhere with him **(p. 116)**

peninsular: white person who was born in Spain or Portugal but who lived in Latin America **(p. 563)**

perestroika: Soviet restructuring policy designed to completely overhaul the Soviet political and economic systems **(p. 866)**

perspective: art technique that involves making distant objects smaller than those in the foreground and arranging them to create the illusion of depth on a flat surface **(p. 329)**

phalanx: (FAY • langks) military formation composed of 16 rows of soldiers equipped with lances **(p. 133)**

pharaoh: Egyptian ruler's title **(p. 20)**

philology: history of words **(p. 457)**

philosophes: (fee • luh • ZAWFS) thinkers or philosophers of the Enlightenment **(p. 422)**

philosophy: study of the most fundamental questions of reality and human existence **(p. 128)**

physical science: science that deals with the inanimate, or nonliving, aspects of nature **(p. 518)**

planned economy: governmental regulation and direction of natural resources to meet a definite goal **(p. 674)**

plebeian: (pli • BEE • yuhn) citizen in Rome not of the aristocratic class **(p. 146)**

plebiscite: (PLEB • uh • syt) procedure used by Napoleon to submit the constitution of his new government to the people for a vote **(p. 439)**

pogrom: (POH • gruhm) massacre of Jews in Russia **(p. 589)**

polis: term that in Greece originally meant a fort, but later included the surrounding city **(p. 105)**

polygamy: marriage to more than one wife **(p. 64)**

polytheism: (PAHL • i • thee • iz • uhm) belief in many gods **(p. 22)**

pop art: style used by artists who painted popular objects such as soup cans, pictures from comic books, or flags **(p. 884)**

pope: title assumed by the patriarch of Rome and head of the Catholic Church; from the Latin word meaning "father" **(p. 166)**

popular government: idea that people can and should rule themselves and not be ruled by others **(p. 110)**

popular sovereignty: governmental principle based on just laws and on a government created by and subject to the will of the people **(p. 423)**

praetor: (PREET • uhr) military commander and judge in ancient Rome **(p. 146)**

predestination: belief that in the beginning of time God decided who would be saved and who would be damned **(p. 336)**

prehistory: long period of time before people kept written records **(p. 3)**

prime minister: chief minister of the cabinet, leader of the government **(p. 408)**

primogeniture: (pri • moh • JEN • uh • chuhr) French law under which only the eldest son could inherit his father's property **(pp. 228, 425)**

process art: art style focusing on the arrangement of "environments," composed of objects and people, that emphasize the creation of art as being more important than the actual art **(p. 885)**

Prohibition: law forbidding the manufacture, sale, and transportation of alcoholic beverages **(p. 671)**

proletariat: (proh • luh • TAYR • ee • uht) working class **(p. 510)**

propaganda: ideas, facts, or rumors spread deliberately to further one's cause or to damage an opposing cause **(p. 648)**

prophet: person who speaks of divinely inspired revelations **(p. 43)**

protectorate: colony in which the native ruler keeps his title, but officials of the foreign power actually control the region **(p. 602)**

psychoanalysis: process of revealing and analyzing the unconscious **(p. 532)**

purge: act of forcing people to leave an organization or an area **(p. 686)**

Q

quantum theory: Planck's theory that energy can only be released in definite "packages" **(p. 520)**

queue: (KYOO) single braid that characterized hair style for Chinese men during the Qing dynasty **(p. 455)**

quipu: (KEE • poo) type of knotted string the Incas used to assist the memory **(p. 311)**

R

rabbi: Jewish scholar learned in scriptures and in commentaries on religious law **(p. 162)**

radical: person who wants far-reaching changes **(p. 433)**

radioactivity: process in which atoms of uranium and radium constantly disintegrate and release energy on their own **(p. 520)**

radiocarbon dating: technique that allows the age of organic matter to be identified by measuring its rate of decay **(p. 4)**

rajah: prince who ruled an Aryan city-state **(p. 57)**

rationalism: characteristic of the Enlightenment; rose from the belief that truth can be arrived at solely by reason **(p. 421)**

reaction: desire to return to the conditions of an earlier period **(p.447)**

reactionary: extremist who not only opposes change, but generally would like to turn the clock back to the way things were before **(p. 447)**

realism: realities of everyday life characterized in literature and art in the mid-1800s **(p. 536)**

recession: period of temporary business slowdown and increased unemployment **(p. 769)**

Reformation: religious revolution that split the Christian church in western Europe **(p. 333)**

regionalism: portrayal of everyday life in different parts of a large country **(p. 538)**

reincarnation: Hindu belief in transmigration of the soul **(p. 58)**

Renaissance: movement following the Middle Ages that centered on revival of interest in the classical learning of Greece and Rome **(p. 325)**

reparation: payment for war damages **(p. 658)**

representative democracy: form of government in which citizens elect representatives to run the government for them **(p. 115)**

republic: form of government in which voters elect their leaders **(p. 145)**

revolution: violent attempt to change a country's government and society **(p. 395)**

rhetoric: study of oratory, or public speaking **(p. 117)**

Risorgimento: (ree • sor • jee • MEN • toh) Italian word for "resurgence," used as a name for Italian nationalist movement **(p. 574)**

romantic movement; romanticism: trend followed by many writers of the early 1800s whose work appealed to sentiment and imagination and dealt with the romance of life—life as it used to be, or ought to be, rather than as it actually was **(p. 534)**

S

sacrament: special ceremony at which a participant receives the direct favor, or grace, of God to help him or her ward off the consequences of sin **(p. 233)**

salon: gathering of the social, political, and cultural elite in France **(p. 423)**

samizdat: Russian word meaning "self-published"; described editions put out by banned authors **(p. 868)**

samurai: (SAM • uh • ry) Japanese warlord who led local military units **(p. 286)**

satellite country: nation dependent upon the Soviet Union **(p. 758)**

savanna: vast area of relatively dry grassland **(p. 295)**

scholasticism: attempt of medieval philosophers to reconcile faith and reason **(p. 263)**

scientific method: inquiry method that includes carefully conducted experiments and mathematical calculations to verify the results of the experiments **(p. 348)**

Scientific Revolution: transformation of thinking during the 1500s caused by experimentation and by questioning traditional opinions **(p. 347)**

scorched-earth policy: practice of burning or destroying crops and everything else that might be of value to an enemy **(p. 443)**

scribe: clerk who read or wrote for those who could not **(p. 26)**

sea dog: English sea captain who was both trader and pirate **(p. 410)**

secede: to withdraw from a union **(p. 554)**

sect: society of a few people, usually with a preacher as their leader **(p. 335)**

sectionalism: rivalry among the various sections of a country **(p. 554)**

sepoy: (SEE • poy) local troop in India trained and led by a British officer **(p. 474)**

seppuku: (se • POO • koo) form of ceremonial suicide known as hara-kiri, or "belly-slitting" **(p. 286)**

serf: person bound to the land **(p. 230)**

shire: governmental district in early England **(p. 238)**

shogun: chief officer of the Japanese emperor and the agent of powerful families **(p. 286)**

shuttle diplomacy: process in which a negotiator moves back and forth between countries for the purpose of reaching a peace agreement **(p. 821)**

silt: fertile soil carried as sediment in river water **(pp. 18, 71)**

simony: purchase of a church position during feudal times **(p. 236)**

social Darwinism: application of Darwin's theory stating that society, like plant and animal worlds, had evolved from lower to higher forms through natural selection. If so-called inferior types were allowed to die out, then society would be made up exclusively of superior people **(p. 531)**

social science: field of study dealing with economic development, political institutions, history, and relations among people **(p. 529)**

socialism: political and economic system based on the belief that the means of production should be owned by the government and should be operated for the welfare of all the people **(p. 507)**

sole proprietorship: business owned and controlled by one person **(p. 500)**

special theory of relativity: Einstein's theory that no particle of matter can move faster than the speed of light and that motion can be measured only relative to some particular observer **(p. 520)**

sphere of influence: region where one nation has special economic and political privileges that are recognized by other nations **(p. 602)**

stagflation: combination of decreased economic activity and continued price increases **(p. 853)**

standard of living: measure of the quality of life of a people or a country **(p. 345)**

steppe: vast, grassy plain in eastern Europe **(p. 196)**

strike: bargaining method involving the refusal of workers to work until their demands have been met **(p. 506)**

stupa: hemispherical or dome-shaped shrine that held objects associated with Buddha **(p. 64)**

subsidy: government grant of money **(p. 359)**

suffrage: voting rights **(p. 544)**

suffragette: woman who wanted voting rights for all women **(p. 547)**

sultan: Turkish ruler **(p. 215)**

summit conference: meeting involving the highest officials of participating nations **(p. 761)**

surrealism: art movement that attempted to portray and interpret life as if it took place in a dream **(p. 666)**

suttee: ritual suicide by Indian widows **(p. 64)**

T

taiga: (TY • guh) forest zone in northern region of Kievan states **(p. 198)**

tariff: import tax on foreign goods **(p. 359)**

tax farming: selling the right to collect taxes to private individuals **(p. 377)**

Ten Commandments: moral laws of the Hebrews revealed to Moses by their god Yahweh **(p. 42)**

tepee: cone-shaped tent made of buffalo hide **(p. 306)**

terracing: creating small, flat plots of land by building low walls around the hillsides and filling the space behind them with soil **(p. 115)**

terrorism: bombings, assassinations, and kidnappings by political groups to force governments to meet their demands **(pp. 588, 824)**

theocracy: government ruled by the clergy **(p. 336)**

tithe: church tax collected from Christians in early times that represented one-tenth of their income; today a tithe is a gift to a church that represents one-tenth of a person's income **(pp. 236, 425)**

totalitarian regime: highly centralized government that allows no opposition and holds total control **(p. 665)**

trade deficit: situation in which a country imports more than it exports **(p. 853)**

tragedy: form of Greek drama showing the major character struggling against fate **(p. 132)**

triangular trade: system through which European merchants shipped goods to Africa in exchange for slaves who were transported to America and sold to plantation owners **(p. 365)**

tribune: Roman official elected by the Assembly of Tribes **(p. 146)**

tropical rain forest: vast, forested region receiving more than 100 inches of annual rainfall **(p. 294)**

troubadour: traveling singer who entertained people during the Middle Ages **(p. 259)**

tyrant: someone who seizes power by force rather than by inheriting it and rules alone **(p. 110)**

U

ujamaa: local cooperative village organized to increase productivity and improve standards of living in Tanzania **(p. 814)**

ultimatum: demand that puts forth the final terms ordered for a settlement **(p. 643)**

union: association of workers that plans actions and coordinates demands for workers **(p. 507)**

universal manhood suffrage: the right of every man to vote, regardless of whether he owned property **(p. 434)**

usury: (YOOZH • uh • ree) policy of charging interest on loans **(p. 253)**

utilitarianism: belief that the principle of utility, or usefulness, was the standard by which to measure a society and its laws **(p. 504)**

utopia: an ideal place or society **(p. 331)**

utopian socialist: person who believes that people can live at peace with each other if they live in small cooperative settlements, owning all of the means of production in common and sharing the products **(p. 510)**

V

vassal: person granted land from a lord in return for services *(p. 228)*

vernacular language: "everyday" speech that varies in different places *(p. 259)*

veto: to refuse to approve a measure *(p. 145)*

veto power: power to defeat a measure by a single vote *(p. 755)*

viceroy: representative of the Spanish monarch *(p. 367)*

W

war of attrition: slow wearing-down process in which each side tries to outlast the other *(p. 650)*

welfare state: nation in which the government undertakes primary responsibility for the social welfare of its citizens *(p. 764)*

Western civilization: civilization that evolved in Europe and in recent centuries spread to the Americas *(p. 101)*

Y

yoga: Hindu religious practice of physical and mental discipline that harmonizes the body with the soul *(p. 59)*

Z

ziggurat: Sumerian temple built in layers *(p. 30)*

Zionism: movement to resettle Jews in Palestine *(p. 692)*

Page numbers in *italics* that have *c* before them refer to charts, diagrams, or graphs; *f*, to special features; *m*, to maps; *n*, to notes; and *p*, to pictures. The index employs two kinds of cross-references. *See* references lead the reader from a subject term to an alternate term under which page numbers will be found. An example of a *see* reference is

Catholic church. *See* Roman Catholic church

See also references lead the reader from one term, under which page numbers will appear, to another term under which additional information may be found. An example of a *see also* reference is

free enterprise, 502. *See also* laissez-faire

Congo. *See* Belgian Congo; Zaire
Congo River. *See* Zaire River
Congress (United States), *p172*
Conrad III (Holy Roman Emperor): and Crusades, *m250*, 251
conscription, military. and French Revolutionary Wars, 435; in United States, during World War II, 725
conservatism, *f548*; in Latin America, 569
Conservative Party: in Canada, 550; in Great Britain, 544–45, 547, 764, 858. *See also* Tories
conservatives: in French Revolution, 433
Constable, John, 536
Constantine (emperor), 165, 167–68
Constantine II (king of Greece), 863
Constantinople, 187, 190, *m191*, 193–94, 469, *m594*, 595, 642, 645, 650, 660, 695; Arab attempt to capture, 208; and Crusades, 250–52, *m250*; founding of, 168; and Ottomans, 214; and trade, 253–54. *See also* Istanbul
constitution: definition of, 402; Fifth Republic in France, 765; in Great Britain, 241, 408; Japan, 612–13, 783–84; Second Republic in France, 558
Constitution (United States), 416–417; and Montesquieu's checks and balances, 423
Constitution of 1791, 431, *f432*, 433
constitutional amendments, 556–57
Constitutional Convention, 417
constitutional monarchy: in England, 403–05, 407–08; France, 431; and George III, 413; and Montesquieu, 423; in Spain, 442, 713
Consulate: of Napoleon I, 439–40
consulates: in Japan, 468
consuls: in Rome, 145
containment policy, 758, 769
Continental Army, 416
Continental Congresses, 414, 416
Continental System, 440–43
contraband: definition of, 651
Contras: in Nicaragua, 839, 856
Convention People's Party (CPP), 808, 810
convicts. *See* prisoners
convoys: in World War II, 729, 732
Cook, James, 551–52
Cooper, James Fenimore, 535
cooperative societies, 507, 510
Copernicus, Nicolaus, 348–50
copper: use of, 10
copper mining, *p815*
Copts: and art, *f190*
Coral Sea, Battle of the, 732, *m733*
Corday, Charlotte, 435, *f435*
Cordova, 210, *p211*, 213, *m267*
Corinth: rivalry with Athens, 120
Corn Laws, 544
Cornwallis, Charles, as governor general of India, 474
corporate state, 680–81; in Franco's Spain, 715
corporations, 500–01
Corregidor, *m733*
Corsica, *m326*, 438
Cortes (parliament), 713, 862
Cortés, Hernando, 367
Cossacks, 383, 387, 443

Costa Rica, 566, *m837*, 840
costume: and influence of French Revolution, *n433*
Côte d'Ivoire, 606, *m607*, *m809*, 810
cotton, 24, *f25*, *p25*, 491–92, 501; and Anglo-Chinese trade, 460
cotton cloth, 253
cotton weaving: in India, 610
Council for Mutual Economic Assistance (CMEA), 768, *m864*, 870; and Asia, 802
Council of Constance, 271
Council of Foreign Ministers: after World War II, 752–53
Council of Nicaea, 166
Council of the Indies, 367
Council of Trent, 337, *p337*, 339
Counter-Reformation, 337, 339–41
counterrevolution: and French Revolution, 435
country music, 888
coup d'état: of Napoleon I, 439
Courbet, Gustave, 538
Court of Common Pleas, 242
Court of King's Bench, 242
Court of the Exchequer, 242
courts: in England, 239–40; and Charles I of England, 399–400. *See also* juries
covenant, 400
Coventry, 723
cowpox, 523
craft guilds, 257–58
Cranmer, Thomas, 396
Crassus, Marcus Licinius, 152
Crécy, Battle of, *m265*
Creel, H. G., *f462*
creoles, 563–64, 566, 569
Crete, *m594*, 595; and Minoans, 102, 104, *m106*
Crick, Francis, 880
Crimea, *m385*, 386, *m594*
Crimean War, 559–60, *p560*; Sardinian participation, 575
Croats: in Austria-Hungary, *m592*, 593
Cro-Magnon people, *p2, m6, f7*
Crompton, Samuel, 491
Cromwell, Oliver, 401–02, *p401*
Cromwell, Richard, 402
crop rotation, 490
crops: in China, 456
crucifixion: of Jesus Christ, 164; of Spartacists, 151
Crusades, 249–53, *m250*, *m251*; and Byzantine Empire, 194; Muslim culture, 213; Renaissance, 326. *See also* Children's Crusade
cryptography, *f649*. *See also* ciphers
Cuba, *p362*, 367, 567, *m568*, *m624*, *p706*, 707, *m837*; and Africa, 814, 855; Fidel Castro, 841–42; military occupation, 624; and Nicaragua, 839; Spanish-American War, 620–21
Cuban Missile Crisis, 842
cubism, *f667*, *p667*, 668
cultural diffusion, 135, *f136*; and Asia, 803; and Byzantines, 193; definition of, 11; and Phoenicians, 39
Cultural Revolution, 778–79
culture: in Africa, 815–16; in Europe, 528. *See also* popular culture

Cunard, Samuel, 494
Cunard Line, 494
cuneiform: in Sumer, 29
Curie, Marie, 520
Curie, Pierre, 520
currency. *See* money
Cush, *m21*, 297–98, *p297*, *m298*, 300
customs union: in Germany, 578
Cuxi (empress dowager of China), 697
Cuzco, *m307*, 311
Cybele, cult of, 164
cyclops: in *Odyssey*, *f107*
Cynics, 138
Cyprus, *m594*, 595, 603, 726, *m727*, *m823*, 863, 865
Cyril (saint), 193
Cyrillic alphabet, 193, 383
Cyrus (king of Persia), 36, 118; and Hebrews, 43
czar (title), 200
Czechoslovakia, 659–60, *m659*, 675, 678, 870; and CMEA, 768; Communist takeover, 759; Nazi Germany, 716–20, *m717*, *p718*; reforms under Dubcek, 768; Sudeten Germans after World War II, 752. *See also* Bohemia; Hapsburg, House of; Slovakia
Czechs: in Austria-Hungary, *m592*, 593
Czernowitz, Battle of, *m648*

D

Dachau, 729
Dadaism, *f656*, *p656*
Dahomey, 606
daily life: in Athens, 115–17; in medieval Europe, 230–31, 258; and Netherlands, *p374*, 374–75; in Rome, 157–59; and Song China, 280; after World War II, 891
Daimler, Gottlieb, 517
daimyo, 286–87, *c288*, 289, 463–65, 467–68
Daladier, Edouard, 718
Dalai Lama, 789
Dali, Salvador, 669
Dallas, *p885*
Dalton, John, 518
Dam, Peter Van, *f380*
Damascus, *m820*, 826; capture by Tamerlane, 216; and Crusades, 251, *m251*, 253
dancing: in Europe, *p346*; in United States, 671; after World War II, 888–89. *See also* ballet
Danelaw, 238
Danish War, 580
Dante, 261
Danton, Georges-Jacques, 434–36
Danzig, 658; before World War II, *m717*, 720
Daoism, 82, *f83*, 84; and Buddhism, 277; and Indochina, 283
Dardanelles, *m106*, *m110*, 642, 645, 650, 660; 726–27
Darius (king of Persia), 36, 118–19, 471; and invasion of India, 62
Darwin, Charles, 521–22, *p522*; and interpretation of history, 530
Daumier, Honoré, *f537*, *p537*, 538

0
C 1
D 2
E 3
F 4
G 5
H 6
I 7
J 8